Table of Contents

Microsoft

Microsoft® Office Project 2003 Inside Out

Teresa Stover
Award-winning author and instructional designer

PUBLISHED BY
Microsoft Press
A Division of Microsoft Corporation
One Microsoft Way
Redmond, Washington 98052-6399

Library of Congress Cataloging-in-Publication Data
Stover, Teresa S.
Microsoft Office Project 2003 Inside Out / Teresa Stover.
p. cm.
Includes index.
ISBN 0-7356-1958-1
1. Microsoft Project. 2. Project management--Computer programs. I. Title.

HD69.P75S758 2003
658.4'04'02855369--dc22 2003059956

Printed and bound in the United States of America.

4 5 6 7 8 9 QWT 8 7 6 5 4

Distributed in Canada by H.B. Fenn and Company Ltd.

A CIP catalogue record for this book is available from the British Library.

Microsoft Press books are available through booksellers and distributors worldwide. For further information about international editions, contact your local Microsoft Corporation office or contact Microsoft Press International directly at fax (425) 936-7329. Visit our Web site at www.microsoft.com/mspress. Send comments to *mspinput@microsoft.com.*

Acquisitions Editor: Alex Blanton
Project Editor: Dick Brown
Technical Editor: Brian Kennemer

Body Part No. X10-00045

Contents at a Glance

Chapter 7
Assigning Resources to Tasks 199

Chapter 8
Planning Resource and Task Costs 231

Part 5
Managing Multiple Projects

Chapter 14
Managing Master Projects and Resource Pools 427

Chapter 15
Exchanging Information Between Project Plans 451

Part 6
Integrating Microsoft Project with Other Programs

Chapter 16
Exchanging Information with Other Applications 469

Part 8
Customizing and Managing Project Files

Appendix B
Field Reference 967

Appendix C
Online Resources for Microsoft Project 1003

Appendix D
Keyboard Shortcuts 1007

Acknowledgments

It takes a great team to put out a great book, and I've been fortunate to work with the very best. I'm genuinely grateful to the good people at Microsoft Press: Dick Brown, Alex Blanton, Barbara Moreland, and Sandra Haynes.

For her first-rate editing talents, I'm indebted to Nancy Sixsmith of ConText Editorial Services. I'm sincerely grateful for the brainpower and user advocacy of technical editor Brian Kennemer (MVP) of QuantumPM, who checked, clarified, and confirmed everything, especially the finer points.

For their exceptional ability to communicate their expertise, I thank contributors James Scott and Steve Adams. (Please read more about them in "About the Authors" following the Index.) Many thanks also to Bonnie Biafore and Ken Speer for their fine contributions to the previous edition of the book.

Thanks as well to my persistent supporters at Moore Literary Agency: Claudette Moore and Debbie McKenna.

A thousand thanks to my blessed life preservers—my unique community of friends and family who keep me balanced and smiling. Thanks most of all to Craig Stover for his steady support and brilliant flashes of insight, and for helping me find Internet cafes to continue work on the book during our grand tour of England.

We'd Like to Hear from You

Our goal at Microsoft Press is to create books that help you find the information you need to get the most out of your software.

The *Inside Out* series was created with you in mind. As part of our ongoing effort to ensure that we're creating the books that meet your learning needs, we'd like to hear from you. Let us know what you think. Tell us what you like about this book and what we can do to make it better. When you write, please include the title and author of this book in your e-mail message, as well as your name and contact information. We look forward to hearing from you!

How to Reach Us

E-Mail: nsideout@microsoft.com
Mail: Inside Out Series Editor
Microsoft Press
One Microsoft Way
Redmond, WA 98052

Note: Unfortunately, we can't provide support for any software problems you might experience. Please go to http://support.microsoft.com *for help with any software issues.*

About the CD

The Companion CD that ships with this book contains many tools and resources to help you get the most out of your *Inside Out* book.

What's on the CD

Your *Inside Out* CD includes the following:

- **Complete eBook.** In this section, you'll find an electronic version of *Microsoft Office Project 2003 Inside Out*. The eBook is in PDF format.
- **Project Standard Trial.** In this section, you'll find a trial version of Microsoft Office Project 2003 Standard Edition.
- ***Computer Dictionary*, Fifth Edition eBook.** Here you'll find the full electronic version of the *Microsoft Computer Dictionary*, Fifth Edition. Suitable for home and office, the dictionary contains more than 10,000 entries.
- **Insider Extras.** This section includes files the author selected for you to install and use as additional reference material.
- **Microsoft Resources.** In this section, you'll find information about additional resources from Microsoft that will help you get the most out of Microsoft Office Project and other business software from Microsoft.
- **Extending Project.** In this section, you'll find great information about third-party utilities and tools you use to further enhance your experience with Office Project 2003.

The Companion CD provides detailed information about the files on this CD and links to Microsoft and third-party sites on the Internet. All the files on this CD are designed to be accessed through Microsoft Internet Explorer (version 5.01 or later).

> **Note** The links to third-party sites are not under the control of Microsoft Corporation, and Microsoft is therefore not responsible for their content, nor should their inclusion on this CD be construed as an endorsement of the product or the site. Software provided on this CD is in English language only and may be incompatible with non-English language operating systems and software.

Using the CD

To use this Companion CD, insert it into your CD-ROM drive. If AutoRun is not enabled on your computer, click Index.htm in the WebSite folder in the root of the CD.

Caution This book also contains a trial version of the Microsoft Office Project 2003 Standard Edition software. This software is fully functional, but it expires 60 days after you install it. You should not install the trial version if you have already installed the full version of either Microsoft Office Project 2003 Standard Edition or Microsoft Office Project 2003 Professional Edition.

System Requirements

Following are the minimum system requirements necessary to run the CD:

- Microsoft Windows XP or later or Windows 2000 Professional with Service Pack 3 or later.
- 266-MHz or higher Pentium-compatible CPU
- 64 megabytes (MB) RAM
- 8X CD-ROM drive or faster
- Microsoft Windows–compatible sound card and speakers
- Microsoft Internet Explorer 5.01 or later
- Microsoft Mouse or compatible pointing device

Note System requirements might be higher for the add-ins available via links on the CD. Individual add-in system requirements are specified at the sites specified. An Internet connection is necessary to access the some of the hyperlinks. Connect time charges might apply.

Support Information

Every effort has been made to ensure the accuracy of the book and the contents of this Companion CD. For feedback on the book content or this Companion CD, please contact us by using any of the addresses listed in the "We'd Like to Hear from You" section.

Microsoft Press provides corrections for books through the World Wide Web at *http://www.microsoft.com/mspress/support/*. To connect directly to the Microsoft Press Knowledge Base and enter a query regarding a question or issue that you might have, go to *http://www.microsoft.com/mspress/support/search.asp*.

For support information regarding Windows XP, you can connect to Microsoft Technical Support on the Web at *http://support.microsoft.com/*.

Conventions and Features Used in This Book

This book uses special text and design conventions to make it easier for you to find the information you need.

Text Convention

Convention	Meaning
Abbreviated menu commands	For your convenience, this book uses abbreviated menu commands. For example, "Click Tools, Track Changes, Highlight Changes" means that you should click the Tools menu, point to Track Changes, and click the Highlight Changes command.
Boldface type	**Boldface** type is used to indicate text that you enter or type.
Initial Capital Letters	The first letters of the names of menus, dialog boxes, dialog box elements, and commands are capitalized. Example: the Save As dialog box.
Italicized type	*Italicized* type is used to indicate new terms.
Plus sign (+) in text	Keyboard shortcuts are indicated by a plus sign (+) separating two key names. For example, Ctrl+Alt+Delete means that you press the Ctrl, Alt, and Delete keys at the same time.

Design Conventions

NEW FEATURE! This icon identifies a new or significantly updated feature in this version of the software.

Inside Out

This statement illustrates an example of an "Inside Out" problem statement.

These are the book's signature tips. In these tips, you'll get the straight scoop on what's going on with the software—inside information about why a feature works the way it does. You'll also find handy workarounds to deal with software problems.

Tip Tips provide helpful hints, timesaving tricks, or alternative procedures related to the task being discussed.

Troubleshooting

This statement illustrates an example of a "Troubleshooting" problem statement.

Look for these sidebars to find solutions to common problems you might encounter. Troubleshooting sidebars appear next to related information in the chapters. You can also use the Troubleshooting Topics index at the back of the book to look up problems by topic.

Cross-references point you to other locations in the book that offer additional information about the topic being discussed.

ON THE CD This icon indicates information or text found on the companion CD.

Caution Cautions identify potential problems that you should look out for when you're completing a task or problems that you must address before you can complete a task.

Note Notes offer additional information related to the task being discussed.

Sidebars

The sidebars sprinkled throughout these chapters provide ancillary information on the topic being discussed. Go to sidebars to learn more about the technology or a feature.

Part 1

Project Fundamentals

Chapter 1

Introducing Microsoft Project 2003

What kind of project manager are you, anyway?

Let's say you're an accomplished project management professional who manages projects for several departments in your organization at any given time. You're responsible for managing thousands of tasks, hitting hundreds of deadlines, and assigning scores of resources. You need to plan and monitor each project, work with different managers, and make the best use of team members—some of whom might work on only one project and others who might be shared among several of your projects.

On the other hand, suppose you're a multitasking product specialist for a small startup company. You handle research, development, material procurement, marketing, and staff development. On top of all this, you have just been assigned the responsibility of managing the project for the launch of your company's newest product.

As these two scenarios illustrate, project management is a process and a discipline that can be the full focus of your career or one of many aspects of your job description.

Numerous industries rely on sound project management for their success:

- Construction
- Filmmaking
- Computer system deployment
- Logistics
- Engineering
- Publishing
- Events planning
- Software development

Effective project management is vital at the start of a project when you're determining what needs to be done, when, by whom, and for how much money. Effective project management is also essential after you kick off the project, when you are continually controlling and managing the project details. You frequently analyze the project—tracking the schedule, the budget, resource requirements, and the scope of tasks. In addition, you're managing the level of quality in the project, planning for risks and contingencies, and communicating with the members of the project team as well as upper management or customers.

Throughout this intricate process of planning and tracking your project, Microsoft Office Project 2003 is a smart and trustworthy assistant that can help you manage the many responsibilities associated with your project. Many software applications can help you work toward producing a specific result that you can print, publish, or post. And it's true that you use Microsoft Project 2003 to set up a project schedule and print reports that reflect that schedule. However, Microsoft Project goes far beyond just the printed outcome. This is a tool that helps you brainstorm, organize, and assign your tasks as you create your plan in the planning phase. Microsoft Project then helps you track progress and control the schedule, your resources, and your budget during the execution phase. All this so you can achieve your real objective—to successfully achieve the goals of your project on schedule and under budget.

Using this Book

This book is designed for intermediate to advanced computer users who manage projects. Even if you have never used Microsoft Project or managed a project before, this book assumes you have experience with Microsoft Windows and at least a couple of programs in Microsoft Office; for example, Microsoft Word, Microsoft Excel, or Microsoft Outlook.

- If you are completely new to project management and Microsoft Project, this book will give you a solid grounding in the use of Microsoft Project as well as basic project management practices and methodologies. It will help you understand the phases of project management, including the controlling factors in the project life cycle.
- If you're an experienced project manager, this book integrates common project management practices with the use of the software tool. This helps you see how you can use Microsoft Project to carry out the project management functions you're accustomed to.
- If you're already an experienced Microsoft Project user, this book will help you better understand the inner workings of Microsoft Project, so you can use it more effectively to do what you need it to do. This book also introduces the new features of Project 2003, giving you ideas and tips as to whether and how you can use those features.

Regardless of your previous experience, this book will help you work with Microsoft Project as a facilitator for your project's processes and phases. Read the chapters and parts you feel are appropriate for your needs right now. Familiarize yourself with the topics available in the other chapters. Then, as you continue to manage your projects with Microsoft Project, keep the book within arm's reach so you can quickly find the answers to questions and problems as they come up. As you master your current level of knowledge, use this book to help you get to the next level, whether it's working with multiple projects at one time, customizing Microsoft Project, or programming Microsoft Project functions to automate repetitive activities. This book is your comprehensive Microsoft Project reference, in which you can quickly find answers and then get back to work on your project plan. The book is organized into the following parts:

Part 1: Project Fundamentals If you want a primer on project management in general or Microsoft Project in particular, read the chapters in this part. Here, you find an overview of Microsoft Project, including what's new in Microsoft Project 2003. There's an overview of project management processes and how Microsoft Project facilitates those processes. You also find a discussion of the various kinds of people involved in your project, as well as some keys to successful project management.

Part 2: Developing the Project Plan Everything you need to know about starting a new project and creating a new project plan is found here. You get details about working with the Microsoft Project workspace, scheduling tasks, setting up resources, assigning resources to tasks, establishing costs, and adjusting the project plan to be an accurate model of your project's reality.

Part 3: Tracking Progress After you create the perfect project plan, you're ready to execute it. To keep the project plan working for you, it needs to be up to date. This part provides details about setting and working with baselines so you can track and compare your progress toward deadlines. It covers important aspects of updating and tracking costs as well as adjusting the schedule, resource workload, and costs to reflect ongoing changes in your project.

Part 4: Reporting and Analyzing Project Information Microsoft Project provides a wide range of options for setting up and printing views and reports. This part outlines these methods—from simply printing your current view to designing a custom report and publishing it to the Web. This part also describes how you can export data to Excel for calculation and other analysis, as well as how you can use earned value data to analyze progress and costs.

Part 5: Managing Multiple Projects As a project manager, it's likely that you're managing more than one project at a time. This part explains the concepts and practices of master projects, subprojects, and resource pools. It also explains how you can exchange information between different project plans; copy or link information; and leverage customized views, reports, groups, and other Microsoft Project elements you might have created.

Part 6: Integrating Microsoft Project with Other Programs Microsoft Project is designed to work seamlessly with other programs. You can copy, embed, link, hyperlink, import, and export information. This part describes these methods in detail and also devotes chapters to the specific integration techniques for working with Excel and Outlook.

Part 7: Managing Projects Across Your Enterprise Microsoft Project helps to facilitate collaboration in project teams across your enterprise. If you're using Microsoft Office Project Professional 2003, Microsoft Office Project Server 2003, and Microsoft Office Project Web Access 2003, you and your organization have access to the robust project team collaboration and enterprise project management features. In this part, you see how you can exchange project-related messages with members of your resource team. You can assign tasks, obtain task progress updates, and receive status reports. This part also describes how you can set up and use the enterprise features to standardize and customize Microsoft Project and project management throughout your organization. It also covers enterprise resource management and executive summaries.

Part 8: Customizing and Managing Project Files With Microsoft Project, you can create and customize your own views, tables, groups, reports, formulas, toolbars, dialog boxes, macros, and more. This part covers the details of these custom elements. This part also discusses methods for closing a project at the end of its life cycle and continuing to use what you learn by creating templates that can become the basis for the next project of its kind. Along these lines, this part details project file management issues, including file locations, backups, and multiple versions.

Part 9: Programming Custom Solutions You have access to a number of programming tools that can help you fully customize and automate Microsoft Project to meet your specific requirements. This part provides the information you need about the programming tools, including a primer on Visual Basic, using the Visual Basic Editor, creating Visual Basic for Applications (VBA) macros, and working with the Microsoft Project Database.

Part 10: Appendixes This part includes ancillary information you'll find useful in your work with Microsoft Project. For example, there are installation guidelines, a reference of Microsoft Project fields, and a list of online resources to expand your knowledge of Microsoft Project and project management. Also included is a handy keyboard shortcut reference.

Throughout the book, you'll find tips providing shortcuts or alternate methods for doing certain tasks. The Inside Out tips give you information about known issues or idiosyncrasies with Microsoft Project and possible methods of working around them.

There are also Troubleshooting tips, which alert you to common problems and how to avoid or recover from them.

This book is designed to be referenceable, so you can quickly find the answers you need at the time you have the question. The comprehensive table of contents is a good starting point. Another excellent place to start finding your solution is in one of the two indexes at the end of the book. Use the special Troubleshooting index to solve specific problems. Use the master index to help you find the topics you're looking for when you need them.

Using Microsoft Project—An Overview

Microsoft Project is a specialized database that stores and presents thousands of pieces of data related to your project. Examples of such data include tasks, durations, links, resource names, calendars, assignments, costs, deadlines, and milestones.

These pieces of information interrelate and affect each other in a multitude of ways. Underlying this project database is the scheduling engine, which crunches the raw project data you enter and presents the calculated results to you (see Figure 1-1). Examples of such calculated results include the start and finish dates of a task, the resource availability, the finish date of the entire project, and the total cost for a resource or for the project.

You can then manipulate and display this calculated data in various views to analyze the planning and progress of your project. This information helps you make decisions vital to the project's success.

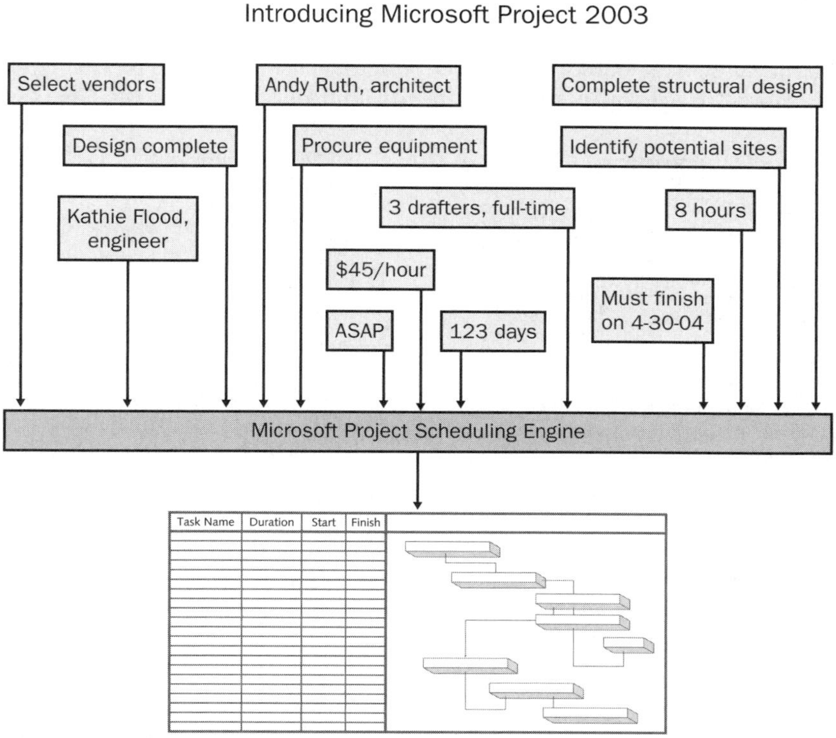

Figure 1-1. Use Microsoft Project as your database of project management information.

You can also communicate your progress and provide the feedback necessary to keep your team and other stakeholders informed of essential project information, create and print reports for status meetings or distribution to stakeholders, and print or publish certain views or reports to your team's Web site.

Microsoft Project 2003 Editions

With Microsoft Project 2003, you have a choice of two editions: Microsoft Office Project Standard 2003 and Microsoft Office Project Professional 2003.

Microsoft Project Standard 2003 is the basic desktop edition of Microsoft Project. It no longer connects in any way to Microsoft Project Server 2003 and strictly stands alone. Microsoft Project Standard consists of all the essential features for individual project management, including the following:

- Task scheduling
- Resource management
- Tracking
- Reporting
- Customization

With this substantial tool set, you can start planning, managing, and reporting your project information "straight out of the box"—that is, immediately upon installation (see Figure 1-2).

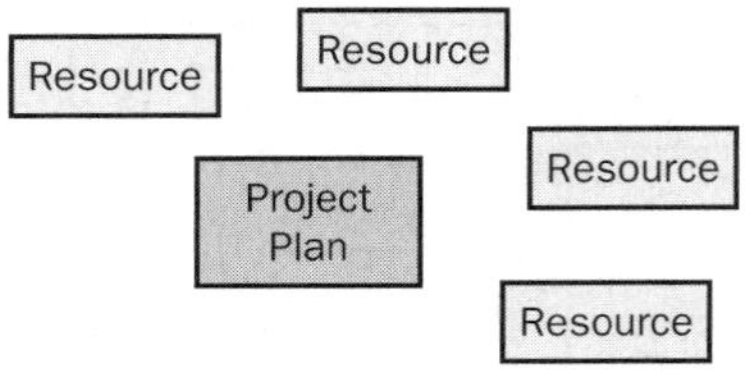

With Microsoft Project Standard, you can plan and track your project and resources as your standalone desktop tool.

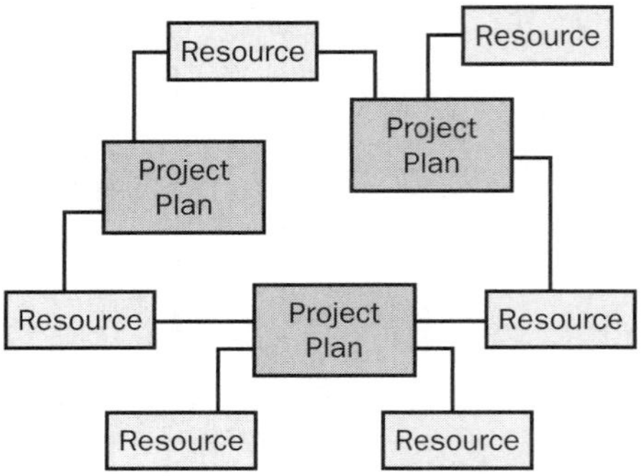

Figure 1-2. Develop and execute single or multiple project plans with Microsoft Project Standard.

Microsoft Project Professional 2003 provides everything that Microsoft Project Standard does. In addition, Microsoft Project Professional provides for team collaboration with a Web interface (see Figure 1-3).

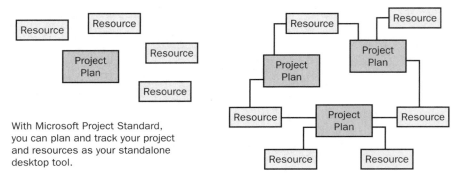

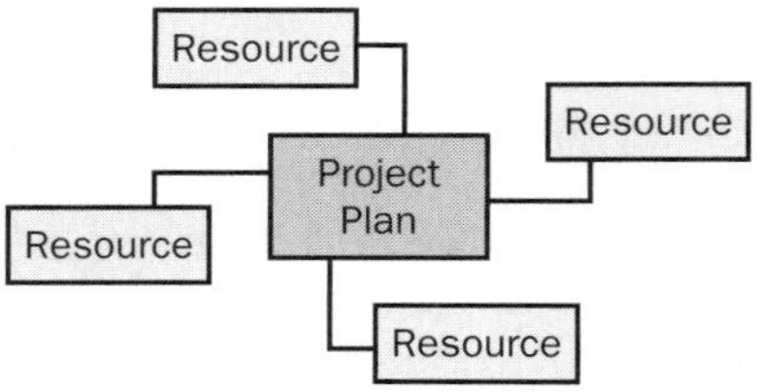

Figure 1-3. Using Microsoft Project Professional, Microsoft Project Server, and Microsoft Project Web Access, you and your team members can communicate and update project information electronically.

Microsoft Project Professional also provides enterprise capabilities for project standardization, resource management, and executive analysis. With Microsoft Project Professional, project management is fully scalable across multiple departments and divisions in an organization (see Figure 1-4).

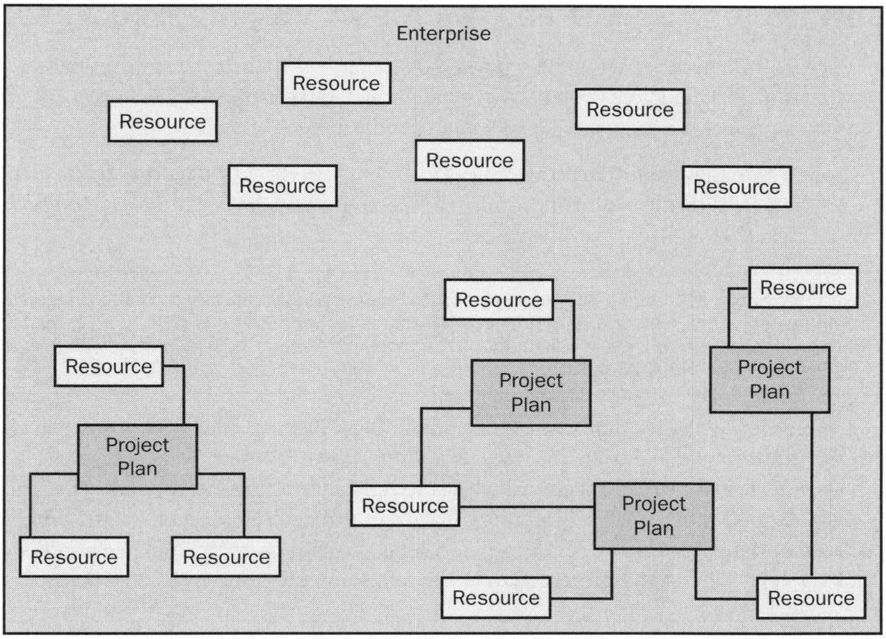

Figure 1-4. Develop and execute project plans across an enterprise with Microsoft Project Professional.

Microsoft Project Professional includes the following features:

- Team collaboration through Microsoft Project Server 2003 and Microsoft Project Web Access 2003. From Microsoft Project Professional, the project manager can send assignments to Microsoft Project Server, and team members can view and update their assignments using Microsoft Project Web Access, the Web-based project management interface.
- Global templates, enterprise fields, and other elements, enabling your project administrator to standardize and customize the use of Microsoft Project for the way your enterprise manages projects.
- The ability to choose and manage resources from the pool of a specific group or the entire company. You can see resource availability across multiple projects and have Microsoft Project automatically find resources that will appropriately fill project team requirements.
- High-level overviews of all the projects taking place throughout the organization. With the enterprise capabilities of Microsoft Project Professional , all information is gathered, organized, and reported consistently throughout the organization, providing a complete and accurate picture of all projects.

For more information about the workgroup collaboration and enterprise project management features provided through Project Professional, see Chapter 20, "Understanding the Project Workgroup and Enterprise Model."

Microsoft Project Server and Microsoft Project Web Access

Microsoft Project Server is the separately licensed companion program that accompanies Microsoft Project Professional. Microsoft Project Server provides for team collaboration among project managers, team members, and other stakeholders.

Project managers use Microsoft Project to enter, store, and update project information. They can then send project information, such as assignments or task updates, to specific team members through Microsoft Project Server.

For more information about setting up Project Server and Project Web Access, see Chapter 21, "Administering Project Server and Project Web Access for Your Enterprise." For project manager information on enterprise and collaboration features, see Chapter 22, "Managing with Project Professional and Project Server."

Team members and other associated stakeholders in the project can view and work with the information held in Project Server through the use of Project Web Access, the Web-based user interface for project team collaboration and messaging. Team members can review their assigned tasks and other project information in Project Web Access. In addition, they can add tasks, update progress information, and send status reports through Project Server, which ultimately updates the project plan being maintained by the project manager.

For more information about functions for team members and resource managers, see Chapter 23, "Participating on a Team Using Project Web Access." Upper management and other stakeholders should see Chapter 24, "Making Executive Decisions Using Project Web Access."

What's New in Microsoft Project 2003

The new features in Microsoft Project 2003 revolve around the following initiatives:

- Improving collaboration among members of the project team.
- Increasing support and tools for resource managers.
- Expanding application customization, integration, and programmability for IT professionals and solution providers.

As in Microsoft Project 2002, there are two editions of Microsoft Project 2003: Project Standard and Project Professional. A major change is that Project Server and Project Web Access work only with Project Professional. Therefore, Project Standard becomes strictly the single-project manager desktop solution, whereas Project Professional builds on that solution with workgroup and enterprise capabilities.

This section summarizes the new features in Project Standard and Project Professional. Cross-references indicate where these new features are covered in more detail elsewhere in the book. In those locations, the discussion is marked with the 2003 New Feature icon.

What's New in Project Standard 2003

The new version of Project Standard includes closer integration with Microsoft Office, including the way online Help is delivered. This version also brings enhancements to the Project Guide and changes to e-mail workgroup collaboration.

Copying a Picture of Project

You can copy a static picture from Microsoft Project and paste it into a Microsoft PowerPoint presentation or Microsoft Word document using the Copy Picture To Office Wizard (see Figure 1-5).

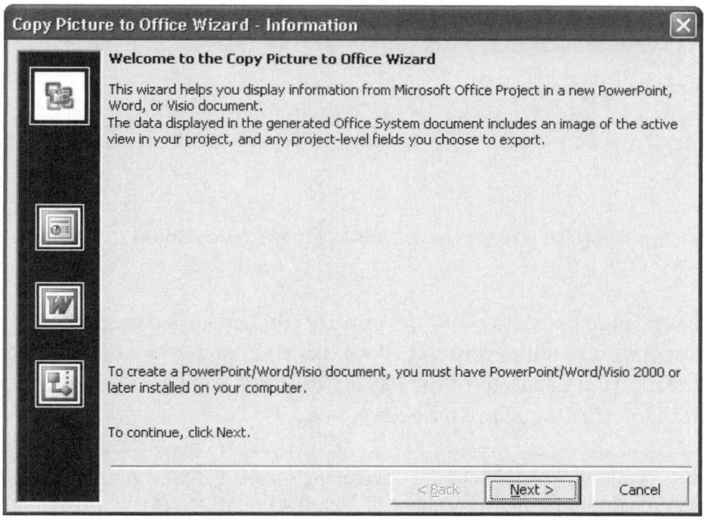

Figure 1-5. Use the Copy Picture To Office Wizard to take a snapshot of a Project view for use in a Microsoft Office application.

For more information about the Copy Picture To Office Wizard, see "Copying from Microsoft Project to Another Application," on page 471.

Reviewing Specific Types of Information Using the Project Guide

The Project Guide was introduced in Microsoft Project 2002, appearing as the interactive task pane to the left of the Microsoft Project workspace. The Project Guide steps you through specific goal-oriented processes. These processes included setting up tasks, setting up and assigning resources, tracking progress, and reporting.

In Project 2003, the Report set of processes is enhanced in the Project Guide (see Figure 1-6).

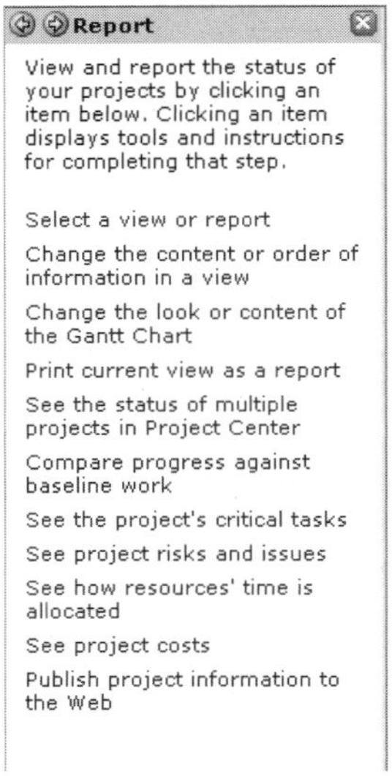

Figure 1-6. You can now use links and controls on the Project Guide to help you set up your views and reports.

The Report Project Guide includes steps and controls for setting up your project to view specific types of information, such as critical tasks, risks and issues, resource allocation, project costs, and so on. Although the focus of the Report Project Guide is to set up and print views, there's also a guide for selecting a predefined report.

> **For more information about the Project Guide, see "Learning As You Go," later in this chapter. For more information about working with views, see Chapter 4, "Viewing Project Information." For more information about working with reports, see Chapter 12, "Reporting Project Information."**

Working with COM Add-Ins

In Project 2002, you had to download the following Project Component Object Model (COM) add-ins from the Web:

- Visio WBS Chart Wizard
- Euro Currency Converter
- XML Reporting Wizard
- Compare Project Versions
- Database Upgrade Utility

These add-ins are now automatically installed with Project, and are accessed from the Analysis toolbar (see Figure 1-7).

Figure 1-7. COM add-ins are now automatically installed with Microsoft Project.

The other COM add-ins have their own dedicated toolbars.

For more information about the Visio WBS Chart Wizard, see "Charting your WBS in Visio" on page 90.

For more information about the Euro Currency Converter, see "Converting an EMU Currency to Euro" on page 245.

For more information about the XML Reporting Wizard, see "Generating Reports from Project XML data" on page 395.

Collaborating with Your Workgroup via E-Mail

In previous versions of Microsoft Project, you could install a set of files that enable basic workgroup collaboration features via your organization's MAPI-based e-mail system. This was the low-tech alternative to using Project Professional, Project Server, and Project Web Access to exchange task information with team members (see Figure 1-8).

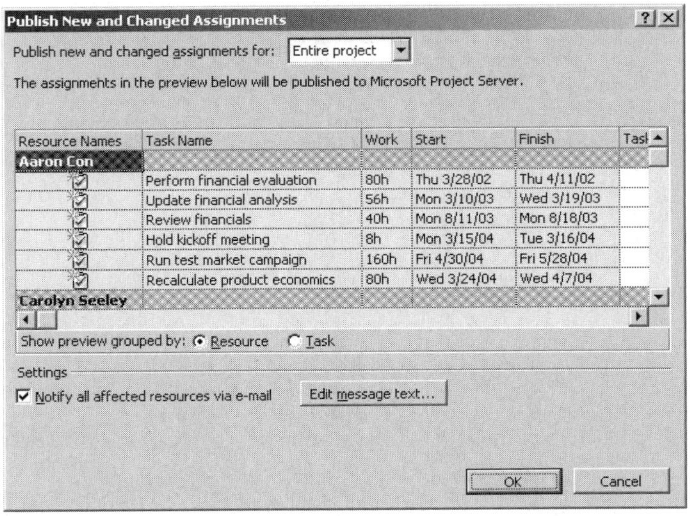

Figure 1-8. You can exchange basic task information using e-mail workgroup collaboration.

In Project 2003, the workgroup program files are no longer provided with the CD. You need to download the workgroup files from the Web and change a registry setting to enable the e-mail workgroup features in Project.

For more information about e-mail workgroup collaboration, see Chapter 19, "Collaborating Using E-Mail."

Getting Help and Training

In Project 2003, goal-based Help is replaced by Project Help in the task pane on the left (see Figure 1-9). As in traditional Help systems, you can browse a table of contents or enter a phrase to search for a Help topic. Review conceptual or reference information, or follow the steps in a specific procedure, all with Help topics installed on your computer along with your Microsoft Project files.

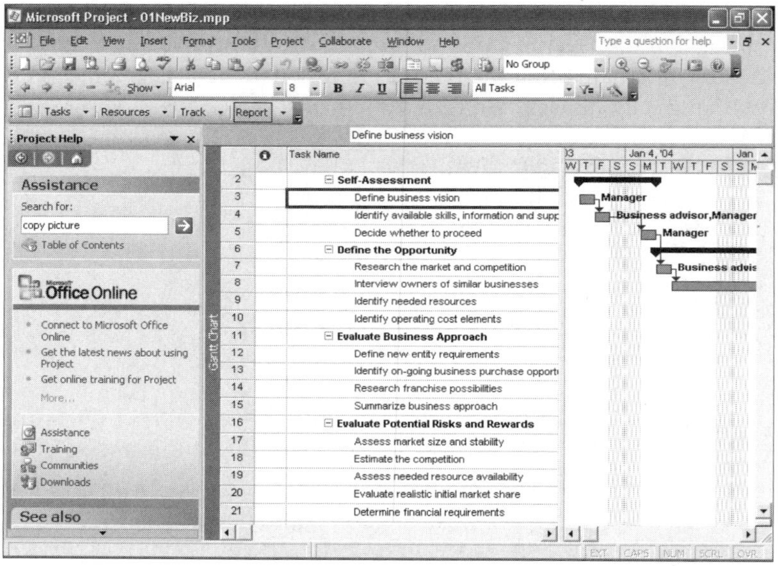

Figure 1-9. The Project Help pane is the new environment for local and Web Help resources.

But in addition to the traditional Help topics installed on your local computer, with Project 2003, you can now access supplemental Help topics, Web articles, and interactive training. Through the Assistance Center, you can search for information in Office Online, the Project Knowledge Base, and Microsoft TechNet. You can find and download additional Project templates onto your computer and access a store of Project information through Office.NET.

Whether you're connected to the Web or not, you can easily take advantage of a variety of Project Help resources.

For more information about using Help, see "Learning As You Go," later in this chapter on page 22.

What's New in Project Professional 2003

Project Professional 2003 includes all the new features of Project Standard, plus a set of features that improve collaboration and information integrity between the project manager and team members.

Specifying Multiple Traits for One Resource

With Project Professional 2002 came the introduction of enterprise resource outline codes, which could be used to specify traits or properties associated with resources, such as skills, locations, certifications, languages, and so on. Now with Project Professional 2003, 10 of the enterprise resource outline codes can be used to each define multiple traits with a single code. Instead of using a separate outline code for each trait, multiple traits can be combined in a single resource field to show all pertinent properties of a resource at once.

The project administrator creates the Enterprise Resource Multi-Value (ERMV) fields and assigns them to the resources as appropriate. The project manager then can add one of the defined ERMV fields to a resource view to show resource properties at a glance. The information contained in this field can also be used with the Resource Substitution Wizard, Team Builder, and Portfolio Modeler.

For more information about setting up enterprise resources, see "Administering the Enterprise Resource Pool" on page 598. For more information about working with fields and outline codes, see "Working with Outline Codes" on page 806.

Soft-Booking Proposed Resources

If you're using Microsoft Project to bid or estimate a project, you might want to add actual enterprise resources to the proposed project. Adding actual resources can help you figure real costs. It can also help you estimate the schedule based on real resources' working times and availability. However, as soon as you add a resource to your plan, that resource's availability is now reserved for the period of time your proposed project encompasses. If the project does not come through, the resources you added to your project might be left without any work.

To allow for proposal situations such as this, in Project Professional 2003, you can now specify that a resource is proposed or committed in your project.

This "soft booking" can also be useful if you're considering possible resources for additional scope or to help with resource overallocation in a project that's currently under way.

For more information about adding unconfirmed resources to your project plan, see "Proposing Tentative Resources" on page 178 and "Building Your Enterprise Project Team" on page 655.

Protecting Baseline Information

Many organizations rely on project baseline information and want to maintain the absolute integrity of that information, allowing no edits after the baseline is saved. The project administrator can specify which project managers have permission to edit their baselines (see Figure 1-10). By default, baseline editing of enterprise projects is not allowed.

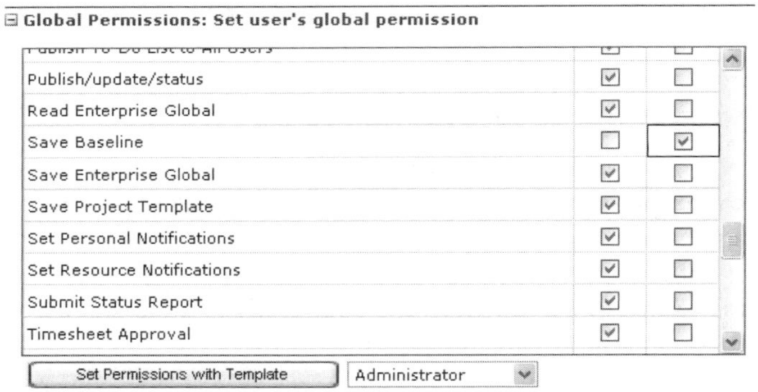

Figure 1-10. Specify whether a project manager has the permission to save baselines.

Protecting your baseline information is especially important if you track variances closely or if your project management methodology relies on earned value calculations.

For more information about working with baselines, see "Saving Original Plan Information Using a Baseline" on page 298. For more information about project administrator responsibilities and permissions, see "Managing Users and System Security" on page 583.

What's New in Project Server and Project Web Access 2003

In the separately licensed Project Server 2003 and Project Web Access 2003, a multitude of new features facilitate collaboration with team members, support for resource managers, and expanded customization and programmability.

Collaborating with Team Members

Through task integration with the Microsoft Outlook calendar, and document version control and risk management capabilities of Windows Sharepoint Services, team members have more access to sophisticated tools to help them carry out and report on their assignments.

Displaying and Updating Tasks in Microsoft Outlook Team members using Project Web Access can now display their assigned tasks in their Microsoft Outlook calendars. They can also update progress on those calendar entries and report status back to Project Server directly from Outlook. Nonworking time noted in the Outlook calendar can also be reported back to Project Server.

This Project Web Access to Outlook integration is accomplished through the Outlook Integration Component Object Model (COM) add-in provided with Project Web Access 2003.

For more information about using Microsoft Project and Project Web Access with Microsoft Outlook, see Chapter 18, "Integrating Microsoft Project with Microsoft Outlook." For more information about team member task assignments and status reporting, see Chapter 23.

Controlling Document Versions Project documents, including needs analyses, scope definition, project deliverable documents, and narrative reports can all be stored in the Project Web Access document library that was introduced with the previous version. The capability of the document library is taken a step further with version control (see Figure 1-11). Document versions can now be controlled using checkin and checkout processes.

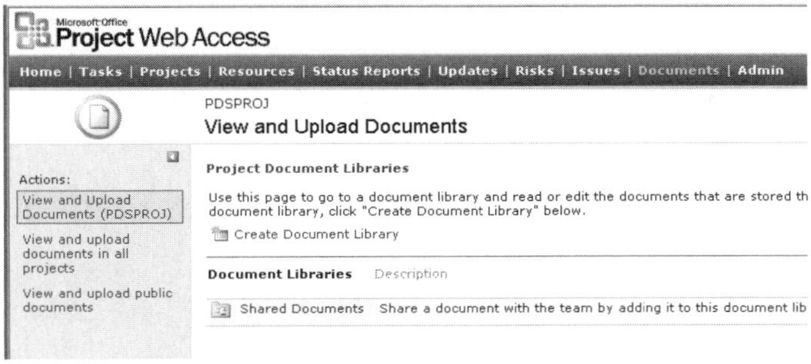

Figure 1-11. Control project documents in the Document Library in Project Web Access.

The document version control capabilities are provided through integration with Windows SharePoint Services 2.0. SharePoint Team Services 1.0 is no longer supported.

For more information about working with the document library in Project Web Access, see "Controlling Project Documents" on page 691.

Managing Risk Project management and risk management go hand-in-hand. Much of what we do in project management is essentially managing risk. Straightforward risk management functionality is now provided in Project Web Access. Users can record information about risks, update this information, and track the risk. Risks can be escalated to the right person for mitigation.

Risks can also be associated with specific tasks, resources, documents, issues, and other risks. The risk-management capabilities are provided through integration with Windows Sharepoint Services.

Managing Resources

With the new resource management features in Project Server 2003 and Project Web Access 2003, more tools and support are provided for resource managers. They can build a team based on skills and availability, and also tentatively add resources to the team. More controls are available to protect the integrity of project information. Team members find that working with the timesheet in Project Web Access has become more convenient, with pick lists for enterprise custom fields and timesheet printing capabilities.

Matching Resource Skills and Availability with Task Requirements The Build Team feature was introduced in Project Professional 2002 to help project managers find resources in the organization who match the skills and availability needed for their project plans. A version of the Build Team feature is now available to resource managers using Project Web Access 2003 (see Figure 1-12).

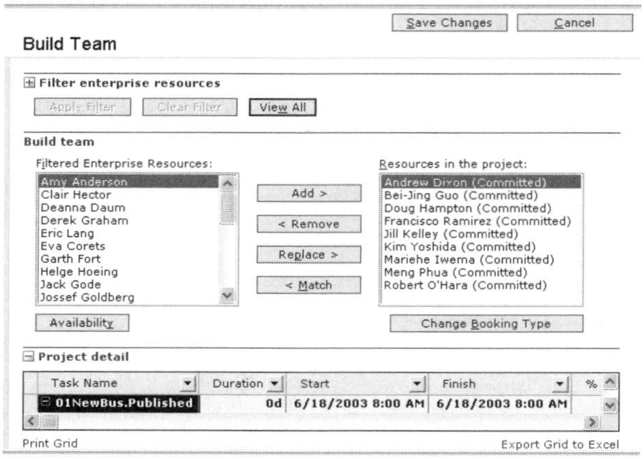

Figure 1-12. Resource managers working in Project Web Access can find resources who have the appropriate skills and availability for the project.

In the Build Team window, resource managers can filter enterprise resources by their enterprise outline codes and view availability graphs.

For more information about the Build Team feature in Project Web Access, see "Managing Resources in Project Web Access" on page 726.

Booking Proposed Resources Just as the project manager can add a resource to a project plan as a proposed or tentative resource, so can the resource manager working in Project Web Access. By booking proposed resources, the resource managers can set up a "what-if" situation using possible real resources.

Using proposed resources, the resource manager can better estimate schedules, costs, and resource availability without locking up a resource's availability on other projects.

For more information about adding proposed resources using Project Web Access, see "Managing Resources in Project Web Access" on page 726.

Locking the Timesheet Periods If your project is tracked by hours of work per time period, you can have those timesheet periods locked (see Figure 1-13). This timesheet lockdown ensures that team members can report hours only for current time periods, not for time periods in the past or future. Locking the timesheet period contributes to the integrity of progress information being submitted by team members.

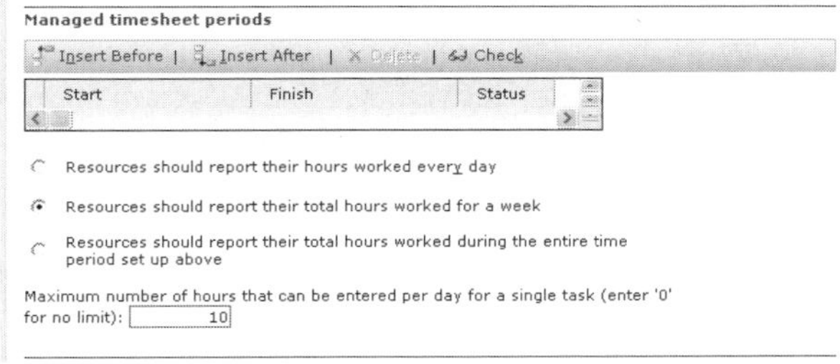

Figure 1-13. The project administrator sets whether non-current timesheet periods are to be locked.

The project administrator sets up the timesheet period lock using the Administrator page in Project Web Access.

> **For more information about tracking actual work in Microsoft Project, see "Updating Progress Using Resource Work" on page 316. For more information about having the project administrator set up the timesheet period lock, see "Setting Up Team Member Timesheets" on page 629. For more information about team members submitting actual work from Project Web Access, see "Updating Assignments in the Outlook Calendar" on page 721.**

Protecting Actual Information Actual progress information sent by team members using Project Web Access to the project manager using Project Professional can be protected. That is, if your organization chooses, any differences between the actuals submitted by team members and the actuals showing in the project plan can be audited. Protecting actuals in this manner contributes to the integrity of progress information being submitted by team members.

The project administrator sets up the protected actuals option using the Administrator page in Project Web Access. Project managers can still edit actuals for local tasks or for those tasks that have no resources assigned.

> **For more information about tracking actual work in Microsoft Project, see "Updating Progress Using Resource Work" on page 316. For more information about having the project administrator set up protected actuals, see "Managing Users and System Security" on page 583. For more information about team members submitting actual work from Project Web Access, see "Updating Assignments in the Outlook Calendar" on page 721.**

Choosing from Lists in Custom Fields In addition to basic task and assignment information in a team member's timesheet, custom fields might also be added to the timesheet by the project manager and project administrator. If an enterprise custom field or outline code field for tasks has been added, they can be set up with a pick-list or lookup table from which to choose the appropriate option.

With the availability of a pick-list or lookup table, it's easy for the team member to quickly enter the correct form of information while maintaining project data integrity.

For more information about setting up enterprise custom fields, including enterprise outline codes, see "Standardizing Enterprise Project Elements" on page 621. For more information about fields in general, see "Customizing Fields" on page 788. For more information about outline codes, see "Working with Outline Codes" on page 806.

Printing Project Web Access Pages In Project Web Access 2003, team members can now print the grid on the following pages:

- Tasks
- Projects
- Resources
- Updates
- Risks
- Issues
- Documents

You can also arrange and format the columns in the grid the way you want, and export the information in the grid to Microsoft Excel.

For more information about working with the Timesheet, see Chapter 23.

Experimenting with Enterprise Projects using the Sample Database A sample project database is provided with Project Server 2003. You can use this database to demonstrate or experiment with enterprise project functionality and evaluate custom Microsoft Project solutions.

This database can also be used for training project managers, team members, and other stakeholders in your organization on the effective use of your implementation of Microsoft Project without having to use live project data.

For more information about the sample database, see "Working with the Sample Database" later in this chapter.

Manipulating Microsoft Project the Way You Want

New capabilities are provided for customizing, integrating, and programming Microsoft Project 2003. By partitioning the Project Server database, you can accommodate the size of your organization. By installing Web Parts in Project Web Access, you can add detailed information to user views. Through the use of Active Directory synchronization and the new set of application interfaces (APIs), you can set up Project Server to automatically pull or display information from other systems throughout your organization.

Partitioning the Database Server scalability and performance are improved in Project Server 2003, through database partitioning. The Project Server database can be divided among two or three servers using the linked server capability of Microsoft SQL Server 2000. During setup, the Views database tables can go on one server while the Project database and services can go on one or two other servers. This distribution increases the number of users

that the database can accommodate by dividing the workload of the Project Server application across a greater number of servers.

For more information about the Project Server database, see Chapter 32, "Working with Microsoft Project Data."

Viewing Project Details Using Web Parts Through the Windows SharePoint Services with Project Server 2003, you can install Web Parts that provide for greater task and project detail in Project Web Access views. Web Parts you can add include the following:

- My tasks
- My projects
- Project summary
- Task changes
- Resource assignments
- Portfolio Analyzer view

For more information about working with Windows SharePoint Services and Web Parts, see "Microsoft Office Project Server 2003 Setup Issues" on page 962.

Synchronizing with Active Directory If your organization uses Active Directory, project server administrators can synchronize Active Directory with Microsoft Project. The project administrator can map resources from the Active Directory to the enterprise resource pool.

In addition, Active Directory security groups can be synchronized with Project Server security groups. These synchronization services run automatically on a regular basis as determined by the project administrator.

For more information about synchronizing Active Directory resources with your enterprise resource pool, see "Administering the Enterprise Resource Pool" on page 598. For more information about synchronizing Active Directory security groups with Project Server security groups, see "Establishing User Accounts and Permissions" on page 583.

Interacting with Different Systems Within an organization, the full project management picture incorporates multiple management disciplines and systems, such as accounting, procurement, and human resources. Microsoft Project 2003 facilitates integration among organizational systems through the inclusion of several additional APIs (application program interfaces).

The following APIs are provided with Project 2003:

API for Timesheets. Provides a programmatic interface from Project Server and Project Web Access to a third-party timesheet program. This API can also enable information to be sent from the Project Web Access Timesheet to your organization's general ledger system. This can be done through the Project Data Service (PDS).

API for Project Data Creation. Provides a programmatic interface to easily create the minimum required elements of a valid enterprise project, including tasks, resources, and assignments, through the PDS.

API for Enterprise Resource Pool Creation. Provides a programmatic interface to easily create and edit enterprise resources from systems in other organizational lines of business.

API for Enterprise Custom Fields. Provides a programmatic interface to edit value lists for enterprise text fields, particularly integrating and synchronizing with systems in other organizational lines of business.

API for Enterprise Outline Code Fields. Provides a programmatic interface to edit and integrate value lists for enterprise outline codes, particularly integrating and synchronizing with systems in other organizational lines of business. A developer can use this API to include a list of hierarchical values and a set of PDS methods for transforming such a list into an enterprise outline code value list.

Learning As You Go

NEW FEATURE! As you work in your project plan, you can quickly get assistance when you need it. This section details the different types of information accessible to you through Microsoft Project.

Getting Started with Office Online

When you first start Microsoft Project, Office Online appears in the task pane on the left (see Figure 1-14).

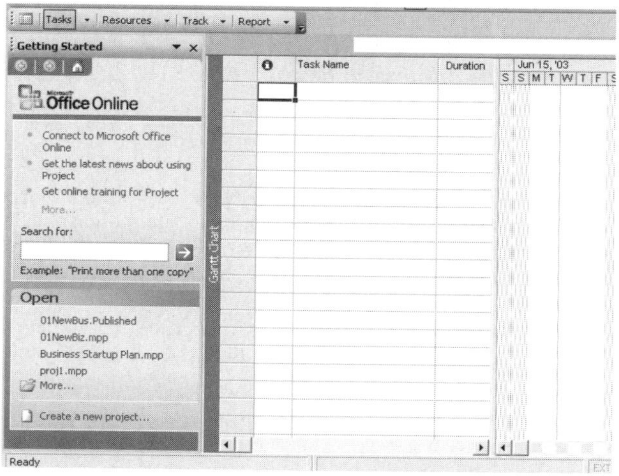

Figure 1-14. With Office Online, you can easily connect to Web sources for Project assistance.

Office Online provides links to Web resources having to do with Microsoft Project, including news, downloads, and templates. For example, click the Connect To Microsoft Office Online link, and the associated Web site appears in a new window (see Figure 1-15). You might see Spotlight links that provide information about highlighted services and features having to do with Microsoft Project or Microsoft Office.

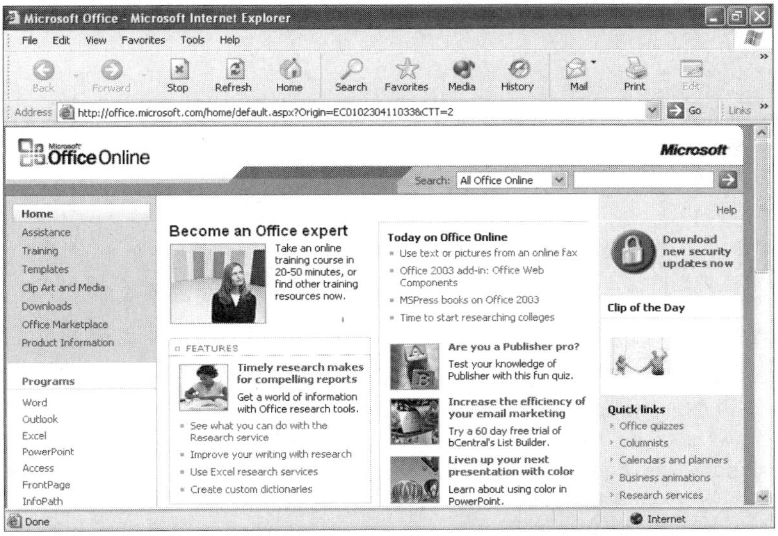

Figure 1-15. Find spotlighted features, downloadable templates, and user assistance from Microsoft Office Online on the Web.

Back in the Office Online pane in Microsoft Project, you can enter a word or phrase in the Search For box. If you're not connected to the Internet, Microsoft Project searches through your local installed Help system for topics matching your search phrase. If you're connected to the Internet, Microsoft Project also searches through Web resources. Either way, a list of Help topics appears in the Search Results pane.

Under the Open section, your four most recently opened project files are listed. If you click More, the Open dialog box appears. You can also click the Create A New Project link, and the New Project task pane appears.

In Microsoft Project 2002, the Project Guide was the first window we saw in the task pane. Now in Microsoft Project 2003, the Office Online pane is the first window. If you want to see the Project Guide, click the Close button in the upper-right corner of the Office Online pane. The Project Guide appears.

Any time you want to see Office Online, click Help, Project Help, or simply press F1. The Project Help pane appears; the Office Online links appear below the Assistance section (see Figure 1-16).

Figure 1-16. Press F1 to open the Project Help pane with its Office Online links.

> **Tip** **Turn off Office Online**
> If you don't want to use Office Online and want to go straight to the Project Guide content in the task pane, you can turn it off. Click Tools, Options and then click the General tab. Clear the Show Startup Task Pane check box.
>
> With this check box cleared, the task pane still appears whenever you start up Microsoft Project. However, the Project Guide will show instead of Office Online.

Working with the Project Guide

The Project Guide is the interactive interface element, introduced in Microsoft Project 2002, which helps you work through your project from the standpoint of project management processes and goals. The Project Guide complements the existing menus and toolbars, which allow you to approach your project plan from a strictly feature-oriented point of view.

The Project Guide resides in a pane on the left side of the screen that provides topics, instructions, and controls that assist your current work in your plan (see Figure 1-17). The Project Guide takes note of your current view and your current activities and presents a list of relevant topics and tools.

For example, while you're working in the Gantt Chart, the Project Guide displays the Tasks guide, which contains topics directly related to entering and scheduling tasks. If you then switch to a resource view, the Project Guide displays the Resources guide, now presenting topics and controls related to entering and assigning resources. There are also groups of topics for tracking and reporting.

Helping to control the Project Guide is the Project Guide toolbar just above the Project Guide pane. Use the buttons on this toolbar to display any Project Guide list or topic you want to see. You can view the Tasks, Resources, Track, or Report lists; display any topic on those lists; and toggle the display of the Project Guide pane on or off.

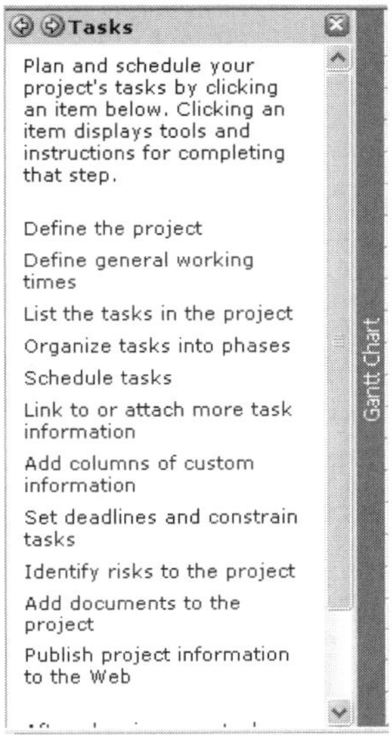

Figure 1-17. The Project Guide is on the left side of the screen.

When you click a topic in the Project Guide, you might find concise text about how to carry out the activity. Or you might click a control in the Project Guide, and the activity is done for you on the spot.

Troubleshooting

The Project Guide toolbar is not available

By default, the Project Guide and its toolbar are showing. You can close the Project Guide pane using the Close button and open it when you need it by clicking any of the buttons on the Project Guide toolbar.

If the Project Guide toolbar is hidden, you can add it back. Click View, Toolbars, Project Guide.

If the Project Guide toolbar is not listed on the Toolbars menu, the Project Guide has been completely turned off. Click Tools, Options and then click the Interface tab. Under Project Guide Settings, select the Display Project Guide check box.

NEW FEATURE! In Microsoft Project 2003, the Project Guide has an enhanced reporting section. The Project Guide now includes steps and controls for setting up your project to view specific types of information, such as critical tasks, risks and issues, resource allocation, project costs, and more.

Show/ Hide Project Guide

Tip Temporarily turn off the Project Guide

If you're concerned about the real estate that the Project Guide is taking up on your screen, you can temporarily turn the Project Guide off and then turn it on again whenever you like. Click the Close button in the Project Guide pane or click the Show/Hide Project Guide button on the Project Guide toolbar. When you want it back, click the button again.

The Project Guide also includes wizards to help automate certain processes. With a wizard, the Project Guide asks you specific questions about the activity you want to carry out. As you answer the questions, the wizard pulls together your answers and executes the task automatically, without your having to search and complete the appropriate dialog boxes in the appropriate views. The following is a list of Project Guide wizards:

Define The Project Wizard. Helps you create a new project plan, either from scratch or from an existing template (see Figure 1-18). This wizard integrates all the tasks you need to create a new project: entering basic project information, setting team collaboration options, adding supporting documentation, and saving the project file.

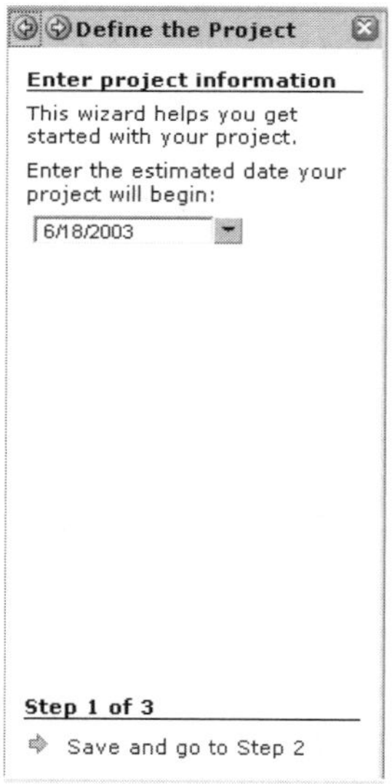

Figure 1-18. Start creating your plan with the Define The Project Wizard.

Project Working Times Wizard. Simplifies the methods of specifying and changing working days and hours, nonworking days and hours, and time units. You can use the Project Working Times Wizard for the project as a whole, in alternative calendars such as a weekend shift, and for specific resources.

Setup Tracking Wizard. Determines how you collect and enter progress information about tasks. Based on the information you provide, the Setup Tracking Wizard designs a tracking view for your specific purposes.

Print Current View Wizard. Sets up the current view to be printed the way you want. You can specify the length of the view to be printed as a report, preview the view as it will be printed, change the dimensions of the report, and modify the content to be included. You can also set the header, footer, and legend for the view.

> **Tip** **Permanently turn off the Project Guide**
> If you don't want to use the Project Guide at all, you can turn it off so it doesn't appear when you start Microsoft Project. Click Tools, Options and then click the Interface tab. Clear the Display Project Guide check box. The Project Guide and its toolbar are hidden. The Project Guide no longer opens when you start up Microsoft Project, and the Project Guide toolbar is not even listed on the Toolbars menu.

Getting Help

You can find Help topics to assist you with your project plan. A large set of Help topics is installed and available on your local computer. Another set of Help topics and other forms of assistance are available on the Web through Office Online. You can do the following:

- Search for topics using key words or phrases.
- Browse the Help table of contents.
- Work through Microsoft Project training modules.
- Join and ask questions from a Microsoft Project community.
- Download Microsoft Project resources, including project plan templates.

Search for a Specific Topic

NEW FEATURE!

Rather than going through a particular structure of ordered goals and topics, it's often faster to just ask a direct question and get a direct answer. If you prefer to get your Help that way, do a search as follows:

1. Open Microsoft Project.
2. On the Standard toolbar, click Project Help.

   Project Help

   The Project Help window appears in the task pane.
3. In the Search For box, type your word, phrase, or question, and then press Enter.
4. Review the list of topics that appears in the Search Results pane, and click the one that matches what you're looking for.

   The Project Help topic window appears in its own pane, separate from the task pane (see Figure 1-19).

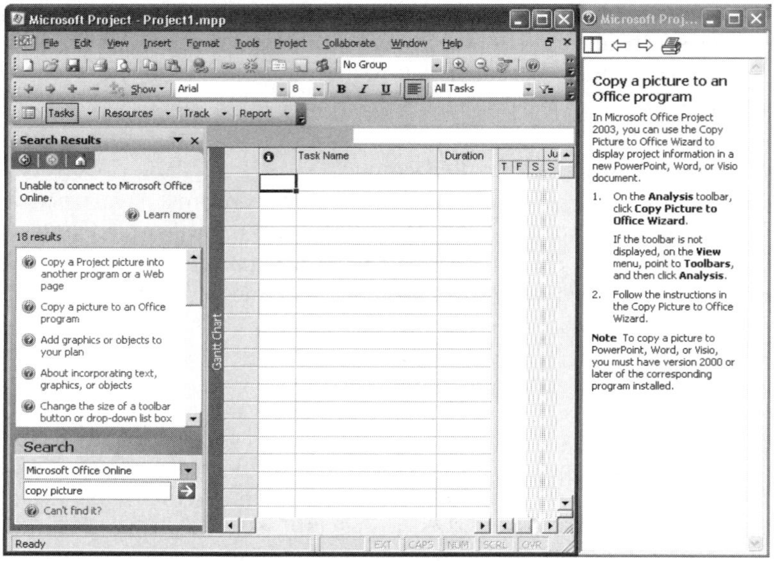

Figure 1-19. The Search Results pane remains in the task pane, whereas the Help pane on the right displays the selected topic.

5. If you want to review a different Help topic, click it in the Search Results pane on the left.

   The Help pane on the right changes to display the new topic.

> **Tip** **Ask a question**
>
> Instead of using the Search For box in the Office Online pane, you can get help from the Type A Question For Help box in the upper-right corner of the Microsoft Project window. Type your question in the box and then press Enter. The Search Results pane appears with a list of related Help topics. Searching for Help this way is especially useful if you don't keep the task pane open on a regular basis.
>
> 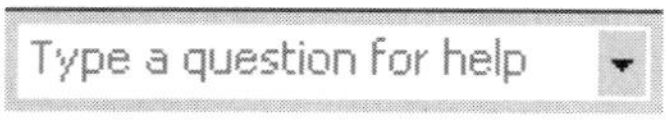
>

If you're connected to the Internet, you can expand your keyword search to Help available on Office Online, as follows:

1. At the bottom of the Search Results pane, under Search, click Microsoft Office Online, or Assistance.

Start Searching

2. Make sure your key word or phrase appears in the second box; then press Enter or click the Start Searching button.

   Microsoft Project searches for related topics on Office Online on the Web. Any topics found, either on the Web or locally on your computer, appear in the Search Results pane. As usual, click a topic name to view it in the Project Help pane.

Troubleshooting

The Help pane is covering your Project view

When you click a Help topic in the task pane, the Project Help topic window appears in a separate pane, which should dock on the right side of the Microsoft Project workspace. However, it's possible that the Help pane might float in the middle of your Project workspace.

If this happens, drag the Help pane's title bar to the right edge of the Microsoft Project window until it docks. The Microsoft Project workspace resizes itself to accommodate the Help pane. Every time you launch Project Help thereafter, the Help pane should appear neatly as the right pane.

Browsing Help Contents

NEW FEATURE!

1. With Microsoft Project open, click Project Help on the Standard toolbar.
   The Project Help window appears in the task pane.
2. In the Assistance section, click Table Of Contents.
   The Help Table Of Contents appears in the task pane (see Figure 1-20).

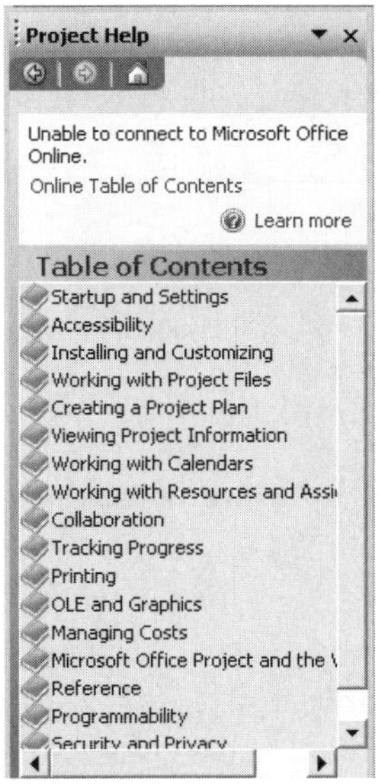

Figure 1-20. Use the Help Table Of Contents to browse through a logical sequence of related Help topics.

Book

3. Click a book link to open that category.

Question mark

4. Click a question mark link to view the Help topic.

   The Project Help topic window appears in its own pane and displays the Help topic you clicked.

Tip **Press F1 to launch Project Help**
In addition to clicking the Project Help button on the Standard toolbar, you can launch the Project Help pane by simply pressing F1. You can also click Help, Project Help.

If your computer is connected to the Internet, and if you want to see any recent additions to Help, click Online Table Of Contents in the Project Help pane on the left.

Inside Out

Goal-based Help has disappeared

In the effort to march to the Microsoft Office drumbeat, Microsoft Project Help has lost the goal-based Help that was a showpiece for Project 2000 and Project 2002. That Help structure laid out topics according to specific project management–oriented goals. The Help Table of Contents in Project 2003 is rather less prescriptive. You have better luck when you know what you're looking for.

The good news is some of that project management information and process guidance is being made available through articles on Office Online. Enter searches or look at the online Table of Contents to find the broader-based Web articles about Microsoft Project and project-management solutions.

Getting Help for Project Fields

There is a Help topic for each and every field in Microsoft Project. One way to find such topics is from the Help Table Of Contents, as follows:

1. On the Standard toolbar, click Project Help.
2. In the Assistance section of the Project Help pane, click Table Of Contents.
3. Click the Reference book link.
4. Click the Fields Reference book link.

   Categories of fields appear as topics.
5. Click a category you want and then click the field you want to learn more about.

   Each field reference topic includes best uses, examples, calculations if applicable, and any special notes to be aware of when working with this field.

You can also open a field reference Help topic if the field is showing in a table. Rest your mouse pointer over the column heading for a field. A ToolTip appears, indicating the name of the field as a link (see Figure 1-21). Click the field name link. The Help topic for that field appears.

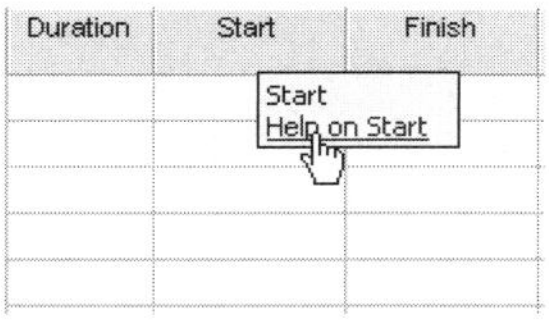

Figure 1-21. Click a field's ToolTip to launch the field's reference topic.

Getting Help for Dialog Boxes

There is a Help topic for many of the more complex dialog boxes in Microsoft Project. One way to find such topics is from the Help Table Of Contents, as follows:

1. On the Standard toolbar, click Project Help.
2. In the Assistance section of the Project Help pane, click Table Of Contents.
3. Click the Reference book link.
4. Click the Dialog Box Reference book link.

   The dialog boxes are listed in alphabetical order. Each dialog box reference topic includes steps on how to open the dialog box, and contains descriptions of each field and control in the dialog box.

NEW FEATURE!

You can also open a dialog box reference Help topic if you already opened the dialog box. Many dialog boxes include a Help button. Click that Help button and the topic for that dialog box appears.

Surfing the Web for Project Assistance

If you're connected to the Internet, use Office Online to browse for more information about Microsoft Project. To do this:

1. Open Microsoft Project and make sure your computer is connected to the Internet.
2. On the Standard toolbar, click Project Help.
3. In the Project Help pane, click Assistance.

   If necessary, your Web browser is launched, and the Microsoft Office Assistance Web site appears.
4. Under Browse Assistance, click Project 2003.

   The Project Assistance Web page appears (see Figure 1-22).

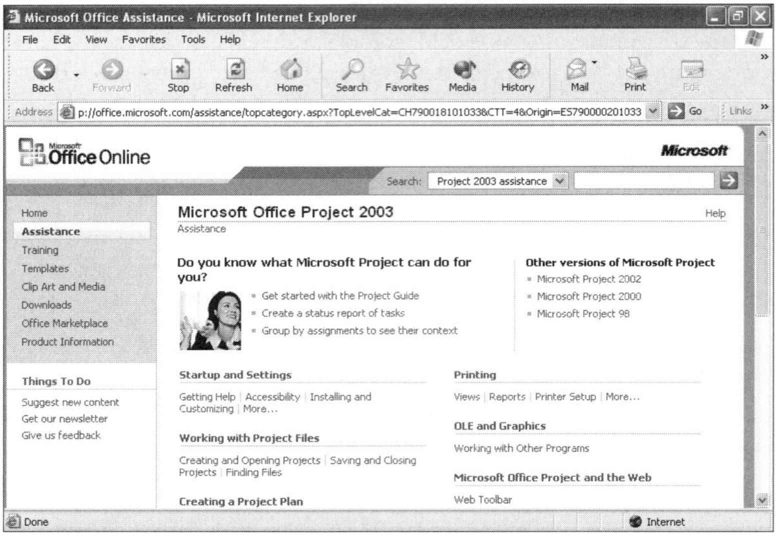

Figure 1-22. Use the Project Assistance page to browse through articles about various aspects of Microsoft Project.

Some articles are step-by-step instructions. Other articles have conceptual information about Microsoft Project features. Still others provide advice about project management solutions using Microsoft Project. There is also access to information in the Microsoft Project Knowledge Base and Microsoft TechNet.

Teaching Yourself Microsoft Project and Project Management

NEW FEATURE!

Web-based online training for Microsoft Project is now available. These training modules include text instructions along with graphics and voiceover. If you're connected to the Internet, use Office Online to browse for your Microsoft Project training options. Where applicable, training modules appear in your Search Results pane.

To browse Web training, do the following:

1. Open Microsoft Project and make sure your computer is connected to the Internet.
2. On the Standard toolbar, click Project Help.
3. In the Project Help pane, click Training.

   If necessary, your Web browser is launched, and the Microsoft Office Training Home page appears.
4. Under Browse Training Courses, click Microsoft Project.

   The Project Courses Training page appears, showing the list of training courses, their estimated length, and current user rating.

5 Click the training module, or course, you want to use, and it starts up, showing the course goals and other information about the course. The course narration begins as well.

6 Click Next to navigate to each succeeding page in the course.

Joining Project Communities

NEW FEATURE!

It's often easiest to learn from your more experienced buddies. A built-in group of knowledgeable friends willing to help can be found in Microsoft Project communities. Use your Internet connection and Office Online to find the Microsoft Project community that can help you find answers to your questions and also learn from questions posed by other users. To find and join a Microsoft Project community:

1 Open Microsoft Project and make sure your computer is connected to the Internet.

2 On the Standard toolbar, click Project Help.

3 Click Communities.

The Microsoft Newsgroups Web site appears in your Web browser.

4 In the left pane, click the plus sign next to Microsoft Project.

5 Click the type of community, or newsgroup, you're interested in.

Choices include General Questions, Professional And Server, Standard And Server, and Programming.

6 Review the newsgroup topics and click any that you're interested in (see Figure 1-23).

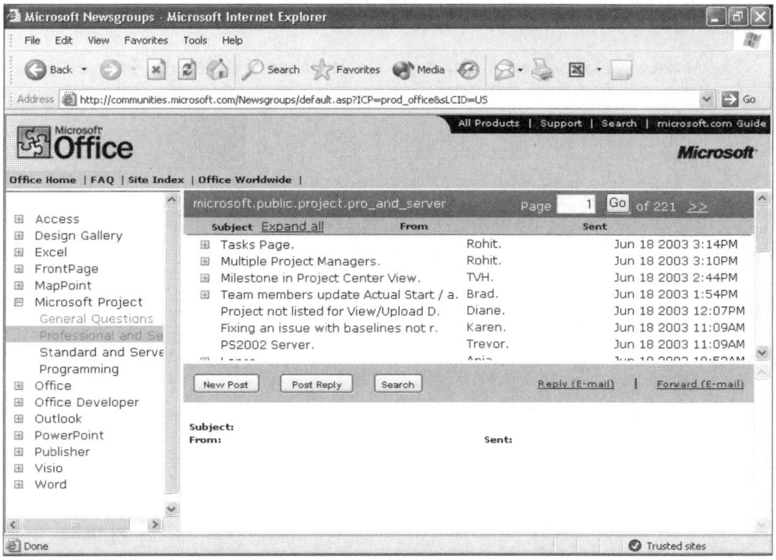

Figure 1-23. The Project newsgroups represent a community of Project users and experts who ask and answer questions.

7 To see whether your question has been asked (and answered) previously, click Search.

It's a great idea to do this before posting a new question, especially if you're new to this newsgroup.

8 If you don't find anything in the archives about your question, click the New Post button and enter and post your question to the newsgroup.

You'll soon find that you're knowledgeable enough to answer others' questions. To reply to an existing question, click the Post Reply button. Enter your answer and post it to the newsgroup.

Finding Project Downloads

NEW FEATURE! Templates, clip art, and other resources are available on Office Online. More downloadable resources are being added all the time. To find and download resources available on the Web:

1 Open Microsoft Project and make sure your computer is connected to the Internet.
2 On the Standard toolbar, click Project Help.
3 Click Downloads.

The Downloads Home page appears in your Web browser.

4 Browse for any Microsoft Project downloads you might be interested in.
5 If you're interested in downloading a Microsoft Project template, click Templates in the left pane of the Downloads page.
6 In the Templates Home page, under Meetings And Projects, click Project Management.

A set of project management templates is listed (see Figure 1-24).

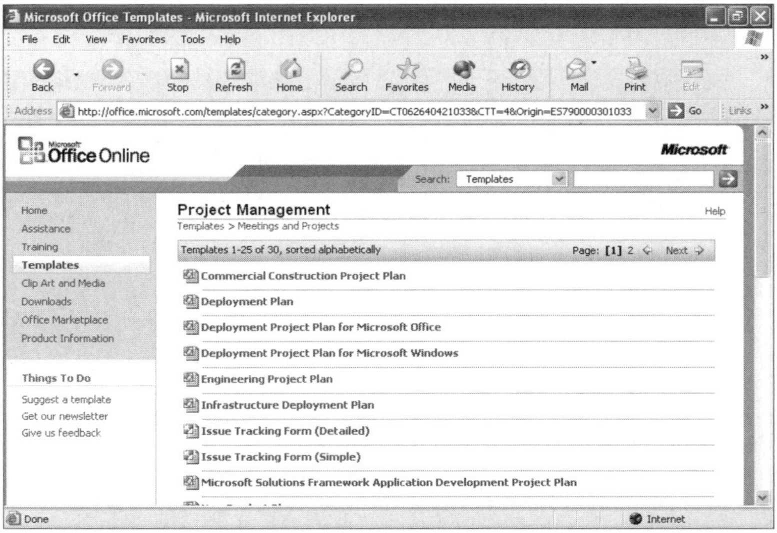

Figure 1-24. Templates marked with the Microsoft Project logo can be downloaded and instantly deployed in Microsoft Project on your desktop.

7 Click a template to see what it looks like.

8 If you like the looks of a template, click Download Now. Follow the steps to copy the template onto your hard drive.

For more information about working with Microsoft Project templates, see "Working with Project Templates" on page 851.

Setting Your Preferences for Project Assistance

NEW FEATURE!

You can set up how you want to obtain your assistance from Office Online. To set these assistance options:

1 On the Standard toolbar, click Project Help.

2 In the Project Help pane, under See Also, click Online Content Settings.

The Service Options dialog box appears (see Figure 1-25).

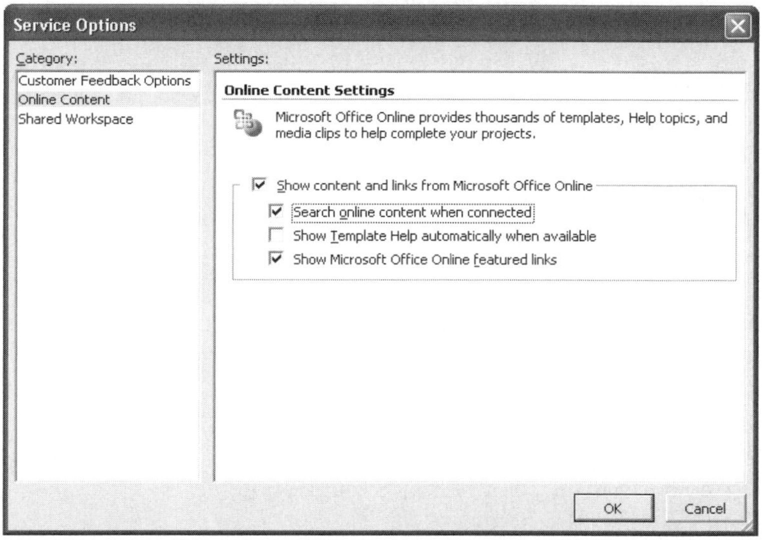

Figure 1-25. Use the Service Options dialog box to set your assistance options, as well as your customer feedback preferences.

3 Review the settings, which indicate whether and what kind of information you want delivered from the Office Online Web site.

4 Select the settings you want, and clear the ones you don't.

5 When finished, click OK.

Note These settings, which apply to all Microsoft Office products, will take effect the next time you open any Office product.

Reporting Crashes

NEW FEATURE! When Microsoft Project experiences a problem and crashes, a message appears, asking whether you want to send information about the malfunction to Microsoft developers. This feature was introduced with Microsoft Project 2002. New with Microsoft Project 2003 is the integration of the more confusing errors with appropriate Help content. In some cases, there are links to Knowledge Base articles for more information.

For more information about Microsoft Project crash reporting, see "Responding to a Microsoft Project Problem" on page 877.

Working with Project Smart Tags

When you make certain types of adjustments to your project plan, Microsoft Project can present Smart Tag indicators with option buttons (see Figure 1-26). These Smart Tags specify the action you've just taken, along with any possible implications that action might have. You get information, especially in certain ambiguous situations, to make sure that the result is really your intention. You also see options to switch to a different action if your intention was for a different outcome.

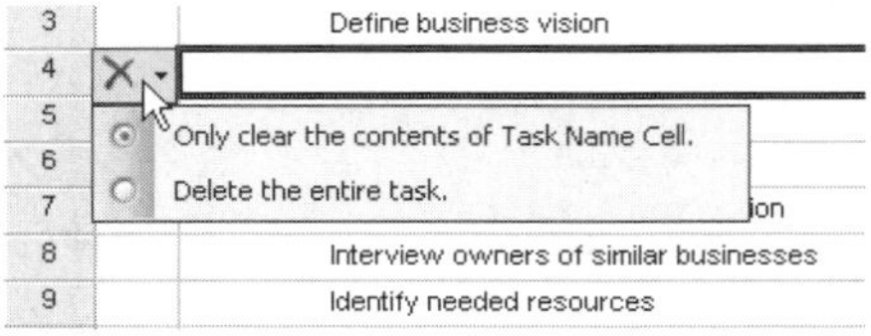

Figure 1-26. A Smart Tag is first marked with a triangle marker in the affected cell. When you move your mouse pointer over the marker, the Smart Tag indicator appears. Click the indicator, and the options appear.

There are four areas in which indicators and option buttons might appear:

- Adding, changing, or removing resource assignments
- Changing start or finish dates
- Editing work, duration, or units
- Deleting a task or resource in the Name column

The indicator appears in the cell as long as the edit is available for an Undo operation. After you make a new edit, the indicator disappears.

Unlike Microsoft Office Smart Tags, you can't change or create your own feedback messages in Microsoft Project.

You can turn off the display of indicators and option buttons. Click Tools, Options and then click the Interface tab. Under Show Indicators And Options Buttons For, clear the check boxes for the category of changes for which you don't need indicators.

Working with the Sample Database

NEW FEATURE!

If you're working with enterprise features in Microsoft Project Professional and Project Server, you can use the new sample database to experiment and evaluate features. The sample database contains the following elements:

- Projects
- Tasks
- Resources
- Assignments
- Views
- Enterprise global settings
- Issues
- Document libraries
- Custom Project Guide

Use the sample database to train project managers, team members, and other stakeholders in your organization on the effective use of your implementation of Microsoft Project without having to use live project data.

Chapter 2

Understanding Projects and Project Management

You use a word processing program to create a text document. You use a spreadsheet program to calculate sales data. You use a publishing program to design and lay out a brochure. In these cases, the application helps you create the end result.

With Microsoft Office Project 2003, this isn't so. Although Project 2003 helps you create a *project plan*, the actual project is being executed by you and your team, who are carrying out the tasks to fulfill the overarching goals of the project. It's up to you to track and control the actual project, using the project plan as your essential road map. When effectively maintained, the project plan is a model providing an accurate picture of what's currently going on in your project, what has happened in the past, and what will happen in the future.

This chapter describes project basics and the phases of the project management process. It also outlines how Microsoft Project fits into the world of your project. You'll understand how you can use Microsoft Project as your project information system; that is, the essential tool for modeling your project and helping you efficiently and successfully manage it.

If you're new to project management, read this entire chapter. If you're an experienced project manager but new to Microsoft Project, skip ahead to "Facilitating Your Project with Microsoft Project" later in this chapter on page 45.

Understanding Project Management Basics

Although it might overlap with other types of management, project management is a specific management process.

What Is a Project?

There are two types of work performed by organizations: operations and projects. An *operation* is a series of tasks that are routine, repetitive, and ongoing throughout the life of the organization. Operations are typically necessary to sustain the business. Examples of operations are accounts receivable, employee performance reviews, and shipping and receiving. Employee performance reviews might take place every six months, for example, and although the names and circumstances of employees and supervisors might change, the process of preparing and conducting employee reviews is always the same. In addition, it's expected that there will continue to be employee reviews throughout the life of the organization.

On the other hand, *projects* are not routine or ongoing. That is, projects are unique and temporary and are often implemented to fulfill a strategic goal of the organization. A project is a series of tasks that will culminate in the creation or completion of some new initiative, product, or activity by a specific end date. Some project examples include an office move, a new product launch, the construction of a building, and a political campaign. It is never the same project twice—for example, this year's product launch is different from last year's product launch. There's a specific end date in mind for the launch, after which the project will be considered complete. After the project is complete, a new and unique product will be on the market.

Projects come in all sizes. One project might consist of 100 tasks; another, 10,000. One project might be implemented by a single resource; another by 500. One project might take two months to complete; another might take 10 years. There can be projects within projects, linked together with a master project consolidating them all. These subprojects, however, are all unique and temporary, and all have a specific outcome and end date.

What Is Project Management?

Project management is the coordinating effort to fulfill the goals of the project. The *project manager*, as the leader of the project team, is responsible for this effort and its ultimate result. Project managers use knowledge, skills, tools, and methodologies to do the following:

- Identify the goals, objectives, requirements, and limitations of the project.
- Coordinate the different needs and expectations of the various project stakeholders, including team members, resource managers, senior management, customers, and sponsors.
- Plan, execute, and control the tasks, phases, and deliverables of the project based on the identified project goals and objectives.
- Close the project when completed and capture the knowledge accrued.

Project managers are also responsible for balancing and integrating competing demands to implement all aspects of the project successfully, as follows:

Project scope. Specifying the specific work to be done for the project.

Project time. Setting the finish date of the project as well as any interim deadlines for phases, milestones, and deliverables.

Project cost. Calculating and tracking the project costs and budget.

Project human resources. Signing on the team members who will carry out the tasks of the project.

Project procurement. Acquiring the material and equipment resources with which to carry out project tasks.

Project communication. Conveying assignments, updates, reports, and other information with team members and other stakeholders.

Project quality. Identifying the acceptable level of quality for the project goals and objectives.

Project risk. Analyzing potential project risks and response planning.

Inside Out

Microsoft Project and the project management disciplines

Microsoft Project supports many, but not all, of the management areas associated with project management. For example, it provides only minimal support for project procurement and project quality.

The solution is to combine Microsoft Project with other tools and resources. Use Microsoft Project to provide the initial information you need. Then draw upon other tools and resources as needed to more fully handle responsibilities specifically associated with procurement or quality. Finally, come full circle with Microsoft Project by adding notes to tasks or resources, inserting related documents, or linking to other locations.

For example, use Microsoft Project to help estimate your initial equipment and material resource requirements. Work through your organization's procurement process and compile the relevant data. Add notes to the resources or tasks in your project plan, making the information easy to reference. Use a tool such as Microsoft Excel, or another program especially designed for this purpose, to help track the depletion of materials to the point where reorder becomes necessary. Even though Microsoft Project can't manage every aspect of your project, it can still be the repository for all related information.

Balancing scope, time, and money is often among the biggest responsibilities of the project manager (see Figure 2-1).

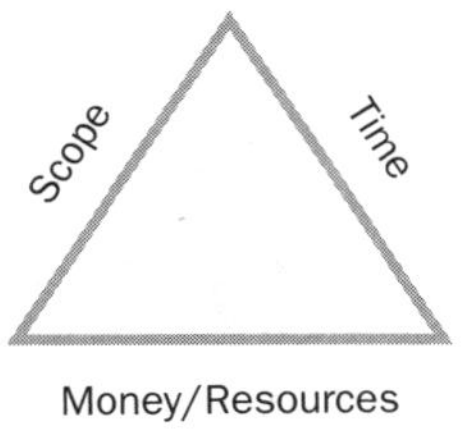

Figure 2-1. The project triangle is an effective model for thinking about your project's priorities.

If you increase the scope, the time or money side of the triangle will also be increased. If you need to reduce time, that is, bring in the project finish date, you might need to decrease the scope or increase the cost through the addition of resources.

Note There's some debate about how to accurately describe the key controlling elements that make up a project. Some believe that it's best described as a triangle—the three sides representing time, money, and resources. Others say that it's a square—with scope, time, money, and resources being the four sides, each one affecting the others. This book approaches money and resources as synonymous in this context because resources cost money. Adding resources adds money, and the only thing you'd need more money for would be resources. So in this book, the project is conceptualized as a triangle with the three sides being scope, time, and money/resources.

For information about working with the project triangle to help control your project, see Chapter 11, "Responding to Changes in Your Project."

Project Management Practices: Balancing and Integrating Competing Demands

Depending on the priorities and standards set for your project and by your organization, certain demands carry more weight than others in your project. Knowing these priorities and standards will help you make sound decisions about the project as issues arise. Although scope, time, and cost tend to be the most prevalent demands, the following is the full list of project controls:

- Scope
- Human resources
- Quality
- Time
- Procurement
- Risk
- Cost
- Communications

Understanding Project Management Processes

It might seem daunting when you realize that, as a project manager, you're responsible for such a tremendous balancing act. However, this responsibility can be broken down into four manageable processes:

1. Initiating and planning the project
2. Executing the project
3. Controlling the project
4. Closing the project

Most of the chapters in this book are structured with these four processes in mind. For each process, you use Microsoft Project in specific ways. There are also standard project management practices related to planning, executing, controlling, and closing the project. Throughout this book, the Microsoft Project procedures and project management practices are described in the context of the relevant project process.

Project Management Processes

These are the four processes of project management, as well as the key elements within each process:

- Initiating and planning the project:
  Examine the big picture
  Identify the project's milestones, deliverables, and tasks
  Develop and refine the project schedule
  Identify skills, equipment, and materials needed
- Executing the project:
  Have assigned resources execute the project
  Save a baseline plan for comparison
  Track progress on tasks
- Controlling the project:
  Analyze project information
  Communicate and report
- Closing the project:
  Identify lessons learned
  Create a project template

Planning the Project

You're ready to begin the planning process after an authoritative stakeholder has decided to implement this project with you as the project manager. The outcome of this planning process will be a workable project plan and a team ready to start working the project. When planning the project, do the following:

Look at the big picture. Before you get too far into the nuts and bolts of planning, you need a comprehensive vision of where you're going with your project. You shape this vision by first identifying the project goals and objectives. This practice helps you set the scope of the project. You learn the expectations, limitations, and assumptions for this project, and they all go into the mix. You also identify possible risks and contingency plans for the project.

Identify the project's milestones, deliverables, and tasks. Subdivide the project into its component tasks and then organize and sequence the tasks to accurately reflect the project scope.

Develop and refine the project schedule. To turn the task list into a workable project schedule, specify task durations and relate tasks to each other. You can create task dependencies, that is, a model of how the start of one task depends on the completion of another task, for example. If you have any specific dates for deliverables, you can enter them as deadlines, or if really necessary, task constraints. At that point, Microsoft Project can start to calculate a realistic schedule for tasks in particular and the project as a whole. With this plan, you can accurately forecast the scope, schedule, and budget for the project. You can also determine which resources are needed, how many, and at what time.

Identify skills, equipment, and materials needed. After the tasks are identified, you can determine the skills, equipment, and materials needed to carry out the work for those tasks. You obtain the needed resources and assign them to the appropriate tasks. You can now calculate when the project can be completed and how much it will cost. If it looks like you're exceeding the allowable deadline or budget, you can make the necessary adjustments.

For more detailed information about planning the project, see the chapters in Part 2, "Developing the Project Plan."

Executing the Project

The second project management process is execution. At this point, you have your project plan in hand. The tasks are scheduled and the resources are assigned. Everyone's at the starting gate waiting for you to say "Go!"

You give the word, and the project moves from planning to the execution and controlling process. In the course of executing the project, you perform the following:

Save a baseline plan for comparison. To get good tracking information, keep a copy of certain project plan information on hand so you can compare your plan to actual progress as the project moves along.

Monitor the resources as they carry out their assigned tasks. As the project manager, you keep an eye on their progress in completing their tasks.

Track task progress. You can track progress in terms of percent complete, how long a task takes from beginning to end, or how many hours a resource spends on a task. As you gather this information, you can see whether tasks and milestones will finish on time. You can also gather information about costs of resources, tasks, and the project as a whole.

For more information about tracking progress, see Chapter 10, "Saving a Baseline and Updating Progress."

Controlling the Project

While your project team is executing the tasks, you're making sure that the project stays within the prescribed deadline and budget while maintaining the scope outlined in the project goals. In project management, this process is referred to as "controlling the project." In the controlling process, you monitor all task activities, compare the plan to actual progress, and make adjustments as needed. To control the project, you do the following:

Analyze project information. Analyze the information you're gathering and use this analysis to solve problems and make decisions. Often, you need to decide how to recover a slipped schedule or a budget overrun. Sometimes, you're in the happy position of deciding what to do with extra time or money.

For more information about controlling the project, see Chapter 11.

Communicate and report. Throughout the execution of the project, you will be in constant communication with your team members and other stakeholders. You need to keep upper management, customers, and other stakeholders informed of any potential problems, new decisions, and your overall progress.

For more informaiton about views and reports, see Chapter 12, "Reporting Project Information."

Closing the Project

In the final process of the project, you have successfully fulfilled the goals of the project and it's now complete. Before you move on to the next project, it's a good idea to capture the knowledge you gained from this one. When closing the project, you do the following:

Identify lessons learned. Work with your project team and conduct a "postmortem" meeting to learn what went well and what could be improved.

Create a project template. Save the project plan along with tasks, duration metrics, task relationships, resource skills, and the like, so the next time you or someone else manages a similar project, your wheel will not need to be reinvented.

For more information about closing the project, see Chapter 28, "Standardizing Projects Using Templates."

Facilitating Your Project with Microsoft Project

Because a project involves a myriad of tasks, resources, assignments, dates, and more, it's clear that you need some kind of tool to help you keep track of the details. By using a spreadsheet or word processing program, you could create a table that lists your tasks, durations, start and finish dates, and assigned resources. In fact, that might very well get you started. But it's likely that you'll end up working harder than you have to in an attempt to make the tool work right. Such a table would not be able to perform the following functions:

- Calculate the start and finish dates for you.
- Indicate whether assigned resources are actually available.
- Inform you if assigned resources are underallocated or overworked.

- Alert you if you have an upcoming deadline.
- Calculate how much of the budget you've spent so far.
- Draw your project tasks as a Gantt chart or network diagram so you can get a visual picture of your project.

To do this and more, you can create a similar table in Microsoft Project. You can then use the project database, schedule calculation, and charting capabilities to help facilitate your project management processes (see Figure 2-2).

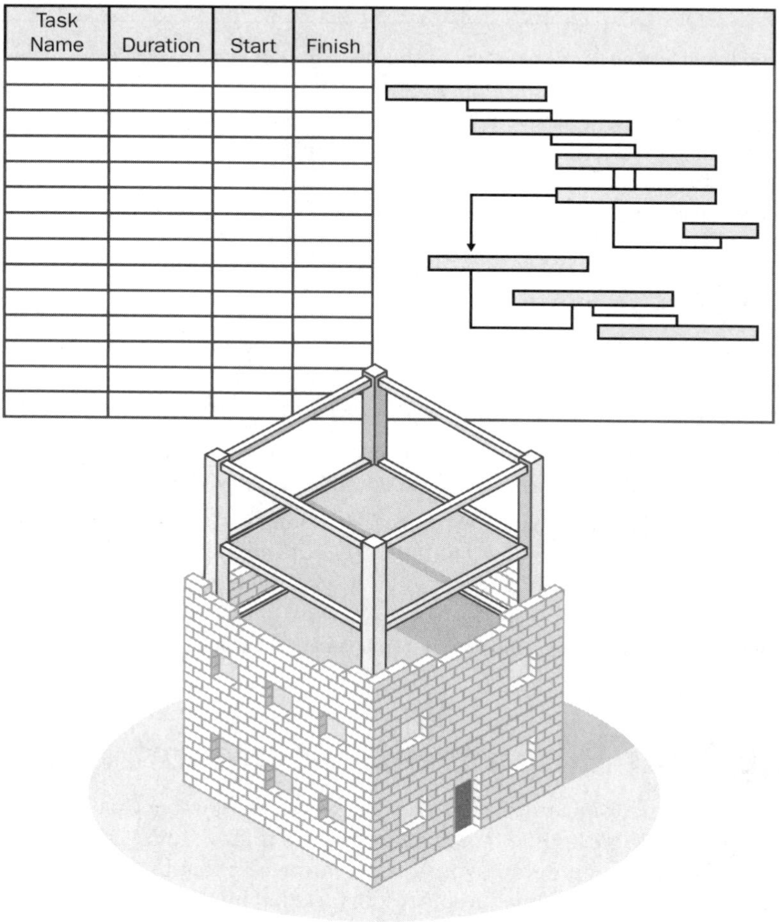

Figure 2-2. The project plan helps you manage your project.

Although Microsoft Project can't negotiate a more reasonable finish date, it can help you determine what you have to sacrifice to make that date. Although Microsoft Project won't complete a difficult and time-consuming task for your team, it will help you find extra time in the schedule or additional resources for that task. And although Microsoft Project can't motivate an uninspired team member, it can tell you if that team member is working on critical tasks that will affect the finish date of the entire project.

In short, Microsoft Project can help you facilitate all processes in the project management life cycle, from developing your scope, modeling your project schedule, and tracking and communicating progress to saving knowledge gained from the closed project. Furthermore, with Microsoft Office Project Professional 2003, project management standards can be established and disseminated throughout your enterprise.

Creating a Model of Your Project

You can use Microsoft Project to create a model, or blueprint, of your project. This model reflects the reality of your project. You enter your tasks, resources, assignments, and other project-related information into Microsoft Project. You can then organize and manage the copious and very detailed bits of project information that otherwise can be quite overwhelming.

With all the necessary information stored in Microsoft Project, the exact project information you need at any given time is always available at your fingertips. You can manipulate and analyze this information in various ways to solve problems and make decisions to successfully manage the project. As you take action and move forward in your project, you update information in Microsoft Project so that it continues to reflect reality (see Figure 2-3).

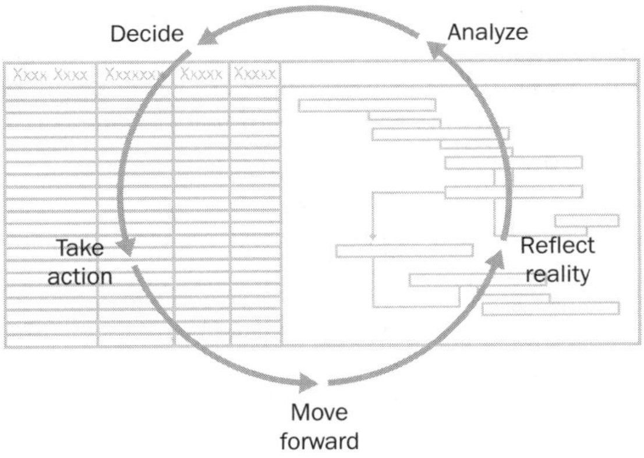

Figure 2-3. Model your project's reality.

Specifically, in the planning process, you use Microsoft Project to do the following:

Create your project phases, milestones, and task list. Microsoft Project uses your task list as the basis for the project database it creates for you. You can organize tasks within phases or subtasks within summary tasks so you can break your project down into manageable segments.

Estimate task durations. One task might take 2 hours to complete; another might take 4 days. Microsoft Project uses these durations to help build your schedule.

Link tasks with their appropriate relationships to other tasks. Often, a task cannot begin until a previous task has been completed. For example, for an office move project, you schedule the "Design office space" task before the "Order new furniture" task. The two tasks are linked because the second task cannot be done until the first task is complete. Microsoft Project uses these task relationships to build your schedule. The durations and task relationships are also shown in the Gantt Chart and Network Diagram views of your project.

Enter any imposed deadlines or other date constraints. If you know that you must be out of your current office space by the end of August, for example, you work with that date as one of the important constraints of your project. Microsoft Project schedules according to such constraints and informs you if there's a conflict between a constraint and the durations or task relationships you have also set.

Set up the resources and assign them to tasks. Not only does Microsoft Project keep track of which resources are assigned to which tasks, it also schedules work on assignments according to the resource's availability and lets you know if a resource is overloaded with more tasks than can be accomplished in the resource's available time.

Establish resource costs and task costs. You can specify hourly or monthly rates for resources. You can specify per-use costs for resources and other costs associated with tasks. Microsoft Project calculates and adds these costs, so you can get an accurate view of how much your project will cost to execute. You can often use this calculation as a basis for the project budget.

Adjust the plan to achieve a targeted finish date or budget amount. Suppose that your project plan initially shows a finish date that's two months later than required or a cost that's $10,000 more than the allocated budget. You can make adjustments to scope, schedule, cost, and resources in order to bring the project plan in line. While working through your inevitable project tradeoffs, Microsoft Project recalculates your schedule automatically until you have the result you need.

For more information about using Microsoft Project to plan your project, see the chapters in Part 2, "Developing the Project."

In the execution and control process of the project, use Microsoft Project to do the following:

Save the baseline plan. For comparison and tracking purposes, you need to take a snapshot of what you consider your baseline project plan. As you update task progress through the life of the project, you can compare current progress with your original plan. These comparisons provide valuable information about whether you're on track with the schedule and your budget.

Update actual task progress. With Microsoft Project, you can update task progress by entering percent complete, work complete, work remaining, and more. As you enter actual progress, the schedule is automatically recalculated.

Compare variances between planned and actual task information. Using the baseline information you saved, Microsoft Project presents various views to show your baseline against actual and scheduled progress, along with the resulting variances. For example, if your initial project plan shows that you had originally planned to finish a task on Thursday but the resource actually finished it on Monday, you'd have a variance of 3 days in your favor.

Review planned, actual, and scheduled costs. In addition to seeing task progress variances, you can compare baseline costs against actual and currently scheduled costs and see the resulting cost variances. Microsoft Project can also use your baseline and current schedule information for earned value calculations you can use for more detailed analyses.

Adjust the plan to respond to changes in scope, finish date, and budget. What if you get a directive in the middle of the project to cut $5,000 from your budget? Or what if you learn that you must bring the project in a month earlier to catch a vital marketing window? Even in the midst of a project, you can adjust scope, schedule, cost, and resources in your project plan. With each change you make, Microsoft Project recalculates your schedule automatically.

For more information about using Microsoft Project to track and control your project, see the chapters in Part 3, "Tracking Progress."

Report on progress, costs, resource utilization, and more. Using the database and calculation features of Microsoft Project, you can generate a number of built-in reports. For example, there are reports for project summary, milestones, tasks starting soon, overbudget tasks, resource to-do lists, and many more. You can modify built-in reports to suit your own needs or create custom reports entirely from scratch.

For more information about using Microsoft Project to report progress, see Chapter 12.

In the closing process of the project, use Microsoft Project to accomplish the following:

Capture actual task duration metrics. If you track task progress throughout the project, you end up with solid, tested data for how long certain tasks actually take.

Capture successful task sequencing. Sometimes, you're not sure at the outset of a project whether a task should be done sooner or later in the cycle. With the experience of the project behind you, you can see whether your sequencing worked well.

Save a template for the next project of this kind. Use your project plan as the boilerplate for the next project. You and other project managers will have a task list, milestones, deliverables, sequence, durations, and task relationships already in place that can be easily modified to fit the requirements of the new project.

For more information about using Microsoft Project to close a project and create templates, see Chapter 28.

You can also use Microsoft Project to work with multiple projects, and even show the task or resource links among them. In the course of modeling your project in this way, Microsoft Project serves as your project information system. Microsoft Project arranges the thousands of bits of information in various ways so you can work with it, analyze your data, and make decisions based on coherent and soundly calculated project management information. This project information system carries out three basic functions:

- It stores project information including tasks, resources, assignments, durations, task relationships, task sequences, calendars, and more.
- It calculates information including dates, schedules, costs, durations, critical path, earned value, variances, and more.

- It presents views of information you're retrieving. You can specify the views, tables, filters, groups, fields, or reports, depending on what aspect of your project model you need to see.

Project Management Terminology

The following is a list of project management–related terms:

Baseline. A snapshot of key project information for tasks, such as their start dates, finish dates, durations, and costs. With baseline information, you have a means of comparison against actual progress on tasks.

Date Constraint. A specific date associated with a specific task. A date constraint dictates that a task must be finished by a certain date, for example, or started no earlier than a certain date.

Deliverable. A tangible outcome, result, or item that must be produced to mark the completion of a project or a project phase. Often, the deliverable is subject to approval by the project sponsor or customer.

Dependency. The reliance of one task upon another. When one task cannot start or finish until a related task starts or finishes, the tasks are dependent upon one another, or related. Also referred to as a *task link* or *task relationship*.

Gantt Chart. A graphic representation of a project. The left half of a Gantt chart is a table listing task names and other task-related information. The right half of the Gantt chart is a bar chart along a timeline in which each bar represents a task, its start and finish date, and its duration. Links to other tasks can also be represented.

Milestone. A significant event in the project, often the completion of a major deliverable or phase. Milestones are represented as part of a project's task list.

Network Diagram. A graphic representation of a project, characterized by nodes representing tasks and link lines showing the relationship among the tasks. Also sometimes called a PERT (Program Evaluation and Review Technique) chart.

Phase. A grouping of tasks that represents a major stage in the life cycle of the project. The outcome of a phase is typically a major deliverable.

Scope. The specific work that needs to be done in a project to deliver the product or service.

Stakeholders. Individuals or organizations who have a vested interest in the outcome of the project and who can influence those project outcomes. Stakeholders include the project manager, members of the project team, the sponsoring organization, and customers.

Working with Your Team through Microsoft Project

In addition to helping you create your project plan, Microsoft Project helps with resource management, cost management, and team communications.

With Microsoft Project resource management features, you can perform the following tasks:

- Enter resources in the Microsoft Project resource list.
- Enter resources from your organization's e-mail address book, Active Directory, or Project Server accounts.
- Maintain a reusable pool of resources available across multiple projects.
- Specify skills required for a task, and have Microsoft Project search for available resources with those skills.
- Schedule tasks according to assigned resources' availability.
- Check for resource overload or underutilization and make adjustments accordingly.
- Book a proposed resource in your project (using Project Professional 2003).

For more information about managing resources, see Chapter 6, "Setting Up Resources in the Project," and Chapter 7, "Assigning Resources to Tasks."

With Microsoft Project's cost management features, you can do the following:

- Enter resource rates including multiple rates for different task types.
- Enter fixed costs for tasks.
- Estimate costs for the project while still in the planning process.
- Compare planned cost variances to actual cost variances.
- View cost totals for tasks, resources, phases, and the entire project.
- Analyze earned value calculations, including budgeted cost of work performed (BCWP), schedule variance (SV), and cost variance percent (CV%).

For more information about setting and managing costs, see Chapter 8, "Planning Resource and Task Costs," and Chapter 11. For information about working with earned value, see Chapter 13, "Analyzing Project Information."

Your communications requirements might be as simple as printing a Gantt chart or resource list for a weekly status meeting. Or, you might prefer to electronically exchange task updates with your resources every day and publish high-level project information to your company's intranet.

With Microsoft Project, you can communicate with others in just the way you need, as follows:

- Print a view as it looks on your screen.
- Generate and print a predesigned report.
- Create a custom view or report.
- Copy a project view as a static picture in another Microsoft Office application.
- Exchange task assignments, updates, and status reports with your team members through Microsoft Office Project Server 2003 and Microsoft Office Project Web Access 2003.

- Allow team leads to delegate tasks to other team members.
- Track issues and documents through Windows SharePoint Services, Project Server 2003, and Project Web Access 2003.
- Publish views or the entire project through Project Server and Project Web Access for review by team members, senior management, customers, and other stakeholders.

For more information about working with resources across an enterprise, see Chapter 22, "Managing with Project Professional and Project Server."

Using Microsoft Project in Your Enterprise

Through the use of Project Server, as accessed by Project Professional and Project Web Access, an entire portfolio of projects can be standardized across your enterprise. Numerous Microsoft Project elements, including views, filters, groups, fields, and formulas, can be designed and included in the enterprise global template that reflects your organization's specific project management methodology. This customization and design is done by a *project server administrator*. This project server administrator is the person who sets up and manages the installation of Microsoft Project for your organization. The project server administrator knows the requirements of project management and the features of Microsoft Project well enough to design custom solutions and is often a programmer or other information technology professional. The project server administrator might also be a technically oriented lead project manager.

When your project server administrator designs a common enterprise project template, all project managers in the organization can then work with the same customized project elements that support organizational initiatives. In addition, senior managers can review summary information from multiple projects throughout the organization.

The project server administrator also sets up the enterprise resource pool, which contains all the resources available to the enterprise, from which the various project managers can draw to staff their projects. The enterprise resource pool includes key resource information such as cost, availability, and skill set.

Some organizations might divide the duties between a project server administrator and *portfolio manager*. While the project server administrator can handle installation, server, network, and database issues, the portfolio manager can be responsible for designing custom project elements, managing the enterprise resource pool, and setting up users and permissions.

For more information about enterprise capabilities, see Part 7, "Managing Projects Across Your Enterprise."

Understanding Project Stakeholders

Every project has a set of stakeholders associated with it. *Project stakeholders* are individuals or organizations who are somehow connected to the project and can influence the project's outcome. As the project manager, you need to be able to work with different types of stakeholders in various ways. A stakeholder can do the following:

- Be actively involved in the work of the project.
- Exert influence over the project and its outcome (also known as *managing stakeholders*).
- Have a vested interest in the outcome of a project.

There are a variety of stakeholder categories, each supported in its own way by Microsoft Project. The categories are as follows:

Project manager. Microsoft Project directly supports the project manager with its scheduling, tracking, and communication capabilities.

Team members. The stakeholders executing the project are supported minimally through e-mail communication with their project manager. In a more comprehensive manner, team members are supported through Project Web Access, in which they can view their assigned tasks, send and receive task updates, send status reports, and review the project as a whole.

Team leads. Team leads can use Project Web Access to delegate and manage tasks.

Project resource manager. A resource manager might work in concert with the project manager to help acquire and maintain necessary resources. Through Project Web Access, a resource manager can analyze resource utilization information.

Senior managers, executives, or sponsors. People who lead the organization in implementing the project or supply the project budget or other resources can use Project Web Access to review high-level project summaries. In an enterprise environment, executives can review a summary comparing multiple projects being carried out throughout the organization. Such individuals are also known as managing stakeholders.

Inside Out

Project support for customers and end users

Other possible stakeholders include customers or end users. There's no direct Microsoft Project support for such stakeholders. However, you can provide them with Project Web Access or periodically publish a view designed for them on a Web site.

For more information about Project Web Access, see Chapters 23 and 24. For more information about publishing project information, see Chapter 12.

Managing stakeholders can influence the planning processes of a project and help set the expectations and assumptions of the project. Sometimes the expectations of different stakeholders conflict with one other. It's the job of the project manager to balance and reconcile these conflicts well before project execution begins.

Managing stakeholders might also impose new requirements that require adjustments to the finish date, budget, or scope. Even if this happens in the midst of execution, you can use Microsoft Project to make adjustments responding to the new demands.

Keys to Successful Project Management

Being well-versed in project management processes and using a powerful tool such as Microsoft Project puts you well ahead in the project management game. For an even greater edge toward a successful project, follow these guidelines:

Develop the goals and objectives. Know the overarching goals as well as the specific, measurable objectives of your project. They are your guiding principles.

Learn the scope. Know the scope (including tasks, quality, and deliverables) of your project and exactly what is expected of it. The scope includes how much you're doing (quantity) and how well you're doing it (quality).

Know your deadlines. Find out any deadlines—final as well as interim milestone and deliverable deadlines. If these deadlines are up to you to suggest, lucky you. But often this isn't your luxury. Often, you might propose one reasonable date only to have upper management or your customers suggest another, not-so-reasonable date. The sooner you learn about these dates, the better you can plan for them by adjusting the scope, the budget, and the resources.

Know your budget. If the project finish date is not your limitation, the budget might very well be. Again, it might be up to you to tell upper management how much the proposed project will cost. But it's also likely that the budget will be imposed upon you, and you'll need to be able to fulfill the goals of the project within a specific and unrelenting dollar amount. Again, the sooner you know the real budget of the project, the more realistic and accurate your plan can be. You can adjust scope, time, and resources in order to meet the budget.

Find the best resources. Gather input about who the best candidates for certain tasks are so you can get the best resources. Although the more experienced resources will likely be more expensive, they'll also be more likely to complete tasks more quickly and with a higher level of quality (likewise with equipment or consumable material resources.) Determine the acceptable level of quality for the project, balance this determination with your budget constraints, and procure the best you can get.

Enter accurate project information. You can enter tasks and durations, link them together, and assign them to resources, making it seem like you have a real project plan. But suppose the data you entered doesn't reflect the real tasks that will be done, how much time resources will really be spending on these tasks, and what needs to be done before each task can start. Then all you have is a bunch of characters and graphics on a screen or in an impressive-looking report. You don't have a project plan at all. The "garbage-in, garbage-out" maxim applies. As you're planning the project, draw upon previous experience with a similar type of project. Solicit input from resources already earmarked for the project—they can provide excellent information about which tasks need to be done, how long they take, and how tasks relate to each other.

Adjust the project plan to meet requirements. Look at the plan's calculated finish date and the total cost. See if they match your limitations for project deadline or budget. If they do not, make the necessary adjustments. This must all be done before you actually start the project—probably even before you show the project plan to any of your managing stakeholders.

Save a baseline and go. After you have a project plan that solidly reflects reality, take a "snapshot" of the plan and begin project execution. This snapshot, which is called the baseline, is the means for determining whether you're on track and how far you might have strayed if you need to recover the schedule later.

Track progress. Many project planners take it only this far: They enter and calculate all the tasks, durations, relationships, and resources to where they can see a schedule and budget. They say "go" and everyone charges, but the plan is left behind. As project variables change (and they always do), the project plan is now useless as a blueprint for managing the project. If you want the project plan to be useful from the time you first enter, assign, and schedule tasks until the time you close the project on time and on budget, you need to maintain the project plan as a dynamic tool that accompanies you every step of the way. Maintaining the plan means tracking progress information. Suppose a task planned for 5 days takes 10 days instead. You can enter that the task actually took 10 days, and the schedule will be recalculated. Your plan will still work, and you'll still be able to see when succeeding tasks should be completed.

Make necessary adjustments. As project variables change during project execution, you can see whether an unplanned change affects key milestones, your resources' schedules, your budget, or your project finish date. For example, suppose that 5-day task took 10 days to complete, and it changes the project finish date and also causes the project to exceed its budget. If this happens, you can take steps well ahead of time to make the necessary adjustments and avert the impending crisis. Use the power of Microsoft Project to recalculate the project plan when actual project details vary from the plan. Then you can analyze the plan, decide on the best course of action to keep the project on track, and take action. This action might be within the project plan or outside the confines of the plan in the real world of the real project itself.

Communicate. Make sure that your team members know what's expected of them. Pay attention when they alert you to potential problems with their tasks. Keep upper management and customers informed of your progress and of any changes to the original plan.

Close the completed project and capture information. When a project goes well, we're often so happy that we don't think to capture all the information we should. When a project is completed with much difficulty, sometimes we're just relieved that we're done with it and can't wait to get on with the next project and forget about this unhappy nightmare. But whether a project is simple or difficult, a radiant success or a deplorable failure, there's always much to be learned. Even if you're not involved in any other projects of this type, other people might be. It's important to record as much information about the project as possible. Narrative and evaluative information can be captured through a postmortem or "lessons learned" document. Project information such as tasks, resources, durations, relationships, and calendars can be recorded in a project plan itself. If the project went very well, you can even save your project plan as a template to be used for future similar projects, thereby enabling future project managers to benefit from your hard-won experience.

Part 2

Developing the Project Plan

Chapter 3

Starting a New Project

In the planning processes of a new project, you do a substantial amount of work to set the stage. You define the big picture and get stakeholder approval for the project, in terms of the product or service you're creating as well as the overall project scope.

After this vision is in place, you're ready to create your project blueprint—the project plan—using Microsoft Office Project 2003. You create a new project file and enter foundation information.

Then you begin to break down your project goals and objectives into the actual phases, milestones, and tasks that form the backbone of your project information system. You sequence the phases and tasks, and organize them into a hierarchy that maps to your project.

If your project or organization has more specialized or advanced requirements, you can use work breakdown structure codes that organize your task list by each deliverable.

You can add your supporting documentation, such as the vision or strategy document, to the project plan. Likewise, you can add other supplementary information such as notes or hyperlinks to individual tasks, milestones, and phases. All this information makes your project plan the central repository of all project information.

Focusing the Project Vision

You might already have a clear picture in your mind of what your project is about and what it will be when it is complete. On the other hand, the project might still seem a little fuzzy, at least around the edges. It's not uncommon for other stakeholders to have a clear vision when you're not sure if you get it just yet.

And don't be surprised if one stakeholder's expectations seem clear enough, but another stakeholder's expectations sound entirely contradictory.

The challenge at this important starting point is to clearly define the project without ambiguity, so that everyone involved is talking about the same project, the same expectations, and the same results. Defining the vision clearly at the beginning prevents redirection (and the attendant wasted effort) in the middle of the project or disappointment at the end.

So how do you create a vision? You work with key stakeholders such as the customers, potential users, sponsors, executives, and project team members to get their project expectations. You might have to reconcile conflicting views and opposing agendas. Throughout this process, you'll identify the goals of the project as well as their measurable objectives. You'll identify project assumptions, spell out potential risks, and make contingency plans for those risks. You'll also identify known limitations, such as budget, time, or resources.

By the time you finish this high-level project planning and get the necessary approval, everyone involved will know exactly what they're signing up for.

Defining Scope

A defined scope articulates the vision of the product you're creating and the project that will create it. As your project is executed and issues arise, your defined scope can help you make decisions. The scope is your guideline for whether or not the direction you're considering is really the job of this project or not. If you don't stay focused on the scope, you're likely to experience "scope creep," in which you end up spending time, money, and resources on tasks and deliverables that are not part of the original vision.

This is not to say that scope can't change during the course of a project. Business conditions, design realities, budgets, time, resource availability, and many other factors can make it necessary to change project scope midway through. Nonetheless, your scope document helps you manage those changes so that you change in the proper direction—in line with your organization's overall strategy, the product's reason for being, and the project's goals.

Understanding Product Scope and Project Scope

There are two types of scope: product scope and project scope. First, you define the product scope, unless it has already been defined for you. The *product scope* specifies the features and functions of the product that will be the outcome of the project. The product scope might well be part of the product description in your charter. The product can be tangible, such as the construction of a new office building or the design of a new aircraft. The product can also be the development of a service or event, for example, deployment of a new computer system or implementation of a new training initiative.

Regardless of the type of product, the product scope indicates the specifications and parameters that paint a detailed picture of the end result. For example, the product scope of the construction of a new office building might include square footage, number of stories, location, and architectural design elements.

The *project scope* specifies the work that must be done to complete the project successfully, according to the specifications of the associated product scope. The project scope defines and controls what will and will not be included in the project. If there will be multiple phases of product development, the project scope might specify which phase this project is handling. For example, a computer system deployment project might specify that its scope encompass the infrastructure development and installation of the new computer system, but not the documentation and training for new system users. Or it might specify that the project handle all aspects of the product, from concept through completion of the final stage.

Developing the Scope Statement

To define the project scope and communicate it to other key stakeholders, you develop and record the *scope statement*. Depending on your organization's planning methods, certain elements of the scope statement might be defined very early, sometimes even before you've been assigned as project manager. Other elements might be defined just before you begin identifying and sequencing the project's tasks. Your scope statement should include the following:

Project justification. The scope statement should define the business need or other stimulus for this project. This justification provides a sound basis for evaluating future decisions, including the inevitable tradeoffs.

Product description. The scope should characterize the details of the product or service being created. The project justification and product description together should formulate the goals of the project.

Project constraints or limitations. The scope should include any limiting factors to the project. Factors that can limit a project's options include a specific budget, contractual provisions, a precise end date, and so on.

Note Because we use the term *constraints* throughout this book to mean task constraints, in this chapter we're using the term *limitations* to refer to overall project constraints.

Project assumptions. The scope should list any elements considered to be true, real, or certain—even when they might not be—for the sake of being able to continue developing the project plan and moving forward. By their nature, assumptions usually carry a degree of risk. For example, if you don't know whether the building for a commercial construction project will be 10,000 or 15,000 square feet, you have to assume one or the other for the sake of planning. The risk is that the other choice might end up being correct. You can adjust the plan after the facts are known, but other project dependencies might already be in place by then.

Note Although the project justification and product description are typically broad statements that remain unchanged through the iterative planning process, that's not necessarily the case with project limitations and assumptions. As the scope becomes more tightly defined, the limitations and assumptions come to light and are better exposed. Likewise, as you continue down the road in the planning process, the entire project scope tends to become more and more focused.

Project deliverables. The scope should list the summary-level subproducts created throughout the duration of the project. The delivery of the final subproject deliverable marks the completion of the entire project. This list might bring into focus major project phases and milestones, which will be valuable when you start entering tasks into your project plan.

Project objectives. The scope should enumerate the measurable objectives to be satisfied for the project to be considered successful. The objectives map to the deliverables and are driven by the project goals, as described by the project justification and product description. To be meaningful, the project objectives must be quantifiable in some way, for example, in terms of a specific dollar amount, a specific timeframe, a specific value, or a specific level of quality.

Note Your scope statement might also address other project planning issues such as communications, quality assurance, and risk management. The scope statement can define the reporting requirements and the collaboration tools to be implemented. The scope statement can also specify the minimum level of quality acceptable, define the potential risks associated with the itemized limitations and assumptions, and stipulate methods of countering the risks.

Product scope and project scope are intricately linked. The project scope relies on a clear definition of the product scope. The project scope is fulfilled through the completion of work represented in the project plan. Likewise, product scope is fulfilled by meeting the specifications in the product requirements.

With the draft of the scope statement in hand, you have a document you can use to clearly communicate with other project stakeholders. This draft helps you flush out any cross-purposes, mistaken assumptions, and misplaced requirements. As you continue to refine the scope statement, the project vision is honed to the point where all the stakeholders should have a common understanding of the project. And because all the stakeholders participated in the creation of the vision, you can feel confident that everyone understands exactly what they're working toward when you begin to execute the project plan.

Creating a New Project Plan

You're now at the point where you can start Project 2003 and actually create your project plan. When you create a new project file, you first decide whether you're scheduling from a start date or finish date. You set your overall project calendar that the tasks will be scheduled against. If you like, you can attach project documentation such as your all-important scope statement and possibly other project-related documents.

Creating a Project File

To start creating your new project plan, you simply start Microsoft Project and choose whether you're creating a new project from scratch or from a template.

If you haven't installed Microsoft Project yet, refer to Appendix A, "Installing Microsoft Project 2003," for installation details and guidelines.

To start Microsoft Project, click the Windows Start menu. Point to All Programs, point to Microsoft Office, and then click Microsoft Project. Microsoft Project starts (see Figure 3-1).

> **Note** If you're working with enterprise projects using Microsoft Office Project Professional 2003, you might first be prompted to enter your account name to connect to Microsoft Office Project Server 2003.

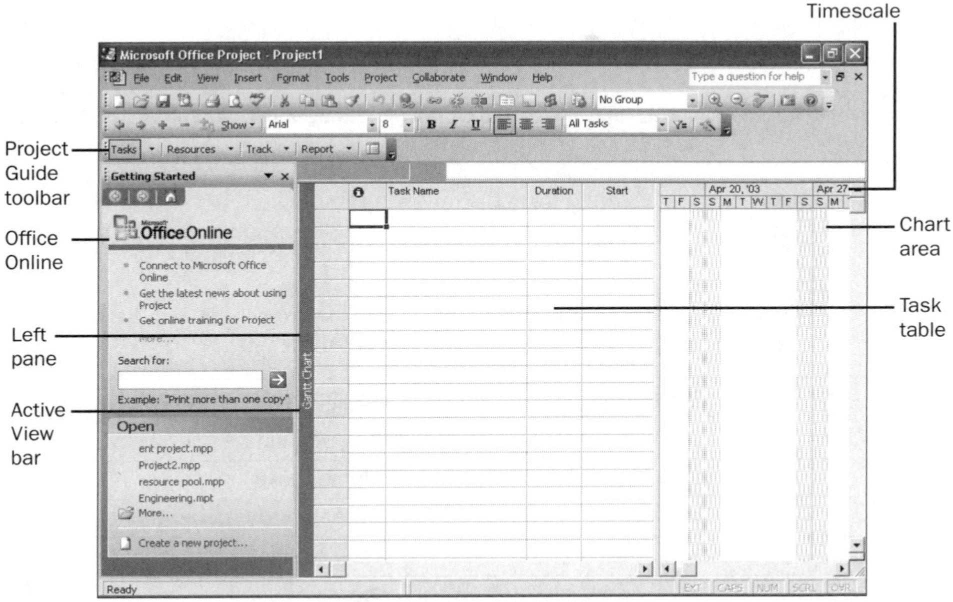

Figure 3-1. A blank project file appears in Microsoft Project.

> **Note** Depending on how you customize your setup, you might also be able to open Microsoft Project from an icon on your Windows desktop.

The Microsoft Project workspace is called the *view*, and the view that comes up by default when you first open Microsoft Project is the Gantt Chart. The Gantt Chart is a *single view*; it has a task table on the left side and the chart with Gantt bars on the right.

> **For more information about working with views such as the Gantt Chart and others, see Chapter 4, "Viewing Project Information."**

You can use the blank project file to start creating your project plan from scratch. If you prefer to do this, skip to the section, "Scheduling from a Start or Finish Date."

You can also create a new project from a template. A *template* is a type of project file that contains existing project information that helps you start your project more quickly. The template usually contains a list of tasks, already sequenced and organized. The task list might be further detailed with phases, milestones, and deliverables. There might be additional task information in the template as well, such as task durations and task dependencies. You can use this task list as the basis for your project. You can add, remove, and rearrange tasks and adapt the task information as needed to correspond to your project requirements. A template can also include resource information, customized views, calendars, reports, tables, macros, option settings, and more.

The template file has an extension of .mpt, indicating that it is the Microsoft Project template file type. When you open and modify a template file, it is saved as a normal .mpp (Microsoft Project plan) file by default.

For more information about file types and project file management, see Chapter 29, "Managing Project Files."

Templates can be generated from the following sources:

- The set of templates built in to Microsoft Project reflecting various types of products or services in different industries.

  These templates are provided with Microsoft Project 2003 and are based on widely accepted industry standards for projects of these types:

General use templates	Commercial construction
	Engineering
	Home move
	Infrastructure deployment
	New business
	New product
	Office move
	Project office
	Residential construction
Software-related project templates	Microsoft Active Directory deployment
	Microsoft Exchange 2000 deployment
	Microsoft Office XP corporate deployment
	Microsoft SharePoint Portal Server deployment
	Microsoft Windows XP deployment
	Microsoft Solutions Framework application development
	Software development
	Software localization

- Any previous projects you have saved as project template files.

For more information about using completed projects as templates, see Chapter 28, "Standardizing Projects Using Templates."

- The templates standard to project management within your specific industry. Professional organizations, standards organizations, and industry groups might have resources, possibly on their Web sites, which include such templates.
- Templates available on Office Online. New Microsoft Project templates are continually added to the Templates page on Office Online.

> **Note** If you use the enterprise features of Project Professional 2003, you use the enterprise global template. This is a different kind of template that's set up by the project server administrator, and it includes customized elements that reflect the project standards for your organization. These elements can include a set of customized views, tables, fields, and more.

Creating a New Project with a Template

New

To create a new project from a template, follow these steps:

1. Click File, New.

> **Note** If you just click the New button on the Standard toolbar, a new blank project is created by default, and you don't see the template choices you need in the Project Guide.

2. In the left pane, under Templates, click the On My Computer link.
3. In the Templates dialog box, click the Project Templates tab (see Figure 3-2).

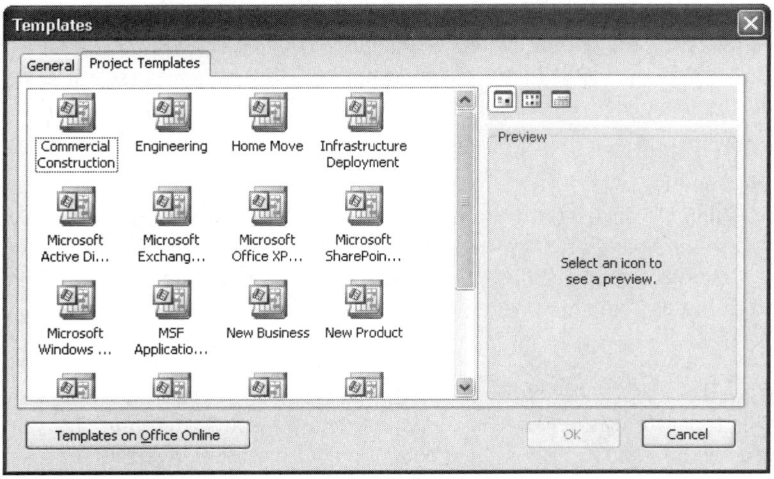

Figure 3-2. The Project Templates tab lists all templates provided with Microsoft Project.

4 Click the project template you want to use and then click OK (see Figure 3-3).

The first time you choose a template, Microsoft Project might need to install it. This takes only a few moments.

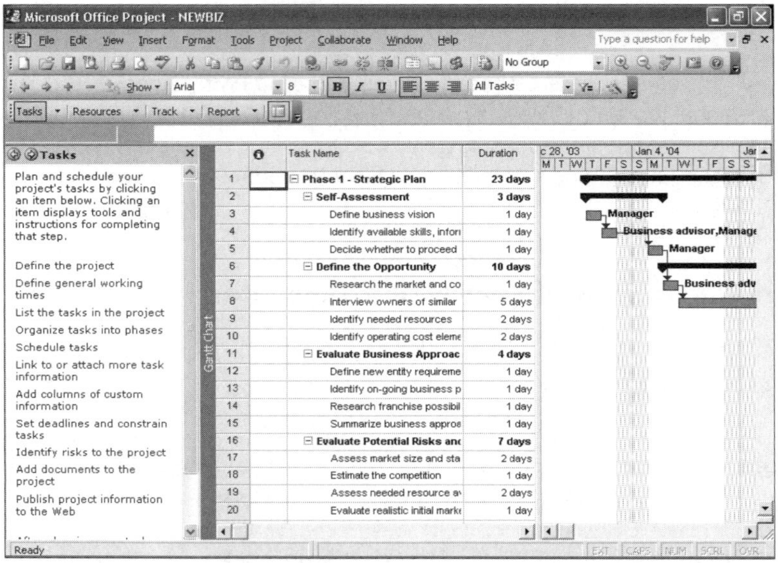

Figure 3-3. A new project file is created based on the chosen template.

> **Tip** **Find more templates online**
> New Microsoft Project templates are continually being added to the Templates page on the Office Online Web site. To see these templates, first be sure that you're connected to the Internet. Click File, New. In the left pane under Templates, click the Templates On Office Online link. The Office Online Web page appears in your Internet browser.
>
> Under Meetings And Projects, click Project Management. A list of project management templates appear. Click a template, and a preview of the template appears. If you want to download the template, click Download Now, and follow the instructions. When finished, the downloaded template is loaded into Microsoft Project as a new file based on that template. Return to this Templates page periodically to check for new templates you can use.

> **Note** Looking for the old New dialog box? As of Microsoft Project 2002, the New dialog box is replaced by the New Project pane in the Project Guide area. This is true even if you close the Project Guide pane and completely turn off the Project Guide.

Creating a New Project from an Existing Project

If you have an existing project that you want to use as a starting point for your new project, you can simply copy and modify it for your current purposes. You will save it under a different filename, creating a completely new file. Follow these steps:

Open

1. On the Standard toolbar, click Open.
2. Browse to the existing project file and then click Open.

Saving Your New Project

Whether you are creating a new project from scratch, from a template, or from an existing project file, your next step is to save your new project. To do this:

1. Click File, Save As.

> **Tip** **Saving a new project**
> If you're creating a new project from scratch or from a template, you can simply click the Save button on the Standard toolbar to open the Save As dialog box.

2. In the Save As dialog box, choose the drive and folder in which you want to save the new project.

   If you're set up for enterprise project management using Project Professional 2003 and Project Server 2003, you'll see the Save To Project Server dialog box instead.

3. In the File Name box, enter a descriptive name for your project and then click the Save button.

   If you're working with Project Server, and you want to save the project to the server, click the Save button. Depending on how your organization has set up enterprise project management standards, you might need to add information in custom enterprise fields.

   If you want to save the project locally on your own computer instead, click the Save As File button.

For more information about working with enterprise projects, see "Creating a New Enterprise Project" on page 645.

Use the Define The Project Wizard

The Define The Project Wizard can walk you through the setup of your new project and complete the necessary dialog boxes quickly for you. To set up a new project by using the Define The Project Wizard, do the following:

1. Create your new project file, either from a blank project or from a template.

2. In the Project Guide, open the Tasks side pane by clicking the Tasks button on the Project Guide toolbar.

   The Project Guide side pane is similar to the task pane in other Microsoft Office XP applications.
3. Click the Define The Project link.

   The Define The Project Wizard starts in the side pane.
4. Enter the estimated start date for your project and then click the Save And Go To Step 2 link at the bottom of the pane.
5. Continue working through the Define The Project Wizard, clicking the Save And Go To link after each step.
6. At the final step, click the Save And Finish link.
7. In the Tasks pane again, click the Define General Working Times link and work through the Project Working Times Wizard.

Scheduling from a Start or Finish Date

Your first scheduling decision is whether you want Microsoft Project to calculate the schedule of your new project from a start date or from a finish date. Often, you have a finish date in mind, but you can still schedule from the start date and then make sure you hit the targeted finish date. You'll get more predictable results when you schedule from a start date.

For example, suppose you set up a project with 100 tasks. You specify task durations and sequence, link the tasks in the order they are to be done, and indicate whether any tasks have specific dates by which they must be completed. When you do not enter specific task start or finish dates, Microsoft Project schedules tasks to be done as soon as possible. Using task durations, links, and date constraints, Microsoft Project schedules the first task to start on your project start date and the remaining tasks from that point forward until the last task is completed. If that last task is done on a date that is too late for your project requirements, you can adjust the duration and sequencing, as well as the scope and resources assigned, to bring in the finish date where you need it to be.

However, you might know the project finish date but not when your project will begin because you're receiving work from another source that could be delayed. Or the project management methodology you use might require you to schedule from a finish date.

Inside Out

Beware of scheduling from the finish date

If you must schedule from the finish date, be aware that your task constraints and leveling tools will behave differently than in a project that is scheduled from the start date.

For more information about task constraints, see "Scheduling Tasks to Achieve Specific Dates" on page 157.

For more information about resource leveling, see "Balancing Resource Workloads" on page 271.

Consider that same project of 100 tasks. In a project scheduled from the finish date, any tasks that do not require a specific date are scheduled to be done as late as possible, rather than as soon as possible. Microsoft Project schedules the last task to be finished on your project finish date and works backward from that point until the first task is started. If that first task is scheduled before the current date or too early for your project requirements, you can adjust the tasks and other aspects of the schedule.

To set up your project plan to be scheduled from the project start date, follow these steps:

1. Click Project, Project Information.

   The Project Information dialog box appears (see Figure 3-4).

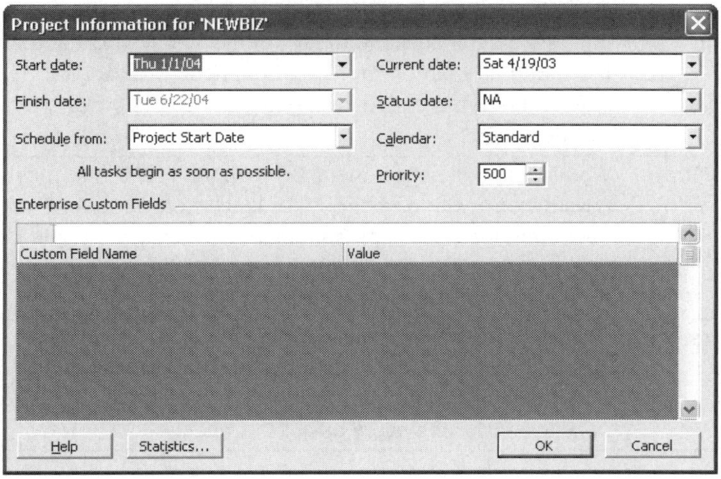

Figure 3-4. Use the Project Information dialog box to specify settings for the entire project.

2. In the Start Date box, enter the project start date.

   By default, the Start Date box shows today's date.

3. In the Schedule From box, click Project Start Date.

   Leave the Project Finish Date box as is. Microsoft Project will calculate this date for you later.

To set up your project plan to be scheduled from the project finish date, follow these steps:

1. Click Project, Project Information.
2. In the Schedule From box, click Project Finish Date.
3. In the Finish Date box, enter the project finish date.

   Leave the Project Start Date box as is. Microsoft Project will calculate this date for you later.

Setting Your Project Calendar

Your *project calendar* sets the working days and times for your project and its tasks. The project calendar is also the default calendar for any resources working on your project. The project calendar indicates when your organization typically works on project tasks and when it's off work. By setting your project calendar, you're establishing one of the fundamental methods for scheduling the tasks in your project.

Working with Base Calendars in Microsoft Project

Microsoft Project comes with three *base calendars*. These base calendars are like calendar templates that you can apply to a set of resources, a set of tasks, or the project as a whole.

Standard	Working time is set to Monday through Friday, 8:00 A.M. until 5:00 P.M., with an hour off for lunch from noon until 1:00 P.M. each day. This is the default base calendar used for the project, for tasks, and for resources.
Night Shift	Working time is set to an 11:00 P.M. until 8:00 A.M. night shift, five days a week, with an hour off for lunch from 3:00 A.M. until 4:00 A.M. each morning. This base calendar is generally used for resources who work a graveyard shift. It can also be used for projects that are carried out only during the night shift.
24 Hours	Working time is set to midnight until midnight seven days a week; that is, work never stops. This base calendar is typically used for projects in a manufacturing situation, for example, which might run two or three back-to-back shifts every day of the week.

You can modify the base calendar in any way you need. To modify an existing base calendar, follow these steps:

1. Click Tools, Change Working Time.
2. In the For box, click the name of the base calendar you want to modify (see Figure 3-5).

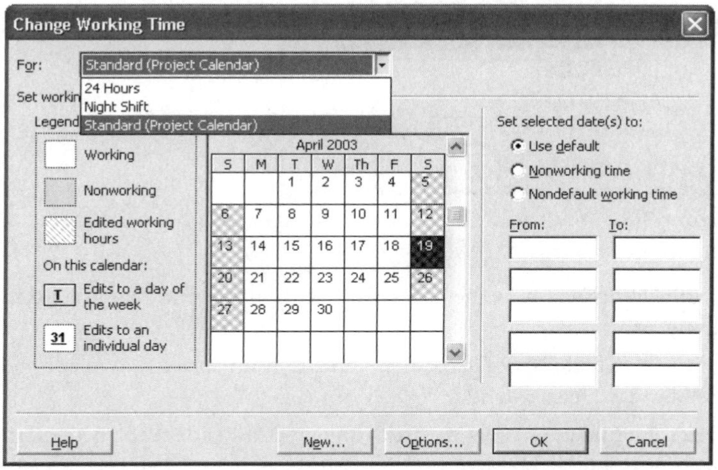

Figure 3-5. Use the Change Working Time dialog box to modify a base calendar.

3. To change the working time of a single day, click that day.

   If you're changing working time to nonworking time, select the Nonworking Time option.

   If you're changing the working time to something other than the default, select the Nondefault Working Time option. Then, change the times in the From and To boxes as needed.
4. To change the working time of a particular day of each week, click the day heading.

   For example, click the M heading to select all Mondays. Select the Nonworking Time or Nondefault Working Time option and then change the times in the From and To boxes as needed.
5. To change the working time of a day in another month, scroll down in the Select Dates box until you see the correct month.
6. As before, click the Nonworking Time or Nondefault Working Time option and then change the working times as needed.

   This is a good method for setting holidays as nonworking time.
7. When you finish changing the selected base calendar, click OK.

To create a new base calendar, follow these steps:

1. Click Tools, Change Working Time.
2. Click the New button.

   The Create New Base Calendar dialog box appears (see Figure 3-6).

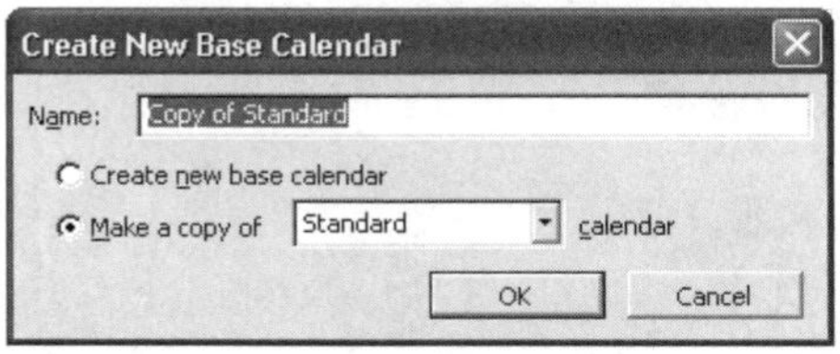

Figure 3-6. You can create a new base calendar from scratch or adapt it from an existing one.

3. In the Name box, type the name you want for the new base calendar; for example, Swing Shift.
4. Select the Create New Base Calendar option if you want to adapt your calendar from the Standard base calendar.

   Select the Make A Copy Of option if you want to adapt the new calendar from a different base calendar, such as the Night Shift calendar. Click the name of the existing calendar you want to adapt and click OK.
5. Make the changes you want to the working days and times of individual days or of a particular day of every week, as needed.
6. When finished with your new base calendar, click OK.

Applying a Base Calendar to the Project Calendar

If you're using the Standard base calendar as your project calendar, you don't need to do much—the Standard calendar is the project calendar by default. Just make sure to modify the Change Working Times dialog box to reflect your team's working times and days off, as well as any holidays you'll all be taking.

If you want to use a different base calendar, you must select it as your project calendar. Follow these steps:

1. Click Project, Project Information.
2. In the Calendar box, select the name of the base calendar.
3. Click OK.

Calendars in Microsoft Project

Microsoft Project uses three types of calendars as tools for scheduling the project, as shown in the following table.

Project calendar	Governs when tasks are scheduled to be worked on and when resources are scheduled to work on assigned tasks.
Resource calendar	Governs when resources are scheduled to work on assigned tasks. One group of resources (for example, day shift resources) can be assigned to a different base calendar than another group of resources (for example, swing shift resources). Each resource can have his or her own individual resource calendar, which can reflect special work schedules, personal days off, and vacation time. By default, the resource calendar is the Standard calendar.
Task calendar	Governs when tasks are scheduled to be worked on. As a rule, tasks are scheduled according to the project calendar and the calendars of any assigned resources. However, sometimes a task has special scheduling requirements that are different from the norm. For example, a task might be carried out by a machine running 24 hours a day. In such a case, it's useful for a task to have its own calendar.

You can use any of the three base calendars (Standard, Night Shift, or 24 Hours) as the basis for the project calendar, resource calendars, or task calendars.

All three of these calendars can easily be customized for specialized working days and times. If you need to apply a common working schedule to a group of resources or a set of tasks and it isn't built in to Microsoft Project already, you can create your own base calendar.

For more information about the task calendar, see "Working with Task Calendars" on page 169. For more information about the resource calendar, see "Setting Resource Working Time Calendars" on page 187.

Attaching Project Documentation

You can make Microsoft Project the central repository for all your important project documentation. For example, you might want to attach or link your scope statement to your project plan, as well as other documents such as the needs analysis, market study, and product specifications.

Showing the Project Summary Task

To attach planning documentation to your project, the first step is to display the project summary task. Not only does the project summary task eventually provide summary date and cost information for the project as a whole, it can serve as the location for your attached or linked planning documents. To display the project summary task, follow these steps:

1. Click Tools, Options and then click the View tab.
2. Under Outline Options, select the Show Project Summary Task check box.
3. Click OK.

   A summary task appears in Row 0 of the Gantt Chart (see Figure 3-7), adopting the name of the file as the project summary task name.

   If you want to change the name, click in the Task Name field for the project summary task. Edit the name in the entry field above the task sheet.

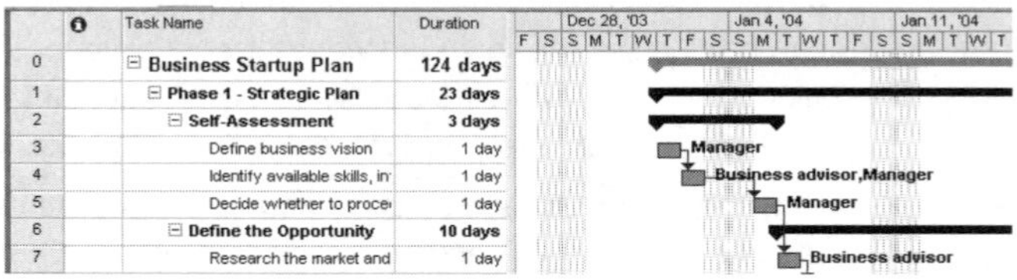

Figure 3-7. Use the project summary task to attach or link planning documents.

Copying a Document into Your Project File

You can include documents created in other programs within Microsoft Project. Although this can significantly increase your file size, you'll know that all your project information is stored in one place. To include the documents, follow these steps:

Task Information

1. With the project summary task selected, click Task Information on the Standard toolbar and then click the Notes tab.

   You can also double-click the task to open the Summary Task Information dialog box.

Insert Object

2. On the Notes tab, click the Insert Object button.
3. In the Insert Object dialog box, select the Create From File option and then click the Browse button.
4. In the Browse dialog box, select the project planning document you want to attach or embed into your project file. Click the Insert button.
5. Back in the Insert Object dialog box again (see Figure 3-8), select the Display As Icon check box.

   If the document is small, consider clearing the Display As Icon check box. Clearing this check box embeds the content of the file into your project Notes box, so you can read it directly from there.

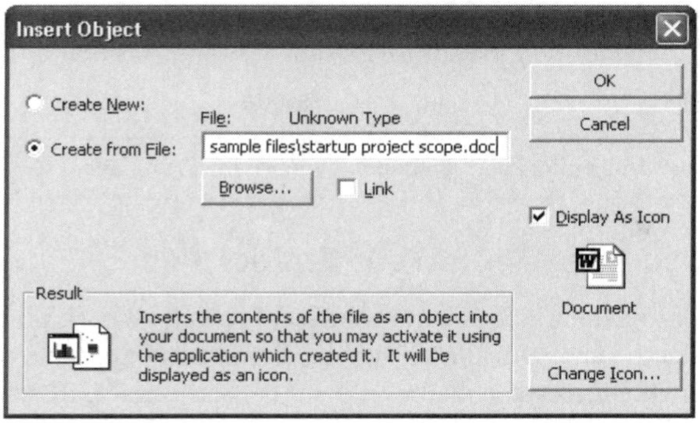

Figure 3-8. The selected document will be embedded in your project plan.

6 Click OK.

The document's icon appears in the Notes area of the Summary Task Information dialog box (see Figure 3-9).

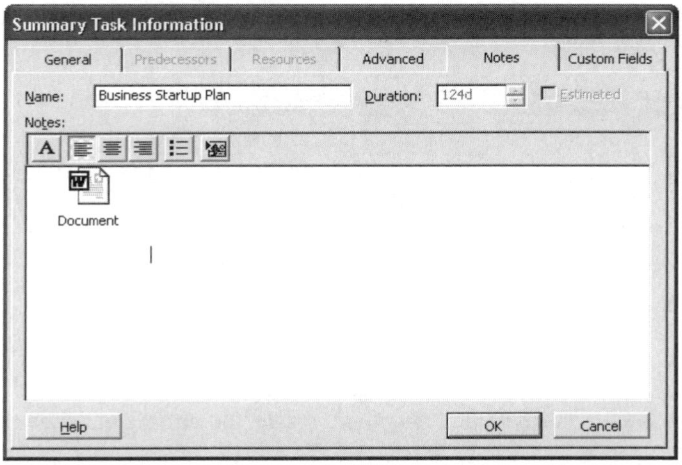

Figure 3-9. Double-clicking the icon opens it in its originating application.

7 In the Summary Task Information dialog box, click OK.

The Notes indicator appears in the Gantt Chart (see Figure 3-10).

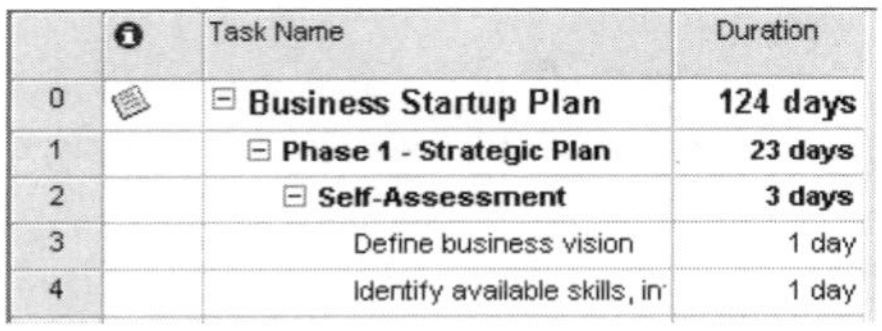

		Task Name	Duration
0		Business Startup Plan	124 days
1		Phase 1 - Strategic Plan	23 days
2		Self-Assessment	3 days
3		Define business vision	1 day
4		Identify available skills, in	1 day

Figure 3-10. When you store something in a Notes tab, the Notes indicator appears in the corresponding row of the Gantt Chart.

Chapter 3

Now, whenever you need to review the document, just double-click the Notes indicator to open the Notes tab of the Summary Task Information dialog box. Then double-click the document icon.

For more information about embedding, see "Embedding Information" on page 479.

Hyperlinking a Document from Your Project File

You can also hyperlink to a document from Microsoft Project. Hyperlinking is a preferred method when you want to keep your file size trimmer and you know that your project plan and associated planning documents will always be in the same place. It's also a very efficient method for opening associated documents quickly. To insert a hyperlink, follow these steps:

Insert Hyperlink

1. With the project summary task selected, click Insert Hyperlink on the Standard toolbar.
2. In the Text To Display box, type a descriptive name for the document to which you are linking; for example, Project Scope Statement.
3. Find and select the project planning document you want to link to your project file (see Figure 3-11).

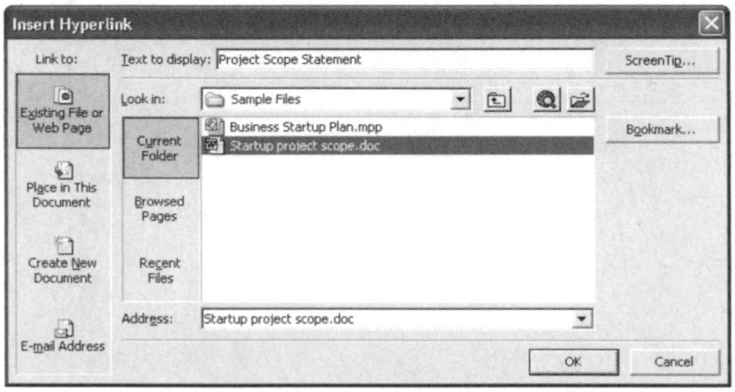

Figure 3-11. The path and name of the selected document appear in the Address box.

4. Click OK.
5. The Hyperlink indicator appears in the Indicators field of the Gantt Chart.

Hyperlink indicator

Now, whenever you need to review the document, just click the Hyperlink indicator. The document opens in its own application window.

For more information, see "Hyperlinking to Documents in Other Applications" on page 492.

If you're using Project Professional with Project Server for enterprise project management, the preferred method for keeping all project documents together is to use the *document library*. By setting up Microsoft Office Project Web Access 2003 with Windows SharePoint Services, you can set up and maintain a document library. This way, all your team members and other stakeholders can view the documents through their Web browsers. They can also check documents in and out, providing vital version control.

For more information about setting up a document library with Windows SharePoint Services, see "Controlling Project Documents" on page 691.

Entering Tasks

Now that your project file is set up with all the necessary basics, you're ready to get down to the real business of entering tasks.

> **Note** If you're working with a template or a copy of an existing project plan, you already have tasks in place. In this case, you can skip this section.

There are several approaches you can take to fill in the Gantt Chart. The following are some examples:

Brainstorming. Enter tasks as you think of them, without regard to sequence or grouping of related tasks. You can move and organize the tasks later.

Sequential. Think through the project from beginning to end, and enter tasks sequentially.

Phases. Think of the overall phases of the project. For example, in a commercial construction project, you might enter the phases of Procurement, On-Site Mobilization, Site Grading, Foundations, Steel Erection, and so on. After those phases are in place, you can add tasks and subtasks beneath them.

Milestones and deliverables. Consider what the project is producing in terms of the milestones and deliverables. Enter those events as tasks and then add tasks and subtasks beneath them to flesh out the project. Your scope statement can be a valuable guide in this process.

Team collaboration. Ask team members to list the tasks they believe will be necessary to the areas under their responsibility (assuming, of course, that you already have team members in place and available). Team members can do this informally, for example, through e-mail. Or, team members can submit tasks and their estimated durations in a Microsoft Excel spreadsheet, which you can then easily import into Microsoft Project. If you're using Project Server, team members can send you tasks from Project Web Access 2003 and then you can incorporate them automatically into your project plan.

For more information about creating new tasks through automated team collaboration, see "Assigning Tasks to Enterprise Resources" on page 666.

Archived projects. Review completed projects of a similar type done in your organization. With such historical information, you might find that much of the "legwork"—in terms of phases, task sequencing, resource assignments, and more—has been done for you. If the archived projects contain solid tracking information, you'll have excellent data on durations and costs.

For more information about using an old project as a starting point for a new one, see "Starting a New Project Using a Template" on page 851.

For more information about saving a completed project for future reference, see "Closing a Project" on page 860.

Expert consultation. Ask known experts what tasks are needed for various aspects of the project. This is particularly useful if you're the manager of a project in which you're not necessarily an expert. This happens frequently enough, and it's not necessarily a bad thing, but you will need dependable experts to help provide reliable task information. Even if you're well-versed in the project knowledge area, you might not know all the necessary details for each phase. Experts can come from within your own group, from stakeholders, from other groups or project managers within your organization, or from colleagues in your profession or industry.

Project Management Practices: Activity Definition

The stage of the project management process in which you're entering tasks is often referred to as *activity definition*. Here, the planning team identifies the specific activities, or tasks, that must be done to produce the project deliverables and meet the project objectives as specified in the scope statement.

Activity definition is typically done with the guidance provided in the scope statement and the work breakdown structure (WBS). The deliverables, or work packages, described in the WBS are divided and subdivided into smaller tasks that can be better managed and controlled in the project.

For more information about work breakdown structures in Microsoft Project, see "Setting Up Your Work Breakdown Structure" later in this chapter on page 88.

In some organizations, the project management methodology dictates that the WBS is developed first and the task list is developed next. Other organizations develop both at the same time.

In any case, the task list must include all activities that will be performed in the project, but it does not include any activities that are not required as part of the project scope. Each task should be descriptive enough to communicate to responsible team members what is required by the task.

Adding Tasks to Your Project Plan

To enter tasks directly into your project plan, follow these steps:

1. Make sure you're working in the Gantt Chart.

You can see the name of the current view in the Active View bar that runs vertically along the left side of the view. If it doesn't say *Gantt Chart*, click View, Gantt Chart.

You can enter tasks in any task view, of course. For more information about views, see Chapter 4.

2 Type the name of the task in the Task Name field.

3 Press Enter or the down arrow key to move to the next row.

The task name isn't recorded and other commands remain unavailable until you press Enter.

4 To edit a task that's already entered, click the task name and then make your changes in the entry box just above the task sheet. Or click in the selected task name until the cursor appears and edit it directly in the Task Name field.

For more information about entering durations, links, and start and finish dates, see Chapter 5, "Scheduling Tasks."

Tips for Entering Tasks

Keep the following in mind when entering tasks:

- Don't be overly concerned about sequence when first entering tasks. You can worry about that after you have a "first draft" of tasks in place.
- Enter duration estimates either at the same time you enter your new tasks or later. The default duration estimate is 1 day, and estimates are formatted with a question mark to remind you that they are not confirmed yet.
- Don't enter a start or finish date in the Start or Finish fields in the Gantt Chart, although it might be tempting to do so. In most cases, you'll want Microsoft Project to calculate those dates for you, based on other task information you'll be entering.
- Name the task with sufficient description to communicate to team members and stakeholders what the task is about. A task called simply "Review" or "Edit" might not be enough information.
- Decide whether you want the context of the task to be understood if it's ever separated (by being in a separate view, report, filter, or grouping, for example) from its surrounding tasks. For example, you might have several tasks in different phases for "Administer contracts." But one task might relate to procurement, one to the architects, and another one to the builders.
- Note whether you have sets of tasks that are repeated in different phases of the project. You might want to give them more general names so you can copy and paste these sets of tasks under their respective phases, instead of repeatedly typing them individually.

Inside Out

Don't fill in the Start and Finish fields

By default, the Gantt Chart table includes the Task Name, Duration, Start, Finish, Predecessors, and Resource Names fields as columns. A natural impulse when entering tasks is to enter project information into each of these fields. However, you can get yourself into some trouble if you enter dates in the Start and Finish fields. Not only would you be struggling to calculate start and finish dates for each task while Microsoft Project could more easily do it for you, but you'd be putting undue restrictions on your schedule and possibly creating scheduling conflicts.

The best approach is to enter the task names first and then the durations if you know them. Leave the Start and Finish fields as they are for now, and let Microsoft Project calculate them for you as you add other project information. The Predecessors field is filled in for you when you start creating links between tasks. At that point, with durations and links in place, Microsoft Project calculates the Start and Finish dates. If you then need to constrain the dates, you can edit them as you need.

Importing Tasks from an Excel Worksheet

Many project managers do well by having others on the team develop a task list of their specific areas of responsibility. A great way to automate this process is to have these individuals use Microsoft Excel to create their task lists and then import the worksheets into the Microsoft Project Gantt Chart.

The standard Excel importing process involves mapping the Excel columns to the corresponding Project columns to ensure that the right information ends up in the right places in your Gantt Chart task table. Microsoft Project comes with an Excel Task List template set up for this very purpose.

To use Excel and the Excel Task List template on the same computer on which Microsoft Project is installed, follow these steps:

1. Start Microsoft Excel.
2. In the New Workbook task pane, click General Templates.

   The Templates dialog box appears. If you don't see the New Workbook task pane, click File, New.
3. Click the Spreadsheet Solutions tab.
4. Double-click Microsoft Project Task List Import Template.

   The template creates a new file with columns that correspond to the default Gantt Chart in Microsoft Project (see Figure 3-12).

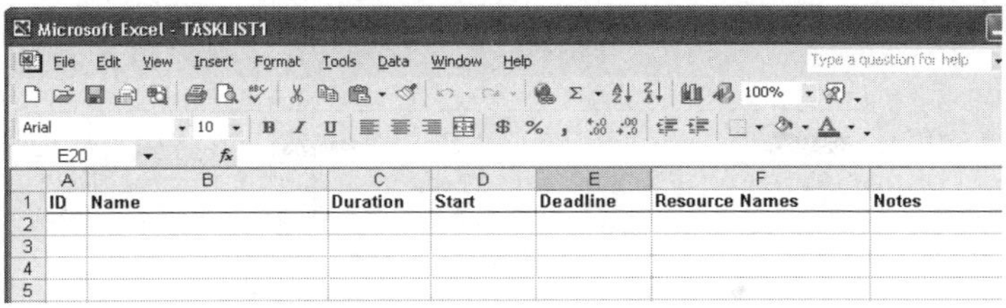

Figure 3-12. Share the Excel Task List template with your team to help build your project plan.

5 Enter tasks and other task information as needed and then save the file.

> **Note** If you're working with a version of Microsoft Excel 2000 or earlier, you can still use the Microsoft Project Task List Import template. Open Excel and then click File, New. Click the Spreadsheet Solutions tab. Double-click the Microsoft Project Task List Import Template.

When you're ready to import the task list into your project plan, follow these steps:

1. Open the project plan into which you want to import the Excel task list.
2. On the Standard toolbar, click Open.
3. Go to the location on your computer or network where the Excel task list is saved.
4. In the Files Of Type list, click Microsoft Excel Workbooks (*.xls).

   The task list appears in the list of folders and files.
5. Click the task list workbook and then click Open.

   The Import Wizard appears.
6. Click Next.
7. Click Project Excel Template and then click Next.
8. Specify whether you want to import the file as a new project, append the tasks to the currently active project, or merge the data into the active project.
9. Click Finish.

   The tasks are imported into Microsoft Project as you specified.
10. If you need to provide this template to others on your team, by default, it's located in the C:\Program Files\Microsoft Office\Templates\1033 folder, and it's named tasklist.xlt.

    Those who want to use this template should copy this file to the same location on their computers.

For more information about using Microsoft Project with other applications, see "Importing and Exporting Information" on page 497, and Chapter 17, "Integrating Microsoft Project with Microsoft Excel."

Entering Recurring Tasks

You might have certain tasks that need to be scheduled at regularly occurring intervals. For example, suppose that you have a project team meeting every Thursday morning. Or perhaps you gather information and generate a resource management report the first Monday of each month. Instead of entering the same task every week or every month throughout the span of the project, you can create a *recurring task*. To do this, follow these steps:

1. Make sure that you're working in the Gantt Chart.

   If necessary, click View, Gantt Chart.
2. In the Task Name field, click in the row below where you want the recurring task to appear.
3. Click Insert, Recurring Task.
4. In the Recurring Task dialog box, type the name of the recurring task in the Task Name field; for example: **Generate resource management report** (see Figure 3-13).

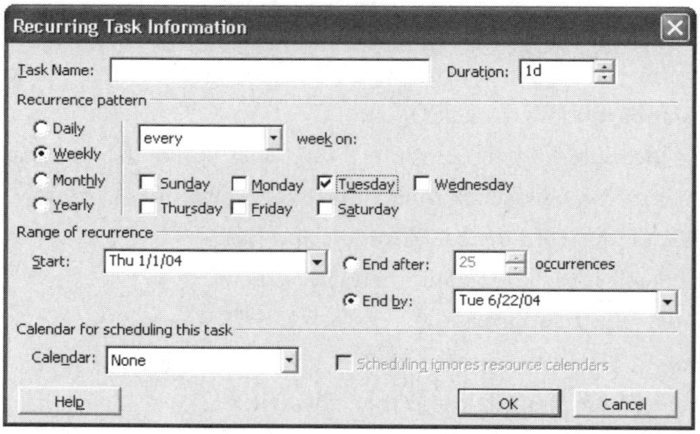

Figure 3-13. Specify the name and scheduling details of your recurring task.

5. Under Recurrence Pattern, specify how often the task is to be scheduled; that is, daily, weekly, or monthly.
6. Specify the details of when the task is to take place during that frequency; for example, every other Thursday or the first Monday of every month.
7. Under Range Of Recurrence, specify when the recurring task is to start and end.
8. When finished, click OK.

   The recurring task is marked with a recurring task indicator. It's represented with a summary task with all occurrences of the task as subtasks.

Recurring indicator

Tip **View recurring task information**

Review the recurrence pattern and range by resting your pointer over the recurring task indicator. Double-click the recurring task to open the Recurring Task Information dialog box.

Troubleshooting

You enter project information in Gantt Chart view and your menus and toolbars have all gone gray

When you're in the middle of entering a task or any other task information in a Gantt Chart, the menus and toolbars become temporarily unavailable and are therefore grayed out.

Finish entering the task by pressing Enter. If you want to do something to that task, click it to select it again and then choose the command or button you want.

Sequencing and Organizing Tasks

With the Gantt Chart in your project file now full of tasks, it's time to put these tasks in a logical order. It's also time to add any forgotten tasks or delete duplicated ones.

Moving Tasks

To move a task from one row to another, follow these steps:

1. In the table portion of the Gantt Chart, select the entire task row by clicking the gray row heading, which includes the task number.
2. With your mouse pointer still over the row heading (the pointer should appear as a black crosshair), drag the task to the location in the Gantt Chart where you want to place it.

   A gray line along the row border follows your mouse movements, indicating where the task will be inserted when you release the mouse button.
3. Release the mouse button to insert the task in the new location.

Tip **Drag and drop; don't cut and paste**
Dragging tasks is the best method for reordering tasks in your project plan. If you use the Cut and Paste commands, the Task Unique ID field for the tasks is renumbered. This can cause problems if you integrate the project with other applications, including third-party timesheet systems.

Inserting Additional Tasks

To add a new task to other existing tasks, follow these steps:

1. In the table portion of the Gantt Chart, click anywhere in the row below where you want the new task to be inserted.
2. Click Insert, New Task. (You can also simply press the Insert key.)
3. Type the name of the new task and then press Enter.

Copying Tasks

You can copy one or more tasks to use as the basis for other tasks. The following list describes the various copy techniques:

Copy Cell

Paste

Copy a single task name. Click in the Task Name field and then click Copy Cell on the Standard toolbar. Click the Task Name field in a blank row and then click Paste.

Copy multiple adjacent task names. Click the first task name you want to select, hold down the Shift key, and then click the last task name. All task names between the first and last are selected. Click Copy Cell. Click the first Task Name field where you want the selected tasks to be pasted, and then click Paste. You can also simply drag to select the tasks. If you want to copy the selected tasks to empty rows directly under a particular task, drag the fill handle in the lower-right corner of the cell into those empty rows (see Figure 3-14).

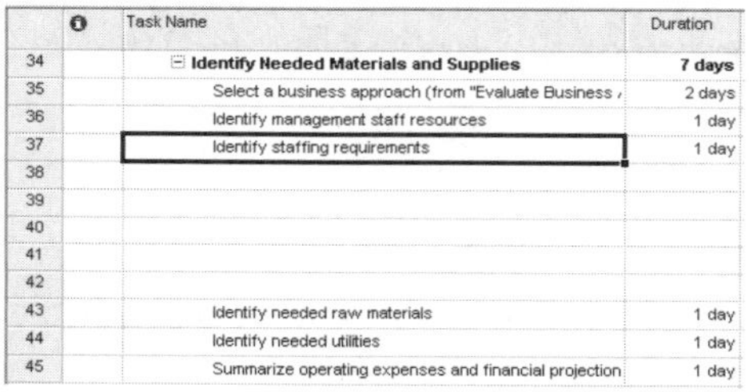

Task Name
Duration
34 Identify Needed Materials and Supplies 7 days
35 Select a business approach (from "Evaluate Business 2 days
36 Identify management staff resources 1 day
37 Identify staffing requirements 1 day
38
39
40
41
42
43 Identify needed raw materials 1 day
44 Identify needed utilities 1 day
45 Summarize operating expenses and financial projection 1 day

Figure 3-14. Copy tasks using the fill handle.

Copy multiple nonadjacent task names. Click the first task name you want to select, hold down the Ctrl key, and then click any additional task names you want to add to the selection (see Figure 3-15). Click Copy Cell. Select the Task Name field where you want the selected tasks to start to be added and then click the Paste button. The tasks are added in the order that you selected them.

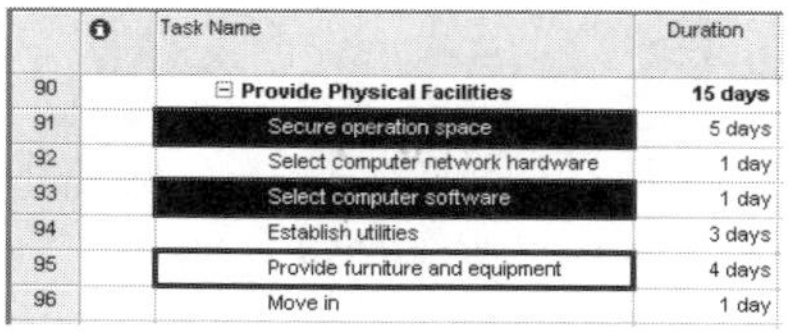

Task Name
Duration
90 Provide Physical Facilities 15 days
91 Secure operation space 5 days
92 Select computer network hardware 1 day
93 Select computer software 1 day
94 Establish utilities 3 days
95 Provide furniture and equipment 4 days
96 Move in 1 day

Figure 3-15. Copy multiple task names at once to save yourself some keyboard entry.

Chapter 3

Copy a single task and its task information. Click the row heading of the task you want to copy, which selects the entire task and its associated information. Click Copy Task. To add the task into an empty row, select the row and then click Paste. To insert the task between two existing tasks, select the lower task (below where you want the copied task to appear) and then click Paste.

Copy multiple adjacent tasks and their task information. Click the row heading of the first task you want to copy. Hold down the Shift key and then click the row heading of the last task (see Figure 3-16). Click Copy Task. Select the task below where you want the copied tasks to start to be added and then click Paste.

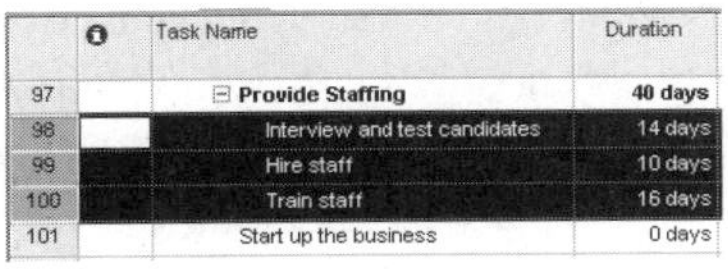

Figure 3-16. Copy multiple tasks along with all their associated information.

Copy multiple nonadjacent tasks and their task information. Click the row heading of the first task you want to copy. Hold down the Ctrl key and then click the row headings of all the tasks you want to copy. Click Copy Task. Select the task below where you want the copied tasks to be added. Click Paste. The tasks are added in the order that you selected them.

Chapter 3

Deleting Tasks

To delete a task you don't need, select the row heading and then press the Delete key.

In Microsoft Project 2000 and earlier, when you clicked a task name and pressed the Delete key, the entire task row was deleted. Now the Delete indicator appears in the Indicators column, enabling you to choose whether to delete the entire task or just the task name (see Figure 3-17).

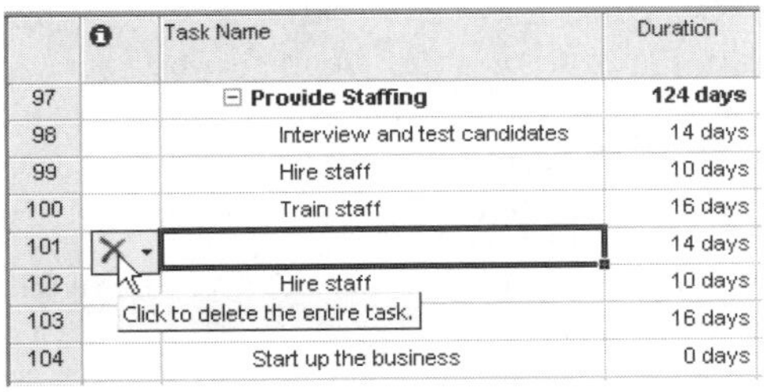

Figure 3-17. Click the down arrow next to the Delete indicator to choose what you want to delete.

If you want to delete the entire task, click the indicator. If you simply want to clear the task name, press Enter or click elsewhere in the view.

Organizing Tasks into an Outline

Now that your task list is sequenced to your satisfaction, you're ready to organize the tasks into a structure representing the hierarchy of tasks from the broader perspective to the deep and detailed perspective where the real work actually takes place.

A task at a higher outline level than other tasks is called a summary task; the tasks beneath that summary task are called subtasks (see Figure 3-18). Summary tasks typically represent phases in a project. For example, in a new business startup project, you might have summary tasks for developing the strategic plan, defining the business opportunity, planning for action, and proceeding with the startup plan.

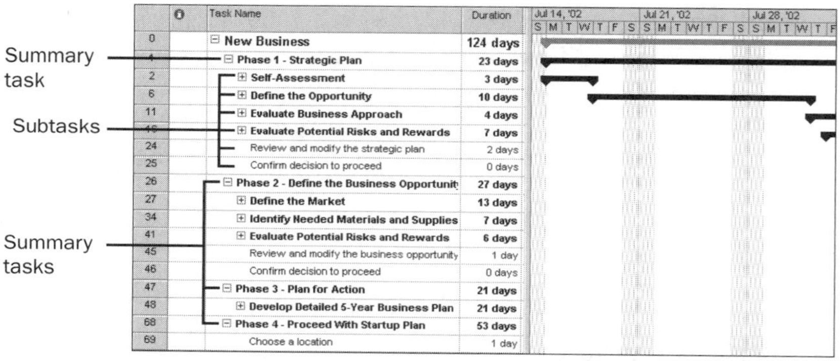

Figure 3-18. Use summary tasks and subtasks to combine related tasks into manageable chunks.

The subtasks under those phases can be actual tasks that are assigned to resources. Or they could be another set of summary tasks. For example, the "Define the business opportunity" summary task could have subtasks such as "Define the market," "Identify needed materials and supplies," and "Evaluate potential risks and rewards." These subtasks in turn can be summary tasks to still more subtasks. You can have up to nine outline levels.

Many project managers use the outline levels to correspond to their WBS, in which the lowest-level subtask corresponds to the work package.

> **For more information about WBSs in Microsoft Project, see "Setting Up Your Work Breakdown Structure" later in this chapter on page 88.**

As you create the outline structure in your task list, you might find that you need to refine the task list even more by inserting, moving, and deleting tasks.

All your tasks are initially at the first outline level. To make a summary task, you need to indent subtasks beneath it. The following list describes various outlining techniques:

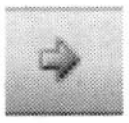

Indent

Make a task a subtask. Click the task. On the Formatting toolbar, click Indent. The task is indented, and the task above it becomes its summary task. Summary tasks are highlighted in bold in the table portion of the Gantt Chart and are marked with a black bar spanning the summary tasks in the chart portion of the Gantt Chart.

Create a subtask under a subtask. Click a task under a subtask. Click Indent twice. It's now in the third outline level, as a subtask of a subtask.

Outdent

Move a subtask to a higher level. Click a subtask and then click Outdent.

Indent several tasks at one time. Drag the mouse pointer across several adjacent tasks to select them and then click Indent. Use the Ctrl key to select several nonadjacent tasks at once and then click Indent. This method also works for tasks that will become subtasks to different summary tasks.

Show

Show the tasks at a specified outline level. If you want tasks only at the first and second outline levels to be visible throughout your entire project plan, for example, on the Formatting toolbar, click Show and then click Outline Level 2. You can select any outline level you want. You can also click All Subtasks to see all outline levels.

Show Subtasks

Hide Subtasks

Hide or show the subtasks for a selected summary task. Next to each summary task is a plus or minus sign. The plus sign indicates that there are hidden subtasks for this summary task. Click the plus sign, and the subtasks appear. The minus sign indicates that the subtasks are currently displayed. Click the minus sign, and the subtasks will be hidden. You can also use Show Subtasks and Hide Subtasks on the Formatting toolbar to do the same thing.

Summary tasks show rolled-up task information that is an aggregate of the information in the associated subtasks. For example, if there are four subtasks, each with a duration of 2 days, the summary task shows the total of 8 days. You can also see rolled-up summary information for costs, start dates, finish dates, and more.

You can also display a summary task for the project as a whole. The project summary task shows rolled-up summary information for the project as a whole; for example, total costs, total duration, project start, and project finish. To show the project summary task, follow these steps:

1. Click Tools, Options.
2. On the View tab, under Outline Options, select the Show Project Summary Task check box.

The project summary task name is adopted from the project filename.

Setting Up Your Work Breakdown Structure

Many project managers and organizations use a WBS as an essential element of their project management methodology. Similar to the outline structure of your project task list, the WBS is a hierarchical chart view of deliverables in a project in which each level down represents an increasingly detailed description of the project deliverables. Each level has its own code set, such as 2.1.3.a. Levels in the hierarchy represent summary tasks, subtasks, work packages, and deliverables. You can define a project's scope and develop its task lists with the WBS.

Industries, application areas, and organizations experienced with a particular type of project tend to have WBSs developed to represent the life cycles of their typical types of projects; for example, the design of a new vehicle or the construction of an office building.

Understanding Work Breakdown Structure Codes

Each item and level in a work breakdown structure is described by a unique WBS code. Each digit in the code typically represents a level in the structure's hierarchy, such as 2.1.4.3 or 5.B.c.3. A WBS code such as 1.2.3 might represent the third deliverable for the second activity in the first phase of the project.

Note In some industries or application areas, the work breakdown structure is also known as the *project breakdown structure*, or *PBS*.

In Microsoft Project, any outline structure you set up for your tasks is assigned a set of unique outline numbers. The outline number for the first summary task is 1; the outline number for the first subtask under the first summary task is 1.1 (see Figure 3-19).

	ℹ	Outline Number	WBS	Task Name	Duration
1		**1**	**1**	⊟ **Phase 1 - Strategic Plan**	**23 days**
2		**1.1**	**1.1**	⊟ **Self-Assessment**	**3 days**
3		1.1.1	1.1.1	Define business vision	1 day
4		1.1.2	1.1.2	Identify available skills, information and support	1 day
5		1.1.3	1.1.3	Decide whether to proceed	1 day
6		**1.2**	**1.2**	⊟ **Define the Opportunity**	**10 days**
7		1.2.1	1.2.1	Research the market and competition	1 day
8		1.2.2	1.2.2	Interview owners of similar businesses	5 days
9		1.2.3	1.2.3	Identify needed resources	2 days
10		1.2.4	1.2.4	Identify operating cost elements	2 days
11		**1.3**	**1.3**	⊟ **Evaluate Business Approach**	**4 days**
12		1.3.1	1.3.1	Define new entity requirements	1 day
13		1.3.2	1.3.2	Identify on-going business purchase opportunities	1 day
14		1.3.3	1.3.3	Research franchise possibilities	1 day
15		1.3.4	1.3.4	Summarize business approach	1 day
16		**1.4**	**1.4**	⊟ **Evaluate Potential Risks and Rewards**	**7 days**
17		1.4.1	1.4.1	Assess market size and stability	2 days
18		1.4.2	1.4.2	Estimate the competition	1 day

Figure 3-19. The outline number specifies the task's position in your project plan's task outline hierarchy.

By default, Microsoft Project creates WBS codes that are derived from these outline numbers, and you can't change the code scheme of the outline numbers. However, if you and your organization have a specific WBS coding scheme, you can change the WBS numbering. When working with WBS codes, keep the following in mind:

- You can have only one set of WBS codes. However, if you use additional coding schemes, you can create up to ten sets of outline codes and then sort or group your tasks by those codes.

Note Certain project management methodologies use other structured and hierarchical codes that can describe your project from different viewpoints. Examples include the *organizational breakdown structure (OBS)*, the *resource breakdown structure (RBS)*, and the *bill of materials (BOM)*.

For more information about outline codes, see "Working with Outline Codes" on page 806.

- You can include ordered numbers, uppercase letters, and lowercase letters as part of your custom WBS code format. You can also include unordered characters in the code format.
- You can automatically generate your custom WBS codes for tasks as you add them.

Setting Up Work Breakdown Structure Codes

To set up your custom WBS code scheme, including any prefix and *code mask*, follow these steps:

1. Click Project, WBS, Define Code.
2. If you use a prefix for the project in front of the WBS code to distinguish it from other projects using the same code format, enter that prefix in the Project Code Prefix box.
3. In the Sequence field in the first row, select whether the first digit of the code (representing the first level of the hierarchy) is an ordered number, ordered uppercase letter, ordered lowercase letter, or unordered character.
4. In the Length field in the first row, specify whether there is a length limit for the first code.
5. In the Separator field in the first row, specify the character that separates the first and second code.
6. Repeat the procedure in the Sequence field in the second row.

   Continue these steps until all the levels of your custom WBS code are set up (see Figure 3-20). As you enter the code mask for each succeeding level, the Code Preview box shows an example of the code.

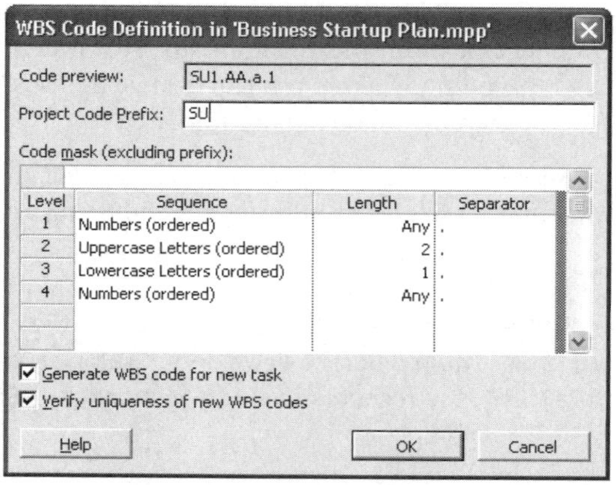

Figure 3-20. Define your organization's WBS code format.

7 When finished, click OK. The WBS codes for your tasks are reset to conform to your custom structure (see Figure 3-21).

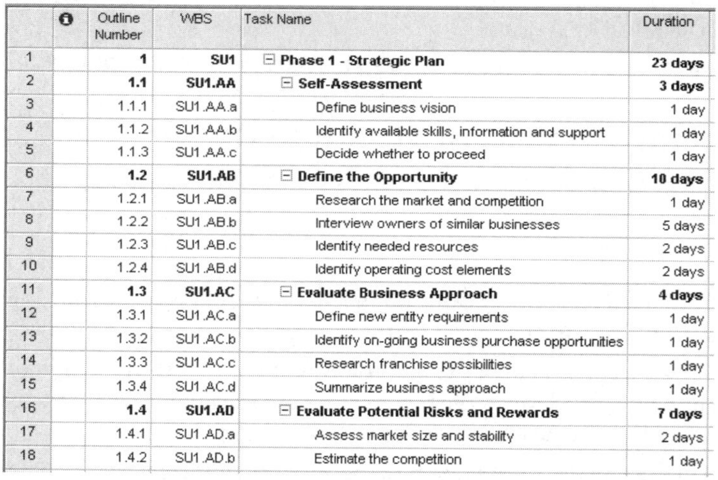

		Outline Number	WBS	Task Name	Duration
1		**1**	**SU1**	**Phase 1 - Strategic Plan**	**23 days**
2		**1.1**	**SU1.AA**	**Self-Assessment**	**3 days**
3		1.1.1	SU1.AA.a	Define business vision	1 day
4		1.1.2	SU1.AA.b	Identify available skills, information and support	1 day
5		1.1.3	SU1.AA.c	Decide whether to proceed	1 day
6		**1.2**	**SU1.AB**	**Define the Opportunity**	**10 days**
7		1.2.1	SU1.AB.a	Research the market and competition	1 day
8		1.2.2	SU1.AB.b	Interview owners of similar businesses	5 days
9		1.2.3	SU1.AB.c	Identify needed resources	2 days
10		1.2.4	SU1.AB.d	Identify operating cost elements	2 days
11		**1.3**	**SU1.AC**	**Evaluate Business Approach**	**4 days**
12		1.3.1	SU1.AC.a	Define new entity requirements	1 day
13		1.3.2	SU1.AC.b	Identify on-going business purchase opportunities	1 day
14		1.3.3	SU1.AC.c	Research franchise possibilities	1 day
15		1.3.4	SU1.AC.d	Summarize business approach	1 day
16		**1.4**	**SU1.AD**	**Evaluate Potential Risks and Rewards**	**7 days**
17		1.4.1	SU1.AD.a	Assess market size and stability	2 days
18		1.4.2	SU1.AD.b	Estimate the competition	1 day

Figure 3-21. Your newly defined WBS codes replace the default WBS codes derived from the outline numbers.

Charting Your WBS in Visio

NEW FEATURE! You can use the Microsoft Project Gantt Chart to set up and rearrange your tasks according to your custom WBS. If you use Microsoft Visio 2000 or later, you can take this a step further and use Visio's charting features for your WBS structure. You can then display project information in a Visio WBS chart by using the Visio WBS Chart Wizard, which is installed with Microsoft Project.

To create a Microsoft Visio WBS chart from your project tasks, do the following:

1. Open the project that contains the WBS codes.

   The WBS codes must be identified and applied to the tasks before running the Visio WBS Chart Wizard.

2. If necessary, show the Visio WBS Chart toolbar.
3. On the View menu, point to Toolbars and then click Visio WBS Chart.
4. On the Visio WBS Chart toolbar, click Visio WBS Chart Wizard.
5. Click Launch Wizard.

   The Visio WBS Chart Wizard appears (see Figure 3-22).

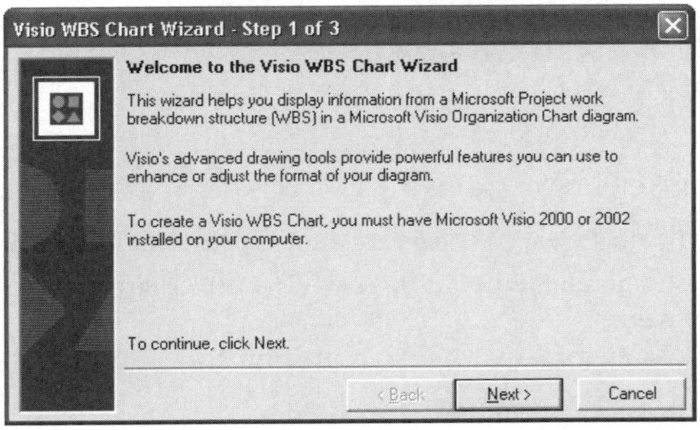

Figure 3-22. The Visio WBS Chart Wizard consists of three steps.

6. Follow the instructions to create the Visio WBS Chart.

   This procedure creates a chart for all tasks or for all tasks based on a selected outline level (see Figure 3-23).

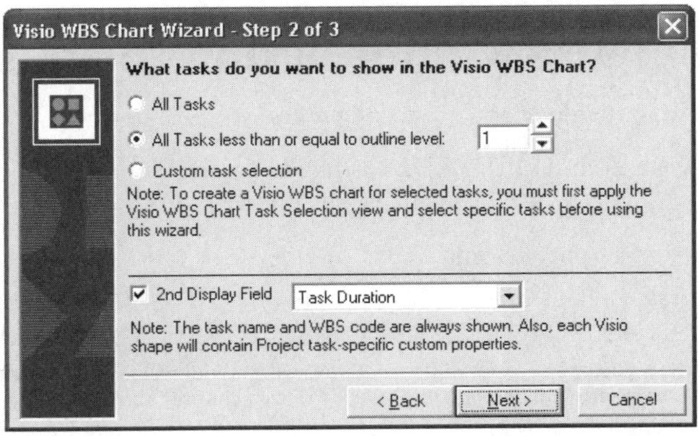

Figure 3-23. Specify which tasks and information you want the Visio WBS chart to include.

Chapter 3

You can also create a chart for specific selected tasks. Follow these steps to do this:

1. On the toolbar, click Visio WBS Chart Wizard and then click Apply Task Selection View (see Figure 3-24).

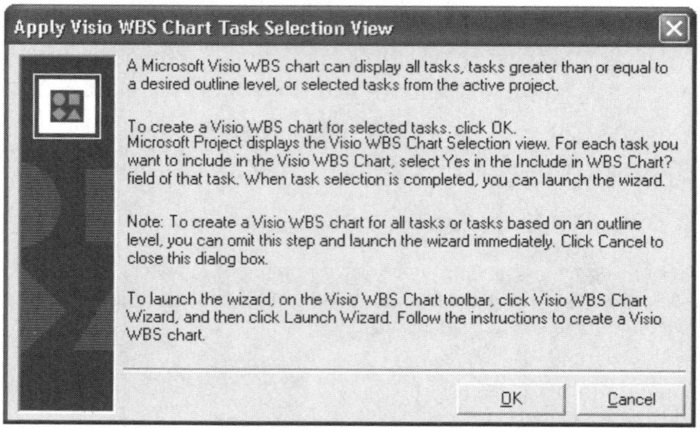

Apply Visio WBS Chart Task Selection View
A Microsoft Visio WBS chart can display all tasks, tasks greater than or equal to a desired outline level, or selected tasks from the active project.
To create a Visio WBS chart for selected tasks, click OK.
Microsoft Project displays the Visio WBS Chart Selection view. For each task you want to include in the Visio WBS Chart, select Yes in the Include in WBS Chart? field of that task. When task selection is completed, you can launch the wizard.
Note: To create a Visio WBS chart for all tasks or tasks based on an outline level, you can omit this step and launch the wizard immediately. Click Cancel to close this dialog box.
To launch the wizard, on the Visio WBS Chart toolbar, click Visio WBS Chart Wizard, and then click Launch Wizard. Follow the instructions to create a Visio WBS chart.
OK
Cancel

Figure 3-24. Click OK to add the Include In WBS Chart field to the current task sheet.

2. Click OK. The Include In WBS Chart column appears in the current task sheet.
3. For each task you want to include in your Visio WBS chart, click Yes in the Include In WBS Chart field.
4. On the Visio WBS Chart toolbar, click Visio WBS Chart Wizard and then click Launch Wizard.
5. Click Next. The Custom Task Selection option is selected in the wizard page.
6. Click Next. The WBS Chart of your selected tasks is created in Visio.
7. Click Finish.
8. To remove the Include In WBS Chart field from the task sheet, click the column heading and then press Delete.

Adding Supplementary Information to Tasks

You can annotate an individual task by entering notes. To add a note to a task, do the following:

1. Click the task and then click Task Information on the Standard toolbar.
2. Click the Notes tab.
3. In the Notes area, type the note.
4. When finished, click OK.

You can insert an entire document as a note associated with an individual task. For more information, see "Copying a Document into Your Project File" earlier in this chapter on page 74.

Note You can also hyperlink from a task to a document on your computer or on a Web site. For more information, see "Hyperlinking a Document from Your Project File" earlier in this chapter on page 76.

Chapter 4
Viewing Project Information

To plan, track, and manage your project with Microsoft Office Project 2003, you enter a variety of detailed information regarding tasks, resources, assignments, durations, resource rates, and more. Project 2003, in turn, calculates certain entries to create even more information, including start dates, finish dates, costs, and remaining work. In Microsoft Project, more than 400 distinct pieces of information, including your own custom information, are available for tasks, resources, and assignments. The more tasks, resources, and assignments you have in your project, and the more custom capabilities you use, the more these pieces of information are multiplied.

There's no way you could look at this mass of project information at one time and work with it in any kind of meaningful or efficient way. To solve this problem, Microsoft Project organizes and stores the information in a *database*. All information associated with an individual task, for example, is a single *record* in that database. Each piece of information in that record is a separate *field* (see Figure 4-1).

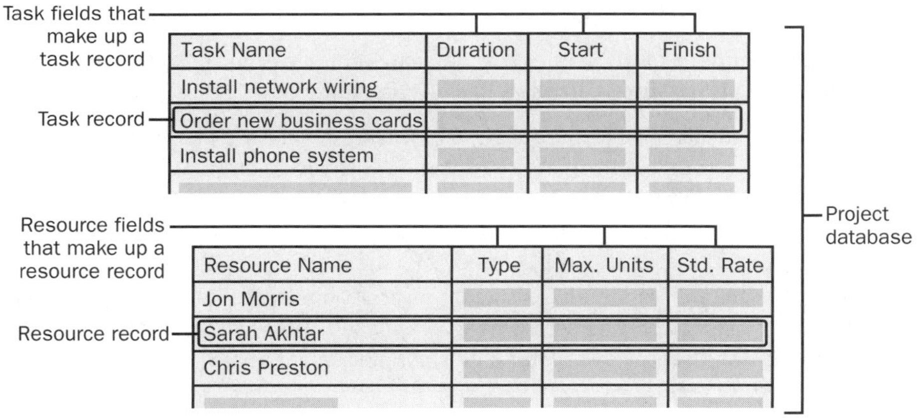

Figure 4-1. Each task represents a single record in your project database, with all associated information represented by individual fields.

Note The project database is distinct from the SQL Server database that Microsoft Project uses to store data. In the SQL Server database, information about one task can actually be spread across multiple tables in multiple records.

When you need to look at or work with a particular set of information, you choose a particular *view* to be displayed in the Microsoft Project workspace. A view filters the project information in a specific way according to the purpose of the view and then presents that layout of information in the Microsoft Project workspace so you can easily work with it. More than 25 views are built into Microsoft Project.

You can rearrange the project information presented in a view. You can sort information in many views by name, date, and so on. You can group information, for example, by complete versus incomplete tasks. You can filter information to see only the information you want, for example, only tasks that are assigned to a particular resource. These concepts and techniques are all presented in this chapter.

Understanding Project Information Categories

The means for organizing, managing, and storing the thousands of pieces of project information is the Microsoft Project database. There are three major categories in the project database:

- Task information
- Resource information
- Assignment information

When you start entering project information, typically you enter tasks and associated information such as duration, date constraints, deadlines, and task dependencies. These all fall under the task information category.

Then you enter resource names and associated information such as standard rate, overtime rate, and working times calendar. These all fall under the resource information category.

As soon as you assign a resource to a task, you create an assignment, which is the intersection of task and resource. Information associated with an assignment includes the amount of work, the assignment start and finish dates, the cost for the assignment, and so on. These fall under the assignment information category.

Note There are also three subcategories of project information: task-timephased, resource-timephased, and assignment-timephased. These subcategories are covered in "Working with Usage Views" later in this chapter on page 105.

Understanding these three categories is important when viewing project information. There are task views and resource views. The individual fields that make up all views are also classified as task, resource, or assignment fields, and can only be seen in their respective views. Likewise, there are filters and groups designed just for task views and other filters and groups designed just for resource views.

For more information about working with your Microsoft Project database, see Chapter 32, "Working with Microsoft Project Data."

Accessing Your Project Information

You view and work with information in Microsoft Project by selecting a specific view to be displayed in your Microsoft Project workspace. Of the many views built into Microsoft Project, some have to do with tasks, others with resources, and still others with assignments. Certain views are a spreadsheet of tables and columns. Others are graphs or forms. Other views are a blend; for example, the Gantt Chart includes both a sheet and a graph.

You can switch tables in a view, and add and remove fields shown in a view, and so modify these views to present your project information exactly the way you need.

Using Views

When you first start using Microsoft Project, typically the first view you use is the Gantt Chart, which is the default view. Here, you enter information such as tasks, durations, and task relationships. Then you might use the Resource Sheet, in which you enter resource information. As you continue to plan your project, your requirements become more sophisticated, and you find you need other views. For example, you might want to see all your tasks with their current percent complete, along with the critical path. Or you might need a graph showing a particular resource's workload throughout April and May.

Tip **Change the default view**

To change the view that opens when you first open Microsoft Project and create a new project file, click Tools, Options and then click the View tab. In the Default View box, click the view you want to appear by default whenever you create a new project file.

This setting changes the view only for any new project files. For an existing project file, the last view shown when you saved and closed the file is the one that appears when you open it again.

For more information about other view options, see "Arranging Your Microsoft Project Workspace" later in this chapter on page 132.

The most commonly used views are available on the View menu. All views are available on the More Views submenu. To switch to a different view, do the following:

1. Click View and then look for the view you want.
2. If the view you want is listed, click its name. If the view is not listed, click More Views. The full list of available Microsoft Project views appears (see Figure 4-2).

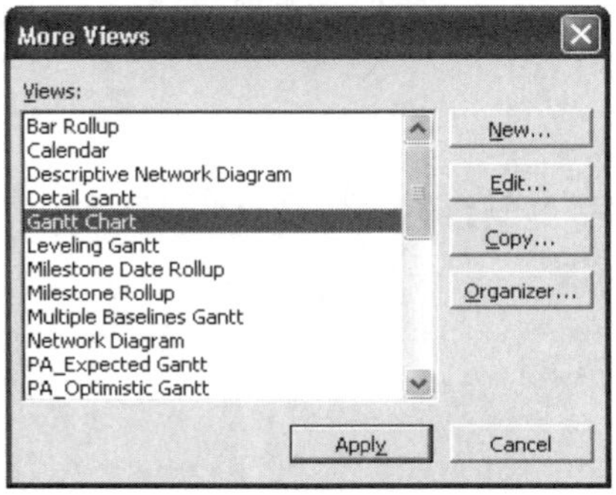

Figure 4-2. The More Views dialog box lists all available views in alphabetical order.

3 Double-click the view you want. It appears in your Microsoft Project workspace, replacing the previous view.

Keep in mind that when you switch from one view to another, you're not changing the data; you're just getting a different look at the data in your project database.

If you display the View bar, you can use it to quickly switch views. To show the View bar, do the following:

1 Click View, View Bar. The View bar appears on the far left edge of the Microsoft Project window (see Figure 4-3). The same views that appear on the View menu are listed on the View bar.

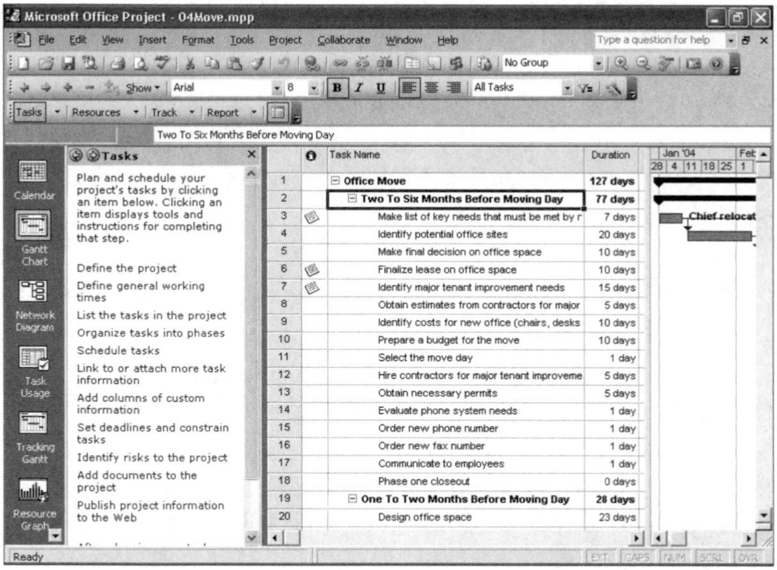

Figure 4-3. The View bar lists icons for the same views shown in the View menu.

Chapter 4

2 Click a view's name or icon to switch to that view. If you can't see the view's name, click the arrow at the bottom of the list to see more views.

If the view isn't listed on the View bar, click More Views to see the full list.

Tip **Switch views with Active View bar**
To hide a showing View bar, click View, View Bar.

When the View bar is hidden, a blue vertical bar appears between the Project Guide side pane and the current view. This is the Active View bar, and it shows the name of the current view. To change the current view, right-click the Active View bar. If the view you want appears in the shortcut menu, click it. Otherwise, click More Views to display the More Views dialog box and then click the view you want.

Inside Out

Add your favorite views to the View menu

Although the most commonly used views are listed on the View menu and the View bar, they might not be *your* most commonly used views. For example, you might use the Task Entry view and the Detail Gantt daily, and you don't want to click More Views every time you need it.

You can add your frequently used views to the View menu and View bar. To do this, follow these steps:

1 Click View, More Views.
2 Click the view you want to add to the View menu and then click Edit.
3 In the View Definition dialog box, select the Show In Menu check box

You can use this technique to remove views you never use from the View menu and View bar as well. Simply select the view, click Edit, and clear the Show In Menu check box.

You can also rearrange the order of views listed. The task views are listed first, in alphabetical order, and then the resource views are listed in alphabetical order. In the More Views dialog box, click the view you want to rearrange and then click Edit. In the Name box, add a number in front of the name; it is then brought to the top of its respective list. Prefix all the displayed views with a sequential number, and they'll appear in that sequential order.

You can fully customize your views and create entirely new views. For more information, see “Customizing Views” on page 761.

You can think of Microsoft Project views in the following categories:

- Gantt charts
- Network diagrams
- Graph views
- Sheet views
- Usage views
- Forms
- Combination views

Working with Gantt Charts

Gantt charts are a special type of view used extensively in project management. The left side of a Gantt chart contains a sheet view and the right side contains a bar graph along a timescale (see Figure 4-4).

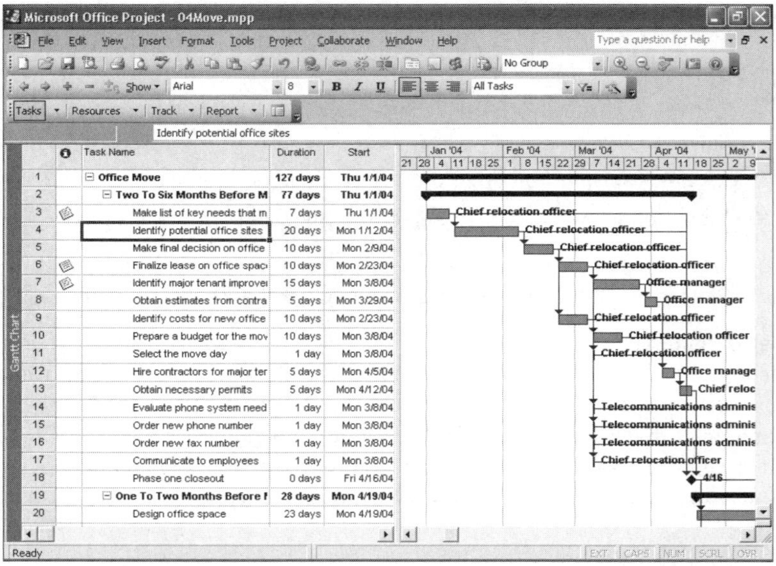

Figure 4-4. A Gantt chart shows task information in the sheet portion of the view; the corresponding bar graph shows the task’s duration, start and finish dates, and task relationships.

Table 4-1 describes the Microsoft Project Gantt charts.

Table 4-1. Microsoft Project Gantt Charts

Type of Gantt chart	How you can use it	For more information
Bar Rollup (task view)	View summary tasks with labels for all subtasks. Use the Bar Rollup view with the Rollup_Formatting macro to see all tasks concisely labeled on summary Gantt bars.	"Organizing Tasks into an Outline" on page 86
Detail Gantt (task view)	View tasks and associated information in a sheet, and see slack and slippage for tasks over time in a bar graph on a timescale. Use the Detail Gantt to check how far a task can slip without affecting other tasks.	Chapter 9, "Checking and Adjusting the Project Plan"
Gantt Chart (task view)	View tasks and associated information in a sheet, and see tasks and durations over time in a bar graph on a timescale. Use the Gantt Chart to enter and schedule a list of tasks. This is the view that appears by default when you first start Microsoft Project.	"Creating a New Project Plan" on page 62.
Leveling Gantt (task view)	View tasks, task delays, and slack in a sheet, and the before-and-after effects of the Microsoft Project leveling feature. Use the Leveling Gantt to check the amount of task delay caused by leveling.	"Balancing Resource Work-loads" on page 271
Milestone Date Rollup (task view)	View summary tasks with labels for all subtasks. Use the Milestone Date Rollup view with the Rollup_Formatting macro to see all tasks concisely labeled with milestone marks and dates on summary Gantt bars.	"Creating Mile-stones in Your Schedule" on page 167
Milestone Rollup (task view)	View summary tasks with labels for all subtasks. Use the Milestone Rollup view with the Rollup_Formatting macro to see all tasks concisely labeled with milestone marks on the summary Gantt bars.	"Creating Mile-stones in Your Schedule" on page 167
Multiple Baselines Gantt (task view)	View different colored Gantt bars for the first three base-lines (Baseline, Baseline1, and Baseline2) on summary tasks and subtasks in the chart portion of the view. Use the Multiple Baselines Gantt to review and compare the first three baselines you saved for your project.	"Saving Original Plan Information Using a Base-line" on page 298.
PA_Expected Gantt (task view)	View your schedule's expected scenario based on dura-tions calculated from a PERT analysis.	"Calculating Your Most Probable Duration" on page 145
PA_Optimistic Gantt (task view)	View your schedule's best-case scenario based on dura-tions calculated from a PERT analysis.	"Calculating Your Most Probable Duration" on page 145

Chapter 4

Table 4-1. Microsoft Project Gantt Charts

Type of Gantt chart	How you can use it	For more information
PA_Pessimistic Gantt (task view)	View your schedule's worst-case scenario, based on durations calculated from a PERT analysis.	"Calculating Your Most Probable Duration" on page 145
Tracking Gantt (task view)	View tasks and task information in a sheet, and a chart showing a baseline and scheduled Gantt bars for each task. Use the Tracking Gantt to compare the baseline schedule with the actual schedule.	Chapter 10, "Saving a Baseline and Updating Progress"

You can change the look and content of bars on a Gantt chart. You can:

- Change the pattern, color, and shape of the Gantt bar for a selected task.
- Change the text accompanying the Gantt bar for a selected task.
- Change the format and text for all Gantt bars of a particular type.
- Change the text style for all Gantt bars of a particular type.
- Change the layout of links and bars on a Gantt chart.
- Change the gridlines in the view.

Troubleshooting

You can't find the PERT analysis views

If you haven't used PERT (Program Evaluation and Review Technique) analysis since installing Project 2003, you might not see the PA_Expected Gantt, PA_Optimistic Gantt, PA_Pessimistic Gantt, or PA_PERT Entry Sheet in the More Views dialog box.

Click View, Toolbars, PERT Analysis. On the PERT Analysis toolbar (see Figure 4-5), click the button for the PERT analysis view (for example, Optimistic Gantt) you need. From this point forward, that PERT analysis view is listed in the More Views dialog box.

Figure 4-5. A PERT analysis view does not become available in the More Views dialog box until you select it on the PERT Analysis toolbar.

For more information about changing the look and content of Gantt bars, see "Formatting a Gantt Chart View" on page 766.

To change the timescale in a Gantt Chart, see "Working with Timescales" later in this chapter on page 111.

You can also change the content or look of the sheet portion of a Gantt chart. For details, see "Customizing Views" on page 761.

You can print views with the content and format you set up in the Microsoft Project window. For more information, see "Setting Up and Printing Views" on page 358.

Working with Network Diagrams

Network diagrams are a special type of graph view that presents each task and associated task information in a separate box, or *node*. The nodes are connected by lines that represent task relationships. The resulting diagram is a flowchart of the project. Network Diagram views (see Figure 4-6) are also referred to as PERT charts. They are *Activity on Node diagrams*, as contrasted with *Activity on Arrow diagrams*.

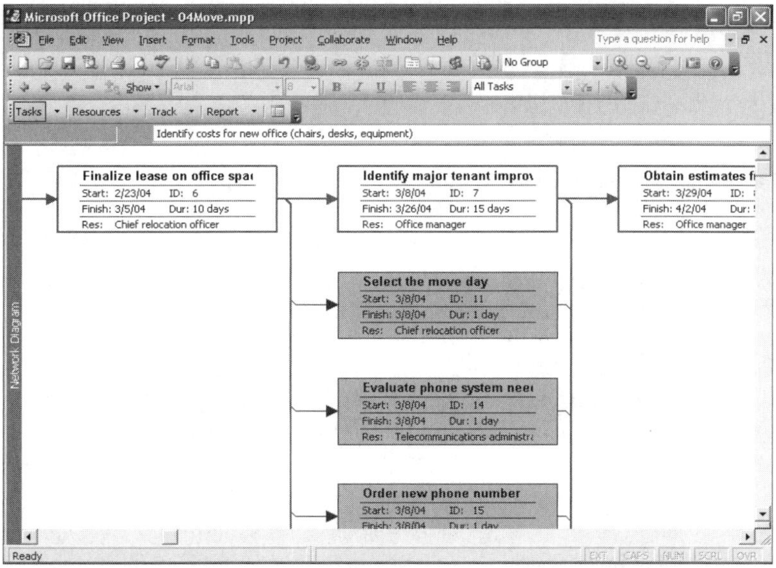

Figure 4-6. You can enter, edit, and review tasks and their dependencies in the Network Diagram view.

Table 4-2 describes the Microsoft Project network diagram views.

Table 4-2. Microsoft Project Network Diagram Views

Type of Network diagram	How you can use it	For more information
Descriptive Network Diagram (task view)	View all tasks and task dependencies. Use the Descriptive Network Diagram to create and fine-tune your schedule in a flowchart format. This view is similar to the regular Network Diagram, but the nodes are larger and provide more detail.	"Establishing Task Dependencies" on page 149
Network Diagram (task view)	Enter, edit, and review all tasks and task dependencies. Use the Network Diagram to create and fine-tune your schedule in a flowchart format.	"Establishing Task Dependencies" on page 149
Relationship Diagram (task view)	View the predecessors and successors of a single selected task. In a large project or any project with more complex task linking, use this task view to focus on the task dependencies of a specific task.	"Establishing Task Dependencies" on page 149

To learn about modifying the content or format of a Network Diagram, see "Modifying a Network Diagram" on page 772.

Working with Graph Views

Graph views present project information in a pictorial representation that more readily communicates the data (see Figure 4-7).

Table 4-3 describes the Microsoft Project graph views.

Table 4-3. Microsoft Project Graph Views

Type of graph view	How you can use it	For more information
Calendar (task view)	View tasks and durations for a specific week or range of weeks in a monthly calendar format (see Figure 4-8).	Chapter 5, "Scheduling Tasks"
Resource Graph (resource view)	View resource allocation, cost, or work over time for a single resource or group of resources at a time. Information is displayed in a column graph format (refer to Figure 4-7). When used in combination with other views, the Resource Graph can be very useful for finding resource overallocations.	"Balancing Resource Workloads" on page 271

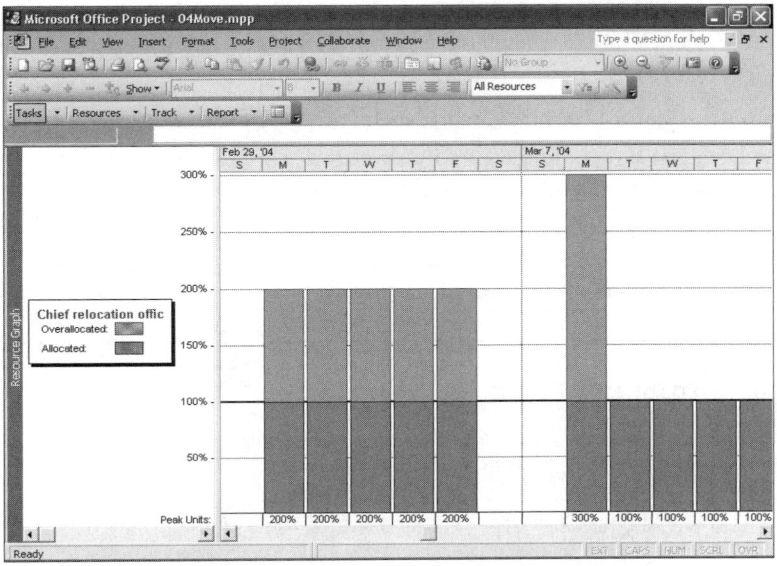

Figure 4-7. You can use the Resource Graph to review resource allocation levels.

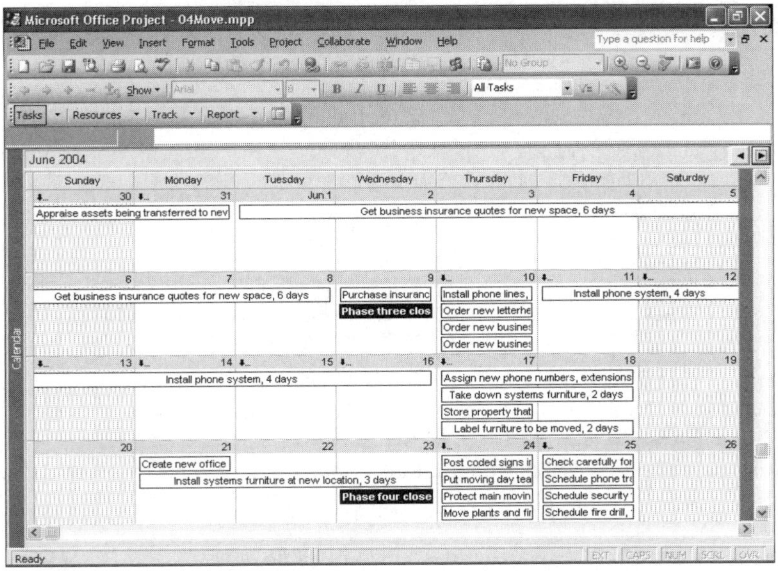

Figure 4-8. In the Calendar view, you can quickly see which tasks are scheduled on particular days, weeks, or months.

The Resource Graph shows peak units by resource, including the percentage of allocation and overallocation. You can change the type of information being shown in the Resource Graph by doing the following:

1. With the Resource Graph showing, click Format, Details.

   The Details submenu lists the various categories of information that the Resource Graph can chart, including Work, Percent Allocation, and Cost.

2. Click the category of information you want charted on the Resource Graph.

For information about modifying the format of the Resource Graph or Calendar view, see "Customizing Views" on page 761.

Working with Sheet Views

Sheet views are spreadsheet-type views that are divided into columns and rows, and in which each individual field is contained in a cell (see Figure 4-9).

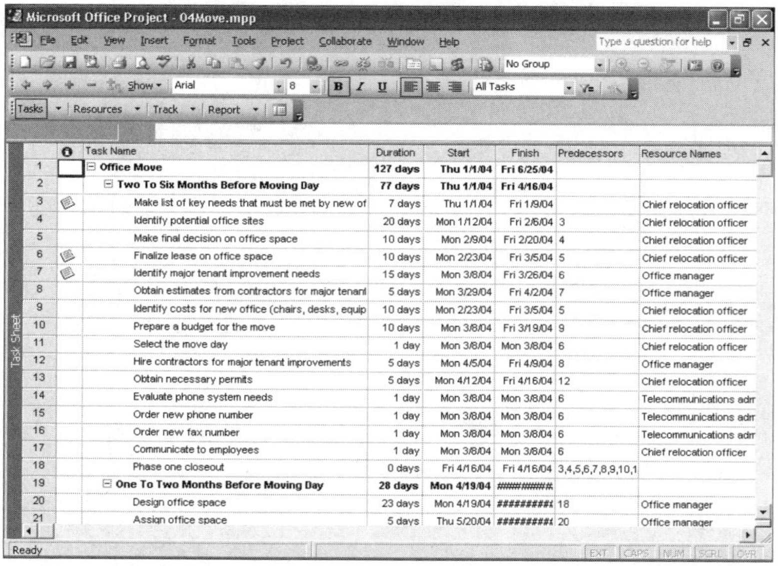

Figure 4-9. Use the Task Sheet to enter tasks and durations, and to review calculated start and finish dates.

The Microsoft Project sheet views are described in Table 4-4.

Table 4-4. **Microsoft Project Sheet Views**

Type of sheet view	How you can use it	For more information
PA_PERT Entry Sheet (task view)	Enter your schedule's best-case, expected-case, and worst-case scenarios for a task's duration in preparation of calculating the most probable duration using a PERT analysis, which helps you consider and reconcile disparities between different task estimates.	"Calculating Your Most Probable Duration" on page 145
Resource Sheet (resource view)	Enter, edit, and review resource information in a spreadsheet format.	Chapter 6, "Setting Up Resources in the Project"
Task Sheet (task view)	Enter, edit, and review task information in a spreadsheet format.	"Creating a New Project Plan" on page 62

For information about modifying the content or format of a sheet view, see "Modifying a Sheet View" on page 780.

Working with Usage Views

Usage views are made up of a sheet view on the left side and a timesheet on the right. Together with the timescale, the timesheet can show work, cost, availability, and other data broken out by time, that is, *timephased* (see Figure 4-10).

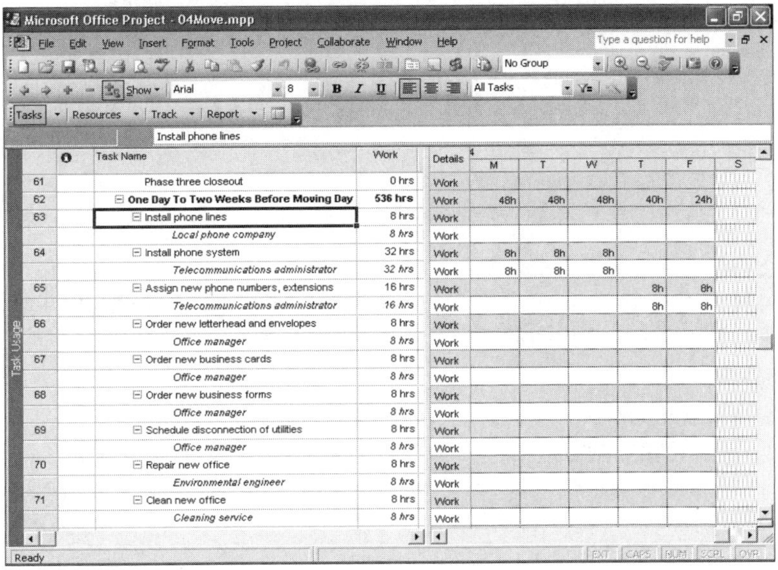

Figure 4-10. Display the Task Usage view to review assignments by task.

The Microsoft Project usage views are described in Table 4-5.

Table 4-5. Microsoft Project Usage Views

Type of usage view	How you can use it	For more information
Resource Usage (assignment view)	Review, enter, and edit assignments by resource. In the sheet portion of the Resource Usage view, each resource is listed with all associated task assignments indented beneath it (see Figure 4-11). In the timesheet portion of the view, information such as work or costs for the resource and the assignment is listed according to the timescale, for example, by week or month.	Chapter 7, "Assigning Resources to Tasks"
Task Usage (assignment view)	Review, enter, and edit assignments by task. In the sheet portion of the Task Usage view, each task is listed with the assigned resources indented beneath it (see Figure 4-12). In the timesheet portion of the view, information such as work or costs for the task and the assignment is listed according to the timescale, for example, by day or by week.	Chapter 7

⊟ **Network support manager**	**144 hrs**
Order systems furniture	*8 hrs*
Evaluate server room needs	*16 hrs*
Evaluate computer networking needs	*16 hrs*
Order internet phone lines	*8 hrs*
Inventory existing computers	*40 hrs*

Figure 4-11. In the Resource Usage view, each resource is listed with its assigned tasks.

⊟ Design office space	276 hrs
Office manager	*92 hrs*
Chief relocation officer	*92 hrs*
Environmental engineer	*92 hrs*
⊟ Assign office space	40 hrs
Office manager	*40 hrs*

Figure 4-12. In the Task Usage view, each task is listed with its assigned resources.

Because the timesheet portion of the usage views breaks down information from certain fields and from specific time periods, there are three subcategories to the major field categories of tasks, resources, and assignments:

- Task-timephased
- Resource-timephased
- Assignment-timephased

You can review task-timephased and assignment-timephased fields in the timesheet portion of the Task Usage view. You can review resource-timephased and assignment-timephased fields in the timesheet portion of the Resource Usage view.

Note Timephased information is used in many earned-value analysis calculations. For more information about earned value, see "Analyzing Progress and Costs Using Earned Value" on page 401.

The Work field is shown by default in the timephased fields in the timesheet portion of a usage view. Multiple fields of information can be "stacked" in the view at one time. To change the type of information shown, do the following:

1. With a usage view showing, click Format, Details.

   The Details submenu lists the different timephased fields that the timesheet portion of the usage view can display, for example, Actual Work, Baseline Work, and Cost. Any fields currently displayed are noted with a check mark.
2. Click the field you want to add to the timesheet. Another row of timephased information is added to the timesheet for each task.
3. To remove a row of information from the timesheet, click Format, Details and then click the item you want to remove.

Note For information about modifying the format of a usage view, see "Modifying a Usage View" on page 781.

Working with Forms

Forms are specialized views that include text boxes and grids in which you can enter and review information in a way similar to a dialog box (see Figure 4-13). Although you can display a form on its own and click the Previous and Next buttons to cycle through the different tasks or resources in your project, a form is most useful when included as part of a combination view (see "Working with Combination Views" in the next section).

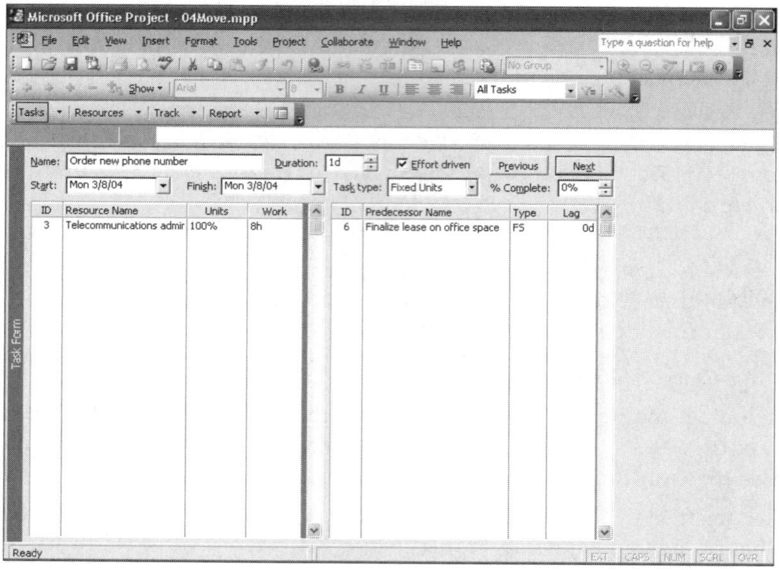

Figure 4-13. This Task Form shows fundamental information about the task, along with information about assigned resources and predecessor tasks.

The Microsoft Project forms are described in Table 4-6.

Table 4-6. Microsoft Project Forms

Type of form	How you can use it	For more information
Resource Form (resource view)	Enter, edit, and review all resource, task, and schedule information about a selected resource, one resource at a time. The grid area can show information about the resource's schedule, cost, or work on assigned tasks. It is most useful when used as part of a combination view (see Figure 4-14).	Chapter 7
Resource Name Form (resource view)	Enter, edit, and review the selected resource's schedule, cost, or work on assigned tasks. The Resource Name Form is a simplified version of the Resource Form.	Chapter 7
Task Details Form (task view)	Enter, edit, and review detailed tracking and scheduling information about a selected task, one task at a time. The grid area can show information about assigned resources, predecessors, and successors.	Chapter 5
Task Form (task view)	Enter, edit, and review information about a selected task, one task at a time. The grid area can show information about the task's assigned resources, predecessors, and successors.	Chapter 5

Table 4-6. Microsoft Project Forms

Type of form	How you can use it	For more information
Task Name Form (task view)	Enter, edit, and review the selected task's assigned resources, predecessors, and successors. The Task Name Form is a simplified version of the Task Form.	Chapter 5

You can change the categories of information shown in a form view. To do this, follow these steps:

1. Click View, More Views. In the More Views dialog box, click the form you want. Click the Apply button.
2. Right-click the blank area on the form. A shortcut menu appears, which shows different types of information that can be shown in the form. A check mark appears next to the information currently shown in the form.
3. Click the information you want to display in the form. You can choose only one item from the shortcut menu at a time.

Working with Combination Views

Combination views are groupings of two views in a split screen. Typically, the information in one portion of the split screen controls the content in the other portion (see Figure 4-14).

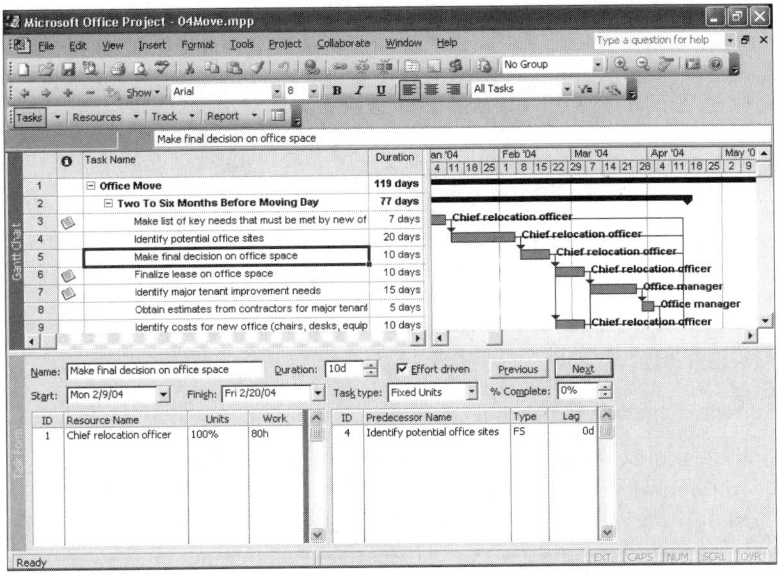

Figure 4-14. When you click a task in the upper Gantt Chart portion of the Task Entry view, the task, assignment, and predecessor information for that selected task appear in the lower Task Form portion of the view.

The predefined Microsoft Project combination views are described in Table 4-7.

Table 4-7. Microsoft Project Combination Views

Type of combination view	How you can use it	For more information
Task Entry (task view)	Enter, edit, and review detailed information about the task selected in the Gantt Chart. The Gantt Chart appears in the upper portion of the view, and the Task Form appears in the lower portion. The information shown in the Task Form corresponds with the task selected in the Gantt Chart.	Chapter 5
Resource Allocation (resource view)	Review and resolve resource overallocations. The Resource Usage view appears in the upper portion of the view, and the Leveling Gantt appears in the lower portion. The information shown in the Leveling Gantt corresponds with the resource or assignment selected in the Resource Usage view.	"Balancing Resource Workloads" on page 271

You can create your own combination view by simply splitting the view. For example, if you split the Gantt Chart view, the Task Form appears in the lower pane, instantly resulting in the Task Entry view. Likewise, if you split the Resource Sheet, the Resource Form appears in the lower pane.

The split bar is located in the lower-right corner of the Microsoft Project window, just below the vertical scroll bar. To split a view, drag the split bar up to about the middle of the view or wherever you want the split to occur. Or click Window, Split.

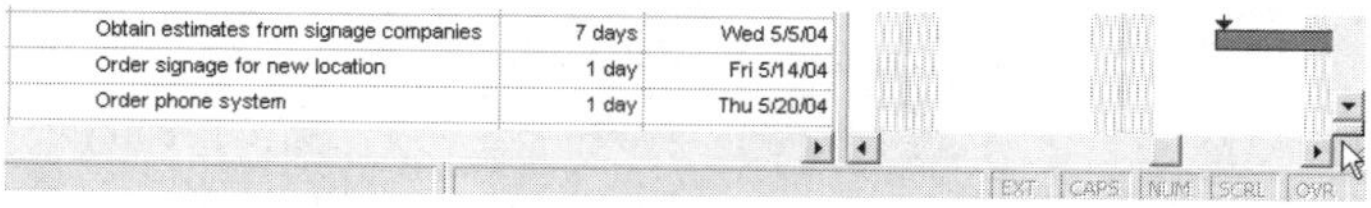

Troubleshooting

The current view doesn't have a split bar

By their nature, graph views and forms do not have a split bar. However, you can still create a combination view with these views in the upper pane. Click Window, Split. The view splits, with the Task Form or Resource Form appearing in the lower pane.

To remove the split and return to a single view, double-click the split bar, which is now the gray dividing bar between the two views. Or click Window, Remove Split.

20	Design office space	23 days	Mon 4/19/04
21	Assign office space	5 days	Thu 5/20/04
22	Order chairs	1 day	Thu 5/20/04

Name: Communicate to employees Duration: 1d ☑ Effort driven Previous Next

Start: Mon 3/8/04 Finish: Mon 3/8/04 Task type: Fixed Units % Complete: 0%

| ID | Resource Name | Units | Work | | ID | Predecessor Name | Type | Lag |
| 1 | Chief relocation officer | 100% | 8h | | 6 | Finalize lease on office space | FS | 0d |

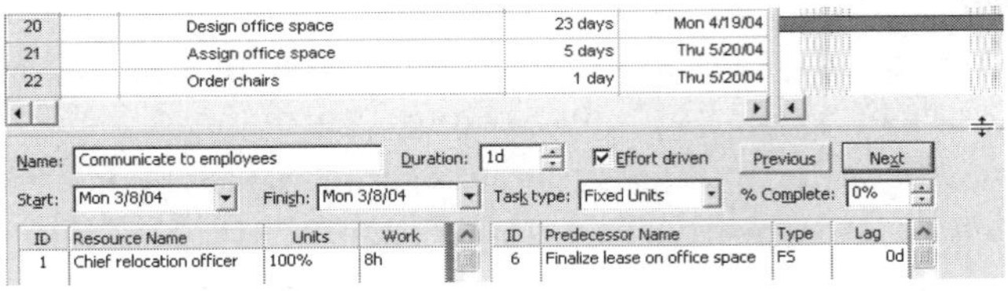

To modify a combination view, simply modify one component of the combination view as if it were in its own view.

 For more information about combination views, see "Customizing Views" on page 761.

Troubleshooting

You can't get the combination view to be a single view again

In a combination view such as Task Entry or Resource Allocation, one of the two views always has focus; that is, it's the currently active view. When you switch to another view, only the active view switches.

Before switching to another view, make the combination view a single view. To do this, click Window, Remove Split. Or double-click the split bar—the gray dividing bar between the two views. Then switch to the other view.

Working with Timescales

Many Microsoft Project views, including Gantt charts and usage views, use a timescale to indicate time in the project. The timescale appears above the chart or timesheet area of a view. Starting with Project 2002, you can now display up to three timescales (see Figure 4-15), each timescale in a tier. The highest tier shows the broadest period of time, and the lowest tier shows the most detailed period of time. For example, you can show days within weeks within months, or you can show weeks within quarters.

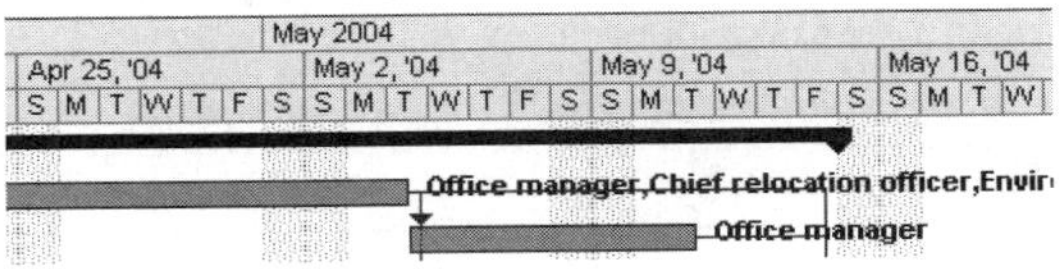

Figure 4-15. You can zoom your timescales up or down while you're working.

The default timescale is two tiers: days within weeks. To set your timescale options, do the following:

1. Show a view that contains a timescale; for example, the Gantt Chart, Task Usage view, or Resource Graph.

2. Click Format, Timescale. The Timescale dialog box appears.

3 The Timescale dialog box has four tabs: Top Tier, Middle Tier, Bottom Tier, and Non-Working Time. The Middle Tier tab is displayed by default. In the Show box, click the number of timescale tiers you want to display (one, two, or three).

4 In the Units box, specify the time unit you want to display at the middle tier, for example, quarters, months, or weeks.

5 In the Label box, click the format in which you want to display the time unit, for example, Mon Jan 26, '04; Mon January 26; or Mon 1/26.

6 If you chose to display more than one tier, click the Top Tier and/or Bottom Tier tabs and repeat steps 4 and 5.

Using Tables

Any sheet view, including the sheet portion of any Gantt chart or usage view, has a default table defined for it. You can change the table for these types of views. Or you can modify an existing table to add, change, or remove the fields in the columns.

Views that Use Tables

Table 4-8 shows the default table for each view.

Table 4-8. Default Table Views

View	Default table	View	Default table
Bar Rollup	Rollup Table	PA_PERT Entry Sheet	PA_PERT Entry
Detail Gantt	Delay	PA_Pessimistic Gantt	PA_Pessimistic Case
Gantt Chart	Entry	Resource Allocation	Usage (Resource Usage view) Delay (Leveling Gantt view)
Leveling Gantt	Delay	Resource Sheet	Entry
Milestone Date Rollup	Entry	Resource Usage	Usage
Milestone Rollup	Rollup Table	Task Entry	Entry
Multiple Baselines Gantt	Entry	Task Sheet	Entry
PA_Expected Gantt	PA_Expected Case	Task Usage	Usage
PA_Optimistic Gantt	PA_Optimistic Case	Tracking Gantt	Entry

Table 4-9 lists a description of the task tables and their default fields.

Table 4-9. **Task Tables and Their Default Fields**

Information displayed	Default fields included	For more information
Baseline		
Specific baseline values reflecting the schedule as originally planned.	ID, Task Name, Baseline Duration, Baseline Start, Baseline Finish, Baseline Work, and Baseline Cost	"Saving Original Plan Information Using a Baseline" on page 298
Constraint Dates		
The specific constraint types for each task, along with associated dates where applicable. You can use these fields to review or change the constraint type and date.	ID, Task Name, Duration, Constraint Type, Constraint Date	"Scheduling Tasks to Achieve Specific Dates" on page 157
Cost		
Cost information for each task, helping you analyze various types of cost calculations.	ID, Task Name, Fixed Cost, Fixed Cost Accrual, Total Cost, Baseline, Variance, Actual, and Remaining	"Monitoring and Adjusting Costs" on page 338
Delay		
Information to help you determine how long it will take to complete your tasks, given the resources you have and the amount of time they have for a given task.	ID, Indicators, Task Name, Leveling Delay, Duration, Start, Finish, Successors, and Resources	"Balancing Resource Workloads" on page 271
Earned Value		
Earned value information that compares the relationship between work and costs based on a status date.	ID, Task Name, BCWS, BCWP, ACWP, SV, CV, EAC, BAC, and VAC.	"Analyzing Progress and Costs Using Earned Value" on page 401
Earned Value Cost Indicators		
Earned-value cost information, including the ratio of budgeted to actual costs of work performed.	ID, Task Name, BCWS, BCWP, CV, CV%, CPI, BAC, EAC, VAC, and TCPI.	"Analyzing Progress and Costs Using Earned Value" on page 401
Earned Value Schedule Indicators		
Earned-value schedule information, including the ratio of work performed to work scheduled.	ID, Task Name, BCWS, BCWP, SV, SV%, and SPI.	"Analyzing Progress and Costs Using Earned Value" on page 401

Table 4-9. Task Tables and Their Default Fields

Information displayed	Default fields included	For more information
Entry		
Fundamental information regarding tasks. This table is most useful for entering and viewing the most essential task information.	ID, Indicators, Task Name, Duration, Start, Finish, Predecessors, Resource Names.	"Entering Tasks" on page 77
Export		
A large set of fields from which to export task fields to other applications such as Microsoft Excel or Microsoft Access.	ID, Unique ID, Task Name, Duration, Type, Outline Level, Baseline Duration, Predecessors, Start, Finish, Early Start, Early Finish, Late Start, Late Finish, Free Slack, Total Slack, Leveling Delay, % Complete, Actual Start, Actual Finish, Baseline Start, Baseline Finish, Constraint Type, Constraint Date, Stop, Resume, Created, Work, Baseline Work, Actual Work, Cost, Fixed Cost, Baseline Cost, Actual Cost, Remaining Cost, WBS, Priority, Milestone, Summary, Rollup, Text1–10, Cost1–3, Duration1–3, Flag1–10, Marked, Number1–5, Subproject File, Contact, Start1–5, and Finish1–5.	"Importing and Exporting Information" on page 497
Hyperlink		
Hyperlink information to associate linked shortcuts with your tasks.	ID, Indicators, Task Name, Hyperlink, Address, and SubAddress.	"Hyperlinking to Documents in Other Applications" on page 492
PA_Expected Case		
Expected scheduling information based on PERT analysis of task durations.	ID, Indicators, Task Name, Expected Duration, Expected Start, and Expected Finish.	"Calculating Your Most Probable Duration" on page 145
PA_Optimistic Case		
The best-case scheduling information based on PERT analysis of task durations.	ID, Indicators, Task Name, Optimistic Duration, Optimistic Start, and Optimistic Finish.	"Calculating Your Most Probable Duration" on page 145
PA_PERT Entry		
The most probable duration information for a project based on PERT analysis of task durations.	ID, Task Name, Duration, Optimistic Duration, Expected Duration, and Pessimistic Duration.	"Calculating Your Most Probable Duration" on page 145

Table 4-9. Task Tables and Their Default Fields

Information displayed	Default fields included	For more information
PA_Pessimistic Case		
The worst-case scheduling information based on PERT analysis of task durations.	ID, Indicators, Task Name, Pessimistic Duration, Pessimistic Start, and Pessimistic Finish.	"Calculating Your Most Probable Duration" on page 145
Rollup Table		
Summarized task information that appears after you run the Rollup_Formatting macro.	ID, Indicators, Task Name, Duration, Text Above, Start, Finish, Predecessors, Resource Names.	"Organizing Tasks into an Outline" on page 86
Schedule		
Detailed scheduling information that can help you see when a task is scheduled to begin and how late it can actually begin without jeopardizing the project's finish date.	ID, Task Name, Start, Finish, Late Start, Late Finish, Free Slack, and Total Slack.	"Understanding Slack Time and Critical Tasks" on page 252
Summary		
Overview project information to analyze durations, dates, progress, and costs.	ID, Task Name, Duration, Start, Finish, % Complete, Cost, and Work.	"Bringing In the Project Finish Date" on page 258
Tracking		
Actual progress and cost information, as contrasted with scheduled or baseline information.	ID, Task Name, Actual Start, Actual Finish, % Complete, Physical % Complete, Actual Duration, Remaining Duration, Actual Cost, and Actual Work.	"Updating Task Progress" on page 308
Usage		
The most fundamental task schedule information.	ID, Indicators, Task Name, Work, Duration, Start, and Finish.	Chapter 5
Variance		
Gaps between baseline start and finish dates and the actual start and finish dates, enabling a comparison between your original planned schedule and actual performance.	ID, Task Name, Start, Finish, Baseline Start, Baseline Finish, Start Variance, and Finish Variance.	Chapter 11, "Responding to Changes in Your Project"
Work		
A variety of measurements for analyzing the level of effort for each task.	ID, Task Name, Work, Baseline, Variance, Actual, Remaining, and % Work Complete.	"Updating Task Progress" on page 308

Table 4-10 lists a description of all resource tables and their default fields.

Table 4-10. Resource Tables and Their Default Fields

Information displayed	Default fields included	For more Information
Cost		
Cost information about resources in a project.	ID, Resource Name, Cost, Baseline Cost, Cost Variance, Actual Cost, and Remaining Cost.	"Monitoring and Adjusting Costs" on page 338
Earned Value		
Earned value information that compares the relationship between work and costs for resources based on a status date.	ID, Resource Name, BCWS, BCWP, ACWP, SV, CV, EAC, BAC, and VAC.	"Analyzing Progress and Costs Using Earned Value" on page 401
Entry		
Essential information regarding resources. This table is most useful for entering and viewing fundamental resource information.	ID, Indicators, Resource Name, Type, Material Label, Initials, Group, Maximum Units, Standard Rate, Overtime Rate, Cost/Use, Accrue At, Base Calendar, and Code.	Chapter 6
Entry – Material Resources		
Essential information about consumable material resources.	ID, Resource Name, Type, Material Label, Initials, Group, Standard Rate, Cost/Use, Accrue At, and Code.	"Adding Material Resources to the Project" on page 186
Entry – Work Resources		
Essential information about work (people and equipment) resources.	ID, Resource Name, Type, Initials, Group, Maximum Units, Standard Rate, Overtime Rate, Cost/Use, Accrue At, Base Calendar, and Code.	"Adding Work Resources to the Project" on page 175
Export		
A large set of fields from which to export resource fields to other applications, such as Microsoft Excel or Microsoft Access.	ID, Unique ID, Resource Name, Initials, Maximum Units, Standard Rate, Overtime Rate, Cost Per Use, Accrue At, Cost, Baseline Cost, Actual Cost, Work, Baseline Work, Actual Work, Overtime Work, Group, Code, Text1–5, and Email Address.	"Importing and Exporting Information" on page 497
Hyperlink		
Hyperlink information to associate linked shortcuts with your resources.	ID, Indicators, Resource Name, Hyperlink, Address, and SubAddress.	"Hyperlinking to Documents in Other Applications" on page 492

Table 4-10. Resource Tables and Their Default Fields

Information displayed	Default fields included	For more Information
Summary		
Overview resource information.	ID, Resource Name, Group, Maximum Units, Peak, Standard Rate, Overtime Rate, Cost, and Work.	Chapter 6
Usage		
The most essential resource scheduling information.	ID, Indicators, Resource Name, and Work.	Chapter 7
Work		
A variety of measurements for analyzing work, or the level of effort, for resources and their assigned tasks.	ID, Resource Name, % Complete, Work, Overtime, Baseline, Variance, Actual, and Remaining.	"Updating Progress Using Resource Work" on page 316

> **Tip See the name of the current table**
> You can quickly see the name of the current table. Simply rest your mouse pointer in the All Cells box where the row and column headings intersect. The ToolTip containing the table name (and view name) appears.

Changing the Table in a View

To switch to a different table, follow these steps:

1. Display the view containing the table you want to change. This could be the Task Sheet, Resource Sheet, Gantt Chart, Task Usage view, and so on.
2. Click View, Table.
3. If the table is listed on the submenu, click it. If the table is not listed on the submenu, click More Tables (see Figure 4-16) and then double-click the table you want.

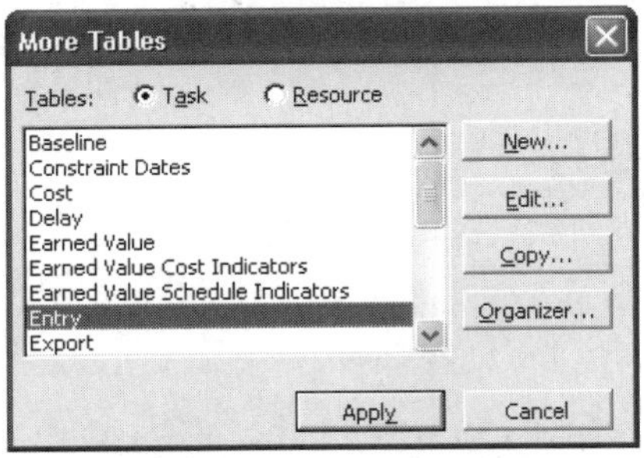

Figure 4-16. The More Tables dialog box contains the full list of built-in tables.

The table is replaced by the table you clicked.

Note If a task view is currently displayed, task tables are listed. If a resource view is currently displayed, resource tables are listed. You cannot apply a resource table to a task view, and vice versa.

Tip **Quickly change a table**
Another method for changing tables is to right-click the All Cells box where the row and column headings intersect. The Tables shortcut menu appears.

Modifying a Table

Suppose that the Entry task table provides all the information you need except baseline values. You can easily add another column to any table, and you can just as easily remove superfluous columns. There are also certain changes you can make to the columns themselves.

Note When working with columns in a table, you're working with fields in your project database. Fields are discussed in more detail in "Using Fields," later in this chapter on page 120.

To add a column to a table, follow these steps:

1. Display the view and table to which you want to add a new column.
2. Right-click the column heading to the left of where you want the new column to be inserted and then click Insert Column. The Column Definition dialog box appears.

Note You can also open the Column Definition dialog box (see Figure 4-17) by clicking in a column and then clicking Insert, Column.

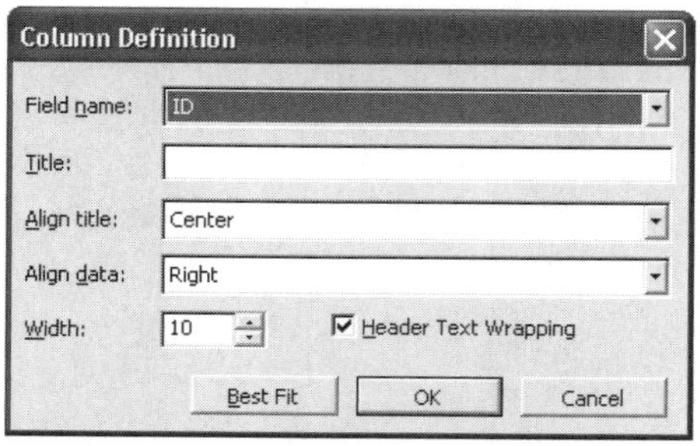

Figure 4-17. You can also open the Column Definition dialog box by clicking a column heading and then pressing the Insert key.

3. In the Field Name box, click the field representing the information you want in the new column.

Tip **Scroll quickly to a field**
With the Field Name box selected, you can just type the first letter of the field's name to scroll close to its name in the list.

Troubleshooting

The field you're looking for is not in the Field Name list

When you display a task view and table, only task fields are listed in the Column Definition dialog box. Likewise, when you display a resource view and table, only resource fields are listed. Assignment fields are available only in the Task Usage and Resource Usage views.

To remove a column from a table, follow these steps:

1. Display the view and table from which you want to remove a column.
2. Right-click the heading of the column you want to remove, and then click Hide Column.

Tip **Remove a column**
You can also remove a column by selecting the column heading and then clicking Edit, Hide Column. Or simply select the column heading and press the Delete key.

The column is removed. The field and its contents still exist in the database, however, and can be displayed again in this or other tables.

Tip **Hide a column temporarily**
You can hide a column in your table while keeping it in place. Position your mouse pointer over the right edge of the column heading border. The mouse pointer changes to a black crosshair. Drag the right border past the column's left border. The column disappears.

To show the column again, position your mouse pointer on the edge where your column is hidden. Drag to the right, and your column appears again.

To use this method, you need to know where you hid the column because there's no visual indication that it's there.

You can change the title of the column to something other than the actual field name. You can also modify the column text alignment and the column width. To modify a column, follow these steps:

1. Display the view and table containing the column you want to modify.
2. Double-click the heading of the column you want to change. The Column Definition dialog box appears.

3. To change the field information appearing in the column, click the field you want in the Field Name list.
4. To change the title of the column heading, type a new title in the Title box.
5. Use the Align Title list to change the alignment of the column title.
6. Use the Align Data list to change the alignment of the field information itself.
7. Enter a number in the Width box to change the column width.

> **Tip** **Change the column width by dragging**
> You can also change the column width directly on the table. Click the column's heading to select the column. Then move the mouse pointer to the right edge of the column until the pointer changes to a black crosshair. Drag to the right to widen the column. Drag to the left to make the column narrower. Double-click the edge to widen the column to the same size as the longest entry in the column.

You can move a column to another location in the table simply by dragging. To move a column, follow these steps:

1. Display the view and table containing the column you want to move.
2. Click the heading of the column you want to move.
3. With the black crosshair mouse pointer over the column heading, drag to the new location for the column. As you drag, a gray line moves with the mouse pointer to indicate where the column will be inserted when you release the mouse button.

> **Tip** In addition to adding and removing columns in existing tables, you can also create entirely new tables. For more information about tables, see "Customizing Tables" on page 785.

Using Fields

Fields are the smallest piece of data in the vast collection of information that makes up your project database. For example, one task comprises a single record in this database. This record consists of a number of task fields, such as the task name, duration, start date, finish date, assigned resource, deadline, and more.

Whether you see them in a view or not, there are numerous fields for your tasks, resources, and assignments, as well as for the project as a whole.

> **For more information about the project database, see Chapter 32.**

Some fields are entered by you, such as task name and duration. Other fields are calculated for you by Microsoft Project, such as start date, finish date, and total cost. Still other fields can either be entered by you or calculated by Microsoft Project.

You're already familiar with the different field categories:

- Task fields
- Task-timephased fields
- Resource fields
- Resource-timephased fields
- Assignment fields
- Assignment-timephased fields

The timephased fields break down field information—such as work, costs, and availability—by time periods. This breakdown gives you more information to work with in your project. In the Task Usage and Resource Usage views, for example, you can see task cost by day or resource work by week. You can break either of those down further into the component assignments. The timephased fields also give you more tools for analysis through earned-value calculations.

For more information about earned value analysis, see "Analyzing Progress and Costs Using Earned Value" on page 401.

Another way that fields are categorized is by *data type*. The data type indicates how a field can be used, for example, as a currency-type field, or a date-type field. The following are the field data types:

Currency. Information is expressed as a cost.

Date. Information is expressed as a date.

Duration. Information is expressed as a span of time.

Enumerated. Information is selected from a list of predefined choices.

Indicator. Information is shown as graphical indicators about a task, resource, or assignment.

Integer. Information is expressed as a whole number.

Outline code. Information is defined with a custom tag for tasks or resources that enables you to show a hierarchy of tasks in your project.

Percentage/Number. Information is displayed as a value that can be expressed as either a percentage or decimal number, such as 100 percent or 1.00.

Text. Information is expressed as unrestricted characters of text.

Yes/No. Information is set to either Yes or No, that is, a Boolean or True/False value.

Fields make up your project database, the whole of which you might never view. Fields are also seen throughout your project plan. You see field information in the following locations:

- Columns in a table
- Rows in a timesheet
- Information in a network diagram node
- Gantt bars and associated text in a Gantt chart

- Fields in a form view
- Fields in a dialog box

Some of these locations, such as columns in a table and rows in a timesheet, can be changed to suit your needs. Others, such as the fields in a form view or dialog box, are fixed.

You can create your own custom fields and add them to tables in your views. There are custom fields you can define for currency, dates, durations, finish dates, start dates, text, numbers, outline codes, and more. Microsoft Office Project Professional 2003 includes an additional set of enterprise custom fields as well, so an enterprise can design a robust set of fields that standardizes how the enterprise manages projects.

For more information about defining custom fields, see "Customizing Fields" on page 788. For a complete list of fields, see Appendix B, "Field Reference."

Learn More About Microsoft Project Fields

You can immediately get comprehensive information about any field in a table. Position your mouse pointer over the column heading; a ToolTip pops up that contains a link to online Help for this field. Click the link, and the Help topic appears.

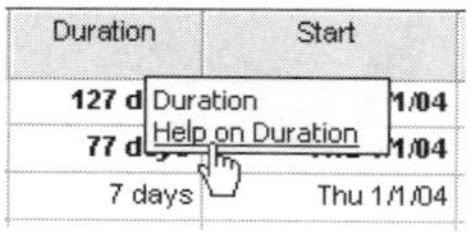

You can also get lists of field categories and find information about fields by following these steps:

1. Click Help, Microsoft Project Help.
2. In the Project Help pane, click Table Of Contents.
3. Click Reference and then click Fields Reference.
4. Click one of the field types, for example, Duration Fields. A complete list of fields of that type appears in a separate Help pane.
5. Click a field name, and its Help topic appears (see Figure 4-18).

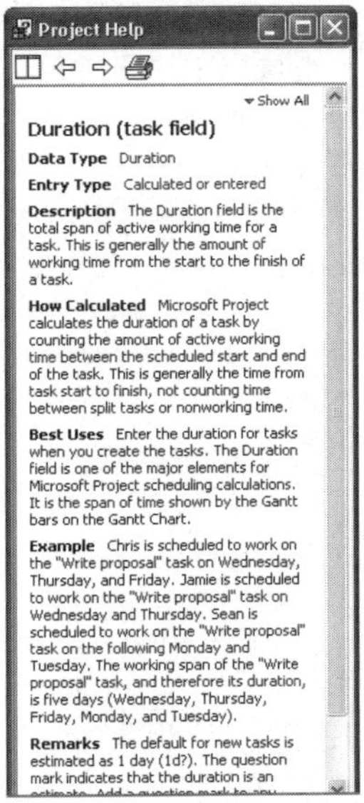

Figure 4-18. The Fields Reference Help topics each contains comprehensive information about the field.

These online Help topics about the fields contain the following information:

- Data type (duration, cost, text, and so on)
- Entry type (entered, calculated, or both)
- Description (a general overview of the field's function)
- How Calculated (for calculated fields)
- Best Uses (the purpose of the field)
- Example (how this field might be used to facilitate a project plan)
- Remarks (any additional information)

Rearranging Your Project Information

The ability to switch from one view to another, to switch tables in a sheet view, and to add or remove fields in a view gives you tremendous versatility in how you see your project information. You can take it a step further by sorting, grouping, and filtering the information in a view.

Sorting Project Information

By sorting information in a table, you can arrange it in alphabetical or numerical order by a particular field. For example, you might sort your tasks by start date so you can see tasks that are due to start next week. Or you might sort your tasks by duration so you can see the tasks with the longest durations and how you might break them up and bring in the project finish date.

You can also sort resources. For example, in the Resource Sheet, you might have originally entered all resources as they came on board, but they might be easier for you to manage if they were in alphabetical order. You can easily sort by the resource name. Better yet, you can sort by department or group name, and then by resource name.

To sort items in a sheet view, do the following:

1. Display the sheet view whose information you want to sort.
2. Click Project, Sort.
3. In the submenu that appears, commonly used sort fields are presented. For example, if you're working in the Gantt Chart, you can sort by Start Date, Finish Date, Priority, Cost, or ID. If you're working in the Resource Sheet, you can sort by Cost, Name, or ID.
4. If you want to sort by a different field than what's presented in the submenu, click Sort By. The Sort dialog box appears (see Figure 4-19).

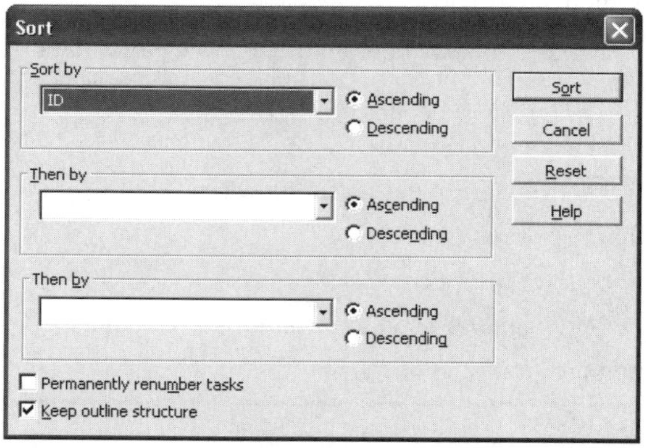

Figure 4-19. Use the Sort dialog box to choose the fields you want to sort by.

5. Under Sort By, click the name of the field you want to sort by and then specify whether you want the sort to be ascending (lowest to highest) or descending (highest to lowest). If you want to sort within the sort, add another field in one or both of the Then By boxes.
6. Make sure that the Permanently Renumber check box is cleared. You will likely want to clear this check box in the majority of the cases. However, if you really want this sort to be permanent and you're certain that you won't ever want to return to the original order of the tasks or resources, go ahead and select this check box. The ID numbers for the tasks or resources are changed, and the tasks or resources will be sorted by order of the ID numbers when you don't have any other sort order applied.
7. Click Sort.

Inside Out

Don't accidentally renumber tasks when sorting

If you select the Permanently Renumber Tasks or Permanently Renumber Resources check box for the current sort operation, the check box remains selected for your subsequent sort operation. This is true whether your next sort operation is for resources or tasks. This can be a problem if you want to do a temporary sort—which is likely to be the case most of the time—and you're not in the habit of looking at that check box.

To prevent unwittingly jumbling up your project plan, whenever you do a permanent renumber sort, immediately open the Sort dialog box again, clear the Permanently Renumber check box, and then click Reset.

To return a sorted sheet view to its original order, click Project, Sort, and then click By ID.

Note If you choose to permanently renumber your tasks or resources according to a new sort order, remember that this renumbering will affect the order of tasks and resources in all other task or resource views. This is not the case with temporary sorting operations.

Grouping Project Information

Think of grouping as a more sophisticated kind of sorting, in which a graphical layout is applied to the sheet to segregate the groupings you've chosen. For example, suppose you group your task sheet by complete and incomplete tasks. Tasks that are 0 percent complete (not started yet) are grouped first and marked by a yellow band (see Figure 4-20). Tasks that are 1–99 percent complete (in progress) are grouped next, bounded by another yellow band. Tasks that are 100 percent complete are grouped last.

112		Schedule fire drill	1 day	Tue 6/15/04	Tue 6/15/04
113		Periodically visit old office to pick up mail	1 day	Tue 6/15/04	Tue 6/15/04
114		Schedule open house for clients	1 day	Tue 6/15/04	Tue 6/15/04
115		Office move project complete	0 days	Tue 6/15/04	Tue 6/15/04
		⊟ % Complete: 1% - 99%	40 days	Mon 2/23/04	Fri 4/16/04
9		Identify costs for new office (chairs, desks, equipment	10 days	Mon 2/23/04	Fri 3/5/04
10		Prepare a budget for the move	10 days	Mon 3/8/04	Fri 3/19/04
11		Select the move day	1 day	Mon 3/8/04	Mon 3/8/04
12		Hire contractors for major tenant improvements	5 days	Mon 4/5/04	Fri 4/9/04
13		Obtain necessary permits	5 days	Mon 4/12/04	Fri 4/16/04
14		Evaluate phone system needs	1 day	Mon 3/8/04	Mon 3/8/04
		⊟ % Complete: 100%	67 days	Thu 1/1/04	Fri 4/2/04
3	✓	Make list of key needs that must be met by new office	7 days	Thu 1/1/04	Fri 1/9/04
4	✓	Identify potential office sites	20 days	Mon 1/12/04	Fri 2/6/04
5	✓	Make final decision on office space	10 days	Mon 2/9/04	Fri 2/20/04
6	✓	Finalize lease on office space	10 days	Mon 2/23/04	Fri 3/5/04
7	✓	Identify major tenant improvement needs	15 days	Mon 3/8/04	Fri 3/26/04
8	✓	Obtain estimates from contractors for major tenant impi	5 days	Mon 3/29/04	Fri 4/2/04

Figure 4-20. Groups graphically separate categories of information in a view.

The grouping band shows the title of the group, for example, Percent Complete: 0% or 100% Complete. Where appropriate, the grouping band also rolls up information summarized from the group, such as the total duration for the grouping, the earliest start date for all tasks in the grouping, the latest finish date for all tasks in the grouping, and so on.

Built-in Task Groups

All built-in task groups appear on the Group By submenu on the Project menu when a task view is showing. The following is a complete list of these built-in task groups:

- Complete And Incomplete Tasks
- Constraint Type
- Critical
- Duration
- Duration Then Priority
- Milestones
- Priority
- Priority Keeping Outline Structure

You can also group resources in a resource sheet. For example, you might want to group resources by their department or code or by resource type (work or material).

Built-in Resource Groups

All built-in resource groups appear on the Group By submenu on the Project menu when a resource view is showing. The following is a complete list of these built-in task groups:

- Assignments Keeping Outline Structure
- Complete And Incomplete Resources
- Resource Group
- Standard Rate
- Work vs. Material Resources

You can also group nodes in the Network Diagram view (see Figure 4-21).

To group task or resource information in a sheet view or Network Diagram, follow these steps:

1. Display the view whose information you want to group.
2. Click Project, Group By.
3. In the submenu that appears, click the grouping you want.

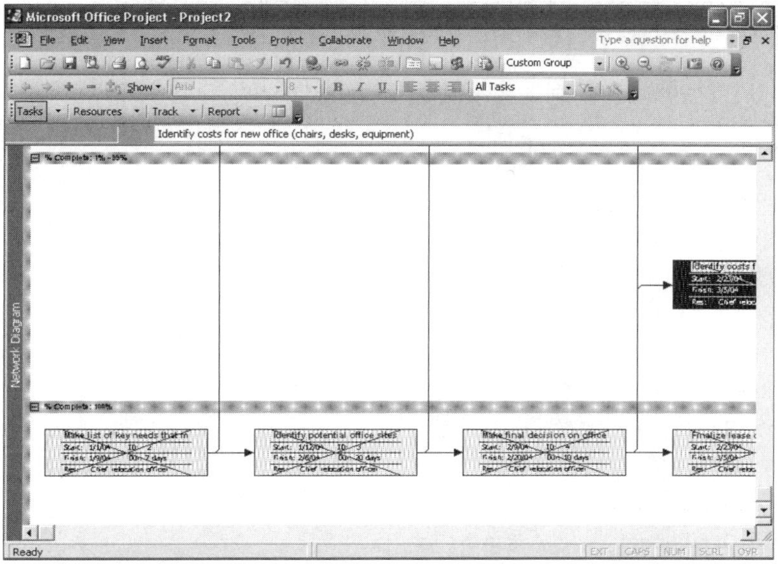

Figure 4-21. Nodes are collected and rearranged when you group them by a particular category.

To remove a grouping, click Project, Group By and then click No Group.

Tip **Use the Group By tool on the Standard toolbar**

You can also use the Group By tool on the Standard toolbar. With a sheet view displayed, click the grouping you want to apply.

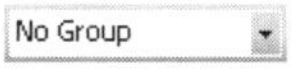

When you want to restore the view to its original order, click the arrow in the Group By tool and select No Group.

You can customize built-in groups and create entirely new groups as well. You can group by fields, including custom outline codes that you create.

For more information about groups, see "Customizing Groups" on page 795.

Filtering Project Information

When you filter a view, you're excluding information you don't need to see so you can focus on what you do need to see. For example, if you want to see only tasks that use a particular resource so you can more closely analyze the workload, you can apply the Using Resource filter. Or if you're about to attend a status meeting and you want to discuss tasks that are either in progress or not started, you can apply the Incomplete Tasks filter to a task sheet.

Built-in Task Filters

The most commonly used task filters appear on the Filtered For submenu of the Project menu. All built-in filters are accessible in the More Filters dialog box. The following is a complete list of the built-in task filters:

- Completed Tasks
- Confirmed
- Cost Greater Than
- Cost Overbudget
- Created After
- Critical
- Date Range
- In Progress Tasks
- Incomplete Tasks
- Late/Overbudget Tasks Assigned To
- Linked Fields
- Milestones
- Resource Group
- Should Start By
- Should Start/Finish By
- Slipped/Late Progress
- Slipping Tasks
- Summary Tasks
- Task Range
- Tasks With A Task Calendar Assigned
- Tasks With Attachments
- Tasks With Deadlines
- Tasks With Estimated Durations
- Tasks With Fixed Dates
- Tasks/Assignments With Overtime
- Top Level Tasks
- Unconfirmed
- Unstarted Tasks
- Update Needed
- Using Resource In Date Range
- Using Resource
- Work Overbudget

You can also apply filters to a resource sheet. If you want to examine all resources that are running over budget, for example, you can apply the Cost Overbudget filter. Or if you want to see only your material resources, you can apply the Resources – Material filter to a resource sheet.

Built-in Resource Filters

The most commonly used resource filters appear on the Filtered For submenu of the Project menu. All built-in filters are accessible in the More Filters dialog box. The following is a complete list of the built-in resource filters:

- Confirmed Assignments
- Cost Greater Than
- Cost Overbudget
- Date Range
- Group
- In Progress Assignments
- Linked Fields
- Overallocated Resources
- Resource Range
- Resources – Material
- Resources – Work
- Resources With Attachments
- Resources/Assignments With Overtime
- Should Start By
- Should Start/Finish By
- Slipped/Late Progress
- Slipping Assignments
- Unconfirmed Assignments
- Unstarted Assignments
- Work Complete
- Work Incomplete
- Work Overbudget

To filter information in a view, follow these steps:

1. Display the view whose information you want to filter. You can filter information in all views.
2. Click Project, Filtered For.

3 If the filter you want is listed on the submenu, click it. If the filter is not in the submenu, click More Filters and then find and click it in the More Filters dialog box (see Figure 4-22). Click Apply.

Figure 4-22. The More Filters dialog box lists all built-in filters.

4 Some filters require you to enter more information. For example, if you choose the Should Start/Finish filter, you need to enter start and finish dates and click OK.

Tip **Apply a highlighting filter**

By default, a filter excludes tasks or resources that do not meet the conditions of that filter. If you prefer, you can instead have the filter highlight tasks or resources that do meet the filter conditions. Click Project, Filtered For, More Filters. Click the filter you want and then click the Highlight button.

To remove a filter and show all tasks or all resources again, click Project, Filtered For and then click All Tasks.

Tip **Use the Filter tool on the Formatting toolbar**

You can also use the Filter tool on the Formatting toolbar. Display the view you want to filter; then use the tool to click the filter you want to apply. When finished, click the arrow in the Filter tool and select All Tasks (or All Resources).

Using AutoFilter, you can quickly filter by a value in a particular field. To do this, follow these steps:

1 Display the sheet view whose information you want to autofilter.

2 On the Formatting toolbar, click AutoFilter. The AutoFilter arrows appear in each column heading in the sheet view.

Duration	Start	Finish	Predecessors
20 days	Mon 1/12/04	Fri 2/6/04	3
10 days	Mon 2/9/04	Fri 2/20/04	4
10 days	Mon 2/23/04	Fri 3/5/04	5

3 Click the arrow in the column whose information you want to filter by and then click the value you want to filter by.

For example, suppose you are displaying the Gantt Chart with the Entry table applied. If you want to filter for all tasks scheduled to start next month, click the AutoFilter arrow in the Start column and then click Next Month.

When an AutoFilter is applied, the column heading changes color.

4 To show all tasks or resources again, click the AutoFilter arrow in the applied column heading and then click All.

The AutoFilter arrows remain handy in the column headings for all views throughout your project plan until you turn AutoFilter off. With AutoFilter on, you can always quickly filter tasks or resources in a sheet. If you want to turn AutoFilter off, click the AutoFilter button again.

Troubleshooting

Some of your project information is missing

It's easy to apply a filter, work with your project information for a while, and then forget that the filter is applied. Then, when you look for certain tasks or resources that you know are there, you can't see them.

Check whether a filter is applied. Click the Project menu and look at the Filtered For command. If it says Filtered For: All Tasks Or All Resources, you know you're seeing it all. If it says Filtered For: Critical, for example, you know you have a filter applied. Click All Tasks or All Resources to show your information again.

When you have an AutoFilter applied, the Project menu might still indicate that you're showing all tasks or resources. If the Project menu indicates that you're displaying everything (but you're not), check whether AutoFilter is on. If it is, review your column headings and find the one that's blue. Click the arrow, and then click All to show all tasks or resources.

Note You can customize built-in filters and create entirely new filters as well. You can also create custom AutoFilters. For more information, see "Customizing Filters" on page 799.

Learn More about Microsoft Project Views, Tables, Filters, and Groups

In Microsoft Project online Help, you can get more information about all available views, tables, filters, and groups. To do this, follow these steps:

1. Click Help, Microsoft Project Help.
2. In the Project Help pane, click Table Of Contents.
3. Click Viewing Project Information.
4. Click categories and topics you want to see.

Arranging Your Microsoft Project Workspace

The more you work with Microsoft Project, the stronger your preferences become about various workspace options. You can make changes to the Microsoft Project workspace that will persist across your working sessions with the project plan as well as to other projects you create. For example, you can reset which view should be the default when you first start a new project plan. You can also show or hide different elements in the default Microsoft Project window. In making these changes, you can set up your Microsoft Project workspace to be the most efficient for your own working methods.

On the other hand, sometimes you need to rearrange the workspace temporarily to accomplish a specific task. For example, maybe you need to see the same window in two different panes. You can arrange open windows to do this. You can also easily switch among multiple open projects.

Setting Your Default View

The Gantt Chart is the default view that appears whenever you start Microsoft Project or create a new project file. This is because the Gantt Chart is the view used by most project managers. However, if a different view is your favorite, you can make that one the default view. To do this, follow these steps:

1. Click Tools, Options.
2. Click the View tab.
3. In the Default View box, click the name of the view you want as your default view.

Inside Out

Not always the default view

Setting the default view does not control the view that appears when you open an existing project plan. When you open an existing project plan, it displays the last view you were working with when you closed it. If you want your project plan to open in a particular view each time, make sure you end your working session in that view.

Showing and Hiding Workspace Elements

Certain workspace elements are displayed by default in your Microsoft Project workspace. To expand your working area, you can hide elements you don't use much. (You can still use these elements when you need them.) This also frees up more space if you want to add a different element in its place.

Table 4-11 lists the workspace elements you can show or hide, along with the procedure for doing so.

Table 4-11. Workspace Elements

NEW FEATURE!

Workspace element	How to display or hide it
Microsoft Office Online	To close Microsoft Office Online for the current project only, simply click the Close (X) button in the upper-left corner of the pane. When you want it to show again, click Help, Project Help. Or, simply press F1.
Project Guide	To close the Project Guide for the current project only, simply click the Close (X) button in the upper-left corner of the pane. When you want it to show again, click the Show/Hide Project Guide button on the Project Guide toolbar. To show or hide the Project Guide for all projects, click Tools, Options. On the Interface tab, under Project Guide Settings, select or clear the Display Project Guide check box.
View bar	Click View, View Bar.
Online Help	To show Help, click Help, Project Help or press F1. Project Help appears in the task pane. Enter a term or phrase in the Search For box, or click Table Of Contents to browse through listed categories and topics. To close the Help window, simply click its Close button.
Toolbars	Click View, Toolbars and then click the name of the toolbar you want to show or hide.
Entry bar (the bar above the view)	Click Tools, Options. On the View tab, under Show, select or clear the Entry Bar check box.
Scroll bars	Click Tools, Options. On the View tab, under Show, select or clear the Scroll Bars check box.
Status bar (the bar below the view)	Click Tools, Options. On the View tab, under Show, select or clear the Status Bar check box.

Splitting a Window

You might be familiar with the Split function in Microsoft Excel or Microsoft Word, in which you can divide a single window into two panes and scroll each pane independently. In Microsoft Project, you might need to refer to different parts of the same Microsoft Project view. Perhaps you want to show different parts of the same view in a split screen because you're modeling a new section of a project on an existing section farther up the view. Or maybe you want to see two different views at the same time.

The problem is that when you split a screen in Microsoft Project (using Window, Split), a form appears that gives you a combination view. You can switch to a different view, but the lower view is designed to show information relevant to the information selected in the upper view.

The solution is to open a second instance of the same window and then arrange them side by side in your Microsoft Project window. To see two independent panes of your project plan at the same time, follow these steps:

1. Click Window, New Window. In the New Window dialog box, click the name of your project plan, and click OK. This opens a second instance of your project plan. The two instances are marked in the title bar with a "1" and "2," indicating that these are separate windows of the same project. Any changes you make in one window are simultaneously made in the other.
2. Click Window, Arrange All. Any open project plans are tiled in your project window (see Figure 4-23).

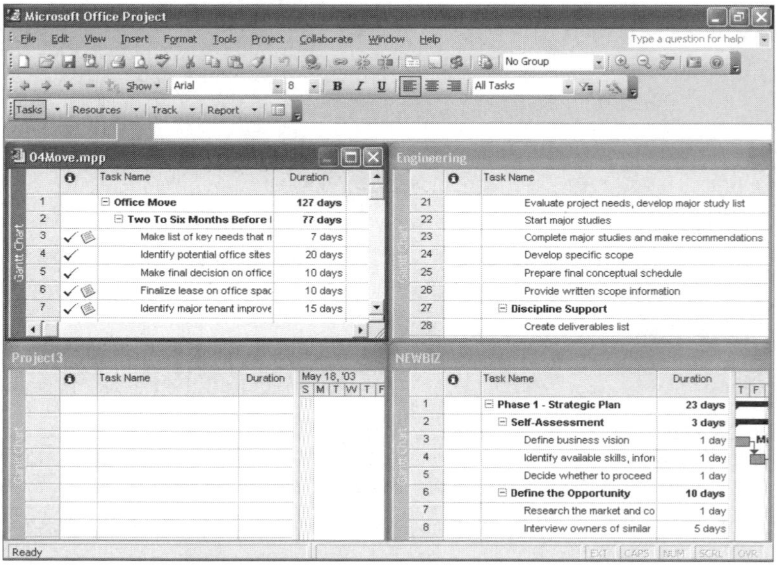

Figure 4-23. Clicking Arrange All makes all open projects visible.

3. If you have other project plans open besides the two you want to work with, either close them or select each one and click Window, Hide. When only the two instances of the project plan are displayed, click Window, Arrange All again. The two open projects are tiled horizontally: one above and the other below (see Figure 4-24). Now you can scroll the two windows independently of each other and also look at different views independently.

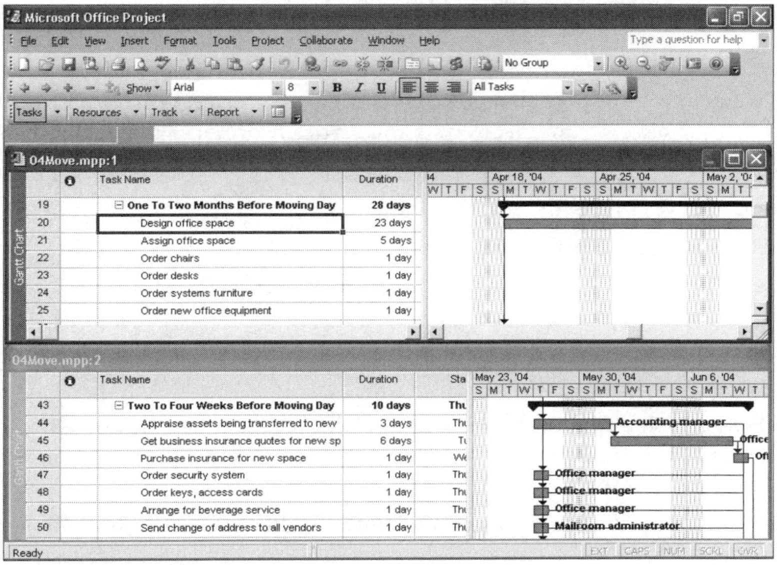

Figure 4-24. You can independently scroll or change views in the two tiled project windows.

> **Tip** **Hide toolbars temporarily to add space**
> To give yourself more working space while viewing two project windows at one time, hide a toolbar or two. Click View, Toolbars and then click the name of the checked toolbar you want to hide. By default, the Standard, Formatting, and Project Guide toolbars are showing.

Switching Among Open Projects

If you have multiple projects open at the same time, there are several ways to switch among them. You can do the following:

- Click the project's button on the Windows taskbar.
- Press Alt+Tab to cycle through all open programs and windows.
- Press Ctrl+F6 to cycle through all open projects.

> **Note** **Multiple Project files on a single Windows taskbar button**
> By default, multiple open Microsoft Project files are represented as individual buttons on the Windows taskbar. You can change this so that there's just a single Microsoft Project button on the taskbar, regardless of the number of open project files. Click Tools, Options and then click the View tab. Clear the Windows In Taskbar check box.

Navigating to a Specific Location in a View

With a long list of tasks, dozens of resources, and dates spanning months or even years, the different views in your project plan probably cover a lot of space. When you're trying to get to a specific place in a view, you can always scroll vertically or horizontally. But there are shortcuts, as follows:

Ctrl+Home. Moves to the first row in a sheet.

Ctrl+End. Moves to the last row in a sheet.

Alt+Home. Moves to the beginning of the project timescale (Gantt Chart, Resource Graph, usage view).

Alt+End. Moves to the end of the project timescale (Gantt Chart, Resource Graph, usage view).

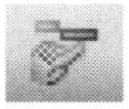

Go To Selected Task button, or Ctrl+Shift+F5. Moves the timescale portion of a view (Gantt Chart or usage view) to the location of the task or assignment selected in the sheet portion of the view.

F5, "Today". Moves the chart portion of a timescaled view (Gantt Chart, usage view, or Resource Graph) to the location of today's date. You can either click today's date in the Date box, or type the word "**Today**" in the box.

Chapter 5

Scheduling Tasks

You've developed your task list, and it's sequenced and outlined. Perhaps you've even applied a work breakdown structure. You have a good task list, but you don't have a schedule...yet.

Although there are many knowledge areas (including scope management, cost management, and resource management) that contribute to successful project management, time management is most related to development of your project schedule—your roadmap for completing tasks, handing off deliverables, passing milestones, and finally achieving the goals of your project in a timely manner.

To develop an accurate and workable schedule that truly reflects how your project will run, you need to do the following:

- Enter task durations.
- Identify the relationships, or dependencies, among tasks.
- Schedule certain tasks to achieve specific dates when necessary.

When you've done these three things, you begin to see the basic outline of a real project schedule. You have not yet added and assigned resources, which further influence the schedule. Nor have you refined the project plan to make the project finish date and costs conform to your requirements. However, at this point, you can start to see how long certain tasks will take and how far into the future the project might run.

To learn about adding and assigning resources, see Chapter 7, "Assigning Resources to Tasks." For information about refining your project, see Chapter 9, "Checking and Adjusting the Project Plan."

You can incorporate handy scheduling cues to help keep you focused and on track as you and your team work your way through the project. You can do the following:

- Create reminders to alert you as deadlines are approaching.
- Add milestones to your schedule as conspicuous markers of producing a deliverable, completing a phase, or achieving another major event in your project.
- Apply a calendar to a task that is independent of the project calendar or the calendars of resources assigned to the task, so that the task can be scheduled independently.

Setting Task Durations

When your task list is entered, sequenced, and outlined in Microsoft Office Project 2003 (see Figure 5-1), you're ready to start the work of creating a schedule.

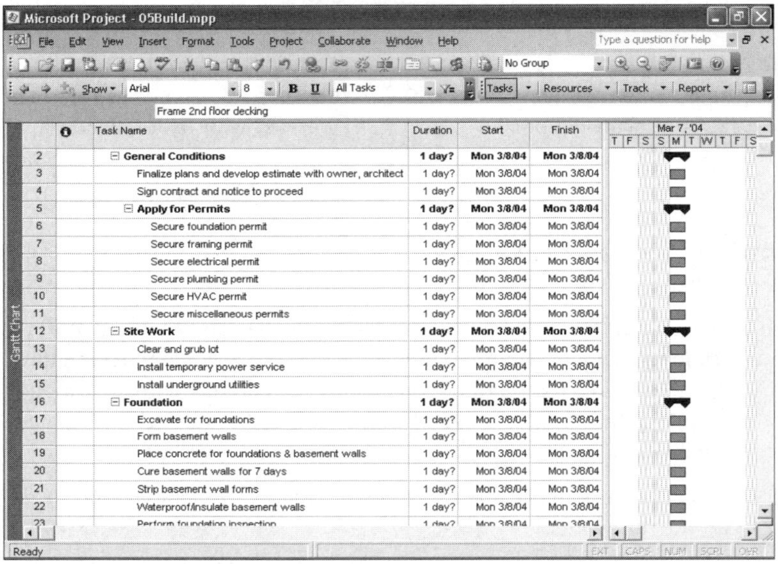

Figure 5-1. Your project schedule displays all tasks starting on the project start date, each with an estimated duration of 1 day.

To create a realistic schedule, you can start by entering the amount of working time you believe each task will take to complete; that is, the task *duration*. As soon as you enter a task, Project 2003 assigns it an estimated duration of 1 day, just to have something to draw in the Gantt chart. You can easily change that duration.

Entering accurate durations is very important for creating a reliable project schedule. Microsoft Project uses the duration of each task to calculate the start and finish dates for the task. If you will be assigning resources, the duration is also the basis for the amount of work for each assigned resource.

Developing Reliable Task Durations

As the project manager, you can start by entering a broad duration estimate based on your experience. Then, you can refine the estimate by soliciting input from others who are more directly involved or experienced with the sets of tasks. There are four possible sources for developing reliable task durations, as follows:

Team knowledge Suppose that you're managing a new business startup project and you already have your team in place. The business advisor can provide durations for tasks such as creating a market analysis, researching the competition, and identifying the target market niche. The accountant can provide durations for tasks such as forecasting financial returns, setting up the accounting system, and obtaining needed insurance. Team members ready to work on the project can also provide duration estimates for tasks based on their previous experience as well as their projection of how long they expect the tasks to take for this particular project.

Expert judgment If you don't have a team in place yet from whom you can get durations, or if you want reliable input from impartial specialists in the field, you might call upon experts such as consultants, professional associations, or industry groups. These can help you establish task durations.

Project files Similar projects that have been completed can be an excellent source of durations. If Microsoft Project files are available, you can see the initial durations. If the project manager tracked actuals diligently throughout the life of the project, you have valuable information about how long certain tasks actually took, as well as any variances from their planned durations.

Industry standards Historical duration information for tasks typical to an industry or discipline is sometimes available commercially through professional or standards organizations. You can adapt such information for tasks and durations to fit the unique requirements of your project.

You might use a combination of these methods to obtain durations for all the tasks in your project. It's often very useful to have durations based on established metrics. For example, suppose that you know the industry standard for the number of hours it takes to develop certain types of architectural drawings as well as the number of those drawings you need. You can multiply these figures to develop a reasonable duration for your specific task.

Project Management Practices: Building in a Buffer

Building in a duration *buffer* is a method that many project managers use as a contingency against project risk. Some say that the durations should be as "real" and accurate as possible, already taking into account any possible risk. Others say it just isn't realistic to believe that you can account for all possible problems while you're still in the project planning processes. To build in a buffer, also known as *reserve time*, you can do one or more of the following:

- Add a percentage of the duration itself as a buffer to each duration. For example, if a duration estimate is 10 days, adding 10 percent of that as a buffer makes the duration 11 days.
- Add a fixed number of work periods (hours, days, or weeks) to each duration.
- Add a "buffer task" close to the end of the project, with a duration that represents a percentage of the total project duration.
- Add a buffer task close to the end of the project, with a duration that represents a fixed work period; for example, two weeks.

You might not want to tell your resources about the buffer. (Work always expands to fit into the available time!) You can publish individual task deadlines to resources, but publish your post-buffer deadline to management.

The reserve time can later be reduced or eliminated as more precise information about the project becomes available. For example, suppose you initially enter a duration of 5 days to set up the accounting system. Later on, more concrete information indicates that it will actually take 8 days. You can "transfer" that time from your buffer without pushing out your project finish date.

Understanding Estimated vs. Confirmed Durations

Any value in the Duration field that's followed by a question mark is considered a duration estimate. Technically, all planned durations are only estimates because you don't know how long a task takes until it's completed and you have an actual duration. However, the question mark indicates what you might consider an "estimate of a duration estimate." Estimated durations are calculated into the schedule the same as confirmed durations; they simply serve as an alert that a duration is still more of a guess.

Tip **Turn off estimated durations**
If you have no use for the estimated durations question mark, you can turn it off. Click Tools, Options, and then click the Schedule tab. Clear the Show That Tasks Have Estimated Durations check box. Also, clear the New Tasks Have Estimated Durations check box.

By default, a duration estimate of 1 day is entered for any newly added task (*1d?*). Use this value as a flag to indicate that the duration still needs to be entered for this task. You can also enter a question mark (?) after a duration; for example, *2w?*. Any durations with question marks can serve as a flag to indicate that the duration is still under consideration and might change after you receive more solid information. When you remove the question mark from a duration, the duration is confirmed; that is, you're now confident of this duration.

Tip **Rearrange your view by estimated durations**
You can sort, group, or filter tasks by whether a task has an estimated or confirmed duration. For more information, see "Rearranging Your Project Information" on page 123.

Entering Durations

You can enter duration in different time period units, as follows:

- Minutes (m or min)
- Hours (h or hr)
- Days (d or dy)
- Weeks (w or wk)
- Months (mo or mon)

Note Whether you type **h**, **hr**, or **hour** in your duration entry, by default Microsoft Project enters "hr". You can change which abbreviation of the time unit appears in the Duration field. Click Tools, Options and then click the Edit tab. In each of the fields under View Options For Time Units, set the abbreviation of the time unit you want to see. This setting applies to that project file only. If you want it to apply to all new projects you create, click the Set As Default button.

You can use different duration units throughout your plan. One task might be set with a duration of 2w, and another task might be set for 3d.

Tip **Specify the time unit you use most often**
If you don't specify a duration unit, by default Microsoft Project assumes that the unit is days and automatically enters "days" after your duration amount. If you want the default duration unit to be something different, such as hours or weeks, you can change it. Click Tools, Options and then click the Schedule tab. In the Duration Is Entered In box, select the time unit you want as the default.

To enter a duration, follow these steps:

1. Display the Gantt chart.
2. In the Duration field for each task, type the duration; for example, *1w* or *4d.*
3. If a duration is an estimate, add a question mark after it; for example, *1w?* or *4d?.*
4. Press Enter. The Gantt bar is drawn to represent the time period for the task (see Figure 5-2). In addition, the Finish field is recalculated for the task. Microsoft Project adds the duration amount to the Start date to calculate the Finish date.

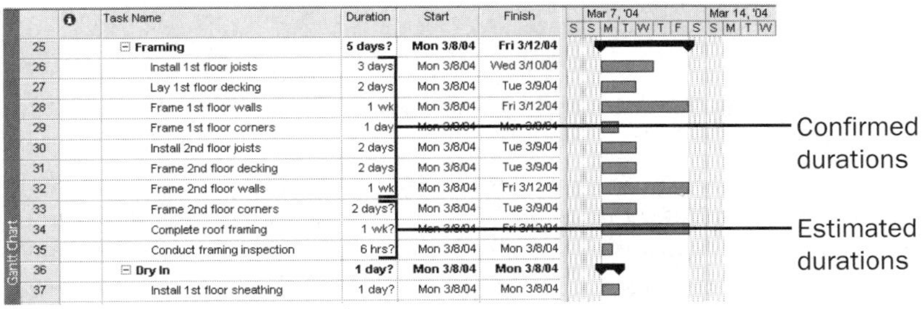

Figure 5-2. Confirmed as well as estimated durations are drawn with the Gantt bars.

Tip In a Gantt chart, you can also drag the right edge of a Gantt bar to change the task duration.

Chapter 5

Task Information

Tip **Quickly confirm estimated durations**
You can change the estimated durations of multiple tasks to confirmed durations. Select all the tasks containing estimated durations. On the Standard toolbar, click Task Information and then click the Advanced tab. Clear the Estimated check box.

Understanding How Durations Affect Scheduling

When you enter a duration, the task is scheduled according to its assigned calendar. Initially, this is the project calendar. When resources are assigned, the task is scheduled according to the resource's working times calendar. If a task calendar is applied, the task is scheduled according to the task's working times calendar.

For more information about task calendars, see "Working with Task Calendars," later in this chapter on page 169.

For example, suppose you enter a 2d duration for the "Create market analysis plan" task, and the task starts Monday at 8:00 A.M. Based on the default Standard calendar and its options, and assuming that the resource is assigned full-time to the task, Microsoft Project counts the 16 working hours in the 2-day duration to arrive at a finish date of Tuesday at 5:00 P.M.

Note Until you set task dependencies by linking predecessors and successors, the Start date of all your tasks is the same as the project start date by default.

You can make any new tasks adopt the current date (today) as the start date. Click Tools, Options and then click the Schedule tab. In the New Tasks list, click Start On Current Date.

In a schedule-from-finish project, the Finish date of all your tasks is the same as the Project finish date.

If you're working in a schedule-from-finish task and you enter a duration, Microsoft Project subtracts the duration amount from the Finish date to calculate the Start date.

If you want a task to take a set amount of time regardless of any working times calendars, you can enter an *elapsed duration.* An elapsed duration can be useful for tasks such as "Paint drying" or "Cement curing" that can't be stopped after they've started or that are independent of project schedules or resource assignments. Elapsed durations are scheduled 24 hours a day, 7 days a week, until finished. That is, one day is always considered 24 hours long (rather than 8 hours), and one week is always 7 days (rather than 5 days). To specify an elapsed duration, simply enter an **e** before the duration unit; for example, **3ed** for three elapsed days (see Figure 5-3).

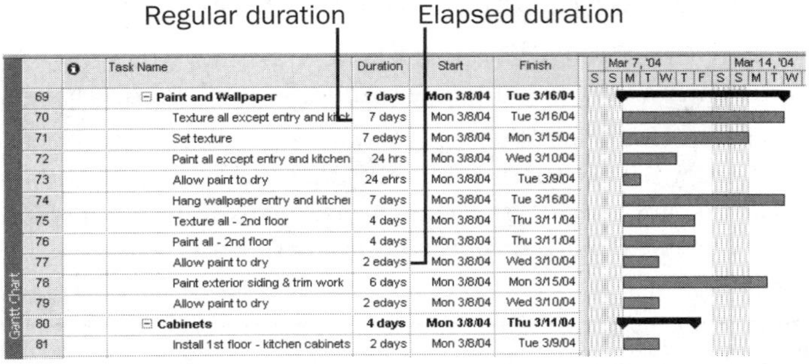

Regular duration
Elapsed duration
Task Name
Duration
Start
Finish
Mar 7, '04
Mar 14, '04
S S M T W T F S S M T W
69 Paint and Wallpaper 7 days Mon 3/8/04 Tue 3/16/04
70 Texture all except entry and kitch 7 days Mon 3/8/04 Tue 3/16/04
71 Set texture 7 edays Mon 3/8/04 Mon 3/15/04
72 Paint all except entry and kitchen 24 hrs Mon 3/8/04 Wed 3/10/04
73 Allow paint to dry 24 ehrs Mon 3/8/04 Tue 3/9/04
74 Hang wallpaper entry and kitchen 7 days Mon 3/8/04 Tue 3/16/04
75 Texture all - 2nd floor 4 days Mon 3/8/04 Thu 3/11/04
76 Paint all - 2nd floor 4 days Mon 3/8/04 Thu 3/11/04
77 Allow paint to dry 2 edays Mon 3/8/04 Wed 3/10/04
78 Paint exterior siding & trim work 6 days Mon 3/8/04 Mon 3/15/04
79 Allow paint to dry 2 edays Mon 3/8/04 Wed 3/10/04
80 Cabinets 4 days Mon 3/8/04 Thu 3/11/04
81 Install 1st floor - kitchen cabinets 2 days Mon 3/8/04 Tue 3/9/04
Gantt Chart

Figure 5-3. Regular durations are scheduled according to applied working times calendars, whereas elapsed durations are based on 24 hours per day, 7 days per week.

For regular (non-elapsed) durations, we need a way to specify the number of working hours in a day and week, the number of working days in a month, and so on. This way, when we specify 2 weeks as a duration, for example, we can be assured that this means the same thing as 80 hours, or 10 days. To set these options, follow these steps:

1. Click Tools, Options, and then click the Calendar tab (see Figure 5-4).

   You can also click Tools, Change Working Time and then click the Options button.

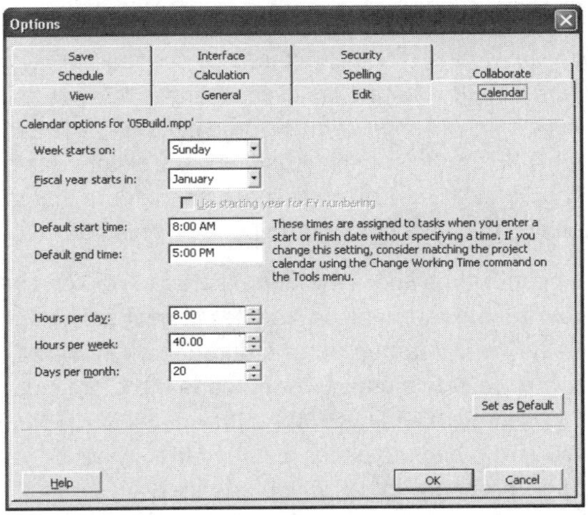

Figure 5-4. On the Calendar options tab, you can specify the details of your working time units, including the hours, days, and weeks.

Chapter 5

2 Select the options on this tab to reflect the way your team works.

The Default Start Time (8:00 A.M.) and Default End Time (5:00 P.M.) are assigned to tasks when you enter a start or finish date without specifying a time.

The Hours Per Day, Hours Per Week, and Days Per Month values serve as your time unit specifications when needed. If you specify that a task has a duration of 1 month, does that mean 20 days or 30 days? These settings are used in conjunction with the working times calendars to dictate how your tasks are scheduled.

Troubleshooting

You set the calendar for 20 hours per week, but the tasks are still being scheduled for 40 hours per week

Or you thought you set the calendar for 8:00 A.M. to 12:00 P.M., for the project to be scheduled only in the mornings, but the tasks are still being scheduled 8:00 A.M. to 5:00 P.M.

Sometimes, the Calendar options tab confuses more readily than it assists. The Hours Per Day, Hours Per Week, and Days Per Month settings can easily be misinterpreted to make us think we're using them to set the schedule for the project. What we're actually doing is setting start and end times and specifying how duration entries are to be converted to assignment work.

Suppose you want to specify that work on this project is to be scheduled only in the mornings, from 8:00 A.M. until 12:00 P.M. To affect actual task scheduling in this way, you'd need to edit the working times for each day in the Change Working Time calendar. The Default Start Time only specifies the time that Microsoft Project should enter if you enter a start date without a corresponding start time. The Default End Time only specifies the time that Microsoft Project should enter if you enter a finish date without a corresponding finish time.

Also, suppose you want to specify that work on this project is to be scheduled only 20 hours per week because your team is working on another project at the same time. If you enter ***20*** in the Hours Per Week box and then enter a duration of 2 weeks, it is scheduled as 40 hours—according to the project calendar. That means if the project's working times calendar is still set for Monday through Friday, 8:00 A.M. through 5:00 P.M., the 2 weeks is scheduled as two sets of 20 hours back to back, resulting in "2 weeks" taking place in 1 actual week in your schedule—probably not what you intended.

The solution is to make the corresponding change in the working times calendar. Set the working and nonworking times in the Change Working Time calendar so that there are 20 hours of working time per week. Then, when you enter 2 weeks as a duration, the first 20 hours are scheduled in the first week, and the second 20 hours are scheduled in the second week.

The settings in the Calendar Options tab also determine how durations are translated into work time units when you assign resources to tasks. Think of this as a "Conversions" tab, and it might be more clear.

Reviewing Durations

Any Gantt Chart view can give you a closer look at your task durations graphically across the timescale. The Calendar view also shows each task as a bar on the days and weeks in which it's scheduled.

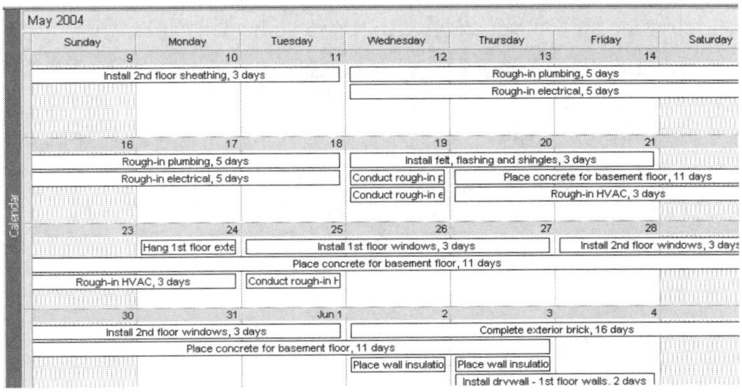

Calculating Your Most Probable Duration

In the course of researching task duration information, you might get conflicting results. Maybe the team member who will carry out a major task says it will take 3 weeks. Perhaps an expert stakeholder says it should take 2 weeks. And maybe the industry standard states that the same task should take 4 weeks. These are large discrepancies and they're all coming from credible sources. How do you schedule a task with three possible durations?

Or maybe you have a single reliable duration or a duration range such as 2 weeks +/- 10 percent for all tasks in your task list, and you want your project plan to model a best-case scenario, a worst-case scenario, and an expected scenario for all durations. This way, you can learn the earliest possible project finish date, the latest possible date, and the most probable finish date.

To help resolve discrepancies or to model alternative scenarios, you can run a *PERT analysis*. A PERT (Program Evaluation and Review Technique) analysis uses a weighted average of optimistic, pessimistic, and expected durations to calculate task durations and therefore the project schedule. This analysis can be an effective risk management tool. It can also help if you're working out a project proposal or estimating time, cost, or resource requirements.

Caution When you run a PERT analysis, the resulting calculated values in the Optimistic Duration, Expected Duration, and Pessimistic Duration fields will be stored in the custom fields Duration1, Duration2, and Duration3, respectively. In addition, the resulting optimistic start and finish dates are stored in the custom fields Start1 and Finish1. The expected start and finish dates are stored in the custom fields Start2 and Finish2. The pessimistic start and finish dates are stored in the custom fields Start3 and Finish3. Any values in any of these custom fields are overwritten by the results of the PERT analysis. This can be significant if you were storing interim plan information in these fields.

Chapter 5

For more information about interim plans, see "Saving Additional Baselines" on page 304. For more information about using custom fields, see "Customizing Fields" on page 788.

To set up a PERT analysis, follow these steps:

1. Click View, Toolbars, PERT Analysis.

PERT Entry Sheet

2. On the PERT Analysis toolbar, click PERT Entry Sheet.
3. For each task, enter the optimistic, expected, and pessimistic durations in the appropriate fields (see Figure 5-5). You can also think of these fields as minimum, probable, and maximum durations for each task.

PA_PERT Entry Sheet

	Task Name	Duration	Optimistic Dur.	Expected Dur.	Pessimistic Dur.
16	⊟ **Foundation**	**1 day?**	**0 days**	**0 days**	**0 days**
17	Excavate for foundations	1 day?	2 days	3 days	4 days
18	Form basement walls	1 day?	11 days	13 days	18 days
19	Place concrete for foundations & basement walls	1 day?	10 days	12 days	16 days
20	Cure basement walls for 7 days	1 day?	5 days	7 days	10 days
21	Strip basement wall forms	1 day?	1 day	2 days	4 days
22	Waterproof/insulate basement walls	1 day?	2 days	2 days	4 days
23	Perform foundation inspection	1 day?	1 day	1 day	3 days
24	Backfill foundation	1 day?	1 day	2 days	5 days
25	⊟ **Framing**	**1 day?**	**0 days**	**0 days**	**0 days**
26	Install 1st floor joists	1 day?	1 day	2 days	3 days
27	Lay 1st floor decking	1 day?	2 days	2 days	4 days
28	Frame 1st floor walls	1 day?	3 days	4 days	8 days
29	Frame 1st floor corners	1 day?	1 day	1 day	2 days

Figure 5-5. Use the PERT Entry Sheet to specify the optimistic, expected, and pessimistic durations for each task.

If you do not expect a duration for a particular task to vary at all, enter the same value in all three fields.

Calculate PERT

4. On the PERT Analysis toolbar, click Calculate PERT.
5. The estimated durations are calculated, and the results change the value in the Duration field (see Figure 5-6).

PA_PERT Entry Sheet

	Task Name	Duration	Optimistic Dur.	Expected Dur.	Pessimistic Dur.
16	⊟ **Foundation**	**13.5 days?**	**11 days**	**13 days**	**18 days**
17	Excavate for foundations	3 days?	2 days	3 days	4 days
18	Form basement walls	13.5 days?	11 days	13 days	18 days
19	Place concrete for foundations & basement walls	12.33 days?	10 days	12 days	16 days
20	Cure basement walls for 7 days	7.17 days?	5 days	7 days	10 days
21	Strip basement wall forms	2.17 days?	1 day	2 days	4 days
22	Waterproof/insulate basement walls	2.33 days?	2 days	2 days	4 days
23	Perform foundation inspection	1.33 days?	1 day	1 day	3 days
24	Backfill foundation	2.33 days?	1 day	2 days	5 days
25	⊟ **Framing**	**4.5 days?**	**3 days**	**4 days**	**8 days**
26	Install 1st floor joists	2 days?	1 day	2 days	3 days
27	Lay 1st floor decking	2.33 days?	2 days	2 days	4 days
28	Frame 1st floor walls	4.5 days?	3 days	4 days	8 days
29	Frame 1st floor corners	1.17 days?	1 day	1 day	2 days

Figure 5-6. The recalculated durations based on the PERT analysis replace the values in the Duration field for each task.

Inside Out

PERT analysis and critical path method

In addition to the PERT method for calculating task durations, there is the Critical Path Method (CPM). In fact, standard Microsoft Project calculations are based on CPM. With CPM, project duration is forecasted by analyzing which sequence of project activities has the least amount of scheduling flexibility. An early start and early finish are calculated, as are the late start and late finish.

Many project managers use PERT analyses for their duration estimates and then use CPM to manage the importance of tasks in their schedule, given their level of scheduling flexibility.

For more information about the Critical Path Method, see "Working with the Critical Path and Critical Tasks" on page 251.

You can review Gantt charts using each of the three sets of durations, as follows:

Optimistic Gantt

- For the optimistic durations, click Optimistic Gantt on the PERT Analysis toolbar (see Figure 5-7).

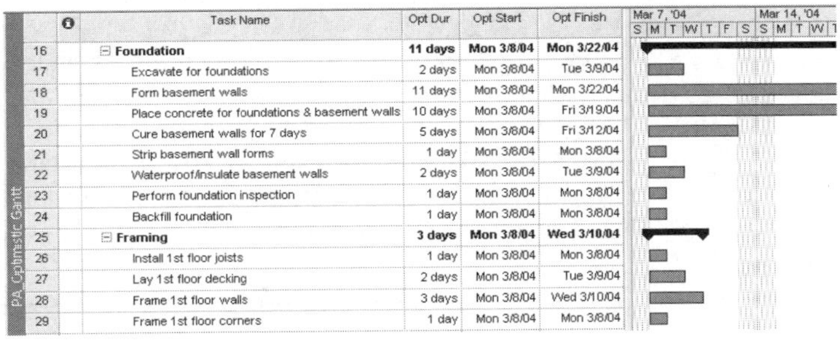

	Task Name	Opt Dur	Opt Start	Opt Finish
16	**Foundation**	**11 days**	**Mon 3/8/04**	**Mon 3/22/04**
17	Excavate for foundations	2 days	Mon 3/8/04	Tue 3/9/04
18	Form basement walls	11 days	Mon 3/8/04	Mon 3/22/04
19	Place concrete for foundations & basement walls	10 days	Mon 3/8/04	Fri 3/19/04
20	Cure basement walls for 7 days	5 days	Mon 3/8/04	Fri 3/12/04
21	Strip basement wall forms	1 day	Mon 3/8/04	Mon 3/8/04
22	Waterproof/insulate basement walls	2 days	Mon 3/8/04	Tue 3/9/04
23	Perform foundation inspection	1 day	Mon 3/8/04	Mon 3/8/04
24	Backfill foundation	1 day	Mon 3/8/04	Mon 3/8/04
25	**Framing**	**3 days**	**Mon 3/8/04**	**Wed 3/10/04**
26	Install 1st floor joists	1 day	Mon 3/8/04	Mon 3/8/04
27	Lay 1st floor decking	2 days	Mon 3/8/04	Tue 3/9/04
28	Frame 1st floor walls	3 days	Mon 3/8/04	Wed 3/10/04
29	Frame 1st floor corners	1 day	Mon 3/8/04	Mon 3/8/04

Figure 5-7. The Optimistic Gantt shows the optimistic durations for the PERT Analysis.

Expected Gantt

Pessimistic Gantt

- For the expected durations, click Expected Gantt on the PERT Analysis toolbar.
- For the pessimistic durations, click Pessimistic Gantt on the PERT Analysis toolbar.

You can also display one of the PERT Analysis Gantt charts or the PERT Entry Sheet by clicking View, More Views and then selecting it in the dialog box. However, be aware that a PERT Analysis view does not appear in the More Views dialog box until you click the button for that view on the PERT Analysis toolbar the first time after installing Microsoft Project.

Inside Out

Adjust PERT analysis weighting

Set PERT Weights

Sometimes, the PERT analysis results appear to be skewed or exaggerated. You can adjust how Microsoft Project weights duration estimates for the PERT analysis. On the PERT Analysis toolbar, click Set PERT Weights. Change the number in at least two of the three fields—Optimistic, Expected, and Pessimistic—so that the sum of all three numbers equals six (see Figure 5-8). Then, enter the durations in the PERT Entry Sheet as described previously. Finally, click Calculate PERT.

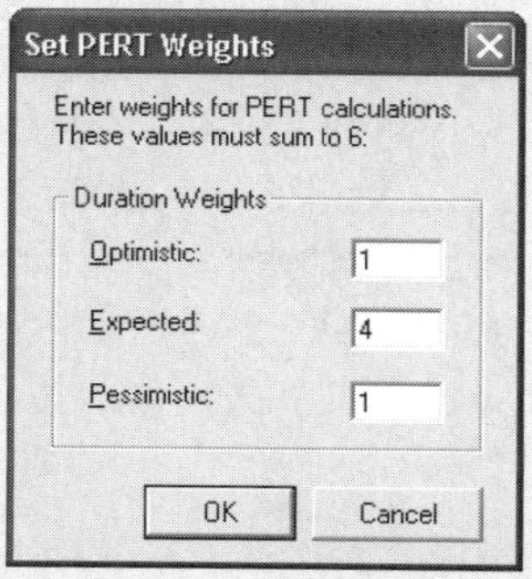

Figure 5-8. Use the Set PERT Weights dialog box to change the weighting of optimistic, expected, and pessimistic durations for the PERT Analysis calculation.

By default, the PERT weights are 1-4-1; that is, heavily weighted toward the expected duration, and lightly and equally weighted for the pessimistic and optimistic durations. Although 1-4-1 is the standard PERT weighting, 1-3-2 can build in a little more pessimism for better risk management.

Tip **Use your PERT analysis to check how you're progressing**
A good use of the PERT analysis is for a quick check of how your project is going. Has your critical path or resource leveling pushed the project schedule beyond your worst-case PERT analysis? If so, it can tell you it's time to replan your project.

Establishing Task Dependencies

Now task durations are entered in your Gantt chart (see Figure 5-9).

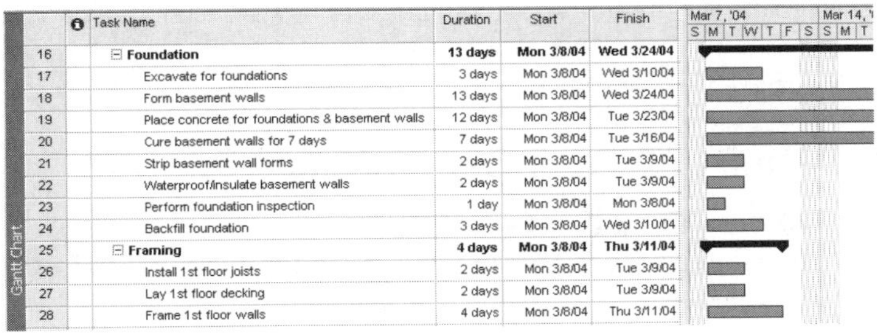

	Task Name	Duration	Start	Finish
16	Foundation	13 days	Mon 3/8/04	Wed 3/24/04
17	Excavate for foundations	3 days	Mon 3/8/04	Wed 3/10/04
18	Form basement walls	13 days	Mon 3/8/04	Wed 3/24/04
19	Place concrete for foundations & basement walls	12 days	Mon 3/8/04	Tue 3/23/04
20	Cure basement walls for 7 days	7 days	Mon 3/8/04	Tue 3/16/04
21	Strip basement wall forms	2 days	Mon 3/8/04	Tue 3/9/04
22	Waterproof/insulate basement walls	2 days	Mon 3/8/04	Tue 3/9/04
23	Perform foundation inspection	1 day	Mon 3/8/04	Mon 3/8/04
24	Backfill foundation	3 days	Mon 3/8/04	Wed 3/10/04
25	Framing	4 days	Mon 3/8/04	Thu 3/11/04
26	Install 1st floor joists	2 days	Mon 3/8/04	Tue 3/9/04
27	Lay 1st floor decking	2 days	Mon 3/8/04	Tue 3/9/04
28	Frame 1st floor walls	4 days	Mon 3/8/04	Thu 3/11/04

Figure 5-9. Durations are graphed in the Gantt chart, and all tasks start on the project start date.

The next step in creating your schedule is to link tasks that are dependent upon each other. Often, one task cannot begin until a previous task has been completed. Sometimes, several tasks are dependent upon the completion of one task; sometimes, several tasks must finish before a single later task can begin. You can link the previous, or *predecessor* task, to its succeeding, or *successor* task, and thereby set up the *task dependency* between the two.

> **Note** A task dependency is also referred to as a *task relationship* or a *link*.

With your task dependencies and durations in place, your project plan really starts to look like a real schedule. You can start to see possible start dates and finish dates, not only for the individual tasks, but also for major phases, milestones, and the project as a whole. When you create a link between two tasks, Microsoft Project calculates the successor's start and finish dates based on the predecessor's start or finish date, the dependency type, the successor's duration, and any associated resource assignments. There's still more information and refinement to be done, but you're getting closer to a schedule you can work with.

Project Management Practices: Real vs. Preferred Task Dependencies

When building your project schedule, bear in mind whether the task dependencies you're creating are really required or whether they simply reflect a preference on your part.

For example, in a construction project, a task such as "Build house" *must* be the predecessor to "Paint house." This is a true task dependency.

On the other hand, you might make a task such as "Finish interior" a predecessor to "Install landscaping." They don't need to be linked to each other, but might only reflect a preference you or your team has for a variety of reasons.

> Be careful of these kinds of preferred but unnecessary dependencies because they can cause unnecessary problems later when you're trying to fine-tune the project plan or respond to problems that arise in the midst of tracking the project. At that point, you want as much scheduling flexibility in the project as possible. Any artificial task dependencies reduce that flexibility.

Creating the Finish-to-Start Task Dependency

The most typical link is the finish-to-start task dependency. With this link, the predecessor task must finish before the successor task can begin. To link tasks with the finish-to-start task dependency, follow these steps:

1. Display the Gantt chart. You can set task dependencies in any task sheet, but you can see the effects of the links immediately in the Gantt Chart.
2. In the task sheet, select the two tasks you want to link. Drag from the predecessor to the successor task if they are right next to each other. If they are not adjacent tasks, click the predecessor, hold down the Ctrl key, and then click the successor.
3. On the Standard toolbar, click Link Tasks. The tasks are linked in the chart portion of the Gantt chart. In addition, the Predecessor field of the successor task lists the task number for its predecessor (see Figure 5-10).

Link Tasks

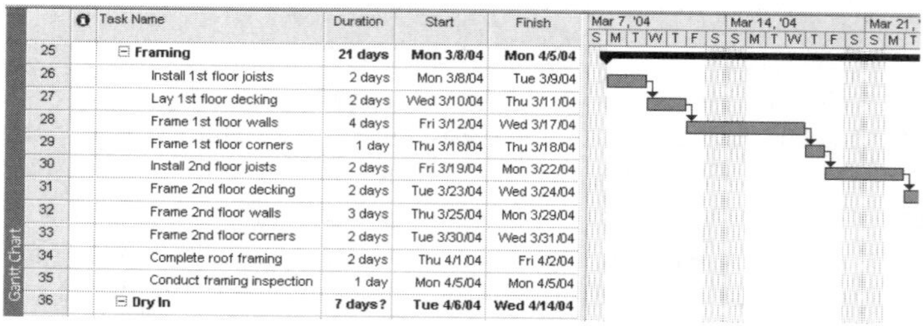

	Task Name	Duration	Start	Finish
25	Framing	21 days	Mon 3/8/04	Mon 4/5/04
26	Install 1st floor joists	2 days	Mon 3/8/04	Tue 3/9/04
27	Lay 1st floor decking	2 days	Wed 3/10/04	Thu 3/11/04
28	Frame 1st floor walls	4 days	Fri 3/12/04	Wed 3/17/04
29	Frame 1st floor corners	1 day	Thu 3/18/04	Thu 3/18/04
30	Install 2nd floor joists	2 days	Fri 3/19/04	Mon 3/22/04
31	Frame 2nd floor decking	2 days	Tue 3/23/04	Wed 3/24/04
32	Frame 2nd floor walls	3 days	Thu 3/25/04	Mon 3/29/04
33	Frame 2nd floor corners	2 days	Tue 3/30/04	Wed 3/31/04
34	Complete roof framing	2 days	Thu 4/1/04	Fri 4/2/04
35	Conduct framing inspection	1 day	Mon 4/5/04	Mon 4/5/04
36	Dry In	7 days?	Tue 4/6/04	Wed 4/14/04

Figure 5-10. Linked tasks in the Gantt chart.

> **Tip** **Link multiple tasks at once**
> You can link multiple tasks at one time, as long as they all have the same type of task dependency. Select all the tasks that are to be linked, either by dragging across adjacent tasks or by clicking nonadjacent tasks while holding down the Ctrl key. On the Standard toolbar, click Link Tasks.

> **Tip** **Set multiple links to a single task**
> You can have multiple links to and from a single task. One task might be the predecessor for several other tasks. Likewise, one task might be the successor for several tasks. There's no difference in how you set the links. Select the two tasks and click Link Tasks on the Standard toolbar. Or select the successor and then set the predecessor and link type on the Predecessors tab in the Task Information dialog box.

Chapter 5

Tip Link tasks by dragging between Gantt bars
In the chart portion of the Gantt chart, drag from the middle of the predecessor Gantt bar to the middle of the successor Gantt bar. Before you drag, be sure that you see a crosshair mouse pointer. This method creates a finish-to-start task dependency between them.

Inside Out

Link in or out of order

When you drag across a series of tasks and then click Link Tasks, the tasks are linked in order from the task higher in the task list (lower Task ID number) to the task lower in the task list (higher Task ID number). It doesn't matter whether you drag from top to bottom or bottom to top—the resulting links are the same. This is also true if you select adjacent tasks using the Shift key—the order of selection does not matter.

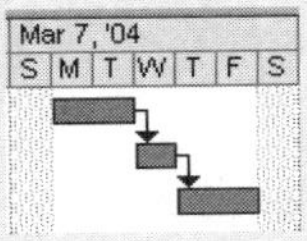

However, if you hold down Ctrl and click each task, the tasks are linked in precisely the order in which you selected each individual task. Using this method, you can make a task lower in the list and the predecessor of a task higher in the list.

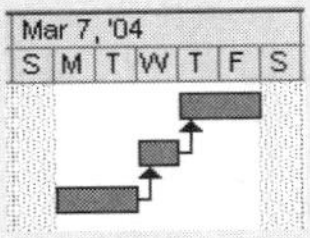

Understanding the Dependency Types

Although the finish-to-start task dependency is the most common, there are a total of four types of dependencies that help you model your task relationships. These dependency types are as follows:

Finish-to-Start (FS) As soon as the predecessor task finishes, the successor task can start.

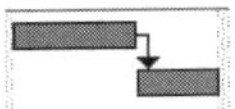

Finish-to-Finish (FF) As soon as the predecessor task finishes, the successor task can finish.

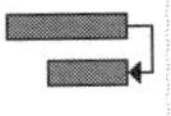

Start-to-Start (SS) As soon as the predecessor task starts, the successor task can start.

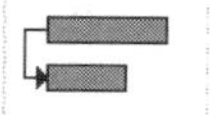

Start-to-Finish (SF) As soon as the predecessor task starts, the successor task can finish. This type of link is rarely used, but still available if you need it.

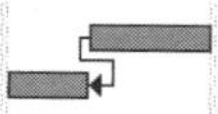

Tip **Link tasks with the Project Guide**

You can use the Project Guide to help you set task dependencies. On the Project Guide toolbar, click the Tasks button. In the Project Guide pane, click the Schedule Tasks link. Read the information, and use the controls provided to link tasks. When finished, click the Done link.

Tip **Automatically link tasks**

By default, when you move a task from one location to another in your task sheet or when you insert a new task, that task is automatically linked like its surrounding tasks. You can control this setting. Click Tools, Options and then click the Schedule tab. Select or clear the Autolink Inserted Or Moved Tasks check box.

To apply a task dependency, follow these steps:

1. Display the Gantt Chart or other view with a task sheet.
2. Select the task that is to become the successor in the dependency you will be setting.
3. On the Standard toolbar, click Task Information.

   You can also simply double-click a task to open the Task Information dialog box.
4. Click the Predecessors tab (see Figure 5-11).
5. Click the first blank row in the Task Name field and then click the down arrow. The list of tasks in the project appears.
6. Click the task that is to be the predecessor to the current task.
7. Click the Type field and then select the type of task dependency: Finish-to-Start (FS), Start-to-Start (SS), Finish-to-Finish (FF), Start-to-Finish (SF), or None.
8. Click OK.

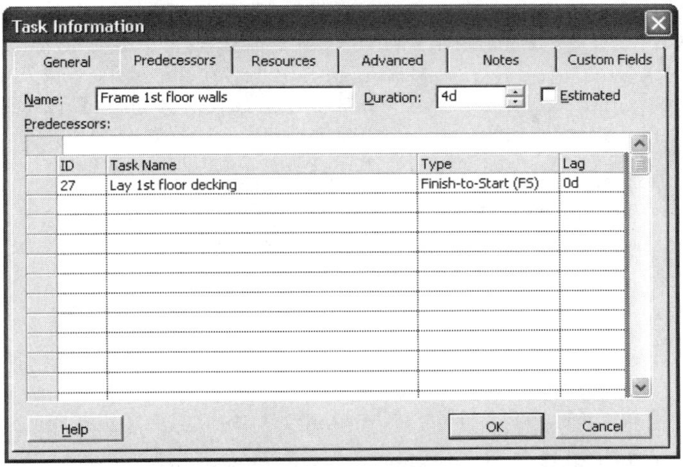

Figure 5-11. Use the Predecessors tab in the Task Information dialog box to set different types of task dependencies.

Tip **Change the task link directly in the Gantt chart**
You can also apply the Finish-to-Start task link to a pair of tasks and then quickly change the link on the chart portion of the Gantt chart. Double-click the task link line on the chart. The Task Dependency dialog box appears, as shown in Figure 5-12. In the Type box, change the dependency type and then click OK.

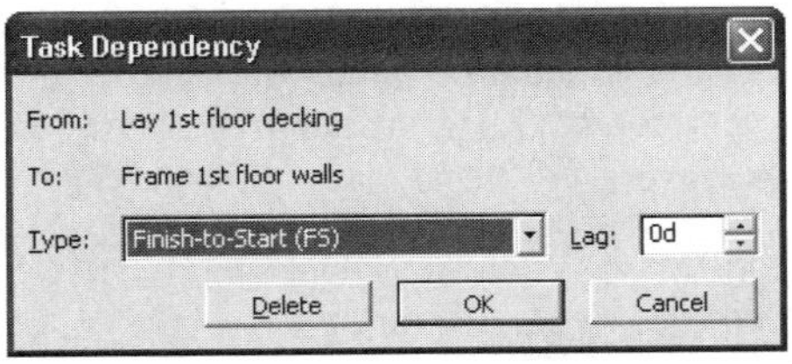

Figure 5-12. Double-click the task link line to open the Task Dependency dialog box and change the dependency type.

Tip **Link between projects**
Not only can you link tasks within one project, you can link tasks in different projects. For more information, see Chapter 15, "Exchanging Information Between Project Plans."

Overlapping Linked Tasks by Adding Lead Time

One way to make your project schedule more efficient is to overlap linked tasks where possible. Suppose you have a task that isn't scheduled to begin until a previous task is finished. You realize that the predecessor doesn't actually have to be finished—the successor can really begin when the predecessor is only 50 percent complete. The successor essentially gets a 50 percent head start, hence the term *lead time*. For example, "Construct walls" is the predecessor to "Plaster walls." Although plastering cannot be done until the walls are constructed, the final wall does not need to be constructed before plastering of the first wall can begin. You can set an amount of lead time for the "Plaster walls" task.

Lead time is expressed as a negative value. If you think of it as reducing time in the schedule, the minus sign makes sense. Lead time can be expressed as a percentage of the predecessor; for example, *-25%*. Or, it can be a specific time period, for example, *-4d* or *-1ew*.

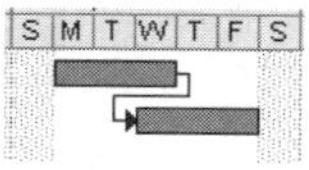

To enter lead time for a linked task, follow these steps:

1. Display the Gantt Chart or other view with a task sheet.
2. Select the successor task that is to have the lead time.
3. On the Standard toolbar, click Task Information.
4. In the Task Information dialog box, click the Predecessors tab.
5. In the Lag field for the existing Predecessor, type the amount of lead time you want for the successor. Use a negative number, and enter the lead time as a percentage or duration amount.

Tip **Enter lead time directly in the task sheet**
You can also enter lead time in the sheet portion of the Gantt chart. Click in the Predecessors field for the successor task. The field should already contain the Task ID of the predecessor task. After the Task ID, enter the code representing the link type and then enter the amount of lead time; for example, *9FS-1 day*, or *14FF-20%*.

Delaying Linked Tasks by Adding Lag Time

Suppose you have a pair of tasks with a finish-to-start link. And then you realize that the successor really can't start when the predecessor is finished—there needs to be some additional delay. This is usually the case when something needs to happen between the two tasks that isn't another task. For example, suppose the "Order equipment" task is the predecessor to the "Install equipment" task. Although the equipment cannot be installed until after the equipment is ordered, it still cannot be installed immediately after ordering. Some *lag time* is needed to allow for the equipment to be shipped and delivered. In such a case, the successor needs to be delayed, and you can enter lag time in the schedule to accurately reflect this condition.

Just like lead time, lag time can be a percentage of the predecessor; for example, *75%*. Or it can be a specific time period; for example, *16h* or *3ed*. Because it's adding rather than reducing time in the schedule, however, lag time is expressed as a positive number.

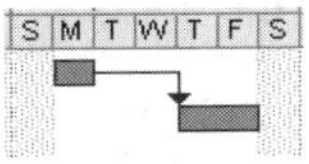

> **Note** Don't confuse the delay afforded by lag time with *assignment delay*. With lag time, the delay is from the end of the predecessor to the beginning of the successor task. With assignment delay, there is a delay from the task start date to the assignment start date.

For more information about adjusting assignments using delay, see "Adjusting Assignments" on page 278.

To enter lag time for a linked task, follow these steps:

1. Display the Gantt Chart or other view with a task sheet.
2. Select the successor task that is to have the lag time.
3. On the Standard toolbar, click Task Information and then click the Predecessors tab.
4. In the Lag field for the existing Predecessor, type the amount of lag time you want for the successor. Use a positive number and enter the lag time as a percentage or duration amount.

> **Tip** **Enter lag time directly in the task sheet**
> You can also enter lag time values in the sheet portion of the Gantt chart. Click in the Predecessors field of the successor task. The field should already contain the Task ID of the predecessor task. After the Task ID, enter the code representing the link type and then enter the amount of lag time; for example, *9FS+1 day*, or *14FF+20%*.

Changing or Removing Links

To change or remove an existing task dependency, follow these steps:

1. Display the Gantt Chart or other view with a task sheet.
2. Select the successor task whose link you want to change.
3. On the Standard toolbar, click Task Information and then click the Predecessors tab.
4. Click in the Type field for the predecessor you want to change and then select the type of task dependency you want it to be: Finish-to-Start (FS), Start-to-Start (SS), Finish-to-Finish (FF), Start-to-Finish (SF), or None. If you select None, the link is removed entirely.

Troubleshooting

You're trying to remove just the predecessor link from a task, but the successor link is removed at the same time

Unlink Tasks

When you click a task and then click Unlink Tasks, all links are removed: predecessor, successor, and any multiples. As a result, the scheduling of this task returns to the project start date or a start date entered as a constraint.

To remove just a single predecessor, click the task and then click Task Information on the Standard toolbar. In the Task Information dialog box, click the Predecessors tab. Click the task name of the predecessor you want to delete and then press the Delete key.

Reviewing Task Dependencies

When needed, the following views can give you a closer look at the task dependencies in your project:

- The Gantt Chart shows task dependencies with link lines between the Gantt bars. In fact, all Gantt Chart views show task dependencies this way.

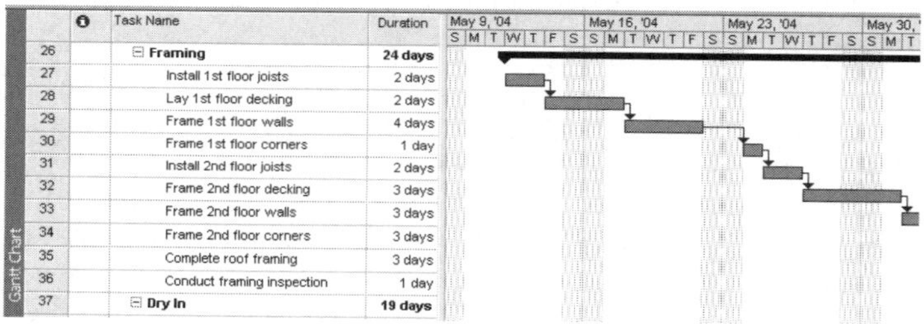

- The Network Diagram shows each task as an individual node with link lines between them. The Descriptive Network Diagram shows the same, but the nodes are larger and provide more detail.

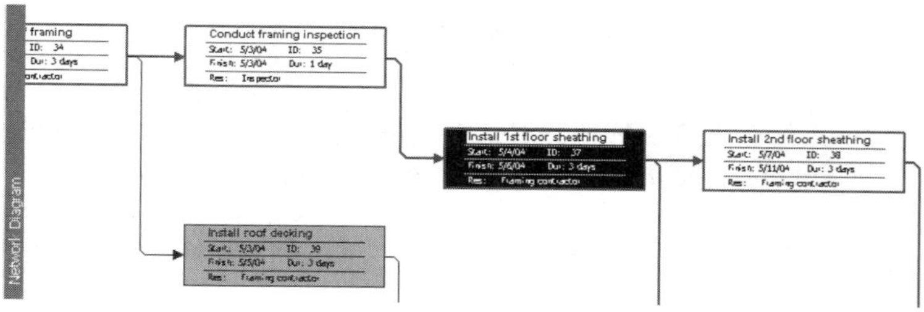

- The Relationship Diagram shows the predecessors and successors of a single selected task. This view is particularly useful for a large project or any project with complex linking.

- The Task Details Form, Task Form, and Task Name Form can show predecessors and successors of a single selected task as part of a combination view. For example, you can display the Gantt chart in the upper pane and one of the task forms in the lower pane. In fact, the Task Entry view is the built-in combination view of Gantt Chart and Task Form. By default, these forms show assigned resource information in the left grid, and the predecessor information in the right grid. To show predecessor and successor information in the form, first click the form pane. Click Format, Details, and then click Predecessors & Successors.

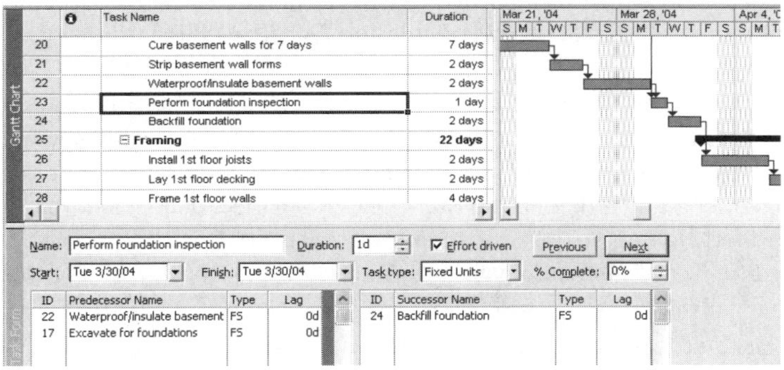

Scheduling Tasks to Achieve Specific Dates

With task dependencies established, your project schedule is taking shape and looking more and more realistic (see Figure 5-13).

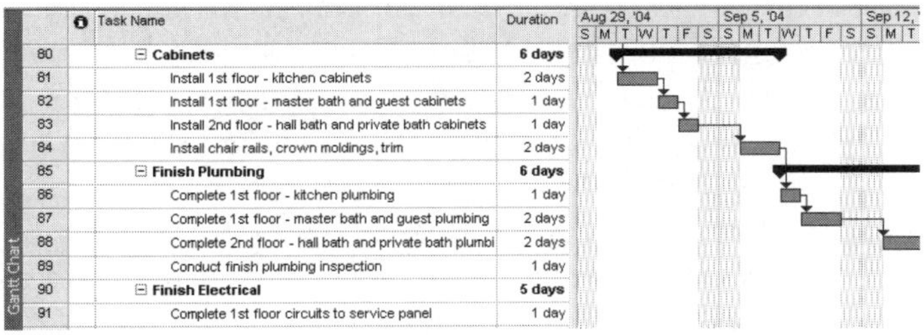

Figure 5-13. With durations entered and tasks linked, the Gantt chart is starting to show meaningful schedule information.

Microsoft Project uses the task information and controls that you enter to schedule your project from start to finish. By default, Microsoft Project schedules each task to start "As Soon As Possible."

However, you might have additional dates to consider. For example, maybe certain pivotal supplies will not be ready for use in the project until after April 6. Perhaps an important review meeting is taking place on June 29 that will set the stage for work toward the final milestones. Maybe one of your deliverables is a presentation at a key professional conference held on August 22.

To schedule around these important dates, you can set a *constraint*, which is a restriction on the start or finish date of a task. All tasks have a constraint applied—at the very least, the default "As Soon As Possible" constraint. The As Soon As Possible constraint indicates that the task should be scheduled according to its working times calendars, duration, task dependencies, and any resource assignments—without regard to any specific date.

Understanding Constraint Types

The As Soon As Possible constraint is applied by default to all tasks in a project scheduled from the start date. In a project scheduled from the finish date, the As Late As Possible constraint is applied. The As Soon As Possible and As Late As Possible constraints are considered flexible constraints.

> **Note** Different types of constraints are applied in certain situations, depending on whether you're working with a project scheduled from the start date or from the finish date. For example, entering a date in the Start field of a project scheduled from the start date causes a Start No Earlier Than constraint to be applied. Doing the same thing in a project scheduled from the finish date causes a Start No Later Than constraint to be applied.

When a task needs to be scheduled in relation to a specific date, there are additional constraints you can apply, each of which is associated with a date. The following is a list of all the date constraints you can use to refine your project schedule:

Start No Earlier Than (SNET) A moderately flexible constraint that specifies the earliest possible date that a task can begin. For projects scheduled from a start date, this constraint is automatically applied when you enter a start date for a task.

Finish No Earlier Than (FNET) A moderately flexible constraint that specifies the earliest possible date that this task can be completed. For projects scheduled from a start date, this constraint is automatically applied when you enter a finish date for a task.

Start No Later Than (SNLT) A moderately flexible constraint that specifies the latest possible date that this task can begin. For projects scheduled from a finish date, this constraint is automatically applied when you enter a start date for a task.

Finish No Later Than (FNLT) A moderately flexible constraint that specifies the latest possible date that this task can be completed. For projects scheduled from a finish date, this constraint is automatically applied when you enter a finish date for a task.

Must Start On (MSO) An inflexible constraint that specifies the exact date when a task must begin. Other scheduling controls such as task dependencies become secondary to this requirement.

Must Finish On (MFO) An inflexible constraint that specifies the exact date on which a date must be completed. Other scheduling controls such as task dependencies become secondary to this requirement.

Inside Out

Beware of entering dates

If you enter a date in the Start field (in a project scheduled from the start date), the Start No Earlier Than constraint is applied. The Finish date is recalculated based on the new Start date and the existing duration.

If you then enter a date in the Finish field of the same task, the constraint changes to Finish No Earlier Than. The Start date remains as you set it, but the duration is recalculated to reflect the difference between your entered Start and Finish dates.

Always be aware that any dates you enter change the As Soon As Possible or As Late As Possible constraints to something more inflexible. If you enter both the Start and Finish dates for a task, Microsoft Project recalculates the duration.

Entering your own start and finish dates imposes often unnecessary restrictions on Microsoft Project's capability to create the best possible schedule. It can also adversely affect results when you have Microsoft Project level overallocated resources. In the majority of cases, you get the best results when you enter durations and task dependencies and then let Microsoft Project figure out the best start and finish dates for tasks to be done as soon as possible. Use date constraints only when there is a hard and fast date that you must work toward.

Project Management Practices: Working with Date Constraints

When developing your project schedule, you might contend with one of two major categories of date constraints: externally imposed dates and milestone dates.

An externally imposed date reflects situations outside the project that influence the project schedule. Examples include the following:

- A shipment of material needed for the project
- A market window for a new product
- A product announcement date at a trade conference

- Weather restrictions on outdoor activities
- A special event important to the project but scheduled by forces outside the project

You can reflect externally imposed dates as constraints on the tasks they affect. You can also add a task note as a reminder of the source of this date.

Milestone dates are typically dates set internally. As the project manager, you might set them yourself as goals to work toward. The project sponsor, customer, or other stakeholder might request certain dates for certain milestones, deliverables, or events being produced by the work of your project. You can set constraints on milestones as well as on regular tasks.

Changing Constraints

Remember, tasks always have a constraint applied—even if it's just As Soon As Possible or As Late As Possible. So we never think of *adding* or *removing* constraints. When making a change, we're typically changing a constraint from a flexible one to a more inflexible one or vice versa.

There are several methods for changing constraints, as follows:

- In the Gantt Chart or similar view with a task sheet, type or select dates in the Start or Finish fields. In a project scheduled from the start date, this causes a Start No Earlier Than or Finish No Earlier Than constraint to be applied. In a project scheduled from the finish date, this causes a Start No Later Than or Finish No Later Than constraint to be applied.
- In any task view, select the task whose constraint you want to change and then click Task Information on the Standard toolbar. In the Task Information dialog box, click the Advanced tab (see Figure 5-14). In the Constraint Type box, click the constraint type you want to apply to this task. If applicable, enter the date in the Constraint Date box.

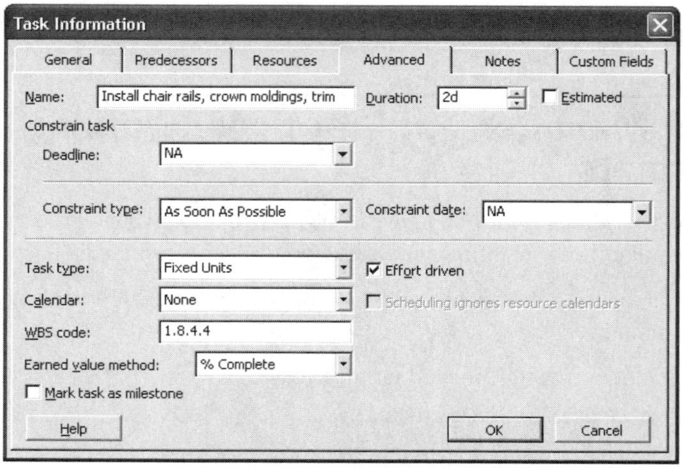

Figure 5-14. On the Advanced tab of the Task Information dialog box, you can set constraints, deadlines, milestones, and task calendars.

- On the Project Guide toolbar, click the Tasks button. In the Project Guide pane, click the Set Deadlines And Constrain Tasks link. Read the information under Constrain A Task and use the controls that are provided to set constraints.
- In the Gantt Chart or other view with a task sheet, apply the Constraint Dates table. Click View, Table, More Tables. In the More Tables dialog box, click Constraint Dates and then click the Apply button (see Figure 5-15). In the Constraint Type field, click the constraint type you want to apply to this task. If applicable, enter the date in the Constraint Date box.

	Task Name	Duration	Constraint Type	Constraint Date
80	**Cabinets**	**9 days**	**As Soon As Possible**	**NA**
81	Install 1st floor - kitchen cabinets	2 days	Start No Earlier Than	Tue 8/31/04
82	Install 1st floor - master bath and guest cabinets	1 day	As Soon As Possible	NA
83	Install 2nd floor - hall bath and private bath cabinets	1 day	As Soon As Possible	NA
84	Install chair rails, crown moldings, trim	2 days	Must Finish On	Fri 9/10/04
85	**Finish Plumbing**	**6 days**	**As Soon As Possible**	**NA**
86	Complete 1st floor - kitchen plumbing	1 day	As Soon As Possible	NA
87	Complete 1st floor - master bath and guest plumbing	2 days	As Soon As Possible	NA
88	Complete 2nd floor - hall bath and private bath plumbing	2 days	As Soon As Possible	NA
89	Conduct finish plumbing inspection	1 day	Finish No Later Than	Fri 9/24/04
90	**Finish Electrical**	**5 days**	**As Soon As Possible**	**NA**
91	Complete 1st floor circuits to service panel	1 day	As Soon As Possible	NA

Figure 5-15. Apply the Constraint Dates table to review or change constraint types and dates.

Tip **Change constraints for multiple tasks at once**
Select all the tasks that will have the same constraint applied. Drag across adjacent tasks to select them or hold down Ctrl while clicking nonadjacent tasks. Click Task Information on the Standard toolbar and then click the Advanced tab in the Multiple Task Information dialog box. Change the Constraint Type, and if applicable, the Constraint Date. Click OK. The constraint is changed for all selected tasks.

This method works best if you're changing date constraints to As Soon As Possible or As Late As Possible, because it's rare for multiple tasks to have the same constraint date.

Troubleshooting

You can't delete a constraint

By their nature, constraints are not deleted. A constraint is applied to every task. If you're thinking of deleting a constraint, what you probably want to do is change it from a date constraint such as Must Start On or Finish No Later Than to a flexible constraint such as As Soon As Possible.

Double-click the task to open the Task Information dialog box and then click the Advanced tab. In the Constraint Type box, click As Soon As Possible or As Late As Possible.

Working with Flexible and Inflexible Constraints

There are three levels of flexibility associated with task constraints: flexible, moderately flexible, and inflexible.

Flexible Constraints

The flexible constraints are As Soon As Possible and As Late As Possible. These constraints work with task dependencies to schedule a task as soon or as late as the task dependency and other scheduling considerations will accommodate. These default constraints allow Microsoft Project maximum flexibility in calculating start and finish dates for the tasks. For example, a task with an ASAP constraint and a finish-to-start dependency is scheduled as soon as the predecessor task finishes.

Moderately Flexible Constraints

The moderately flexible constraints (Start No Earlier Than, Start No Later Than, Finish No Earlier Than, and Finish No Later Than) have a range of dates to work within. That is, the task is restricted to starting or finishing before or after the date you choose, which provides some room for flexibility, even though a date is in place. For example, a task with a Start No Later Than constraint for November 14 and a finish-to-start dependency to another task can begin any time its predecessor is finished up until November 14, but it cannot be scheduled after November 14.

Inflexible Constraints

The inflexible constraints, Must Start On and Must Finish On, have an absolute single date that the schedule must accommodate, which means that other scheduling considerations must fall by the wayside if necessary to meet this date. By default, constraints take precedence over task dependencies when there's a conflict between the two. For example, a task with a Must Finish On constraint for April 30 and a finish-to-start dependency to another task is always scheduled for April 30, regardless of whether the predecessor finishes on time.

Inside Out

Conflicts between dependencies and constraints

If you set a moderately flexible constraint, such as Start No Earlier Than or an inflexible constraint, such as Must Finish On, you run the risk of a conflict with task dependencies. Suppose the "Hang wallpaper" task has a Must Finish On constraint for June 25. Because of various delays, the task's finish-to-start predecessor task, "Texture walls," actually finishes on June 29.

This situation creates a scheduling conflict. According to the task dependency, you can't hang wallpaper until the walls are textured, which won't finish until June 29. But according to the constraint, the wallpaper must be hung by June 25.

By default, where there's a conflict like this between a task dependency and a constraint, the constraint takes precedence. In this case, there would be 4 days of *negative slack*, which essentially means that the predecessor task is running 4 days into the time allotted to the successor task. You might see a Planning Wizard message regarding this, especially if you're still in the planning processes and are setting up tasks with such a conflict before actual work is even reported.

To resolve this conflict, you can change the constraint to a more flexible one, such as Finish No Earlier Than. You can change the Must Finish On date to a later date that will work. You can also change the scheduling precedence option. If you want task dependencies to take precedence over constraints, click Tools, Options. In the Options dialog box, click the Schedule tab, and then clear the Tasks Will Always Honor Their Constraint Dates check box.

Reviewing Constraints

With the right constraints in place, you have the beginnings of a schedule. The Gantt chart can provide a great deal of information about your constraints and other scheduling controls.

You can sort tasks by Start Date, Finish Date, Constraint Type, or Constraint Date. You can group tasks by Constraint Type. You can filter tasks by the Should Start By date or the Should Start/Finish By date.

Such task arrangements can provide overviews of the big picture of start and finish dates across many tasks at a time. If you want to review details, you can review the Task Information dialog box for a task. The General tab includes the scheduled start and finish dates, and the Advanced tab includes the constraint type and constraint date.

You can apply the Task Entry view. The task details for any task you select in the Gantt chart in the upper pane are shown in the Task Form in the lower pane. The default Resources & Predecessors details show task dependencies as well as any lead or lag time (see Figure 5-16).

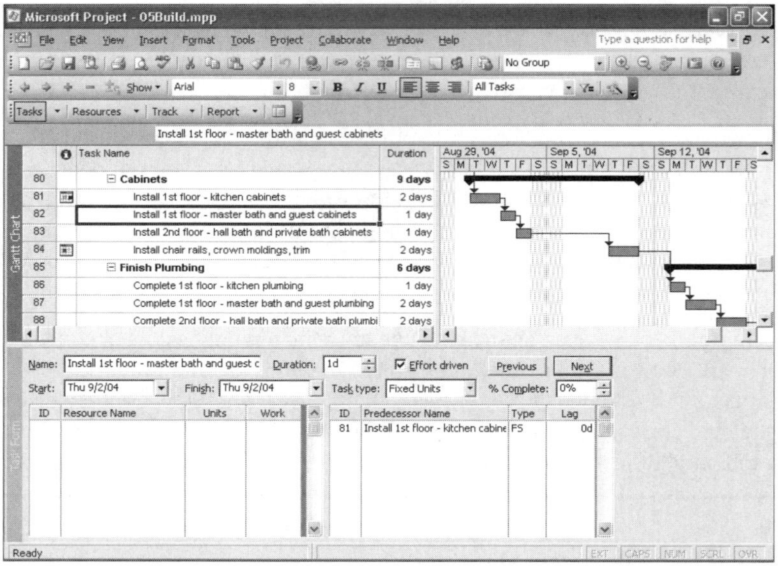

Figure 5-16. With the Task Entry view, you can review details of an individual task selected in the Gantt Chart.

Getting Scheduling Feedback

NEW FEATURE!

After you assign tasks to resources, Microsoft Project 2003 employs Microsoft Office Smart Tags technology to provide scheduling feedback. When you make certain kinds of changes that affect scheduling—such as changes to duration, start date, or finish date—a green triangle might appear in the corner of the edited cell in a Gantt Chart, task sheet, or usage view.

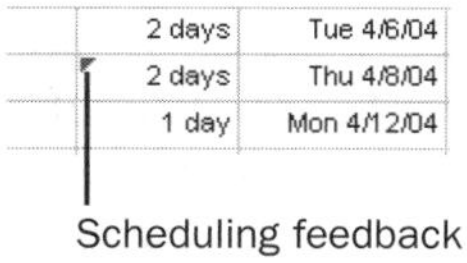

When you move your mouse pointer over the cell containing the feedback indicator, the Smart Tag icon appears.

Chapter 5

Click the Smart Tag icon. A message explains the scheduling ramifications of your edit. The message usually gives you the opportunity to change the edit so that the result is closer to your expectation.

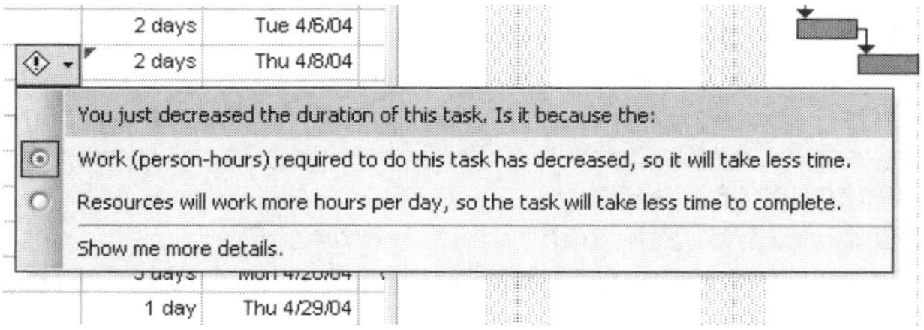

Feedback message

The indicator appears in the cell as long as the edit is available for an Undo operation. After you make a new edit, the indicator disappears.

Unlike Microsoft Office Smart Tags, you cannot change or create your own feedback messages in Microsoft Project. However, you can turn them off. Click Tools, Options, and then click the Interface tab. Clear any of the check boxes under Show Indicators And Options Buttons.

For more information about feedback indicators in resource assignments, see "Changing Resource Assignments" on page 220.

Setting Deadline Reminders

Suppose you want a task or milestone to be completed by a certain date, but you don't want to limit the schedule calculations by setting a date constraint. Set a *deadline* instead. A deadline appears as an indicator on your Gantt chart as a target or goal, but does not affect the scheduling of your tasks.

To set a deadline, follow these steps:

1. Select the task for which you want to set a deadline.
2. On the Standard toolbar, click Task Information and then click the Advanced tab.
3. In the Deadline box, enter or select the deadline date.

The deadline marker appears in the chart area of the Gantt chart (see Figure 5-17). Repeat Steps 1–3 to change or remove a deadline if necessary. If you're removing a deadline, select the date and press the Delete key.

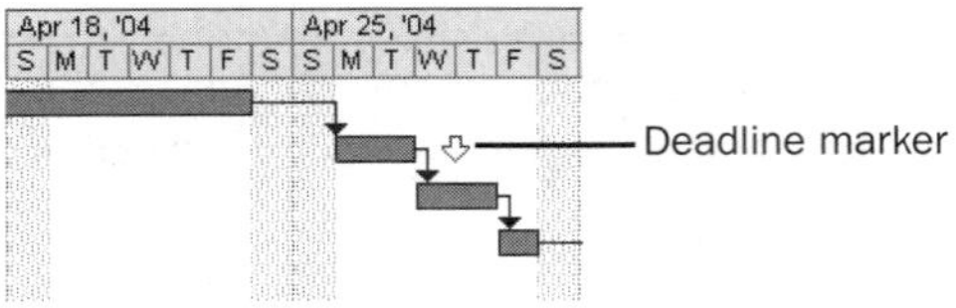

Figure 5-17. The deadline does not affect scheduling but simply provides a guideline for important dates.

> **Tip** **Use the Project Guide to set deadlines**
> On the Project Guide toolbar, click the Tasks button. In the Project Guide pane, click the Set Deadlines And Constrain Tasks link. Read the information under Set A Deadline and use the controls provided to set deadlines.

You can show deadlines in your task sheet as well, by adding the Deadline field as a column. Follow these steps:

1. Right-click the column heading to the right of where you want your new Deadline column to be inserted, and then click Insert Column.

   Or you can click the column heading and then click Insert, Column. The Column Definition dialog box appears.

2. In the Field Name box, click Deadline. You can type the first one or two letters to go straight to it in the list.

   The Deadline field shows any deadline dates that are already set and shows "NA" for tasks without deadlines. You can enter deadlines directly in this field.

If the schedule for a task moves beyond its deadline date, either because of normal scheduling calculations or because of actual progress information entered, an alert appears in the Indicators field, specifying that the task is scheduled to finish later than its deadline (see Figure 5-18).

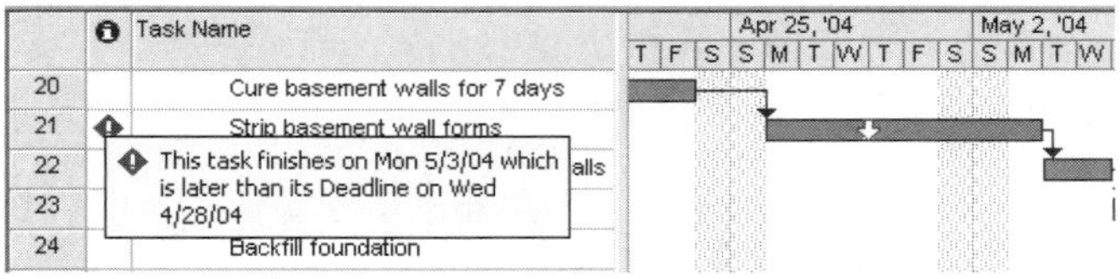

Figure 5-18. If a deadline will be missed, the deadline indicator provides the details.

You can set deadlines for summary tasks as well as individual tasks. If the summary task's deadline conflicts with the finish dates of any of the subtasks, the deadline indicator specifies a missed deadline among the subtasks. You can also set deadlines for milestone tasks as well as for normal tasks.

Inside Out

A deadline might affect scheduling after all

There are two instances in which a deadline can indeed affect task scheduling. The first is if you enter a deadline that falls before the end of the task's *total slack*. The total slack is recalculated using the deadline date rather than the task's late finish date. If the total slack reaches 0, the task becomes critical.

The second instance is if you set a deadline on a task with an As Late As Possible constraint. Suppose the task is scheduled to finish on the deadline date. However, if any predecessors slip, the task could still finish beyond its deadline.

For more information about the critical path, slack, and late finish dates, see "Working with the Critical Path and Critical Tasks" on page 251.

Creating Milestones in Your Schedule

You can designate certain tasks as *milestones* in your project plan. Having milestones flagged in your project plan and visible in your Gantt chart helps you see when you've achieved another benchmark. Milestones often indicate the beginning or ending of major phases or the completion of deliverables in your project. As you complete each milestone, you come ever closer to completing the project. Milestones are also excellent reporting points.

A milestone, as such, has no additional calculation effect on your schedule. However, you typically link a milestone to other tasks. You might also set a date constraint on a milestone.

The simplest method for entering a milestone is to create the task that's worded like a milestone (for example, "First floor construction complete") and enter a duration of 0. Any task with a 0 duration is automatically set as a milestone. The milestone marker and date are drawn in the chart area of the Gantt chart (see Figure 5-19).

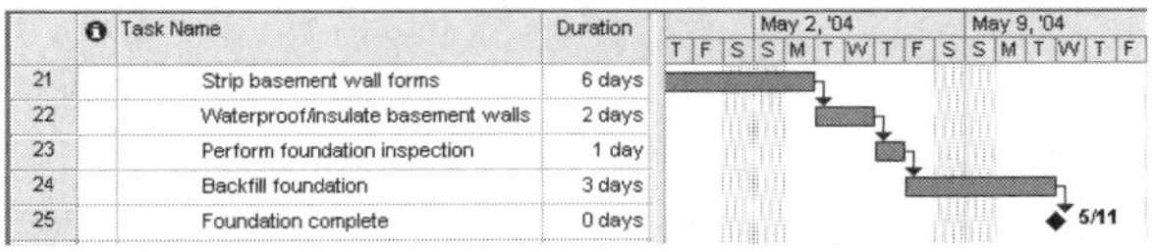

Task Name
Duration
May 2, '04
May 9, '04
21 Strip basement wall forms 6 days
22 Waterproof/insulate basement walls 2 days
23 Perform foundation inspection 1 day
24 Backfill foundation 3 days
25 Foundation complete 0 days
5/11

Figure 5-19. Microsoft Project interprets any task with a 0 duration as a milestone.

However, a milestone doesn't have to have a 0 duration. You might want to make the final task in each phase a milestone, and these are real tasks with real durations. To change a regular task into a milestone, follow these steps:

1. Select the task you want to become a milestone.
2. On the Standard toolbar, click Task Information and then click the Advanced tab.

3 Select the Mark Task As Milestone check box.

The Gantt bar for the task changes to the milestone marker in the chart area of the Gantt chart (see Figure 5-20).

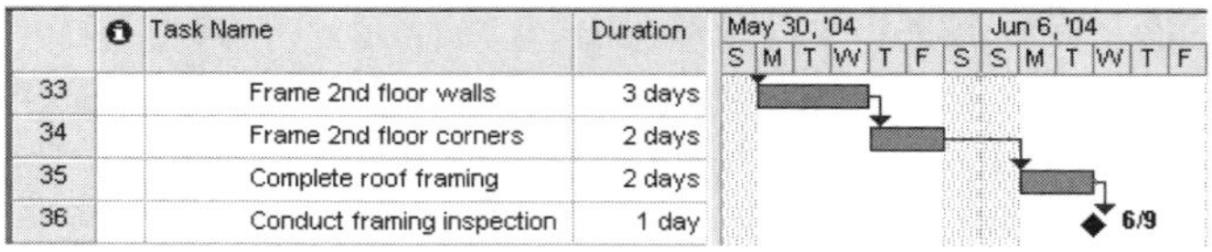

Task Name
Duration
May 30, '04
Jun 6, '04
S M T W T F S S M T W T F
33 Frame 2nd floor walls 3 days
34 Frame 2nd floor corners 2 days
35 Complete roof framing 2 days
36 Conduct framing inspection 1 day
6/9

Figure 5-20. You can set any task as a milestone.

Inside Out

Misleading milestone markers

By default, milestones markers are set to appear on their Start date. Suppose you have a 4-day task with a Start date of December 12 and a Finish date of December 16. If you change this task to a milestone, the duration, start date, and finish dates remain the same. However, the Gantt bar for the task in the chart area of the Gantt chart changes to a milestone marker on December 12. The position of the milestone marker can be misleading because there's no longer anything drawn to show the end of the task.

You can change the bar style for the milestone marker. By default, the style is drawn From Start To Start, but you can change it to be From Finish To Finish. Click Format, Bar Styles. In the grid, click in the From field for the Milestone style and then click Finish. Click in the To field for the Milestone style and then click Finish, which causes the milestone marker to sit on the Finish date (see Figure 5-21).

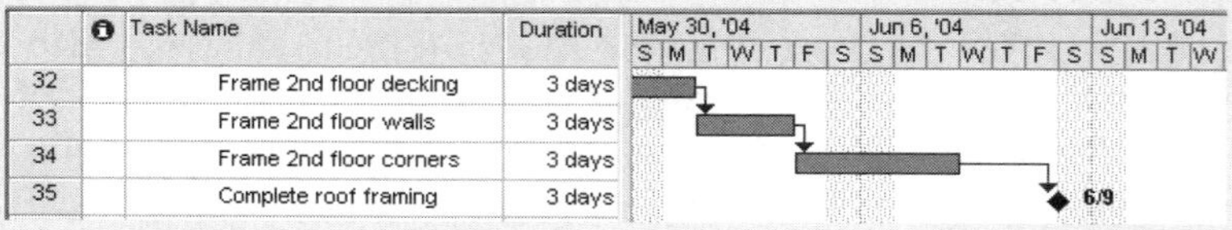

Task Name
Duration
May 30, '04
Jun 6, '04
Jun 13, '04
S M T W T F S S M T W T F S S M T W
32 Frame 2nd floor decking 3 days
33 Frame 2nd floor walls 3 days
34 Frame 2nd floor corners 3 days
35 Complete roof framing 3 days
6/9

Figure 5-21. You can change the milestone marker to appear on the Finish date rather than the Start date.

Or you can change the bar style to include a bar showing duration, with the milestone marker at the end of the bar. In the Bar Styles dialog box, click the Appearance field for the Milestone style. Below the grid, under Middle, enter a shape, pattern, and color for the Gantt bar you want to represent the milestone bar. Under End, enter the shape, type, and color for the end marker for the milestone Gantt bar. In the grid, change the From field to Start and the To field to Finish, which gives you a Gantt bar showing the duration of the milestone task as well as a symbol to mark the end of the task and the completion of the milestone (see Figure 5-22).

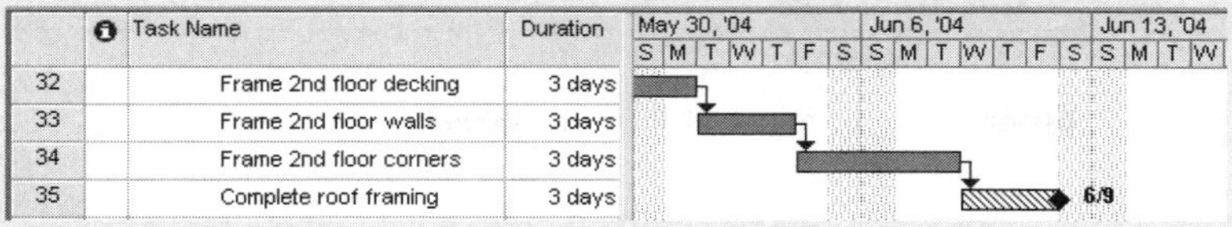

Figure 5-22. You can create a milestone Gantt bar to show the milestone's duration as well as its end point.

> **Tip** **Use milestone Gantt charts**
> You can review specialized milestone Gantt charts to take a closer look at project milestones. First run the Rollup_Formatting macro. Then switch to the Milestone Rollup or Milestone Date Rollup view.

Working with Task Calendars

The scheduling of your tasks is driven by task duration, task dependencies, and constraints. It's also driven by the project calendar. If your project calendar dictates that work is done Monday through Friday, 8:00 A.M. until 5:00 P.M., initially that's when your tasks are scheduled.

For more information about calendars, see "Setting Your Project Calendar" on page 70.

However, if a task is assigned to a resource who works Saturday and Sunday, 9:00 A.M. until 9:00 P.M., the task is scheduled for those times instead. That is, the task is scheduled according to the assigned resource's working times calendar rather than the project calendar.

Sometimes, you have a task that needs to be scheduled differently from the working times reflected in the project calendar or the assigned resource calendars. For example, you might have a task that specifies preventive maintenance on equipment at specified intervals. Or you might have a task being completed by a machine running 24 hours a day. In any case, the task has its own working time, and you want it to be scheduled according to that working time rather than the project or resource working time so it can accurately reflect what's really happening with this task.

Creating a Base Calendar

Microsoft Project comes with three *base calendars*, which are like calendar templates that you can apply to the project as a whole, as a set of resources, or in this case, as a set of tasks. The three base calendars are described in Table 5-1.

Table 5-1. Base Calendar Types

Calendar Type	Description
Standard	Working time is set to Monday through Friday, 8:00 A.M. until 5:00 P.M., with an hour off for lunch from 12:00 P.M. until 1:00 P.M. each day. The Standard is the default base calendar used for the project, for tasks, and for resources.
Night Shift	Working time is set from 11:00 P.M. until 8:00 A.M. five days a week, with an hour off for lunch from 3:00 A.M. until 4:00 A.M. each morning. This base calendar is generally used for resources who work a graveyard shift. It can also be used for projects that are carried out only during the night shift.
24 Hours	Working time is set to 12:00 A.M. until 12:00 A.M. seven days a week; that is, work never stops. This base calendar is typically used for projects in a manufacturing situation, for example, which might run two or three back-to-back shifts every day of the week.

> **Note** If you are running Microsoft Office Project Server 2003, the Night Shift and 24 Hours calendars are available only to project administrators.

If you want to apply a task calendar, you often need to create a special base calendar for the purpose. To create a new base calendar, follow these steps:

1. Click Tools, Change Working Time.
2. Click the New button. The Create New Base Calendar dialog box appears (see Figure 5-23).

Figure 5-23. Create a new base calendar to set a unique working times schedule for a specific task.

3. In the Name box, type the name you want for the new base calendar, for example, **Equipment Maintenance**.

4. Select Create New Base Calendar if you want to adapt your calendar from the Standard base calendar.

   Select Make A Copy Of if you want to adapt the new calendar from a different existing base calendar, such as the Night Shift. Select the name of the existing calendar you want to adapt.
5. Click OK.
6. Make the changes you want to the working days and times for individual days or entire days of the week, as needed.
7. When finished with your new base calendar, click OK.

Assigning a Base Calendar to a Task

To assign a base calendar to a task, follow these steps:

1. Select the task to which you want to assign a base calendar.
2. On the Standard toolbar, click Task Information and then click the Advanced tab.
3. In the Calendar box, click the name of the calendar you want to assign to this task. All base calendars are listed, including ones you have created yourself.

A calendar indicator appears in the Indicator column. If you rest your mouse pointer over the indicator, a ScreenTip displays the name of the assigned calendar (see Figure 5-24). Follow this same procedure to change to a different task calendar or to remove the task calendar.

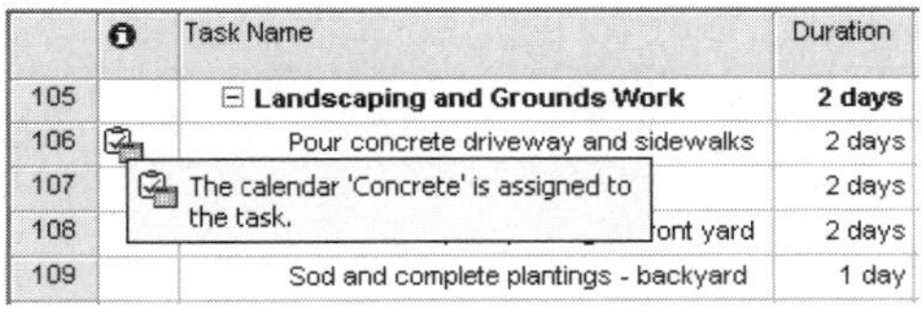

Figure 5-24. Assign a calendar to a task to schedule it independently from the project or resource calendars.

Don't confuse the task calendar with the Calendar view. A task calendar reflects working days and times for one or more selected tasks. The Calendar view is a graphical representation of tasks and durations in a monthly calendar format.

For more information about the Calendar view, see "Working with Graph Views" on page 104.

Troubleshooting

You assigned a task calendar, but it's not scheduling tasks in all the times it should

The task probably also has a resource assigned, and the resource calendar is conflicting with what you want the task calendar to accomplish.

When you assign a task calendar, it takes the place of the project calendar. However, suppose resources are assigned to the task as well. Resources are all associated with their own resource calendars as well. Although a resource's calendar might be the same as the project calendar, it can be customized for the resource's specific working times.

When resources are assigned, the task is scheduled not just for the working times indicated in the task calendar. Instead, by default, Microsoft Project schedules the task according to the common working times between the task calendar and the resource calendar.

For example, suppose the 24-hour base calendar is assigned to a task that's also assigned to a resource who works Friday through Sunday, 9:00 A.M. until 7:00 P.M. The only times the two calendars have in common are Friday through Sunday, 9:00 A.M. until 7:00 P.M., so by default, those are the only times when work will be scheduled for this task.

If you want the resource calendar to be ignored on a task, open the Task Information dialog box for the task and click the Advanced tab. Select the Scheduling Ignores Resource Calendars check box.

Chapter 6

Setting Up Resources in the Project

As soon as you're assigned as manager of the project, you might already have certain resources in mind whom you know would be right for this project. As the scope becomes more defined and as you develop the task list along with the milestones and deliverables, you're likely to have even more ideas. If you have specific people in mind, you might start inquiring about their availability. You might also start investigating sources, specifications, and prices for material and equipment.

By the time you develop the durations of the tasks, you have very concrete information in front of you—you now know exactly which tasks need to be done and what kinds of resources you need to do them.

There might be a team in place already—the full-time members of a department who are waiting to sink their teeth into a good project. There might be no team at all, and you'll have to hire some people and contract others. Or you might have a core staff, but for this project you'll need to contract additional temporary workers to fill out the skills needed for the team.

You can add the names of resources who will be working on this project as you acquire them. These might be the names of actual people. Or they might be generic resource names that describe the skills and competencies needed to fulfill the task. Where applicable, you can enter the names of equipment or material resources that will also help implement the project. You can enter additional resource information, such as availability, cost, and notes.

How Many Resources Do You Need?

Although you know the tasks that need to be done and the kinds of resources you need to be able to do them, you might not know *how many* of a particular type of resource you need just yet.

Here's the process: First, you identify the tasks that need to be done. Second, you identify the resources needed to do those tasks. Third, you assign resources to the tasks. At that point, you can see whether the resulting schedule meets your target date or target budget.

You need to have tasks in place to find out how many resources you need. You also need resources to assign to those tasks to create an accurate schedule and cost estimate. After assigning resources, if the schedule calculates a finish date later than the target finish date, you might have to go back and add more resources to your team. Or if the project costs are over budget and you haven't even started work yet, you might have to forgo additional resources or scramble to replace expensive resources with less expensive ones.

As you can see, tuning your project plan to get the right number of resources to meet your schedule, costs, and workload requirements is an iterative process. You might need to go through several cycles of refinement before you arrive at the perfect plan.

For more information about refining the project plan to meet a target date or budget, see Chapter 9, "Checking and Adjusting the Project Plan."

Understanding the Impact of Resources in the Project Plan

Resources carry out the work of your project. However, with your tasks defined and scheduled, why is it necessary to actually specify resources in your project plan? You could just print the schedule and tell people which tasks they're responsible for: Here are your due dates; now go make them happen.

This procedure might seem like a simple way of managing a project, but if you do it this way, you'll miss out on the tremendous scheduling, tracking, and communication capabilities provided by Microsoft Office Project 2003. By adding resources to your project, you can do the following:

- Increase the accuracy of your schedule. In addition to scheduling according to the project calendar, durations, task dependencies, and constraints, when you assign resources, Project 2003 adds the working times and availability of your resources into the scheduling calculations.
- Know ahead of time whether any resources are overloaded with too much work in the allotted time. You can also see whether anyone is underallocated and shift responsibilities accordingly as you refine your schedule. Later, when work is being done and you're getting progress information on each task, you can find bottlenecks or any new overallocations or underallocations due to shifts in the schedule.

- Track progress according to resource work. Your resources can tell you how much time they've spent on their tasks for a given week and how much more time they will need. This tracking can help you make any necessary adjustments to keep the project moving in the right direction. Recording actual progress data also captures historical information that will be invaluable for future projects.
- Record the use, cost, and consumption of materials in your project. These details can help you monitor your budget performance as well as give you advance notice as to when you need to reorder supplies.
- Exchange task assignments, task updates, progress information, and status reports with your resources, via Microsoft Office Project Server 2003 and Microsoft Office Project Web Access 2003.
- Make sure that all tasks are assigned to a responsible and accountable resource, so nothing inadvertently slips through the cracks to be forgotten until it's too late.

Adding Work Resources to the Project

The following types of resources can accomplish work on your tasks:

- People
- Equipment
- Materials

Microsoft Project consolidates these resources into two resource types. *Work resources* consist of people and equipment, which use time as a measure of effort on a task. *Material resources* are consumable supplies, which use quantity as a measure of effort on a task.

For more information about material resources, see "Adding Material Resources to the Project," later in this chapter on page 186.

Add resources to your project simply by entering their names into your project plan. To automate the process, you can select resource names from your company's e-mail address book. If you have a resource list in a Microsoft Excel workbook, you can import it into your project plan. After your resources are in place, you can add information regarding their availability, costs, notes, and more.

Project Management Practices: Staffing Management

Ongoing operations such as accounts payable or shipping and receiving always need to be staffed "forever." In projects, however, that's not the case: Because projects have a specific beginning and ending point, there's a definite starting point when you begin to need resources. There's also a definite ending point when resources are no longer needed because the project is complete. In between the start and finish dates, there are likely to be ramp-up and ramp-down periods, which often take place at a variety of times for different phases or functions.

Given this condition of project staffing, it's important to have a clear sense of when you actually need people to work on projects, what you need them for, at what point you don't need them anymore, and what happens to them after that point.

A staffing management plan is considered a subset of your project plan. It describes when and how your human resources will be brought on and taken off your project team. An excellent way to develop your staffing management plan is to develop your task list and preliminary schedule using generic resources, which can help you to determine your staffing needs based on specific tasks in the schedule.

Adding Resource Names Manually

To add resources to your project by simple data entry, follow these steps:

1. Click View, Resource Sheet to switch to the Resource Sheet view (see Figure 6-1).

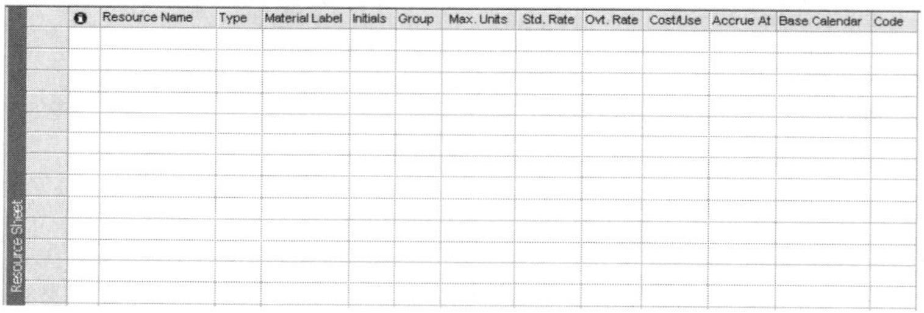

Figure 6-1. Enter Resource information on the Resource Sheet.

2. Make sure the Entry table is applied. Click View, Table, Entry.
3. In the first Resource Name field, type the name of a resource and then press Enter.
4. Enter the names of other resources in the same way.

If a piece of equipment will be integral to the successful completion of a task, enter its name as a work resource, just as you would a human resource.

Tip **Sort your resource names**

When you have all the resources entered, you might want to sort them in a particular order and keep them in that order. In the Resource Sheet, click Project, Sort, Sort By. In the Sort By field, click the field you want the resources sorted by; for example, Name, or Group. Select the Permanently Renumber Resources check box and then click Sort. This procedure makes this particular order permanent because it renumbers the Unique ID for each resource.

Whenever you select the Permanently Renumber Resources check box and click Sort, it's a very good idea to open the Sort dialog box again, click Reset and then click Cancel. This process clears the Permanently Renumber Resources check box. This way, the next time you sort your resources for some temporary need, you won't inadvertently renumber the resources again.

You can enter actual names of resources or you can enter *generic resources.* A generic resource is a title or other similar description of the resource instead of an actual name; for example, Accountant, Marketing Specialist, Sales Representative (see Figure 6-2).

	i	Resource Name	Type	Material Label	Initials	Group	Max. Units	Std. Rate	Ovt. Rate	Cost/Use	Accrue At	Base Calendar
1		Pilar Ackerman	Work		P		100%	$0.00/hr	$0.00/hr	$0.00	Prorated	Standard
2		Amy S. Recker	Work		A		100%	$0.00/hr	$0.00/hr	$0.00	Prorated	Standard
3		Jae B. Pak	Work		J		100%	$0.00/hr	$0.00/hr	$0.00	Prorated	Standard
4		Frank Martinez	Work		F		100%	$0.00/hr	$0.00/hr	$0.00	Prorated	Standard
5		Designer	Work		D		100%	$0.00/hr	$0.00/hr	$0.00	Prorated	Standard
6		Project Engineer	Work		P		100%	$0.00/hr	$0.00/hr	$0.00	Prorated	Standard
7		Drafter	Work		D		100%	$0.00/hr	$0.00/hr	$0.00	Prorated	Standard

Figure 6-2. Use either actual resource names or generic categories of resources to get started.

As you bring resources into the project, you can either leave the generic names or you can replace the generic names with the actual names. Whenever you change resource names in the Resource Sheet, the names are changed on any assigned tasks automatically.

Tip **Apply the Entry – Work Resources table**

If you're entering a significant number of work resources or if you don't expect to enter any material resources, apply the Entry – Work Resources table. This table has only those resource fields applicable to work resources.

With the Resource Sheet showing, click View, Table, More Tables. Click Entry – Work Resources and then click Apply.

Troubleshooting

You have duplicate resource names, and information is being tracked separately for each instance

Whether you enter actual names or generic names, be aware that Microsoft Project allows duplicate entries of the same name. Through the use of a unique identifier (Unique ID) for each resource record you enter, the duplicate entries appear unique to the Microsoft Project database. The problem is that when you assign tasks to a duplicated resource, you might assign some tasks to one instance of the resource and other tasks to another instance. Microsoft Project tracks the resource and assignment information as if they are separate resources, so your information is skewed.

If you've entered a long list of resources, it's a good idea to sort the resource list and review the sorted list to check for duplicates. In the Resource Sheet, click Project, Sort, By Name.

Tip **Mark generic resources and automatically substitute them**

If you're using Microsoft Office Project Professional 2003 with Project Server 2003 and the enterprise features, you can mark generic resources as such. Double-click the resource name to open the Resource Information dialog box. Make sure that the General tab is displayed and then select the Generic check box.

When your project is connected to Project Server, you can use the Resource Substitution Wizard to search throughout the enterprise resource pool to find the resources with the skill set and availability you need. When the right resource is found, the Resource Substitution Wizard replaces the generic resource with the real resource who can now work on your project.

For information about the Resource Substitution Wizard and the Team Builder, see "Building Your Team Using Enterprise Resources" on page 655.

Estimate Resource Requirements Using Generic Resources

Entering generic resources can help you estimate which resources and how many of a type of resource you need to meet your project finish date within a targeted budget. Enter your generic resources in the Resource Sheet and then assign them to tasks.

For more information about associating resources with specific tasks, see Chapter 7, "Assigning Resources to Tasks."

Check the calculated project finish date to see if you need additional resources to meet the targeted project finish date. Check the total project costs to see if you need to change your resource mix to meet your budget.

When you finish tweaking your project plan to meet your requirements, you'll know which resources you need.

Proposing Tentative Resources

NEW FEATURE!

If you're using Project Professional 2003, you can specify that a resource be proposed or committed to your project. Adding proposed resources and assigning them to tasks can help you decide whether a particular resource is needed without locking up their availability on other projects. You and other project managers and resource managers can search for resources and include or exclude proposed resources.

All resources you add are booked as committed to your project by default. To specify that a resource be proposed rather than committed, follow these steps:

Resource Information

1. Display the Resource Sheet.
2. Click the resource you want to specify as proposed.
3. On the Standard toolbar, click Resource Information.
4. In the Resource Information dialog box, be sure the General tab is showing.
5. In the Booking Type box, click Proposed.

Adding Resources from Your E-Mail Address Book

If Microsoft Project is installed on the same computer as your company's Microsoft Exchange e-mail connection, you can add resources to your project plan from the e-mail address book. To do this:

1. Click Insert, New Resource From, Address Book.

   If the Choose Profile dialog box appears, click the profile name for your e-mail system.

   The Select Resources dialog box appears.
2. Click the resources you want and then click the Add button to add the selected resources to your project plan.

   You can add all resources contained in a group or distribution list. Add the name of the group to your list, just as you would add an individual resource. When you click OK, Microsoft Project asks whether you want to expand the group to list the individual resources in the project plan.

> **Tip** **Add resources from Project Server**
> If you're connected to Project Server to use the enterprise features, Project Web Access 2003, or both, you have access to all existing resources identified in the server. Click Insert, New Resource From, Microsoft Project Server. The Build Team dialog box appears. Under Enterprise Resource, select the team members you want to add to your project and then click Add. The names are added to the Team Resource table. When finished, click OK.

Add Resources Using the Project Guide

Resources

You can also use the Project Guide to help add resources to your project plan. It can walk you through the steps to enter resources manually; to add them from your company address book or directory, or from Project Server. To add resources using the Project Guide:

1. On the Project Guide toolbar, click Resources.
2. In the Project Guide pane, click the Specify People And Equipment For The Project link.
3. Read the succeeding panes and make choices as directed (see Figure 6-3).

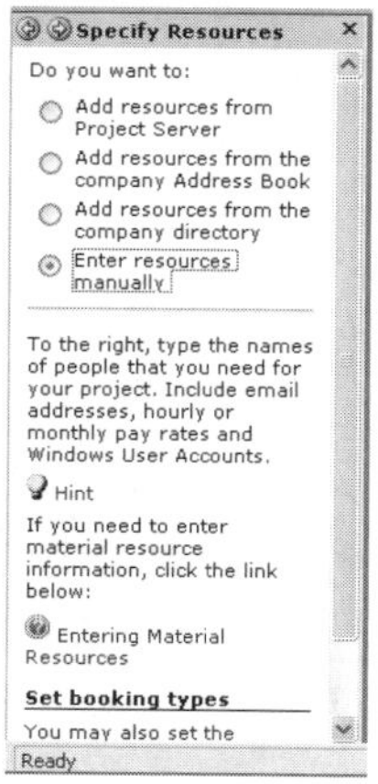

Figure 6-3. Make the choices you want, follow any directions, and click the controls provided. The Project Guide walks you through the process.

Using Resource Information from Microsoft Excel

Suppose you have a list of resources in a Microsoft Excel workbook. You can easily use it to populate your project's Resource Sheet. You can copy information or you can import the file.

To copy a resource list from an Excel workbook, follow these steps:

Copy

Paste

1. Open the Excel workbook that contains the resource list.
2. Select the resource names. On the Standard toolbar in Excel, click Copy.
3. Open the project plan. If necessary, click View, Resource Sheet.
4. In the Resource Name column, click the cell where you want to begin inserting the copied resources.
5. On the Standard toolbar in Microsoft Project, click Paste.

You can also use the Microsoft Project Plan Import Export Template to import resources from Excel to Microsoft Project. The standard Excel importing process involves mapping the Excel columns to the corresponding Microsoft Project columns to ensure that the right information ends up in the right locations in your Resource Sheet. The Microsoft Project Plan Import Export Template is set up to enter more detailed resource information in the format needed by Microsoft Project. To do this, make sure that Excel and the Microsoft Project Plan Import Export Template are installed on the same computer as Microsoft Project, and then follow these steps:

1. Start Microsoft Excel.
2. Click File, New.
3. In the New Workbook task pane, click General Templates.

   The Templates dialog box appears.
4. Click the Spreadsheet Solutions tab (see Figure 6-4).

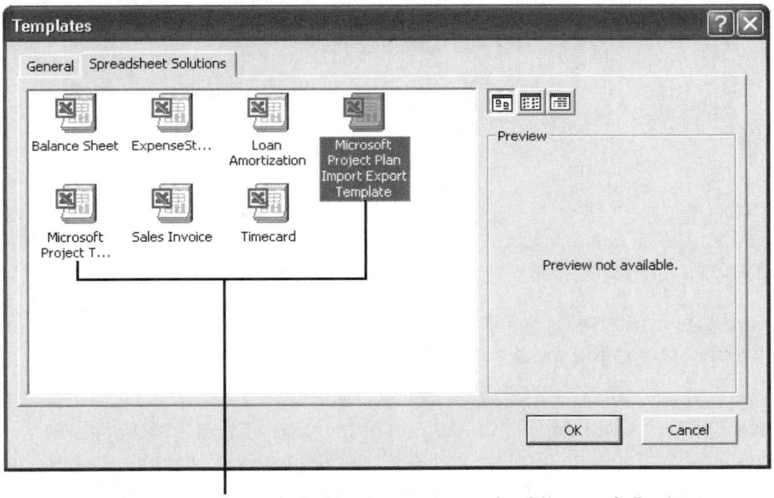

Figure 6-4. Two templates are available in Microsoft Excel to facilitate entering information in Microsoft Project.

5. Double-click the Microsoft Project Plan Import Export Template.

   The template creates a new file with columns that correspond to the most commonly used fields in Microsoft Project.
6. At the bottom of the workbook window, click the Resource_Table tab.
7. Enter resources and any other resource information in the columns provided (see Figure 6-5). Save the file.

Chapter 6

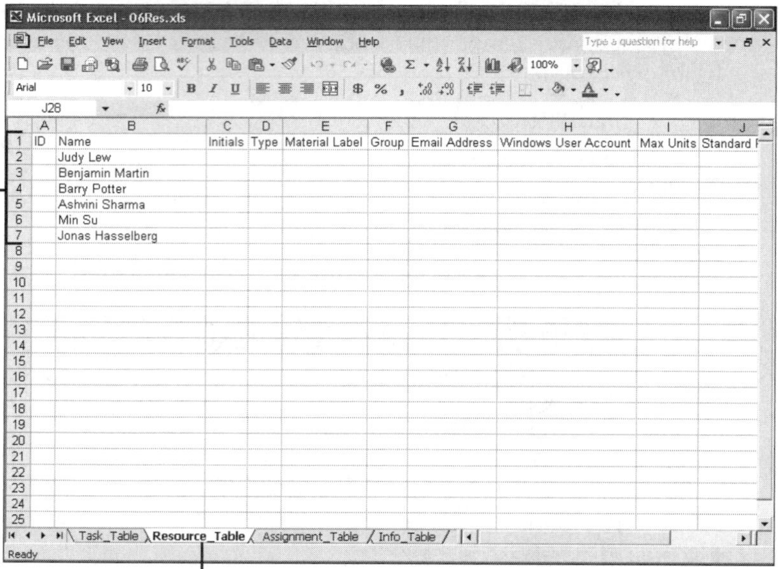

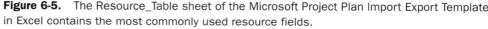

Figure 6-5. The Resource_Table sheet of the Microsoft Project Plan Import Export Template in Excel contains the most commonly used resource fields.

> **Note** If you're working with a version of Microsoft Excel 2000 or earlier, you can still use the Microsoft Project Plan Import Export template. Open Excel and then click File, New. Click the 1033 or Spreadsheet Solutions tab. Double-click the Microsoft Project Plan Import Export Template.

When you're ready to import the resource list into your project plan, follow these steps:

Open

1. If necessary, open the project plan.
2. On the Standard toolbar, click Open.
3. Go to the location on your computer or network where the Excel workbook is saved.
4. In the Files Of Type list, click Microsoft Excel Workbooks (*.xls).

   The task list appears in the list of folders and files.
5. Click the task list workbook and then click the Open button.

   The Import Wizard appears (see Figure 6-6).

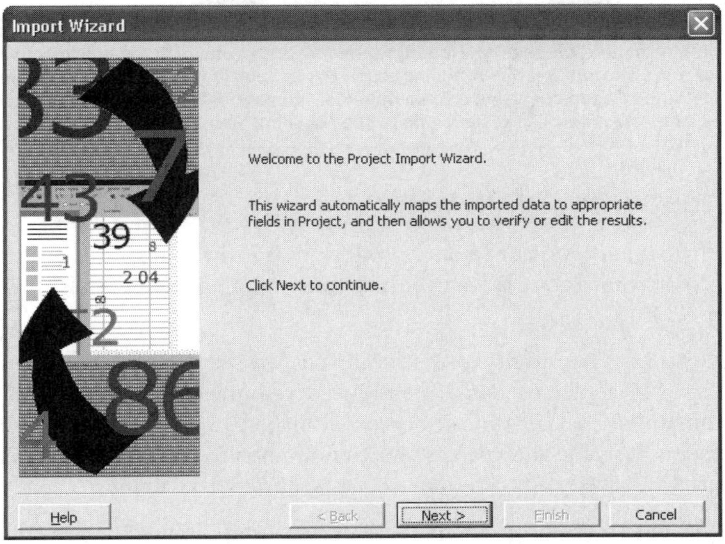

Figure 6-6. The Import Wizard helps you import the resource information from your Excel workbook into your project plan.

6 In the first wizard page, click Next.

7 Click Project Excel Template and then click Next.

8 Specify whether you want to import the file as a new project, append the resources to the currently active project, or merge the data into the active project.

9 Click Finish (see Figure 6-7).

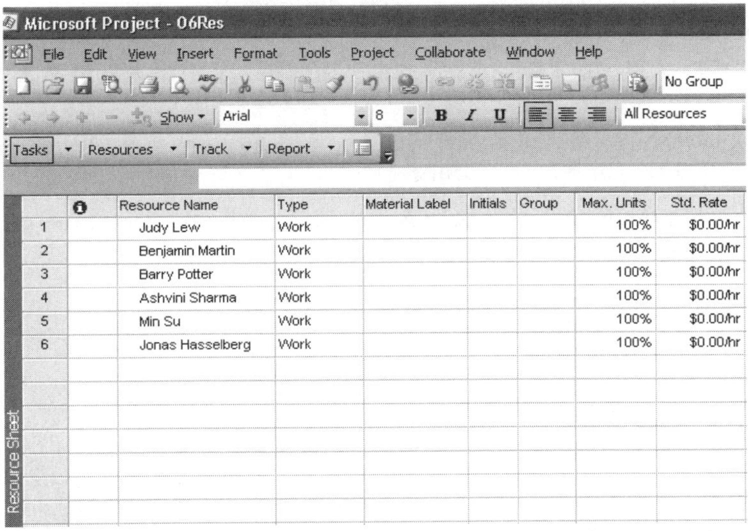

Figure 6-7. The resource information is imported into Microsoft Project as you specified.

For more information about using Microsoft Project with other applications, see "Importing and Exporting Information" on page 497 and Chapter 17, "Integrating Microsoft Project with Microsoft Excel." For more information about adding resources to your project plan from a shared resource pool file, see "Sharing Resources Using a Resource Pool" on page 441. For more information about adding resources from the enterprise resource pool, see "Building Your Enterprise Project Team" on page 655.

Specifying Resource Availability

It's likely that many of your resources will work full-time on your project. But suppose you have two part-timers: one is available half-time, and the other is available three out of the five working days.

You can specify this kind of resource availability by setting the resource's *maximum units*, also referred to as *resource units*. The full-time resources are each available at 100 percent maximum units. The half-time resource is available at 50 percent maximum units. The other part-timer is available at 60 percent maximum units. When you assign resources to tasks, those tasks are scheduled according to that resource's availability.

But 50 percent of what, you might ask? The maximum units is the percentage of time shown as available in the resource's working time calendar. If a resource calendar shows working time of Monday through Friday, 8:00 A.M. until 5:00 P.M., with an hour off for lunch, then 100% maximum units means a 40-hour workweek. 50% maximum units means a 20-hour workweek. Likewise, if a resource calendar shows working time of Monday through Friday, 9:00 A.M. until 1:00 P.M., then 100% maximum units means a 20-hour workweek. 50% maximum units for this resource would be a 10-hour workweek.

Here's another scenario: suppose that you have three engineers, two architects, and four drafters, all working a full-time schedule. Instead of naming them individually, you decide you want to name your resources by their functions and consolidate them into a single resource representing multiple individuals. You can do that with maximum units as well. The three engineers together are available at 300 percent, the two architects at 200 percent, and the four drafters at 400 percent.

If you have three full-time drafters and one half-time drafter, your *Drafters* resource is available at 350 percent maximum units.

To enter maximum units, simply type the percentage in the Max. Units field in the Resource Sheet (see Figure 6-8).

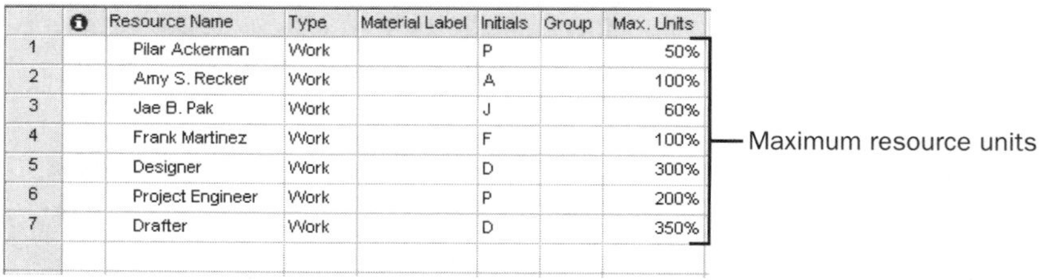

	ℹ	Resource Name	Type	Material Label	Initials	Group	Max. Units
1		Pilar Ackerman	Work		P		50%
2		Amy S. Recker	Work		A		100%
3		Jae B. Pak	Work		J		60%
4		Frank Martinez	Work		F		100%
5		Designer	Work		D		300%
6		Project Engineer	Work		P		200%
7		Drafter	Work		D		350%

Figure 6-8. You can enter maximum units when you enter resource names, or come back to it later. The default for the Max. Units field is 100%.

Chapter 6

Now, suppose your staffing plan specifies that you'll start the project life cycle needing four drafters. After three months, you'll need only three drafters. Two months later, you'll need only one. To specify variable resource quantity or availability over time, follow these steps:

1. In the Resource Sheet, click the resource whose maximum units you want to adjust.
2. On the Standard toolbar, click Resource Information. Or simply double-click the resource name.

   The Resource Information dialog box appears. Make sure the General tab is displayed (see Figure 6-9).

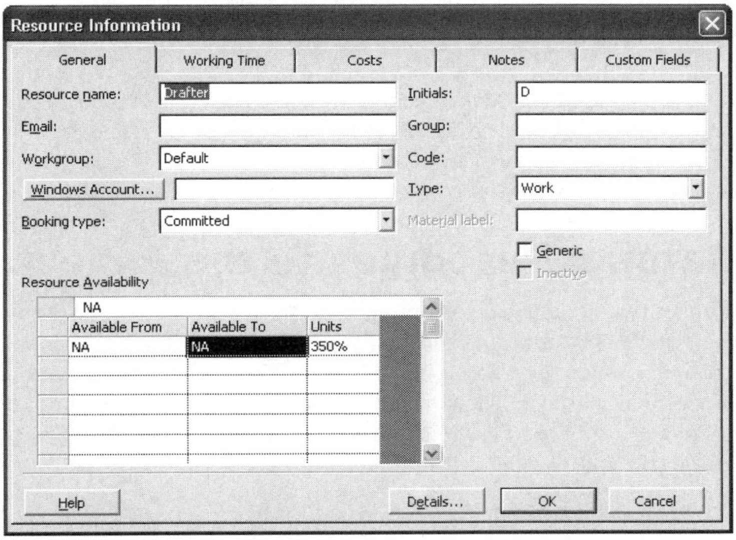

Figure 6-9. Use the Resource Information dialog box to enter detailed information about an individual or consolidated resource.

3. Under Resource Availability, enter the first date range for the resource's units specification.

   That is, enter the beginning date, the ending date, and the maximum units that will be available during those dates. For example, in the first row enter **1/5/04** under Available From; enter **3/26/04** under Available To; enter **400%** under Units.
4. In the second row, enter the second date range for the resource's units specification.

   For example, enter **3/29/04** under Available From; enter **6/25/04** under Available To; enter **300%** under Units.
5. Continue in this manner until your entire resource availability specification is set.

   For example, enter **6/28/04** under Available From; enter **8/27/04** under Available To; enter **100%** under Units (see Figure 6-10).

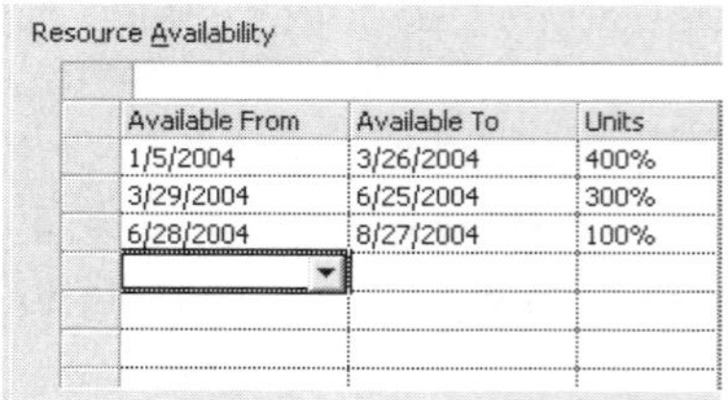
Resource Availability

Available From	Available To	Units
1/5/2004	3/26/2004	400%
3/29/2004	6/25/2004	300%
6/28/2004	8/27/2004	100%

Figure 6-10. Use the Resource Availability table in the Resource Information dialog box to specify multiple levels of maximum units throughout the project.

Tip **Switch units from percentage to decimal**
By default, maximum units are expressed as a percentage. You can represent them as a decimal if you prefer. Click Tools, Options and then click the Schedule tab. In the Show Assignment Units As A box, select Decimal. Now, instead of 100 percent, one full-time resource is shown as having 1 max unit.

Adding Material Resources to the Project

Any supplies that are integral to completing tasks can be added to your project plan as a material resource. Examples of such material resources might be steel for a building structure, roofing material for a home, and bricks for a landscaping project. You might have a task "Lay brick sidewalk," to which a bricklayer is assigned for a certain amount of time. You can also assign a quantity of bricks to the task. The bricklayer and the bricks are both essential resources to the completion of the task.

To enter a material resource:

1. Display the Resource Sheet with the Entry table applied.
2. In the next available Resource Name field, type the name of the material resource (for example, **Bricks**) and then press Tab.
3. In the Type field, click Material.
4. In the Material Label field, enter the unit of measurement for the material.

   This measurement will differ depending on the nature of the material. It might be tons, yards, feet, cartons, and so on.

When you specify that a resource is a material rather than a work resource, be aware of the following points:

- Maximum units (or resource units) and the associated variable availability are not applicable to material resources. You'll specify units (for example, 50 yards or 100 feet per day) when you assign the material resource to a task. With these assignment units, you can track the usage of materials and possibly the depletion rate of materials.

For more information about material resource assignments, see "Assigning Material Resources to Tasks" on page 213.

- Resource calendars are not available for material resources.
- Workgroup fields such as Workgroup and Windows Account are not available for material resources. The Overtime field is also disabled.

Tip **Apply the Entry – Material Resources table**
If you're entering a significant number of material resources, apply the Entry – Material Resources table. This table has only those resource fields applicable to material resources. With the Resource Sheet showing, click View, Table, More Tables. Click Entry – Material Resources and then click Apply.

You can right-click the All Cells box that sits between the first column and first row. In the shortcut menu that appears, click More Tables, click Entry – Material Resources, and then click Apply.

Removing a Resource from the Project

If you've added a resource by mistake or have found duplicates of the same resource, you can delete a resource.

Note If you're working with enterprise features using Project Professional and Project Server, you cannot delete an enterprise resource from your project. Enterprise resources can be deleted only by the project administrator using Project Web Access.

To completely delete a resource:

1. Display the Resource Sheet.
2. Click somewhere in the row of the resource you want to delete.
3. Click Edit, Delete Resource.

   The resource row, along with any associated resource or assignment information, is removed from your project.

Tip You can also delete a resource by clicking the row header for the resource and then pressing Delete.

Setting Resource Working Time Calendars

With maximum units (resource units), you can specify resource availability in terms of part-time or full-time resources, or the number of individuals or machines available. The basis of setting resource availability is the resource's working time calendar, also simply known as the *resource calendar*. The resource calendar starts out the same as the project calendar, which you can then customize to reflect the individual resource's specific working times. Because the resource calendar indicates when a resource is available to work on assigned tasks, it affects the manner in which tasks are scheduled.

> **Note** If you're working with enterprise projects and enterprise resources, the calendars are set by the project administrator. Therefore, your ability to assign different calendars to resources might be limited.

Viewing a Resource Calendar

As soon as you create a resource, the project calendar is assigned by default as the resource's working time calendar. To view a resource's working time calendar:

1. Display the Resource Sheet or other resource view.
2. Click the resource whose working time calendar you want to view.
3. On the Standard toolbar, click Resource Information.
4. In the Resource Information dialog box, click the Working Time tab.

   The working time calendar for the selected resource appears (see Figure 6-11). By default, it's identical to the project calendar until you change it. The Base Calendar field indicates which base calendar is the origin of the resource calendar.

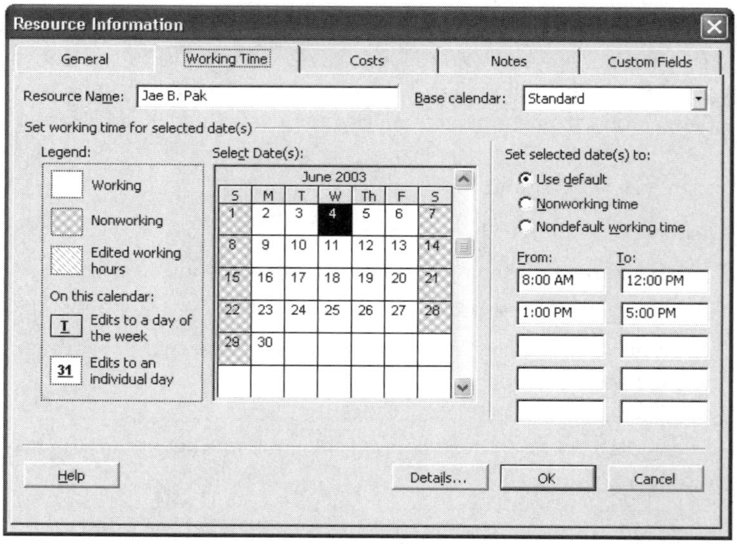

Figure 6-11. Use the Working Time tab in the Resource Information dialog box to view or modify an individual resource's working times. These are the days and times when assigned tasks can be scheduled for this resource.

> **Note** Microsoft Project comes with three *base calendars*: Standard, Night Shift, and 24 Hours. These base calendars are like calendar templates that you can apply to a set of resources, a set of tasks, or the project as a whole.

Chapter 6

Modifying a Resource Calendar

You can change an individual resource's calendar to reflect a different work schedule from others on the project team. For example, most everyone on your team might work Monday through Friday, 8:00 A.M. until 5:00 P.M. But suppose one team member works just three days a week, and another team member works weekend nights. You can change their resource calendars to fit their actual work schedules. This way, their assigned tasks will be scheduled only when they're actually available to work on them.

You can also update resource calendars to reflect vacation time, personal time off, sabbaticals, and so on. Updating the resource calendars helps keep your schedule accurate. To modify a resource's working time calendar:

1. Display the Resource Sheet or other resource view.
2. Double-click the resource whose working time calendar you want to modify.

   The Resource Information dialog box appears.
3. Click the Working Time tab.
4. To change the working time of a single day, click that day.
5. If you're changing working time to nonworking time, select the Nonworking Time option.

   If you're changing the working time to something other than the default, select the Nondefault Working Time option. Then, change the times in the From and To boxes as needed.

   To change the working time of a particular day of each week, click the day heading. For example, click the M heading to select all Mondays. Select the Nonworking Time or Nondefault Working Time option and then change the times in the From and To boxes as needed.
6. To change the working time of a day in another month, scroll down in the Select Dates box until you see the correct month. As before, select the Nonworking Time or Nondefault Working Time option and then change the working times as needed.
7. When finished, click OK.

Creating a New Base Calendar for Resources

If you find you're making the same modifications to individual resource calendars repeatedly, you might do well to create an entirely new base calendar and apply it to the applicable resources. If you have a group of resources who work a different schedule, for example, a weekend shift or "four-tens," create a new base calendar and apply it to those resources. To create a new base calendar:

1. Click Tools, Change Working Time.
2. Click the New button.

   The Create New Base Calendar dialog box appears (see Figure 6-12).

Figure 6-12. You can create a new base calendar from scratch or adapt it from an existing one.

3. In the Name box, type the name you want for the new base calendar; for example, **Weekend Shift.**
4. Select the Create New Base Calendar option if you want to adapt your calendar from the Standard base calendar.

   Select the Make A Copy Of option if you want to adapt the new calendar from a different base calendar, such as the Night Shift. Click the name of the existing calendar you want to adapt and click OK.
5. Make the changes you want to the working days and times of individual days or of a particular day of every week, as needed.
6. When finished with your new base calendar, click OK.

When you create a new base calendar, it becomes available in any of the three calendar applications: project calendar, task calendar, or resource calendar. To assign the new base calendar to a resource, follow these steps:

1. Display the Resource Sheet or other resource view.
2. Double-click the resource to whom you want to assign the new base calendar.

   The Resource Information dialog box appears.
3. Click the Working Time tab.
4. In the Base Calendar field, select the base calendar you want to apply to the selected resource.
5. Make any additional changes to the calendar as needed for this resource.

   These changes apply only to the selected resource; they do not change the original base calendar.

Inside Out

Base calendar for multiple resources

You cannot change the base calendar for multiple resources at once. You have to select each resource individually and then change his or her calendar. The fastest way to do this is to work in the Resource Sheet. For each resource, select the new calendar in the Base Calendar field.

You can also set your resource working times using the Project Guide. On the Project Guide toolbar, click Resources. In the Project Guide pane, click the Define Working Times For Resources link. Read the succeeding panes and make choices as directed (see Figure 6-13).

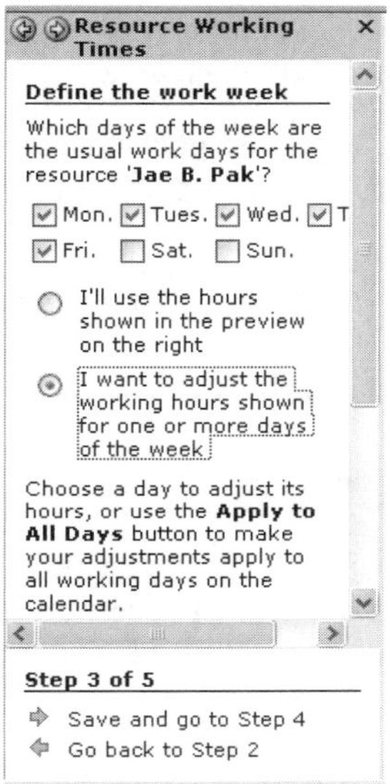

Figure 6-13. The Resource Working Times pane of the Project Guide assists you through the process of setting resource calendars.

Tip **Specify availability for equipment resources**
You can enter maximum units with varying availability and a customized resource calendar for equipment resources just as you can for human resources. Both equipment and human resources are considered work resources. Setting equipment working times and availability can help account for other projects using the same equipment at different times, and schedule downtime for preventive maintenance.

Allow for Non-Project Work

It's a reality that your resources are not likely to spend every minute of every work day devoted to project tasks. To allow for department meetings, administrative tasks, and other non-project work, you can adjust the project calendar, the resource calendar, or max units.

First, determine how much non-project work there is. If you're thinking of the project as a whole, adjust the project calendar. If you think of non-project work in terms of individual resources, adjust their individual resource calendars. For example, instead of defining a day as 8 hours long, you might define it as 6 or 7 hours. Changing the calendar directly affects the days and times when tasks are scheduled.

You can also adjust max units for resources. Instead of setting up full-time resources with 100% max units, set them up with 75% max units. This method distributes task scheduling over time, without regard to specific days and hours.

With either method, you can keep from having every single hour of the day being scheduled for project work and allow for the realities of daily overhead and administrative tasks.

If you're set up for enterprise project management using Project Professional and Project Server, you can use the Administrative Project feature to formalize and track resources' non-project activities.

For more information about Administrative Projects, see "Assigning Tasks to Enterprise Resources" on page 666.

Adding Detailed Resource Information

Along with the basic resource information such as the resource name, type, units, and calendar, you can add supplementary information to either work or material resources. This data can include additional fields of resource information, notes, or hyperlinks.

Working with Supplemental Resource Fields

You can add initials, group designations, or a code to a resource using the appropriate field in the Resource Sheet or the General tab in the Resource Information dialog box. The following list provides examples of how you might use these fields:

Initials If you want a resource's initials, rather than his or her entire name, to appear in certain fields in your project plan, enter the initials in the Initials field in the Resource Sheet or on the General tab in the Resource Information dialog box.

Group Use the Group field to specify any categories of resources that might be useful for sorting, grouping, or filtering. For example, you can specify the department the resources come from, such as Product Development or Marketing. If you are using contracted resources, you can enter their company's name in the Group field. Or you can use the Group field to specify the resource's title or skill set; for example, Engineer, Architect, or Designer.

Note You cannot assign a group name to a task. The group simply provides more information about a resource so you can sort, group, or filter resources.

Code Enter any code meaningful to you or your company in the Code field. It can be any alphanumeric designation you want. In fact, you can use it the way you use the Group field. You can enter job codes or skill codes, for example. Like the Group field, you can then sort, group, or filter these codes.

Identify Resource Skill Sets

If the Group field is not robust enough to identify your resource skill sets, create and assign resource *outline codes*. Not only can you use outline codes to identify resource skill sets, you can also reflect the levels of your organization's human resource structure. This can be useful when you want to apply a code-based hierarchical or outline structure to your resources that reflects resource properties or attributes in your organization.

After your outline codes are set up and assigned to resources, you can sort, group, or filter by outline codes to see the resources displayed in that structure. These techniques can help you find resources that are appropriate for specific kinds of tasks. You can also search for resources that have a certain outline code (or group) using the Assign Resources dialog box.

If you're using Project Professional with the enterprise features through Project Server, you can identify multiple skills for enterprise resources.

Note For more information about outline codes, see "Working with Outline Codes" on page 806. For more information about finding resources with skills for specific assignments using the Assign Resources dialog box, see "Finding the Right Resources for the Job" on page 205. For more information about identifying multiple skills for enterprise resources, see "Creating the Enterprise Resource Pool" on page 599.

Cost-related fields are an important part of the Resource Sheet. The Resource Information dialog box also includes a Cost tab.

For more information about resource cost information for both work and material resources, see "Planning Resource Costs" on page 232.

Other tables containing different collections of resource fields are available. To apply a different table to the Resource Sheet:

1. Display the Resource Sheet.
2. Click View, Table. Click the table you want.

   If the table you want is not listed, click More Tables. Click the table in the list (see Figure 6-14) and then click Apply.

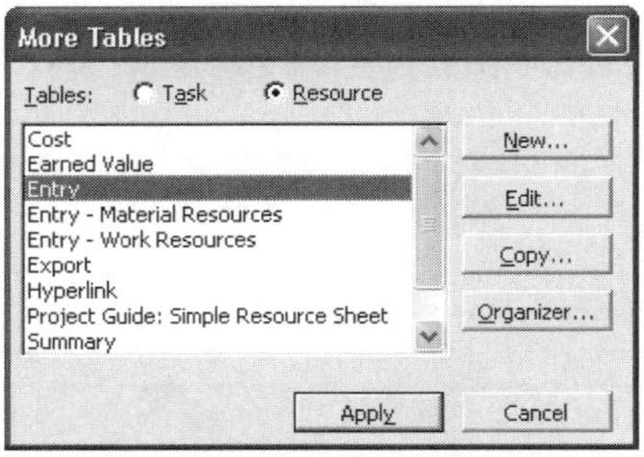

Figure 6-14. Apply any table that fits what you're trying to do.

Dozens of additional resource fields are available for you to add to your Resource Sheet. To add a new field to your current table:

1. Click the column heading to the right of where you want the new column to be inserted.
2. Click Insert, Column or simply press the Insert key.

   The Column Definition dialog box appears.
3. In the Field Name box, click the field you want to add.

   The fields listed are all resource fields. You can quickly move to a field by typing the first one or two letters of its name.

To hide a field you don't need, follow these steps:

1. Click the column heading you want to hide.
2. Click Edit, Hide Column or simply press the Delete key.

   The column is hidden, but the information is not deleted. It's still in the database and can be shown again whenever you display its column.

Tip **Hide a column by making it very narrow**

You might frequently hide and insert certain columns; for example, when you print a view for presenting at a status meeting. If you're getting tired of constantly deleting and then inserting these columns, you can just make them very narrow. Position your mouse pointer on the right edge of the heading for the column you want to hide. When the pointer becomes a black crosshair, drag to the left to narrow the column until the contents cannot be seen.

If you drag past the left column edge, the column will be completely hidden, although it is actually still there.

When you're ready to display the narrow column again, drag the edge of the column heading to the right until you can read the contents of the column.

There's no indication that a column you hid completely is there—you just have to remember.

Adding Initials of Assigned Resources to the Gantt Bar

By default, the full resource name appears next to the Gantt bars in the Gantt Chart, displaying the resources assigned to this task. To help make your Gantt Chart look a little less cluttered or to enable you to fit more task details in a small space, set a resource's initials as text next to a Gantt bar instead of the full name.

For more information about resource assignments, see Chapter 7.

To change the text style of your Gantt bar to include resource initials rather than the full resource name:

1. In the Resource Sheet, make sure that all resources have initials identified for them.

   It doesn't necessarily have to be their actual initials—it can be a short name, a first or last name, a nickname, or whatever you want.
2. Click View, Gantt Chart.
3. Click Format, Bar Styles.
4. In the table area of the Bar Styles dialog box, make sure the Task row is selected.
5. In the lower half of the dialog box, click the Text tab. By default, Resource Names appears in the Right field.
6. Click the Right field and then click Resource Initials (see Figure 6-15). Click OK.

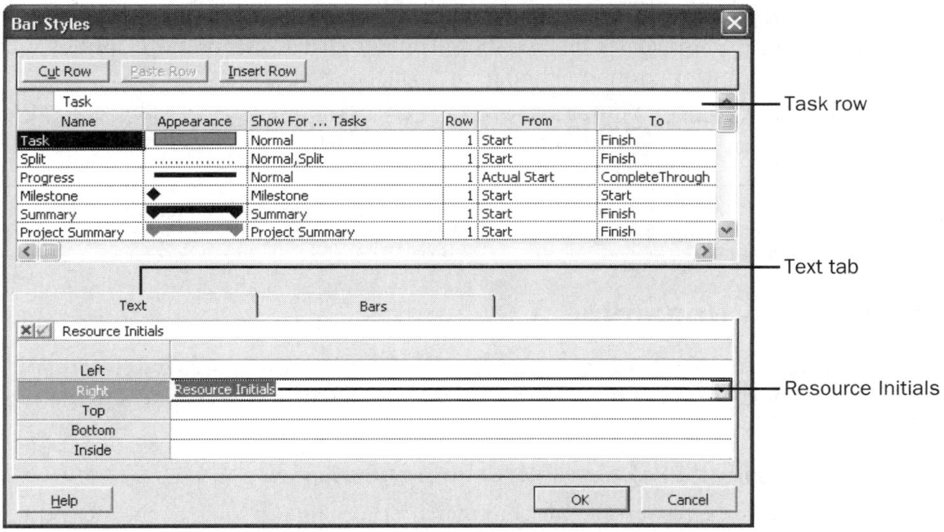

Figure 6-15. Use the Text tab in the Bar Styles dialog box to change the text that appears with the selected Gantt bar.

The resource initials you defined replace the full resource names next to the Gantt bars in the chart (see Figure 6-16).

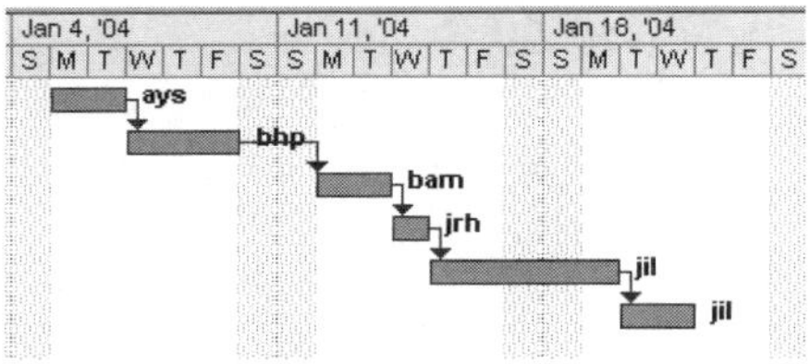

Figure 6-16. Resource initials replace the full resource names next to the Gantt bars.

Chapter 6

Specifying Workgroup Information

If you will communicate project information electronically with resources, you might need to complete one or more of the following fields on the General tab in the Resource Information dialog box:

E-mail Specifies the resource's e-mail address, which is essential if you exchange e-mail messages or project files with team members. If the resource is outside your company—that is, using a different e-mail system than you—be sure to specify the full e-mail address; for example, *someone@microsoft.com.*

For more information about communicating project information through e-mail, see Chapter 18, "Integrating Microsoft Project with Microsoft Outlook," and Chapter 19, "Collaborating Using E-Mail."

Workgroup Specifies the workgroup method for this resource. The choices are Microsoft Office Project Server, None, or Default. Depending on how your implementation of Project is set up, you might also see a choice for E-mail Only. To set the default workgroup choice, click the Collaborate menu, click Collaboration Options, and click your default workgroup method in the Collaborate Using list.

Windows Account Finds the resource's user account in the local address book and places it in that resource's Windows User Account field.

For more information about using e-mail as a workgroup communication method, see Chapter 19. For guidelines on setting up Project Server options, see Appendix A, "Installing Microsoft Office Project 2003."

Adding a Note Regarding a Resource

Use notes to add comments regarding a resource. Notes might include information about the skills or experience of the resource or anything you believe is pertinent to this resource working on this project. To add a note to a resource:

Resource Notes

1. Display the Resource Sheet or other resource view.
2. Click the resource name, and then on the Standard toolbar, click Resource Notes (see Figure 6-17).

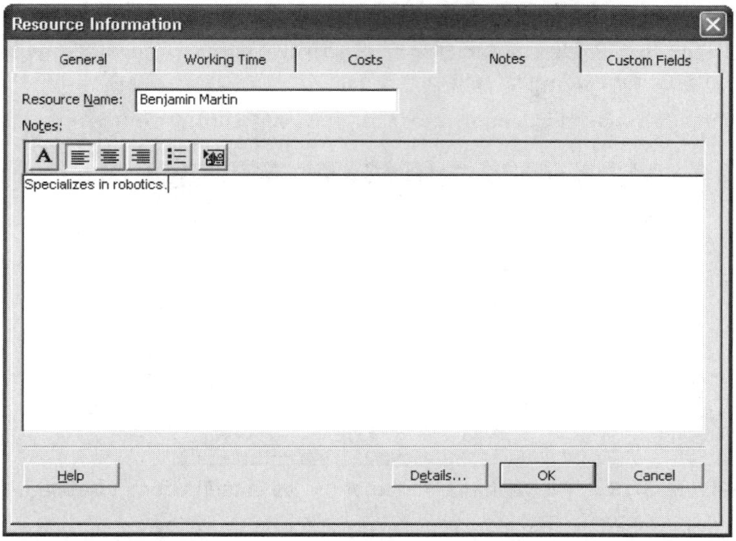

Figure 6-17. Enter relevant notes about a resource in the Notes tab of the Resource Information dialog box. You can also attach outside documents in the Notes tab.

3 In the Notes area, type the note.

4 When finished, click OK.

The Note indicator appears next to the resource name in the Indicators field of the Resource Sheet (see Figure 6-18). You can double-click this icon when you want to read the note.

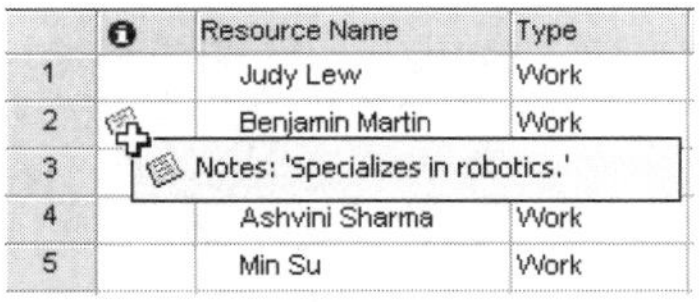

Resource Name
Type
1
Judy Lew
Work
2
Benjamin Martin
Work
3
Notes: 'Specializes in robotics.'
4
Ashvini Sharma
Work
5
Min Su
Work

Figure 6-18. Position your mouse pointer over the Note indicator to read the note. Double-click the indicator to open the Notes tab in the Resource Information dialog box.

Hyperlinking to Resource Information

If there's a document or Web site relevant to a resource, you can create a hyperlink to reference it. This is a very efficient method of opening associated documents quickly. To insert a hyperlink, follow these steps:

1 Display the Resource Sheet or other resource view.

2 Click the resource to which you want to link an outside document or Web page.

Insert Hyperlink

3 On the Standard toolbar, click Insert Hyperlink.

4 In the Text To Display box, type a descriptive name for the document to which you are linking; for example, **Quarterly Goals.**

5 Find and select the document or site you want to link to your project file (see Figure 6-19).

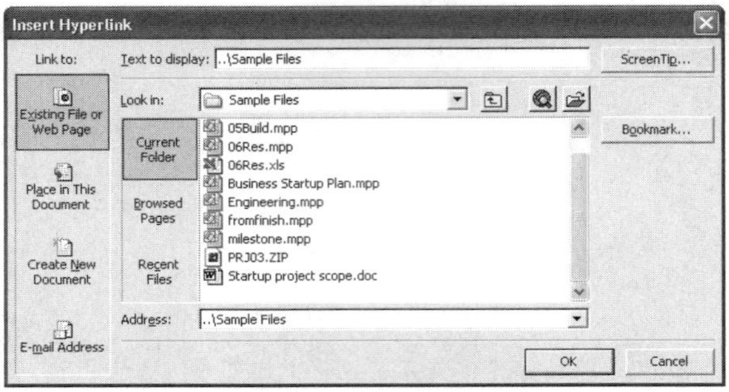

Figure 6-19. The path and name of the selected document appear in the Address box.

6 Click OK.

The Hyperlink indicator appears in the Indicators field of the Resource Sheet (see Figure 6-20).

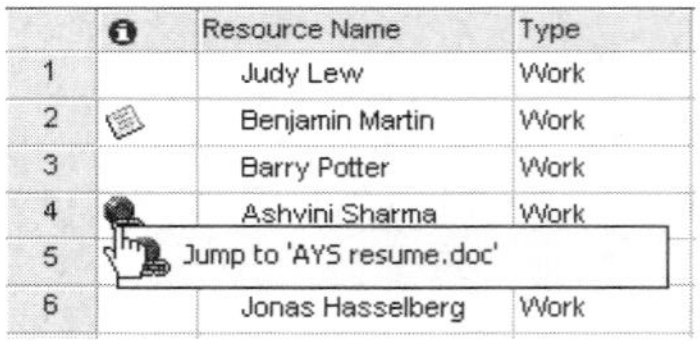

Figure 6-20. Position your mouse pointer over the Hyperlink indicator to read the link. Click the indicator to jump to the link's location.

Whenever you need to review the target of the hyperlink, just click the Hyperlink indicator. The contents open in their own application window.

You can use the Project Guide to help you add notes or hyperlinks to resources. On the Project Guide toolbar, click Resources. In the Project Guide pane, click the Link To Or Attach More Resource Information link. Read the succeeding panes and make choices as directed.

Chapter 7

Assigning Resources to Tasks

You have tasks. You have resources. Now you need to match them up. Tasks + resources = assignments. With human, equipment, and material resources assigned to tasks, Microsoft Office Project 2003 can create a project schedule that reflects not only the project calendar, task durations, dependencies, and constraints, but also the calendars and availability of assigned resources.

Assigning Work Resources to Tasks

When you assign a work resource, you are attaching the resource name to a task and then indicating how much of the resource's total availability is to be devoted to this task.

When you first add a resource to the project plan, through the use of maximum units (also known as *resource units*), you specify how available this resource will be to this project. For example, if the resource is available full time on the project, say, 40 hours a week, you would probably specify that the resource has 100 percent maximum units. If another resource is available 20 hours a week, you would probably specify that this resource has 50 percent maximum units. If you have three of the same type of resource (for example, three graphic designers), you could indicate that there are 300 percent maximum units.

When you assign these resources to tasks, you take the idea of availability a step further by using *assignment units*. With maximum units, you specify resource availability to the project as a whole. With assignment units, you specify resource availability to the specific task to which the resource is assigned.

For example, one resource might be available full time to perform one task. When that's finished, she'll be assigned full time to the next task, and so on. Upon assigning this resource to the task, you therefore indicate 100 percent assignment units for this resource.

You might have another full-time resource, however, who is spending 40 percent of his time on one task and 60 percent of his time on another task that takes place at the same time. For the first task, you specify 40 percent assignment units; and for the second task, 60 percent. The assignment units specify the percentage of the full 100 percent maximum units being used for the task in question.

Now, take the case of a half-time resource (50 percent maximum units) who is spending all available time on one task. The maximum assignment units you can have for this resource is

50 percent. If this resource is spending half her time on one task and half on another, the assignment units are 25 percent for each task.

Finally, let's look at the case of the three graphic artists whose max units are 300 percent. When you start to assign tasks to a *consolidated resource* such as this one, Project 2003 does not assume that you want to use all three on one task. You can, but the default assignment units are 100 percent. You can change it to anything up to 300 percent.

Inside Out

Max units vs. assignment units

Because maximum units and assignment units are both called "units," the terms can be confusing. They're related but different. It would be nice if the respective names were a little more different and a little more descriptive. However, they're vital to our assignment scheduling, and they're what we have to work with. So we need to keep them straight in our minds.

The Max. Units field applies to resources. Think of max units as total *resource units*. The value you enter in the Max. Units field tells Microsoft Project how much of a particular resource you have available for work on this project, whether it's half of full time (50 percent), full time (100 percent), or three full-time equivalents (300 percent).

On the other hand, the Units field applies to assignments. Think of the Units field as *assignment units*. The value you enter in the Units field tells Microsoft Project how much of the resource you can use to work on this specific assignment.

Another way to differentiate the two kinds of units is to pay attention to the context in which you see them. If you see a Units field in the Resource Sheet, it's referring to the resource's units on the entire project. If you see a Units field in the Assign Resources dialog box or the Assignment Information dialog box, it's referring to the resource's units on the individual assignment.

Both kinds of units can be expressed in either percentages or decimals.

Tip **Switch assignment units from percentage to decimal**
By default, assignment units are expressed as a percentage, but you can express them as a decimal if you prefer. Click Tools, Options, and in the Options dialog box, click the Schedule tab. In the Show Assignment Units As A box, click Decimal. A resource working full time on an assignment is shown as having 1 assignment unit instead of 100 percent. This setting also changes how maximum units are displayed in the Resource Sheet.

Creating Work Resource Assignments

By creating an assignment, you specify both the resources assigned to a task and their associated assignment units. Using the Assign Resources dialog box, you can assign one resource to a task, multiple resources to a task, or multiple resources to multiple tasks. To assign a work resource to a task, follow these steps:

1. In the Gantt Chart or other task sheet, click the task to which you want to assign resources.

Assign Resources

2. On the Standard toolbar, click Assign Resources.

   The Assign Resources dialog box appears (see Figure 7-1).

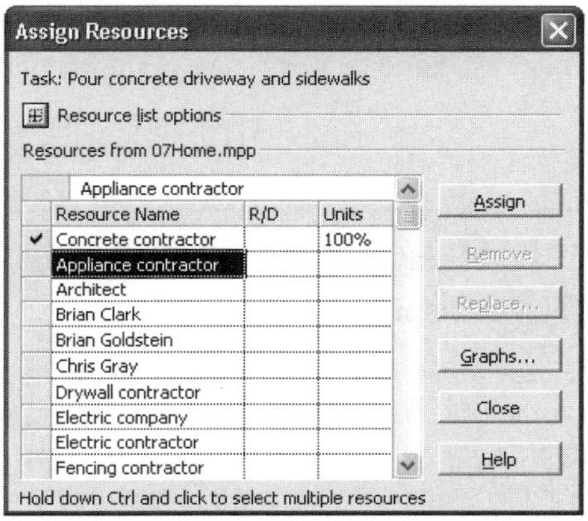

Figure 7-1. Use the Assign Resources dialog box to specify which resources are to be assigned to which tasks, and for how much of their available time.

3. In the dialog box, click the name of the work resource you want to assign to the task and then click the Assign button.

   The resource name moves to the top of the Resources list in the table, and a default percentage appears in the Units field for the resource. For individual resources, the default assignment units are the same as the resource's maximum units. For consolidated resources with more than 100 percent maximum units, the default assignment units are 100 percent.

4. Review the Units field to make sure that it's appropriate for this assignment.

5. If you want to assign a second resource, click that resource name and then click the Assign button. Modify the Units field as necessary. If you change the Units field, you need to press Enter or click another field.

   This procedure ends the edit mode for the field, sets your change, and makes the Assign button available.

> **Tip** **Assign multiple resources in one operation**
> You can select all resources to be assigned to a task and assign them at once. Click the first resource, hold down Ctrl, and then click all other resources. Click the Assign button.

6. Repeat Step 5 for all resources you want to assign to the selected task.

7 To assign resources to a different task, click the next task for which you want to make assignments.

You don't have to close the Assign Resources dialog box to select a different task.

8 Repeat Steps 3–6 to assign resources to all tasks as necessary.

9 When finished assigning resources to tasks, click the Close button.

Tip **Keep the Assign Resources dialog box open as long as you like**
Unlike other dialog boxes, you can switch back and forth between the task sheet and the Assign Resources dialog box. It's handy to keep it open while you're working out all the details you need to finish making your assignments.

Project Management Practices: Assigning the Right Resources to Tasks

As the project manager, you consider several factors when deciding whom to assign to which tasks. One of the most important factors is the resource's skill set, competencies, and proficiencies. His or her ability to carry out the assigned task is essential to the success of the task. You can set up your resources in Microsoft Project so that you can find and assign resources based on their skill sets.

Another important factor is the resource's availability. If the perfect resource is 100 percent committed to another project during the same timeframe as your project, you can't use this resource. Microsoft Project can help you find resources that are available to work on your project.

There are other factors as well:

Experience Have the resources you're considering for the assignment done similar or related work before? How well did they do it? Perhaps you can use this assignment as an opportunity to pair a more experienced team member with a less-experienced one. This pairing can set up a mentoring situation in which both team members can benefit, and in which your team is strengthened in the long run.

Enthusiasm Are the resources you're considering personally interested in the assignment? In many cases, a resource with less experience but more enthusiasm can be more effective than a seasoned but bored resource.

Team dynamics Do certain tasks require several resources to work together? If so, are the resources you're considering likely to work well together? Do they have a history of conflicts with each other? Do certain team members have good synergy with one another?

Speed Is alacrity important to your project, all other things being equal? Some resources work faster than others. This speed can be a function of experience. Or it can be a function of working style or level of quality. Determine how important speed is to your project, and assign tasks accordingly.

Cost Are you hiring contractors for the project? If you have specific budget limitations, cost is definitely a factor. Sometimes, the rework required by an inexpensive resource can negate any cost savings. Conversely, sometimes more-expensive resources can be a bargain, especially if they work faster than the norm.

Quality What are your quality standards for the project? Try to assign resources who can match those standards.

Adding and Assigning Resources at the Same Time

Suppose that you want to assign a specific resource to a task, but that resource isn't listed in the Assign Resources dialog box because you haven't added him or her to your Resource Sheet yet. You can add new resources to your project plan while working in the Assign Resources dialog box and then immediately assign the newly added resource to tasks. You can then go to the Resource Sheet and complete any detailed resource information you want. To add new resources in the Assign Resources dialog box, follow these steps:

1. In the Gantt Chart or other task sheet, click the task to which you want to assign resources.
2. On the Standard toolbar, click Assign Resources to display the Assign Resources dialog box.
3. In the Resources table, type the resource name in the next available blank Resource Name field and then press Tab to enter the name and stay in the same field.
4. Click the Assign button.

   The resource name moves to the top of the Resources list in the table, and 100% appears in the Units field for the resource.
5. Adjust the assignment units if necessary. Assign any additional tasks you want.
6. When finished, click the Close button.
7. Click View, Resource Sheet.

   The new resources you added are listed. Modify any resource fields as necessary; for example, Group, Max. Units, Calendar, and so on.

Tip **Add resource information from the Assign Resources dialog box**
Double-click any resource name in the Assign Resources dialog box, and the Resource Information dialog box appears. Enter detailed resource information as appropriate.

You can add an entire group of resources from your e-mail address book, Microsoft Office Project Server 2003, or your Windows Server Active Directory to the Assign Resources dialog box, just as you can in the Resource Sheet. To add resources from a server, follow these steps:

1. With the Gantt Chart or other task sheet open, click Assign Resources on the Standard toolbar.
2. In the Assign Resources dialog box, click the Add Resources button.

If you don't see the Add Resources button (see Figure 7-2), click the + Resource List Options button. The dialog box expands to include the Add Resources button.

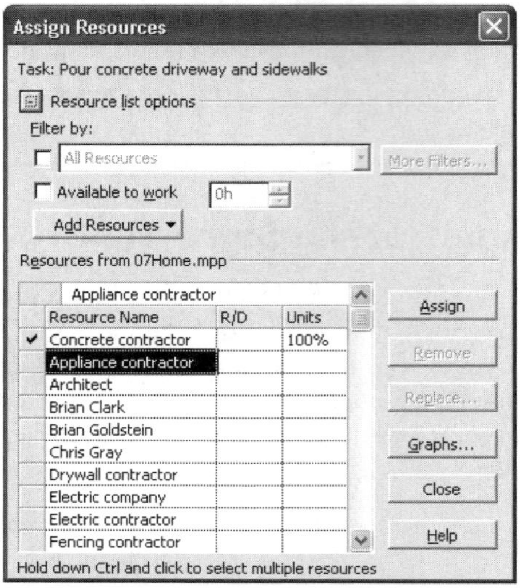

Figure 7-2. Click the – Resource List Options button to collapse the Assign Resources dialog box; click the + Resource List Options button to expand it.

3 Click From Active Directory if you are working with a Windows Server and want to add resources from the Active Directory.

Click From Address Book if you want to add resources from your e-mail program's address book.

Click From Microsoft Project Server if you want to add the resources who are listed as Project Server 2003 users.

4 Click the resources you want from the source you chose and then click the Add button to add the selected resources to the Assign Resources dialog box.

5 After the resources are added, you can immediately assign them to tasks.

Caution **Avoid assigning resources to summary tasks**

Be very careful about assigning resources to summary tasks. Technically you can do it, and in some cases it's beneficial. However, having resources assigned to summary tasks can cause confusion when reviewing rolled up values for work, actual work, cost, and so on. By default, the summary task Gantt bar does not show the resource name, so that can cause still more confusion.

Also take care when you create additional tasks and make them subtasks under existing tasks that have resources assigned. This creates a situation where resources are now assigned to summary tasks.

Filtering for Resources

In addition to filtering for resources in the Assign Resources dialog box, you can filter for tasks and assignments using particular resources. To do this, follow these steps:

1. Display the task or assignment view in which you want to filter for certain assignments, for example, the Gantt Chart or Resource Usage view.
2. Click Project, Filtered For, Using Resource.
3. In the Using Resource dialog box, click the name of the resource whose assignments you want to see.

To filter for a resource's assignments within a particular date range, do the following:

1. Display the task or assignment view in which you want to filter.
2. Click Project, Filtered For, More Filters.
3. In the More Filters dialog box, click Using Resource In Date Range and click the Apply button.
4. In the Using Resource In Date Range dialog box, click the name of the resource whose assignments you want to see and then click OK.
5. Enter the beginning of the date range you want to see and then click OK.
6. Enter the end of the date range you want to see and then click OK.

To see all tasks or assignments again, click Project, Filtered For, All Tasks.

Finding the Right Resources for the Job

You can use the Assign Resources dialog box to narrow your list of resources to only those who meet the criteria needed for the tasks you're assigning. You can filter the resource list to show only those resources who belong to the Marketing department, for example, or only those resources who have a particular job code or skills definition. Using resource fields such as Group or Code comes in handy in these types of scenarios.

If you create and apply resource outline codes, you can also filter for a particular outline code level.

To find resources that meet certain criteria, follow these steps:

1. With the Gantt Chart or other task sheet open, click Assign Resources on the Standard toolbar.
2. In the Assign Resources dialog box, select the check box next to the Filter By box.

   If you don't see the Filter By box, click the + Resource List Options button. The dialog box expands to include the Filter By box.
3. In the Filter By list, click the filter that applies to the type of resource you want to find. For example, Group or Resources – Work.

   For additional filters, click the More Filters button.

Any filter that requires additional information includes an ellipsis (...) after its name. Click the filter, enter the requested information in the dialog box that appears, and click OK.

As soon as you select a filter, the list in the Resources table changes to show only those resources that meet the filter's criteria (see Figure 7-3).

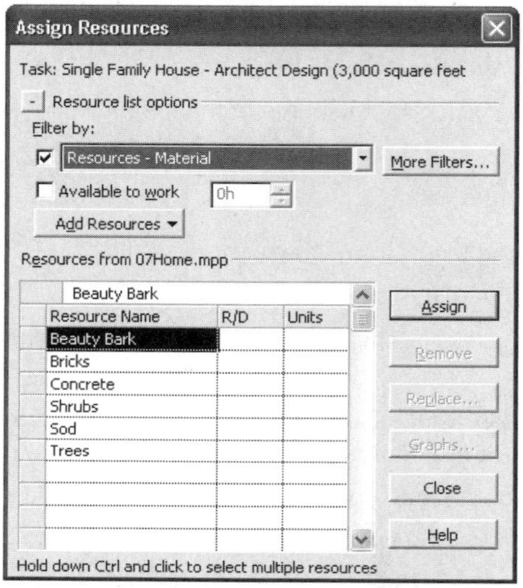

Figure 7-3. By filtering your resource list, you can choose from a set of targeted resources that meet the criteria for the tasks you are currently assigning.

4 Assign resources to tasks as usual.

5 When you want to review the full list of resources again, click All Resources in the Filter By list, or simply clear the Filter By check box.

Defining a Resource Skill Set

If you set up a resource field that defines certain skill sets, you can use the Assign Resources dialog box to filter for resources with specific skills. For example, you can use the Group field in the Resource Sheet to specify the type of resource; for example, "Writer," "Editor," "Designer," or "Programmer." To assign writing tasks, you can filter for Writer in the Group field. To assign programming tasks, you can filter for Programmer in the Group field. Filtering by the Group field can be especially useful if you have a large number of resources.

Other fields you can use to define skill sets include Code and Outline Code. You can also use custom fields such as Text1 or Number1 to specify skills descriptions or numbers. The Code field is present by default on the Entry table of the Resource Sheet. You can enter any alphanumeric string you like in the Code field. Enter the set of skill codes that correspond with how you identify skills in your organization or develop your own scheme. For example, you can have a set of codes for Designer-1, Designer-2, Programmer-1, and so on. As long as you enter your codes consistently for your resources, you can successfully sort, group, and filter resources by their code.

For a more sophisticated and hierarchical code scheme, set up an outline code for skill sets. With an outline code, you can have a higher level, such as Designer; and sub-levels of 1, 2, and 3. You can then filter or group on the upper-level Designer or find just designers at level 3. You first set up your outline code and then apply the appropriate outline code to resources. With outline codes, you have the added advantage of setting up pick lists and lookup tables, so you don't have to remember the proper method for entering the code.

Note For more information about working with custom fields, see "Customizing Fields" on page 788. For more information about outline codes, see "Working with Outline Codes" on page 806.

If you're using Microsoft Office Project Professional 2003 with Project Server and the enterprise features, you can work with your project administrator to define skill sets for everyone in your enterprise resource pool using the resource breakdown structure code, enterprise resource outline codes, and the new multi-value resource outline codes. With these skills defined, you can then use the Resource Substitution Wizard and Team Builder to search throughout the enterprise resource pool to find the resources with the skill set and availability you need.

For information about the Resource Substitution Wizard and the Team Builder, see "Building Your Enterprise Project Team" on page 655.

Inside Out

Missing resource filters

There is no built-in resource filter for Code or Outline Code. You can create your own filters by clicking New in the More Filters dialog box and then specifying the field name, test, and value for the filter. For example, you can create a filter that finds all resources that have a Code field greater than 9100. Or you can create a filter that finds all resources that have an Outline Code equal to Engineer-1.

NEW FEATURE! If you're using Project Professional 2003, you might have added certain resources to your project as *proposed resources*. It would be nice, therefore, to have a filter to find only confirmed resources or to find just proposed resources when setting up assignments. But such resources are not built in, and you need to create them yourself.

For more information about adding proposed resources, see "Proposing Tentative Resources" on page 178. For more information about creating custom filters, see "Customizing Filters" on page 799.

You can filter your resources to see only those who actually have enough time available for more work. For example, suppose that you assigned all your resources to tasks. Then you add several more tasks and you want to assign only resources who have time for them. To filter for resources with a certain amount of available time, do the following:

1. With the Gantt Chart or other task sheet open, click Assign Resources on the Standard toolbar.
2. In the Assign Resources dialog box, select the Available To Work check box.

   If you don't see the Available To Work check box, click the + Resource List Options button. The dialog box expands to include the Available To Work check box.

   In the Available To Work box, enter the amount of time needed for the task you're about to assign. For example, if you need a resource with 4 days of available time, enter **4d** in the box.

   As soon as you enter the amount of time, the list in the Resources table changes to show only those resources who have the specified availability.
3. Assign resources to tasks as usual.
4. When you want to see the full list of resources again, simply clear the Available To Work check box.

Tip **Filter resources and availability at the same time**
You can find resources in the category you want who have the right amount of available time for your assignments. Under Resource List Options in the Assign Resources dialog box, select both check boxes under Filter By. First, select the resource filter you want to use in the first box and then enter the amount of time in the Available To Work box.

Troubleshooting

Your Filter By or Available To Work boxes are dimmed

It might look like the Filter By box and its More Filters button are unavailable to you because they're dimmed. They don't look available until you select the check box next to the Filter By box.

> The same applies to the Available to Work box. It's dimmed until you select the Available To Work check box.
>
> Selecting the check boxes is necessary because it helps you specify what kind of filter you want to apply. You can apply a resource filter only, or just check for available time. And of course, you can combine the two—applying a filter to find only those resources who meet the filter criteria *and* have a certain amount of available time.

You can review graphs of resource availability from the Assign Resources dialog box. This can help you decide which work resource should be assigned to a task. To review the resource availability graph, follow these steps:

1. With the Gantt Chart or other task sheet open, click Assign Resources on the Standard toolbar.
2. In the Assign Resources dialog box, click the work resource whose availability graph you want to view. Note that availability does not apply to material resources.
3. Click the Graphs button. The Resource Availability Graph for the selected resource appears (see Figure 7-4). By default, the work graph is displayed.

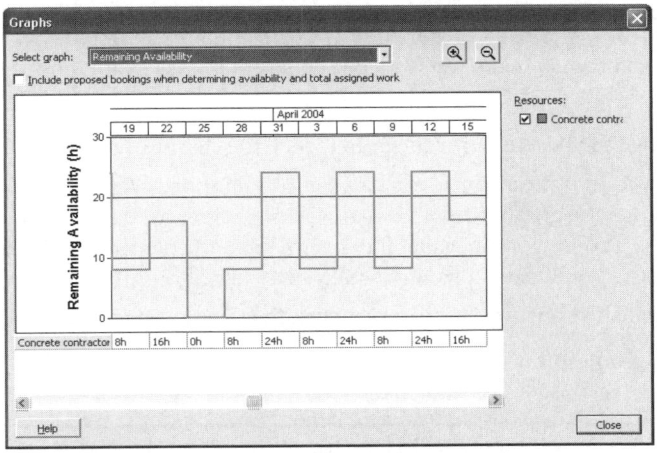

Figure 7-4. In the Work version of the Resource Availability Graph, you can review the selected resource's remaining availability over time.

4. To change the field on which the graph is based, click Remaining Availability or Assignment Work in the Select Graph list.

The Work graph shows the total work for all the selected resource's assignments. The Assignment Work graph breaks down the work on the currently selected tasks in relation to the selected resource's total work assigned (see Figure 7-5). The Remaining Availability graph shows when the selected resource has any available time for more assignments.

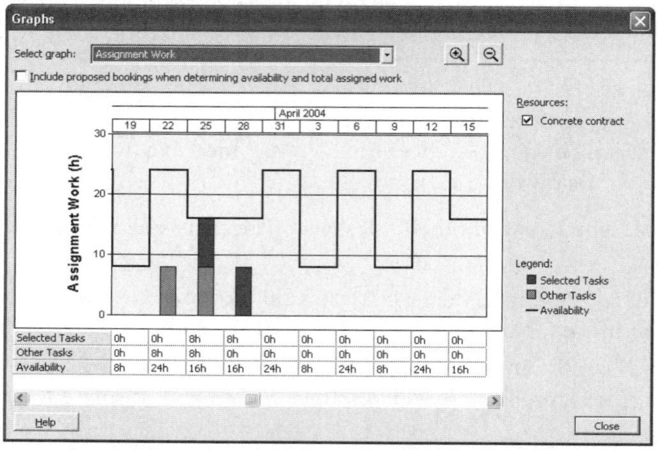

Figure 7-5. With the Assignment Work version of the Resource Availability Graph, you can compare the workload of selected tasks with those of other tasks.

5 To change the timescale for the graph, click the Zoom In or Zoom Out buttons.

The Zoom In button provides a closer look at a shorter time period. For example, it can change the graph from a view of weeks to a view of days. The Zoom Out button provides an overview of availability over a longer time period. For example, it can change the graph from a view of weeks to a view of months.

6 When finished reviewing the graph, click the Close button.

The Assign Resources dialog box appears again.

Review Availability Graphs for Multiple Resources

Select multiple resources in the Assign Resources dialog box and then click the Graphs button. The Resource Availability Graph shows graphs for each resource at the same time, using different colors for each resource (see Figure 7-6).

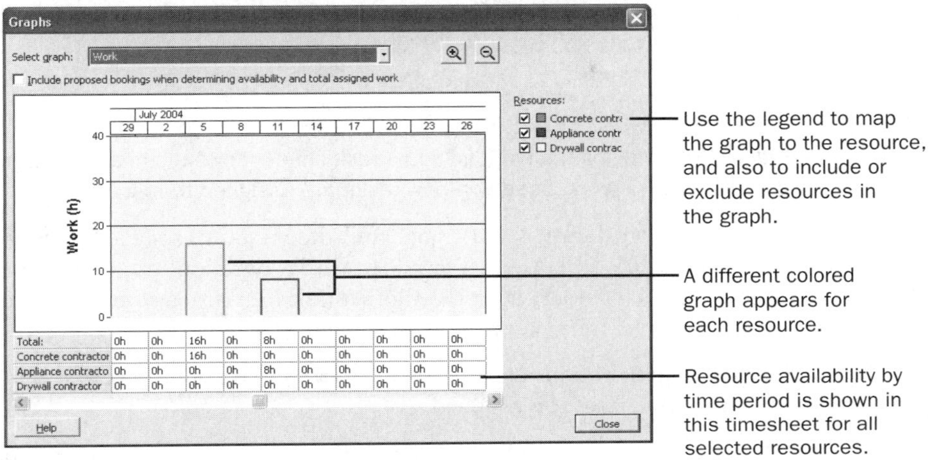

Figure 7-6. View the availability graphs and timesheets for several resources at one time.

In the upper-right corner of the graph window, clear the check box for any resource whose graph you want to hide. The timesheet for all resources still shows below the graph.

Understanding Assignment Calculations

Work is the amount of effort it takes to complete a task. As soon as you assign a resource to a task, the duration is translated into work. A simple example: If you have a task with a 3-day duration and you assign a single full-time resource to it, that resource now has an assignment with 24 hours of work spread across three days (assuming default calendar settings).

You can see this principle in action by adding the Work field to the Gantt Chart or other task sheet, as follows:

1. Display the Gantt Chart or other task sheet that contains the Duration field.
2. Click the heading of the column to the right of the Duration field. For example, if you are working with the default Gantt Chart with the default Entry table applied, click the Start column heading.
3. Click Insert, Column.
4. In the Field Name box, click Work. To move quickly to the fields that begin with "W," type **W**.
5. Click OK.

   The Work field appears next to the Duration field, and you can see comparisons between the two (see Figure 7-7).

Task Name	Duration	Work	Resource Names
⊟ **Landscaping and Grounds Work**	**12 days**	**56 hrs**	
Pour concrete driveway and sidewalks	2 days	16 hrs	Concrete contractor
Install backyard fence	2 days	16 hrs	Fencing contractor
Sod and complete plantings - front yard	2 days	16 hrs	Landscape contractor
Sod and complete plantings - backyard	1 day	8 hrs	Landscape contractor

Figure 7-7. Adding the Work field to a task sheet shows the relationship of task duration to task work, based on how tasks are assigned to resources.

That task with a 3-day duration and a single full-time resource assigned translates (by default) to 24 hours of work. Another task with a 3-day duration and two full-time resources assigned translates to 48 hours of work. Another task with a 3-day duration and three full-time resource assigned translates to 72 hours of work.

Duration is the length of time it takes from the start to finish of the task, but work equates to person-hours for the resources assigned.

These calculations are based on the *initial assignment;* that is, assigning one, two, or three resources at one time to a task that previously had no assigned resources. That is, if you assign two full-time resources to that same 3-day task, both resources are assigned 24 hours of work, also spread across 3 days (see Figure 7-8). When you assign multiple resources *initially*, Microsoft Project assumes that you intend for the resources to have the same amount of work across the original task duration.

Task Name	Work	Duration	Details	M	T	W
⊟ Pour concrete driveway and sidewalks	24 hrs	3 days	Work	8h	8h	8h
Concrete contractor	*24 hrs*		Work	8h	8h	8h
⊟ Install backyard fence	48 hrs	3 days	Work	16h	16h	16h
Brian Clark	*24 hrs*		Work	8h	8h	8h
George Jiang	*24 hrs*		Work	8h	8h	8h

Figure 7-8. In the first task with a single resource assigned, the total work is 24 hours. In the second task with two resources assigned, the total work is 48 hours.

Tip Let Microsoft Project calculate duration from work

Instead of entering duration and having Microsoft Project calculate work amounts upon assigning tasks, you can do this the other way around. You can enter tasks, assign resources, and then enter work amounts from estimates those resources provide. From those work amounts, Microsoft Project can calculate duration.

Just as work is calculated from the duration and assigned resource availability, duration can be calculated from work amounts and assigned resource availability.

Translate Duration to Work Amounts

You can control how Microsoft Project translates duration to work amounts. By default, if you specify a 1-day duration, Microsoft Project translates this to 8 hours of work. However, if you want 1 day to mean 6 hours to account for non-project work, you can change your calendar options.

Click Tools, Options, and in the Options dialog box, click the Calendar tab. Change the settings in Hours Per Day, Hours Per Week, or Days Per Month, as needed to fit your requirements.

If you want the project or resource calendar to reflect the changes you made to the duration to work-amount settings, you must change the appropriate working time calendars to match. If the calendars don't match the calendar option settings, you'll see odd results.

For more information about changing the project calendar, see "Setting Your Project Calendar" on page 70. For information about resource calendars, see "Setting Resource Working Time Calendars" on page 187.

Troubleshooting

You assign two resources to a task, but the work is doubled rather than halved

When you assign multiple resources *initially*, Microsoft Project assumes that you intend for the same amount of work to be applied to all assigned resources across the time span represented by the task duration.

If you want the duration to be reduced because multiple resources are assigned, set the duration accordingly. Or start by assigning just one resource at first. Then assign the additional resources in a separate operation. As long as the task is not a *fixed-duration task*, the duration is reduced based on the number of additional resources added.

The calculations for work and duration can change if you assign one resource *initially* and then *later* assign a second resource. This might also be true if you initially assign two resources and later remove one of them.

For more information about these schedule recalculations, see "Changing Resource Assignments" later in this chapter on page 220.

Tip **Specify the work time unit you use most often**
If you don't specify a work unit, by default Microsoft Project assumes the unit to be hours, and automatically enters "hrs" after your work amount. You can change the default work unit if you like. Click Tools, Options and then click the Schedule tab. In the Work Is Entered In box, select the time unit you want as the default.

Assigning Material Resources to Tasks

When you assign a material resource, you are attaching the material resource name to a task and then indicating the quantity of material to be used in fulfilling this task.

Material resources are supplies consumed in the course of fulfilling a task. As with work resources, there are units of measurement to specify how much of the resource is available to carry out the task. With work resources, this measurement is time: number of hours or days, for example. With materials, however, the measurement, and therefore the material resource assignment units, is quantity. When you assign a material resource to a task, you specify the quantity of resource that this task will consume.

For example, suppose that you have a landscaping project that includes the "Lay down beauty bark" task. The material resource for this task is obviously beauty bark. Because beauty bark is measured in cubic yards, you would have set the material's unit of measurement, or label, as **cubic yards** when you added beauty bark as a material resource in the Resource Sheet. Now, when you assign beauty bark as a material resource to the "Lay down beauty bark" task, you can specify the assignment units as **6**, to indicate 6 cubic yards of beauty bark.

Other examples of material labels include tons, linear feet, packages, cartons, pounds, crates, and so on.

The quantity of material consumed in the course of performing a task can be fixed or variable, based on duration. That is, if the same amount of material will be used whether the task takes 2 days or 2 weeks, the material is said to have a *fixed material consumption*. However, if more material will be used if the duration increases and less material used if the duration decreases, the material is said to have a *variable material consumption*. To specify variable material consumption, enter a per-time period specification in the assignment Units field: for example, 1/week or 3/day. This will be translated with the material's label: for example, 1 ton/week or 3 yards/day.

Inside Out

Specify a variable consumption rate

You might think that a material with a variable consumption rate can be set as such in the Label field of the Resource Sheet. Not so. You can enter any string you want in the Label field, including something like ***yards/day***. But when you assign the material to a task, the expected per-day calculations are not made.

To specify the variable consumption rate, always specify it in the Units field in the Assign Resources dialog box rather than in the Label field in the Resource Sheet.

To assign a material resource to a task, follow these steps:

1. In the Gantt Chart or other task sheet, click the task to which you want to assign a material resource.

2 On the Standard toolbar, click Assign Resources.

3 In the Assign Resources dialog box, click the name of the material resource you want to assign to the task and then click the Assign button.

The material resource name moves to the top of the Resources list in the table, and the label appears in the Units field, defaulting to a quantity of 1, for example, **1 yards.**

4 Change the *1* in the Units field to the correct quantity for this assignment; for example, **3 yards** (see Figure 7-9).

If you change the Units field, you need to press Tab or Enter, or click another field. This process ends the edit mode for the field and sets your change.

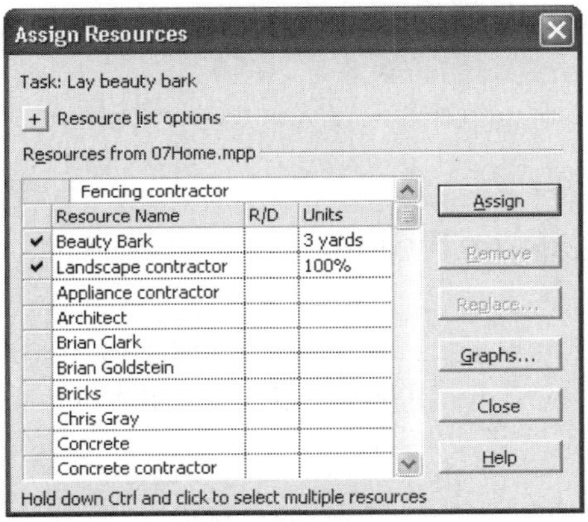

Figure 7-9. Change the default of 1 unit to the appropriate quantity of material to be used to complete the selected task.

5 If necessary, change the material from the default fixed consumption rate to variable consumption rate (see Figure 7-10). After the material's label, enter a slash and time period abbreviation, for example, **3 yards/d.**

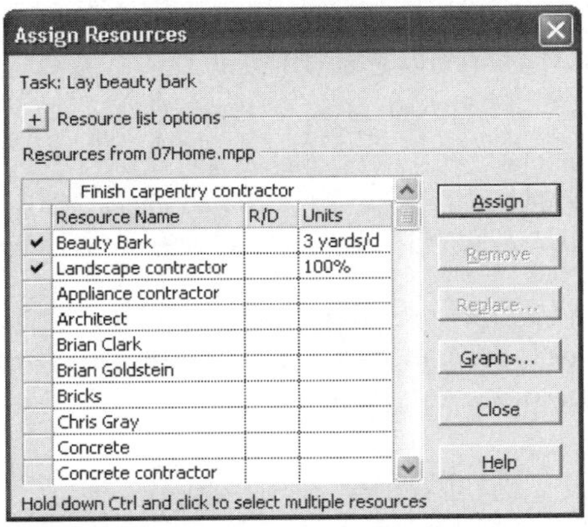

Figure 7-10. Use the standard time period abbreviations (h, d, w, and so on) to specify the quantity per time period for a material resource with a variable consumption rate.

6. If you want to assign another resource to the selected task, click the name and then click the Assign button. Modify the Units field as necessary.

   You can assign material and work resources in the same operation.
7. To assign material resources to a different task, click the next task to which you want to assign a material resource. You don't have to close the Assign Resources dialog box to select a different task.
8. When finished assigning resources to tasks, click the Close button.

Reviewing Assignment Information

There are several ways to look at resource assignments. You can switch to a usage view, which shows assignments for each task or assignments for each resource. You can also add a form to your Gantt Chart or other task view, and review assignment information in relation to selected tasks.

Showing Assignments by Task or Resource

You can see work assigned to resources in either the Task Usage or Resource Usage views. The Task Usage view shows assignments by tasks (see Figure 7-11). The information for each assignment is rolled up, or summarized, in the row representing the task. To switch to the Task Usage view, click View, Task Usage.

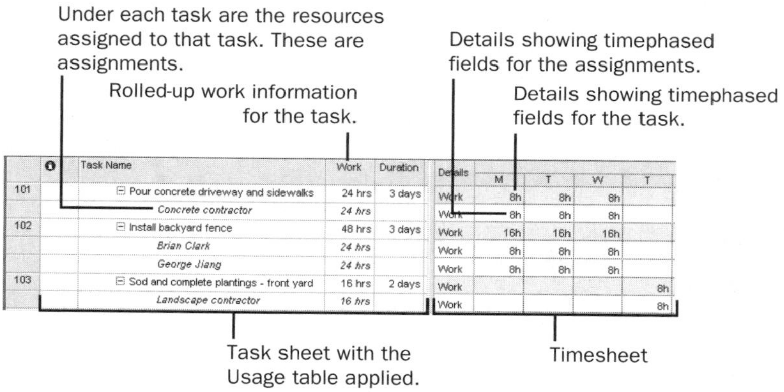

Figure 7-11. The Task Usage view shows task duration as well as assignment work.

The Resource Usage view shows assignments by resources (see Figure 7-12). The information for each assignment is rolled up, or totaled, in the row representing the resource. To switch to the Resource Usage view, click View, Resource Usage.

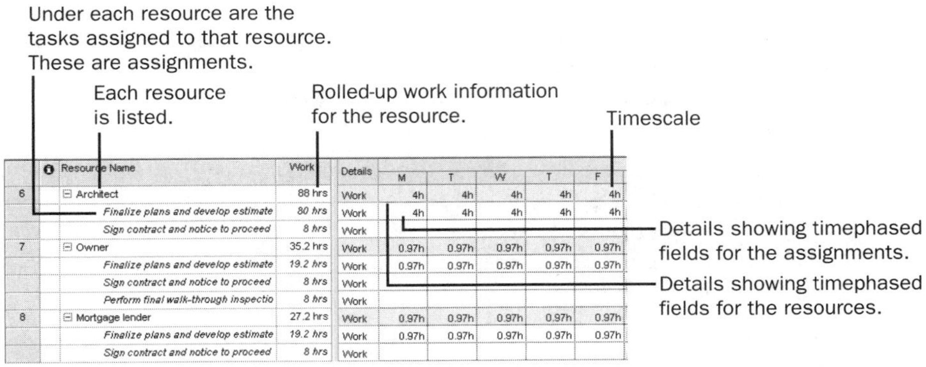

Figure 7-12. The Resource Usage view focuses on resource and assignment work.

Either usage view is great for reviewing assignment information. Which one you use depends on whether you want to see assignments within the context of tasks or resources.

The usage views are the only two views in which you can see detailed assignment information. From these two views, you can also access the Assignment Information dialog box (see Figure 7-13). Just double-click the assignment whose information you want to see.

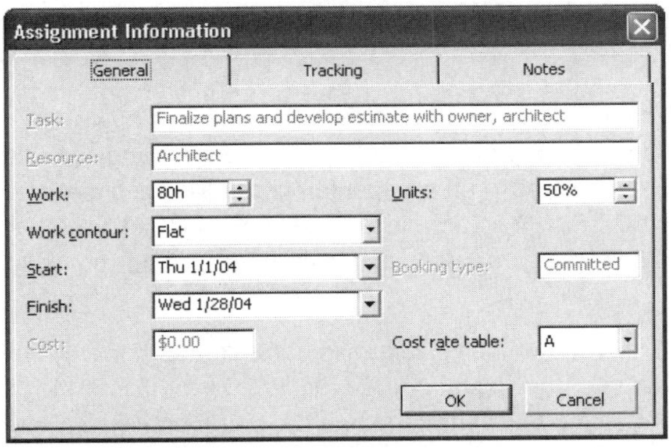

Figure 7-13. You can open the Assignment Information dialog box by double-clicking an assignment in the Task Usage or Resource Usage views.

Assignment Notes

Tip **Add a note about an assignment**

In the Task Usage or Resource Usage view, click the assignment, and click Assignment Notes on the Standard toolbar. The Notes tab in the Assignment Information dialog box appears. Enter the note and click OK when finished. The Notes icon appears in the Indicators column of the usage view.

Troubleshooting

The Assignment Information dialog box does not open

If you're in the Task Usage view or Resource Usage view, and you want to open the Assignment Information dialog box, be sure that you actually have selected an assignment. In the usage views, the assignments appear under the task name or resource name. If you double-click the task or resource name at the summary level, the Task Information or Resource Information dialog box opens.

Instead, double-click the assignment under that summary level. In the Task Usage view, the summary level shows the task name, and the subordinate assignment level shows the resource names. Those are the resources assigned to the task; that is, the task's assignments. If you double-click a resource name in the Task Usage view, the Assignment Information dialog box appears.

In the Resource Usage view, the same principle applies. The summary level shows the resource name, and the subordinate assignment level shows the task names. Those are the tasks to which this resource is assigned; that is, the resource's assignments. If you double-click a task name in the Resource Usage view, the Assignment Information dialog box appears.

Show/Hide Assignments

Tip **Show and hide assignments**

If you want to just want to see summary information in a usage view, you can temporarily hide assignments. Click the All Cells box in the upper-left corner of the sheet view (between the first column and first row): select the entire sheet. On the Formatting toolbar, click Hide Assignments. To show assignments again, click the same button, which is now Show Assignments.

You can hide and show assignments for individual tasks or resources. Click the task in the Task Usage view or the resource in the Resource Usage view. On the Formatting toolbar, click Hide Assignments. Clicking Hide Assignments has the same effect as clicking the – sign next to the summary task or resource for the assignments. To show the assignments again, click Show Assignments or the + sign.

Showing Assignment Information Under a Task View

You can use different types of forms under the Gantt Chart or other task view to see detailed information about assignment information. The easiest way to do this is to apply the Task Entry view, which is a built-in combination view made up of the Gantt Chart and the Task Form (see Figure 7-14).

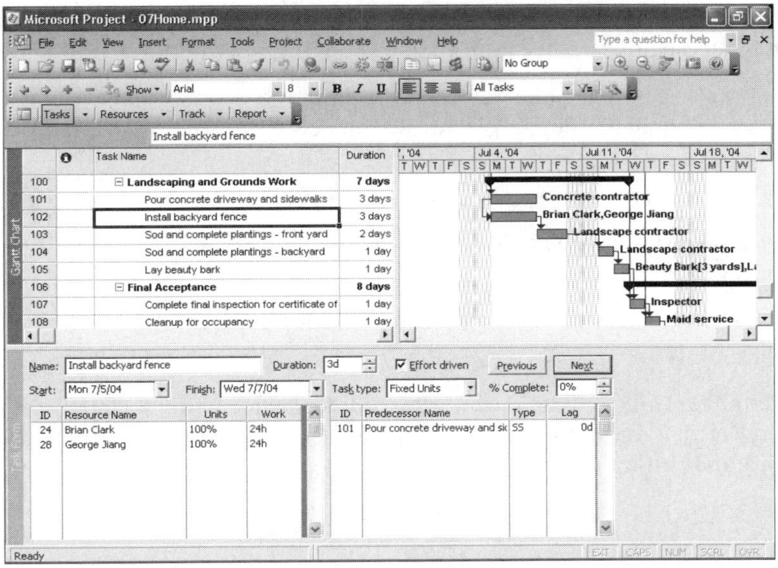

Figure 7-14. Detailed task and assignment information is shown in the Task Form in the lower pane for the task selected in the Gantt Chart in the upper pane.

With the Task Form, you can easily see all schedule-related information, including duration, task type, units, and work. Click the Previous or Next button to move to different tasks.

An abbreviated version of the Task Form is the Task Name Form, which dispenses with the task details and includes only the Task Name with the two tables of information (see Figure 7-15).

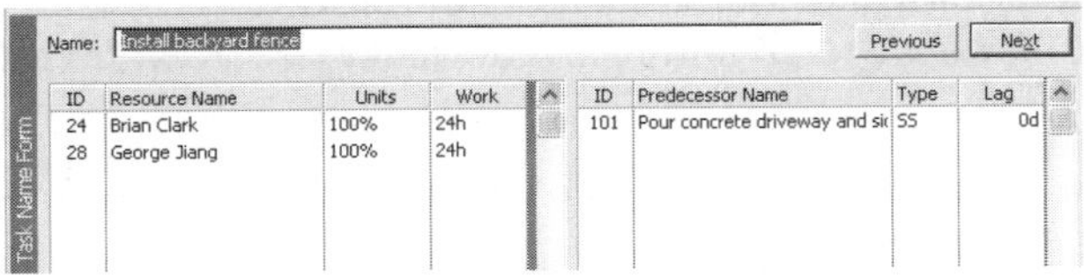

Figure 7-15. Use the Task Name Form if you're interested only in the table information.

To apply the Task Name Form:

1. Click in the lower pane to make the form the active pane.
2. Click View, More Views, Task Name Form.
3. Click Apply.

In either the Task Form or the Task Name Form, the default table information includes resources on the left and predecessors on the right. You can change which categories of information are shown. To do this:

1. Click in the lower pane to make the form the active pane.
2. Click Format, Details.

You can simply right-click in the form, and then click the categories you want to see.

3 In the submenu, click the information you want to see in the form's tables.

You can see more detailed information about resources assigned to the selected task by applying the Resource Form or Resource Name Form as the lower pane under a task sheet.

To apply the Resource Form or Resource Name Form:

1 Click in the lower pane to make the form the active pane.
2 Click View, More Views.
3 In the submenu, click Resource Form or Resource Name Form.
4 Click Apply.

In the Resource Form, you can review detailed information about the resources assigned to the task selected in the task sheet in the upper pane (see Figure 7-16). This data includes availability and cost information.

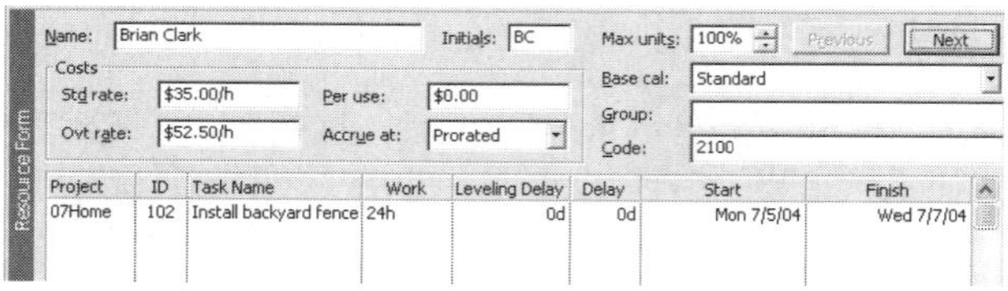

Figure 7-16. Use the Resource Form to review detailed information about assigned resources.

By default, schedule information is shown in the table area. To change the category of table information, right-click the form and then click one of the other categories; for example, Cost or Work. Click the Previous or Next button to move to the resources assigned to the current task.

The Resource Name Form is a condensed version of the form, showing just the Resource Name with the table of information.

Note To return to a single-pane view, double-click the split bar dividing the two panes. Or click Window, Remove Split.

Changing Resource Assignments

There are three ways you can change resource assignments:

- You can add more resources to the existing resources assigned to a task.
- You can replace one resource with another.
- You can remove a resource from a task.

To add more resources to the existing ones initially assigned to a task, follow these steps:

1. In the Gantt Chart or other task sheet, click the task to which you want to add more resources.
2. On the Standard toolbar, click Assign Resources. The Assign Resources dialog box appears, showing a check mark next to the names of resources already assigned.

   You can also open the Assign Resources dialog box by pressing Alt+F10.
3. Click the name of the resource you want to add to the task and then click the Assign button.

   The resource name moves to the top of the Resources list in the table, and the default percentage appears in the Units field for the resource.
4. Review the Units field and make sure that it's appropriate for this assignment.

   If you change the Units field, you need to press Enter or click another field. Pressing Enter ends the edit mode for the field, sets your change, and makes the Assign button available.
5. When finished working with resource assignments, click the Close button.

In the task sheet, you'll see that the task has been updated to include the new resource. Depending on the task type (fixed units, fixed work, or fixed duration), you might see changes in the duration or work amount as a result of the newly assigned resource. You'll also see the green feedback triangle in the task cell. Position your mouse pointer over the triangle, and the Smart Tag icon appears in the Indicators field. Click the Smart Tag icon. A menu appears (see Figure 7-17).

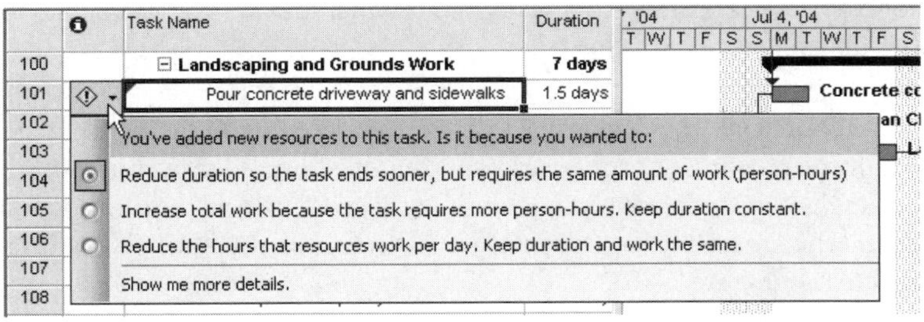

Figure 7-17. The Smart Tag informs you of the ramifications of adding a resource to the task. These results are based on the task type.

The Smart Tag disappears as soon as you carry out another operation, and therefore cannot undo the previous operation.

To replace one resource with another, follow these steps:

1. In the Gantt Chart or other task sheet, click the task to which you want to add more resources.
2. On the Standard toolbar, click Assign Resources.

   The Assign Resources dialog box appears, showing a check mark next to the names of resources already assigned.

3 Click the name of the assigned resource you want to replace and then click the Replace button.

The Replace Resource dialog box appears, showing the same resources that are displayed in the Assign Resources dialog box, according to any filters you might have applied.

4 Click the name of the replacement resource and then click OK.

The name of the replacement resource moves to the top of the Resources list in the table, and the default percentage appears in the Units field for the resource.

5 Review the Units field and make sure that it's appropriate for this assignment.

6 When finished replacing resources, click the Close button.

To remove a resource assignment, follow these steps:

1 In the Gantt Chart or other task sheet, click the task from which you want to remove a resource.

2 On the Standard toolbar, click Assign Resources.

The Assign Resources dialog box appears, showing a check mark next to the names of resources already assigned.

3 Click the name of the assigned resource you want to remove and then click the Remove button.

4 When finished working with resource assignments, click the Close button.

Note When you remove a resource assignment, you're removing only the assignment, not the resource itself. The resource is still assigned to other tasks, and is available for assignment to other tasks.

In the task sheet, you'll see that the task has been updated to exclude the deleted resource. If there were multiple resources assigned and you removed one of them but left others intact, you'll also see the green feedback triangle in the task cell. Position your mouse pointer over the triangle, and the Smart Tag icon appears in the Indicators field. Click the Smart Tag icon. A menu appears (see Figure 7-18).

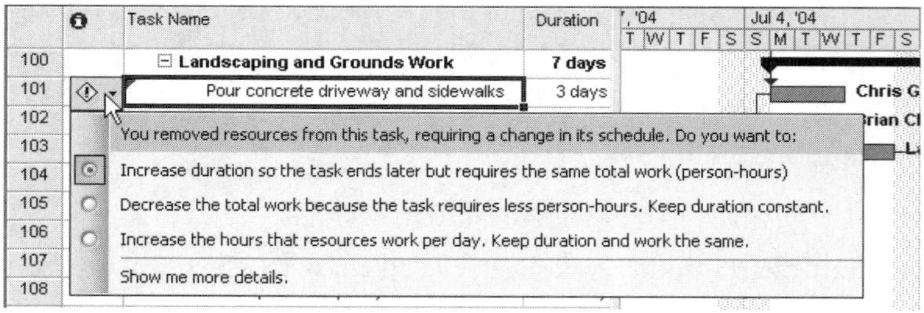

Figure 7-18. The Smart Tag informs you of the ramifications of removing a resource from the task. These results are based on the task type.

Tip **Use the Task Information dialog box to assign or change resources**
As an alternative to the Assign Resources dialog box, you can double-click a task to open the Task Information dialog box and then click the Resources tab (see Figure 7-19). Although the Task Information dialog box doesn't have all the options of the Assign Resources dialog box, you can still assign, replace, and remove assigned resources (as well as set the assignment units) for a single task.

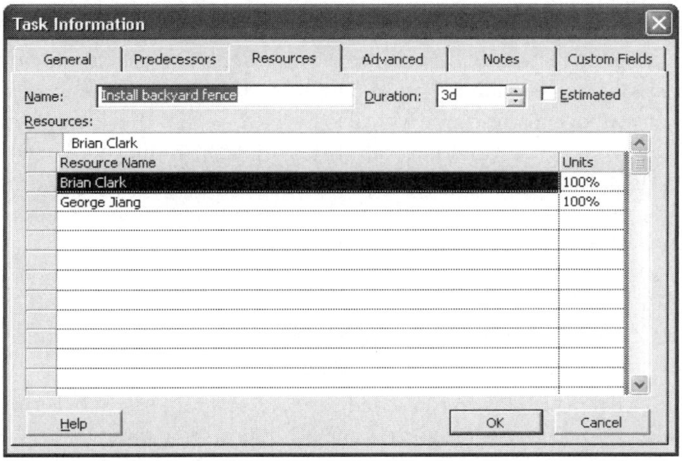

Figure 7-19. Use the Resources tab in the Task Information dialog box to create or modify resource assignments on a single task.

Tip **Turn off Smart Tags**
Smart Tags provide feedback for users who are still getting used to the ways Microsoft Project schedules tasks. This feedback helps users understand the impact of their scheduling changes.

If you understand the impact of your scheduling changes, you might not need Smart Tags, so you can turn them off. To do this, click Tools, Options and then click the Interface tab. Under Show Indicators And Option Buttons For, clear the Resource Assignments and the Edits To Work, Units Or Duration check boxes.

Controlling Changes with Effort-Driven Scheduling

When you assign an additional resource to a task that already has assigned resources, by default, the amount of work scheduled for each assigned resource decreases. Likewise, suppose that you remove a resource from a task, leaving at least one remaining resource assigned. By default, the amount of work scheduled for each remaining assigned resource increases.

These changes in work amounts are a function of *effort-driven scheduling*, which dictates that as more resources are added, there is less work for each resource to perform, although the total work to be performed by all resources stays constant. If resources are removed, each remaining resource needs to do more work—again, with the total work remaining constant.

The results of effort-driven scheduling operate in conjunction with the task type. If the task type is set to fixed units or fixed work, adding resources decreases the duration. If the task type is set to fixed duration, adding resources decreases the units for each assigned resource.

By default, effort-driven scheduling is enabled for all tasks. This makes sense because, in the majority of cases, the primary reason for adding resources to a task is to bring in its finish date.

However, you might have certain tasks whose work should not change regardless of the addition or removal of assigned resources. For example, you might have a 4-day document review task. You want all resources assigned to have 4 days to review the document. Suppose that you realize later that you forgot a resource who also needs to review the document. When you add this resource to the task, you wouldn't want the work to be reduced—you still want everyone to have 4 days. Because each resource is reviewing different aspects of the document, it isn't the type of task that can be completed more quickly if more resources are added. For such a task, it's best to turn off effort-driven scheduling.

To turn off effort-driven scheduling for selected tasks, follow these steps:

1. In the Gantt Chart or other task sheet, click the task for which you want to turn off effort-driven scheduling.

   If you want to turn off effort-driven scheduling for several tasks at one time, click the first task, hold down Ctrl, and then click the other tasks you want.

Task Information

2. On the Standard toolbar, click Task Information.
3. In the Task Information dialog box, click the Advanced tab.
4. Clear the Effort Driven check box.

To turn off effort-driven scheduling for all new tasks in this project plan:

1. Click Tools, Options and then click the Schedule tab.
2. Clear the New Tasks Are Effort Driven check box.

> **Tip** **Use Smart Tag feedback when adding or removing resources**
> When you add or remove resources assigned to a task, the Smart Tag feedback icon appears so you'll get the scheduling results you want. Click the Smart Tag icon to read your options and then make any changes you want. If you click Show Me More Details, the Customize Assignment pane in the Project Guide appears.

Controlling Schedule Changes with Task Types

Adding or removing resources after the initial assignment can change the task and assignment scheduling based on whether the task is effort-driven.

The scheduling for a task or assignment can also change when one of the following items is changed:

- Task duration
- Assignment units
- Work

Duration, units, and work are interrelated and interdependent. When you change one of the three, at least one of the others is affected. For example, by default, if you revise duration, work is recalculated. If you revise assignment units, duration is recalculated. This is based on the basic Microsoft Project scheduling formula:

*Duration * Units = Work*

You need to be able to control how the schedule is affected when you change duration, assignment units, or work. This control is the *task type*. Think of the task type as the one anchor among the three elements of duration, units, and work. When you make a change, the task type dictates which of the three elements must remain fixed and which of the other two can flex to accommodate the change (see Figure 7-20).

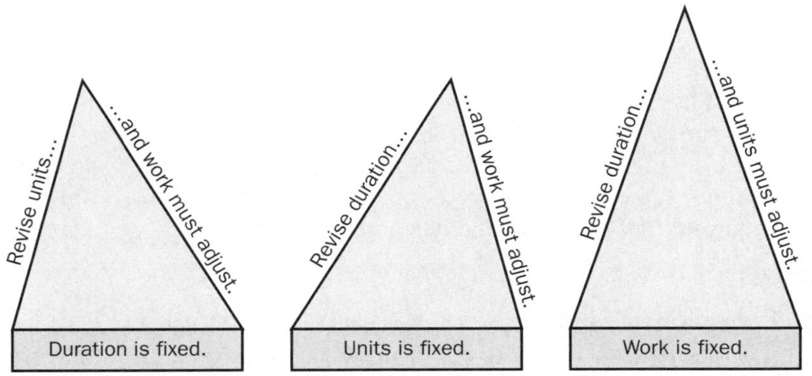

Figure 7-20. When you change one of the three elements, at least one of the others is affected, which changes your task or assignment scheduling.

Therefore, the three task types are as follows:

- Fixed Units
- Fixed Duration
- Fixed Work

Which task type you choose for your project default and change for individual tasks has to do with how you develop your project and the scheduling rules you have in mind as you set your task durations and assign your resources.

> **Tip** **Use Smart Tag feedback when you change scheduling controls**
> When you change units, work, or duration, the Smart Tag feedback icon appears so that you'll get the scheduling results you want. Click the Smart Tag icon to read your options and then make any changes you want. If you click Show Me More Details, the Customize Assignment pane in the Project Guide appears.

Understanding the Fixed Units Task Type

When you assign a resource to a task, you specify the assignment units in the Units field of the Assign Resources dialog box. You can see the units in the chart portion of the Gantt Chart (see Figure 7-21). By default, the units appear with the resource name next to the Gantt bar if it's anything other than 100 percent.

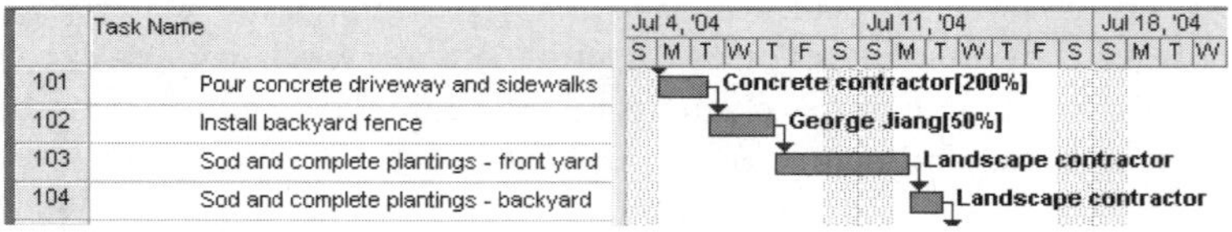

Figure 7-21. Assignment units other than 100 percent are shown next to the relevant Gantt bars.

The Fixed Units task type dictates that the percentage of assignment units on an assignment should remain constant regardless of changes to duration or work. This is the default task type because it's the task type that fits the majority of project tasks. If you increase task duration, Microsoft Project shouldn't force you to find another resource or force a 50 percent resource to work 100 percent on the assignment.

Changes to a Fixed Unit task have the following results:

- If you revise the duration, work also changes, and units are fixed.
- If you revise work, duration also changes, and units are fixed.
- If you revise units, duration also changes, and work is fixed.

Understanding the Fixed Work Task Type

When you assign a resource to a task, the task's duration is translated into work. You can see the amount of work in the Task Usage or Resource Usage view.

The Fixed Work task type dictates that the amount of work on an assignment should remain constant regardless of changes to duration or units.

Changes to a Fixed Work task have the following results:

- If you revise the duration, units also change, and work is fixed.
- If you revise units, duration also changes, and work is fixed.
- If you revise work, duration also changes, and units are fixed.

Understanding the Fixed Duration Task Type

When you create a task, you specify the task's duration in the Duration field of the Gantt Chart or other task sheet. The Gantt bar for the task is drawn according to the duration you set.

The Fixed Duration task type dictates that the task duration should remain constant, regardless of changes to units or work.

Changes to a Fixed Duration task have the following results:

- If you revise units, work also changes, and duration is fixed.
- If you revise work, units also change, and duration is fixed.
- If you revise the duration, work also changes, and units are fixed.

Changing the Task Type

As you gain more experience working with Microsoft Project, you'll see the impact of the schedule recalculations engendered by the changes you make. You can control the way changes to the resource assignments of tasks are made by choosing a default task type, and you can make occasional exceptions when needed.

By default, all tasks are Fixed Units. To change the task type of selected tasks, follow these steps:

1. In the Gantt Chart or other task sheet, click the task for which you want to change the task type.

   If you want to change the task type for several tasks at one time, click the first task, hold down Ctrl, and then click the other tasks you want.
2. On the Standard toolbar, click Task Information.
3. In the Task Information dialog box, click the Advanced tab.
4. In the Task Type box, click the task type you want to apply to the selected tasks.

To set the default task type for all new tasks in this project plan, follow these steps:

1. Click Tools, Options, and in the Options dialog box, click the Schedule tab.
2. In the Default Task Type box, click the task type you want to apply to all new tasks.

All the tasks in your schedule can have the same task type, or they can be intermixed.

Contouring Resource Assignments

When you assign a resource to a task, typically the work time allotted for the task is spread equally across the task duration. For example, if Pat is the only resource assigned full-time to a 4-day task, Pat is assigned 8 hours of work in each of the 4 days.

If you want to adjust how the hours are assigned, however, you can shape the work amounts. You can assign 1 hour on the first day, 2 hours on the second day, 5 hours on the third day, 8 hours on the fourth and fifth day, 5 hours on the sixth day, 2 hours on the seventh day, and 1 hour on the eighth day. You still have 32 hours of work, but the duration has stretched to 8 days. The assignment is shaped like a bell: It has a ramp-up period, a full-on period, and a ramp-down period. A shape applied to the work is called a work *contour* (see Figure 7-22).

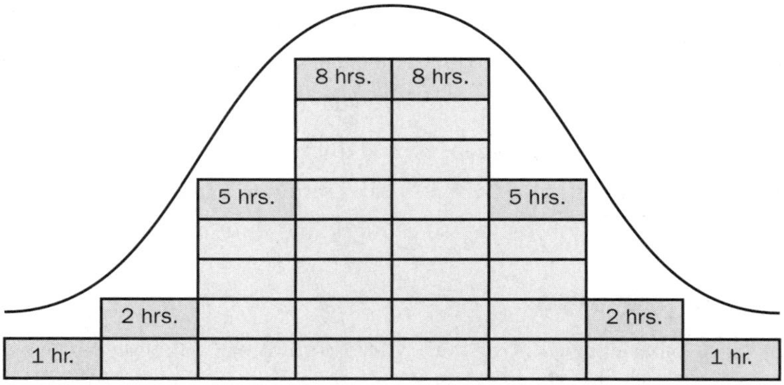

Figure 7-22. Apply the Bell work contour to shape the work amounts to reflect ramp-up, peak, and ramp-down periods, in the shape of a bell.

You can apply this shape by manually adjusting work amounts for the assignment in the timesheet portion of the Task Usage view. Or you can apply the built-in bell contour, which converts the default flat contour into different shapes of time, such as back loaded, front loaded, early peak, and more.

The available built-in work contours are the following:

- Flat (the default)
- Back Loaded

- Front Loaded

- Double Peak

- Early Peak

- Late Peak

- Bell

- Turtle

To apply a built-in work contour to an assignment, follow these steps:

1. Display the Task Usage or Resource Usage view so you can see assignments.

Assignment Information

2. Click the assignment to which you want to apply a work contour and then click Assignment Information.

   The Assignment Information dialog box appears.

3. If necessary, click the General tab.
4. In the Work Contour box, click the work contour you want to apply (see Figure 7-23).

   Work for the assignment is redistributed in the shape of the selected contour.

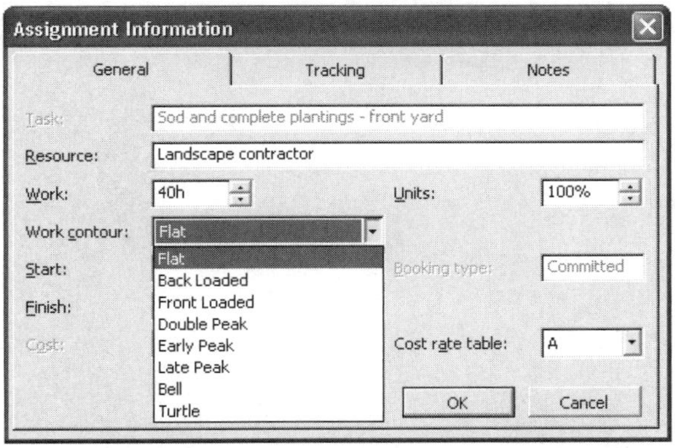

Figure 7-23. Use the General tab in the Assignment Information dialog box to set work contours.

Edited work indicator

You can also reshape the work for an assignment manually by editing work amounts in the timesheet portion of the Task Usage or Resource Usage view. When you do this, an icon appears in the Indicators column, alerting you to the fact that work amounts have been edited.

Any assignment with a work contour applied shows the specific contour icon in the Indicators field of the Task Usage or Resource Usage view.

> **Tip** **Apply a work contour to material resources**
> You can also apply a work contour to material resources. In this case, the quantity of material used is distributed over the task span according to the selected contour.

Chapter 8

Planning Resource and Task Costs

Microsoft Office Project 2003 can help you plan, forecast, and track costs associated with the performance of the project. The bulk of your costs is likely to be generated by the resources assigned to tasks. There might also be costs directly associated with tasks.

The starting point is to enter unit resource costs and any fixed costs for tasks. As resources are assigned to tasks, Project 2003 calculates these unit costs to forecast the cost for each assignment, each resource, each task, and the project as a whole.

Use this cost estimate to develop your project's budget. Or if the budget has already been imposed, see whether the project plan is in line with the realities of the budget. If it isn't, use Microsoft Project to make the necessary adjustments.

Cost planning involves estimating your costs and setting your budget, which is the subject of this chapter. If necessary, you can adjust the project plan to conform to the budget. As soon as you start executing the project, you start tracking and managing costs. At that point, you can compare actual costs to your original planned costs and analyze any variances between the two.

For information about tracking costs, including setting cost baselines and entering actual costs, see Chapter 10, "Saving a Baseline and Updating Progress." For information about managing costs, see "Monitoring and Adjusting Costs" on page 338. For more information about adjusting the project plan to conform to the budget, see "Reducing Project Costs" on page 267.

Working with Costs and Budgeting

Project cost management is one of the many knowledge areas, or disciplines, required for a successful project execution. Simply put, effective project cost management ensures that the project is completed within the approved budget. Processes associated with project cost management include the following:

Resource planning After you determine the types and quantities of resources needed for the project, you can estimate costs for those resources. You obtain work resources by hiring staff through human resources processes. You obtain contract staff, material resources, and equipment resources through procurement processes. You then enter those resources into your project plan and assign them to tasks.

Cost estimating *Top-down cost estimating* is the practice of using the actual cost of a previous similar project as the basis for estimating the cost of the current project. *Bottom-up cost estimating* involves estimating the cost of individual tasks and then summarizing those estimates to arrive at a project cost total. The estimate should take into consideration labor, materials, supplies, and any other costs. With Microsoft Project, you can see the planned costs of resources, as well as the fixed costs associated with tasks. Microsoft Project can total all costs to give you a reliable estimate of how much it will cost to implement the project.

Cost budgeting The budget can allocate certain amounts to individual phases or tasks in the project. Or the budget can be allocated to certain time periods in which the costs will be incurred. The cost estimate and the project schedule—with the scheduled start and finish dates of the different phases, tasks, milestones, and deliverables—are instrumental to developing the project budget.

Cost control This process controls changes to the project budget. Cost control addresses the manner in which cost variances will be tracked and managed, and how cost information will be reported. A cost management plan can detail cost control procedures and corrective actions.

Planning Resource Costs

The key to planning project costs is entering resource costs. The majority of your costs come from resources carrying out their assignments. When you enter resource cost rates and assign resources to tasks, those resource cost rates are multiplied by the work on assignments. The result is the cost of the assignment.

You can set costs for work resources as well as material resources. Cost rates might be variable, such as $40/hour, or $200/ton. Or they might be a fixed per-use cost, such as $300 per use.

Setting Costs for Work Resources

You can set pay rates for work resources: people and equipment. When these resources are assigned to tasks, Microsoft Project multiplies the pay rates by the amount of assigned work to estimate the planned cost for the assignment. You can also set per-use costs for work resources. If a resource has different costs for different types of assignments or during different periods of time, you can enter multiple costs for one resource.

> **Tip** **Enter costs when entering resources**
> You can enter cost information for resources at the same time you add resources to the project. Simply complete all the fields in the Resource Sheet at the same time.

Specifying Variable Work Resource Costs

To set pay rates for work resources, follow these steps:

1 Click View, Resource Sheet.

2 If the Entry table is not already applied to the Resource Sheet, click View, Table, Entry.

3 Make sure that the work resource is set up.

It should be designated as a Work resource in the Type field.

For more information about setting up work resources, see "Adding Work Resources to the Project" on page 175.

4 In the Std. Rate field for the first work resource, enter the resource's standard pay rate; for example, *$30/hour*, or *$400/day*.

5 If the resource is eligible for overtime, enter the resource's overtime pay rate in the Ovt. Rate field.

Tip **Set default rates**
You can set a default standard rate and overtime rate for all work resources. Click Tools, Options and then click the General tab. Enter values in the Default Standard Rate and Default Overtime Rate boxes. Default rates ensure that there's at least an estimated value in the work resource rate fields, which can help you approximate project costs in broad terms until you have confirmed all resource rates.

Note If you're working with Microsoft Office Project Professional 2003 in an enterprise environment, enterprise resource rate information can be updated by the project server administrator, portfolio manager, or other user with the proper permissions.

For more information about setting up enterprise resource information, see "Creating the Enterprise Resource Pool" on page 599.

Inside Out

Specify overtime work yourself

Microsoft Project does not automatically assign the overtime pay rate when a resource's work exceeds 8 hours in a day or 40 hours in a week. Although it seems as if this overtime assignment would be the expected behavior, Microsoft Project can't make that assumption. If it did, you might end up with higher costs than you actually incurred.

For the overtime rate to be used, you must specify overtime work in addition to regular work for the resource. For example, if a person is scheduled to work 50 hours in a week, which includes 8 hours of regular work and 2 hours of overtime work per day, you should assign 10 hours of regular work per day and designate 2 hours of it as overtime work. The cost of the hours specified as overtime work is then calculated with the overtime rate you entered for the resource.

For more information about working with overtime, see "Balancing Resource Workloads" on page 271.

Specifying Fixed Resource Costs

Some work resources incur a cost each time you use them. This *per-use cost* might be instead of or in addition to a cost rate, and is often associated with equipment. It's a set, one-time fee for the use of the resource. For example, rental equipment might have a delivery or setup charge every time they're used, in addition to their day rate.

Per-use costs never depend on the amount of work to be done. They're simply one-time costs that are incurred each time the resource is used.

To specify a per-use cost, follow these steps:

1. Click View, Resource Sheet.
2. If the Entry table is not already applied to the Resource Sheet, click View, Table, Entry.
3. In the Cost/Use field for the work resource, enter the resource's per-use cost; for example, *$100*.

Tip **Set options for how currency is displayed**
You can set the currency symbol, the placement of the symbol to the number, and the number of digits after the decimal point. Click Tools, Options and then click the View tab. Under Currency Options, set the fields as appropriate to your project. The changes apply to your current project plan.

Setting Costs for Material Resources

To set resource costs for consumable materials, follow these steps:

1. Click View, Resource Sheet.
2. If the Entry table is not already applied to the Resource Sheet, click View, Table, Entry.
3. Make sure the material resource is set up in your Resource Sheet.

   It should be designated as a material resource in the Type field and have a unit of measurement, such as yards, tons, feet, and so on, in the Material Label field.

For more information about setting up material resources, see "Adding Material Resources to the Project" on page 186.

4. In the Std. Rate field for the material resource, enter the cost per unit.

   For example, if you have a material resource that is measured in tons, and each ton of this material costs $300, enter **$300** in the Std. Rate field.

5 If there's a per-use cost for the material, such as a setup fee or equipment rental fee associated with using the material, enter it in the Cost/Use field.

Project Management Practices: Procurement Management

When you need to hire contract staffing or use vendors for certain phases of your project, procurement management comes into play. Procurement is also necessary when you need to purchase materials and equipment from selected suppliers.

You use procurement planning to identify which project requirements are best satisfied by purchasing products or services outside the project organization. Through procurement planning, you decide what you need, how much you need, when you need it, and who you're purchasing it from.

The procurement process includes the following:

- Bid solicitation planning
- Bid solicitation
- Vendor selection
- Contract administration
- Contract closing

Because contracting and procurement are specialized knowledge areas, it's best to get experts enlisted and involved on the project team as soon as possible.

Setting Multiple Costs for a Resource

Suppose that you know that certain work resources will get a 5 percent raise on September 1. Maybe the contract for an equipment resource stipulates a discount for the first month of use and then the cost returns to normal for the second month and beyond. Or perhaps a resource has one rate for one type of work and another rate for another type of work. You can specify different costs at different times by using the *cost rate tables*. To specify different costs, follow these steps:

1 In the Resource Sheet, click the work or material resource for which you want to specify multiple cost rates.

Resource Information

2 On the Standard toolbar, click Resource Information.

3 In the Resource Information dialog box, click the Costs tab (see Figure 8-1).

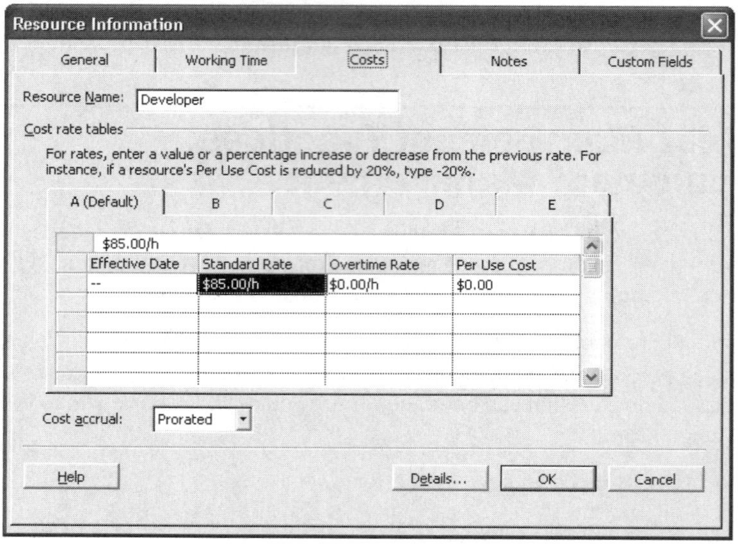

Figure 8-1. Use the cost rate tables in the Resource Information dialog box to specify up to 25 different resource rates.

4 On the A (Default) tab, you see the standard rate, overtime rate, and per-use cost you might have already entered in the Resource Sheet.

5 To specify a change in rate after a certain period of time, click in the next blank Effective Date field, and enter the date the change is to take effect. Enter the cost changes as applicable in the Standard Rate, Overtime Rate, and Per Use Cost fields (see Figure 8-2).

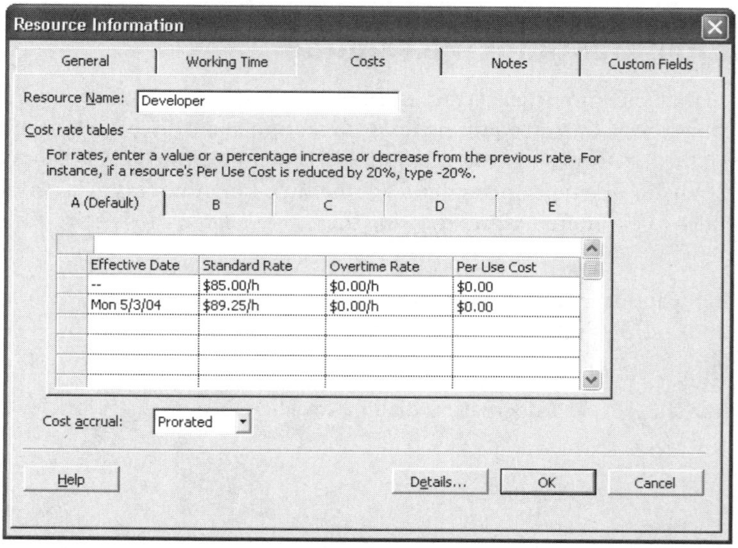

Figure 8-2. If new costs are to take effect on a certain date, add the date and costs in the A (Default) cost rate table.

6 To specify different costs based on different types of activities, enter the different costs in a different tab, such as B or C.

Click the B tab, for example; and enter the Standard Rate, Overtime Rate, and Per Use Cost for the other activity as applicable. When you assign this resource to a task that uses the different rates, you can specify them with the assignment.

> **Tip** **Specify rate changes in percentages**
> If a percentage rate change goes into effect on a certain date, you can have Microsoft Project calculate the new rate for you. Enter the date in the Effective Date field; and then in the Standard Rate, Overtime Rate, or Per Use Cost fields, enter the percentage change: for example, +10% or -15%. The actual rate representing that change is immediately calculated and entered in the field.

Cost Rate Table A for resources is applied to the resource's assignments by default. If you defined a different cost rate table for another category of work, specify which cost rate table is to be used for the assignment. To do this, follow these steps:

1. In a task view such as the Gantt Chart view, assign the resource to the task using the Assign Resources dialog box.
2. Click View, Task Usage or View, Resource Usage to switch to an assignment view.
3. Click the assignment that needs a different cost rate table applied and then click Assignment Information on the Standard toolbar.
4. If necessary, click the General or Tracking tab.
5. In the Cost Rate Table list, click the cost rate table you want to apply to this assignment (see Figure 8-3).

Assignment Information

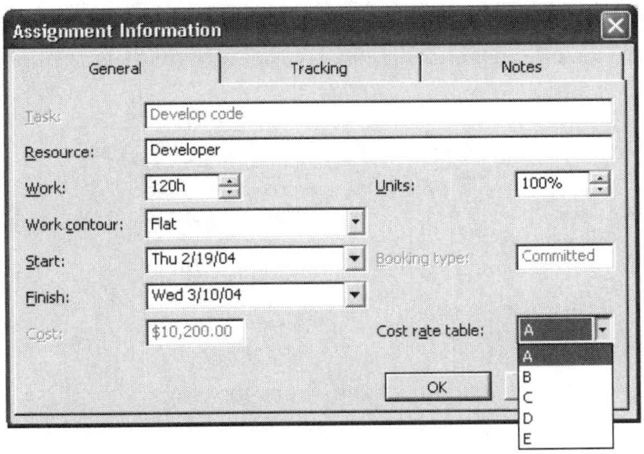

Figure 8-3. Select which cost rate table should be used for this assignment in the Assignment Information dialog box.

Setting Cost Accrual

The point in time when costs are incurred, or charged, is the *cost accrual method*. You can have costs incurred at the beginning of the assignment or after the end of the assignment. Or you can have the costs *prorated* across the time span of the assignment, which is the default method. Specifying the cost accrual method is important for budget cash flow planning.

To specify the cost accrual method, follow these steps:

1. Click View, Resource Sheet.
2. If the Entry table is not already applied to the Resource Sheet, click View, Table, Entry.
3. In the Accrue At field for the work or material resource, click the method: Start, Prorated, or End.

You can also specify the cost accrual method on the Costs tab in the Resource Information dialog box. Although different resources can have different cost accrual methods, you cannot set different cost accrual methods for different cost rate tables.

Planning Fixed Task Costs

Most of your costs are associated with resources and are calculated based on resource rates and assigned work. However, sometimes you have a cost associated with a task that's independent of any resource. In this case, you can enter a fixed cost for a task. Examples might include printing costs associated with the completion of a document deliverable or the travel costs associated with a milestone conference or event. To enter a fixed cost for a task, follow these steps:

1. Display the Gantt Chart or other task sheet.
2. Click View, Table, Cost.

   The Cost table with the Fixed Cost and Fixed Cost Accrual fields is applied to the task sheet (see Figure 8-4).

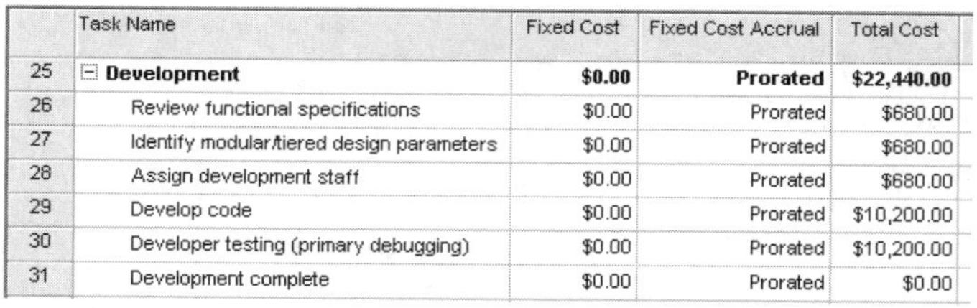

	Task Name	Fixed Cost	Fixed Cost Accrual	Total Cost
25	⊟ **Development**	**$0.00**	**Prorated**	**$22,440.00**
26	Review functional specifications	$0.00	Prorated	$680.00
27	Identify modular/tiered design parameters	$0.00	Prorated	$680.00
28	Assign development staff	$0.00	Prorated	$680.00
29	Develop code	$0.00	Prorated	$10,200.00
30	Developer testing (primary debugging)	$0.00	Prorated	$10,200.00
31	Development complete	$0.00	Prorated	$0.00

Figure 8-4. Apply the Cost table to enter fixed costs for tasks.

3. In the Fixed Cost field for the task, enter the cost.
4. In the Fixed Cost Accrual field, specify when the cost should be accrued: at the beginning of the task, at the end, or prorated throughout the duration of the task. The planned fixed cost for the task is added to the planned cost for the task based on assigned resources, and is shown in the Total Cost field.

> **Tip Set the default fixed cost accrual method**
> To set the default fixed cost accrual method, click Tools, Options and then click the Calculation tab. In the Default Fixed Costs Accrual list, select your preferred accrual method. This default accrual applies only to fixed costs for tasks, not resource costs.

You can also enter a fixed cost for the project as a whole. To do this, follow these steps:

1. Display the Gantt Chart or other task sheet.
2. Click View, Table, Cost.

   The Cost table is applied.
3. Click Tools, Options.
4. In the Options dialog box, click the View tab.
5. Under Outline Options, select the Show Project Summary Task check box and then click OK.

   The project summary task row appears at the top of the view, and includes rolled-up costs for tasks (see Figure 8-5).

	Task Name	Fixed Cost	Fixed Cost Accrual	Total Cost
0	⊟ **Software Development**	**$0.00**	**Prorated**	**$89,580.00**
1	⊟ **Scope**	**$0.00**	**Prorated**	**$2,240.00**
2	Determine project scope	$0.00	Prorated	$320.00
3	Secure project sponsorship	$0.00	Prorated	$640.00
4	Define preliminary resources	$0.00	Prorated	$640.00
5	Secure core resources	$0.00	Prorated	$640.00
6	Scope complete	$0.00	Prorated	$0.00
7	⊟ **Analysis/Software Requirements**	**$0.00**	**Prorated**	**$9,220.00**
8	Conduct needs analysis	$0.00	Prorated	$3,000.00

Figure 8-5. Add the project summary task to add a fixed cost for the project.

6. In the Fixed Cost field for the project summary task, enter the fixed cost for the project.
7. In the Fixed Cost Accrual field, specify when the cost should be accrued: at the beginning of the project, at the end, or prorated throughout the duration of the project.

   The planned fixed cost for the project is added to all other costs calculated for assignments and tasks throughout the project. This total is shown in the Total Cost field of the project summary task.

Troubleshooting

The rolled-up value for fixed task costs looks wrong

If you have fixed costs for individual tasks, and possibly a fixed cost for the project as a whole, these values are not rolled up into the project summary task or outline summary tasks.

Instead, the fixed costs for tasks and any resource costs are calculated and displayed in the Total Cost field for the individual tasks. In turn, the Total Cost field is rolled up in the project summary task, and that's where you can see project cost totals.

The reasoning is that you might need to enter a fixed cost for a project phase, represented in a summary task. Likewise, you might need to enter a fixed cost for the project as a whole. Not rolling up totals in the Fixed Cost field makes it possible for you to do this, although at first glance it looks wrong. Keep your eye on the Total Cost field instead.

Reviewing Planned Costs

The planned costs for your project become reliable figures that you can use for a budget request or a project proposal when the following information is entered in your project plan:

- All required work and material resources, even if they're just generic resources
- Costs rates and per-use costs for all work and material resources
- All tasks, complete with reliable duration estimates
- Assignments for all tasks
- Any fixed costs for tasks

After this information has been entered, you can review planned assignment costs, resource costs, task costs, and total project costs.

Reviewing Assignment Costs

Review assignment costs by applying the Cost table to the Task Usage or Resource Usage view, as follows:

1. Click View, Task Usage or View, Resource Usage to display one of the assignment views.
2. Click View, Table, Cost. The Cost table is applied to the view (see Figure 8-6).

	Task Name	Fixed Cost	Fixed Cost Accrual	Total Cost	Details	T	W	T
7	**Analysis/Software Requirements**	**$0.00**	**Prorated**	**$9,220.00**	Work	4h	8h	8h
8	Conduct needs analysis	$0.00	Prorated	$3,000.00	Work	4h	8h	8h
	Analyst			*$3,000.00*	Work	4h	8h	8h
9	Draft preliminary software specifice	$0.00	Prorated	$1,800.00	Work			
	Analyst			*$1,800.00*	Work			
10	Develop preliminary budget	$0.00	Prorated	$1,280.00	Work			
	Project manager			*$1,280.00*	Work			

Figure 8-6. Apply the Cost table to the Task Usage view to see assignment costs.

In the Task Usage view, you can see individual assignment costs, as well as the total cost for each task. In the Resource Usage view, you can see individual assignment costs with the total cost for each resource.

You can review timephased costs by adding cost details to the timesheet portion of the Task Usage or Resource Usage view, as follows:

1. Display either the Task Usage or Resource Usage view.
2. Click Format, Details, Cost. The Cost field is added to the Work field in the timesheet portion of the view (see Figure 8-7).

	Task Name	Fixed Cost	Fixed Cost Accrual	Total Cost	Details	T	W	T
7	**Analysis/Software Requirements**	**$0.00**	**Prorated**	**$9,220.00**	Work	4h	8h	8h
					Cost	$300.00	$600.00	$600.00
8	Conduct needs analysis	$0.00	Prorated	$3,000.00	Work	4h	8h	8h
					Cost	$300.00	$600.00	$600.00
	Analyst			*$3,000.00*	Work	4h	8h	8h
					Cost	$300.00	$600.00	$600.00

Figure 8-7. Review assignment costs over time by adding the Cost field to the Task Usage or Resource Usage timesheet.

Zoom In

3. To see more or less time period detail, click the Zoom In or Zoom Out buttons on the Standard toolbar.

Reviewing Resource Costs

You can review resource costs to see how much each resource is costing to carry out assigned tasks. To get total costs for a resource's assignments, add the Cost field to the Resource Sheet, as follows:

1. Click View, Resource Sheet.
2. Click the column heading to the right of where you want to insert the Cost field.
3. Click Insert, Column.
4. In the Field Name list, click Cost and then click OK.

   The Cost field is added to the table and shows the total planned costs for all assignments for each individual resource.

You can sort, filter, and group resources by cost information. In the Resource Sheet with the Cost field added, you can rearrange the view by cost information as follows:

- Click Project, Sort, By Cost.

  To return your Resource Sheet to its original order, click Project, Sort, By ID.
- Click Project, Filtered For, More Filters. Click Cost Greater Than and then click the Apply button. Enter an amount and then click OK.

  To see all resources again, click Project, Filtered For, All Resources.
- Click Project, Group By, Standard Rate.

  To ungroup your resources, click Project, Group By, No Group.

Reviewing Task Costs

You can review task costs to see how much each task will cost to carry out. This cost is the sum of all the costs of resources assigned to this task, as well as any fixed costs for tasks. To view total costs for tasks, do the following:

1. Display the Gantt Chart or other task sheet.

2 Click View, Table, Cost.

3 Review the Total Cost field to see the cost for each task.

There are two built-in reports you can run that show planned costs. To generate the Budget report, do the following:

1 Click View, Reports.

2 Double-click Costs.

3 Double-click Budget.

The Budget report appears (see Figure 8-8).

Budget Report as of Mon 6/23/03
Software Development

Task Name	Fixed Cost	Fixed Cost Accrual	Total Cost
Develop code	$0.00	Prorated	$10,200.00
Developer testing (primary debugging)	$0.00	Prorated	$10,200.00
Develop Help system	$0.00	Prorated	$5,760.00
Develop user manuals	$0.00	Prorated	$5,760.00
Develop training materials	$0.00	Prorated	$5,160.00
Conduct needs analysis	$0.00	Prorated	$3,000.00
Develop functional specifications	$0.00	Prorated	$3,000.00
Develop prototype based on functional specifications	$0.00	Prorated	$2,400.00
Draft preliminary software specifications	$0.00	Prorated	$1,800.00
Review modular code	$0.00	Prorated	$1,800.00
Test module integration	$0.00	Prorated	$1,800.00

Figure 8-8. The Budget report shows the task name, fixed costs, and total planned costs.

4 To print the report, click the Print button.

To generate the Cash Flow report, do the following:

1 Click View, Reports.

2 Double-click Costs.

3 Double-click Cash Flow.

The Cash Flow report appears (see Figure 8-9).

Cash Flowas of Mon 6/23/03
Software Development

	12/28/03	1/4/04	1/11/04
Software Development			
Scope			
Determine project scope	$320.00		
Secure project sponsorship	$640.00		
Define preliminary resources	$320.00	$320.00	
Secure core resources		$640.00	
Scope complete			
Analysis/Software Requirements			
Conduct needs analysis		$2,100.00	$900.00
Draft preliminary software specifications			$1,800.00
Develop preliminary budget			$320.00
Review software specifications/budget with team			

Figure 8-9. The Cash Flow report shows planned costs by task, with totals for tasks and for weekly periods.

4 To print the report, click the Print button.

For more information about reports, see "Generating Reports" on page 363.

You can sort and filter tasks by cost. In the Gantt Chart or other task sheet, rearrange your view by cost information as follows:

- Click Project, Sort, By Cost.

  To return your task list to its sort original order, click Project, Sort, By ID.
- Click Project, Filter For, More Filters. Click Cost Greater Than and then click the Apply button. Enter an amount and then click OK.

  To see all tasks again, click Project, Filter For, All Tasks.

Reviewing the Total Planned Cost for the Project

You can see the total planned cost for the entire project. This cost is the sum of all task costs, as well as any fixed costs you might have entered for the project. To see the total cost for the project, add the Project Summary Task to the Gantt Chart or other task sheet, as follows:

1. Display the Gantt Chart or other task sheet.
2. Click View, Table, Cost.

   The Cost table is applied.
3. Click Tools, Options and then click the View tab.
4. Under Outline Options, select the Show Project Summary Task check box and then click OK.

   The project summary task row appears at the top of the view. The total project cost is displayed in the Total Cost field.

Another way to see the total project cost is in the Project Statistics dialog box. To display the Project Statistics dialog box, follow these steps:

1. Click Project, Project Information.
2. Click the Statistics button. The Project Statistics dialog box appears (see Figure 8-10).

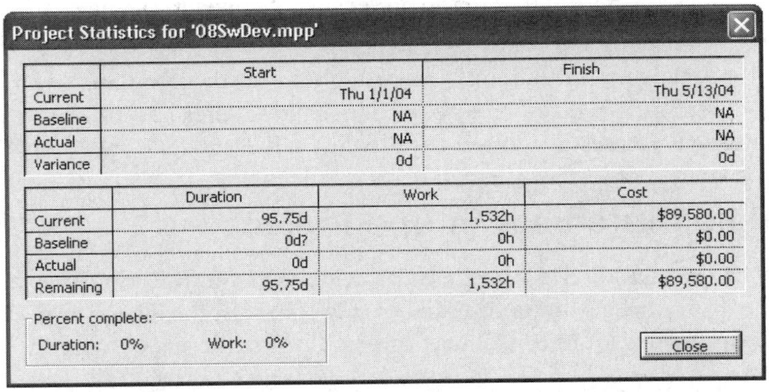
Project Statistics for '08SwDev.mpp'

	Start	Finish
Current	Thu 1/1/04	Thu 5/13/04
Baseline	NA	NA
Actual	NA	NA
Variance	0d	0d

	Duration	Work	Cost
Current	95.75d	1,532h	$89,580.00
Baseline	0d?	0h	$0.00
Actual	0d	0h	$0.00
Remaining	95.75d	1,532h	$89,580.00

Percent complete:
Duration: 0% Work: 0%

Close

Figure 8-10. The Project Statistics dialog box shows the overall project cost; as well as the project start and finish dates, total duration, and total work.

Working with Multiple Currencies

You can set up your project to work with a different currency, and now even to work with multiple currencies in a single plan. These capabilities facilitate cost planning and management for projects that span multiple countries and their currencies.

Setting Up a Different Currency

The currency used in Microsoft Project is the one you have set in your computer system's Regional And Language Options. To set up a different currency:

1. On the Windows taskbar, click Start, Control Panel and then double-click Regional And Language Options.
2. On the Regional Options tab, click the country whose currency you want to add.

   Under Samples, the formats for currency, time, and date for the selected country are displayed.
3. Click OK.

Currencies are set for individual plans, not for Microsoft Project globally. To apply the new currency in your project:

1. In Microsoft Project, open the project in which you want to use the new currency.
2. Click Tools, Options and then click the View tab.
3. Under Currency Options, enter the new currency symbol in the Symbol box.

   There is no list of currency symbols in Microsoft Project. You need to access it from your keyboard, or paste it in from another source. You can find the currency symbols you need from symbol fonts loaded with Microsoft Word or Microsoft Excel.
4. Make any necessary changes to the Decimal Digits box and Placement box and then click OK.

   Any currencies already entered in the project are changed to the new currency. Note, however, that currencies are not converted; the symbol is just switched.

Using this method, the one currency applies throughout the project plan. If you consolidate projects using different currencies, be sure to change the settings in each one to a common currency, and make the necessary conversions to cost values.

Setting Up Multiple Currencies in One Project

NEW FEATURE!

In the past, using the method described in the previous section, you could display only a single currency per project. This limitation can be truly cumbersome if your project spans multiple countries or if you want to consolidate projects using different currencies.

However, with the Euro Currency Converter Component Object Model (COM) add-in, you can now display costs in multiple currencies. Microsoft Project can also convert currencies between different currencies in the European Monetary Union (EMU). If you're converting from a currency not in the EMU (such as the United States dollar), you can add a currency, symbol, placement, and exchange rate; and then use it in your project along with the other currencies.

In Microsoft Project 2002, the Euro Currency Converter COM add-in had to be downloaded from the Web. It's now built in to Microsoft Project 2003, with its functions on a single taskbar. To show the Euro Currency Converter toolbar, click View, Toolbars, Euro Currency Converter. The toolbar appears, as shown in Figure 8-11.

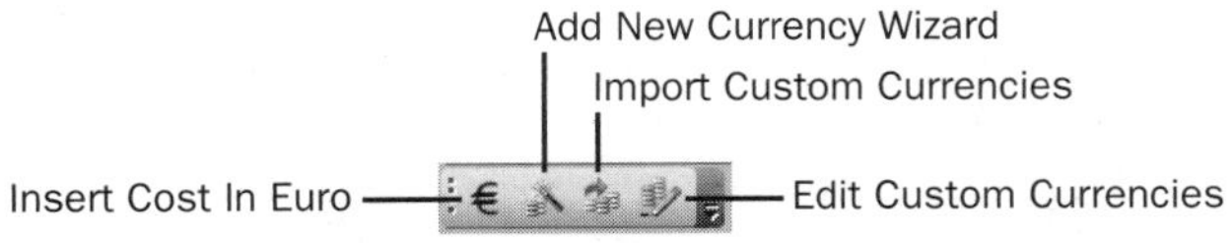

Figure 8-11. Use the Euro Currency Converter to work with multiple currencies in your project.

Note To use the Euro Currency Converter toolbar, you need to turn the Project Guide off. It's not enough just to close the Project Guide window. Click Tools, Options and then click the Interface tab. Clear the Display Project Guide check box.

Converting an EMU Currency to Euro

If you're working with a currency from a country that's part of the EMU, you can select a set of cost fields in your project and create a second set of fields with those costs converted to euros. The calculations are made for the exchange rate from your currency into euros. To add euro-converted costs to your project:

1. Display the view and apply the table you want to use.

   If necessary, add the currency field to the table.

2. Select the currency fields you want to convert.

   You can either drag across the fields or select the entire column by clicking the column heading.

Insert Cost In Euro

3. On the Euro Currency Converter toolbar, click Insert Cost In Euro.

   The Insert Euro Cost dialog box appears, as shown in Figure 8-12.

Figure 8-12. Select your original EMU currency from the list to convert it to euros.

4 In the list, select the currency you're converting from.

The list includes only currencies in the EMU. If you want to convert from a different currency, you need to set up the exchange rate yourself using the Add New Currency Wizard.

For more information, see the next section, "Converting One Currency to Another."

5 Click OK.

A new column appears in your table next to the selected column containing the original currency fields. The new column adopts its name from the original column, and adds the euro symbol (see Figure 8-13).

Original currencies in the French Franc

Std. Rate	Standard Rate [€]
F448.00/hr	€68.30/hr
F400.00/hr	€60.98/hr
F420.00/hr	€64.03/hr
F476.00/hr	**€72.57/hr**
F252.00/hr	**€38.42/hr**
F250.00/hr	**€38.11/hr**
F260.00/hr	**€39.64/hr**
F253.00/hr	€38.57/hr

Francs converted to euros

Figure 8-13. The new column shows the currency converted to euros.

You cannot directly edit the euro field because it's a field calculated by Microsoft Project. However, as you add or change costs in the original currency field, the conversions are instantly updated in the corresponding euro field.

Converting One Currency to Another

If you're working with a currency from a country that's not part of the EMU (for example, Great Britain or the United States), you can set up the currency conversion so you can still work with multiple currencies in a single project. You can convert to or from the euro, or between two non-EMU currencies. To do this, use the Add New Currency Wizard, as follows:

Add New Currency Wizard

1 Open the project in which you want to use the new currency.
2 On the Euro Currency Converter toolbar, click Add New Currency Wizard.
3 Read the first page of the wizard and then click Next.
4 In the Step 2 wizard page, click No and then click Next.
5 In the Step 3 wizard page, enter the symbol, placement, decimal digits, and exchange rate. Enter the exchange rate of the currency in the project to the currency you're adding and converting to (see Figure 8-14).

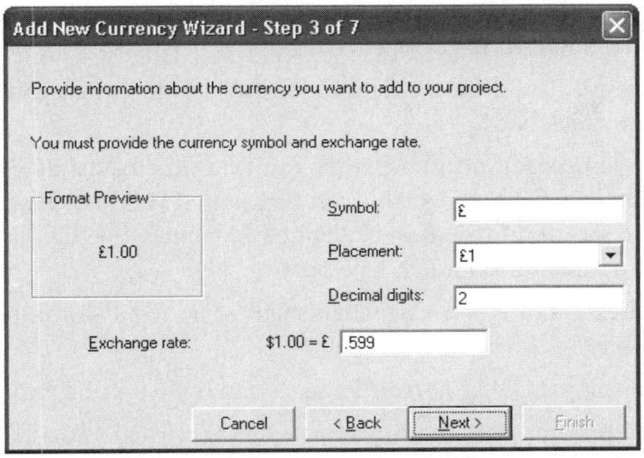

Figure 8-14. In the wizard, specify the details of the new currency you're adding to the project.

6 Click Next to display the Step 4 wizard page, in which you select the cost fields to be created.

7 Select the Task Fields or Resource Fields option.

This option provides a list of cost fields for tasks or cost fields for resources. If you want both, you'll need to work through the wizard twice.

8 Under Cost Fields Available, select all the cost fields that you want to make copies of for the new currency and then click Add.

Use Ctrl or Shift to select multiple fields and then click Add. The selected fields are added to the Fields To Be Created box (see Figure 8-15).

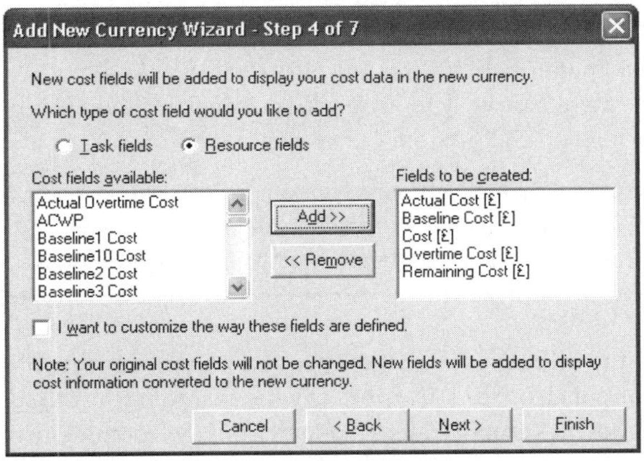

Figure 8-15. In the wizard, select the cost fields you want to copy and convert to the new currency.

Remember, your original cost information remains intact in the original fields. Copies of these fields are being made for the new currency.

9. Click Next. If you selected the I Want To Customize The Way These Fields Are Defined, the Step 5 wizard page appears.

   Use this page to specify a different field name and a different custom field to contain the information. Click Next.

10. In the Step 6 wizard page, specify whether you want to create a new table containing just the new currency fields. This table can be useful if you're converting several fields, and you want to see all information in the new currency together. If you click the Yes option, enter a name in the Table Name box.

    Whether you click Yes or No, the new fields will be added as columns at the end of your current table.

11. Click Next to display the Step 7 wizard page. Read the page and then click Finish.

    The currencies are converted and the new fields are created and added to the current table. The new fields are available to be added to any table you want. Apply the table, click a column heading and then click Insert, Column. Find the new currency field and then click OK.

> **Note** To apply the new table, click View, Table, More Tables. In the More Tables dialog box, click the Task or Resource option as applicable and then click the name of the new table. Click Apply.

You cannot directly edit the field containing the new currency because it's a field calculated by Microsoft Project. However, as you add or change costs in the original currency field, the conversions are instantly updated in the corresponding currency field.

Update the exchange rate

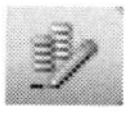

Edit Custom Currencies

If you added a non-EMU currency using the Add New Currency Wizard, you might need to change the exchange rate periodically to keep your currencies accurate. On the Euro Currency Converter toolbar, click Edit Custom Currencies.

In the dialog box, select the Task or Resource option. Select the field you want to change and then click Modify. The Modify Custom Currency dialog box appears, in which you can update the exchange rate. You can also change the symbol, placement, and decimal digits.

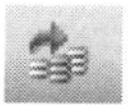

Import Custom Currencies

You can import custom currency information you've set up in another project. Open the project you want to import from and the project you want to import to. On the Euro Currency Converter toolbar, click Import Custom Currencies. Select the source project and then click OK. Follow the steps to import the currencies from one project to the other.

Chapter 9

Checking and Adjusting the Project Plan

In a perfect world, you'd define the project scope, schedule tasks, assign resources, and presto! The project plan would be finished and ready to execute.

In reality, however, this is rarely the case. After you've scheduled tasks and assigned resources, you generally need to check the results and see whether they meet expectations and requirements. Ultimately, you might need to answer one or all of the following questions to your satisfaction and to the satisfaction of your managing stakeholders:

- Will the project be finished on time?
- Is the project keeping to its budget?
- Do the resources have the appropriate amount of work?

If you get the wrong answers to any of these questions, you need to adjust your project plan until you get the right answers. For example, if the finish date is too far away, you can add more resources to major tasks.

After you make such adjustments, you need to check the project plan again. Adding resources to tasks might bring in the finish date, but it also might add cost if you hired additional resources or authorized overtime. And if you assigned more tasks to existing resources, those resources might be overallocated.

To save time as well as money, you might decide to cut certain tasks, a deliverable, or a phase. But if this means you're cutting project scope, you probably need to get approval from your managing stakeholders.

This relationship between time, money, and scope is sometimes referred to as the *project triangle* (see Figure 9-1). When you change one side of the triangle, it affects at least one of the other sides of the triangle.

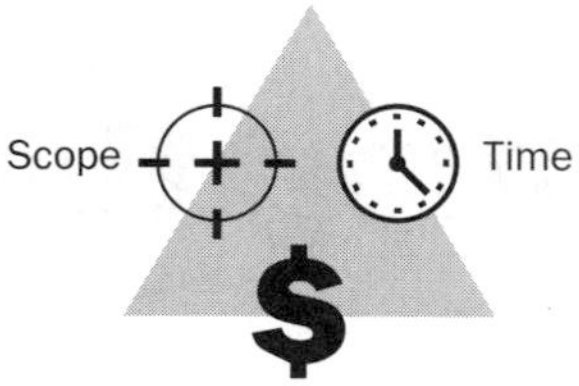

Figure 9-1. Managing your project requires balancing time, money, and scope.

You need to know which side of the triangle is your most important consideration. Is it schedule—you definitely have to finish by November 14? Is it budget—there is absolutely $264,300 for this project, and not a penny more? Is it scope—it is imperative that each and every task in your project plan be implemented? Only one side of the triangle can be "absolute." The other two sides must be flexible so you can adjust the project plan to hit that one absolute.

Depending on which side of your project triangle is your absolute, you might adjust your project plan to do one of the following:

- Bring in the project finish date
- Reduce project costs
- Cut project scope

Although not strictly a part of your project triangle, it's likely that you also will check resource workloads. Resources are the biggest part of your project costs. If any resources are overallocated, you might be facing more overtime than your budget will allow. If resources are grossly overallocated, you run the risk that the tasks won't be done on time and the entire project will slip. If any resources are underallocated, you might be paying more for resources than you should, which also affects your budget.

After you make your adjustments and balance your project triangle to meet the project requirements, you'll be ready for stakeholder buyoff. After you have buyoff, you'll be ready to start the execution phase of the project.

Sources of your project scope, finish date, and budget

Your project scope, finish date, and budget can be imposed on you for various reasons, depending on the type of project and the specific situation. The following are a few examples:

- You are a seller or potential subcontractor bidding on a project whose scope has been defined in the Request for Proposal (RFP). You need to provide the full scope, but your costs and finish date must be competitive with other bidders. If possible, you'll want to include value-added items to give your proposal an advantage while still making a good profit.

- You are a subcontractor and you have been awarded the contract based on a proposal including broad assumptions of scope, finish date, and cost. Having taken this risk, now you must create a detailed project plan that will actually implement that finish date, cost, and scope.
- You've been assigned as project manager of a project within your company. The scope, budget, or finish date have been handed down as one or more of the project assumptions. Your success is predicated upon your ability to implement the project within those limitations.
- You've been assigned as project manager of a project within your company. You and other stakeholders developed the scope to a fair level of detail. It's up to you to propose the budget and finish date for the project.
- You are the project manager and you've balanced your project triangle the way you believe is best. However, after you submitted the project plan for client review, certain new project requirements or limitations surfaced. You have to readjust the project triangle to take the new limitations or requirements into account.

Working with the Critical Path and Critical Tasks

In most projects, there are multiple sets of tasks, which have task relationships with one another, taking place at any one time. In an office move project, for example, the facilities manager and her team might be researching new office sites and then working out the lease terms. At the same time, the office manager and his team might be ordering new office furniture and equipment and then arranging for movers. These two sets of activities are not dependent on each other and use different sets of resources. Therefore, they can be scheduled on parallel tracks. There can be any number of sets of tasks on these parallel tracks, or *paths*, depending on the size and complexity of the project, as well as the number of resources involved.

At any time, there's one task that has the latest finish date in the project. This task, along with its predecessors, dictates the finish date of the project as a whole. The finish date of this path is critical to the finish date of the project itself; therefore we call it the *critical path*. In turn, the tasks that make up each step along the critical path are called the *critical tasks*. Because the critical path dictates the finish date of the project, we pay a tremendous amount of attention to it in project management.

Note The term "critical task" refers only to tasks that are on the "critical path." These terms reflect the scheduling of the tasks, not their relative importance. There can be very important tasks that don't happen to be on the critical path.

In the planning phase, you identify a particular critical path. After you begin the execution phase and actual progress begins to be reported, the critical path might change from one set of linked tasks to another. For example, task progress is likely to differ in various ways from the original schedule. Perhaps one task in the critical path finishes early, but a task in a second path is delayed. In this case, the second path might become the critical path if that is now the path with the latest finish date in the project.

If you need to bring in the finish date, one of the most effective things you can do is focus on the critical path. If you can make critical tasks along that path finish sooner, you can make the project itself finish sooner.

For more information about strategies to bring in a project's finish date, see "Bringing In the Project Finish Date," later in this chapter on page 258.

Understanding Slack Time and Critical Tasks

Many tasks have some amount of scheduling buffer—an amount of time that a task can slip before it causes a delay in the schedule. This scheduling buffer is called *slack*, or *float*. The following describes the two types of slack:

- *Free slack* is the amount of time a task can slip before it delays another task, typically its successor task.
- *Total slack* is the amount of time a task can slip before it delays the project finish date.

Note Sometimes you run into a situation in which you have negative slack; that is, the opposite of slack time. An example of negative slack would be when a successor task is due to begin before the predecessor is finished. This can happen when the task duration of a predecessor task conflicts with a successor task that must begin on a date specified by an assigned constraint, for example.

Because critical tasks cannot slip without delaying the project finish date, critical tasks have no slack, and tasks with no slack are critical.

If a noncritical task consumes its slack time, it usually causes its successor to use some or all of its total slack time. The task becomes a critical task and causes its successor tasks to become critical as well.

Maybe you don't want just those tasks with total slack of 0 to be critical. For example, perhaps you want your critical tasks to be those that still have 1 day of slack. In this case, you can change the definition of a critical task. To do this:

1. Click Tools, Options, and in the Options dialog box, click the Calculation tab.
2. Enter your preference for a critical task in the Tasks Are Critical If Slack Is Less Than Or Equal To box (see Figure 9-2).

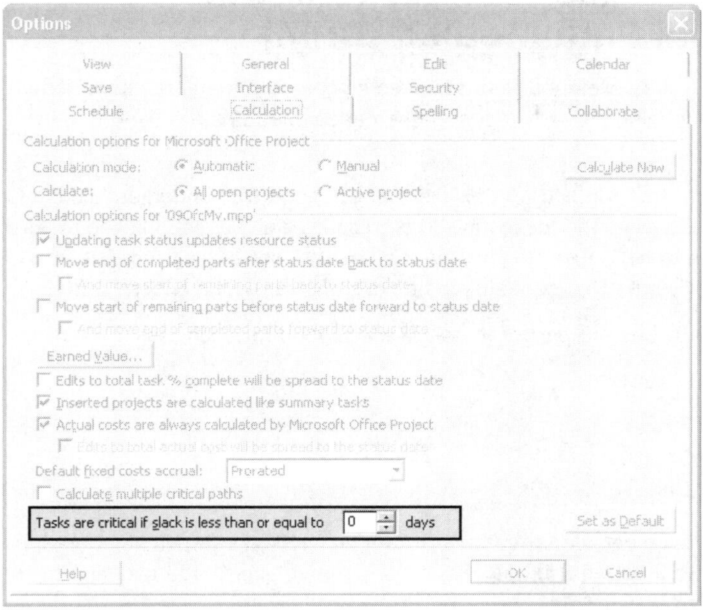

Figure 9-2. Specify the amount of slack that should define a critical task in your project plan.

To see how much free slack and total slack each task has, you can apply the Schedule table to a task sheet, as follows:

1. Click View, Gantt Chart. Or display any other task sheet you want.
2. Click View, Table, Schedule.

   The Schedule table is applied (see Figure 9-3). You might need to drag the vertical divider to the right to see some of the columns in this table.

	Task Name	Start	Finish	Late Start	Late Finish	Free Slack	Total Slack
22	Order chairs	Thu 5/20/04	Thu 5/20/04	Wed 5/26/04	Wed 5/26/04	4 days	4 days
23	Order desks	Thu 5/20/04	Thu 5/20/04	Wed 5/26/04	Wed 5/26/04	4 days	4 days
24	Order systems furniture	Thu 5/20/04	Thu 5/20/04	Wed 5/26/04	Wed 5/26/04	4 days	4 days
25	Order new office equipment	Thu 5/20/04	Thu 5/20/04	Wed 5/26/04	Wed 5/26/04	4 days	4 days
26	Obtain estimates from moving companies	Mon 4/19/04	Tue 5/4/04	Thu 4/29/04	Fri 5/14/04	0 days	8 days
27	Hire movers	Wed 5/5/04	Wed 5/5/04	Wed 5/26/04	Wed 5/26/04	15 days	15 days
28	Evaluate server room needs	Thu 5/20/04	Fri 5/21/04	Tue 5/25/04	Wed 5/26/04	3 days	3 days
29	Evaluate computer networking needs	Thu 5/20/04	Fri 5/21/04	Tue 5/25/04	Wed 5/26/04	3 days	3 days
30	Order change of address labels for notifice	Wed 5/5/04	Wed 5/5/04	Wed 5/26/04	Wed 5/26/04	15 days	15 days

Figure 9-3. The Schedule table shows free slack and total slack, as well as late start and late finish dates.

Critical Path Method (CPM)

Schedules are developed from task sequences, durations, resource requirements, start dates, and finish dates. Various mathematical methods are used to calculate project schedules.

The *Critical Path Method*, or *CPM*, is the technique that underlies Microsoft Office Project 2003 scheduling. The focus of CPM is to analyze all series of linked tasks in a project and determine which series has the least amount of scheduling flexibility; that is, the least amount of slack. This series becomes designated as the critical path.

Four date values are part of the slack calculation for each task:

- Early start
- Early finish
- Late start
- Late finish

The difference between the late start and early start dates is compared, as is the difference between late finish and early finish. The smaller of the two differences becomes the value for total slack.

Viewing the Critical Path

The easiest way to see the critical path in a Gantt chart is to click View, Tracking Gantt. The Tracking Gantt highlights the critical path in red in the chart portion of the view (see Figure 9-4). The Entry table is applied by default to the Tracking Gantt, just as in the regular Gantt Chart.

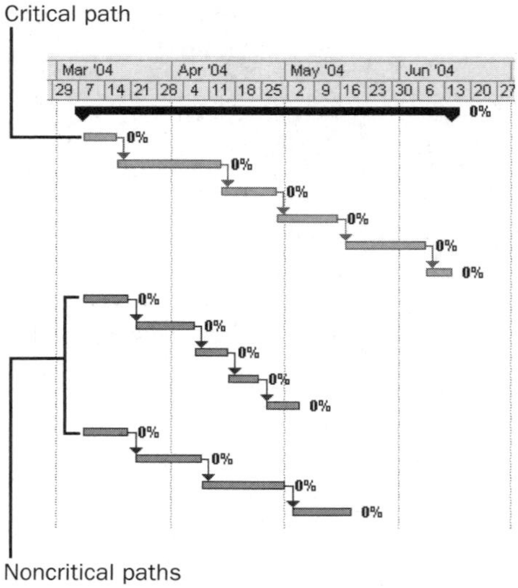

Figure 9-4. The Tracking Gantt highlights the critical path.

Go To Selected Task

Tip **Move the Gantt chart to the selected task**

When you first open a Gantt chart, the timescale is at today's date. If the tasks you're reviewing are in the past or future, you might not see the Gantt bars in the chart. Click a task whose Gantt bar you want to see. On the Standard toolbar, click Go To Selected Task.

You can also use the Gantt Chart Wizard, which formats the chart portion of any Gantt Chart view to highlight the critical path. To do this, follow these steps:

1. Click View, Gantt Chart.

   If you want to modify another Gantt Chart view, such as the Leveling Gantt or Tracking Gantt, display that view instead.

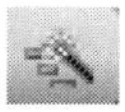

Gantt Chart Wizard

2. On the Formatting toolbar, click Gantt Chart Wizard.
3. On the first page of the Gantt Chart Wizard, click Next.
4. On the second page, select the Critical Path option (see Figure 9-5). Then click Next.

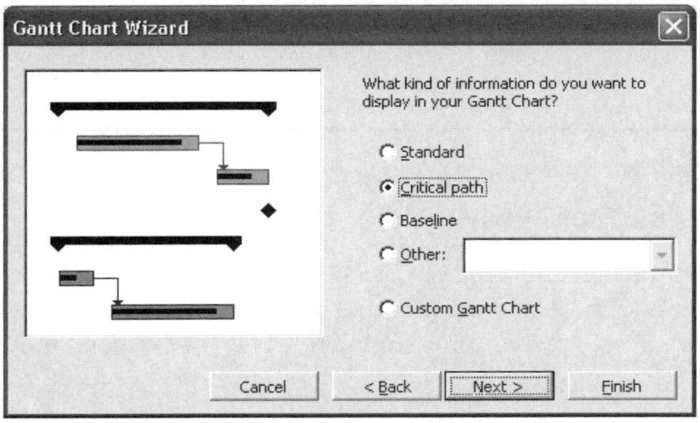

Figure 9-5. To highlight the critical path Gantt bars, select the Critical Path option.

5. On the third page, select the option for any text you want to accompany the Gantt bars, such as resource names, dates, and so on. Click Next.
6. On the fourth page, select whether you want the link lines for task dependencies to show. Click Next.
7. On the final page, click the Format It button.

   Microsoft Project 2003 formats your Gantt Chart according to your specifications.
8. Click the Exit Wizard button to view your new Gantt Chart format, which displays red Gantt bars for critical tasks (see Figure 9-6).

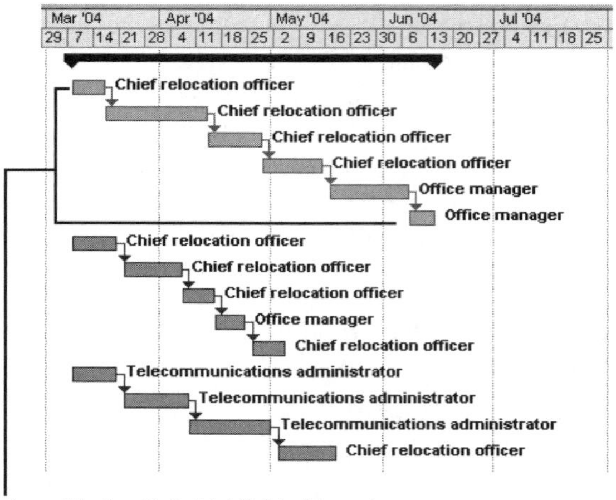

The critical path is highlighted in red.

Figure 9-6. Use the Gantt Chart Wizard to instantly highlight critical path tasks in any Gantt Chart view.

Inside Out

Alternatives to the Gantt Chart Wizard

The Gantt Chart Wizard is convenient for quickly changing the Gantt bar format of certain types of tasks. However, if you use the wizard to do your formatting, you might lose certain standard Gantt bar formatting that you want to preserve. For example, the Deadline bar style is lost.

If you want to see only critical tasks in a Gantt Chart view, switch to the Detail Gantt or Tracking Gantt.

If you want to highlight critical tasks in the Gantt Chart, customize the bar styles.

For more information, see "Formatting a Gantt Chart View" on page 766.

Although displaying the Detail Gantt or using the Gantt Chart Wizard can display the Gantt bars for the critical path at a glance, you can also look at the details for individual critical tasks. The following list details different methods for viewing critical tasks:

Display the Detail Gantt. Click View, More Views, Detail Gantt. This view shows the critical path tasks in red Gantt bars (see Figure 9-7). By default, the Delay table is applied to the sheet portion of the view.

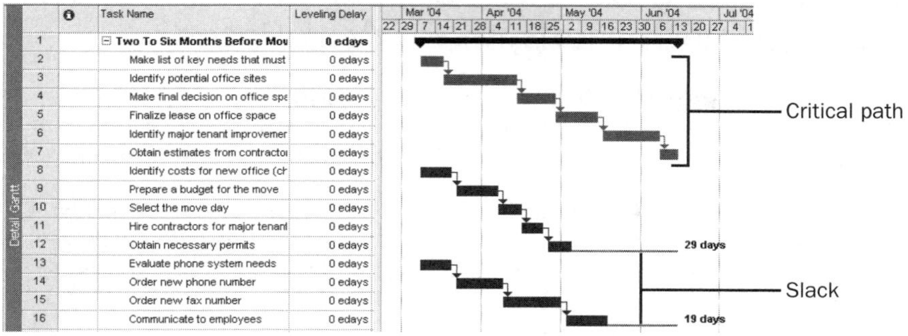

	Task Name	Leveling Delay
1	Two To Six Months Before Mov	0 edays
2	Make list of key needs that must	0 edays
3	Identify potential office sites	0 edays
4	Make final decision on office spa	0 edays
5	Finalize lease on office space	0 edays
6	Identify major tenant improvemer	0 edays
7	Obtain estimates from contracto	0 edays
8	Identify costs for new office (ch	0 edays
9	Prepare a budget for the move	0 edays
10	Select the move day	0 edays
11	Hire contractors for major tenant	0 edays
12	Obtain necessary permits	0 edays
13	Evaluate phone system needs	0 edays
14	Order new phone number	0 edays
15	Order new fax number	0 edays
16	Communicate to employees	0 edays

Figure 9-7. The Detail Gantt shows the critical path as well as available slack.

Review the Critical Tasks report. Click View, Reports. Double-click Overview, and then double-click Critical Tasks.

Group tasks by critical and noncritical tasks. Click Project, Group By, Critical (see Figure 9-8). To return tasks to their original order, click Project, Group By, No Group. You can also use the Group By tool on the Standard toolbar.

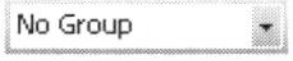

Group By

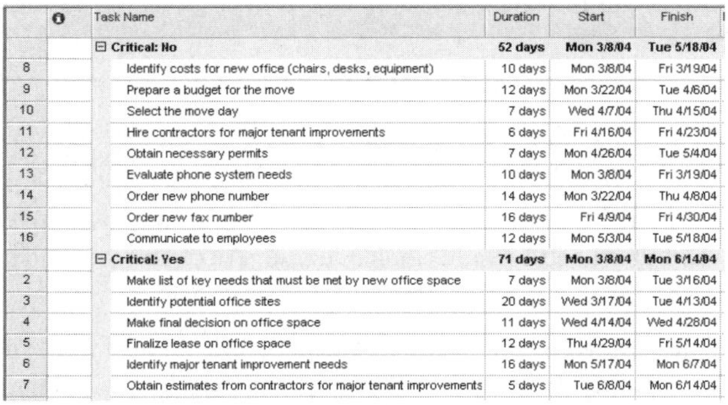

	Task Name	Duration	Start	Finish
	Critical: No	52 days	Mon 3/8/04	Tue 5/18/04
8	Identify costs for new office (chairs, desks, equipment)	10 days	Mon 3/8/04	Fri 3/19/04
9	Prepare a budget for the move	12 days	Mon 3/22/04	Tue 4/6/04
10	Select the move day	7 days	Wed 4/7/04	Thu 4/15/04
11	Hire contractors for major tenant improvements	6 days	Fri 4/16/04	Fri 4/23/04
12	Obtain necessary permits	7 days	Mon 4/26/04	Tue 5/4/04
13	Evaluate phone system needs	10 days	Mon 3/8/04	Fri 3/19/04
14	Order new phone number	14 days	Mon 3/22/04	Thu 4/8/04
15	Order new fax number	16 days	Fri 4/9/04	Fri 4/30/04
16	Communicate to employees	12 days	Mon 5/3/04	Tue 5/18/04
	Critical: Yes	71 days	Mon 3/8/04	Mon 6/14/04
2	Make list of key needs that must be met by new office space	7 days	Mon 3/8/04	Tue 3/16/04
3	Identify potential office sites	20 days	Wed 3/17/04	Tue 4/13/04
4	Make final decision on office space	11 days	Wed 4/14/04	Wed 4/28/04
5	Finalize lease on office space	12 days	Thu 4/29/04	Fri 5/14/04
6	Identify major tenant improvement needs	16 days	Mon 5/17/04	Mon 6/7/04
7	Obtain estimates from contractors for major tenant improvements	5 days	Tue 6/8/04	Mon 6/14/04

Figure 9-8. Use the Critical grouping to group critical tasks together and noncritical tasks together.

Filter

Filter for critical tasks. Click Project, Filtered For, Critical. Only critical tasks are shown. To show all tasks again, click Project, Filtered For, All Tasks. You can also use the Filter tool on the Formatting toolbar.

Report

Use the Project Guide. On the Project Guide toolbar, click Report. Click the See The Project's Critical Tasks link. The view changes to a Critical Tasks Gantt generated by the Project Guide. Additional information is provided in the Project Guide side pane.

Chapter 9

Working with Multiple Critical Paths

By default, you have one path through your project that constitutes your critical path. That one critical path constitutes the series of tasks whose end date is closest to affecting the end date of the project. When the last task is completed, the project is completed.

However, you can display multiple critical paths if you like. Although they might finish earlier than the one "real" critical path, each critical path can show the different networks of tasks throughout your project; for example, for different phases or parallel efforts. To do this, follow these steps:

1. Click Tools, Options and then click the Calculation tab.
2. Select the Calculate Multiple Critical Paths check box.

To create multiple critical paths, Microsoft Project changes the calculation of the critical path so that any task without a successor (that is, the last task in any series of linked tasks) becomes a critical task. The task's late finish date is set to be the same as its early finish date. This setting gives the task 0 slack, which in turn makes it a critical task. Any series of predecessors before this final task becomes a critical path, thereby providing multiple critical paths.

This calculation contrasts with that of a single critical path, in which a task without a successor has its late finish date set to the project finish date. This gives the task slack and therefore makes it a noncritical task.

Bringing in the Project Finish Date

A *time-constrained project* is one in which the project finish date is the most important factor in your project plan. Although you still need to balance budget constraints and satisfy the project scope, the finish date reigns supreme over those other considerations.

If your project plan calculates that your finish date will be beyond your all-important target finish date, focus on the critical path. Shorten the critical path and you bring in the finish date.

Viewing Finish Dates and the Critical Path

Before you analyze the critical path, you just need to see your bottom line: what's the project finish date? Follow these steps:

1. Click Project, Project Information.
2. In the Project Information dialog box, click the Statistics button.

   The Project Statistics dialog box appears. The current, or scheduled, finish date appears in the Finish column (see Figure 9-9).

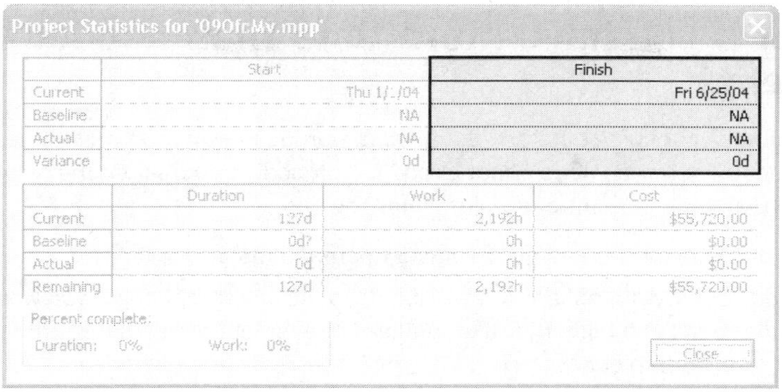

Figure 9-9. The Project Statistics dialog box shows overall project information: project start date, project finish date, total duration, total work, and total cost.

Another way to keep your eye on the project finish date at all times is to add the project summary task row, as follows:

1. Click Tools, Options and then click the View tab.
2. Select the Show Project Summary Task check box.

The project summary task appears at the top of any task sheet view, including the Gantt Chart (see Figure 9-10). Task information is rolled up for the entire project and its summary total is displayed in the project summary row. Specifically, the Finish field in the project summary row shows the latest finish date in the project.

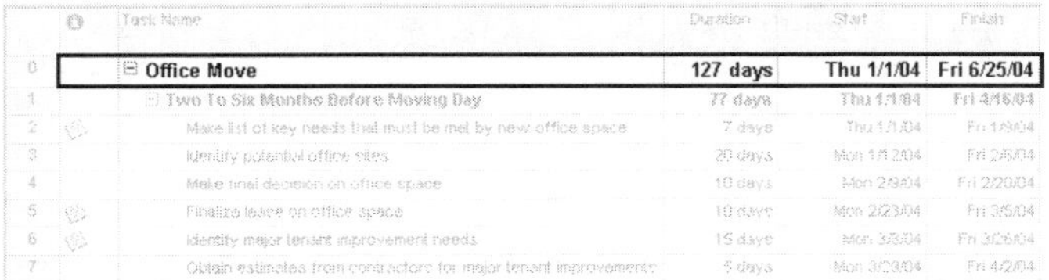

Task Name
Duration
Start
Finish
Office Move
127 days
Thu 1/1/04
Fri 6/25/04
Two To Six Months Before Moving Day
77 days
Thu 1/1/04
Fri 4/16/04

Figure 9-10. The Project Summary row rolls up task information to display the totals for the entire project.

To see the critical path, click View, Tracking Gantt.

For more information about viewing the critical path, see "Viewing the Critical Path," earlier in this chapter.

By viewing the finish date or the critical path, you can easily see whether you're hitting your target finish date. If you need to bring in the finish date, you might want to focus on the critical tasks. You can filter your task sheet to show only critical tasks by clicking Project, Filtered For, Critical. To show all tasks again, click Project, Filtered For, All Tasks.

What if you have more time than needed for the project?

You reviewed your finish date and got a happy surprise—you have more time available than your schedule says you need. What to do? It depends, of course, on the type of project, the situation, and the amount of surplus time. You can:

- Use the extra time as buffer against potential risks.
- Add scope. Add tasks you were hoping to include, but thought you wouldn't have the time. Build in a higher level of quality. Increase quantities being produced, if applicable to your project.
- Use the extra time to save money. For example, you might be able to be able to hire two designers instead of three and have those two designers carry out the design tasks in the longer available time.
- Inform your manager or client that you can complete the project sooner than expected.

Checking Your Schedule Assumptions

If you've determined that you need to bring in the finish date, look first at the schedule itself. Make sure that all the scheduling controls you put into place are accurate and required. The fewer controls you impose, the more flexibility Microsoft Project can have with scheduling, and that added flexibility can give you an earlier finish date. In the Gantt Chart or other task sheet, review and update the following:

- Date constraints
- Task dependencies
- Durations
- Task calendars

You can look at all tasks in the project, but to affect the finish date you need only make adjustments to critical tasks. If you shorten the sequence of critical path tasks to the point at which a different sequence is now the critical path, check to see if that path finishes before your target finish date. If it does, switch your focus to that new critical path until you achieve the planned project finish date you need.

Note If you change aspects of your schedule to bring in the finish date, the good news is that you probably won't adversely affect your project triangle. That is, adjusting your schedule to meet your schedule requirements affects only the schedule side of the triangle. Costs and scope will probably stay as they are.

Checking and Adjusting Date Constraints

First, look at any date constraints you've set in your schedule, particularly for your critical tasks. This is where you can potentially make a significant impact on your finish date. To look at the constraints you've applied, follow these steps:

1. Display the Gantt Chart or other task sheet.
2. Click View, Table, More Tables.
3. In the More Tables dialog box, click Constraint Dates and then click Apply.

   The table shows the constraint type and constraint dates for all tasks.

If you have the tasks sorted by Task ID; that is, in their outline sequence, you can review constraints for each task within the context of its surrounding tasks. If you like, you can sort the tasks by constraint type, as follows:

1. Apply the Constraint Dates table to the Gantt Chart or other task sheet.
2. Click Project, Sort, Sort By.
3. In the Sort By dialog box, click Constraint Type and then click Sort.

   The tasks are sorted by constraint type, so you can see where you might have applied a Must Finish On or Start No Later Than constraint, for example. You can also see their associated dates.

To see only the constraints for critical tasks, follow these steps:

1. Apply the Constraint Dates table to the Gantt Chart or other task sheet.
2. Click Project, Filtered For, Critical.

   Only critical tasks are shown. When you want to see all tasks again, click Project, Filtered For, All Tasks.

Make sure that the constraint types and dates you have applied are truly necessary. Wherever you can, change a date constraint to a flexible one such as As Soon As Possible or As Late As Possible. Even changing an inflexible date constraint such as Must Start On or Must Finish On to a moderately flexible date constraint such as Start No Later Than or Finish No Earlier Than can improve your schedule. To change the constraint, do the following:

1. Apply the Constraint Dates table to the Gantt Chart or other task sheet.
2. Click the Constraint Type field, click the arrow, and then click the constraint you want in the list.

Task Information

Tip **Changing all constraints at one time**
Maybe you applied too many date constraints to too many tasks and you just want to start fresh. Select all tasks in the project, either by dragging them or by clicking the Select All box just above the row 1 heading in the upper-left corner of the table. On the Standard toolbar, click Task Information and then click the Advanced tab. In the Constraint Type box, click As Soon As Possible or As Late As Possible. The constraints on all selected tasks are changed.

For more information about constraints, see "Scheduling Tasks to Achieve Specific Dates" on page 157.

Checking and Adjusting Task Dependencies

The second place to check your schedule for critical path-shortening opportunities is your task dependencies. A Gantt Chart is the best view for reviewing task dependencies and their impact on your schedule. View the Tracking Gantt or Detail Gantt so you can see critical tasks highlighted. Focusing on the task dependencies of critical tasks helps you bring in the finish date.

Specifically, examine whether the task dependencies are required. If two tasks don't really depend on each other, remove the link. Or consider whether two tasks can begin at the same time. If so, you can change a finish-to-start dependency to a start-to-start dependency. Change a task dependency as follows:

1. Click the successor task.
2. On the Standard toolbar, click Task Information and then click the Predecessors tab.
3. To change the link type, click in the Type field for the predecessor.
4. Click the arrow and then click the link type you want in the list.

   To remove the link entirely, click anywhere in the predecessor row, and press the Delete key.

Unlink Tasks

Tip **Removing all links**
If you want to start over with your task dependency strategy, you can remove all links in the project. Be sure that this is really what you want to do because it can erase a lot of the work you've done in your project plan.

Click the Select All box just above the row 1 heading in the upper-left corner of the table. On the Standard toolbar, click Unlink Tasks. All links on all tasks are removed.

For more information about task dependencies, see "Establishing Task Dependencies" on page 149.

Checking and Adjusting Durations

After adjusting date constraints and task dependencies, if the finish date is still beyond your target, look at task durations. However, be aware that it's risky to be too optimistic about durations, especially if you used reliable methods such as expert judgment, past project information, industry metrics, or PERT analysis to calculate your current durations.

You can look at durations in the Gantt Chart or most task sheets. If your tasks are sorted by Task ID (that is, in their outline sequence), you can review durations for each task within the context of its surrounding tasks. However, you can also sort tasks by duration so you can see the longer durations first. These longer durations might have more buffer built in, so they might be a good place to trim some time. To sort tasks by duration, follow these steps:

1 Display the Gantt Chart with the Entry table applied, or display another task sheet that includes the Duration field.

2 Click Project, Sort, Sort By.

   The Sort dialog box appears.

3 In the Sort By list, click Duration and then click Sort.

   The tasks are sorted by duration.

4 To see only the durations for critical tasks, click Project, Filtered For, Critical.

   When you want to see all tasks again, click Project, Filtered For, All Tasks.

5 To change a duration, simply type the new duration into the task's Duration field.

   The schedule is recalculated with the new duration.

6 To return to the original task order, click Project, Sort, By ID.

For more information about duration, see "Setting Task Durations" on page 138.

Project Management Practices: Duration Compression

In project management, there are two commonly used methods of shortening a series of tasks without changing the project scope. These two *duration compression* methods are as follows:

Crashing the schedule. The schedule and associated project costs are analyzed to determine how a series of tasks (such as the critical path) can be shortened, or *crashed*, for the least additional cost.

Fast tracking. Tasks normally done in sequence are rescheduled to be done simultaneously (for example, starting to build a prototype before the specifications are approved).

By their nature, both of these methods are risky. It's important to be aware that these methods can increase cost or increase task rework.

Tip **Check and adjust assigned task calendars**
Task calendars can be applied to tasks that can be scheduled beyond the normal project working times calendar; however, sometimes a task calendar indicates a specific frequency with which a task is performed. Examine tasks with their own task calendars to make sure they're accurately reflecting reality and not holding up progress.

Tasks with task calendars assigned display a calendar icon in the Indicators column next to the task name. Place the mouse pointer over the icon to see more information.

For more information about task calendars, see "Working with Task Calendars" on page 169.

Adjusting Resource Settings to Bring in the Finish Date

Another way to bring in the finish date is to adjust your resource settings. You can check that the resource availability affecting assigned task scheduling is accurate. You can also add resources to tasks to decrease task duration. Be aware that increasing resource availability as well as adding resources to tasks usually means an increase in costs.

Checking and Adjusting Resource Availability

The more availability your resources have, the sooner their assigned tasks can be completed. For example, a 4-day task assigned to a resource who works a regular 5-day week will be completed in 4 days. The same 4-day task assigned to a resource who works a 2-day week will be completed in 2 weeks. For resources assigned to critical tasks, review and update the following:

- Resource calendars
- Resource (maximum) units
- Assignment units

The Task Entry view is best for checking these three items. Apply the view, set the Task Form to show the resource information you need, and filter for critical tasks, as follows:

1. Click View, More Views.
2. In the More Views dialog box, click Task Entry and then click Apply.
3. To view critical tasks, click in the Gantt Chart (upper) portion of the view. Click Project, Filtered For, Critical.

   Only critical tasks are displayed. You can also click View, Tracking Gantt. Critical tasks are shown in red.
4. Click in the Task Form (lower) portion of the view. Click Format, Details, Resource Work (see Figure 9-11).

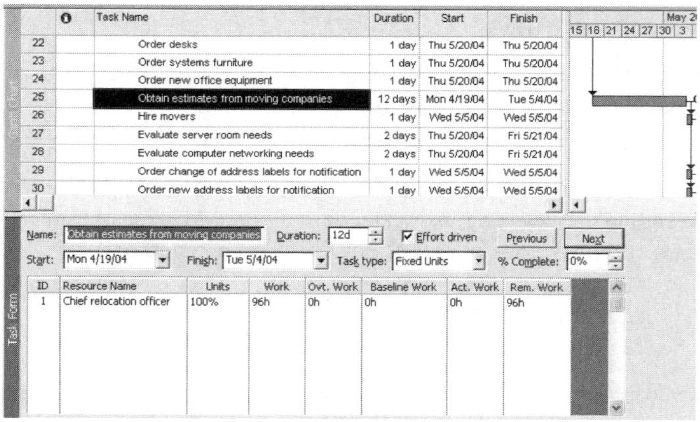

Figure 9-11. The Task Entry view is now set up to check resource and assignment availability.

5 Click a critical task in the Gantt chart portion of the view.

The resources assigned to the selected task are listed in the Task Form portion of the view.

6 To check the resource calendar for this assigned resource, double-click the resource name. The Resource Information dialog box appears. Click the Working Time tab. Check the working times set for this resource and make sure they're correct.

For more information about resource calendars, see "Setting Resource Working Time Calendars" on page 187.

7 To check resource units, click the General tab in the Resource Information dialog box. Under Resource Availability, check the resource units and associated dates, if applicable, and make sure they're correct.

For more information about resource units, see "Specifying Resource Availability" on page 184.

8 To check assignment units, review the Units field next to the resource name in the Task Form and make sure the setting is correct.

Tip See if your resources have more to give

You can check your resources' working time calendar, their resource units, and their assignment units—and everything might look correct. Find out if your resources can provide any more time on this project or on critical tasks to help bring in the finish date. It doesn't hurt to ask, at least.

Adding Resources to Decrease Duration

A key method of shortening the critical path and bringing in the project finish date is to add resources to critical tasks in such a way that it decreases the task's duration. For example, two people working together might be able to complete a development task in half the time it takes either of them individually. For this to be the case, the tasks must be either fixed-units and effort-driven, or fixed-work tasks. They cannot be fixed-duration tasks, for obvious reasons.

With fixed-units effort-driven scheduling, which is the default for tasks in Microsoft Project, when you assign an additional resource to a task that already has assigned resources, the amount of work scheduled for each assigned resource decreases. Likewise, when you remove a resource from an effort-driven task, the amount of work scheduled for each assigned resource increases.

The same is true for fixed-work tasks, which are effort-driven by definition. When you add or remove resources (that is, assignment units) on a fixed-work task, duration changes but work remains fixed, of course.

For more information about effort-driven scheduling, see "Controlling Changes with Effort-Driven Scheduling" on page 223. For more information about task types, see "Controlling Schedule Changes with Task Types," on page 224.

To check the task type of an individual task, follow these steps:

1. In a task sheet, such as the Gantt Chart, double-click the task.
2. In the Task Information dialog box, click the Advanced tab.
3. Review the Task Type list and the Effort Driven check box. Make any changes necessary.

You can add the task type and effort-driven fields to a task sheet so you can see the scheduling methods for all tasks at a glance, as follows:

1. Display the task sheet to which you want to add the new columns.
2. Click the column heading to the right of where you want the new column to be inserted.
3. Click Insert, Column.
4. In the Field Name box, select Type.

   Type **ty** to move quickly to the Type field in the list.
5. Click OK, and the task types are shown in the task sheet.

   You can use this field to quickly change task types.
6. Follow steps 1–5 to add the Effort Driven field to the task sheet.

   This field displays Yes or No, indicating whether the task is effort-driven.

When you assign additional resources to your fixed-units and effort-driven or fixed-work critical tasks, the duration of those critical tasks is reduced, and therefore the length of the critical path is reduced.

Note Be aware that as you add resources to critical tasks, you run the risk of reduced productivity. There might be additional overhead associated with bringing on additional resources. More support might be needed to get those resources up to speed on the tasks, and you might lose whatever time savings you thought you might gain. Take care to add resources who are experienced enough to hit the ground running so your efforts don't backfire on you.

Project Management Practices: The Right Resources for Critical Tasks

Having overallocated resources assigned to critical tasks can push out your finish date. If you level overallocated resources, their assignments are rescheduled to times when they can perform them. Even if you do not level overallocated resources, and even if your schedule shows that there's no slip, this doesn't mean it will not happen. An overallocated resource has to let something slip..By leveling, you can see realistically when tasks can be done and make the necessary adjustments to make sure critical tasks are not late.

As much as possible, shift assignments to evenly distribute the resource workload and to ensure that resources working on critical tasks are not overallocated.

For more information about leveling, see "Leveling Assignments," later in this chapter on page 285.

If you have an overallocated resource assigned to critical tasks and an underallocated resource with the right skills and availability, you can switch to or add the underallocated resources to the critical tasks to shorten their durations.

Also, check that the fastest and more experienced resources are assigned to the longer or more difficult critical tasks. Although adjusting assignments might or might not actually reduce the duration, it significantly reduces the risk of critical tasks needing rework or being otherwise delayed.

Note You can also adjust scope to bring in the finish date.

For more information about cutting scope, see "Changing Project Scope" later in this chapter on page 293.

Reducing Project Costs

A budget-constrained project is one in which costs are the most important factor in the project plan. Although you still need to balance schedule requirements and satisfy the project scope, the costs are at the forefront of your decision-making processes as you plan and execute the project.

If your project plan calculates that your total costs are above the allowed budget, you need cost-cutting strategies. Your best approach will involve cutting resources because resources and costs are virtually synonymous in projects. As described in the previous section, when you want to bring in the finish date, you focus on tasks in the critical path. In the same way, when you want to cut costs, you focus on resources to gain the biggest cost savings.

Viewing Project Costs

Review your cost picture first, compare it with your budget, and then make any necessary adjustments. To review total project costs using Project Statistics, do the following:

1. Click Project, Project Information.
2. In the Project Information dialog box, click the Statistics button.

   The Project Statistics dialog box appears. The current or scheduled total project cost appears in the Cost column.

You can also see the total project cost in the Project Summary Task when you apply the Cost table, as follows:

1. Display the Gantt Chart or other task sheet.
2. Click View, Table, Cost. The Cost table is applied.
3. Click Tools, Options and then click the View tab.
4. Under Outline Options, select the Show Project Summary Task check box and then click OK.

   The project summary task row appears at the top of the task sheet. The total project cost, as currently scheduled, is displayed in the Total Cost field.

Two cost reports can help you analyze project costs, as follows:

Budget report. Click View, Reports. Double-click Costs and then double-click Budget (see Figure 9-12). The Total Cost column is a summary of the resource costs and fixed costs for each task.

Office Move

Task Name	Fixed Cost	Fixed Cost Accrual	Total Cost
Identify potential office sites	$0.00	Prorated	$4,800.00
Obtain estimates from moving compan	$0.00	Prorated	$2,880.00
Design office space	$0.00	Prorated	$2,760.00
Make final decision on office space	$0.00	Prorated	$2,400.00
Finalize lease on office space	$0.00	Prorated	$2,400.00
Identify costs for new office (chairs, de	$0.00	Prorated	$2,400.00
Prepare a budget for the move	$0.00	Prorated	$2,400.00
Inventory existing computers	$0.00	Prorated	$2,000.00
Identify major tenant improvement nee	$0.00	Prorated	$1,800.00
Make list of key needs that must be m	$0.00	Prorated	$1,680.00
Install phone system	$0.00	Prorated	$1,600.00
Obtain necessary permits	$0.00	Prorated	$1,200.00
Pack up desks, personal spaces	$0.00	Prorated	$1,200.00

Figure 9-12. Run the Budget report to view costs for each task.

Cash Flow report. Click View, Reports. Double-click Costs and then double-click Cash Flow (see Figure 9-13). This report forecasts the funding needed for each period of time, enabling you to see whether budgeted costs will be exceeded at a particular point.

Cash Flow
Office Move

	12/28/03	1/4/04	1/11/04	1/18/04
Office Move				
Two To Six Months Before Moving Day				
Make list of key needs that must be met by new office space	$480.00	$1,200.00		
Identify potential office sites			$1,200.00	$1,200.00
Make final decision on office space				
Finalize lease on office space				
Identify major tenant improvement needs				

Figure 9-13. Run the Cash Flow report to see cost forecasts by time period.

You can sort a sheet view by costs. To review task or resource costs in order of amount, do the following:

1. Display a task sheet or resource sheet, depending on whether you want to see costs by resource or by task.

2. Click View, Table, Cost.
3. Click Project, Sort, By Cost.

   The sheet is sorted by the Total Cost field. To return to the original sort order, click Project, Sort, By ID.

You can filter a sheet view to display only tasks or resources that have costs exceeding a specified amount. To do this, follow these steps:

1. Display a task sheet or resource sheet, depending on whether you want to see costs by resource or by task.
2. Click View, Table, Cost.
3. Click Project, Filtered For, More Filters.
4. In the More Filters dialog box, click Cost Greater Than and then click Apply.
5. In the Cost Greater Than dialog box, enter the amount (see Figure 9-14).

   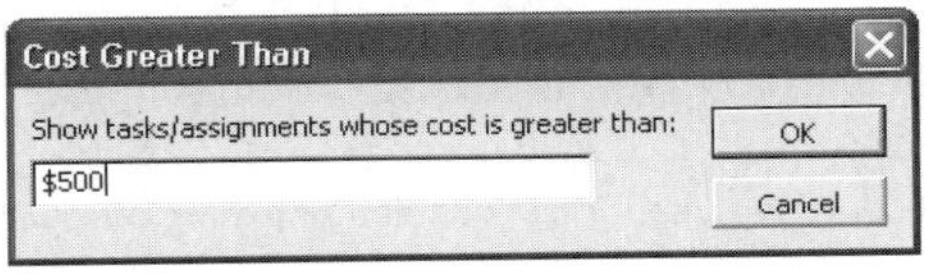

   Figure 9-14. To see only those tasks or assignments that have a scheduled cost exceeding a certain amount, enter the amount in this dialog box.

   To see all tasks or all resources again, click Project, Filtered For, All Tasks or All Resources.

What if you have more money than you need?

If you investigate your total project costs and discover that you have more budget than costs, you have some decisions to make. Depending on the type of project, the situation, and the amount of extra budget, you can:

- Reserve the buffer. Use the extra funds as insurance against potential risks.
- Add resources. Use the money to hire resources and take some of the load off overallocated resources or bring in the finish date.
- Add scope. Add tasks you were hoping to include, but thought you wouldn't have enough money to do. Build in a higher level of quality. If applicable, increase quantities being produced.
- Inform your manager or client that you can complete the project well under budget.

Checking Your Cost Assumptions

If you find that your scheduled costs are higher than your budget, first review the individual costs themselves. Check the resource rates as well as fixed costs for tasks and make sure they're accurate.

To check resource rates, review the Resource Sheet with the Entry table applied. With the default fields in the Entry table, you can see each resource's standard rate, overtime rate, and cost per use.

To check fixed costs for tasks, review a task sheet such as the Gantt Chart with the Cost table applied. The Fixed Cost field displays any costs associated with the tasks that are independent of resource costs.

Adjusting the Schedule to Reduce Costs

If many of your resource costs are based on time periods such as an amount per hour or per day, you might be able to cut costs if you can reduce task durations. For example, suppose you have a 2-day fixed-units task assigned to a $100/hour resource. By default, this resource is assigned to 16 hours of work, for a cost of $1600. If you reduce the duration to 1 day, the work is reduced to 8 hours, and the cost is reduced to $800.

When you reduce task duration in a fixed-units or fixed-duration task, the amount of work is also reduced. However, if you reduce duration for a fixed-work task, work stays the same and assignment units increase. In this case, resource costs would not be reduced.

For more information about changing durations, see "Checking and Adjusting Durations" earlier in this chapter.

Adjusting Assignments to Reduce Costs

Another way to reduce work and therefore cut costs is to reduce work directly. In effect, you're cutting the amount of time that resources are spending on assigned tasks.

The manner in which a work reduction affects your task and resource scheduling depends on the individual task types. When you decrease work in a fixed-units or fixed-work task, duration is reduced. When you decrease work in a fixed-duration task, units are decreased.

To change work amounts for individual resources, display the Task Usage view or Resource Usage view, and edit the Work field for the assignment.

Strategies for Reducing Resource Costs

The following are suggestions for reducing resource costs by adjusting assignments:

- If you have assignments with multiple resources assigned, reduce the work for the more expensive resources and assign the work to less expensive resources. By shuffling work around on an assignment, you won't risk changing duration or units inadvertently.
- If you have resources with the same skills and availability, replace the more expensive work or material resources with less expensive ones. Although this replacement can introduce some risk into your project, it can also ensure that you're using your expensive resources where you really need them.

- If you have resources with the same skills and availability, replace slower work or equipment resources with faster ones. If one resource is faster than another, you might save money, even if the faster resource's rate is higher.
- If you have material resources whose costs are based on assignment units, for example, 3 tons or 100 yards, decrease the assignment units; that is, use less of the material.

Note You can also adjust scope to cut costs.

For more information about cutting scope, see "Changing Project Scope" later in this chapter on page 293.

Balancing Resource Workloads

Sometimes, the use of resources is the most important limitation on a project. In the resource-constrained project, you need to make sure that all the resources are used well, are doing the right tasks, and are neither underallocated nor overallocated. That is, you need to examine workloads and allocations and then fix any problems you find. You still need to keep your eye on the schedule and your costs, but schedule and costs are secondary to resource utilization in this type of project.

Balancing resource workloads isn't really part of the project triangle. However, you can adjust scope—add or remove tasks—to balance workload. You can also adjust the schedule—split or delay tasks until resources have time to work on them. Finally, you can adjust costs—add more money to pay for additional resources to help balance the workload.

Inside Out

Project's prime directive

Although resource management is typically a large part of the project manager's job, it's important to keep in mind that the primary job of Microsoft Project is to schedule and track tasks. Traditionally, the resource management functions of Microsoft Project have been more rudimentary. However, starting with Microsoft Project 2002 and certainly with Microsoft Project 2003, there are more features devoted to resource management than in past versions. The new resource availability features attest to this, as do the continuing improvements in team collaboration and delegation capabilities through Microsoft Office Project Server 2003 and Microsoft Office Project Web Access 2003. The Resource Substitution Wizard, Enterprise Resource Pool, Team Builder, and other enterprise resource features available through Microsoft Office Project Professional 2003 have taken resource management in projects to a higher level.

Viewing Resource Workloads

When you analyze resource workloads, you're actually reviewing the way resources are assigned. The optimum situation is when all resources in your project are assigned at their full availability, no more and no less, throughout their time on the project.

However, there might be resources for whom you are not able to fill every hour. These resources are said to be *underallocated*. You might have to pay for these resources' time even when they're not directly carrying out project tasks, and therefore can adversely affect your project budget.

Other resources might consistently have more work than time. These resources are *overallocated*. Such a situation represents risk to the project. If there's more work than available time, it's highly probable that deadlines will be missed, quality will suffer, costs will increase, or scope will have to be cut.

At this point in the project, just before work actually begins, you can look at scheduled underallocations and overallocations, make the necessary changes to maximize your resource contributions, and reduce your risk from overallocation. The goal is to balance the workload as much as possible so that you're not wasting resource dollars and burning out a handful of key resources.

Troubleshooting

Tasks scheduled at the same time are causing overallocations

You influence how tasks and assignments are scheduled by specifying resource availability through their working time calendars, resource units (maximum units), and assignment units. Within those limitations, however, Microsoft Project might still schedule multiple tasks for the same time frame, which can cause overallocations.

For example, suppose there's a resource with a working time calendar specifying that she works on this project only on Tuesdays. When you assign a task to her, that task is scheduled to accommodate the fact that work will be done only on Tuesdays. When you assign a 5-day task to her, by default, this assignment will take 40 hours, which will stretch across 5 weeks.

Likewise, suppose there's another resource who works half-time. His resource units are 50 percent. When you assign a task to him, by default, his assignment units are also 50 percent. So by default, a 5-day task does not translate to 40 hours in a week, but rather 20 hours.

However, if you have two 1-day tasks assigned to the same resource at the same time, both assignments will be scheduled for the resource at the same time, and therefore that resource will be overallocated.

You can resolve overallocations by following the strategies outlined in "Adjusting Assignments" on page 278 and "Leveling Assignments" on page 285.

You can use one of several Microsoft Project views to review how much work is assigned to a resource in any selected time period, as follows:

Resource Graph. Click View, Resource Graph (see Figure 9-15). In the default Peak Units format, the Resource Graph displays how much the resource is being utilized, in terms of maximum units, for the time period specified in the timescale.

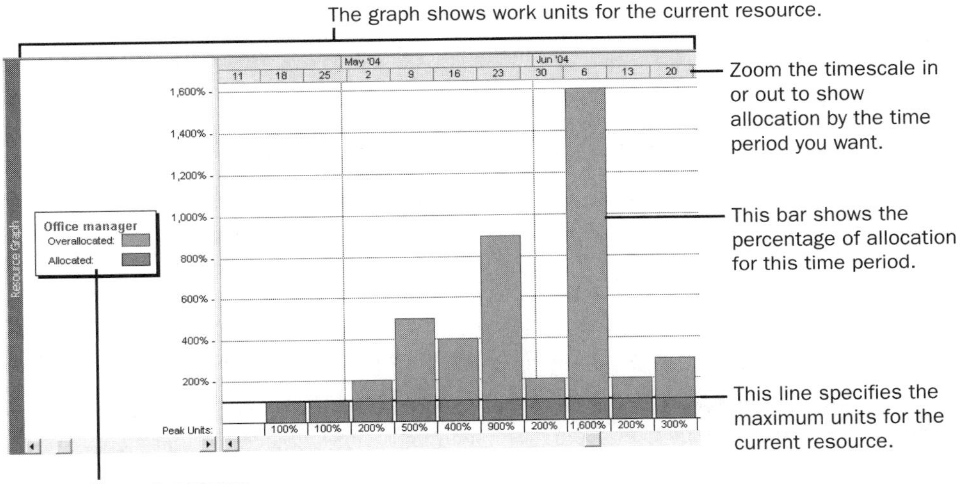

Figure 9-15. The Resource Graph displays resource utilization, one resource at a time.

Zoom In

Zoom Out

To see resource allocation information by different measures, click Format, Details, and then pick a different format such as Overallocation or Percent Allocation.

To change the timescale, click the Zoom In or Zoom Out buttons.

To see information for a different resource, press the Page Down or Page Up buttons.

Resource Usage view. Click View, Resource Usage. Each resource is listed with all assigned tasks (see Figure 9-16). The timesheet portion of the view shows how work is allocated over the selected time period. As in all resource views, overallocated resources are shown in red. In the timesheet portion, any work that exceeds the resource availability for the time period is also shown in red.

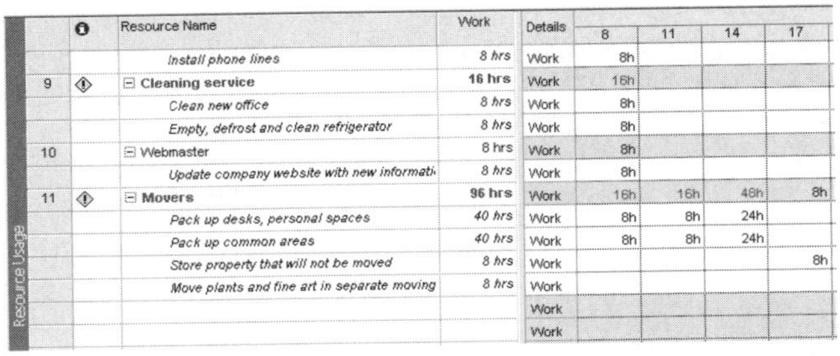

		Resource Name	Work	Details	8	11	14	17
		Install phone lines	8 hrs	Work	8h			
9		⊟ Cleaning service	16 hrs	Work	16h			
		Clean new office	8 hrs	Work	8h			
		Empty, defrost and clean refrigerator	8 hrs	Work	8h			
10		⊟ Webmaster	8 hrs	Work	8h			
		Update company website with new informati	8 hrs	Work	8h			
11		⊟ Movers	96 hrs	Work	16h	16h	48h	8h
		Pack up desks, personal spaces	40 hrs	Work	8h	8h	24h	
		Pack up common areas	40 hrs	Work	8h	8h	24h	
		Store property that will not be moved	8 hrs	Work				8h
		Move plants and fine art in separate moving	8 hrs	Work				
				Work				
				Work				

Figure 9-16. The Resource Usage view can help you notice periods of overallocation.

Resource Allocation view. Click View, More Views and then click Resource Allocation. This is a combination view, with the Resource Usage view in the upper portion of the view and the Leveling Gantt in the lower portion (see Figure 9-17).

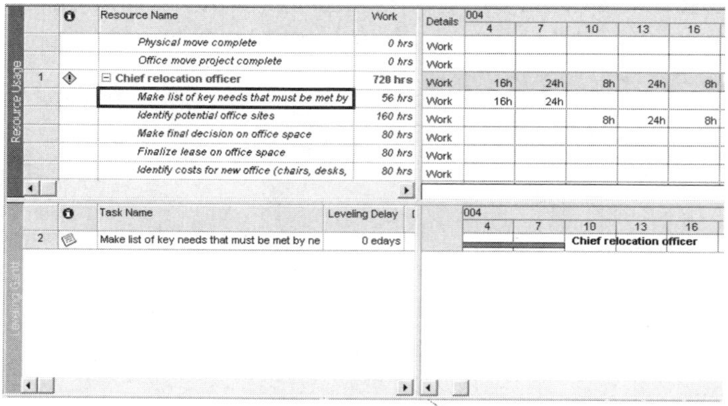

Figure 9-17. The Leveling Gantt portion displays details about the tasks assigned to the resource selected in the Resource Usage view.

Go To Next Overallocation

Tip Use the Resource Management toolbar to find overallocated resources
Click View, Toolbars, Resource Management. The Resource Management toolbar (see Figure 9-18) includes a variety of functions that help you work with your resources. As you're analyzing resource overallocations, click the Go To Next Overallocation button to find and review the assignments for each overallocated resource in turn.

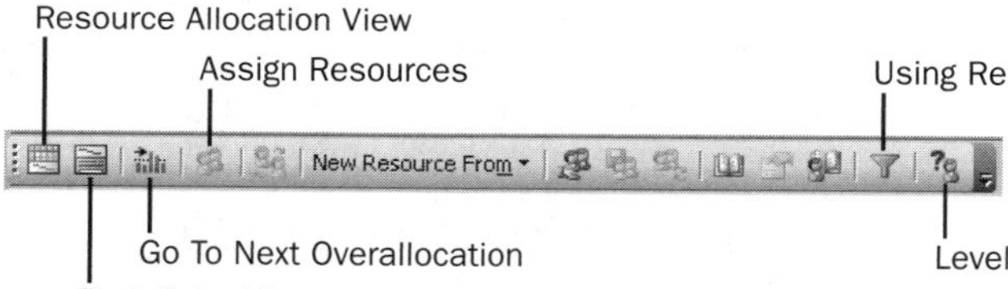

Figure 9-18. The Resource Management toolbar includes a variety of functions that help you work with your resources.

Note When you want to switch to another view from a combination view, remember to remove the split in the window. Click Window, Remove Split, or double-click the split bar. When you switch to the view you want, it'll appear in the full screen.

Resource Form. With a resource sheet view displayed, such as the Resource Sheet or Resource Usage view, click Window, Split. The Resource Form appears in the lower portion of the view with the resource sheet in the upper portion (see Figure 9-19).

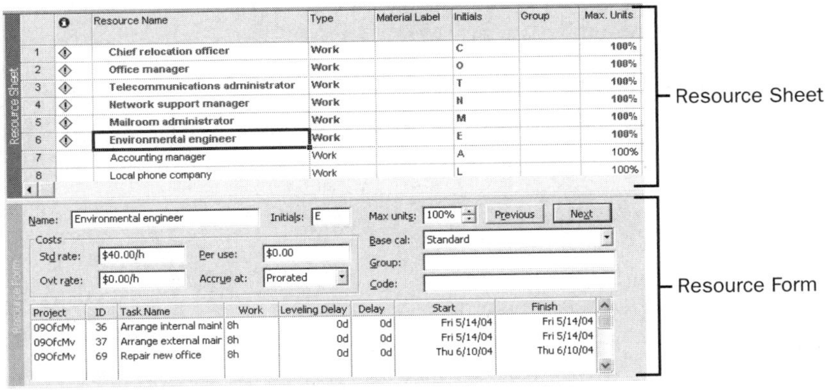

Figure 9-19. The Resource Form displays details about the resource selected in the upper portion of the view.

Inside Out

No clue about overallocations in task views

Task views do not indicate when resources are overallocated, which can be a problem because you're assigning tasks in a task view. Even the Assign Resources dialog box doesn't give an indication unless you apply the Available To Work filter.

To see which resources have too much work assigned, switch from a task view to a resource view. Overallocated resources are highlighted in red.

To see at a glance which tasks have overallocated resources assigned, add the Overallocated column to a task sheet. To do this, click the column heading to the left of where you want to insert the Overallocated column. Click Insert, Column. In the Field Name box, click Overallocated. This is a Yes/No field. Any tasks that have overallocated resources assigned display a Yes. You can sort by the Overallocated field so you can better focus on balancing the assignments for those tasks. Be aware that by default, even resources overallocated by a couple hours in just one week are marked as overallocated.

Another means of seeing how your resources are allocated is to run assignment-related reports, as follows:

Who Does What When report. Click View, Reports. Double-click Assignments and then double-click Who Does What When. This report displays the amount of work for each resource by day and by assignment (see Figure 9-20).

Who Does What When
Office Move

	3/13	3/14	3/15	3/16	3/17	3/18
Chief relocation officer			8 hrs	8 hrs	8 hrs	8 hrs
Make list of key needs that must be met by new office space						
Identify potential office sites						
Make final decision on office space						
Finalize lease on office space						
Identify costs for new office (chairs, desks, equipment)						
Prepare a budget for the move			8 hrs	8 hrs	8 hrs	8 hrs
Select the move day						
Obtain necessary permits						
Communicate to employees						
Obtain estimates from moving companies						
Hire movers						
Create a moving day team to provide direction to movers						
Put moving day team in place						
Schedule open house for clients						
Office manager			8 hrs	8 hrs	8 hrs	8 hrs
Identify major tenant improvement needs			8 hrs	8 hrs	8 hrs	8 hrs
Obtain estimates from contractors for major tenant improvements						
Hire contractors for major tenant improvements						
Design office space						

Figure 9-20. Run the Who Does What When report to see assignment details by day.

Overallocated Resources report. Click View, Reports. Double-click Assignments and then double-click Overallocated Resources. This report displays only overallocated resource information (see Figure 9-21). If there are no overallocated resources, no report is generated.

Overallocated Resources
Office Move

ID		Resource Name	Work
1	◆	Chief relocation officer	720 hrs

ID	Task Name	Units	Work	Delay	Start
2	Make list of key needs that must be met by new office space	100%	56 hrs	0 days	Thu 1/1/04
3	Identify potential office sites	100%	160 hrs	0 days	Mon 1/12/04
4	Make final decision on office space	100%	80 hrs	0 days	Mon 2/9/04
5	Finalize lease on office space	100%	80 hrs	0 days	Mon 2/23/04
6	Identify costs for new office (chairs, desks, equipment)	100%	80 hrs	0 days	Mon 2/23/04
9	Prepare a budget for the move	100%	80 hrs	0 days	Mon 3/8/04
10	Select the move day	100%	8 hrs	0 days	Mon 3/8/04
12	Obtain necessary permits	100%	40 hrs	0 days	Mon 4/12/04
16	Communicate to employees	100%	8 hrs	0 days	Mon 3/8/04
25	Obtain estimates from moving companies	100%	96 hrs	0 days	Mon 4/19/04
28	Hire movers	100%	8 hrs	0 days	Wed 5/5/04
99	Create a moving day team to provide direction to movers	100%	8 hrs	0 days	Thu 6/10/04
103	Put moving day team in place	100%	8 hrs	0 days	Thu 6/24/04
113	Schedule open house for clients	100%	8 hrs	0 days	Fri 6/25/04

ID		Resource Name	Work
9	◆	Cleaning service	16 hrs

ID	Task Name	Units	Work	Delay	Start	Finish
70	Clean new office	100%	8 hrs	0 days	Thu 6/10/04	Thu 6/10/04
97	Empty, defrost and clean refrigerator	100%	8 hrs	0 days	Thu 6/10/04	Thu 6/10/04

ID		Resource Name	Work
6	◆	Environmental engineer	24 hrs

ID	Task Name	Units	Work	Delay	Start	Finish
36	Arrange internal maintenance service	100%	8 hrs	0 days	Fri 5/14/04	Fri 5/14/04
37	Arrange external maintenance service	100%	8 hrs	0 days	Fri 5/14/04	Fri 5/14/04
69	Repair new office	100%	8 hrs	0 days	Thu 6/10/04	Thu 6/10/04

Figure 9-21. Run the Overallocated Resources report to see assignment information about units and work for each overallocated resource.

Resource Usage report. Click View, Reports. Double-click Workload and then double-click Resource Usage. This report displays the amount of work each week by resource and assignment. Totals are included for the resource, assignment, and week (see Figure 9-22).

Resource Usage
Office Move

	5/2/04	5/9/04	5/16/04	5/23/04	5/30/04	6/6/04
Order new address labels for notification	8 hrs					
Send change of address to all vendors				8 hrs		
Send change of address to all customers				8 hrs		
Send change of address to all subscriptions				8 hrs		
Identify closest overnight drop off boxes						8 hrs
Get shipping labels						8 hrs
Notify post office of change of address						8 hrs
Order moving boxes						8 hrs
Periodically visit old office to pick up mail						
Environmental engineer		16 hrs				8 hrs
Arrange internal maintenance service		8 hrs				
Arrange external maintenance service		8 hrs				
Repair new office						8 hrs
Accounting manager				16 hrs	8 hrs	
Appraise assets being transferred to new location				16 hrs	8 hrs	
Local phone company						8 hrs
Install phone lines						8 hrs
Cleaning service						16 hrs
Clean new office						8 hrs
Empty, defrost and clean refrigerator						8 hrs
Webmaster						8 hrs
Update company website with new information						8 hrs
Movers						32 hrs
Pack up desks, personal spaces						16 hrs
Pack up common areas						16 hrs
Store property that will not be moved						
Move plants and fine art in separate moving van						
Total	104 hrs	120 hrs	128 hrs	168 hrs	56 hrs	320 hrs

Figure 9-22. Run the Resource Usage report to see assignment details by week.

Reports are particularly useful for resource management meetings or team status meetings. Remember that you can also print views for hardcopy distribution.

You can filter a view to examine task allocation, as follows:

- In a resource sheet like the Resource Usage view, click Project, Filtered For, Overallocated Resources.
- In a task sheet like the Gantt Chart, click Project, Filtered For, Using Resource.

  Enter the name of the resource whose tasks you want to see.
- When you want to see all resources or tasks again, click Project, Filtered, For, All Resources or All Tasks.

Tip **Use the Project Guide to review resource allocation**
On the Project Guide toolbar, click Report. Click the See How Resources' Time Is Allocated link. The view changes to a combination view, including the Resource Usage view and Gantt Chart. Additional information is provided in the Project Guide side pane.

What If You Have More Resources Than You Need for the Project?

If you have more resources than needed for the project, you need to determine whether this is a help or a hindrance. Depending on the type of project, the situation, and the number of extra resources, you can do one of the following:

- If the underallocated resources have the same skills and availability as other resources that are overallocated, you can use them to balance the workload.

Chapter 9

- Even if you have no overallocations, consider assigning multiple resources to tasks to shorten the schedule.
- If you can't use the resources, find another project for them. Having extra people without work can get in the way of progress on the project. It can also place an unnecessary burden on your budget.

Adjusting Resource Availability

If you find that resources are overallocated or underallocated, check with the resources to see whether their availability can be modified to reflect how they're needed on the project. For example, if a full-time resource is consistently 50 percent underallocated throughout the life of the project, you might consider changing his units to 50 percent and making him available as a 50 percent resource on another project. Or if a part-time resource is consistently 20 percent overallocated, ask her if she can add more time to her availability on the project.

To change resource units, in a resource sheet, double-click the resource name to open the Resource Information dialog box. Click the General tab. In the Resource Availability table, specify the units in the Units field. If necessary, enter the starting and ending dates of the new levels of availability.

To change a resource's working time calendar, click the Working Time tab in the Resource Information dialog box. Make the necessary changes to increase or decrease the resource's working time on the project.

Adjusting Assignments

You can shift assignments around to fix overallocations and underallocations. This shifting assumes, however, that you have resources with similar skills and availability who can fulfill the necessary tasks.

If you can't add or replace resources to take the burden off overallocated resources, you might be able to delay tasks or assignments until the resources have time to work on them. Or you can simply add overtime work to account for the overallocation.

Adding More Resources to Tasks

You can add underallocated resources to tasks to assist overallocated resources. Depending on the task type, you can distribute the work or the assignment units among the assigned resources, thereby balancing the workload better.

For more information about adding resources to tasks, including the impact of effort-driven scheduling and the different task types, see "Adjusting Resource Settings to Bring in the Finish Date" earlier in this chapter.

Replacing Overallocated Resources

You can replace an overallocated resource on an assignment with an underallocated one as long as they have the same skills and availability. To replace a resource on a task, do the following:

1. In a task sheet such as the Gantt Chart, select the task for which you want to replace resources.
2. On the Standard toolbar, click Assign Resources.

Assign Resources

3. In the Assign Resources dialog box, click the resource you want to replace.

   The currently assigned resources have check marks next to their names.
4. Click the Replace button.

   The Replace Resource dialog box appears (see Figure 9-23).

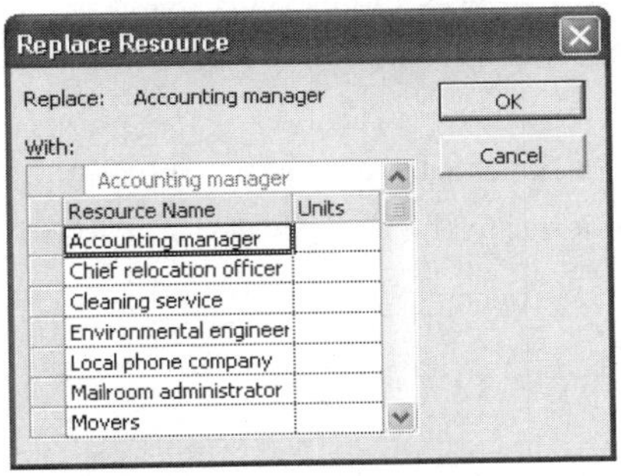

Figure 9-23. Use the Replace Resource dialog box to remove one resource and add a different one in a single operation.

5. Click the resource you want to add to the task and then click OK.

   The old resource is replaced with the new one.

Delaying a Task or Assignment

You can delay a task or assignment until the assigned resource has time to work on it, as follows:

Leveling delay. This is a *task delay*—the amount of time that should pass from the task's scheduled start date until work on the task should actually begin. It delays all assignments for the task. *Leveling delay* can also be automatically calculated and added by the Microsoft Project leveling feature.

For more information about leveling, see "Leveling Assignments" later in this chapter on page 285.

Note Don't confuse lag time with task delay. Lag time is the amount of time to wait after the predecessor is finished (or has started, depending on the link type) before a successor task should start.

For more information about lag time, see "Delaying Linked Tasks by Adding Lag Time" on page 154.

Assignment delay. This is the amount of time that should pass from the task's scheduled start date until the assignment's scheduled start date.

Because it's best to delay within available slack time, review the tasks or assignments in context of their slack time and then add delay as time is available. Otherwise, you could push out the finish date of the task (or even of the project) if it's a critical task. To check available slack, do the following:

1. Click View, More Views. In the More Views dialog box, click Resource Allocation and then click Apply.
2. Click the Resource Usage portion of the view and then click the resource or assignment for which you want to examine slack and possibly delay.
3. Click the Leveling Gantt portion of the view.
4. Click View, Table, Schedule.
5. Review the Free Slack and Total Slack fields to find tasks that have slack (see Figure 9-24).

   You need to drag the vertical split bar to the right to see these fields.

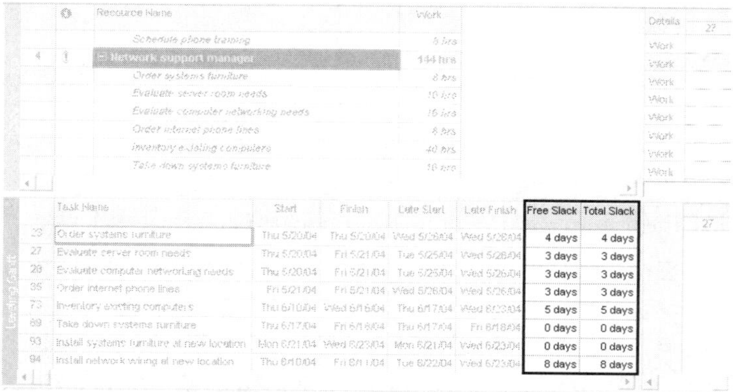

Figure 9-24. Use the Schedule table in the Resource Allocation view to find available slack in which to add task delay.

6. Also review the chart portion of the Leveling Gantt. The thin bars to the right of the regular Gantt bars show any available slack (see Figure 9-25).

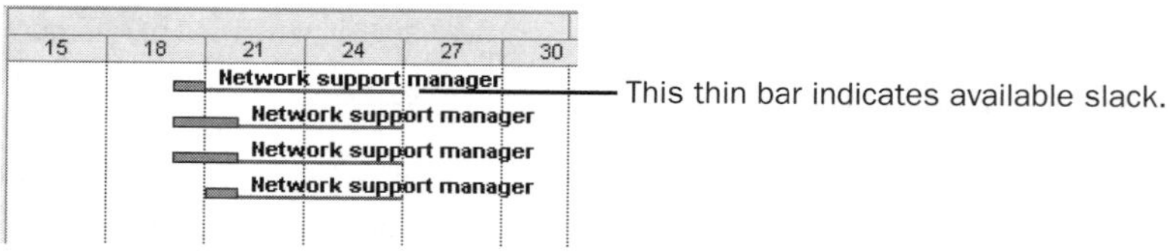

Figure 9-25. Use the Leveling Gantt portion of the Resource Allocation view to find available slack in which to add task delay.

After you find tasks with slack that you can use, add leveling delay as follows:

1. With the Resource Allocation view displayed, click the Leveling Gantt portion of the view.
2. Click View, Table, More Tables. In the More Tables dialog box, click Delay, and then click Apply.
3. In the Resource Usage portion of the view, click the assignment whose task you want to delay.
4. In the Leveling Gantt portion of the view, enter the amount of time you want to delay the task in the Leveling Delay field.

If you want to delay an individual assignment for a task that has multiple resources assigned, add assignment delay instead of leveling delay, as follows:

1. With the Resource Allocation view displayed, click the Resource Usage portion of the view.
2. Click the column heading to the right of where you want to insert the Assignment Delay column.
3. Click Insert, Column.
4. In the Field Name box, click Assignment Delay and then click OK.
5. In the Assignment Delay field of the assignment you want to delay, enter the length of the delay.

   This entry indicates how much time after the task's start date the resource is to wait before starting work on this assignment.

Specifying Overtime Work to Account for Overallocations

Often, you can't reassign overallocated work to other resources or delay a task until later. In this case, overtime might be the answer.

Microsoft Project does not automatically assign overtime or the associated overtime pay rate when a resource's work exceeds your definition of a normal workday (for example, 8 hours) or a normal workweek (for example, 40 hours). You need to specify overtime work, in addition to total work, for the resource.

For example, suppose a resource is assigned to 10 hours of work in a day. You can specify 2 of those hours as overtime work. The work still totals 10 hours, but 8 hours are regular work and 2 hours are overtime.

Regular work, overtime work, and total work

When working with overtime, it's important to keep your work terminology straight; otherwise, it can get confusing. The Work field is actually *total work*, that is, the total amount of time that this resource is assigned to this task.

When you add overtime on an assignment, that amount is stored in the Overtime Work field, and the (total) Work amount stays the same.

Another field, Regular Work, contains the amount of regular (non-overtime) work, based on your amount of total work and overtime work, according to the following calculation:

Regular Work + Overtime Work = (total) Work.

You can add the Regular Work field to a sheet view if you want to see the amount of regular work schedules for a resource, in relation to overtime work and (total) work.

To specify overtime work for overallocated resources, first set up a view containing overtime work fields, as follows:

1. Click View, Resource Usage.
2. Click the column heading for the Work field.
3. Click Insert, Column.
4. In the Field Name box, click Overtime Work. Click OK.

   The Overtime Work field is added to the Resource Usage view.
5. Click Format, Detail Styles.

   The Detail Styles dialog box appears (see Figure 9-26).

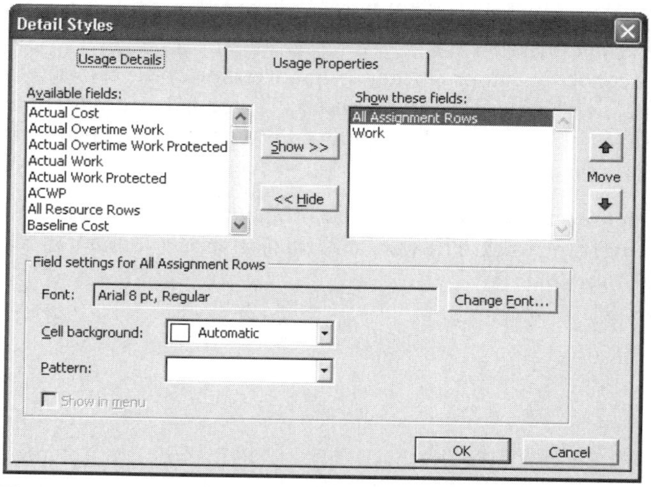

Figure 9-26. Use the Detail Styles dialog box to add another row of timephased information to the timesheet portion of the Resource Usage or Task Usage view.

6 In the Available Fields box, click Overtime Work and then click Show.

The Overtime Work field appears in the Show These Fields box.

7 Click OK.

The Overtime Work field is added to the timesheet portion of the view (see Figure 9-27).

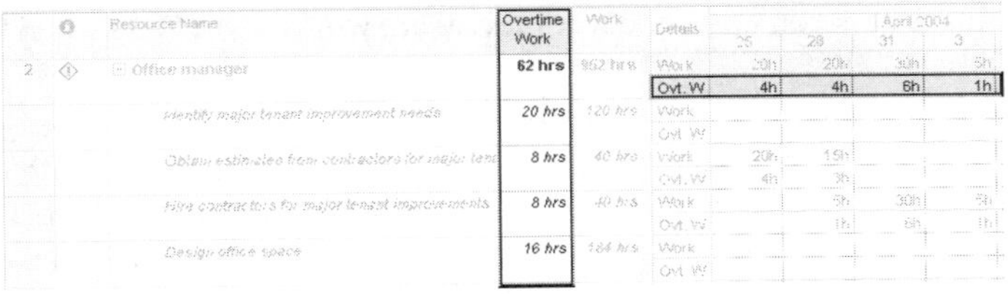

Figure 9-27. Add the Overtime Work field to the sheet and timesheet portion of the Resource Usage view.

> **Tip** **Adding the Regular Work field**
> You might also find it helpful to add the Regular Work field to the sheet portion of the Resource Usage view. Click the Work field and then click Insert, Column. In the Field Name box, click Regular Work and then click OK.

To specify overtime work for overallocated resources, follow these steps:

1. In the Resource Usage view containing the Overtime Work field, find the first overallocated resource (highlighted in red) for whom you want to add overtime work.
2. Under the overallocated resource, review the assignments and the hours in the timesheet portion of the view. Find the assignments that are contributing to the overallocated work amounts.
3. In the sheet portion of the view, in the Overtime Work field for the assignment, enter the amount of overtime you want to designate.

   You do not change the work amount because the overtime work amount is a portion of the total work. The amount you enter in the Overtime Work field is distributed across the time span of the assignment, which you can see in the timesheet portion of the view. For example, if an assignment spans 3 days, and you enter 6 hours of overtime, an amount of overtime is added to each day for the assignment.

   In the timesheet portion of the view, you can view how the overtime work you enter is distributed across the assignment's time span. However, you cannot edit the amount of overtime in the individual time periods.
4. Repeat this process for any other assignments causing the resource to be overallocated.

When you enter overtime work, the duration of the task is shortened. Overtime work is charged at an overtime rate you enter for the resource, either in the Resource Sheet or in the Resource Information dialog box. The resource name is still shown in red as overallocated, but now you've accounted for the overallocation using overtime.

Chapter 9

Splitting Tasks

Sometimes a resource needs to stop working on one task, start work on a second task, and then return to the first task. This can happen, for example, when an overallocated resource needs to work on a task with a date constraint. In this situation, you can split a task. With a *split task*, you can schedule when the task is to start, stop, and then resume again. As with delay, splitting a task can ensure that resources are working on tasks when they actually have time for them.

> **Note** In a split task, the task duration is calculated as the value of both portions of the task, not counting the time when the resource is working on something else. However, if you split a task with an elapsed duration, the duration is recalculated to include the start of the first part of the task through the finish of the last part of the task.

To split a task, follow these steps:

1. Display the Gantt Chart by clicking View, Gantt Chart.

Split Task

2. On the Standard toolbar, click Split Task. Your mouse pointer changes to the split task pointer, and a small pop-up window appears.
3. In the chart portion of the view, position your mouse pointer on the Gantt bar of the task you want to split, on the date when you want the split to occur.
4. Drag the Gantt bar to the date when you want the task to resume (see Figure 9-28).

   While you drag, the pop-up shows the start and finish dates.

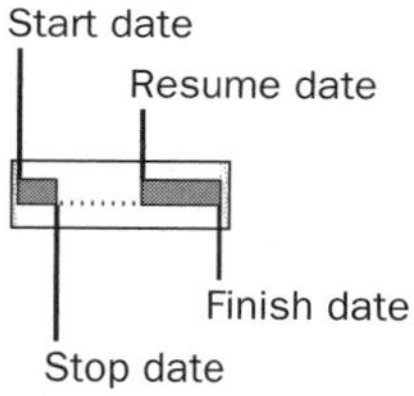

Figure 9-28. Drag the Gantt bar to represent when the task stops and when it resumes again.

You can split the task multiple times. Click Split Task on the Standard toolbar to activate each new split.

To remove the split in a split task, drag the right portion of the split Gantt bar toward the left portion until both sides of the bar touch and join.

> **Tip** **Split a task after work has started**
> After you begin the execution and tracking phase of the project, you can also split a task on which a resource has started working.

For more information on rescheduling, see "Rescheduling the Project" on page 321.

Note You can also adjust scope to balance the workload.

For more information about cutting scope, see "Changing Project Scope" later in this chapter on page 293.

Leveling Assignments

The previous sections described how you can delay and split tasks to balance or *level* resource assignments. Microsoft Project can balance the workload for you with the leveling feature, which adds delay and splits in your project plan according to specifications that you set.

You can have Microsoft Project level assignments whenever you give the command. You also have the option to keep the leveling feature on all the time. If you leave leveling on all the time, whenever you change the schedule in some way, Microsoft Project levels assignments at that time.

Note that leveling does not reassign tasks or units. It does not change work amounts. It causes the start date to move later by delays, or it splits a task so that it finishes later when the assigned resources have available time. Also, leveling works only on actual work resources—that is, material resources and generic resources are not leveled.

When you level resources, you carry out some or all of these major process steps, which are detailed in the following sections.

Inside Out

Resource leveling on demand

Through automatic resource leveling, Microsoft Project has the capability to automatically schedule assignments only when the resources actually have time available. However, if you set up automatic leveling, your schedule will be recalculated every time you make a single change that affects scheduling or assignments. If you have a large or complex project file, you are likely to find that this constant recalculation significantly slows down work in your project file. Because of this performance problem, automatic resource leveling is not recommended.

Instead, have Microsoft Project level resources only when you explicitly give the command. Click Tools, Level Resources. Make sure that the leveling options are what you want, and click the Level Now button.

An advantage to directing when Microsoft Project levels is that you can immediately review the results of leveling in the Leveling Gantt and undo the operation if you don't like the results. Having Microsoft Project level only when you say also ensures that you have control over when task splits and delays are being made.

Another alternative, which is not recommended, is to turn on automatic leveling and turn off automatic recalculation. If you want to do this, click Tools, Options and then click the

Calculation tab. For Calculation Mode, select the Manual option. Any time you want Microsoft Project to recalculate values in your project based on scheduling changes you've made, press the F9 key, which calculates all open projects. (If you want to calculate just the active project, press Shift+F9.) Whenever you've made changes that require calculation, the status bar says Calculate.

Whether or not you use automatic resource leveling, be aware that Manual calculation brings with it its own slough of problems. You have to remember that the data you're looking at might not be accurate at any given time, and that can cause you or others to make decisions based on faulty data.

For the best performance, most accurate data, and the most control over task splits and delays, make sure that resource leveling is set to Manual, and calculation is set to Automatic.

Setting Leveling Priorities

You can set a priority for each task if you like. The priority levels range from 0 (the lowest priority) to 1000 (the highest). All tasks start with a default priority of 500; that is, they are all equal in priority. Microsoft Project uses the task priority setting as a leveling criterion. If you have certain tasks that are so important that you never want the leveling feature to split or delay them, you should set them for a priority of 1000, which ensures that Microsoft Project will never level resources using that task. You might have other tasks that, although important, enjoy more potential flexibility as to when they can be completed. Those tasks can be set with a lower priority, such as 100. Having tasks set with lower priorities gives Microsoft Project the flexibility it needs to effectively level resource assignments.

To change the priority of an individual task, do the following:

1. In the Gantt Chart or other task sheet, double-click the task whose priority you want to change from the default of 500.
2. In the Task Information dialog box, click the General tab.
3. In the Priority box, enter the number representing the priority you want for this task.

Inside Out

Priorities apply only to resource leveling and substitution

Although it seems that priorities can help influence Microsoft Project's scheduling decisions throughout your project, priorities are actually used only in the context of leveling. If you're working with Project Professional 2003, priorities also play a part in the Resource Substitution Wizard. When Microsoft Project is determining whether to split or delay one task versus another in order to level resources, it can use priority as one of its criteria, in addition to the other criteria you have set in the Resource Leveling dialog box.

You can still set up your own uses of priorities. You can sort and group tasks by priority. You can also create a filter to see only tasks above a certain priority.

For more information about how priorities work with the Resource Substitution Wizard, see "Assigning Tasks to Enterprise Resources" on page 666.

Suppose there are ten tasks throughout your project that you want to set with a higher priority than the average. You can select those tasks and then change their priority in one operation, as follows:

1. In the Gantt Chart or other task sheet, select all the tasks whose priority you want to change to the same number. To select adjacent tasks, click the first task, hold down the Shift key, and then click the last task. To select nonadjacent tasks, click the first task, hold down the Ctrl key, and then click each task you want to include.
2. On the Standard toolbar, click Task Information.
3. In the Multiple Task Information dialog box, click the General tab.
4. In the Priority box, enter the number representing the priority you want for all selected tasks.

You can add the Priority field to a task sheet and change the priority for tasks individually throughout the sheet. To do this, follow these steps:

1. In the Gantt Chart or other task sheet, click the column to the right of where you want the new Priority column to be inserted.
2. Click Insert, Column.
3. In the Field Name box, click Priority, and then click OK. The Priority column appears in your sheet (see Figure 9-29).

Figure 9-29. Type or select the priority you want in the Priority field.

4. For any task whose priority should be other than the default, enter the number in the Priority field.

Tip **How many levels of priority do you need?**
Having 1000 levels of priority might seem like overkill, but the number of levels you use depends on what you're trying to do with your project, and how much control you want to wield over the leveling process.

If you feel you only need 10 levels of priority, use 0, 100, 200, 300, and so on as your priorities. Or use 495 through 505.

If you need only three priorities—low, medium, and high, for example—use 0, 500, and 1000. Or use 499, 500, and 501.

However, remember that tasks with a priority of 1000 are never leveled.

Leveling Resources with Standard Defaults

You use the Resource Leveling dialog box to set your leveling preferences and give the command to level. The default settings of the dialog box work for the majority of resource-leveling needs. It's a good idea to try leveling with those settings first and see how they work for you. Then you'll have a better idea of the kinds of controls you want to impose on the leveling operation. Follow these steps to level resources using the default settings:

1. If you want to level only selected resources rather than all resources, switch to a resource sheet and select the resource(s) you want to level.

   To select multiple adjacent resources, drag from the first to the last resource.

   To select multiple nonadjacent resources, click the first resource, hold down the Ctrl key, and then click each of the others.

2. Click Tools, Level Resources.

   The Resource Leveling dialog box appears (see Figure 9-30).

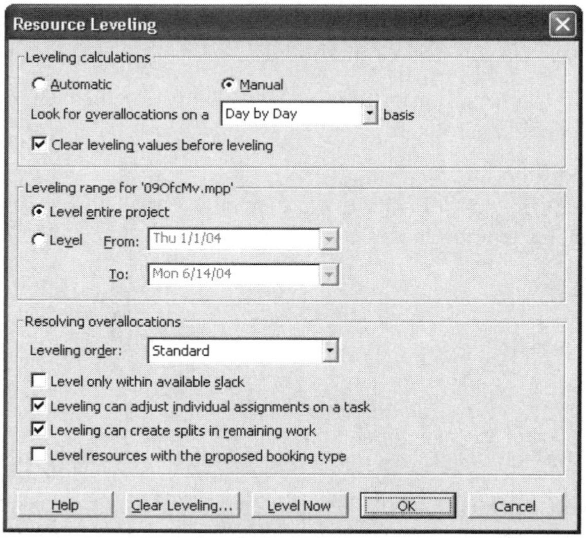

Figure 9-30. You can do a standard leveling operation using the defaults or you can set your own options.

3. Click the Level Now button.

4. If you selected resources, the Level Now dialog box appears (see Figure 9-31). Select the Entire Pool or Selected Resources option and then click OK.

Figure 9-31. Specify whether you want to level all or selected resources.

This dialog box does not appear if you had a task selected. In that case, all resources are leveled for the entire project.

Your resources are leveled according to the default dialog box settings.

To see the changes that leveling has made, see "Checking the Results of Leveling" later in this chapter on page 292.

Inside Out

Rein in the extent of resource leveling

By default, Microsoft Project levels on a day-by-day basis. That means even if resources are assigned just one hour over their availability as determined by their resource calendar or maximum units, their assignments will be leveled.

You might think this is somewhat nit-picky, and maybe you'd rather not split tasks or add delays unless there are larger overallocations. In this case, click Tools, Level Resources; and then under Leveling Calculations, change the Day By Day setting to Week By Week or Month By Month.

If you set leveling to Week By Week, for example, this means that a resource set up with a 40-hour work week is only leveled if she is assigned more than 40 hours in a week. However, her assignments are not leveled if she is assigned 14 hours in a single day.

Setting Leveling Options

If you've leveled your project a few times and want to take more control over how Microsoft Project levels, click Tools, Level Resources and then change the options you want in the Resource Leveling dialog box. The following list describes the available options:

Calculate automatically or manually. Under Leveling Calculations, select the Automatic option if you want Microsoft Project to level resources whenever you make a change that affects scheduling. Select the Manual option if you want resources leveled only when you give the Level Now command. If you select the Automatic option, clear the Clear Leveling Values Before Leveling check box to improve performance.

Specify the overallocation leveling time period. Resources are considered overallocated if they have even one minute of work scheduled beyond their availability, as determined by their resource calendars and maximum units. You can set the time period at which leveling is triggered with the Look For Overallocations On A Basis box. By default, the time period basis is a day, so if resources are overallocated by a minute or hour within a day, they'll be leveled. If you set the overallocation leveling time period basis to the week, resources that are scheduled for more work than can be accomplished by their weekly availability will be leveled. The choices are Minute By Minute, Day By Day (the default), Week By Week, and Month By Month.

Clear leveling. The Clear Leveling Values Before Leveling check box is selected by default. This setting specifies that any delays previously entered as a result of leveling or as a result of manually entering leveling delay are to be cleared before the next leveling operation is performed. The Clear Leveling button does the same thing. Use the check box if you're about to level again and you want to start fresh. Use the button if you're not planning to level right now, but want to remove any leveling delay from your project plan.

Level certain tasks or the entire project. Under Leveling Range, you can specify that only those tasks falling within a date range you enter should be leveled. This can be particularly useful in projects that take place over a long period of time or that are subject to many changes. The default is for all tasks in the project to be leveled.

Set the order of leveling operations. The first part of the leveling process is to determine which tasks are causing overallocations. Then Microsoft Project works through the project, splitting tasks and adding delays to remove the overallocation. You can control the order in which Microsoft Project levels through the project by setting the leveling order. By default, Microsoft Project uses the Standard leveling order, which looks at task relationships, slack, start dates, priorities, and constraints to determine whether and how tasks should be leveled (see Table 9-1). If you choose the ID Only leveling order, Microsoft Project delays tasks with the higher ID numbers before considering any other criteria. If you choose the Priority, Standard leveling order, Microsoft Project first looks at any priorities you've set and then all the factors of the Standard leveling order.

Level within available slack. By default, the Level Only Within Available Slack check box is cleared. Select this check box if you need to ensure that leveling will not push out the finish date. However, unless your project has a fair amount of built-in slack, if this check box is selected, you might not see many changes to your project.

Adjust individual assignments on a task. By default, the Leveling Can Adjust Individual Assignments On A Task check box is selected. This setting controls adjustments to when a resource works on a task, independent of other resources working on the same task.

Create splits in remaining work. By default, the Leveling Can Create Splits In Remaining Work check box is selected. This means that not only can leveling split tasks that haven't started yet, it can also split tasks that are currently in progress.

NEW FEATURE!

Level proposed resources. If you're working with Project Professional, you can add resources tentatively to your project and assign them to tasks. Such resources have a proposed booking type. By default, proposed resources are not included in a leveling operation; only committed resources are. If you want to include proposed resources in the leveling operation, select the Level Resources With The Proposed Booking Type.

For more information about working with proposed and committed resources, see "Proposing Tentative Resources" on page 178.

If you're working with proposed enterprise resources, see "Building Your Enterprise Project Team" on page 655.

After you change the leveling options to your satisfaction, level the resources in your project plan by clicking the Level Now button.

Table 9-1. Order of Operations for Resource Leveling

With this leveling order...	These fields are examined...
Standard	Task relationships Slack Start date Priority Constraint
ID Only	Task ID
Priority, Standard	Priority Task relationships Slack Start date Constraint

Inside Out

Delay in projects scheduled from the finish date

If you level tasks in a project scheduled from the finish date, negative delay values are applied from the end of the task or assignment, which causes the task or assignment's finish date to happen earlier.

Also, if you switch a project to be scheduled from the finish date from one to be scheduled from the start date, any leveling delays and splits are removed.

Troubleshooting

Leveling delay you entered manually has disappeared

Suppose you entered leveling delay to manually delay tasks. When you use the Microsoft Project leveling feature, by default, any previously entered leveling delay is removed. This is true whether the delay was entered automatically or manually.

To prevent manual leveling delay from being removed in the future, always clear the Clear Leveling Values Before Leveling check box in the Resource Leveling dialog box. And don't click the Clear Leveling button.

You might also consider entering assignment delay rather than leveling delay when manually entering delay values. Whereas leveling delay values delay all assignments on a task, assignment delay values delay individual assignments. Therefore, it might be a little more cumbersome and repetitious to enter initially, but you never have to worry about losing the values to a new leveling operation.

To get your leveling back, click Edit, Undo, which will reverse the leveling operation only if it's the very last operation you've done in your project. Otherwise, you might need to enter the leveling delay again or use a backup project file.

For more information about manually entering delay, see "Delaying a Task or Assignment" earlier in this chapter.

Checking the Results of Leveling

To see the changes made to your project plan as a result of leveling, use the Leveling Gantt. Display the Leveling Gantt as follows:

1. Click View, More Views.
2. In the More Views dialog box, click Leveling Gantt.

   The Gantt bars in this view display the task schedule as it looked before the leveling operation in addition to the task schedule as it looks after leveling, so you can compare the changes made (see Figure 9-32). It also shows any new task delays and splits.

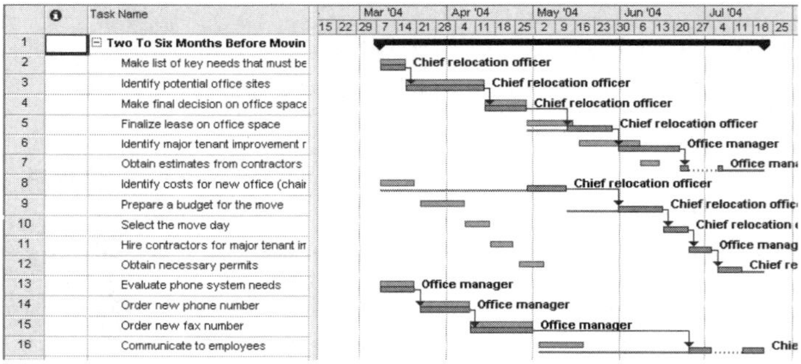

Figure 9-32. The green Gantt bars show the preleveled task schedule; whereas the blue bars, delays, and splits show the results of the leveling operation.

3. If you don't like the results of leveling, click Tools, Level Resources, and then click Clear Leveling.

Troubleshooting

Microsoft Project performance has slowed since you last leveled

You probably set resource leveling to Automatic. Every time you make a scheduling change that affect assignments, Microsoft Project automatically levels resources. Although this is a nice feature and is often what we expect Microsoft Project to do for us, it can significantly slow down performance in larger or more complex projects.

There are three ways to resolve the slowdown. In the Resource Leveling dialog box, select the Manual option under Leveling Calculations. Then click Level Now whenever you want resources to be leveled. This is the most effective solution, providing the most reliable results throughout your project.

Another solution is to maintain automatic leveling but turn off automatic calculation. Click Tools, Options, and then click the Calculation tab. Under Calculation Options, select the Manual option. Now, whenever you make schedule changes, your schedule won't be recalculated until you come back to this tab and click the Calculate Now button, or press F9 to calculate all open projects or Shift+F9 to calculate only the active project.

Here's the third method for improving performance. If you want to keep automatic leveling as well as automatic calculation, clear the Clear Leveling Values Before Leveling check box in the Resource Leveling dialog box. This procedure can help improve performance because previous leveling values are not cleared before the new leveling is done.

Tip **Switch to the Leveling Gantt before leveling**
If you go to the Leveling Gantt first and then level your project, you can see the results immediately in the Leveling Gantt. If you don't like the results, you can click Edit, Undo to reverse the changes made by leveling.

Troubleshooting

You told Microsoft Project to level your resources, but nothing changed

You set up all your options in the Resource Leveling dialog box and then click OK. But if leveling is set to Manual, nothing happens in your project plan. In the Manual leveling mode, your resources are not leveled until you click the Level Now button. Therefore, instead of clicking OK, click the Level Now button, and your resources will be leveled.

Another alternative is to select the Automatic leveling option. In this case, as soon as you click OK, Microsoft Project levels your project plan. In addition, every time you make a scheduling change that affects assignments, Microsoft Project levels resources again.

Changing Project Scope

In the course of checking and adjusting your project plan, you might need to cut scope. For example, you might need to cut tasks you perceive as optional to meet the finish date. To bring project costs in line with your allotted budget, you might cut tasks associated with increased quality or quantity that you think you can live without. Or maybe you need to cut an entire phase or deliverable in order to alleviate resource overallocation.

Note Your task list is likely based on the scope statement that all the stakeholders, including customers, originally approved. If you need to cut scope, you might have to go back and obtain stakeholder approval for these changes.

To delete a task, simply click its row heading and press the Delete key. You can also delete a summary task that represents an entire phase or group of related tasks. To delete a summary task, click its row heading and press the Delete key. A message appears and warns you that deleting the summary task will delete all of its subtasks as well. Click OK to confirm that you want to do this.

Reviewing the Impact of Changes

After you adjust your project plan to bring in your finish date, reduce costs, or balance your workload, check that you've succeeded in hitting your target. Look at the Project Statistics dialog box or review the project summary task, as described earlier in this chapter.

When you're content with one aspect of your project plan, such as your finish date, it's a good idea to see whether you've "broken" any other aspect of your project, such as your costs. Keep an eye on your finish date, total project costs, and resource allocation while always remembering your highest priority of the three. Continue to adjust and balance until all aspects of the project are just the way you want them.

Obtaining Buyoff on the Project Plan

Typically, before you even start Microsoft Project, you have a defined scope for the project. This scope drives the development of deliverables, milestones, phases, and tasks; and it was also probably developed in conjunction with various stakeholders.

If you were forced to cut scope as a result of adjusting the project plan to meet finish date, cost, or resource requirements, you need to go back to those stakeholders and get their approval for your scope changes.

You might need to justify your changes and specify the tradeoffs that are being made to meet the finish date, reduce costs, or balance workload to a reasonable level. You can also point out that the scope is now defined more precisely, based on the project limitations. With this more precise definition, you lower potential risks. The plan is solid and realistic. The project is less apt now to incur unexpected delays, costs, or other changes that can disrupt the project, cause rework, or lower productivity.

As soon as you obtain the buyoff from your stakeholders, you have officially completed the planning phase of your project. You're finally ready to tell your team "Go!" and enter the execution phase of the project.

Part 3

Tracking Progress

Chapter 10

Saving a Baseline and Updating Progress

By now, you've completed the planning phase of your project. The scope is set, along with the project goals and objectives. The tasks and deliverables are scheduled. The budget is approved, and you've procured the necessary human, equipment, and material resources. Your project plan reflects all these details and has been signed off by upper management or by your customers.

After all this, you're ready to charge forward with your team and actually start doing the work prescribed by the project. You are now leaving the planning phase and entering the execution phase.

The execution phase consists of four major activities:

Tracking. You track progress on tasks so you know when tasks are actually completed by their assigned resources.

Analyzing. You examine any differences between your original plan and how it's actually progressing. You monitor the differences in schedule or cost to anticipate any potential problems.

Controlling. You take any necessary corrective actions to keep the project on a steady course toward completion by its deadline and on its budget.

Reporting. You keep stakeholders informed. Whether you're providing the big picture to your team members or presenting high-level progress information to executives, you regularly report various aspects of project information.

You used Microsoft Office Project 2003 in the planning phase to organize, schedule, and budget your project. Now you can use it in the execution phase to enter progress information, analyze performance, and generate status reports. With a close eye on progress and performance, you can adjust the project plan as necessary to ensure that your scope, schedule, costs, and resources are all balanced the way you need.

To execute your project with Project 2003, do two things:

- Save baseline information on your project as planned.
- Enter progress information as your resources begin to complete tasks.

With both baseline and progress information in hand, you can use the power of Microsoft Project to execute your project toward a successful outcome.

Are You a Charter or a Tracker?

Some project managers set up a project plan, painstakingly enter tasks, and create a schedule with meticulously accurate durations, task dependencies, and constraints. They acquire and assign exactly the right resources and calculate costs to the last penny. However, after they have their plan perfected, they execute the project and leave the project plan behind. What started out as an excellent roadmap of the project is now little more than a bit of planning history.

To be an effective project manager, take your project plan with you as you move to the execution phase of your project. Maintain the plan and enter actual progress information. By tracking progress in this way, your schedule and costs are updated so you know what to expect as you work through the weeks and months of your project. Use the calculating power of Microsoft Project to:

- Calculate variances between your original plan and your current schedule.
- Perform *earned value* analyses.
- Generate reports you can share at status meetings.

Most importantly, you'll always have the up-to-date details you need at your fingertips. If you need to adjust the plan, either to recover a slipping phase or to respond to a directive to cut 10 percent of the project budget, Project serves as your project management information system to help you make those adjustments.

Saving Original Plan Information Using a Baseline

The project plan, having been adjusted to perfection, is considered your *baseline*. Think of it as your *original* plan. It represents the most ideal balance between scope, schedule, and cost.

The project plan, at this point in time, is also your *scheduled* plan. Think of it as your *current* plan. This is the only point in the project when the original plan and the current plan are exactly the same.

They're identical only at this time because the current project plan is fluid. As soon as you enter progress information, such as one task's actual start date or another task's percent complete, your project plan is recalculated and adjusted to reflect the new information from those *actuals*.

For example, suppose that Task A has a scheduled finish date of May 3. It's linked with a finish-to-start task dependency to Task B, so Task B's scheduled start date is also May 3. However, Task A finishes 2 days early on May 1. So after entering the actual finish date of Task A, the scheduled start date of Task B, which has the default ASAP constraint, changes to May 1. The scheduled start dates of any other successor tasks are recalculated as well.

This constant recalculation is essential for you to always know where your project stands in the current reality. But what if you want to know what your original start dates were? What if you want to compare the original baseline plan with the *current schedule* to analyze your progress and performance?

The answer is to save baseline information. By saving a baseline, you're basically taking a snapshot of key scheduling and cost information in your project plan at that point in time; that is, before you enter your first actuals and the scheduled plan begins to diverge from the original baseline plan. With fixed baseline information saved, you'll have a basis for comparing the current or actual project plan against your original baseline plan.

The difference between baseline and current scheduled information is called a *variance*. Baselines, actuals, and variances are used in a variety of ways, including earned value analyses, to monitor project schedule and cost performance. In fact, you cannot perform earned value analyses at all unless you have first saved a baseline.

Saving a baseline is not the same as saving the entire project plan. When you save a baseline, you save the following specific fields for all tasks, resources, and assignments:

- Cost, in the Baseline Cost field
- Duration, in the Baseline Duration field
- Finish, in the Baseline Finish field
- Start, in the Baseline Start field
- Work, in the Baseline Work field

These are the fields that will give you a good basis for schedule and budget performance as you execute your project.

Saving a Baseline

To save the first set of baseline information for your project plan, follow these steps:

1. Click Tools, Tracking, Save Baseline.

   The Save Baseline dialog box appears (see Figure 10-1).

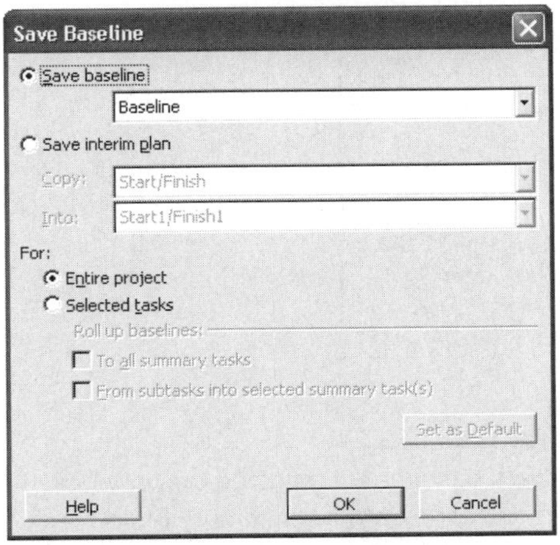

Figure 10-1. Use the Save Baseline dialog box to save up to 11 baselines or up to 10 interim plans.

2 Make sure that the Save Baseline option is selected.
3 In the box under the Save Baseline option, make sure that Baseline (not Baseline 1 or Baseline 2) is selected.
4 Under For, make sure that the Entire Project option is selected.
5 Click OK.

Although nothing appears to happen, as soon as you click OK, all your scheduled fields are copied into their corresponding baseline fields. The value stored in the Cost field is copied into the Baseline Cost field. The value stored in the Work field is copied into the Baseline Work field, and so on.

But what if you save a baseline and later add another set of additional tasks? Even after you save the baseline initially, you can still add tasks to it, as follows:

1 In the Gantt Chart or another task sheet, select the tasks that you want to add to the baseline.
2 Click Tools, Tracking, Save Baseline to display the Save Baseline dialog box. Make sure that the Save Baseline option is selected.
3 Under the Save Baseline option, make sure that Baseline is selected.

   The Baseline box lists the date you last saved the baseline. If you want to add tasks to a different baseline, for example, Baseline 1 or Baseline 2, click that baseline in the list.
4 Under For, select the Selected Tasks option.

   When you select the Selected Tasks option (see Figure 10-2), the Roll Up Baselines check boxes become available. This option ensures that the summarized baseline data shown in summary tasks are accurate and rolled up the way you expect.

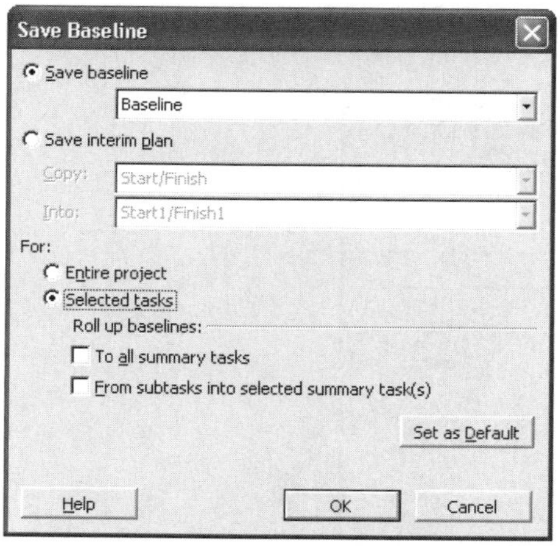

Figure 10-2. When you save a baseline for selected tasks, you can choose how to update the corresponding baseline data on summary tasks.

5 Select the check box that reflects how you want the baseline information of the selected task to be rolled up to summary tasks.

By default, after the initial baseline is saved, a summary task is not updated when a subtask is modified, added, or deleted.

If you want the selected tasks to be rolled up to all associated summary tasks, select the To All Summary Tasks check box.

If you want the selected tasks to be rolled up only to a selected summary task, select the From Subtasks Into Selected Summary Task(s) check box.

6 Click OK and then click Yes to confirm that you want to change the existing baseline.

Tip **Overwrite existing baseline information**
When saving a baseline, click the name of the baseline that has a Last Saved date. Under For, select Entire Project or Selected Tasks to specify whether you want to overwrite the baseline information of the entire project or only of selected tasks. The current schedule information in your project plan overwrites the baseline information in the selected baseline.

Protecting Baseline Information

NEW FEATURE!

If you're using Microsoft Office Project Professional 2003 with Microsoft Office Project Server 2003 and the enterprise project management features, your project server administrator grants or denies the ability to save baselines in enterprise projects. Only those who have the Save Baseline permission set by the administrator can save or potentially overwrite a baseline in your project. This baseline protection feature, new in Project 2003, is used by organizations who want to lock down baseline information and ensure it's never changed through the life of the project without the proper stakeholder approvals.

For example, the project manager builds the project and obtains buy-off from all managing stakeholders. When that buy-off is achieved, the project server administrator might check out the project and save the baseline. Or the administrator might temporarily grant the project manager permission to save the baseline. After it's saved, the administrator removes that permission. Either way, the baseline is saved and cannot be edited or changed. Additional baselines cannot be saved either.

For more information about project server administrator responsibilities, see "Chapter 21, "Administering Project Server and Project Web Access for Your Enterprise."

Reviewing Baseline Information

After you save baseline information, you can review it in various ways. Initially, baseline information is identical to the scheduled information. As your team starts to complete work on the project, the two might diverge. It is this deviation, and the amount of it, that you'll be interested in as you monitor and control the project.

The following lists methods of reviewing baseline information:

Apply the Tracking Gantt. Click View, Tracking Gantt. The Tracking Gantt shows the baseline Gantt bars underneath the scheduled Gantt bars (see Figure 10-3).

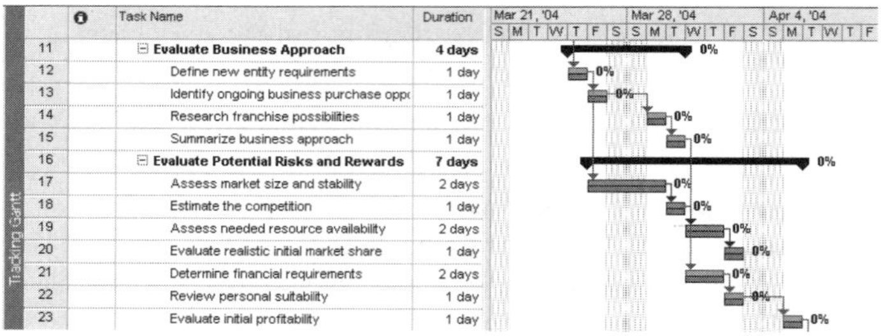

Figure 10-3. The Tracking Gantt shows baseline start, duration, and finish in its Gantt bars, in relation to the scheduled Gantt bars.

Apply the Baseline table to a task sheet. Click View, Table, More Tables; click Baseline and then click Apply. This table shows baseline information for duration, start, finish, work, and cost (see Figure 10-4). This table is also useful if you ever need to edit baseline information.

	Task Name	Baseline Dur.	Baseline Start	Baseline Work	Baseline Finish	Baseline Cost
81	**Establish the Operating Control Base**	**12 days**	**Fri 7/2/04**	**144 hrs**	**Mon 7/19/04**	**$6,880.00**
82	Choose and set up the accounting system	2 days	Fri 7/2/04	16 hrs	Mon 7/5/04	$720.00
83	Obtain required licenses and permits	4 days	Tue 7/6/04	64 hrs	Fri 7/9/04	$2,720.00
84	Obtain needed insurance	4 days	Mon 7/12/04	32 hrs	Thu 7/15/04	$1,440.00
85	Establish security plan	2 days	Fri 7/16/04	32 hrs	Mon 7/19/04	$2,000.00
86	**Develop Marketing Program**	**4 days**	**Thu 6/17/04**	**40 hrs**	**Tue 6/22/04**	**$2,800.00**
87	Establish an advertising program	2 days	Thu 6/17/04	16 hrs	Fri 6/18/04	$1,200.00
88	Develop a logo	1 day	Mon 6/21/04	16 hrs	Mon 6/21/04	$1,000.00
89	Order promotional materials	1 day	Tue 6/22/04	8 hrs	Tue 6/22/04	$600.00
90	**Provide Physical Facilities**	**15 days**	**Tue 7/20/04**	**120 hrs**	**Mon 8/9/04**	**$6,080.00**
91	Secure operation space	5 days	Tue 7/20/04	40 hrs	Mon 7/26/04	$2,000.00
92	Select computer network hardware	1 day	Tue 7/27/04	8 hrs	Tue 7/27/04	$440.00

Figure 10-4. The Baseline table shows many of the baseline fields.

Tip Editing a baseline

Technically, a baseline field should never be edited. The baseline information is a snapshot of the project plan information at a particular point in time. When you change a baseline field, you're probably changing a variance or results of an earned value analysis.

If you need different values in baseline fields because of changed circumstances, save a new baseline, for example, Baseline 1 or Baseline 2. You can retain the values in your original baseline and choose which baseline is to be used for earned value analyses.

Add baseline fields to an existing table. You might like to add a baseline field next to the equivalent scheduled field in the Entry table, for example (see Figure 10-5). You can add the Baseline Duration field next to the Duration field and the Baseline Start field next to the Start field. Click Insert, Column. In the Field Name box, click the baseline field you want to add. The names of all baseline fields begin with the word "Baseline."

Task Name	Baseline Duration	Duration	Baseline Start	Start	Baseline Finish	Finish
⊟ **Establish the Operating Control Base**	**12 days**	**12 days**	**Fri 7/2/04**	**Wed 7/7/04**	**Mon 7/19/04**	**Thu 7/22/04**
Choose and set up the accounting system	2 days	2 days	Fri 7/2/04	Wed 7/7/04	Mon 7/5/04	Thu 7/8/04
Obtain required licenses and permits	4 days	4 days	Tue 7/6/04	Fri 7/9/04	Fri 7/9/04	Wed 7/14/04
Obtain needed insurance	4 days	4 days	Mon 7/12/04	Thu 7/15/04	Thu 7/15/04	Tue 7/20/04
Establish security plan	2 days	2 days	Fri 7/16/04	Wed 7/21/04	Mon 7/19/04	Thu 7/22/04
⊟ **Develop Marketing Program**	**4 days**	**4 days**	**Thu 6/17/04**	**Thu 6/17/04**	**Tue 6/22/04**	**Tue 6/22/04**
Establish an advertising program	2 days	2 days	Thu 6/17/04	Thu 6/17/04	Fri 6/18/04	Fri 6/18/04
Develop a logo	1 day	1 day	Mon 6/21/04	Mon 6/21/04	Mon 6/21/04	Mon 6/21/04
Order promotional materials	1 day	1 day	Tue 6/22/04	Tue 6/22/04	Tue 6/22/04	Tue 6/22/04

Figure 10-5. Showing baseline fields next to the equivalent scheduled fields in a table can help you see at a glance whether and how much of a variance exists.

Tip **Review current and baseline summary information**

Open the Project Statistics dialog box to compare current schedule information with baseline information in terms of Start, Finish, Duration, Work, and Cost. Click Project, Project Information and then click the Statistics button.

Troubleshooting

You see nothing in the baseline fields

Baseline fields show a value of 0 or NA until you save a baseline. If you add baseline fields to a table, apply the Baseline table, or show the Tracking Gantt before you have saved a baseline, you'll see no information. Click Tools, Tracking, Save Baseline and then click OK. The baseline fields are now populated.

For more information about using baseline information to analyze variance and monitor progress, see Chapter 11, "Responding to Changes in Your Project."

For more information about earned value, see "Analyzing Progress and Costs Using Earned Value" on page 401.

Troubleshooting

Your baseline information doesn't roll up

When you first save your baseline plan, any baseline fields you display show the proper rollup amounts, whether it's duration, start date, finish date, cost, and so on.

As you adjust the schedule or enter tracking information, your scheduled information changes, whereas the baseline information remains the same. It's supposed to stay the same. The job of the baseline is, of course, to always show information from your original plan so you can make the necessary comparisons.

Now suppose that you edit a baseline field, even if you know you shouldn't. Although Microsoft Project allows you to edit an individual baseline field, its associated summary tasks are not recalculated to reflect your edit. Every change that's made to the baseline chips away at the integrity of the baseline information and dilutes the purpose of having the baseline in the first place.

A more likely scenario is that you've added or removed tasks in the plan, and these changes are not reflected in the baseline. Strictly speaking again, such changes are not supposed to be in the baseline because it is a different state from your original plan.

In any case, if you do have a legitimate reason for updating baseline information, you can add selected tasks to the baseline and have the summary information recalculated, as follows:

1. Select the tasks with the changed information. If applicable, select the summary task(s) you want updated as well.
2. Click Tools, Tracking, Save Baseline. Make sure the Save Baseline option is selected, and that the baseline you want to use is selected in the box.
3. Under For, click the Selected Tasks option.

   The Roll Up Baselines section becomes available.
4. Select the To All Summary Tasks check box if you want all changed information in the selected tasks to roll up to all associated summary tasks.

   Select the From Subtasks Into Selected Summary Task(s) if you want the changed information in selected subtasks to roll up only into your selected summary tasks.

Saving Additional Baselines

Sometimes, you track your project for a period of time and then a big change occurs. Maybe your company undergoes a major shift in priorities. Maybe an emergency project comes up that takes you and your resources away from this project. Maybe funding was stalled and then started up again. In such cases, your original baseline might not be as useful a tool as it once was. And although you don't want to replace it entirely, you want to use another more up-to-date baseline for your everyday tracking requirements.

Even if nothing catastrophic happened to your project, you might still have good uses for multiple baselines. In addition to taking that snapshot at the beginning of your execution phase, you might want to take another snapshot at the end of each month or each quarter. This snapshot can show more exact periods of time when you experienced greater variances between baseline and scheduled information.

You can now save up to 11 different baselines. If you use earned value analyses, you can use one of 11 baselines for the earned value calculations.

To save an additional baseline, do the following:

1. Click Tools, Tracking, Save Baseline.
2. Make sure that the Save Baseline option is selected.
3. In the Save Baseline list, click Baseline 1, for example (see Figure 10-6).

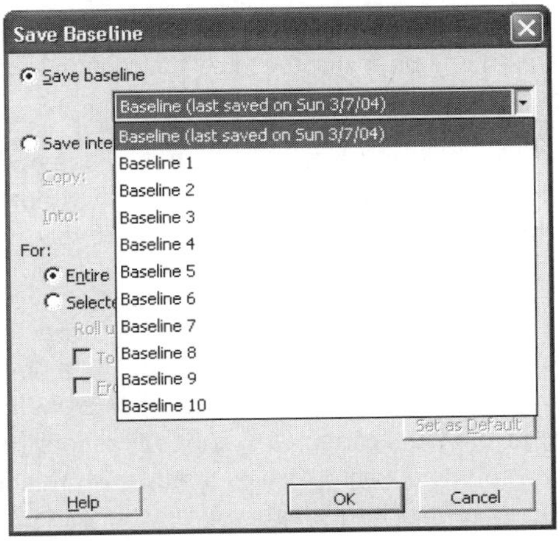

Figure 10-6. To save an additional baseline, choose any of the baselines in the list.

If a baseline has a Last Saved date after it, you already saved information in that baseline. If you select a baseline with a Last Saved date, you'll overwrite the previous baseline information with current schedule information.

4. Under For, make sure that the Entire Project option is selected.

To review the contents of additional baseline fields, click Insert, Column in a task sheet. In the Field Name box, click the name of the additional baseline field you want to add to the table; for example, Baseline1 Duration or Baseline5 Start. The column and the contents of the field for each task are displayed in the table.

Tip **View multiple baseline Gantt bars**
Using the Multiple Baselines Gantt, you can view Gantt bars reflecting different baselines. Multiple Gantt bars for multiple baselines can give you a visual representation of schedule changes from one set of baseline information to another. Click View, More Views and then click Multiple Baselines Gantt. Each baseline is represented as a different color Gantt bar.

Project Management Practices: Working with the Baseline

The primary schedule baseline is the approved project schedule. This plan has been adjusted and refined to the point where it meets the scope, the targeted finish date, and the budget of the project. The baseline plan has been deemed technically feasible given available resources. The baseline plan has been approved as the plan of record by the managing stakeholders.

This baseline plan is a component of the overall project plan. It provides the basis for measuring the schedule and cost performance of the project. In turn, any variances found can drive decisions about whether corrective actions should be taken and what those corrective actions should be.

In the course of project execution, if the schedule variance becomes very large, perhaps because of major scope changes or lengthy delays, *rebaselining* might be needed to provide realistic information from which to measure performance. Prior to Microsoft Project 2002, rebaselining was a painful decision for project managers using Microsoft Project because only one set of baseline information could be saved. However, now the project manager can save up to 11 baselines. There should always be a single primary baseline, however, which serves as the definitive baseline to be used for analysis and authoritative historical data.

Saving Additional Scheduled Start and Finish Dates

In addition to saving up to 11 baselines, you can also save up to 10 different sets of start and finish dates, or *interim plans*. Think of these plans as mini-baselines. Instead of saving the full set of schedule information (such as duration, work, cost, and so on), an interim plan saves only the current start and finish dates and stores them in the custom Start1-10 and Finish1-10 fields.

To save an interim plan, follow these steps:

1. Click Tools, Tracking, Save Baseline.
2. Select the Save Interim Plan option.
3. By default, the Copy box displays Start/Finish.

   This display indicates that the dates in the currently scheduled Start and Finish fields will be saved as this interim plan. You can copy from a different set of Start and Finish fields. In the Copy list, click the set you want.
4. By default, the Into box displays Start1/Finish1.

   This display specifies where the start and finish dates of this interim plan will be stored. You can copy the start and finish fields into a different set of Start and Finish fields. In the Into box, click the set you want.
5. Under For, click Entire Project or Selected Tasks.

You can copy start and finish dates from other baselines into an interim plan. This process can be useful if you have an old baseline you want to reuse, but you want to retain the start and finish dates. To do this, click the old baseline in the Copy list and then click the set of Start and Finish fields in the Into list.

You can also copy start and finish dates from an interim plan to one of the baselines, which can be useful if you used interim plans as a substitute for baselines in the past. Now that multiple baselines are available, you can take advantage of them by using your interim plan information. To do this, click the interim plan containing the start and finish dates in the Copy list. Then in the Into list, click the baseline to which you want the information to be moved.

Inside Out

Do we need interim plans any more?

Interim plans seem to be a vestige of previous versions of Microsoft Project in which only one baseline was available. Interim plans were just a "bone" thrown to project managers who really needed multiple baselines. With interim plans, at least multiple sets of Start and Finish dates could be saved.

We finally have multiple baselines now, so interim plans don't seem to have much use anymore. They need to stick around, however, for those project managers who are updating project plans created in previous versions of Microsoft Project.

Interim plans might also be useful for project managers who like to create periodic snapshots, maybe once a month or once a quarter. With 11 baselines, you might run out of baseline fields in less than a year. With 10 interim plans, you have more fields to work with, even if they are limited to just the Start and Finish dates.

Clearing a Baseline

You can clear baseline and interim plan fields, as follows:

1. Click Tools, Tracking, Clear Baseline.

   The Clear Baseline dialog box appears.
2. Select the Clear Baseline Plan or Clear Interim Plan option.
3. In the corresponding box, click the name of the sets of fields you want to clear; for example, Baseline 3, or Start5/Finish5.
4. Select the Entire Project or Selected Tasks option.

   The selected fields are cleared.

Updating Task Progress

So the resources are digging into their assignments and progress is being made. At regular intervals, you want to record their progress in Microsoft Project. Depending on how much time you want to spend entering progress information (and how much time you want your team members to spend doing that), you can choose a simple, high-level method; a comprehensive, detailed method; or something in-between.

Entering actual progress information into Microsoft Project ensures that you'll always know how the project's going. You can keep an eye on the critical path and your budget. You can monitor key tasks and know exactly when you'll be handing off an important deliverable. With actual information coming into your project plan, you can also anticipate potential problems and take corrective actions as necessary.

If you're using Microsoft Office Project Server 2003 with Microsoft Office Project Web Access 2003, updating task progress can become highly automated. You set up the types of progress information you want to receive from your team members, and that information is integrated with the assignments in the timesheet that team members use in Project Web Access 2003. Every week (or however often you specify), team members send you an update regarding their actual progress toward completing tasks. You can have the progress information automatically integrated into your project plan or you can review the information before incorporating it.

For more information about exchanging task updates using Project Web Access, see Chapter 22, "Managing with Project Professional and Project Server."

Project Management Practices: Scope and Quality Verification

As you meet milestones in your project and hand off deliverables, be sure to obtain formal acceptance of the project scope from the appropriate stakeholders; for example, the sponsor or customer. The sponsor reviews the deliverables and signs off that they're completed to his or her satisfaction.

At the same time, the sponsor should also check the correctness, or quality standards, of the work results.

It's important to have this acceptance process at various interim stages throughout the project—for each deliverable or at the end of each major phase, for example, rather than waiting until the end of the project.

You can also exchange task update messages with your team members through e-mail, although the features are more limited.

For more information about using e-mail for team collaboration, see Chapter 19, "Collaborating Using E-Mail."

Whether you're exchanging updates electronically, getting a status update in a weekly meeting, using paper timesheets, or making the rounds to hear team members' progress, you can enter the following actual progress information in your project plan:

- Percent complete
- Actual duration and remaining duration
- Actual start and actual finish
- Percent work complete
- Actual work complete and remaining work
- Actual work complete by time period

Tip **Collect progress information to set future benchmarks**
When you enter actuals in your project plan, you're not just keeping your project on track. You're also building historical information that you can use as metrics for other similar project plans. You're tracking solid, tested data about how long these tasks actually take.

When you enter one piece of status information, often other pieces of information are calculated by Microsoft Project. Certainly the schedule and costs are automatically recalculated.

Turn Automatic Calculation On or Off

By default, Microsoft Project recalculates information in your project plan as soon as you make a change that warrants recalculation. Such changes include assigning a resource, linking tasks, adding a cost, and so on.

If your project plan is very large or complex, you might find that constant recalculation slows down system performance. You can have Microsoft Project calculate your changes only when you give the command. To do this, click Tools, Options and then click the Calculation tab. Next to Calculation Mode, select the Manual option.

Whenever you make a change that requires a calculation, the word Calculate appears in the status bar. Press F9 to calculate all open projects. Press Shift+F9 to calculate just the active project.

Choosing the Best Method for Entering Actuals

There are several methods of tracking actual progress information in your project plan. How do you decide which method to use?

The first consideration is the level of detail you need. Your managing stakeholders might expect you to report at a certain level of detail at the weekly status meetings. Or you might need reliable historical information from this project because it's serving as a benchmark for similar future projects.

The second consideration is time. Will you have time to enter detailed progress information, or will you be so busy managing the project and perhaps working on your own assigned tasks that you won't be able to keep track of everything with an adequate amount of detail? What about your team members? Are they going to be too stretched to complete an electronic or paper timesheet? If you're using Project Server and Project Web Access, certain processes are automated for you, but they might still take time for your team members.

The third consideration is whether you've assigned resources to tasks in your project plan. Obviously, resources will carry out the tasks one way or the other. But if you've chosen not to include resources in your project plan, you have fewer available tracking methods.

Tailoring Project Web Access Timesheet Fields

If you're collaborating with your team members using Project Server and Project Web Access, you can tailor the fields shown in the team members' electronic timesheet. Depending on the progress information you want to track, you might want to add any of the following fields to the team members' timesheet:

- % Work Complete
- Actual Work Complete
- Actual Duration
- Remaining Duration
- Actual Finish
- Remaining Work
- Actual Start

These fields are task progress fields, so they can be most useful in a team member's timesheet. However, you can add any task or assignment field available in Microsoft Project. The timesheet becomes part of the periodic task update that the team members send you.

For more information about setting up Project Web Access options, see Chapter 21, "Adminstering Project Server and Project Web Access for Your Enterprise."

There's also a simplistic e-mail collaboration method. For more information, see Chapter 19, "Collaborating Using E-Mail."

Using one primary method of tracking actuals does not prevent you from using other methods for other tasks. Although you might achieve more consistent results if you stick to one method, sometimes other tasks simply lend themselves to a different type of progress information. Certain tasks are so important that you want to track them very closely. You can do that—you're never locked into a single tracking method.

Using the Tracking Toolbar

Many of your tracking functions are available on the Tracking toolbar (see Figure 10-7). To display the Tracking toolbar, click View, Toolbars, Tracking. You can also right-click an empty spot in the toolbars area and then click Tracking.

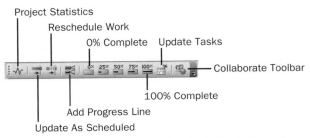

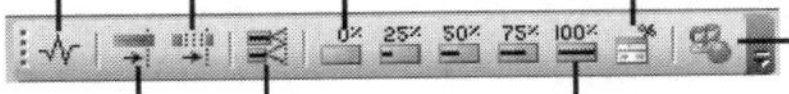

Figure 10-7. The Tracking toolbar includes buttons for setting percent complete, updating multiple tasks at once, and more.

As soon as you enter the tracking and monitoring phase of your project, it's a great idea to continuously display the Tracking toolbar, which contains many of the tools you need to quickly review and update task status throughout the life of the project.

The following list describes the functions available on the Tracking toolbar:

Project Statistics. Opens the Project Statistics dialog box, which shows the current, baseline, actual, variance, and remaining information for overall project start, finish, duration, work, and cost.

Update As Scheduled. Enters actual information to show that the selected tasks are proceeding exactly as planned. This is a shortcut to using the Update Project dialog box with the default settings.

Reschedule Work. Reschedules the entire project to start any uncompleted work after the current date. This is a shortcut to using the Update Project dialog box to reschedule uncompleted work.

Add Progress Line. Changes your cursor to a selection tool for you to select the status date for the progress line. Click the date in the chart portion of the Gantt Chart, and the progress line is drawn according to that date. This is a shortcut to using the Progress Lines dialog box.

0% Complete through 100% Complete. Enters actual progress for the selected tasks to the selected percent complete. This is a shortcut to using the Update Tasks dialog box.

Update Tasks. Opens the Update Tasks dialog box.

Collaborate Toolbar. Displays the Collaborate toolbar, which you can use to publish assignments, update project progress, request progress information, and use various features associated with Project Server, Project Web Access, and enterprise project management.

Updating Progress Using Task Scheduling Controls

You can update progress by entering actual information from task scheduling controls such as percent complete, duration, start date, and finish date. You can use these methods whether or not resources are assigned in Microsoft Project.

Updating the Project as Scheduled

Probably the easiest method of entering tracking information is to provide information to Microsoft Project that shows that your project is going exactly according to plan. You can use today's date or another date as the reference *complete through* date. With this method, tasks are updated as follows:

- Any tasks with a scheduled finish date before your complete through date are shown as completed on that scheduled date. In other words, your scheduled finish dates become your actual finish dates up to today's date or whichever date you specify.
- Any tasks with a scheduled start date before your complete through date (and a finish date after your date) are shown to be in progress through that date.
- Any tasks with a scheduled start date after your complete through date are untouched.

To update the project as scheduled, follow these steps:

1. Click Tools, Tracking, Update Project.

   The Update Project dialog box appears (see Figure 10-8).

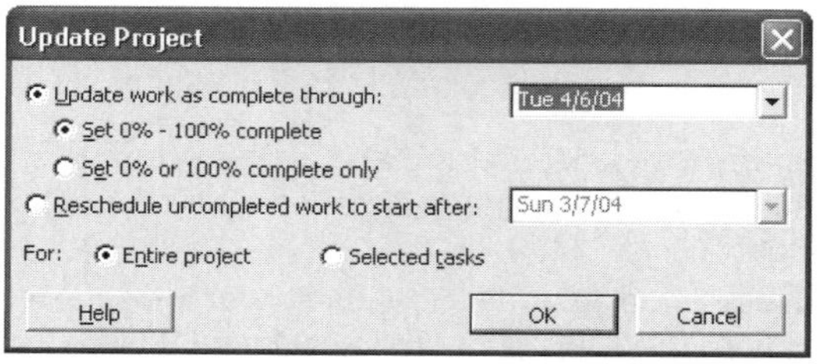

Figure 10-8. Update your project as scheduled through a specified date.

2. Make sure that the Update Work As Complete Through option is selected.
3. Enter the complete through date in the box. By default, today's date appears.
4. Select the Set 0% - 100% Complete option if you want Microsoft Project to calculate whether the task is not started, 100% complete, or in progress.

   If a task's scheduled start date is after your complete through date, the task remains 0% complete.

   If a task's scheduled finish date is before your complete through date, the task is set to 100% complete.

   If a task's scheduled start date is before your complete through date, and the scheduled finish date is after your complete through date, Microsoft Project calculates a percent complete value (see Figure 10-9).

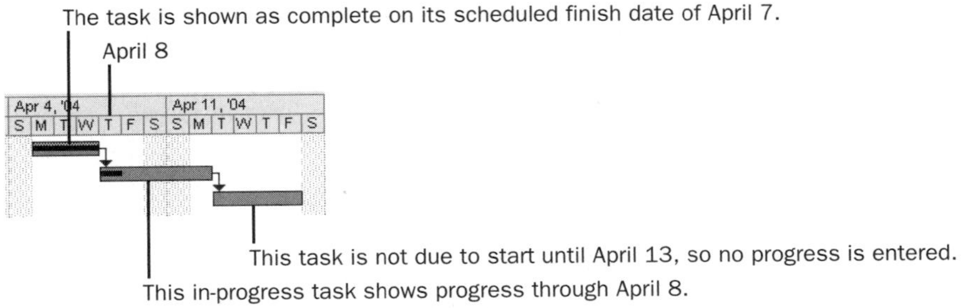
The task is shown as complete on its scheduled finish date of April 7.
April 8
Apr 4, '04
Apr 11, '04
S M T W T F S S M T W T F S
This task is not due to start until April 13, so no progress is entered.
This in-progress task shows progress through April 8.

Figure 10-9. If your complete through date is April 8 and you want the Update Project function to calculate current progress of completed and in-progress tasks, your Gantt Chart shows progress bars looking like this.

5 Select the Set 0% or 100% Complete Only option if you want in-progress tasks to remain at 0% (see Figure 10-10). That is, any tasks whose scheduled finish date is after your complete through date do not have any progress entered for them.

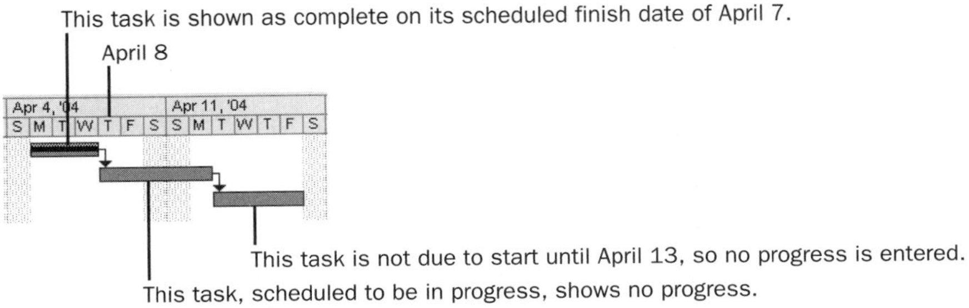
This task is shown as complete on its scheduled finish date of April 7.
April 8
Apr 4, '04
Apr 11, '04
S M T W T F S S M T W T F S
This task is not due to start until April 13, so no progress is entered.
This task, scheduled to be in progress, shows no progress.

Figure 10-10. If you want the Update Project function to display in-progress tasks as 0% complete, this is the result when your complete through date is April 8.

You can use this method to update the entire project or selected tasks. Select the Entire Project or Selected Tasks option to specify your choice.

Entering Percent Complete

Another relatively simple method of tracking task progress is to specify percent complete. When you enter percent complete, Microsoft Project calculates actual duration and remaining duration.

To enter percent complete for one or more tasks, do the following:

1 In a task sheet view, such as the Gantt Chart or Tracking Gantt, select the task(s) whose percent complete you want to update.

Task Information

2 On the Standard toolbar, click Task Information and then click the General tab.

3 In the Percent Complete box, enter the percent complete that applies to all selected tasks.

Chapter 10

The tasks are updated to reflect the percent complete. In the Gantt Chart, the percent complete is represented as a thin black line within Gantt bars (see Figure 10-11).

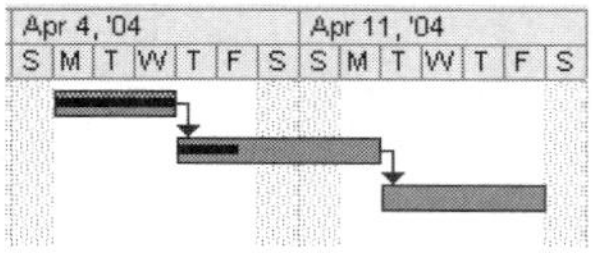

Figure 10-11. Gantt bars display how much of the task has been completed.

50% Complete

Tip **Use the Tracking toolbar to update percent complete**
To display the Tracking toolbar, click View, Toolbars, Tracking. Click the tasks whose percent complete you want to update. Click the 0%, 25%, 50%, 75%, or 100% buttons as appropriate.

Note By default, when you enter percent complete for a task, this percentage is distributed evenly across the actual duration of the task. You can change this to distribute to the status date instead. Click Tools, Options and then click the Calculation tab. Select the Edits To Total Task % Complete Will Be Spread To The Status Date check box.

Entering Actual Duration

If you enter the actual duration of a task, Microsoft Project calculates the percent complete. You can change remaining duration, if necessary.

To enter actual duration of one or more tasks, do the following:

1. In a task sheet view, such as the Gantt Chart or Tracking Gantt, select the task(s) whose actual duration you want to update.
2. Click Tools, Tracking, Update Tasks. The Update Tasks dialog box appears (see Figure 10-12).

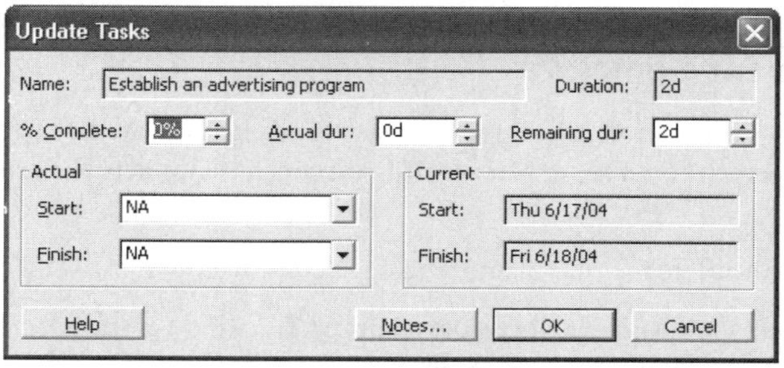

Figure 10-12. Use the Update Tasks dialog box to enter different types of progress information for one or more selected tasks.

3. In the Actual Dur box, enter the actual duration value.
4. If you expect the task to take more or less time than currently scheduled, update the remaining duration in the Remaining Dur box.

Note By default, when you enter progress information for tasks, Microsoft Project automatically calculates the actual and remaining work and cost for assigned resources. This is the case when you update Percent Complete, Actual Duration, or Remaining Duration of tasks or assignments.

If you prefer to enter values for actual and remaining work and cost yourself rather than have Microsoft Project calculate it for you based on entered task progress, you can turn this option off. Click Tools, Options and then click the Calculation tab. Clear the Updating Task Status Updates Resource Status check box.

Entering Actual Start and Actual Finish

When you enter actual start and finish dates for tasks, you can better monitor the finish date of the project as whole, especially when working with critical tasks. When you enter an actual start date, the scheduled start date changes to match the actual start date. Likewise, when you enter an actual finish date, the scheduled finish date changes to match the actual finish date. Any successor tasks are rescheduled as needed.

To enter an actual start or finish for one or more tasks, do the following:

1. In a task sheet view, such as the Gantt Chart or Tracking Gantt, select the task(s) whose actual start or finish you want to update.
2. Click Tools, Tracking, Update Tasks.
3. Under Actual, enter the actual start date in the Start box or the actual finish date in the Finish box.

   The scheduled start and finish dates are shown under Current.

Troubleshooting

Your scheduled start and finish dates change when you enter actuals

When you enter actual start or actual finish dates, your scheduled (current) start or finish dates change to match. Microsoft Project recalculates the scheduled dates so that you can see any effects the change might have on the rest of your schedule. For example, if Task A was scheduled to finish on May 15 but it finished on May 20 instead, you'd need to know how its successor Task B is now scheduled. This update is especially important when critical tasks are involved.

If you want to keep your scheduled start and finish dates for comparison purposes, save a baseline or interim plan before you enter the actuals. With a baseline, not only can Microsoft Project remember the original start and finish dates; it can also calculate the differences between the original and scheduled information. These differences are stored in the Variance fields, which are empty until you save a baseline and start entering progress information.

Design a Custom Tracking View

Use the Tracking Setup Wizard in the Project Guide to help you set up a custom tracking view tailored to work-related progress information and how you're receiving it. The Tracking Setup Wizard facilitates your tracking efforts, whether progress information comes in automatically through Project Server and Project Web Access or you're entering information manually. Either way, the Tracking Setup Wizard helps you set up the tracking of work-related progress information.

To start the Tracking Setup Wizard, click Track on the Project Guide toolbar and then click the Prepare To Track The Progress Of Your Project link. Read the information in the Project Guide side pane and work through the steps, clicking the Save And Go To link at the bottom of the page when you're ready to move to the next step (see Figure 10-13). When finished, click the Save And Finish link.

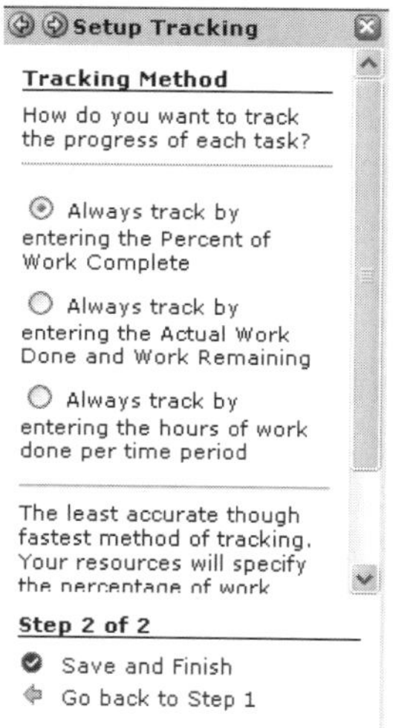

Figure 10-13. The Project Guide walks you through the steps for setting up a custom tracking view.

When you want to enter progress information, click Track on the Project Guide toolbar. Click the Incorporate Progress Information Into The Project link. Your custom view appears, and the Project Guide side pane provides guidelines and controls to help you through the process.

You can also access your custom tracking view on the View menu.

Updating Progress Using Resource Work

If resources are assigned in Microsoft Project, you can update progress information based on *work* for the task or the assignment. Work doesn't exist in your project plan unless you assign resources, at which time task duration is translated into assignment work time. Work can be further divided among multiple assigned resources, depending on the task type. Updating progress using work can be more precise than updating with percent complete or actual duration.

The following work tracking methods are listed in order from the quickest and simplest to the most sophisticated.

Updating Progress Around the Status Date

As you enter actual progress, you can choose the status date to be the reference point for actual and remaining portions of the task. Changing the status date can be helpful if you received actuals on Friday, but you don't enter them into the project plan until the next Wednesday. If you were to use Wednesday's date as the status date, some of your actuals could be skewed. By default, the status date is the current date; that is, today. To set the status date, do the following:

1. Click Project, Project Information.
2. In the Status Date box, enter the status date you want to use for the actual progress information you're about to enter.

You have additional options about how actual progress is to be entered in your project plan. Click Tools, Options and then click the Calculation tab. Under Calculation Options for your project file, a series of four check boxes provides options for handling actual and remaining task information in your schedule in relation to the status date. These options are as follows:

- Move End Of Completed Parts After Status Date Back To Status Date
- And Move Start Of Remaining Parts Back To Status Date
- Move Start Of Remaining Parts Before Status Date Forward To Status Date
- And Move End Of Completed Parts Forward To Status Date

Entering Percent Work Complete

If resources are assigned in Microsoft Project, you can enter their reports of what percentage of work they've completed so far. Remember, *work* comes into existence only when resources are assigned to tasks. To enter percent work complete for a task (as contrasted with an assignment), follow these steps:

1. Display a task sheet view, such as the Tracking Gantt or Task Usage view.
2. Apply the Work table. Click View, Table, Work.
3. In the % W. Comp. field of the task you want to update, enter the value of percent work complete.

Follow these steps to enter percent work complete for an assignment (as contrasted with a task):

1. Display the Task Usage view.
2. Select the assignment (the resource name beneath the task) whose percent work complete you want to update.

   If you want to update several assignments at once with the same percent work complete, select them all.

Assignment Information

3. On the Standard toolbar, click Assignment Information and then click the Tracking tab (see Figure 10-14).

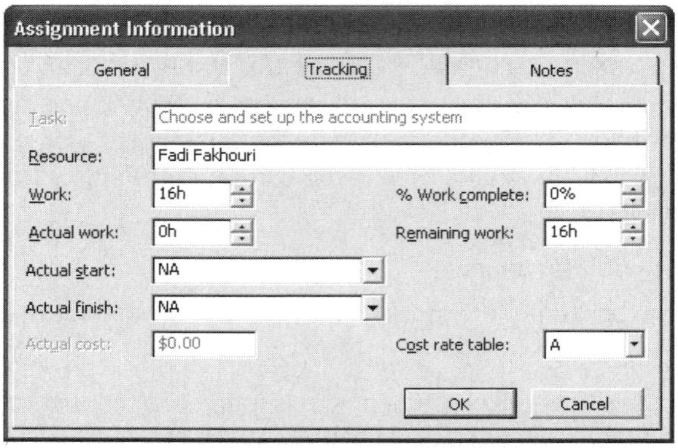

Figure 10-14. Use the Tracking tab in the Assignment Information dialog box to update progress for an assignment.

4. In the % Work Complete box, enter the value.

If entering percent work complete will be your primary method of updating progress information, use the Project Guide to create a custom tracking view. A view similar to the Tracking Gantt is created with the % Work Complete field added as a column in the sheet portion of the view (see Figure 10-15).

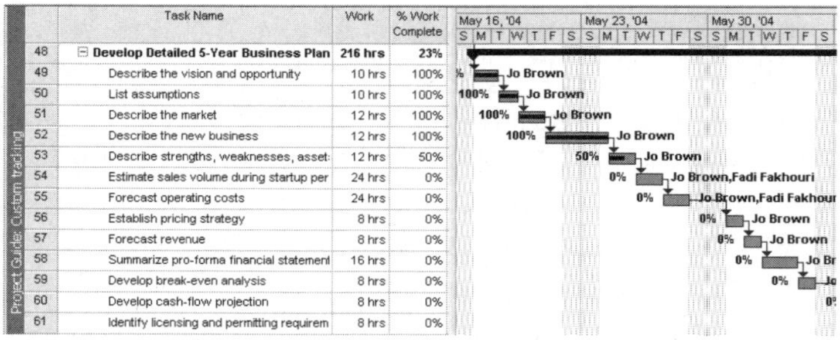

Figure 10-15. The Project Guide can create a custom view for updating percent work complete, which is considered the quickest method of entering work-related actuals.

Entering Actual Work Complete and Remaining Work

If resources are assigned in Microsoft Project, you can enter their reports of actual work completed. If they believe that there is more or less work (than originally scheduled) remaining to be done, you can adjust remaining work as well.

If you have multiple resources assigned to a task, and you enter actual work completed for the task, the work amounts are evenly distributed among the assigned resources. To enter total amounts for actual work completed on a task (as contrasted with an assignment), do the following:

1. Display a task sheet, such as the Task Usage view or Tracking Gantt.
2. Click View, Table, Work.
3. If necessary, drag the divider bar to see the Actual (work) field (see Figure 10-16).

	Task Name	Work	Baseline	Variance	Actual	Remaining	% W. Comp.
27	⊟ **Define the Market**	**100 hrs**	**104 hrs**	**-4 hrs**	**36 hrs**	**64 hrs**	**36%**
28	Access available information	10 hrs	8 hrs	2 hrs	10 hrs	0 hrs	100%
29	Create market analysis plan	14 hrs	16 hrs	-2 hrs	10 hrs	4 hrs	71%
30	Implement market analysis plan	40 hrs	40 hrs	0 hrs	16 hrs	24 hrs	40%
31	Identify competition	16 hrs	16 hrs	0 hrs	0 hrs	16 hrs	0%
32	Summarize the market	12 hrs	16 hrs	-4 hrs	0 hrs	12 hrs	0%
33	Identify target market niche	8 hrs	8 hrs	0 hrs	0 hrs	8 hrs	0%

Figure 10-16. Use the Work table to update actual work on a task.

4. In the Actual (work) field of the task you want to update, enter the actual work value.

   The values in the Remaining (work) and % W. Comp fields are recalculated.

To enter total amounts of actual work completed on an assignment (as contrasted with a task), do the following:

1. Display the Task Usage view.
2. Click View, Table, Work.
3. If necessary, drag the divider bar to see the Actual (work) field.
4. In the Actual (work) field of the assignment (the resource name under the task) you want to update, enter the actual work value.

   The values in the Remaining (work) and % W. Comp fields for the assignment are recalculated.

> **Tip Update actual work in the Assignment Information dialog box**
> You can also double-click the assignment to open the Assignment Information dialog box. Click the Tracking tab. Update the value in the Actual Work box. This is also a good method of updating actual work for multiple assignments if they all have the same value.

If entering actual work will be your primary method of updating progress information, use the Project Guide to create a custom tracking view. A view similar to the Tracking Gantt is created with the Tracking table applied. This method is considered a happy medium—moderately detailed and moderately time-consuming.

Automate Tracking with Project Web Access

If you use Project Professional 2003 with Project Server and Project Web Access, you can automate the gathering and entry of actuals so you don't have to enter actuals on assignments yourself. With the help of your project server administrator, you can set up your team members' timesheets in Project Web Access to enter and submit their actuals on a periodic basis.

You can then review these actuals and accept them for incorporation into the project plan. If you prefer, you can set a rule to have these actuals automatically accepted and incorporated. You can also use the Project Guide to set up the timesheet and options.

For more information about setting up team member timesheets for progress tracking in Project Web Access, see "Setting Up Team Member Timesheets" on page 629.

Entering Actual Work Complete by Time Period

The most comprehensive method of updating actual progress information is to enter actual work on assignments by time period. This is the smallest unit of information you can enter because you're entering information about the assignment, and you're probably entering hours worked in a day.

With this method, you're using the timesheet portion of the Task Usage view to enter actuals. To do this, follow these steps:

1. Display the Task Usage view.
2. Click Format, Details, Actual Work.

   The timesheet portion of the view changes to include Act. Work as a row under (scheduled) Work.
3. If you want to show rolled-up actual work totals for assignments, apply the Work table to the sheet portion of the view. Click View, Table, Work (see Figure 10-17).

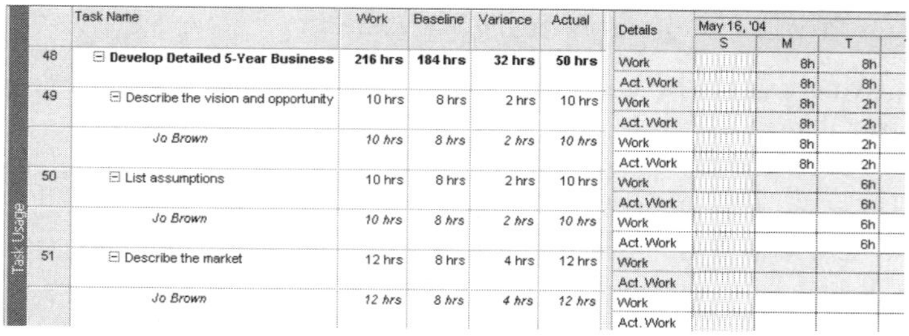

Task Usage
Task Name
Work
Baseline
Variance
Actual
Details
May 16, '04
S
M
T
48
Develop Detailed 5-Year Business
216 hrs
184 hrs
32 hrs
50 hrs
49
Describe the vision and opportunity
10 hrs
8 hrs
2 hrs
10 hrs
Jo Brown
50
List assumptions
51
Describe the market
12 hrs
4 hrs
Work
Act. Work
8h
2h
6h

Figure 10-17. Use the Task Usage view to enter daily values of actual work on assignments.

Chapter 10

4 In the Act. Work field for the assignment and the day, enter the actual work value.

5 If you want to enter actual work for different time periods, click Zoom Out or Zoom In on the Standard toolbar.

Zoom Out

Zoom In

If entering actual work by time period will be your primary method of updating progress information, use the Project Guide to create a custom tracking view. A view similar to the Task Usage view is created with the Act. Work field added as a row in the timesheet portion of the view and the Work and Actual Work fields added as columns in the sheet portion of the view.

Protecting Actuals Information

NEW FEATURE!

Using Project Professional, Project Server, and Project Web Access to automatically gather and enter actuals, you can protect the integrity of actuals submitted by team members. Maintaining true actuals can be crucial if those actuals are directly submitted to your organization's general ledger system to produce customer invoices.

Your project server administrator first sets up the Project Web Access progress method to track hours of work per day or per week. Then the administrator sets the open reporting time period. Team members can enter actuals only during the open reporting period, not long after the period is past.

Furthermore, options can be set so that if the project manager or another user changes actual hours that have been submitted and incorporated into the project plan, those changes can be audited against what was originally submitted by the team member.

You can review the protected actuals submitted by the team member by adding the Actual Work Protected and Actuals Overtime Work Protected fields to a task sheet. You can also return actuals edited in the project plan back to their value as submitted and stored on Project Server. Click Tools, Tracking, Sync To Protected Actuals.

For more information about setting up team member timesheets for progress tracking in Project Web Access, see "Setting Up Team Member Timesheets" on page 629.

Rescheduling the Project

Suppose that you and your team started executing a project a few months ago. Some tasks were completed and some were in progress when your team's efforts were redirected onto a different urgent priority. Now, you're all back to work on this project again, ready to pick up where you left off.

What do you do with your project plan? The scheduled dates of tasks you need to work on now are two months old. Do you have to readjust all the tasks to align them with the current calendar?

No, you just need to reschedule incomplete tasks for the current date. Microsoft Project will shift any incomplete tasks forward to a date you specify, and you can continue forward from there (see Figure 10-18).

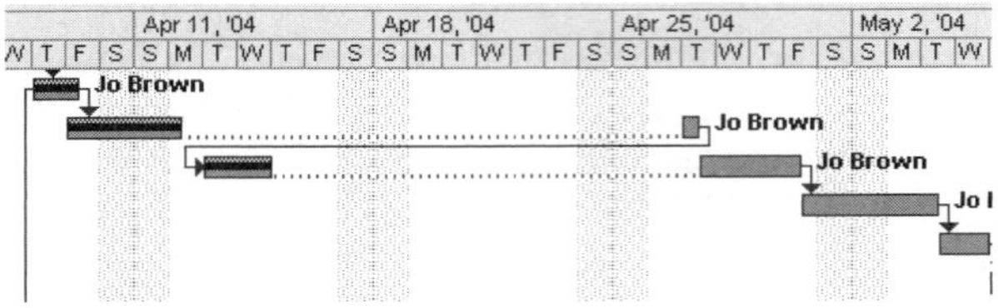

Figure 10-18. This project stalled in early April, and then was rescheduled to continue about two weeks later.

> **Note** In a situation like this, it might be a good idea to save a new baseline. Keep the old one, but use the new baseline for your everyday variance measurements.

To reschedule uncompleted tasks, follow these steps:

1. Click Tools, Tracking, Update Project.
2. Select the Reschedule Uncompleted Work To Start After option.
3. Enter the start after date in the box.

   By default, today's date appears.

You can use this method to reschedule the entire project or just selected tasks. Select either the Entire Project or the Selected Tasks option to specify your choice.

By default, any tasks that were in progress are split so that remaining work is scheduled after the date you specify. If you don't want in-progress tasks to be split, click Tools, Options and then click the Schedule tab. Clear the Split In-Progress Tasks check box.

When you rescheduled uncompleted work in Microsoft Project 2000 and earlier, date constraints were removed and changed to As Soon As Possible or As Late As Possible. Starting with Microsoft Project 2002, uncompleted tasks that have a date constraint (such as Must Start On or Finish No Earlier Than) are not rescheduled, which preserves the constraint and gives you the option of deciding how to handle it.

Also in previous versions of Microsoft Project, when you rescheduled uncompleted work, you could not enter a date in the past; you could only enter the current or future date. As of Microsoft Project 2002, you can enter any reschedule date you want, even one in the past. If a task is in progress, the date does need to be after the task's existing stop date or actual start date.

Manually Updating Project Costs

If resources are assigned to tasks in your project plan and those resources also have their costs entered in Microsoft Project, costs are updated whenever you enter actual progress information. For example, suppose that a $25/hour resource is assigned to 8 hours of work on a task. When you enter that the task is 50 percent complete, $100 of actual cost is recorded for this task.

If you do not want Microsoft Project to calculate costs for you in this manner, you can turn off this option and enter costs yourself. To turn off automatic cost calculation, follow these steps:

1. Click Tools, Options and then click the Calculation tab.
2. Clear the Actual Costs Are Always Calculated By Microsoft Office Project check box.
3. By default, any edits you make to cost will be distributed evenly across the actual duration of a task.

   If you would rather distribute the costs to the status date, select the Edits To Total Actual Cost Will Be Spread To The Status Date check box.

To enter task costs manually, display a task sheet and click View, Table, Cost to apply the Cost table. Enter total actual costs in the Actual field for the task.

To manually enter timephased costs for tasks or assignments, display the Task Usage view. Click Format, Details, Actual Cost to add the Actual Cost field to the timesheet portion of the view.

Tip **Don't enter costs manually**
It can be very cumbersome and tricky to update costs manually. You'll experience more accurate results if you enter resources and their costs in your project plan, along with any fixed costs of tasks. When you assign those resources to tasks, costs are forecasted. When you enter progress on tasks, actual costs are calculated.

Chapter 11

Responding to Changes in Your Project

During the execution phase of your project, your resources are working on their tasks, and you're tracking their progress by entering actuals into your project plan. Those actuals, combined with your baseline information, give you the means to compare your current progress against your original plan. As part of your project control responsibilities, you use this information to keep an eye on project progress. In this way, you can analyze project performance, see how you're doing, and take any corrective action that you might deem necessary.

As you monitor and analyze project performance day to day, occasionally you'll need to make adjustments. Perhaps one task finishes a few days early, and this affects its successors and their assigned resources. Maybe another task took longer than expected and went over budget. Suppose that various changes in the schedule caused a resource to become overallocated and another one to be underutilized.

You might need to adjust your project plan to account for such variances. Sometimes, the differences work in your favor, as when a task finishes early. Other times, the differences point to a potential problem, which you can prevent if you catch it soon enough.

The nature of the changes you make to your project plan depends on your project priorities. Remember the one fixed side of your project triangle (finish date, budget/resources, or scope), and adjust your project accordingly.

For more information about the project triangle, see Chapter 9, "Checking and Adjusting the Project Plan."

In addition to the day-to-day monitoring and adjusting of a project in progress, sometimes larger modifications are needed because of external changes imposed on the project. For example, your customers might announce that you must move the finish date up six weeks. Or a new corporate edict might cut $8,000 from your budget or reduce your staff by 10 percent.

Sometimes, wholesale changes to the project are needed because the scheduled finish date, overall cost, or resource allocation has somehow gotten way off track. In this case, radical measures might be needed to bring the project into conformance again.

With large, externally imposed changes or a temporarily derailed project, you might need to *replan* or reschedule the project. The techniques used are similar to those you used to hit your targets when you were first planning the project. You make adjustments to the schedule, costs, resources, or scope in your project plan; and Microsoft Office Project 2003 recalculates your schedule so you can quickly see the results of your replanning.

Baseline, Scheduled, and Actual Project Information

In the course of monitoring project performance, there are four terms to keep in mind:

Baseline. Baseline dates, costs, durations, and so on, are your project plan's values at the time you saved baseline information. This is also referred to as *planned* information.

Scheduled. The current project combines the project's *actual* performance on past and current tasks with the *planned schedule* for current and future tasks. The combination of the actual and scheduled information forms the current plan as scheduled. In other words, Actual + Remaining = Scheduled.

Actual. Actual progress information reflects real data about task status. *Actuals* include data such as percent complete, actual work, actual finish date, actual costs, and so on.

Variance. The difference between baseline information and scheduled information is the *variance*. Project 2003 subtracts the baseline value from the scheduled value (which incorporates any actuals you have entered) to calculate the variance. Therefore, a positive variance means you're behind in your schedule or over budget, whereas a negative variance means you're ahead of the game—finishing faster or under budget. A variance of 0 indicates that your baseline and scheduled values are exactly the same. If actuals have been entered, this means that everything went exactly according to plan. If the task is still in the future, this means that projections forecast that the task will still go according to plan.

Whether you're making large adjustments to respond to large issues or small adjustments to keep a healthy project well on its way, you can always keep a close eye on progress. You can analyze the current status of the project and decide on any corrective actions necessary.

Inside Out

Variances calculated from scheduled values

It might seem odd that variances are calculated from scheduled values rather than actual values. However, because the scheduled values incorporate any actual values, it makes sense. And by not requiring actual values to make the calculation, you can see variances in future tasks as well. If you see any large variances projected for future tasks or for the project as a whole, you'll still have time to take corrective action and head off the problems.

Tip **Show the Tracking toolbar**
Now that you're in the execution phase of your project, you might find it convenient to display the Tracking toolbar. It contains many of the tools you need to quickly review and update task status. Click View, Toolbars, Tracking. You can also right-click an empty spot in the toolbars area and then click Tracking.

Monitoring and Adjusting the Schedule

If you're managing a time-constrained project, there are a few pieces of task information you'll want to keep a close eye on, including the following:

- Project finish date
- Critical path
- Start and finish dates of critical tasks
- Current progress of critical tasks

If actuals have changed task scheduling to the point where your target project finish date is projected to be late, you'll need to adjust the schedule to bring that finish date back in line.

Project Management Practices: Schedule Control

It's understood that very few projects run precisely as planned. Tasks take more or less time than planned, resources discover new information, forgotten tasks are remembered, and outside forces influence the project implementation. When changes to the project schedule take place, you might have to revise durations, rearrange task sequences, or analyze what-if scenarios for your project.

Microsoft Project is an excellent tool for schedule control because it can calculate and predict the effects of any schedule changes, whether the change comes as a result of entering actual information or what-if information. Microsoft Project tracks your planned dates against your actual dates (and other schedule information). This variance analysis is key to schedule control. Analyzing variances in dates, durations, and other schedule information helps you detect where the project is diverging from your original plan. You can then predict possible delays in the schedule further down the line and take corrective actions now to offset those delays.

Monitoring Schedule Progress

Use one or more of the following techniques to help you monitor progress toward your finish date:

- Review finish dates and the critical path.
- Check and adjust task constraints, dependencies, and durations.
- Add resources to tasks.

For more information about monitoring and adjusting the schedule to achieve a specific finish date, see "Bringing In the Project Finish Date" on page 258.

Another method for monitoring schedule progress is to save a baseline and then compare it with the current schedule. For example, you can see baseline finish dates for tasks next to their scheduled finish dates, based on actuals you entered. Then, you can look at the variances between the baseline and scheduled finish. The finish date variance, for example, is calculated as follows:

(Scheduled/Current) Finish – Baseline Finish = Finish Variance

Tip **Evaluate your schedule variances and performance with earned value analysis**
You can use earned value calculations, such as the Schedule Performance Index (SPI) and Schedule Variance (SV) earned value fields, to analyze your project performance so far.

For more information on examining project performance, see "Analyzing Progress and Costs Using Earned Value" on page 401.

Note Because baseline information is vital to tracking and analyzing progress on your project, be sure to save a baseline early in the project. The ideal time to save a baseline is after you build your project plan and adjust all values to hit your target finish date, budget, and resource workload levels.

Even if you realize you hadn't saved a baseline until you're well into tracking, go ahead and save a baseline at that time. Better late than never.

For more information about saving baseline information, see "Saving Original Plan Information Using a Baseline" on page 298.

Reviewing Overall Schedule Progress

Review your project statistics to get a broad view of how your project status compares with your baseline. Project statistics show your currently scheduled start and finish dates, along with their baseline, actual, and remaining values. To review your project statistics, follow these steps:

1. Click Project, Project Information.

   The Project Information dialog box appears.

2. Click the Statistics button.

   The Project Statistics dialog box appears. The current (scheduled) finish date appears in the Finish column (see Figure 11-1).

Project Statistics for '11SwDev.mpp'

	Start	Finish
Current	Thu 1/1/04	Mon 5/24/04
Baseline	Thu 1/1/04	Thu 5/13/04
Actual	Thu 1/1/04	NA
Variance	0d	7.25d

	Duration	Work	Cost
Current	103d	1,668h	$72,528.00
Baseline	95.75d	1,532h	$64,888.00
Actual	15.39d	252h	$12,420.00
Remaining	87.61d	1,416h	$60,108.00

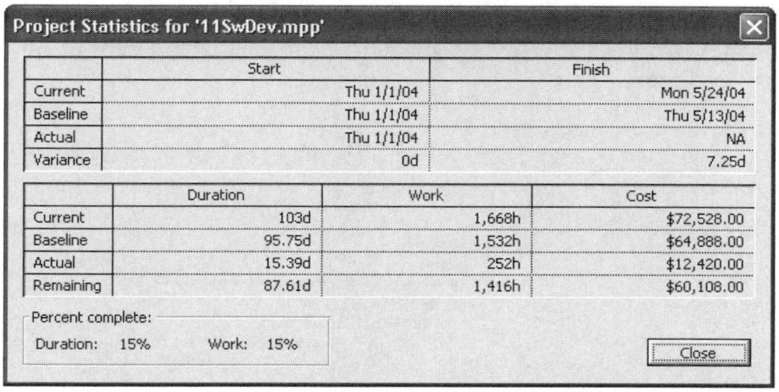

Percent complete:

Duration: 15% Work: 15% [Close]

Figure 11-1. The Project Statistics dialog box shows overall project information with its currently scheduled values, baseline values, actual values, and more.

Tip Click the Project Statistics button

Project Statistics

You can also use the Tracking toolbar to quickly open the Project Statistics dialog box. On the Tracking toolbar, click Project Statistics.

Another way to keep your eye on the schedule at all times is to add the project summary task row, as follows:

1 Display the Gantt Chart or other task sheet.

2 Click Tools, Options, and then click the View tab.

3 Select the Show Project Summary Task check box.

The project summary task appears at the top of any task sheet view, including the Gantt Chart (see Figure 11-2). Task information is rolled up for the entire project, and its summary total is displayed in the project summary row. Specifically, the Finish field in the project summary row shows the latest finish date in the project. If you added additional fields or applied different tables, information is also rolled up for those fields as appropriate.

	ⓘ	Task Name	Duration	Start	Finish		Jan 4, '04	Jan 11
						W T F S S M T W T F S S M		
0		⊟ **Software Development**	**103 days**	**Thu 1/1/04**	**Mon 5/24/04**			
1	✓	⊟ Scope	3.5 days	Thu 1/1/04	Tue 1/6/04			
2	✓	Determine project scope	8 hrs	Thu 1/1/04	Thu 1/1/04	Eva Corets		
3	✓	Secure project sponsorship	1 day	Thu 1/1/04	Fri 1/2/04	Eva Corets		
4	✓	Define preliminary resources	1 day	Fri 1/2/04	Mon 1/5/04	Clair Hector		
5	✓	Secure core resources	1 day	Mon 1/5/04	Tue 1/6/04	Clair Hector		
6	✓	Scope complete	0 days	Tue 1/6/04	Tue 1/6/04	1/6		
7	✓	⊟ Analysis/Software Requireme	14.5 days	Tue 1/6/04	Mon 1/26/04			
8	✓	Conduct needs analysis	7 days	Tue 1/6/04	Thu 1/15/04			
9	✓	Draft preliminary software spe	4 days	Tue 1/13/04	Mon 1/19/04			
10	✓	Develop preliminary budget	2 days	Fri 1/16/04	Tue 1/20/04			
11	✓	Review software specification/	4 hrs	Tue 1/20/04	Tue 1/20/04			
12	✓	Incorporate feedback on softw	1 day	Wed 1/21/04	Wed 1/21/04			

Figure 11-2. The Project Summary row rolls up task information to display the totals for the entire project.

By default, the regular Gantt Chart shows progress as a thin black line through the Gantt bar. To also see percent complete next to the Gantt bars, apply the Tracking Gantt. Click View, Tracking Gantt (see Figure 11-3).

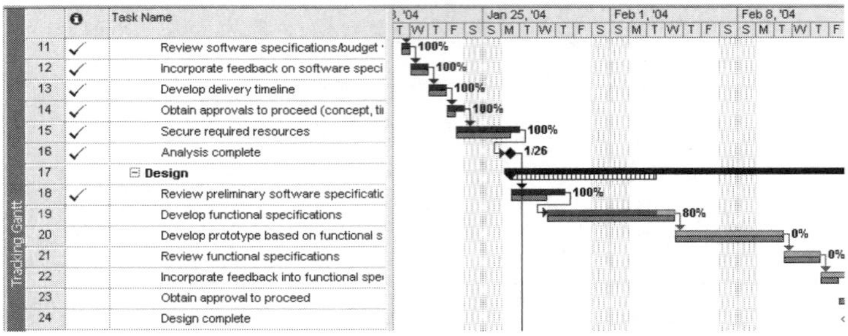

Figure 11-3. The Tracking Gantt shows the progress, the percent complete, the baseline, and the critical path in the chart area of the view.

Reviewing Schedule Variances

To review the differences between your original baseline plan values and your currently scheduled values, apply the Variance table, as follows:

1. Display the Gantt Chart or other task sheet.
2. Click View, Table, Variance.

   The Variance table is applied to the current view (see Figure 11-4).

	Task Name	Start	Finish	Baseline Start	Baseline Finish	Start Var.	Finish Var.
0	**Software Development**	**Thu 1/1/04**	**Mon 5/24/04**	**Thu 1/1/04**	**Thu 5/13/04**	**0 days**	**7.25 days**
1	**Scope**	**Thu 1/1/04**	**Tue 1/6/04**	**Thu 1/1/04**	**Tue 1/6/04**	**0 days**	**0 days**
2	Determine project scope	Thu 1/1/04	Thu 1/1/04	Thu 1/1/04	Thu 1/1/04	0 days	0.5 days
3	Secure project sponsorship	Thu 1/1/04	Thu 1/1/04	Thu 1/1/04	Fri 1/2/04	0 days	-0.5 days
4	Define preliminary resources	Fri 1/2/04	Fri 1/2/04	Fri 1/2/04	Mon 1/5/04	0 days	-0.5 days
5	Secure core resources	Mon 1/5/04	Tue 1/6/04	Mon 1/5/04	Tue 1/6/04	0 days	0 days
6	Scope complete	Tue 1/6/04	Tue 1/6/04	Tue 1/6/04	Tue 1/6/04	0 days	0 days
7	**Analysis/Software Requirements**	**Tue 1/6/04**	**Mon 1/26/04**	**Tue 1/6/04**	**Mon 1/26/04**	**0 days**	**0.5 days**
8	Conduct needs analysis	Tue 1/6/04	Thu 1/15/04	Tue 1/6/04	Tue 1/13/04	0 days	2 days
9	Draft preliminary software specifice	Tue 1/13/04	Mon 1/19/04	Tue 1/13/04	Fri 1/16/04	0 days	1 day

Figure 11-4. The Variance table shows the currently scheduled start and finish dates as compared with the baseline start and finish dates (including the differences between them).

> **Tip** **Quickly switch tables**
>
> To quickly change to a different table, right-click the Select All box in the upper-left corner of the table in a sheet view. The list of tables appears.
>
> To quickly see the name of the current view and table, position your mouse pointer over the Select All box. A ScreenTip lists the name of the current view and table.

Troubleshooting

Your scheduled values change whenever you enter actuals

Whenever you enter actual progress information, Microsoft Project recalculates your scheduled information based on these actuals, so you can see any effect the actual progress information has on the rest of your schedule. This also enables you to continue to see scheduled projections for the project finish date and total cost, based on performance to this point. For example, if Task A was scheduled to be finished on May 15, but it is finished on May 20 instead, you'd need to know how its successor Task B is now scheduled. This information is especially important if these are critical tasks.

If you want to keep your original start and finish dates for comparison purposes, save a baseline or interim plan before you enter the actuals. Then, add the Baseline Start and Baseline Finish to a task sheet, perhaps right next to your scheduled Start and Finish fields. If you're using start and finish dates saved with your interim plan, add Start1 and Finish1 (or whichever custom fields you used for your interim plan) to a task sheet.

For more information about saving baselines, saving interim plans, and adding original field information to your task sheet, see "Saving Original Plan Information Using a Baseline" on page 298.

Reviewing the Critical Path

By viewing the finish date or the critical path, you can easily see whether you're still scheduled to hit your target finish date, given the actuals you've entered. To see the critical path, click View, Tracking Gantt. If you need to bring in the finish date, you might want to focus on the critical tasks. You can filter your task sheet to show only critical tasks by clicking Project, Filtered For, Critical. To show all tasks again, click Project, Filtered For, All Tasks.

Tip **Click the Filter tool**
To select a filter, you can also click the Filter tool on the Formatting toolbar. In the Filter list, click Critical. When finished, click All Tasks in the Filter list.

For more information about viewing the critical path, see "Viewing the Critical Path" on page 254.

Note After a critical task is completed, it becomes noncritical because it can no longer affect the completion of future tasks.

Reviewing Task Progress

Reviewing the progress of critical tasks is the most effective means of learning quickly whether your project is staying on track with its target finish date. The following filters can help you focus on any potential problems with task progress:

- Late/Overbudget Tasks Assigned To
- Should Start By
- Should Start/Finish By
- Slipped/Late Progress
- Slipping Tasks (see Figure 11-5)
- Tasks With Deadlines
- Tasks With Fixed Dates

	Task Name	Start	Finish	Baseline Start	Baseline Finish	Start Var.	Finish Var.
26	Review functional specifications	Tue 2/17/04	Tue 2/17/04	Mon 2/16/04	Mon 2/16/04	1 day	1 day
27	Identify modular/tiered design parar	Wed 2/18/04	Wed 2/18/04	Tue 2/17/04	Tue 2/17/04	1 day	1 day
28	Assign development staff	Thu 2/19/04	Thu 2/19/04	Wed 2/18/04	Wed 2/18/04	1 day	1 day
29	Develop code	Fri 2/20/04	Thu 3/18/04	Thu 2/19/04	Wed 3/10/04	1 day	6 days
30	Developer testing (primary debuggir	Fri 2/27/04	Thu 3/25/04	Tue 2/24/04	Tue 3/16/04	2.25 days	7.25 days
31	Development complete	Thu 3/25/04	Thu 3/25/04	Tue 3/16/04	Tue 3/16/04	7.25 days	7.25 days

Figure 11-5. Apply the Slipping Tasks filter to quickly see which tasks are in jeopardy.

To apply one of these filters, follow these steps:

1. Display the Gantt Chart or other task sheet you want to filter.
2. On the Formatting toolbar, click the arrow in the Filter tool.

   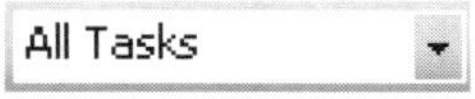

   In the Filter list, click the filter you want.
3. When you want to show all tasks again, click All Tasks in the Filter list.

You can also run reports that provide information about the progress of tasks, such as the following:

- Unstarted Tasks
- Tasks Starting Soon
- Tasks In Progress
- Completed Tasks
- Should Have Started Tasks
- Slipping Tasks

To run a report, follow these steps:

1. Click View, Reports.
2. Double-click Current Activities.

3 Double-click the report you want.

4 If a dialog box appears asking for more information, enter the information and then click OK.

The report appears in a preview window. You can zoom or print the report for a closer look.

Review Status Indicators

You can add the Status Indicator field to any task sheet. This field displays icons that indicate whether a task is completed, on schedule, or behind schedule.

Select the column heading next to which you want to insert the Status Indicator column. Click Insert, Column. In the Field Name list, click Status Indicator.

If you prefer to show current task status as text rather than icons, insert the Status column instead. For every task, the status of "Future Task," "On Schedule," "Late," or "Complete" appears (see Figure 11-6).

	Status Indicator	Status	Task Name
1	✓	Complete	Review preliminary software specifications
2	✓	Complete	Develop functional specifications
3		On Schedule	Develop prototype based on functional specifications
4	✓	Complete	Review functional specifications
5		Late	Incorporate feedback into functional specifications
6		On Schedule	Obtain approval to proceed
7		Future Task	Review functional specifications
8		Future Task	Identify modular/tiered design parameters

Figure 11-6. Add the Status Indicator or the Status fields to a task sheet to see task status at a glance.

Working with Progress Lines

You can add *progress lines* to your Gantt Chart that provide a graphic means of seeing whether tasks are ahead of schedule, behind schedule, or exactly on time. Progress lines are shown for tasks that have been completed, are in progress, or are currently due. They are not shown for tasks in the future.

For any given progress date, which you can set as the status date, you can have Microsoft Project draw a progress line connecting in-progress tasks and tasks that should have started (see Figure 11-7). You can set the progress date to be the current date, the project status date, or any other date you select. You can also set multiple progress dates at recurring intervals; for example, on the first Monday of every month.

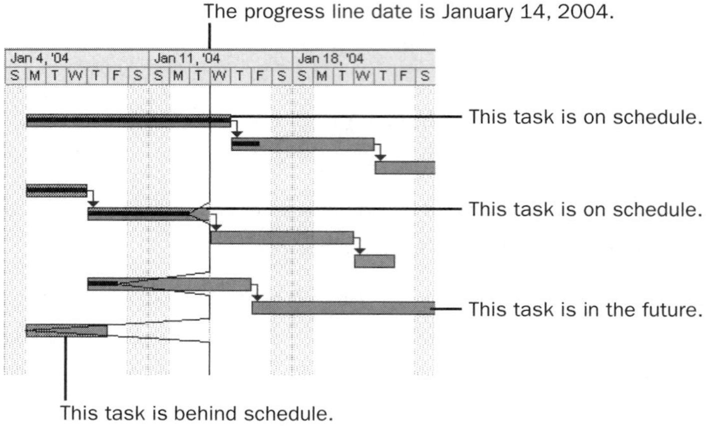

Figure 11-7. The left-pointing peaks indicate a negative schedule variance, whereas straight lines show tasks that are exactly on schedule.

Progress lines create a graph on the Gantt Chart that provides valuable progress information, as follows:

- A progress line angled to the left indicates work that's behind schedule as of the progress line date.
- A straight progress line indicates a task on schedule as of the progress line date.
- Tasks untouched by the progress line are tasks starting in the future from the progress line date.

To add a progress line to a Gantt chart:

1. Display the Gantt Chart, Tracking Gantt, or any other Gantt view.
2. Click Tools, Tracking, Progress Lines.

   The Progress Lines dialog box appears (see Figure 11-8).

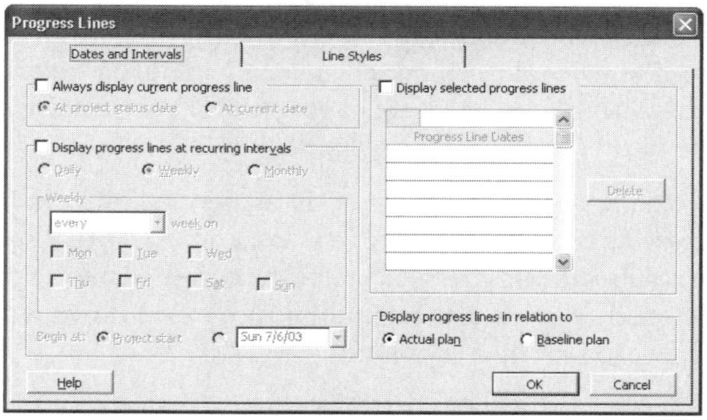

Figure 11-8. Set progress lines in the Gantt Chart using the Progress Lines dialog box.

3 On the Dates And Intervals tab, select the Always Display Current Progress Line check box. Then select whether you want the progress line to be displayed at the project status date or the current date.

The project status date, as well as the current date, is set in the Project Information dialog box (Project, Project Information). If no status date is set there, the current date (today) is used instead.

4 Under Display Progress Lines In Relation To, select whether you want progress lines to reflect the actual plan or your baseline.

5 Set any other preferences for the way you want dates and intervals of dates to be represented with your progress lines.

You can enter specific progress line dates, display progress lines at selected date intervals, and so on (see Figure 11-9).

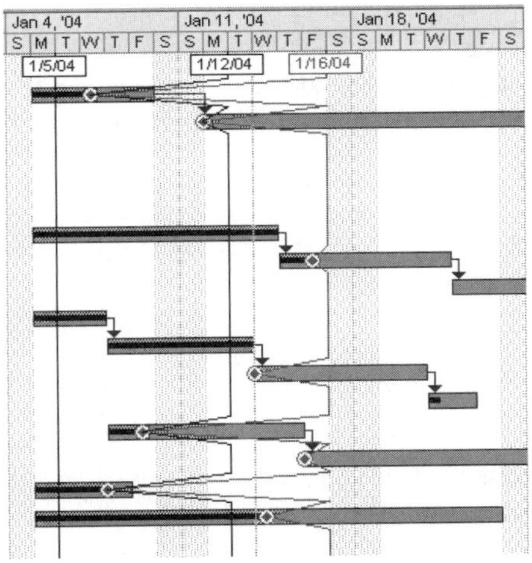

Figure 11-9. Specify as many progress lines as you need for your purposes.

6 Click the Line Styles tab, and set your preferences for the way you want the progress lines to appear in the Gantt Chart.

You can specify the line type and color and the progress point shape and color for the current progress line and other progress lines (see Figure 11-10 on the following page).

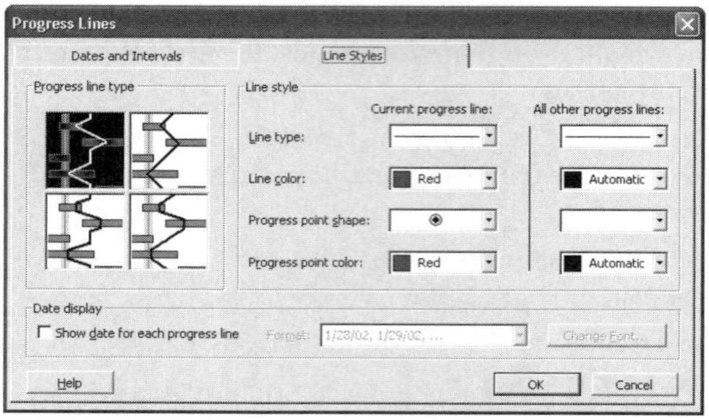

Figure 11-10. Use the Line Styles tab in the Progress Lines dialog box to customize the way progress lines appear in your Gantt Chart.

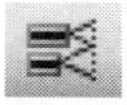

Add Progress Line

Tip **Click the Add Progress Line button**

You can also use the Tracking toolbar to quickly add a progress line. On the Tracking toolbar, click Add Progress Line. A pop-up appears, and the mouse pointer changes to the progress line icon:

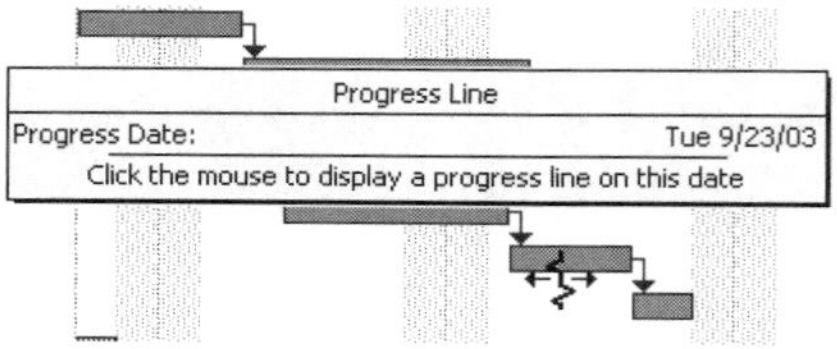

In the chart area of the Gantt Chart, click where you want the progress line to be added. The Progress Line pop-up shows the exact date you're pointing at.

If you have defined progress line dates in addition to the status date or current date, you can choose to show them only when you want. For example, you might want to show progress lines in a printed view for a status meeting, but hide them while updating progress. To temporarily hide progress lines:

1. Click Tools, Tracking, Progress Lines.
2. Make sure the Dates And Intervals tab is showing.
3. Clear the Display Selected Progress Lines check box.

   The defined progress lines are removed from your Gantt Chart, but the dates remain in the Progress Lines dialog box for when you want to show them again.

You can remove one or more of your defined progress lines. To delete a progress line:

1. Click Tools, Tracking, Progress Lines.

   Make sure the Dates And Intervals tab is showing.

2. Under Progress Line Dates, select the progress line you want to remove from the Gantt Chart and then click the Delete button.

To hide the current progress line reflecting the project status date or the current date:

1. Click Tools, Tracking, Progress Lines.

   The Progress Lines dialog box appears.

2. On the Dates And Intervals tab, clear the Always Display Current Progress Line check box.

Correcting the Schedule

Suppose that you reviewed your schedule details and found that your project isn't going as quickly as planned and the finish date is in jeopardy. Or perhaps upper management has imposed a schedule change, and you need to work toward a different finish date.

If you need to take corrective actions in your project plan to bring in the scheduled finish date, you can do the following:

- Check schedule assumptions—such as duration, constraints, and task dependencies—to see whether any adjustments can be made.
- Add resources to recover a slipping schedule (this will likely add costs).
- Cut scope to recover a slipping schedule (this will probably require stakeholder approval).

For more information about using any of these techniques to adjust the schedule to meet the current or new finish date, see "Bringing In the Project Finish Date" on page 258.

Create a What-If Project

Suppose that an external change is being proposed, or you just want to see the effect of a potential change to your project plan. You can save another version of your project plan and make the necessary adjustments to reflect the potential change. You can then examine specifically what the imposed changes will do to your project plan in terms of schedule, cost, and resource allocation.

To save a what-if project, click File, Save As. In the File Name box, enter a name for the what-if project and then click OK.

You can change the what-if project as much as you like. Because you saved it under a different filename, your working version of the project plan remains intact, but you gained valuable information about the impact of potential change.

If you or other stakeholders decide to go ahead with the change, you can adopt the what-if project as your new working project.

Tip **Check the adjustments**
When you adjust your project plan to achieve the finish date you need, be sure to check costs, resource allocation, and scope. You need to know how your changes affect other areas of the project plan.

You might also think you need to save a new baseline, especially if there have been major schedule changes.

For more information on new baselines, see "Need a New Baseline?" later in this chapter on page 352.

Monitoring and Adjusting Costs

If your project is a budget-constrained project, you'll want to keep a close eye on the resource and task costs, and on estimated costs for the project as a whole. You'll also want to adjust your project plan if you receive any actuals that are likely to blow the budget.

Project Management Practices: Cost Control

Cost control is the means for a project to stay within the bounds of the prescribed project budget. It involves continual monitoring of the project plan, tracking actual work and cost information, and taking corrective action where needed. If a task early in the project costs more than expected, costs might have to be trimmed in later tasks. In addition, outside forces might affect the project budget. For example, certain material costs might have gone up from the time you developed your plan to the time you're actually procuring the material. Or your company might undertake a cost-cutting initiative that requires you to cut all project costs by 15 percent.

When changes to project costs take place, you might have to adjust assignments or scope to bring costs in line with the budget. If you have a positive cost variance, the scheduled or current cost is more than your planned baseline cost. If you have a negative cost variance, the scheduled cost is less than your baseline cost. Although you certainly need to know why costs are higher than planned, you also should look into costs that are lower than planned. Lower costs can point to potential problems with increased risk, and perhaps with quality issues.

Earned value analysis is particularly useful for cost control. With variances and earned value analysis, you can assess the differences between planned and scheduled costs, determine their causes, and decide whether corrective actions are needed.

Monitoring Project Costs

Use one or more of the following techniques to monitor and adjust costs so you can continue to work within your budget:

- Display specialized views and tables to review project costs.
- Adjust the schedule to reduce costs.
- Adjust assignments to reduce costs.

For more information about monitoring and adjusting costs to achieve a specific budget, see "Reducing Project Costs" on page 267.

Using baseline information you saved, you can review your current costs and compare them with baseline costs. For example, you can see baseline costs for tasks (including their resource costs) next to their scheduled costs, based on actuals you entered. Then, you can review the variances between the baseline and scheduled cost. The cost variance is calculated as follows:

(Scheduled/Current) Cost – Baseline Cost = Cost Variance

Tip **Evaluate your cost variances and performance with earned value analysis**
You can use earned value calculations, such as the Budgeted Cost of Work Scheduled (BCWS) and Cost Variance (CV) earned value fields to analyze your project performance against the budget so far.

For more information, see "Analyzing Progress and Costs Using Earned Value" on page 401.

Reviewing Overall Cost Totals

There are two ways to review your overall cost totals, as follows:

- Review project statistics. Click Project, Project Information and then click the Statistics button. Under Cost, review the current, baseline, actual, and remaining cost for the project. You can also click Project Statistics on the Tracking toolbar.
- Add the project summary task row. In the Gantt Chart or other task sheet, click Tools, Options and then click the View tab. Select the Show Project Summary Task check box. Summary totals for task information in the current table are displayed in the project summary task row at the top of the sheet. If a table containing cost information is applied, the project summary task row shows project cost totals.

Reviewing Cost Variances

Use the Cost table to review the differences between your original baseline costs and your currently scheduled costs. The Cost table includes fields containing baseline costs, total scheduled costs, actual costs, remaining costs, and cost variances. To apply the Cost table:

1. Display the Gantt Chart or other task sheet.
2. Click View, Table, Cost.

   The Cost table is applied to the current view (see Figure 11-11).

	Task Name	Fixed Cost	Fixed Cost Accrual	Total Cost	Baseline	Variance	Actual	Remaining
0	Software Development	$0.00	Prorated	$72,068.00	$64,888.00	$7,180.00	$15,140.00	$56,928.00
1	Scope	$0.00	Prorated	$1,380.00	$1,600.00	($220.00)	$1,160.00	$220.00
2	Determine project scope	$0.00	Prorated	$480.00	$240.00	$240.00	$480.00	$0.00
3	Secure project sponsorship	$0.00	Prorated	$240.00	$480.00	($240.00)	$240.00	$0.00
4	Define preliminary resources	$0.00	Prorated	$220.00	$440.00	($220.00)	$110.00	$110.00
5	Secure core resources	$0.00	Prorated	$440.00	$440.00	$0.00	$330.00	$110.00
6	Scope complete	$0.00	Prorated	$0.00	$0.00	$0.00	$0.00	$0.00
7	Analysis/Software Requirement	$0.00	Prorated	$7,620.00	$5,860.00	$1,760.00	$3,240.00	$4,380.00
8	Conduct needs analysis	$0.00	Prorated	$2,520.00	$1,800.00	$720.00	$1,890.00	$630.00
9	Draft preliminary software specif	$0.00	Prorated	$1,440.00	$1,080.00	$360.00	$720.00	$720.00
10	Develop preliminary budget	$0.00	Prorated	$880.00	$880.00	$0.00	$440.00	$440.00

Figure 11-11. Apply the Cost table to a task sheet to see the most important cost data for tasks.

With the project summary task row applied, you can also review rolled up cost totals.

There's also a cost table for resources, which includes cost information for all the resource's assignments. With the Resource Sheet or Resource Usage view displayed, apply the Cost table. The Resource Cost table includes the baseline cost, scheduled cost, actual cost, remaining cost, and cost variance for all the resource's assignments (see Figure 11-12).

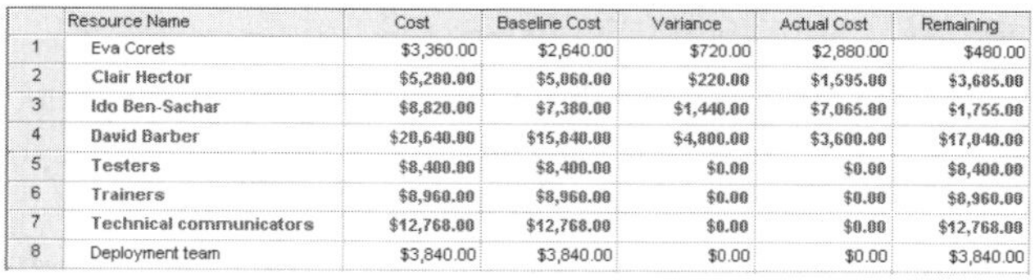

	Resource Name	Cost	Baseline Cost	Variance	Actual Cost	Remaining
1	Eva Corets	$3,360.00	$2,640.00	$720.00	$2,880.00	$480.00
2	Clair Hector	$5,280.00	$5,060.00	$220.00	$1,595.00	$3,685.00
3	Ido Ben-Sachar	$8,820.00	$7,380.00	$1,440.00	$7,065.00	$1,755.00
4	David Barber	$20,640.00	$15,840.00	$4,800.00	$3,600.00	$17,040.00
5	Testers	$8,400.00	$8,400.00	$0.00	$0.00	$8,400.00
6	Trainers	$8,960.00	$8,960.00	$0.00	$0.00	$8,960.00
7	Technical communicators	$12,768.00	$12,768.00	$0.00	$0.00	$12,768.00
8	Deployment team	$3,840.00	$3,840.00	$0.00	$0.00	$3,840.00

Figure 11-12. Apply the Cost table to a resource sheet to see the most important cost data for resources.

Reviewing Overbudget Costs

You can apply a filter to a task or resource sheet to see only those tasks or resources associated with overbudget costs, as follows:

1. Display the view and apply the table that contains the information you want to review in the context of overbudget costs.
2. Click Project, Filtered For, More Filters.
3. In the More Filters dialog box, click Cost Overbudget and then click Apply.

If you prefer to see all tasks or resources, but have the overbudget tasks or resources highlighted, click Highlight instead.

Microsoft Project filters for any tasks or resources whose scheduled or actual costs are higher than the baseline costs.

4. Review the tasks or resources to analyze the extent of the cost overages.
5. When you finish, show all tasks again by clicking the Filter tool on the Formatting toolbar and then clicking All Tasks.

Reviewing Cost Performance Using Earned Value Analysis

If you saved a baseline and are entering actuals, you can evaluate current cost and schedule performance using earned value calculations. To generate most earned value information, you must have the following items in your project plan:

- A saved baseline
- Resources assigned to tasks
- Costs associated with assigned resources
- Actual progress information

To review earned value information, follow these steps:

1. Display the Gantt Chart or other task sheet.
2. Click View, Table, More Tables.
3. Click Earned Value, Earned Value Cost Indicators, or Earned Value Schedule Indicators, depending on the type of earned value information you want to review (see Figure 11-13).

	Task Name	BCWS	BCWP	CV	CV%	CPI	BAC	EAC	VAC	TCPI
0	⊟ **Software Development**	**$4,300.00**	**$2,915.00**	**($195.00)**	**-6%**	**0.94**	**$64,888.00**	**$69,228.71**	**($4,340.71)**	**1**
1	⊟ **Scope**	**$1,600.00**	**$1,430.00**	**$390.00**	**27%**	**1.38**	**$1,600.00**	**$1,163.64**	**$436.36**	**0.3**
2	Determine project scope	$240.00	$180.00	($180.00)	-100%	0.5	$240.00	$480.00	($240.00)	-0.5
3	Secure project sponsorshi	$480.00	$480.00	$240.00	50%	2	$480.00	$240.00	$240.00	0
4	Define preliminary resourc	$440.00	$440.00	$330.00	75%	4	$440.00	$110.00	$330.00	0
5	Secure core resources	$440.00	$330.00	$0.00	0%	1	$440.00	$440.00	$0.00	1
6	Scope complete	$0.00	$0.00	$0.00	0%	0	$0.00	$0.00	$0.00	0
7	⊟ **Analysis/Software Require**	**$2,700.00**	**$1,485.00**	**($585.00)**	**-39%**	**0.72**	**$5,860.00**	**$8,168.48**	**($2,308.48)**	**1.15**
8	Conduct needs analysis	$1,800.00	$1,350.00	($540.00)	-40%	0.71	$1,800.00	$2,520.00	($720.00)	-5
9	Draft preliminary software	$900.00	$135.00	($45.00)	-33%	0.75	$1,080.00	$1,440.00	($360.00)	1.05
10	Develop preliminary budget	$0.00	$0.00	$0.00	0%	0	$880.00	$880.00	$0.00	1
11	Review software specifica	$0.00	$0.00	$0.00	0%	0	$400.00	$400.00	$0.00	1

Figure 11-13. The Earned Value Cost Indicators table displays earned value fields related to budget performance.

Chapter 11

Tip **See all available earned value fields**
You can see a list of all earned value fields available in Microsoft Project. Click Help, Microsoft Project Help (or press F1). In the Search For box, type **fields** and then press Enter. Click Earned Value Fields. The list of all available earned value fields appears in a separate Help window.

Click a field name to open a Help topic that gives a description of each field, how it's calculated, its best uses, and an example of its use.

Table 11-1 lists the default contents of each of the three earned value tables.

Table 11-1. Earned Value Tables

Table name	Included fields
Earned Value	BCWS (Budgeted Cost of Work Scheduled)
	BCWP (Budgeted Cost of Work Performed)
	ACWP (Actual Cost of Work Performed)
	SV (Schedule Variance)
	CV (Cost Variance)
	EAC (Estimate At Completion)
	BAC (Budget At Completion)
	VAC (Variance At Completion)
Earned Value Cost Indicators	BCWS (Budgeted Cost of Work Scheduled)
	BCWP (Budgeted Cost of Work Performed)
	CV (Cost Variance)
	CV% (Cost Variance Percent)
	CPI (Cost Performance Index)
	BAC (Budget At Completion)
	EAC (Estimate At Completion)
	VAC (Variance At Completion)
	TCPI (To Complete Performance Index)
Earned Value Schedule Indicators	BCWS (Budgeted Cost of Work Scheduled)
	BCWP (Budgeted Cost of Work Performed)
	SV (Schedule Variance)
	SV% (Schedule Variance Percent)
	SPI (Schedule Performance Index)

For more information about analyzing project performance with earned value, see "Analyzing Progress and Costs Using Earned Value" on page 401.

Chapter 11

Troubleshooting

Your earned value fields are all $0.00

If you applied an Earned Value table or inserted an earned value field only to find all the values to be $0.00, it likely that you're missing one or more of the pieces of information needed by Microsoft Project to calculate earned value fields.

For earned value to be calculated, you must have all the following items in your project plan:

- A saved baseline
- Resources assigned to tasks
- Costs associated with assigned resources
- Actual progress information

Reviewing Budget Status

The following filters can help you focus on any potential problems with project costs and budget:

- Cost Greater Than
- Cost Overbudget (see Figure 11-14)
- Late/Overbudget Tasks Assigned To
- Work Overbudget

	Task Name	Fixed Cost	Fixed Cost Accrual	Total Cost	Baseline	Variance
0	**Software Development**	**$0.00**	**Prorated**	**$72,068.00**	**$64,888.00**	**$7,180.00**
1	**Scope**	**$0.00**	**Prorated**	**$1,380.00**	**$1,600.00**	**($220.00)**
2	Determine project scope	$0.00	Prorated	$480.00	$240.00	$240.00
7	**Analysis/Software Requirements**	**$0.00**	**Prorated**	**$7,620.00**	**$5,860.00**	**$1,760.00**
8	Conduct needs analysis	$0.00	Prorated	$2,520.00	$1,800.00	$720.00
9	Draft preliminary software specific	$0.00	Prorated	$1,440.00	$1,080.00	$360.00
14	Obtain approvals to proceed (conc	$0.00	Prorated	$920.00	$460.00	$460.00
15	Secure required resources	$0.00	Prorated	$660.00	$440.00	$220.00
17	**Design**	**$0.00**	**Prorated**	**$6,700.00**	**$5,860.00**	**$840.00**
18	Review preliminary software spec	$0.00	Prorated	$1,080.00	$720.00	$360.00
22	Incorporate feedback into function	$0.00	Prorated	$960.00	$480.00	$480.00
25	**Development**	**$0.00**	**Prorated**	**$20,640.00**	**$15,840.00**	**$4,800.00**
29	Develop code	$0.00	Prorated	$9,600.00	$7,200.00	$2,400.00
30	Developer testing (primary debugg	$0.00	Prorated	$9,600.00	$7,200.00	$2,400.00

Figure 11-14. Apply the Cost Overbudget filter to quickly see which tasks are or are projected to be over budget.

Apply a filter by clicking the arrow beside the Filter tool on the Formatting toolbar. In the Filter list, click the name of the filter you want. To show all tasks again, click All Tasks in the Filter list.

You can also run reports that provide information about costs and budget status, as follows:

- Cash Flow
- Budget
- Overbudget Tasks
- Overbudget Resources (see Figure 11-15)
- Earned Value

Overbudget Resources
Software Development

Resource Name	Cost	Baseline Cost	Variance	Actual Cost
David Barber	$20,640.00	$15,840.00	$4,800.00	$3,600.00
Ido Ben-Sachar	$8,820.00	$7,380.00	$1,440.00	$7,065.00
Eva Corets	$3,360.00	$2,640.00	$720.00	$2,760.00
Clair Hector	$5,280.00	$5,060.00	$220.00	$1,595.00
	$38,100.00	$30,920.00	$7,180.00	$15,020.00

Figure 11-15. Run the Overbudget Resources report to see which resource costs are greater than the baseline resource costs.

To run a cost report, click View, Reports. Double-click Costs and then double-click the report you want.

Realigning the Project with the Budget

Suppose that you reviewed your budget details against the current project costs and found that you will end up significantly over budget. Or perhaps upper management has asked you to cut costs by 10 percent, and you need to work toward a different total project cost.

If you need to take corrective actions in your project plan to reduce project costs, you can do the following:

- Recheck your cost assumptions such as resource rates, per-use costs for resources, and fixed costs for tasks.
- Adjust the schedule to reduce costs. Reducing task durations and adjusting task dependencies can help reduce costs.
- Adjust assignments to reduce costs. Add, remove, or replace resources on assignments as appropriate to cut costs.
- Cut scope to reduce costs (which will probably require stakeholder approval).

> **Tip** **Check the adjustments**
> When you adjust your project plan to achieve the budget you need, be sure to check your finish date, resource allocation, and scope. You need to know how your changes affect other areas of the project plan.
>
> You might also think you need to save a new baseline, especially if there have been major cost changes or changes that have affected the schedule.

For more information about using any of these strategies to trim project costs, see "Reducing Project Costs" on page 267.

For more information on saving a new baseline, see "Need a New Baseline?" later in this chapter on page 352.

Monitoring and Adjusting Resource Workload

If you're a resource manager or if your biggest project priority is to maintain a balanced workload among your resources, monitor your resources' workload and see if anyone is unexpectedly overallocated or underallocated. As you receive information from resources about their assigned tasks and enter actuals, you can see whether you need to take any action to prevent potential resource allocation problems in the near future.

Monitoring Resource Workload

Use one or more of the following techniques to help you monitor and adjust the schedule to achieve a balanced resource workload:

- Review resource workloads.
- Adjust resource availability.
- Adjust assignments.
- Split tasks to reschedule remaining work for when resources have available time.
- Level assignments.

Because work is the measure of resource effort on tasks, you can use the baseline value for work to help review how well resources are utilized according to actual and scheduled values. For example, you can see Maureen's baseline work for tasks next to her values for scheduled work, based on actuals she has submitted regarding her progress. Then, you can review the variances between the baseline and scheduled work. Work variance is calculated as follows:

(Scheduled/Current) Work – Baseline Work = Work Variance

If actual work values are considerably higher than originally planned, you can anticipate some problems with resource overallocation now or in the near future.

For more information about balancing the resource workload, see "Balancing Resource Workloads" on page 271.

Tip **Analyze your work variances and performance with earned value**
You can use earned value calculations, such as the Budgeted Cost of Work Scheduled (BCWS) and Actual Cost of Work Performed (ACWP) earned value fields, to analyze project performance based on resource work.

For more information, see "Analyzing Progress and Costs Using Earned Value" on page 401.

Reviewing Overall Work Totals

There are two ways to review your overall work totals, as follows:

- Review project statistics. Click Project, Project Information and then click the Statistics button. Under Work, review the current, baseline, actual, and remaining work for the project. You can also click Project Statistics on the Tracking toolbar.
- Add the project summary task row. In the Gantt Chart or other task sheet, click Tools, Options and then click the View tab. Select the Show Project Summary Task check box. Summary totals for task information in the current table are displayed in the project summary task row at the top of the sheet. If a table containing work information is applied, the project summary task row shows project work totals.

Reviewing Work Variances

To review the differences between your original baseline work and your currently scheduled work, apply the Work table, as follows:

1. Display the Gantt Chart or other task sheet.
2. Click View, Table, Work.

   The Work table is applied to the current view (see Figure 11-16).

	Task Name	Work	Baseline	Variance	Actual	Remaining	% W. Comp.
0	**Software Development**	**1,660 hrs**	**1,532 hrs**	**128 hrs**	**277 hrs**	**1,383 hrs**	**17%**
1	**Scope**	**24 hrs**	**28 hrs**	**-4 hrs**	**21 hrs**	**3 hrs**	**88%**
2	Determine project scope	8 hrs	4 hrs	4 hrs	8 hrs	0 hrs	100%
3	Secure project sponsorship	4 hrs	8 hrs	-4 hrs	4 hrs	0 hrs	100%
4	Define preliminary resources	4 hrs	8 hrs	-4 hrs	3 hrs	1 hr	75%
5	Secure core resources	8 hrs	8 hrs	0 hrs	6 hrs	2 hrs	75%
6	Scope complete	0 hrs	0 hrs	0 hrs	0 hrs	0 hrs	0%
7	**Analysis/Software Requirements**	**156 hrs**	**120 hrs**	**36 hrs**	**52 hrs**	**104 hrs**	**33%**
8	Conduct needs analysis	56 hrs	40 hrs	16 hrs	28 hrs	28 hrs	50%
9	Draft preliminary software specifications	32 hrs	24 hrs	8 hrs	16 hrs	16 hrs	50%
10	Develop preliminary budget	16 hrs	16 hrs	0 hrs	4 hrs	12 hrs	25%
11	Review software specifications/budget with tea	8 hrs	8 hrs	0 hrs	2 hrs	6 hrs	25%
12	Incorporate feedback on software specification:	8 hrs	8 hrs	0 hrs	2 hrs	6 hrs	25%
13	Develop delivery timeline	8 hrs	8 hrs	0 hrs	0 hrs	8 hrs	0%
14	Obtain approvals to proceed (concept, timeline, l	16 hrs	8 hrs	8 hrs	0 hrs	16 hrs	0%
15	Secure required resources	12 hrs	8 hrs	4 hrs	0 hrs	12 hrs	0%

Figure 11-16. Apply the Work table to a task sheet to see scheduled, baseline, and actual work—along with any variances.

With the project summary task row applied, you can also review rolled up work totals.

Reviewing Overbudget Work

You can apply a filter to a task or resource sheet to see only those tasks or resources who have more actual work reported than was planned, as follows:

1. Display the view and apply the table that contains the information you want to review in the context of overbudget work.

2 Click Project, Filtered For, More Filters.

3 In the More Filters dialog box, click Work Overbudget and then click Apply.

If you prefer to see all tasks or resources, but have the overbudget tasks or resources highlighted, click Highlight instead.

Microsoft Project filters for any tasks or resources whose actual work reported is higher than the baseline work.

4 Review the tasks or resources to analyze the extent of the work overages.

5 When you finish, show all tasks again by clicking the Filter tool on the Formatting toolbar and then clicking All Tasks.

Reviewing Resource Allocation

If a resource is overallocated, his or her name appears in red in any resource view. In resource sheets, a leveling indicator is also displayed next to the resource name, recommending that the resource be leveled.

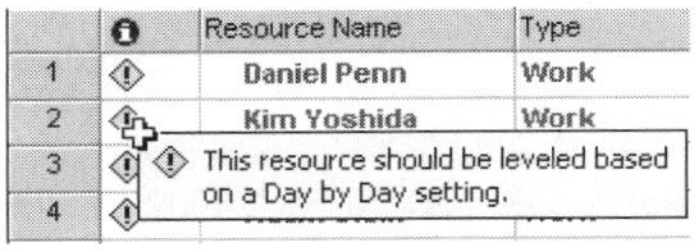

Resource Name
Type
Daniel Penn
Work
Kim Yoshida
Work
This resource should be leveled based on a Day by Day setting.

To see the extent of overallocation or underallocation for a resource, use the Resource Graph, as follows:

1 Click View, Resource Graph (see Figure 11-17).

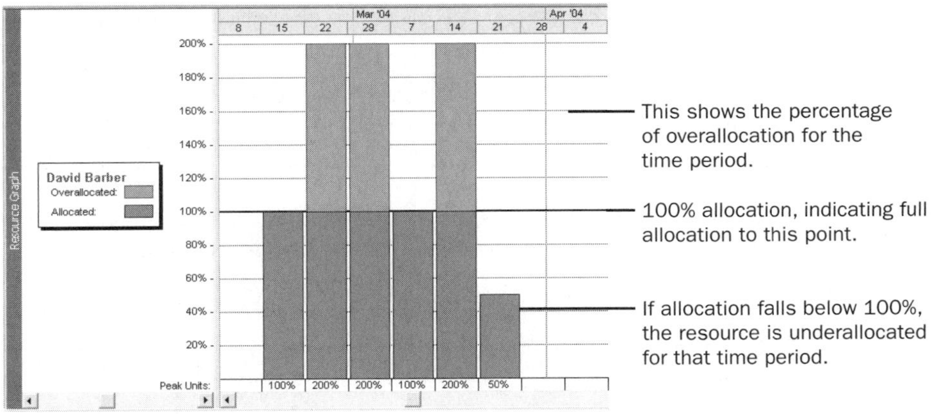

Figure 11-17. The Resource Graph can show whether a resource is fully allocated, overallocated, or underallocated for a selected period of time.

2 Review the allocation for the first resource.

Chapter 11

By default, the Resource Graph shows *peak units* for each time period, including the percentage allocated and the percentage overallocated. You can show different types of information in the Resource Graph. Click Format, Details and then click another type of information (for example, Work or Remaining Availability).

Zoom Out

3 On the Standard toolbar, click the Zoom Out button to see the Resource Graph for a longer period of time. Click the Zoom In button to see details about a shorter period of time.

Zoom In

4 To see information for the next resource, press the Page Down key or click in the horizontal scroll bar in the left pane of the view.

Tip **Resource Graph in combination**

Adding the Resource Graph as the lower pane in a combination view can be very useful in finding resource overallocations.

Inside Out

Relieve the leveling hair-trigger

The leveling indicator often suggests that the resource be leveled on a Day By Day basis because Microsoft Project has found that this resource is overallocated by at least one minute over the resource availability for a day.

You might find that level of detail too fine for your purposes. It might be more effective to level resources on a Week By Week basis or a Month By Month basis. Although the overallocation is still detected when you're overallocated by just one minute, looking at the entire week or the entire month instead of just one day provides more "wiggle room" for overallocations to take care of themselves.

To change the leveling trigger, click Tools, Level Resources. In the Look For Overallocations On A Basis box, click Week By Week or Month By Month. Click OK.

You can also see the details about which assignments are causing resource overallocations (or underallocations) by using the Resource Usage view, as follows:

1 Click View, Resource Usage (see Figure 11-18).

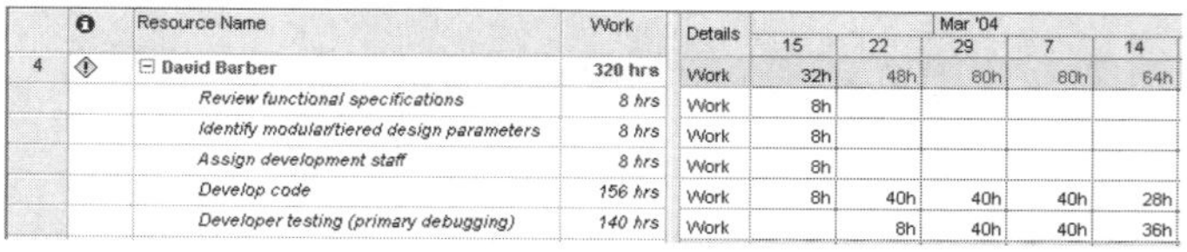

	ⓘ	Resource Name	Work	Details	Mar '04 15	22	29	7	14
4	◈	⊟ **David Barber**	**320 hrs**	Work	32h	48h	80h	80h	64h
		Review functional specifications	*8 hrs*	Work	8h				
		Identify modular/tiered design parameters	*8 hrs*	Work	8h				
		Assign development staff	*8 hrs*	Work	8h				
		Develop code	*156 hrs*	Work	8h	40h	40h	40h	28h
		Developer testing (primary debugging)	*140 hrs*	Work		8h	40h	40h	36h

Figure 11-18. The Resource Usage view shows how resources are allocated for each time period, as well as the specific assignments that contribute to that allocation.

Any resource whose name appears in red or with a leveling indicator is overallocated.

2 Review the timesheet portion of the view to see where the overallocation occurs.

You might need to scroll to move to a different time period.

3 On the Standard toolbar, click the Zoom Out button to see the Resource Usage view for a longer period of time. Click the Zoom In button to see details about a shorter period of time.

4 Review the sheet portion of the view to see the assignments for each resource.

5 You can add the Overallocation field to the timesheet portion of the view, which you can use to learn how many hours or days, for example, a resource is overallocated. To do this, click Format, Details, Overallocation (see Figure 11-19).

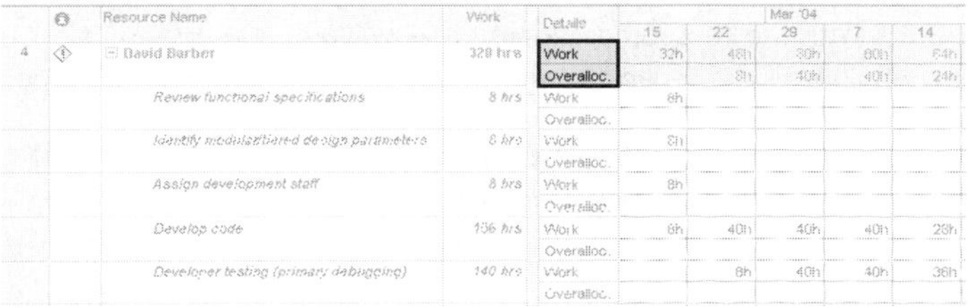

Figure 11-19. Add the Overallocation field to the Resource Usage view to see the number of hours (or other time period) by which each resource is overallocated.

6 To see underallocations or the amount of time that a resource is available for more assignments, add the Remaining Availability field to the timesheet portion of the view. Click Format, Details, Remaining Availability.

> **Tip** **Apply the Work table to the Resource Usage view**
> If you apply the Work table to the Resource Usage view, you can see work details and tracking information for each resource and assignment—including baseline work, the variance between the baseline and scheduled work, any actual work reported, remaining work, and percent complete.

Use the Resource Allocation view to see the Resource Usage view in combination with the Leveling Gantt. This view helps you see which resources are overallocated in conjunction with the tasks that are causing the overallocation. Click View, More Views. In the More Views dialog box, click Resource Allocation and then click Apply (see Figure 11-20).

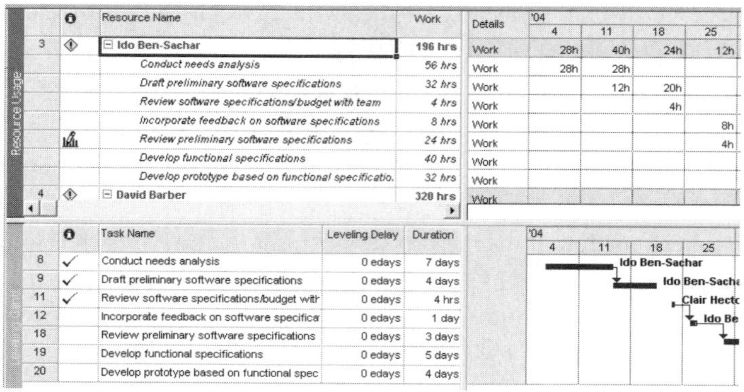

Figure 11-20. With the Resource Allocation view, you can see task information in the lower pane for any assignment you click in the Resource Usage view in the upper pane.

With the Summary table applied to a resource view, you can see the Peak field, which can quickly tell you whether resources are allocated to their maximum availability (100 percent), overallocated (more than 100 percent), or underallocated (less than 100 percent). Click View, Table, Summary (see Figure 11-21).

	Resource Name	Group	Max. Units	Peak	Std. Rate	Ovt. Rate	Cost	Work
1	Eva Corets		100%	100%	$60.00/hr	$0.00/hr	$3,360.00	56 hrs
2	**Clair Hector**		**100%**	**200%**	**$55.00/hr**	**$0.00/hr**	**$5,280.00**	**96 hrs**
3	**Ido Ben-Sachar**		**100%**	**200%**	**$45.00/hr**	**$0.00/hr**	**$8,820.00**	**196 hrs**
4	**David Barber**		**100%**	**200%**	**$60.00/hr**	**$0.00/hr**	**$19,200.00**	**320 hrs**
5	**Testers**		**100%**	**200%**	**$30.00/hr**	**$0.00/hr**	**$8,400.00**	**280 hrs**
6	**Trainers**		**100%**	**300%**	**$35.00/hr**	**$0.00/hr**	**$8,960.00**	**256 hrs**
7	**Technical communicators**		**100%**	**200%**	**$38.00/hr**	**$0.00/hr**	**$12,768.00**	**336 hrs**
8	Deployment team		100%	100%	$40.00/hr	$0.00/hr	$3,840.00	96 hrs

Figure 11-21. By reviewing the Peak field for resources, you can quickly see how many resources are allocated and whether they're available to take on more assignments.

The following filters can help you focus on any potential problems with overallocated resources:

- Overallocated Resources (see Figure 11-22)
- Work Overbudget
- Resources/Assignments With Overtime
- Slipping Assignments

	Resource Name	% Comp.	Work	Overtime	Baseline	Variance	Actual	Remaining
2	**Clair Hector**	**30%**	**96 hrs**	**0 hrs**	**92 hrs**	**4 hrs**	**29 hrs**	**67 hrs**
3	**Ido Ben-Sachar**	**62%**	**196 hrs**	**0 hrs**	**164 hrs**	**32 hrs**	**122 hrs**	**74 hrs**
4	**David Barber**	**19%**	**320 hrs**	**0 hrs**	**264 hrs**	**56 hrs**	**60 hrs**	**260 hrs**
5	**Testers**	**0%**	**280 hrs**	**0 hrs**	**280 hrs**	**0 hrs**	**0 hrs**	**280 hrs**
6	**Trainers**	**0%**	**256 hrs**	**0 hrs**	**256 hrs**	**0 hrs**	**0 hrs**	**256 hrs**
7	**Technical communicators**	**0%**	**336 hrs**	**0 hrs**	**336 hrs**	**0 hrs**	**0 hrs**	**336 hrs**

Figure 11-22. Apply the Overallocated Resources filter to a resource view to quickly see a list of resources who have more work assigned than time available for that work.

With a resource view displayed, apply a filter by clicking the Filter tool on the Formatting toolbar. In the Filter list, click the name of the filter you want.

You can also run the following reports that provide information about resource usage:

- Who Does What
- Who Does What When
- To-Do List
- Overallocated Resources (see Figure 11-23)
- Task Usage
- Resource Usage

Overallocated Resources
Software Development

	Resource Name	Work
◆	Clair Hector	96 hrs

ID	Task Name	Units	Work	Delay	Start
4	Define preliminary resources	100%	4 hrs	0 days	Fri 1/2/04
5	Secure core resources	100%	8 hrs	0 days	Mon 1/5/04
10	Develop preliminary budget	100%	16 hrs	0 days	Wed 1/21/04
11	Review software specifications/budget with team	100%	4 hrs	0 days	Fri 1/23/04
13	Develop delivery timeline	100%	8 hrs	0 days	Tue 1/27/04
14	Obtain approvals to proceed (concept, timeline, budget)	100%	8 hrs	0 days	Wed 1/28/04
15	Secure required resources	100%	12 hrs	0 days	Thu 1/29/04
23	Obtain approval to proceed	100%	4 hrs	0 days	Mon 2/16/04
80	Identify test group	100%	8 hrs	0 days	Mon 1/26/04
82	Document lessons learned	100%	8 hrs	0 days	Thu 5/20/04
83	Distribute to team members	100%	8 hrs	0 days	Fri 5/21/04
84	Create software maintenance team	100%	8 hrs	0 days	Mon 5/24/04

	Resource Name	Work
◆	David Barber	320 hrs

ID	Task Name	Units	Work	Delay	Start	Finish
26	Review functional specifications	100%	8 hrs	0 days	Tue 2/17/04	Tue 2/17/04
27	Identify modular/tiered design parameters	100%	8 hrs	0 days	Wed 2/18/04	Wed 2/18/04
28	Assign development staff	100%	8 hrs	0 days	Thu 2/19/04	Thu 2/19/04
29	Develop code	100%	156 hrs	0 days	Fri 2/20/04	Thu 3/18/04
30	Developer testing (primary debugging)	100%	140 hrs	0 days	Fri 2/27/04	Thu 3/25/04

Figure 11-23. Run the Overallocated Resources report to get detailed information about resources who have too much work assigned.

To run an assignments or workload report, click View, Reports. Double-click Assignments or Workload and then double-click the report you want.

Balancing the Resource Workload

Suppose that you reviewed information about assignments and workload throughout your project plan and found that some resources are overallocated and others are underallocated. Or perhaps your company had a reduction in force, and your project staffing was reduced by 15 percent.

If you need to take corrective actions in your project plan to balance the resource workload, you can:

- Adjust resource availability.
- Adjust assignments, for example, add resources, replace resources, delay a task or assignment, or specify overtime.

- Split tasks to balance the workload.
- Use the Microsoft Project leveling feature to balance the workload.
- Adjust scope (this will probably require stakeholder approval).

For more information about using any of these strategies to better allocate your resources, see "Balancing Resource Workloads" on page 271.

Note When you adjust your project plan to achieve the resource allocation levels you need, be sure to check the scheduled finish date, costs, and scope. You need to know how your changes affect other areas of the project plan.

Need a New Baseline?

If you made substantial changes to the schedule or costs in your project plan, consider whether you should save a new baseline. Your decision depends on how you intend to use baseline information, in terms of variance monitoring, earned value calculations, and archival data. Which will give you the more meaningful data: the original baseline or a new one based on recent changes?

You can retain the original baseline (usually the best idea in terms of project data integrity) and save the new information as Baseline 1, for example.

Another alternative is to copy the original baseline information to Baseline 1, for example, and then make the new baseline the primary. The primary baseline (that is Baseline, rather than Baseline 1 or Baseline 2) is always used for earned value calculations.

For more information about copying baseline fields from one set to another, see "Saving Additional Baselines" on page 304.

Part 4

Reporting and Analysis

Chapter 12

Reporting Project Information

By now, you've built your project plan and you're using it to track progress and display project information. Because you're now in the execution and control processes of the project, you'll need to share important data with stakeholders. For example, your new test procedure might have worked better than expected, but your materials testing ran into some unanticipated slowdowns. All this information is reflected in the project plan. However, for different audiences and different purposes, you want to highlight certain information and filter out other information to present a particular focus with professional panache.

You can print views and generate reports built in to Microsoft Office Project 2003 and use them as an integral part of your project communication plan. These views and reports leverage the power of Project 2003 by presenting the specific focus and clarity required by corporate and program departments. By tailoring the views and reports to the interests of different groups (finance, human resources, and procurement, among others), you can feed the right information to the right people, avoid misunderstandings, and mitigate problems. Microsoft Project views and reports are often used for:

- Weekly project team meetings
- Monthly department status conferences
- Quarterly or annual executive reviews

In addition to printing views and generating built-in reports, you can design custom reports to meet your specific project communication needs. You can publish project information to the Web. You can also generate reports using project data saved as XML.

Establishing Your Communications Plan

Reports are instrumental in effective project management. As a part of the initial project planning, you'll determine the requirements for reporting, including:

Report recipients. Who needs to see the reports? Stakeholders throughout the organization and within the project team need to see certain reports tailored to their areas of responsibility. For example, you might generate one report for your team members, another one for team leads and resource managers, and yet another for executives and customers.

Specific content of the reports. What type of information is included? The reports can focus on any aspect of the project, for example, tasks, resource allocation, assignments, costs, and so on. Reports might focus on past successes or current progress. They might provide a forecast of upcoming tasks, costs, or workloads. They might present a high-level summary. They can point out areas of risk or current problems that need resolution.

Frequency of report publication. How often should you generate reports? Regularly scheduled project meetings or status reporting often drive the generation of reports. Certain important issues that are being closely watched might warrant report generation more frequently than usual. Be sure to strike a balance between providing up-to-date information often enough and overloading a stakeholder with too detailed or too frequent reporting.

Establishing your communications strategy for a project helps you effectively communicate realistic progress and estimates. You can point to unexpected changes that present risks. You can avoid larger problems and understand root causes. Specifically, with reports you can:

- Review status.
- Compare data.
- Check progress on the schedule.
- Check resource utilization.
- Check budget status.
- Watch for any potential problems looming in the future.
- Help stakeholders make decisions affecting the project.

Using the appropriate Microsoft Project views and reports on a regular basis for progress analysis and communication is a key component of effective project management. By implementing a communications plan, including regular presentations of reports to stakeholders, you can keep interested parties aware of crucial information and trends.

Project Management Practices: Communications Management

Communication is a vital element of successful project management. Effective project communication ensures that the appropriate information is generated, collected, and distributed in a timely manner to the appropriate project stakeholders. Different stakeholders need different kinds of project information—from the team members carrying out the project tasks, to customers sponsoring the project, to executives making strategic decisions regarding the project and the organization. Your stakeholders don't just receive project information; they also generate it. When all your stakeholders share project information, people are linked and ideas are generated—all of which contributes to the ultimate success of the project.

The first stage of effective project communications management is communications planning. This stage should take place in the initiating and planning processes for the project, in conjunction with scope and activity development. As you develop and build your project plan, you also need to determine what types of communication will be necessary throughout the life of the project.

Determine what tools you have at your disposal and how your project team communicates most effectively. You might have weekly meetings and weekly status reports. Perhaps you'll also have monthly resource management and cost management reviews. Other possible communication vehicles include presentations, e-mail, letters, and an intranet site. You'll likely use a combination of these vehicles for different aspects of project management and different audiences.

If you're using Microsoft Office Project Server 2003 and Microsoft Office Project Web Access 2003, you have a very effective and targeted means of communicating electronically with your team members and other stakeholders. You can automate the flow of progress information about the project, including status reporting. You'll post certain views of the project periodically to Project Web Access 2003 for all stakeholders to review. If you're also using Windows SharePoint Services with your Project Server 2003 implementation, you can store reports, manage risks, and track issues.

While the project is being executed, you'll be executing your communications plan. You'll report on current project status, describing where the project stands at that point in time, especially as it relates to the schedule, budget, scope, and resource utilization. You'll also report on overall progress, describing the accomplishments of the project team to date and what is yet to be done. Finally, you'll make forecasts by using project plan information to predict future progress on tasks and anticipating potential problems.

Tasks will be completed, milestones met, deliverables handed off, and phases concluded. Your communications management strategy provides the means for documenting project results and the receipt of deliverables as each stage of the project is completed.

Setting Up and Printing Views

Suppose that you've been tracking and managing your project for some time now by using the Gantt Chart, the Resource Sheet, and other Microsoft Project views. You can set up one of these views to contain exactly the fields of information you need and then print it to create a kind of report. By printing views, you can share pertinent information with team members and stakeholders. You can include printed views in project status reports and in progress meetings.

Note Form views, such as the Task Form or Resource Form, cannot be printed. Neither can combination (split-screen) views. You can print one part of a split screen at a time, but if one part of the split screen is a form (such as Task Entry), it cannot be printed.

To set up and print a view, follow these steps:

1 Open the view and arrange the data as you want it to appear when printed.

For more information about available views, and arranging information on those views, see Chapter 4, "Viewing Project Information."

2 Click File, Page Setup to display the Page Setup dialog box (see Figure 12-1).

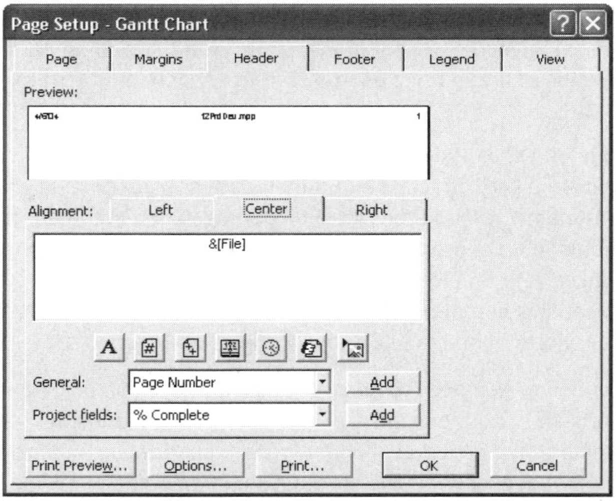

Figure 12-1. Use the Page Setup dialog box to set your margins, legend, headers, and more.

3 Specify the options you want for the printed view using controls on the different tabs of this dialog box.

You can adjust the view orientation, page scaling, margins, header and footer, and so on. When finished, click OK.

Print Preview

4 On the Standard toolbar, click Print Preview.

A picture of the view as printed appears, reflecting your Page Setup options (see Figure 12-2).

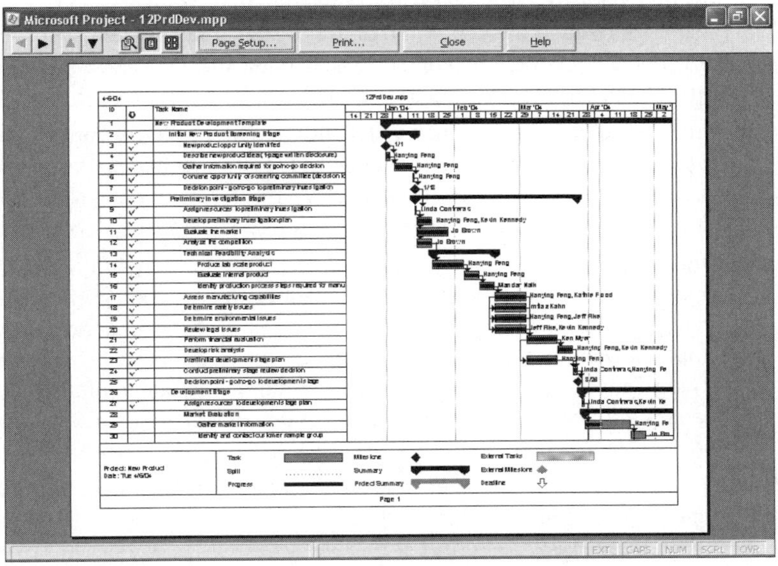

Figure 12-2. The Print Preview window shows the printable layout of the current view.

5 To make further adjustments to the print options, click Page Setup at the top of the Print Preview window.

6 To make further adjustments to the view itself, click Close on the Print Preview toolbar and work in the view.

Print

7 When finished with your adjustments, print the view by clicking Print on the Standard toolbar.

Page Setup Options

The following list describes the options available on the six tabs of the Page Setup dialog box, which controls how your view looks when printed. To display this dialog box, click File, Page Setup:

Page tab. Specifies whether the view should be printed in portrait or landscape orientation and whether the view should be scaled up or down to fit on a page.

Margins tab. Specifies the size of each of the four margins and whether a border should be printed around the page.

Insert File Name

Header tab. Specifies the content and location of header information. You can add the page number, current date and time, or the filename. You can also add a picture (such as a company or project logo) as part of your left, center, or right header. For example, next to Alignment, click the Center tab and then click Insert File Name to display the project filename in the center top of every page. You can also specify that a project field should be part of the header. You can enter your own text as well. Simply click the Left, Center, or Right tab and then click the text box and type the text you want.

Insert Current Date

Footer tab. Specifies the content and location of footer information. The same information available for headers is available for footers. For example, click the Left tab in the Alignment area and then click Insert Current Date to display the date in the lower-left corner of every page. The Preview box shows what your footer will look like.

Legend tab. Specifies the content and location of a view's legend, which specifies what symbols or bars on the view represent. For example, when printing the Gantt Chart, the legend includes a key for the task bars, summary bars, deadlines, and milestone symbols. By default, the legend appears on the bottom two inches of every page and includes the project's title and the current date. The same information available for headers and footers is available for legends. You can also enter your own information.

View tab. Specifies which elements you want printed on each page, for example, notes, blank pages, sheet columns, and so on.

Note Divided views, such as Task Usage, have a table on the left and the timephased information sheet on the right. Such divided views are not split screens, so you can print both sides of these views.

Inside Out

The date and time printed

Insert Current Time

The Insert Current Date and Insert Current Time buttons take their information from your computer's system clock. This date and time will change to reflect the date or time that you print the view. If you want a fixed date or time, in the Alignment area of the Page Setup dialog box, simply type the date or time on the Left, Center, or Right tab text box itself.

Getting Assistance from the Report Project Guide

Report

Use the Report Project Guide to help you set up key views presenting important progress and cost information. On the Project Guide toolbar, click Reports. The Report pane appears.

Note If your Project Guide toolbar is not showing, click View, Toolbars, Project Guide.

The Report Project Guide includes improved steps and controls for setting up your project to view specific types of information, such as critical tasks, risks and issues, resource allocation, project costs, and so on.

The updated Report Project Guide focuses on view setup and printing options. Click the Print Current View As A Report link to start the Print Current View Wizard. This wizard provides options for printing the current view, with optimum print spacing and scaling (see Figure 12-3).

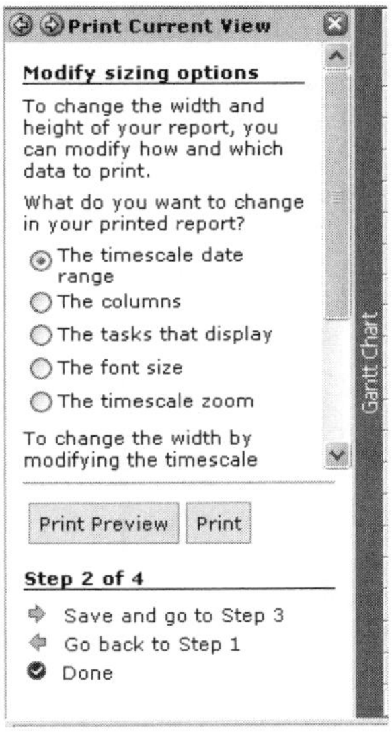

Figure 12-3. Use the Print Current View Wizard to set options for printing the current view.

For more information about the Project Guide, see "Working with the Project Guide" on page 24.

Copying a Picture of a View

Suppose that you're creating a formal narrative project status report or preparing a presentation for a high-profile project status meeting. You can copy a view in Microsoft Project and paste it into a Microsoft Word document or a Microsoft PowerPoint presentation slide.

Note To use the Copy Picture To Office Wizard, you must have Microsoft Word, Microsoft PowerPoint, or Microsoft Visio 2000 or later installed on your computer.

To copy a picture of a Microsoft Project view to Microsoft Word, Microsoft PowerPoint, or Microsoft Visio, follow these steps:

1. Click View, Toolbars, Analysis.
2. On the Analysis toolbar that appears, click Copy Picture To Office Wizard.

3 Read the first page of the wizard and then click Next.

4 Select options on the second page of the wizard to reflect how you want the Project view to appear in the Office application (see Figure 12-4).

These options will differ depending on the type of view. For example, a Gantt Chart will present options different from the Resource Graph.

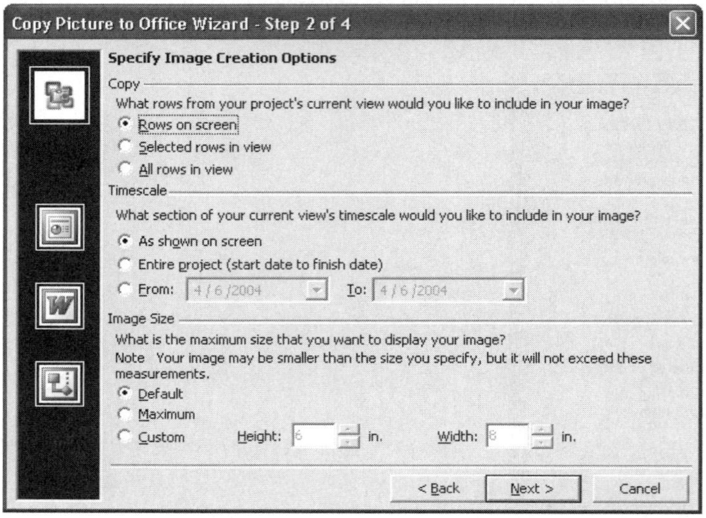

Figure 12-4. Specify options in the Copy Picture To Office Wizard to indicate how you want the picture of the Project view to appear.

5 Click Next. Review the third page of the wizard, which you can use to preview the picture and then select the target Office application.

6 Click the Preview button.

A picture of the view is exported and saved according to the options you selected. A browser window appears, showing the generated picture.

7 Return to Microsoft Project and the wizard. Under Application, click the program the picture is intended for. If necessary, select whether the picture should be presented in portrait or landscape orientation. Click Next.

The option for any program not installed on your computer is dimmed.

8 Select any Microsoft Project fields you want to export along with the picture of the view. The available fields are listed in the Microsoft Office Project Fields box. Click one or more fields (using Shift or Ctrl to select multiple fields) and then click Add. Click the Move buttons if necessary to rearrange the positions of selected fields listed in the Fields To Export box. Then click Finish.

The picture of the Microsoft Project view with any selected fields is exported and saved to the selected Microsoft Office application.

9 In the final window of the wizard, click Close.

The selected Office application opens and displays the picture (see Figure 12-5).

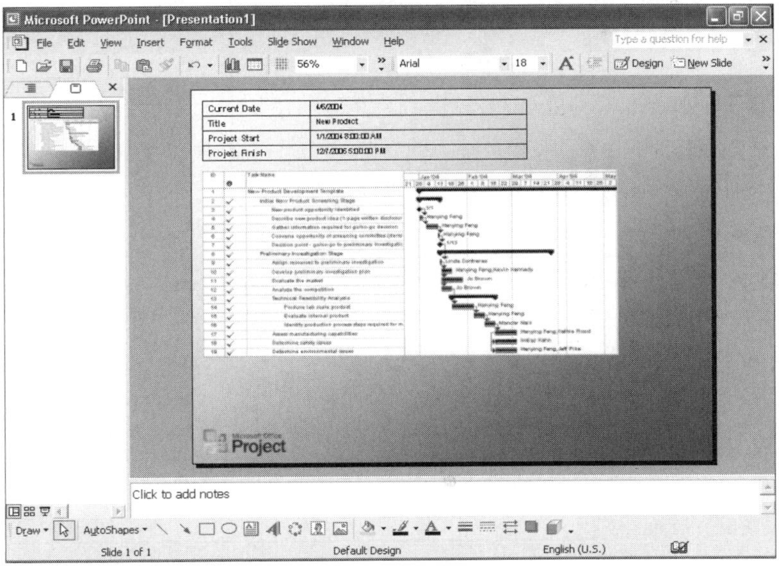

Figure 12-5. The selected Project View and fields appear in the Office application you selected.

> **For more information about other methods of moving project data to different programs, see Chapter 16, "Exchanging Information with Other Applications."**

Generating Reports

In addition to printing views, Microsoft Project comes with more than 20 built-in reports that you can simply select, preview, and print. These reports compile the most commonly used sets of information needed to manage a project, coordinate resources, control costs, analyze potential problems, and communicate progress.

When you select and generate a report, information is drawn from selected fields throughout your project. That information is laid out in the report design, in either discrete or summarized form, depending on the specific report. You can generate an up-to-date report mere minutes before the start of a meeting, and the report instantly reflects the very latest changes you made or that team members have submitted.

To see the list of available built-in reports, click View, Reports. The Reports dialog box appears, showing six report categories (see Figure 12-6).

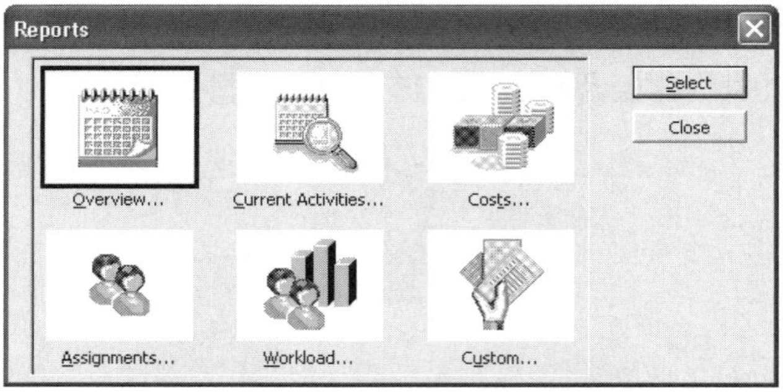

Figure 12-6. There are five categories for 22 built-in reports, plus a Custom category for designing your own report.

The report categories are as follows:

- Overview
- Current Activities
- Costs
- Assignments
- Workload
- Custom

Each category focuses on a specific type of information. You might find that certain reports are best-suited to one type of audience, whereas other reports are better for another type of audience. For example, Cost reports might be most appropriate for meetings with the finance department, whereas you might prefer to distribute Assignment reports to team leads.

To generate these reports, Microsoft Project gathers information from a particular time period, from certain tables, and with a particular filter applied as appropriate for the requirements of the specific report. Information is formatted with bands, highlights, fonts, and other professional layout considerations.

Inside Out

The Report Project Guide for views, not reports

The Report Project Guide is somewhat misnamed. Only one link takes you to a built-in generated report. The rest of the links display a view displaying a certain type of information often needed in progress reports or status meetings. These links walk you through setting up the view for optimum printing.

However, there's nothing here that tells you the best report to use or how to customize it for your own purposes. It would also be nice if there were a guide, or even a wizard, to walk you through the steps of creating a new report from scratch.

The Report Project Guide does get you to the point of opening the Reports dialog box. On the Project Guide toolbar, click Report. In the Project Guide pane, click Select A View Or Report, click Print A Project Report, and then click Display Reports.

To select and print a report, follow these steps:

1. Click View, Reports.
2. In the Reports dialog box, double-click the category you want.
3. In the dialog box that appears, double-click the report you want.
4. If a dialog box prompts you for more information, such as a date range, enter it and then click OK.

   The report appears in a Print Preview window (see Figure 12-7). Click any portion of the report to zoom in on it. Click a second time to zoom back out again. Click Page Setup to change the page orientation, scaling, margins, header, or footer.

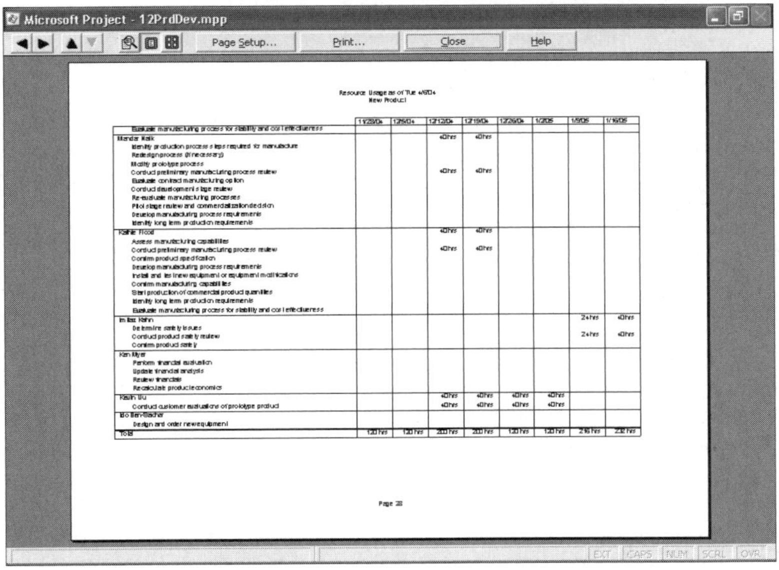

Figure 12-7. A picture of the report shows how it will look when printed.

5. When ready to print the report, click Print on the Print Preview toolbar.
6. In the Print dialog box that appears, select the page range and number of copies you want to print and then click OK.

Inside Out

Reports are not "saved"

Each Microsoft Project report has a preset format and is generated from current project data, so you cannot save a built-in report as such. Essentially, it's already saved. As long as your project file is saved, you can always quickly generate the report again using current information.

However, if you do want to save an instance of a report, perhaps for an historical record of a moment in time or for a series of certain reports throughout the project life cycle, you have two options—both of which take a bit of effort. But if you generate and want to save data from the same report each week, it might be worth it to you.

NEW FEATURE! One option is to use the new XML Reporting Wizard, which enables you to save your project as an XML file. You apply an XSL template that you've created or one that's provided with Microsoft Project to generate a report. The data in the report is saved at that moment in time.

For more information about the XML Reporting Wizard, see "Generating Reports from Project XML Data" later in this chapter on page 395.

The other option is to create an export map consisting of the fields in the report. Export the data to Microsoft Excel, Microsoft Access, or whichever program you want to capture and maintain your project data in the format you want.

For more information about exporting project data to another program, see "Exporting Information from Microsoft Project" on page 500.

Note **Create a report macro**
If your weekly routine has you generating your status report, exporting the data, and saving it, consider creating a macro to do this for you each week.

For more information about creating macros, see Chapter 27, "Automating Your Work with Macros."

Summarizing with Overview Reports

The Overview reports are well-suited for executives and upper management who need more generalized project information and status. The Overview reports provide summary project information at a glance.

To see the available Overview reports, follow these steps:

1. Click View, Reports.
2. In the Reports dialog box, click Overview and then click Select. The Overview Reports dialog box appears (see Figure 12-8).

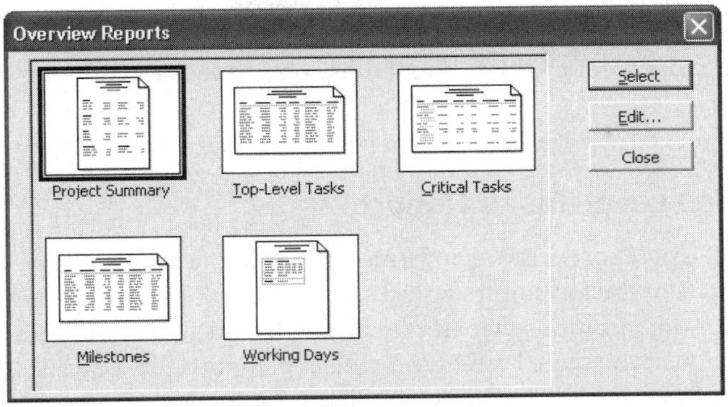

Figure 12-8. The Overview Reports dialog box shows the available summary reports.

3 Double-click the report you want. A preview of the report appears, showing how the report will look when printed.

Using the Project Summary Report

The Project Summary report focuses on the most important information in the project plan and is particularly useful to upper management because of its concise presentation of overall project data.

The information in the Project Summary report is the same as that available in the Project Statistics dialog box. It includes a high-level summary of rolled-up dates, duration, work, costs, work and resource status, and notes (see Figure 12-9). The format is designed for easy comparison of baseline (planned) versus actual data.

New Product

as of Tue 4/6/04

Dates			
Start:	Thu 1/1/04	Finish:	Thu 12/7/06
Baseline Start:	Thu 1/1/04	Baseline Finish:	Thu 12/7/06
Actual Start:	Thu 1/1/04	Actual Finish:	NA
Start Variance:	0 days	Finish Variance:	0 days
Duration			
Scheduled:	766 days	Remaining:	675.41 days
Baseline:	766 days	Actual:	90.59 days
Variance:	0 days	Percent Complete:	12%
Work			
Scheduled:	15,688 hrs	Remaining:	14,208 hrs
Baseline:	15,688 hrs	Actual:	1,480 hrs
Variance:	0 hrs	Percent Complete:	9%
Costs			
Scheduled:	$568,400.00	Remaining:	$515,520.00
Baseline:	$568,400.00	Actual:	$52,880.00

Figure 12-9. The Project Summary report shows overall project duration, dates, and cost.

The header of this report shows the company name, the project title, the date produced, and the project manager's name. The source of this header information is the properties data entered for the project.

> **Tip** **Enter project properties**
> To enter project properties, click File, Properties. Complete the information on the Summary tab.

Using the Top-Level Tasks Report

The Top-Level Tasks report presents information about the project plan's summary tasks. It displays the results of the top summary tasks, rolling up all the data from any subtasks. This is most useful for organizations that are clearly divided into functional groups. If each group has its own section at the same level in the project plan, the Top-Level Tasks report quickly shows the status of each group's efforts (see Figure 12-10).

Top Level Tasks as of Tue 4/6/04
New Product

Task Name	Duration	Start
Initial New Product Screening Stage	9 days	Thu 1/1/04
Preliminary Investigation Stage	53 days	Wed 1/14/04
Development Stage	264 days	Mon 3/29/04
Pilot Stage	115 days	Fri 4/1/05
Commercialization Stage	195 days	Fri 9/9/05
Post Commercialization Review	130 days	Fri 6/9/06

Figure 12-10. The Top-Level Tasks report shows summary task information.

The Top-Level Tasks report is based on the Summary table for tasks, with the Top Level Tasks filter applied. The report includes the top-level summary tasks and their rolled-up durations, start and finish dates, percentage complete, cost, and work.

> **Note** If you have applied the project summary task, that's the only task that will show in this report. To hide the project summary task, click Tools, Options and then click the View tab. Clear the Show Project Summary Task check box. Generate the report again. Then show the project summary task again.

For more information about summary tasks and subtasks, see "Organizing Tasks into an Outline" on page 86.

Using the Critical Tasks Report

The Critical Tasks report filters your project information to show only those tasks that are most likely to affect the project finish date; that is, critical tasks. In addition to displaying task notes, this report provides a subtable containing successor task information under each task, which shows the other tasks that will be affected by progress on the critical task.

Because task information is always changing, it's a good idea to print the Critical Tasks report very shortly before presenting it for review. For example, on the day of the report's presentation, a predecessor task to a critical task might finish early, thus allowing the critical task to start earlier and no longer *be* critical. This report also lists any summary tasks to the critical tasks and any indicators from the Task Entry view (see Figure 12-11).

Inside Out

Decipher subtables in a report

Certain tables include additional task, resource, or assignment information. For example, the Critical Tasks report adds successor information after each critical task listed in the table. The Tasks Starting Soon report adds assignment schedule information after each upcoming task listed.

At first, this additional detail looks like so much clutter in the report. The details are in italics in a subtable below the name of the associated task or resource. This format takes some getting used to, but it's worth the time because it contains such pertinent and useful information.

If you really hate the additional detail, however, you can get rid of it. Select the report name and then click Edit. Click the Details tab; under Task, Resource, or Assignment, clear the check box that represents the additional detailed information you want to remove.

Critical Tasks as of Tue 4/6/04
New Product

Task Name	Duration	Start	Finish
Development Stage	264 days	Mon 3/29/04	Thu 3/31/05
Technical Product Evaluation	204 days	Tue 3/30/04	Fri 1/7/05
Develop prototype process	10 days	Thu 4/1/04	Wed 4/14/04
Successor Name / Type / Lag			
Produce prototype product / FS / 0 days			
Produce prototype product	25 days	Thu 4/15/04	Wed 5/19/04
Successor Name / Type / Lag			
Conduct internal product review / FS / 0 days			
Conduct internal product review	5 days	Thu 5/20/04	Wed 5/26/04
Successor Name / Type / Lag			
Conduct marketing/technical review / FS / 0 days			
Conduct marketing/technical review	92 days	Thu 5/27/04	Fri 10/1/04
Successor Name / Type / Lag			
Redesign process (if necessary) / FS / 0 days			
Redesign process (if necessary)	10 days	Mon 10/4/04	Fri 10/15/04

Figure 12-11. The Critical Tasks report shows only those tasks whose finish dates affect the overall project finish date.

The Critical Tasks report is typically used to explain why problems are occurring in a project. This report does an excellent job of showing the source of some problems, but it must be used with the understanding that the listing of critical tasks can change easily and often. The inclusion of summary and successor tasks in the report helps present a more expanded description of how the critical tasks relate to other tasks in the project. If the list becomes too lengthy, you can filter it down further:

1. In the Overview Reports dialog box, click Critical Tasks and then click Edit.
2. Be sure that the Definition tab is showing in the Task Report dialog box.
3. In the Filter list, click any of the filters to define the type of critical tasks you want to see in the report.

The Critical Tasks report is based on the task Entry table with the Critical filter applied. The report includes durations, start and finish dates, indicators, notes, and successor fields for all critical tasks.

For more information about critical tasks, see "Working with the Critical Path and Critical Tasks" on page 251.

Using the Milestones Report

The Milestones report filters your project tasks to show only milestone tasks and associated information (see Figure 12-12). This high-level report helps you focus on key events and dates in your project.

Milestones as of Tue 4/6/04
New Product

ⓘ	Task Name	Duration	Start	Finish
✓	Initial New Product Screening Stage	9 days	Thu 1/1/04	Tue 1/13/04
✓	New product opportunity identified	0 days	Thu 1/1/04	Thu 1/1/04
✓	Decision point-go/no-go to preliminary investigation	0 days	Tue 1/13/04	Tue 1/13/04
✓	Preliminary Investigation Stage	53 days	Wed 1/14/04	Fri 3/26/04
✓	Decision point-go/no-go to development stage	0 days	Fri 3/26/04	Fri 3/26/04
	Development Stage	264 days	Mon 3/29/04	Thu 3/31/05
	Decision point-go/no-go to pilot stage	0 days	Thu 3/31/05	Thu 3/31/05

Figure 12-12. The Milestones report shows only milestone tasks and related information.

The Milestones report is based on the task Entry table with the Milestone filter applied. The report includes durations, start and finish dates, indicators, and notes for all milestone tasks.

For more information about milestones, see "Creating Milestones in Your Schedule" on page 167.

Using the Working Days Report

The Working Days report specifies which days are working days and which are nonworking days for each base calendar used in the project (see Figure 12-13). You might use several base calendars to reflect the scheduled working days of different functional groups or to reflect working times specified by labor contracts.

Base Calendar as of Tue 4/6/04
New Product

BASE CALENDAR:	Standard
Day	Hours
Sunday	Nonworking
Monday	8:00 AM - 12:00 PM, 1:00 PM - 5:00 PM
Tuesday	8:00 AM - 12:00 PM, 1:00 PM - 5:00 PM
Wednesday	8:00 AM - 12:00 PM, 1:00 PM - 5:00 PM
Thursday	8:00 AM - 12:00 PM, 1:00 PM - 5:00 PM
Friday	8:00 AM - 12:00 PM, 1:00 PM - 5:00 PM
Saturday	Nonworking
Exceptions:	None

Figure 12-13. The Working Days report shows working days for each base calendar used in the project.

The Working Days report is formatted as a table; with columns for day of the week, hours of the day, and nonworking days. One table is drawn for each calendar. The data in this report might not change very often, so it would be appropriate to include it in a comprehensive project review or a quarterly or annual report.

For more information about calendars, see "Setting Your Project Calendar" on page 70.

Focusing on Tasks with Current Activity Reports

The Current Activity reports are intended for more frequent usage and geared toward audiences more directly involved with the work of the project. For example, project teams can use these reports at weekly status meetings. Functional groups in a project can use these reports to quickly check how they are measuring up against the project plan. You might rely on these reports toward the end of projects, when current task status must be monitored frequently. There are six standard reports in the Current Activity category (see Figure 12-14).

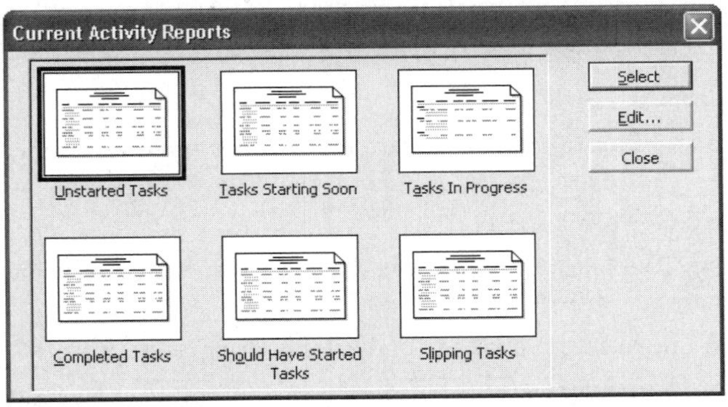

Figure 12-14. The Current Activity Reports dialog box shows the available reports for this category.

Using the Unstarted Tasks Report

Tasks in the project that have not had any actual progress reported are displayed in the Unstarted Tasks report. Generally, the number of tasks displayed decreases as the project progresses, so this report can be especially useful toward the end of the project. This information can help with planning expenditures, deploying tools and materials, and assessing quickly the amount of the work yet to be done. This report is also effective at showing functional leads and team members the scope of their required efforts.

The Unstarted Tasks report is based on the Entry table with the Unstarted Tasks filter applied. The report includes the task duration, start and finish dates, predecessors, and indicators. Assigned resource information is listed in a subtable under the associated task (see Figure 12-15).

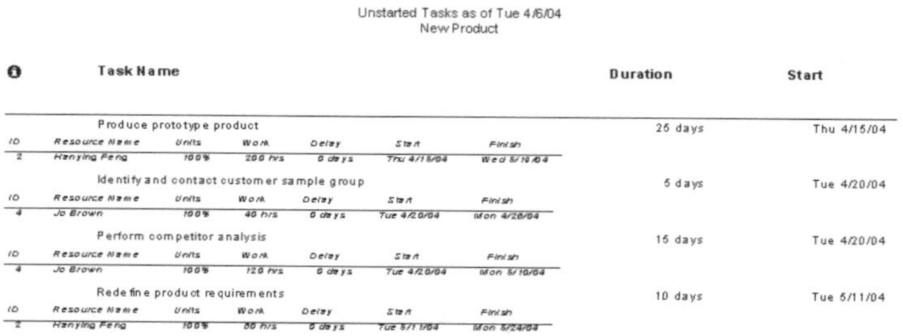

Unstarted Tasks as of Tue 4/6/04
New Product

ⓘ	Task Name	Duration	Start
	Produce prototype product	25 days	Thu 4/15/04
	Identify and contact customer sample group	5 days	Tue 4/20/04
	Perform competitor analysis	15 days	Tue 4/20/04
	Redefine product requirements	10 days	Tue 5/11/04

ID	Resource Name	Units	Work	Delay	Start	Finish
2	Hanying Feng	100%	200 hrs	0 days	Thu 4/15/04	Wed 5/19/04
4	Jo Brown	100%	40 hrs	0 days	Tue 4/20/04	Mon 4/26/04
4	Jo Brown	100%	120 hrs	0 days	Tue 4/20/04	Mon 5/10/04
2	Hanying Feng	100%	80 hrs	0 days	Tue 5/11/04	Mon 5/24/04

Figure 12-15. The Unstarted Tasks report shows all tasks that have no progress reported on them.

Using the Tasks Starting Soon Report

The Tasks Starting Soon report is actually a subset of the Unstarted Tasks report. The format is similar to the Unstarted Tasks report (see Figure 12-15). The difference is that the Date Range filter is applied. You specify the dates for the tasks you want to see in the report.

To generate the Tasks Starting Soon report, follow these steps:

1. Click View, Reports.
2. In the Reports dialog box, double-click Current Activities and then double-click Tasks Starting Soon.

   The Date Range dialog box appears.
3. In the Show Tasks That Start Or Finish After box, enter the date after which you want to see tasks that are scheduled to start or finish.

   This is the beginning of the date range of tasks for your report. Click OK.
4. In the And Before box, enter the date before which you want to see tasks that are scheduled to start or finish.

   This is the ending of the date range of tasks for your report. Click OK to see the results.

> **Note** The date range can yield a surprisingly large number of tasks. For example, if there are many summary divisions in a large project plan, each subgroup will have several tasks in a certain date range. The functional managers are aware of all these tasks, but when the entire project is displayed, the total number of tasks in that range can be an eye-opener. Conversely, if a large date range is entered and few tasks reported, this can indicate a high-risk time period.

Using the Tasks In Progress Report

The Tasks In Progress report is a handy tool that enables you to keep close track of work currently being done. This report quickly shows the amount of work that has started; it also points out tasks that are behind schedule. The in-progress tasks are grouped by month (see Figure 12-16).

Tasks In Progress as of Tue 4/6/04
New Product

ID		Task Name	Duration	Start	Finish
March 2004					
28		Gather market information	15 days	Tue 3/30/04	Mon 4/19/04

ID	Resource Name	Units	Work	Delay	Start	Finish
2	Hanying Feng	100%	120 hrs	0 days	Tue 3/30/04	Mon 4/19/04
4	Jo Brown	100%	120 hrs	0 days	Tue 3/30/04	Mon 4/19/04

ID		Task Name	Duration	Start	Finish
April 2004					
28		Gather market information	15 days	Tue 3/30/04	Mon 4/19/04

ID	Resource Name	Units	Work	Delay	Start	Finish
2	Hanying Feng	100%	120 hrs	0 days	Tue 3/30/04	Mon 4/19/04
4	Jo Brown	100%	120 hrs	0 days	Tue 3/30/04	Mon 4/19/04

ID		Task Name	Duration	Start	Finish
34		Develop prototype process	10 days	Thu 4/1/04	Wed 4/14/04

ID	Resource Name	Units	Work	Delay	Start	Finish
2	Hanying Feng	100%	80 hrs	0 days	Thu 4/1/04	Wed 4/14/04

ID		Task Name	Duration	Start	Finish
37		Document patent application process	10 days	Thu 4/1/04	Wed 4/14/04

ID	Resource Name	Units	Work	Delay	Start	Finish
2	Hanying Feng	100%	80 hrs	0 days	Thu 4/1/04	Wed 4/14/04

Figure 12-16. The Tasks In Progress report shows all tasks currently in progress, grouped by the month in which progress is reported.

Grouping tasks by the month of their start dates helps managers see the longest ongoing tasks that are still unfinished. Using this report regularly helps prevent managers from overlooking (or forgetting) the status updates and long-overdue tasks.

The Tasks In Progress report is based on the Entry table with the Tasks In Progress filter applied. The report includes the task duration, start and finish dates, predecessors, indicators, and assignment schedule information.

Using the Completed Tasks Report

The other end of the spectrum of status reports about current progress is the report showing all 100% completed tasks, as grouped by month (see Figure 12-17).

Completed Tasks as of Tue 4/6/04
New Product

ID	Task Name	Duration	Start	Finish	% Comp.	Cost
January 2004						
2	New product opportunity identified	0 days	Thu 1/1/04	Thu 1/1/04	100%	$0.00
3	Describe new product idea (1-page wr	2 days	Thu 1/1/04	Fri 1/2/04	100%	$560.00
4	Gather information required for go/no-	6 days	Mon 1/5/04	Mon 1/12/04	100%	$1,680.00
5	Convene opportunity of screening com	1 day	Tue 1/13/04	Tue 1/13/04	100%	$280.00
6	Decision point - go/no-go to prelimina	0 days	Tue 1/13/04	Tue 1/13/04	100%	$0.00
8	Assign resources to preliminary invest	1 day	Wed 1/14/04	Wed 1/14/04	100%	$320.00
9	Develop preliminary investigation plan	5 days	Thu 1/15/04	Wed 1/21/04	100%	$3,000.00
10	Evaluate the market	10 days	Thu 1/15/04	Wed 1/28/04	100%	$2,800.00
11	Analyze the competition	5 days	Thu 1/15/04	Wed 1/21/04	100%	$1,400.00
13	Produce lab scale product	10 days	Thu 1/22/04	Wed 2/4/04	100%	$2,800.00
February 2004						
13	Produce lab scale product	10 days	Thu 1/22/04	Wed 2/4/04	100%	$2,800.00
14	Evaluate internal product	5 days	Thu 2/5/04	Wed 2/11/04	100%	$1,400.00
15	Identify production process steps requ	5 days	Thu 2/12/04	Wed 2/18/04	100%	$1,800.00
16	Assess manufacturing capabilities	10 days	Thu 2/19/04	Wed 3/3/04	100%	$5,600.00
17	Determine safety issues	10 days	Thu 2/19/04	Wed 3/3/04	100%	$2,800.00
18	Determine environmental issues	10 days	Thu 2/19/04	Wed 3/3/04	100%	$5,600.00
19	Review legal issues	10 days	Thu 2/19/04	Wed 3/3/04	100%	$6,000.00
March 2004						
16	Assess manufacturing capabilities	10 days	Thu 2/19/04	Wed 3/3/04	100%	$5,600.00
17	Determine safety issues	10 days	Thu 2/19/04	Wed 3/3/04	100%	$2,800.00
18	Determine environmental issues	10 days	Thu 2/19/04	Wed 3/3/04	100%	$5,600.00
19	Review legal issues	10 days	Thu 2/19/04	Wed 3/3/04	100%	$6,000.00
20	Perform financial evaluation	10 days	Thu 3/4/04	Wed 3/17/04	100%	$2,400.00

Figure 12-17. The Completed Tasks report shows all tasks that are reported as complete so far.

The Completed Tasks report is significant for both historical reference and as a record of the team's accomplishment. It provides real data about "lessons learned," helps estimate task durations for future projects, and gives you a general idea of how much work is left to do in the current project. Another important use of this report is to boost team morale, increase motivation, and foster pride in team accomplishments. Although the project goal is paramount, accomplishments to date can be recognized.

The Completed Tasks report is based on the Summary table with the Completed Tasks filter applied. The report includes the task duration, start and finish dates, total cost, and total work.

Using the Should Have Started Tasks Report

The Should Have Started Tasks report, most effective when used regularly, alerts you to all tasks whose scheduled start dates have passed but for which no progress information has been reported to indicate that work on the task has begun. Sometimes, the data shown in this report reflects missing status updates, making this report an effective tool for optimizing the flow of communication on project progress.

When you select this report, you're prompted to enter a Should Start By date. Any tasks that do not have an actual start date entered and that are scheduled to start on or before a given date (usually the current date) are displayed in this report (see Figure 12-18).

Should Have Started Tasks as of Tue 4/6/04
New Product

Task Name	Start	Finish	Baseline Start	Baseline Finish
Development Stage	Mon 3/29/04	Thu 3/31/05	Mon 3/29/04	Thu 3/31/05
Assign resources to developmen	Mon 3/29/04	Mon 3/29/04	Mon 3/29/04	Mon 3/29/04

ID	Successor Name	Type	Lag
28	Gather market information	FS	0 days
33	Establish product characteristics (performance criteria)	FS	0 days

Task Name	Start	Finish	Baseline Start	Baseline Finish
Market Evaluation	Tue 3/30/04	Mon 5/24/04	Tue 3/30/04	Mon 5/24/04
Gather market information	Tue 3/30/04	Mon 4/19/04	Tue 3/30/04	Mon 4/19/04

ID	Successor Name	Type	Lag
29	Identify and contact customer sample group	FS	0 days
30	Perform competitor analysis	FS	0 days

Task Name	Start	Finish	Baseline Start	Baseline Finish
Technical Product Evaluation	Tue 3/30/04	Fri 1/7/05	Tue 3/30/04	Fri 1/7/05
Establish product characteristics	Tue 3/30/04	Wed 3/31/04	Tue 3/30/04	Wed 3/31/04

ID	Successor Name	Type	Lag
34	Develop prototype process	FS	0 days
37	Document patent application process	FS	0 days

Figure 12-18. The Should Have Started Tasks report shows all tasks that are due to start, but have no actual start date reported.

The Should Have Started Tasks report is based on the Variance table with the Should Start By filter applied and sorted by start date. The report includes the baseline and scheduled start and finish dates, along with the start variance field. It also includes task notes and subtables for successor task to show the tasks immediately affected by those starting late.

Using the Slipping Tasks Report

The Slipping Tasks report is used only with projects that have a saved baseline. That is, the report cannot be generated unless baseline information exists. The emphasis of this report is a list of tasks that have started, but that will finish after their baseline finish date. This slipping of the finish date can be caused by the start date occurring later than originally planned or by an increase in the duration.

This report helps you determine which tasks might require added resources, which tasks might require replanning of their duration, and which tasks have become (or might soon become) critical.

The Slipping Tasks report is based on the Variance table with the Slipping Tasks filter applied and is sorted by start date. The report includes the baseline and scheduled start and finish dates, along with the start variance field. It also includes task notes and subtables for successor task to show the tasks immediately affected by the slipping tasks.

For more information about saving and using a baseline, see Chapter 10, "Saving a Baseline and Updating Progress."

Troubleshooting

You can't adjust report column sizes

When you're generating a report, you have no control over column widths. You can specify the content, change font sizes of report elements, adjust the timescale, and modify the headers and footers. This is true whether you're generating a built-in report or one that you've created yourself.

However, you can adjust the scale of the report so you can fit more columns on a page. You can also switch a report between portrait and landscape page orientation.

For more information on changing page setup options, see "Adjusting the Page Setup of a Report" later in this chapter on page 393.

You might also consider printing a sheet view instead of a generated report. When you print a view, you can apply the same table that the report is based on and adjust the column sizes by dragging the edges of the column headings. You can also add and remove columns.

For example, suppose that you want to generate the Unstarted Tasks report, but you don't like that it goes across two pages. You can change the page setup to reduce the left and right margins to 0.5 inch each, and the scaling to 80 percent.

If this change makes the report too small, look at the table and filter the report is based on. In the Current Activity Reports dialog box, select the report and then click Edit. The Definition tab shows that the report is based on the Entry table with the Unstarted Tasks filter applied. Close the dialog boxes and display the Gantt Chart or Task Sheet view. If necessary, apply the Entry table. Then, apply the Unstarted Tasks filter. Adjust the column sizes the way you want; add or remove columns as necessary. Set the page setup for the page orientation, scaling, and margins you want. This way, you can print the information you want with full control over the column widths and content.

For more information about printing views, see "Setting Up and Printing Views" earlier in this chapter on page 358.

Analyzing Budget Status with Cost Reports

The Cost reports in Microsoft Project are a powerful and very effective means of tracking the fiscal health of a project. By using these reports, you can quickly and accurately focus on the pressing cost issues and catch potential problems early.

The Cost reports category provides five reports for reviewing your project's costs and budget (see Figure 12-19).

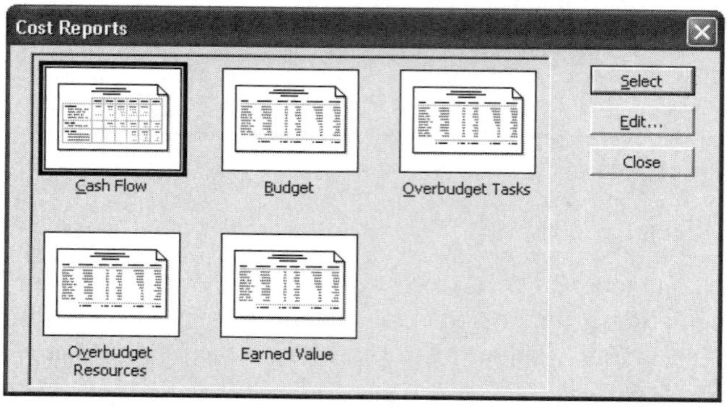

Figure 12-19. Choose one of the available cost-related reports in the Cost Reports dialog box.

Using the Cash Flow Report

The Cash Flow report is a *crosstab* report that displays total scheduled costs by each task and by each week in the project timespan (see Figure 12-20).

Cash Flowas of Tue 4/6/04
NewProduct

	12/28/03	1/4/04	1/11/04
Initial New Product Screening Stage			
New product opportunity identified			
Describe new product idea (1-page written disclosure)	$560.00		
Gather information required for go/no-go decision		$1,400.00	$280.00
Convene opportunity of screening committee (decision to pursue idea or not)			$280.00
Decision point - go/no-go to preliminary investigation			
Preliminary Investigation Stage			
Assign resources to preliminary investigation			$320.00
Develop preliminary investigation plan			$1,200.00
Evaluate the market			$560.00
Analyze the competition			$560.00
Technical Feasibility Analysis			
Produce lab scale product			
Evaluate internal product			

Figure 12-20. The Cash Flow report shows costs for each task by each week in the project.

Use this report to see the costs of tasks per time period. The information shown also enables quick comparisons with baseline budgets or projections, especially when used in conjunction with others, such as the Overbudget Tasks Report, the Tasks In Progress Report, and the Slipping Tasks Report—both to show cost impacts and to clarify budget and earned value figures.

All the costs that go into the performance of a task (assigned human resources, materials, equipment, fees, and fixed costs) are aggregated for each task. The scheduled costs shown also include any actual costs that have accrued as a result of tasks started, in progress, or completed. The date when the task cost is incurred is also reflected in the Cash Flow report, reflecting the cost accrual method you've defined. Costs can accrue at the start of a task, at the end of the task, or be prorated throughout the task duration.

The tasks are listed in order, along with their summary tasks. Rolled-up costs for the summary tasks are included so you can see interim totals for phases or types of work. The costs for each week and each task are totaled.

For more information about establishing project costs, see Chapter 8, "Planning Resource and Task Costs."

Using the Budget Report

The Budget report lists all project tasks in order of total cost. Use the Budget report to quickly focus on your "big ticket" tasks (see Figure 12-21).

Budget Report as of Tue 4/6/04
New Product

Task Name	Fixed Cost	Fixed Cost Accrual	Total Cost	Baseline	Variance
Conduct marketing/technical review	$0.00	Prorated	$51,520.00	$51,520.00	$0.00
Determine if product is meeting customer cost/performance expectations	$0.00	Prorated	$38,400.00	$38,400.00	$0.00
Determine if sales have met projections	$0.00	Prorated	$36,000.00	$36,000.00	$0.00
Produce product for customer evaluation	$2,140.00	Prorated	$24,140.00	$22,000.00	$2,140.00
Evaluate manufacturing process for stability and cost effectiveness	$0.00	Prorated	$24,000.00	$24,000.00	$0.00
Start production of commercial product quantities	$0.00	Prorated	$22,400.00	$22,400.00	$0.00
Monitor customer acceptance testing	$0.00	Prorated	$18,000.00	$18,000.00	$0.00
Determine if product is sustaining its position against competitive response	$0.00	Prorated	$18,000.00	$18,000.00	$0.00
Install and test new equipment or equipment modifications	$873.00	Prorated	$17,673.00	$16,800.00	$873.00
Design and order new equipment	$0.00	Prorated	$15,600.00	$15,600.00	$0.00
Evaluate opportunities to expand product or product line	$0.00	Prorated	$13,200.00	$13,200.00	$0.00
Conduct customer evaluations of prototype product	$0.00	Prorated	$12,000.00	$12,000.00	$0.00
Produce prototype product	$3,592.00	Prorated	$10,592.00	$7,000.00	$3,592.00
Identify long term production requirements	$0.00	Prorated	$9,600.00	$9,600.00	$0.00
Review production performance results	$0.00	Prorated	$9,200.00	$9,200.00	$0.00
Perform evaluate/predict product cycle time	$0.00	Prorated	$9,000.00	$9,000.00	$0.00

Figure 12-21. The Budget report lists all tasks in order of total cost, highest cost to lowest.

The Budget report is based on the Cost table for tasks, and is sorted by cost. The total scheduled costs for each task are listed. The total costs include forecasted costs as well as any actual costs that have accrued as a result of tasks started, in progress, or completed. Also included are any task fixed costs and fixed cost accrual (start, end, prorated). The baseline costs and variances between baseline and total costs show whether you're over budget or under budget, or exactly as originally planned. The actual and remaining cost fields show costs for completed and in-progress tasks. Each column of cost data is totaled.

Using the Overbudget Tasks Report

The Overbudget Tasks report provides a quick look at all tasks in the project whose actual or scheduled costs are higher than their baseline costs. Obviously, this report can be used only for projects with saved baselines. The columns of data are the same as those in the Budget report (see Figure 12-21), but the report filter selects only those tasks whose costs are higher than the baseline.

The Overbudget Tasks report is based on the Cost table with the Cost Overbudget filter applied. The amount of cost variance is listed, and the tasks are sorted in order of the highest variance first. This report is most useful for analyzing the extent of cost overruns for specific tasks.

For more information about adjusting costs to conform to your budget, see "Reducing Project Costs" on page 267.

Using the Overbudget Resources Report

Like the Overbudget Tasks report, the Overbudget Resources report shows the resources whose actual costs exceed those in the baseline plan (see Figure 12-22).

Overbudget Resources as of Tue 4/6/04
New Product

Resource Name	Cost	Baseline Cost	Variance	Actual Cost	Remaining
Haiying Feng	$198,730.00	$197,680.00	$1,050.00	$19,530.00	$179,200.00
Kevin Kennedy	$94,800.00	$94,400.00	$400.00	$7,440.00	$87,360.00
Jeff Pike	$16,310.00	$15,960.00	$350.00	$5,950.00	$10,360.00
Linda Contreras	$65,680.00	$65,600.00	$80.00	$1,040.00	$64,640.00
	$375,520.00	$373,640.00	$1,880.00	$33,960.00	$341,560.00

Figure 12-22. The Overbudget Resources report lists all resources in descending order of cost variance.

The Overbudget Resources report is based on the Cost table for resources with the Cost Overbudget filter applied and sorted by cost variance. The Cost, Baseline Cost, Variance, Actual Cost, and Remaining Cost columns are included and totaled for all over-budget resources.

Usually, the reason these resources are over budget is that their tasks are requiring more work than originally planned. This report is most useful for analyzing the extent of cost overruns for specific resources.

For more information about reviewing and controlling costs in your project, see "Monitoring and Adjusting Costs" on page 338.

Troubleshooting

Project says there is no data to print

If you try to generate a report, and you get a message saying that there is no data to print, it typically means that the filter that the report is based on is not returning any fields (see Figure 12-23).

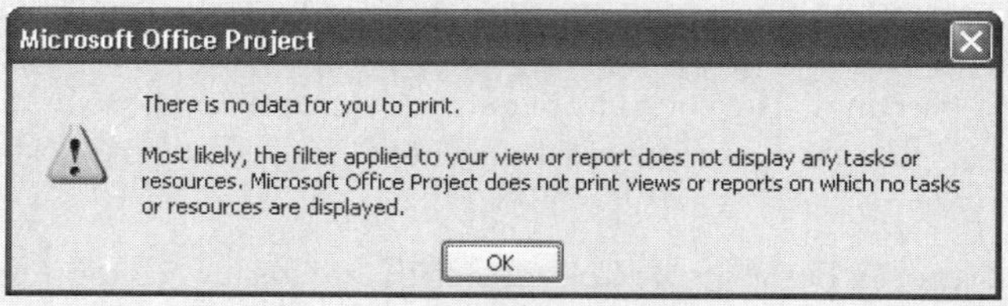

Microsoft Office Project
There is no data for you to print.
Most likely, the filter applied to your view or report does not display any tasks or resources. Microsoft Office Project does not print views or reports on which no tasks or resources are displayed.
OK

Figure 12-23. This error message indicates that a filter to which your selected report is based on is returning no fields to show.

Single-click the name of the report you want and then select Edit. The dialog box that appears shows how the report is defined, including the fields and filters the report is based on. If there are no data in those fields, or if the applied filter finds no match in your project, this might explain why the report is not generated on your project data.

If you get this message when you're trying to generate the Overbudget Tasks or Overbudget Resources, either all your tasks and resources are under budget or right on target. It can also indicate that:

- You haven't entered costs for assigned resources. These costs become a part of your baseline to determine your target budget figures. Display the Resource Sheet, and enter costs for resources in the Std. Rate field. You might need to save a new baseline.
- You haven't entered fixed costs for tasks. These costs become a part of your baseline to determine your target budget figures. Apply the Cost table to a task sheet, and make any necessary entries in the Fixed Cost field for the tasks. You might need to save a new baseline.
- You haven't saved a baseline yet. The baseline determines your target budget figures. Click Tools, Tracking, Save Baseline.
- You haven't entered any tracking data for in-progress or completed tasks. Select the task(s), click Tools, Tracking, Update Tasks.

The Should Have Started Tasks or Slipping Tasks report are also based on variances between the current scheduled start dates and the baseline start dates. If no baseline has been saved, or if there is no variance between the baseline start and scheduled start, there are no data to print for this report.

Using the Earned Value Report

The Earned Value report is based on the concept of comparisons between planned and actual costs. More specifically, *earned value* is the analysis of cost performance based on comparisons between the baseline and actual costs and between the baseline and actual schedule.

The earned value analysis always uses a specific date as the reference point for the comparisons being made. This date is referred to as the *status date*, or sometimes the *cutoff date*. To set a status date that's different from today's date, click Project, Project Information and then enter a date in the Status Date box.

The Earned Value report is based on the Earned Value table for tasks. Every non-summary task is listed along with its earned value calculations for BCWS, BCWP, ACWP, SV, CV, EAC, BAC, and VAC (see Figure 12-24).

Earned Value as of Tue 4/6/04
New Product

Task Name	BCWS	BCWP	ACWP	SV	CV	EAC
New product opportunity identified	$0.00	$0.00	$150.00	$0.00	($150.00)	$150.00
Describe new product idea (1-page wr	$560.00	$560.00	$700.00	$0.00	($140.00)	$700.00
Gather information required for go/no-	$1,680.00	$1,680.00	$1,750.00	$0.00	($70.00)	$1,750.00
Convene opportunity screening com	$280.00	$280.00	$350.00	$0.00	($70.00)	$350.00
Decision point-go/no-go to preliminar	$0.00	$0.00	$0.00	$0.00	$0.00	$0.00
Assign resources to preliminary invest	$320.00	$320.00	$320.00	$0.00	$0.00	$320.00
Develop preliminary investigation plan	$3,000.00	$3,000.00	$3,000.00	$0.00	$0.00	$3,000.00
Evaluate the market	$2,800.00	$2,800.00	$2,800.00	$0.00	$0.00	$2,800.00
Analyze the competition	$1,400.00	$1,400.00	$1,400.00	$0.00	$0.00	$1,400.00
Produce lab scale product	$2,800.00	$2,800.00	$4,200.00	$0.00	($1,400.00)	$4,200.00
Evaluate internal product	$1,400.00	$1,400.00	$1,400.00	$0.00	$0.00	$1,400.00
Identify production process steps requ	$1,800.00	$1,800.00	$1,800.00	$0.00	$0.00	$1,800.00
Assess manufacturing capabilities	$5,600.00	$5,600.00	$4,200.00	$0.00	$1,400.00	$4,200.00
Determine safety issues	$2,800.00	$2,800.00	$2,800.00	$0.00	$0.00	$2,800.00
Determine environmental issues	$5,600.00	$5,600.00	$5,600.00	$0.00	$0.00	$5,600.00
Review legal issues	$6,000.00	$6,000.00	$6,750.00	$0.00	($750.00)	$6,750.00
Perform financial evaluation	$2,400.00	$2,400.00	$2,400.00	$0.00	$0.00	$2,400.00
Develop risk analysis	$3,000.00	$3,000.00	$3,000.00	$0.00	$0.00	$3,000.00
Draft initial development stage plan	$2,800.00	$2,800.00	$2,800.00	$0.00	$0.00	$2,800.00
Conduct preliminary stage review deci	$1,840.00	$1,840.00	$1,840.00	$0.00	$0.00	$1,840.00
Decision point-go/no-go to developm	$0.00	$0.00	$0.00	$0.00	$0.00	$0.00
Assign resources to development stag	$640.00	$0.00	$0.00	($640.00)	$0.00	$640.00
Gather market information	$1,680.00	$0.00	$0.00	($1,680.00)	$0.00	$8,400.00
Identify and contact customer sample	$0.00	$0.00	$0.00	$0.00	$0.00	$2,675.00
Perform competitor analysis	$0.00	$0.00	$0.00	$0.00	$0.00	$4,300.00

Figure 12-24. The Earned Value report shows a summary of all task costs, based on your specified status date.

Tip **Positive is good; negative is bad**

When you see positive numbers in the variance columns of the Earned Value table (that is, the SV, CV, and VAC columns), you're ahead of schedule or under budget so far.

When you see negative numbers in these columns, the task is behind schedule or over budget.

When you see $0.00 in SV, CV, or VAC, the associated task is exactly on target with the schedule or budget.

Interpret the Earned Value Figures

So what are you looking at when you see those earned value calculations? Are they good numbers or bad numbers? Or are they just right? The following list can help you interpret, in a general way, the calculations you see in your Earned Value report.

Budgeted Cost of Work Scheduled (BCWS). The cost amount originally defined for a task, up to the status date. By this date, this much of the budget should have been spent. Review this amount in conjunction with the BAC and EAC.

Budgeted Cost of Work Performed (BCWP). The baseline cost of a task, multiplied by the calculated percent complete, up to the status date. Based on the amount of work reported by this date, this much of the budget should have been spent. Compare this amount with the BCWS and ACWP.

Actual Cost of Work Performed (ACWP). The costs incurred from the actual amount of work done on a task and any fixed costs accrued for that task. Based on the amount of work reported by this date, this much budget has actually been spent. Compare this amount with the BCWS and BCWP.

Schedule Variance (SV). The result of subtracting the BCWS from the BCWP. Even though it's called "Schedule Variance," the variance really calculated is cost resulting from schedule considerations. This dollar amount indicates the difference between the baseline costs for scheduled tasks and actual progress reported on those tasks. A positive SV means the task is ahead of schedule in terms of cost. A negative SV means the task is behind schedule in terms of cost. An SV of $0.00 means the task is exactly on schedule in terms of cost. Although SV does not necessarily specify whether you're under or over budget, it can be an indicator that budget should be looked at more closely. Compare this figure with CV and VAC.

Cost Variance (CV). The result of subtracting the ACWP from the BCWP. If the number is positive, the actual costs are less than what was budgeted. This dollar amount indicates the difference between the baseline and actual costs for tasks. A positive CV means the task is currently under budget. A negative CV means the task is currently over budget. A CV of $0.00 means the task is exactly on budget. Compare this figure with SV and VAC.

Estimate At Completion (EAC). The amount calculated from the ACWP, BCWP, and the Cost Performance Index (CPI), resulting in a composite forecast total of costs for the task upon completion. Also known as Forecast At Completion (FAC). This dollar amount indicates the current best guess of what this task will cost by the time it's finished. Compare this amount with the BAC.

Budgeted At Completion (BAC). The cost for the task as planned. This is exactly the same as the baseline cost, which includes assigned resource costs and any fixed costs for the task.

Variance At Completion (VAC). The result of subtracting EAC from BAC. A negative VAC indicates that the forecasted cost for the task is currently over budget. A positive VAC indicates that the forecasted cost for the task is currently under budget. A VAC of $0.00 indicates that the task is right on budget. Compare this figure with SV and CV.

For more detailed information, including the underlying calculations, about earned value analysis, see "Analyzing Progress and Costs Using Earned Value" on page 401.

Troubleshooting

My earned value fields are showing $0.00

If you run the Earned Value report, and see nothing but zeros except in the EAC and VAC columns, you probably have yet to save a baseline. All earned value calculations are based on comparisons between your baseline and scheduled costs and dates. Click Tools, Tracking, Save Baseline.

If you've saved a baseline, and you're seeing all zeros except in the EAC and BAC columns, this indicates that you're probably close to the beginning of your project and you haven't entered any tracking information yet. As time goes by and you start entering task progress data, those numbers will start changing to reflect the schedule and current progress.

If you've saved a baseline, and you're seeing all zeros in the SV, CV, and VAC columns, your project is running exactly as planned, with no positive or negative variances recorded at all. Make sure that all your tracking information is entered and up to date. If it is and you're still seeing all those zeros, pat yourself on the back. You're exactly on schedule and on budget—great job!

Evaluating Resource Allocation with Assignment Reports

There are four standard reports in Microsoft Project relating to assignments (see Figure 12-25). You can use these reports to generate to-do lists for resources and their assigned tasks, to follow up with resources and their current task progress, or to determine who has too many assignments in the available time.

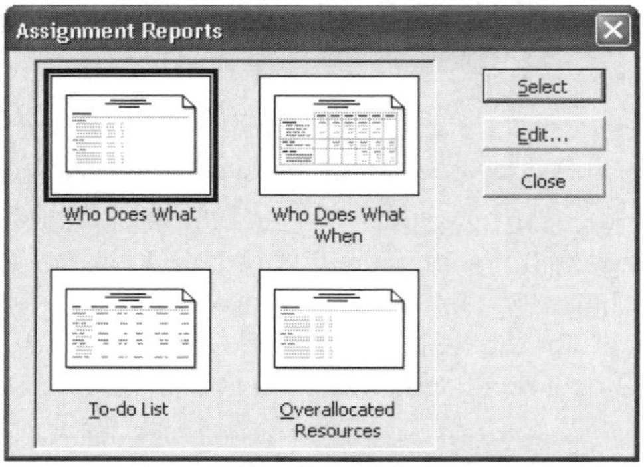

Figure 12-25. The Assignment Reports dialog box lists the reports for resources and their assigned tasks.

Using the Who Does What Report

The Who Does What report lists the tasks assigned to each resource (see Figure 12-26). It clearly shows the relative number of assignments for all the project resources. This report can also help you or a resource manager plan for coverage when a resource becomes unavailable.

Who Does What as of Tue 4/6/04
New Product

ID	Resource Name / Task Name	Work / Units	Work	Delay	Start	Finish
◆	Linda Contreras	1,642 hrs				
ID	Task Name	Units	Work	Delay	Start	Finish
2	New product opportunity identified	100%	2 hrs	0 days	Thu 1/1/04	Thu 1/1/04
6	Decision point - go/no-go to preliminary investigation	100%	0 hrs	0 days	Tue 1/13/04	Tue 1/13/04
8	Assign resources to preliminary investigation	100%	8 hrs	0 days	Wed 1/14/04	Wed 1/14/04
23	Conduct preliminary stage review decision	100%	16 hrs	0 days	Thu 3/25/04	Fri 3/26/04
24	Decision point - go/no-go to development stage	100%	0 hrs	0 days	Fri 3/26/04	Fri 3/26/04
28	Assign resources to development stage plan	100%	8 hrs	0 days	Mon 3/29/04	Mon 3/29/04
36	Conduct internal product review	100%	40 hrs	0 days	Thu 5/20/04	Wed 5/26/04
46	Conduct marketing/technical review	100%	16 hrs	0 days	Mon 1/10/05	Tue 1/11/05
49	Review legal and patent considerations	100%	80 hrs	0 days	Wed 1/12/05	Tue 1/25/05
55	Review preliminary investigation criteria	100%	16 hrs	0 days	Wed 3/16/05	Thu 3/17/05
58	Decision point - go/no-go to pilot stage	100%	0 hrs	0 days	Thu 3/31/05	Thu 3/31/05
66	Assign pilot stage resources	100%	8 hrs	0 days	Fri 4/1/05	Fri 4/1/05
76	Assign commercialization leadership responsibility and resources	100%	16 hrs	0 days	Mon 9/5/05	Tue 9/6/05
79	Pilot stage review and commercialization decision	100%	16 hrs	0 days	Wed 9/7/05	Thu 9/8/05
93	Review production performance results	100%	80 hrs	0 days	Wed 5/3/06	Tue 5/16/06
96	Affirm decision to continue commercialization program	100%	16 hrs	0 days	Wed 6/7/06	Thu 6/8/06
98	Determine if product is meeting customer cost/performance expectations	100%	480 hrs	0 days	Fri 6/9/06	Thu 8/31/06
99	Determine if sales have met projections	100%	480 hrs	0 days	Fri 6/9/06	Thu 8/31/06
100	Determine if product is sustaining its position against competitive response	100%	240 hrs	0 days	Fri 9/1/06	Thu 10/12/06
103	Evaluate opportunities to expand product or product line	100%	120 hrs	0 days	Fri 11/17/06	Thu 12/7/06
◆	Hanying Feng	5,678 hrs				
ID	Task Name	Units	Work	Delay	Start	Finish
2	New product opportunity identified	100%	2 hrs	0 days	Thu 1/1/04	Thu 1/1/04
3	Describe new product idea (1-page written disclosure)	100%	20 hrs	0 days	Thu 1/1/04	Mon 1/5/04
4	Gather information required for go/no-go decision	100%	50 hrs	0 days	Mon 1/5/04	Tue 1/13/04
5	Convene opportunity of screening committee (decision to pursue idea or not)	100%	10 hrs	0 days	Tue 1/13/04	Wed 1/14/04
6	Decision point - go/no-go to preliminary investigation	100%	0 hrs	0 days	Tue 1/13/04	Tue 1/13/04
9	Develop preliminary investigation plan	100%	40 hrs	0 days	Thu 1/15/04	Wed 1/21/04

Figure 12-26. The Who Does What report shows which resources are assigned to which tasks.

The Who Does What report is based on the Usage table for work resources, and also shows assignment schedule information.

For more information about making and changing resource assignments, see Chapter 7, "Assigning Resources to Tasks."

Using the Who Does What When Report

The Who Does What When report is an amplification of the information given in the Who Does What report, adding the daily breakdown of hours of work assigned. Who Does What When is a crosstab report that shows a tabular presentation of work assigned by resource, by assignment, and by day (see Figure 12-27).

Who Does What When as of Tue 4/6/04
New Product

	2/15	2/16	2/17	2/18	2/19	2/20
Evaluate manufacturing process for stability and cost effectiveness						
Mandar Naik		8 hrs	8 hrs	8 hrs		
Identify production process steps required for manufacture		8 hrs	8 hrs	8 hrs		
Redesign process (if necessary)						
Modify prototype process						
Conduct preliminary manufacturing process review						
Evaluate contract manufacturing option						
Conduct development stage review						
Re-evaluate manufacturing processes						
Pilot stage review and commercialization decision						
Develop manufacturing process requirements						
Identify long term production requirements						
Kathie Flood					8 hrs	8 hrs
Assess manufacturing capabilities					8 hrs	8 hrs
Conduct preliminary manufacturing process review						
Confirm product specification						
Develop manufacturing process requirements						
Install and test new equipment or equipment modifications						
Confirm manufacturing capabilities						
Start production of commercial product quantities						
Identify long term production requirements						
Evaluate manufacturing process for stability and cost effectiveness						
Imtiaz Kahn					8 hrs	8 hrs
Determine safety issues					8 hrs	8 hrs
Conduct product safety review						

Figure 12-27. The Who Does What When report is a daily accounting of resources and their assigned tasks.

Down the left side, you see a list of all resources with all their assigned tasks. Across the top is each day in the project. All work hours for each of those assignments are listed by resource and by day. Not only does this show you how resources are assigned, but you can also easily see when a resource is assigned to excessive amounts of work on a given day.

Inside Out

The voluminous Who Does What When report

Because it is so detailed, the Who Does What When report requires a large amount of paper when printed. Also, generating the data needed to create the report might take some time. Thus, it might be best to use this report less frequently than others or to view it in Print Preview rather than printing it.

You cannot print a date range with this report unless you create a new custom report based on the data this report generates. However, you can easily modify the report to show work amounts by weeks or by months rather than by days. To do this, follow these steps:

1. Click View, Reports.
2. Double-click Assignments.
3. Click Who Does What When and then click Edit.

   The Crosstab Report dialog box appears (see Figure 12-28).

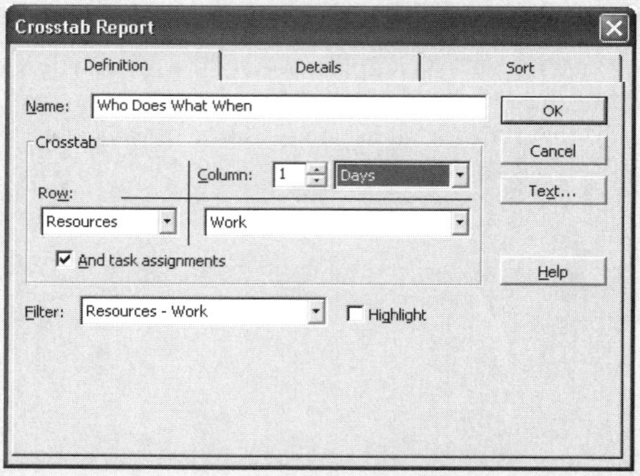

Figure 12-28. Edit the Who Does What When report using the Crosstab Report dialog box.

4. Next to Column, change Days to Weeks or Months, for example.

   You can also change the number next to Column to indicate that data should be shown for every two weeks, for example.
5. Click OK.

6 Double-click the Who Does What When report, and you'll see that your changes have taken effect (see Figure 12-29).

Who Does What When as of Tue 4/6/04
New Product

	Feb 15, '04	Feb 22, '04	Feb 29, '04
Evaluate manufacturing process for stability and cost effectiveness			
Mandar Naik	24 hrs		
Identify production process steps required for manufacture	24 hrs		
Redesign process (if necessary)			
Modify prototype process			
Conduct preliminary manufacturing process review			
Evaluate contract manufacturing option			
Conduct development stage review			
Re-evaluate manufacturing processes			
Pilot stage review and commercialization decision			
Develop manufacturing process requirements			
Identify long term production requirements			
Kathie Flood	16 hrs	40 hrs	4 hrs
Assess manufacturing capabilities	16 hrs	40 hrs	4 hrs
Conduct preliminary manufacturing process review			
Confirm product specification			
Develop manufacturing process requirements			
Install and test new equipment or equipment modifications			
Confirm manufacturing capabilities			
Start production of commercial product quantities			
Identify long term production requirements			
Evaluate manufacturing process for stability and cost effectiveness			
Imtiaz Kahn	16 hrs	40 hrs	24 hrs
Determine safety issues	16 hrs	40 hrs	24 hrs
Conduct product safety review			
Confirm product safety			

Figure 12-29. You can change the timescale in the Who Does What When report.

The change you made to this report is saved with this project file.

Using the To-Do List

Use the To-Do List to generate a list of tasks to provide to assigned resources (see Figure 12-30). This can be especially useful if you're not using Project Server and Project Web Access to exchange assignment information electronically with your resources.

To Do List as of Tue 4/6/04
New Product

Task Name	Duration	Start	Finish	Predecessors	Resource Names
Evaluate the market	10 days	Thu 1/15/04	Wed 1/28/04	8	Jo Brown
Analyze the competition	5 days	Thu 1/15/04	Wed 1/21/04	8	Jo Brown
Evaluate the market	10 days	Thu 1/15/04	Wed 1/28/04	8	Jo Brown
Analyze the competition	5 days	Thu 1/15/04	Wed 1/21/04	8	Jo Brown
Evaluate the market	10 days	Thu 1/15/04	Wed 1/28/04	8	Jo Brown
Gather market information	15 days	Tue 3/30/04	Mon 4/19/04	26	Hanying Feng,Jo Brow
Gather market information	15 days	Tue 3/30/04	Mon 4/19/04	26	Hanying Feng,Jo Brow

Figure 12-30. The To-Do List is generated for a single resource at a time, showing all task information for that resource's assignments.

The To-Do List is based on the Entry table for tasks with the Using Resource filter applied. It's grouped by week and sorted by task start date. The To-Do List shows the names of all tasks to which the selected resource is assigned, the task durations, and the start and finish dates.

Inside Out

Reports can't be e-mailed

It would be nice to be able to e-mail a report like the To-Do List to team members or a report like the Project Summary to your boss. But that capability is not available (for many of the same reasons why you can't save a report from a moment in time).

Note You might consider using a third-party screen capture application that allow you to "print" your report to a .gif or .jpg file. You can then e-mail that file to team members or other stakeholders.

What you can do, however, is e-mail selected tasks or selected resources from your project plan to your team members. This works if you're using a MAPI-compliant 32-bit e-mail application such as Microsoft Outlook. You must also have your resources' e-mail addresses entered in the Resource Information dialog box.

To e-mail selected tasks or resources to your resources:

1. Display a sheet view that contains the tasks or resources you want to e-mail.
2. If necessary, apply a filter to show just the tasks or resources you want.
3. Select the tasks or resources whose information you want to e-mail.
4. Click File, Send To, Mail Recipient.
5. In the Send Schedule Note dialog box, select the Resources check box.
6. Click the Selected Tasks or Selected Resources option.
7. Under Attach, select the Picture Of Selected Tasks or Picture of Selected Resources check box.
8. Click OK. Your e-mail program's message form appears with address information filled in and the picture of tasks or resources already attached.
9. Adjust the recipients of the message, add a comment if you like, and then click Send.

For more information about using e-mail to exchange project information, see "Exchanging Project Information Using E-Mail" on page 563.

Using the Overallocated Resources Report

The Overallocated Resources report lists only the resources that have been assigned work in excess of their availability, as reflected in their resource calendars (see Figure 12-31). For example, if a resource's availability is based on the default Standard calendar, the resource will become overallocated when scheduled for more than eight hours per day or more than five days per week.

The list includes every task assigned to a resource, not just the tasks for which the resource is overallocated. Overallocated resources have an overallocated indicator by their name, but the report does not show which specific tasks are actually causing the overallocation. Analyze the task start and finish dates and the amount of work scheduled during those timespans to find the periods of overallocation.

Overallocated Resources as of Tue 4/6/04
New Product

	Resource Name	Work
	Kevin Kennedy	2,370 hrs

ID	Task Name	Units	Work	Delay	Start	Finish
9	Develop preliminary investigation plan	100%	40 hrs	0 days	Thu 1/15/04	Wed 1/21/04
19	Review legal issues	100%	80 hrs	0 days	Thu 2/19/04	Fri 3/5/04
21	Develop risk analysis	100%	40 hrs	0 days	Thu 3/18/04	Wed 3/24/04
23	Conduct preliminary stage review decision	100%	16 hrs	0 days	Thu 3/25/04	Fri 3/26/04
24	Decision point - go/no-go to development stage	100%	0 hrs	0 days	Fri 3/26/04	Fri 3/26/04
26	Assign resources to development stage plan	100%	8 hrs	0 days	Mon 3/29/04	Mon 3/29/04
41	Develop plan for customer product testing	100%	40 hrs	0 days	Mon 11/8/04	Fri 11/12/04
42	Produce product for customer evaluation	100%	200 hrs	0 days	Mon 11/8/04	Fri 12/10/04
44	Conduct customer evaluations of prototype product	100%	160 hrs	0 days	Mon 12/13/04	Fri 1/7/05
52	Perform evaluate/predict product cycle time	100%	120 hrs	0 days	Wed 2/9/05	Tue 3/1/05
56	Develop pilot stage plan	100%	40 hrs	0 days	Wed 1/12/05	Tue 1/18/05
57	Conduct development stage review	100%	16 hrs	0 days	Wed 3/30/05	Thu 3/31/05
58	Decision point - go/no-go to pilot stage	100%	0 hrs	0 days	Thu 3/31/05	Thu 3/31/05
60	Assign pilot stage resources	100%	8 hrs	0 days	Fri 4/1/05	Fri 4/1/05
61	Secure customer commitment to participate in commercialization trials	100%	40 hrs	0 days	Mon 4/4/05	Fri 4/8/05
63	Schedule/reserve pilot production facility	100%	40 hrs	0 days	Mon 4/11/05	Fri 4/15/05
64	Resolve raw material and finish products logistics	100%	40 hrs	0 days	Mon 4/18/05	Fri 4/22/05
65	Review trial plan and requirements	100%	40 hrs	0 days	Mon 4/11/05	Fri 4/15/05
66	Review preliminary trial results	100%	80 hrs	0 days	Mon 5/23/05	Fri 6/3/05
72	Confirm sales and marketing strategies	100%	40 hrs	0 days	Mon 7/4/05	Fri 7/8/05
73	Confirm product safety	100%	40 hrs	0 days	Mon 7/4/05	Fri 7/8/05
76	Assign commercialization leadership responsibility and resources	100%	16 hrs	0 days	Mon 9/5/05	Tue 9/6/05
83	Confirm customer specification acceptance and trial participation	100%	80 hrs	0 days	Wed 9/14/05	Tue 9/27/05
86	Develop and review production trial plan (resolve logistics issues)	100%	40 hrs	0 days	Wed 1/18/06	Tue 1/24/06
90	Monitor customer acceptance testing	100%	240 hrs	0 days	Wed 3/22/06	Tue 5/2/06
93	Review production performance results	100%	80 hrs	0 days	Wed 5/3/06	Tue 5/16/06
96	Affirm decision to continue commercialization program	100%	16 hrs	0 days	Wed 6/7/06	Thu 6/8/06
98	Determine if product is meeting customer cost/performance expectations	100%	480 hrs	0 days	Fri 6/9/06	Thu 8/31/06
101	Evaluate manufacturing process for stability and cost effectiveness	100%	320 hrs	0 days	Fri 9/1/06	Thu 10/26/06

	Resource Name	Work
	Linda Contreras	1,642 hrs

ID	Task Name	Units	Work	Delay	Start
2	New product opportunity identified	100%	2 hrs	0 days	Thu 1/1/04
6	Decision point - go/no-go to preliminary investigation	100%	0 hrs	0 days	Tue 1/13/04
8	Assign resources to preliminary investigation	100%	8 hrs	0 days	Wed 1/14/04

Figure 12-31. The Overallocated Resources report lists all overallocated resources along with their assignments.

The Overallocated Resources report is based on the Usage table for resources, with the Overallocated Resources filter applied. This report includes the resource's name and total work hours on the summary level and the resource's assignment schedule information in a subtable.

For more information about resolving overallocated resources, see "Balancing Resource Workloads" on page 271.

Reports That Identify Problems

You can generate reports that will help you identify problems in the project. This can help mitigate and address issues before they become disasters. The following reports help you look at potential or current problems:

- Critical Tasks (Overview)
- Should Have Started Tasks (Current Activity)
- Overbudget Tasks (Cost)
- Overbudget Resources (Cost)
- Earned Value (Cost)
- Overallocated Resources (Assignment)

For more information about resolving project problems, see Chapter 9, "Checking and Adjusting the Project Plan," and Chapter 11, "Responding to Changes in Your Project."

Reviewing Resource Usage with Workload Reports

There are two reports in the Workload report category: the Task Usage report and the Resource Usage report (see Figure 12-32).

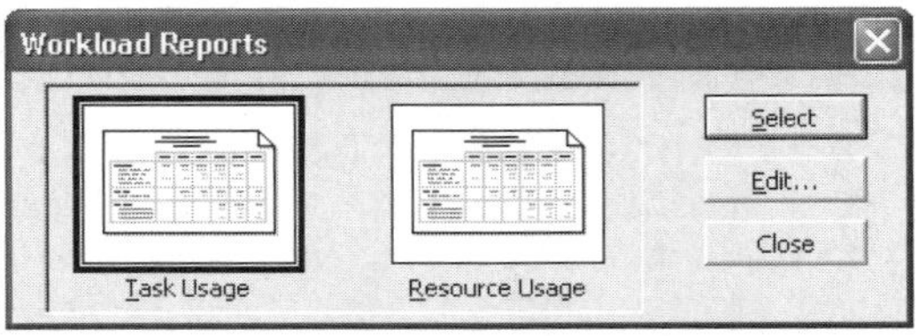

Figure 12-32. The Workload Reports dialog box shows the available reports in this category.

These reports are excellent tracking tools for seeing the amount of work per task or per resource, on a weekly basis. Both are crosstab reports, showing a tabular presentation of work assigned by assignments along the left and by week across the top.

Using the Task Usage Report

The Task Usage report emphasizes assignment hours by task and by week. Under the task names are the assignments, shown as the names of the assigned resources (see Figure 12-33).

Task Usage as of Tue 4/6/04
New Product

	12/28/03	1/4/04	1/11/04	1/18/04
Initial New Product Screening Stage				
New product opportunity identified	4 hrs			
Linda Contreras	2 hrs			
Hanying Feng	2 hrs			
Describe new product idea (1-page written disclosure)	16 hrs	4 hrs		
Hanying Feng	16 hrs	4 hrs		
Gather information required for go/no-go decision		40 hrs	10 hrs	
Hanying Feng		40 hrs	10 hrs	
Convene opportunity of screening committee (decision to pursue idea or not)			10 hrs	
Hanying Feng			10 hrs	
Decision point - go/no-go to preliminary investigation				
Linda Contreras				
Hanying Feng				
Preliminary Investigation Stage				
Assign resources to preliminary investigation			8 hrs	
Linda Contreras			8 hrs	
Develop preliminary investigation plan			32 hrs	48 hrs
Hanying Feng			16 hrs	24 hrs
Kevin Kennedy			16 hrs	24 hrs
Evaluate the market			16 hrs	40 hrs
Jo Brown			16 hrs	40 hrs

Figure 12-33. The Task Usage report shows assignments by task.

The Task Usage report is very similar to the Task Usage view. Summary tasks are shown so the logical groupings of tasks within the project are easy to follow. Totals are shown for each week and each task. This is a clear way to show the full extent of how work and material resources are assigned to every task.

Using the Resource Usage Report

The Resource Usage report emphasizes assignment hours by resource and by week. Under the resource names are the assignments, shown as the names of the tasks to which the associated resource is assigned.

The Resource Usage report is very similar to the Resource Usage view. For each resource, all assigned tasks are listed along with weekly totals of the hours of work assigned for that task. The report layout is the same as the Task Usage report (see Figure 12-33).

More Built-in Reports

If these reports weren't enough, there are several more available that aren't listed in the Reports dialog box. These additional reports are as follows:

- Base Calendar
- Resource
- Resource (material)
- Resource (work)
- Resource Usage (material)
- Resource Usage (work)
- Task

To generate these reports, follow these steps:

1. Click View, Reports.
2. In the Reports dialog box, double-click Custom.

   The Custom Reports dialog box appears, showing a single list of all built-in reports.
3. In the Reports box, scroll to and select the report you want to use.
4. Click Preview.

Revising a Built-in Report

After using the standard built-in reports for several reviews and meetings, you might come up with some new ideas for customizing the presentation and content. You can tweak a built-in report a little (or a lot) to make it suit your needs better. A great method is to copy an existing report and change the copy, leaving the original intact. If you're certain about the changes you want to make, you can directly modify the existing report itself.

Copying an Existing Report

Copying an existing report and modifying the copy is the easiest and most non-threatening method for creating a new report. The original report remains unfettered, and you can feel free to go wild with the copy. It will probably turn out great, but it's good to know you can experiment without dire consequences. You can always delete the copy and start over again with a fresh copy.

To copy and modify an existing report, follow these steps:

1. Click View, Reports.
2. Double-click Custom.

   The Custom Reports dialog box appears (see Figure 12-34).

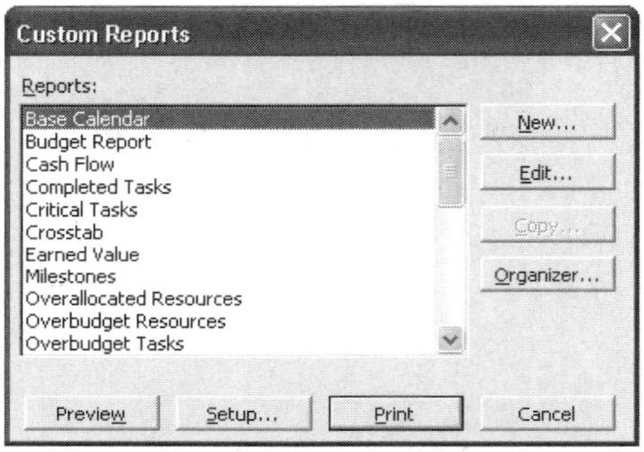

Figure 12-34. The Custom Reports dialog box shows all built-in reports and report formats.

3. In the Reports box, click the report you want to copy and then click Copy.

   One of three possible dialog boxes appears, depending on the format of the report you're copying: Task Report, Resource Report, or Crosstab Report (see Figure 12-35).

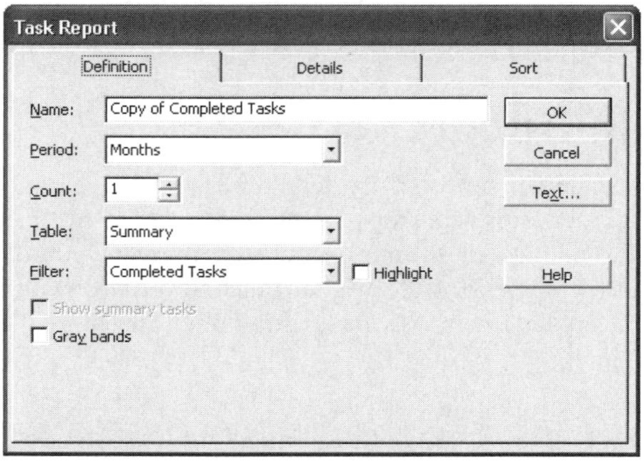

Figure 12-35. The Task Report dialog box appears for any report based on task information.

4 In the Name box, which shows Copy Of <Report Name>, enter the name of your new custom report.

Make sure it's a unique name in the Reports list.

5 Make any changes you want to the report content.

Use the Definition tab to set the fields, time periods, and filters to be used. Use the Details tab to specify additional information you want to add to the report. Use the Sort tab to specify which field should dictate the order of information in the report.

6 Make any changes you want to the report fonts by clicking the Text button.

The Text Styles dialog box appears (see Figure 12-36).

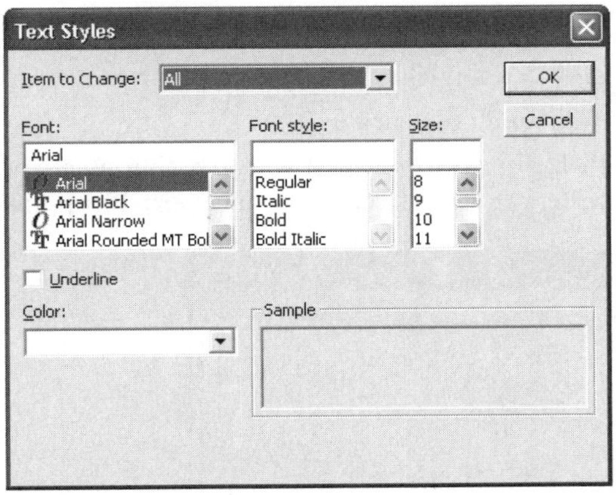

Figure 12-36. Change the font of various items in the report using the Text Styles dialog box.

In the Item To Change box, click the report element whose text you want to format and then specify the changes throughout the rest of the dialog box. When finished, click OK.

7 When finished with your new report's definition and changes, click OK in the report definition dialog box.

The name of your new report appears in the Reports list in the Custom Reports dialog box.

8 Select your new report if necessary and then click Preview to generate the report and see what it looks like.

9 If you want to make further changes, click the Close button in the Preview window and then click Edit.

The report definition dialog box appears again.

Your new report is saved with your project file and is available whenever you work in this particular project.

Modifying an Existing Report

You can directly edit the definition properties of a built-in report. The elements available for editing vary by report. In some reports, all you can change is the font. In other reports, you can change the reporting period, filter for specific types of information, specify that information be drawn from a specific table, and more.

When you change an existing report, your changes are saved only with the project file. If you open the same report in any other project file, the original default report properties will still be present there.

To edit a report, follow these steps:

1. Click View, Reports.
2. In the Reports dialog box, double-click the report category you want.
3. Click the report you want and then click Edit.

   One of four possible dialog boxes appears, showing the options available for this report: Task Report, Resource Report, Crosstab Report, or Report Text (see Figure 12-37).

   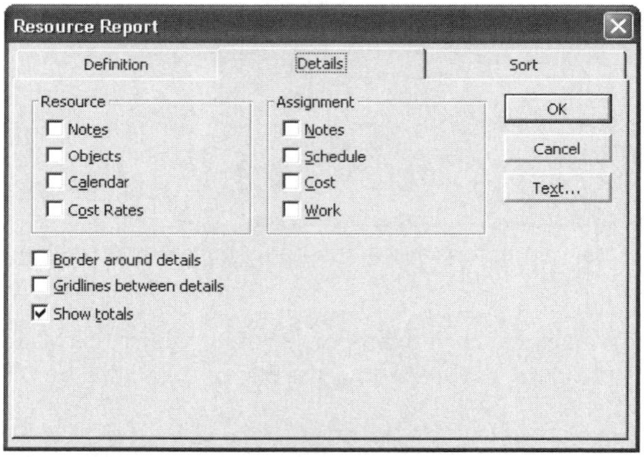

   Figure 12-37. You can edit different types of information depending on the report you choose.

4. Make the changes you want to the report content or format.

   If available, use the Definition tab to set the fields, time periods, and filters to be used. Use the Details tab to specify additional information you want to add to the report. Use the Sort tab to specify which field should dictate the order of information in the report.
5. Make any changes you want to the report fonts by clicking the Text button.
6. When finished editing the report, click OK in the report definition dialog box.
7. Select the edited report if necessary and then click Preview to generate the report and see what it now looks like.

8. If you want to make further changes, click the Close button in the Preview window and then click Edit again to reopen the report definition dialog box.

Adjusting the Page Setup of a Report

You can modify the header, footer, page numbering, and other general page setup elements of a built-in report, a copied report, or a brand-new report. To do this, follow these steps:

1. Click View, Reports.
2. Double-click Custom.
3. In the Reports box, click the report whose page setup you want to modify and then click Preview.
4. In the Preview window, click Page Setup.
5. Use the options on the Page, Margins, Header, and Footer tab to make the changes you want.

For more information about page setup options, see "Page Setup Options" earlier in this chapter on page 359.

Building a Custom Report

You might have a specialized report requirement that none of the built-in reports fulfills. If you don't think you can even copy and modify an existing report to meet your needs, you need to create a new report from scratch.

Well, it's not entirely from scratch. Microsoft Project provides four report templates that give you the framework in which to build a good report. These templates, or *report types*, are:

- Task
- Resource
- Crosstab
- Monthly Calendar

If you've edited or copied any existing reports, or just looked at a report's definition out of curiosity, you're probably already familiar with at least some of these report types. They're also the basis for all the built-in reports. You can preview any of these report formats. In the Custom Reports dialog box, select its name and click Preview.

To build a custom report, follow these steps:

1. Click View, Reports.
2. In the Reports dialog box, double-click Custom.
3. In the Custom Reports dialog box, click New.

   The Define New Report dialog box appears (see Figure 12-38).

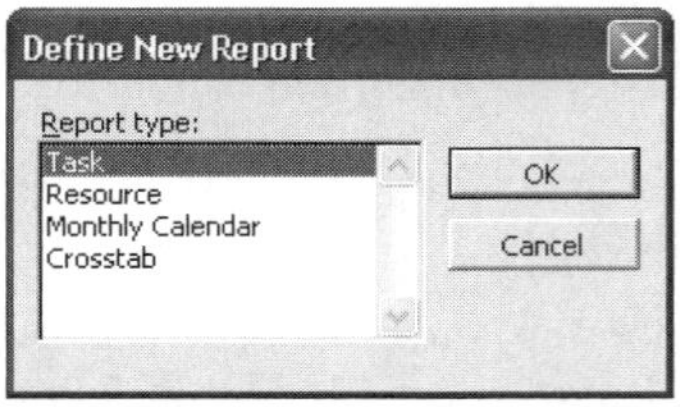

Figure 12-38. Select the format for your new report.

4 In the Report Type box, select the type of report you're creating and then click OK.

The report definition dialog box appears. The dialog box you see depends on the report type you select (see Figure 12-39).

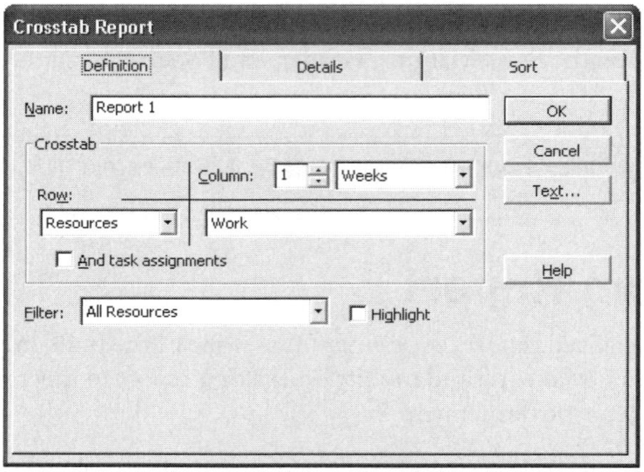

Figure 12-39. The Crosstab Report dialog box appears for any report that displays a tabular format of intersecting information along vertical and horizontal fields of information.

5 In the Name box, enter the name of your new custom report.

Make sure that it's a unique name in the Reports list.

6 Define your report. Specify any fields, filters, or formatting as the report definition.

If you're defining a task, resource, or crosstab report, also use the Details tab to specify additional information you want to add to the report. Use the Sort tab to specify which field should dictate the order of information in the report.

7 Make any changes you want to the report fonts by clicking the Text button.

In the Item To Change box, click the report element whose text you want to format and then specify the changes you want. When finished, click OK.

8 When finished with your new report's definition and changes, click OK in the report definition dialog box.

The name of your new report appears in the Reports list in the Custom Reports dialog box.

9 Select your new report if necessary and then click Preview to generate the report and see what it looks like.

10 If you want to make further changes, click the Close button in the Preview window and then click Edit.

The report definition dialog box appears again.

Your new report is saved with your project file and is available whenever you work in this particular project.

> **Note** **Copy reports to your global template**
> If you want your changed or newly created reports to be present in all your project files, you can use the Organizer to copy those reports from your current project to your *global.mpt* project template.
>
> You can go the other direction as well. If you've changed a built-in report and want to return to the original default report, you can copy it from the global.mpt back into the project file.
>
> For more information about copying project elements using the Organizer, see "Sharing Customized Elements Among Projects" on page 812.

Generating Reports from Project XML Data

You can export project information as XML data and create reports in other applications. You can generate this information as an HTML file for viewing on a Web site. You can send this information to a Microsoft Excel spreadsheet. In short, you can use this project XML data in any application that recognizes XML.

This function can be useful if you want to save a snapshot of report information in another program or if you want to manipulate project data in different ways than are available in Microsoft Project.

NEW FEATURE! In Microsoft Project 2002, the XML Reporting Wizard Component Object Model (COM) add-in was available as a Web download. Now the wizard is built in to Microsoft Project and available on the Analysis toolbar.

With the XML Reporting Wizard, you can save your project as an XML file. You can apply an XSL template to that data. Two sample XSL templates for HTML files are provided with Microsoft Project. You can also create your own XSL template to make the XML data appear exactly the way you need. If you're using your own XSL template for your project report, be sure it's created and ready on your computer or network before running the wizard.

To generate a report using the XML Reporting Wizard, follow these steps:

1 Click View, Toolbars, Analysis to show the Analysis toolbar.

2 On the Analysis toolbar, click XML Reporting Wizard.

3 Read the first page of the XML Reporting Wizard and then click Next.

XML Reporting Wizard

4 In the Specify XML File Wizard page, make sure that the New File option is selected and then click Next.

5 In the browser window that appears, navigate to the location on your computer or network where you want to save the new XML file containing your project data. In the File Name box, enter a filename and then click Save.

The Select The Transform To Apply Wizard page appears (see Figure 12-40).

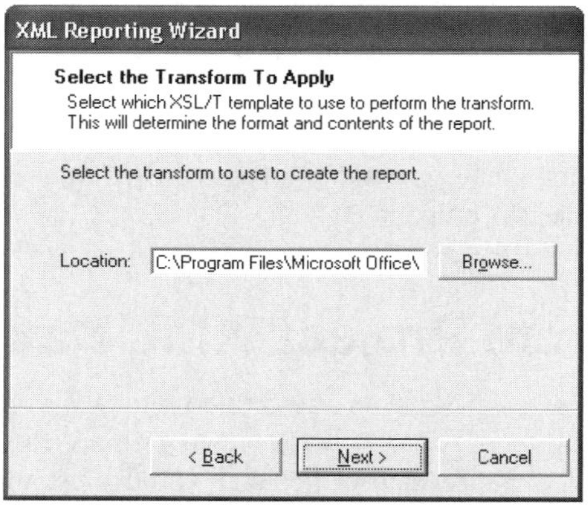

Figure 12-40. Find the XSL template to apply to your project XML data and create your report.

6 Click the Browse button to find and select the XSL template to apply to your data.

The template you choose will determine the format and content of your project XML report.

Click Open.

Two XSLs are provided with Microsoft Project: CRITTASK.XSL and RESOURCE.XSL.

7 In the wizard again, with the path to your selected XSL in the Location box, click Next.

8 In the Complete The Report Wizard page, click Preview.

Your browser opens with the new XML report.

9 Review your report in your Web browser (see Figure 12-41).

10 Return to Microsoft Project.

If you're happy with the report, click Save. Navigate to the location you want, enter a name for the report, and then click Save.

If you want to change the report before saving it, click the Back button to return to previous wizard pages.

When you're finished previewing and saving your new report, click Finish.

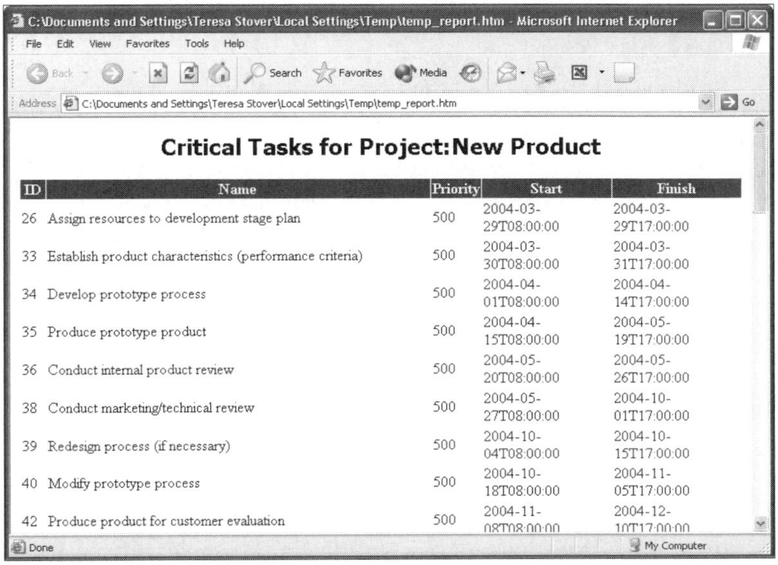

ID	Name	Priority	Start	Finish
26	Assign resources to development stage plan	500	2004-03-29T08:00:00	2004-03-29T17:00:00
33	Establish product characteristics (performance criteria)	500	2004-03-30T08:00:00	2004-03-31T17:00:00
34	Develop prototype process	500	2004-04-01T08:00:00	2004-04-14T17:00:00
35	Produce prototype product	500	2004-04-15T08:00:00	2004-05-19T17:00:00
36	Conduct internal product review	500	2004-05-20T08:00:00	2004-05-26T17:00:00
38	Conduct marketing/technical review	500	2004-05-27T08:00:00	2004-10-01T17:00:00
39	Redesign process (if necessary)	500	2004-10-04T08:00:00	2004-10-15T17:00:00
40	Modify prototype process	500	2004-10-18T08:00:00	2004-11-05T17:00:00
42	Produce product for customer evaluation	500	2004-11-	2004-12-

Figure 12-41. Use the XML Reporting Wizard and an XSL template to create an XML report from your project data.

Publishing Project Information to the Web

With the pervasive use of the World Wide Web and company intranets, you might find it very useful to publish your project information as a Web page, which is made much easier in Microsoft Project since the addition of the Export Wizard.

> **Note** Project reports cannot be converted to HTML because they are designed for previewing and printing only and cannot be saved. This goes for the built-in reports as well as any custom reports you have created.

Follow these steps to publish the project information:

1. Open the project plan containing the information you want to publish.

   It is not necessary to set up the views or fields you want to publish. You'll do this as part of the export process.
2. Click File, Save As Web Page.

   The Save As dialog box appears.
3. In the Save In box, select the drive or folder where you store your HTML files.

   If you have access to it, select the actual folder for your intranet Web site files.
4. In the File Name box, name your new html file.
5. Be sure that Web Page (*.html; *.htm) appears in the Save As Type box.

Chapter 12

6 Click Save.

The Export Wizard opens.

7 Read the welcome page of the Export Wizard and then click Next.

8 On the Map page, click New Map and then click Next.

The Map Options Page opens.

9 Under Select The Types Of Data You Want To Export, select the Tasks check box. Under HTML Options, select Export Header Row/Import Includes Headers. Click Next.

The Task Mapping page opens.

10 In the Destination HTML Table Title box, give the table a name or just use the default, for example, "Task_Table1."

11 In the Export Filter box, click All Tasks.

12 Click the Base On Table button and then choose the table that you want exported, for example, the Entry table.

This process fills in the From: Microsoft Project Field and To: HTML Table Field columns. The Preview area shows what the HTML table will look like (see Figure 12-42). Click Next.

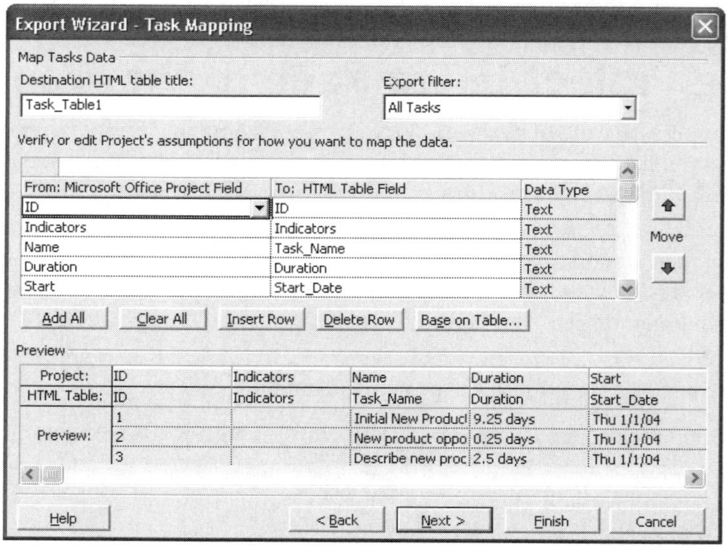

Figure 12-42. On the Task Mapping page, specify which fields should be exported to the Web page.

13 The End Of Map Definition page opens.

If you want to save this map for future use, click Save Map. Save the map if you expect to repeat this same export operation from time to time.

14 Click Finish.

Your customized table of the selected view is now saved as an HTML Web page. You can view it in a Web browser to see how it looks. You'll see that Microsoft Project has added some title and project information, including the project name and project start and finish dates (see Figure 12-43).

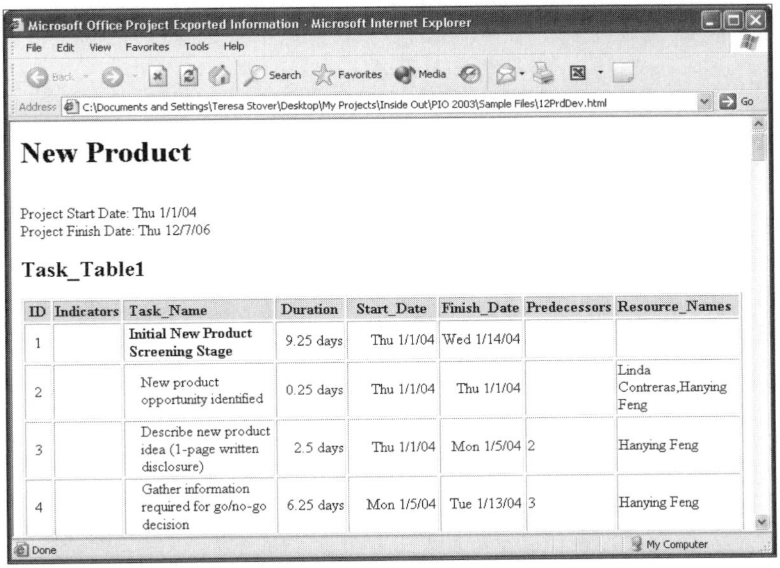

Figure 12-43. Review the project HTML Web page in a Web browser.

> **Tip** **Automatic Web page formatting**
> Summary tasks are shown in bold and subtasks retain their indentation as in Microsoft Project. The table is sized to fit the Web page, so task names will be text wrapped as necessary.

After you save your newly built HTML Web page, you're ready to upload it to your Web server.

Chapter 13

Analyzing Project Information

As part of your efforts in tracking and controlling your project, you might want to analyze certain aspects of project performance. Project analysis can give you a closer look at the overall execution of the project. For first-time efforts at managing a particular kind of project or for new variations on an established project theme, you and the stakeholders might want to see performance indicators and estimates for the remainder of the project. These indicators help assess the effectiveness of the plan and define the amount of corrective action needed to make actual performance in the project conform to the baseline.

The starting point for any project analysis is to decide what you want to evaluate. You can examine:

- Work required for task or project completion.
- Cost required for task or project completion.
- Schedule adherence.

In the course of tracking your project, you probably analyze the data in various views or reports in Microsoft Office Project 2003. You might even have created custom views and reports to show specific types of project information, such as schedule slippage.

In addition, there are specialized techniques you can use with Project 2003 to analyze project information. These techniques include performing earned value calculations, creating formulas in custom fields, and exporting data to Microsoft Excel and calculating figures there.

Analyzing Progress and Costs Using Earned Value

Earned value calculation is a systematic method of measuring and evaluating schedule, cost, and work performance in a project. Earned value provides a variety of comparisons between baseline and actual information. The basis of earned value calculations are the following:

- The project baseline, including schedule and cost information for assigned resources
- Actual work and costs reported
- Variances between actuals and baseline information
- A status date, often the current date

As soon as you save a baseline, Project 2003 begins calculating and storing earned value data. You can view this data using three earned value tables and an earned value report.

Generating Earned Value Data

Earned value data begin to be generated as soon as you save a project baseline. Then as you start entering progress information, such as actual start or finish dates, actual percentage completed, and so on, Microsoft Project compares the actuals against the baseline, calculates variances, and plugs those variances into earned value calculations. There are three categories of earned value fields, each with a different focus:

- Cost
- Schedule
- Work

Saving the Baseline

Save the project *baseline* when you have built and refined the project plan to your satisfaction and just before you start entering progress information against tasks. The project plan should show all tasks and resources assigned, and costs should be associated with those resources. The project plan should reflect your target schedule dates, budget amounts, and scope of work.

To save a baseline, click Tools, Tracking, Baseline.

Starting with Project 2002, you can now save up to 11 different baselines. However, earned value is calculated on only a single baseline. To specify which baseline should be used for earned value analyses, follow these steps:

1. Click Tools, Options and then click Calculation.
2. Click the Earned Value button.

   The Earned Value dialog box appears (see Figure 13-1).

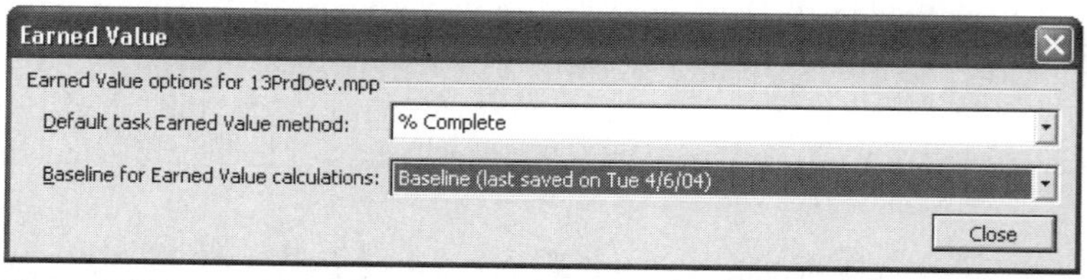

Figure 13-1. Specify which of 11 possible saved baselines should be used for the earned value calculations.

3. In the Baseline For Earned Value Calculations list, click the baseline you want to use.

For a complete discussion of baselines, see "Saving Original Plan Information Using a Baseline" on page 298.

Entering Actuals

The counterpart to baseline information for earned value calculations is the *actuals* information. To enter task progress information manually, click Tools, Tracking, Update Tasks and then complete one or more of the progress fields indicating percentage complete, actual and remaining duration, or actual start and finish dates.

To enter true timephased actuals, enter actuals in the timesheet portion of the Task Usage or Resource Usage view. Otherwise, Microsoft Project derives timephased actuals by dividing any total amount entered into the timespan of the assignment.

If you're set up for enterprise project management using Microsoft Office Project Professional 2003 and Microsoft Office Project Server 2003, progress information is probably automatically updated in your project plan as team members submit task updates from their use of Microsoft Office Project Web Access 2003.

If you and your project server administrator have set up Project Web Access to record actual work performed per time period (days or weeks), you'll receive true timephased actuals from the team members. However, if Project Web Access records actuals by percent complete or total actual work and remaining work, again, Microsoft Project derives timephased actuals by dividing any total amount entered into the timespan of the assignment.

For more information about manually entering progress information, see "Updating Task Progress" on page 308.

Microsoft Project can calculate *variances* as soon your project plan contains baseline as well as actuals information. With variances, the earned values fields begin to populate.

Specifying the Status Date

Earned value data are calculated based on a particular cutoff date, or *status date*. Unless you specify otherwise, the status date is today's date. You can specify a different status date, for example, if you want to see figures based on the end of the month, which was last Thursday. To enter a status date, do the following:

1. Click Project, Project Information.
2. In the Status Date box, enter the status date you want.

Because Microsoft Project stores *timephased* data for values such as baseline and actual work, cost, and so on, earned value can be calculated based on the specified status date.

Tip **Calculate earned value based on physical percent complete**
You can change the basis of earned value calculations from percent complete, based on task duration, to *physical percent complete*, based on a physical rather than time measurement. Click Tools, Options, and then click Calculation. Click the Earned Value button. In the Default Task Earned Value Method list, click Physical % Complete.

Reviewing Earned Value Data

To study and analyze project performance, you can apply one of three earned value tables to a sheet view. You can run the Earned Value report. You can also add selected earned value fields to any sheet view.

Working with Earned Value Tables

With a baseline saved and actuals entered, you can evaluate current cost and schedule performance through earned value. To review your earned value information in a view, do the following:

1. Click View, More Views. Click Task Sheet and then click Apply.
2. Click View, Table, More Tables.

   The More Tables dialog box appears.
3. In the Tables list, click Earned Value, and then click Apply.

   The earned value data for your project displays (see Figure 13-2).

	Task Name	BCWS	BCWP	ACWP	SV	CV	EAC	BAC	VAC
1	**Initial New Product Screening Stage**	**$2,520.00**	**$2,520.00**	**$2,950.00**	**$0.00**	**($430.00)**	**$2,950.00**	**$2,520.00**	**($430.00)**
2	New product opportunity identified	$0.00	$0.00	$150.00	$0.00	($150.00)	$150.00	$0.00	($150.00)
3	Describe new product idea (1-page writter	$560.00	$560.00	$700.00	$0.00	($140.00)	$700.00	$560.00	($140.00)
4	Gather information required for go/no-go d	$1,680.00	$1,680.00	$1,750.00	$0.00	($70.00)	$1,750.00	$1,680.00	($70.00)
5	Convene opportunity of screening committ	$280.00	$280.00	$350.00	$0.00	($70.00)	$350.00	$280.00	($70.00)
6	Decision point - go/no-go to preliminary inv	$0.00	$0.00	$0.00	$0.00	$0.00	$0.00	$0.00	$0.00
7	**Preliminary Investigation Stage**	**$43,560.00**	**$43,560.00**	**$44,310.00**	**$0.00**	**($750.00)**	**$44,310.00**	**$43,560.00**	**($750.00)**
8	Assign resources to preliminary investigati	$320.00	$320.00	$320.00	$0.00	$0.00	$320.00	$320.00	$0.00
9	Develop preliminary investigation plan	$3,000.00	$3,000.00	$3,000.00	$0.00	$0.00	$3,000.00	$3,000.00	$0.00
10	Evaluate the market	$2,800.00	$2,800.00	$2,800.00	$0.00	$0.00	$2,800.00	$2,800.00	$0.00
11	Analyze the competition	$1,400.00	$1,400.00	$1,400.00	$0.00	$0.00	$1,400.00	$1,400.00	$0.00
12	**Technical Feasibility Analysis**	**$6,000.00**	**$6,000.00**	**$7,400.00**	**$0.00**	**($1,400.00)**	**$7,400.00**	**$6,000.00**	**($1,400.00)**
13	Produce lab scale product	$2,800.00	$2,800.00	$4,200.00	$0.00	($1,400.00)	$4,200.00	$2,800.00	($1,400.00)
14	Evaluate internal product	$1,400.00	$1,400.00	$1,400.00	$0.00	$0.00	$1,400.00	$1,400.00	$0.00
15	Identify production process steps requ	$1,800.00	$1,800.00	$1,800.00	$0.00	$0.00	$1,800.00	$1,800.00	$0.00
16	Assess manufacturing capabilities	$5,600.00	$5,600.00	$4,200.00	$0.00	$1,400.00	$4,200.00	$5,600.00	$1,400.00
17	Determine safety issues	$2,800.00	$2,800.00	$2,800.00	$0.00	$0.00	$2,800.00	$2,800.00	$0.00
18	Determine environmental issues	$5,600.00	$5,600.00	$5,600.00	$0.00	$0.00	$5,600.00	$5,600.00	$0.00
19	Review legal issues	$6,000.00	$6,000.00	$6,750.00	$0.00	($750.00)	$6,750.00	$6,000.00	($750.00)
20	Perform financial evaluation	$2,400.00	$2,400.00	$2,400.00	$0.00	$0.00	$2,400.00	$2,400.00	$0.00

Figure 13-2. Use the Earned Value table to review earned value fields.

Tip **Review earned value by resources**
To analyze earned value data by resources instead of tasks, show the Resource Sheet. Click View, Table, More Tables and then click Earned Value.

Make Earned Value Tables and Views More Accessible

If you review the earned value table often, you might do well to add it to the Table menu. To do this, follow these steps:

1. Click View, Table, More Tables.
2. In the More Tables dialog box, click Earned Value or one of the other earned value tables you want to add to the Table menu.
3. Click Edit.
4. At the top of the Table Definition dialog box, select the Show In Menu check box.

   The selected table is now listed in the Table menu in the current project, and you can get to it with fewer clicks.

You can also create a custom earned value view, perhaps with the Earned Value table applied to the Task Sheet. You can then add your new view to the Views menu as well.

For information about creating custom views, see "Customizing Views" on page 761.

Although the Earned Value table shows the majority of the earned value fields, two other tables (added with Project 2002) help you focus on specific types of earned value information. Apply the Earned Value Cost Indicators table to analyze your project for budget performance. Apply the Earned Value Schedule Indicators table to analyze schedule and work performance. The fields included by default in each of the three earned value tables are shown in Table 13-1.

Table 13-1. Earned Value Tables

Table Name	Included Fields
Earned Value	BCWS (Budgeted Cost of Work Scheduled)
	BCWP (Budgeted Cost of Work Performed)
	ACWP (Actual Cost of Work Performed)
	SV (Schedule Variance)
	CV (Cost Variance)
	EAC (Estimate At Completion)
	BAC (Budget At Completion)
	VAC (Variance At Completion)
Earned Value Cost Indicators	BCWS (Budgeted Cost of Work Scheduled)
	BCWP (Budgeted Cost of Work Performed)
	CV (Cost Variance)
	CV% (Cost Variance Percent)

Table 13-1. Earned Value Tables

Table Name	Included Fields
	CPI (Cost Performance Index)
	BAC (Budget At Completion)
	EAC (Estimate At Completion)
	VAC (Variance At Completion)
	TCPI (To Complete Performance Index)
Earned Value Schedule Indicators	BCWS (Budgeted Cost of Work Scheduled)
	BCWP (Budgeted Cost of Work Performed)
	SV (Schedule Variance)
	SV% (Schedule Variance Percent)
	SPI (Schedule Performance Index)

Tip **Add an earned value field to another table**
Add one or more earned value fields to other task or resource tables if you want to keep a close eye on one or two calculations without having to apply an entire earned value table. Display the view and table you want and then click the column header where you want the earned value field to be added. Click Insert, Column. In the Field Name box, click the earned value field you want and then click OK.

Understanding the Earned Value Fields

Measuring earned value helps you see the adherence to the baseline plan or deviation from it, in terms of cost and schedule. The following list details each earned value field in Microsoft Project and how they're calculated:

Budgeted Cost Of Work Scheduled (BCWS). The original planned cost of a task, up to the status date. BCWS indicates the amount of budget that should have been spent by now on this task (or for this resource). For example, if a task *should be* 50 percent finished according to the schedule, the BCWS would be 50 percent of the original planned cost of that task. Microsoft Project determines the values by adding the timephased baseline dates for the task up to the status date.

Budgeted Cost Of Work Performed (BCWP). The cost of the task work *actually* done, according to the original budget. BCWP indicates the amount of budget that should have been spent by now on this task (or this resource), based on the amount of actual work reported by this date. If the task is actually 50 percent complete, the BCWP will be the originally planned cost of the work on the task multiplied by 50 percent. Because this is a measure of actual work costs incurred, BCWP is sometimes called the *earned value* of a task.

Actual Cost Of Work Performed (ACWP). The sum of all costs actually accrued for a task to date. It includes standard and overtime costs for assigned resources, any per-use costs, and fixed costs for tasks. ACWP indicates the amount of budget that should have been spent by now on this task (or this resource), based on the actual work reported by this date.

Cost Variance (CV). The difference between the budgeted costs and the actual costs of a task (ACWP–BCWP). The CV dollar amount indicates the difference between the baseline and actual costs for tasks. A positive CV means that the task is currently under budget. A negative CV means that the task is currently over budget. A CV of $0.00 means that the task is exactly on budget.

Schedule Variance (SV). The measure of the difference between the cost as planned and the cost as performed (BCWP–BCWS). Even though it's called "schedule variance," the variance really calculated is the cost resulting from schedule considerations. The SV dollar amount indicates the difference between the baseline costs for scheduled tasks and actual progress reported on those tasks. A positive SV means that the task is ahead of schedule in terms of cost. A negative SV means that the task is behind schedule in terms of cost. An SV of $0.00 means that the task is exactly on schedule in terms of cost. SV does not necessarily specify whether you're under or over budget; however, it can be an indicator that budget should be looked at more closely. SV shows clearly how much schedule slippage and duration increases affect cost.

Estimate At Completion (EAC). The projected cost of a task at its completion, also known as Forecast At Completion (FAC). EAC is the amount calculated from the ACWP, BCWP, and the Cost Performance Index (CPI), resulting in a composite forecast total of costs for the task upon completion. This dollar amount indicates the current best guess of what this task will cost by the time it's finished. The projection is based on current schedule performance up to the status date.

Budgeted At Completion (BAC). The baseline cost of a task at its completion. BAC is the cost for the task as planned. BAC is exactly the same as the baseline cost, which includes assigned resource costs and any fixed costs for the task. The budgeted cost is based on the baseline planned schedule performance.

Variance At Completion (VAC). The difference between actual cost at completion and baseline cost at completion, or BAC–EAC. VAC is the cost variance for a completed task. A negative VAC indicates that the forecasted cost for the task is currently over budget. A positive VAC indicates that the forecasted cost for the task is currently under budget. A VAC of $0.00 indicates that the task is right on budget.

Cost Performance Index (CPI). The ratio of budgeted to actual cost of work performed. CPI is also known as Earned Value for Cost. When the CPI ratio is 1, the cost performance is now exactly as planned, according to current work performance. A ratio greater than 1.0 indicates that you're under budget; less than 1.0 indicates that you're over budget. CPI is calculated by dividing BCWP by ACWP.

Schedule Performance Index (SPI). The ratio of budgeted cost of work performed to budgeted cost of work scheduled. SPI, which is also known as Earned Value for Schedule, is often used to estimate the project completion date. When the SPI ratio is 1.0, the task is precisely on schedule. A ratio greater than 1.0 indicates that you're ahead of schedule; less than 1.0 indicates that you're behind schedule. SPI is calculated by dividing BCWP by BCWS.

Cost Variance Percent (CV%). The difference between how much a task should have cost and how much it has actually cost to date, displayed in the form of a percentage. CV is calculated as follows: [(BCWP–ACWP)/BCWP]*100. A positive percentage indicates an under-budget condition, whereas a negative percentage indicates an overbudget condition.

Schedule Variance Percent (SV%). The percentage of how much you are ahead of or behind schedule for a task. SV is calculated as follows: (SV/BCWS) * 100. A positive percentage indicates that you're currently ahead of schedule, whereas a negative percentage indicates that you're behind schedule.

To Complete Performance Index (TCPI). The ratio of the work yet to be done on a task to the funds still budgeted to be spent on that task. TCPI is calculated as follows: (BAC–BCWP)/(BAC–ACWP). TCPI helps you estimate whether you will have surplus funds or a shortfall. Values over 1.0 indicate a potential shortfall. Increased performance for remaining work would be needed to stay within budget.

Physical Percent Complete. This is a user-entered value that can be used in place of % Complete when calculating earned value or measuring progress. It represents a judgment that overrides the calculations based on actual duration. To use this option, click Tools, Options and then click Calculation. Click the Earned Value button. In the Default Task Earned Value Method list, click Physical % Complete.

Tip **See all available earned value fields**

You can see a list of all earned value fields available in Microsoft Project. Click Help, Microsoft Project Help (or press F1). In the Search For box, type **fields** and then press Enter. Click Earned Value Fields. The list of all available earned value fields appears in a separate Help window.

Click a field name to open a Help topic that gives a description of each field, how it's calculated, its best uses, and an example of its use.

Generating the Earned Value Report

The Earned Value report is based on the Earned Value table for tasks. Every non-summary task is listed, along with its earned value calculations for BCWS, BCWP, ACWP, SV, CV, EAC, BAC, and VAC. To run the Earned Value report, follow these steps:

1. Click View, Reports.
2. Double-click Costs.
3. Double-click Earned Value.

   A preview of the Earned Value report appears (see Figure 13-3).

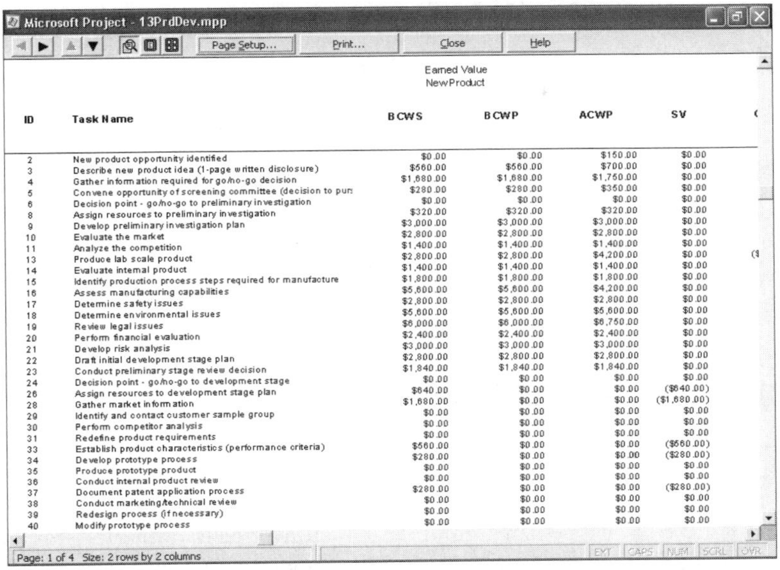

Earned Value
New Product

ID	Task Name	BCWS	BCWP	ACWP	SV
2	New product opportunity identified	$0.00	$0.00	$150.00	$0.00
3	Describe new product idea (1-page written disclosure)	$560.00	$560.00	$700.00	$0.00
4	Gather information required for go/no-go decision	$1,680.00	$1,680.00	$1,750.00	$0.00
5	Convene opportunity of screening committee (decision to pur	$280.00	$280.00	$350.00	$0.00
6	Decision point - go/no-go to preliminary investigation	$0.00	$0.00	$0.00	$0.00
8	Assign resources to preliminary investigation	$320.00	$320.00	$320.00	$0.00
9	Develop preliminary investigation plan	$3,000.00	$3,000.00	$3,000.00	$0.00
10	Evaluate the market	$2,800.00	$2,800.00	$2,800.00	$0.00
11	Analyze the competition	$1,400.00	$1,400.00	$1,400.00	$0.00
13	Produce lab scale product	$2,800.00	$2,800.00	$4,200.00	$0.00
14	Evaluate internal product	$1,400.00	$1,400.00	$1,400.00	$0.00
15	Identify production process steps required for manufacture	$1,800.00	$1,800.00	$1,800.00	$0.00
16	Assess manufacturing capabilities	$5,600.00	$5,600.00	$4,200.00	$0.00
17	Determine safety issues	$2,800.00	$2,800.00	$2,800.00	$0.00
18	Determine environmental issues	$5,600.00	$5,600.00	$5,600.00	$0.00
19	Review legal issues	$6,000.00	$6,000.00	$6,750.00	$0.00
20	Perform financial evaluation	$2,400.00	$2,400.00	$2,400.00	$0.00
21	Develop risk analysis	$3,000.00	$3,000.00	$3,000.00	$0.00
22	Draft initial development stage plan	$2,800.00	$2,800.00	$2,800.00	$0.00
23	Conduct preliminary stage review decision	$1,840.00	$1,840.00	$1,840.00	$0.00
24	Decision point - go/no-go to development stage	$0.00	$0.00	$0.00	$0.00
26	Assign resources to development stage plan	$640.00	$0.00	$0.00	($640.00)
28	Gather market information	$1,680.00	$0.00	$0.00	($1,680.00)
29	Identify and contact customer sample group	$0.00	$0.00	$0.00	$0.00
30	Perform competitor analysis	$0.00	$0.00	$0.00	$0.00
31	Redefine product requirements	$0.00	$0.00	$0.00	$0.00
33	Establish product characteristics (performance criteria)	$560.00	$0.00	$0.00	($560.00)
34	Develop prototype process	$280.00	$0.00	$0.00	($280.00)
35	Produce prototype product	$0.00	$0.00	$0.00	$0.00
36	Conduct internal product review	$0.00	$0.00	$0.00	$0.00
37	Document patent application process	$280.00	$0.00	$0.00	($280.00)
38	Conduct marketing/technical review	$0.00	$0.00	$0.00	$0.00
39	Redesign process (if necessary)	$0.00	$0.00	$0.00	$0.00
40	Modify prototype process	$0.00	$0.00	$0.00	$0.00

Figure 13-3. The Earned Value report shows earned values for all tasks, based on your specified status date.

4 To print the report, click the Print button at the top of the report preview window.

Your Earned Value Fields Are All $0.00

If you applied an earned value table or inserted an earned value field, only to find all the values to be $0.00, it's likely that you're missing one or more of the pieces of information needed by Microsoft Project to calculate earned value fields.

For an earned value to be calculated, you must have all of the following items in your project plan:

- A saved baseline
- Resources assigned to tasks
- Costs associated with assigned resources
- Actual progress information

If you saved a baseline and you're seeing all zeros except in the EAC and BAC columns, you're probably close to the beginning of your project and haven't entered any tracking information yet. As time goes by and you start entering task progress data, those numbers will start changing to reflect the schedule and current progress.

If you saved a baseline and you're seeing all zeros in the SV, CV, and VAC columns, your project is running exactly as planned, with no positive or negative variances recorded at all. Make sure that all your tracking information is entered and up to date. If it is, and you're still seeing all those zeros, you're precisely on schedule and on budget.

Calculating Project Information in Microsoft Excel

Because Microsoft Excel is such a powerful tool for manipulating and calculating numeric data, in some cases you might find it beneficial to move some of the numeric data from Microsoft Project for more in-depth analyses in Excel.

For example, you can export project cost or earned value data to Excel. Or perhaps you want to crunch tracking data or assignment information. You can also create pivot tables and generate graphs such as S-curves to show project performance information.

Exporting information from Microsoft Project to Excel has been made particularly easy with the Excel Export Wizard, introduced with Project 2002.

Analyzing Numeric Project Data in Excel

Although you can export most information types from Microsoft Project to Excel, it's most useful to export numeric data for further analysis in Excel. *Numeric data* are any data that can be used in calculations and mathematical operations. Examples of such data include cost and work data. Work data (such as hours) can be converted to numeric fields, but are stored in Microsoft Project as text because of the unit names such as hours, days, or weeks. On the other hand, dates are not considered numeric data, even though they consist mostly of numbers.

When preparing to export information from Microsoft Project to Excel for numerical analysis, first decide which tasks, resources, and fields you want to export to Excel. You can export only selected or filtered tasks or resources to Excel. You can export the same fields you see in a given table—such as the Earned Value, Cost, or Tracking table—or you can export just three or four fields that you select. You can also export a large representation of all your project data with the different types of project, task, resource, and assignment data appearing in different worksheets within the Excel workbook.

> **Tip** **Calculating Project Information Using Custom Formulas**
> You can set up formulas to calculate specified data within Microsoft Project. You create a custom field, such as Cost1 or Number3, and then build the formula to operate on the data in or related to that field.

For more information about creating a custom field containing a formula, see "Creating a Calculated Field" on page 792.

Exporting Selected Data to Excel

To specify the project data you want to export and then send it to Excel, follow these steps:

1. Apply the view that contains the task, resource, or assignment information you want to export.

   The table or fields applied to the view does not matter at this point because you choose the fields you want as part of the export process.

2 If you want to export only certain tasks, resources, or assignments, select them using the Shift or Ctrl keys. If you want to export all tasks, all resources, or all assignments, click the Select All cell in the upper-left cell in the view, above the ID number.

Later, as part of the export process, you can apply a task or resource filter if you want.

3 Click File, Save As.

The Save As dialog box appears.

4 Browse to the drive and folder where you want to save your information.

5 In the Save As Type box, select Microsoft Excel Workbook (*.xls).

6 In the File Name box, enter a name for your new Excel file.

By default, the project file name is adopted with the *.xls* extension.

7 Click Save.

The first page of the Export Wizard appears.

8 On the Welcome page of the wizard, click Next.

9 On the Export Wizard – Data page, be sure that the Selected Data option is selected. Click Next.

10 On the Export Wizard – Map page, be sure that the New Map option is selected. Click Next.

11 On the Map Options page of the wizard, select the check box for the type of data you want to map: Tasks, Resources, or Assignments. Under Microsoft Excel Options, select the Export Includes Headers check box (see Figure 13-4). Click Next.

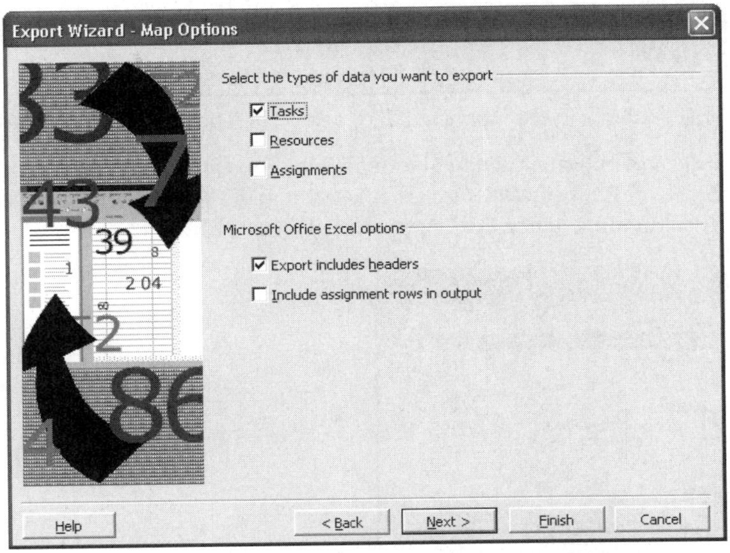

Figure 13-4. In the Export Wizard, select the type of data you're exporting to Excel.

12 On the Mapping page of the wizard, in the Destination Worksheet Name box, you can enter a name for the destination worksheet within the workbook you're creating.

You can also just use the default name provided; for example, Task_Table1.

13 In the Export Filter box, click any filter you want to apply to the tasks or resources you're exporting.

14 In the Verify Or Edit Microsoft Project's Assumptions For How You Want To Import The Data table, specify which project fields are to be exported and how they should be defined. In the From: Microsoft Office Project Field, click the arrow and then click the name of the field you want to export. Be sure to start with the Name field, to make sure the task name or resource name is exported. Type the first one or two characters of the field name to move to it quickly (see Figure 13-5).

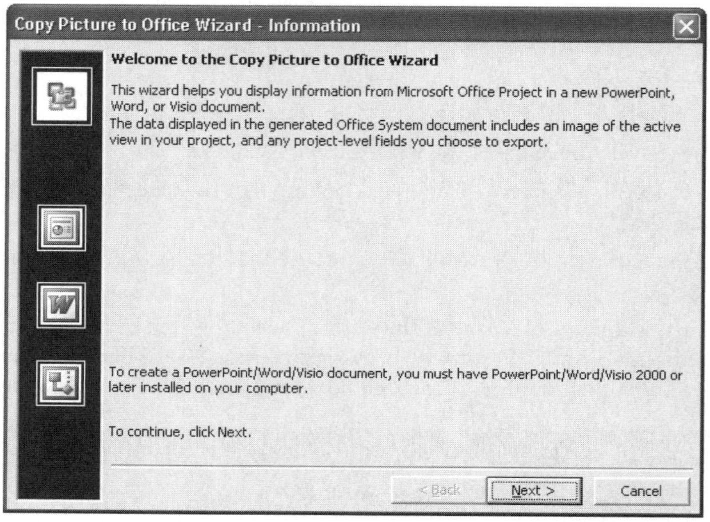

Figure 13-5. In the Mapping page, select the specific fields you want to export.

Instead of entering each field individually, you can add all fields from a particular Microsoft Project table. Click the Base On Table button. The Select Base Table For Field Mapping dialog box appears (see Figure 13-6).

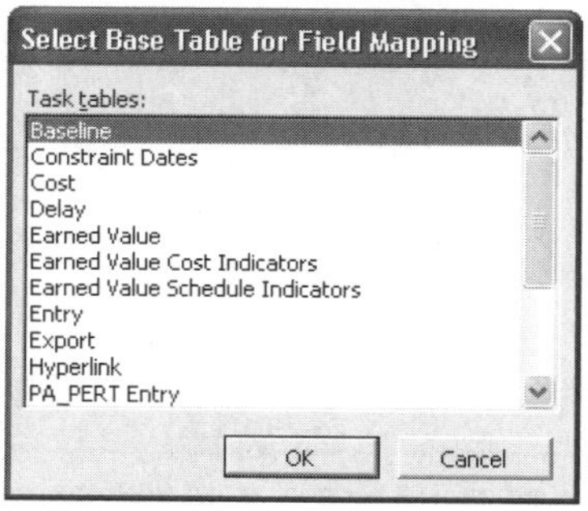

Figure 13-6. Select the Project table that contains the fields you want to use as your export data source.

Click the Microsoft Project table you want to export (for example, Earned Value or Cost) and then click OK. The fields that define that table appear in the Task Mapping table.

As soon as you enter a field in the From column, its default equivalent appears in the To: Excel Field column, showing the name of the field as it will appear in the Excel workbook column heading (see Figure 13-7). You can change the Excel column heading here if you want (for example, from ***Baseline Cost*** to ***Task Budget***).

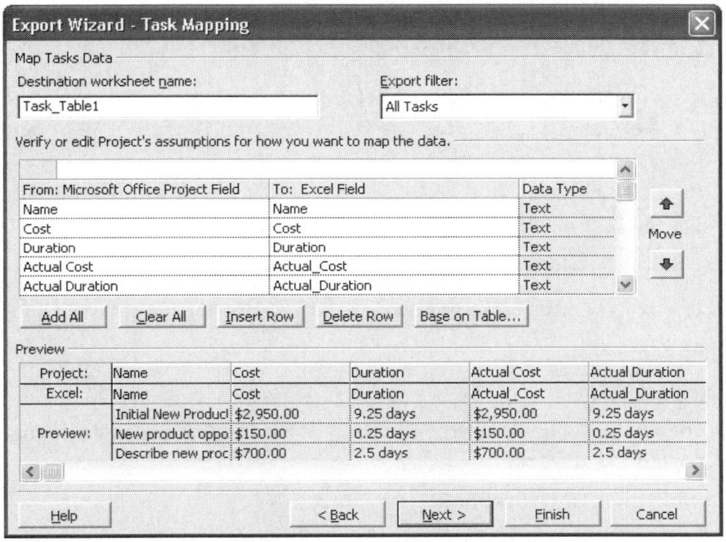

Figure 13-7. The Microsoft Project field, its Excel equivalent, and the data type as exported show in the table.

Because you want to work with numeric project data, you can use this table to select only those fields containing numeric values. For example, you might select Name, Cost, and Duration.

The Data Type column shows the data type of the field. Incidentally, these data all come in as Text fields, even though they might really be number, date, or currency fields in Microsoft Project. To simplify the export process, all fields are changed to text fields. Then you can easily convert the data type for any of these fields in Excel, which is especially important for numeric data on which you want to run calculations.

Use the command buttons below the table to add and remove fields in the table. Use the Move up and down buttons to the right of the table to rearrange the order of the fields, which represents the order the columns will appear in Excel.

The data is shown as it will appear in Excel in the Preview area at the bottom of the Mapping page. Use the scroll bar to view all the columns. When ready, click Next.

15 On the End Of Map Definition page, click the Save Map button if you expect to export this same information again. Otherwise, click Finish.

Your specified project data is exported to Excel in the exact layout you defined.

Troubleshooting

I can't find a field I want in the Mapping table

The list of Microsoft Project fields changes depending on whether you're exporting tasks or resources. Tasks and resources have different fields associated with them.

If you're looking specifically for the BAC (Budgeted At Completion) earned value field, find and apply the Baseline Cost field instead—they are the same field.

If you're looking for a Variance field, look for the specific type of variance—for example, Cost Variance or earned value CV (Cost Variance). There's also Work Variance, SV (Schedule Variance), and VAC (Variance At Completion).

Refer to Appendix B, "Field Reference" for a complete listing of all Microsoft Project fields.

To open and review your exported project data in Excel, follow these steps:

1. Start Microsoft Excel.
2. Click File, Open.
3. In the Open dialog box, browse to the drive and folder in which you saved your exported Excel workbook.
4. Double-click the workbook.

   Your project data appears in the workbook using the tasks (or resources), filter, and table or fields you selected in the export process (see Figure 13-8).

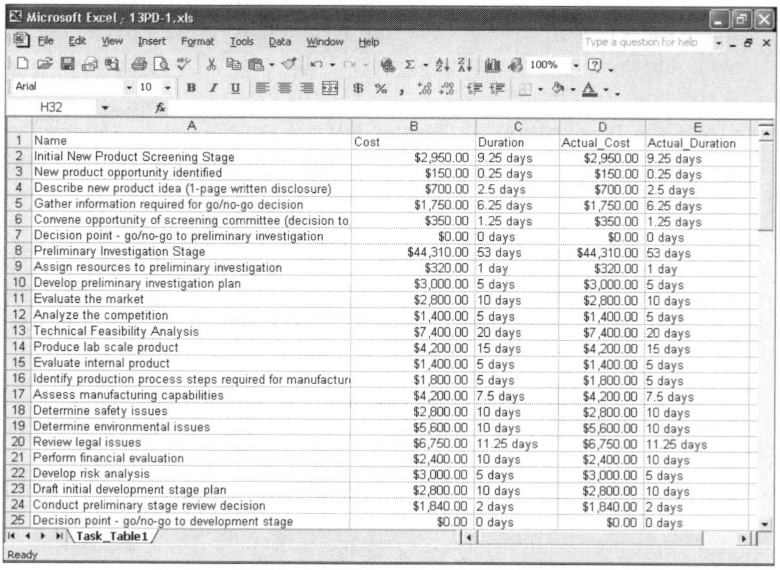

	A	B	C	D	E
1	Name	Cost	Duration	Actual_Cost	Actual_Duration
2	Initial New Product Screening Stage	$2,950.00	9.25 days	$2,950.00	9.25 days
3	New product opportunity identified	$150.00	0.25 days	$150.00	0.25 days
4	Describe new product idea (1-page written disclosure)	$700.00	2.5 days	$700.00	2.5 days
5	Gather information required for go/no-go decision	$1,750.00	6.25 days	$1,750.00	6.25 days
6	Convene opportunity of screening committee (decision to	$350.00	1.25 days	$350.00	1.25 days
7	Decision point - go/no-go to preliminary investigation	$0.00	0 days	$0.00	0 days
8	Preliminary Investigation Stage	$44,310.00	53 days	$44,310.00	53 days
9	Assign resources to preliminary investigation	$320.00	1 day	$320.00	1 day
10	Develop preliminary investigation plan	$3,000.00	5 days	$3,000.00	5 days
11	Evaluate the market	$2,800.00	10 days	$2,800.00	10 days
12	Analyze the competition	$1,400.00	5 days	$1,400.00	5 days
13	Technical Feasibility Analysis	$7,400.00	20 days	$7,400.00	20 days
14	Produce lab scale product	$4,200.00	15 days	$4,200.00	15 days
15	Evaluate internal product	$1,400.00	5 days	$1,400.00	5 days
16	Identify production process steps required for manufactur	$1,800.00	5 days	$1,800.00	5 days
17	Assess manufacturing capabilities	$4,200.00	7.5 days	$4,200.00	7.5 days
18	Determine safety issues	$2,800.00	10 days	$2,800.00	10 days
19	Determine environmental issues	$5,600.00	10 days	$5,600.00	10 days
20	Review legal issues	$6,750.00	11.25 days	$6,750.00	11.25 days
21	Perform financial evaluation	$2,400.00	10 days	$2,400.00	10 days
22	Develop risk analysis	$3,000.00	5 days	$3,000.00	5 days
23	Draft initial development stage plan	$2,800.00	10 days	$2,800.00	10 days
24	Conduct preliminary stage review decision	$1,840.00	2 days	$1,840.00	2 days
25	Decision point - go/no-go to development stage	$0.00	0 days	$0.00	0 days

Figure 13-8. View and manipulate your project data in Excel.

5 Adjust columns, change data types, and then set up formulas or charts as you wish to analyze this data further.

Change the Data Type in an Excel Column

After exporting your project information to Excel, if you need to, you can change the data type of a field of information from text, for example, to numbers. For example, Duration fields are exported as text. You can easily change that text to numbers so you can run calculations on them.

In Excel, select the column heading and then click Format, Cells. Click the Number tab if necessary. Under Category, select General, Number, or Currency, as appropriate (see Figure 13-9). Set any number attributes you want and then click OK.

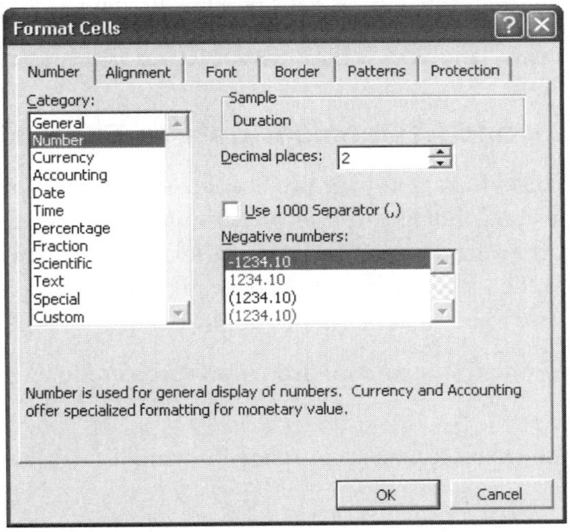

Figure 13-9. Use the Number tab in the Format Cells dialog box in Excel to change the data type or number format of a set of exported project fields.

Even though the Task Mapping page of the Microsoft Project Export Wizard says they're Text fields, currency fields (such as Cost and Actual Cost) and earned value currency fields (such as BCWS and VAC) are automatically formatted as currency in Excel.

Inside Out

Overwrite Excel format

Suppose that you changed information or formatting in your new Excel workbook containing your exported project information, and now you're ready to save your changes. After you click the Save button, you might get a prompt asking whether you want to overwrite an older Excel format (see Figure 13-10).

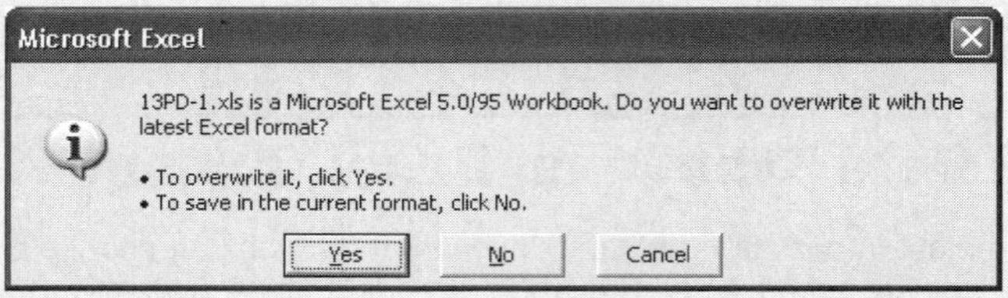

Figure 13-10. Click Yes to update the Excel 5.0 Workbook format to the latest Excel format.

To ensure compatibility with older versions of Excel, Microsoft Project exports to the Microsoft Excel 5.0/Excel 95 file format. When you go to save the new Excel file the first time, Excel prompts you to update the format to the current version you have installed on your computer, which might be Microsoft Excel 2000 or Excel XP, for example.

Click Yes to update the workbook format, which ensures that you can use the latest features of your current Excel version on your exported project data.

Exporting Task, Resource, and Assignment Data to Excel at Once

For certain kinds of analyses, you need to look at your project data by general type; that is, by task, resource, or assignment. You can export project information to Excel as a *template*. With this type of export, Microsoft Project organizes data into Task, Resource, and Assignment data types. Each data type is then presented with its relevant information in its own separate worksheet within the single Excel workbook.

To export task, resource, and assignment information from your project file to Excel all at once, follow these steps:

1. In Microsoft Project, open the project whose complete information you want to analyze in Excel.
2. Click File, Save As.
3. Browse to the drive and folder in which you want to save your information.
4. In the Save As Type box, click Microsoft Excel Workbook (*.xls).
5. In the File Name box, enter a name for the Excel file.
6. Click Save.

   The Export Wizard appears.
7. On the Welcome page of the wizard, click Next.
8. In the Export Wizard – Data page, select the Project Excel Template option and then click Finish.

Open the new Excel workbook you just created. The workbook contains four worksheets of discrete information: Task_Table, Resource_Table, and Assignment_Table. Info_Table provides general instructions for using this workbook (see Figure 13-11).

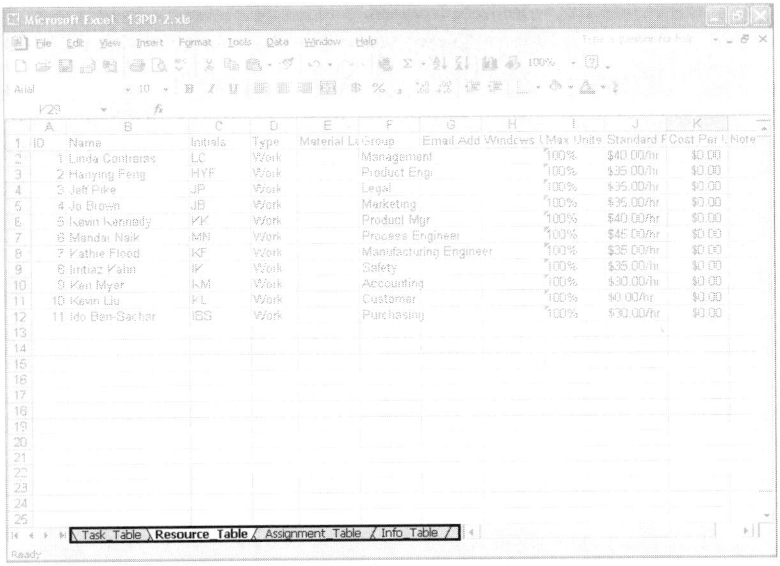

Figure 13-11. Separate worksheets are created to hold key task, resource, and assignment information from your project.

> **Tip** **Change the date format**
>
> When you export date fields from Microsoft Project to Excel, the Excel date fields also include the time. If you prefer, you can change the Excel date format. To do this, first click the column headings for the date fields; then click Format, Cells. The Format Cells dialog box appears. Click the Number tab. Under Category, click Date. Click the date format you prefer and then click OK.

Analyzing Timephased Project Data in Excel

In addition to exporting task, resource, and assignment field information to Excel, you can also export timephased data from Microsoft Project to Excel. To do this, follow these steps:

1. In Microsoft Project, open the project plan whose timephased data you want to export to Excel.
2. Display a task view if you want to export timephased task information. Display a resource view to export timephased resource information.
3. If you want to export data only for selected tasks or resources, display and select those items. Use the Ctrl or Shift keys to select multiple tasks or resources.
4. Click View, Toolbars, Analysis to display the Analysis toolbar.
5. On the Analysis toolbar, click Analyze Timescaled Data In Excel.

6 In the first page of the Analyze Timescaled Data Wizard, select the Entire Project or Currently Selected Tasks (or Currently Selected Resources) to specify which set of timephased data is to be exported. Click Next.

The second page of the wizard appears, showing the list of all available timephased fields for either tasks or resources, depending on whether you're showing a task or resource view.

7 Under Available Fields, select the timephased fields you want to export; for example, Actual Cost, Baseline Cost, and Cost. Click Add to move the selected fields to the Fields To Export box (see Figure 13-12).

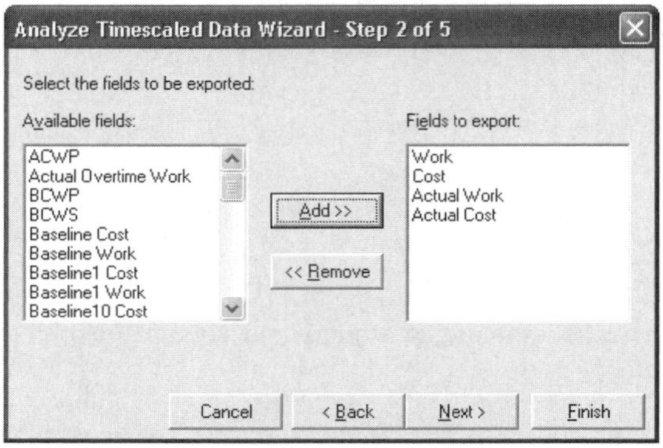

Figure 13-12. Select the timephased fields you want to export to Excel.

Use the Ctrl or Shift keys to select multiple fields at one time. You can select fields and click Add as many times as you need to.

8 When you finish adding fields to the Fields To Export box, click Next.

9 In the third page of the wizard, enter the date range and time unit you want to use for the exported data (see Figure 13-13). Click Next.

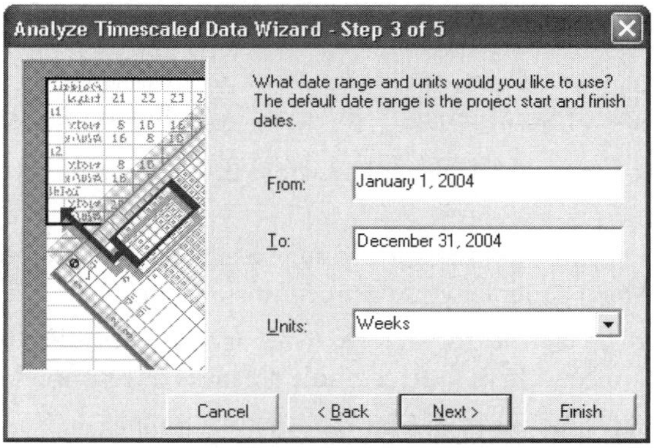

Figure 13-13. Enter the date range and time unit for the exported timephased data.

When choosing your date range and time unit, keep in mind that Excel can display only 256 columns of data.

10 In the fourth page of the wizard, specify whether you want the timescaled data to be graphed in Excel. Click Next.

11 In the fifth page of the wizard, click the Export Data button.

Microsoft Excel starts up, and the selected timephased data is exported. This process might take several minutes, depending on the amount of data to be exported and the speed of your computer. This export works with Microsoft Excel version 5.0 or later.

If the data you have chosen results in more than 256 columns of timephased data, an error message appears. To fit your data into fewer columns, you can specify a shorter date range or a different timescale; for example, weeks instead of days. Or you can simply have the export process cut off the data at 256 columns.

12 Review your timephased data in Excel.

When the export is complete, Excel appears, showing your data. If you chose to chart the data, the Timescaled Data Graph appears first (see Figure 13-14).

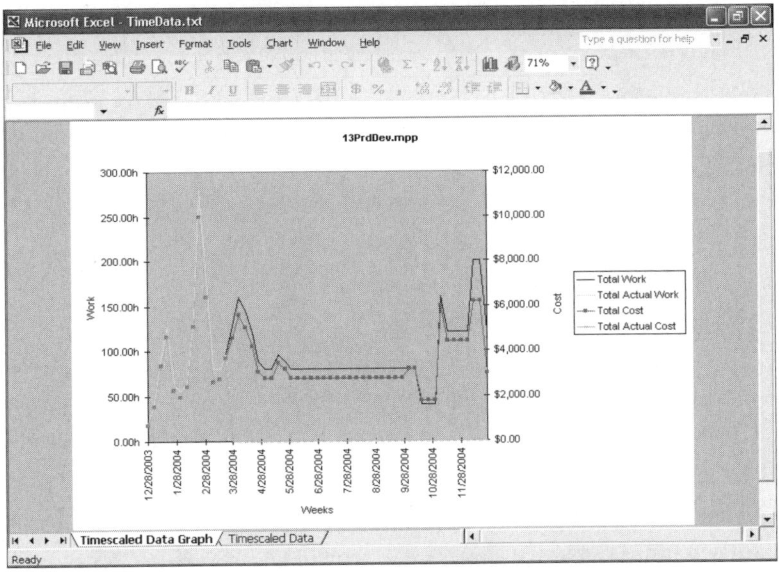

Figure 13-14. Review the exported timephased fields in Excel as a line chart.

Click the Timescaled Data worksheet tab at the bottom of the Excel workbook to review the data in an Excel worksheet (see Figure 13-15).

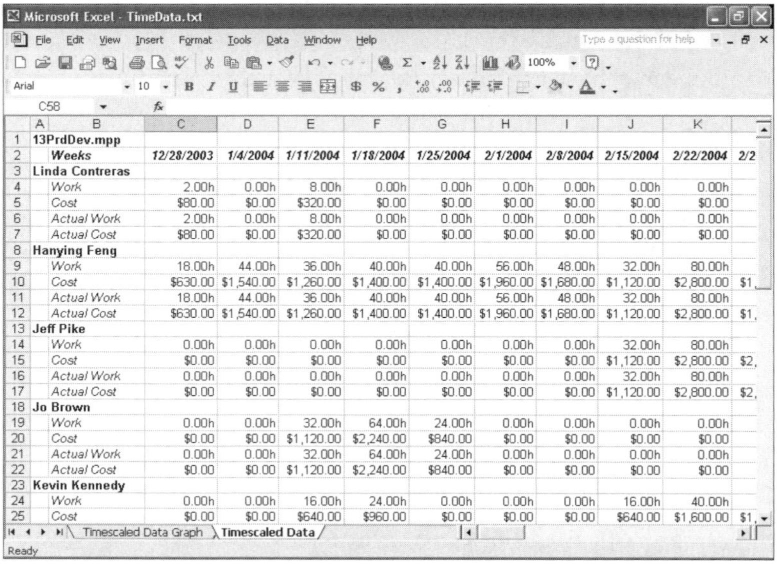

	A / B	C	D	E	F	G	H	I	J	K	
1	13PrdDev.mpp										
2	*Weeks*	*12/28/2003*	*1/4/2004*	*1/11/2004*	*1/18/2004*	*1/25/2004*	*2/1/2004*	*2/8/2004*	*2/15/2004*	*2/22/2004*	*2/2*
3	**Linda Contreras**										
4	*Work*	2.00h	0.00h	8.00h	0.00h	0.00h	0.00h	0.00h	0.00h	0.00h	
5	*Cost*	$80.00	$0.00	$320.00	$0.00	$0.00	$0.00	$0.00	$0.00	$0.00	
6	*Actual Work*	2.00h	0.00h	8.00h	0.00h	0.00h	0.00h	0.00h	0.00h	0.00h	
7	*Actual Cost*	$80.00	$0.00	$320.00	$0.00	$0.00	$0.00	$0.00	$0.00	$0.00	
8	**Hanying Feng**										
9	*Work*	18.00h	44.00h	36.00h	40.00h	40.00h	56.00h	48.00h	32.00h	80.00h	
10	*Cost*	$630.00	$1,540.00	$1,260.00	$1,400.00	$1,400.00	$1,960.00	$1,680.00	$1,120.00	$2,800.00	$1,
11	*Actual Work*	18.00h	44.00h	36.00h	40.00h	40.00h	56.00h	48.00h	32.00h	80.00h	
12	*Actual Cost*	$630.00	$1,540.00	$1,260.00	$1,400.00	$1,400.00	$1,960.00	$1,680.00	$1,120.00	$2,800.00	$1,
13	**Jeff Pike**										
14	*Work*	0.00h	0.00h	0.00h	0.00h	0.00h	0.00h	0.00h	32.00h	80.00h	
15	*Cost*	$0.00	$0.00	$0.00	$0.00	$0.00	$0.00	$0.00	$1,120.00	$2,800.00	$2,
16	*Actual Work*	0.00h	0.00h	0.00h	0.00h	0.00h	0.00h	0.00h	32.00h	80.00h	
17	*Actual Cost*	$0.00	$0.00	$0.00	$0.00	$0.00	$0.00	$0.00	$1,120.00	$2,800.00	$2,
18	**Jo Brown**										
19	*Work*	0.00h	0.00h	32.00h	64.00h	24.00h	0.00h	0.00h	0.00h	0.00h	
20	*Cost*	$0.00	$0.00	$1,120.00	$2,240.00	$840.00	$0.00	$0.00	$0.00	$0.00	
21	*Actual Work*	0.00h	0.00h	32.00h	64.00h	24.00h	0.00h	0.00h	0.00h	0.00h	
22	*Actual Cost*	$0.00	$0.00	$1,120.00	$2,240.00	$840.00	$0.00	$0.00	$0.00	$0.00	
23	**Kevin Kennedy**										
24	*Work*	0.00h	0.00h	16.00h	24.00h	0.00h	0.00h	0.00h	16.00h	40.00h	
25	*Cost*	$0.00	$0.00	$640.00	$960.00	$0.00	$0.00	$0.00	$640.00	$1,600.00	$1,

Figure 13-15. Review the exported timephased fields in Excel as a worksheet.

The timescaled data in Excel is initially exported from Microsoft Project as a text (.txt) file and saved in a temporary folder. To retain this timephased information in the Excel format, follow these steps:

1. In Excel, click File, Save As.
2. In the Save As Type box, click Microsoft Excel Workbook (*.xls).
3. In the File Name box, enter a name for the new file.

   Its default name is *TimeData.xls.*
4. Use the Save In box and Up One Level button to browse to the drive and folder in which you want to save the new workbook.
5. Click Save.

Analyzing Project Data with Crosstab Tables

Another technique for analyzing project data in Excel is to use *crosstab tables* of information, which are tabular presentations of intersecting information along vertical and horizontal fields of information. In Excel, these crosstabs are known as *pivot tables.* Pivot tables are a flexible way to reorganize data in comparative form, with one category of information being filtered and populated into another category of information. Microsoft Project has a built-in method for exporting project data into Excel pivot tables.

For example, you can use an Excel pivot table to analyze information regarding the relative cost performance of different groups of team members and to also see how that performance varies according to the different phases of your project.

To build an Excel pivot table, do the following:

1. In Microsoft Project, open the project plan from which you want to create a Microsoft Excel pivot table.
2. Click File, Save As.
3. In the Save As dialog box, browse to the drive and folder in which you want to save the Excel pivot table file.
4. In the Save As Type box, click Microsoft Excel PivotTable (*.xls).
5. In the File Name box, enter a name for the new Excel pivot table file you'll be creating.
6. Click Save.

   The first page of the Export Wizard appears.
7. On the Welcome page, click Next.
8. On the Map page, click the New Map option and then click Next.
9. On the Map Options page, click Tasks, Resources, or Assignments to specify the type of data you're using to create the pivot table. Read the explanation on this page of how PivotTable mapping is done, and then click Next.

   The Task Mapping, Resource Mapping, or Assignment Mapping page appears, depending on the type of data you chose to export.
10. If you want, specify the destination worksheet name and an export filter. Specify the field to be exported, either by selecting it individually in the table or by clicking Base On Table and selecting the project table that contains the fields you want to include. Click Finish.

    The project information is exported and saved in the Excel pivot table.

In Excel, open your newly created PivotTable workbook. You see that there are two worksheets: one contains the field data specified, and the other holds the actual pivot table, which you can now modify (see Figure 13-16 on the following page).

Your choices for working with the pivot table are extensive, including graphic charting of your results. There is also a handy floating PivotTable toolbar. You can change the preformatted pivot table to see different groupings and summaries.

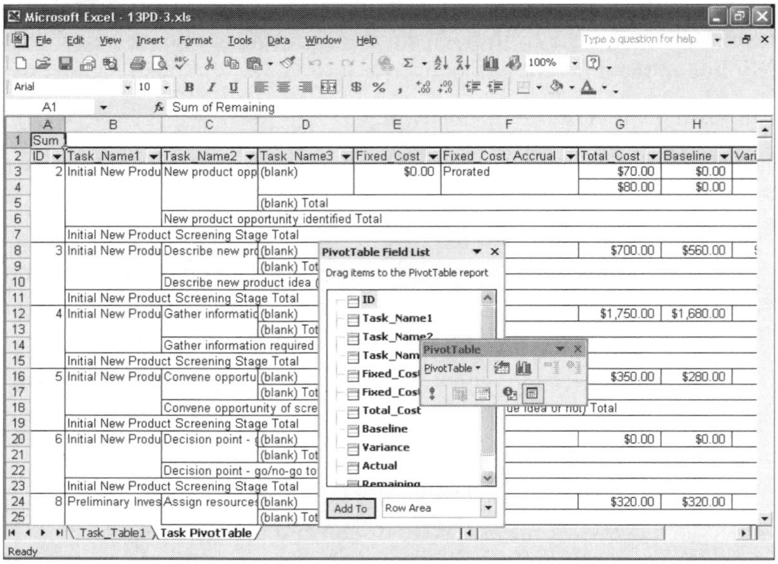

Figure 13-16. Examine your project information in the Excel pivot table.

Refer to Excel's online Help for detailed information on working with your new pivot table.

Charting Project Data Using S-Curves

Suppose that you exported numerical project data into Excel, and the worksheets show you what you need to know. Now you want to share information—for example, the actual cost of work for a task—in a more graphical format. One popular format for graphing performance trends is the *S-Curve graph*. Use the charting and graphing capabilities of Excel to build an S-Curve graph of your project data, as follows:

1. Export project information to Excel using the methods described earlier in this chapter.
2. Open the Excel workbook you just created. Select the data you want charted, for example, Task Name and Cost.

   You can select multiple columns or rows at once by holding down the Ctrl key as you click them (see Figure 13-17).

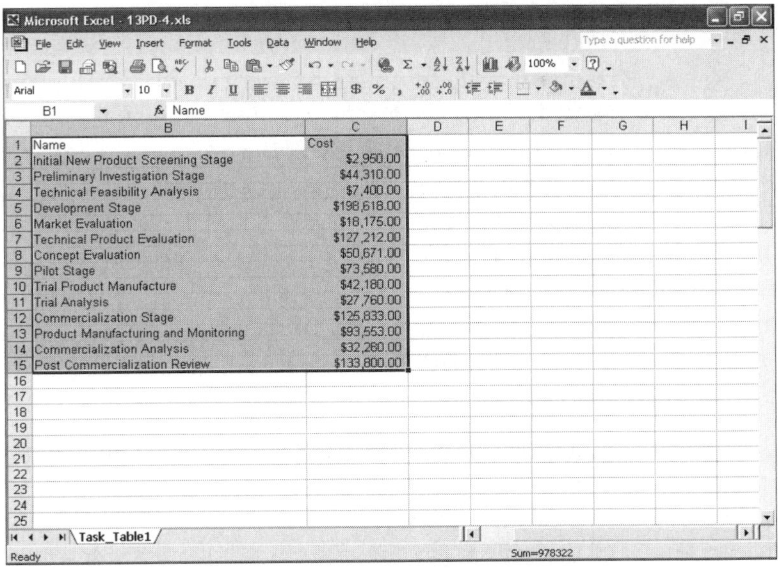

Figure 13-17. Select the data you want to be included in your S-Curve graph.

Chart Wizard

3 On the Formatting toolbar in Excel, click Chart Wizard.

4 In the first page of the Chart Wizard, click the Custom Types tab and then select the Smooth Lines chart type (see Figure 13-18). Click Next.

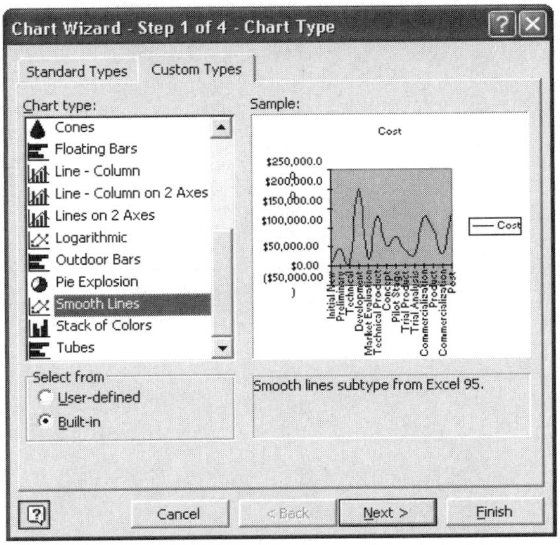

Figure 13-18. Choose the Smooth Lines chart type to create an S-Curve graph.

Data Range

5 In the second page of the wizard, ensure that the Data Range contains the two columns you chose in Step 2.

You should see the moving "marquee" around your selected columns in the worksheet behind the wizard. Use the Data Range selection button if needed.

6 Click the Columns option and then click Next.

7 In the third page of the wizard, make any changes you want to the chart formatting on the various tabs and then click Next.

8 In the fourth and final page of the wizard, click As New Sheet. Leave the name as Chart1 and then click Finish.

The S-Curve graph appears in a separate sheet of your workbook (see Figure 13-19). You can create a wide variety of Excel charts and graphs from different aspects of your Microsoft Project data.

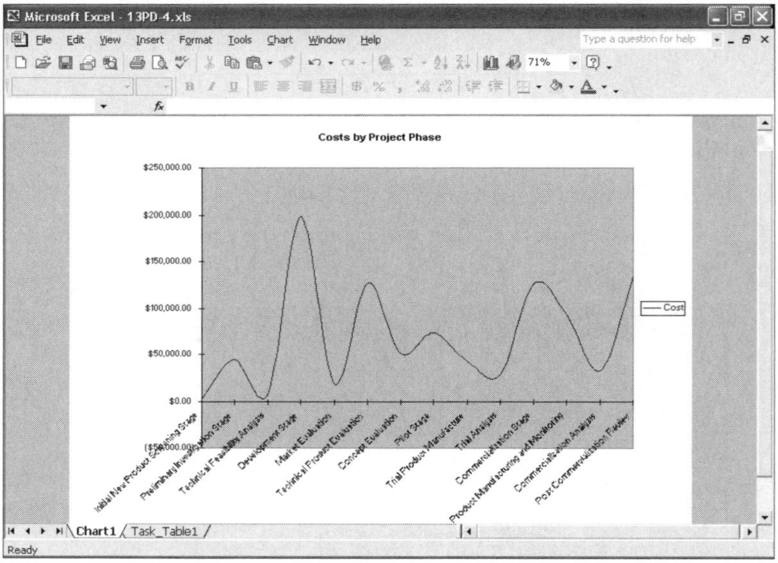

Figure 13-19. Review graphic representations of your project data in Microsoft Excel.

Part 5

Managing Multiple Projects

Chapter 14

Managing Master Projects and Resource Pools

As a project manager, you juggle time, money, resources, and tasks to carry out and complete a project successfully. Often, however, you're juggling not only multiple elements of a single project, you're also juggling multiple projects—each with its own associated challenges. The following are three typical scenarios involving multiple projects:

- Katherine manages a large project containing many phases or components for which other project managers are responsible. In Microsoft Office Project 2003, she can set up a master project with subprojects representing those subphases. She can keep an eye on the overall picture while the project managers responsible for the individual phases have complete control over their pieces of the project.
- Frank manages several unrelated projects and keeps the information for each in separate project files. Occasionally, however, he needs to see information about all of them in relation to one other. He might need to print a view or report that temporarily combines the projects. With Project 2003, Frank can consolidate information from multiple related or unrelated projects, and can do so either temporarily or permanently.
- Sarah, Dennis, and Monique are project managers in the same organization. Although they manage different projects, they use many of the same resources. Sometimes, their projects conflict with one another because of demands on the same resources at the same time. In Microsoft Project, they can create a resource pool file that contains the resources they all use. They can then link their individual project files to that resource pool. The resource availability and usage information is available through that resource pool. When one project assigns tasks to a resource in the resource pool, the resource pool is updated with that resource's allocation information.

Structuring Master Projects with Subprojects

With Microsoft Project, you can insert one project into another. Inserted projects look and act like summary tasks in any task view, with their subordinate tasks readily available. You can view and change all tasks within that inserted project. The task information is changed in the source project file as well, because the two projects are linked by default.

Although you might insert projects for a variety of reasons, the most effective use of this capability is to create a *master project* structure with *subprojects* inserted within that master project. This structure is most useful when you have a large project containing a number of subcomponents, especially if those subcomponents are managed by other project managers. If you're managing the overall project, your master project can give you the view you need into the planning and execution of all the subprojects.

Reviewing multiple projects' information in a master project structure is analogous to using the enterprise Portfolio Analyzer feature. If you're set up for enterprise project management using Microsoft Office Project Professional 2003 and Microsoft Office Project Server 2003, you can use the Portfolio Analyzer to see a high-level overview of multiple enterprise projects. With the Portfolio Analyzer, you can review schedule information, cost performance, and resource allocation, for example.

For more information about the Portfolio Analyzer, see "Examining Projects Using Portfolio Analyzer" on page 749.

Even if you're the sole project manager, you might find the master project-subprojects structure helpful for alternating between project details and the overall project picture.

Information in the master project and subprojects are interactively linked to each other. When project managers of the subprojects make changes, by default, you see those changes reflected in your master project. The reverse is true as well—you can change subproject information in your master project, and those changes are updated in the source subproject.

Your master project can also contain regular tasks. Tasks and subprojects can be organized in relation to one another, and your inserted subprojects can be part of an outline structure and have dependencies, just like regular "native" tasks.

Note Instead of inserting and linking projects together, you might need to just link an individual task in one project to a task in another project.

For information about linking tasks between projects, see "Linking Information Between Project Plans" on page 451.

Setting Up a Master Project

When you want to set up a master project with subprojects, first decide where all the files are going to reside. If you're the sole user of the projects and subprojects, the files can all be stored on your own computer. If you're handling the master project, and other project managers are responsible for subprojects, you'll need to store the projects on a central file server or in a shared folder to which all the managers have access.

Inserting Projects into a Master Project

Creating a master project is simply a matter of inserting subordinate projects into what you're designating as the central controlling project; that is, the master project. To insert a subproject into a master project, follow these steps:

1. Open the project that you want to become the master project.
2. Display the Gantt Chart or other task sheet.
3. Click the row below where you want to insert the project.

   You can insert the project at any level in an existing outline structure. The inserted project adopts the outline level of the task above the location where it's inserted.
4. Click Insert, Project. The Insert Project dialog box appears (see Figure 14-1).

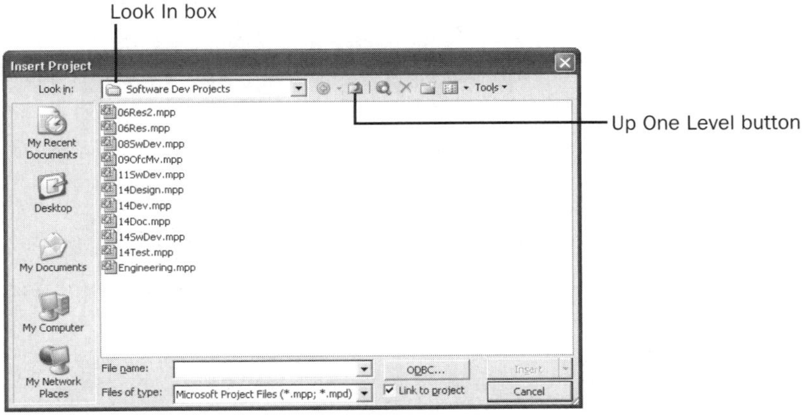

Figure 14-1. Use the Look In box and the Up One Level button in the Insert Project dialog box to find the location of the project you want to insert.

5. Browse to the drive and folder in which the subproject is stored.
6. Click the project file and then click the Insert button.

   The project is inserted and its filename appears as the summary task name in the selected row. The inserted project icon appears in the Indicators field (see Figure 14-2).

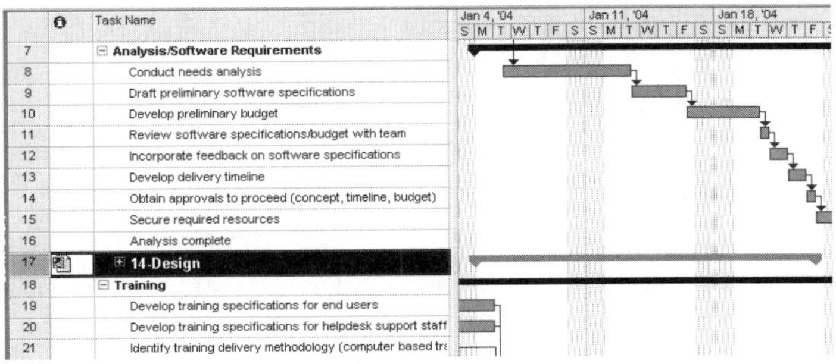

Figure 14-2. The inserted project looks like a summary task among your regular tasks.

7 To see the tasks in the inserted project, click the plus sign next to the project name in the Task Name field.

The subproject expands to show all tasks (see Figure 14-3). They look and behave exactly as if you created them in this project.

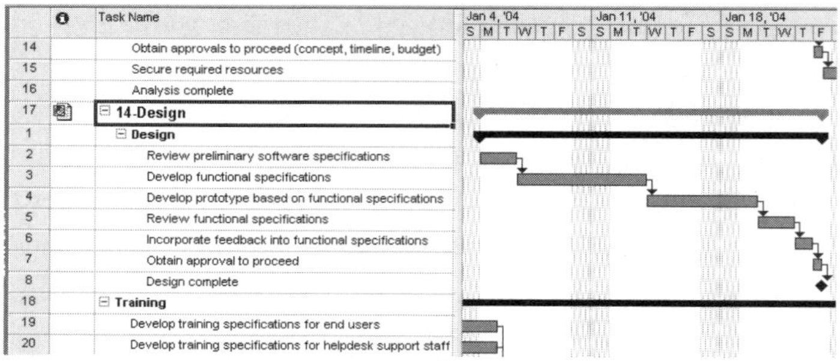

Figure 14-3. You can view and edit the tasks of an inserted project in the same way as those that were originally created in the master project.

The summary task Gantt bar for the inserted project is formatted with a different color. On the other hand, the inserted project's Gantt bars for subordinate tasks are formatted exactly the same as native tasks.

To hide the tasks in the inserted project, click the minus sign next to the project name.

8 Repeat Steps 3–6 for any other projects you want to insert into your master project (see Figure 14-4).

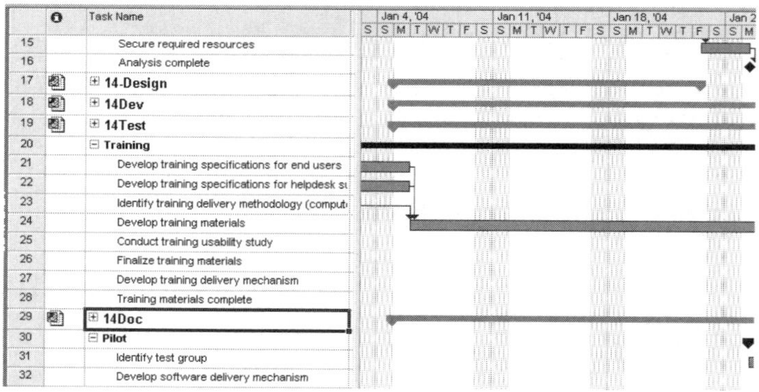

Figure 14-4. This master project contains four subprojects, each one containing the plan for a major project phase.

9 Indent or outdent the inserted project as appropriate. Also link inserted projects or tasks to native tasks as needed to reflect task dependencies.

In the Network Diagram view, the summary task representing the subproject is formatted differently from other tasks and includes the path and name of the source project file (see Figure 14-5). The subproject tasks themselves look the same as regular tasks.

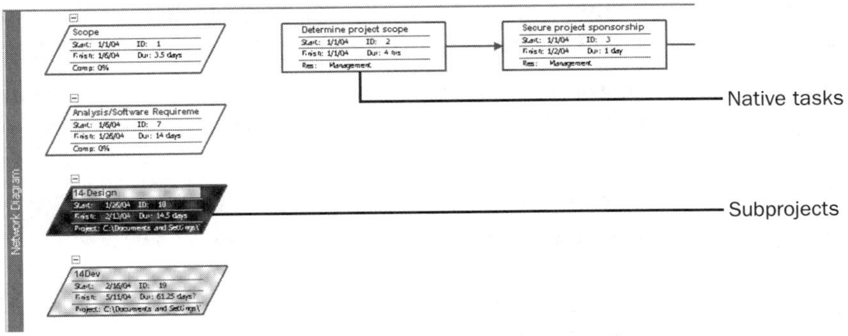

Figure 14-5. In the Network Diagram view, the node representing the subproject summary task shows the name of the source project file as well as its start and finish dates.

In the Calendar view, the name of the subproject appears with the individual subproject tasks (see Figure 14-6). If you don't see the subproject name, drag the bottom edge of a calendar row to increase its height.

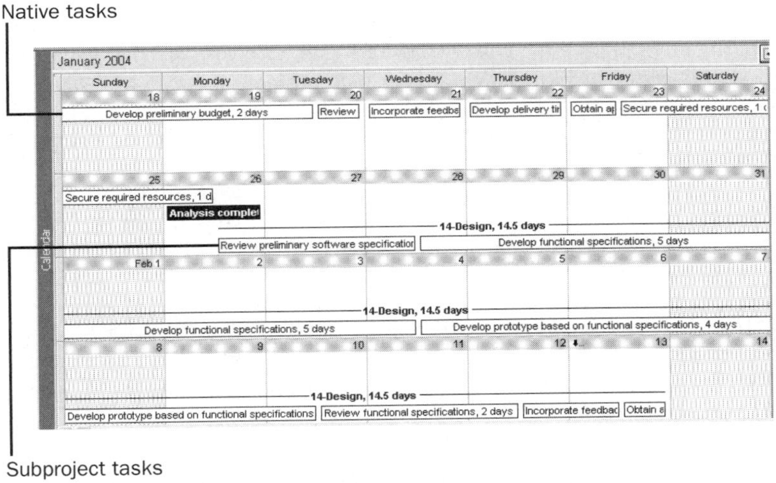

Figure 14-6. The Calendar view displays the subproject name above the individual subproject tasks.

Breaking Up a Large Project into Subprojects

You might know during the preplanning stage of your project that you want your project set up as a master project with subprojects, which makes things easier. On the other hand, you might not know until you're in the middle of project execution that a master project is just the solution you need. You can still set it up without having to significantly rework your project files.

If you already have multiple project files that you want to bring together with a master project, it's pretty simple. Create a new project file, insert the projects, and you're all set.

If you have a single large project file and you want to break it up into more manageable subproject files, it's a little trickier, but still very doable. In this case, you need to do some reverse engineering. The overall process for doing this is as follows:

1. Create a new project file for each new subproject you want to insert.
2. In each new file, set the project start date (or project finish date if you're scheduling from the finish date) for the project.
3. Set the project calendar to match the project calendar in the original file.

For information about copying calendars and other project elements from one project file to another, see "Copying Project Elements Using the Organizer" on page 462.

4. Move tasks from the large project file into the subproject file using the Cut and Paste commands.

   Be sure to select all task information by selecting the row headers, not just the task names. When just the cell is selected, the command name is Copy Cell; when the entire row is selected, the command name is Copy Task, which is what you want. Selecting and copying the entire task copies all necessary task information, including any actual progress information, to the new project file.

For more information about moving project information, see "Copying and Moving Information Between Projects" on page 459.

5. After you have all your separate project files set up, as well as the proper project start and finish dates and calendars, you can insert those files as subprojects into your master project.

If you're set up for enterprise project management using Project Professional 2003 and Project Server 2003, only subprojects are published to the server unless the server has been explicitly set up to accept master projects. You create and maintain your master project on your local computer.

For more information about importing and publishing projects to the enterprise server, see "Creating a New Enterprise Project" on page 645.

Working with Subproject Information

You can edit any task, resource, or assignment in a subproject. By default, any change you make to subproject information is instantly made in the source project file. Likewise, any change made in the source project file updates the information in your master project because the subproject and source project are *linked*. This updating is convenient because you never have to worry about whether you're synchronized with the most current subproject information.

Troubleshooting

There are duplicate resource names in your master project

Often, your master project contains a set of tasks and a set of resources assigned to those tasks. When you insert a project, the resources from that inserted project are added to your master project. Resource information appears in the resource views, and task information from the subproject appears in the task views just as if you had entered it in the master project originally. You can review and edit the information normally.

If you inserted a project that contains some of the same resources as your master project, you see their names listed twice in your resource sheets. One instance of the resource name is associated with the master project, and the other instance is associated with the subproject. If that resource is a part of other projects you insert, that name can appear additional times.

You can assign resources from a particular subproject to tasks only in that subproject. That is, you cannot assign resources from one subproject to tasks in a different subproject.

To see which resources are associated with which project, add the Project column to the Resource Sheet or Resource Usage view.

If you want to work with a single set of resources across all your projects, consider setting up a resource pool.

For more information, see "Sharing Resources Using a Resource Pool" later in this chapter on page 441.

Changing Subproject Information to Read-Only

In some cases, you might not want subproject information to be changed from the master project. Maybe you want to view it only in the master project—which might be the case when you have several project managers in charge of their own subprojects—and you need to see only the high-level view of all integrated project information. In this case, you can change a subproject to be read-only information in your master project, as follows:

1. Display the Gantt Chart or other task view.
2. Click the subproject summary task name.
3. On the Standard toolbar, click Task Information.
4. In the Inserted Project Information dialog box, click the Advanced tab (see Figure 14-7).

Task Information

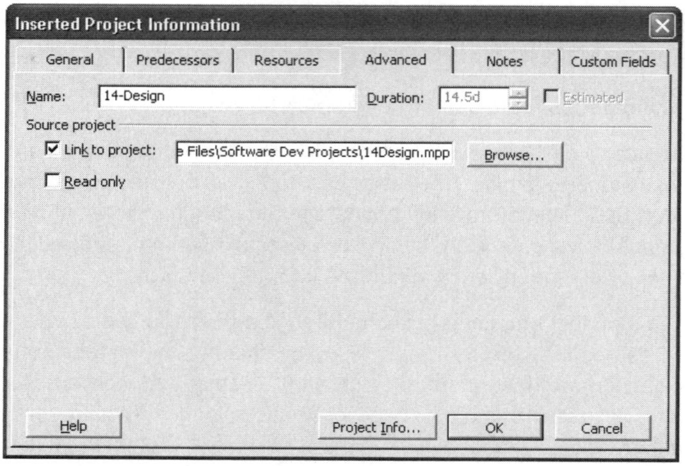

Figure 14-7. Use the Advanced tab in the Inserted Project Information dialog box to change a subproject to read-only or to remove the link to the subproject.

5. Select the Read Only check box.

   Now, if you make changes to any subproject information and then try to save the master project, you'll see a message reminding you that the subproject is read-only.

Whether you make a subproject read-only or not, whenever you change subproject information in a master project and save the master project, you are given the choice to save the subproject information to the subproject file. You can always discard those changes.

Inside Out

Is the subproject read-only or isn't it?

If you set your subproject as read-only in your master project, be aware of certain exceptions to read-only subproject enforcement.

If you work in the master project without opening the subproject file, everything behaves as expected: If you change subproject information in the master project, when you try to save the file, Microsoft Project reminds you that the subproject is read-only, and gives you the opportunity to save the subproject as a new file or discard the changes. You can still save changes to other tasks in the master project that are not read-only.

But suppose that you want to open both the master project file and subproject file. The enforcement of the read-only setting depends on which file you open first. If you open the subproject file first and then the master project file, you can make changes to subproject information in the master project, it's reflected in the subproject file, and you can save them.

To be sure that your read-only settings are enforced, therefore, open only your master project, or open the master project first and then the subproject file. In this case, not only can you not save subproject information changed from the master project, you can't save edits made directly in the subproject file.

Work with subproject-related fields

You might find it helpful to add certain subproject-related fields to a task sheet or resource sheet. You can add the Project, Subproject File, and Subproject Read Only fields to a task sheet (see Figure 14-8). In addition, if you want to know which project a resource is associated with, add the Project field to the Resource Sheet.

		Task Name	Project	Subproject File	Subproject Read Only
19		⊟ **14Dev**	**14SwDev**	**:cts\14Dev.mpp**	**Yes**
2		Review functional specifications	14Dev		No
3		Review functional specifications	14Dev		No
4		Identify modular/tiered design parameters	14Dev		No
5		Assign development staff	14Dev		No
6		Develop code	14Dev		No
7		Developer testing (primary debugging)	14Dev		No
8		Development complete	14Dev		No
20		⊟ **14Test**	**14SwDev**	**cts\14Test.mpp**	**No**
2		Develop unit test plans using product spec	14Test		No
3		Develop integration test plans using produ	14Test		No
4		⊞ **Unit Testing**	**14Test**		**No**
11		⊞ **Integration Testing**	**14Test**		**No**
21		⊟ **Training**	**14SwDev**		**No**
23		Develop training specifications for end use	14SwDev		No
24		Develop training specifications for helpdes	14SwDev		No

Figure 14-8. Add subproject-related fields to a table in the master project.

To add a field, click the column heading to the right of where you want the new field to be inserted. Click Insert, Column. In the Field Name list, click the field you want.

If you make a subproject read-only, and you add the Subproject Read Only column to a task sheet, you'll see that the subproject summary task is marked Yes, whereas the subtasks are marked No. However, they're all read-only.

You can also sort, group, or filter tasks or resources by these fields.

For more information about the ways you can view project data, see "Rearranging Your Project Information" on page 123.

Viewing the Critical Path in a Master Project

By default, Microsoft Project calculates a single critical path across all your projects. If you prefer, you can change your settings to see the critical path for each subproject, as follows:

1. In your master project, click Tools, Options and then click the Calculation tab.
2. Clear the Inserted Projects Are Calculated Like Summary Tasks check box.

   This procedure results in a critical path being calculated for the master project independent of the subprojects. In addition, the critical path for each subproject is shown.

   You can easily see the critical path(s) in the Tracking Gantt chart.

Tip **Review overall project information for an inserted project**

You can review project information and statistics for a subproject in a master project. Double-click the subproject summary task. The Inserted Project Information dialog box appears. Click the Project Info button. The Project Information dialog box appears for the inserted project, showing the project start, finish, and status dates, as well as the name of the project calendar.

To see overall project information for the inserted project—including the project start, finish, and cost—click the Statistics button in the Project Information dialog box.

Troubleshooting

You lose text and bar formatting when you insert projects

The formatting of the master project is adopted by any inserted projects, so if you changed the styles for text, Gantt bars, or Network Diagram nodes in the subproject, you won't see those customizations in the master project. However, any formatting changes you made to the master project are adopted by subprojects being inserted. Also, any formatting changes are retained in the subproject file, even if the subproject and master project are linked.

Unlinking a Subproject from Its Source File

You can keep a subproject in a master project but unlink the subproject from its source project file. When you unlink a subproject from its source project file, changes to the source file won't affect the subproject in the master project, and vice versa. To disconnect a subproject from its source, follow these steps:

1. Display the Gantt Chart or other task view.
2. Click the subproject summary task.
3. On the Standard toolbar, click Task Information.
4. In the Inserted Project Information dialog box, click the Advanced tab.
5. Clear the Link To Project check box.

The subproject is now disconnected from its source, and all the tasks are adopted as native to the master project. The inserted project icon is removed from the Indicators field. Although the project filename still appears in the summary task name field, it's now just a regular summary task—not an inserted project (see Figure 14-9).

	❶	Task Name	Project
7		Obtain approval to proceed	14Design
8		Design complete	14Design
19		⊟ **14Dev**	**14SwDev**
21		Review functional specifications	14SwDev
22		Review functional specifications	14SwDev
23		Identify modular/tiered design parameters	14SwDev
24		Assign development staff	14SwDev
25		Develop code	14SwDev
26		Developer testing (primary debugging)	14SwDev
27		Development complete	14SwDev
29		⊟ **14Test**	**14SwDev**
2		Develop unit test plans using product spec	14Test
3		Develop integration test plans using produ	14Test
4		⊞ **Unit Testing**	**14Test**
11		⊞ **Integration Testing**	**14Test**
30		⊟ **Training**	**14SwDev**
32		Develop training specifications for end use	14SwDev
33		Develop training specifications for helpdes	14SwDev

Figure 14-9. The tasks from the disconnected subproject remain in the project, but they no longer have a link to the source project file.

Removing a Subproject from the Master Project

You can completely delete a subproject from the master project and keep the subproject file intact. To remove a subproject from the master project:

1. Display the Gantt Chart or other task view.
2. Select the heading of the row containing the subproject summary task.
3. Click Edit, Delete Task, or simply press the Delete key.

   A Planning Wizard message reminds you that you're about to delete a summary task along with all of its subtasks.
4. Make sure that the Continue option is selected and then click OK.

   The subproject is removed from the master project. However, the source file for the subproject is still intact.

Consolidating Project Information

You can join information from multiple projects into a *consolidated project*, which can be useful if you're managing several unrelated projects at one time. Sometimes you need to see information from several projects in relation to one another, particularly when you want to view, organize, or work with project information from all projects as a single unit.

You can consolidate projects temporarily, for example, to print a specific view based on information in the projects. You can sort, group, or filter the tasks or resources of the combined projects. If this is a combination you use frequently, you can make it permanent and save the consolidated file for future use.

What's the difference between a consolidated project and a master project?

A consolidated project is simply another implementation of the Insert Project feature. The differences are as follows:

- The consolidated project is not necessarily structured as a hierarchy, as are the master project and subprojects. With a consolidated project, you might bring all the projects together at the same outline level. With subprojects, some projects might be subordinate to others, and you're likely to need them to be laid out in a specific sequence.
- The projects might be completely unrelated to one another. The consolidated project might simply be a repository for multiple project files.
- The consolidation of projects in a single file might be temporary—just long enough for you to review certain information or generate a report.

To combine multiple projects into a single consolidated project file, follow these steps:

New

1. On the Standard toolbar, click New.

   A new project window appears.
2. Click Insert, Project.
3. Select the project files you want to include in the consolidated project.

   If the project files are all stored on the same drive and in the same folder, open that location. Hold down the Shift key to select multiple adjacent project files. Hold down the Ctrl key to select multiple nonadjacent project files.
4. Click the Insert button. The projects are inserted into the new file (see Figure 14-10).

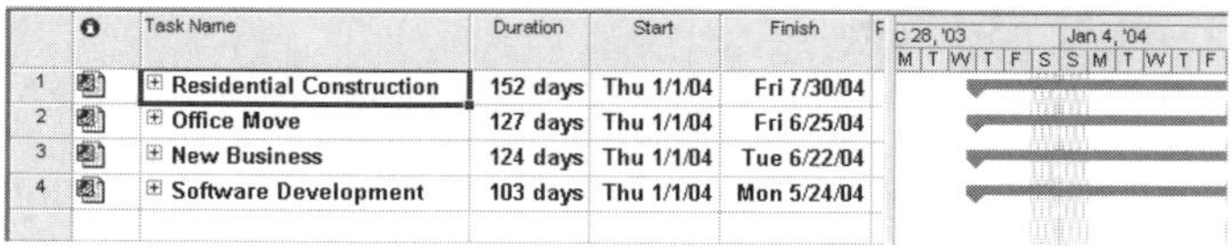

Figure 14-10. The selected projects are inserted into a new window.

5. If you need to consolidate project files located on other drives or folders, repeat Steps 2–4 until all the files you want are consolidated into your new project file.
6. To keep this file permanently, click File, Save. Select the drive and folder in which you want to store the consolidated file. Enter a name for the consolidated file in the File Name box and then click the Save button.

   If you're just using this file temporarily, you don't need to save it.

If the project files are already open, you can use the following alternative method to consolidate them:

1. Make sure that all the project files you want to consolidate are open.
2. Click Window, New Window.
3. In the Projects list, click the names of the project files you want to consolidate (see Figure 14-11).

   Hold down the Shift key (for adjacent project files) or the Ctrl key (for nonadjacent project files) to select the other projects.

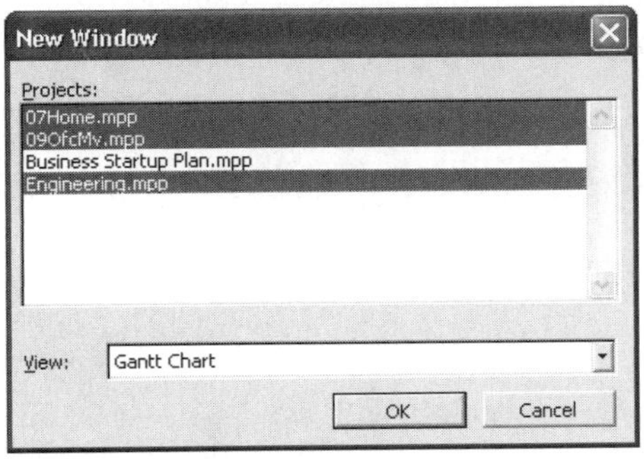

Figure 14-11. Select the projects you want to consolidate in the New Window dialog box.

4. In the View list, click the view in which you want to display the consolidated information initially.

   After you click OK, a new project window appears with the multiple project files inserted and expanded to show all tasks (see Figure 14-12).

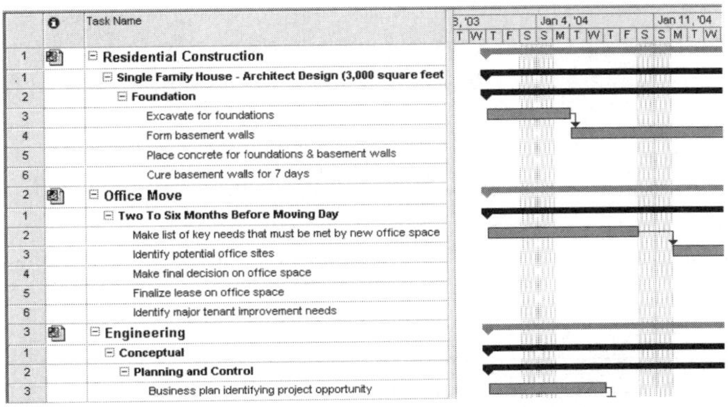

Figure 14-12. The selected projects are inserted into a new window and consolidated in alphabetical order.

Opening Multiple Project Files as a Set

If you always open the same set of project files, you can put those files together in a project *workspace*. Without creating a master project or consolidating the files into a single project file, you can simply associate the projects together. When you open the workspace file, all projects that are a part of that workspace open at once. To save a project workspace, follow these steps:

1. Open all project files you want to be a part of the workspace.
2. Close any project files you do not want to save in the workspace.
3. Click File, Save Workspace.

   The Save Workspace As dialog box appears (see Figure 14-13).

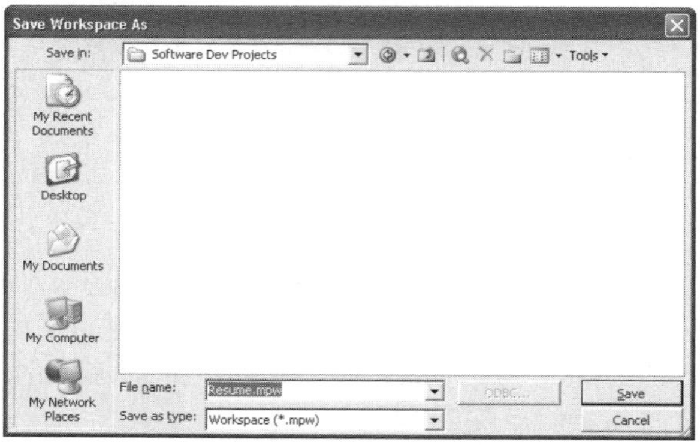

Figure 14-13. Use the Save Workspace As dialog box to group project files that should always be opened at the same time.

4. Select the drive and folder in which you want to save the workspace file and then enter the name for the workspace in the File Name box.
5. Click the Save button. Workspace files are saved with the *.mpw* extension.

> **Tip** **Open multiple projects using Project Web Access**
> If you're set up for enterprise project management using Project Professional and Project Server, you can use Microsoft Office Project Web Access 2003 to group projects the way you need. For example, in the Project Center, you can select several projects and then click Open Into Project.

For more information about working with multiple projects in Project Web Access 2003, see "Opening Multiple Projects in Project Professional" on page 745.

Sharing Resources Using a Resource Pool

Typically, when you create a project file, you set up and schedule your tasks and then add resources and assign tasks to them. Often however, resources are assigned to tasks in multiple projects. You might be the manager of these different projects and use the same resources in all of them. Or multiple project managers might share the same resources for their projects.

To prevent conflicts between projects and avoid resource overallocation among multiple projects, you can create a resource pool. A *resource pool* is a project file that's devoted to maintaining information about resources, including their availability, costs, and current usage or allocation.

Any project manager who wants to use the resources in the resource pool file can link the project file to the resource pool file and make the project file a *sharer file*. When you link a project file to the resource pool file, the resource names and other information appear in your project file. You can then assign those resources to tasks as if you originally created them in this project file.

The Enterprise Resource Pool

Using this local resource pool for multiple projects is similar in concept to using the enterprise resource pool. If you're set up for enterprise project management using Project Professional and Project Server, your enterprise resource pool consists of all resources identified as part of the organization. With the enterprise resource pool, you can check skill sets, availability, costs, and other resource information to find the right resources for your project.

Because of this access to the enterprise resource pool, local resource pool functionality is disabled whenever you work with enterprise projects.

For more information about the project administrator setting up the enterprise resource pool, see "Creating the Enterprise Resource Pool" on page 599. For information about project managers using the enterprise resource pool, see "Building Your Enterprise Project Team" on page 655.

Setting Up a Resource Pool

Resource pools are easier to manage in the long run if you have a project file whose only job is to serve as the resource pool file. However, if all the resources you need for the pool are already in a project you're executing, for example, you can use that as your resource pool file as well.

To create a resource pool in its own dedicated project file, follow these steps:

1. On the Standard toolbar, click New.

   A new project window appears.

2 Click View, Resource Sheet.

3 Enter the information for all work or equipment resources you want to be included in the resource pool.

This information includes at least the resource name, maximum units, and standard rate. If different from the default, also enter the cost per use, cost accrual method, and calendar. Enter the initials, group, and overtime rate if applicable to your projects.

4 If you want material resources to be a part of your resource pool, enter at least the material resource names, identify them as material resources; then enter the material labels and the unit costs.

Save

5 On the Standard toolbar, click Save. Select the drive and folder in which you want to store the resource pool file.

If other project managers will be using this resource pool, make sure that you save the file in a location to which you all have access, such as a central file server or a shared folder.

6 Enter a name for the resource pool file in the File Name box and then click the Save button.

Give the resource pool file a name that identifies it as such; for example, **ResPool.mpp** or **Marketing Resources.mpp**.

For more information about entering resource information, see Chapter 6, "Setting Up Resources in the Project."

If you already have resource information in an existing project file, you can use it to create your resource pool file and cut down on your data entry. One method for doing this is to copy the existing project file and then delete the task information from the new copy. To do this, follow these steps:

1 Open the project file that contains the resource information you want to use.

2 Click File, Save As.

3 Select the drive and folder in which you want to store the resource pool file.

4 Enter a unique name for the resource pool file in the File Name box and then click the Save button.

5 Display the Gantt Chart or other task sheet.

6 Click the Select All box in the upper-left corner of the sheet, above the row 1 header.

The entire sheet is selected.

7 Press the Delete key.

All task information is deleted.

8 Display the Resource Sheet and check the resource information.

Update any information as necessary, including adding or removing resources.

9 On the Standard toolbar, click Save.

Another method of using existing resource information is to copy and paste information from the existing project files to the new resource pool file. To do this, follow these steps:

1. Open the project file that contains resource information you want to copy.
2. Display the Resource Sheet.
3. Select resource information by selecting the row headers.

   To select adjacent resource rows, drag from the first to the last row header. Or click the first row, hold down the Shift key, and then click the last row.

   To select nonadjacent resource rows, click the first row header. Hold down the Ctrl key and then click all other rows you want to select.

   Be sure to select the row headers, not just the task names. Selecting row headers copies all the necessary information—including maximum units and costs—associated with the resource, even if that information isn't displayed in the sheet.

Copy

4. On the Standard toolbar, click Copy.
5. On the Standard toolbar, click New.

   A new project window appears.
6. Display the Resource Sheet.

Paste

7. On the Standard toolbar, click Paste.

   The resource information you copied from the other project file is inserted into the appropriate fields in the Resource Sheet.
8. Click File, Save As.
9. Select the drive and folder in which you want to store the resource pool file.

   Enter a name for the resource pool file in the File Name box and then click Save on the Standard toolbar.

Linking a Project to Your Resource Pool

After the resource pool is set up, you can link project files to it. The project file that uses a resource pool is called the *sharer file*. As long as the resource pool and the sharer file are open at the same time, the resources in the resource pool file appear in the sharer file as if they were originally entered there. Even if you have resources in your project file, you can still use resources from the resource pool.

To link your project to a resource pool, follow these steps:

1. Open the resource pool file.
2. Open your project file that you want to share resources from the resource pool.

   In this project file, click Tools, Resource Sharing, Share Resources (see Figure 14-14).

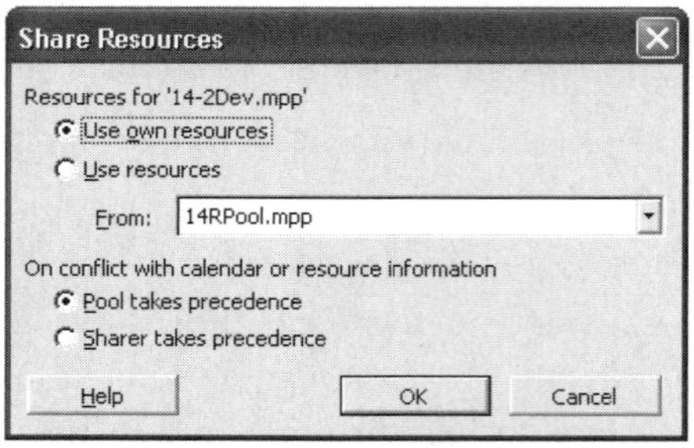

Figure 14-14. Use the Share Resources dialog box to specify that you want your project file to use the resource pool.

3 Select the Use Resources option.

4 In the From list, click the name of the resource pool file. All open files are displayed in this list.

5 Specify how you want any resource information conflicts to be handled.

If you want the resource pool information to be the final authority in a conflict, select the Pool Takes Precedence option. This is the default, and it is the recommended option.

If you want the resource information in the sharer file (your project file) to be the final authority, select the Sharer Takes Precedence option.

6 Click OK. Your project file is now designated as a sharer file of the resource pool, thereby linking the two.

Now all resource information in the resource pool appears in your project file (see Figure 14-15), and any resource information in your project file is added to the resource pool.

Resource Sheet

	ℹ	Resource Name	Type	Material Label	Initials	Group	Max. Units	Std. Rate
1		David Barber	Work		DB		100%	$25.00/hr
2		Ido Ben-Sachar	Work		IBS		100%	$35.00/hr
3		Eva Corets	Work		EC		100%	$28.00/hr
4		Clair Hector	Work		CH		100%	$39.00/hr
5		Brenda Diaz	Work		BD		100%	$45.00/hr
6		Brian Groth	Work		BG		100%	$20.00/hr
7		Andrew Dixon	Work		AD		100%	$25.00/hr
8		David Wright	Work		DW		100%	$45.00/hr
9		Wendy Wheeler	Work		WW		100%	$46.00/hr
10		Tony Wang	Work		TW		100%	$43.00/hr
11		Jeff Pike	Work		JP		100%	$30.00/hr
12		Barry Potter	Work		BP		100%	$32.00/hr
13		Daniel Shimshoni	Work		DS		100%	$32.00/hr
14		Alan Shen	Work		AS		100%	$32.00/hr

Figure 14-15. With the resource pool and sharer file linked, the resource information for both files is merged.

Troubleshooting

The resource sharing commands are dimmed

If the Resource Sharing and Share Resources commands are grayed-out, it indicates that you are working with an enterprise project. Enterprise projects do not use local resource pools. They use the enterprise resource pool instead.

To access the enterprise resource pool, click Tools, Build Team From Enterprise.

For more information about working with the enterprise resource pool, see "Building Your Enterprise Project Team" on page 655.

Even if your organization is set up for enterprise project management, you can still create a local (non-enterprise) project using a local resource pool. Start a new project file. When you click File, Save, the Save To Project Server dialog box appears. Click Save As File. The Save As dialog box appears, in which you can save the project on your own computer, making it a local rather than enterprise project. With this project, you can create and use a local resource pool.

Troubleshooting

You don't see an open project file in the Share Resources dialog box

Typically, any open project files are shown in the Use Resources From list in the Share Resources dialog box. Sharer files are the exception, however. You are never given the choice to use a sharer file as a resource pool.

You can now work with your project file and the resources as usual, including assigning resources from the pool to tasks. Be sure to save both the sharer file and the resource pool file because you're saving the link between the two. You're also saving any resource information from your sharer file as additional resources in the resource pool.

Note You can make a regular project file into a resource pool file. Open the project file you want to use as a resource pool file. Also open the project file that is to become the sharer file. In the sharer file, click Tools, Resource Sharing, Share Resources. Select the Use Resources option and then select the other project file in the From list.

Although making a regular project file into a resource pool can be convenient at first, keep in mind that when the project ends, the assignments will still be a part of the resource pool file, even though they're no longer relevant.

The next time you open your sharer file, you'll be prompted to open the resource pool also (see Figure 14-16).

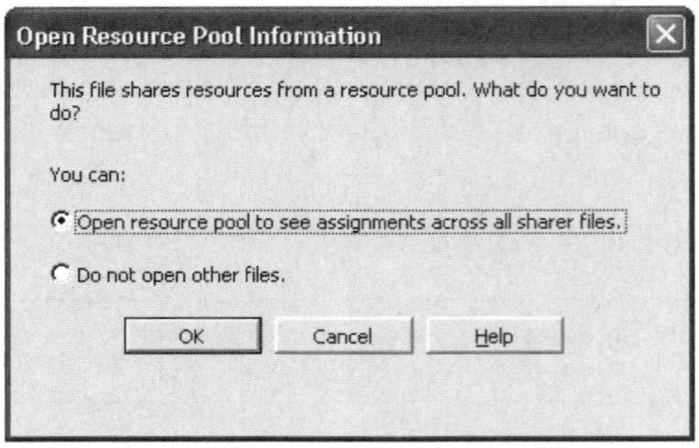

Figure 14-16. If you choose to open the resource file, you'll be able to see all resources, including their assignments, in your sharer file.

Click OK to open the resource file. It's opened with read-only privileges. If you select the Do Not Open Other Files option, the resources you're using from the resource pool do not appear.

If you open a resource pool file before opening any of its sharer files, you are prompted to select whether you want read-only or read-write privileges in the resource pool file (see Figure 14-17).

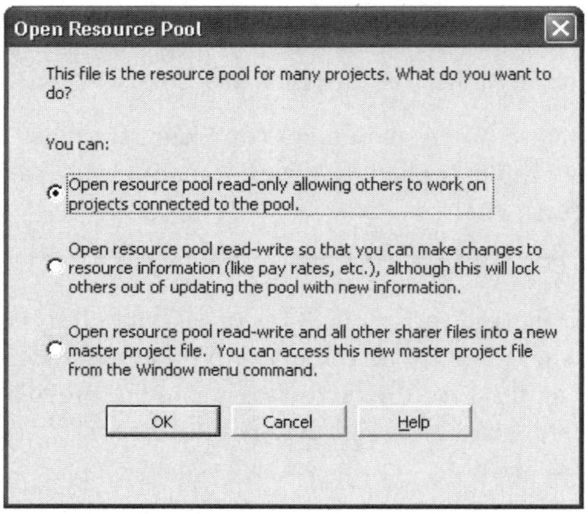

Figure 14-17. You see this alert whenever you directly open a resource pool file. Specify whether you want to open the resource pool as read-only or read-write.

Select the first option to open the resource pool as a read-only file. This is the default, and you should use this option in most cases. You can still update assignment information when working with a read-only resource pool.

Chapter 14

Select the second option to open the resource pool as a read-write file. Choose this option when you need to explicitly change basic resource information such as cost or group information. Only one user can open a resource pool as a read-write at a time.

Select the third option to open the resource pool as a read-write file along with all of its sharer files. These files will be combined into a master project file.

Troubleshooting

The resources are missing from your sharer file

Suppose that you already linked your project file to a resource pool, thereby making the file a sharer file. But when you close the resource pool, the resources no longer show up in your sharer file.

Open the resource pool, and the resources appear again.

Checking Availability of Resource Pool Resources

Display the Resource Usage view or the Resource Graph in the resource pool file to check the availability of resources across all sharer projects. In these views, you can see all the assignments for all the resources in the resource pool. You can see the amount of time they're assigned, if they're overallocated, or if they have time available to take on more assignments.

For more information about checking resource allocation, see "Monitoring and Adjusting Resource Workload" on page 345.

Inside Out

Where did all these assignments come from?

When reviewing assignments across multiple projects in the Resource Usage view of the resource pool file, there's no way to discern which assignments are from which projects.

If you want to see the projects responsible for each assignment, add the Project field to the sheet portion of the Resource Usage view. Click the Work column heading, for example, and then press the Insert key. In the Field Name box of the Column Definition dialog box, click Project and then click OK. The Project field is listed. The project filename for each assignment is listed (see Figure 14-18).

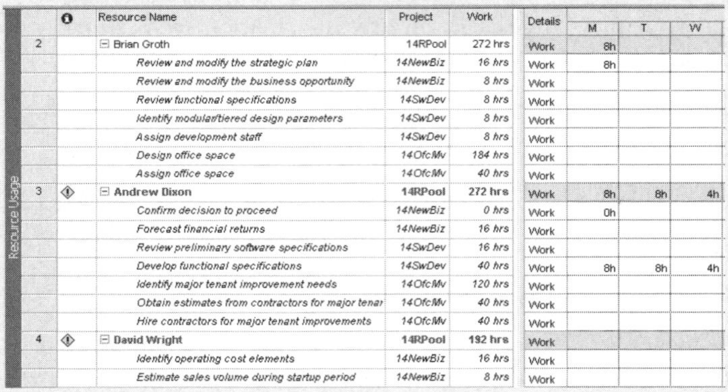

Figure 14-18. Add the Project field to the Resource Usage view to see the source of resources and their assignments.

When assigning resources to tasks, you can also use the filters in the Assign Resources dialog box to find resources with the right skills and availability (see Figure 14-19).

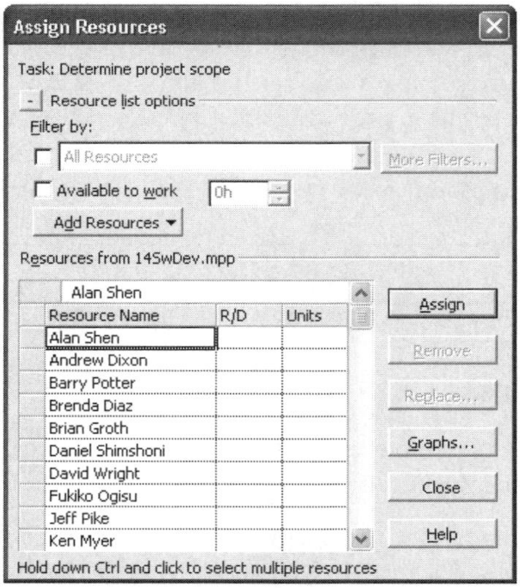

Figure 14-19. Check resource availability while making assignments using the Assign Resources dialog box.

For example, you can find only those resources from the resource pool who are associated with a particular defined group. Or you can list only material resources. You can also specify that you just want to see a list of resources who have at least 16 hours of availability across all the projects to which they're assigned.

For more information about filtering resources and reviewing availability graphs, see "Assigning Work Resources to Tasks" on page 199.

Chapter 14

You can see more availability information about a resource by selecting the name in the dialog box and then clicking the Graphs button. Review the Work, Remaining Availability, or Assignment Work graphs.

Updating Resource Pool Information

If you need to change resource-specific information—such as cost information, notes, maximum units, working time calendar, and so on—you need to open the resource pool file with read-write privileges and change the information. After you save these changes, the next time any users of the sharer files open the resource pool or refresh their resource pool information, they'll see the updated information.

If you're changing resource assignments, there's more flexibility. You can open the resource pool file with read-only privileges, access all your resource information, and change assignment information as needed. When you start to save the sharer file, a message appears, asking if you want to update the resource pool with your changes (see Figure 14-20). Click OK. Even though the resource pool is read-only, it's updated with your changes at that moment. Any other users of the resource pool will see the changes the next time they open the resource pool or when they refresh the open resource pool.

Figure 14-20. This message appears when you're working with a read-only resource pool and you make changes that affect resources in the pool.

Another way to update the resource pool after making assignment changes is to click Tools, Resource Sharing, Update Resource Pool.

If you're working with a sharer file and the resource pool that others also use, it's a good idea to periodically refresh the resource pool to make sure that you have the latest changes to resource and assignment information. Click Tools, Resource Sharing, Refresh Resource Pool.

Inside Out

The resource pool and system performance

Sometimes project managers find that Microsoft Project runs slower when there are large resource pools linked with large or complex project files.

If you experience system performance problems such as these, open the sharer file without the resource pool file. If you can get by without the resource information, you'll be able to work faster.

Another alternative is to divide your project into a master project with subprojects. Then, link the resource pool with the smaller subprojects.

Disconnecting a Resource Pool from a Project Plan

If you no longer need the resource pool and the sharer file to be linked, you can disconnect them, as follows:

1. Open both the resource pool and the sharer file.
2. Display the sharer file.
3. Click Tools, Resource Sharing, Share Resources.
4. Select the Use Own Resources option.

The resources assigned to tasks in the sharer project remain in the project file. Any assignment information for these resources is removed from the resource pool file.

You can also disconnect the link from within the resource pool, as follows:

1. Open the resource pool.
2. Click Tools, Resource Sharing, Share Resources (see Figure 14-21).

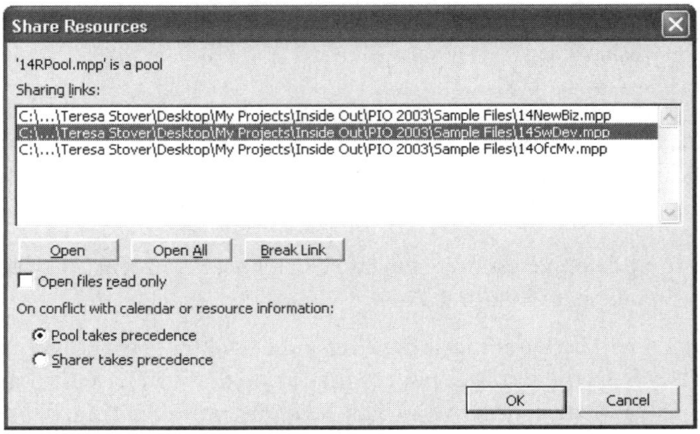

Figure 14-21. In the resource pool, the Share Resources dialog box shows the path of all sharer files.

3. In the Sharing Links box, click the name of the sharer file that you want to disconnect from the resource pool.
4. Click the Break Link button.

Chapter 15

Exchanging Information Between Project Plans

You might occasionally find it necessary to share information between project plans, especially when you're working with multiple projects or adapting information from an old, finished project to a new project you're beginning to plan. There are a variety of situations in which you might need to share information, as follows:

- A task in one project might depend on the start or finish of a task in another project.
- Task or resource information or specific fields might need to be copied or moved from one project to another.
- Customized project elements, such as views, reports, or calendars, might need to be copied from one project to another.

With Microsoft Office Project 2003, you can easily exchange different types of information between project plans, enabling you not only to model your project appropriately, but also to increase your efficiency by decreasing duplicated entries or development.

Linking Information Between Project Plans

When you link two tasks, you're creating a task dependency or task relationship between them. In the most common link type (finish-to-start), as soon as a predecessor task finishes, its successor task can start.

Tasks don't have to be in the same project to be linked. You can have *external links*. An *external predecessor* is a task in another project that must be finished (or started) before the current task can start (or finish). Likewise, an *external successor* is a task in another project that cannot start (or finish) until the current task is finished (or started). Creating task relationships with external tasks like these is also referred to as *cross-project linking*.

Linking Tasks Between Different Projects

There are two methods for linking tasks between different projects. One method uses a temporarily consolidated project. The other has you typing a path.

To link tasks between consolidated projects:

1. Open both projects.
2. Click Window, New Window.
3. Under Projects, select the two projects that you want to link between.

   Use the Ctrl or Shift key to select them both at the same time.
4. In the View list, click the name of the view you want the consolidated projects to appear in.

   The Gantt Chart is the default.
5. Click OK.

   The two projects are consolidated into one.
6. Click the task in the one project you want to become the external predecessor.
7. Scroll to the task in the other project that you want to become the external successor.
8. When you find the task, hold down Ctrl, and click the task.

   Now both the predecessor from one project and the successor from the other project are selected.
9. On the Standard toolbar, click Link Tasks.

   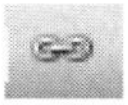

   Link Tasks

   The tasks are linked with a Finish-To-Start task dependency (see Figure 15-1). You can change the dependency type later.

   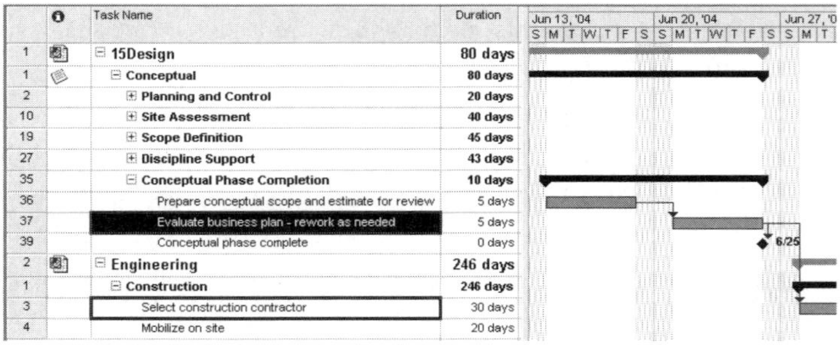

   Figure 15-1. By consolidating projects, you can use the mouse to link tasks in different projects.

   If you're linking tasks between two enterprise projects, the projects must both be of the same enterprise *version*, for example, "published" or "published1," according to the enterprise version control protocol.
10. Close the consolidated project without saving it.

    Review the two projects that are still open. You'll see that they now have external predecessors and external successors, as shown by the gray tasks in both projects (see Figure 15-2).

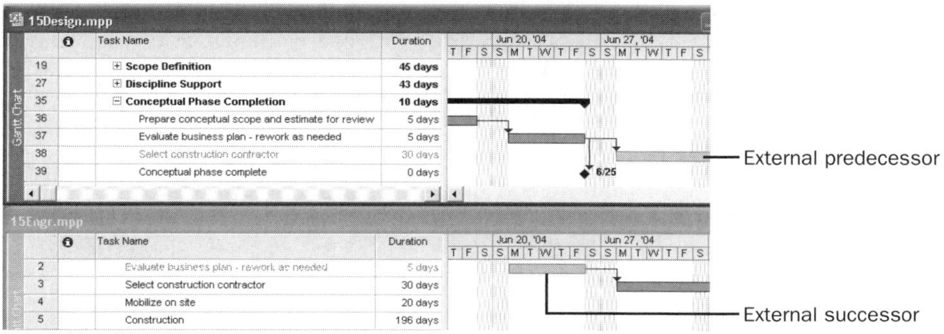

Figure 15-2. Any external predecessors or external successors are displayed in gray.

To link a task in one project to a task in another project by entering a path name:

1. Open both projects.

   Close any other projects.
2. Click Window, Arrange All.

   This isn't required to link, but it enables you to see the tasks in both projects.
3. In the Task Name field, double-click the task that is to be the successor to the external predecessor.
4. In the Task Information dialog box, click the Predecessors tab.
5. In the ID column, type the project path name and ID number of the external predecessor, separated by a backslash (see Figure 15-3).

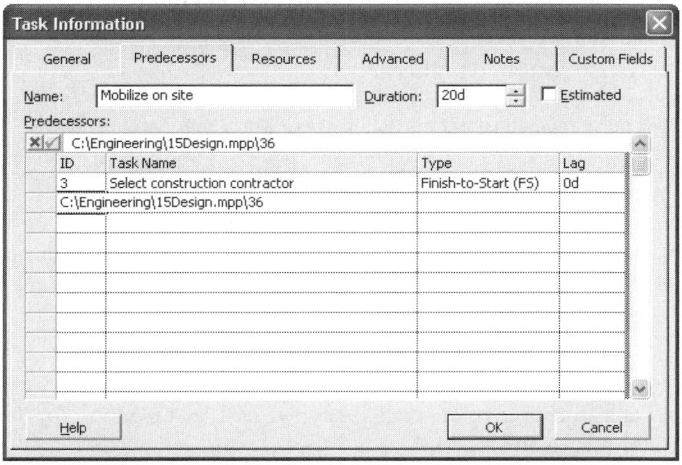

Figure 15-3. On the Predecessors tab in the Task Information dialog box, enter the path, name, and task ID of the external predecessor in the ID field.

For example, suppose that the path name of the project containing the predecessor is **C:\Engineering\Design Project.mpp**, and the ID for the predecessor task is 15 (see Figure 15-4). In the ID field of the Predecessor tab, you'd type:

C:\Engineering\Design Project.mpp\15

Then press Enter.

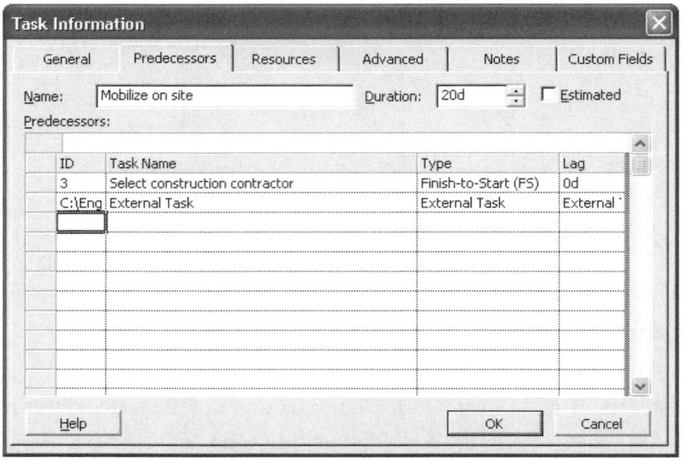

Figure 15-4. After you enter the name and ID of the external task, the other fields contain the words "External Task" and are temporarily not editable.

If you're linking tasks between two enterprise projects, the projects must both be of the same enterprise *version*, for example, "published" or "published1," according to the enterprise version control protocol. Plus, you need to precede the string with two angle brackets: <>. For example:

<>**\Design Project.mpp.published\15**

For more information about enterprise project versions, see "Creating a New Enterprise Project" on page 645.

6 Click OK.

The name of the external predecessor appears in the current project just above the successor task. By default, table text, Gantt bars, and Network Diagram nodes of external predecessors are formatted in gray.

Just as with regular predecessors, you can change the link type from the default finish-to-start to any of the other three link types (finish-to-finish, start-to-start, or start-to-finish). You can also enter lead time or lag time. Use the Predecessors tab in the Task Information dialog box to do this, as follows:

1 In the Task Name field, double-click the successor task to the external predecessor.
2 In the Task Information dialog box, click the Predecessors tab.

The name of the external task appears in the Task Name field, and the Type and Lag fields are now editable (see Figure 15-5).

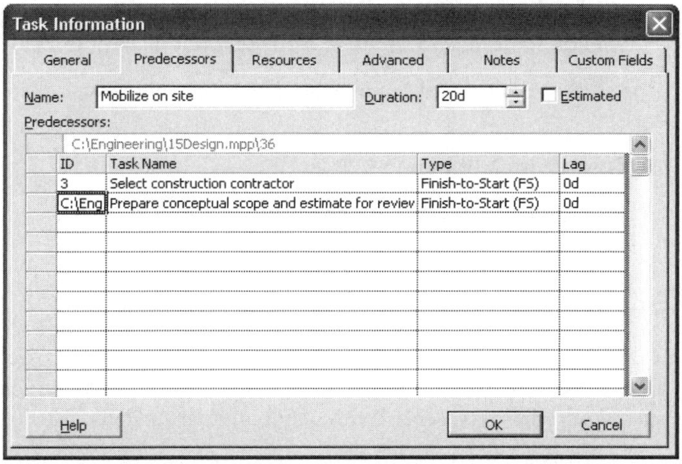

Figure 15-5. The second time you open the Task Information dialog box, the name of the external task appears in the Predecessors table.

3 To change the task dependency to a type other than finish-to-start, select it in the Type field.

4 To enter any lead or lag time for the dependency, enter the value in the Lag column.

Lag time is entered as a positive number, whereas lead time is entered as a negative number.

For more information about task dependencies in general, including lead and lag time, see "Establishing Task Dependencies" on page 149.

Inside Out

Change a link: open, close, and open

When you first enter an external predecessor in the Task Information dialog box, you can't immediately change the link type or enter lead or lag time. Those fields contain the words "External Task" and are not editable.

Click OK to close the dialog box and then open it again. When you click OK, Project 2003 finds the external task information and checks that it's valid. When you open the dialog box again, the name of the external task appears on the Predecessors tab, and the Type and Lag fields are now editable.

Tip **Enter external link information in the Predecessor field of the Entry table**
You can enter the information about an external predecessor directly in the Predecessor field of the Entry table or any other table showing the Predecessor field. If you want to change the link type or enter lead or lag time, you can do it all in one step.

For example, for an external task with a finish-to-finish task link and 2 days of lead time, you could enter:

C:\Engineering\Design Project.mpp\15FF-2d

There are no spaces between the task ID, link type, and lead time.

Reviewing Cross-Project Links

You can see your external links in the different views throughout your project. Whether they're external predecessors or external successors, by default external tasks are highlighted in gray in sheets. External tasks are also represented with gray Gantt bars and gray Network Diagram nodes.

If you double-click an external task, the project containing that task opens and the task is selected. You can then review its task information and current schedule. The other project is still open, and you can return to it by double-clicking the corresponding external task in the second project.

Chapter 15

Tip **Hide external tasks**
If you don't want external tasks to be visible in your project, you can hide them. Click Tools, Options and then click the View tab. Under Cross Project Linking Options, clear the Show External Successors and the Show External Predecessors check boxes. This setting applies only to the current project.

To review the details about links throughout your project, click Tools, Links Between Projects. The Links Between Projects dialog box shows information about all external predecessors on the External Predecessors tab (see Figure 15-6). Likewise, the External Successors tab shows information about all external successors.

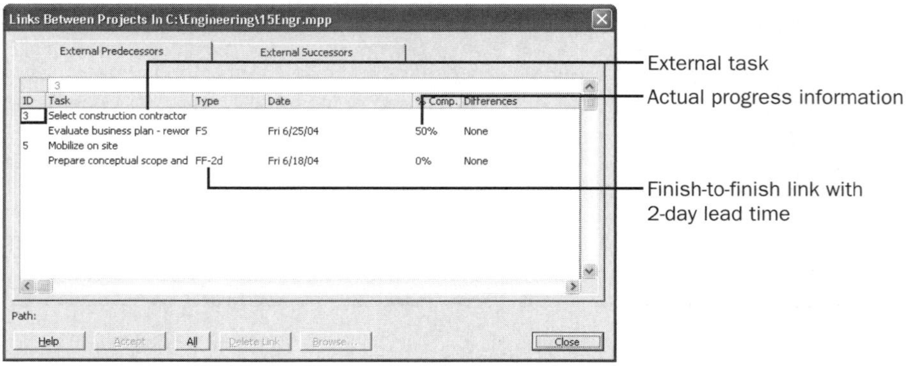

Figure 15-6. The Links Between Projects dialog box shows the pairs of linked tasks along with their link types, finish dates, current percent complete, and any available updates.

To see the path and name of an external task, click the task name in the Task field. The path and name appear in the lower-left corner of the dialog box.

There are two fields related to external tasks that you can add to a table or use for sorting, grouping, or filtering. The External Task field, which is a Yes/No (Boolean) field, simply indicates whether or not the task is external. The Project field contains the name of the project to which this task belongs. For external tasks, the project field also contains the full path (see Figure 15-7).

Task Name	External Task	Project
⊞ **Discipline Support**	**No**	**15Design**
⊟ **Conceptual Phase Completion**	**No**	**15Design**
Prepare conceptual scope and estimate for review	No	15Design
Mobilize on site	Yes	C:\Engineering\15Engr.mpp
Evaluate business plan - rework as needed	No	15Design
Select construction contractor	Yes	C:\Engineering\15Engr.mpp
Conceptual phase complete	No	15Design

Figure 15-7. You can add the External Task or Project fields to a task table to provide information about your cross-project linking.

To add a field to a task table, click Insert, Column and then click the field in the Field Name column.

Whether you add the External Task or Project fields to a table or not, you can sort, group, or filter by these fields. This capability can be handy when you want to see all your external tasks together.

For more information about sorting, grouping, or filtering by a particular field, see "Rearranging Your Project Information" on page 123 and Chapter 25, "Customizing Your View of Project Information."

Linking Projects

Sometimes, an entire project cannot start or finish until another entire project has finished or started. You can set up this relationship between projects by using a master project and subprojects.

For more information about setting up a master project with subprojects, see "Structuring Master Projects with Subprojects" on page 427.

You can also simply create a task dependency between key tasks in the two projects. For example, if Project1 can't start until Project2 is completely finished, set up a finish-to-start task dependency from the final task or milestone in Project2 with one of the first tasks in Project1.

Updating Cross-Project Links

By default, the Links Between Projects dialog box appears whenever you open a project file that contains external links that have changed since the last time you opened the file. The Differences field alerts you to any changed information, such as a changed name, schedule change, new progress information, and so on (see Figure 15-8).

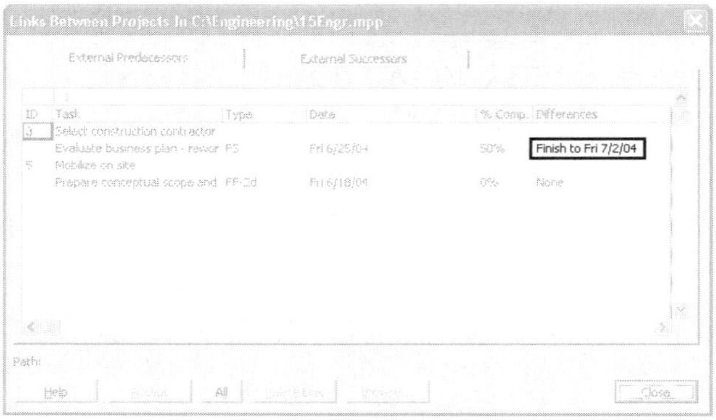

Figure 15-8. The Links Between Projects dialog box appears when you open a project whose external links have changed, and the change is noted in the Differences field.

To incorporate changes from external tasks into your project plan, follow these steps:

1. In the Links Between Projects dialog box, review the change in the Difference field.
2. Click the name of the task that has changed and then click the Accept button.

   To incorporate multiple changes all at once, click the All button.

   When finished accepting changes, click the Close button.

   If you click the Close button without accepting the changes, the changes are not yet incorporated into the project. As long as there are differences between the linked task information in the two projects, this dialog box will appear every time you open the project.

You can modify the way differences between projects are updated, as follows:

1. Open the project containing external links.
2. Click Tools, Options.

   The Options dialog box appears.
3. Click the View tab.
4. Under Cross Project Linking Options, clear the Show Links Between Projects Dialog On Open check box.

   If this check box is cleared, the Links Between Projects dialog box does not appear when you open the project. Whenever you want to synchronize information between the two projects, you'll need to click Tools, Links Between Projects and then update links.

5 If you want external task changes to automatically be updated in your project, select the Automatically Accept New External Data check box.

Removing Cross-Project Links

To remove an external link, do the following:

1. Click Tools, Links Between Projects.
2. In the Links Between Projects dialog box, click the External Predecessors tab or External Successors tab.
3. Click the link you want to remove.
4. Click the Delete Link button.

Copying and Moving Information Between Projects

Suppose that there's a set of resources in a project you just finished, and you want to use them in a new project you're starting to plan. You can copy the resource information from one project to another using the Copy and Paste commands.

Maybe you're working with a huge project, and you need to break it up into a master project and subprojects. Or maybe several people are managing different pieces of a single project, and you're trying to pull together fragments of different project files related to that one project. You can move task information from one project to another using the Cut and Paste commands.

You can copy or move entire sets of task or resource information. You can also copy individual fields of information, such as task names and durations, or resource names.

Copying and Moving Task and Resource Information

When you want to copy or move all task information—including the task name, duration, predecessors, dates, notes, progress information, resource assignments, and so on—you need to select the entire task. Likewise, you can copy or move all resource information—including maximum units, availability dates, costs, and calendars—by selecting the entire resource, not just the resource name.

To copy or move task or resource information from one project to another, follow these steps:

1. In the source project, apply a task sheet or resource sheet.

   It doesn't matter whether the sheet contains all the information fields you want to copy or move. All information associated with the task or resource will be copied or moved.
2. Click the row heading for all tasks or resources you want to copy or move.

   If the tasks or resources are adjacent, simply drag across the row headings to select them. Or click the first row heading, hold down the Shift key, and then click the last row heading (see Figure 15-9).

	ⓘ	Task Name	Duration	Start	Finish
9		Develop management model and staff plan	5 days	Mon 3/29/04	Fri 4/2/04
10		⊟ **Site Assessment**	**40 days**	**Mon 3/29/04**	**Fri 5/21/04**
11		Identify potential sites	10 days	Mon 3/29/04	Fri 4/9/04
12		Define infrastructure requirements	15 days	Mon 4/12/04	Fri 4/30/04
13		Define utility needs	10 days	Mon 4/12/04	Fri 4/23/04
14		Identify project site	5 days	Mon 4/12/04	Fri 4/16/04
15		Assess regulatory and environmental impacts	10 days	Mon 4/12/04	Fri 4/23/04
16		Identify permitting requirements	3 days	Mon 4/26/04	Wed 4/28/04
17		Recommend site	10 days	Mon 5/3/04	Fri 5/14/04
18		Site and planning review	5 days	Mon 5/17/04	Fri 5/21/04
19		⊟ **Scope Definition**	**45 days**	**Mon 3/29/04**	**Fri 5/28/04**
20		Develop general scope for project objectives	5 days	Mon 3/29/04	Fri 4/2/04
21		Evaluate project needs, develop major study list	5 days	Mon 4/5/04	Fri 4/9/04

Figure 15-9. Drag or use the Shift key to select adjacent tasks or resources.

If the tasks or resources are nonadjacent, click the row heading of the first task or resource you want to select, hold down the Ctrl key, and then click the row headings of all other tasks or resources to be copied or moved (see Figure 15-10).

	ⓘ	Resource Name	Type	Material Label	Initials	Group	Max. Units	Std. Rate
6		Kevin Kennedy	Work		KK		100%	$60.00/hr
7		Kevin Liu	Work		KL		100%	$65.00/hr
8		Christie Moon	Work		CM		100%	$45.00/hr
9		Salman Mughal	Work		SM		100%	$45.00/hr
10		Frank Martinez	Work		FM		100%	$50.00/hr
11		Bart Duncan	Work		BD		100%	$25.00/hr
12		Annette Hill	Work		AH		100%	$25.00/hr
13		Fadi Fakhouri	Work		FF		100%	$45.00/hr
14		Suroor Fatima	Work		MS		100%	$30.00/hr
15		Hanying Feng	Work		FO		100%	$30.00/hr

Figure 15-10. Use the Ctrl key to select nonadjacent resources or tasks.

Copy

3 On the Standard toolbar, click Copy.

If you're moving the information, on the Standard toolbar, click Cut.

Cut

4 Open the destination project.

5 Display a view compatible with the information you've copied or cut.

That is, if you're copying or moving task information, display a task sheet view, such as the Gantt Chart or Task Usage view. If you're copying or moving resource information, display a resource sheet view; for example, the Resource Sheet or Resource Usage view.

6 Click anywhere in the row where you want the first of your selected tasks or resources to be pasted.

When you paste full rows of task information or resource information, they are inserted among any existing tasks or resources. No information will be overwritten.

Paste

7 On the Standard toolbar, click Paste.

The copied or cut information is pasted into the cells, starting at your anchor cell.

Copying Fields Between Projects

Instead of copying all information about tasks and resources, you can simply copy the contents of a field, such as task names, resource names, or a custom text field. This procedure can be handy if you just need to copy a set of resource names, for example, or a set of task names with their durations.

> **Note** Although you can move (rather than copy) fields from one project to another, it isn't all that useful to do so. For example, if you were to cut resource names from one project, you'd be left with a set of resource information that has no names associated with them.

To copy the contents of a field, do the following:

1. In the source project, apply the view containing the fields you want to copy.
2. Select the fields.

   If the fields are adjacent, simply drag to select them. Or click the first field, hold down the Shift key, and then click the last field (see Figure 15-11).

ⓘ	Resource Name	Type	Material Label	Initials
	Kevin Kennedy	Work		KK
	Kevin Liu	Work		KL
	Christie Moon	Work		CM
	Salman Mughal	Work		SM
	Frank Martinez	Work		FM
	Bart Duncan	Work		BD
	Annette Hill	Work		AH

Figure 15-11. Drag or use the Shift key to select adjacent fields.

   If the fields are nonadjacent, click the first field, hold down the Ctrl key, and then click all other fields to be copied (see Figure 15-12).

	ⓘ	Task Name	Duration	Start
19		⊟ **Scope Definition**	**45 days**	**Mon 3/29/04**
20		Develop general scope for project objectives	5 days	Mon 3/29/04
21		Evaluate project needs, develop major study list	5 days	Mon 4/5/04
22		Start major studies	2 days	Mon 4/12/04
23		Complete major studies and make recommendations	15 days	Wed 4/14/04
24		Develop specific scope	5 days	Wed 5/5/04
25		Prepare final conceptual schedule	10 days	Wed 5/12/04
26		Provide written scope information	5 days	Mon 5/24/04
27		⊟ **Discipline Support**	**43 days**	**Wed 4/14/04**

Figure 15-12. Use the Ctrl key to select nonadjacent fields.

3. On the Standard toolbar, click Copy.
4. Open the destination project.
5. If necessary, apply a table that contains the same or compatible field as the information you're pasting.

   For example, if you're pasting text information, such as task names, make sure that the Task Name or other editable text field is available. If you're pasting cost information, you need to paste it into an editable currency field, such as Standard Rate or Cost1. If necessary, add a field to a current table. Click a column heading and then press the Insert key. In the Field Name list, click the name of the field you want.

6 Click the anchor cell, which is the cell in which you want the first of your selected fields to be pasted.

7 On the Standard toolbar, click Paste. The copied information is pasted into the cells, starting at your anchor cell.

The information overwrites any existing information; it does not insert new cells. Because of this, be sure that you have the right number of blank cells in which to paste your information.

Troubleshooting

Your pasted information deleted existing information

When you paste selected fields of task or resource information, those fields flow into any existing cells, starting with the anchor cell and continuing into the cells below. If any of those cells contain information, that information is overwritten.

If this wasn't your intention, and if you haven't done any other operations yet, quickly press Ctrl+Z to undo the paste operation. Your overwritten information returns.

If you've done other work since you pasted, you might have to re-create the overwritten information or use your backup project file.

Tip **Copying information between your project plan and other applications**
You can copy and paste project information into other applications, and paste information from other applications into your project plan.

For more information about this, see "Copying Information" on page 471.

Copying Project Elements Using the Organizer

In the course of working on a project over a year or so, you might have created a number of efficiencies for yourself. For example, you might have modified and saved a view to display all key cost information at a glance or created a report for a specific meeting you have every other week. Maybe you've created a set of macros to automate a number of repetitive task-tracking activities.

When you start a new project and you're looking at your new project file, you might think you need to do all that modifying, customizing, and creating all over again. Not so. Just as you can copy task information from one project to another, you can copy customized project elements such as tables, calendars, and fields from one project to another. You do this with the Organizer.

Some elements you change in your project also change your Microsoft Project global template, which is applied to all projects on your computer system. Many other elements just stay in the current project. You can use the Organizer to copy elements to the project global template, thereby making them available to all projects. You can also use the Organizer to copy elements from one project to another.

For information about the project global template, see "Working with the Project Global Template" on page 848. Project managers creating new projects based on the enterprise global template can refer to "Creating a New Enterprise Project" on page 645.

With the Organizer, you can copy the following project elements:

- Views
- Custom fields and outline codes
- Tables
- Toolbars
- Groups
- Forms
- Filters
- VBA modules and macros
- Reports
- Import/export maps
- Base calendars

No matter which type of element you copy, the procedure is the same. You select a source file that contains the element that you want to copy, select a destination file into which you want to copy the element, and then copy the element.

Copying an Element from a Project to the Global Template

To copy an element from a project to the project global template, follow these steps:

1. Open the project that contains the element you want to copy.
2. Click Tools, Organizer. The Organizer dialog box appears (see Figure 15-13).

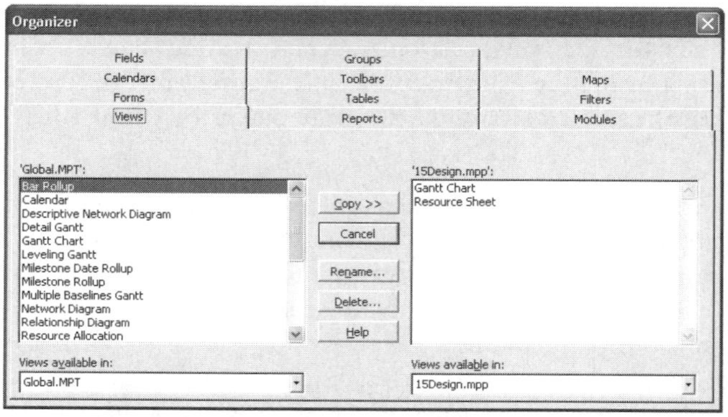

Figure 15-13. Use the Organizer to copy, rename, or delete customized elements between projects or between a project and the project global template.

3 Click the tab for the type of element you want to copy; for example, Views or Reports.

4 In the <Element> Available In list on the right side of the dialog box, click the project that contains the element that you want to copy.

<Element> stands for the name of the current tab.

5 Click the name of the element you want to copy in the list of elements on the right side of the dialog box.

6 Click the Copy button.

If an element with the same name already exists in the project global template, a confirmation message appears. Click Yes if you want to replace the element in the project global template with the one from the source project.

To copy the element with a different name, click the Rename button, and then type a new name.

Copying an Element Between Two Projects

To copy an element between two projects, follow these steps:

1 Open both the source and destination projects.

2 Click Tools, Organizer.

3 In the Organizer dialog box, click the tab for the element you want to copy.

4 In the <Element> Available In list on the right side of the dialog box, click the source project.

5 In the <Element> Available In list on the left side of the dialog box, click the destination project.

6 Click the name of the element you want to copy in the list of elements on the right side of the dialog box.

7 Click the Copy button.

If an element with the same name already exists in the project global template, a confirmation message appears. Click Yes if you want to replace the element in the project global template with the one from the source project.

To copy the element with a different name, click the Rename button and then enter a new name.

For more information about working with the Organizer, including renaming and deleting elements, see "Sharing Customized Elements Among Projects" on page 812.

Part 6

Integrating Microsoft Project with Other Programs

Chapter 16

Exchanging Information with Other Applications

You can exchange data in Microsoft Office Project 2003 with other applications. This capability can save everyone involved an immense amount of time and effort and can also provide for the flexibility of information so essential in an efficient project.

For example, you might want to provide a set of data from your project plan to a stakeholder who doesn't have access to Project 2003, but has another compatible application such as Microsoft Excel or Microsoft Word.

You might want to send project data to a spreadsheet or database application to manipulate the information in ways that those applications specialize in.

In the same way, you can easily bring information into Microsoft Project from other applications. If someone has a list of tasks or resources along with associated information that you need in your project plan, copying or importing this information can save you from rekeying existing data.

Note When referring to the exchange of data between applications, we use the terms *source* and *target* to mean the originating application and the receiving application, respectively.

There are several techniques for exchanging information between applications. The method you use depends on what you're trying to accomplish with the information. Table 16-1 provides some basic guidelines.

Table 16-1. Appropriate Methods for Information Exchange

To Do This	Use This Method
Copy static text, numbers, or pictures between Microsoft Project and another application. The information appears as if it were created originally in the target application.	Copy
Add data along with its source application to another program. When you double-click the embedded information, the source application opens and you can work with it there.	Embed

Table 16-1. Appropriate Methods for Information Exchange

To Do This	Use This Method
Create a dynamic connection between the information in the source and target applications. When the information is updated in one, it's updated in the other as well.	Link
Reference a document at its source, whether it's a Web site or file location. Clicking the hyperlink finds and launches the document in its native application.	Hyperlink
Bring information into Microsoft Project from another application or another file format, making the information appear as if it were created in Microsoft Project to begin with. Similar to copying, but typically used with entire files.	Import
Converts Microsoft Project information into a file format able to be used by another application, making the information appear as if it were created in that other application to begin with. Similar to copying, but typically used with entire files.	Export
Converts Microsoft Project information into Hypertext Markup Language (HTML), typically for use in a Web page.	Export project data as HTML
Converts Microsoft Project information into eXtensible Markup Language (XML) for use in Web pages or any other application that reads or is based on XML.	Export project data as XML

It's important to keep in mind that some methods of exchanging data move the data and then freeze it, so the information transferred cannot be altered after the exchange. Other methods move the data into the other application and allow it to be dynamically manipulated.

Note Microsoft Project has particularly convenient and robust methods for exchanging information with Microsoft Excel and Microsoft Outlook.

These methods are covered in their own chapters: Chapter 17, "Integrating Microsoft Project with Microsoft Excel," and Chapter 18, "Integrating Microsoft Project with Microsoft Outlook."

Creating Server interfaces with Other Applications

NEW FEATURE!

If you're set up for enterprise project management using Microsoft Office Project Professional 2003 and Microsoft Office Project Server 2003, your organization might take advantage of additional means for working with other applications.

New application program interfaces (APIs) allow integration between Project Server 2003 and other organizational systems that interact with project management processes, such as accounting, procurement, human resources, and more. The following is a summary of the new APIs available:

API for Timesheets. Provides an interface from Project Server and Microsoft Office Project Web Access 2003 to a third-party timesheet program or your organization's general ledger system.

API for Project Data Creation. Provides an interface to easily create the minimum required elements of a valid enterprise project, including tasks, resources, and assignments.

API for Enterprise Resource Pool Creation. Provides an interface to easily create and edit enterprise resources from systems in other organizational lines of business.

API for Enterprise Custom Fields. Provides an interface to edit value lists for enterprise text fields, particularly integrating and synchronizing with systems in other organizational lines of business.

API for Enterprise Outline Code Fields. Provides an interface to edit and integrate value lists for enterprise outline codes, particularly integrating and synchronizing with systems in other lines of business.

For more information about setting up Project Server for enterprise project management, see Chapter 21, "Administering Project Server and Project Web Access for Your Enterprise."

Copying Information

You can copy textual as well as graphical data between Microsoft Project and other applications. With one method, you simply use the Copy and Paste commands. With another method, you use a wizard.

Copying from Microsoft Project to Another Application

You can copy field information, such as from a task sheet or resource sheet, to another application, such as Microsoft Word or Microsoft Access. When you need a subset of project information in another application, the best transfer method is usually to simply copy and paste. To copy and paste data from Microsoft Project to another application, follow these steps:

1. In Microsoft Project, display the view and table that contains the information you want to copy. If necessary, insert other columns of information by clicking Insert, Column.
2. Select the data you want to copy to the other application (see Figure 16-1). You can drag across adjacent items (columns, rows, or fields), or hold Ctrl while clicking multiple nonadjacent items.

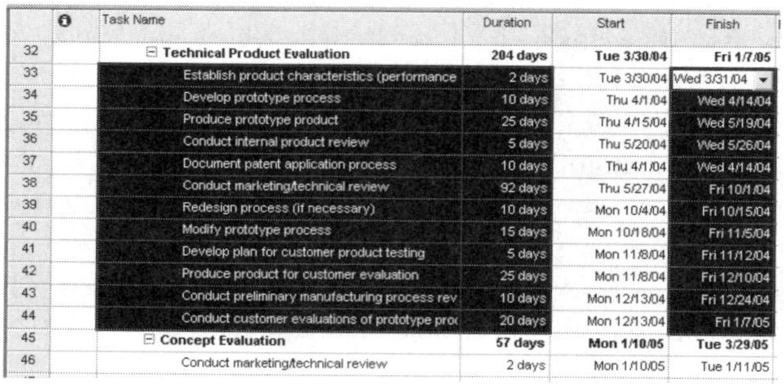

Task Name
Duration
Start
Finish
32 Technical Product Evaluation 204 days Tue 3/30/04 Fri 1/7/05
33 Establish product characteristics (performance 2 days Tue 3/30/04 Wed 3/31/04
34 Develop prototype process 10 days Thu 4/1/04 Wed 4/14/04
35 Produce prototype product 25 days Thu 4/15/04 Wed 5/19/04
36 Conduct internal product review 5 days Thu 5/20/04 Wed 5/26/04
37 Document patent application process 10 days Thu 4/1/04 Wed 4/14/04
38 Conduct marketing/technical review 92 days Thu 5/27/04 Fri 10/1/04
39 Redesign process (if necessary) 10 days Mon 10/4/04 Fri 10/15/04
40 Modify prototype process 15 days Mon 10/18/04 Fri 11/5/04
41 Develop plan for customer product testing 5 days Mon 11/8/04 Fri 11/12/04
42 Produce product for customer evaluation 25 days Mon 11/8/04 Fri 12/10/04
43 Conduct preliminary manufacturing process rev 10 days Mon 12/13/04 Fri 12/24/04
44 Conduct customer evaluations of prototype proc 20 days Mon 12/13/04 Fri 1/7/05
45 Concept Evaluation 57 days Mon 1/10/05 Tue 3/29/05
46 Conduct marketing/technical review 2 days Mon 1/10/05 Tue 1/11/05

Figure 16-1. Select a small number of fields for copying.

Copy Cell

3 On the Standard toolbar, click Copy Cell.

A copy of the selected data is placed on the Clipboard.

4 Open the application into which you want to paste the project information. Select the area in which you want the data to begin being inserted.

Paste

5 In the target application, click Paste on the Standard toolbar. Or click Edit, Paste.

Your copied data is inserted at the selection.

> **Tip** When copying data without column headers, leave room in the target file to add them.

If the workspace of the target application is laid out in columns and rows like the Microsoft Project tables, as is the case with spreadsheet applications, the pasted project information flows into columns and rows without further ado.

However, if the workspace is open, as in a word processing program, the incoming project information comes in looking like a jumbled mess (see Figure 16-2). The information is tab-delimited, though, so it should be fairly easy to switch to a table format.

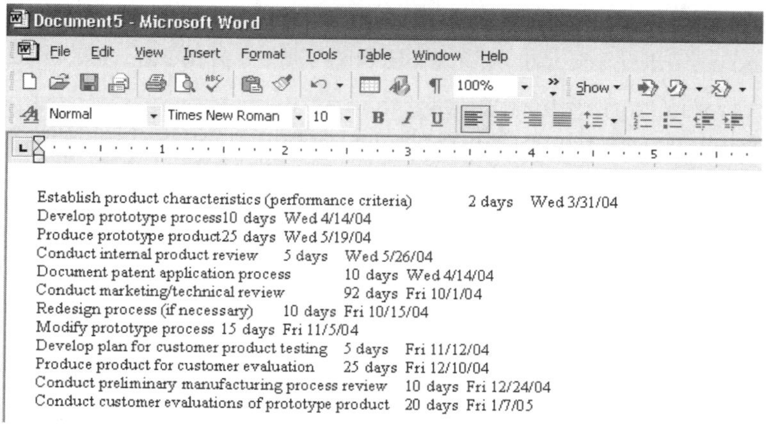

Figure 16-2. Your project data is pasted into the target application.

Chapter 16

In such an application, you need to reformat the text to restore the columns and rows of your project data. To convert column and row information from Microsoft Project to a table in Microsoft Word, follow these steps:

1. In Microsoft Word, select the project data.
2. Click Table, Convert, Text To Table.

   The project information is converted to a table, with the columns and rows separated as they were in Microsoft Project (see Figure 16-3).

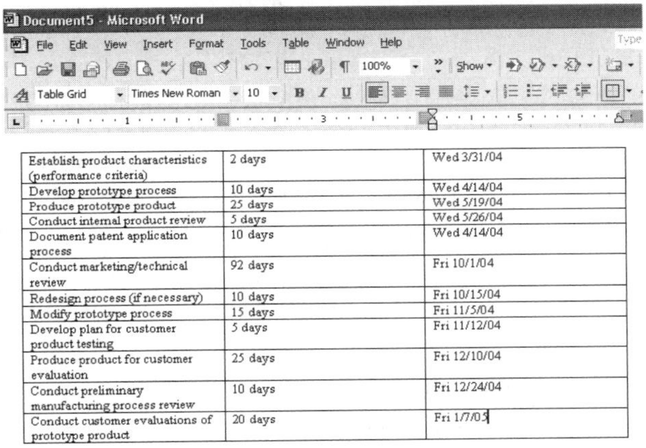

Establish product characteristics (performance criteria)	2 days	Wed 3/31/04
Develop prototype process	10 days	Wed 4/14/04
Produce prototype product	25 days	Wed 5/19/04
Conduct internal product review	5 days	Wed 5/26/04
Document patent application process	10 days	Wed 4/14/04
Conduct marketing/technical review	92 days	Fri 10/1/04
Redesign process (if necessary)	10 days	Fri 10/15/04
Modify prototype process	15 days	Fri 11/5/04
Develop plan for customer product testing	5 days	Fri 11/12/04
Produce product for customer evaluation	25 days	Fri 12/10/04
Conduct preliminary manufacturing process review	10 days	Fri 12/24/04
Conduct customer evaluations of prototype product	20 days	Fri 1/7/05

Figure 16-3. Your project data is converted to a table in Word.

Inside Out

Paste directly into a Word table

You can create a Word table ahead of time with the right number of columns and rows. When you're ready to paste the information in, however, it's different from copying into a spreadsheet.

In a spreadsheet, you select the cell in the upper-left corner, and the information flows into as many rows and columns as it needs.

However, when you paste into a Word table, you need to select exactly the right number of rows and columns ahead of time; then click the Paste button. If you select too few, only the information that is supposed to occupy those cells will be pasted. If you select too many, the information will be repeated.

Chapter 16

Copying from Another Application to Microsoft Project

You can copy information from another application—for example, Microsoft Access or Microsoft Word—and insert it into Microsoft Project. You select and copy the source data, select the cell in Microsoft Project in which you want the data to start being inserted, and then paste the data. This is a good way to get project-related information that was created by others in another application into your Microsoft Project file. For example, suppose that you asked your manufacturing manager to put together a detailed task list of the process that will be used to manufacture your new product. He completes the list, including tasks and resource assignments, using Microsoft Access.

You do need to be mindful of the order in which data is being pasted and inserted into the project table. The type of data you're pasting must match the field type in which the data is being pasted, or you'll get a series of error messages. For example, if you copied a column of text next to a column of numbers, in Microsoft Project it must be pasted into a text field column that's next to a number field column. To make sure the fields match, you can either set up the source information in the proper order or you can rearrange columns in a Microsoft Project table.

To copy the information you need from Microsoft Access into Microsoft Project, follow these steps:

1. Open the source application and file.
2. Select the rows or columns you want to copy and then click Edit, Copy.

   If available, you can also click the Copy button on the Standard toolbar.
3. Open Microsoft Project and the project plan in which you want to insert the copied information.
4. Apply the view and table that represents the closest match to the types of information you'll be pasting.

   If you need to add any columns to match the incoming information, click the column to the left of where you want to insert the new field. Click Insert, Column. In the Field Name list, click the name of the field you want and then click OK.
5. Click the cell in which you want the incoming information to begin to be pasted.
6. On the Standard toolbar, click Paste.

   The copied information is pasted into the columns you've prepared.

   Pasting data into Microsoft Project overwrites data in the target cells. If this is not your intention, insert the appropriate number of empty rows in the sheet before giving the Paste command.

Based on the newly inserted information, other project data might be automatically populated and calculated. Review other fields on this and other tables. Make any necessary adjustments to ensure that your project data is accurate.

Note Any information that can be moved to the Clipboard using the Copy command can be pasted into Microsoft Project, but not all views accept all types of data. For example, you can paste objects such as pictures only into the chart portion of the Gantt Chart. Nothing can be pasted into the Network Diagram.

Troubleshooting

Data isn't pasting into the target file correctly

When you exchange data using the Copy and Paste commands, it's important to remember that fields and columns of data will stay in the order and format of their source file. Before you paste data from another application into your project file, first set up the columns in the source file in the order of the corresponding columns into which they'll be pasted in your project file.

Also be careful that data formats, particularly numbers and dates, are the same in the source file as in your project file. If you want to copy and paste data from another application into a project file that has no project field equivalent, insert columns of generic custom fields (for example, Text1 or Number1) to hold the new type of data. These extra columns must match the column order in the source file. This matching of compatible columns is called manual *data mapping*, and must be done before you give the Paste command. If you paste inappropriate data into Microsoft Project fields, a paste error message alerts you that a mismatch has occurred (see Figure 16-4).

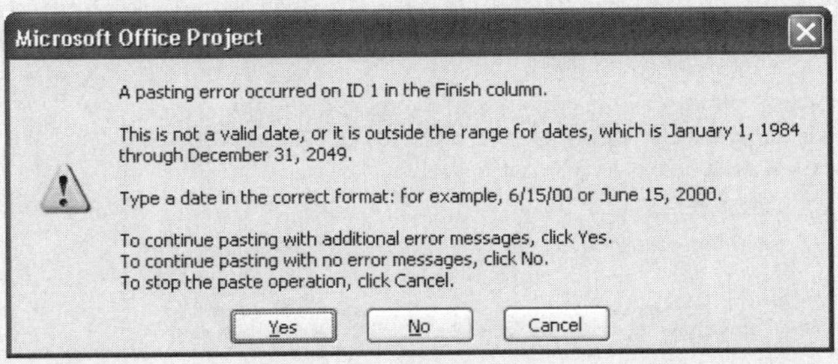

Figure 16-4. The paste error message appears for every field mismatch.

You'll repeatedly see a separate paste error for every mismatch field in the paste operation.

For information about copying information from Excel to Microsoft Project, see "Copying Information from Excel" on page 504.

Copying a Picture of a View

You can copy a picture of any view and then paste it into another application.

Capturing a View for Word, PowerPoint, or Visio

NEW FEATURE!

Using a new wizard in Project 2003, you can now easily copy a view in Microsoft Project and paste it into a file in Microsoft Word, Microsoft PowerPoint, or Microsoft Visio. This procedure works for version 2000 or later for all these applications.

To copy a picture of a Microsoft Project view to Microsoft Word, Microsoft PowerPoint, or Microsoft Visio, follow these steps:

1. Click View, Toolbars, Analysis.

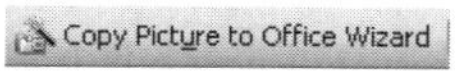

Copy Picture To Office Wizard

2. On the Analysis toolbar that appears, click Copy Picture To Office Wizard.
3. Read the first page of the wizard and then click Next.
4. Select options on the second page of the wizard to reflect how you want the Project view to appear in the Office application.

   These options differ depending on the type of view. For example, a Gantt Chart presents different options from the Resource Graph.
5. Click Next.

   Review the third page of the wizard, which you can use to preview the picture and then select the target Office application (see Figure 16-5).

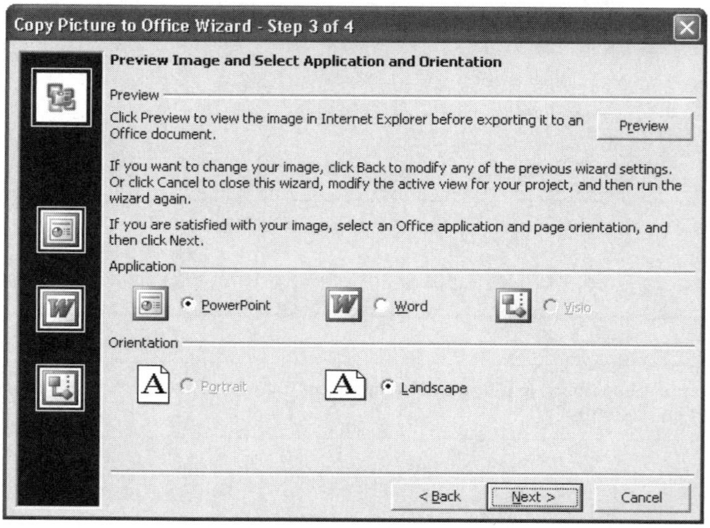

Figure 16-5. Use the Copy Picture To Office Wizard to create an image of a Microsoft Project view for Word, PowerPoint, or Visio.

6 Click the Preview button.

A picture of the view is exported and saved according to the options you selected. A browser window appears, showing the generated picture.

7 Return to Microsoft Project and the wizard. Under Application, click the program the picture is intended for.

If necessary, select whether the picture should be presented in portrait or landscape orientation. Click Next.

The option for any program not installed on your computer is dimmed.

8 Select any Microsoft Project fields you want to export along with the picture of the view. The available fields are listed in the Microsoft Office Project Fields box. Click one or more fields (using Shift or Ctrl to select multiple fields) and then click Add. Click the Move buttons if necessary to rearrange the position of selected fields listed in the Fields To Export box. Then click Finish.

The picture of the Microsoft Project view with any selected fields is exported and saved to the selected Microsoft Office application.

9 In the final window of the wizard, click Close.

The selected Office application opens and displays the picture.

Capturing a View for Other Applications

If you're copying a picture into an application other than Word, PowerPoint, or Visio 2000, follow these steps:

1 In your project plan, display the view you want to copy to the other application.

2 Manipulate the view to show the information the way you want it to initially appear in the target application.

3 Click Edit, Copy Picture.

4 In the Copy Picture dialog box, select the options you want (see Figure 16-6).

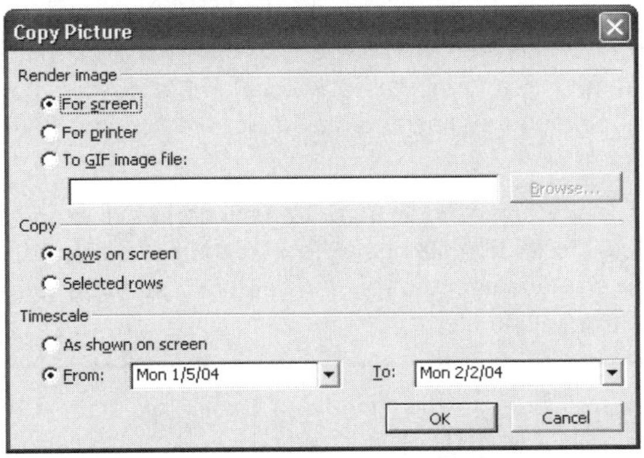

Figure 16-6. Choose the options you want for the picture you're copying.

Chapter 16

In the Render Image section, select whether the image is to be viewed on a computer screen (the default), to be printed, or to be used in a GIF image file.

In the Copy section, select the Rows On Screen option (the default) if you want the rows currently showing on the screen to be copied or if only selected rows should be copied.

In the Timescale section, select the As Shown On Screen option (the default) if you want the timescale to be represented as set in the current view. Select the From and To boxes if you want to specify the timescale and date range now.

When finished setting the Copy Picture options, click OK.

5 Open the target application. Click the place on the page where you want to paste the object.

6 Click Edit, Paste.

A static picture of the Microsoft Project view as you had set it up is pasted into the target application. If needed, you can resize the image by dragging any of the edges.

Using Microsoft Visio with Microsoft Project

Many of the processes and structures reflected in your project plan can be represented in a graphical format and illustrated to help readers visualize them. You already are using a Gantt Chart and Network Diagram for depiction of your project work. By using Microsoft Visio, you can create more extensive visual graphic representations of the flows, concepts, structure, and organization involved with your project. The unique capabilities of Microsoft Visio make it a great tool to use in conjunction with Microsoft Project. You can use Microsoft Visio as a standalone tool that provides visual depiction of your project information or as a source of embedded illustrations within your project plan.

In Microsoft Project, you can use the Visio WBS Chart Wizard to generate a work breakdown structure (WBS) chart of your project.

For more information about creating a WBS chart in Visio using Microsoft Project data, see "Charting Your WBS in Visio" on page 90.

Using the Copy command in Visio and the Paste Special, Paste As Picture command in Microsoft Project, you can embed the diagram in a vacant area of your Gantt Chart to illustrate the organization of your work.

Using the same commands, you can build an organization chart in Visio and embed it in the Notes box of the Resource Information dialog box for a resource you want to show in a hierarchy. As described in the previous section, you can capture a static picture of a Microsoft Project view and include it in a Visio file.

Embedding Information

An *object* is a class or a group of data that gets its format from another application. When you *embed* an object in one application that originated in a different application, you're basically inserting an entire file, with all of its source application's capabilities, into the target application.

For example, suppose that you embed a graphic illustration object created in a graphics application. The object appears in Microsoft Project as if you created it there. If you double-click the object, the graphics application in which it was created is launched; you can make changes to the illustration on the spot, save them, and close the application. The changes you made are reflected instantly in the illustration in Microsoft Project.

For embedding to work properly, both the source and target applications must be installed on the same computer or have ready network access to it. Also, because embedding inserts an entire file within another file, embedding uses a large amount of memory while the project is open and makes the target file much larger.

> **Note** Embedding objects between different applications is made possible by the Object Linking and Embedding (OLE) technology. Any application that employs the OLE standard can embed and link information from another application employing that standard.

Embedding from Microsoft Project to Another Application

You can embed the Microsoft Project file in another application—for example, Word or PowerPoint. When you double-click the object in the target application, Microsoft Project is launched on the spot, and you can switch views and manipulate data.

Embedding an Existing Microsoft Project File

To embed an existing Microsoft Project file in another application, follow these steps:

1. Open the target application and the file in which you want to embed the existing Microsoft Project file.
2. Select the location where you want the Microsoft Project object to be embedded.
3. Click Insert, Object.

   If the target application does not have an Insert Object command, embedding is probably not supported. Look in the application's online Help or other documentation to see if it's called something else.
4. In the Insert Object dialog box, click the Create From File option or tab.

5 Click the Browse button.

The Browse window appears. Navigate through your computer's filing system (and onto your network if applicable) to find the drive and folder in which the project file is located.

6 Find and double-click the file.

Its path and name are entered in the File box in the Insert Object dialog box (see Figure 16-7).

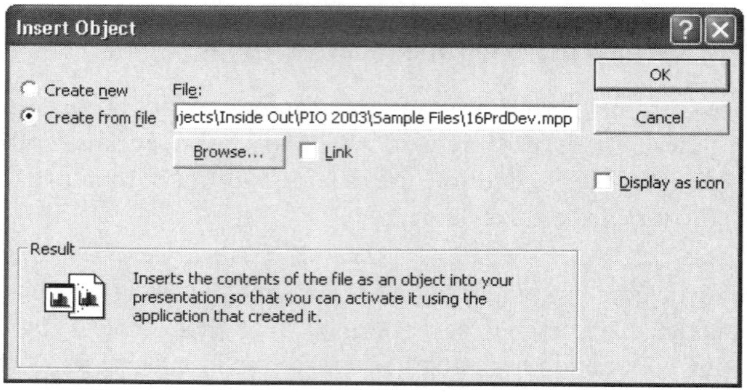

Figure 16-7. Use the Insert Object dialog box to embed a Microsoft Project file into another application's file.

7 If you want the embedded object to be linked to the source, select the Link check box.

If you link the object, any changes in the original update the embedded object. Likewise, any changes made in the embedded object are reflected in the original.

If you don't link the object, you're essentially making a copy of the original object, which becomes a separate entity from the original. You can change the embedded version without affecting information in the original.

8 If you want the embedded project to be displayed as an icon in the target application, rather than showing as a Gantt Chart or other view, select the Display As Icon check box.

9 Click OK.

Part of a view of the selected project file appears in the location you selected (see Figure 16-8).

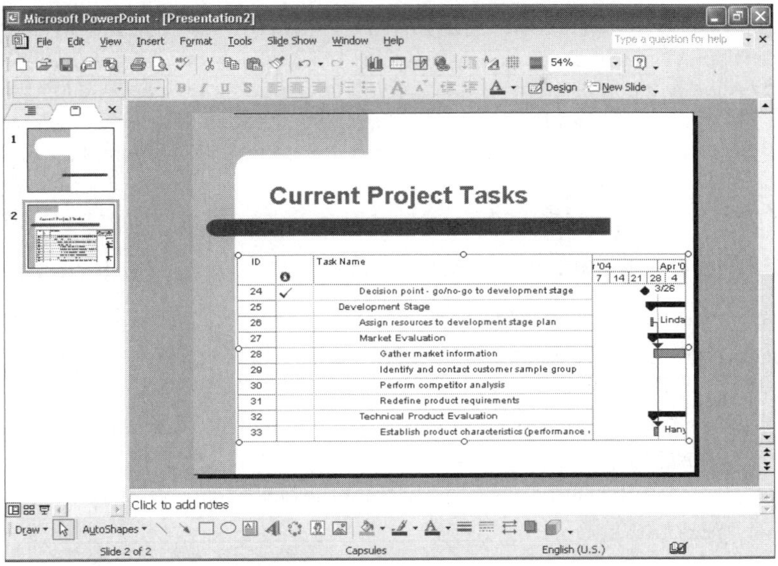

Figure 16-8. The selected project is embedded in PowerPoint.

If you selected the Display As Icon check box, the embedded project file appears as the Microsoft Project icon (by default) in the selected location (Figure 16-9).

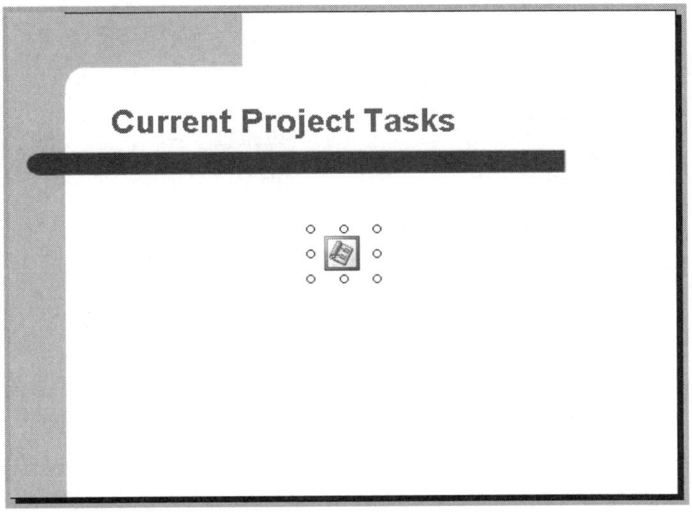

Figure 16-9. The selected project is embedded in PowerPoint, displayed as an icon.

Tip **Display an embedded file as an icon**
The Display As Icon check box in the Insert Object dialog box is useful when you are embedding a large document. When the object is displayed as an icon, you just double-click the icon to open the linked file. With files such as databases and worksheets, this is the most efficient way to embed an object in Microsoft Project. The filename is included with the icon, as well as the shortcut arrow symbol.

Creating a New Microsoft Project File as an Embedded Object

You can create a new Microsoft Project file as an embedded object in another application. In this case, the object exists only within the target application. To create a new Microsoft Project file within another application, follow these steps:

1. Open the target application and the file in which you want to create a new Microsoft Project file as an embedded object.
2. Select the location in which you want the new Microsoft Project object to be embedded.
3. Click Insert, Object.
4. In the dialog box, click the Create New option or tab.
5. Scroll through the list and click Microsoft Project Document (see Figure 16-10).

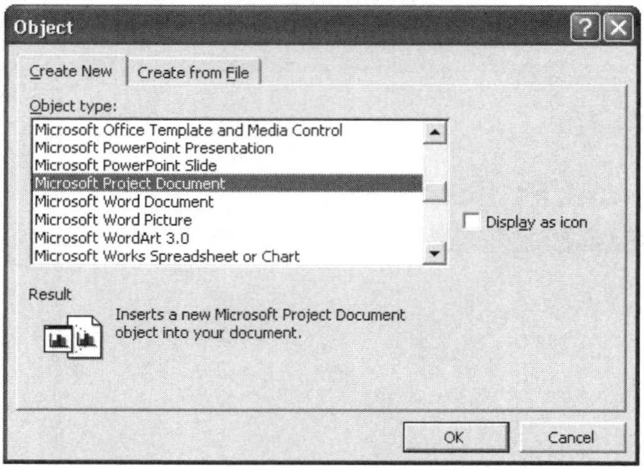

Figure 16-10. Use the Insert Object dialog box to create a Microsoft Project file as an embedded object.

6. If you want the embedded project to be displayed as an icon in the target application rather than showing as a Gantt Chart or other view, select the Display As Icon check box.
7. Click OK.

   Part of a view of the new project file appears (see Figure 16-11).

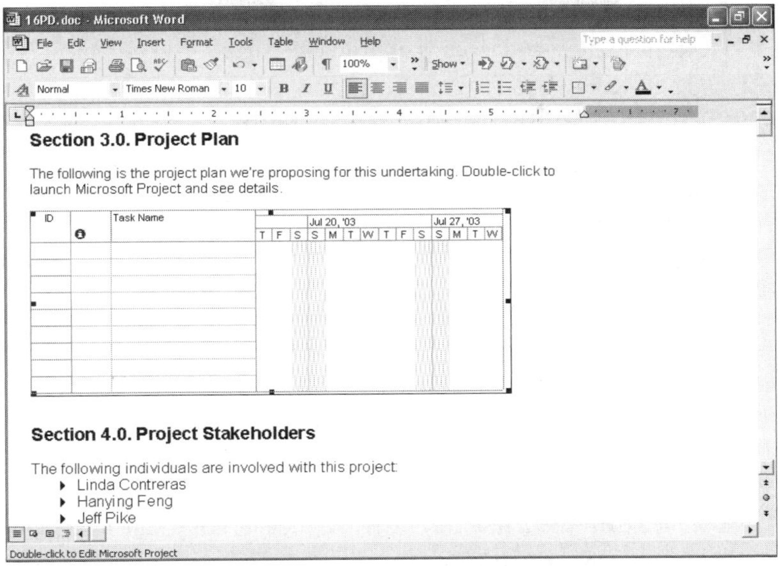

Figure 16-11. The new project is embedded in Word.

If you selected the Display As Icon check box, the embedded project file appears as the Microsoft Project icon (by default) in the selected location.

8 Double-click the new project to add information to it on the spot.

Working with the Embedded Microsoft Project File

Whenever you want to work with the embedded project file, just double-click the object. Microsoft Project launches and the embedded project file appears. You can use Microsoft Project as normal, switching views, applying tables and filters, changing data, running calculations, and so on.

For information about embedding a Microsoft Project file in Excel, see "Embedding Between Microsoft Project and Excel" on page 510.

Embedding from Another Application to Microsoft Project

Objects can be embedded into Microsoft Project from other applications, but only in a limited number of places. For the best visibility, project managers often embed objects in the chart portion of the Gantt Chart. Other available locations for embedding objects in Microsoft Project are as follows:

- The Notes portion of the Task Form or Task Information dialog box
- The Notes portion of the Resource Form or Resource Information dialog box
- The Notes tab in the Assignment Information dialog box
- The Objects box in the Task Form

Chapter 16

- The Objects box in the Resource Form
- Headers, footers, and legends of printable pages

Embedding an Object in the Gantt Chart

Objects you might find useful for embedding in the Gantt Chart include graphic charts of the data, symbols to show significant points, and even cartoons and drawings. Other media forms can be embedded as appropriate, such as sounds and video. To embed an object from another application into the chart portion of the Gantt Chart, follow these steps:

1. Open Microsoft Project and the project plan in which you want to embed the object.
2. Display the Gantt Chart and click in the chart portion of the view to make it active.
3. Click Insert, Object.
4. In the Insert Object dialog box, select the Create From File option.
5. Click the Browse button and find the location of the object you want to embed. Double-click the file.

   The file's path and name are entered in the File box in the Insert Object dialog box.
6. If you want the embedded object to be linked to the source, select the Link check box.

   If you link the object, any changes in the original update the embedded object. Likewise, any changes made in the embedded object are reflected in the original.

   If you don't link the object, you're essentially making a copy of the original object, which becomes a separate entity from the original. You can change the embedded version without affecting information in the original.
7. If you want the embedded object to be displayed as an icon in your project rather than showing as the item itself, select the Display As Icon check box.
8. Click OK.

   The object appears in the upper-left corner of the Gantt Chart. Move the object to the location you want on the Gantt Chart and resize the image as needed (see Figure 16-12).

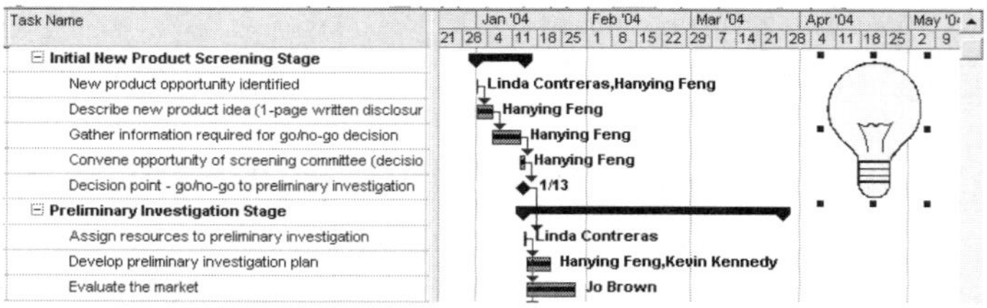

Figure 16-12. Embed an object in your project's Gantt Chart to add more information or to dress it up for a presentation.

Tip **Embed an object in a header, footer, or legend**
You can add an object (for example, a company or project logo) to the project file header, footer, or legend so the object appears when you print a view.

Click File, Page Setup; then click the Header, Footer, or Legend tab. Select the location (Left, Center, Right) for the object; then click Insert Picture. Find and double-click the picture.

Embedding an Object in a Note

If the object you want to embed is associated with a particular task, resource, or assignment, you might prefer to embed it in a note. To do this, follow these steps:

1. Display a view that contains the task, resource, or assignment you want to associate with an object.

   For example, for tasks, display the Gantt Chart. For resources, display the Resource Sheet. For assignments, display the Task Usage or Resource Usage view.
2. Double-click the task, resource, or assignment to which you want to associate the object.

   The Task Information, Resource Information, or Assignment Information dialog box appears.
3. Click the Notes tab.
4. Click the Insert Object button.
5. In the Insert Object dialog box, select the Create From File option.
6. Click the Browse button, find the file you want to embed as an object in the note, and double-click its name.
7. Specify whether you want the embedded object to be linked to the source or displayed as an icon and then click OK.

   The object appears in the upper-left corner of the object area in the Task Form (see Figure 16-13).

Insert Object

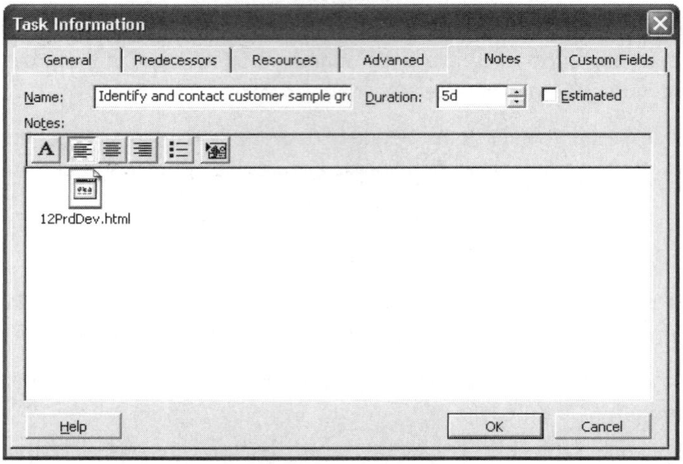

Figure 16-13. Embed an object in a task note, resource note, or assignment note.

Depending on the object's file type, it might be displayed as the file itself; for example, the actual bitmap or the first page of a presentation. Or it might just show the filename. Either way, the object is embedded in your project, associated with the selected task, resource, or assignment. When you double-click the object, the source application opens and the object is displayed.

Notes

As with any note, the Notes indicator appears in the indicators column in a sheet view when a note is present. Double-click the Notes indicator to quickly open the Notes tab and see the object.

Tip **Embed an object in a project note**

You can embed an object in a note associated with the project as a whole. First, add the project summary task by clicking Tools, Options, View and then selecting the Show Project Summary Task check box.

Double-click the project summary task. In the Summary Task Information dialog box, click the Notes tab. Click the Insert Object button and add the object.

Inside Out

Bury an object in a form

You can also embed an object associated with a task or resource into the Task Form or Resource Form.

Select the task or resource in the form. Click Format, Details, Objects. Click Insert, Object and then find and add the object as usual. The object appears in the upper-left corner of the object area in the Task Form.

However, be aware that objects in a form are not as flexible as those inserted in the Gantt Chart or in a note. The object cannot be moved or resized. Plus, it takes a lot of clicks to get to it, so it's pretty buried.

Creating a New Object to Embed in the Project

You can create a new file as an embedded object in your project. In this case, the new object exists only within your project file. To do this, follow these steps:

1. In your project plan, go to the location where you want to embed the object, for example, the Gantt Chart or the Notes area of the Resource Information dialog box.
2. Click Insert, Object.
3. In the Insert Object dialog box, be sure that the Create New option is selected.
4. Scroll through the Object Type box and click the name of the application with which you want to create the new object, for example, Microsoft WordArt 3.0 or Paintbrush Picture.
5. Specify whether you want the new object to be displayed as an icon in the project and then click OK.

   A miniature version of the application either appears in the location you selected, or the application launches immediately (see Figure 16-14).

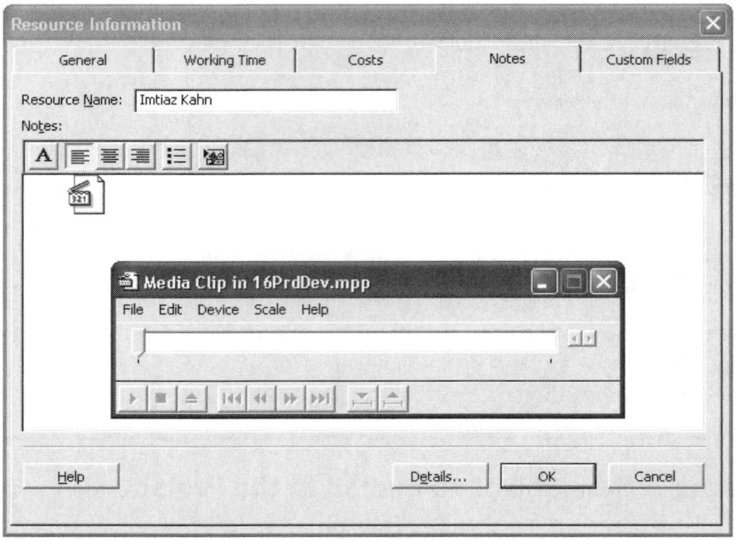

Figure 16-14. Create a new object in your project.

6 Start creating the new file on the spot.

If necessary, double-click the application to launch it.

Working with the Embedded Object in the Project

If an object embedded in your project is a graphic that's displayed in its proper place, you might never need to do anything with it. With other objects, however, you need to open and work with them. This is particularly true of new objects you created within the project file. They contain nothing until you add your own data.

To open and work with an embedded object, simply double-click the object. The source application opens, and you can use its commands and tools to work with the object as needed. When finished, on the File menu, click the Close or Exit command. The source application closes, and the object appears in your project file showing the changes you just made.

Tip Delete an embedded object

To delete an embedded object anywhere in your project plan, simply click it and press Delete.

For information about embedding information from Excel to Microsoft Project, see "Embedding Between Microsoft Project and Excel" on page 510.

Linking Information

Linking is another method of exchanging data between applications. By linking information, you maintain a connection to the source application. When a change is made to the information, it's reflected in the target application.

A major advantage of linking is that the file size is much smaller than it would be if the information in the linked file were embedded. A potential difficulty with linking is that you always need to know the current location of the linked file and its update status. If the linked file is moved, the link is broken. If the information in the linked file becomes obsolete, the linked information also becomes out of date.

Linking from Microsoft Project to Another Application

You can create a link from Microsoft Project information in another application using the Copy and Paste Special commands. Follow this procedure:

1. In Microsoft Project, display the view that contains the information you want to copy and link to another application.

   If it's text-based information—such as tasks, resources, or assignment fields—select the information. If it's graphical information—such as a Gantt Chart, Resource Graph, or Network Diagram—arrange the view to contain the information you want represented in the other application.
2. Click Edit, Copy or Copy Task.
3. Open the target application; for example, Microsoft Word. Place the cursor where you want the information to be inserted.
4. In the target application, click Edit, Paste Special.
5. In the Paste Special dialog box, select the Paste Link option (see Figure 16-15).

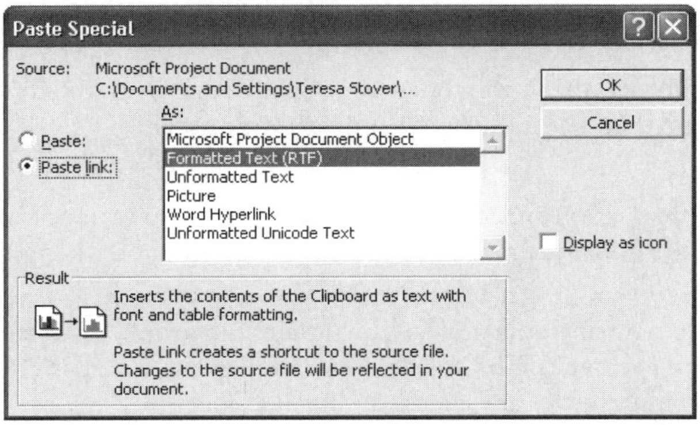

Figure 16-15. Use the Paste Special dialog box to create a link from Microsoft Project.

6. Review the choices available in the As box. Click each one to read its description in the Result box and then select the one that meets your needs.

   The choices vary depending on the type of information that was copied in Microsoft Project. One of the choices is always Microsoft Project Document Object, which creates an embedded object that's linked.

7. Click OK.

   The linked information appears in the target application. When changes are made to the information in Microsoft Project, those changes are reflected in the target application.

For information about linking information from Microsoft Project to Excel, see "Linking Between Microsoft Project and Excel" on page 516.

Linking from Another Application to Microsoft Project

The data connection of a linked object can be made using another application as the source and Microsoft Project as the target, which can be a handy way to show currently updated information from a different origin. Linked graphical information can be pasted only in select locations in Microsoft Project; for example, the Gantt Chart, Notes areas, and the Task and Resource Forms. Linked textual information can also be pasted into the table cell.

To link data from another application, follow these steps:

1. In the source application, select the information to be linked in Microsoft Project, and click Edit Copy.
2. In Microsoft Project, display the view and select the location to contain the linked information.
3. Click Edit, Paste Special.
4. In the Paste Special dialog box, click the Paste Link option.

   The As box changes to present the options for linking the copied information into Microsoft Project.

5. Review the choices available in the As box. Click each one to read its description in the Result box and then select the one that meets your needs.
6. Click OK.

   The linked information appears at your selection point in your project. When changes are made to the information in the source application, those changes can be reflected in this project file.

By default, whenever you open the project file containing the link, a message appears, asking whether you want to re-establish the link between the files (see Figure 16-16). Clicking Yes re-establishes the link and updates any changed information.

Figure 16-16. Each time you open a linked project, you are prompted to re-establish the link.

If you do not want to see this alert each time you open the project, click Tools, Options and then click the View tab. Clear the Show OLE Links Indicators check box.

To review and work with links in your project, follow these steps:

1. Click Edit, Links.

   The Links dialog box appears, showing all links existing in your project file (see Figure 16-17).

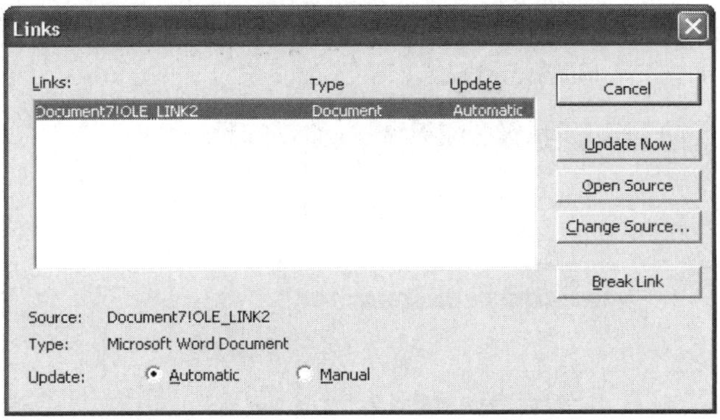

Figure 16-17. Review the status of links in your project file.

2. If you chose not to update a link when opening the project file or if you're not prompted, you can select a link and click Update Now.
3. If the linked document location has changed, you can update the information in the project by clicking Change Source.
4. To break the link with the source application, click Break Link.

For information about linking information from Excel to Microsoft Project, see "Linking Between Microsoft Project and Excel" on page 516.

Hyperlinking to Documents in Other Applications

In your project file, you can insert a hyperlink to jump to a Web site or another file on your computer or network. Inserting a hyperlink can be useful for including relevant reference material for tasks and resources in your project plan. It's also useful for linking project-related documents, such as the scope document and bill of materials, to your project plan.

> **Note** Although it's called a *hyperlink*, the item you're linking to does *not* have to be a Web page, and it does not have to be in HTML or XML format. It can be any document in any file format. You do need to have the application for that file on your computer, and it does need to be in a stable location.

To create a hyperlink in your project:

1. In Microsoft Project, display the view that contains the task, resource, or assignment to which you want to add a hyperlink.
2. Click the task, resource, or assignment name to select it.
3. On the Standard toolbar, click Insert Hyperlink.

   Insert Hyperlink

   The Insert Hyperlink dialog box appears.
4. In the Text To Display box, type a short description of the page you're linking to.
5. In the Look In list, locate and select the source file (see Figure 16-18).

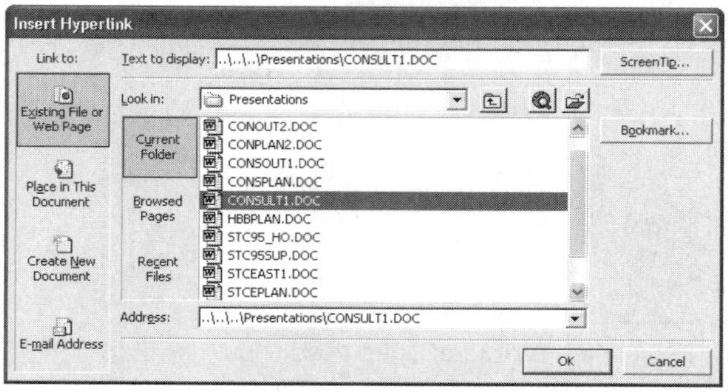

Figure 16-18. The path and name of the selected document appear in the Address box.

6. Click OK.

   Hyperlink indicator

   The Hyperlink indicator appears in the Indicators column of the current view. If you rest your mouse pointer over the hyperlink indicator, the name of the link appears.

> **Tip** **Review all hyperlink information**
> If you want to review all your hyperlink information in a table, apply the Hyperlink table. There's a version for task hyperlinks and another one for resource hyperlinks.
>
> Apply a sheet view, such as the Gantt Chart or the Resource Sheet. Click View, Table, Hyperlink.

Whenever you want to review the file pointed to by the hyperlink, simply click the Hyperlink indicator. The hyperlinked document appears in its own application window.

Set up a document library

If you're using Project Professional 2003 with Project Server for enterprise project management, the preferred method for keeping all project documents together is to use the document library. By setting up Project Web Access 2003 with Windows SharePoint Services, you can set up and maintain a document library. This way, all your team members and other stakeholders can view the documents through their Web browsers. They can also check documents in and out, providing vital version control.

For information about setting up a document library with Windows SharePoint Services, see "Controlling Project Documents" on page 691.

Publishing Project Information to the Web

Suppose that one of your managing stakeholders asked you to publish key project information on her department's intranet Web page. You can do this by exporting a Microsoft Project view to HTML format.

To convert Microsoft Project information to HTML format, follow these steps:

1. In Microsoft Project, open the project that contains the information you want to publish to the Web.

   You do not have to display the exact information being published to the Web; you'll specify this in the export process.
2. Click File, Save As Web Page.

   The Save As dialog box appears.
3. In the Save In list, select the drive and folder where your HTML files are stored. This might be the folder for your intranet Web server. Make a note of the full path to the file, including server name, folder name, and filename.
4. In the File Name box, enter a name for the Web page you're creating.
5. Make sure that Web Page (*.html, *.htm) appears in the Save As Type box.
6. Click Save.

   The Export Wizard opens.
7. On the Welcome page, click Next.
8. On the Map page, click New Map and then click Next.
9. On the Map Options page, click the Tasks, Resources, or Assignments check box to indicate the type of data you're exporting. Under HTML Options, click Export Header Row/Import Includes Headers (see Figure 16-19). Click Next.

   The Mapping page opens.

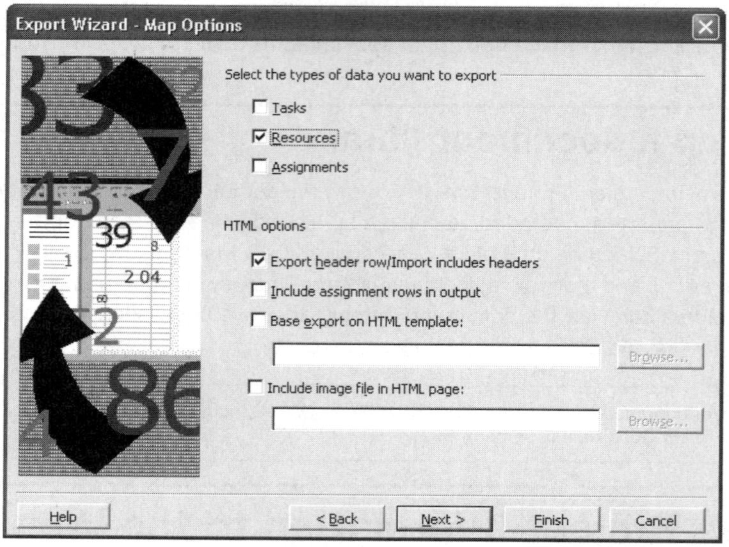

Figure 16-19. Specify whether you're including tasks, resources, or assignments to your new Web page.

10 In the Export Filter box, click All Tasks, All Resources; or apply any appropriate filter for the information you want to publish.

11 Click the Base On Table button and then choose the table that contains the fields of information you want to publish to the Web, for example, the Entry table. This procedure fills in the From: Microsoft Project Field and To: HTML Table Field columns. The Preview area shows what the HTML table will look like. Click Next.

12 On the End of Map Definition page, click Save Map if you will be publishing this information to the Web on a periodic basis.

13 Click Finish.

Your specified project information is now saved as an HTML file. You can view it in a Web browser to see how it looks. Microsoft Project adds title and project information (see Figure 16-20).

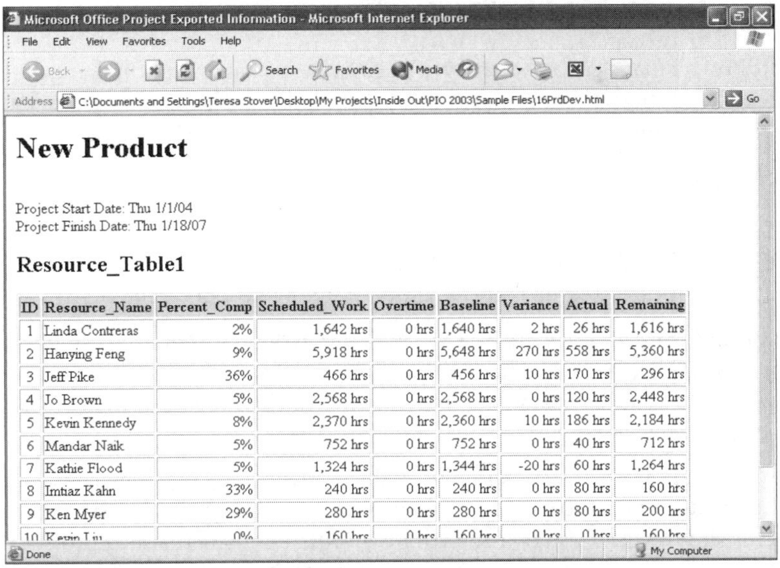

ID	Resource_Name	Percent_Comp	Scheduled_Work	Overtime	Baseline	Variance	Actual	Remaining
1	Linda Contreras	2%	1,642 hrs	0 hrs	1,640 hrs	2 hrs	26 hrs	1,616 hrs
2	Hanying Feng	9%	5,918 hrs	0 hrs	5,648 hrs	270 hrs	558 hrs	5,360 hrs
3	Jeff Pike	36%	466 hrs	0 hrs	456 hrs	10 hrs	170 hrs	296 hrs
4	Jo Brown	5%	2,568 hrs	0 hrs	2,568 hrs	0 hrs	120 hrs	2,448 hrs
5	Kevin Kennedy	8%	2,370 hrs	0 hrs	2,360 hrs	10 hrs	186 hrs	2,184 hrs
6	Mandar Naik	5%	752 hrs	0 hrs	752 hrs	0 hrs	40 hrs	712 hrs
7	Kathie Flood	5%	1,324 hrs	0 hrs	1,344 hrs	-20 hrs	60 hrs	1,264 hrs
8	Imtiaz Kahn	33%	240 hrs	0 hrs	240 hrs	0 hrs	80 hrs	160 hrs
9	Ken Myer	29%	280 hrs	0 hrs	280 hrs	0 hrs	80 hrs	200 hrs
10	Kevin Liu	0%	160 hrs	0 hrs	160 hrs	0 hrs	0 hrs	160 hrs

Figure 16-20. Review the project HTML Web page in a Web browser.

After you save your newly built HTML Web page, you or the Web master can upload it to your Web server.

Using Web Parts to Create a Project Information Web Page

You can use *Web Parts* to develop Web page components that convey key project information efficiently to your team or organization. Web Parts are self-contained, reusable components that consist of types of information varying from sophisticated dynamic Web page content embedded in a frame to concise text messages in HTML. Generally, most features and content that can be seen on a Web page can be included as a Web Part.

Web Parts group and position all key information logically and consistently; the information is accessed through hyperlinks. In addition, Web Parts can be enhanced and customized to suit your organization's needs.

Because you can use just about any type of Web page as a Web Part, you can save Microsoft Project information as a Web page and then include it as a Web Part.

For more information about building a Web page using Web Parts, refer to the Project Software Development Kit (SDK) and navigate to the "Creating Web Parts" section. To access the SDK, go to *http://msdn.microsoft.com/project*, click Microsoft Office Project 2003, and then click SDK Documentation.

Chapter 16

Creating Project XML Data

Microsoft Project plans can now be saved in XML (eXtensible Markup Language) format. XML is a self-defining, adaptable language that's used to define and interpret data between different applications, particularly in Web documents. With XML, you can:

- Define the structure of data used.
- Have your data be platform-independent.
- Automatically process data defined by XML.
- Define your own unique markup tags that hold your data elements.

NEW FEATURE! The simple and consistent nature of XML makes it very useful for exchanging data between many types of applications. Use the XML Reporting Wizard Component Object Model (COM) add-in to save your project as an XML file. You can use this project XML data in any applications that recognize XML.

By creating and applying an XSL template to the XML data, you can determine which project data is used and how it's formatted. Two sample XSL templates for HTML files are provided with Microsoft Project. If you're using your own XSL template for your project report, be sure that it's created and ready on your computer or network before running the wizard.

To generate a report using the XML Reporting Wizard, follow these steps:

1. Click View, Toolbars, Analysis to show the Analysis toolbar.

XML Reporting Wizard

2. On the Analysis toolbar, click XML Reporting Wizard.
3. On the first page of the XML Reporting Wizard, click Next.
4. In the Specify XML File wizard page, make sure that the New File option is selected and then click Next.
5. In the browser window that appears, navigate to the location on your computer or network where you want to save the new XML file containing your project data. In the File Name box, enter a filename, and then click Save.

   The Select The Transform To Apply Wizard page appears.
6. Click the Browse button to find and select the XSL template to apply to your data. The template you choose will determine the format and content of your project XML report. Click Open.
7. In the wizard again, with the path to your selected XSL in the Location box, click Next.
8. In the Complete The Report Wizard page, click Preview.

   Your browser opens with the new XML report.

9 In the Windows taskbar, click the browser button to review your report.

10 Return to Microsoft Project. If you're happy with the report, click Save. Navigate to the location you want, enter a name for the report, and then click Save.

If you want to change the report before saving it, click the Back button to return to previous wizard pages.

When you finish previewing and saving your new report, click Finish.

Inside Out

Data Access Pages are defunct

With earlier versions of Microsoft Project and Microsoft Access, you could create a Data Access Page (DAP), which enabled dynamic Web page reports that could be viewed in Microsoft Internet Explorer. DAP was made possible by the Microsoft Office Project OLE DB Provider. However, as of Project 2003, the Project OLE DB Provider is not installed, therefore DAP is no longer available.

There is an alternative, though. If you're set up with Microsoft Office Project Server 2003, you can use the Project Web Access to create dynamically updated Web reports for project information. All the reporting that a DAP could do is built in to Project Server, through the use of the SQL Server OLE DB Provider.

For more information about creating dynamic Web reports for project information in Project Web Access, download the online book "Microsoft Office Project Server 2003 Administrator's Guide." Go to *http://www.microsoft.com.downloads*, and then search for Project Server 2003.

Also refer to the Microsoft Project Software Development Kit (SDK). Go to *http://msdn.microsoft.com/project*, click Microsoft Project 2003, and then click SDK Documentation.

Importing and Exporting Information

When you import or export information between Microsoft Project and other applications, you're transferring information so that it appears as if the source information were originally created in the target application. Importing and exporting essentially converts the information from the *file format* of the source application to that of the target application.

Microsoft Project supports importing and exporting with the file formats shown in Table 16-2.

Table 16-2. Supported File Types

File Format	Filename Extension
Microsoft Project files	*.mpp*
Microsoft Project templates	*.mpt*
Microsoft Project databases	*.mpd*
Web pages	*.html* or *.htm*

Table 16-2. Supported File Types

File Format	Filename Extension
Microsoft Access databases	*.mdb*
Microsoft Excel workbooks	*.xls*
Microsoft Excel PivotTables	*.xls*
Text files (tab delimited)	*.txt*
CSV Text files (comma delimited)	*.csv*
XML format files	*.xml*

Information can also be exported to or imported from an ODBC (Open Database Connectivity) database, which is a protocol used to access data in SQL database servers. With ODBC drivers installed, it is possible to connect a Microsoft Project database to SQL databases.

Importing Information into Microsoft Project

You can bring information into Microsoft Project from another application and another file format by *importing* it. Importing converts another application's file format into the Microsoft Project file format. You start an import process by simply using the File, Open command.

To import data to Microsoft Project, follow these steps:

1. In Microsoft Project, click File, Open.
2. In the Files of Type list of the Open dialog box, click the file format of the file you are importing; for example, Microsoft Access Databases (*.mdb), or Text (tab delimited) (*.txt).
3. Browse to the drive and folder that contain the file you want to import.
4. Click the filename of the file you are importing and then click the Open button.
5. Read the Import Wizard welcome page and then click Next.
6. On the Map page, select the New Map option. Click Next.
7. On the Import Mode page, select how you want to import the data (see Figure 16-21). Click Next.

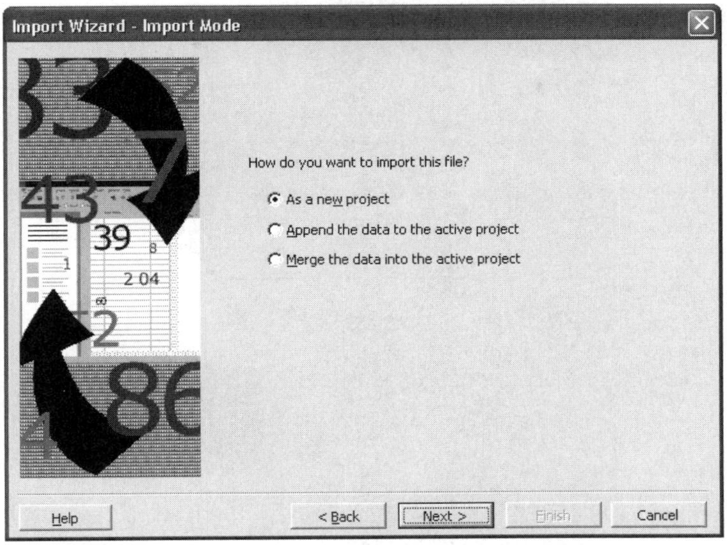

Figure 16-21. Select how you want the imported data to be brought into Microsoft Project.

8 On the Map Options page, under Select The Types Of Data You Want To Import, click the Tasks, Resources, or Assignments check box as appropriate. Click Next.

You see separate Mapping pages for each data type you select on this page.

9 On the Mapping page, complete the fields to specify the information to be imported. In the To: Microsoft Office Project Field column of the table, specify how fields from the source application are to map to specific Microsoft Project fields (see Figure 16-22). Any unmapped data appears in red and will not be imported. Click Next.

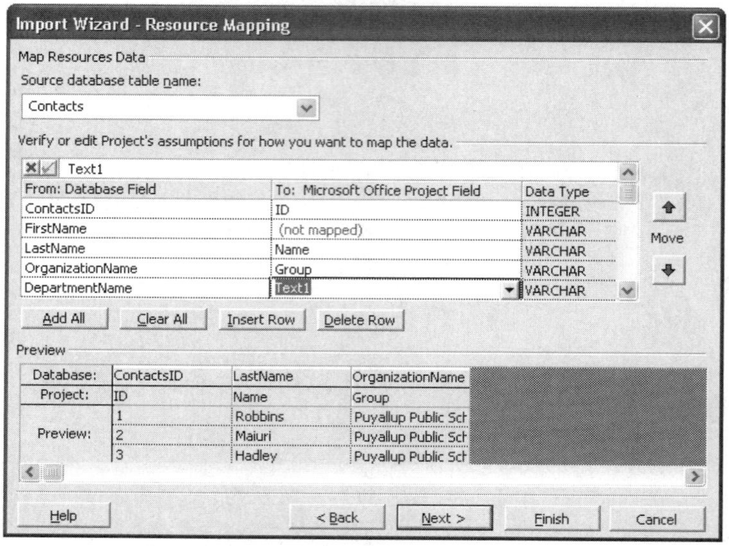

Figure 16-22. Specify how fields from the source application are to be mapped to Microsoft Project fields.

10 On the End of Map Definition page, click Finish.

The imported data appears in your project plan as you specified. This process might take a few minutes, depending on the source of the information and the speed of your computer. However, after the information is imported, it's set in your project plan. Save the project and the information is there for you to work with instantly, as if you had originally created it in Microsoft Project.

For information about importing information from Excel to Microsoft Project, see "Importing and Exporting with Excel" on page 521.

Exporting Information from Microsoft Project

You can use information from Microsoft Project in another application and another file format by *exporting* it. Exporting converts your Microsoft Project information into the file format of another application. You start an export process by simply using the File, Save As command.

To export data from Microsoft Project, follow these steps:

1 In Microsoft Project, open the project that contains the information you want to export.

2 Click File, Save As.

3 In the Save In list, select the drive and folder where you want to save the new exported file.

4 In the File Name box, enter the name for the new exported file.

By default, the name of the project is adopted, and the extension representing the new file format will be added.

5 In the Save As Type list, click the file format to which you want to export your project information. For example, if you want to export your project information to XML, click XML Format (*.xml).

If you want to export your data to a Microsoft SQL Server or an Oracle Server, click the ODBC button and then skip to Step 6.

6 Click the Save button.

The Export Wizard opens and guides you step by step through selecting the specifics of data mapping what you want from Microsoft Project to the target file. Some of the specific steps and choices of the Export Wizard vary depending on the file type you are exporting to.

7 Work through each page of the Export Wizard, clicking Next after making your selections on each page.

8 On the final page, click Finish. Microsoft Project exports your project information to the selected file format.

Tip **Use the Export table**

If you want to export a wide and representative range of fields, click in the Export Wizard Task Mapping or Resource Mapping page, click the Base On Table button, and then click Export. The task Export table contains more than 70 task fields. The resource Export table contains more than 20 resource fields.

For information about exporting information from Microsoft Project to Excel, see "Importing and Exporting with Excel" on page 521.

Chapter 17

Integrating Microsoft Project with Microsoft Excel

Several techniques for information interchange are at your disposal to exchange information in Microsoft Office Project 2003 with Microsoft Excel. Not only can you integrate Excel information into your project plan, but you can also feed information from Project 2003 to an Excel workbook. Such capabilities provide for a greater ease of information sharing among team members and project stakeholders. Transferring data between Microsoft Project and Excel can simplify aspects of building your project plan, tracking progress, reporting status, and communicating with stakeholders

Using the special Excel-to-Project templates, you can have stakeholders build task lists and even a more elaborate project plan using Excel, and import those files seamlessly into Project. You can copy resource lists from an Excel worksheet. You can embed an Excel chart into a Gantt chart. You can even link Excel information in Microsoft Project to automatically update when that information changes.

Going the other direction, you can easily transfer portions of your project data into Microsoft Excel, so you can take advantage of the formatting and calculation options available there. For example, you can export project cost or earned value data to Excel. You might want Excel to crunch tracking data or assignment information in a particular way. For example, you can create pivot tables with project data. You can also create graphs, such as S-curves, showing project performance information.

For more information about creating pivot tables and S-curves using project data in Excel, see "Calculating Project Information in Microsoft Excel" on page 410. For information about exchanging information with other applications besides Excel, see Chapter 16, "Exchanging Information with Other Applications."

The methods for transferring information between Microsoft Project and Excel are as follows:

- Copy and paste sheet or graphic information.
- Insert, or embed, a Microsoft Project file into an Excel file.
- Insert, or embed, an Excel workbook or chart into a Microsoft Project file.

- Link information dynamically between the Microsoft Project and Excel files, so that when that information changes in one file, the same information in the other file automatically updates to reflect that change.
- Open, or import, an Excel file as a Microsoft Project file.

  You can also import a Microsoft Project file as an Excel file.
- Save, or export, a Microsoft Project file as an Excel file. The file is converted to the Excel file format so it can simply be opened in Excel. You can also export an Excel file as a Microsoft Project file.

These techniques are all covered throughout this chapter.

Copying Between Microsoft Project and Excel

By using the Copy and Paste commands, you can easily exchange sheet data and static graphics between Microsoft Project and Excel.

You can also use the Copy command to insert an embedded object.

See "Embedding Between Microsoft Project and Excel" later in this chapter on page 510.

Copying Information from Excel

You can copy information from Excel worksheets and graphs and paste it into your project plan.

Copying Sheet Information from Excel

Anything in Excel worksheet cells can easily be copied and pasted into a Microsoft Project table. However, you need to prepare either the Excel workbook or the Microsoft Project table ahead of time. The order and data type of the columns of information must match.

Match the Columns

Copying and pasting information is one of the easiest ways to get information from Excel to Microsoft Project. However, to paste successfully, the columns of Excel information must match the Microsoft Project columns into which you're pasting.

For example, suppose that your Excel worksheet contains four columns you want to copy to your project plan: Task Name, Resource, Duration, and Fixed Cost. Add, remove, and rearrange columns in a Microsoft Project task table so that these four columns appear next to each other (see Figure 17-1).

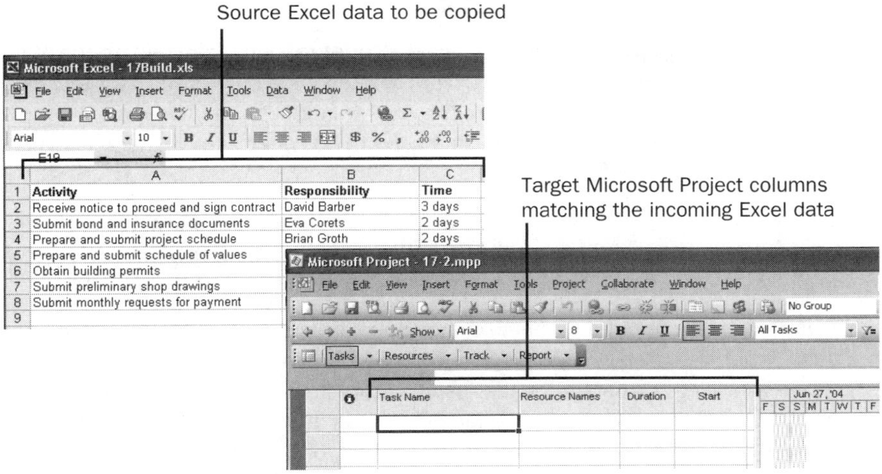

Figure 17-1. Make sure that the order and type of Microsoft Project columns match the Excel data being copied and pasted.

The following is a list of techniques you can use to arrange your Microsoft Project view to match the incoming Excel data:

- Apply a different table to a Microsoft Project sheet view. Click View, Table and then click the table you want.
- Add a column to a Microsoft Project table. Click in the column to the right of where you want the new column to appear. Click Insert, Column. In the Field Name box, click the field you want to add and then click OK.
- Remove a column from a table. Click the column heading and then click the Delete key.
- Move a column to a different location. Click the heading to select the entire column. Drag the left or right edge of the column body (not the heading) to the location you want.

  A vertical gray marker appears to show where the column will be moved.

To copy and paste Excel worksheet cells into Microsoft Project, do the following:

1. Arrange the source Excel columns to match the target Microsoft Project field order and data type. Or, arrange the target columns in Microsoft Project to match the incoming Excel data.
2. In Microsoft Excel, select the set of cells to be copied.
3. On the Standard toolbar, click Copy.

Copy

4. In Microsoft Project, select the *anchor cell* in the table where you want the incoming information to begin to be pasted.

   This anchor cell will become the location of the upper-left cell of data selected in Excel.
5. On the Standard toolbar, click Paste.

Paste

Match the Data Types

There's no law that says you have to paste a set of resource names into the Microsoft Project Resource Name column. Although you probably wouldn't want to, technically you can paste those resource names into the Task Name field, the Group field, the Contact field, or even the WBS field because all these are *text fields*. Any of these fields can accept any text field information.

However, you could not paste that same set of resource names into the Work field or the Start field, for example, because they are incompatible *data types*. Work is a *duration field*, and Start is a *date field*. Those resource names need to go into a text field.

So when we say you need to match the columns of information from Excel to Microsoft Project, what we're really saying is that you need to match the data types. The data type specifies the kind of information that can be stored in a field; for example, text, number, or percentage. The data type also specifies the format that information can take; for example, **14d** for a duration field, **6/29/04** for a date field, or **$35.90** for a currency field.

If you don't want to use the exact Microsoft Project fields, you can use custom fields that are of the matching *data type*, such as text, duration, currency, date, number, and so on. Examples of custom fields are Text1, Duration5, Currency3, and so on.

To add a custom field to a Microsoft Project table, click in the column to the right of where you want the new column to appear. Click Insert, Column. In the Field Name box, click the field you want to add and then click OK.

For more information about working with custom fields, see "Customizing Fields" on page 788. For a list of custom fields available in Microsoft Project, see "Custom Fields and Custom Outline Codes" in Appendix B.

Copying Graphics from Excel

You can copy an Excel graph and paste it into certain areas of Microsoft Project as a picture. You can even copy Excel worksheet cells, and instead of pasting those cells into table cells, you can paste them as a picture in Microsoft Project.

To paste Excel information as a static picture, do the following:

1. In Excel, select the chart or other data you want to insert as a picture in Microsoft Project.
2. On the Standard toolbar, click Copy.
3. In your Microsoft Project file, display the location where you want to place the picture. The following specific locations in Microsoft Project can accept pictures:
   - Chart area of a Gantt chart
   - Notes tab on the Task Information, Resource Information, or Assignment Information dialog box
   - Objects box in the Task Form or Resource Form

- Notes box in the Task Form or Resource Form
- Header, footer, or legend of a printable view or report

4 Click Edit, Paste Special.

The Paste Special dialog box appears (see Figure 17-2).

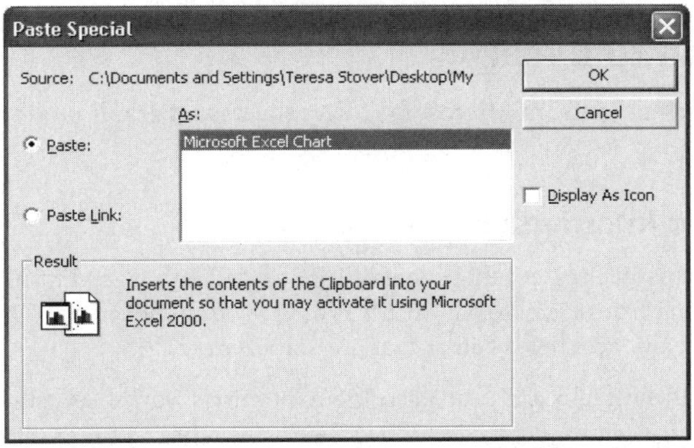

Figure 17-2. Use the Paste Special dialog box to specify that you want to insert the Excel information as a picture.

5 Select the Paste option.

6 In the As box, click Picture or Picture (Bitmap).

This option ensures that the data, whether it's a chart or a set of worksheet cells, is pasted as a graphic rather than as an embedded graphic or straight text.

> **Note** If the Paste Special command is not available for the location where you want to paste the picture, press Ctrl+V instead.

7 Click OK.

The new picture is pasted in Microsoft Project at your selected location (see Figure 17-3).

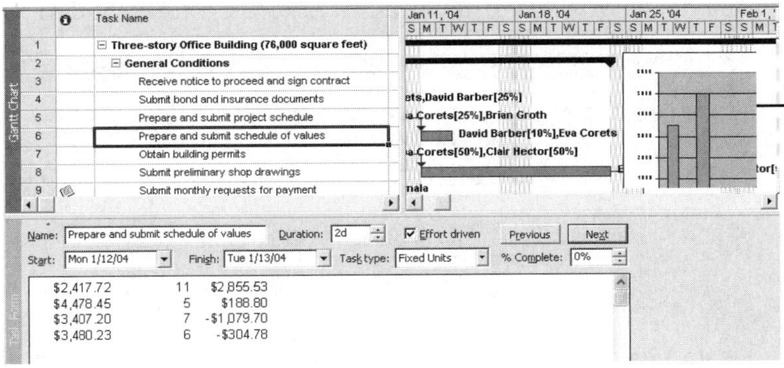

Figure 17-3. The Excel information appears as a picture in your selected Microsoft Project location.

Although static pictures look like embedded objects, they cannot be opened and edited. However, they can be moved and resized.

For more information about embedded objects, see "Embedding an Excel Object in Project" later in this chapter on page 510.

Copying Information to Excel

You can copy information from Microsoft Project sheets and graphs and paste it into Excel worksheets.

Copying Sheet Information to Excel

Anything in a Microsoft Project table can easily be copied and pasted into Excel worksheet cells. Unlike copying from Excel to Microsoft Project, you do not need to match columns or data types because all Excel fields can accept any data types.

To copy Microsoft Project table cells and paste them into Excel worksheet cells, follow these steps:

1. In Microsoft Project, display the view that contains the information you want to copy to Excel. If necessary, apply a different table or add a column that contains the information you need.
2. Select the cells or columns you want to copy.

   To select a column, click its heading. Select multiple adjacent columns by dragging across the column headings. Select multiple nonadjacent columns by holding down Ctrl while you click each column heading.
3. On the Standard toolbar, click Copy Cell.
4. In Excel, select the anchor cell in the worksheet where you want the incoming information to begin to be pasted. This anchor cell will become the location of the upper-left cell of data selected in Microsoft Project.
5. On the Standard toolbar, click Paste.

   The selected project data is inserted into the Excel worksheet starting at the anchor cell. Adjust column widths in the worksheet as necessary to see the data (see Figure 17-4).

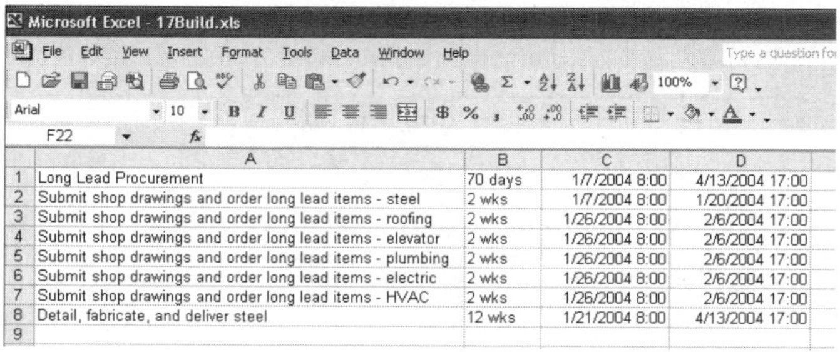

	A	B	C	D
1	Long Lead Procurement	70 days	1/7/2004 8:00	4/13/2004 17:00
2	Submit shop drawings and order long lead items - steel	2 wks	1/7/2004 8:00	1/20/2004 17:00
3	Submit shop drawings and order long lead items - roofing	2 wks	1/26/2004 8:00	2/6/2004 17:00
4	Submit shop drawings and order long lead items - elevator	2 wks	1/26/2004 8:00	2/6/2004 17:00
5	Submit shop drawings and order long lead items - plumbing	2 wks	1/26/2004 8:00	2/6/2004 17:00
6	Submit shop drawings and order long lead items - electric	2 wks	1/26/2004 8:00	2/6/2004 17:00
7	Submit shop drawings and order long lead items - HVAC	2 wks	1/26/2004 8:00	2/6/2004 17:00
8	Detail, fabricate, and deliver steel	12 wks	1/21/2004 8:00	4/13/2004 17:00
9				

Figure 17-4. Your project data is pasted into the Excel worksheet.

Copying Graphics to Excel

You can copy a picture of any Microsoft Project view and then paste it into Excel. To do this, follow these steps:

1. In Microsoft Project, display the view you want to capture as a picture for Excel.
2. Manipulate the view to show the information the way you want it to appear in the target application.
3. Click Edit, Copy Picture.
4. In the Copy Picture dialog box, select the options you want.

   In the Render Image section, select whether the image is to be viewed on a computer screen (the default), to be printed, or to be used in a GIF image file.

   In the Copy section, select the Rows On Screen option (the default) if you want the rows currently showing on the screen to be copied, or if only selected rows should be copied.

   In the Timescale section, select the As Shown On Screen option (the default) if you want the timescale to be represented as set in the current view. Select the From and To boxes if you want to specify the timescale and date range now.

   When finished setting the Copy Picture options, click OK.
5. In Excel, select the location in the worksheet where you want to paste the picture of the view.
6. On the Standard toolbar, click Paste.

   A static picture of the Microsoft Project view is pasted into Excel (see Figure 17-5). You can move the image by dragging it. You can also resize the image by dragging any of the edges.

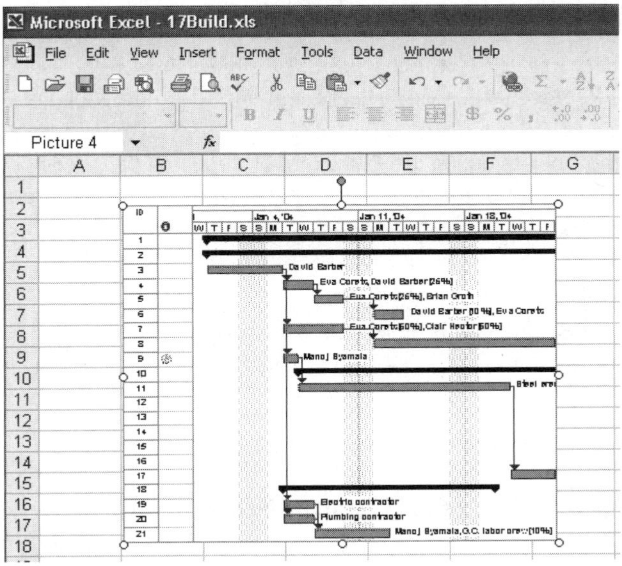

Figure 17-5. The copied picture of your Microsoft Project view is pasted into Excel.

Embedding Between Microsoft Project and Excel

You can exchange information between Microsoft Project and Excel by embedding the source application as an *embedded object* in the target application. When you embed an object in one application that originated in a different application, you're basically inserting an entire file, with all of its source application's capabilities, into the target application.

This means that not only can you have a picture of a Gantt chart in an Excel worksheet, but you can double-click that Gantt Chart picture to access Microsoft Project commands to change data in the Gantt Chart. You can then switch to the Resource Sheet and change information there as well.

Likewise, in Microsoft Project, not only can you have just a picture of an S-curve graph generated by Excel, but you can double-click it to launch Excel and edit the format of the graph or even the underlying data for the graph.

Embedding an Excel Object in Project

You can insert all or part of an Excel worksheet or chart into Microsoft Project as an embedded object.

Embedding Copied Excel Information in a Project File

To copy and paste selected Excel information as an embedded object, follow these steps:

1. In Excel, select the data or chart you want to insert as an embedded object in Microsoft Project.
2. On the Standard toolbar, click Copy.
3. In your Microsoft Project file, display the location where you want to place the object.

   Only the chart area of a Gantt chart and the Objects box in the Task Form or Resource Form can accept a chart or worksheet fragment as an embedded object.

> **Note** To apply the Objects box in the Task Form or Resource Form, click in the form area to make it active (if it's part of a combination view such as the Task Entry view). Click Format, Details, Objects.

4. Click Edit, Paste Special.
5. In the Paste Special dialog box, select the Paste option.
6. In the As box, click Microsoft Excel Worksheet or Microsoft Excel Chart.
7. Click OK.

   The data or chart is pasted in Microsoft Project.

Embedding an Entire Excel File in a Project File

To embed an entire existing Excel file into the chart portion of the Gantt Chart, follow these steps:

1. In Microsoft Project, open the project plan in which you want to embed the Excel file.
2. Display the location where you want to insert the file.

   Only the chart area of a Gantt chart and the Notes tab in the Task Information, Resource Information, or Assignment Information dialog box can accept an Excel file as an embedded object.
3. Click Insert, Object.
4. In the Insert Object dialog box, select the Create From File option.
5. Click the Browse button and find the location of the Excel file you want to insert. Double-click the file.

   The file's path and name are entered in the File box in the Insert Object dialog box.
6. If you want the embedded Excel file to be linked to the source, select the Link check box.

   If you link the file, any changes to the file in Excel update the embedded object in Microsoft Project. If you try to change the embedded object, you'll see a message indicating that the object is linked, and if you change information, the link will be removed. In this way, the linked information is protected.

   If you don't link the object, you're essentially making a copy of the original object that becomes a separate entity from the original. You can change information in the embedded version without affecting the source data.
7. If you want the embedded object to be displayed as an Excel icon in your project, rather than showing as part of the worksheet, select the Display As Icon check box.
8. Click OK.

   The Excel file appears in the area you selected. Drag to move or resize the object as needed (Figure 17-6).

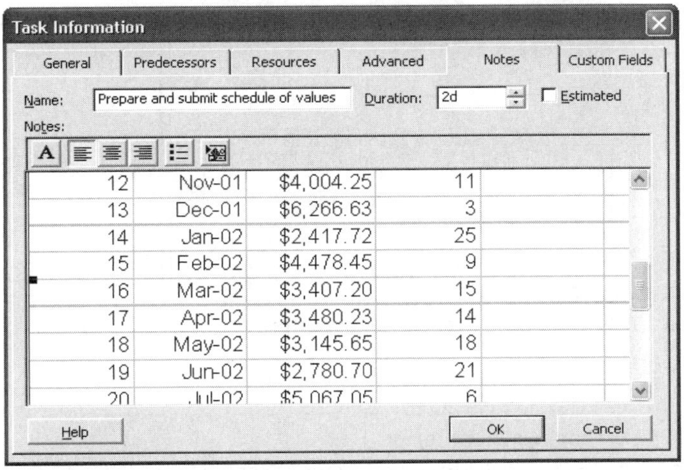

Figure 17-6. The selected Excel file is embedded in the Notes tab in the Task Information dialog box.

Tip **Embed an object in a project note**
You can embed an Excel file in a note associated with the project as a whole. First, add the project summary task by clicking Tools, Options, View and then selecting the Show Project Summary Task check box.

Double-click the project summary task. In the Summary Task Information dialog box, click the Notes tab. Click the Insert Object button and add the Excel file.

Creating a New Excel Object in Project

You can create a new Excel workbook or chart as an embedded object in your project. In this case, the new Excel object exists only within your project file. To do this, follow these steps:

1. In your project plan, display the location where you want to embed the object.

   Only the chart area of a Gantt chart and the Notes tab in the Task Information, Resource Information, or Assignment Information dialog box can accept an Excel file as an embedded object.
2. Click Insert, Object.
3. In the Insert Object dialog box, be sure that the Create New option is selected.
4. In the Object Type box, click Microsoft Excel Chart or Microsoft Excel Worksheet.
5. Specify whether you want the new object to be displayed as an icon in the project, and then click OK.

   An Excel worksheet or chart appears in the location you selected (see Figure 17-7).

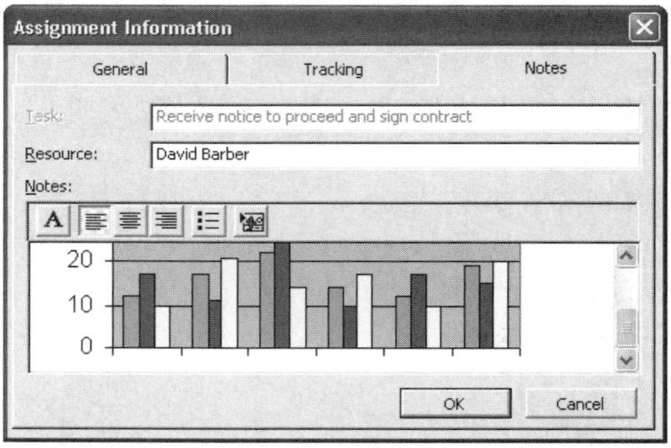

Figure 17-7. Embed a new chart in your project plan.

6. Double-click the Excel object to start adding your information.

Tip **Delete an embedded Excel object**
To delete an embedded object anywhere in your project plan, click it and then press Delete.

Working with the Embedded Excel Object

To open and work with an embedded Excel object, simply double-click the object. The Microsoft Project menus and toolbars change to Excel menus and toolbars (see Figure 17-8). Use these controls to work with the Excel object as needed.

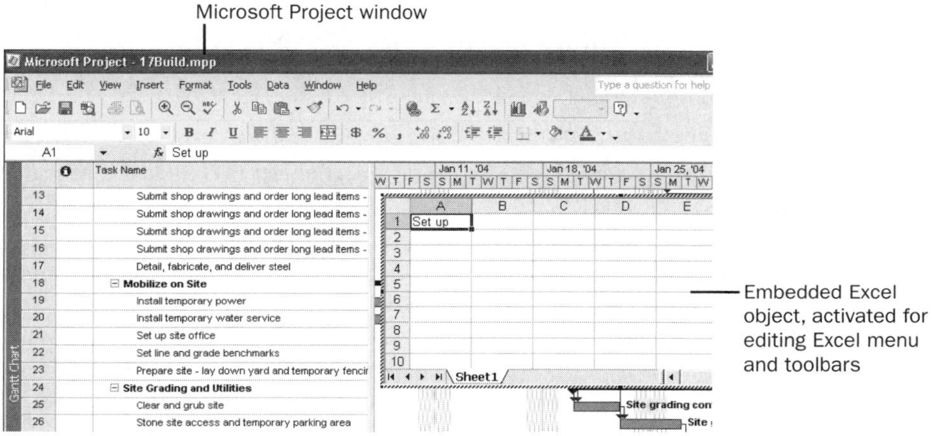

Figure 17-8. When you double-click an embedded Excel object, the Microsoft Project menus and toolbars change to those of Excel.

When finished editing the Excel object, click outside the object frame. The menus and toolbars return to those of Microsoft Project again.

> **Tip Show an embedded file in a form**
> You cannot insert an object in the Notes box of a Task Form or Resource Form. However, after you have embedded an Excel file on the Notes tab in the Task Information or Resource Information dialog box, you can work with it from the Notes box in a form. You can also delete the object from the Notes box.
>
> To apply the Objects box in the Task Form or Resource Form, first click in the form area to make it active if necessary. Click Format, Details, Notes.

Embedding a Project File in Excel

You can embed a new or existing Microsoft Project file as an object in an Excel worksheet. When you double-click the Microsoft Project object in Excel, Microsoft Project menus and commands temporarily replace those of Excel, so you can create or edit project information without leaving the Excel file.

Embedding an Existing Project File in Excel

To embed an existing Microsoft Project file in Excel, follow these steps:

1 Open the Excel file in which you want to embed the existing Microsoft Project file.
2 Select the location where you want the Microsoft Project object to be embedded.
3 Click Insert, Object.
4 In the Insert Object dialog box, click the Create From File tab.
5 Click the Browse button. The Browse window appears. Navigate through your computer's filing system (and onto your network if applicable) to find the drive and folder where the project file is located.
6 Find and double-click the file.

   Its path and name are entered in the File box in the Insert Object dialog box.
7 If you want the embedded Microsoft Project object to be linked to the source file, select the Link check box.

   If you link the object, any changes in the source project plan update the embedded object. If you try to change the embedded object, you'll see a message indicating that the object is linked, and you cannot change the information (which protects the integrity of the source information).

   If you don't link the object, you're making a copy of the original object, which becomes a separate entity from the original. You can change the embedded project without affecting information in the original project.
8 If you want the embedded project to be displayed as a Microsoft Project icon in Excel, rather than showing a part of the Gantt Chart or other view, select the Display As Icon check box.
9 Click OK.

   Part of a view of the selected project file appears in the location you selected (see Figure 17-9).

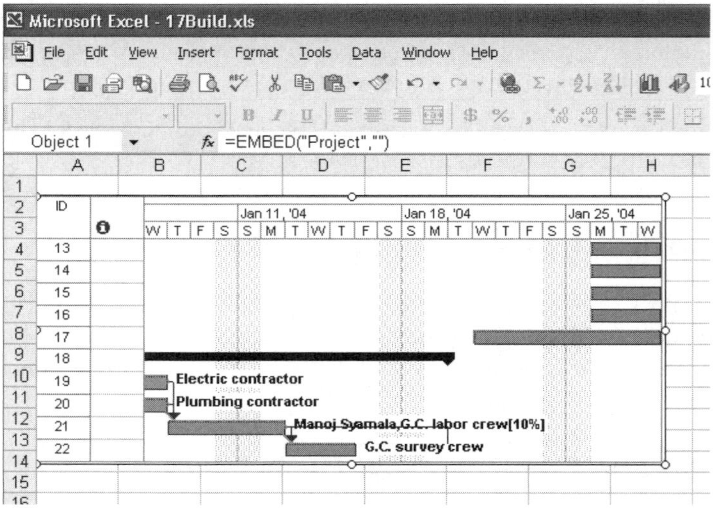

Figure 17-9. The selected project is embedded in Excel.

If you selected the Display As Icon check box, the embedded project file appears as the Microsoft Project icon (by default) in the selected location. This is most useful when you have limited space in your Excel worksheet.

Creating a New Project File in Excel

You can create a new Microsoft Project file as an embedded object in Excel. In this case, the object exists only within the Excel file. To create a new Microsoft Project file within Excel, follow these steps:

1. Open the Excel file in which you want to create a new Microsoft Project file as an embedded object.
2. Select the location where you want the new Microsoft Project object to be embedded.
3. Click Insert, Object.
4. In the dialog box, click the Create New tab.
5. In the Object Type box, click Microsoft Project Document (see Figure 17-10).

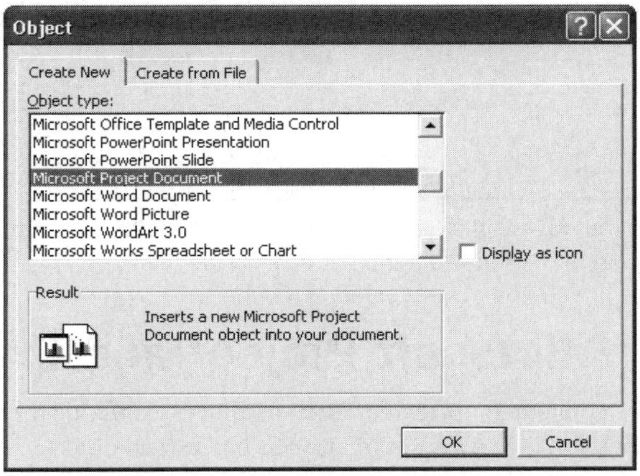

Figure 17-10. Use the Insert Object dialog box to create a Microsoft Project file as an embedded object.

6. If you want the embedded project to be displayed as an icon in Excel, rather than showing a part of the Gantt Chart or other view, select the Display As Icon check box.
7. Click OK.

   Part of a view of the new project file appears.

   If you selected the Display As Icon check box, the embedded project file appears as the Microsoft Project icon (by default) in the selected location.
8. Double-click the new project to add information to it on the spot.

Working with the Embedded Project File

Whenever you want to work with the embedded project file, just double-click the object. The Excel menus change to reflect the relevant Microsoft Project menus (see Figure 17-11). You can use Microsoft Project in the usual way: switching views, applying tables and filters, changing data, running calculations, and so on.

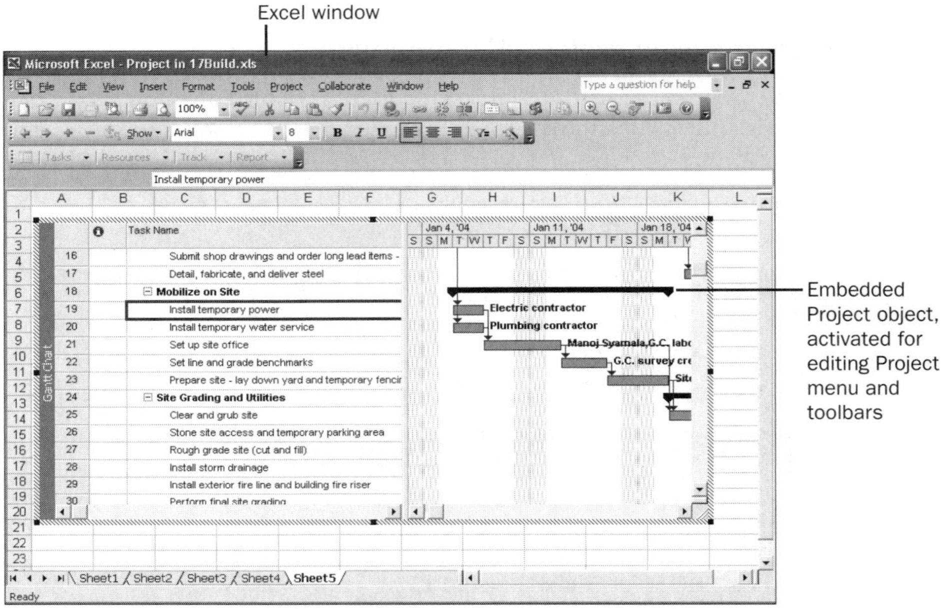

Figure 17-11. When you double-click an embedded Project object, the Excel menus and toolbars change to those of Microsoft Project.

Linking Between Microsoft Project and Excel

You can take the use of embedded objects one step further—by *linking* them to their source. With a dynamic link between source and target, your embedded object can be updated whenever the source changes. The source and target information are essentially the same file, rather than just a separate copy, which is the case when they are not linked.

Creating a link between embedded objects is as easy as selecting a check box when you're embedding the object, whether it's a fragment you're inserting using the Paste Special dialog box or an entire file you're embedding using the Insert Object dialog box.

Be aware that when you link information between Microsoft Project and Excel, you always need to know the current location of the linked file and its update status. If the linked file is moved, the link is broken. If the information in the linked file becomes obsolete, the linked information also becomes out-of-date. However, when the conditions are right, linking is an excellent means of maintaining comprehensive and current information.

Linking from Excel to Project

In Microsoft Project, you can link an Excel worksheet fragment or chart in the chart area of a Gantt chart or the Objects box in the Task Form or Resource Form. To do this, follow the steps listed under "Embedding Copied Excel Information in a Project File" earlier in this chapter. In the Paste Special dialog box, select the Paste Link option.

You can link an entire existing Excel file in the chart area of a Gantt chart and the Notes tab in the Task Information, Resource Information, or Assignment Information dialog box. To do this, follow the steps listed under "Embedding an Entire Excel File in a Project File" earlier in this chapter. In the Insert Object dialog box, select the Link check box.

You can also copy worksheet cells and link them into Microsoft Project table cells. The data looks as if they were originally typed in Microsoft Project, but they're actually linked to Excel data. To link worksheet cell data in a Microsoft Project table, follow these steps:

1. Arrange the source Excel columns to match the target Microsoft Project field order and data type. Or, arrange the target columns in Microsoft Project to match the incoming Excel data.
2. In Excel, select the information to be linked in Microsoft Project and then click Copy on the Standard toolbar.
3. In Microsoft Project, display the view and click the cell that is to become the anchor cell for the linked information.

   This anchor cell becomes the location of the upper-left cell of data selected in Excel.
4. Click Edit, Paste Special.
5. In the Paste Special dialog box, click the Paste Link option.
6. In the As box, click Text Data (see Figure 17-12).

   If you select Microsoft Excel Worksheet, a picture of the selected cells is embedded and linked, rather than flowing into the table cells as text.

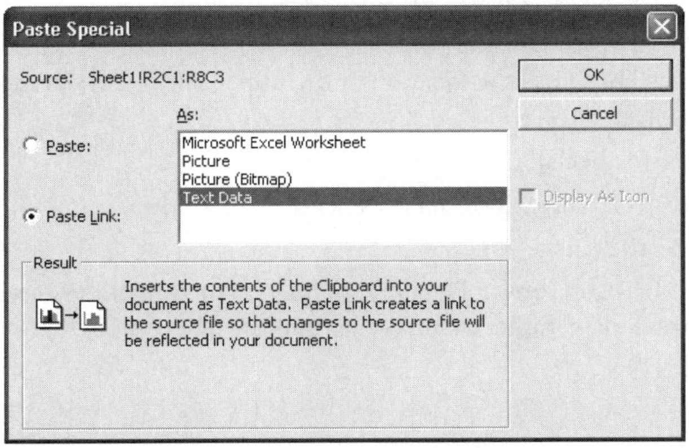

Figure 17-12. Choose these options in the Paste Special dialog box to link worksheet data with project table data.

7. Click OK.

   The linked information appears at your selection point in your project. When changes are made to the information in the source application, those changes can be reflected in this project file.

Troubleshooting

You're getting paste error messages

Paste error messages are the result of a mismatch between the data type of the incoming Excel data and the Microsoft Project columns into which they're supposed to go. Click through the paste error messages to dismiss them.

Then review the order and type of the Excel data and the order and type of the Project sheet and see where the problem is. Make any necessary corrections, and repeat the Copy and Paste Special operation again.

Linking from Project to Excel

In Excel, you can link to an embedded Microsoft Project file. To do this, follow the steps listed under "Embedding an Existing Project File in Excel" earlier in this chapter. In the Insert Object dialog box, select the Link To File option.

You can also copy a set of table cells in Microsoft Project and link them into Excel worksheet cells. The data looks as if they were originally typed in Excel, but they're actually linked to Microsoft Project data. To link Microsoft Project table data to Excel worksheet cells, follow these steps:

1. In Microsoft Project, select the table data to be linked in Excel.
2. On the Standard toolbar, click Copy.
3. In Excel, click the cell that is to become the anchor cell for the linked information.

   This anchor cell becomes the location of the upper-left cell of data selected in Microsoft Project.
4. Click Edit, Paste Special.
5. In the Paste Special dialog box, click the Paste Link option.
6. In the As box, click Text.

   If you select Microsoft Project Document Object, a picture of the selected project data is embedded and linked, rather than flowing into the table cells as text (see Figure 17-13).

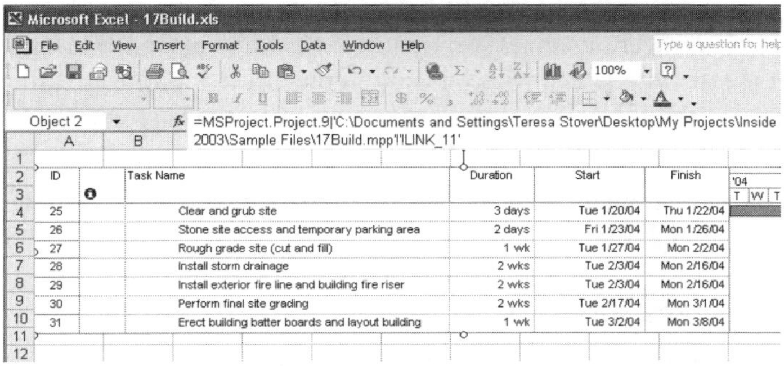

Figure 17-13. Selected project data inserted into Excel as a linked picture.

7 Click OK.

The linked information appears at the worksheet selection (see Figure 17-14). When changes are made to the data in the project plan, those changes are reflected in this linked data in Excel.

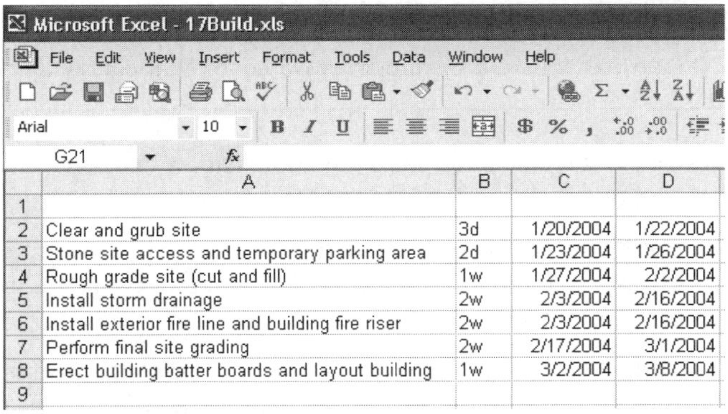

Microsoft Excel - 17Build.xls
File Edit View Insert Format Tools Data Window Help
Arial 10
G21
Clear and grub site 3d 1/20/2004 1/22/2004
Stone site access and temporary parking area 2d 1/23/2004 1/26/2004
Rough grade site (cut and fill) 1w 1/27/2004 2/2/2004
Install storm drainage 2w 2/3/2004 2/16/2004
Install exterior fire line and building fire riser 2w 2/3/2004 2/16/2004
Perform final site grading 2w 2/17/2004 3/1/2004
Erect building batter boards and layout building 1w 3/2/2004 3/8/2004

Figure 17-14. Selected project data inserted into Excel as linked sheet text.

Working with a Linked Object

After you have linked information in Microsoft Project or Excel, you can manipulate the information in certain ways. You can edit the source information and also accept updates in the target file from the source. You can review a list of all linked information in the file and then redirect or break the link if needed.

Editing Linked Information

If you try to change information in an embedded object, a message indicates that you cannot do so from within the target application without breaking the link, therefore protecting the linked information.

However, you can double-click a linked object to launch the source file in the source application so you can make the changes you want. This is different from working with an unlinked embedded object, with which you can work in the target application, using the temporarily changed menus and tools. With linked information, you always need to work in the source because the source always updates the target.

When finished updating the source, click Save and then return to the target application. Your changes are reflected there.

Updating Linked Objects

In both Microsoft Project and Excel, when you open the file that contains links, by default you will see a dialog box prompting you to update the file using the link (see Figure 17-15).

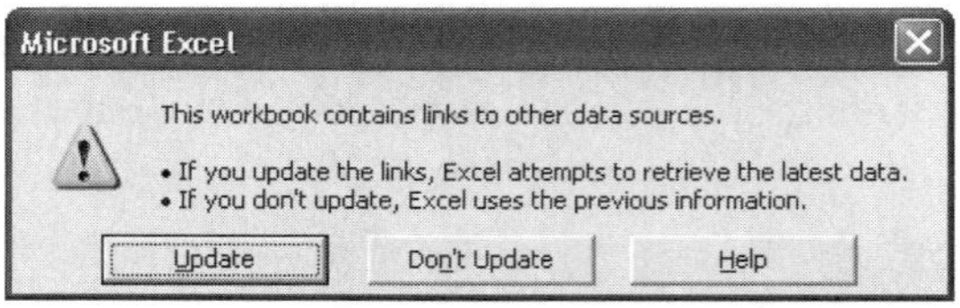

Figure 17-15. When you open a project plan or workbook that contains links, you'll see a message like this.

Click Yes to re-establish the link and update any information that has changed since the last time you opened and updated this file.

In Microsoft Project, if you do not want to see this alert each time you open the project containing links, click Tools, Options and then click the View tab. Clear the Show OLE Links Indicators check box.

In Excel, if you do not want to see this alert each time you open the workbook, click Tools, Options and then click the Edit tab. Clear the Ask To Update Automatic Links check box.

Viewing Links

In Microsoft Project, to review and work with links in your project, follow these steps:

1. Click Edit, Links.

   The Links dialog box appears, showing all links existing in your project file.
2. If you chose not to update a link when opening the project file or if you turned the prompt off, you can select a link and click Update Now.
3. If the location of the linked workbook has changed, you can update the location information in the project by clicking Change Source.
4. To break the link with the source application, click Break Link.

   When you break a link, the information remains in the project file as a separate embedded object. You can still view and edit the Excel information; it's simply no longer linked.

To review and work with links in Excel, follow these steps:

1. In Excel, open the workbook containing the links.
2. Click Edit, Links.

   The Edit Links dialog box appears, showing all links existing in the workbook (see Figure 17-16).

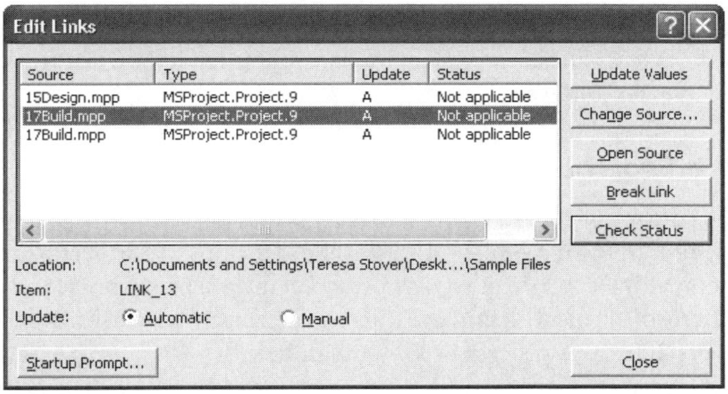

Figure 17-16. Use the Edit Links dialog box in Excel to review and update the links in the current workbook.

3. If you chose not to update a link when opening the workbook or if you turned the prompt off, you can select a link and click Update Values.
4. If the location of the linked project has changed, update the location information in the workbook by clicking Change Source.
5. To break the link with the source application, click Break Link.

   When you break a link, the project information remains in the workbook file as a separate embedded object. You can still view and edit the project information; it's simply no longer linked.

Importing and Exporting with Excel

You can *import* information from Excel into Microsoft Project. You can also *export* information from Microsoft Project into Excel. When you import information, you're bringing information in a foreign file format (for example, the Excel .xls file format) into the current application (for example, Microsoft Project, which uses the .mpp file format). When you export information, you're saving information in the current application in a different file format, so that it can be easily opened by another application. In both cases, the information will look as if it were created originally in the target application.

Importing from Excel to Microsoft Project

Using two templates specifically designed for integration, importing task, resource, and even assignment information from Excel to Microsoft Project is a breeze. With these templates, the most commonly used fields are present and the fields are already recognized and mapped in Microsoft Project. All you have to do is open the Excel file and make a couple of choices, and the data is imported into your project plan.

One template is designed just for task information being imported into the default Entry table of the Gantt Chart. Another template allows for more detailed project information, including resources and assignments.

If a team member or other stakeholder has created project information in Excel without using one of these templates, never fear. You can still import an Excel workbook into Microsoft Project the "old way."

Importing a Project Task List from Excel

You can make your project plan more accurate and inclusive by integrating the suggestions and concrete input of team members and stakeholders into the project plan. Specifically, you can have others on the team create a task list from an Excel workbook and quickly incorporate it into Microsoft Project. Using the Microsoft Project Task List template in Excel, introduced in Project 2002, this process becomes seamless.

The standard Excel importing process involves mapping the Excel columns to the corresponding Microsoft Project columns to ensure that the right information ends up in the right places in your Gantt Chart task table. Microsoft Project is supplied with an Excel Task List template set up for this very purpose.

For example, suppose that the marketing department is suggesting an addition to the project plan that will provide more detail for their test marketing efforts. They want to develop a list of detailed tasks in Excel. You have them use the Microsoft Project Task List Template in Excel, as follows:

1. In Microsoft Excel, click File, New.
2. In the New Workbook task pane, click General Templates.
3. In the Templates dialog box, click the Spreadsheet Solutions tab.
4. Click Microsoft Project Task List Import Template and then click OK.

   A new file is created that contains columns that correspond to the default Gantt Chart in Microsoft Project.
5. Enter the task information in the Task_Table sheet (see Figure 17-17).

   The columns in this Excel template are specifically designed for integration with Microsoft Project. For example, the ID, Duration, Start, and Deadline fields are all set up to flow in to the Microsoft Project fields in the correct format and data type.

   Also, the second worksheet, labeled either "Info_Table" or "Microsoft Project," contains a brief explanation of how Microsoft Project can use and augment the template.

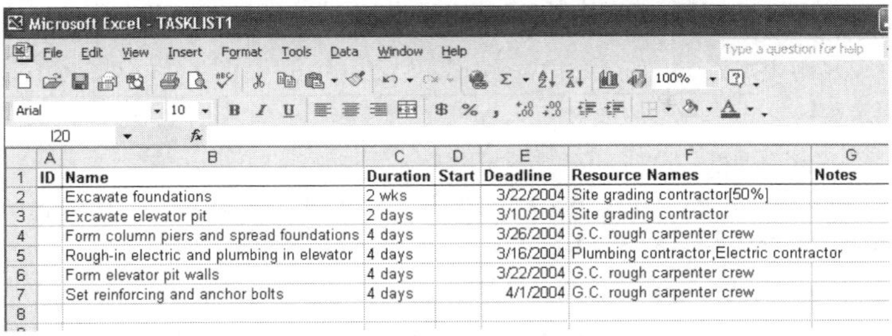

ID	Name	Duration	Start	Deadline	Resource Names	Notes
	Excavate foundations	2 wks		3/22/2004	Site grading contractor[50%]	
	Excavate elevator pit	2 days		3/10/2004	Site grading contractor	
	Form column piers and spread foundations	4 days		3/26/2004	G.C. rough carpenter crew	
	Rough-in electric and plumbing in elevator	4 days		3/16/2004	Plumbing contractor,Electric contractor	
	Form elevator pit walls	4 days		3/22/2004	G.C. rough carpenter crew	
	Set reinforcing and anchor bolts	4 days		4/1/2004	G.C. rough carpenter crew	

Figure 17-17. Share the Excel Task List template with your team to help build your project plan.

Save

6 When you finish entering task information, click Save on the Standard toolbar and give the file a name.

Make sure that you're saving the new task list as an Excel workbook (*.xls), not overwriting the template (*.xlt).

7 Close the file.

Troubleshooting

You can't find the Excel Task List template

There might be two reasons why the Task List template is not available in the Templates dialog box.

You might be working with Microsoft Excel 2000 or earlier. For these versions, the template is stored in a different location. In Excel, click File, New. Click the 1033 or Spreadsheet solutions tab. Double-click Microsoft Project Task List Import Template.

If you still can't find it, click File, Open. Browse to the Office template directory, which is typically \Program Files\Microsoft Office\Templates\1033. In the Files Of Type list, click Templates. Double-click the Tasklist.xlt file.

The other reason why you might not see the Task List template is that the computer you're working on might not have Microsoft Project installed on it. The Task List template is installed with Microsoft Project. If you have Microsoft Excel installed on the same computer as Microsoft Project, those templates then become available in Excel.

On a computer running Microsoft Project and Excel, use Windows Explorer to find the template file. Its typical location is \Program Files\Microsoft Office\Templates\1033. Copy the file to a disk or network location so you can make it available for use on other computers. This is particularly useful when you want to provide the template to various team members and other stakeholders to use Excel to build parts of the project plan.

At this point, the new Excel task list is ready to be imported into Microsoft Project, as follows:

1. In Microsoft Project, open the project plan into which you want to import the Excel task list.

Open

2. On the Standard toolbar, click Open.
3. In the Open dialog box, browse to the location on your computer or network where the Excel task list is saved.
4. In the Files Of Type list, click Microsoft Excel Workbooks (*.xls).

   The task list workbook appears in the list of folders and files.
5. Click the task list workbook and then click Open.

   The Import Wizard appears.
6. On the Welcome page of the Import Wizard, click Next.
7. On the Data Type page, click Project Excel Template and then click Next.
8. On the Import Mode page, specify whether you want to import the file as a new project, append the tasks to the currently active project, or merge the data into the active project. Click Finish.

   The tasks are imported into Microsoft Project as you specified (see Figure 17-18).

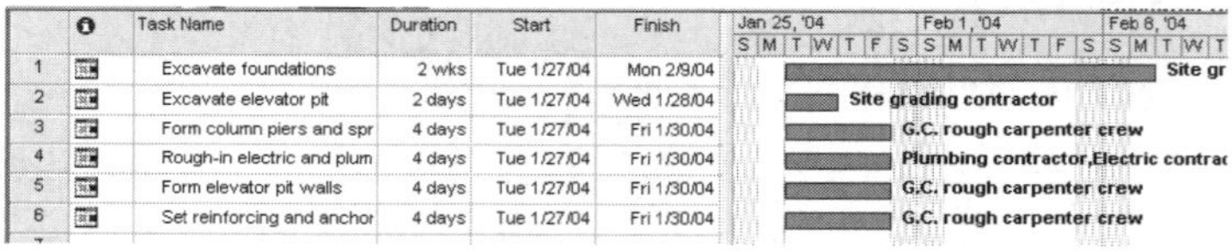

Figure 17-18. Task information from the Excel template is imported into Microsoft Project.

If you scroll to the right, you see that the resources have all been placed in the proper column, but the Predecessors column is empty. The imported tasks still need to be organized, outlined, and linked.

For more information about inserting and organizing tasks, see Chapter 3, "Starting a New Project."

Inside Out

Remove the SNET constraints

All tasks imported from the Excel task list template come in to the project plan with a Start No Earlier Than (SNET) constraint. If a date was entered in the workbook's Start field, that becomes the SNET constraint date. If no date was entered, the SNET date is today's date.

Be sure to review those imported start dates. If there are any dates entered besides today's date, the originator might have intended a SNET constraint. Check with the originator. Because the column is included in the template, originators might be led to believe they're supposed to enter a start date, not realizing that Microsoft Project figures it out for them.

To provide for the best scheduling flexibility, you need to change those imposed (and arbitrary) date constraints to the most flexible As Soon As Possible constraint. To change the constraints all at once, do the following:

1. In the Gantt Chart, select the names of all tasks with date constraints.

   You can select the Start column if you're changing all tasks in the project to an ASAP constraint.

   If you want to change only certain tasks, select their row headings while holding the Ctrl key.

Task Information

2. On the Standard toolbar, click Task Information.
3. In the Multiple Task Information dialog box, click the Advanced tab. In the Constraint Type box, click As Soon As Possible.

When asking others to enter task information using the Excel Task List template, ask them to enter any important finish dates in the Deadline column and any important start dates in the Notes column. This way, you can change all the SNET constraints to ASAP without having to examine every imported data to see whether it's a real date constraint.

For more information about setting constraints, see "Scheduling Tasks to Achieve Specific Dates" on page 157.

Importing Detailed Project Information from Excel

If certain team members or other project stakeholders are doing more than just building a task list in Excel, have them use the Microsoft Project Import Export Template. This template can be used in Excel to build a project with tasks, resources, and assignments. Then you have a properly formatted worksheet for many of the essential elements of a plan for importing into Microsoft Project.

The standard Excel importing process involves mapping the Excel columns to the corresponding Microsoft Project columns to ensure that the right information ends up in the right locations in your Resource Sheet. The Microsoft Project Plan Import Export Template is set up to enter more detailed resource information in the format needed by Microsoft Project. To use this template, make sure that Excel is installed on the same computer as Microsoft Project and then follow these steps:

1. In Microsoft Excel, click File, New.
2. In the New Workbook task pane, click General Templates.
3. In the Templates dialog box, click the Spreadsheet Solutions tab.
4. Click Microsoft Project Plan Import Export Template and then click OK.

> **Note** If the Template is not in the Templates dialog box (which might be the case if you're working with Excel 2000 or earlier), close the dialog box and then click File, Open. Browse to the Office template directory, which is typically \Program Files\Microsoft Office\Templates\1033. In the Files Of Type list, click Templates. Double-click the Projplan.xlt file.

The template creates a new file with columns that correspond to many commonly used fields in Microsoft Project. There is one worksheet each for tasks, resources, and assignments. A fourth worksheet, labeled Info_Table, provides general information on how to use the template.

The data fields are set up so that when you fill in the worksheets and export them into Microsoft Project, you don't need to map your data. If you decide to add data in extra columns (fields), Microsoft Project will map that data to an appropriate field in the Microsoft Project data tables for you.

5 At the bottom of the workbook window, click the tab for the worksheet you want to use.

6 Enter the data in the fields you want. You don't have to use all the fields in all the sheets; just the ones you need (see Figure 17-19).

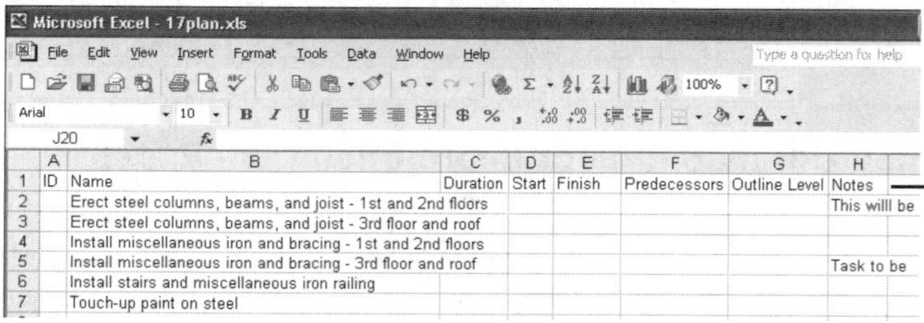

Figure 17-19. Use the Microsoft Project Plan Import Export Template to develop task, resource, and assignment information in Excel.

7 When finished, click Save on the Standard toolbar, and give the file a name.

Make sure you're saving the new file as an Excel Workbook (*.xls), rather than overwriting the template (*.xlt).

8 Close the file.

This workbook will become the source file when you import the data into Microsoft Project.

To import the information from this new Excel workbook into Microsoft Project, do the following:

1 On the Standard toolbar in Microsoft Project, click Open.

2 Go to the location on your computer or network where the Excel workbook is saved.

3 In the Files Of Type list, click Microsoft Excel Workbooks (*.xls).

The workbook appears in the list of folders and files.

4 Click the workbook file and then click Open.

The Import Wizard appears.

5 Read the Welcome page and then click Next.

6 On the Data Type page, click Project Excel Template and then click Next.

7 On the Import Mode page, specify whether you want to import the file as a new project, append the resources to the currently active project, or merge the data into the active project.

8 Click the Finish button.

The new project opens with all the data populated from the template (see Figure 17-20).

		Task Name	Duration	Start	Jan 25, '04 S S M T W T F S
1		Erect steel columns, beams, and joist - 1st and 2nd floors	1 day	Tue 1/27/04	■
2		Erect steel columns, beams, and joist - 3rd floor and roof	1 day	Tue 1/27/04	■
3		Install miscellaneous iron and bracing - 1st and 2nd floors	1 day	Tue 1/27/04	■
4		Install miscellaneous iron and bracing - 3rd floor and roof	1 day	Tue 1/27/04	■
5		Install stairs and miscellaneous iron railing	1 day	Tue 1/27/04	■
6		Touch-up paint on steel	1 day	Tue 1/27/04	■

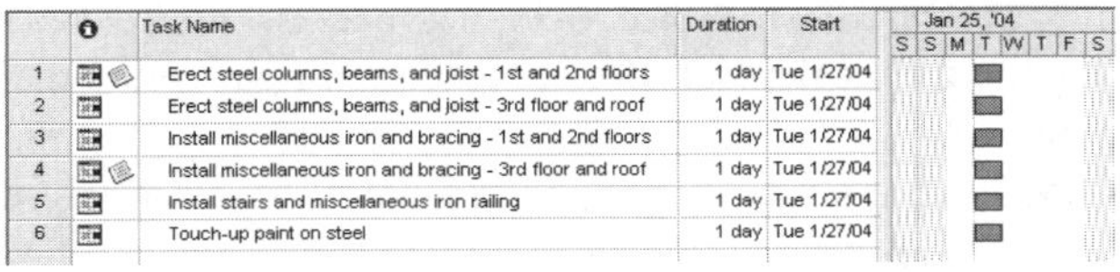

Figure 17-20. Using the template, you can import the project information from Excel to Microsoft Project without having to map individual fields.

Importing from Excel without a Template

If team members or other project stakeholders created an Excel workbook containing project information before they knew of the existence of the templates, you can still import Excel worksheets.

To do this, follow these steps:

1 On the Standard toolbar in Microsoft Project, click Open.

2 Go to the location on your computer or network where the Excel workbook is saved.

3 In the Files Of Type list, click Microsoft Excel Workbooks (*.xls).

The workbook appears in the list of folders and files.

4 Click the workbook file and then click Open.

The Import Wizard appears.

5 Read the Welcome page and then click Next.

6 On the Map page, select New Map and then click Next.

7 On the Import Mode page, specify whether you want to import the file as a new project, append the resources to the currently active project, or merge the data into the active project. Click Next.

8 On the Map Options page, select the types of data you want to import. You can select multiple types if you need to. If your workbook file includes column headings, select the Import Includes Headers check box. Click Next.

9 On the Mapping page, under Source Worksheet Name, select the sheet that contains the data you're importing, even if it's just **Sheet1**.

The fields from the Excel sheet appear in the From: Excel Field column. If there is an obvious match to a Microsoft Project field, it appears in the To: Microsoft Office Project Field column. If Microsoft Project could not figure out a match, the field indicates (**not mapped**).

10 For any fields that are not mapped, click in the box and select the Microsoft Project field in which you want to store the corresponding imported field. Scroll down through the entire table and make sure that all the Excel fields you want to import are mapped to a Microsoft Project field.

The Preview area shows a sample of how your table data is mapped (see Figure 17-21).

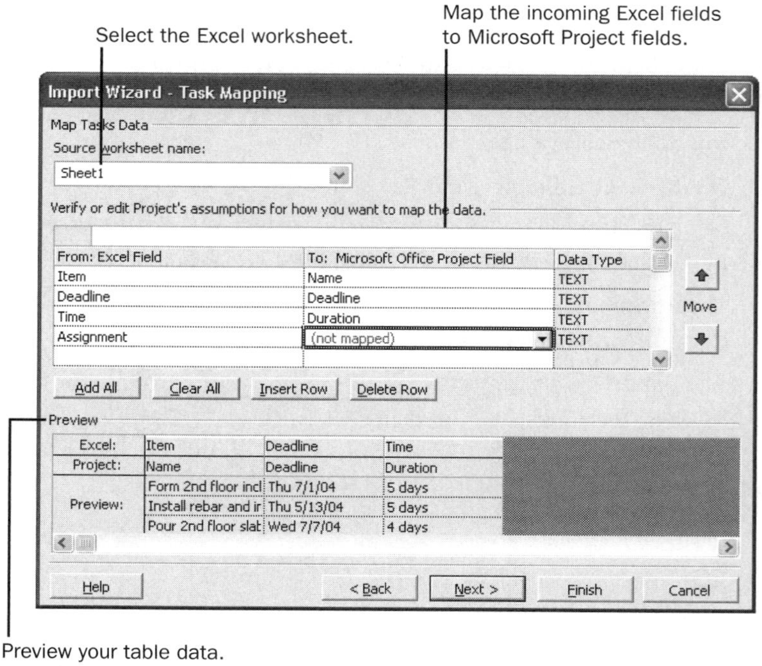

Figure 17-21. Use the Mapping page to specify the Microsoft Project fields that are to contain each category of incoming Excel data.

11. When finished mapping, click Next.

    If you selected multiple types of data to import on the Map Options page (for example, Tasks and Resources), another Mapping page will appear. You can potentially work through a Task Mapping, Resource Mapping, and Assignment Mapping page.

12. On the End Of Map Definition page, specify whether you want to save the map for future use. Then click Finish.

    The project opens with all the data imported from the workbook in the fields you specified.

Exporting from Project to Excel

Suppose that your company's accounting department wants to analyze your project cost information in conjunction with those of other projects taking place throughout the company. The department uses Excel to analyze project cost data, so you'll need to export your Microsoft Project information to an Excel workbook.

When exporting from Microsoft Project, you use the Export Wizard introduced in Project 2002. With the Export Wizard, you can export information you select or export key information from the entire project.

Exporting Selected Data to Excel

To export only information you choose, follow these steps:

1. In Microsoft Project, open the project plan that contains the project information you want to export.
2. Click File, Save As.

   The Save As dialog box appears.
3. Browse to the drive and folder where you want to save your information.
4. In the Save As File Type list, click Microsoft Excel Workbook (*.xls).
5. In the File Name box, enter a name for your new Excel file.

   By default, the project file name is adopted with the *.xls* extension.
6. Click Save.

   The first page of the Export Wizard appears.
7. On the Welcome page of the wizard, click Next.
8. On the Data page, be sure that the Selected Data option is selected and then click Next.
9. On the Map page, be sure that the New Map option is selected and then click Next.
10. On the Map Options page, select the check box for each type of data you want to map and export: Tasks, Resources, and Assignments. Under Microsoft Excel Options, select the Export Includes Headers check box. Click Next.

11 On the Mapping page of the wizard, in the Destination Worksheet Name box, you can enter a name for the target worksheet within the workbook you're creating.

You can also just use the default name provided; for example, Task_Table1.

12 In the Export Filter box, click any filter you want to apply to the tasks or resources you're exporting.

13 In the table, specify how each field of data should be defined when it is exported to Excel.

You can change the column heading for a given field, for example, from ***Duration*** to ***Task Length***. The Data Type field shows how the field will be exported, for example, as text, currency, date, and so on.

Use the command buttons below the table to help with the process. If you're not interested in editing each field individually, click the Base On Table button. The Select Base Table For Field Mapping dialog box appears (see Figure 17-22).

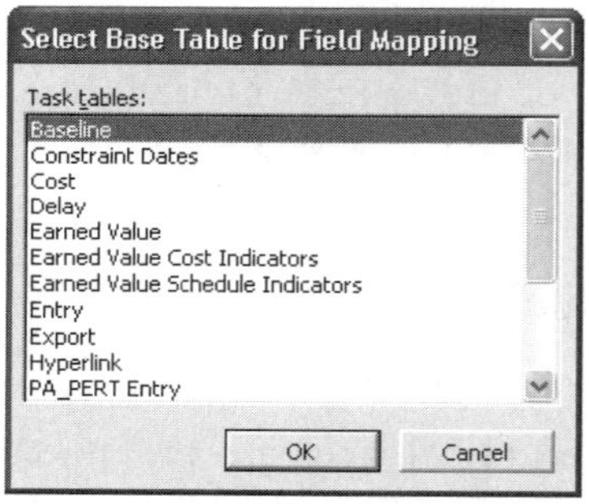

Figure 17-22. Select the Project table that contains the fields you want to use as your export data source.

Click the Microsoft Project table you're exporting and then click OK. The fields that define that table appear in the Mapping table.

A preview of the data is shown as it will appear in Excel in the Preview area at the bottom of the Mapping page. Use the scroll bar to view all the columns. When ready, click Next.

14 On the End Of Map Definition page, click the Save Map button if you expect to export this same information again. Otherwise, click Finish.

Your specified project data is exported and saved as a complete Excel workbook in the exact layout you defined.

To open and review your exported project data in Microsoft Excel, follow these steps:

1 In Microsoft Excel, open the Excel file that you created by exporting project data.

Your project data appears in the workbook, using the tasks (or resources or assignments), filter, and table you selected in the export process (see Figure 17-23).

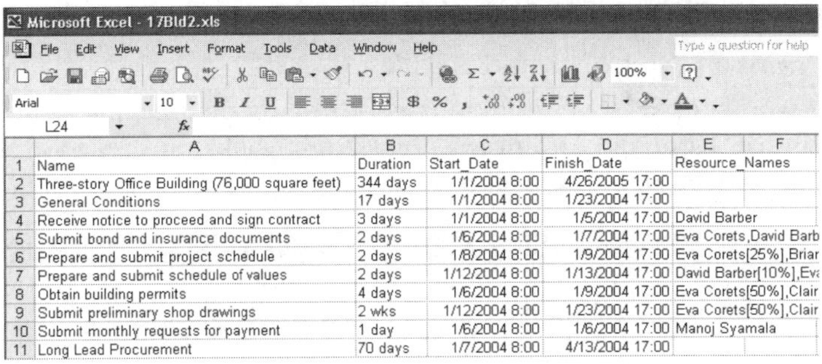

	A	B	C	D	E	F
1	Name	Duration	Start_Date	Finish_Date	Resource_Names	
2	Three-story Office Building (76,000 square feet)	344 days	1/1/2004 8:00	4/26/2005 17:00		
3	General Conditions	17 days	1/1/2004 8:00	1/23/2004 17:00		
4	Receive notice to proceed and sign contract	3 days	1/1/2004 8:00	1/5/2004 17:00	David Barber	
5	Submit bond and insurance documents	2 days	1/6/2004 8:00	1/7/2004 17:00	Eva Corets,David Barb	
6	Prepare and submit project schedule	2 days	1/8/2004 8:00	1/9/2004 17:00	Eva Corets[25%],Briar	
7	Prepare and submit schedule of values	2 days	1/12/2004 8:00	1/13/2004 17:00	David Barber[10%],Ev	
8	Obtain building permits	4 days	1/6/2004 8:00	1/9/2004 17:00	Eva Corets[50%],Clair	
9	Submit preliminary shop drawings	2 wks	1/12/2004 8:00	1/23/2004 17:00	Eva Corets[50%],Clair	
10	Submit monthly requests for payment	1 day	1/6/2004 8:00	1/6/2004 17:00	Manoj Syamala	
11	Long Lead Procurement	70 days	1/7/2004 8:00	4/13/2004 17:00		

Figure 17-23. View and manipulate your project data in Microsoft Excel.

2 Resize and reformat the date fields, as needed.

Note the Smart Tags on some cells and the formatting of durations such as "53.d."

3 Click File, Save.

A message appears, indicating that the file is in the Excel 5.0/95 format. To ensure compatibility with older versions of Excel, Microsoft Project exports to the Microsoft Excel 5.0/Excel 95 file format. When you open the new Excel file and save it the first time, Excel prompts you to update the format to the current version you have installed on your computer, which might be Microsoft Excel 2000 or Excel XP, for example.

4 Click Yes to save your Excel file in the latest Excel format.

Updating the format ensures that you can use the latest features of your current Excel version on your exported project data.

Exporting Complete Project Data to Excel

You can export more complete information about tasks, resources, and assignments. With this method, Microsoft Project organizes data into Task, Resource, and Assignment data types, which in turn are presented in their own separate worksheets in the single Excel workbook. To create a complete Excel workbook of project information from your project file, follow these steps:

1 In Microsoft Project, open the project whose information you want to export to Excel.
2 Click File, Save As.
3 Browse to the drive and folder where you want to save your information.
4 In the Save As File Type list, click Microsoft Excel Workbook (*.xls).
5 In the File Name box, enter a name for the Excel file and then click Save.
6 On the Export Wizard Welcome page, click Next.
7 On the Data page, click Project Excel Template and then click Finish.

Your data is saved as a complete Excel workbook.

To open and review your exported project data in Microsoft Excel, follow these steps:

1 In Microsoft Excel, open the Excel file.

The workbook is created with four worksheets of discrete information: Task_Table, Resource_Table, and Assignment_Table. Info_Table provides general instructions for using this workbook (see Figure 17-24).

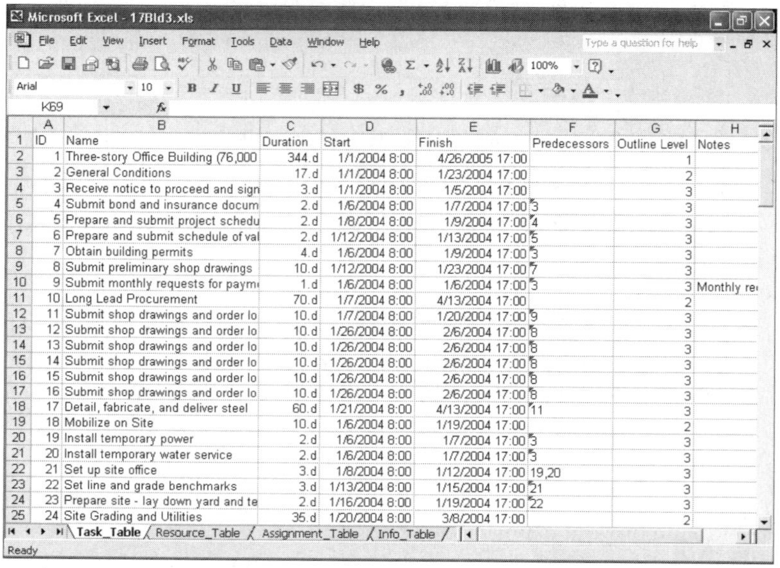

ID	Name	Duration	Start	Finish	Predecessors	Outline Level	Notes
1	Three-story Office Building (76,000	344.d	1/1/2004 8:00	4/26/2005 17:00		1	
2	General Conditions	17.d	1/1/2004 8:00	1/23/2004 17:00		2	
3	Receive notice to proceed and sign	3.d	1/1/2004 8:00	1/5/2004 17:00		3	
4	Submit bond and insurance docum	2.d	1/6/2004 8:00	1/7/2004 17:00	3	3	
5	Prepare and submit project schedu	2.d	1/8/2004 8:00	1/9/2004 17:00	4	3	
6	Prepare and submit schedule of val	2.d	1/12/2004 8:00	1/13/2004 17:00	5	3	
7	Obtain building permits	4.d	1/6/2004 8:00	1/9/2004 17:00	3	3	
8	Submit preliminary shop drawings	10.d	1/12/2004 8:00	1/23/2004 17:00	7	3	
9	Submit monthly requests for paym	1.d	1/6/2004 8:00	1/6/2004 17:00	3	3	Monthly re
10	Long Lead Procurement	70.d	1/7/2004 8:00	4/13/2004 17:00		2	
11	Submit shop drawings and order lo	10.d	1/7/2004 8:00	1/20/2004 17:00	9	3	
12	Submit shop drawings and order lo	10.d	1/26/2004 8:00	2/6/2004 17:00	8	3	
13	Submit shop drawings and order lo	10.d	1/26/2004 8:00	2/6/2004 17:00	8	3	
14	Submit shop drawings and order lo	10.d	1/26/2004 8:00	2/6/2004 17:00	8	3	
15	Submit shop drawings and order lo	10.d	1/26/2004 8:00	2/6/2004 17:00	8	3	
16	Submit shop drawings and order lo	10.d	1/26/2004 8:00	2/6/2004 17:00	8	3	
17	Detail, fabricate, and deliver steel	60.d	1/21/2004 8:00	4/13/2004 17:00	11	3	
18	Mobilize on Site	10.d	1/6/2004 8:00	1/19/2004 17:00		2	
19	Install temporary power	2.d	1/6/2004 8:00	1/7/2004 17:00	3	3	
20	Install temporary water service	2.d	1/6/2004 8:00	1/7/2004 17:00	3	3	
21	Set up site office	3.d	1/8/2004 8:00	1/12/2004 17:00	19,20	3	
22	Set line and grade benchmarks	3.d	1/13/2004 8:00	1/15/2004 17:00	21	3	
23	Prepare site - lay down yard and te	2.d	1/16/2004 8:00	1/19/2004 17:00	22	3	
24	Site Grading and Utilities	35.d	1/20/2004 8:00	3/8/2004 17:00		2	

Figure 17-24. By exporting tasks, resources, and assignments to Excel, separate worksheets are created to hold key task, resource, and assignment information from the selected project.

2 Resize and reformat the date fields, as necessary.

3 Click File, Save.

A message appears, indicating that the file is in the Excel 5.0/95 format (see Figure 17-25). To ensure compatibility with older versions of Excel, Microsoft Project exports to the Microsoft Excel 5.0/Excel 95 file format. When you open the new Excel file and save it the first time, Excel prompts you to update the format to the current version you have installed on your computer, which might be Microsoft Excel 2000 or Excel XP, for example.

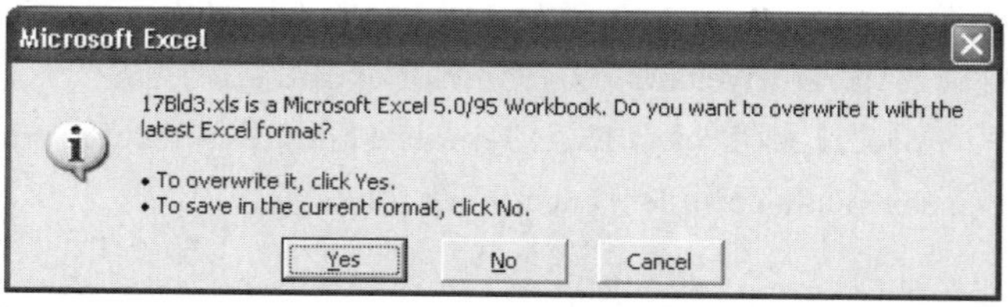

Figure 17-25. Click Yes to upgrade the exported project information to your current installed version of Excel.

Chapter 17

4. Click Yes to save your Excel file in the Excel format you have installed on your computer.

   Updating the format ensures that you can use the latest features of your current Excel version on your exported project data.

Exporting Timephased Information to Excel

NEW FEATURE!

In previous versions of Microsoft Project, if you wanted to work with *timephased* task, resource, or assignment information in another application, you had to copy and paste it. However, in Microsoft Project 2003, there's now a method for exporting timephased information to Microsoft Excel. To do this, follow these steps:

1. In Microsoft Project, open the project plan whose timephased data you want to export to Excel.
2. Display a task view if you want to export timephased task information. Display a resource view to export timephased resource information.
3. If you want to export data only for selected tasks or resources, display and select those items.

   Use the Ctrl or Shift keys to select multiple tasks or resources.
4. Click View, Toolbars, Analysis to display the Analysis toolbar.
5. On the Analysis toolbar, click Analyze Timescaled Data In Excel.
6. In the first page of the Analyze Timescaled Data Wizard, select the Entire Project or Currently Selected Tasks (or Currently Selected Resources) to specify which set of timephased data is to be exported. Click Next.

   The second page of the wizard appears, showing the list of all available timephased fields for either tasks or resources, depending on whether you're showing a task or resource view.
7. Under Available Fields, select the timephased fields you want to export; for example, Actual Cost, Baseline Cost, and Cost. Click Add to move the selected fields to the Fields To Export box.

   Use the Ctrl or Shift keys to select multiple fields at one time. You can select fields and click Add as many times as you need to.
8. When finished adding fields to the Fields To Export box, click Next.
9. In the third page of the wizard, enter the date range and time unit you want to use for the exported data. Then click Next.

   When choosing your date range and time unit, keep in mind that Excel can display only 256 columns of data.
10. In the fourth page of the wizard, specify whether you want the timescaled data to be graphed in Excel. Then click Next.
11. In the fifth page of the wizard, click the Export Data button.

    Microsoft Excel starts up, and the selected timephased data is exported. This might take several minutes, depending on the amount of data to be exported and the speed of your computer. This export works with Microsoft Excel version 5.0 or later.

If the data you chose results in more than 256 columns of timephased data, an error message appears. Excel can only display up to 256 columns of data. To fit your data into fewer columns, you can specify a shorter date range or a different timescale; for example, weeks instead of days. Or you can simply have the export process cut off the data at 256 columns.

12 Review your timephased data in Excel.

When the export is complete, Excel appears and shows your data. If you chose to chart the data, the Timescaled Data Graph appears first.

Click the Timescaled Data worksheet tab at the bottom of the Excel workbook to review the data in an Excel worksheet.

The timescaled data in Excel is initially exported from Microsoft Project as a text (.txt) file and saved in a temporary folder. To retain this timephased information in the Excel format, follow these steps:

1. In Excel, click File, Save As.
2. In the Save As Type box, click Microsoft Excel Workbook (*.xls).
3. In the File Name box, enter a name for the new file. Its default name is ***TimeData.xls.***
4. Use the Save In box and Up One Level button to browse to the drive and folder where you want to save the new workbook.
5. Click Save.

Chapter 18

Integrating Microsoft Project with Microsoft Outlook

Microsoft Office Project 2003 and Microsoft Office Outlook 2003 are partners well-suited for one another. A Project 2003 plan is made up of tasks, and Outlook 2003 includes the Tasks list. Microsoft Project schedules when tasks should be started and finished; Outlook has its Calendar. You use Microsoft Project to set up resource information; Outlook has its Address Book listing information about people in your organization. You need to communicate project information with team members and other stakeholders; Outlook can send messages and files to these people.

When you use Microsoft Project and Outlook together, you can do the following:

- Add tasks from your Outlook Tasks list to your Microsoft Project plan.
- Add resource information to your project plan from your Outlook address book.
- Integrate resources' tasks between Microsoft Project Web Access 2003 and the Outlook Calendar.
- Exchange messages, including assignments and actuals, with team members.
- Send or route an entire project file to others.
- Publish a project file to an Exchange folder.

Some of these techniques work only with Microsoft Outlook. With other techniques, you can use any 32-bit Messaging Application Programming Interface (MAPI)–based e-mail system. These distinctions are made throughout the chapter.

Exchanging Task Information with Outlook

You can bring tasks into your project plan from your Outlook Tasks list. In addition, your team members can bring non-project tasks from their Outlook Calendar into their task list in Project Web Access 2003. This process works the other way as well: Team members can send assigned tasks from Project Web Access to their Outlook Calendar and work with them there.

Adding Outlook Tasks to Microsoft Project

You might have started brainstorming tasks for a new project in your Outlook Tasks list, and you're now ready to import them into Microsoft Project (see Figure 18-1).

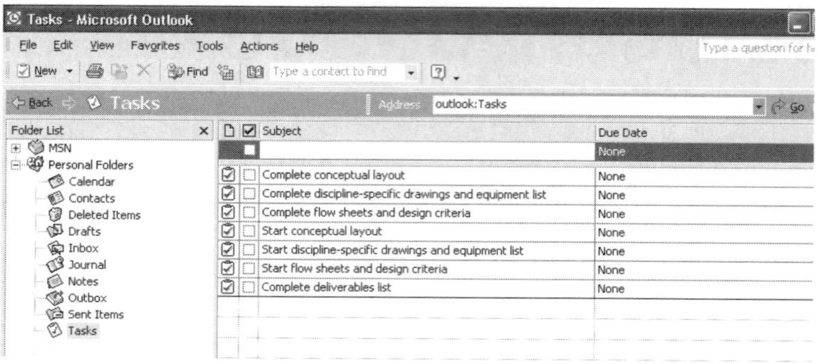

Figure 18-1. Tasks entered in your Outlook Tasks view can be imported to your project plan.

To import Outlook tasks into Microsoft Project, follow these steps:

1. In Microsoft Project, open the project plan in which you want to import the Outlook tasks.
2. Click Tools, Import Outlook Tasks.

   The Import Outlook Tasks dialog box appears (see Figure 18-2). Outlook does not necessarily need to be already running. However, at least one incomplete task must be present in your Outlook Tasks list. Any tasks marked complete in Outlook are not made available for import into Microsoft Project.

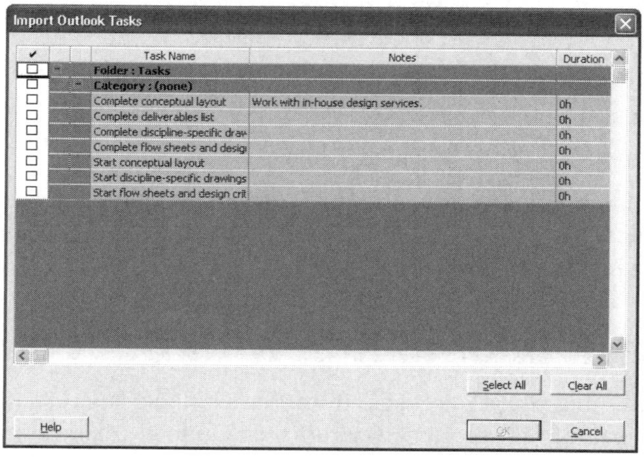

Figure 18-2. Use the Import Outlook Tasks dialog box to bring tasks from Outlook to your project plan.

3. Select the check box for each task you want to import. Click the Select All button to select all tasks.

Items listed with the darker background are folders or summary tasks, and you might not want to import them. If the same tasks are saved in multiple folders, be careful to select just one instance of the task for import. Clear the check box for any Outlook tasks not relevant to your project plan.

4 After you selected the tasks you want, click OK.

The tasks you selected are appended to the end of the last task in your project plan (see Figure 18-3).

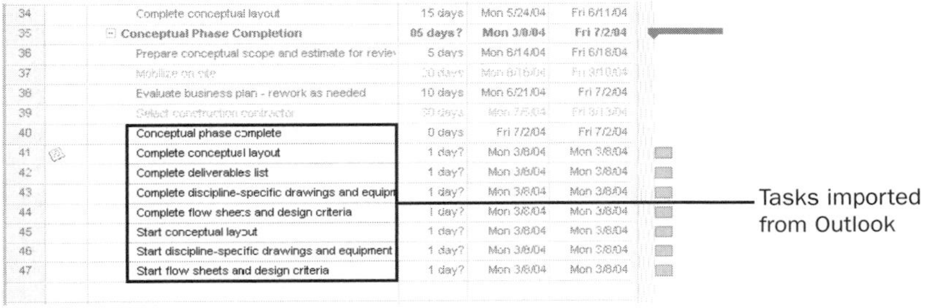

34 Complete conceptual layout 15 days Mon 5/24/04 Fri 6/11/04
35 Conceptual Phase Completion 85 days? Mon 3/8/04 Fri 7/2/04
36 Prepare conceptual scope and estimate for reviev 5 days Mon 6/14/04 Fri 6/18/04
38 Evaluate business plan - rework as needed 10 days Mon 6/21/04 Fri 7/2/04
40 Conceptual phase complete 0 days Fri 7/2/04 Fri 7/2/04
41 Complete conceptuel layout 1 day? Mon 3/8/04 Mon 3/8/04
42 Complete deliverables list 1 day? Mon 3/8/04 Mon 3/8/04
43 Complete discipline-specific drawings and equipn 1 day? Mon 3/8/04 Mon 3/8/04
44 Complete flow sheets and design criteria 1 day? Mon 3/8/04 Mon 3/8/04
45 Start conceptual layout 1 day? Mon 3/8/04 Mon 3/8/04
46 Start discipline-specific drawings and equipment 1 day? Mon 3/8/04 Mon 3/8/04
47 Start flow sheets and design criteria 1 day? Mon 3/8/04 Mon 3/8/04
Tasks imported from Outlook

Figure 18-3. The selected Outlook tasks and associated notes are appended to the current project plan.

The imported Outlook tasks have the following characteristics:

Note

- Any notes entered in Outlook become task notes. Double-click the Note icon in the indicator column to review the note.
- Durations entered in Outlook are lost. The imported Outlook tasks have the default estimated duration of 1 day.
- The start date of all imported tasks adopt the project start date, with the ASAP constraint.
- There are no predecessors or assigned resources.

Adding Microsoft Project Tasks to Outlook Tasks

You might want to add certain key tasks from your project plan to your *Outlook Tasks*. Adding them can be helpful if there are certain tasks that you want to keep a closer eye on; for example, critical tasks or milestone tasks. Or, they might be tasks that you're assigned to, and you're tracking your own tasks in Outlook. To add project tasks to Outlook, simply use the Copy and Paste commands, as follows:

1 In your project plan, display a task view such as the Gantt Chart.

2 Select the name of the task you want to copy to Outlook.

You can copy and paste only one task at a time from Microsoft Project to Outlook. Also, it's best to only select the task name. If you select multiple fields, the information is all pasted together in the task Subject field in Outlook.

Copy

3 On the Standard toolbar, click Copy.

4 Switch to Outlook and display the Tasks view.

5 Click in the Subject entry box labeled Click Here To Add A New Task.

6 Click Edit, Paste.

The copied task from Microsoft Project appears in the box (see Figure 18-4).

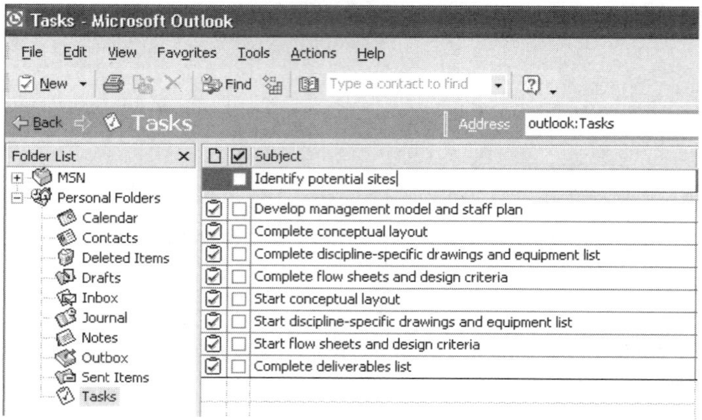

Figure 18-4. Use Copy and Paste to add a project task to Outlook.

7 Press Enter.

The task is added to the top of the Tasks list.

8 Repeat Steps 2–7 for any additional tasks you want to copy to Outlook.

Integrating Tasks Between Project Web Access and the Outlook Calendar

NEW FEATURE!

Through the use of the Outlook Integration Component Object Model (COM) add-in provided with Project Web Access 2003, team members using Project Web Access can now keep track of their assigned tasks in their *Outlook Calendars*, along with their other appointments. They can update progress on those project assignments in the Calendar and report the status back to Microsoft Project Server 2003 directly from Outlook.

Project tasks can be displayed as free or busy time, just like any other Calendar entries.

Note Outlook integration with Project Web Access allows integration with the Outlook Calendar, but not Outlook Tasks.

Team members receive their assignments from Microsoft Project into Project Server, and then from Project Server into Outlook. While team members must still use Project Web Access to use custom fields, project views, status reports, and other project-related features, they now have a choice to work in Project Web Access or Outlook to review, track, and update their project assignments.

The team members can update their assignments and send actual progress information back to the project manager via Project Server. The project manager uses Project Web Access to approve transactions and incorporate these updates into the project plan.

Setting Up Outlook Calendar Integration

To set up Project Web Access integration with Outlook, follow these steps:

1. Log on to Project Web Access.
2. On the Tasks page, in the side pane, click View And Report On Your Tasks From Your Outlook Calendar.

   The Work With Outlook page appears (see Figure 18-5).

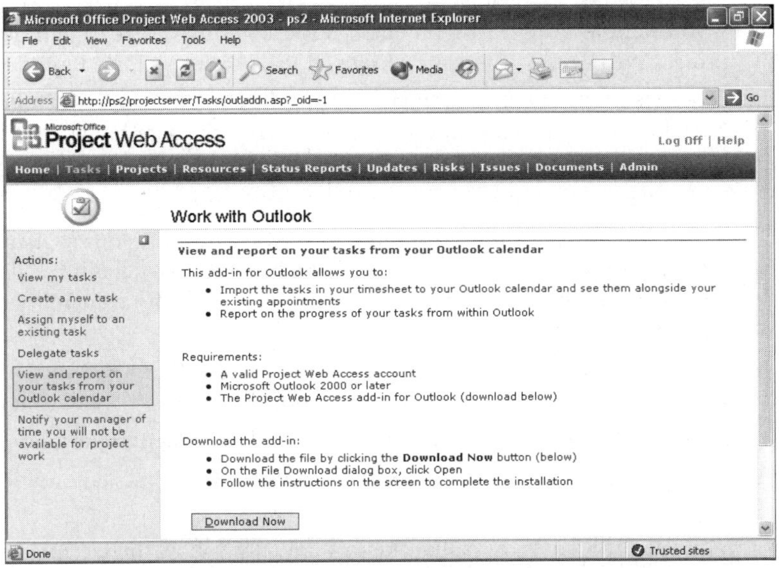

Figure 18-5. Go to the Work With Outlook page in Project Web Access to download the Outlook Integration COM add-in.

3. Click Download Now.

   The COM add-in is installed.

To establish the connection between Outlook and Project Web Access, follow these steps:

1. In Outlook, click Tools, Options.

   The Options dialog box appears.
2. Click the new Microsoft Project Web Access tab.
3. Click the Enter Login Information button.
4. In the Microsoft Project Server URL box, enter the address to your project server; for example, ***http://servername/projectserver***.

If you click the Test Connection button, Outlook tests the URL you entered and makes sure that it's a valid project server.

5. Under When Connecting, specify whether you should be validated with your Windows user account or if you're using a separate Project Server account name.

Importing Project Assignments into the Outlook Calendar

To import assignments from Project Web Access into your Outlook Calendar, follow these steps:

1. In Outlook, click Tools, Options and then click the Microsoft Project Web Access tab.
2. Under Date Range, specify the time period from which you want assignments to be imported.

   If you want to import assignments from the standard reporting time period set up in Project Web Access, select the Microsoft Project Server Date Range option.

   If you want to import assignments from a different time period (for example, the next 2 weeks), select the Next option and then select the date range.
3. In the Show Availability For Project Assignment Appointment, specify your availability for other appointments during the time of your assignments.

   Just as with other Outlook appointments, you can show your availability as free, busy, tentative, or out of the office. This setting becomes the default for all project assignments in the Outlook Calendar. You can still change the availability for individual assignments as needed.
4. Under Import From Microsoft Project Web Access To Your Outlook Calendar, specify whether you want assignments to be imported manually or automatically.

   Select the Manually option if you want to import assignments yourself.

   Select the Every option if you want to import assignments automatically on a time schedule that you set in the associated boxes.

To import Project Web Access assignments manually, follow these steps:

1. Open the Outlook Calendar view.
2. Show the Project Web Access toolbar by clicking View, Toolbars, Project Web Access.
3. On the Project Web Access toolbar, click Import New Assignments.

   The Import Assignments From Project Web Access dialog box appears, listing project assignments within the date range set in the Options dialog box.

   If you never need to see this dialog box, select the Don't Show The Dialog In The Future, Just Import check box.
4. Click OK.

   The listed assignments are imported into your Outlook Calendar.

Updating Assignments in the Outlook Calendar

To set up how you want to update assignment progress information from the Outlook Calendar to Project Web Access and Project Server, follow these steps:

1. In Outlook, click Tools, Options and then click the Microsoft Project Web Access tab.
2. Under Assignment Update, specify whether you want assignment updates to be sent manually or automatically.

   Select the Manually option if you want to send assignment updates only upon your explicit command.

   Select the Every option if you want to update assignment progress automatically at regular time periods that you set in the associated boxes.

To record progress on a project assignment from Outlook, follow these steps:

1. Open the Outlook Calendar view.
2. Double-click the assignment for which you want to record progress.

   The appointment form appears, showing assignment details. In addition to the normal Appointment and Scheduling tabs, the Project Web Access tab is added.
3. Click the Project Web Access tab.

   This tab shows your timesheet as it looks in Project Web Access, so you can update progress information.
4. Depending on the tracking method used in your project, enter the hours worked per time period, percent complete, or actual work and remaining work.
5. To send the updated information to Project Server, click the Update Project Manager button.

   To save the changes for an update at a later time, click the Save Changes button. Click Save Changes if you have other assignments to update and you want to send all updates at once, or if you chose the automated update option and Outlook will be sending all updates at that scheduled time.

To update assignment progress to Project Server manually, follow these steps:

1. Open the Outlook Calendar view.
2. Make sure that the Project Web Access toolbar is displayed. If it is not, click View, Toolbars, Project Web Access.
3. On the Project Web Access toolbar, click Update Project Web Access.

   The dialog box lists all project assignments. In the Update column, select the check boxes of the assignments you want to update.

Building Your Resource List with Outlook

You can quickly and accurately add resource names and e-mail addresses to your project plan by pulling them into Microsoft Project from your Outlook Address Book or Contacts list.

> **Note** If you're set up for enterprise project management using Microsoft Office Project Professional 2003 and Microsoft Office Project Server 2003, don't use this feature to build your resource list. Use the enterprise resource pool instead.

To import resource names from Outlook into Microsoft Project, follow these steps:

1. In Microsoft Project, open the project to which you want to add resources from Outlook.
2. Click View, Resource Sheet. Select the row where you want the new resources to start being added.
3. Click Insert, New Resource From, Address Book. The Select Resources dialog box appears. In the Show Names From The list, choose the name of the area where you've stored the contact information for the resources you want to add.
4. On the left side of the Select Resources dialog box, select the names of resources you want to add to your project. Hold down the Shift key to select multiple adjacent resources or the Ctrl key to select multiple nonadjacent resources.
5. Click the Add button.

   The selected resources are added to your project and listed in the Resource Sheet.

Exchanging Workgroup Messages

If you use a 32-bit MAPI-based e-mail system, such as Microsoft Outlook, Microsoft Exchange, Microsoft Mail, Lotus cc:Mail, or Lotus Notes, you can exchange project workgroup messages with your project team members.

Through e-mail workgroup messaging, you can send resources information about their assigned tasks. You can also send any changes to those assignments, along with requests for progress updates or status reports.

In turn, the resources can send progress updates on those assignments, which can then be automatically incorporated into your project plan. The resources can also send you additional tasks, task information changes, and narrative status reports.

> **Planning** For details about e-mail workgroup messaging, see Chapter 19, "Collaborating Using E-Mail."

Inside Out

Phasing out e-mail workgroup messaging

The e-mail workgroup messaging solution has been peripheral to Microsoft Project for the past several versions. However, with the advent and increasing acceptance of Project Server and Project Web Access, e-mail workgroup messaging is woefully outmoded. Even small project management teams in small companies are finding Project Server and Project Web Access to be the right collaboration solution, which can be scaled to their size and purpose.

For these and other reasons, word has it that Project 2003 is the last version for which e-mail workgroup messaging will be available.

Sending Project File Information

You can send information from your project file to others using Outlook or any other MAPI-based e-mail system. You can send project file information in the following ways:

- Send the entire project file as an attachment.
- Send a selected set of tasks or resources as a Microsoft Project file attachment.
- Send a set of tasks or resources as a picture to a set of predefined recipients.
- Route a project file to a group of recipients to obtain their input.
- Publish a project file to a Microsoft Exchange public folder.

Sending an Entire Project File

You can quickly send an entire file to selected recipients directly from within your project file. To do this, follow these steps:

1. In Microsoft Project, open the project file you want to send.
2. Click File, Send To, Mail Recipient (As Attachment).

   Your MAPI e-mail application is launched, if necessary. The new e-mail message form appears, showing your project file already attached and the name of the project in the Subject field.
3. In the To box (and Cc box, if necessary), add the e-mail addresses of the recipients.
4. In the message area, add any necessary comments regarding the project file (see Figure 18-6).

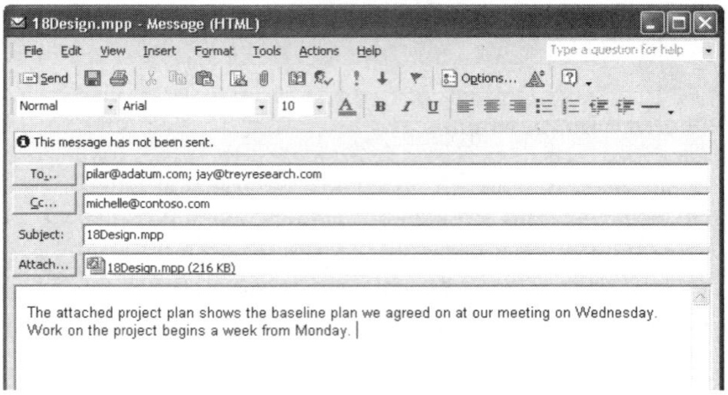

Figure 18-6. Quickly send the project file as an e-mail attachment.

5 Click the Send button.

Your message and the attached project file are sent to the specified recipients.

Send a Project File to Predefined Recipients

You can also send the project file by clicking File, Send To, Mail Recipient (As Schedule Note). Under Attach, select the File check box. Clear the Picture Of Selected Tasks check box. Under Address Message To, specify the group of recipients associated either with the entire project or the currently selected tasks.

If you're using a non-MAPI e-mail program, you can still send a project file as an attachment. You just can't do so from within Microsoft Project. Start in your e-mail program, select the attachment function, and then select the Microsoft Project file.

Sending Selected Tasks or Resources

Note You can send a schedule note if you're using Outlook or any other 32-bit MAPI-based e-mail program.

You can send a picture of selected tasks or resources in any given view to the assigned resources and other associated contacts by using the Send Schedule Note dialog box. Send a Schedule Note when you want to do the following:

- Send information about critical tasks to the assigned resources.
- Send information about tasks leading up to a major milestone to the assigned resources.
- Ask assigned resources about progress on late tasks.
- Ask assigned resources to report on the status of current tasks.

- Alert contacts in human resources, procurement, or accounting about their responsibilities related to a set of resources.
- Report current status of selected tasks to a managing stakeholder.

To send a Schedule Note, do the following:

1. In Microsoft Project, open the project file that contains the information you want to send.
2. Display the view, including the table and fields, you want to send.
3. Select the tasks or resources whose information you want to send.
4. Click File, Send To, Mail Recipient (As Schedule Note).

   The Send Schedule Note dialog box appears (see Figure 18-7).

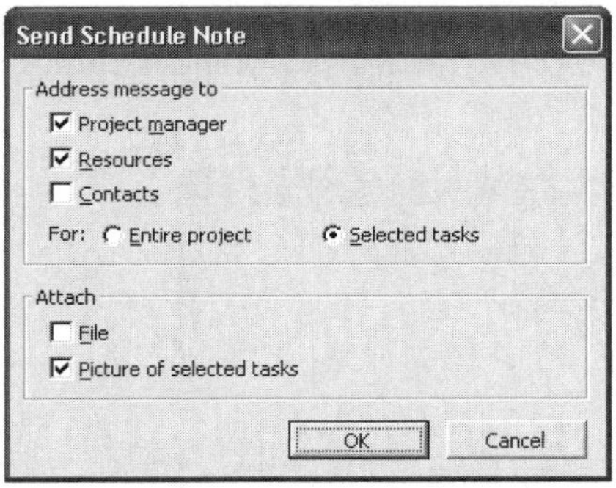

Figure 18-7. You can transmit a selected update with a Schedule Note.

5. Under Address Message To, select the Resources check box.

   The e-mail addresses for resources must be identified. This can be done by adding the Email Address field to the Resource Sheet or by entering it in the Resource Information dialog box.

   If you are using the Contacts field in a task view to include the e-mail addresses of stakeholders or other individuals associated with tasks, you can also select the Contacts check box to send a schedule note to them.
6. Under Attach, be sure that the Picture Of Selected Tasks check box is selected.

   If you also want to send the entire project file, select the File check box.
7. Click OK.

   Depending on the settings in your e-mail program or virus protection program, you might see a message specifying that an outside program is attempting to access your e-mail addresses (see Figure 18-8). Specify that you do want to allow this. You might see this message for each recipient of your schedule note.

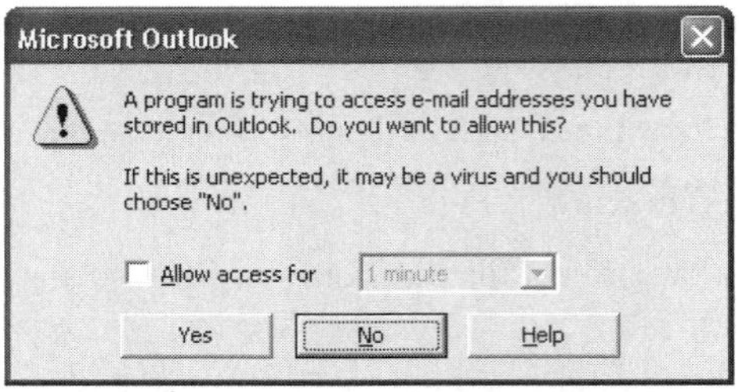

Figure 18-8. Your e-mail security settings or virus protection program might present an alert.

Your MAPI e-mail application is launched, if necessary. The new e-mail message form appears with address information filled in and the title bar reflecting the name of the project file. The specified attachment is included. If you are sending a picture of selected tasks or resources, a .bmp file is attached. If you are sending the entire project file, an .mpp file is attached (see Figure 18-9).

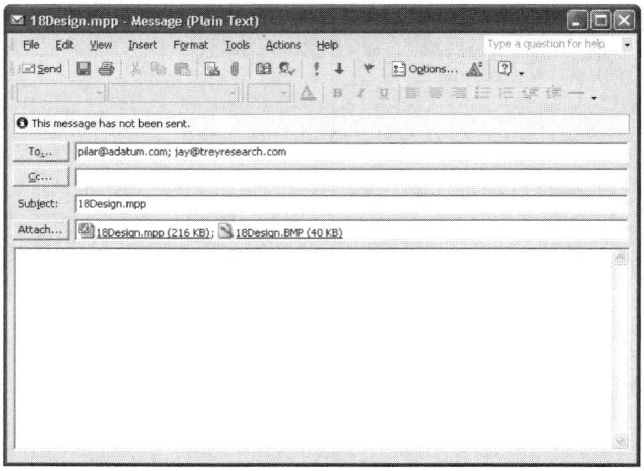

Figure 18-9. A new e-mail message is created with the recipients and attachments you specified.

8. In the To and Cc boxes, add any additional recipients as necessary.
9. In the Subject box, enter a subject.
10. In the message area, type a message to inform your recipients of your intentions with the project attachments.
11. Click Send.

If your schedule note consists of a picture of selected tasks or resources, recipients can double-click the .bmp attachment to open it (see Figure 18-10).

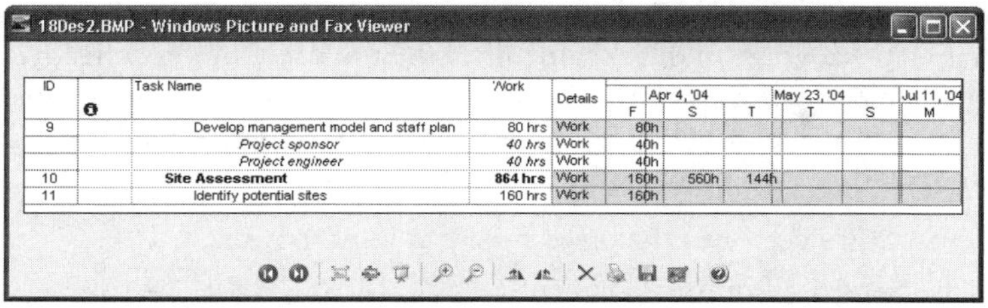

Figure 18-10. The schedule note sends a picture of selected tasks or resources via e-mail.

If your schedule note consists of the project file, recipients can double-click the .mpp attachment to open the project file in Microsoft Project, as long as they have it installed on their computer.

Tip **E-mail report information**
It would be nice to be able to e-mail a report like the To-Do List to team members or a report like the Project Summary to your boss. But that capability is not available, for many of the same reasons that you can't save a report from a moment in time.

What you can do, however, is use your MAPI-compliant e-mail application to send selected tasks or selected resources from your project plan to your team members.

Troubleshooting

Only a fragment of the project file is being sent

Suppose that you're using the Send Schedule Note dialog box to send a project file, but only a few of the tasks or resources are showing up in the e-mail attachment.

When you select the Entire Project option in the Address Message To section, this refers to the recipients associated with the entire project. This does not indicate that the entire project is being sent.

Check the setting under Attached. By default, the Picture Of Selected Tasks check box is selected. If you want to send the entire project, select the File check box.

Routing a Project File

Note You can route a project file if you're using Outlook or any other 32-bit MAPI-based e-mail program.

Sometimes you need specific information from certain individuals regarding the project plan. Maybe one team member is developing the task list, someone else is adding the resources, and someone else is assigning those resources to tasks. Or perhaps you want various leads to update progress on their segments of the project. One very effective way to give a comprehensive picture of your work is to route your project plan through e-mail to a list of individuals. You can specify whether your addressees receive your e-mail message one at a time or all at once. To route a project file, follow these steps:

1. In Microsoft Project, open the project file you want to route.
2. Click File, Send To, Routing Recipient.

   The Routing Slip dialog box appears (see Figure 18-11).

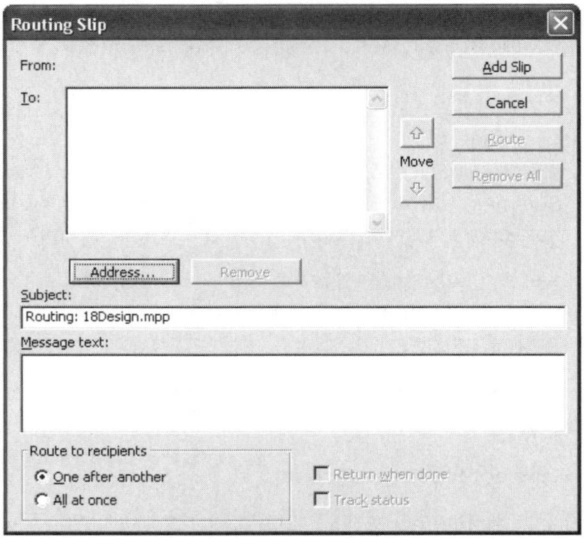

Figure 18-11. Complete the Routing Slip dialog box to send the project file to multiple recipients.

3. Click the Address button.

   The Address Book dialog box appears.
4. In the left window, click the names of the individuals you want on the distribution list and then click the To button.

   Note that each individual on the distribution list must have access to Microsoft Project on their computer in order to open the project file.
5. If you're routing the project one recipient at a time, designate the order of recipients by rearranging their names on the list using the Move buttons.
6. In the Subject field, change the subject if necessary.
7. In the Message Text box, enter any comments or instructions to accompany the attached project file.
8. Under Route To Recipients, select the One After Another option (the default) or the All At Once option.

Although sequential routing can be time-consuming and impractical for urgent information, it's ideal for review and evaluation. Each recipient edits the project file and adds comments to the routing message. To send it to the next designated addressee, the recipient clicks File, Send To, Next Routing Recipient.

9 Select the Track Status check box to keep an eye on the progress of the project routing and make sure it doesn't get stuck too long with any one recipient. Select the Return When Done check box to make sure the file comes back to you so you can see everyone's changes and comments.

10 Click the Route button.

The message with the project file is routed to your designated recipients through e-mail.

Publishing the Project File to an Exchange Folder

> **Note** You can publish a project file to an Exchange folder if you're using Microsoft Exchange Server and if you have permission to use public folders.

You can send your project file to an Exchange folder, which is most useful for making the project file available to a large number of stakeholders. To send the file to an Exchange folder, do the following:

1 In Microsoft Project, open the project file you want to publish to an Exchange folder.

2 Click File, Send To, Exchange Folder.

The Send To Exchange Folder dialog box appears, displaying the folders available to you (see Figure 18-12).

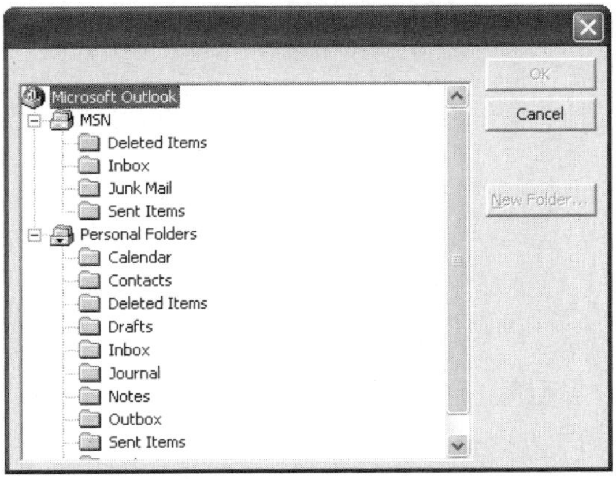

Figure 18-12. Select the public folder for your project file.

3 Click the folder to which you'd like to send the project file and then click OK.

Your project file is copied into the selected folder.

Chapter 19

Collaborating Using E-Mail

In previous versions of Microsoft Project, you had access to a set of files that enabled basic workgroup collaboration features via your organization's MAPI-based e-mail system. Essentially, you linked the tasks and resources in your project plan to your e-mail system in order to exchange basic assignment and progress tracking information in specialized message forms with team members.

Now in Microsoft Office Project 2003, the workgroup program files are no longer provided with the CD. You have to download the workgroup files from the Web and change a registry setting to enable the e-mail workgroup features for your project plan.

The preferred alternative for efficient workgroup collaboration, of course, is Microsoft Office Project Professional 2003 with Microsoft Office Project Server 2003 and Microsoft Office Project Web Access 2003. This suite of products provides everything from sophisticated workgroup collaboration capabilities to robust enterprise project management functionality.

For more information about working with Project Server 2003 and Project Web Access 2003 for workgroup collaboration and enterprise project management, refer to the chapters in Part 7, "Managing Projects Across Your Enterprise."

Inside Out

E-mail workgroup messaging on its way out

The e-mail workgroup messaging solution has been peripheral to Microsoft Project for the past several versions. However, with the availability of Project Server and Project Web Access, e-mail workgroup messaging is woefully outmoded. Even small project management teams in small companies are finding Project Server and Project Web Access to be the right collaboration solution, which can be scaled to their size and purpose.

For these and other reasons, it's expected that Project 2003 is the last version for which e-mail workgroup messaging will be available. So if you've been using e-mail workgroup messaging, now's the time to start transitioning to another method of workgroup collaboration. It might be Project Server and Project Web Access, or it might be a third-party timesheet system that ties in with Microsoft Project.

Setting Up E-Mail Workgroup Messaging

If you used e-mail workgroup messaging in previous versions of Microsoft Project and need a little time to transition to another workgroup collaboration method, you can download the files that install the workgroup files. You can do this with either Microsoft Office Project Standard 2003 or Project Professional 2003.

Understanding System Requirements

System requirements for installing and enabling workgroup e-mail messaging are as follows:

- The project manager must have Project Standard 2003 or Project Professional 2003 installed on his or her computer.
- A network, typically a local area network (LAN), must be in place to transmit e-mail messages.
- The e-mail system must be compliant with the Messaging Application Programming Interface (MAPI) and it must be a 32-bit system. Microsoft Outlook is an example of a MAPI-compliant system. Other examples include Microsoft Exchange Server, Microsoft Mail, Lotus cc:Mail, and Lotus Notes.

Downloading and Installing the Workgroup Message Handler

Files and information for installing and enabling workgroup e-mail messaging are available on the Web. To download and install the workgroup message handler, follow these steps:

1. Open your Web browser and go to the Microsoft Download Center at *www.microsoft.com/downloads*.
2. Under Search For A Download in the Product/Technology box, click Microsoft Project.
3. In the Keywords box, type **workgroup message handler**.

   A list of related downloads appear. Click the download link related to Project 2003.
4. Follow the steps provided to download and install the files for the workgroup message handler on your computer.

After you have installed the workgroup message handler, you need information about specific registry settings that enable the message handler in Microsoft Project. To find the Knowledge Base article and set your registry, follow these steps:

1. Using your Web browser, go to the Microsoft Product Support Services Web site at *support.microsoft.com*.
2. In the Search The Knowledge Base box, type the article ID **818337** or the keywords **project workgroup message handler**.
3. Under Search Results, find and click the article titled "Configuring Workgroup Message Handler for Microsoft Office Project 2003."
4. Follow the instructions provided to configure and enable the workgroup e-mail messaging features in Project 2003. These instructions include registry setting updates.

Note Because the workgroup message handler is being phased out, and the downloadable files and instructions are only an interim solution, be aware that technical support is not available for e-mail workgroup messaging.

Preparing Your Project Plan for E-Mail Collaboration

After you set up the workgroup message handler, be sure that the e-mail addresses for all team members are added in the project plan. To add team member e-mail addresses, follow these steps:

1. In Microsoft Project, click Collaborate, Collaboration Options.

   The Options dialog box appears with the Collaborate tab displayed.
2. In the Collaborate Using list, select E-Mail Only. If you get a warning message, close it. Click OK to close the Options dialog box.

   The E-Mail Only option becomes available only after you install the workgroup message handler and set the registry to enable the message handler in Microsoft Project.
3. Display the Resource Sheet.
4. Select the column to the right of where you want the Email Address column to be inserted.
5. Click Insert, Column.

   The Column Definition dialog box appears.
6. In the Field Name box, click Email Address (see Figure 19-1). Click OK.

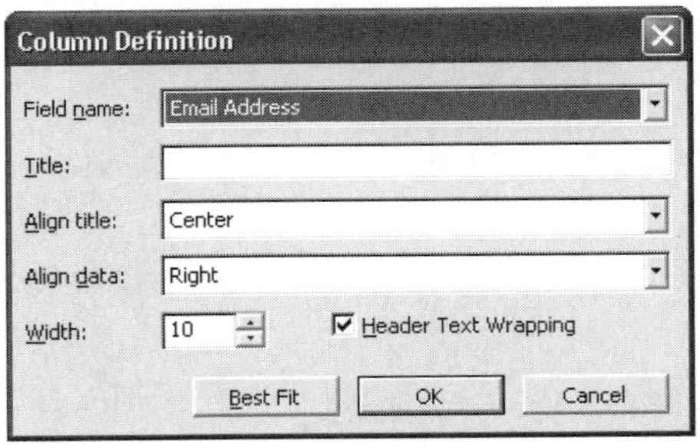

Figure 19-1. Click the Email Address field in the Column Definition dialog box.

7. In the Resource Sheet, enter the resources' e-mail addresses in their corresponding Email Address fields (see Figure 19-2).

Resource Sheet

	Resource Name	Email Address	Type	Initials	Max. Units
1	Brian Groth	brian@adatum.com	Work	BG	100%
2	Andrew Dixon	andrew@adatum.com	Work	AD	100%
3	David Wright	**davidw**	Work	DW	100%
4	Wendy Wheeler	**wendyw**	Work	WW	100%
5	Tony Wang	**tonyw**	Work	TW	100%
6	Jeff Pike	**jeffp**	Work	JP	100%
7	Barry Potter	**barry@adatum.com**	Work	BP	100%
8	Daniel Shimshoni	**daniels**	Work	DS	100%
9	Alan Shen	alans@adatum.com	Work	AS	100%
10	Manoj Syamala	**manojs**	Work	MS	100%
11	Fukiko Ogisu	**fukikoo**	Work	FO	100%
12	Paul Komosinski	**paul@cpandl.com**	Work	PK	100%
13	Ken Myer	**ken@cpandl.com**	Work	KM	100%
14	Mandar Naik	**mandarn@cpandl.com**	Work	MN	100%

Figure 19-2. Enter e-mail addresses in the Resource Sheet.

8 Click File, Save.

Entering E-Mail Addresses Automatically

If you haven't added resource names or other information yet, you can add resource names along with their e-mail addresses automatically. If you use Microsoft Outlook, you can add resource names and e-mail addresses through the Outlook Address Book. The same is true if you use Active Directory.

Use your Outlook Address Book to enter resource names and e-mail addresses as follows:

1 Display the Resource Sheet.

2 Click Insert, New Resource From, Address Book.

Your Outlook Address Book opens.

3 Select the names of the resources you want to add to your project plan and then click the Add button. When done, click OK.

If you use Active Directory, enter resource names and their e-mail addresses as follows:

1 Display the Resource Sheet.

2 Click Insert, New Resource From, Active Directory.

3 Select the names of the resource(s) you want to add to your project and then click the Add button. When done, click OK.

The names and e-mail addresses of the selected resources are added to your project plan.

Sending Assignments and Updates to Team Members

After you enter all the e-mail addresses of your project resources, you're ready to start using e-mail workgroup messaging. You start by sending resources their assignments. When you *publish* an assignment, you're sending the assignment details through e-mail to each assigned resource. The resources can reply to the assignment notice with an acceptance or rejection and add explanatory comments.

As you work through the project, you continue to publish any tasks that have been added or changed so that team members always have the up-to-date assignment information they need.

When you need progress information from the resources, you can use workgroup handling to request updates for assigned tasks. Resources respond with actual progress information such as number of hours worked or percent complete. You can establish a weekly update schedule for your team members to send you e-mail progress reports with their hours worked per task. You can then incorporate this information into the project plan to facilitate your project tracking and monitoring efforts.

For more information about entering actual progress information on tasks, see "Updating Task Progress" on page 308.

Sending Assignments to Team Members

To send all task information to the assigned resources, follow these steps:

1. Click Collaborate, Publish, New And Changed Assignments.
2. If you see a message having to do with saving the project plan (see Figure 19-3), just click OK to proceed.

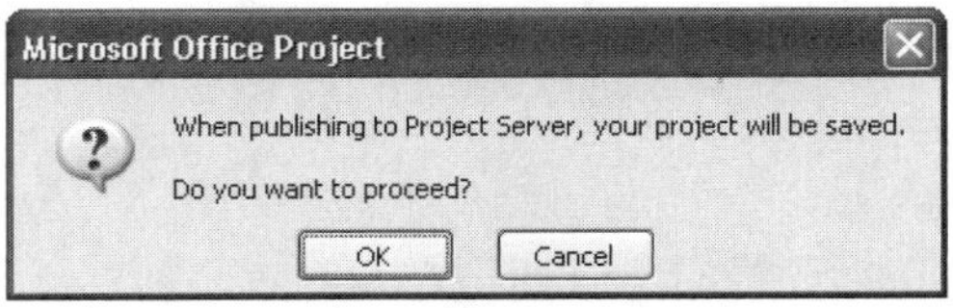

Figure 19-3. When you publish assignments, click OK if you see this alert message.

3. The Publish New And Changed Assignments dialog box appears (see Figure 19-4).

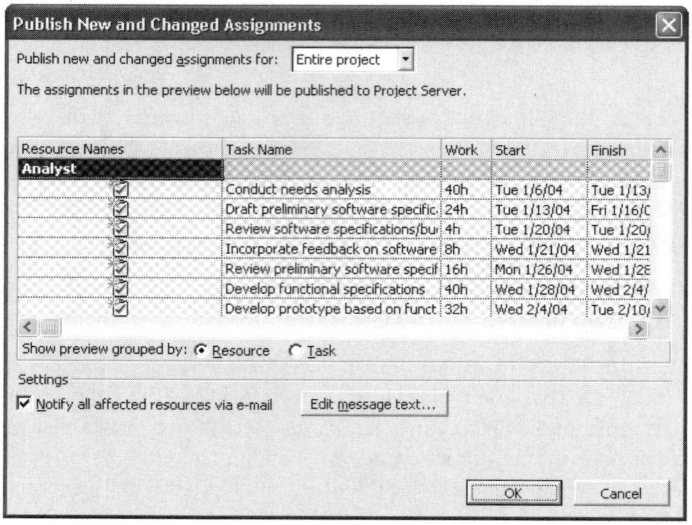

Figure 19-4. Send all project assignments to their assigned resources.

4 In the Publish New And Changed Assignments For list, click Entire Project.

5 Under the task table, select the Resource option next to Show Preview Grouped By.

6 Be sure that the Notify All Affected Resources Via E-Mail check box is selected.

7 Click the Edit Message Text button.

The Edit Message Text dialog box appears (see Figure 19-5).

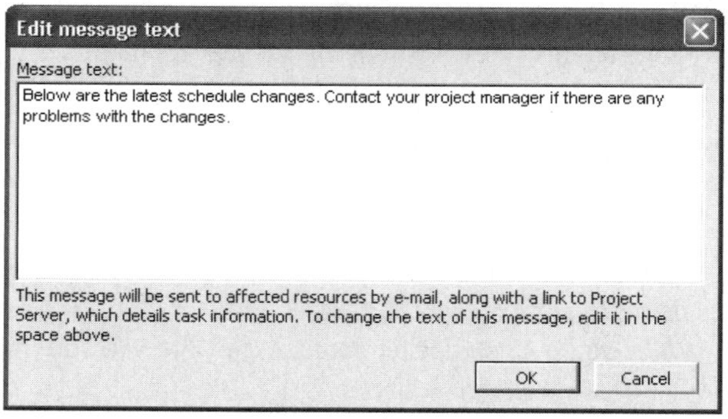

Figure 19-5. Revise the introductory note that accompanies the published assignments.

8 Revise the message as you feel appropriate to explain the process to your team members, and then click OK.

If necessary, your e-mail program launches and then you'll see a message confirming that the assignment messages have been sent.

After your messages are sent, the Gantt Chart will show Unconfirmed indicators (see Figure 19-6) next to each task that was published. They indicate that an assignment has been published for that task, but that you have not yet received a response from the assigned resource.

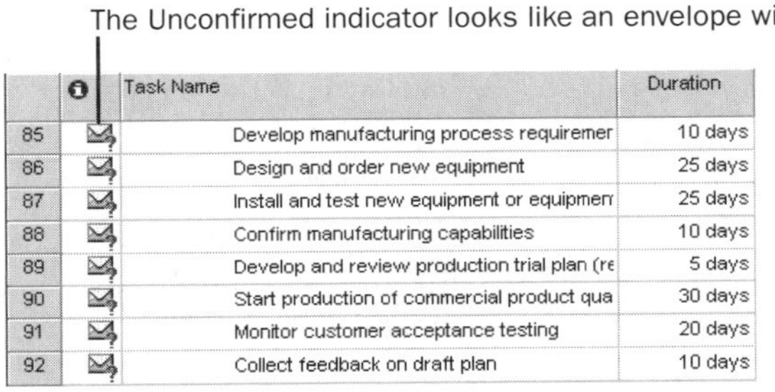

The Unconfirmed indicator looks like an envelope with a question mark.
Task Name
Duration
85 Develop manufacturing process requiremer 10 days
86 Design and order new equipment 25 days
87 Install and test new equipment or equipmen 25 days
88 Confirm manufacturing capabilities 10 days
89 Develop and review production trial plan (re 5 days
90 Start production of commercial product qua 30 days
91 Monitor customer acceptance testing 20 days
92 Collect feedback on draft plan 10 days

Figure 19-6. Unconfirmed indicators mark tasks that have been published and are awaiting acknowledgment by the assigned resources.

Receiving Workgroup Messages from Team Members

When a team member responds to an assignment, you receive an e-mail message from the team member in your e-mail inbox. Depending on the e-mail program you use, the information might be contained in a special e-mail form or in an attachment (see Figure 19-7).

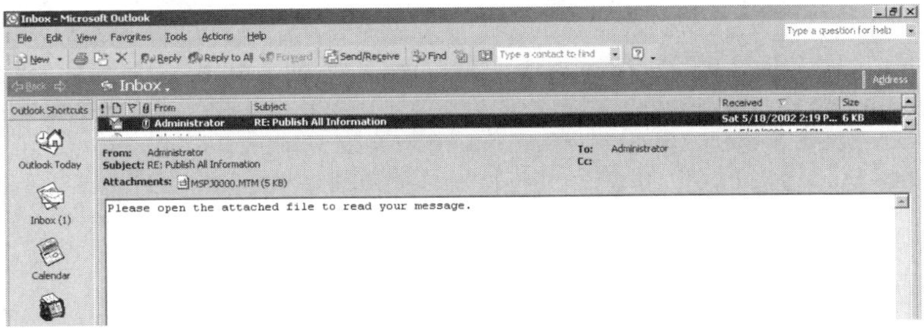

Figure 19-7. You receive assignment confirmations from resources in your e-mail inbox.

To review and incorporate your team members' responses to their assignments, follow these steps:

1 If necessary, open the e-mail attachment. The team member's response to your assignment appears (see Figure 19-8).

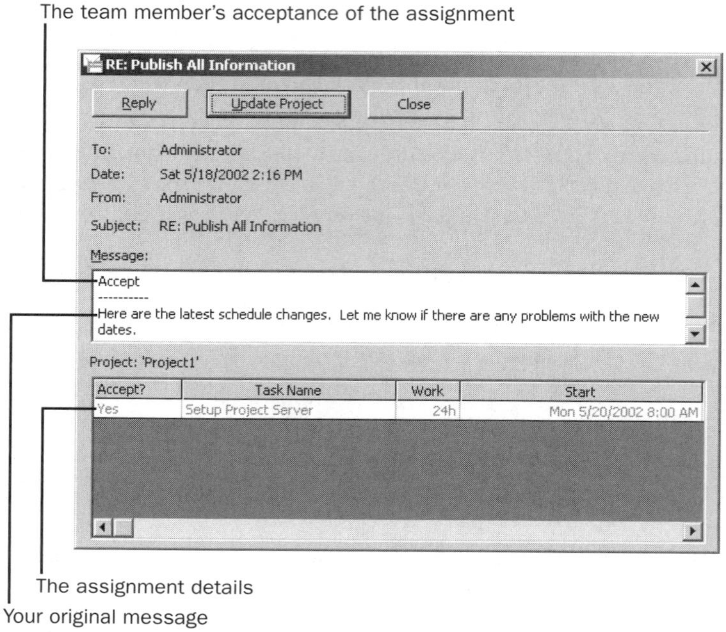

Figure 19-8. The message indicates whether the resource accepts or declines the assignment.

2. To incorporate the team member's response into your project plan, click the Update Project button.

   In your project plan, the Unconfirmed indicator for the assignment disappears.

> **Note** Team members can also send you task updates with changes to task information and progress information with assignment actuals. Open the messages the same way, and either click Update Project to incorporate the information into your project plan or click Reply to have a dialogue with the team member about the information.

Sending Task Updates to Team Members

If you add new tasks or change assigned tasks in any way, you need to publish those specific tasks to the assigned resources. Follow these steps to publish selected tasks to the assigned resources:

1. On the Gantt Chart or other task sheet, click the tasks you want to publish.
2. Click Collaborate, Publish, New And Changed Assignments. If you see the message about saving the project, just click OK.

The Publish New And Changed Assignments dialog box appears (see Figure 19-9). Since you chose specific tasks, Selected Items is the default selection in the Publish New And Changed Assignments For list.

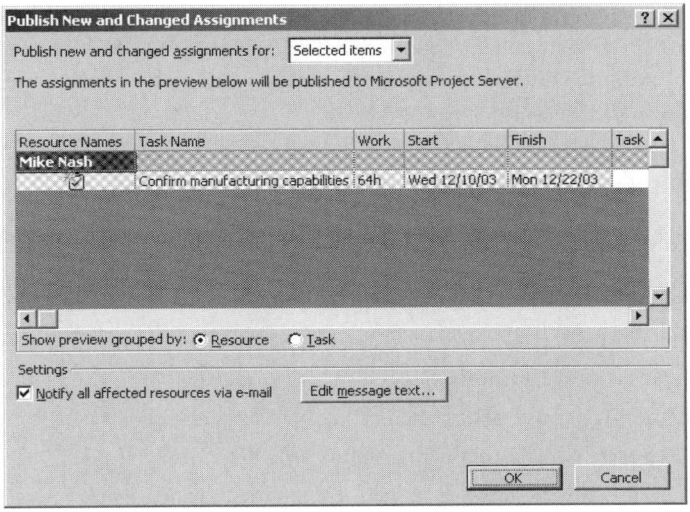

Figure 19-9. Use the Publish New and Changed Assignments dialog box to confirm and send assignments to the resources.

3. Confirm the tasks in the list and then click OK.

   Your message is sent to the resources assigned to the selected tasks.

After you publish a message regarding changed assignments, the Gantt Chart shows the Unconfirmed indicators next to the selected tasks. They indicate that an assignment has been published for that task, but that you have not yet received a response from the assigned resource. When you receive the acknowledgment from the resources and select the Update Project button, the Unconfirmed indicators disappear.

Requesting Progress Information

You can quickly send an e-mail to resources requesting information about an assignment. To do this, follow these steps:

1. In your project plan, display the Gantt Chart or another task view.
2. Select the tasks for which you want progress information.

   To select adjacent tasks, drag across them. To select nonadjacent tasks, click the first task, hold down the Ctrl key, and then click all the other tasks you want to select.
3. Click Collaborate, Request Progress Information.
4. In the message that appears, click OK.

Tip **Quickly request assignment actuals**
You can also right-click a task, click Request Progress Information, and then click OK.

After you request progress information, the Gantt Chart shows an indicator specifying that progress information has been requested and not yet received. When you receive workgroup messages containing actuals information from the team members and select the Update Project button, the indicators disappear.

Resending Task Assignments

Sometimes it's necessary to republish task assignments to the team members. This is typically done when there's a problem with the original assignment e-mail. To republish assignments, follow these steps:

1. In the Gantt Chart or other task sheet, select the tasks you want to republish.
2. Click Collaborate, Publish, Republish Assignments.
3. If the message about saving the project plan appears, click OK.

   The Republish Assignments dialog box appears.
4. In the Publish New And Changed Assignments For box, click Selected Items.

   Your e-mail program sends the assignments to the resources assigned to the selected tasks.

Receiving Assignments from the Project Manager

Note This section describes the process for team members using e-mail workgroup messaging to communicate with the project manager. Project team members should read this section.

As the member of a project team, you can use e-mail to exchange information about your tasks and current status with your project manager. With special e-mail messages from Microsoft Project, you obtain fast notification of changes regarding your tasks. Just as quickly, you can send assignment and status updates back to the project manager.

Receiving and Responding to Assignments

You receive new or changed assignment messages in your e-mail inbox. The subject box of these special e-mails contains a brief description of the assignment action (see Figure 19-10). This subject lets you know that you have important project information to open. Depending on which e-mail application you're using, the assignment e-mail might show the assignment form directly, or it might include an attachment containing the assignment form.

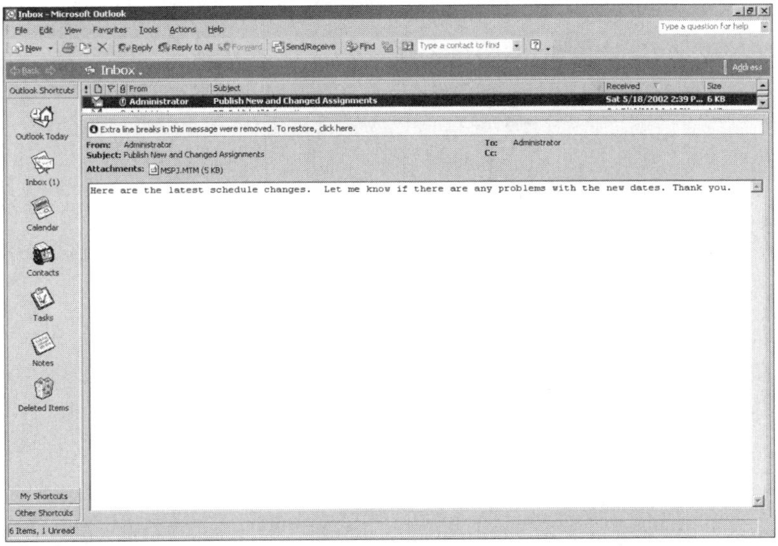

Figure 19-10. Notifications of new and changed assignments are sent through e-mail.

The e-mail message form contains preformatted features enabling quick and direct communication back to the project manager. To read and respond to a Microsoft Project e-mail message, do the following:

1 Double-click the e-mail message to open it.

The specialized Microsoft Project e-mail form appears (see Figure 19-11). You might receive such a message when the project manager sends the initial set of assignments to you. You might also receive it when the project manager adds new assignments to your workload or when there's been a change to assignments you're already working on.

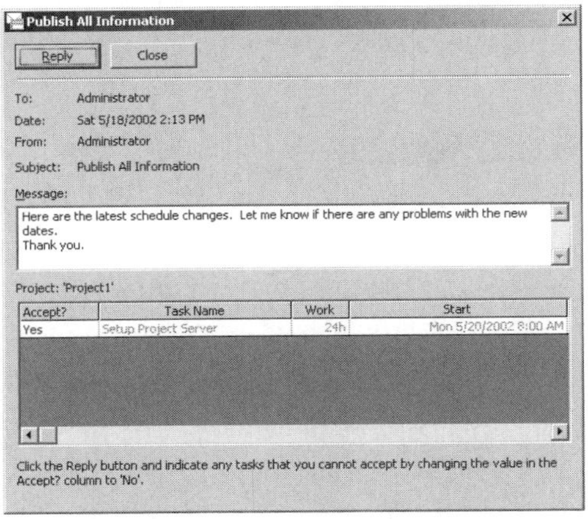

Figure 19-11. You receive e-mail regarding your assignments in a specialized message form.

2 Click Reply.

The Reply form appears (see Figure 19-12).

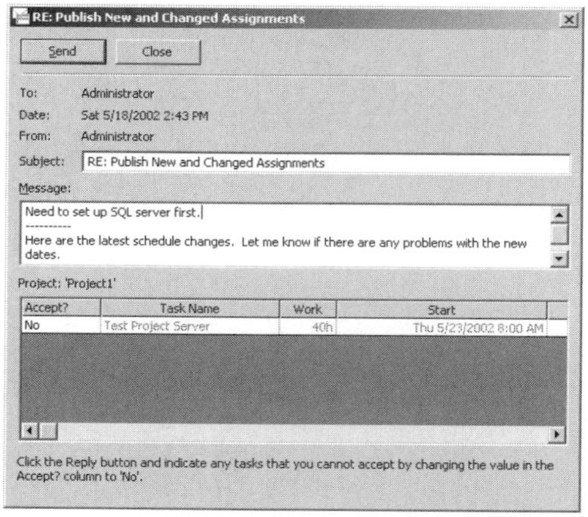

Figure 19-12. Indicate whether you accept or decline the assignment and add any comments as necessary.

3 In the Accept? field, retain the default Yes to accept the assignment. If you need to decline the assignment, double-click on the word Yes to change it to No.

4 If necessary, enter a comment in the Message box.

5 Click the Send button.

The message is sent to the project manager's e-mail inbox. When the project manager accepts your information, the project plan is updated accordingly.

> **Tip** **Add or update tasks in your Outlook Tasks list**
> If you use Outlook, you can add or update the tasks in your Outlook Tasks list. Click the Update Task List button in the Microsoft Project e-mail form.

Providing Assignment Status Updates

Throughout the project, you need to provide actual information reflecting your current progress on assignments to the project manager. The project manager sends you a progress information request message, to which you can respond as follows:

1 In your e-mail program, double-click the status request message.

2 Click the Reply button.

3 In the appropriate fields, enter the information as applicable to your individual assignments.

Depending on how the project manager has customized the status request form, you might be asked to provide percent complete, hours worked, actual start and finish dates, and so on.

4 Enter any comments you want in the Message box.

5 Click the Send button.

The actuals information message is sent to the project manager's e-mail inbox. When the project manager accepts your information, the project plan is updated accordingly.

Exchanging Project Information Using E-Mail

In addition to exchanging specific assignment and status information through your e-mail system, you can also use e-mail to send project information to team members, stakeholders, and other interested parties. If your organization uses a 32-bit MAPI-based e-mail system, you can

- Send your project file as an e-mail attachment.
- Send a picture of selected tasks to a group of recipients.
- Send a picture of selected resources to a group of recipients.
- Route the project file to a group of recipients.
- Post the project file to a public Exchange folder.

For more information about these capabilities, see "Sending Project File Information" on page 543.

Part 7

Managing Projects Across Your Enterprise

Chapter 20

Understanding the Project Workgroup and Enterprise Model

Through the use of Microsoft Office Project Professional 2003, Microsoft Office Project Server 2003, and Microsoft Office Project Web Access 2003, your organization has the capacity to set up dynamic project workgroup collaboration and refined enterprise project management functionality.

Microsoft Office Project 2003 workgroup collaboration is designed to facilitate communication of task assignments and actual progress among members of a project team, using Project Web Access 2003 as the Web-based interface. In addition, team leads and resource managers can delegate tasks and manage resources as needed to accomplish the goals of the project and keep the project manager well-informed. Other stakeholders can also use Project Web Access to view various aspects of the project.

If your organization is set up with Windows SharePoint Services, you can integrate it with Project Web Access to add document check-in and checkout, issues tracking, and risk management to the workgroup collaboration features.

With enterprise project management, hundreds of projects and thousands of resources can be managed in a consistent manner throughout an organization. Project elements such as views, toolbars, fields, and macros can be customized for the organization and standardized across all projects. Resources and their associated skill, cost, and availability information can be built into a common and interactive enterprise resource pool from which all project managers can build their project teams. Executives and other managing stakeholders can do high-level modeling and analyses of tasks, resources, and costs across multiple projects.

Who's Who in Enterprise Project Management

Given the nature of project workgroups and enterprise project management, it's obvious that Project 2003 users represent a variety of roles.

Roles in enterprise project management are as follows:

Project manager. The traditional user of Microsoft Project, the project manager is still the hub around which all other roles rotate. The project manager primarily uses Project Professional 2003 and occasionally also uses Project Web Access. The project manager builds and adjusts the project, assigns resources, tracks progress, responds to changes, mitigates risks, and communicates progress throughout the project's life cycle.

Resource manager. Although the project manager often plays the role of the resource manager, Project Web Access 2003 makes it easy for a separate resource manager to work with the project manager to assign tasks to the right people. The resource manager uses Project Web Access with special resource-related privileges. The resource manager can manage data about users in the enterprise resource pool, review timesheets, and create resource-related views.

Team lead. The team lead is often a user carrying out a set of project tasks while also fulfilling lead responsibilities for a small group of other team members. The team lead uses Project Web Access to do both.

Team member. The team member implements the work of the project, actually completing the tasks that contribute to the goal of the project. Team members use Project Web Access to review, create, and update tasks and to see details of the project as a whole. They also use Project Web Access to enter and submit timesheet information regarding actual progress on assignments.

Executive. Upper management, customers, or other managing stakeholders provide high-level direction and support of the project, and keep an eye on progress through the use of specialized views in Project Web Access. They can also compare aspects of multiple projects against each other for sophisticated modeling or analysis.

Portfolio manager. The portfolio manager is typically a managing stakeholder who manages the priorities and overall resource allocation for entire groups of projects. The portfolio manager has the default permissions necessary to take on some system administrator responsibilities, if needed.

Administrator. The project server administrator configures Project Server 2003 and Project Web Access 2003 to implement the features and permissions needed by the organization. The administrator works mostly in Project Web Access and occasionally in Project Professional.

Although these roles are distinct, it's entirely possible for one person to fulfill two or more overlapping roles and have the permissions in Project Server that reflect these multiple responsibilities.

This chapter provides the overview of the Project 2003 workgroup collaboration and enterprise project management features. Succeeding chapters detail different aspects of these features as they apply to the different types of users, as follows:

- Chapter 21, "Administering Project Server and Project Web Access for Your Enterprise," is written for the project server administrator and the portfolio manager. The chapter includes instructions on configuring Project Server and Project Web Access for workgroup and enterprise, as well as setting user permissions. Creation of custom fields and other standardization elements is covered, as is enterprise resource pool setup. Chapter 21 can also be reviewed by project managers who want a clearer picture of capabilities that are implemented by the administrator.
- Chapter 22, "Managing with Project Professional and Project Server," is the project manager's chapter. It details processes for creating an enterprise project, either from scratch or from an existing local project. Building the project team from the enterprise resource pool is covered, as well as the details for workgroup collaboration from the project manager's standpoint.
- Chapter 23, "Participating on a Team Using Project Web Access," is the chapter designed for the team member, team lead, and resource manager, who all work in Project Web Access. The chapter includes information on accepting and creating new task assignments, reporting on assignment progress, and viewing the overall project picture. Information on building project teams and delegating tasks is for team leads and resource managers.
- Chapter 24, "Making Executive Decisions Using Project Web Access," is directed at the executive or other managing stakeholder who wants to review high-level project and resource information. Information about the Portfolio Modeler and Portfolio Analyzer is included in this chapter.

Understanding Project Server Components

The core components of Microsoft Project workgroup collaboration and enterprise project management are as follows:

Project Professional. The origin of all project data, including tasks, resources, assignments, scheduling dates, costs, and tracking information. The Microsoft Project database stores all project information managed from Project Professional. Through the Microsoft Project database, Project Professional interfaces with Project Server.

Project Server. Essentially a server and database custom-designed to convert data to and from your project plan and to interface with Project Web Access using that data. The Project Server database stores information related to security settings, administrative settings, and all other information related to Project Web Access. Project Server is a separate application containing business logic and functionality to process this data.

Project Web Access. A Web site with unique capabilities to work specifically with Project Server and display targeted project data. It is the view into the Project Server. This Web site typically lives on your organization's intranet and is accessed by project team members entering via some type of user authentication. Some Project Web Access features can also be accessed from within Project Professional.

Note Depending on other resources in use by your organization, you can also integrate these other components for additional functionality:

- Windows SharePoint Services
- Microsoft Outlook
- Active Directory

Here's a description of the interaction between the three Microsoft Project components in a little more detail:

1. Project data saved to the project server using Project Professional is saved to *Project Tables* in a certain area of the Project Server database. This is the only area of the database with which Project Professional reads or writes, and it is not used by Project Web Access.
2. When projects are *published* (rather than simply *saved*), a command is sent to the project server to process the data about the project held in the Project Tables. These data are saved in a separate part of the database: in the *Views Tables*. The Views Tables are accessed by Project Web Access when users view project, resource, or assignment information using their browsers.
3. Both Project Server and Project Web Access use XML to pass data. In addition, Project Web Access uses HTML and ASP to present that data and build interactive features. Other technologies, such as ActiveX controls, contribute to the capabilities of the Project Web Access interface.

When you change data in your project plan, it's changed in the Project Tables area of the Project Server database. When you publish the information to Project Server, relevant data are parsed into XML formats, read into the Project Server database, and then saved to the Views Tables in the Project Server database—where it is converted back from XML into HTML-rendered text (see Figure 20-1). All this in a blink of an eye (or as many blinks as determined by your network configuration and database size).

These components work together to provide team collaboration as well as enterprise project management functionality.

For more information about the Microsoft Project database, the Project Server database, and how the two interact, see Chapter 32, "Working with Microsoft Project Data."

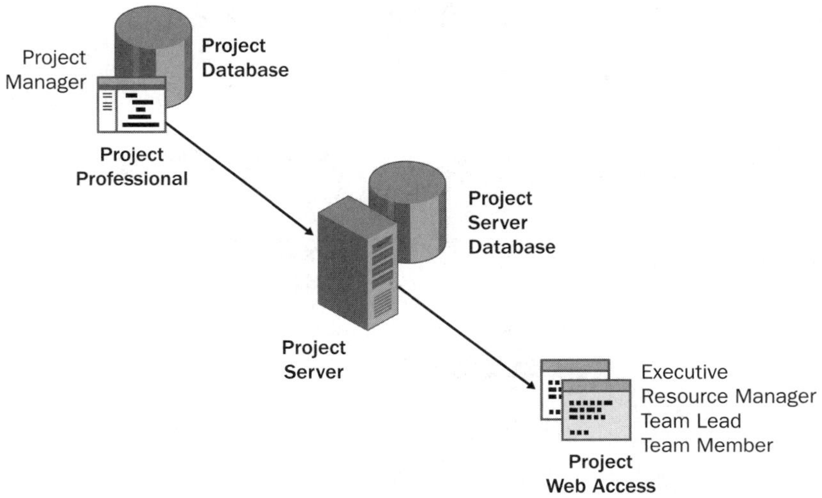

Figure 20-1. Publish information from Project Professional, and it is converted in Project Server to be displayed in Project Web Access.

Understanding Project Workgroup Collaboration

Communication is a critical component of effective project management. There's no question that establishing an effective two-way information flow prevents a host of problems.

Project Server and Project Web Access provide a highly efficient process for exchanging project information with team members. As the project manager working in Project Professional and Project Web Access, you can transmit project information through Project Server to do the following:

- Submit assignments and task changes to assigned resources.
- Request assignment actuals from assigned resources.
- Request, receive, and compile narrative status reports.
- Incorporate actuals submitted by assigned resources directly into the project plan.
- Publish the full project plan for review by team members and other stakeholders.

Note In Project 2002, you could implement workgroup collaboration using either Project Standard or Project Professional. In Project 2003, you must use Project Professional.

For details about workgroup collaboration information for the project manager, see Chapter 22.

With Project Web Access, team members can see all the relevant project information for their assignments. The Web site that is their Project Web Access page (see Figure 20-2) has an easy-to-navigate layout that simplifies information flow.

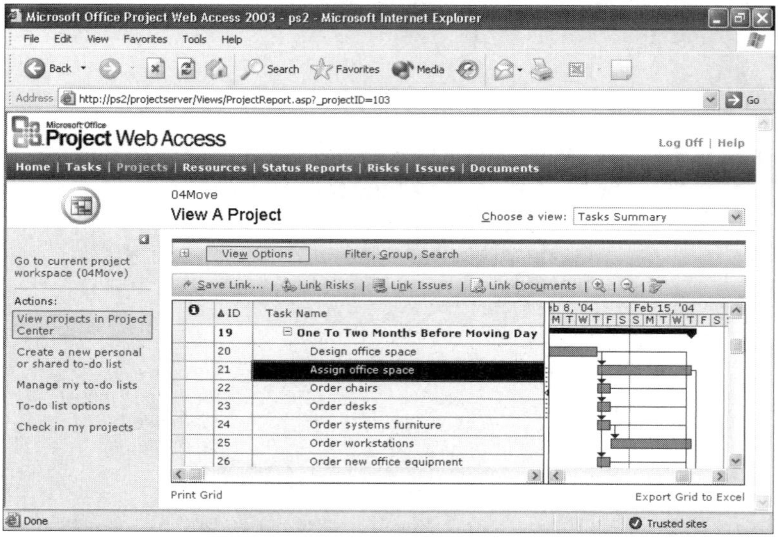

Figure 20-2. Team members use the Project Web Access Timesheet to manage their assignments.

Using Project Web Access, team members can do the following:

- Accept (or reject) task assignments.
- Create and self-assign new tasks for addition to the project plan.
- Add comments to assignments that become part of the project task record.
- Update task information for incorporation in the project plan.
- Enter daily or weekly actuals, specify percent complete, or indicate the amount of completed and remaining work to report progress on assignments and submit them to the project manager for incorporation into the project plan.
- Review assignments in different views, with applied filters, groups, and sorting.
- Review the entire project plan to see the context of individual assignments.

Information updated or changed by team members is stored initially in the Project Server database. As project manager, you can accept or reject changes. If you accept an update, you can incorporate it immediately into your project plan. The Project Server database is then updated to show that the change has been accepted, and team members who review the project plan through Project Web Access can see the updates (see Figure 20-3).

In the Project Web Access intranet site, team members can see different views of project data, review assignments, enter time reports, update tasks, view summary project plans, send information to the project manager, and more. Each Project Web Access user can individually customize his own view to enhance individual efficiencies.

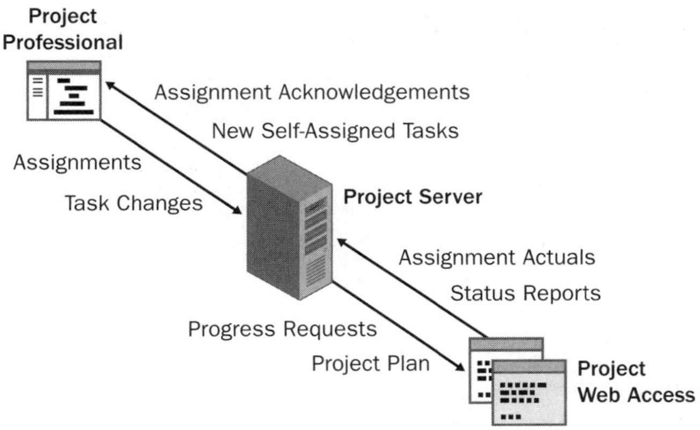

Figure 20-3. The project manager and team members exchange information via Project Server.

For details about workgroup collaboration information for the team member, see Chapter 23.

Project Web Access is not just for team members, though. Any stakeholders—including functional managers, customers, human resources representatives, and finance managers—can be set up with a user name and a personalized set of permissions to access their view of Project Server through Project Web Access.

If your organization also uses Windows SharePoint Services, additional functions can be integrated into the Project Web Access experience:

Document check-in and checkout. You can include project-related documents with the project, and even associate them with individual tasks or phases. You can implement version control through document check-in and checkout processes.

Issues tracking. You can record issues associated with a task or phase. You can then track the issues, assign responsibility, and close them when they're resolved. The issue becomes a part of the task history.

Risk management. You can record potential risks associated with a task or phase, along with mitigation plans should the risk become a reality. You can assign responsibility and track the risk and then close the risk record when appropriate. The risk information becomes a part of the task history, which can be especially helpful when planning another similar project.

Note The implementation of Windows SharePoint Services requires that Project Server run in enterprise mode and use Windows authentication.

Understanding Enterprise Project Management

The enterprise features of Project Professional scale up the power of Microsoft Project beyond the individual project to multiple departments and groups in a mid- to large-size multiple-project business. With enterprise project management, information stored in the Project Server database from every resource and every project in the entire company can be quickly collated and reported. Enterprise project management is implemented through Project Professional together with Project Server, Project Web Access, SQL Server 2000, and Windows SharePoint Services.

For any business that works on multiple projects, rich customization, resource management, reporting, and analysis capabilities become possible through enterprise project management. Executives, customers, and other managing stakeholders can review and analyze information on all projects and all resources in their organization, providing for a comprehensive understanding of the nature and progress of the activity within the organization. In addition, the enterprise features help individual project managers plan and control their projects within the context of their organization.

The following steps detail a typical process for working with multiple projects in an enterprise environment:

1. The project server administrator uses Project Professional to create the *enterprise global template*, the basis for all project plans to be created throughout the enterprise.

   This global template contains standardized project elements such as custom fields, currency format, tables, formulas, and VBA modules created to reflect the organization's requirements. The use of the global template propagates the custom elements as the organizational standard for all projects.
2. The project server administrator or resource manager uses Project Professional to build and manage the enterprise-wide resource pool, which includes vital information such as resource skill sets, costs, and availability for project assignments.
3. Project managers throughout the organization use Project Professional to create and check in brand new enterprise projects based on the enterprise global template.

   Project managers can also import existing local projects as enterprise projects.
4. Project managers submit, or *check in*, their project plans from Project Professional to Project Server as enterprise projects.

   Project Server interfaces with SQL Server, which provides the Project Server database. Project Server also interfaces with Project Web Access, the Web-based view of project information.
5. Project managers use Project Professional to access the enterprise resource pool and find resources in the organization who have the right skill set and availability for their individual project requirements.

   Project managers can specify generic properties for required resources and then automatically build their team and assign real resources to tasks.

6 Executives can use Project Web Access to view multiple projects in the organization using the portfolio view. Using the Portfolio Analyzer, executives can review a high-level summary of projects throughout the enterprise, including information about scheduling, costs, resources, and more.

> **For system requirements for Project Server and the enterprise features, see Appendix A, "Installing Microsoft Office Project 2003."**

Standardizing and Customizing Enterprise Projects

A key element of effective management and control systems is standardization. One purpose of standardization is to ensure that one project is operating with the same ground rules as any other project. Another is consistency throughout the organization.

You can standardize and customize the use of Microsoft Project for the way your enterprise specifically does business, as follows:

- Tailored fields, calendars, views, VBA modules, and other consistent Microsoft Project elements are applied throughout all projects through the use of the enterprise global template.

  Individual project templates are also available in the Project Server.
- Your organization's project server administrator can use enterprise custom fields, create formulas and outlines, and pick lists for skill codes or titles.

  Project management efforts can therefore be tailored to the specific processes of the organization.

Managing Enterprise Resources

The lack of a skilled worker for a job can cause serious delays or loss of business. Likewise, having underutilized resources can be an unnecessary drain on the business treasury and can reduce profits.

Project Professional can provide valuable insight into resource utilization, allocation, and availability throughout the enterprise. Although it's not a human resources management tool, the Microsoft Project enterprise features help project managers, resource managers, and functional managers maximize their resource usage while keeping an eye on overallocations.

You can access, assign, and manage resources to leverage the many skill sets available throughout the enterprise. With Microsoft Project enterprise project management, you can obtain up-to-date information about the availability and utilization of thousands of resources in an enterprise as follows:

- All resource assignments throughout the enterprise are visible to project managers, resource managers, and other authorized stakeholders.

  This enterprise-wide visibility ensures that all parties have access to accurate information regarding resource availability. Resource assignments can be checked out, edited, and checked in again.

- The Team Builder helps you find resources throughout the enterprise who have the right skills and availability to work on your project.

  Filter and query the enterprise resource database to fine-tune your project for the right resources.
- The Resource Substitution Wizard analyzes the skills needed by tasks in a project, matches those with skills possessed by resources in the enterprise, and determines their availability.

  By using the Resource Substitution Wizard while still building the project plan, project managers can find and assign tasks to the right resources in the right project.
- Resource availability graphs enable project managers to quickly identify when and why resources might be underallocated or overallocated.
- With workgroup collaboration features, project managers and team members can automate their communications with each other and get the assignments and actuals they need.

For further information about managing projects with enterprise resources, see "Building Your Enterprise Project Team" on page 655.

Analyzing Your Enterprise Project Activities

A key benefit of implementing Microsoft Project enterprise project management is that a view of all projects, that is, the organization's project *portfolio*, can be presented for a set of summary information that provides a unique view into multiple projects. In such a portfolio summary, executives can analyze schedules, costs, resource utilization, and other factors at a high level across all the projects taking place throughout the organization.

The Portfolio Analyzer presents spreadsheet or graphical summary information through the use of o*nline analytical processing (OLAP) cubes*, used for both projects and resources. This tool enables the user to "mine" the enterprise data for specific kinds of information drawn from the entire organization.

Through the use of the Portfolio Analyzer, management can make informed decisions in support of enterprise priorities and initiatives.

For more information about high-level enterprise project reporting and analysis, see Chapter 24.

Modeling Enterprise Implementations

Because the components are designed to be flexible and scalable, there are probably hundreds of ways in which your organization can implement enterprise project management through Project Professional. The style of the implementation your organization adopts depends largely on your organization's structure and management practices. This section includes three implementation examples, based on modern organizational structures.

Implementing a Pyramid Hierarchy

One example of a straightforward project enterprise implementation is the classic *pyramid hierarchy* model (see Figure 20-4) with a single top point and more connections the further you go down, from CEO to project team member.

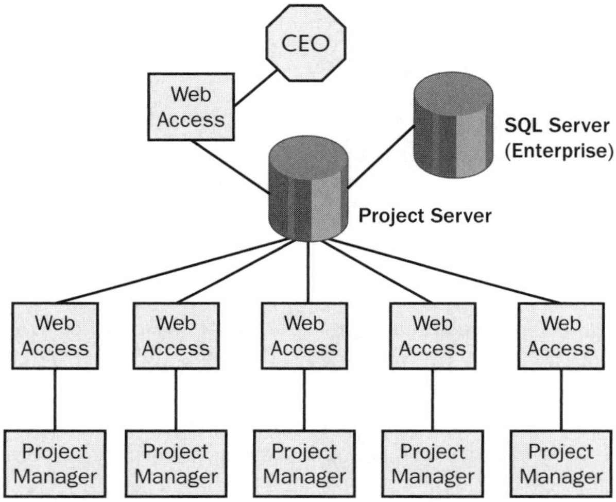

Figure 20-4. You can implement enterprise projects in a classic pyramid hierarchy.

For example, imagine a software development company with five different projects in progress at the same time. The project managers all use Project Professional to manage their projects. Project Server is installed in the central data systems office, along with SQL Server. Each of the five projects has ten team members connected through the Project Server. The CEO of the company has an executive account set up to work with Project Server with Web Access.

The five project managers publish their enterprise project and resource information through Project Server. Their team members and stakeholders use Project Web Access to see their pertinent project information and collaborate effectively. The CEO uses the enterprise account to see and evaluate all the projects in the company in a standardized form and view and analyze all the resources in the company.

Implementing a Tapered Block Hierarchy

A second example involves larger organizations that have dozens of projects being worked on at a given time. This type of implementation is more of a *tapered block* model of information exchange and access.

In the tapered-block model, there are multiple sources of information at the project level and there are multiple (though fewer) connections at the upper enterprise level. This model is effective for large, discretely organized firms, such as telecommunications companies, which make executive decisions based on input from department heads.

For example, suppose that each of the projects is using Project Professional. Project Server is set up for enterprise features, and all the project managers publish their enterprise project and resource data to Project Server. At the enterprise account level, ten vice presidents connect to their Project Server accounts, in which they view and analyze project and resource information, focusing on the projects that are most important to them. They then advise and inform the company president.

Implementing a Straight Block Hierarchy

A third example is a company that uses a pure project management model for its organization. Some construction companies are set up in this way. This model is considered a *straight block*. The level of authority and responsibility below the president is the project manager. All the work in the company is planned, performed, and tracked as projects.

For example, suppose that there are 12 different projects being done, each independent and equal in importance to the company. The 12 project managers all use Project Professional and all are connected to Project Server, which is set up for enterprise project management. All project managers and the company president have enterprise accounts. They see the resource and project information about all or selected projects among the 12. They can quickly resolve prioritization and utilization issues by using the enterprise features. The president also can see the entire company's work and resources in a standardized manner.

Chapter 21

Administering Project Server and Project Web Access for Your Enterprise

To implement the workgroup and enterprise features provided by Microsoft Office Project Professional 2003, Microsoft Office Project Server 2003, and Microsoft Office Project Web Access 2003, a *project server administrator* must configure Project Server 2003 and set up users, permissions, and other options pertinent to your organization.

The project server administrator might be a lead project manager with a good working knowledge of systems and databases. Or, the administrator can be an IT professional with a good working knowledge of project management. In either case, the project server administrator needs to be dedicated and available when Project Server and Project Web Access 2003 are first being set up. This person also needs to be available whenever project managers, team members, or other system users need to change their setup.

Specifically, the project server administration functions include:

- Identifying enterprise and workgroup options.
- Adding users and setting their permissions.
- Establishing the enterprise resource pool and associated resource information.
- Configuring projects for multiple project portfolio review, analysis, and modeling.
- Standardizing project elements included in the enterprise global template.
- Customizing team member timesheets for the requirements of a particular project.

Depending on whether you're implementing enterprise features with workgroup, or workgroup features only (without enterprise project management), you might carry out all or some of these tasks.

Although this chapter is targeted for project server administrators and *portfolio managers*, it's not a bad idea for project managers to review this chapter as well. This chapter can help project managers understand the enterprise and workgroup capabilities available, as well as the effort required to implement certain features.

Configuring Your Enterprise and Workgroup

Your organization can set up Microsoft Office Project 2003 for enterprise project management with workgroup collaboration or for workgroup collaboration only.

As the project server administrator, you configure enterprise and workgroup options on the Admin page in Project Web Access. To go to this page, follow these steps:

1. Open your Web browser, and in the Address bar enter the URL for the location of the project server.
2. In the logon page, enter your user ID and password that was set up for you as the administrator.
3. In the blue navigation bar across the top of the Project Web Access page, click Admin.

   The Admin page appears (see Figure 21-1). Only a user identified as a project server administrator with the associated permissions can open the Admin page in Project Web Access.

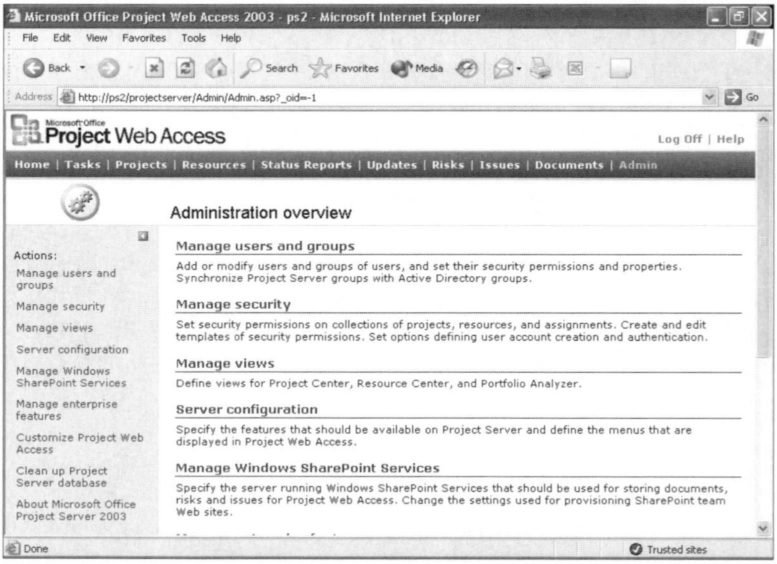

Figure 21-1. Set up enterprise and workgroup options on the Project Web Access Admin page.

For information about installing Project 2003, along with Project Server and enterprise project management setup issues, see Appendix A, "Installing Microsoft Office Project 2003." For detailed guidance, see the Microsoft Project Help file pjsvr.chm, provided on the Companion CD as well as on the Microsoft Project 2003 installation CD.

You can also download the online book from the Microsoft Project Web site entitled "Microsoft Office Project 2003 Installation Guide." Go to *http://www.microsoft.com/downloads*, and then search for **Project Server 2003**.

After installation, one of your first tasks as the project server administrator might be to configure the use of Project Server in your organization. You can configure Project Server for enterprise features along with the workgroup features. Or, you can configure Project Server for workgroup features alone. To configure Project Server:

1. In the Admin page of Project Web Access, click Server Configuration in the left pane.

   You can also click the Start button on the Windows taskbar, point to Programs, point to Microsoft Project Server, and then click Configure Microsoft Project Server.

   The Server Configuration page appears (see Figure 21-2).

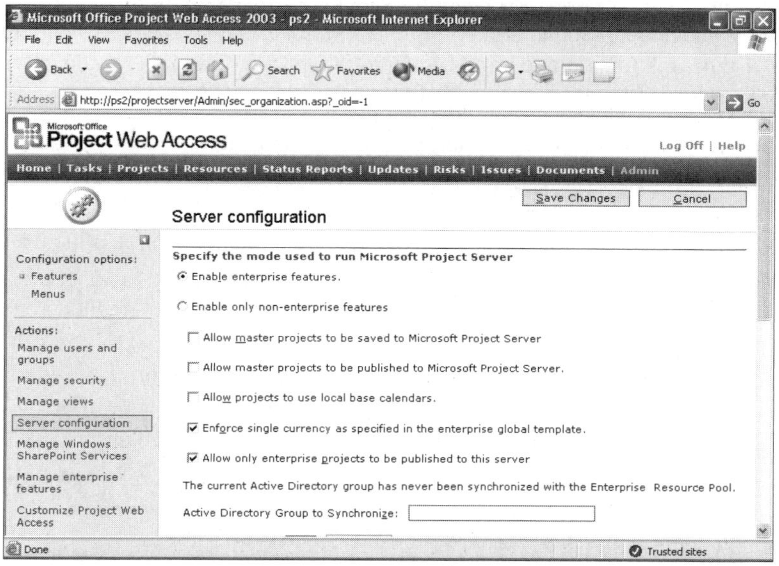

Figure 21-2. Select whether you are using the full features for enterprise project management.

2. Under Specify The Mode Used To Run Microsoft Project Server, select the option that indicates whether you're using enterprise and workgroup together or just workgroup on its own.

   If you select the Enable Enterprise Features, additional configuration settings appear, which have to do with the base calendar, Active Directory, and update scheduling. Set the enterprise options as appropriate. If you don't know whether you want a particular option, leave the default. You can always change these settings later.

3. Under Select The Features That You Want To Make Available To Users In Project Web Access, scroll through the table and select the global permissions you and your organization want for team members and other users of Project Web Access.

   These check boxes set the defaults for all users. You can change these defaults when you set permissions for individual users and groups of users.

4. Under Enter The Intranet And/Or Extranet Address Of Project Server, enter the address (URL) for your project server. Enter the address in the appropriate box.

5. At the top of the page, click the Save Changes button.

For information about configuring Windows SharePoint Services with Project Server, see Appendix A.

For project manager information about using Windows SharePoint Services with Project Server, see "Managing Documents, Risks, and Issues" on page 691.

Carry out administrative duties

The Administration Overview page in Project Web Access contains all the tools and commands you need to administer enterprise and workgroup features for your organization. The links in the left (blue) pane on the Administration Overview page list the different categories of tasks you can carry out, as follows.

Manage Users And Groups Add, modify, or deactivate individual user accounts. Create, modify, or delete groups of users.

Manage Security Manage security-related aspects of Project Web Access. Specifically, create custom *security templates* and additional categories of users.

Manage Views Define the views available to Project Web Access users on pages such as Projects, Resources, Status Reports, Updates, and Timesheets. Create new views as necessary.

Server Configuration Specify whether your organization is using just the workgroup features or is also using the enterprise project management features. Set global default permissions for Project Web Access users. Enter the project server URL.

Manage Windows SharePoint Services Manage the servers running Windows SharePoint Services. These servers store the content that can be viewed on the Documents, Issues, and Risks pages in Project Web Access.

Manage Enterprise Features Set up the check-in and checkout of enterprise projects and enterprise resources. Specify the different enterprise project versions available to users. Set up the *OnLine Analytical Processing (OLAP) cube* for resource and project analysis and modeling.

Customize Project Web Access Set preferences for various aspects of Project Web Access, such as Home page content and links, as well as e-mail notifications and reminders.

Clean Up Project Server Database Delete inactive user records from your project server that are no longer needed.

About Microsoft Office Project Server 2003 Review the version number of your Project Server. Also, see the current number of Project Web Access accounts in your organization and compare this with the number of licenses your organization currently has.

Note If you need assistance while using Project Web Access, click Help in the upper-right corner of the Project Web Access page. Microsoft Project Web Access Help appears on the right side of the window.

Managing Users and System Security

To allow people throughout the organization to use the Microsoft Project enterprise and workgroup features they need, you first need to identify them as users of your project server. At the same time, you also specify the users' permissions that enable them to carry out their category of project responsibilities.

Establishing User Accounts and Permissions

Project Server is loaded with a set of built-in user *groups*, each of which is associated with a set of *permissions* having to do with various aspects of enterprise project management and workgroup collaboration. Consider using the built-in groups and permission sets as a starting point. As you and your organization gain more experience with Project Server and start to get a better idea about how you want to implement enterprise and workgroup features, you can make adjustments and customizations.

The built-in user groups, also known as *roles*, are as follows:

- Administrators
- Executives
- Portfolio Managers
- Project Managers
- Resource Managers
- Team Leads
- Team Members

Each of the user groups is associated with a security *template* that includes the set of permissions most likely to be needed by someone in that user group.

In addition to setting the permissions for a new user, you also set the categories of information that can be accessed by that user. Although you can create your own categories, the built-in categories are as follows:

- My Direct Reports
- My Organization
- My Projects
- My Resources
- My Tasks

Category permissions

Table 21-1 shows the category permissions as set using the built-in templates according to a user's group, or role.

Table 21-1. Category Permissions

Category Permissions	Admin	Exec	Portfolio Mgr	Project Mgr	Resource Mgr	Team Leader	Team Member
Adjust Actuals	X						
Approve Timesheets For Resources	X						
Assign Resource	X		X				
Build Team On Project	X		X	X			
Create New Task Or Assignment	X			X	X	X	X
Edit Enterprise Resource Data	X		X				
Open Project	X		X	X			
Save Project	X		X	X			
See Enterprise Resource Data	X	X	X	X			
See Projects In Project Center	X	X	X	X	X	X	X
See Projects In Project Views	X	X	X	X		X	X
See Resource Assignments In Assign-ment Views	X	X	X	X		X	
View Risks, Issues, and Documents	X	X	X	X	X	X	X

To create a new user account in Project Web Access and set the user's permissions, follow these steps:

1. In the vAdmin page of Project Web Access, click Manage Users And Groups in the left pane.

The Users page appears (see Figure 21-3).

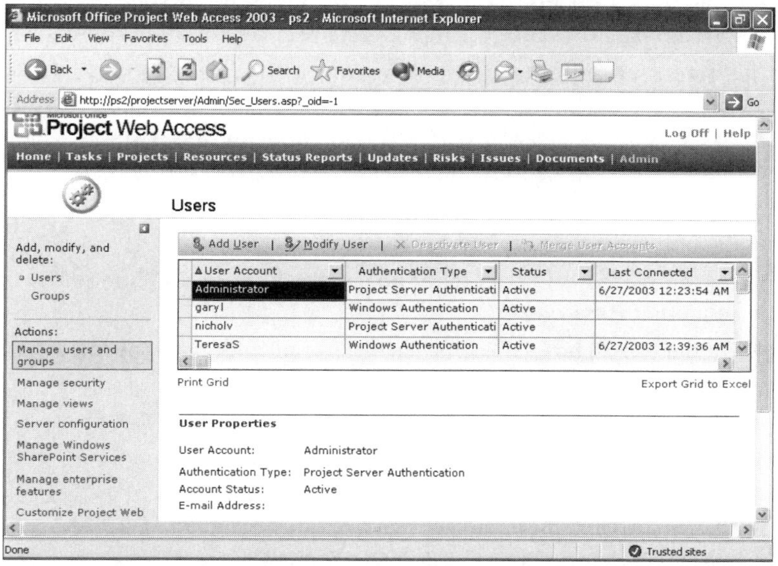

Figure 21-3. Click Manage Users And Groups to open the Users page and add a new user account.

2 Above the table, click Add User.

The Add User page appears (see Figure 21-4).

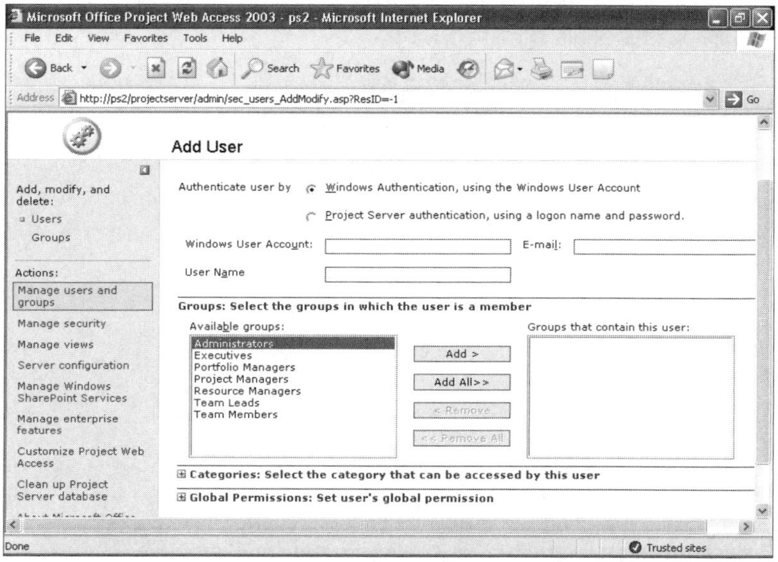

Figure 21-4. In the Add User page, specify the new user's authentication, group, and permissions.

3 Next to Authenticate User By, select the option for this user's authentication method.

Windows Authentication users can log on to Project Web Access using the same user ID and password they use to log on to your organization's Windows network.

Project Server Authentication users log on to Project Web Access using the user ID you set up on this page. They can then set their password in Project Web Access.

If you have added enterprise resources, they are automatically added as Project Web Access users authenticated by Project Server.

4 If you select the Windows Authentication option, complete the Windows User Account, User Name, and E-Mail fields.

In the Windows User Account box, enter the person's Windows account in the format of ***domain\username***.

In the E-mail box, enter the person's e-mail address in the format of ***someone@ microsoft.com***.

In the User Name box, enter the person's first and last names.

5 If you select the Project Server Authentication option, enter the person's User Name.

The first time these users log on to Project Web Access, they'll be prompted to set a password.

6 Under Groups, click the group that this user belongs to and then click Add.

A user can be a member of more than one group.

7 Click the Categories heading to expand the Categories section (see Figure 21-5).

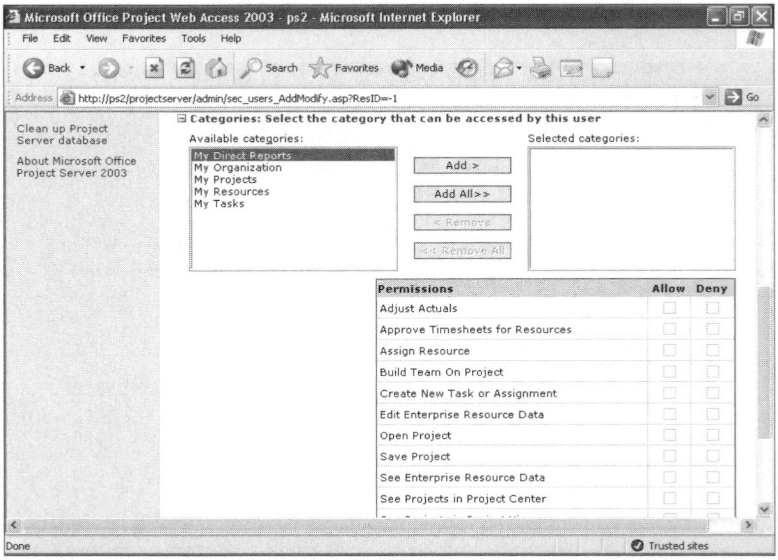

Figure 21-5. In the Categories section, specify the items that can be accessed by this user and then start setting permissions.

8 In the Available Categories box, select the data that should be available for access by this user and then click Add.

A user can access multiple categories as appropriate to his responsibilities.

9 Select the check boxes for the permissions you want to set for this user.

It's easiest to set permissions with a template that corresponds to the user's group and then make any individual adjustments as necessary. To do this, under the permissions table, click the Set Permissions With Template button and then click the user's group, for example, Project Manager or Team Lead. The check boxes in the permissions table are completed as appropriate to the selected group (see Figure 21-6).

To set a permission, select the check box under the Allow column. To deny a permission, clear the check box under the Allow column. You can also select the check box under the Deny column, but it's not necessary—just one or the other is sufficient.

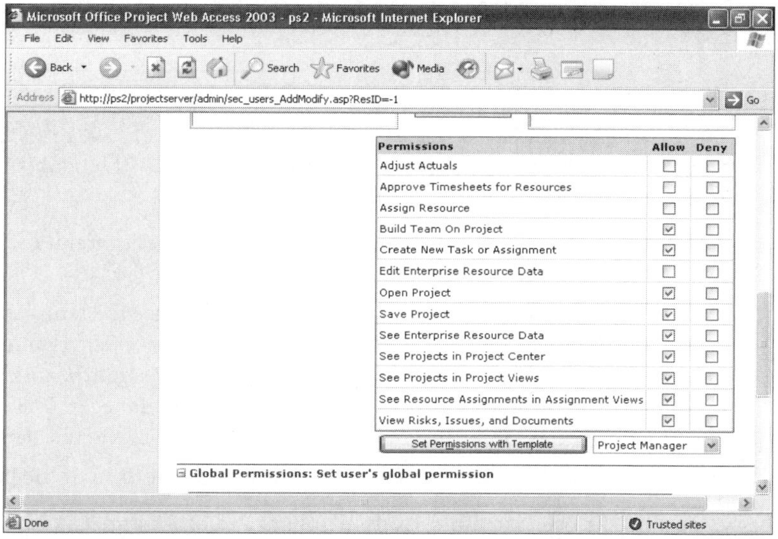

Figure 21-6. These are the permissions set by the built-in Project Manager security template.

10 Click the Global Permissions heading to expand the Global Permissions section (see Figure 21-7).

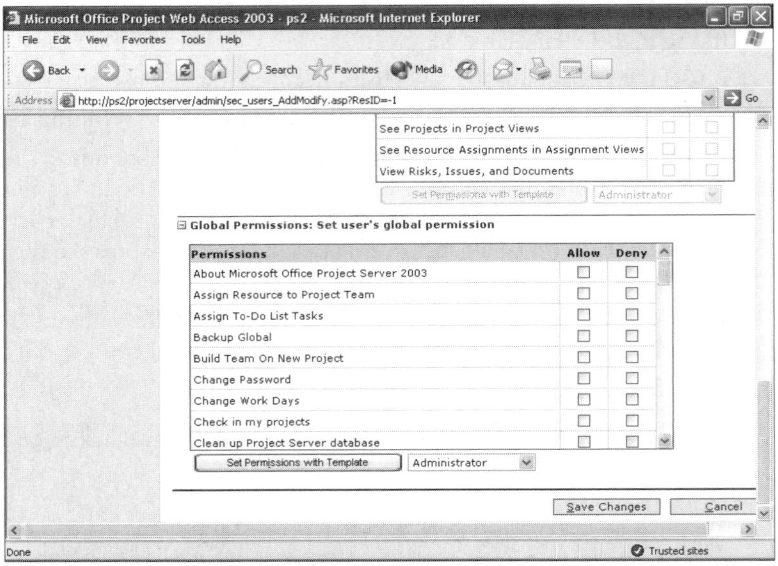

Figure 21-7. In the Global Permissions section, specify the permissions you want to allow or deny for this user.

11 Select the check boxes for the global permissions you want to set for this user. Be sure to scroll to see all the permissions—it's a long list.

As with the category permissions, it's much easier to use the template for the user's group and then make any individual adjustments as necessary. Under the global permissions table, click the Set Permissions With Template button and then click the user's group, for example, Team Member or Resource Manager. The check boxes in the global permissions table are completed as appropriate to the selected group.

12 When finished, click the Save Changes button at the bottom of the page.

After you set up the user accounts, team members and other Project Web Access users just need to use their Web browser to go to the designated URL for your project server location. They enter their user name (and password if necessary), and their own view of Project Web Access appears.

Team members and resource managers needing information about using Project Web Access should refer to Chapter 23, "Participating on a Team Using Project Web Access."

Upper managers using Project Web Access should refer to Chapter 24, "Making Executive Decisions Using Project Web Access."

Global permissions

Table 21-2 shows the global permissions as set using the built-in templates according to a user's group, or role.

Table 21-2. Global Permissions

Global Permissions	Admin	Exec	Portfolio Mgr	Project Mgr	Resource Mgr	Team Leader	Team Member
About Microsoft Office Project Server 2003	X		X				
Assign Resource To Project Team	X			X	X		
Assign To-Do List Tasks	X	X		X	X	X	X
Backup Global	X						
Build Team On New Project	X		X	X	X		
Change Password	X	X	X	X	X	X	X
Change Work Days	X						X
Check In My Projects	X	X	X	X	X	X	X
Clean Up Project Server Database	X						
Connect To Project Server Using Microsoft Project 2002 Or Earlier	X						
Create Accounts From Microsoft Office Project	X			X			

Table 21-2. Global Permissions

Global Permissions	Admin	Exec	Portfolio Mgr	Project Mgr	Resource Mgr	Team Leader	Team Member
Create Accounts When Delegating Tasks	X			X			
Create Accounts When Requesting Status Reports	X			X			
Create Administrative Projects	X				X		
Create And Manage To-Do List	X	X		X	X	X	X
Customize Project Web Access	X						
Delegate Task	X			X			
Go Offline From Project Web Access	X	X	X	X	X	X	X
Hide Task From Timesheet	X			X			X
Integration With External Timesheet System	X	X	X	X	X	X	X
Log On	X	X	X	X	X	X	X
Manage Enterprise Features	X		X				
Manage Rules	X			X			
Manage Security	X						
Manage Server Configuration	X						

Table 21-2. Global Permissions

Global Permissions	Admin	Exec	Portfolio Mgr	Project Mgr	Resource Mgr	Team Leader	Team Member
Manage Status Report Request	X	X		X	X	X	
Manage Task Changes	X			X			
Manage Users And Groups	X						
Manage Views	X		X				
Manage Windows SharePoint Services	X						
New Project	X		X	X			
New Project Task	X			X			X
New Resource	X		X		X		
New Task Assignment	X			X			X
Open Project Template	X		X	X			
Publish To-Do List To All Users	X	X		X	X	X	X
Publish/Update/Status	X		X	X			
Read Enterprise Global	X		X	X	X		
Save Baseline	X			X			
Save Enterprise Global	X		X				
Save Project Template	X		X	X			
Set Personal Notifications	X	X	X	X	X	X	X
Set Resource Notifications	X	X	X	X	X	X	

Table 21-2. Global Permissions

Global Permissions	Admin	Exec	Portfolio Mgr	Project Mgr	Resource Mgr	Team Leader	Team Member
Submit Status Report	X	X		X	X	X	X
Timesheet Approval	X				X		
User Defined 1	X	X	X	X	X	X	X
User Defined 2	X	X	X	X	X	X	X
User Defined 3	X	X	X	X	X	X	X
View Adjust Actuals	X						
View Assignments View	X	X	X	X	X	X	
View Documents	X	X	X	X	X	X	X
View Home	X	X	X	X	X	X	X
View Issues	X	X	X	X	X	X	X
View Models	X	X	X				
View Portfolio Analyzer	X	X	X				
View Project Center	X	X	X	X	X		X
View Project View	X	X	X	X	X		X
View Resource Allocation	X	X	X		X		
View Resource Center	X	X	X		X		
View Risks	X	X	X	X	X	X	X
View Status Report List	X	X		X	X	X	X
View Timesheet	X			X			X

Chapter 21

Managing Security

System security is an all-important administrator responsibility. Anything that can be done to make it easier or more automatic is likely to be welcomed by project server administrators.

In Project Server, you can redefine the built-in groups, categories, permissions, and security templates that contribute toward the establishment of user profiles.

NEW FEATURE! If your organization is set up with Active Directory, you can synchronize the Active Directory security groups with those in Project Server.

Creating a New Group

If your organization uses different roles from those identified as groups in Project Web Access (for example, Project Managers and Team Leaders), you can create your own. To do this, follow these steps:

1. In the Admin page of Project Web Access, click Manage Users And Groups in the left pane.
2. In the left pane, click Groups.

   The Groups page appears (see Figure 21-8)

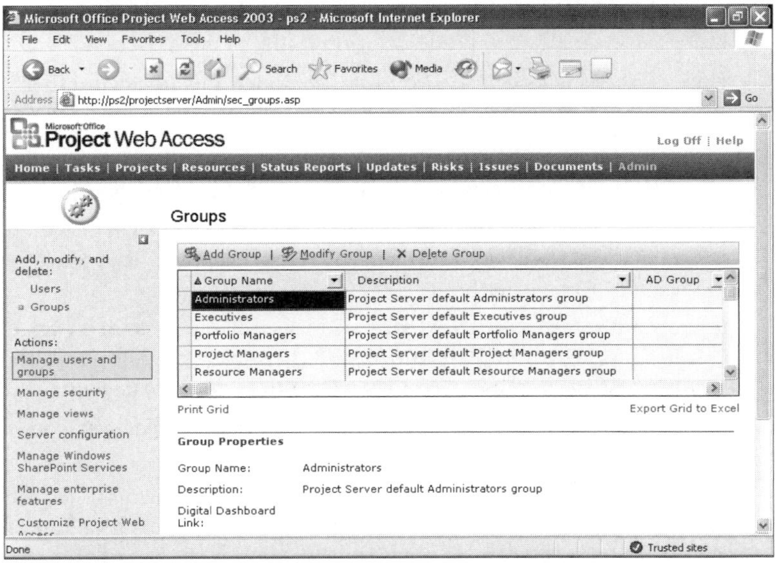

Figure 21-8. Use the Groups page to review, modify, add, or delete groups (roles) in Project Server.

3. Above the table, click Add Group.

   The Add Group page appears (see Figure 21-9).

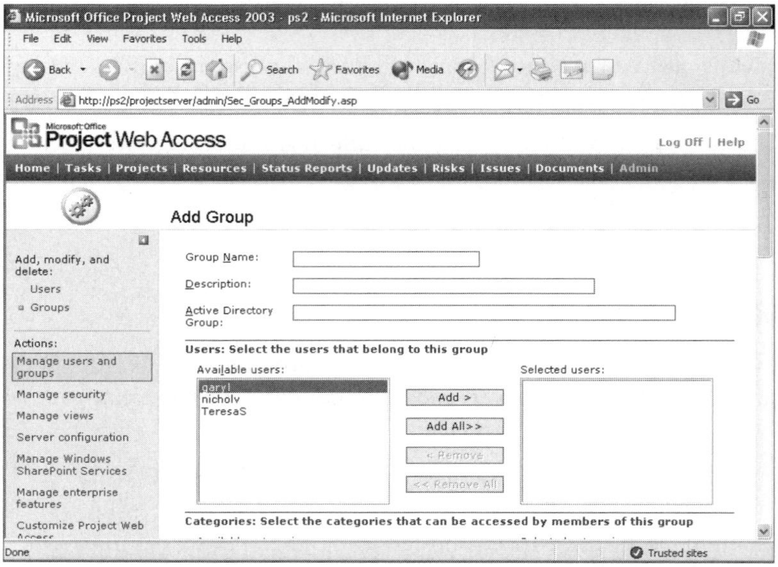

Figure 21-9. Use the Add Group to create a new group to reflect roles in your organization.

4 Enter the group name and description in the first two boxes.

NEW FEATURE!

5 Under Users, click the users you want to add to the group and then click Add.

You can also add users after you've finished defining the group.

6 Under Categories, click any categories (for example, My Tasks or My Resources) that are appropriate to be accessed by members of this group and then click Add.

7 In the Selected Categories box, select each category in turn and then set the permissions for the category in the Permissions box. Repeat this process for each category in the Selected Categories box.

If you want to use a security template to set permissions for a category, click the Set Permissions With Template button and then select the template. Make any adjustments to the permissions as necessary for the selected category.

8 Under Global Permissions, select global permissions that you want to apply to your new group.

If you prefer to use a security template to set global permissions, click the Set Permissions With Template button and then select the template. Make any adjustments to the global permissions as necessary for the group.

9 When finished defining the new group, click the Save Changes button at the bottom of the page.

> **Tip** **Modify an existing group**
> To edit an existing group, click Manage Users And Groups in the left pane of the Admin page. Click Groups in the left pane. In the table, click the group you want to change and then click Modify Group above the table. Work through the rest of the page in which you can add or remove users, change the categories associated with the group, or set options for Active Directory synchronization.

Synchronizing with Active Directory Security Groups

NEW FEATURE!

If your organization uses Active Directory, you can synchronize your project server security groups with the Active Directory ones, as follows.

1. In the Admin page of Project Web Access, click Manage Users And Groups in the left pane.
2. In the left pane, click Groups.
3. In the Groups page, scroll down to the Active Directory section (see Figure 21-10).

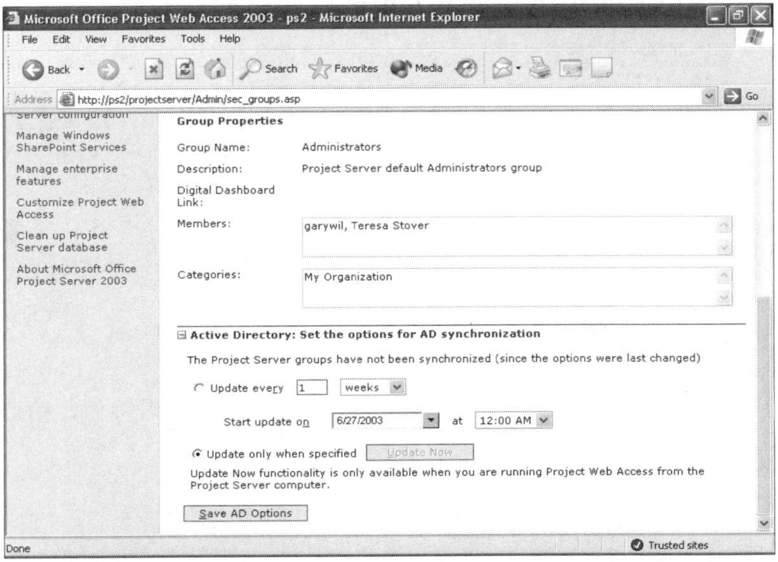

Figure 21-10. Use the Active Directory section on the Groups page to set Active Directory synchronization for security groups.

4. In the Active Directory Group box, enter the name of the Active Directory security group.

Chapter 21

5 Specify when Active Directory updates should take place.

If you select the Update Every option, specify the frequency at which your project server should be synchronized to changed in Active Directory, for example every week or every two months. Also, specify the date when updates should begin and the time at which the update should be done.

If you select the Update Only When Specified option, the Update Now button becomes available when you are running Project Web Access from the project server computer.

6 Click the Save AD Options button.

Customizing Categories

If the built-in categories and associated security templates don't fit the way your organization works with projects, you can customize them or create entirely new ones. To do this, follow these steps:

1 In the Admin page of Project Web Access, click Manage Security in the left pane.

The Categories page appears (see Figure 21-11).

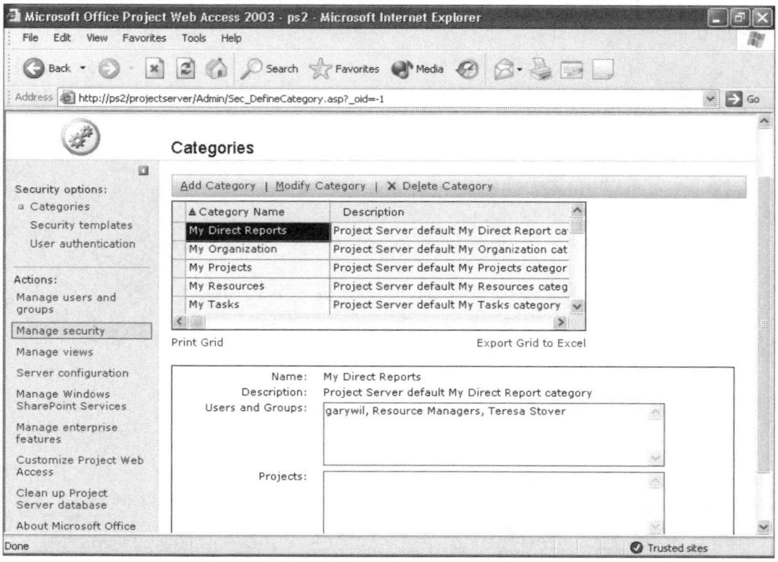

Figure 21-11. Click Manage Security to open the Categories page and customize user categories and security templates.

2 Click any of the categories in the table, such as My Direct Reports or My Tasks, to review the definition for that category in the boxes below the table.

3 To change an existing category, click Modify Category above the table.

To define a new category, click Add Category above the table.

4 In the page that appears, make any changes needed in the Category Name And Description section.

5 In the Users And Groups section, select the users and groups already identified that you want to be a part of the category and then click the Add button.

6 In the Permissions box, specify the permissions that users in this category should have.

7 In the Projects section, specify which projects the users in this category should be able to access: all projects in the Project Server database or just the selected projects.

Select or clear the project-related check boxes to further define the category.

8 In the Available Project Views box, specify the views that the users in this category should be able to see.

9 In the Resources section, specify which resources the users in this category should be able to access: all resources in the Project Server database or just the selected resources (see Figure 21-12).

Select or clear the resource-related check boxes to further define the category.

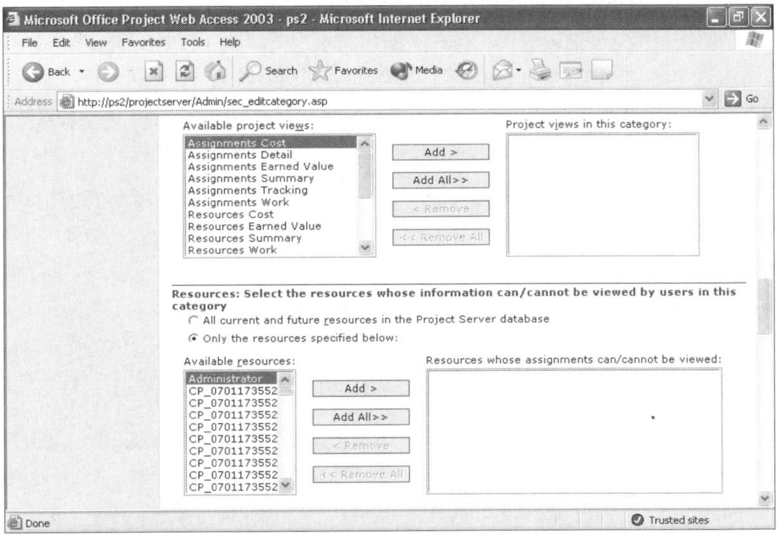

Figure 21-12. Specify the resources whose information can be accessed by users in this category.

10 In the Available Assignment Views and Available Resource Center Views boxes, specify the assignment and resource views that users in this category should be able to see.

11 In the Project Center Views section, specify the views that users in this category should be able to access. These views include Project Center views, any Portfolio Analyzer views, and any Portfolio Modeler models that have been defined.

12 When finished, click the Save Changes button at the bottom of the page.

Chapter 21

Creating a New Security Template

You can set up your own security templates with entirely different sets of permissions. You can then assign the new set of permissions to users, groups, and categories in a single step. To create a new security template, follow these steps:

1. In the Admin page of Project Web Access, click Manage Security in the left pane.
2. In the left pane, click Security Templates.
3. Above the table, click Add Template.
4. Enter a name and description for your new security template.
5. If you want to base your new security template on an existing template, select a template from the Copy Template box.

   Whether or not you base your new security template on another existing template, you'll need to modify the new template to change the permissions.

Modifying a Security Template

You can edit the permissions in an existing security template or set the permissions for a new security template you just created. To do this, follow these steps:

1. In the Admin page of Project Web Access, click Manage Security in the left pane.
2. In the left pane, click Security Templates.
3. In the table, select the name of the security template you want to modify.
4. Above the table, click Modify Template.
5. Next to each permission, select either the Allow check box or the Deny check box to specify the set of permissions for this template.

   The permissions are organized by category, such as Collaboration and Status Reports. You can globally allow or deny all permissions in a category by selecting the Allow or Deny check box for the category.
6. When finished setting permissions for the security template, click the Save Changes button.

Administering the Enterprise Resource Pool

The *enterprise resource pool* is the set of people, equipment, and materials available to be assigned and carry out the work of projects throughout an organization. The organization can be as compact as a small department or as wide ranging as all employees in all regions of a worldwide corporation. The enterprise resource pool contains fundamental information about resources, such as skill sets and availability, that helps project managers find the right resources for their projects. The enterprise resource pool also contains cost information, which not only helps project managers work within their allotted budgets, but also helps accounting and human resources figure costs from their varied points of view.

With the enterprise resource pool, high-level visibility of resource availabilities, skills, roles, and utilization is now possible. Project managers as well as upper management can see when additional staff is needed and where there are underutilized resources. They also can view the basic data for all project resources in one place.

Furthermore, project managers can plan for project staffing needs with accurate and current resource information from the entire enterprise, instead of from just their own team or group. The advantages of the multiple project resource pool, such as resource sharing between project managers, are magnified when applied to the entire enterprise.

Resource managers can use the enterprise resource pool to staff, plan, and budget with more accuracy and confidence. They can see resources by skill level and definition, availability, and organizational hierarchy. In addition, they can assist project managers with current and anticipated resource requirements by analyzing the enterprise resource database. Together with the project managers, resource managers can work with *generic resources* in the enterprise resource pool to perform planning and contingency analyses.

The project server administrator is often the one who sets up and maintains the enterprise resource pool. However, because of the specialized information having to do with resource skills, costs, and availability, other specialists such as the portfolio manager or a human resources representative might be involved in the setup. By default, the project server administrator and portfolio manager are given the permission to add and edit enterprise resource data.

A user with the permission to edit enterprise resource data can do the following:

- Create and add users to the enterprise resource pool.
- Update information on resources in the enterprise resource pool.
- Customize resource fields for use in the enterprise resource pool.
- Specify multiple properties for resources in the enterprise resource pool.

Project managers working with enterprise projects connected to the project server cannot use the regular resource pool because it is replaced by the enterprise resource pool. However, the local resource pool features are available to users working with local, nonenterprise projects.

For more information about working with the resource pool, see "Sharing Resources Using a Resource Pool" on page 441.

Creating the Enterprise Resource Pool

After you create the enterprise resource pool, project managers can access it and build project teams from it. If you can, add the bulk of your resources at once. You can always add individual resources as time goes on. Project managers who have been working with their own resources can import those local resources into the enterprise resource pool.

Adding Multiple Enterprise Resources

The basic way to add resources to your enterprise resource pool is just standard data entry, as follows:

1. Make sure your user profile is set with the Edit Enterprise Resource Data category permission in Project Server.

   If you are the project server administrator or portfolio manager, you have this permission by default.

2. In Project Professional 2003, click Tools, Enterprise Options, Open Enterprise Resource Pool.

   The Open Enterprise Resources dialog box appears (see Figure 21-13).

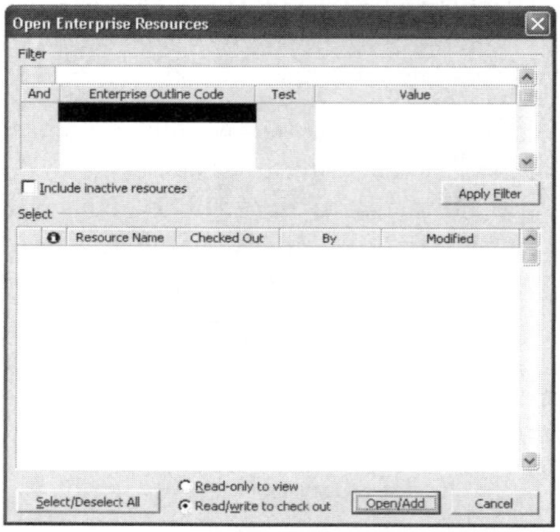

Figure 21-13. Use the Open Enterprise Resources dialog box to add or edit resources in the enterprise resource pool.

3. Click the Open/Add button.

   A new project plan called Checked-Out Enterprise Resources (as shown in the title bar) opens, with the Resource Sheet displayed.

Resource Information

4. In the Resource Name field, type the name of the resource. Enter any other information in the other fields, such as group, maximum units, cost rates, and base calendar.

   If you want to add complete resource information, click the Resource Information button on the Standard toolbar. The Resource Information dialog box appears. Enter information on the various tabs as appropriate to this resource. When finished, click OK.

> **For more information about the different types of resource information that can be added to the Resource Sheet and Resource Information dialog box, see Chapter 6, "Setting Up Resources in the Project."**

5. Repeat Step 4 for all other resources you want to add (see Figure 21-14).

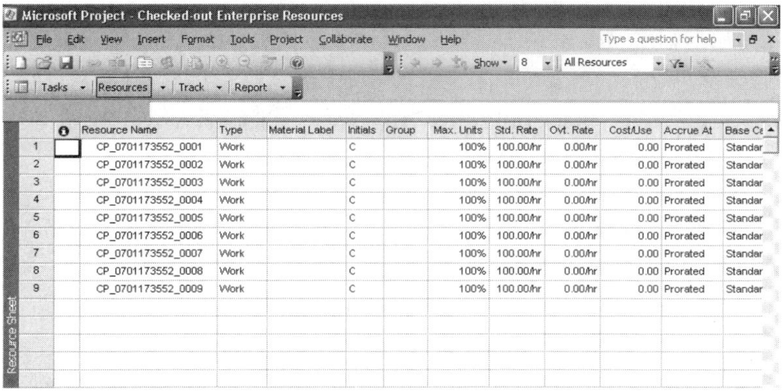

Figure 21-14. Enter resource names and associated information in Checked-Out Enterprise Resources.

6 When you're finished adding resources and you want to check the enterprise resource pool and its new information in to Project Server, click File, Close.

7 In the prompt that appears, click Yes to save your changes.

> **Tip** **Enterprise resources are added automatically as Project Web Access users**
> When you add resources to your enterprise resource pool, Project Server adds them automatically as Project Web Access users with Project Server authentication. Those users have instant access to Project Web Access and just need to set their passwords upon their first login.
>
> However, when you add Project Web Access users, they are not likewise added to the enterprise resource pool. This is because you're likely to have more Project Web Access users, such as executives, resource managers, accountants, and other managing stakeholders who need access to project information, but who are not available to be assigned to a project team.

Synchronizing with Active Directory Resources

NEW FEATURE!

If your organization uses Active Directory, you have the easiest way to generate your enterprise resource pool. You can synchronize an Active Directory group with the Project Server enterprise resource pool, and also schedule periodic synchronization updates or refreshes. In this way, resources from a specific Active Directory group are instantly mapped to the enterprise resource pool. If the resource exists in Active Directory, the resource is automatically added to the enterprise resource pool upon the next scheduled Active Directory update to Project Server. Any resources that no longer exist in Active Directory are likewise removed from the Project Server. This is a one-way synchronization, from Active Directory to Project Server.

The Active Directory synchronization options are set as part of the Project Server configuration. These options can be set during initial configuration, or they can be set anytime afterward, as follows:

1. In the Admin page of Project Web Access, click Server Configuration in the left pane.

   The Server Configuration page appears.

2. In the Active Directory Group To Synchronize box, enter the name of your Active Directory group.

   This box, along with the other Active Directory options, is under Specify The Mode Used To Run Microsoft Project Server (see Figure 21-15).

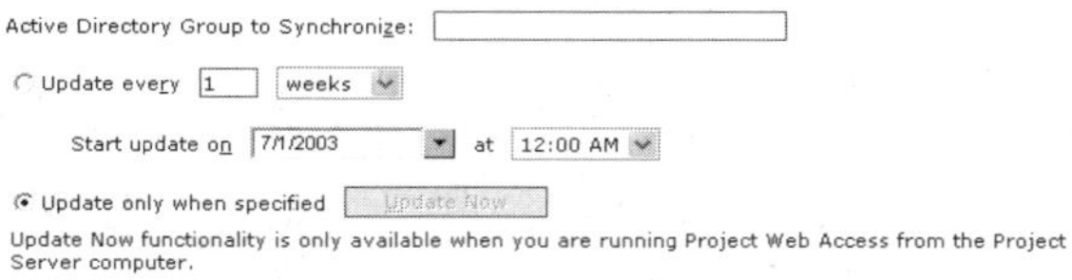

Figure 21-15. Set your Active Directory options on the Server Configuration page in Project Web Access.

3. Specify when Active Directory updates should take place.

   If you select the Update Every option, specify the frequency at which Project Server should be synchronized to be changed in Active Directory, for example, every week or every two months. Also specify the date when updates should begin and the time at which the update should be done.

   If you select the Update Only When Specified option, the Update Now button becomes available when you are running Project Web Access from the project server computer.

Note Active Directory synchronization is available only if you are running enterprise features. It is not available if you're implementing only workgroup features without enterprise project management.

Tip Develop an API to create your enterprise resource pool

NEW FEATURE!

An Application Program Interface (API) can be developed to help you automatically create a programmatic interface to create your enterprise resource pool from existing information in another system, for example, your human resources or general ledger system.

For information about the new APIs, refer to the Microsoft Project Software Development Kit (SDK) and search for "API". To access the SDK, go to *http://msdn.microsoft.com/project*, click Microsoft Project 2003, and then click SDK Documentation.

Adding an Individual Enterprise Resource

Adding an individual resource to the enterprise resource pool entails essentially the same process as adding a bunch of resources at one time.

1. In Project Professional, click Tools, Enterprise Options, Open Enterprise Resource Pool.
2. Without selecting any existing resources in the dialog box, click the Open/Add button.

   The Resource Sheet for the Checked-Out Enterprise Resources project appears in Project Professional. The Resource Sheet is blank.

Note When adding a new resource to an existing enterprise resource pool, it might seem odd to see a blank Resource Sheet, especially because you selected the Open Enterprise Resource Pool command.

In reality, however, you never really check out the entire resource pool unless you select all resources and then click the Open/Add button. Typically, you add one or more new resources or you edit the information for a select group of resources, while the rest of the resources are still safely checked in.

3. Enter the new resource, along with any associated resource information.
4. When finished, click File, Close.
5. In the prompt that appears, click Yes to save your changes.

   The new resource is checked in to Project Server as a new member of the enterprise resource pool.

Importing Existing Local Resources to the Project Server

A number of resources, complete with reliable availability and cost information, might already exist in enterprise and nonenterprise projects. You can easily open those projects and import the resources into the enterprise resource pool using the Import Resource Wizard.

Tip **Import projects and resources at once using the Import Projects Wizard**
If you want to import resources from a nonenterprise project that you need to import to the project server as an enterprise project, you can do both at the same time. The primary job of the Import Projects Wizard is to import tasks in an existing project into a new enterprise project. If you want, you can specify that the resources in that project also be added to the enterprise resource pool and assigned to the newly created enterprise project.

For more information about importing projects with their resources and custom fields, see "Importing a Local Project to the Server" on page 646.

Follow these steps to import local (nonenterprise) resources from an existing project to the enterprise resource pool:

1. Be sure you're logged in to the project server through Project Professional. Also be sure that the project from which you want to import resources is *not* open.
2. Click Tools, Enterprise Options, Import Resources To Enterprise.

   The Import Resources Wizard appears.
3. On the wizard's first page, click the Next button.

   The Open From Microsoft Office Project Server dialog box appears, listing all enterprise projects (see Figure 21-16).

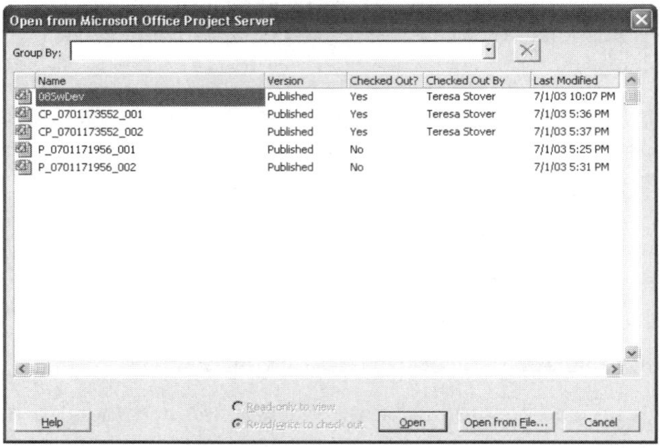

Figure 21-16. Select the project that contains the resource information you want to import.

4. If the resources you want to import are in an enterprise project, click the name of that project and then click Open.

   If the resources are in a local project stored on your computer or network, click Open From File. In the Import Resources dialog box (which looks like a standard Open dialog box), find and open the project file.
5. Click Next.

   The Map Resource Fields wizard page appears. Notice that the Resource Name field appears in the Preview area, along with the first few resource names.
6. Map any custom resource fields from the original project to the enterprise resource pool (see Figure 21-17). If there are no custom resource fields to map and import to the server, you can skip this wizard page.

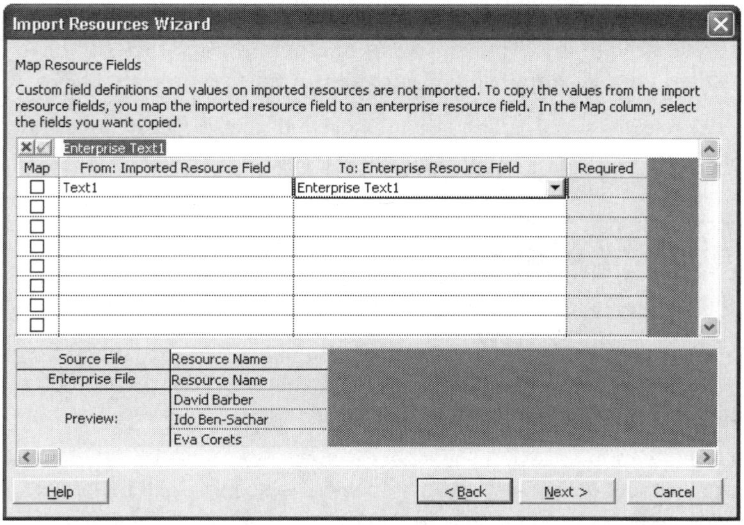

Figure 21-17. Map any custom resource fields to the enterprise resource pool.

7 Click Next.

The next wizard page displays the list of local resources in the selected project who are available for import to the enterprise resource pool

8 Select or clear check boxes in the X column to specify which resources are to be imported. To select (or clear) all resources, click Select/Deselect All (see Figure 21-18). Click Next.

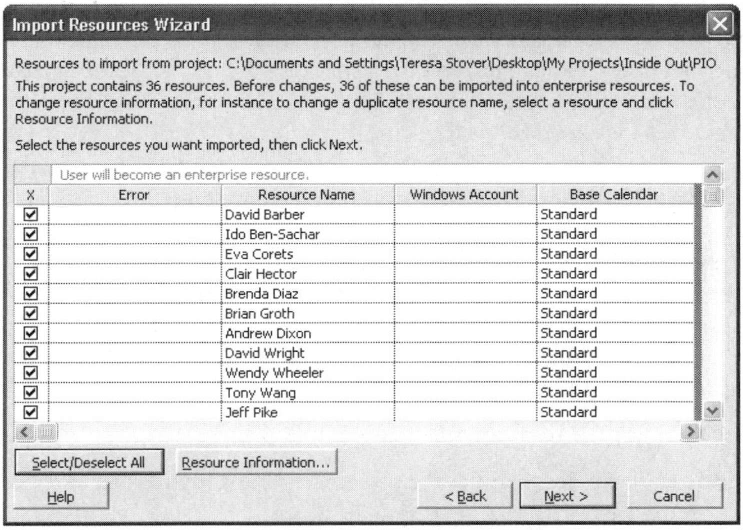

Figure 21-18. Select the resources whose information you want to import to the enterprise resource pool.

The Import Complete page appears.

9 If you need to import resources from other projects, click Import More Resources. When finished importing resources from existing projects, click Finish.

The selected resources and their associated calendar, cost, and other resource information are imported into the enterprise resource pool.

Troubleshooting

You're getting resource import error messages

Suppose you're trying to import resources and you see an error message in the Import Resources Wizard that states, "This project contains a certain number of resources. Before changes, 0 of these can be imported into enterprise resources."

You see this error message if you select a check box in the Map Resource Fields page of the wizard without having any custom resource fields to map. If the project contains no custom resource fields (such as Number1 or Date3), just skip this page by clicking Next.

You might also see this error message if you inadvertently deselect all the resource names. By default, all resources are automatically selected, and there is no need to change that. If you click the Select All/Deselect All button, you might inadvertently deselect the entire list of resources. Check that the resources you want are selected on this page and then click Next.

Updating Resource Information

After you add resources, you can edit resource information by checking the resource(s) out, making the necessary changes, and then checking them in again. Any resource information—such as maximum units, base calendar, group name, cost information, and resource outline codes—is edited this way.

Note Assignment information is changed in the enterprise project itself, not in the enterprise resource pool.

This resource information cannot be changed casually by project managers. Only those granted the Edit Enterprise Resource Data permission can check out and edit this resource information. By default, the project server administrator and portfolio manager are the only ones granted this permission.

To modify enterprise resource information, follow these steps:

1 Be sure you're logged in to the project server through Project Professional.

2 In Project Professional, click Tools, Enterprise Options, Open Enterprise Resource Pool.

The Open Enterprise Resources dialog box appears (see Figure 21-19).

Figure 21-19. Select the enterprise resource(s) you want to check out to edit.

3 If your enterprise resource pool is very large and you want to work with a smaller group of resources, create a filter using the fields in the upper part of the Open Enterprise Resources dialog box.

4 In the Select table, click the names of the resources to be modified.

Select multiple adjacent resources by clicking their names while holding the Shift key. Select multiple nonadjacent resources by clicking their names while holding the Ctrl key.

5 Be sure the Read/Write To Check Out option is selected.

6 Click the Open/Add button.

The Checked-Out Enterprise Resources appears as a project plan. The selected resources are listed in the Resource Sheet.

7 In the Resource Sheet, make the changes you want to the enterprise resource.

If you need to work with additional resource information, select the resource(s) and then click the Resource Information button on the Standard toolbar. The Resource Information dialog box appears. Enter information on the various tabs as appropriate to this resource. When finished, click OK.

8 When you're finished modifying the resource information and you want to check the enterprise resources back in to the server, click File, Close.

9 In the prompt that appears, click Yes to save your changes.

If an enterprise resource is checked out by another user, and you need to check the resource back in to the enterprise resource pool (usually because of some extenuating circumstance), you can force a resource check-in as follows:

1 In the Admin page of Project Web Access, click Manage Enterprise Features in the left pane.

2 Under Enterprise Options in the left pane, click Check In Enterprise Resources.

All resources that are currently checked out are listed in the table.

3 Select the resource for which you want to force a check-in and then click Check-In above the table.

Deactivating Users

You can deactivate users from the project server. You deactivate rather than delete resources because even obsolete resources are probably associated with assignments and actuals that are best retained for your archival and historical project data. You can deactivate a resource using either the Admin page in Project Web Access or by checking out the enterprise resource in Project Professional.

To deactivate users with Project Web Access, follow these steps:

1 In the Admin page of Project Web Access, click Manage Users And Groups in the left pane.

The Users page appears.

2 In the table, select the account for the user you want to deactivate.

3 Above the table, click Deactivate User.

A message appears, asking if you're sure (see Figure 21-20).

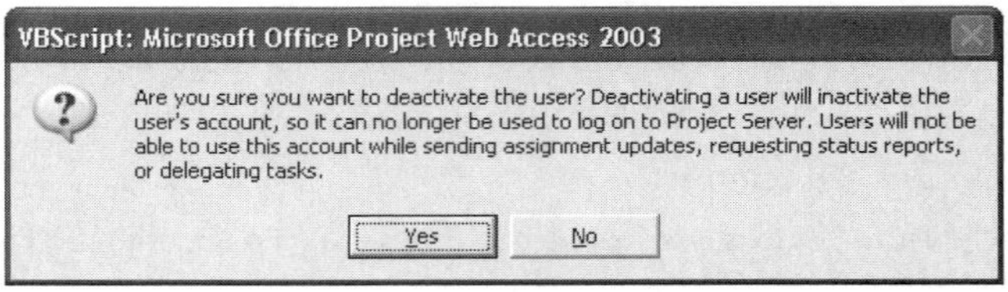

Figure 21-20. Confirm that you really want to deactivate the selected user.

4 Click Yes.

The selected resource is deactivated. The deactivated user cannot log on to the project server, and other users cannot send updates, tasks, or requests to the deactivated user.

To deactivate resources by checking them out in Project Professional, follow these steps:

1 Be sure you're logged in to the project server through Project Professional.

2 In Project Professional, click Tools, Enterprise Options, Open Enterprise Resource Pool.

The Open Enterprise Resources dialog box appears.

3 In the Select table, click the names of the resources to be deactivated.

4 Be sure the Read/Write To Check Out option is selected.

5 Click the Open/Add button.

The Checked-Out Enterprise Resources appears as a project plan. The selected resources are listed in the Resource Sheet.

6. Select one or all of the resources and then click Resource Information on the Standard toolbar.
7. In the Resource Information dialog box, be sure the General tab is active.
8. Select the Inactive check box and then click OK.
9. Click File, Close.
10. In the prompt that appears, click Yes to save your changes.

Customizing Enterprise Resource Fields

Another responsibility of the project server administrator is to set up any custom enterprise resource fields that might be needed to further define and categorize enterprise resources. Custom enterprise resource fields include the following:

- Custom resource fields, such as Enterprise Date1, Enterprise Number3, and Enterprise Text10
- Resource breakdown structure fields, using Enterprise Resource Outline Code30
- Single-value enterprise resource outline codes, using Enterprise Resource Outline Code1 through Enterprise Resource Outline Code19
- Multiple-value enterprise resource outline codes, using Enterprise Resource Outline Code20 through Enterprise Resource Outline Code29

Establishing Custom Resource Fields

If your organization or certain project managers want to capture custom resource information for which there is no built-in Microsoft Project field, you can create one and make it available to all Project Professional users. The custom resource information can then either be entered by the project manager or calculated by Microsoft Project from other Microsoft Project fields.

The following custom fields are available to be defined for enterprise resources:

- Enterprise Cost1 through Enterprise Cost10
- Enterprise Date1 through Enterprise Date30
- Enterprise Duration1 through Enterprise Duration10
- Enterprise Flag1 through Enterprise Flag20
- Enterprise Number1 through Enterprise Number40
- Enterprise Text1 through Enterprise Text40

To define a custom field for enterprise resources and make it available to all projects in your organization, follow these steps:

1. Make sure your user profile is set with the Save Enterprise Global permission in Project Server.

   If you are the project server administrator or portfolio manager, you have this permission by default.

2 Log in to the project server through Project Professional.

3 In Project Professional, click Tools, Open Enterprise Global.

The enterprise global opens as a special project plan called Checked-Out Enterprise Global (see Figure 21-21).

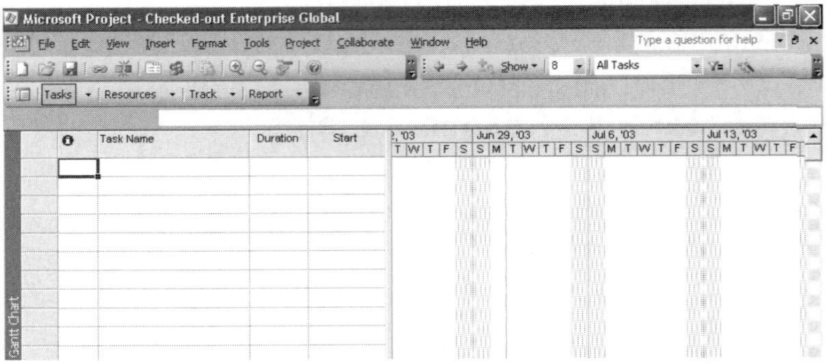

Figure 21-21. Use the enterprise global template to define standards for all projects throughout the enterprise, including custom resource fields.

4 In Project Professional, click Tools, Customize, Enterprise Fields.

The Customize Enterprise Fields dialog box appears (see Figure 21-22).

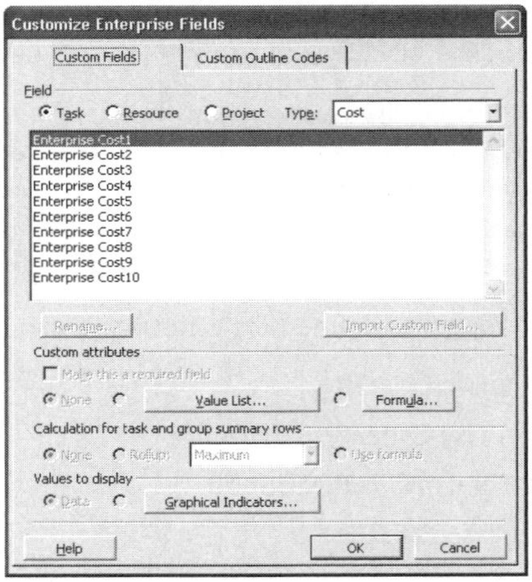

Figure 21-22. Use this dialog box to define custom fields for enterprise resources.

5 If necessary, click the Custom Fields tab.

6 Under Field, select the Resource option.

7 In the Type box, click the type of field you want to define, for example, Date or Flag.

8 In the list of enterprise fields that appears, select the specific custom field you want to use, for example, Enterprise Date1.
9 Click the Rename button to give a descriptive name to the custom field.
10 If you want to specify a value list, formula, or graphical indicator for the custom field, use the sections in the lower half of the dialog box.

For more information about defining custom fields, value lists, formulas, and graphical indicators, see "Customizing Fields" on page 788.

11 When you're finished defining the custom field, click OK.
12 When you're finished working with the enterprise global and you want to check it back in to the project server, click File, Close.
13 In the prompt that appears, click Yes to save your changes.

The enterprise global, along with your new custom resource field, is checked in to the project server and now available to all project managers.

For more information about the enterprise global, see "Working with the Enterprise Global Template" later in this chapter on page 622.

Establishing the Resource Breakdown Structure

If the project managers in your organization will be using the Build Team dialog box or the Resource Substitution Wizard, you need to define the *Resource Breakdown Structure (RBS)* and associate RBS codes to the resources in your organization. The RBS defines the hierarchy of resource positions in your organization. The RBS is a special resource outline code—actually Enterprise Resource Outline Code30. However, the field name as seen in Project Professional is RBS.

For more information about the Build Team feature, see "Building Your Enterprise Project Team" on page 655. For more information about the Resource Substitution Wizard, see "Assigning Tasks to Enterprise Resources" on page 666.

To define the RBS for your organization, follow these steps:

1 Log in to the project server through Project Professional.
2 In Project Professional, click Tools, Open Enterprise Global.
3 In the checked-out enterprise global, click Tools, Customize, Enterprise Fields.
4 Click the Custom Outline Codes tab.
5 Under Field, select the Resource option.

All enterprise resource outline codes are listed, including the RBS at the bottom of the list (see Figure 21-23).

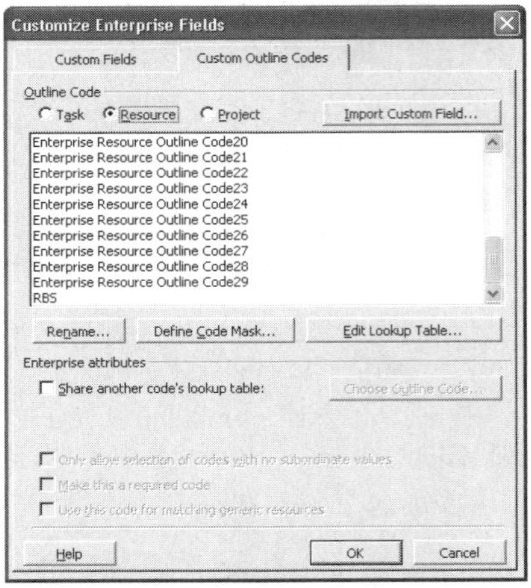

Figure 21-23. Select the RBS outline code to define the RBS for your organization.

6 Scroll to the bottom of the list and click RBS.

7 Click Define Code Mask to specify the hierarchical format of the resource breakdown structure.

8 Click Edit Lookup Table to define the values that can be selected for any level of the RBS and therefore control the RBS data entry for each enterprise resource.

For more information about defining a code mask, controlling entered values, and defining a lookup table, see "Working with Outline Codes" on page 806.

9 Under Enterprise Attributes, select the Use This Code For Matching Generic Resources check box.

This selection enables project manager use of the Build Team and Resource Substitution Wizard features through RBS codes.

10 Select or clear the other check boxes under Enterprise Attributes as appropriate to your organization's implementation of enterprise project management.

11 When you're finished defining the RBS, click OK.

12 When you're finished working with the enterprise global and you want to check it back in to the project server, click File, Close.

13 In the prompt that appears, click Yes to save your changes.

The enterprise global, along with the newly defined RBS, is checked in to the project server.

After defining the RBS, you can assign the appropriate RBS to each enterprise resource. Then users can sort, group, or filter resources by RBS code. More significantly, project managers can use Build Team or the Resource Substitution Wizard to replace generic resources in their project plans with real resources containing the specified RBS code.

Establishing Resource Outline Codes

Your organization might have other ways of looking at resources and resource hierarchy besides the structure provided for in the RBS. You can define outline codes and assign those codes to enterprise resources. Then users can sort, group, or filter resources by the specific outline code.

Use the enterprise resource outline codes 1–19 to define a single-value code. To do this, follow these steps:

1. Log in to the project server through Project Professional.
2. In Project Professional, click Tools, Open Enterprise Global.
3. In the checked-out enterprise global, click Tools, Customize, Enterprise Fields.
4. Click the Custom Outline Codes tab.
5. Under Field, select the Resource option.
6. Select one of the outline codes between Enterprise Resource Outline Code1 and Enterprise Resource Outline Code19.

   These outline codes are single-value enterprise resource outline codes. If you need to define multiple values in each outline code assigned to a resource, see the next section, "Specifying Multiple Properties for a Resources."
7. Click Rename to give the outline code a descriptive name.
8. Click Define Code Mask to specify the hierarchical format of your new outline code.
9. Click Edit Lookup Table to define the values that can be selected for your new outline code.

> **For more information about defining a code mask, controlling entered values, and setting up a lookup table, see "Working with Outline Codes" on page 806.**

10. Select or clear the check boxes under Enterprise Attributes as appropriate to your organization's implementation of enterprise project management.
11. When you're finished defining the new outline code, click OK.
12. When you're finished working with the enterprise global and you want to check it back in to the project server, click File, Close.
13. In the prompt that appears, click Yes to save your changes.

Specifying Multiple Properties for a Resource

NEW FEATURE!

Instead of defining five different resource outline codes related to a single set of resource properties, you can define a single resource code to contain multiple properties that you can assign to a resource. Use multiple-value resource outline codes to define multiple skill sets, certifications, resource locations, resource languages, working arrangements, or any other related set of resource information your organization requires (see Figure 21-24).

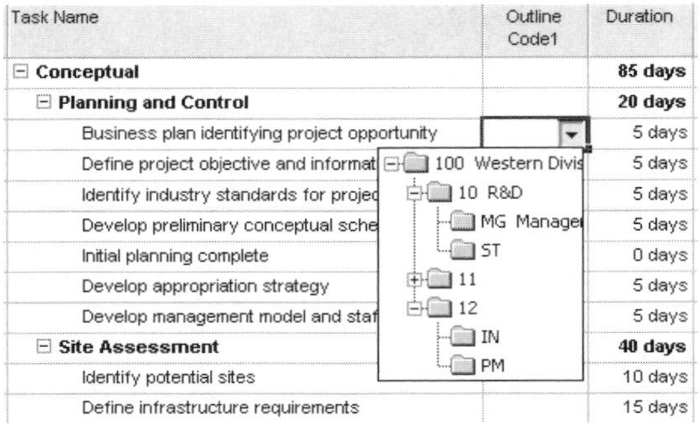

Figure 21-24. Define a multiple value outline code for enterprise resources.

In Microsoft Project, 10 enterprise resource outline codes can be defined with multiple values: enterprise resource outline codes 20–29. These multiple-value resource outline codes are also known as *enterprise resource multivalue fields*, or *ERMV*.

> **Note** Multiple-value codes can be defined only for enterprise resources. They are not available for nonenterprise outline codes or for enterprise task or project outline codes.

To define a multiple-value enterprise resource outline code, follow these steps:

1. Log in to the project server through Project Professional.
2. In Project Professional, click Tools, Open Enterprise Global.
3. In the checked-out enterprise global, click Tools, Customize, Enterprise Fields.
4. Click the Custom Outline Codes tab.
5. Under Field, select the Resource option.
6. Select one of the outline codes between Enterprise Resource Outline Code20 and Enterprise Resource Outline Code29.

   These outline codes are multivalue enterprise resource outline codes. If you need to define single values in each outline code assigned to a resource, see the earlier section, "Establishing Resource Outline Codes."
7. Click Rename to give the outline code a descriptive name.
8. Click Define Code Mask to specify the hierarchical format of your new outline code.
9. Click Edit Lookup Table to define the multiple values that can be selected for your new multivalue outline code (see Figure 21-25).

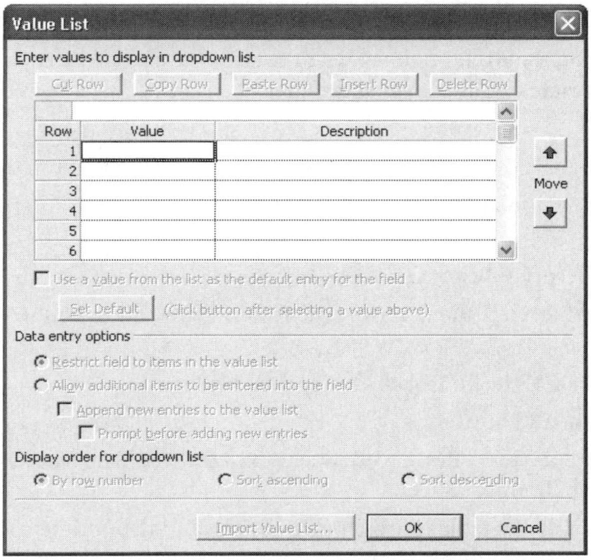

Figure 21-25. Use the Value List dialog box to set up the multiple values for the outline code.

For more information about defining a code mask, controlling entered values, and setting up a lookup table, see "Working with Outline Codes" on page 806.

10 Select or clear the check boxes under Enterprise Attributes as appropriate to your organization's implementation of enterprise project management.

11 When you're finished defining the multiple-value resource outline code, click OK.

12 When you're finished working with the enterprise global and you want to check it back in to the project server, click File, Close.

13 In the prompt that appears, click Yes to save your changes.

Project managers can now add the multivalue enterprise resource outline code to the Resource Sheet to show the defined resource properties at a glance. In addition, the information contained in this field can be used with the Resource Substitution Wizard, Team Builder, and Portfolio Modeler.

For more information about project manager use of the multivalue fields, see "Building Your Enterprise Project Team" on page 655.

Associating Resource Outline Codes with Resources

After you have defined the RBS, single-value, or multivalue enterprise resource outline code, associate the appropriate outline codes and values to enterprise resources by following these steps:

1. Be sure you're logged in to the project server through Project Professional.
2. In Project Professional, click Tools, Enterprise Options, Open Enterprise Resource Pool.

   The Open Enterprise Resources dialog box appears.
3. In the Select table, click the names of the resources to whom you want to assign outline codes.
4. Be sure the Read/Write To Check Out option is selected.
5. Click the Open/Add button.

   Checked-Out Enterprise Resources appears as a project plan. The selected resources are listed in the Resource Sheet.
6. If necessary, apply the table to which you want to add the outline code field.

   By default, the Entry table is displayed.
7. Right-click the column heading to the left of where you want the outline code field to be inserted. Click Insert Column on the shortcut menu.
8. In the Field Name box, click the enterprise resource outline code field.

   Your enterprise resource outline code is listed twice: once using the generic enterprise resource outline code name (for example, *Enterprise Resource Outline Code1*) and again using the name you gave it (for example, *Department Accounting Codes*).
9. In the Insert Column dialog box, click OK.

   A column containing your enterprise resource outline code appears in the Resource Sheet.
10. Click a cell in the enterprise resource outline code column.
11. Enter a value in the outline code field appropriate to the selected resource.

    If you had created a lookup table for the outline code, click the down arrow in the cell, and then click an entry in the list.

    If there is no lookup table, simply type the value in the field.

    If you're completing values for a multiple-value outline code, click the down arrow in the cell and then select any of the multiple values that apply to the selected resource.
12. Repeat Steps 10–11 for all checked-out resources.
13. When you're finished assigning outline codes to resources and you want to check the enterprise resources and their new information back in to the project server, click File, Close.

14 In the prompt that appears, click Yes to save your changes.

The outline code information is now available to project managers and resource managers working with the resources.

Establishing the Enterprise Portfolio

The *enterprise portfolio* is the full set of projects that is stored to your project server. Individual project managers initially add their projects to the project server and then they check their own projects out and in. Team members might participate on one, two, or more projects in the enterprise portfolio at one time, or transition from one to another over time. Executives and other managing stakeholders can review aspects of all projects managed by the project server by using the Portfolio Analyzer and Portfolio Modeler. As the project server administrator, you can control multiple versions as well as archive versions of projects in the portfolio.

Publishing Projects to the Server

Individual project managers are responsible for adding projects to the project server. They can create a new enterprise project entirely from scratch. They can also import a local project; that is, one they've been working on that's stored on their own computer or elsewhere on the network. Importing a local project essentially copies the project to the project server, and that copy becomes the live enterprise version.

After a project is added to the project server, it is considered *published* to the enterprise. The new enterprise project becomes available to be viewed and checked out by users with the proper permissions.

Project managers needing more information about creating a new enterprise project can refer to "Saving a New Enterprise Project to the Server" on page 645. For more information about importing an existing project, refer to "Importing a Local Project to the Server" on page 646.

If a published project is checked out by a project manager or other user, and you need to check it in (usually because of some extenuating circumstance), you can force a project check-in as follows:

1. In the Admin page of Project Web Access, click Manage Enterprise Features in the left pane.
2. Under Enterprise Options in the left pane, click Check In Enterprise Projects.

   All projects that are currently checked out are listed in the table.
3. Select the project for which you want to force a check-in, and then click Check-In above the table.

Protect project baselines

As project server administrator, you might be called upon to intervene in projects when *baselines* are involved.

In many organizations, baseline information is the basis for proposals, contracts, and payment. Variances might be tracked in minute detail. Earned value calculations, which rely on baseline information, might be crucial to measuring project success. In any of these cases, the project is carefully planned and built, and then the details are approved by all the managing stakeholders. At that point, the baseline can be saved and should never be altered.

NEW FEATURE!

By default, project managers are allowed to save and edit baselines using the Save Baseline global permission. However, to protect the integrity of the baseline information, allowing no subsequent edits, your organization might ask you to deny project managers the Save Baseline permission.

Some organizations might choose to prevent project managers from saving baselines at all. When a baseline needs to be saved, you might be instructed to check the project out, save the baseline, and then check the project back in again.

Other organizations might prefer to have the project manager save the baseline, but then instruct you to change the project manager's user profile to deny Save Baseline permission thereafter.

For more information about working with baselines, see "Saving Original Plan Information Using a Baseline" on page 298.

Configuring Portfolio Analyzer and Portfolio Modeler

Through the use of *Portfolio Analyzer*, managing stakeholders can review a high-level picture of tasks, resources, assignments, schedule, progress, costs, and other information across all projects in the enterprise.

With *Portfolio Modeler*, managing stakeholders can create what-if scenarios involving current projects, without impacting live project data.

Both Portfolio Analyzer and Portfolio Modeler are implemented through the use of *online analytical processing (OLAP)* tools provided by SQL Server Analysis Services in conjunction with Project Server and Project Web Access.

For more information about setting up SQL Server Analysis Services with Project Server and configuring the OLAP cube, download the online book from the Microsoft Project Web site entitled "Microsoft Office Project 2003 Administrator's Guide." Go to *http://www.microsoft.com/downloads*, and then search for **Project Server 2003**.

For Portfolio Analyzer and Portfolio Modeler to work properly for users, you need to have the following in place:

- Resources added to the enterprise resource pool
- Enterprise project and resource outline codes defined in the enterprise global template
- Values for any outline code lookup tables stored in the enterprise global template
- Enterprise outline code values associated with enterprise resources as appropriate
- Enterprise projects created and published to the project server
- Enterprise resources assigned as team members to enterprise projects
- Project server user accounts created for users of Portfolio Analyzer and Portfolio Modeler

For more information about carrying out any of these tasks, refer to the appropriate sections throughout this chapter.

After all the prerequisite conditions are met for enterprise projects and enterprise resources, you're ready to configure the *OLAP cube* and enable Portfolio Analyzer and Portfolio Modeler. To do this, follow these steps:

1. In the Admin page of Project Web Access, click Manage Enterprise Features in the left pane.

   The Update Resource Tables And OLAP Cube page appears (see Figure 21-26).

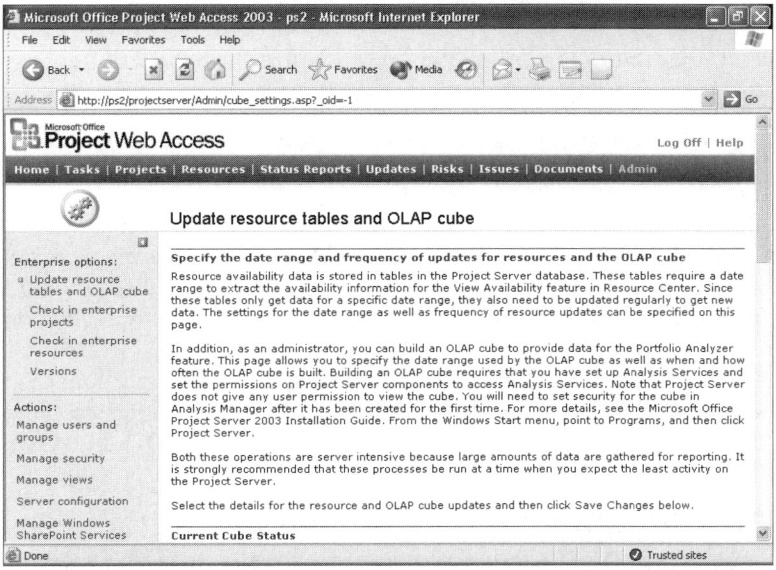

Figure 21-26. Click Manage Enterprise Features to start configuring the OLAP cube.

2. Scroll down to the Build The OLAP Cube section (see Figure 21-27) and make sure the Yes option is selected.

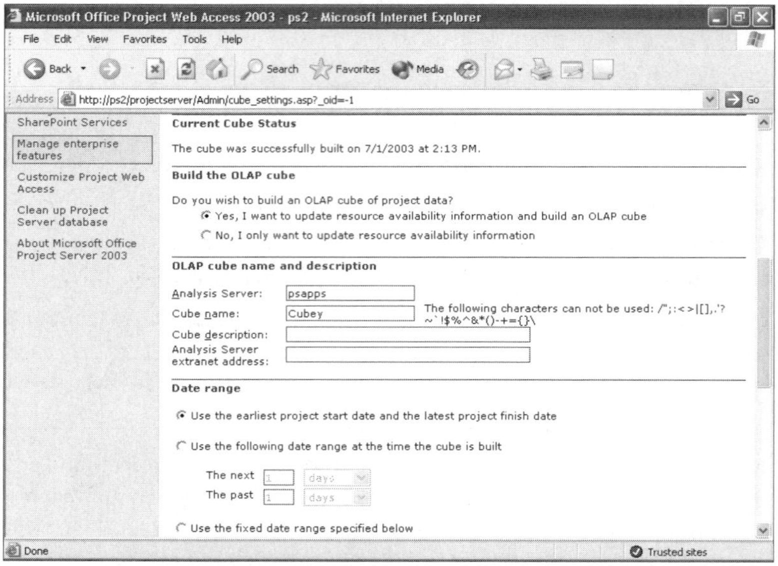

Figure 21-27. Specify that you want to build an OLAP cube.

3 Under OLAP Cube Name And Description, complete the Analysis Server, Cube Name, Cube Description, and Analysis Server Extranet Address boxes.

You might need to obtain some of this information from your SQL Server administrator.

4 Under Date Range, select the date range for which the OLAP cube is to built.

5 Under Update Frequency, specify how often you want the OLAP cube to be refreshed.

You can specify an automatic update at regular intervals or manually when you specify.

6 Click the Save Changes button at the bottom of the page.

At this point, managing stakeholders who are members of the Executives user group or who are allowed the View Portfolio Analyzer and View Models permissions can work with the Portfolio Analyzer and Portfolio Modeler in the Project Center of Project Web Access. By default, users defined as project server administrators, executives, and portfolio managers have these permissions set.

Users wanting more information about working with the Portfolio Analyzer and Portfolio Modeler can refer to Chapter 24.

Setting the Enterprise Project Version

When a project is published to the project server, it is defined with a particular *project version*. By default, the version is *published*. The version is appended to the project name as a second filename extension, for example, *Design.mpp.published*. The version, which must be selected when a new project is published or imported to the project server, specifies all the projects that are a member of a given portfolio of projects.

Users can compare and analyze all projects in a given version. They can also compare the same project in different versions, particularly useful for analyzing what-if scenarios.

As the project server administrator, you can create additional versions, as follows:

1. In the Admin page of Project Web Access, click Manage Enterprise Features in the left pane.
2. Under Enterprise Options in the left pane, click Versions.

   The Versions page appears (see Figure 21-28).

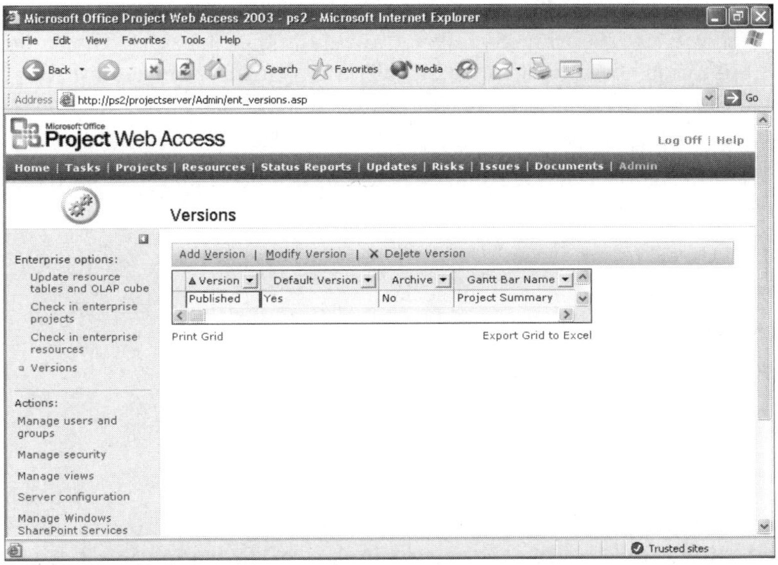

Figure 21-28. Add, modify, or delete a project version using the Versions page.

3. Above the table, click Add Version.
4. In the Version box, type the new version name.
5. In Version Archived, select Yes or No.
6. In the Gantt Bar Name list, select the Gantt bar you want to use to display information about this project version in views showing multiple project versions.
7. Click the Save Changes button.

Standardizing Enterprise Project Elements

As the project server administrator, you have the authority to define customizations needed by your organization and then propagate those customizations to all enterprise projects as the accepted project management standards.

To create and disseminate custom project elements, you use the enterprise global template, also simply known as the *enterprise global*. You check out the enterprise global and then customize any number of Microsoft Project elements as necessary. You can define views, tables, filters, toolbars, macros, custom fields, outline codes, and more. When you check in the enterprise global with your changes, your changed elements become a part of all projects throughout the enterprise.

Working with the Enterprise Global Template

When a project manager or other authorized user checks out an enterprise project, the latest update of the enterprise global is automatically attached. The enterprise global is akin to a global template, or the "global global" over the standard *project global template*. The enterprise global dictates standards being enforced and customizations made available to Microsoft Project interface elements in projects throughout the enterprise. These standards provide for customization and consistency across all projects in an organization. The standards propagated through the enterprise global template also make it possible for project information throughout the enterprise to be compared and analyzed in meaningful ways.

The following list contains examples of tailoring and standardizing you might do for projects in your enterprise:

- Define custom views.
- Apply formulas to enterprise data.
- Design reports.
- Build and apply macros to enterprise data.
- Set up custom calendars.
- Define and customize information tables.

Table 21-3 shows all the Microsoft Project elements that can be modified in the enterprise global and integrated with all enterprise projects. The table also provides a cross-reference to the section in this book where you can find more information about customizing that particular interface element.

Table 21-3. Customizable Project Elements

Project Element	For More Information
Base calendars	"Setting Your Project Calendar" on page 70
Fields	"Customizing Enterprise Resource Fields" on page 609, "Customizing Enterprise Project Fields" on page 625, and "Customizing Fields" on page 788
Filters	"Customizing Filters" on page 799
Forms	"Creating and Customizing Forms" on page 827
Groups	"Customizing Groups" on page 795
Import and export maps	"Importing and Exporting Information" on page 497
Macros	"Automating Your Work with Macros" on page 26xx

Table 21-3. Customizable Project Elements

Project Element	For More Information
Outline codes	"Establishing Resource Outline Codes" on page 613, "Establishing Enterprise Outline Codes" on page 628, and "Working with Outline Codes" on page 806
Reports	"Revising a Built-In Report" on page 389 and "Building a Custom Report" on page 393
Tables	"Customizing Tables" on page 785
Toolbars	"Creating and Customizing Toolbars" on page 817
VBA modules	"Writing Microsoft Project Code with Visual Basic for Applications" on page 905
Views	"Customizing Views" on page 761

Changing the Enterprise Global

By default, only the project server administrator and portfolio manager have the permission to update the enterprise global (using the Save Enterprise Global permission). However, project managers and resource managers are granted the Read Enterprise Global permission.

To check out and change the enterprise global, follow these steps:

1. Log in to the project server through Project Professional.
2. In Project Professional, click Tools, Enterprise Options, Open Enterprise Global.

   The enterprise global opens as a special project plan called Checked-Out Enterprise Global.
3. Define and customize the Microsoft Project elements for the enterprise as needed.

   Refer to Table 21-3 to find specific instructions for customizing a specific element.
4. When you're finished working with the enterprise global and you want to check it back in to the project server, click File, Close.
5. In the prompt that appears, click Yes to save your changes.

   The updated enterprise global is checked in to the project server and is now available to all project managers.

Create an enterprise global change process

It's likely that project managers will have a number of good ideas regarding items that should become part of the enterprise global. Your organization might do well to develop a consistent process for handling such requests. It might be something as simple as having project managers submit a written request to the project server administrator showing an example of the proposed change. The process might be as formal as a periodic change review meeting. It depends entirely on your organization.

Even if you can't implement a change right away (or at all), remind project managers that they can still create and use their own project global templates, as long as there's no conflict between elements in the project global and elements in the enterprise global.

For more information about working with the project global template, see Chapter 28, "Standardizing Projects Using Templates."

Copying a Custom Element from a Project to the Enterprise Global

You might find it a great idea to experiment with certain customized changes using a regular enterprise project or even a local project before checking out the enterprise global and making the changes there. But you don't have to make the change twice. You can simply copy the custom change from the regular project to the enterprise global using the Organizer.

To copy custom elements from a regular project to the enterprise global, follow these steps:

1. Log in to the project server through Project Professional.
2. Open the regular enterprise or nonenterprise project that contains the element you want to copy to the enterprise global.
3. In Project Professional, click Tools, Enterprise Options, Open Enterprise Global.

   The enterprise global opens as the Checked-Out Enterprise Global.
4. Click Tools, Organizer to open the Organizer dialog box (see Figure 21-29).

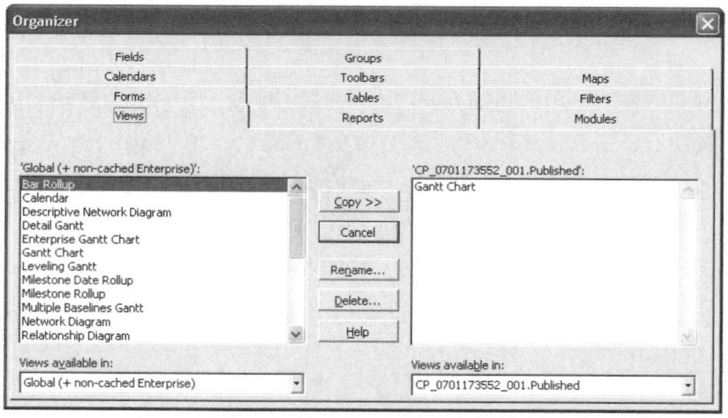

Figure 21-29. Copy customized elements from a project and the enterprise global.

5. Click the tab for the type of element you want to copy, for example, Views or Toolbars.
6. In the <Element> Available In box on the right side of the dialog box, click the project that contains the element you want to copy, if necessary. (<Element> stands for the name of the current tab.)

   The name of the project from which you want to copy the element might already be showing in the box on the right.

7 Make sure the box on the left side of the dialog box is labeled Global (+Non-Cached Enterprise).

   If it is not currently showing, select Global (+Non-Cached Enterprise) from the <Element> Available In box on the left side of the dialog box. This is the name of the enterprise global template.

8 From the list of elements on the right side of the dialog box, click the name of the element you want to copy.

9 Click Copy.

   If an element with the same name already exists in the enterprise global, a confirmation message asks you to confirm that you want to replace the element in the enterprise global. Click Yes to replace the element in the enterprise global with the one from the source project.

   To copy the element with a different name, click Rename, and then type a new name.

10 Check the enterprise global to make sure that your new element is present.

11 When finished working with the enterprise global, click File, Close.

12 In the prompt that appears, click Yes to save your changes and check it in to the project server.

Customizing Enterprise Project Fields

Just as you can set up custom fields for enterprise resources, you can set up custom fields for enterprise projects as a whole as well as individual enterprise tasks and assignments. You can define these custom fields as part of the enterprise global template to hold special information—such as a specific category of costs, dates, or text that is not provided by built-in Microsoft Project fields.

Custom enterprise project and task fields include the following:

- Custom enterprise project fields, such as Enterprise Project Cost1, Enterprise Project Duration3, and Enterprise Project Text15
- Custom enterprise task fields, such as Enterprise Date3 or Enterprise Flag10
- Custom enterprise assignment fields, such as Enterprise Cost4 or Enterprise Number25
- Custom enterprise task outline codes, using Enterprise Task Outline Code1 through Enterprise Task Outline Code30

For more information about enterprise resource fields, including outline codes, see "Customizing Enterprise Resource Fields" earlier in this chapter on page 609.

Establishing Custom Fields

For enterprise projects, you can create a wide range of custom fields. There are different sets of custom fields for the different types of project database information, as follows:

Project fields Store summary project information. Custom project fields can be viewed as part of the project summary row in an individual project plan. They can also be viewed in conjunction with other projects by users of the Portfolio Analyzer and Portfolio Modeler.

Task fields Store information about the tasks in a project. Like the other types of fields, this can include cost, date, text, and number information, to name a few.

Resource fields Store information about the resources in a project. Resource fields are covered in depth in "Customizing Enterprise Resource Fields" earlier in this chapter on page 609.

Assignment fields Store information about the assignments in a project. Assignment information pertains to the intersection of task and resource information.

Custom information can be entered in the fields by the project manager, or calculated by Microsoft Project from other Microsoft Project fields.

Table 21-4 shows the available custom enterprise fields for projects, tasks, resources, and assignments.

Table 21-4. Custom Enterprise Fields

Project Fields	Task Fields	Resource Fields	Assignment Fields
Enterprise Project Cost1–10	Enterprise Cost1–10	Enterprise Cost1–10	Enterprise Cost1–10
Enterprise Project Date1–30	Enterprise Date1–30	Enterprise Date1–30	Enterprise Date1–30
Enterprise Project Duration1–10	Enterprise Duration1–10	Enterprise Duration1–10	Enterprise Duration1–10
Enterprise Project Flag1–20	Enterprise Flag1–20	Enterprise Flag1–20	Enterprise Flag1–20
Enterprise Project Number1–40	Enterprise Number1–40	Enterprise Number1–40	Enterprise Number1–40
Enterprise Project Text1–40	Enterprise Text1–40	Enterprise Text1–40	Enterprise Text1–40
Enterprise Project Outline Code1–30	Enterprise Task Outline Code1–30	Enterprise Resource Outline Code1–29	

To define a custom field in the enterprise global, follow these steps:

1. Log in to the project server through Project Professional.

2. In Project Professional, click Tools, Enterprise Options, Open Enterprise Global.

   The enterprise global opens as the Checked-Out Enterprise Global.
3. In Project Professional, click Tools, Customize, Enterprise Fields.

   The Customize Enterprise Fields dialog box appears.
4. If necessary, click the Custom Fields tab.

For information about defining a custom outline code, see "Establishing Enterprise Outline Codes" in the next section on page 628.

5. Under Field, select the Task, Resource, or Project option.
6. In the Type box, click the type of field you want to define, for example, Date or Flag.
7. In the list of enterprise fields that appears, select the specific custom field you want to use, for example, Enterprise Date1.
8. Click the Rename button to give a descriptive name to the custom field.
9. Under Custom Attributes, specify whether the field is required and whether you want to define a value list or formula for the field.

   Click the Value List button to define a lookup table or drop-down list for the field choices. Click the Formula button to build a formula based on mathematical calculations or logical comparisons of project fields.
10. Under Calculation For Task And Group Summary Rows, specify whether and how you want the field information to be rolled up to task summary and group summary rows.

    This section is available only for task fields.
11. Under Values To Display, specify whether you want alphanumeric data or a graphical indicator to appear in the field.

    If you want a graphical indicator, click the Graphical Indicators button to make further specifications.

For more information about defining custom fields, value lists, formulas, and graphical indicators, see "Customizing Fields" on page 788.

12. When you're finished defining the custom field, click OK.
13. When you're finished working with the enterprise global and you want to check it back in to the project server, click File, Close.
14. In the prompt that appears, click Yes to save your changes.

    The enterprise global, with your new custom field, is checked in to the project server and made available to all project managers.

For more information about the fields used throughout Microsoft Project, refer to Appendix B, "Field Reference."

Establishing Enterprise Outline Codes

Even if you or the project managers have defined a work breakdown structure (WBS) for use with tasks, your organization might have alternative methods for reviewing task structures. These methods can be defined with task outline codes.

In the same way, you can structure project summary information with a project outline code.

Resource outline codes include a set of single-value codes, multiple-value codes, and the resource breakdown structure (RBS). For details about all these, see "Customizing Enterprise Resource Fields" earlier in this chapter on page 609.

To define an enterprise outline code, follow these steps:

1. Log in to the project server through Project Professional.
2. In Project Professional, click Tools, Enterprise Options, Open Enterprise Global.
3. In the checked-out enterprise global, click Tools, Customize, Enterprise Fields.
4. Click the Custom Outline Codes tab.
5. Under Field, select the Task, Resource, or Project option.
6. Select one of the outline codes from the list.

   Each outline code that is currently in use has a name in parentheses beside it.
7. Click Rename to give the outline code a descriptive name.
8. Click Define Code Mask to specify the hierarchical format of your new outline code.
9. Click Edit Lookup Table to define the values that can be selected for your new outline code.

For more information about defining a code mask, controlling entered values, and setting up a lookup table, see "Working with Outline Codes" on page 806.

10. Select or clear the check boxes under Enterprise Attributes as appropriate to your organization's implementation of enterprise project management.
11. When you're finished defining the new outline code, click OK.
12. When you're finished working with the enterprise global and you want to check it back in to the project server, click File, Close.
13. In the prompt that appears, click Yes to save your changes.

Tip **Use regular custom fields**

Only the project system administrator or another user with the proper permissions can save custom enterprise fields to the enterprise global template.

If project managers need custom fields for their individual project plans that don't affect the enterprise, they can define custom fields for their own use in enterprise projects. Instead of using the enterprise custom fields such as Enterprise Cost1-10, they can use Cost1-10, Date1-10, Text1-30, and so on.

For more information about regular custom fields, see "Customizing Fields" on page 788.

Create an interface for enterprise data

NEW FEATURE!

With Project Server 2003, you have a set of APIs you can use to connect with other systems in the organization and facilitate creation and editing of enterprise project data. These APIs are as follows:

Project Data Creation This API provides a programmatic interface to easily create the minimum required elements of a valid enterprise project, including tasks, resources, and assignments, through the Project Data Service (PDS).

Enterprise custom fields This API provides a programmatic interface to edit value lists for enterprise text fields, particularly integrating and synchronizing with systems in other organizational lines of business.

API for Enterprise Outline Code Fields Provides a programmatic interface to edit and integrate value lists for enterprise outline codes, particularly integrating and synchronizing with systems in other organizational lines of business. A developer can use this API to include a list of hierarchical values and a set of PDS methods for transforming such a list into an enterprise outline code value list.

For information about the new APIs, refer to the Microsoft Project Software Development Kit (SDK) and search for "API". To access the SDK, go to *http://msdn.microsoft.com/project*, click Microsoft Project 2003, and then click SDK Documentation.

Setting Up Team Member Timesheets

Whether you're working with enterprise project management or workgroup features only, you need to set up the default team member Timesheets. The Timesheet is the primary view that team members work with to track and update their tasks assigned from one, two, or more projects (see Figure 21-30).

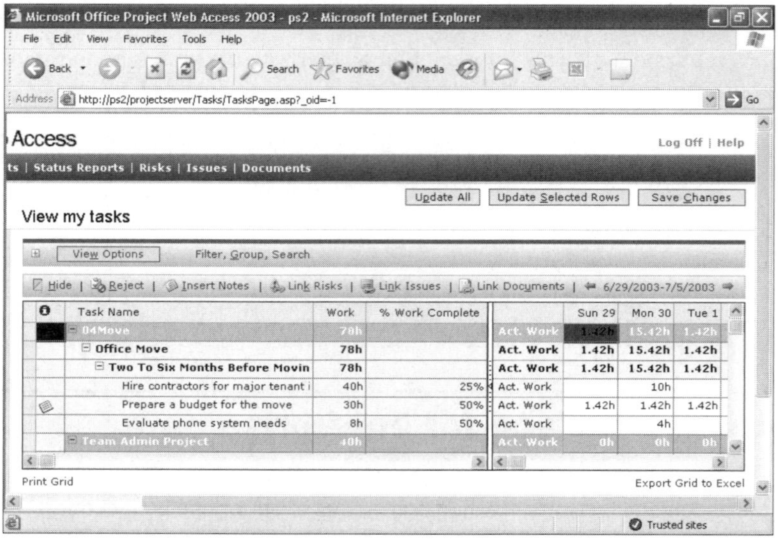

Figure 21-30. Design the Timesheet to fit the needs of the organization and the projects.

Establishing the Update Method and Restrictions

You establish the assignment progress tracking method that is then reflected in the Timesheet. The tracking method can be as simple as noting whether an assignment is not started, in progress, or completed. It can also be as sophisticated as tracking every hour devoted to each assignment.

Depending on the level of project management control that your organization needs, you can set up a number of assignment update restrictions. You can specify an open time period within which assignment updates can be made. You can also specify whether project managers can edit updates submitted by team members.

Work with the project managers and the requirements of the organization to decide on the most appropriate default tracking method. After setting the default, project managers might still be able to switch to a different tracking method, but only if you allow that possibility in your project server configuration.

The three tracking methods are as follows:

Percent of work complete This is the least restrictive and least time-consuming tracking method. The Timesheet includes a field that team members use to update how far along they are with their assignments.

Actual work done and remaining work This tracking method provides a medium level of detail. The Timesheet includes fields for total actual work and remaining work for each assignment. Team members enter those total amounts for each progress update requested.

Hours of work done This is the most detailed tracking method. The Timesheet includes a field for each time period, either days or weeks, for the duration of the project. Team members enter the number of hours worked per day or per week and submit those with each progress update.

In addition to the default tracking method, you can also control when actuals are accepted and whether they can be changed after they've been submitted to the project server.

Use the Customize Project Web Access options on the Admin page to set the default tracking method and any update restrictions, as follows:

1. In the Admin page of Project Web Access, click Customize Project Web Access in the left pane.
2. In the left pane, under Customization Options, make sure that Tracking Settings is selected.

   The Tracking Settings page appears (see Figure 21-31).

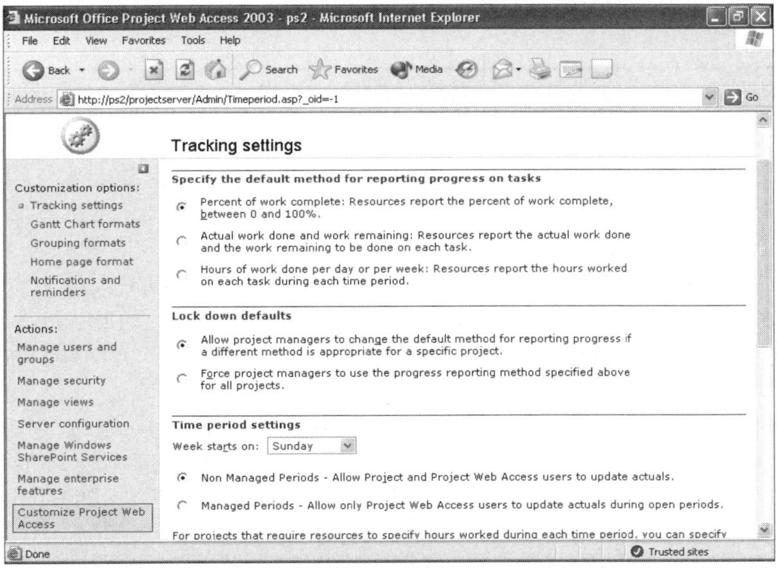

Figure 21-31. Use the Tracking Settings page to specify the default tracking method to be used in the Timesheet.

3. Under Specify The Default Method For Reporting Progress On Tasks, select the option for the tracking method you want to use: Percent Of Work Complete, Actual Work Done And Work Remaining, or Hours Of Work Done Per Day Or Per Week.
4. Under Lock Down Defaults, specify whether you are allowing project managers to change the tracking method in their individual projects, or whether they must always use the default method you selected.

   If you allow project managers to change the default tracking method, they can do so using the Customize Published Fields dialog box in Project Professional.

5. Under Time Period Settings, specify when your work week begins.

NEW FEATURE!

6. If projects are to be tracked by hours of work per time period, you can lock the Timesheet periods.

   Locking the Timesheet periods ensures that team members can report hours only for current time periods, not for time periods in the past or future. Locking the Timesheet period contributes to the integrity of progress information being submitted by team members.

   Select the Non-Managed Periods option if you want to allow team members to enter actuals at any time, no matter how early or late.

   Select the Managed Periods option if you want to allow actuals to update only during a specified open period of time.

7. Click the Save Changes button at the bottom of the page.

For more information about tracking actual work in Microsoft Project, see "Updating Progress Using Resource Work" on page 316.

Protecting actuals information

NEW FEATURE!

Using Project Professional, Project Server, and Project Web Access to automatically gather and enter actuals, you can protect the integrity of actuals submitted by team members. This can be crucial if those actuals are directly submitted to your organization's general ledger system to produce customer invoices.

As the project server administrator, you first set up the Project Web Access progress method to track hours of work per day or per week. Then you set the open reporting time period. Team members can enter actuals only during the open reporting period, not long after the period is past.

Furthermore, you can set an option so that if the project manager or another user changes actual hours that have been submitted and incorporated into the project plan, those changes can be audited against what was originally submitted by the team member.

Only actuals for enterprise resource assignments can be protected. Project managers can still edit actuals for tasks that have local or no resources assigned.

You can review the protected actuals submitted by the team member by adding the Actual Work Protected and Actuals Overtime Work Protected fields to a task sheet. You can also return actuals edited in the project plan back to their value as submitted and stored on the project server. Click Tools, Tracking, Sync To Protected Actuals.

Establishing the Default Timesheet Fields

The Timesheet view is set up with a standard set of task and assignment fields. That set of fields changes according to the tracking method chosen. You or the project manager can change the fields that the team members see in their Timesheets. As the project server administrator, you can choose from the full set of Microsoft Project fields to dictate the set of available Timesheet fields. In turn, project managers start with your selected set of fields to tailor the Timesheets for their individual projects.

NEW FEATURE! If you have defined any custom fields, including custom outline codes, you can include those in the set of default Timesheet fields as well. In fact, as of Project Web Access 2003, outline codes with drop-down value lists (or "pick lists") can be used and displayed as such in the team members' Timesheets.

For more information about defining custom enterprise task fields and task outline codes, see "Customizing Enterprise Project Fields" earlier in this chapter on page 625. For detailed information about defining drop-down value lists, see "Customizing Fields" on page 788.

To modify the set of default Timesheet fields, follow these steps:

1. In the Admin page of Project Web Access, click Manage Views in the left pane.

   The Specify Views page appears (see Figure 21-32).

Figure 21-32. Use the Specify Views page to modify, add, or remove views in Project Web Access.

2. Scroll down the table, almost to the bottom, to find and click the Timesheet view under the Timesheet category.

   The Timesheet view definition appears below the table (see Figure 21-33).

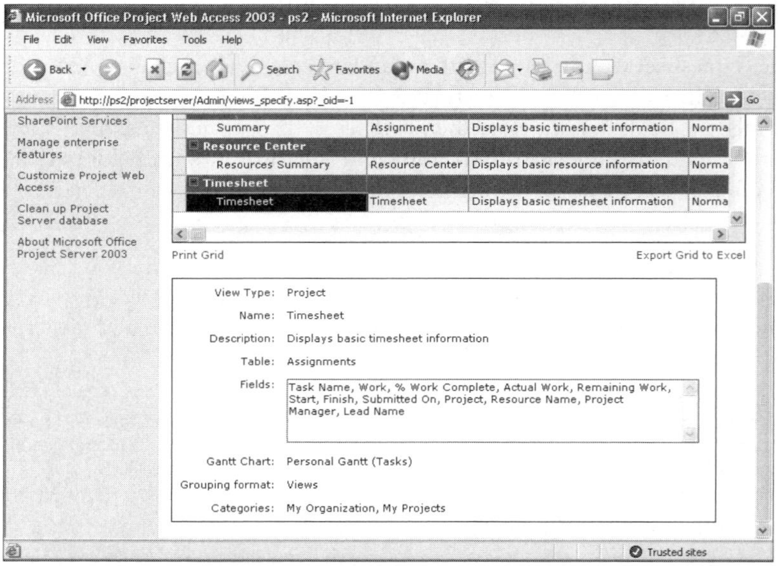

Figure 21-33. The definition for the selected view appears at the bottom of the page.

3 With the Timesheet view selected, scroll all the way back up the page again and then click Modify View.

The Modify Timesheet View page appears (see Figure 21-34).

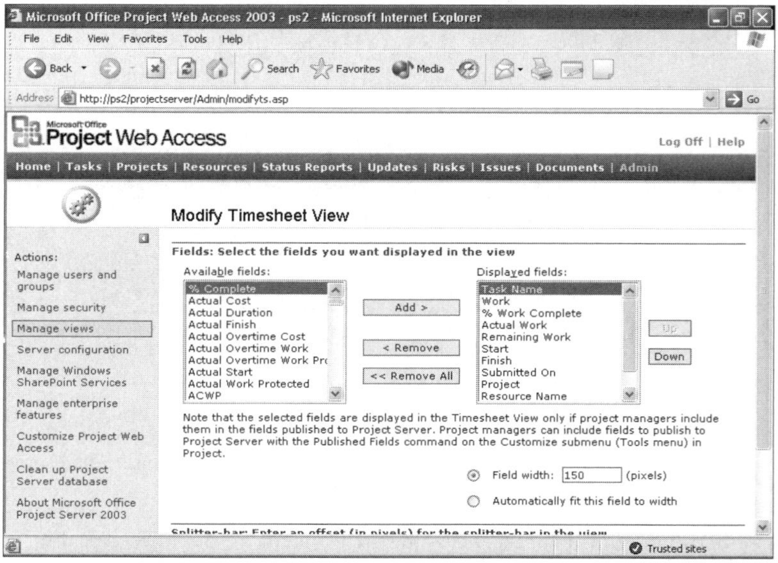

Figure 21-34. Specify the default set of fields from which project managers can choose for their team members' Timesheets.

4 Select one or more fields in the Available Fields box on the left and then click Add to add them to the Displayed Fields box on the right.

   This process adds the selected fields to the default set of available Timesheet fields.

   If you have defined any custom fields in the enterprise global, they are also part of the list of Available Fields.

5 Select one or more fields in the Displayed Fields box on the right, and click Remove to delete them from the default set of available Timesheet fields.

6 When you're finished defining the fields you want in the Displayed Fields box, click the Save Changes button at the bottom of the page.

Project managers setting up their timesheet options using the Customize Published Fields dialog box in Project Professional will see this set as the default Timesheet fields.

NEW FEATURE!

Tip **Develop an API to work with Timesheet information**

An API can be developed to help project managers and team members interface with a third-party system such as a general ledger system or a timesheet application. Information can be sent from your project server to the third-party system. This feature is enabled through the PDS.

For information about the new APIs, refer to the Microsoft Project Software Development Kit (SDK) and search for "API". To access the SDK, go to *http://msdn.microsoft.com/project*, click Microsoft Project 2003, and then click SDK Documentation.

Tailor Project Web Access for users

You can focus the behavior, content, and look of Project Web Access in a wide variety of ways to fit the needs of the entire enterprise as well as those of individual project workgroups. The following list is an overview of Project Web Access customization opportunities:

Home page content Specify any additional links or custom content that should be added to the Project Web Access Home page for all users. In the Admin page, click Customize Project Web Access. Under Customization Options, also in the left pane, click Home Page Format.

Views You can define and customize Project Web Access views, including the Timesheet, Project Center, Resource Center, and Portfolio Analyzer. In the Admin page, click Manage Views in the left pane. In the Specify Views page, scroll through the table to find the views you want to work with. Click Modify View or Copy View to work with the view in more detail.

Gantt bars and grouping formats Customize the look of Gantt bars representing different types of tasks. Make choices about the look of the Gantt Chart timescale. Specify how grouped tasks or resources should appear. In the Admin page, click Customize Project Web Access. Under Customization Options, also in the left pane, click Gantt Chart Formats or Grouping Formats.

Menus You can specify which menus should be displayed or hidden to users in Project Web Access. By customizing menu displays, you can be sure that only the commands needed by the users are present, and you can remove the rest of the clutter. In the Admin page, click Server Configuration in the left pane. Under Configuration Options, also in the left pane, click Menus.

E-mail notification and reminders Set up conditions for when team members and project managers should be alerted via e-mail about changes in task or resource information in Project Web Access. You can set up user's e-mail addresses, if necessary, along with a default e-mail message to accompany any periodic reminders about upcoming tasks, overdue tasks, or status report requests. In the Admin page, click Customize Project Web Access. Under Customization Options also in the left pane, click Notifications And Reminders.

Consider this your invitation to poke around these pages in Project Web Access, armed with your hefty project server administrator permissions. Explore the available functionality, and implement other changes based on the preferences and needs of the organization.

Chapter 22

Managing Enterprise Projects and Resources

As a project manager using Microsoft Office Project 2003, you have probably created projects, assigned resources, tracked progress, and generated your fair share of reports. If you're working with enterprise project management and collaborating with your project team through Microsoft Office Project Professional 2003, Microsoft Office Project Server 2003, and Microsoft Office Project Web Access 2003, there are differences in how you work with your project and resources. This chapter covers these differences as they pertain specifically to the project manager.

Project server administrators and portfolio managers should see Chapter 21, "Administering Project Server and Project Web Access for Your Enterprise." Team members can refer to Chapter 23, "Participating On a Team Using Project Web Access." Managing stakeholders can find pertinent information in Chapter 24, "Making Executive Decisions Using Project Web Access."

Chapter 23 and Chapter 24 are also provided as standalone e-chapters on the Companion CD.

Project 2003 enterprise project management coordinates multiple project managers in an organization dealing with potentially hundreds of projects and thousands of resources. Different stakeholders can plug into the organization's project server to obtain whatever high-level or detailed view of project information they need for their varied functions. But at the heart of this system is the individual project plan—created and controlled by the individual project manager using Project Professional 2003.

To start using the Microsoft Project workgroup and enterprise features, you need to connect your installation of Project Professional to your organization's server running Project Server 2003. You can then log on to your server from Project Professional as well as Project Web Access 2003.

After your setup is configured and connected, you can create new enterprise projects or import existing projects to the project server. You can make full use of the enterprise resource pool to build your project team and assign those resources to the proper tasks based on their skills and availability. As you track progress, you can be in constant communication with your project team members, exchanging assignment and progress information through Project Server 2003.

Note Your project server administrator is responsible for setting up the enterprise resource pool, the associated resource breakdown structure, and any other organizational customizations for project management. This must be done before you, as the project manager, start publishing any of your own projects to your project server.

For more information, talk to your project server administrator. Also, refer to Chapter 21, "Administering Project Server and Project Web Access for Your Enterprise."

Connecting to Your Project Server

After your project server administrator adds you as a user with project manager permissions in Project Server, you can configure your installation of Project Professional to connect to your project server. Then you have all the allowed enterprise and team collaboration features at your disposal.

Setting Up Project Professional for Your Server

To connect your installation of Project Professional to your organization's project server, follow these steps:

1. Start Project Professional.

   At this point, it doesn't matter whether or not a project plan is open.

2. Click Tools, Enterprise Options, Microsoft Office Project Server Accounts.

   The Project Server Accounts dialog box appears (see Figure 22-1).

Figure 22-1. Add your project server location as an account for your installation of Project Professional.

3 In the Project Server Accounts dialog box, click Add.

The Account Properties dialog box appears (see Figure 22-2).

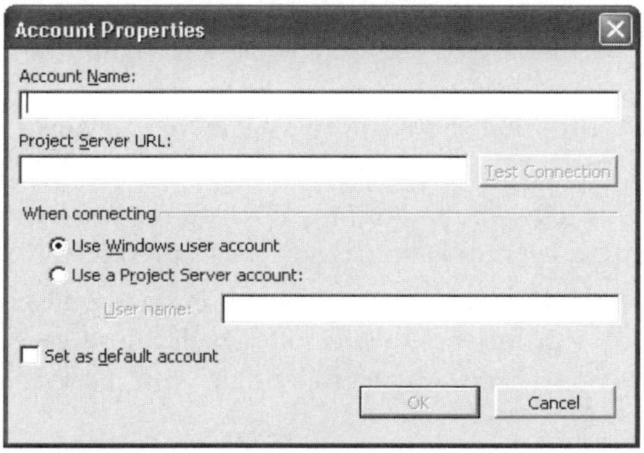

Figure 22-2. Enter the new account name and the project server URL.

4 In the Account Name box, enter the "friendly" name by which you want to identify the project server.

5 In the Project Server URL box, enter the address of your organization's project server, in the format of *http://servername/projectserver*.

Obtain this address from your project server administrator.

6 Click the Test Connection button to verify the connection to the server running Project Server and ensure that the address is correct and actually points to a functioning project server.

A message appears that indicates whether or not the connection was successful. If there is a problem with the connection, verify that you have entered the correct information, or notify your project server administrator.

7 Under When Connecting, specify whether you will be using a Windows or Project Server account.

This account needs to match the way your project server administrator has already set up your user information. If you will be using a Project Server account, enter your user name for that account.

Tip Windows user account or Project Server account?

A Windows user account is generally more versatile and convenient than a Microsoft Project Server account. You use the same user ID and password as you do to log on to your Windows network, which saves time when logging on to the project server and enhances security while maintaining convenience for you.

In addition, several features of Project Server perform better when accessed with a Windows user account, in particular, Portfolio Analyzer and Windows SharePoint Services.

8. Select the Set Default Account check box if you want this account to be automatically selected for connection whenever you start up Project Professional.

   Setting the default account does not necessarily log you into this account when you start up Project Professional; it's simply the account that's selected for logon.

9. Click OK.

   The Project Server Accounts dialog box appears again, listing your new account in the Available Accounts box.

10. Under When Starting, specify whether or not you want to automatically connect to the server running Project Server as soon as you start up Project Professional.

    If you select Automatically Detect Connect State, upon startup Project Professional will connect to the account you set as the default, which can be very convenient if you know that you will always want to connect to a single project server and will rarely work offline.

    If you select Manually Control Connection State, a dialog box will appear upon startup that gives you the choice of which account you want to use for this Project Professional session. This might the most appropriate choice if you sometimes expect to work offline. It is also the right choice if this computer is a shared network computer used by multiple users who have different user names and permissions.

11. When finished, click OK.

    At this point, you are set up to log on to your project server through Project Professional. If you want to log on immediately, exit Project Professional and then start it up again.

Logging On via Project Professional

The first time you log on to your project server from Project Professional, you need to add the project server URL as a trusted site in Internet Explorer. When you restart Project Professional, the Microsoft Project Server Security Login dialog box appears. Follow these steps to make the URL a trusted site in Microsoft Internet Explorer:

1. Start up Project Professional.

   The Microsoft Project Server Security Login dialog box appears, which says you cannot log on to the project server because you have not identified the URL as a trusted site in Internet Explorer.

2. Click the Make Server Trusted button.

   A prompt appears, asking you to confirm the addition of the URL to the list of trusted sites.

3. Click Yes to add the URL to the list of trusted sites.

   The Microsoft Project Server URL is added to the list of trusted sites in Internet Explorer. You need to do this only once.

Troubleshooting

You added an incorrect URL as a trusted site

If you added an incorrect URL to the list of trusted sites, you can remove it. In Internet Explorer, click Tools, Internet Options. In the Internet Options dialog box, click the Security tab. Click the Trusted Sites icon; then click Sites. The Trusted Sites dialog box appears (see Figure 22-3). Under Web Sites, highlight the incorrect URL and then click Remove.

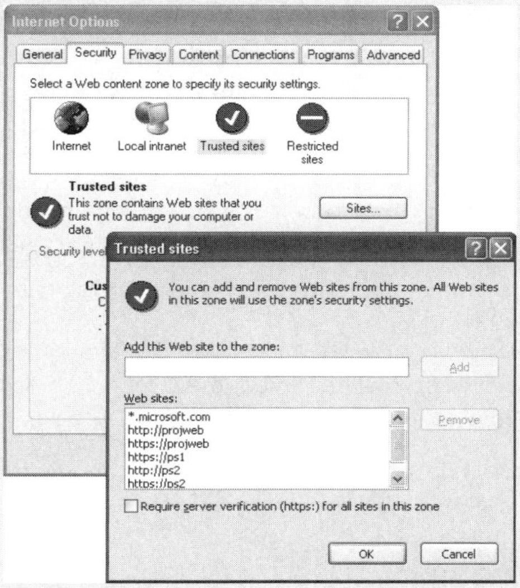

Figure 22-3. Make any changes needed to your list of trusted Web sites.

After the project server URL is listed as a trusted site in Internet Explorer, you can log on. If you specified in the Project Server Accounts dialog box that you want to automatically connect to your project server, all you need to do is start Project Professional. The specified project server location is found, and Project Professional logs you on immediately.

Your user account must be set up by the project server administrator before you can successfully log on to the project server. If you have problems logging on, check with your administrator.

For more information about adding server accounts, see "Establishing User Accounts and Permissions" on page 583.

If you specified that you want to manually connect to the project server, follow these steps:

1. Start up Project Professional.

   The Project Server Accounts dialog box appears (see Figure 22-4).

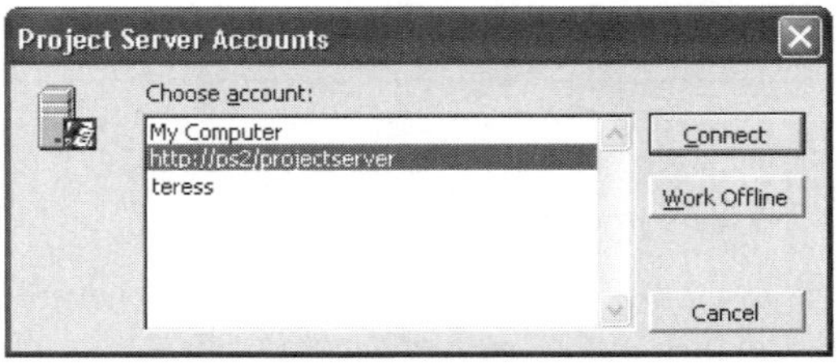

Figure 22-4. Select the project server account, and then click Connect.

2 Click the project server account if necessary and then click Connect.

If you ever want to work offline, or if there's a problem logging on to the project server, click the My Computer account and then click Work Offline.

If you specified in the Account Properties dialog box that you want to use your Windows account to log on, as soon as you open Project Professional, you are immediately authenticated and connected to the server.

If you specified that you want to use a Project Server account to log on, another dialog box appears, asking for your user name and password. Enter them and then click Go.

Tip **Connect across a wide area network**
If you're connecting across a wide area network (WAN) rather than a local area network (LAN), you might need to improve system performance. Select the Connecting Across A WAN check box at the bottom of the Project Server Accounts dialog box.

However, note that you might sacrifice some functionality in the Build Team dialog box.

Logging On via Project Web Access

As the project manager, you can review most of the information stored on your project server having to do with enterprise projects, enterprise resources, and team collaboration from the familiar Project Professional window. However, if you prefer, you can log on to Project Web Access and review the same information there. There are also certain pages of information that you can review only from Project Web Access.

To log on to Project Web Access, follow these steps:

1 Start up Internet Explorer.
2 In the Address box, enter the URL for your project server and then click Go.

This is the same URL you entered in the Account Properties dialog box in Project Professional. However, you do not need to have the account set up in Project Professional to log on to Project Web Access directly using Internet Explorer.

The Project Web Access logon page appears (see Figure 22-5).

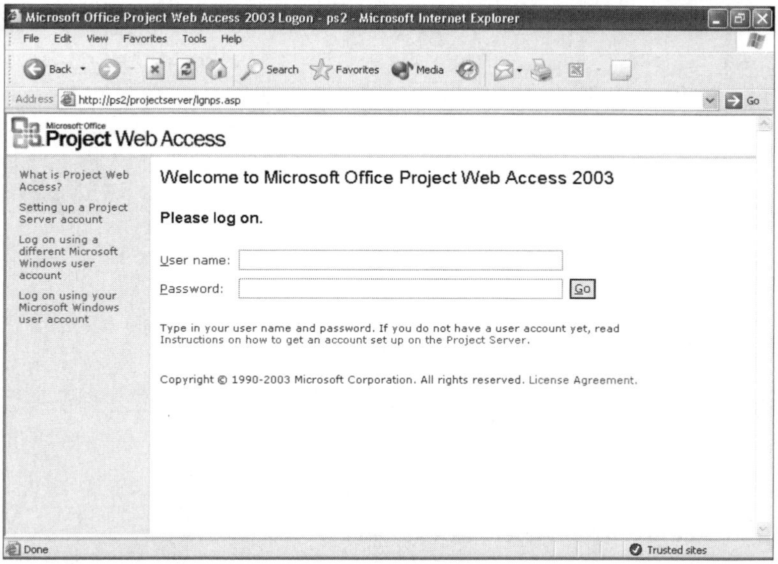

Figure 22-5. Enter your user name and password as set up by the project server administrator.

3 Enter your user name and password and then click Go.

This is the Windows or Project Server account information as specified by the project server administrator.

Your Project Web Access Home page appears (see Figure 22-6). You can carry out many project management activities using Project Web Access features, and they are described throughout the rest of this chapter.

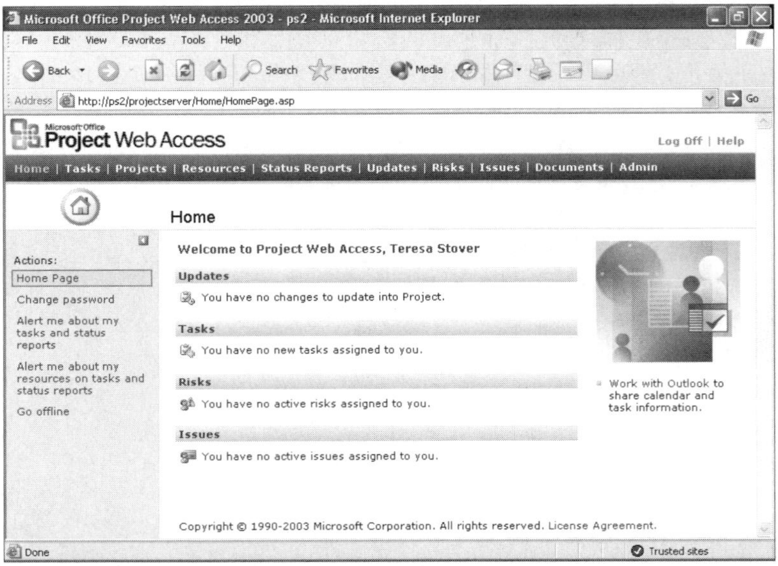

Figure 22-6. After a successful logon, the Project Web Access Home page appears.

> **Tip** **Add Project Web Access as a favorite**
> You probably will be checking Project Web Access from Internet Explorer often enough, so it's a great idea to add the project server URL as a favorite Web site. When the logon page appears in Internet Explorer, click Favorites, Add To Favorites. Enter a name in the Name box and then click OK.

Working with Enterprise Projects

With your user account set up and Project Professional connecting successfully to the project server, you're ready to get down to the nitty-gritty and start creating enterprise projects. You can save a new project to the project server or import an existing local project to the project server. Either way, your new enterprise project is associated with the enterprise global template, which sets the project management standards for your organization.

After your enterprise projects are in place on the server, you can carry out your day-to-day project management tasks. You check out a project from the server, add new tasks, modify existing tasks, work with resources, update progress tracking information, review and add information in custom enterprise fields, generate reports, and more. When done working with the project for the day, you check the project back in to the server.

You can work with multiple versions of a project. In addition, you don't always have to be connected to the project server; you can work with project information offline when needed.

Creating a New Enterprise Project

There are two methods for creating an enterprise project. One way is to start a new project plan in Microsoft Project, make sure you're connected to the project server, and then save it to the server. The other way is to open an existing project and import it to the project server.

As soon as either type of project is saved to the project server, the enterprise global template is applied to the project, and accordingly, the enterprise standards apply.

Saving a New Enterprise Project to the Server

To create a brand-new enterprise project, follow these steps:

1. Start up Project Professional and connect to the project server.
2. Click File, New.
3. In the New Project side pane, click Blank Project or the name of the existing project you want to use as the basis for the new project.

> **To use an enterprise project template set up by your project server administrator, click File, Open Project Template. For more information about creating a new project, see "Creating a Project File" on page 62.**

4. Click File, Save.

   The Save To Project Server dialog box appears (see Figure 22-7).

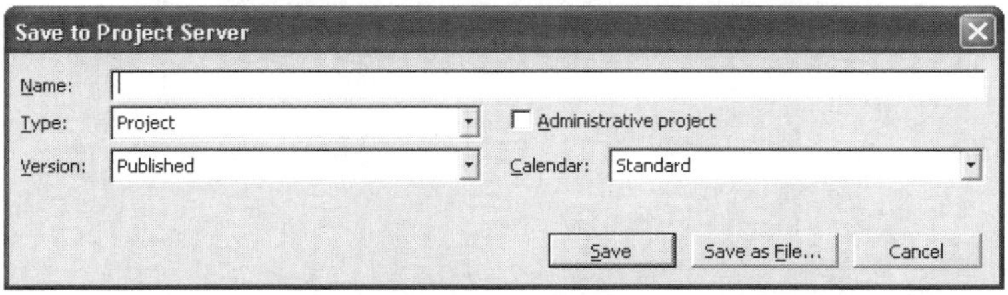

Figure 22-7. When saving a new file while connected to the server, the Save To Project Server dialog box appears.

5. In the Name box, type the project filename.
6. In the Version box, make sure that the version is the one specified by your project server administrator as the correct one to use.

   The default version is *Published*. Your project server administrator might create other versions for various purposes.
7. In the Calendar box, specify the base calendar being used as the project calendar.

   This project calendar is the one specified in the Project Information dialog box.
8. Click Save.

Your new project is saved as a new enterprise project on the project server.

Importing a Local Project to the Server

To import an existing *local* nonenterprise project to the project server, follow these steps:

1. Make sure that Project Professional is connected to the project server.

   A quick way to check whether you're connected to the server is to click the Tools menu. If the Substitute Resources command is available, you're connected. If it's dimmed, you're not. If you're not connected, close Project Professional, start it up again, and then connect to your project server.

   The project you're importing may or may not be open; it doesn't matter to the process.
2. Click Tools, Enterprise Options, Import Project To Enterprise.

   The Import Projects Wizard appears.
3. Read the Welcome page and then click Next.

   A browser window appears, similar to the Open dialog box.
4. Navigate to the drive and folder containing the project you want to import. Click the filename and then click Import.
5. In the message about the currency setting, click OK.
6. In the next wizard page, make any necessary changes to the project's filename, version, calendar, or custom fields (see Figure 22-8). In most cases, you can retain the current settings. Click Next.

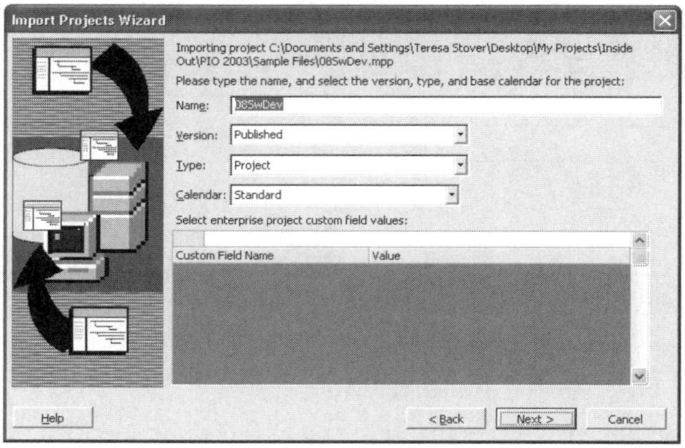

Figure 22-8. Specify any project settings to bring the project into conformance with enterprise standards.

7. In the Map Project Resources Onto Enterprise Resources page, match local resource names from your local project to the corresponding enterprise resource names if possible.

   You can map your local resources to enterprise resources if you know that the resources have already been added to the enterprise resource pool. For each resource name that you want to map, click in the Action On Import field and then click Map To

Enterprise Resource. Then in the Calendar Or Enterprise Resource field, click the down arrow and then select the name of the corresponding enterprise resource.

If your local resource does not exist in the enterprise resource pool, you can import the resource. In the Action On Import field, click Import Resource To Enterprise.

If you don't want to map or import the resource to the enterprise, retain the Action On Import field default of Keep Local With Base Calendar. If necessary, in the Action On Import field, click the name of the base calendar (see Figure 22-9).

Note When in doubt, don't import a resource to the enterprise resource pool. That is, if you're not sure whether certain resources belong in the enterprise resource pool or whether they're already there, bypass this step for now. Once a resource has been added to the enterprise resource pool, they're in semi-permanently. They can be deactivated, but only a database administrator can actually delete an erroneously added resource from the enterprise resource pool.

As long as you have the proper permissions, you can always add a resource later.

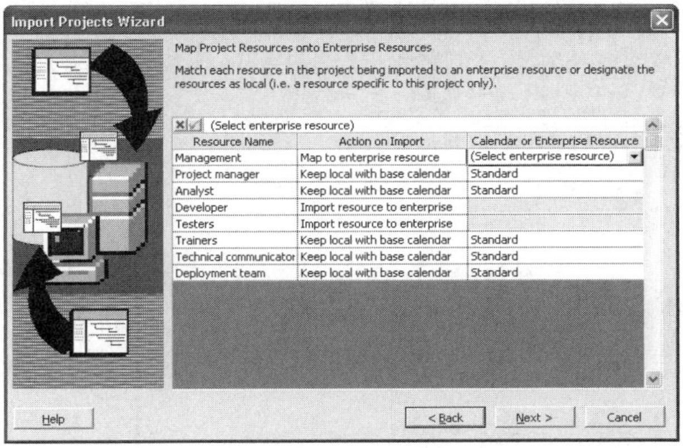

Figure 22-9. Import or map local resources to the enterprise resource pool.

8 When finished mapping resources, click Next.

The Map Task Fields page appears. This page shows any custom fields, such as Cost1 or Text3, you might have defined in the local project. You can map these custom fields to any corresponding enterprise fields that might have been defined for your organization.

9 If you want to map custom task fields, select the field in the From: Task Field column. Then in the To: Enterprise Task Field column, click the down arrow and select the corresponding enterprise task field (see Figure 22-10).

A preview of the enterprise fields appears in the lower part of the page.

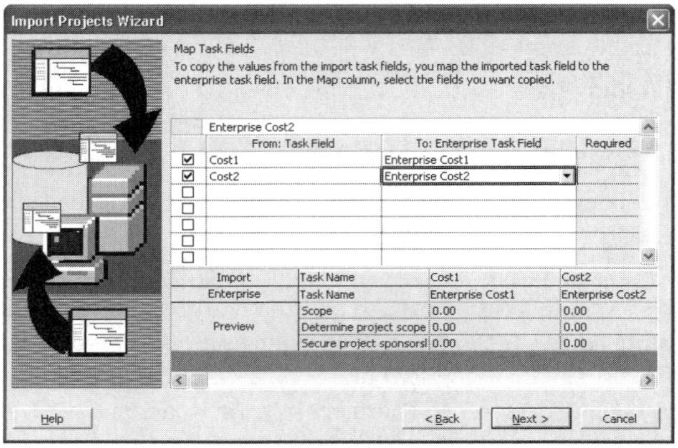

Figure 22-10. Associate custom fields defined in your project with custom enterprise fields.

10 When finished mapping custom task fields, click Next.

A table containing all tasks in the local project appears (see Figure 22-11).

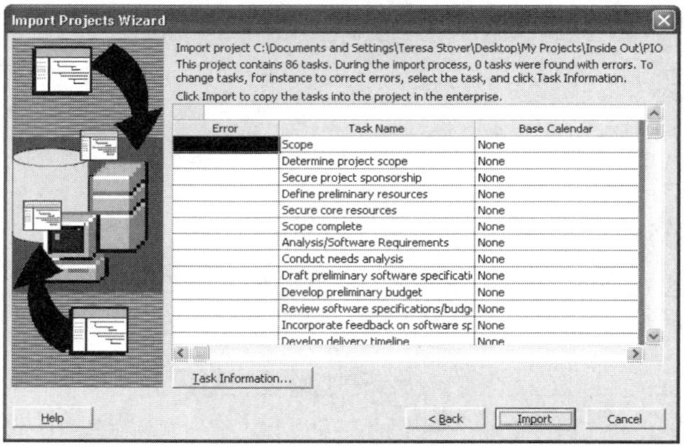

Figure 22-11. Review the table for any possible import problems.

11 Scan through the table of tasks, looking for any problems showing in the Error column.

If there are any errors, click the task and then click Task Information. Modify the task information as needed to make the task acceptable for the import process.

12 Click Import.

The tasks, fields, and resources are imported to a new enterprise project, and the Import Complete page appears.

13 Click Import More Projects if you have more projects to convert to enterprise. Otherwise, click Finish.

Maintaining Your Enterprise Projects

Now that your projects are stored on the project server, you can work with them as enterprise projects. What does that mean to you?

Essentially, it means that you check the project out of the server when you want to work on it and check it back in when you're done for the day, for example. It also means that you're now using the enterprise global template containing any standard project elements that have been defined for your organization, including custom fields, outline codes, macros, views, toolbars, and so on. You also have access to enterprise resources and tools for working efficiently with those resources.

In the wider view, your enterprise projects can be reviewed and analyzed by others to see the big picture of all projects taking place throughout the organization.

Checking Out an Enterprise Project

When you want to open an enterprise project, you check it out of the project server. To check out an enterprise project, follow these steps:

1. With Project Professional connected to the project server, click File, Open.

   The Open From Microsoft Office Project Server dialog box appears (see Figure 22-12). All enterprise projects that you have permission to see are listed, along with their version and current checkout status.

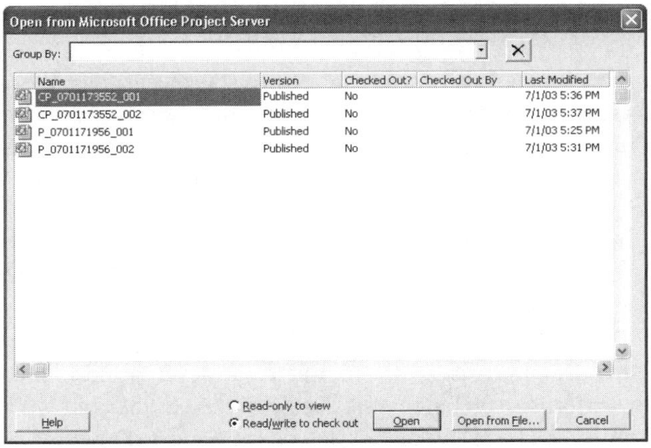

Figure 22-12. Check out your enterprise project from the project server.

2. Click the name of the project you want to check out.

   If there is a great number of projects, you can help yourself find the project by clicking the arrow in the Group By box and choosing a property by which to categorize the projects.

   You can also click any of the table headings to sort projects by that field. By default, the projects are listed in alphabetical order.

3 Make sure that the project you want to check out is not already checked out by someone else.

A project can be checked out by only one user at a time.

4 Make sure that the Read/Write To Check Out option is selected, which is the default.

If someone else has checked out the project you want, you can still open it if you select the Read-Only To View option. You will see the project as it was when it was last saved.

5 Click Open.

The project opens (see Figure 22-13). The enterprise global template is attached to the template, and the enterprise resource pool is available for use in the project.

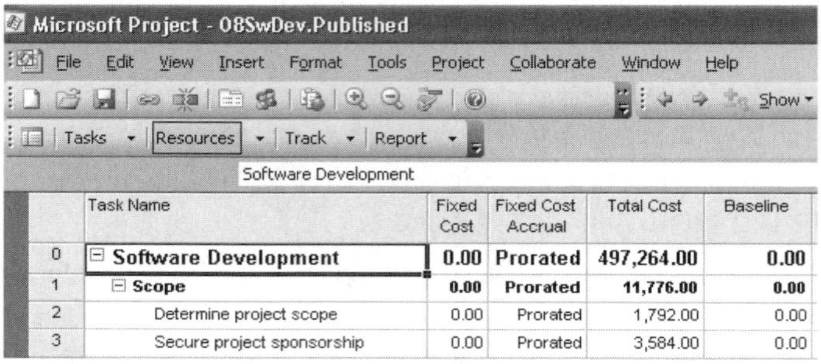

Figure 22-13. Your enterprise project opens in Project Professional.

Reviewing the Enterprise Global Template

When you start Project Professional and connect to your project server, the latest update of the enterprise global template is automatically attached. The enterprise global template is akin to a global template or the "global global" over the standard *project global template*. The enterprise global template dictates standards being enforced and customizations made available to Microsoft Project interface elements in projects throughout the enterprise. These standards provide for customization and consistency across all projects in an organization. The standards propagated through the enterprise global template also make it possible for project information throughout the enterprise to be compared and analyzed in meaningful ways. By default, the portfolio manager and project server administrator are the only users with the permission to modify the enterprise global template. However, project managers have the permission to view the enterprise global template, so you can see the controls behind your individual enterprise projects. The following list details the project elements that can be modified and propagated as standards via the enterprise global template:

- Base calendars
- Fields
- Filters
- Formulas
- Forms
- Groups

- Import and export maps
- Macros
- Outline codes
- Reports
- Tables
- Toolbars
- VBA modules
- Views
- Currency

To review the enterprise global template and see the specific changes that are being enforced for your organization, follow these steps:

1. Make sure that Project Professional is connected to the project server.

   As soon as you connect to the project server, the enterprise global template is loaded into memory for use with your enterprise projects.

2. Click Tools, Enterprise Options, Open Enterprise Global.

   A project plan, which appears to be empty, is displayed (see Figure 22-14).

   Using the default project manager permissions, the enterprise global template is not *checked out* to you in the sense that you can make changes to it; but rather that you're using it as the foundation structure to your own checked-out enterprise projects.

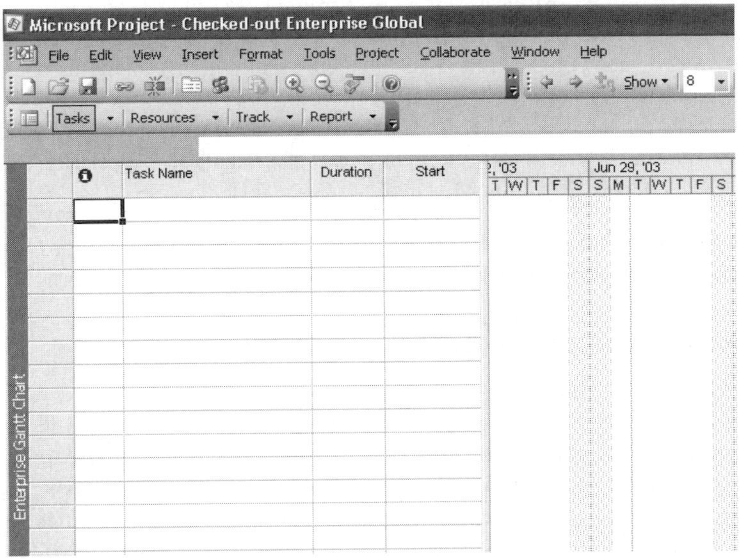

Figure 22-14. Review features in the enterprise global template to see your organization's standards.

3. You can browse around the various interface features—such as the view definitions, filter definitions, custom toolbars, and so on—to see how the enterprise global template has been customized.
4. When finished reviewing the enterprise global template, close it.

   While you can inadvertently enter data in the enterprise global template, they are not saved when you close it. Only specific elements (views, fields, macros, currency, and so on) are saved. Tasks or assignments would never be saved with the enterprise global template.

   The global standards are still present in any enterprise projects you have currently checked out. In fact, if you browse the interface elements in your own enterprise project, you'll see that the same customizations are present there that are in the enterprise global template.

If the enterprise global template changes after you connect to the project server, you only see those changes after you close Project Professional and reconnect.

It's likely that your organization has a system—either formal or informal—for project managers to suggest changes to the enterprise global template. Find out from the project server administrator or portfolio manager how you can suggest changes you want to see implemented. When the enterprise global template is updated, you see the changes take effect the next time you check out an enterprise project.

Even though the enterprise global template affects all your enterprise projects, this doesn't mean that you can't still use your own project global template, which is active on projects on your own computer. As long as there's no conflict between elements in the project global and elements in the enterprise global template, you can create your own sets of standards for all your own projects. For example, you can create and use your own custom toolbar as long as it has a different name from any custom toolbars provided in the enterprise global template.

For more information about working with the project global template, see Chapter 28, "Standardizing Projects Using Templates."

Finally, you can change interface elements to apply to an individual project without it being a part of the enterprise global template or your own project global template.

Working with Custom Enterprise Fields

Custom enterprise fields often constitute a major area of customization and standardization implemented via the enterprise global template. Custom fields can be designed to store a specific category of numbers, durations, or text not provided by built-in Microsoft Project fields. Different data types of custom fields are available for assignments, tasks, and entire projects. The portfolio manager or project server administrator defines these fields as part of the enterprise global template, which are then available to you to add to your project.

Custom enterprise fields include the following:

- Custom enterprise project fields, such as Enterprise Project Cost1, Enterprise Project Duration3, and Enterprise Project Outline Code5
- Custom enterprise task fields, such as Enterprise Date3 or Enterprise Flag10
- Custom enterprise task outline codes, using Enterprise Task Outline Code1 through Enterprise Task Outline Code30

Note There is also an extensive set of custom enterprise resource fields that help define resources in various ways in the enterprise resource pool.

For more information about these enterprise resource fields, see "Working with Enterprise Resource Outline Codes" later in this chapter on page 658.

To add a custom enterprise field to your enterprise project, follow these steps:

1. With Project Professional connected to the project server, check out the enterprise project to which you want to add the custom enterprise field.
2. Display the sheet view and table to which you want to add the custom enterprise field.

   If you're adding an enterprise task field, display a task view. If it's an assignment field, display the Task Usage or Resource Usage view.

   If you're adding an enterprise project field, display the project summary row. To do this, first display a task view. Click Tools, Options and then click the View tab. Select the Show Project Summary Task check box.
3. Right-click the column heading to the left of where you want the custom enterprise field to be inserted. Click Insert Column on the shortcut menu.
4. In the Field Name box, find and click the custom enterprise field.

   You'll know the name of the field from information you've received from your portfolio manager or project server administrator.

   Custom enterprise fields are listed twice: once using the generic enterprise field name (for example, *Enterprise Date1*) and again using the name you gave it (for example, *Deliverable Milestone*).
5. In the Insert Column dialog box, click OK.

   A column containing the selected custom enterprise field appears in the sheet view.

Some custom fields are set up to be calculated from values in other fields in your project. If you added such a *calculated field*, it might already contain values.

Other custom fields are set up for you to simply add the appropriate data. For such *entered fields*, you might just type in data freeform. Entered fields can also be designed to contain a value list for you to choose from. If this is the case, click in the field; click the arrow; and then select the appropriate choice for the task, assignment, or project.

Checking In an Enterprise Project

When you finish working with your enterprise project for now, you check it back in to the project server. Your organization might have specific rules for when you need to check in your projects.

To check in an enterprise project, follow these steps:

1. Make sure that Project Professional is connected to the project server.
2. Click File, Save to save your final changes.
3. Check in the project by simply closing the project: click File, Close.

   As long as the project was already an enterprise project, it is checked back in to the project server.

   If you had not saved final changes, the Save And Check-In dialog box appears. Click Save Any Changes And Then Check-In. If you want to discard your changes, click Check-In Only.

Note If there are any required custom enterprise fields or outline codes that you have not filled in, you'll see a prompt reminding you to do this. You must complete these fields before you can successfully check the project back in.

See "Working with Custom Enterprise Fields" in the previous section for more information.

After you check in your project, it becomes accessible for edit by other project server users with the proper permissions.

Working with Published Versions of Enterprise Projects

When you save or import a new enterprise project to the project server, you select a particular *project version*. By default, the version is *published*. The version is appended to the project name as a second filename extension; for example, *Design.mpp.published*. The version specifies all the projects that are a members of a given portfolio of projects.

The version is used in a variety of ways. Users can compare and analyze all projects in a given version. They can also compare the different versions of the same project, which is particularly useful for analyzing what-if scenarios. Versions can also be used to track different phases or milestones in a project, or different baselines in the same set of project tasks.

The project server administrator can create additional versions, as dictated by the project management requirements of the organization.

Working Offline with Enterprise Projects

You don't always need to be connected to the project server to work with projects. And you don't always need to work with enterprise projects when connected to the project server. This is particularly helpful when you're traveling and need to take a project file with you. It is also helpful if you are working with any projects that don't need to be a part of the published portfolio of enterprise projects.

The following is a list of possible offline scenarios:

- You can save an enterprise project as a local project. To do this, check out the enterprise project. Click File, Save As. In the Save To Project Server dialog box, click Save As File. In the browser window, select the drive and folder where you want to save the local copy. Give the project a new name, if you want, and then click Save. Be aware, however, that the enterprise project is checked back in to the project server, which means that others can make changes to the project while you're working on your local copy.
- You can save an enterprise project as an offline project. With the enterprise project checked out and displayed, click File, Save Offline.
- You can be connected to the project server, but open a local nonenterprise project. To do this, click File, Open. In the Open From Microsoft Office Project Server dialog box, click Open From File. Browse to and select the local project and then click Open.
- You can open Project Professional without connecting to the project server, and open and work with a local nonenterprise project. To do this, you need to have Project Professional set up for manual connection. In the Project Server Accounts dialog box, click My Computer and then click Work Offline. Or click the name of the project server and then click Work Offline.

You can work with an enterprise project without being connected to the project server. This is handy if you are physically away from the network or want to try some contingency scenarios with an enterprise project. When you are ready to reconnect, simply log on to the server, open your enterprise project file, and then save it. Because you are back online and connected to the system, your file will be checked in when you save it.

Building Your Enterprise Project Team

Among the advantages of enterprise project management is the capability to work with the *enterprise resource pool* and the associated functions. The enterprise resource pool is the set of people, equipment, and materials available to be assigned and carry out the work of projects throughout an organization. It contains fundamental information about resources, such as skill sets and availability, which help you find the right resources for your projects. The enterprise resource pool also contains cost information, which not only helps you work within your allotted budget, but also helps accounting and human resources figure costs from their points of view as well.

With the enterprise resource pool, a high-level visibility of resource availabilities, skills, roles, and utilization is now possible. Project managers as well as upper management can see when additional staff is needed and where there are underutilized resources. They also can view the basic data for all project resources in one place.

Resource managers can also use the enterprise resource pool to staff, plan, and budget with more accuracy and confidence. They can see resources by skill level and definition, availability, and organizational hierarchy. In addition, they can assist project managers with current and anticipated resource requirements by analyzing the enterprise resource database. Together with the project managers, resource managers can work with *generic resources* in the enterprise resource pool to perform planning and contingency analyses.

The project server administrator is often the one who sets up and maintains the enterprise resource pool. However, because of the specialized information having to do with resource skills, costs, and availability, other specialists—such as the portfolio manager or a human resources representative—might be involved in the setup. By default, the project server administrator and portfolio manager are given the permission to add and edit enterprise resource data.

For more information about enterprise resource pool setup, see "Administering the Enterprise Resource Pool" on page 598.

The enterprise versus non-enterprise resource pool

When you're working with enterprise projects and enterprise resources, your nonenterprise resource pool functionality is disabled. That is, when you click Tools, Resource Sharing, the commands on the submenu are dimmed. This is because using a local resource pool with an enterprise project can cause unnecessary confusion.

However, if you ever work with nonenterprise projects, the nonenterprise resource pool commands and functionality are available to you.

For more information about working with a non-enterprise resource pool, see "Sharing Resources Using a Resource Pool" on page 441.

Creating Generic Resources as Placeholders

You can create *generic resources* in Microsoft Project to help you define resources of a particular role or skill set, for example, *VB Programmer Expert*. Generic resources can be local, created by the project manager for use in an enterprise or nonenterprise project.

Generic resources can also be created and added to the enterprise resource pool by the project server administrator or other user with the proper permissions. For best results, an organization should define a generic resource for every classification in its resource breakdown structure. Then project managers and resource managers can use those generic resources in their projects for planning and modeling purposes.

Because generic resources are just placeholders for real resources, they are not associated with any availability status. They can be checked out of the enterprise resource pool multiple times by multiple project managers.

Whether local or enterprise, generic resources are invaluable for helping project managers identify team requirements and ultimately find real resources. Generic resources are typically defined by a job title or function, rather than a person's name. What makes generic resources really useful is the association of enterprise resource outline codes, which go a long way toward defining the attributes of the resource.

With generic resources associated with outline codes that define resource attributes, you can populate your project team using the Build Team dialog box. You can assign qualified resources to tasks using the Resource Substitution Wizard. You can run what-if scenarios using the Portfolio Modeler.

> **Caution** Be very careful if you're replacing local generic resources with enterprise resources. You need to be certain that the name of your local generic resource is not used in the enterprise resource pool or even in any other project in your organization.
>
> The best policy is to have your project server administrator create all the generic resources everyone might need. You can then add them to your project when needed, and use the Build Team dialog box to replace them with real resources when you're ready.

To create a local generic resource in your enterprise project and add the appropriate outline codes, follow these steps:

1. Make sure that Project Professional is connected to the project server and that your enterprise project is checked out and displayed.
2. In your enterprise project, display the Resource Sheet and enter information for a new resource. In the Resource Name field, enter a generic name that you'll be able to recognize; for example, ***Web Engineer 3*** or ***Information Architect 4400***.
3. Associate the generic resource with the resource breakdown structure (RBS) or other enterprise resource outline code field. Right-click where you want the new column to be added and then click Insert Column in the shortcut menu. In the Field Name box, click the resource outline code field you want to add and then click OK.

   The selected field is added as a new column in the Resource Sheet.

   The RBS field is simply Enterprise Resource Outline Code30, especially set aside to be defined with an organization's resource breakdown structure.
4. Click in the new enterprise resource outline code field to review the drop-down list of code choices. Select the one appropriate for your generic resource.

   Your project server administrator or other user with permission to edit enterprise resource information has set up these outline codes for your use. For resource matching and substitution to work properly, these outline codes needed to be created with the Use This Code For Matching Generic Resources option.

   If you're using one of the multiple-value enterprise resource outline codes, which are defined as Enterprise Resource Outline Code20-29, you can select multiple attributes in the value drop-down list.

   You can apply enterprise resource outline codes to a local generic resource. However, unless you've been granted the permission to edit enterprise resources, you cannot apply enterprise resource outline codes to enterprise generic resources.

5 Repeat Steps 3–4 if there are additional outline codes you need to use to identify the attributes or qualifications for your generic resource.
6 Double-click the new resource row to open the Resource Information dialog box.
7 In the General tab, select the Generic check box and then click OK.

   Your new generic resource is defined as such, with the attributes identified through the outline code(s).
8 If you want, switch to a task view such as the Gantt Chart and assign tasks to the new generic resource.

   If you assign tasks to your generic resource, later the generic resource can easily be replaced with real enterprise resources possessing the same attributes as defined by the outline codes. You can replace resources this way with either the Build Team dialog box or the Resource Substitution Wizard. The replacing resource is automatically assigned to any tasks to which the generic resource was assigned.

> **Tip** **Use generic resources defined for the enterprise**
> Your organization might have established a set of generic resources as part of the enterprise resource pool. Rather than create your own in this case, use the Build Team dialog box to find the generic resources you want, and add them to your project team.
>
> If you're not sure whether enterprise generic resources have been defined for your organization, check with your project server administrator. Or, just filter and browse the enterprise resource pool in the Build Team dialog box.

Working with Enterprise Resource Outline Codes

Outline codes are custom hierarchical codes that are defined by your project server administrator or other user with permissions to modify the enterprise global template. Just as enterprise project outline codes and enterprise task outline codes can be defined for your organization, so can enterprise resource outline codes.

After the resource outline codes are defined, the project server administrator or other user with the proper permissions associates resources in the enterprise resource pool with the enterprise resource outline codes that define those resources. In this way, the enterprise resources are defined by their job code, qualifications, specialties, locations, or any other attributes needed by an organization.

For more information about enterprise task outline codes, see "Working with Custom Enterprise Fields" earlier in this chapter on page 652.

Because the outline codes are already associated with the enterprise resources, and because most project managers do not modify the enterprise global template by default, you typically use the enterprise resource outline codes to do the following:

- Match or replace resources in your project with others associated with the same values in their outline codes. You do this using the Build Team dialog box.

- Substitute generic, local, or enterprise resources in your project with enterprise resources possessing matching values in their outline codes. You do this using the Resource Substitution Wizard.
- Arrange enterprise resources in your project by their outline codes, so you can review your project team by your organization's resource breakdown structure or other resource hierarchy. You do this by sorting, filtering, or grouping by the outline code.

Adding Enterprise Resource Outline Codes

Your project server administrator is responsible for setting up the enterprise resource outline codes according to the needs of your organization.

For more information about creating enterprise resource outline codes, see Chapter 21.

To add a custom enterprise resource outline code to your enterprise project, follow these steps:

1. With Project Professional connected to the project server, check out the enterprise project to which you want to add the custom enterprise resource field.
2. Display the Resource Sheet and table to which you want to add the custom enterprise field.
3. Right-click the column heading where you want the custom enterprise field to be inserted. Click Insert Column on the shortcut menu.
4. In the Field Name box, find and click the custom enterprise resource field.

   You'll know the name of the field from information you've received from your project server administrator.

   Custom enterprise fields are listed twice: once using the generic enterprise field name (for example, *Enterprise Resource Outline Code1*) and again using the name the project server administrator gave it (for example, *HR Level*).
5. In the Insert Column dialog box, click OK.

   A column containing the selected custom resource enterprise field appears in the sheet view.

Using Multiple-Value Enterprise Resource Outline Codes

NEW FEATURE!

With Project Professional 2002 came the introduction of enterprise resource outline codes, which could be used to specify traits or properties associated with resources, such as skills, locations, certifications, languages, and so on. Now with Project Professional 2003, ten of these enterprise resource outline codes can be used to each define multiple traits within a single code. Instead of using a separate outline code for each trait, multiple traits can be combined in a single resource field to show all pertinent properties of a resource at once.

The project server administrator creates the Enterprise Resource Multi-Value (ERMV) fields and assigns them to the resources as appropriate. The project manager then can add one of the defined ERMV fields to a resource view to show resource properties at a glance. These multiple properties are set up with the ERMV fields, which are the Enterprise Resource Outline Codes20–29.

The information contained in this field can also be used with the Resource Substitution Wizard, Build Team dialog box, and Portfolio Modeler.

For information about administrator setup of the ERMV fields, see "Specifying Multiple Properties for a Resource" on page 613. For more information about working with fields and outline codes, see "Working with Outline Codes" on page 806.

Assembling Your Project Team

You can have Microsoft Project "mine" the entire enterprise resource pool to find resources who have the exact skills, availability, and other traits you need for your project. Specifically, in the planning processes of your project, when putting together the perfect team to carry out your project, you can:

- Find and add resources by name
- Find resources associated with a certain title, code, skill set, or other attribute
- Find resources who are available for work during a certain period of time
- Replace a resource already on your team with another enterprise resource
- Find more resources that have the same traits as a resource already on your team
- Match and replace generic resources in your project with real enterprise resources
- Tentatively add proposed resources to your project

Use the Build Team dialog box to find enterprise resources and add them to your project team. The Build Team process adds resources to your project, but does not necessarily assign tasks (unless you replace a resource who has already been assigned to tasks). After the resources are added, you use the Assign Resources dialog box, as usual, to assign tasks to project team resources.

Note If your project and the enterprise resource pool meet certain conditions, you might be able to use the Resource Substitution Wizard to add resources to your project and assign them to tasks, all in one step.

For more information about this wizard, see "Assigning Tasks to Enterprise Resources" later in this chapter on page 666.

Adding Enterprise Resources by Name

You might already know exactly which enterprise resources you need to add to your team. If this is the case, find and add resources by name as follows:

1. Make sure that Project Professional is connected to the project server and check out the project to which you want to add resources.

2 Click Tools, Build Team From Enterprise.

If there are more than 1000 resources in the enterprise resource pool, a dialog box appears to help you prefilter the enterprise resources. In the Enterprise Outline Code field, select a code or other attribute to help define the list of resources you'll be working with. Click OK.

The Build Team dialog box appears (see Figure 22-15). The upper portion of the dialog box contains filters and options for finding resources that meet certain criteria. The Filtered Enterprise Resource table on the left contains enterprise resources. When no filter is applied, the table lists all members of your organization's enterprise resource pool. The Project Team Resources table on the right lists any enterprise and nonenterprise resources you have already added to the current project.

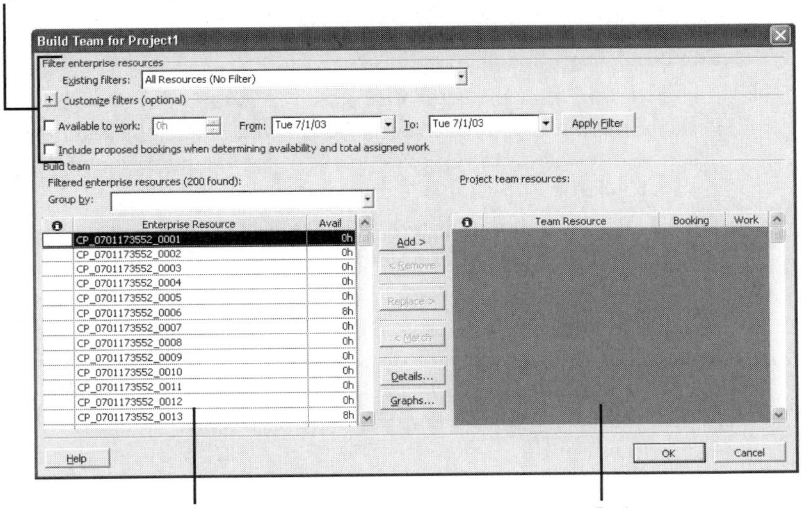

Figure 22-15. Use the Build Team dialog box to add enterprise resources to your project.

By default, the enterprise resources are listed alphabetically by name. To be certain, you can re-sort the list by clicking the Enterprise Resources column heading.

3 Scroll through the Filtered Enterprise Resources table to find and select the resource by name.

You can select multiple resources at once. Use Shift to select multiple adjacent resources; use Ctrl to select multiple nonadjacent resources.

4 Click the Add button.

The selected resources are added to the Project Team Resources table.

Tip **Find more information about an enterprise resource**
You can learn more about a resource by clicking the resource name in either table and then clicking the Details button. The Resource Information dialog box opens for this resource. You can review information about availability, costs, and custom fields. This information is set up by users with special permission to edit resource information, as granted by the project server administrator.

Finding Enterprise Resources that Meet Specific Criteria

If you're looking for a set of enterprise resources who fit a certain set of criteria, you can use the various built-in filters, groups, and other controls in the Build Team dialog box to narrow your search. To find and add resources who possess certain attributes, follow these steps:

1. Click Tools, Build Team From Enterprise.

   The Build Team dialog box appears.

2. If you want to filter the enterprise resource list by a built-in filter, under Filter Enterprise Resources, click the arrow in the Existing Filters box and then select the filter that describes the resources you're looking for, for example, material resources or resource group. Click the Apply Filter button.

   The number of resources listed in the Filtered Enterprise Resources table might change if your applied filter excluded a number of resources from your search and therefore reduced your choices to a more manageable level.

3. If you need to find resources who have a certain amount of time available to work during a specific period of time, you can specify that with the Available To Work controls. Select the Available To Work check box. Enter a work amount in the box if you want. In the From and To boxes, enter the date range when you need the resources. Click the Apply Filter button.

   The resources listed in the Filtered Enterprise Resources table change to show only those resources who meet the filter criteria.

4. You can group the resources in the table by certain attributes such as the Standard Rate or Resource Group. Above the table, click the arrow in the Group By box and then click the group you want to use.

   The list of enterprise resources is rearranged according to your selected group.

For more information about using existing filters and groups, see "Rearranging Your Project Information" on page 123.

You can quickly create your own filter within the Build Team dialog box if you need to filter on a specific field (or two or three) that isn't provided for in the Existing Filters list. Creating your own Build Team filter is particularly useful if you want to find resources that are associated with a certain value in a custom enterprise field such as Enterprise Resource Text1 or Enterprise Resource Outline Code6. Likewise, if RBS codes have been set up and applied to enterprise resources, you can filter for a particular RBS code. To create a Build Team filter, follow these steps:

1. In the Build Team dialog box, click the plus button next to Customize Filters to expand the section.

   A filter definition table appears (see Figure 22-16).

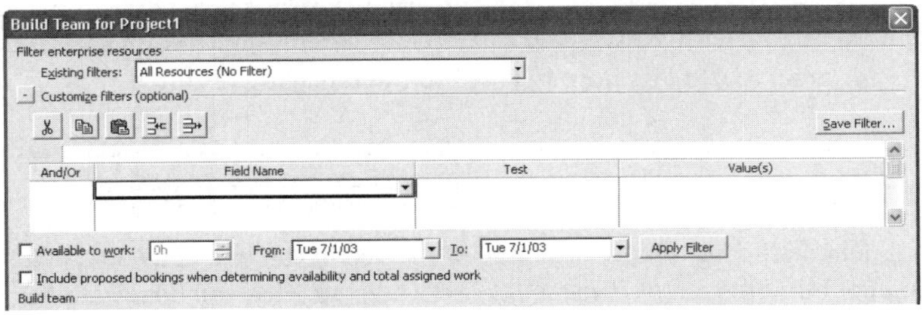

Figure 22-16. Create a filter to find only those resources that meet your criteria.

2. Click in the Field Name column of the first row and select the field you want to filter on.
3. In the Test column, click the test you want to use, such as Equals or Is Greater Than.
4. In the Value(s) field, enter the value that should be stored in the field for the resources found by the filter.
5. If you need to define another set of criteria, in the second row of the table, click in the And/Or field and then click And or Or.
6. In the rest of the row, select the field, test, and value for the second set of criteria.
7. When finished defining the filter, click Save Filter if you want to save it for future use. Otherwise, click the Apply Filter button.

   You can combine the application of your filter with other criteria, including an existing filter or work availability criteria. When you click the Apply Filter button, the list of enterprise resources changes to show only those resources who meet the criteria of your filter(s).

For more information about creating your own filters, see "Customizing Filters" on page 799.

Replacing and Matching Existing Resources

You can use the Build Team dialog box to replace a resource on your project team with one from the enterprise resource pool. This replacement is useful if you have a local resource in the project that you know has been added to the enterprise resource pool. It is also useful if you want to replace generic resources in your project with real enterprise resources. To replace an existing project team resource with an enterprise resource, follow these steps:

1. In the Build Team dialog box, apply any filters or groups you need to find the replacing resource.

2. In the Project Team Resources table, click the name of the resource you want to replace.
3. In the Filtered Enterprise Resources table, click the name of the replacing resource.
4. Click Replace.

   The resource selected in the Filtered Enterprise Resources table replaces the one selected in the Project Team Resources table. If the original resource had reported any actual work on assigned tasks, the original resource remains in the project plan as associated with those assignments. Any remaining work on any tasks assigned to the original resource is now assigned to the replacing resource.

Review a resource's availability graphs

If you find a resource you want to add or replace in your project, you can get more information about that resource's availability and workload. This can help you decide whether this resource really has the time to work on your project.

Select the resource name in either table and then click Graphs. The Graphs dialog box appears. There are three different graphs to choose from in the Select Graph box.

You can also review these same availability graphs for resources in your project plan. In the Assign Resources dialog box, select a resource and then click Graphs.

With the availability graphs, you can see:

- *Timephased* work assignments
- Timephased availability and remaining availability
- Timephased resource data grouped by project

Suppose that you have already added an enterprise resource to your project team and you need five more resources just like him. If the existing resource and enterprise resources have attributes defined for them—such as RBS codes, skill sets, certifications, and so on—you can use the Build Team dialog box to find other resources who have the same attributes. To find more enterprise resources whose defined traits match those of an existing project team resource, follow these steps:

1. In the Build Team dialog box, apply any filters or groups you might need to define matching resources.
2. In the Project Team Resources table, click the name of the resource whose traits you want to match with additional enterprise resources.
3. Click Match.

   The list of filtered enterprise resources is searched for resource matches. The resulting list of resources represents resources whose attributes exactly match with those of your selected resource. The matching attributes used are those outline codes that your project server administrator has set up with the Use For Resource Matching check box.
4. If you want to add any of these resources, click their names and then click Add.

Replacing and Matching Generic Resources

You can combine the Match and Replace functions in the Build Team dialog box to help you find enterprise resources to replace generic resources, as follows:

1. In your project plan, click Tools, Build Team From Enterprise.

   The Build Team dialog box appears.
2. If necessary, apply any filters to better focus the list of resources.
3. In the Project Team Resources table, select your generic resource and then click Match.

   Microsoft Project finds all the resources in the enterprise resource pool that have the same attributes as the ones you defined in your generic resource. Those matching resources are listed in the Filtered Enterprise Resources table.
4. Select the matching resource you want to replace the generic resource and then click Replace.

   The matching enterprise resource is added to your project team. If you had assigned any tasks to the generic resource, the replacing enterprise resource is now assigned to those tasks.
5. Repeat Steps 3–4 to match and replace any other generic resources in your project plan.

Proposing Tentative Resources

As soon as you add enterprise resources to your project team and assign tasks to those resources, their availability information changes in the enterprise resource pool. This availability update ensures that a single resource is not inadvertently booked full-time to two or three different projects, for example.

However, sometimes you need to build a project and its team as a proposal or estimate. You might want to show actual resources in the project, to demonstrate the skill level as well as calculate real costs. However, if the project is just an estimate or model, you probably wouldn't want to tie up the resource's availability in case the project does not actually happen.

In another scenario, you might be working with an approved project and want to run a what-if analysis on the impact of adding certain resources to the project.

NEW FEATURE! For either of these cases, you can *soft-book* resources on your project by adding them as *proposed*, rather than *committed* resources on your team.

> **Note** The booking type, proposed or committed, applies to the resource as a whole on your project. The booking type does not apply to individual assignments within the project.

By default, all resources are booked as committed. To specify that a resource you're adding is to be booked as a proposed resource on your project team, do the following:

1. In the Build Team dialog box, apply any filters or groups you might need to find the resources you want.

2. In the Filtered Enterprise Resources table, click the name of the resource you want to add as a proposed resource.
3. Click Add.
4. In the Project Team Resources table, in the Booking field for the resource, change Committed to Proposed.

   That resource is now considered soft-booked. As you work through your project, you can choose to consider resources' booking types when assigning tasks to resources in your project and when leveling assignments to resolve overallocations.

> **Tip** **Consider proposed bookings for your resource filtering**
> When you're searching for resources who meet certain availability criteria, you can choose whether or not Microsoft Project should consider proposed resource information. In the Build Team dialog box, select or clear the Include Proposed Bookings When Determining Availability And Total Assigned Work.

> **Tip** **Commit a proposed resource**
> A resource's booking type becomes part of the resource information. When you're ready to confirm a resource's place in your project, display the Resource Sheet or other resource view. Double-click the proposed resource's name to open the Resource Information dialog box. On the General tab, in the Booking Type box, change Proposed to Committed.

Assigning Tasks to Enterprise Resources

You can assign enterprise resources to tasks in the more traditional manner—add the resources to your project using the Build Team dialog box. Then use the Assign Resources dialog box to assign tasks to resources on your team.

The newfangled way to assign enterprise resources to tasks in an enterprise project is to find and replace, or substitute, resources that have the qualifications and availability you're looking for. Whether or not you have enterprise resources already added to your project, you can use the *Resource Substitution Wizard* to help you assign project tasks to the right resources.

Essentially, you assign placeholder resources possessing certain attributes to the tasks that need to be staffed. Those placeholder resources can be generic resources, local resources, or other enterprise resources. The attributes are defined through an RBS or other enterprise resource outline codes, and can represent traits such as job codes, skills, specialties, certifications, languages, and so on.

After the placeholder resources are assigned to tasks, you can run the Resource Substitution Wizard, make a number of choices to dictate how you want the substitutions to take place, and then let it do its thing. You review the results and can decide whether you want to update your project with those results, save the results for another time, or discard those results.

For the Resource Substitution Wizard to work successfully, a certain set of conditions must be met. Your project server administrator, portfolio manager, or other user with the permission to modify the enterprise resource pool and enterprise global template needs to have done the following:

- Set up the enterprise resource pool.
- Set up the RBS and any other enterprise resource outline codes in the enterprise global template.
- Apply the RBS and any other enterprise resource outline codes to resources in the enterprise resource pool.

For more information about setting up the enterprise resource pool, creating enterprise outline codes, or applying enterprise outline codes, see "Administering the Enterprise Resource Pool" on page 598.

In addition, you need to prepare your project plan as follows:

- Save or import your project plan as an enterprise project on the project server, if not already done.
- Associate the RBS or other enterprise resource outline codes to the generic resources, local resources, or enterprise resources that you want matched and substituted.
- Assign generic resources, local resources, or enterprise resources to tasks for which you want resources to be matched and substituted.

For more information about saving or importing a project to your project server, see "Creating a New Enterprise Project" earlier in this chapter on page 645. For more information about creating a generic resource and assigning enterprise resource outline codes, see "Replacing and Matching Generic Resources" in the previous section on page 665.

Inside Out

Tracking progress? Don't substitute resources

Use the Resource Substitution Wizard only during the planning stages of a project—before you set the project baseline, initiate work on the project, and start entering actual progress information. The Resource Substitution Wizard is not designed for projects in which actuals have been entered.

You can use the Resource Substitution Wizard to find a resource or do some planning in a project that includes actuals. Just don't save the project or publish the data, and you'll be safe.

If you add a set of tasks after you have begun entering actuals, you can still use the Build Team dialog box to find the right resources for tasks. In your project plan, create generic resources and assign the appropriate RBS code or other custom outline code defined by your organization for identifying resource attributes or qualifications. Assign those resources to the new tasks. Then use the Build Team dialog box to match and replace the generic resources.

See "Replacing and Matching Generic Resources" in the previous section on page 665 for details. For more information about using the Resource Substitution Wizard with projects containing actuals, download the online book "Microsoft Office Project Server 2003 Application Configuration Guide." Go to *http://www.microsoft.com.downloads*, and then search for Project Server 2003.

When all the prerequisite pieces are in place, you're ready to have Microsoft Project find, match, and substitute resources for you. Follow these steps:

1 Make sure that Project Professional is connected to the project server.

2 In your checked-out enterprise project, click Tools, Substitute Resources.

The Welcome page of the Resource Substitution Wizard appears.

3 Read the Welcome page to make sure you have all required components in place. Then click Next.

The Choose Projects page appears (see Figure 22-17), listing all the project files currently open on your computer. This page makes it possible to replace substitutes in multiple enterprise projects at one time.

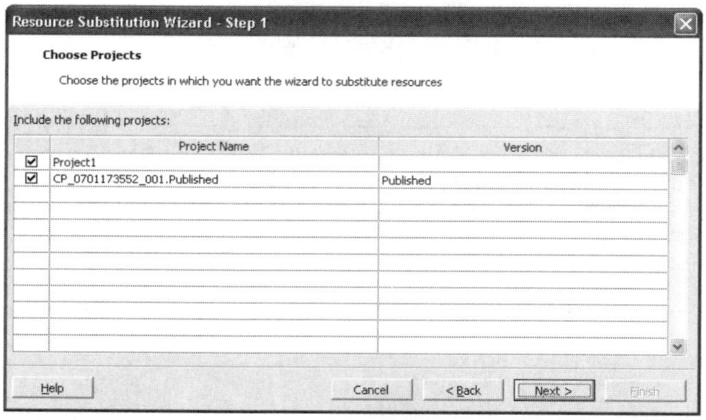

Figure 22-17. Use the Choose Projects page to select the projects in which resources should be substituted.

4 Select the check box next to the project in which resources should be substituted. Then click Next.

The Choose Resources page appears (see Figure 22-18).

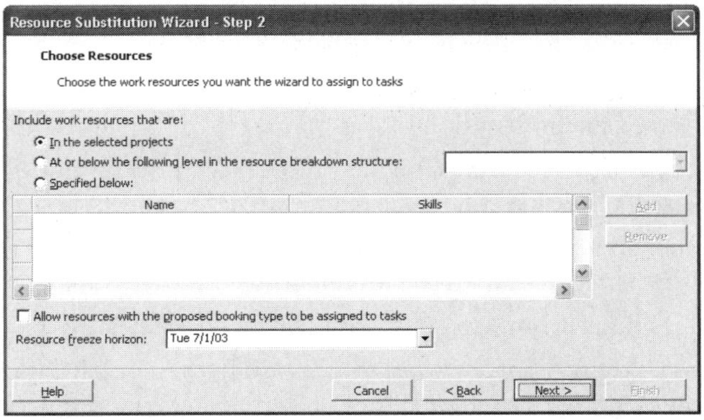

Figure 22-18. Specify the categories of resources that should be substituted in the Choose Resources page.

5 Select the option representing the categories of resources you want substituted.

If you click the In The Selected Projects option, the wizard will try to find substitutions for all resources in the projects selected in the previous Choose Projects page. This option is selected by default.

If you click the At Or Below The Following Level In The Resource Breakdown Structure option, enter the RBS level in the box. The wizard will try to find substitutions for all resources in your selected projects that are at or below your specified RBS level.

If you click the Specified Below option, the Add and Remove buttons become available. Click Add to open the Build Pool For Resource Substitution dialog box, which is similar to the Build Team dialog box and shows the resources in your selected projects. The resources you select are available to be substituted.

6 Select the Allow Resources With The Proposed Booking Type To Be Assigned To Tasks check box if you want resources defined with the proposed booking type in the enterprise resource pool to be suggested as a substitute in your selected project.

7 In the Resource Freeze Horizon box, select the date that represents the earliest start date for tasks being staffed by the Resource Substitution Wizard.

This means that any tasks starting before this date will not be considered for resource substitution.

By default, the Resource Freeze Horizon is today's date.

8 Click Next.

The Choose Related Projects page appears. This page lists any other project files that have some relationship with the selected projects, such as cross-project links or a nonenterprise resource pool.

9 Select the check box next to any related project that you want to be included in the resource substitution process and then click Next.

The Choose Scheduling Options page appears, listing all projects and related projects you have selected for substitution to this point.

10 If you want one project to have a higher precedence in the resources that are substituted, increase its Priority value to be higher than the others.

Projects with higher priority values have their resources substituted first, and therefore tend to get the better resource matches than projects with lower priority values.

Priority values range from 1 to 1000, with 500 being the default.

11 In the Options column, specify whether the resources to be used for substitution are to come from the project itself or from the entire enterprise resource pool.

This option is key to getting a resource substitution with your intended results.

12 Click Next.

The Substitute Resources page appears (see Figure 22-19).

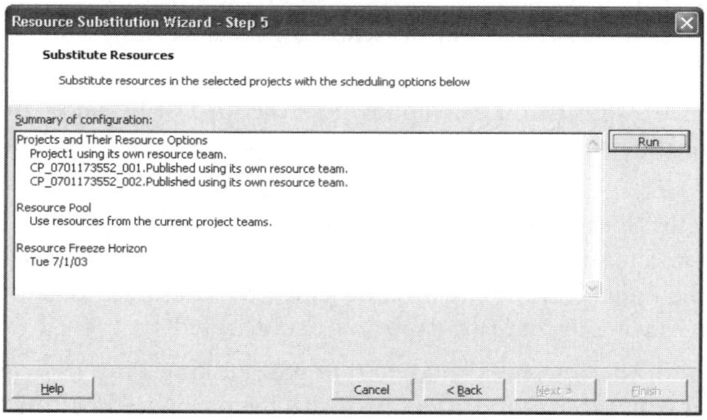

Figure 22-19. Review your resource substitution setup and then click Run.

13 Review the configuration summary, which is based on the selections you have specified so far.

If you want to change one of the specifications, click Back to find the page you need and make the necessary changes.

If everything looks right to you, click the Run button to initiate the resource substitution process. When the process has completed, the Review Results page appears (see Figure 22-20).

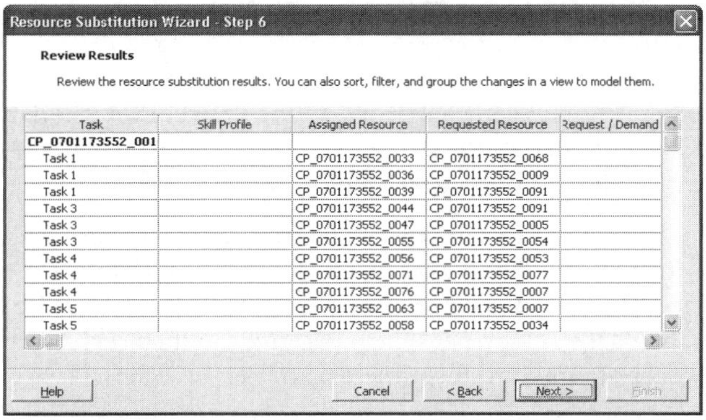

Figure 22-20. Review the resources that have been found.

14 Review the fields for all the tasks in your selected projects.

Each task in each selected project is listed, along with the task's associated skill profile, the currently assigned resource, and the potential substituting resource.

Note that no changes have actually been made to your project(s); this is just a model of potential changes.

> **Note** If you're dissatisfied with the results of the resource substitution and want to change the parameters, click Back to find the page you need and make the necessary changes. Then run the substitution process again.

15 In the Review Results page, click Next.

The Choose Update Options page appears.

16 Specify how you want to proceed with the substitution results.

If you want to change the selected projects with the substitution results, select the Update Projects With Result Of The Wizard check box. This is the default.

If you want to save the results for reference or modeling as a report, rather than changing your project just yet, select the Save Results Of The Wizard check box. Then click the Browse button to find and select the folder where you want to save the results report.

17 Click the Next button.

The Finish page appears, and the progress bar indicates that your projects are being updated or the results report is being created.

18 Read the suggestions on the Finish page and then click Finish.

19 Review the changes in your projects.

If you would rather discard the changes, close the project without saving. If you're happy with the changes, save the project to the project server as usual.

Collaborating with Your Project Team

After you set up your enterprise project team, you have powerful methods of project collaboration and communication at your fingertips. Using Project Professional and Project Web Access, you can assign tasks to resources, receive progress updates, and request narrative status reports—all electronically via publication of information to Project Server.

Among other things, this collaboration process automates the gathering and entry of actuals so you don't have to enter actuals on assignments yourself. With the help of your project server administrator, you can set up your team members' timesheets in Project Web Access to enter and submit their actuals on a periodic basis. You can then review these actuals and accept them for incorporation into the project plan.

To keep a close eye on time usage and project availability, you can also track nonproject tasks and time by assigning an administrative project to team members.

If your organization is also set up with Windows SharePoint Services, you can also control project-related documents, track project issues, and manage project risks.

Designing the Team Member Timesheet

The *Timesheet*, or Tasks View, is the central view used by project team members in Project Web Access. It contains the assignments for each individual team member, along with any additional task and assignment information you want to provide them (see Figure 22-21). The Timesheet also includes fields the team members use to enter progress information—their actuals—that they periodically submit to the project server for you to then incorporate into the project plan.

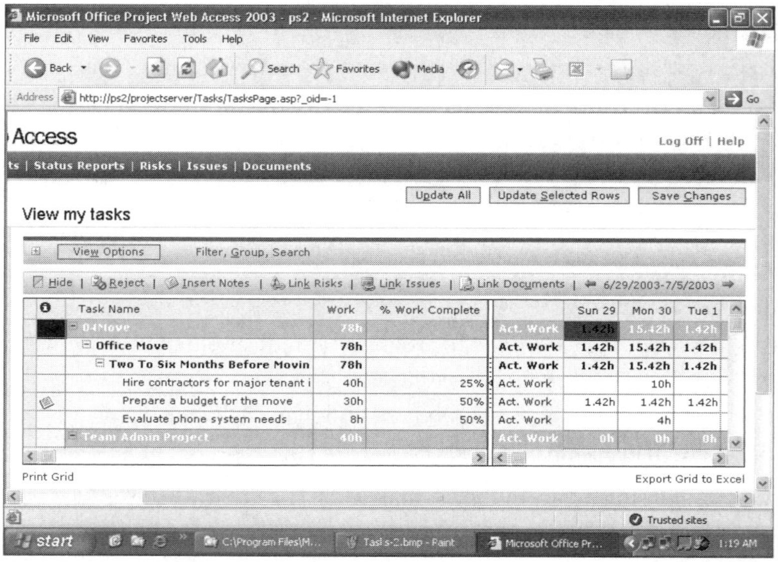

Figure 22-21. Project team members work with their individual Timesheets in Project Web Access.

You can customize the fields that team members see in their Timesheet. Depending on the setup of your enterprise, you might also be permitted to adjust the tracking method for your project.

To set up your team members' Timesheets, you use the Customize Published Fields dialog box in Project Professional as follows:

1. Make sure that Project Professional is connected to the project server, and that your project is checked out and displayed.
2. Click Tools, Customize, Published Fields.

   The Customize Published Fields dialog box appears (see Figure 22-22).

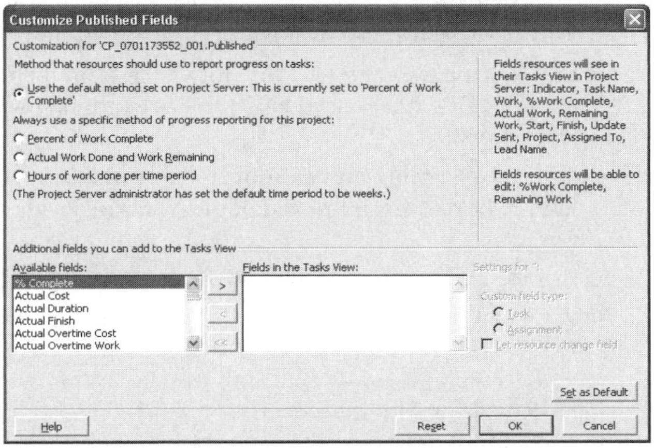

Figure 22-22. Specify the tracking method and fields for your team members' Timesheets.

3. Review the Use The Default Method Set On Project Server to see its current setting.

   This is the setting established by the project server administrator.
4. If this setting matches the method you want to use to track assignment progress, make sure this option is selected.
5. If you want to use a different tracking method, and if the project server administrator allows project managers to change the tracking method, select the one you want under Always Use A Specific Method Of Progress Reporting For This Project.

   Select the Percent Of Work Complete option if you want team members to simply report percent complete on each of their assignments; for example, 15%, 50%, or 100%. This is the least restrictive and least time-consuming tracking method. With this method, the Timesheet includes a % Work Complete field that the team member uses for his assignment updates.

   Select the Actual Work Done And Remaining Work option if you want team members to report the total hours of work completed on an assignment so far, and the number of hours remaining to complete the assignment. This tracking method provides a medium level of detail. The Timesheet includes fields for total actual work and remaining work for each assignment. Team members enter those total amounts for each progress update requested.

Select the Hours Of Work Done option if you want team members to report the number of hours of work completed per day or per week on each assignment. This is the most detailed tracking method, and is required for any organization using the Managed Timesheet Periods feature of Project Server. The Timesheet includes a field for each time period, either days or weeks, for the duration of the project. Team members enter the number of hours worked per day or per week and submit them with each progress update.

6 Review the list of fields in the right side of the dialog box.

These fields are those that are required by the selected tracking method along with any additional fields that have been set up by the project server administrator.

The fields listed in the first paragraph are those for which team members have read-only access. The fields listed in the second paragraph are those for which team members have read-write access.

7 You can add fields to this list using the Additional Fields You Can Add To The Tasks View section. Click any field you want to add in the Available Fields list and then click the > button.

The fields listed include any custom task fields defined by the project server administrator in the enterprise global template (custom fields such as Date1 or Number4, and enterprise task outline codes such as Enterprise Task Outline Code7).

> NEW FEATURE!
> **Tip** **Use custom outline code fields with value lists**
> New in Project Professional 2003, team members can work with value lists in outline codes added to their Timesheets. With the availability of value lists, it's easy for the team member to quickly enter the correct form of information while maintaining project data integrity.

The selected fields are added to the Fields In The Tasks View list. By default, these fields are read-only to the team member.

8 If you want, change a field from read-only to read-write. Select the field in the Fields In The Tasks View list. Then under Settings For, select the Let Resource Change Field check box.

9 When finished defining the progress tracking method and fields, click OK.

> **Note** Work with your project server administrator to help determine the default timesheet fields and permissions.

For more information about administrator responsibilities in customizing the Timesheet, see "Setting Up Team Member Timesheets" on page 629.

Managing the Timesheet periods

NEW FEATURE!

If you're tracking progress by hours per day or per week, the project server administrator can restrict when actuals can be entered in the team members' Timesheet.

Locking the Timesheet periods ensures that team members can report hours only for current time periods, and not for time periods in the past or future. Locking the Timesheet periods contributes to the integrity of progress information being submitted by team members. Furthermore, if your organization is exporting the Project Server timesheet data to your accounting or general ledger system, locking the Timesheet periods that have already been exported becomes essential.

Configuring Update Options

You can specify events that take place relative to your project server and your team members' Timesheets when the following take place:

- You save changes to your project plan.
- You publish new or changed tasks to the project server.
- You accept updates or status reports from team members.

Use settings on the Collaborate tab in the Options dialog box to specify how you want to handle updated task information, as follows:

1. Make sure that Project Professional is connected to the project server and that your project is checked out and displayed.
2. Click Tools, Options and then click the Collaborate tab.

   The Collaborate tab includes various options for you and your team members working with assignments via Project Server (see Figure 22-23).
3. Under On Every Save, specify what information, if any, you want published to the project server whenever you save your project. This applies to saving while you're working on the project as well as saving just before you close the file and check it back in.

   Select the New And Changed Assignments check box if you want to publish all changes that affect any assignments, which ensures that your team members always have the very latest information from your project plan.

   Select the Project Summary check box if you just want to publish the top-level information about the project, including project start and finish date, total duration, total work, and total cost.

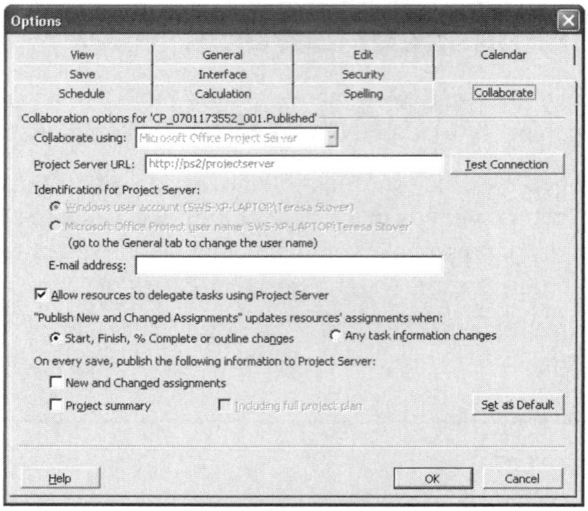

Figure 22-23. Specify your workgroup options on the Collaborate tab.

Select the Including Full Project Plan check box if you want to publish the entire project plan to the project server every time you save.

Which of these check boxes you select depends on how you, your team members, and other stakeholders use the information from your project server. If you prefer, you can keep all these check boxes clear, which is the default. You can have your project information published only when you explicitly specify, using the Publish commands on the Collaborate menu.

4 Under "Publish New And Changed Assignments" Updates Resources' Assignments When, specify the conditions that warrant your team members' assignment information being updated.

Select the Start, Finish % Complete Or Outline Changes option when you want team members' assignments to be updated when you've made these specific types of schedule changes and you've given the Collaborate, Publish, New And Changed Assignments command. This option is selected by default.

Select the Any Task Information Changes option when you want team members' assignments to be updated when you've made any changes to tasks in the project plan and you've given the Collaborate, Publish, New And Changed Assignments command.

5 Select or clear the Allow Resources To Delegate Tasks Using Project Server, depending on whether you want resources to be able to transfer assigned tasks to other project team members.

Other Project Web Access Timesheet update and status options are set through the project server administrator. Work with your administrator to set up the Timesheets the way you need for your project while adhering to organization standards.

Setting Up E-Mail Notifications

When you publish new or changed assignments to the project server, you can specify whether a notification e-mail message is sent to the team members affected by the changes. If you want to send these notifications, make sure that your team members' e-mail addresses are set up in the project plan.

If your organization has implemented the enterprise features of Project Server, your team members are part of the enterprise resource pool, and your project server administrator is responsible for making sure that the e-mail addresses for all resources are present in the enterprise resource pool.

If your organization is implementing the non-enterprise features of Project Server, that is, team collaboration only, you're responsible for setting up the e-mail addresses. If this is the case, add resource e-mail addresses by following these steps:

1. Make sure that Project Professional is connected to the project server and that your project is checked out and displayed.
2. Display the Resource Sheet.
3. Right-click the column heading where you want to add the E-Mail Address field. Click Insert Column on the shortcut menu.
4. In the Field Name box, find and click the Email Address field and then click OK.

   The Email Address field is added in a new column at your selected location in the Resource Sheet.
5. Review the contents of the Email Address field.

   If you added resources to your project using your Outlook Address Book or Active Directory, their e-mail addresses might already be present.
6. As necessary, type your resources' e-mail addresses in their Email Address fields.

You can specify other e-mail notifications to your resources (and to yourself, too) using options in Project Web Access, as follows:

1. Start up Internet Explorer.
2. In the Address box, enter the URL for your project server (or select it from your Favorites list) and then click Go.

   The Project Web Access logon page appears.

3 Enter your user name and password and then click Go.

Your Project Web Access Home page appears.

4 In the side pane of the Home page, click Alert Me About My Resources On Tasks And Status Reports.

The Alert Me page appears (see Figure 22-24).

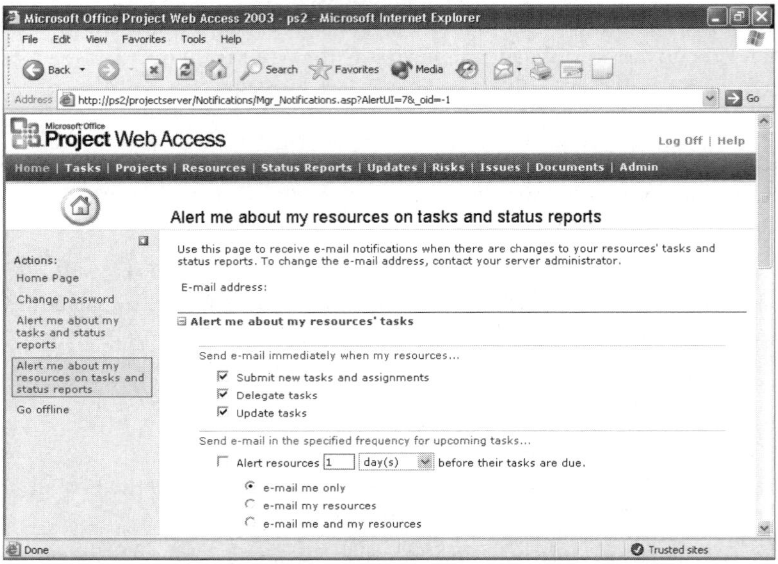

Figure 22-24. Specify any e-mail notifications you want to receive.

5 Review the options throughout this page and select the check boxes for the events for which you want to be notified via e-mail. Clear the check boxes for events for which you do not want an e-mail notification.

There are e-mail notification options for resource activities, upcoming tasks, overdue tasks, tasks requiring progress updates, and status reports.

You can specify whether you should receive the e-mail, whether your affected team members should receive the e-mail, or both (see Figure 22-25).

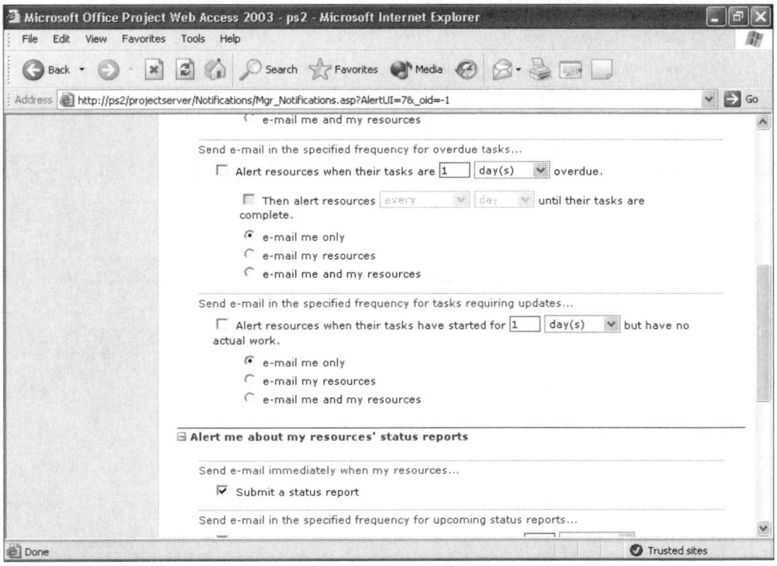

Figure 22-25. You can automate e-mail notifications regarding progress updates or overdue tasks.

6 When finished, click Save Changes at the bottom of the page.

Setting Rules for Accepting Updates

As team members work on, update, and complete their assigned tasks, they submit their task updates to the project server on a periodic basis. You can manually review each task update and accept the information into your project plan, or not. Or, you can set up rules to specify which updates are safe to automatically incorporate into your project plan. Using rules can help keep your project plan up-to-date while significantly reducing the number of updates you have to handle.

To set up rules for accepting changes to the project plan, follow these steps:

1 In Internet Explorer, log on to Project Web Access.
2 In the blue navigation bar across the top of the page, click Updates.
3 In the side pane of the Updates page, click Set Rules For Automatically Accepting Changes.

   The Set Rules page appears (see Figure 22-26).

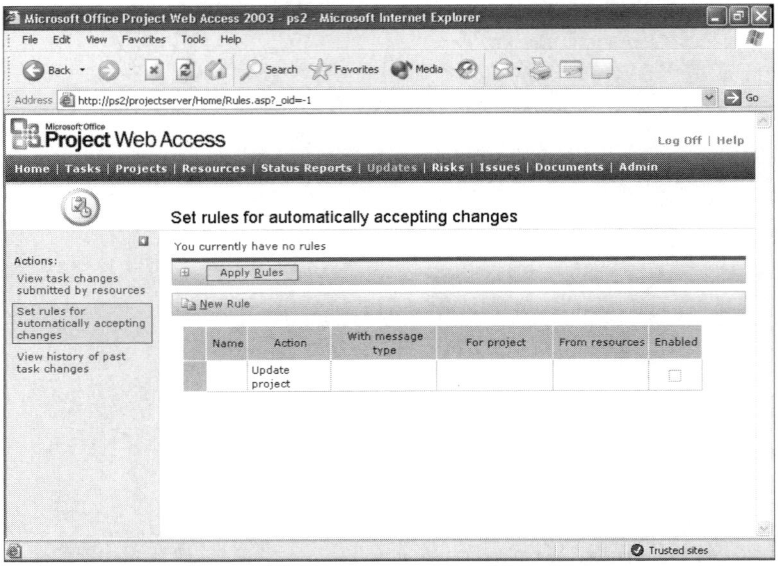

Figure 22-26. Specify the conditions under which updates can be automatically accepted.

4 Above the table, click New Rule.

The Step 1 page appears (see Figure 22-27).

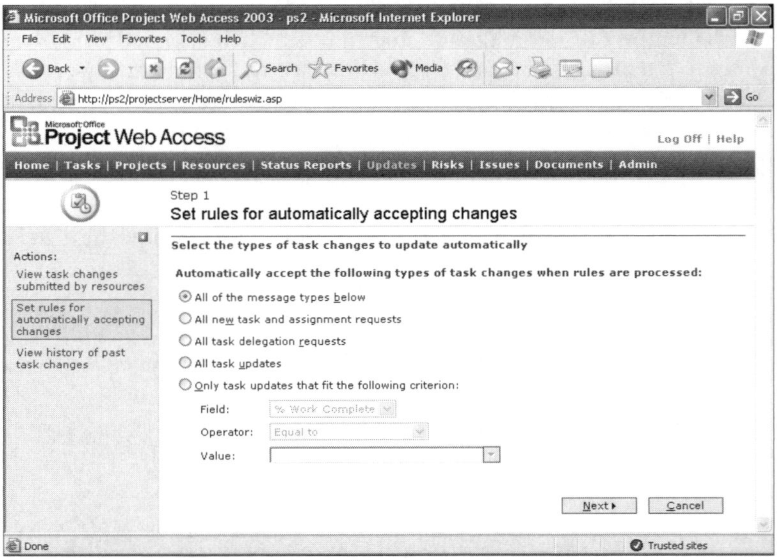

Figure 22-27. Select the types of updates to which you want your new rule to apply.

5 Specify your preferences for your new rule on this page. When finished, click Next.
6 Continue to work through the pages and steps until your new rule is created.

Exchanging Information with Team Members

Your project plan is built, resources are added, and tasks are assigned to those resources. Furthermore, your options for team collaboration using Project Web Access are set up. You're ready to flip the switch and start moving forward on your project.

When using the team collaboration features, there are three fundamental activities you do:

- Publish information, such as assignments or the entire project, to the project server for team members and other Project Web Access users.
- Request information from team members, such as progress updates and status reports.
- Review and accept information from team members, such as task updates and status reports, and incorporate that information into the project plan.

The Collaborate toolbar

As you start publishing assignments, requesting information, and accepting updates, take advantage of the Collaborate toolbar. Click View, Toolbars, Collaborate to show the Collaborate toolbar (see Figure 22-28). This toolbar makes your collaboration commands immediately accessible.

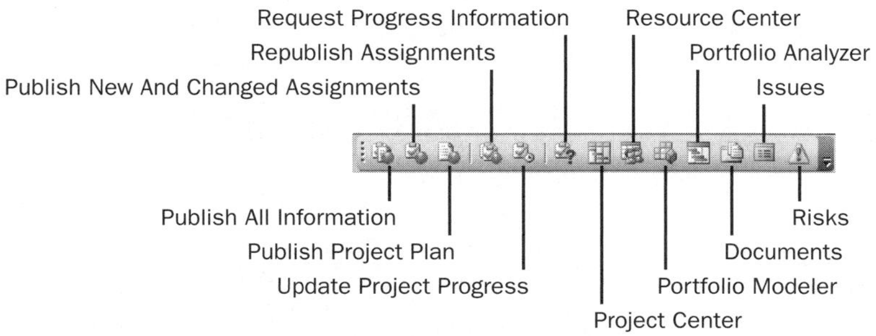

Figure 22-28. Show the Collaborate toolbar to immediately access your workgroup-related commands.

Publishing Information for Team Members

When you *publish* information from your project plan, you're essentially saving it to your project server. The information is stored there and available for viewing in Project Web Access by the users with the right permissions.

There are three categories of project information you habitually publish to the project server for use by your team members:

- New assignments
- Changed assignments
- The entire project schedule

Publishing New Assignments Publishing all the assignments from your project plan to the project server initiates the team collaboration cycle. When your team members log on to Project Web Access, they can instantly view and work with their individual assignments in the Timesheet view.

To submit the initial set of new assignments to the project server and your assigned resources, follow these steps:

1. Make sure that Project Professional is connected to the project server and that your project is checked out and displayed.

Publish New And Changed Assignments

2. Click Collaborate, Publish, New And Changed Assignments. Or, on the Collaborate toolbar, click Publish New And Changed Assignments.

   This procedure will publish all assignments in your project to the project server. Because this is the first time you're publishing assignments, every assignment is considered new.

   A message appears, stating that your project is being saved when publishing to the project server.

3. Click Yes.

   The Publish New And Changed Assignments dialog box appears (see Figure 22-29). The table shows all assignments grouped by resources. You can switch this view to a task grouping by clicking the Task option under the table.

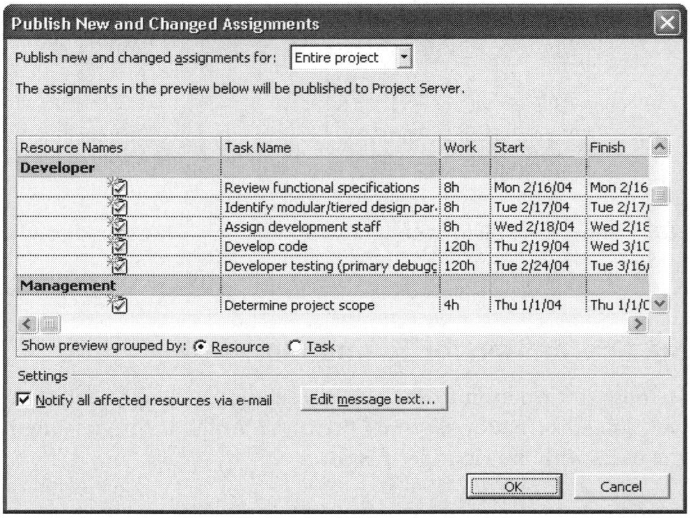

Figure 22-29. All assignments are listed in the Publish New And Changed Assignments dialog box.

4 If you want to send a notification message, make sure that the Notify All Affected Resources Via E-Mail check box is selected.

A standard message will be sent to all assigned resources. If you want to modify the standard message, click Edit Message Text. A dialog box appears in which you can modify the standard message (see Figure 22-30). When finished, click OK.

Regardless of whether team members receive an e-mail notification, they will still see their assignments the next time they log on to Project Web Access.

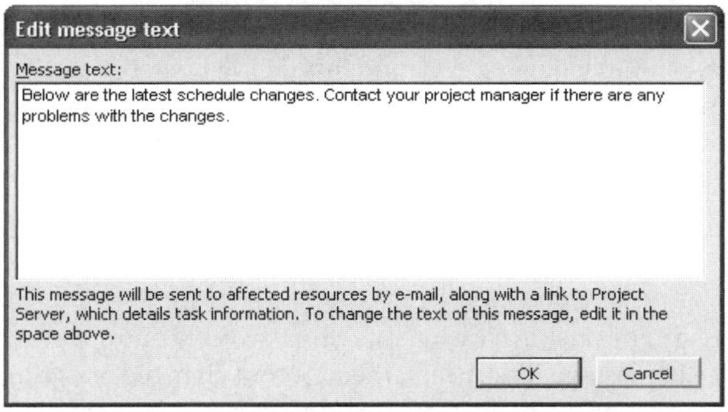

Figure 22-30. Change the standard notification e-mail message text if you want.

5 When you're ready to publish your assignments, click OK in the Publish New And Changed Assignments dialog box.

A message appears, indicating that the entire project plan with summary will be published to the project server.

6 Click OK.

Another message appears, indicating that your project is in the process of being published. When the message disappears, your project has been published and the assignments are now available to the assigned team members.

Any notes and other information associated with assignments are also published. Overall project summary information is published. The full project schedule can also be viewed by users in the Projects view.

For information about collaboration functions used by team members and resource managers, see Chapter 23.

Publishing Changed Assignments So you've published the initial assignments, and the team members are working away on them. But suppose that a new set of tasks is added or the duration on a task is doubled, and the dependencies on these tasks affect several assignments. What now?

All you have to do is publish changed assignments, which is a process similar to publishing the new assignments. The difference is that instead of publishing all assignments in the project, you're publishing only the assignments that have been added or that have changed since the last time you published assignments. To do this, follow these steps:

1. Make sure that Project Professional is connected to the project server and that your project is checked out and displayed.
2. On the Collaborate toolbar, click Publish New And Changed Assignments.

   A message appears, stating that your project is being saved when publishing to the project server.
3. Click Yes.

   The Publish New And Changed Assignments dialog box appears. The table lists only those assignments that have been added or changed since the last time you published assignments. Only these will be published with this operation.
4. Click OK.

   A message appears, indicating that the project is being published to the project server.
5. Click OK.

   Another message appears, indicating that your project is in the process of being published. When the message disappears, the new and changed assignments have been published and are now available to the assigned team members.

Publishing the Project Schedule When you publish assignments, your entire project schedule is also published to the project server. Project Web Access users can then access your schedule view. This can be helpful for team members who want to see the overall context of their tasks. Project views are also essential for other stakeholders, for example, executives, accounting, procurement, human resources, and so on.

You can publish the schedule without publishing assignments, as follows:

1. Make sure that Project Professional is connected to the project server and that your project is checked out and displayed.
2. Click Collaborate, Publish Project Plan. Or, on the Collaborate toolbar, click Publish Project Plan.

   Publish Project Plan

   A message appears, stating that your project is being saved when publishing to the project server.

3 Click Yes.

The Publish Project Plan dialog box appears (see Figure 22-31).

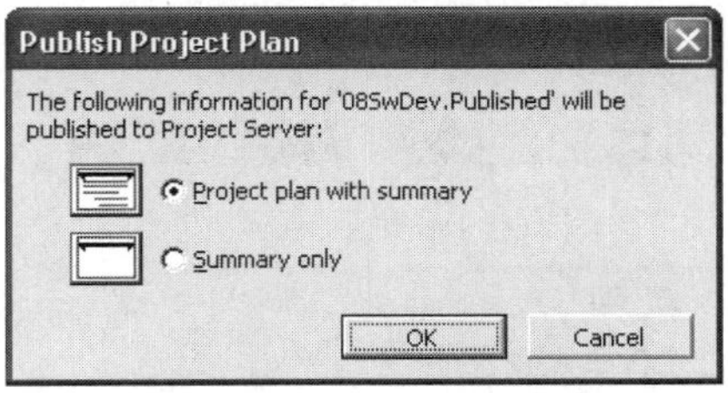

Figure 22-31. Select how much of the project plan you want to publish.

4 To publish the entire project, click OK.

If you just want to publish a project summary, click Summary Only and then click OK. Project Web Access users can see a list of all projects available for viewing in the Project Center (see Figure 22-32).

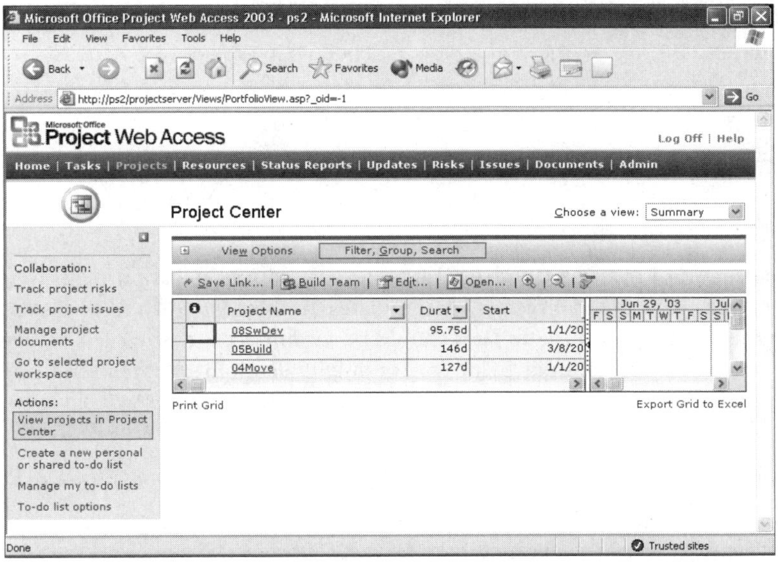

Figure 22-32. Change the standard notification e-mail message text if you want.

They can then open the project by clicking its name in the table (see Figure 22-33).

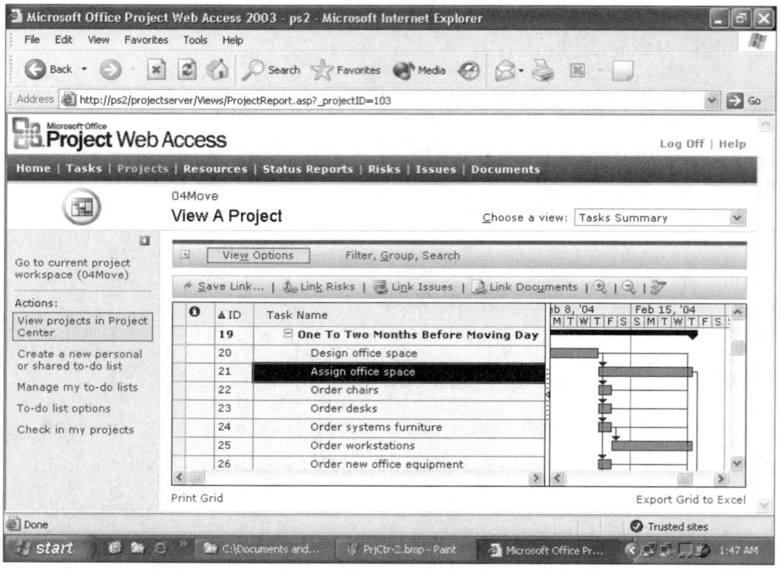

Figure 22-33. View the entire project schedule in Project Web Access.

Submitting Requests to Team Members

While your team members are working on their tasks, you periodically need progress updates of actual work on assignments. If you've also set up narrative status reports, you can request narrative status reports as well.

Requesting Progress Updates As soon as you publish assignments to your team members, they have the ability to submit updates. It's best for you and your project team to agree on the period when task updates should be submitted; for example, every Monday morning, or every other Wednesday by noon. You might also want them to send you a task update whenever there is a significant change or accomplishment, or whenever a major milestone has been completed.

However, you can explicitly request progress updates any time you want, as follows:

1. Make sure that Project Professional is connected to the project server and that your project is checked out and displayed.
2. If you need information on only certain tasks, display a task view and select those tasks.
3. Click Collaborate, Request Progress Information. Or, on the Collaborate toolbar, click Request Progress Information.

   Request Progress Information

   A message appears, stating that your project is being saved when publishing to the project server.
4. Click Yes.

   The Request Progress Information dialog box appears.

5 In the Request Progress Information For box, select Entire Project, Current View, or Selected Items.

6 In the Request Progress Information For Period From and To boxes, enter the dates for the progress updates you want.

7 Click OK.

Your progress update request is published to the project server. Your team members will see this request on their Project Web Access Home page the next time they log on.

Requesting Text-Based Status Reports You can design a status report for team members to complete and submit to you periodically. You set up the time period and the headings. At the designated time periods, your team members write their status report and submit it to the project server. When all team members' reports are in, you can compile them together for a full team status report.

You need to request the status report only when you first set it up. Team members see automated reminders in their Project Web Access Home page when a status report is coming due.

To set up a narrative status report, follow these steps:

1 In your Web browser, log on to Project Web Access and then click Status Reports in the navigation bar (see Figure 22-34).

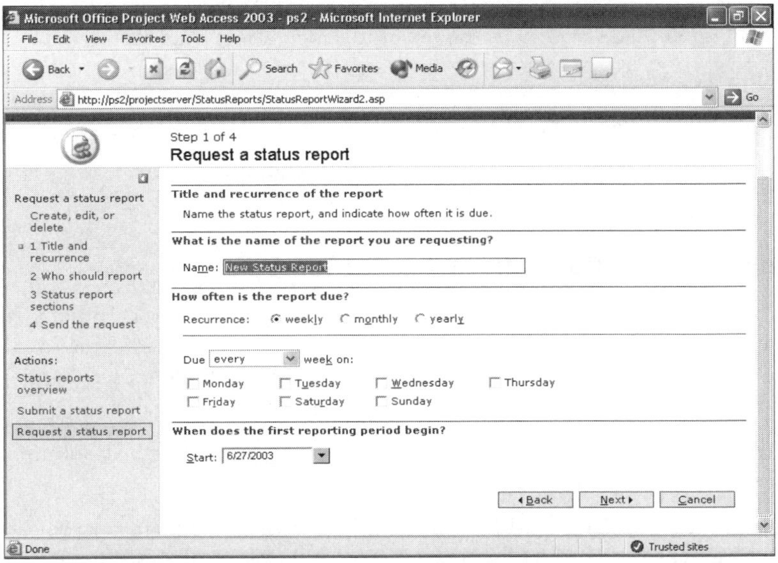

Figure 22-34. Click Request A Status Report to design a narrative periodic status report.

2 In the side pane, click Request A Status Report.

3 Complete the options on the page and then click Next.

Chapter 22

4 Work through the succeeding pages to design the status report the way you need it (see Figure 22-35).

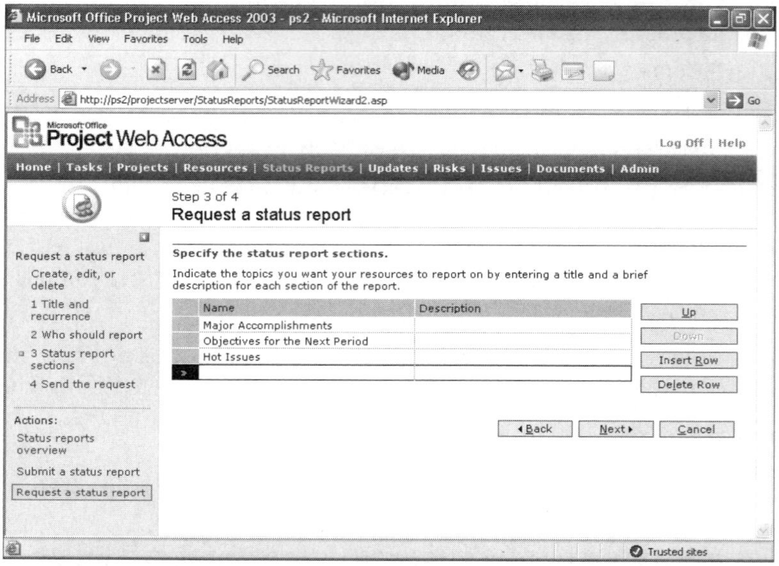

Figure 22-35. Specify the major topics for the status report.

5 Click Next after each page.

6 On the final page, click Send.

The status report request, details, and schedule are sent to your specified team members.

Accepting Updates from Team Members

Just as you publish information to the project server for team members, they publish information to communicate with you as well. You can review the information they're submitting on the Project Web Access Updates page and decide whether to accept and incorporate it into your project plan.

There are three types of information that team members typically submit to the project server for you to accept and incorporate:

Rejected assignments When you publish new assignments to the project server, the next time team members log on to Project Web Access, they see their assignments in their Timesheet view or Gantt Chart in the Tasks view. If necessary, team members can reject an assignment. You see any rejected assignments on your Updates page. Team members can also add a note, which is particularly useful for explaining why they have to reject the assignment.

New self-assigned tasks From Project Web Access, team members can create new tasks, assign themselves to them, and submit them to the project server for inclusion in the project plan, if you approve. This is particularly helpful when you are relying on your team members to fill in the details of tasks that are needed for their areas of expertise.

Assignment progress updates When you send a request for progress information, team members respond by updating their assignment-tracking information according to the tracking method set up by you and the project server administrator. They might update percent complete on their current assignments, enter total work and remaining work hours on assignments, or enter the number of hours per day or per week on each assignment. These updates are the primary reason for using Project Web Access. They keep your project tracking up-to-date, and you always know the current status of tasks without having to collect and enter the information manually.

You can review and process all these updates from team members at once, using your Project Web Access Updates page within Project Professional. To do this, follow these steps:

1. Make sure that Project Professional is connected to the project server.
2. Click Collaborate, Update Project Progress. Or, on the Collaborate toolbar, click Update Project Progress.

Update Project Progress

   The Project Web Access Updates page appears in your Project Professional workspace. All updates submitted by team members are listed in the table.
3. Review each item and then click Accept. Or, if you want to accept all updates in the table at once, click Accept All.

If you prefer, you can review and process your updates directly within Project Web Access, as follows:

1. In your Web browser, log on to Project Web Access.

   Whenever you have updates waiting for you, they're listed on the Project Web Access Home page. You can click the link to go directly to the update.
2. In the blue navigation bar, click Updates.

   The Updates page appears, listing all updates that have been submitted and are awaiting processing. If there are no updates, the page says so (see Figure 22-36).

Figure 22-36. Review any updates submitted by your team members on the Updates page.

3 Review each item and then click Accept. Or, if you want to accept all updates in the table at once, click Accept All.

Protecting Actuals

NEW FEATURE!

Through the team-collaboration features provided by Project Server, the integrity of actuals submitted by team members can be protected. This can be crucial if those actuals are directly submitted to your organization's general ledger system to produce customer invoices.

Your project server administrator first sets up the Project Web Access progress method to track hours of work per day or per week. Then the administrator sets the open reporting time period. Team members can enter actuals only during the open reporting period, not long after the period is past.

Furthermore, options can be set so that if the project manager or another user changes actual hours that have been submitted and incorporated into the project plan, those changes can be audited against what was originally submitted by the team member.

You can compare the protected actuals submitted by the team member by adding the Actual Work Protected and Actuals Overtime Work Protected fields to a task sheet. You can also return actuals edited in the project plan back to their value as submitted and stored on Project Server. Click Tools, Tracking, Sync To Protected Actuals.

For more information about setting up team member timesheets for progress tracking in Project Web Access, see "Setting Up Team Member Timesheets" on page 629.

Managing Documents, Risks, and Issues

If your installation of Project Server is integrated with Windows SharePoint Services, you have three more collaboration features available in Project Web Access, as follows:

- Document control
- Risk management
- Issues tracking

As the project manager, you have access to these features from Project Professional as well as Project Web Access. Your team members also have access to them. Documents, risks, and issues can be added, tracked, linked with tasks, assigned responsibility, and eventually closed. These all become an important aspect of managing the project as well as capturing important project archival information for use in planning future projects.

Controlling Project Documents

Through Windows SharePoint Services and Project Server, you can establish a document library associated with your project. The Project Web Access document library can be an excellent repository for project-related documents, including needs analyses, scope definition, product specifications, deliverable documents, team contact information, change control plan, status reports, and more. By creating a central location for public documents related to the project, you can enhance collaboration and the project management process, ensuring that all team members and other stakeholders have all essential information at their disposal.

Depending on permissions, you and your team members can add a document, view documents, and search for documents in the document library. When adding a new document, you enter the filename and location for the document, specify the owner and status (for example, Draft, Reviewed, Final, and so on), and enter any pertinent comments. You can also associate a document with specific tasks if you want.

After the project server administrator sets up and configures Windows SharePoint Services and the Document Library specific to your team, you can see documents directly from your Microsoft Project Web Access site.

NEW FEATURE! New in Project 2003 is version control. Document versions can now be controlled using check-in and checkout processes. If a document is checked out, only the user who has checked it out can save to it. Multiple versions of a document can be compared and archived separately. When a document is linked to a project or individual tasks, the most current version of the document is linked.

To work with the Project Web Access document management features from Project Professional, follow these steps:

1. Make sure that Project Professional is connected to the project server and that your project is checked out and displayed.

Documents

2. Click Collaborate, Documents. Or, on the Collaboration toolbar, click Documents.

   The Documents page appears (see Figure 22-37).

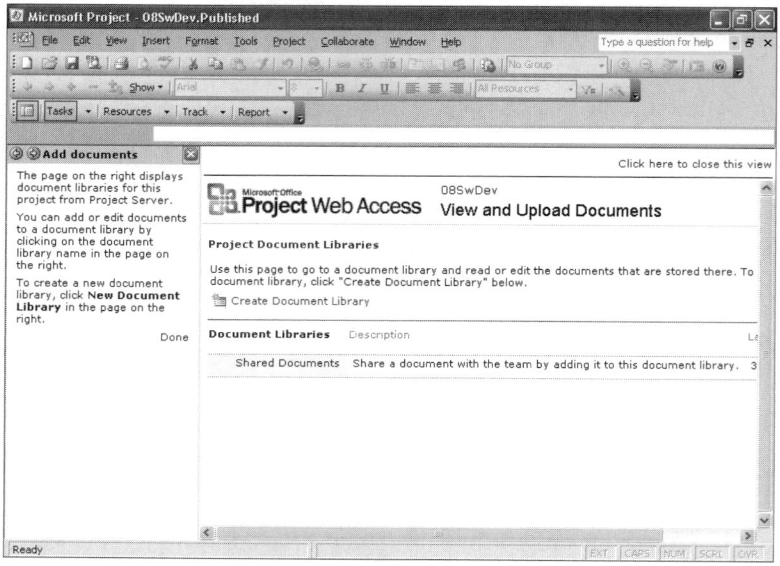

Figure 22-37. View and work with the document library from within Project Professional.

To work with the document-management features in Project Web Access, follow these steps:

1. In your Web browser, log on to Project Web Access.
2. In the blue navigation bar, click Documents.

   The View And Upload Documents In All Projects page appears (see Figure 22-38).

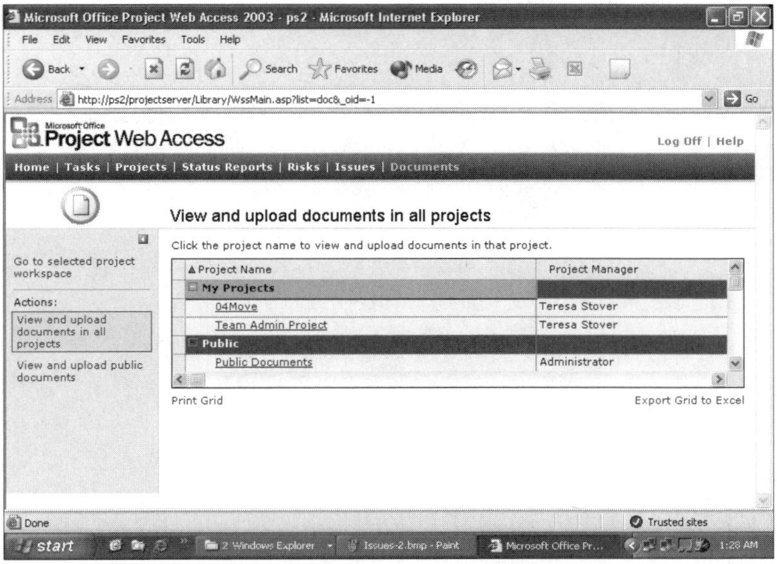

Figure 22-38. View and work with the document library from Project Web Access.

Mitigating Project Risks

NEW FEATURE!

Risks are events or conditions that can have a positive or negative impact on the outcome of a project. Because of this, project management and risk management go hand in hand. Much of what we do in project management is essentially managing risk. Straightforward risk management functionality is now provided in Project Web Access. Users can record information about risks, update this information, and track the risk. Risks can be escalated to the right person for mitigation.

Risks can also be associated with specific tasks, resources, documents, issues, and other risks. The risk-management capabilities are provided through integration with Windows SharePoint Services.

> **Note** Although the new risk management functionality allows you to attach risk assessments to tasks, it does not provide cross-project risk tracking, reporting, or sophisticated risk management, such as MonteCarlo analysis.

To work with the Project Web Access risk-management features from Project Professional, follow these steps:

1. Make sure that Project Professional is connected to the project server and that your project is checked out and displayed.

Risks

2 Click Collaborate, Risks. Or, on the Collaboration toolbar, click Risks.

The Risks page appears (see Figure 22-39).

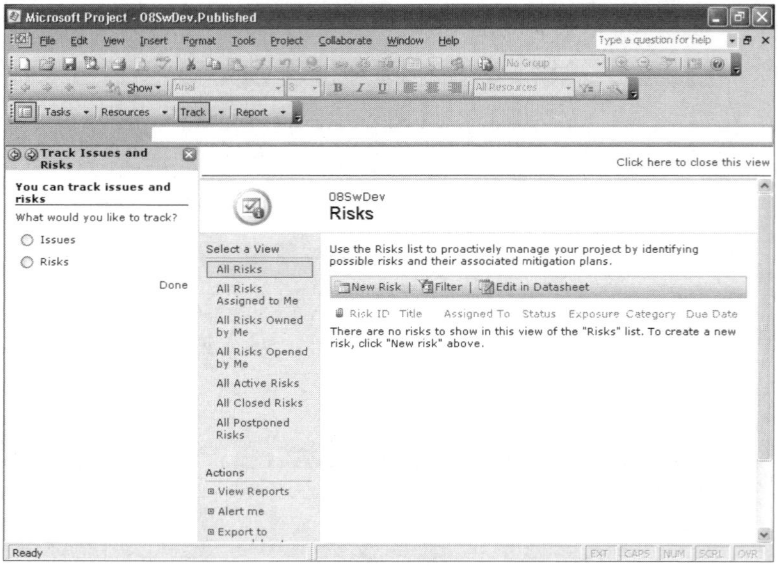

Figure 22-39. Track and manage project risks from within Project Professional.

To work with the risk-management features in Project Web Access, follow these steps:

1 In your Web browser, log on to Project Web Access.

2 In the blue navigation bar, click Risks.

The View And Submit Risks In All Projects appears.

Monitoring Project Issues

Issues tracking is integral to project management and team communication because most issues either arise from task activity or will affect task activity. By tracking issues related to a project, you can improve communication on project-related issues and ensure that problems are handled before they become crises.

With the issue tracker, team members can enter issues, assign ownership, track progress, record resolutions, and create related reports. The issues are stored on Project Server and are accessible through Project Web Access.

Depending on permissions, you and your team members can create an issue, set its priority, and assign responsibility. The issue page includes a due date, discussion of the issue, and date of resolution. Issues can be associated with affected tasks, documents in the document library, or other related issues.

To work with the Project Web Access issues-tracking features from Project Professional, follow these steps:

1. Make sure that Project Professional is connected to the project server and that your project is checked out and displayed.
2. Click Collaborate, Issues. Or, on the Collaboration toolbar, click Issues.

Issues

   The Issues page appears (see Figure 22-40).

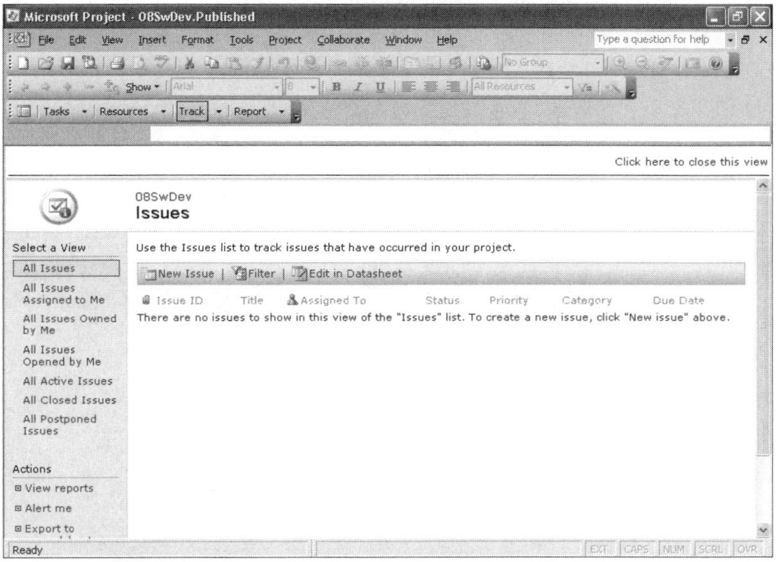

Figure 22-40. Track and manage project issues from within Project Professional.

To work with the issues-tracking features in Project Web Access, follow these steps:

1. In your Web browser, log on to Project Web Access.
2. In the blue navigation bar, click Issues.

   The View And Submit Issues In All Projects appears.

Tracking Non-Project Tasks and Time

No matter how dedicated and conscientious, no one can spend every minute of the workday or workweek devoted to project assignments. There is bound to be time taken for nonproject tasks such as handling e-mail, attending staff meetings, and participating in training workshops.

In addition, there is bound to be some nonworking time happening during the course of a project, such as sick time, vacation time, and holidays.

In past versions of Project Web Access, nonworking time was handled by the resource's working times calendar. Everyday administrative duties were not accounted for formally, although many project managers built in extra time for resources to handle them.

NEW FEATURE! Now in Project Professional, you can create an *administrative project* that can be used to account for and even track nonproject time.

> **Note** By default, the project server administrator and resource manager are granted permission to create an administrative project.

To create an administrative project, follow these steps:

1. Make sure that Project Professional is connected to the project server.
2. Click File, New.
3. Under Templates in the New Project side pane, click On My Computer.
4. In the Templates dialog box, click the Enterprise Templates tab (see Figure 22-41).

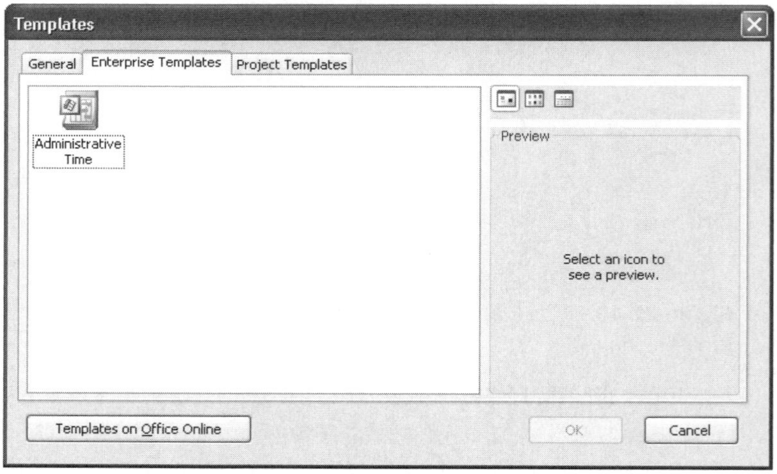

Figure 22-41. Select the Administrative Time template.

5. Click the Administrative Time template and then click OK.

   The template opens (see Figure 22-42).

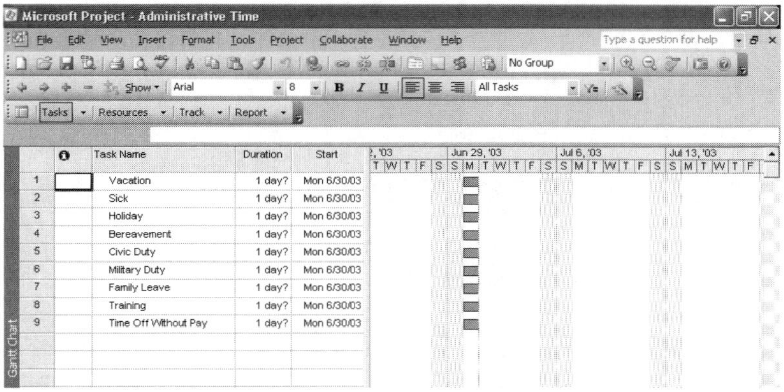

Figure 22-42. Use the Administrative Time template as a basis for your administrative project.

6 Make any modifications you want to the template. Add any additional administrative tasks and delete any you don't want to include.

You can also create your own administrative project from scratch.

7 Display the Resource Sheet and add all your enterprise resources that you want to use the administrative project.

Click Tools, Build Team From Enterprise. Apply filters or groups to narrow the list and find your resources and add them to the administrative project.

These can be enterprise resources from multiple projects. In fact, this can be everyone in a given department. Administrative projects work best with 5–100 resources.

After you have added the resources, don't assign them to any of the administrative tasks. They will later assign themselves to these tasks as needed.

8 Click File, Save.

9 In the Save To Project Server dialog box, enter the filename you want for this administrative project.

10 Select the Administrative Project check box and then click Save.

Publish All Information

11 With the administrative project still open, click Collaborate, Publish, All Information. Or, on the Collaborate toolbar, click Publish All Information.

12 In the message that appears regarding saving the project, click Yes.

13 In the Publish All Information dialog box, click OK.

The administrative project is now published and associated with the team members. Those team members can assign themselves to any of the tasks as they need them. They can enter the dates and duration for any of their self-assigned administrative tasks. This time figures into their overall project availability.

> **Note** Resources should be assigned to only one administrative project, even if they're working on different projects.

You can also work with the administrative project from within Project Web Access.

1. In your Web browser, log on to Project Web Access.
2. In the blue navigation bar, click Projects.

   The Project Center appears (see Figure 22-43).

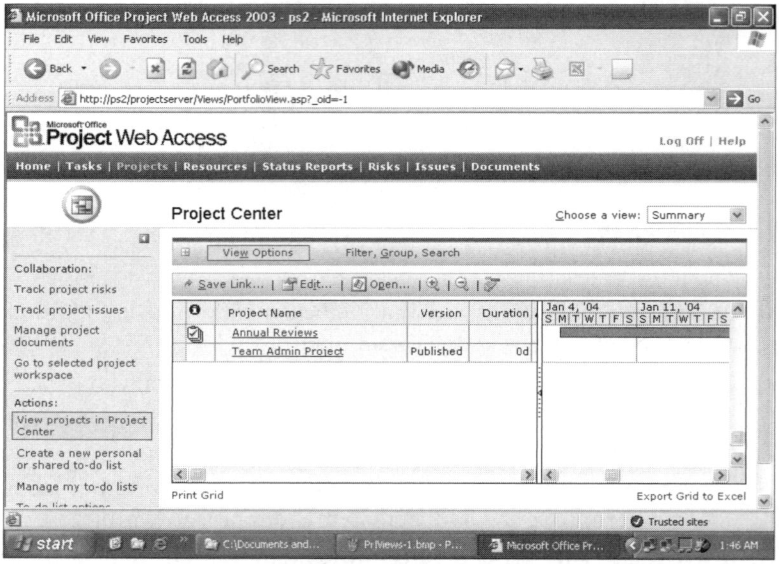

Figure 22-43. The administrative project appears with other projects in the Project Center.

3. Click the link for the administrative project to open it.

Team members needing information about assigning themselves to a project task and about working with an administrative project should refer to Chapter 23.

Tip More Project Web Access functions and views

There are many more Project Web Access functions available to you. As you've already seen, some views are accessible from within Project Professional. Many more views and functions are available in Project Web Access itself. Explore around and see what else you can do with Project Web Access to help you manage your projects and collaborate with your team more efficiently.

Chapter 23

Participating On a Team Using Project Web Access

A project plan might make an impressive report or boardroom presentation. But without resources to implement the tasks, that lovely project plan is nothing more than fiction. As a project team member, you know that it falls to you to help achieve the goals of the task. You also know that it falls to you to regularly inform the powers that be of your progress so that they know how the project is doing overall.

This is where you and Microsoft Office Project Web Access 2003 come into play. As a project team member, you use Project Web Access 2003, the Web-based companion application to Microsoft Office Project Professional 2003 used by the project manager. You use Project Web Access to maintain a detailed list of the tasks under your responsibility, to know when they're due, and to understand how they fit into the larger project picture. You can also use Project Web Access to track your progress on assignments, and submit that information to your project manager.

Project Web Access doesn't limit you to just one project, either, but as many projects as you're contributing to. And if you're working for two or three project managers at a time on these multiple projects, you can keep all this information straight and keep all project managers well informed using Project Web Access.

With project management more automated like this, you can spend more time working on your tasks and less time worrying about keeping management up to date. To this end, this chapter is designed for project team members, team leads, and resource managers, all who use Project Web Access to carry out their project-related responsibilities.

To start using the Microsoft Project workgroup and enterprise features, you use your Web browser to connect to your organization's installation of Microsoft Office Project Server 2003. You can then log on to Project Web Access.

If you're curious about the structure and flow of information among Project Web Access, Project Professional, and Project Server 2003, see Chapter 20, "Understanding the Project Workgroup and Enterprise Model."

After your project manager publishes your set of assignments to the project server, you can see and work with the list of tasks to which you're assigned in Project Web Access. You can add more tasks and assign yourself to other tasks as needed. Project Web Access becomes the central location for all your project tracking activity.

With your assignments in place, your way is set to start working on those assignments, according to the established start and finish dates. While you work, you can record how far along you are on each assignment or even how much time you're spending on each assignment. Then you have progress tracking information in place when your project managers ask for a progress update or status report.

The microcosm of your own tasks draws your focus most of the time. But sometimes it helps you to see the tasks that others on the project team are working on at the same time. You can use Project Web Access to review the full project schedule, which shows who's doing what when.

If your organization is also set up with Windows SharePoint Services, you have access to project-related documents, issues, and risks as well.

In addition to everything else you do, you might have resource management responsibilities. This might be something as simple as needing to delegate a set of tasks to peers on your project team. Or, you might be the team lead or supervisor over a larger group of project team members. You might be a resource manager responsible for building teams and managing all resources on one, two, or many projects in your organization. Resource management features in Project Web Access make sure you have the tools you need.

Project server administrators and portfolio managers should see Chapter 21, "Administering Project Server and Project Web Access for Your Enterprise." Project managers can refer to Chapter 22, "Managing Enterprise Projects and Resources." Managing stakeholders can find pertinent information in Chapter 24, "Making Executive Decisions Using Project Web Access."

Chapter 23, "Participating On a Team Using Project Web Access," and Chapter 24 are also provided as stand-alone e-chapters on the Companion CD.

Getting Started with Project Web Access

The first step, of course, is to start. You use your Web browser to connect to your organization's installation of Project Server. You then log on to the server from Project Web Access using the user identification established for you by the project server administrator.

After you're in Project Web Access, set or change your password. It's a good idea to browse around to orient yourself to the layout of Project Web Access, which will give you some idea of how you can use Project Web Access as a partner in your task-tracking activities.

Logging On

To log on to Project Web Access, follow these steps:

1. Start up Internet Explorer (version 5.01 with Service Pack 3, or later).

Internet Explorer 5.0 or later is required, while Internet Explorer 5.5 or later is recommended.

2 In the Address box, enter the URL for your organization's project server and then click Go.

Your project manager or project server administrator provides you with the URL you need. Enter the URL exactly as provided, including any case sensitivity.

The Project Web Access logon page appears (see Figure 23-1).

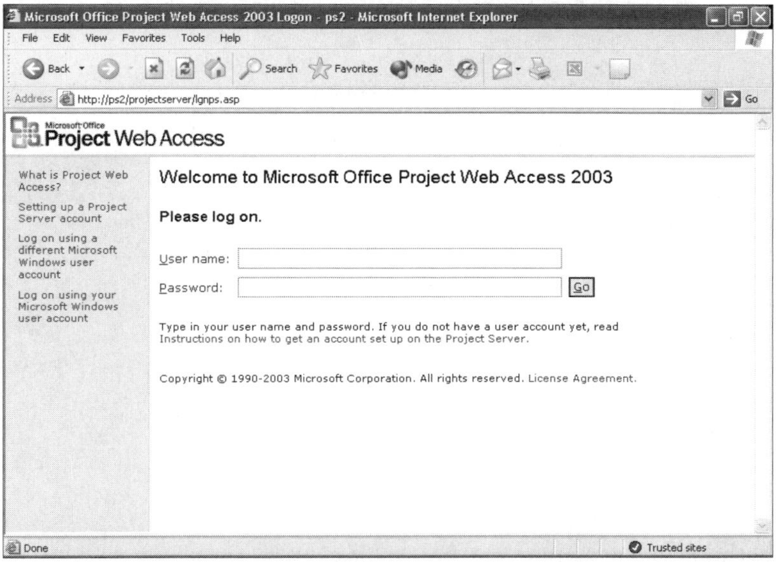

Figure 23-1. Enter your user name and password as set up by the project server administrator.

> **Tip Add Project Web Access as a favorite**
> Because Project Web Access is your "command center" for project activities, it's a great idea to add the project server URL as a favorite Web site. When the Log On page appears in Internet Explorer, click Favorites, Add To Favorites. Enter a name in the Name box and then click OK.

Chapter 23

3 Enter your user name and password and then click Go.

Your user name might be the same as your corporate Windows account that you use to access your corporate network, e-mail, and so on. If your project server administrator set you up to use your Windows account, you are logged in as soon as you enter the Web address.

Alternatively, your project server administrator might have set you up with a separate Project Server account. In this case, you'll need to enter that user name. Leave the password blank. You'll add a password as soon as you gain access.

Your Project Web Access Home page appears (see Figure 23-2).

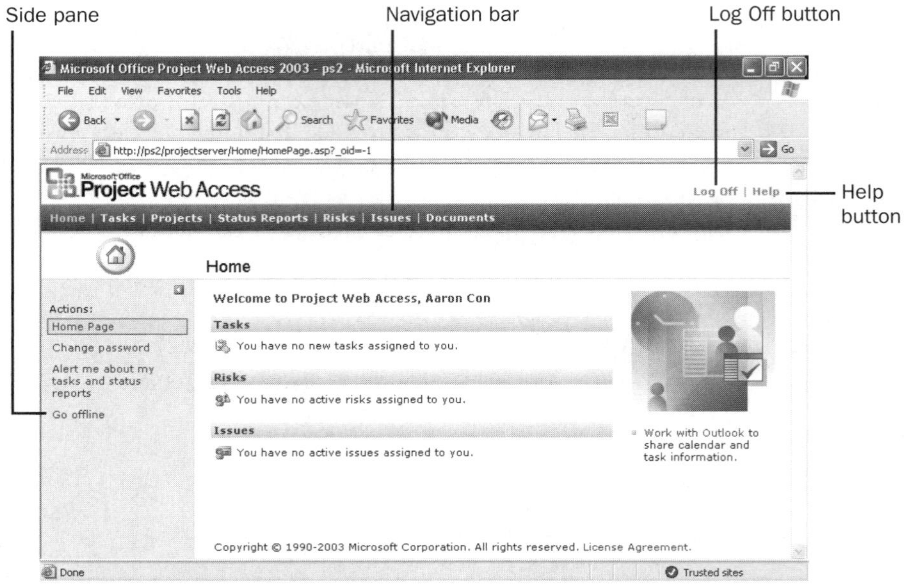

Figure 23-2. After a successful logon, the Project Web Access Home page appears.

Tip **Set your password**

If your project server administrator set you up with a separate Project Server account, add a password the first time you log on to Project Web Access.

In the side pane of the Home page, click Change Password. Follow the instructions in the page that appears.

Chapter 23

Finding Your Way Around

Working with Project Web Access is like working with most Web sites—there's content, there are links, and there are multiple pages.

In the page that's currently displayed, review what's available. Remember to use your scroll bar if it's available.

There are several major areas in Project Web Access, for example, Tasks and Status Reports. You can switch to a different area by clicking one of the buttons in the blue navigation bar toward the top of the page.

To display pages related to the area you're currently in, click one of the links in the side pane on the left side of the page.

To read Help, click the Help button in the upper-right corner. You can read Help about the page that's currently displayed or browse the Help table of contents for another topic.

To end your session with Project Web Access, click the Log Off button in the upper-right corner. Because you have special permissions set up just for you in your Project Web Access user account, and you have access to possibly sensitive or proprietary project information and documents, it's important to practice your normal standards of corporate security.

Working with Assignments

When the project plan is developed and tasks are assigned to resources, the project manager saves, or *publishes*, the project plan to the project server. Then when you log on to Project Web Access, you see the tasks that have been specifically assigned to you.

When working with your assignments, you can do the following:

- Review new assignments as they come in.
- Reject the assignment of a new task.
- Review new updates to your existing assignments.
- Add new tasks to the project plan and assign yourself to them.
- Assign yourself to existing tasks in the project plan.

Accepting New and Changed Assignments

As soon as you log on to Project Web Access, your Home page lists any new notifications that require your attention. Notifications come from new or changed assignments or progress requests published to the project server for you by the project manager. The following are examples of notifications you might see in the Project Web Access Home page:

- New tasks have been assigned to you.
- Task information on an existing assignment has changed.
- The project manager is requesting a progress update on your assignments.
- A status report is coming due.

When you want to see more details about one of the notifications, simply click the notification link. The page containing the details of the notification appears.

One of the first notifications you'll see is that new tasks have been assigned to you. Click the notification link, and the Tasks page appears (see Figure 23-3).

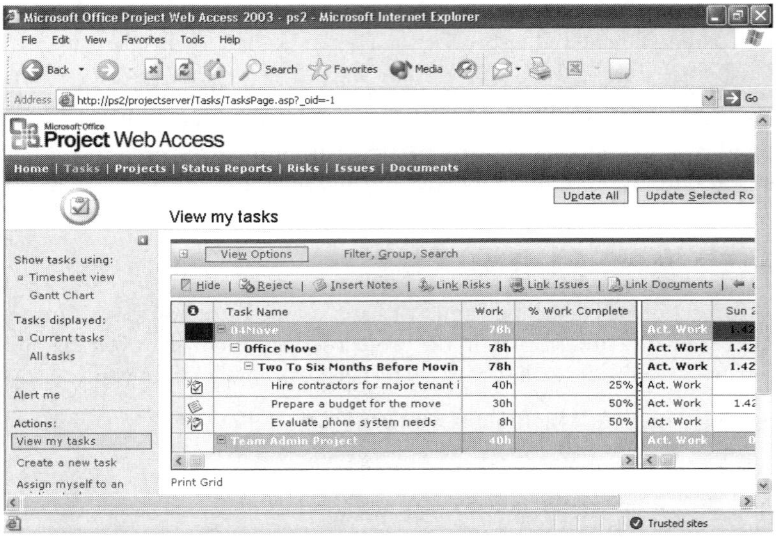

Figure 23-3. New assignments are posted on the Home page.

Look at the blue navigation bar, and you'll see that you are now in the Tasks area. Look at the side pane and the page title, and you'll see that you're in the View My Tasks page. The side pane also shows that you're viewing all tasks for the current time period in the Timesheet view.

The Timesheet view shows your list of tasks along with the fields appropriate to the progress tracking method that has been chosen for this project by the project server administrator and your project manager. Typical fields might include the amount of scheduled work for each assignment, scheduled start date, scheduled finish date, percent complete, and so on. These fields are also customizable by your project manager.

New Assignment

When you receive new task assignments, they are marked with the new assignment icon in the indicators column. You don't need to take any further action to accept your new assignments.

If it's necessary for you to reject an assignment, follow these steps:

1. In the Timesheet view or Gantt Chart, click the assignment in the table.
2. Above the table, click Insert Notes.

   Although this isn't required to reject an assignment, it's a good idea to explain to the project manager your reason for rejecting the assignment.
3. In the Assignment Notes dialog box, enter your explanation and then click OK.
4. Above the table, click Reject and then click Yes.

   The assignment is removed from your Tasks list, and an update is submitted for the project manager. The project manager will then review the rejection. If the project manager accepts the rejected assignment, your name is removed as an assigned resource on this task in the project plan.

updated task

During the course of a project, task information often changes. Maybe new tasks have been added or the duration on a task has doubled, and the dependencies on these tasks affect several other assignments. When this happens, the project manager publishes changed assignments, which then update your tasks list.

When you receive notification of an update to one of your existing assignments, that assignment is marked with a black exclamation point icon in the indicators column. Rest your mouse pointer over the indicator to get more information about the change.

note

If a note icon appears next to a task, the project manager has added a comment about the task. Double-click the icon to read the comment.

Creating New Tasks

Suppose you're performing significant work that doesn't fit the definition of any of your assigned tasks, yet is necessary to the completion of the project and should be tracked. To keep your project manager informed and to ensure that your work on the project is accounted for, you can create and submit a new task to the project manager.

To create and submit a new task, do the following:

1. In the side pane of the Tasks page, click Create A New Task.

   The Create A New Task page appears (see Figure 23-4).

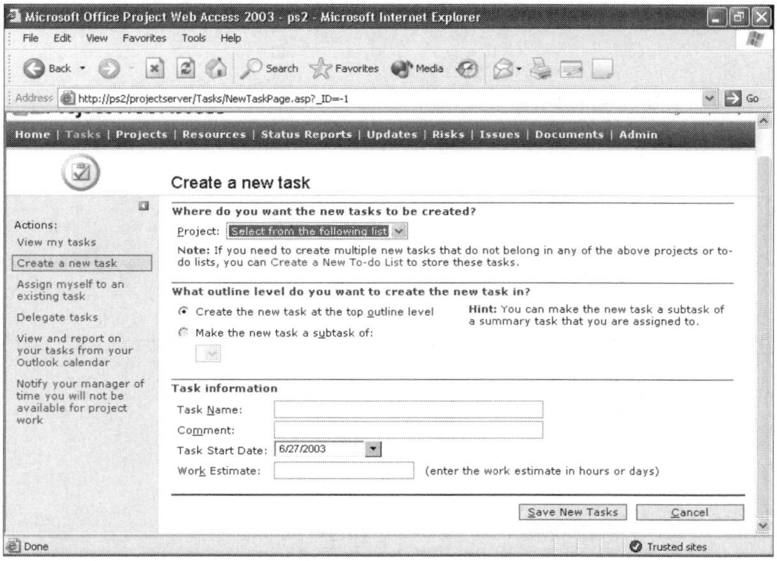

Figure 23-4. Define your new task.

2. In the Project box, select the project to which the new task belongs.

Chapter 23

3. Under What Outline Level, specify where the task should be placed in the project task structure.
4. Under Task Information, specify the new task name, any comment, the task start date, and the work estimate.
5. Click Save New Tasks at the bottom of the page.

   The new task is added to your Tasks list, and is also submitted to the project server. When the project manager for the selected project reviews your update and accepts it, the new task is added to the project plan, with you assigned to it.

> **Note** Creating and self-assigning new tasks is a permission granted according to the user profile set up by your project server administrator.

Assigning Yourself to Existing Tasks

Your project manager might have published project information without assigning tasks to resources. Team members can assign themselves to tasks in a published project. To do this, follow these steps:

1. In the side pane of the Tasks page, click Assign Myself To An Existing Task (see Figure 23-5).

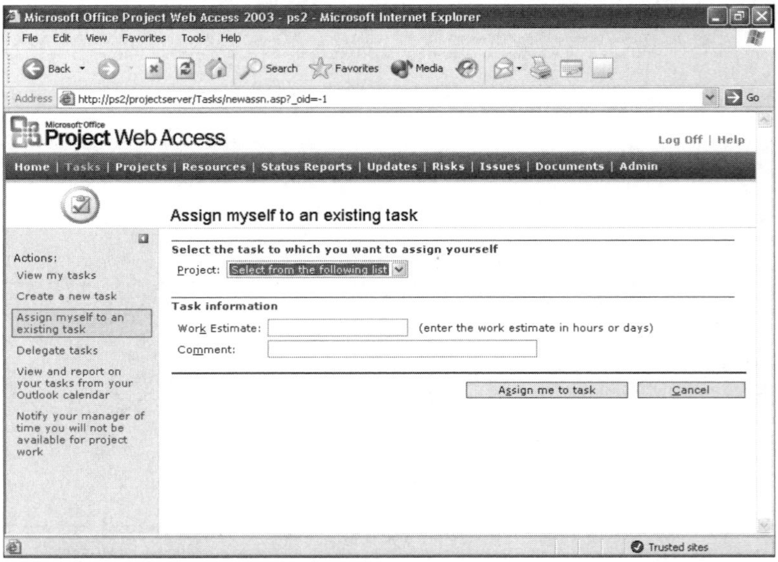

Figure 23-5. Sign up for tasks in a project.

2. In the Project box, select the project to which the task belongs.

   All tasks are grouped by all published projects in which you are listed as a resource, whether or not you're assigned to any tasks.

3 Under Task Information, specify the work estimate and any comment.

4 Click Assign Me To Task.

Your new assignment is added to your Tasks list, and is also submitted to the project server. When the project manager for the selected project reviews and accepts your update, your name is added as assigned to the task in the project plan.

Create a to-do list

In the course of carrying out your assignments, you might have a number of smaller activities that aren't big enough to be tasks. You can create a to-do list for yourself to keep track of these kinds of tasks.

On the navigation bar, click Project. In the side pane, click Create A New Personal Or Shared To-Do List. Click Next to start creating a To-Do List (see Figure 23-6).

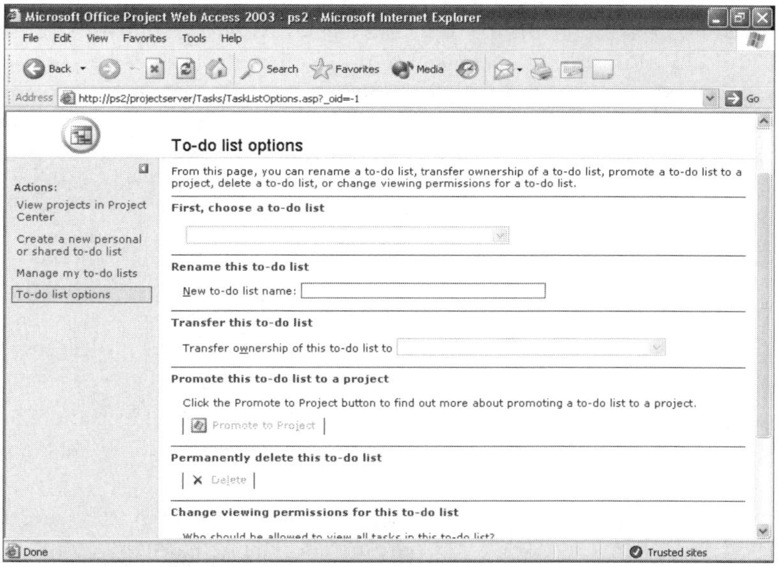

Figure 23-6. Set up a to-do list for yourself.

Your to-do lists are stored only in your own Microsoft Project Web Access site, and are not included in the overall project plan.

Tracking Progress on Your Assignments

After your assignments are established, you're ready to work on those tasks. Of course, your project manager wants to be informed periodically of what you're accomplishing, as well as any snags you might be running into. You will provide one of three categories of progress information, depending on how your project server administrator has configured the Timesheet:

- Specific work hours or percent complete on your individual assignments, also known as actual work, or *actuals*
- Text-based status reports in a format set up by your project manager
- Time spent on nonproject administrative tasks or nonworking time

Submitting Progress Information

Submitting your progress updates, or actuals, on your individual tasks is the heart of Project Web Access functionality. Submitting your assignment actuals ensures that your project manager knows how you're doing on your tasks and also knows whether you have too much on your plate and whether you need more time or assistance. In addition, the actuals you submit help everyone on the project team anticipate potential problems or bottlenecks and head them off before they become crises.

As soon as you have assignments in your Tasks list, you have the ability to submit progress updates. Typically, your project manager and project team have agreed on the period when progress updates should be submitted; for example, every Monday morning or every other Wednesday by noon. You might also submit a task update whenever there is a significant change or accomplishment. Your project manager can also explicitly request progress updates at any time. Such requests appear as a notification on your Project Web Access Home page and possibly as an e-mail notification.

To enter and submit a progress update of assignment actuals, follow these steps:

1. In the side pane of the Tasks page, click View My Tasks.
2. Enter actuals in the fields designated for this purpose by your project server administrator and project manager.

   If your project tracks percent work complete, your Timesheet or Gantt Chart includes the % Work Complete field. Use this field to report percent complete on each of your assignments at this point, for example, 15%, 50%, or 100%.

   If your project tracks total actual work and remaining work for the reporting time period, your Timesheet or Gantt Chart includes the Actual Work and Remaining Work fields. Enter the amount of time you spent on each assignment in the Actual Work field. Enter the estimated number of hours needed to complete the assignment in the Remaining Work field.

   If your project tracks hours of work done per time period, be sure that the Timesheet view is displayed (click Timesheet View in the side pane). Make sure that the proper time period is showing above the table. Click the blue left or right arrows to move back or forward in time to see the correct time period. Use the columns in the time-phased portion on the right side of the Timesheet view to enter the number of hours you spent on each assignment for each day or week (see Figure 23-7).

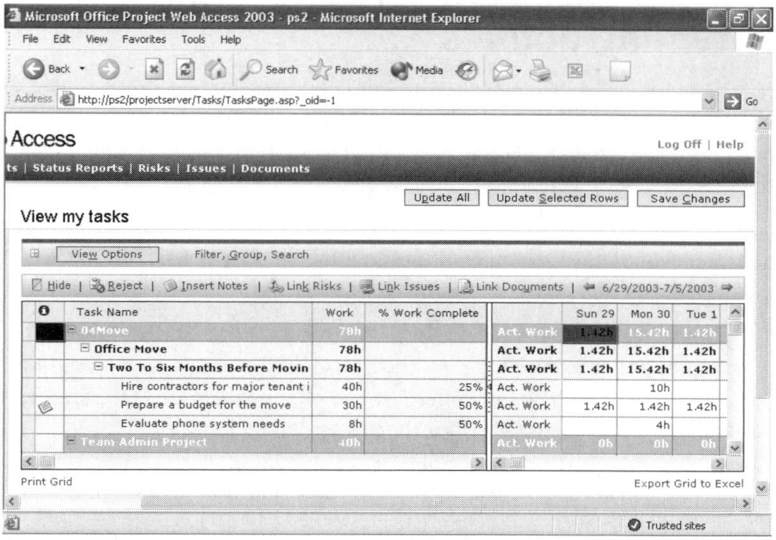

Figure 23-7. Enter actuals in your Timesheet view.

3 When ready to submit your progress updates to the project server and your project manager, click the Update All button above the table.

If you only want to update specific assignments, select the rows containing those assignments and then click Update Selected Rows. To select multiple adjacent rows, click the first row you want to select, hold down the Shift key, and then click the last row. To select multiple nonadjacent rows, click the first row you want, hold down the Ctrl key, and then click all other rows.

Note If you just want to save your changes and update the project server later, click Save Changes—which is useful if you prefer to enter updates every day, for example, or when you switch from working on one assignment to another. You can enter your actuals as you go, and when it's time to submit your update, the information is all ready to go.

Your actuals are submitted to the project server. When your project manager reviews and accepts your update, your actuals update the task progress information in the project plan.

If you're updating multiple projects or multiple project managers, you don't need to do anything special. The tasks for the current period are listed in your Tasks page, regardless of where they came from (by default, they're grouped by project). You can submit updates for tasks in multiple projects and managed by multiple managers. Your project server already knows where the information belongs and which project manager is responsible.

Protecting actuals

NEW FEATURE!

Depending on how your project server administrator has set Project Web Access options, the integrity of actuals that you and other team members submit can be protected. This is crucial if your actuals are directly submitted to your organization's general ledger system to produce customer invoices.

If your project tracks progress by hours of work per time period, your project server administrator can restrict when you can enter actuals in your Timesheet. Locking the Timesheet periods ensures that you report hours only for current time periods, not for time periods in the past or future.

Furthermore, options can be set so that if the project manager or another user changes actual hours that you have submitted, those changes can be compared against what you originally submitted to see whether there's any discrepancy.

For more information about administrator Timesheet setup, see "Setting Up Team Member Timesheets" on page 629.

Writing Text-Based Status Reports

Your project manager might design a status report for you and the other team members to complete and submit periodically. The project manager sets up the time period and the topic headings. At the designated time periods, you write your status report and save it to the project server. When all team members' reports are in, the project manager can compile them together for a full team status report.

After the project manager first sets up the status report, you'll see an automated reminder notification in your Project Web Access Home page whenever a status report is coming due.

To create and submit your text-based status report, follow these steps:

1. In the navigation bar, click Status Reports.

   The Status Reports Overview page appears (see Figure 23-8)

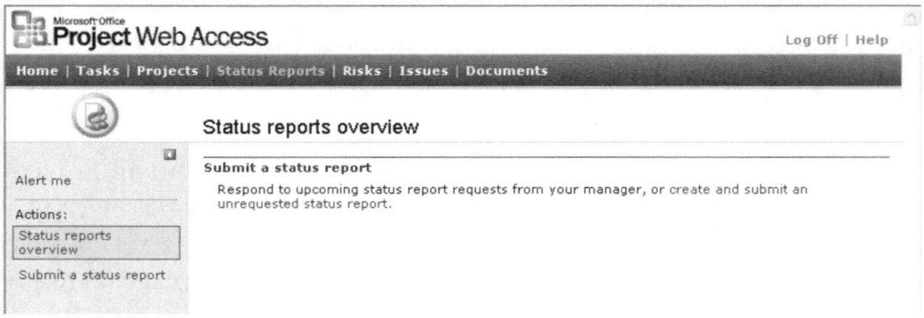

Figure 23-8. Display the Status Reports area.

2. In the side pane, click Submit A Status Report.

3. Complete any fields as needed, and write your report in the sections provided.

   The basic information and topic headings, such as Major Accomplishments, Objectives For The Next Period, and Hot Issues, were set up by the project manager.

4. If you want to add another section of information, click the Click Here To Add Section button. Type a title for the section and then type your report for that topic.

5. If you just want to save your report and update the project server later, click Save.

   This is useful if you're not quite finished with your status report or if it's not time to submit the report yet.

6. When you're ready to submit your status report to the project server and your project manager, click Send.

   Your status report is submitted to the project server. Your project manager might review your status report singly or incorporate it into a group report with the status reports from the other team members.

Tracking Nonproject Tasks and Time

Not every minute of every day can be devoted to your project assignments. You know that you have to take time taken for nonproject tasks such as attending staff meetings and participating in training workshops. And then there are also vacations, holidays, and personal time off.

NEW FEATURE! To handle nonproject tasks and nonworking time, your project server administrator or resource manager creates and publishes a special *administrative project*. This administrative project contains "tasks" such as vacations, sick days, holidays, civic duty, training, and family leave. More tasks can be added by the project server administrator as needed.

You are added as a resource on the administrative project, but you are not assigned to any of its tasks. You assign yourself to an administrative task when you need it. Not only is your time accounted for, but your nonproject time is reflected in your availability data seen throughout the team and organization.

To notify your project manager of upcoming nonproject or nonworking time, follow these steps:

1. In the navigation bar, click Tasks.

2. In the side pane, click Notify Your Manager Of Time You Will Not Be Available For Project Work.

   A timesheet listing all the available nonproject categories appears.

> **Note** If instead you see a message saying that you are not assigned to any tasks on any administrative project, it means that your project server administrator has not yet published an administrative project for you. Contact your administrator or project manager about this.

3. Select the appropriate category and then enter the number of hours in the timephased portion of the view.

4 Click Submit.

Your nonproject task information is added to your Timesheet as a task. The non-project task information is also submitted to the project server for incorporation into the project plan and the enterprise resource pool availability data.

To report the actual time you spent on the non-project task, enter and submit the information in your Timesheet like any other task.

Reviewing Task and Project Information

In your Timesheet and Gantt Chart view, you can review your assignment information in a variety of ways. You can filter and group them; you can even hide assignments temporarily.

When you need to see the big picture of the project schedule as a whole, you can review it in the Project Center.

Working with the Timesheet and Gantt Chart

You have two basic views for working with your own assignments: the Timesheet and the Gantt Chart. They both use the same table with the same set of fields on the left side of the view.

On the right side of the Timesheet, however, is the timephased portion of the view. This view shows work per days or weeks, and is instrumental when your project tracks work closely. Click the blue arrows above the timephased portion of the view to move back or forward in time.

By contrast, on the right side of the Gantt Chart are the Gantt bars showing the start, duration, and finish of each task across the timescale. The current date is shown as a dashed vertical line. Click the Zoom In or Zoom Out buttons to see more or less detail in the time span shown in the chart area.

Use whichever view you prefer for your work. To switch from one to the other, in the left pane of the Tasks area, make your selection under Show Tasks Using.

Working with the Table Fields

You can have either read-write or read-only access for the table fields in the Timesheet or Gantt Chart, which is set by the project server administrator and project manager. At the very least, you have read-write permission for the fields in which you need to enter progress tracking information, for example, % Work Complete or Remaining Work.

If you also have read-write access to other fields that are not necessarily related to progress tracking—for example, Task Name, Duration, or Deadline—it means you have been granted the ability to modify task information. When you submit task updates to the project server and your project manager, these updates can modify tasks in the project plan.

NEW FEATURE! Certain types of custom fields might have been created and added to your Tasks list by the project manager or project server administrator. Some of these custom fields can contain a value list from which you can choose an appropriate option. If such a custom field is part of your Tasks list and if you have read-write permission, click in the field. A drop-down list shows all the choices. Click a choice, and that value now appears in the field. This procedure makes it easy for you to enter the correct form of information while maintaining project data integrity.

Showing and Hiding Information in a View

Whether you're using the Timesheet or Gantt Chart, you can customize your view of assignments to show or hide the information you want, as follows:

- To show only tasks for the current time period in your Tasks list, click Current Tasks in the side pane. This is the default.
- To show all tasks to which you are assigned, click All Tasks in the side pane.
- To hide a selected task, select the task in the table and then click the Hide button above the table, which is useful for moving completed tasks out of the way. When the project manager updates the task, it appears in your list again.
- To specify whether you want to show or hide different types of tasks such as To-Do List tasks or Outlook tasks, or certain types of information with your tasks such as time or scheduled work, click View Options above the table. The View Options section expands to show your choices. Select or clear the check boxes for the items you want to show or hide (see Figure 23-9).

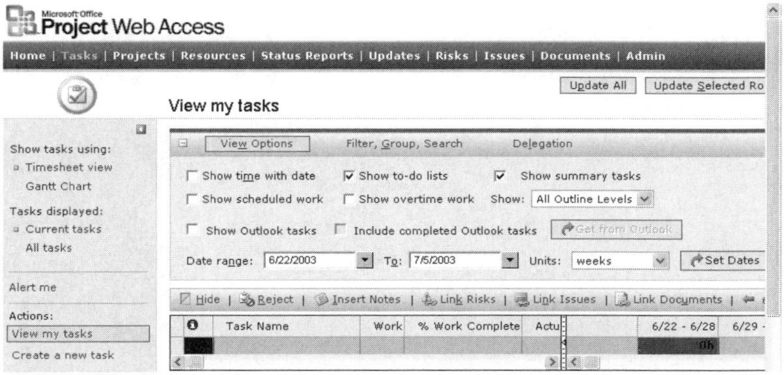

Figure 23-9. Select the items you want to show and clear the items you want to hide.

> **Tip** **Search for task information**
> You can search for information in your Tasks list. In the Timesheet or Gantt Chart, click Filter, Group Search. In the expanded section that appears, enter the series of characters you're searching for in the Search For box. If you want to specify the search in a particular field, click the arrow in the In box and click the field. Click Find Next.

Rearranging Your Assignments

In either the Timesheet or Gantt Chart, you can sort, group, or filter your assignments by criteria you choose.

To sort assignments by a field in the Tasks table—for example, by Task Name or Finish Date—follow these steps:

1. In the Timesheet or Gantt Chart, click the heading of the field column you want to sort by.

   The field is sorted in either ascending or descending order.
2. To sort in the other direction, click the column heading a second time.

To group assignments by a particular field, follow these steps:

1. Display the Timesheet or Gantt Chart.
2. Above the table, click Filter, Group, Search.
3. In the expanded section that appears, click the arrow in the Group By box to see your grouping choices in the dropdown (see Figure 23-10).

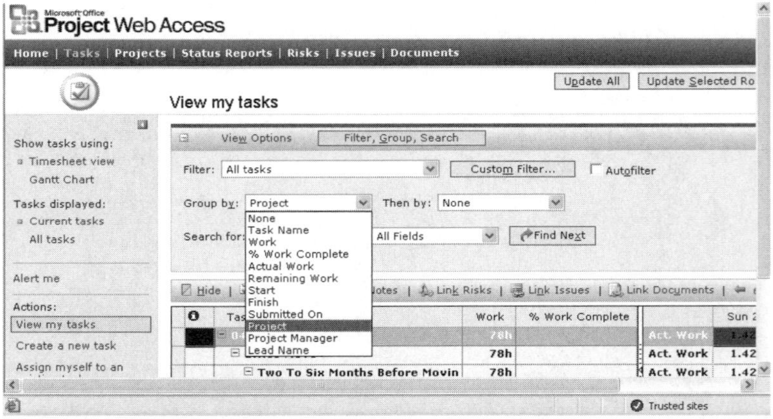

Figure 23-10. Click the field by which you want to group your assignments.

4. Click the field you want to group by.

   The task list changes to reflect your grouping.
5. If you want a subgroup within the group, click the second field in the Then By box.
6. When you want to return to the original nongrouped order, click None in the Group By box.

To filter assignments by a built-in filter, follow these steps:

1. Display the Timesheet or Gantt Chart.
2. Above the table, click Filter, Group, Search.

3 In the expanded section that appears, click the arrow in the Filter box to see your filter choices.

4 Click the filter you want to use; for example, Overdue Tasks or New Tasks Added By Me.

   The task list changes immediately to show only those tasks that meet your filter criteria.

5 To see all tasks again, click All Tasks in the Filter box.

To create a custom filter, follow these steps:

1 Display the Timesheet or Gantt Chart.

2 Above the table, click Filter, Group, Search.

3 In the expanded section that appears, click Custom Filter.

4 In the More Filters dialog box, enter the field you want to filter by in the Field Name box (see Figure 23-11).

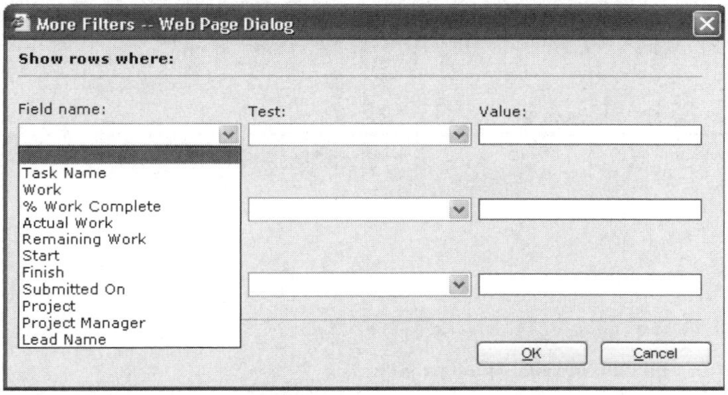

Figure 23-11. Click the field by which you want to filter your assignments.

5 In the Test field, enter the test criteria; for example, Equals or Contains.

6 In the Value field, enter the value for the field and then click OK.

   The task list changes immediately to show only those tasks that meet your filter criteria.

7 To see all tasks again, click All Tasks in the Filter box.

You can also select the AutoFilter check box to add the AutoFilter arrows to each column in the Tasks table.

To collapse the Filter, Group, Search section, click the – (minus) button in the upper-left corner of the section.

Printing or Exporting a Table

NEW FEATURE!

In Project Web Access 2003, you can now print a table on the following pages:

- Tasks
- Projects

- Resources
- Updates
- Risks
- Issues
- Documents

You can also use this function to export the contents of the table to a Microsoft Office Excel 2003 workbook. To print or export a Project Web Access table, follow these steps:

1. Display the view containing the table you want to print.
2. Below the table, click Print Grid on the left or Export Grid To Excel on the right.

   The grid setup page appears (see Figure 23-12).

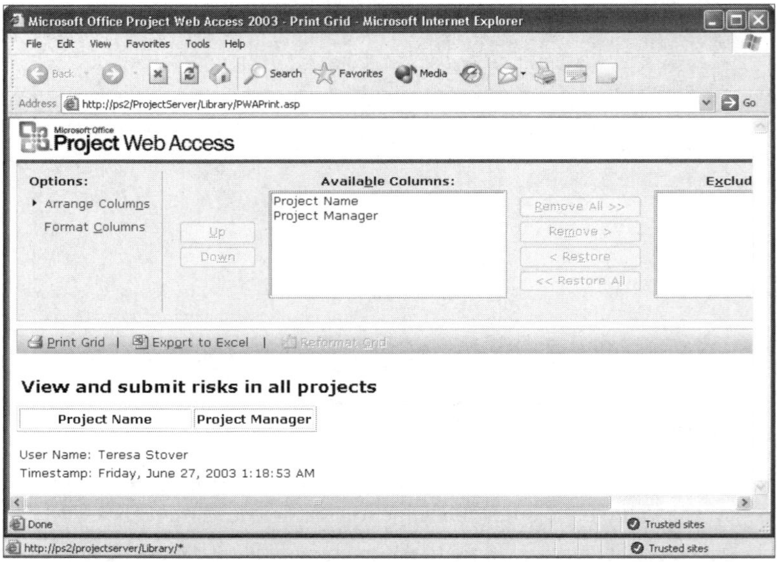

Figure 23-12. Set up the columns you want printed or exported.

3. Select field names in the Available Columns box and use the Up and Down buttons to rearrange the order of the columns as it will be printed or exported.
4. If you want to exclude any fields from the print or export operation, click its name in the Available Columns box and then click the Remove button.

   This removes the column only for the print or export operation. The field is still present in the view itself.

   A preview of the printed report or exported workbook appears in the lower half of the view.
5. Click Print Grid to send the report to the printer. Click Export To Excel to send the report to an Excel workbook.

Glimpsing the Big Project Picture

By default, you can review a list of any published projects in which you're a resource. To do this, follow these steps:

1. In the Project Web Access navigation bar, click Projects.

   The Project Center appears. If you are working with more than one project, the projects are listed in a summary project Gantt Chart (see Figure 23-13).

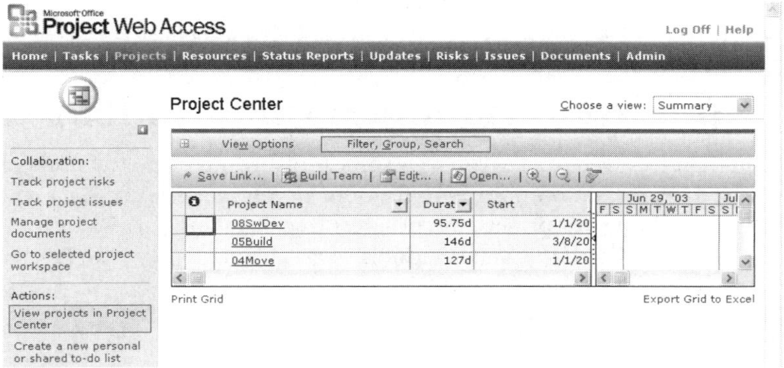

Figure 23-13. Go to the Project Center to review your current projects.

2. Click the link for the project whose tasks you want to review.

   The project view appears (see Figure 23-14).

   If you are working with just a single project, the tasks in the project appear as soon as you go to the Project Center.

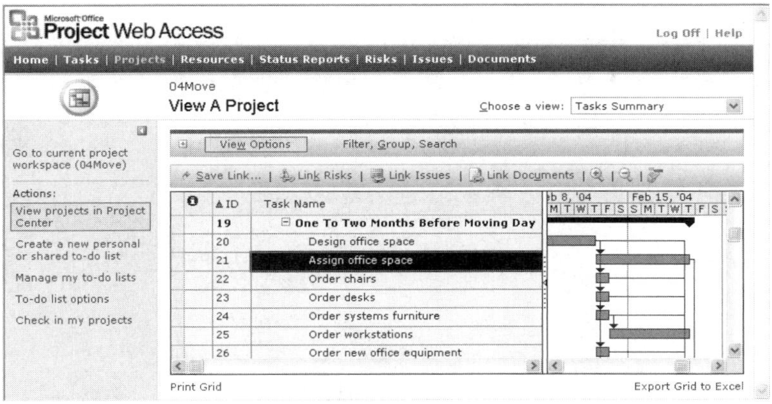

Figure 23-14. View the entire project schedule in Project Web Access.

> **Tip** **Set options and rearrange projects or tasks**
> Whether you're reviewing a project summary or all the tasks within a project, you can set view options, sort, filter, group, and search, just as you can with your assignments. Click View Options or Filter, Group, Search above the table to see your options.

Depending on your user permissions and how your project server administrator has set up views, you might be able to review the project by different sets of information. In the upper-right corner of the Project Center or View A Project page, click the Choose A View box and review your choices.

Setting Up E-Mail Reminders and Calendars

Through Project Web Access, you have some tools at your disposal for making your life a little easier. You can set up automated notifications so you can receive e-mail reminding you about various aspects of your project and progress tracking. You can also integrate your project tasks into your Microsoft Office Outlook 2003 calendar.

Configuring E-Mail Notifications

To configure automated e-mail reminders to yourself, follow these steps:

1. In the Project Web Access navigation bar, click Home.
2. In the side pane of your Home page, click Alert Me About My Tasks And Status Reports.

   The Alert Me page appears (see Figure 23-15).

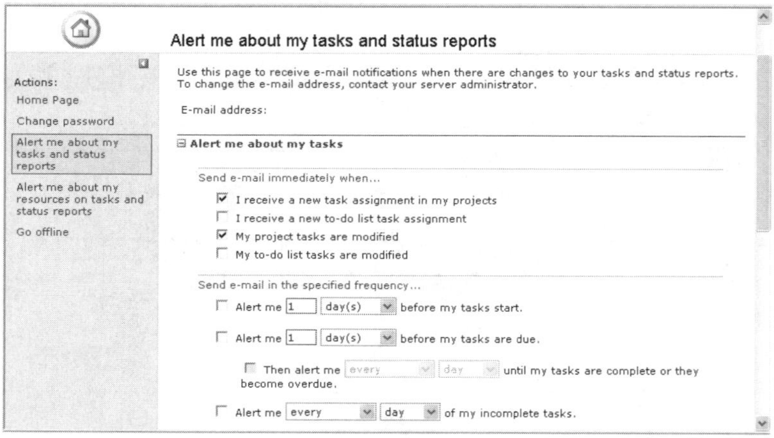

Figure 23-15. Specify any e-mail notifications you want to receive.

3. Review the options throughout this page, and select the check boxes for the events for which you want to be notified via e-mail. Clear the check boxes for events for which you do not want an e-mail notification.

   You can set up e-mail notification options for upcoming tasks, overdue tasks, and for status reports.

4. When finished, click Save Changes at the bottom of the page.

Working with Project Tasks in Your Outlook Calendar

NEW FEATURE! If you use Microsoft Outlook, you can keep track of your assigned tasks in your *Outlook Calendar*, along with your other appointments. You can update progress on your project assignments in the Calendar and report the status back to Project Server directly from Outlook.

Project tasks can be displayed as free or busy time, just like any other Calendar entries.

Note Outlook integration with Project Web Access allows integration with the Outlook Calendar, but not with Outlook Tasks.

If you choose to integrate your project assignments with your Outlook Calendar like this, your assignments are still published from Project Professional to the project server. At that point, your assignments appear in your Outlook Calendar as well as in your Project Web Access Tasks list. You still use Project Web Access for the custom fields, project views, status reports, and other project-related features. However, you now have a choice to work in Project Web Access or Outlook to review, track, and update your project assignments.

From the Outlook Calendar, you can update your assignments and send actual progress information back to the project manager via the project server. As usual, the project manager reviews and approves your updates and incorporates them into the project plan.

Setting Up Outlook Calendar Integration

To set up Project Web Access integration with Outlook, follow these steps:

1. In the Project Web Access navigation bar, click Tasks.
2. In the side pane of the Tasks page, click View And Report On Your Tasks From Your Outlook Calendar.

   The Work With Outlook page appears (see Figure 23-16).

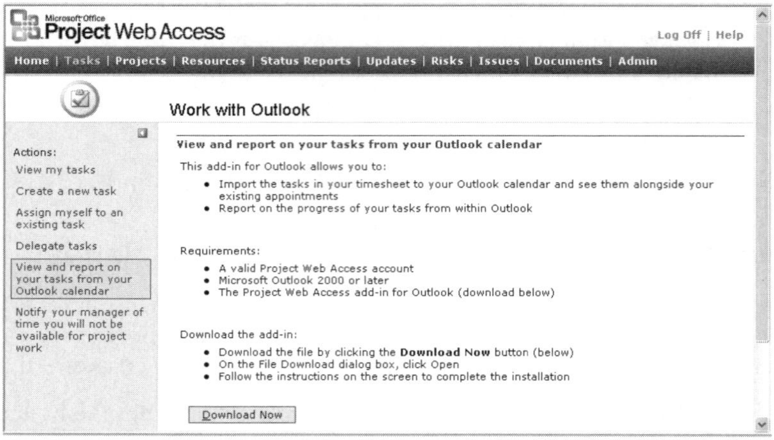

Figure 23-16. Go to the Work With Outlook page to download the Outlook Integration add-in.

3. Review the information about the Outlook Integration add-in.
4. Click Download Now.

   The COM add-in is installed.

To establish the connection between Outlook and Project Web Access, follow these steps:

1. In Outlook, click Tools, Options.
2. In the Options dialog box, click the new Microsoft Project Web Access tab.
3. Click the Enter Login Information button.
4. In the Microsoft Project Server URL box, enter the address to your project server, for example, ***http://servername/projectserver***.

   If you click the Test Connection button, Outlook tests the URL you entered and makes sure that it's a valid project server.
5. Under When Connecting, specify whether you should be validated with your Windows user account or whether you're using a separate Project Server account name.

Importing Project Assignments into the Outlook Calendar

To import assignments from Project Web Access into your Outlook Calendar, follow these steps:

1. In Outlook, click Tools, Options and then click the Microsoft Project Web Access tab.
2. Under Date Range, specify the time period from which you want assignments to be imported.

   If you want to import assignments from the standard reporting time period set up in Project Web Access, select the Microsoft Project Server Date Range option.

If you want to import assignments from a different time period (for example, the next 2 weeks), select the Next option and then select the date range.

3. In the Show Availability For Project Assignment Appointment, specify your availability for other appointments during the time of your assignments.

   Just as with other Outlook appointments, you can show your availability as free, busy, tentative, or out of the office. This setting becomes the default for all project assignments in the Outlook Calendar. You can still change the availability for individual assignments as needed.

4. Under Import From Microsoft Project Web Access To Your Outlook Calendar, specify whether you want assignments to be imported manually or automatically.

   Select the Manually option if you want to import assignments yourself.

   Select the Every option if you want to import assignments automatically on a time schedule that you set in the associated boxes.

To import Project Web Access assignments manually, follow these steps:

1. Open the Outlook Calendar view.
2. Show the Project Web Access toolbar by clicking View, Toolbars, Project Web Access.

3. On the Project Web Access toolbar, click Import New Assignments.

   The Import Assignments From Project Web Access dialog box appears, listing project assignments within the date range set in the Options dialog box.

   If you never need to see this dialog box, select the Don't Show The Dialog In The Future, Just Import check box.

4. Click OK.

   The listed assignments are imported into your Outlook Calendar.

Updating Assignments in the Outlook Calendar

To set up how you want to update assignment progress information from the Outlook Calendar to Project Web Access and Project Server, follow these steps:

1. In Outlook, click Tools, Options and then click the Microsoft Project Web Access tab.
2. Under Assignment Update, specify whether you want assignment updates to be sent manually or automatically.

   Select the Manually option if you want to send assignment updates only upon your explicit command.

   Select the Every option if you want to update assignment progress automatically at regular time periods that you set in the associated boxes.

To record progress on a project assignment from Outlook, follow these steps:

1. Open the Outlook Calendar view.
2. Double-click the assignment for which you want to record progress.

   The appointment form appears, showing assignment details. In addition to the normal Appointment and Scheduling tabs, the Project Web Access tab is added.
3. Click the Project Web Access tab.

   This tab shows your timesheet as it looks in Project Web Access, so you can update progress information.
4. Depending on the tracking method configured for your project, enter the hours worked per time period, percent complete, or actual work and remaining work.
5. To send the updated information to Project Server, click the Update Project Manager button.

   To save the changes for an update at a later time, click the Save Changes button. Click Save Changes if you have other assignments to update and you want to send all updates at once, or if you chose the automated update option and Outlook will be sending all updates at that scheduled time.

To update assignment progress to Project Server manually, follow these steps:

1. Open the Outlook Calendar view.
2. Make sure that the Project Web Access toolbar is displayed.

   If it is not, click View, Toolbars, Project Web Access.

3. On the Project Web Access toolbar, click Update Project Web Access.

   The dialog box lists all project assignments. In the Update column, select the check boxes of the assignments you want to update.

Managing Risks, Issues, and Documents

If your installation of Project Server is integrated with Windows SharePoint Services, you have three more collaboration features available in Project Web Access:

- Risk management, in the Risks area
- Issues tracking, in the Issues area
- Document control, in the Documents area

Risks, issues, and documents can be added, tracked, linked with tasks, assigned responsibility, and eventually closed. They all become an important aspect of managing the project as well as capturing important project archival information for use in planning future projects.

> **Note** By default, team members are set up with the permission to view risks, issues, and documents. Depending on how the administrator has set up Project Server and Windows SharePoint Services, team members might also have the permission to add and edit risks, issues, and documents.

Mitigating Project Risks

NEW FEATURE!

Because *risks* are events or conditions that can have a positive or negative impact on the outcome of a project, project management and risk management go hand in hand. Users can record information about risks, update this information, and track the risk. Risks can be escalated to the right person for mitigation.

Risks can also be associated with specific tasks, resources, documents, issues, and other risks.

To work with the risk management features, follow these steps:

1. In the Project Web Access navigation bar, click Risks.

   The View And Submit Risks In All Projects appears (see Figure 23-17).

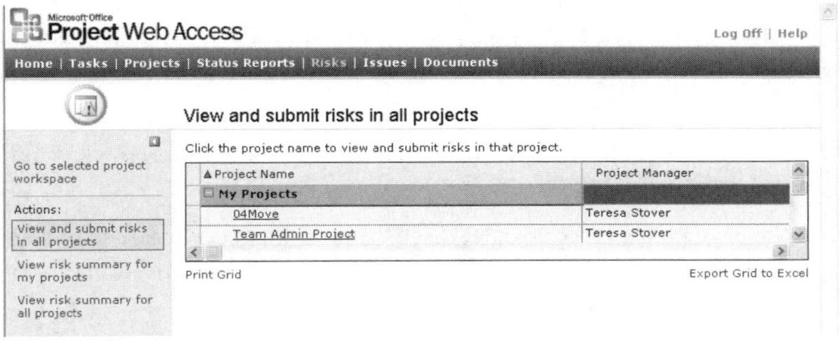

Figure 23-17. Click any of the projects to view or submit risks associated with that project.

2. Click the project to review risks or enter a new risk.

   If no risks are entered yet, the Risks: New Item page appears (see Figure 23-18).

Chapter 23

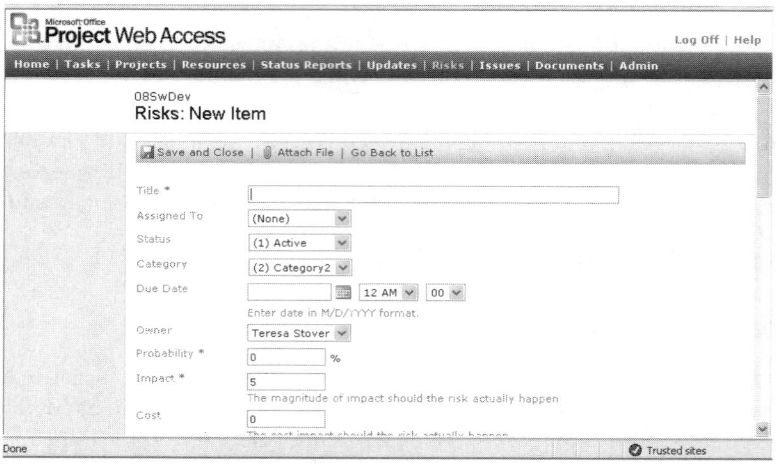

Figure 23-18. Use the Risks: New Item page to enter a new risk associated with the selected project.

3 Complete the page with the risk information. When finished, click Save And Close.

Monitoring Project Issues

Issues tracking is integral to project management and team communication because most issues either arise from task activity or will affect task activity. By tracking issues related to a project, communication is improved on project-related issues, ensuring that problems are handled before they become crises.

With the issues tracker, you can enter issues, assign ownership, track progress, record resolutions, and create related reports.

The issue page includes a due date, discussion of the issue, and date of resolution. Issues can be associated with affected tasks, documents in the document library, or other related issues.

To work with the issues tracking feature, follow these steps:

1 In the Project Web Access navigation bar, click Issues.

The View And Submit Issues In All Projects appears (see Figure 23-19).

2 Click the project to review issues or enter a new issue.

If no issues are entered yet for the selected project, the Issues: New Item page appears.

3 Complete the page with the issue information. When finished, click Save And Close.

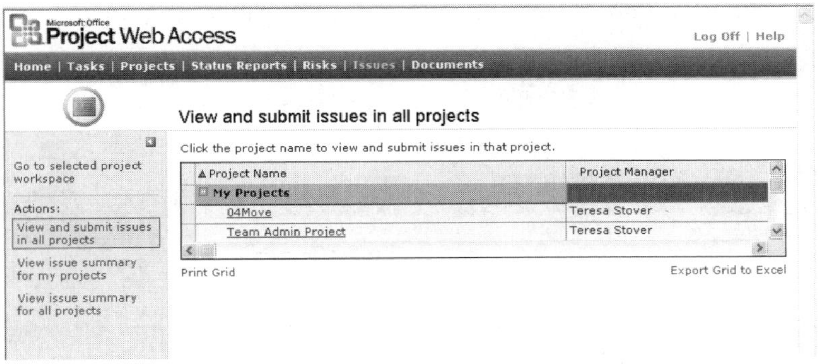

Figure 23-19. View and work with the project issues.

Controlling Project Documents

Through Windows SharePoint Services and Project Server, you can establish a document library associated with your project. The Project Web Access document library can be an excellent repository for project-related documents, including needs analyses, scope definition, product specifications, deliverable documents, team contact information, change-control plan, status reports, and more.

A central location for public documents related to your project can enhance collaboration and the project management process, ensuring that you and other project team members have all essential information at their disposal.

Depending on how your permissions are set, you might be able to add a document, view documents, and search for documents in the document library. When adding a new document, you enter the filename and location for the document, specify the owner and status (for example, Draft, Reviewed, Final, and so on), and enter any pertinent comments. You can also associate a document with specific tasks if you want.

After the project server administrator sets up and configures Windows SharePoint Services and the Document Library specific to your team, you can see documents directly from your Project Web Access site.

NEW FEATURE! New in Project 2003 is version control. Document versions can now be controlled using checkin and checkout processes. If a document is checked out, only the user who has checked it out can save to it. Multiple versions of a document can be compared and archived separately. When a document is linked to a project or individual tasks, the most current version of the document is linked.

To work with the document management features, follow these steps:

1. In the Project Web Access navigation bar, click Documents.

   The View And Upload Documents In All Projects page appears (see Figure 23-20).

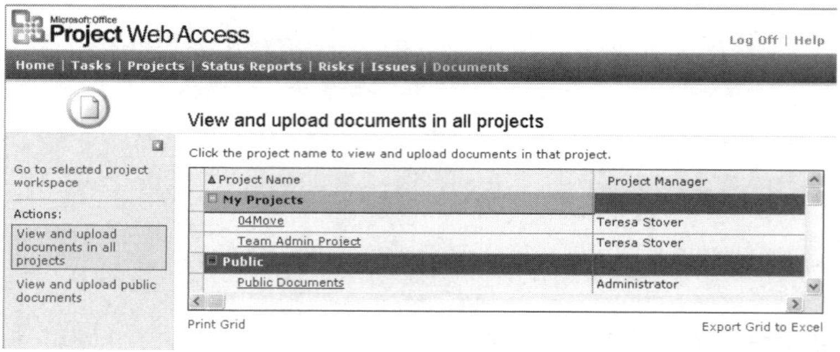

Figure 23-20. View and work with the document library.

2. Click a project to review its documents or to add a new document library.

Managing Resources in Project Web Access

If you're a resource manager or a team leader on a project, you have additional capabilities available to you in Project Web Access. Depending on your permissions, you might be able to do some or all of the following resource management activities:

- Find the right resources for a project team using the Build Team feature.
- Review resource assignments, workload, and availability.
- Delegate or assign tasks to the right resources.
- Update resource information in the enterprise resource pool.
- Create an administrative project to track non-project time.
- Set up e-mail notification for resources.
- Review resource timesheets for incorporation into project plans.

Finding the Right Resources

NEW FEATURE! If you're using the enterprise features of Project Server 2003, and if you're a resource manager with the appropriate permissions, you have access to the Build Team page in Project Web Access.

With the Build Team page, you can search your entire enterprise resource pool to find resources who have the exact skills, availability, resource breakdown structure code, and other traits you need for a given project. Specifically, in the planning processes of your project, when putting together the perfect team to carry out your project, you can:

- Find and add resources to the project by name.
- Find resources associated with a certain title, code, skill set, or other attribute.
- Find resources who are available for work during a certain period of time.
- Replace a resource already on your team with another enterprise resource.
- Find more resources that have the same traits as a resource already on your team.
- Match and replace generic resources in a project with real enterprise resources.
- Tentatively add proposed resources to a project.

Use the Build Team page to find enterprise resources and add them to your project team. The Build Team process adds resources to your project, but does not necessarily assign tasks (unless you replace a resource who has already been assigned to tasks). After the resources are added, they can be assigned to tasks.

Adding Resources to a Project

You might already know exactly which enterprise resources you need to add to a project. If this is the case, find and add resources by name as follows:

1. In the Project Web Access navigation bar, click Projects.

   The Project Center appears. If you are working with more than one project, the projects are listed in a summary project Gantt Chart.
2. Click the project to which you want to add resources.
3. Above the Tasks table, click the Build Team button.

   The Build Team page appears.
4. Click the + button in the Filter Enterprise Resources section.

   The section expands to show filters and options for finding resources that meet certain criteria.
5. Specify any filters you want having to do with the skills, availability, or other resource traits you want to find.

   You can use the filter to find resources who are associated with a particular RBS level or code, with a particular enterprise resource outline code, or even a multiple-value enterprise resource outline code.
6. Click Apply Filter.

   If you want to show all resources in the enterprise resource pool, click View All. All members of your organization's enterprise resource pool are listed in the Filtered Enterprise Resource table.
7. Scroll through the Filtered Enterprise Resources table to find and select the resource you want to add.

   You can select multiple resources at once. Use Shift to select multiple adjacent resources; use Ctrl to select multiple nonadjacent resources.
8. Click the Add button.

The selected resources are added to the Resources In The Project box on the right. This box lists any enterprise and nonenterprise resources that are already added to the selected project.

9. When finished adding resources, click Save Changes.

   The newly selected resources are added to the selected project plan.

Replacing and Matching Existing Resources

You can use the Build Team dialog box to replace one resource on a selected project team with another one from the enterprise resource pool, which is useful if you have a local resource in the project that you know has been added to the enterprise resource pool. This is also useful if you want to replace generic resources in your project with real enterprise resources. To replace an existing project team resource with an enterprise resource, follow these steps:

1. In the Projects area, click the project to which you want to add resources.
2. Above the Tasks table, click the Build Team button.
3. In the Build Team page, apply any filters or groups you need to find the replacing resource.
4. In the Resources In The Project box, click the name of the resource you want to replace.
5. In the Filtered Enterprise Resources box, click the name of the replacing resource.
6. Click Replace.

   The resource selected in the Filtered Enterprise Resources box replaces the one selected in the Resources In The Project box. If the original resource had reported any actual work on assigned tasks, the original resource remains in the project plan as associated with those assignments. Any remaining work on any tasks assigned to the original resource are now assigned to the replacing resource.

Review a resource's availability graphs

If you find a resource you want to add or replace in a selected project, you can get more information about that resource's availability and workload. This can help you decide if this resource really has the time to work on your project.

In the Build Team page, select the resource name in either box and then click the Availability button. The Availability dialog box appears. There are three different graphs to choose from in the Select Graph box.

With the availability graphs, you can see

- Timephased work assignments by project.
- Timephased work assignments by resource.
- Timephased availability and remaining availability.
- Timephased resource data grouped by project.

Suppose that you have already added an enterprise resource to a project team, and the project manager says he needs five more resources just like her. If the existing resource and enterprise resources have attributes defined for them—such as RBS codes, skill sets, certifications, and so on—you can use the Build Team dialog box to find other resources who have the same attributes. To find more enterprise resources whose defined traits match those of an existing project team resource, follow these steps:

1. In the Build Team page, apply any filters or groups you might need to define matching resources.
2. In the Resources In The Project box, click the name of the resource whose traits you want to match with additional enterprise resources.
3. Click Match.

   The list of filtered enterprise resources is searched for resource matches. The resulting list of resources represent resources whose attributes line up with those of your selected resource.
4. If you want to add any of these resources, click their names and then click Add.

Proposing Tentative Resources

As soon as you add enterprise resources to a project's team and assign tasks to those resources, their availability information changes in the enterprise resource pool. This ensures that a single resource is not inadvertently booked full-time to two or three different projects, for example.

However, sometimes you need to build a project and its team as a proposal or estimate. You might want to show actual resources in the project to demonstrate the skill level as well as calculate real costs. However, if the project is just an estimate or model, you probably wouldn't want to tie up the resource's availability in case the project does not actually happen.

In another scenario, you might be working with an approved project and want to run a what-if analysis on the impact of adding certain resources to the project.

NEW FEATURE! For either of these cases, you can *soft-book* resources on your project by adding them as *proposed*, rather than *committed* resources on your team.

> **Note** The booking type, proposed or committed, applies to the resource as a whole on your project. The booking type does not apply to individual assignments within the project.

By default, all resources are booked as committed. To specify that a resource you're adding is to be booked as a proposed resource on your project team, do the following:

1. In the Build Team page in Project Web Access, apply any filters or groups you might need to find the resources you want.
2. In the Filtered Enterprise Resources box, click the name of the resources you want to add as a proposed resource.
3. Click Add.

4. In the Resources In The Project box, in the Booking field for the resource, change Committed to Proposed.

   That resource is now considered soft-booked. As you work through your project, you can choose to consider resources' booking type when assigning tasks to resources in your project and when leveling assignments to resolve overallocations.

> **Tip Consider proposed bookings for your resource filtering**
> When you're searching for resources who meet certain availability criteria, you can choose whether or not Microsoft Project should consider proposed resource information. In the Build Team page, select or clear the Include Proposed Bookings When Determining Availability And Total Assigned Work.

Reviewing Resource Allocation and Availability

As a resource manager, by default you have the necessary permissions for reviewing resource assignments and availability.

To review resource assignments, follow these steps:

1. In the Project Web Access navigation bar, click Resources.

   The Resource Center appears.
2. In the side pane, click View Resource Assignments.

   The View Resource Assignments page appears (see Figure 23-21).

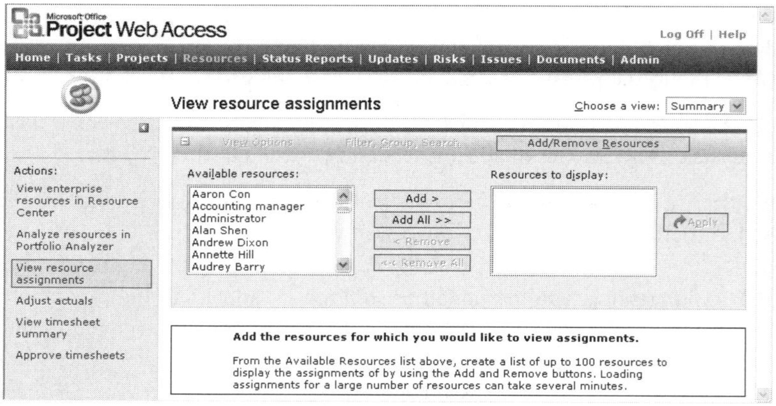

Figure 23-21. Select the resources for whom you want to review assigned tasks.

3. In the Available Resources box, click the names of the resource whose assignments you want to review.

   Use your Shift or Ctrl keys to select multiple resources as needed.
4. Click the Add button.

   The selected resources are added to the Resources To Display box.

5. Click the Apply button.

   A view appears, showing all tasks assigned to the selected resources.

To review resource availability, follow these steps:

1. In the Project Web Access navigation bar, click Resources.

   The Resource Center appears.
2. In the side pane, click View Enterprise Resources In Resource Center.

   All enterprise resources are displayed.
3. Scroll through the table to find the resource whose availability you want to check.

   Click in the Choose A View box to switch to a different resource view, if necessary.

   Click View Options or Filter, Group, Search above the table to arrange the resources in the table to make it easier for you to find and work with the resources.
4. Select the resource whose availability information you want to check and then click View Availability above the table.

Delegating Tasks to Resources

As a resource manager, a project manager might assign all project tasks to you. You are then responsible for passing those tasks on to the resources you have determined to be appropriate.

As a team lead, the project manager or resource manager might assign you a set of tasks in your specialty area. You can then delegate some or all of those tasks to others on your team to make sure that the right resources are working on the right tasks, and that these tasks can be done on time.

The process begins when the project manager assigns tasks to you, and those assignments show up in your Tasks list. To delegate assignments to others, follow these steps:

1. In the Project Web Access navigation bar, click Tasks.
2. In the side pane, click Delegate Tasks.

   The Delegation section opens above the Tasks table (see Figure 23-22).

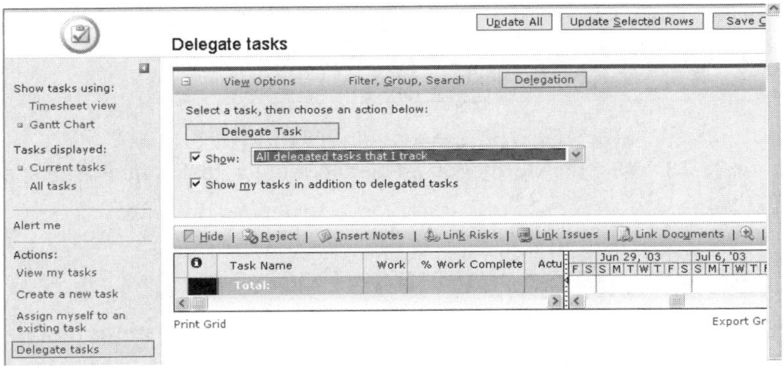

Figure 23-22. Use the Delegation section to set your options for delegating tasks.

3. In the Delegation section, select or clear the check boxes to control which tasks you see in the list.
4. In the table, select the task(s) you want to delegate to a resource.

   Use your Shift or Ctrl keys to select multiple tasks as needed.

   If you don't see all the tasks you want to delegate, click All Tasks in the side pane.

   If you are assigned to tasks from multiple projects, by default the tasks are grouped by project.
5. In the Delegation section, click the Delegate Task button.

   The Delegate Tasks wizard appears.
6. Specify the resource to whom you are delegating the task. Also specify whether you are assuming the lead role on the task and whether you will continue to track the task in your Timesheet. Click Next.
7. In the next wizard page, confirm your changes, and then click the Send button.

   An update regarding this delegation is submitted to the project server for review by the responsible project manager. If the project manager accepts the delegation, it is reflected in the project plan.

After you have delegated tasks, you have additional choices for working with those tasks and the resources to whom you delegated the tasks. Depending on your choices and permissions in tracking the delegated tasks and whether you are retaining the lead role, the Request Task Status and Delegate Lead Role buttons appear in the Delegation section of the Tasks area (see Figure 23-23).

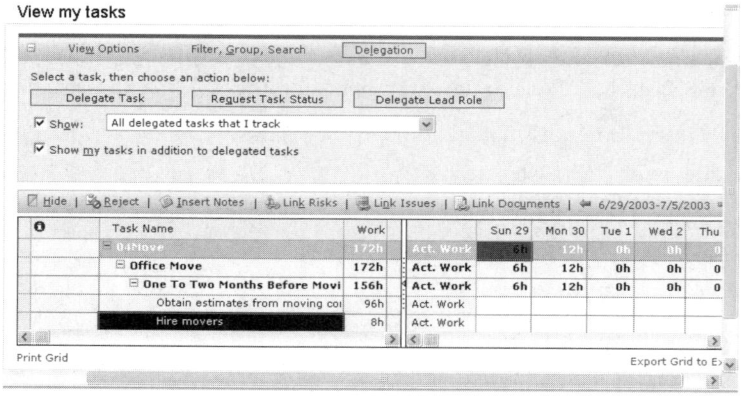

Figure 23-23. Use the Delegation section to request task status and delegate your lead role.

Updating the Enterprise Resource Pool

If you are a resource manager, by default you have the permissions necessary to update resource information in the enterprise resource pool from within Project Web Access.

Note If your organization has set up a resource breakdown structure and applied it to all enterprise resources, you can update only resource information for others within your own RBS level.

1. In the Project Web Access navigation bar, click Resources.
2. In the side pane, click View Enterprise Resources In Resource Center.

   The enterprise resource pool is displayed in the Resource Center (see Figure 23-24).

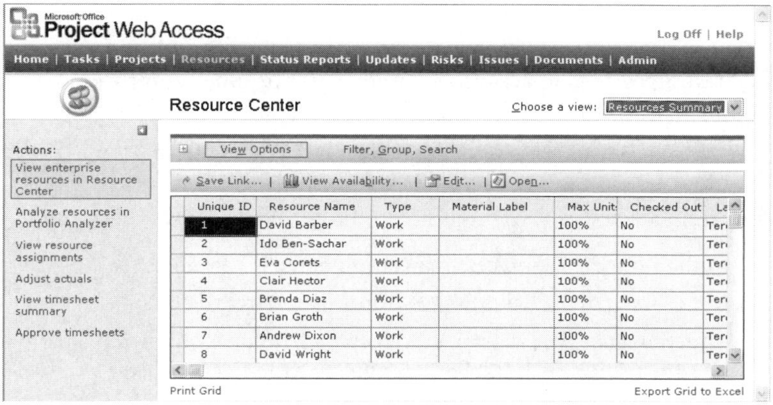

Figure 23-24. All resources in the enterprise resource pool are listed in the Resource Center.

3. Scroll through the table to find the resource whose information you need to update.

   Click in the Choose A View box to switch to a different resource view if necessary.

   Click View Options or Filter, Group, Search above the table to arrange the resources in the table to make it easier for you to find and work with the resources.
4. Select the resource whose information you want to change, and then click Edit above the table.

   You can change a resource's max units, booking type, standard rate, overtime rate, and so on.

   If the RBS, enterprise resource outline codes, and multivalue enterprise resource outline codes have been set up, you can apply the appropriate codes to resources in this table. Click in the outline code field and then click the appropriate code for the resource.
5. Click Save And Close.

For more information about setting up the RBS and other enterprise resource outline codes, see "Customizing Enterprise Resource Fields" on page 609.

Creating an Administrative Project

NEW FEATURE! If you are a resource manager, by default you have the permissions necessary to create and assign an administrative project from Project Web Access. "Tasks" such as vacation, sick days, holidays, personal time, civic duty, training, and family leave are included in the administrative project. You can add other such tasks as needed. You add resources to the administrative project and then save the project.

> **Note** Resources should be assigned to only one administrative project, even if they're working on different projects.

When resources need to account for nonproject or other nonworking time like this, they assign themselves to one of the administrative tasks. In this way, resource time can be accounted for and tracked. Furthermore, a more accurate picture of resource availability is provided.

To create an administrative project from Project Web Access, follow these steps:

1. In the Project Web Access navigation bar, click Projects.
2. In the side pane, click Manage Administrative Projects.

   The Manage Administrative Projects page appears, showing a table with any other administrative projects that have been created.
3. Above the table, click Add Project.

   The administrative project template opens in Project Professional.
4. In the Gantt Chart, make any modifications you want to the template. Add any additional administrative tasks and delete any you don't want to include.
5. In the Resource Sheet, add the resources on the project team who should have access to this administrative project.

   You can use the Build Team dialog box to add the resources. Click Tools, Build Team From Enterprise.
6. Click File, Save. If necessary, name the administrative project file.

   The administrative project is saved to the project server, and Microsoft Project closes.

For information about how team members use the administrative project, see "Tracking Nonproject Tasks and Time" earlier in this chapter on page 711. For more information about working with the administrative project within Project Professional, see "Tracking Nonproject Tasks and Time" on page 695.

Setting Up E-Mail Notifications

You can configure e-mail reminders to be sent to your resources, and to yourself, too. To do this, follow these steps:

1. In the Project Web Access navigation bar, click Home.

2 In the side page of the Home page, click Alert Me About My Resources On Tasks And Status Reports.

The Alert Me page appears (see Figure 23-25).

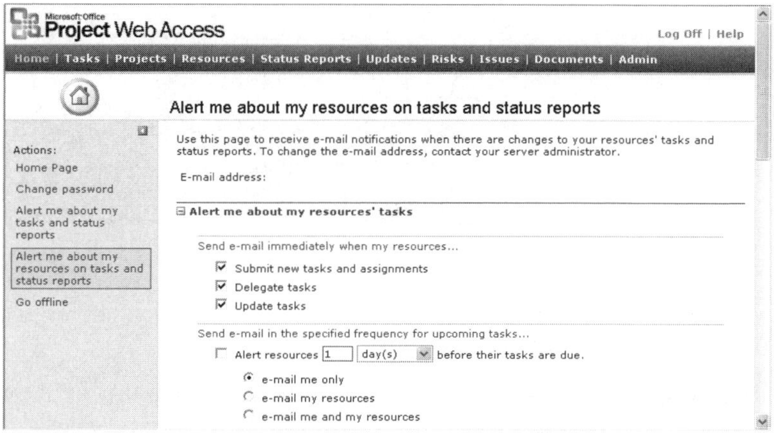

Figure 23-25. Specify any e-mail notifications you want to send to your resources.

3 Review the options throughout this page and select the check boxes for the events for which you want to send or receive e-mail. Clear the check boxes for events for which you do not want an e-mail notification.

There are e-mail notification options for resource activities, upcoming tasks, overdue tasks, tasks requiring progress updates, status reports, and delegated task activity.

You can specify whether you should receive the e-mail, whether your affected team members should receive the e-mail, or both.

4 When finished, click Save Changes at the bottom of the page.

Reviewing Resource Timesheets

Suppose that you're a resource manager who has delegated a set of tasks to the appropriate resources. Those resources submit their updates to you for approval.

Alternatively, the project manager might have directly assigned all tasks, but you've been asked to review timesheets and approve them for incorporation into the project plan.

To approve timesheets, follow these steps:

1 In the Project Web Access navigation bar, click Resources.

The Resource Center appears.

2 In the side pane, click View Timesheet Summary.

The View Timesheet Summary page appears (see Figure 23-26).

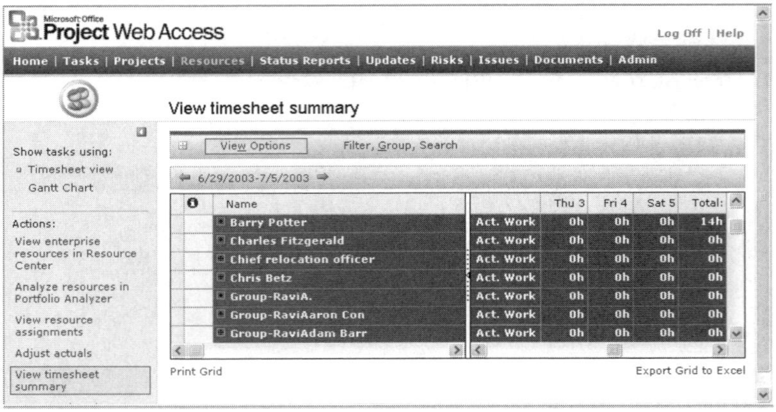

Figure 23-26. Review the summary for each Timesheet that has been sent to you by different resources.

3 Click the name of the resource whose Timesheet you want to review.

The Approve Timesheets page appears (see Figure 23-27).

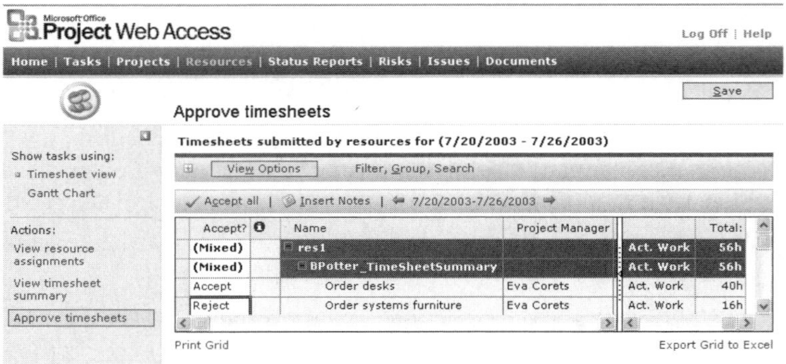

Figure 23-27. Review the tasks and accept or reject the update.

4 Review each updated task. In the Accept column, click Accept or Reject. If you want to accept all updates in the table at once, click Accept All.

5 When finished reviewing the Timesheet for the selected resource, click Save.

Any accepted task information updates the project plan. Any rejected task information is returned to the resource, typically with comments, and the project plan is not updated for that task.

Chapter 24

Making Executive Decisions Using Project Web Access

Executives and other managing stakeholders can use the enterprise features in Microsoft Office Project Web Access 2003 to monitor and measure projects and resources throughout the entire organization. They can see information about dozens of projects and thousands of resources, presented in a manner most relevant to their requirements.

When you are a managing stakeholder identified with executive-level permissions, you can log on to Project Web Access 2003 and view all enterprise resource information, see your entire *portfolio* of projects in one place, and perform analytical functions to compare and evaluate data.

You can compare one project against another, and look at overall resource allocation and availability throughout your organization. Your high-level views of the project portfolio and enterprise resources can be easily adapted and tailored to what you need to see for your particular focus, which can be quite different from what another managing stakeholder might need to see.

By integrating Microsoft Office Project 2003 with Windows SharePoint Services, you can have additional project collaboration and analysis information at your fingertips. Windows SharePoint Services can be set up with your implementation of Microsoft Office Project Server 2003 to provide risk management, issue tracking, and document control services.

Being able to set up e-mail reminders and to-do lists, you can use Project Web Access as an efficiency tool for your project-related activities.

Project Web Access provides clear visibility into your organization's project efforts. You can access vital information which helps you prevent problems and ensure smooth operations. Through the Microsoft Project enterprise project management features, you can see the big project picture, use resources wisely, and make sound decisions for the future of your organization.

Getting Started with Project Web Access

Use your Web browser to connect to Project Server. You then log on to the server from Project Web Access using the user identification established for you by the project server administrator.

After you're in Project Web Access, you can set or change your password if necessary. It's a good idea to browse around to orient yourself to the layout of Project Web Access. This will give you some ideas of how you can use Project Web Access as a partner in your project analysis.

Logging On

To log on to Project Web Access, follow these steps:

1. Start up Internet Explorer (version 5.01 with Service Pack 3, or later).
2. In the Address box, enter the URL for your organization's project server and then click Go.

   Your project manager or project server administrator provides you with the URL you need.

   The Project Web Access log on page appears (see Figure 24-1).

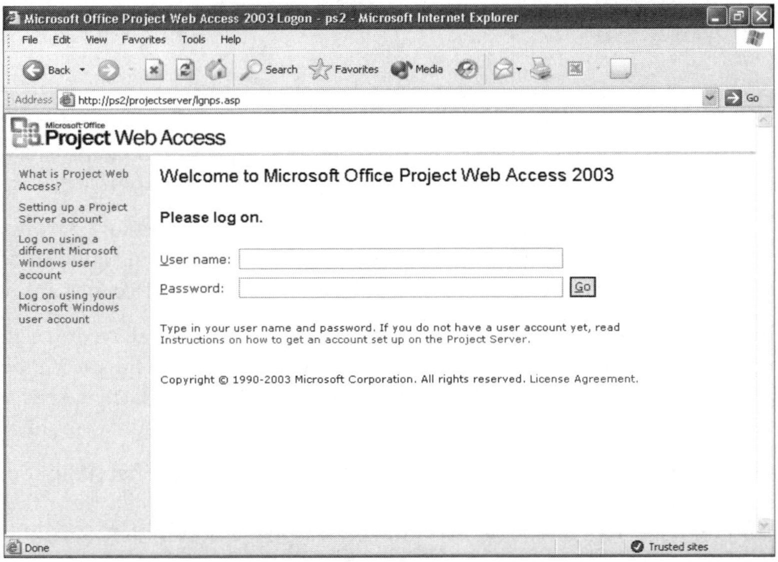

Figure 24-1. Enter your user name and password as set up by the project server administrator.

> **Tip** **Add Project Web Access as a favorite**
> Because you'll be coming to Project Web Access whenever you want a view into your organization's project activities, add the project server URL as a favorite Web site. When the Log On page appears in Internet Explorer, click Favorites, Add To Favorites. Enter a name in the Name box and then click OK.

3. Enter your user name and password and then click Go.

   Your user name might be the same as your corporate Windows account that you use to access your corporate network, e-mail, and so on. If your project server administrator set you up to use your Windows account, you just need to enter your Windows account user name. You might or might not need to also enter your Windows account password.

Alternatively, your project server administrator might have set you up with a separate Project Server account. In this case, you'll need to enter that user name. Leave the password blank. You'll add a password as soon as you gain access.

Your Project Web Access Home page appears (see Figure 24-2).

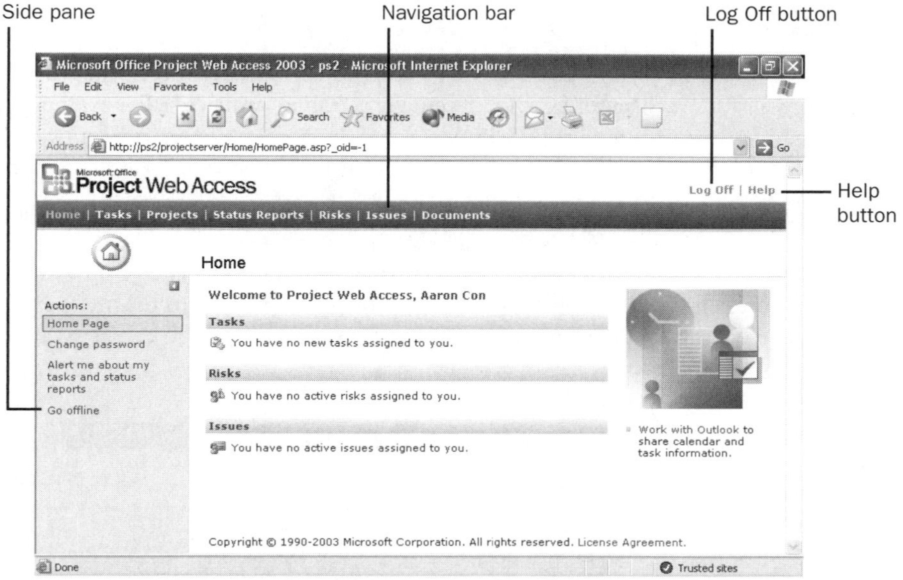

Figure 24-2. After a successful logon, the Project Web Access Home page appears.

> **Tip** **Set your Project Server account password**
>
> If your project server administrator set you up with a separate Project Server account, add a password the first time you log on to Project Web Access.
>
> In the side pane of the Home page, click Change Password. Follow the instructions in the page that appears.

Getting Oriented

Browse around Project Web Access to get a feel for available features and how you might like to use them. You'll find Project Web Access similar to many Web sites, with the content and links on multiple pages.

There are several major areas in Project Web Access; for example, Projects and Resources. You can switch to a different area by clicking one of the buttons in the blue navigation bar toward the top of the page.

To display pages related to the area you're currently in, click one of the links in the side pane on the left side of the page.

To read Help, click the Help button in the upper-right corner. You can read Help about the page that's currently displayed, or browse the Help table of contents for another topic.

To end your session with Project Web Access, click the Log Off button in the upper-right corner.

Working with Views and Fields

As you use Project Web Access to review project, task, resource, and assignment information, you work with a number of different views, tables, and fields. For example, in the Project Web Access navigation bar, click Projects, and the Project Center view appears (see Figure 24-3). In this view is a table, probably with a Gantt chart, showing your enterprise projects.

A variety of views are available, set up by the project server administrator for users with different permission levels. You can switch to another view by clicking in the Choose A View box in the upper-right corner. Alternate views in the same page show different fields for the same category of information, such as this set of projects or the individual project. You'll see these same elements in many of the views you work with in Project Web Access.

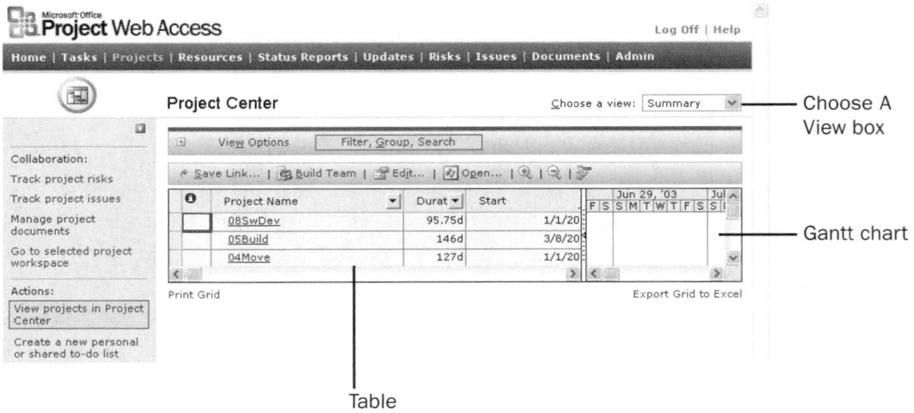

Figure 24-3. Go to the Project Center to review the list of enterprise projects.

Zoom In

Many views you work with are a type of Gantt chart. In a Gantt chart, the left side of the view is a table, and the right side displays the Gantt bars, showing the start, duration, and finish of each item (project, task, resource, assignment) across the timescale. The current date is shown as a dashed vertical line. Click the Zoom In or Zoom Out buttons to see more or less detail in the time span shown in the chart area.

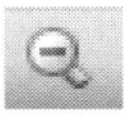

Zoom Out

Understanding Fields

You can have either read-write or read-only access for the table fields in the view. Work with your project server administrator to make sure you have the access to the fields you need in the views you use most often.

NEW FEATURE! Certain types of custom fields might have been created and added to your Tasks list by the project manager or project server administrator. Some of these custom fields can contain a value list from which users can choose an appropriate option. If such a custom field is part of a view that you are modifying, and if you have read-write permission, click in the field. A drop-down list shows all the choices. Click a choice, and that value now appears in the field. This makes it easy for you to enter the correct form of information while maintaining project data integrity.

Rearranging View Information

In project and resource views, you can sort, group, or filter information by criteria you choose.

To sort items in a view by a particular field, follow these steps:

1. In the view, click the heading of the field column you want to sort by.

   The field is sorted in either ascending or descending order.
2. To sort in the other direction, click the column heading a second time.

To group items by a particular field in a view, follow these steps:

1. Display the view you want to work with.
2. Above the table, click Filter, Group, Search.
3. In the expanded section that appears, click the arrow in the Group By box to see your grouping choices in the drop-down list (see Figure 24-4).

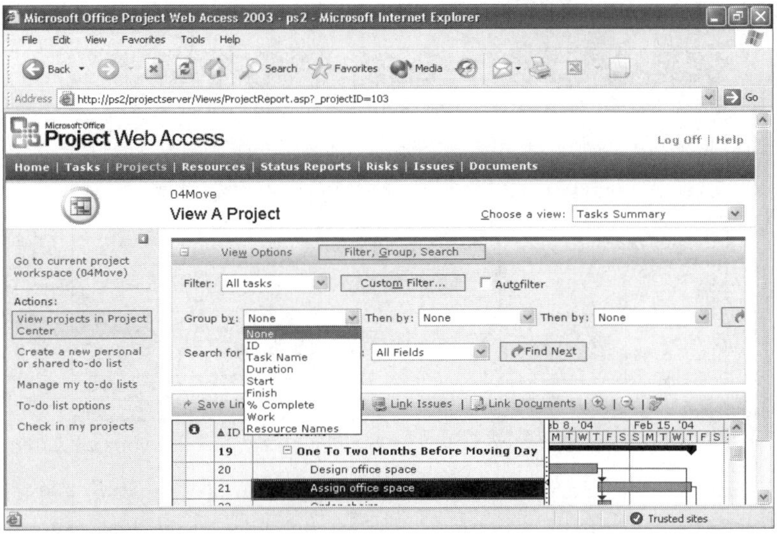

Figure 24-4. Click the field by which you want to group the information.

4. Click the field you want to group by.

   The table changes to reflect your grouping.

5. If you want a subgroup within the group, click Second Field in the Then By box.

   Some views also provide a third Then By box.
6. When you want to return to the original non-grouped order, click None in the Group By box.

To filter items by a built-in filter in a view, follow these steps:

1. Display the view in which you want to filter information.
2. Above the table, click Filter, Group, Search.
3. In the expanded section that appears, click the arrow in the Filter box to see your filter choices.
4. Click the filter you want to use.

   The table changes immediately to show only those items that meet your filter criteria.
5. To see all items in the table again, click All Tasks (or All Resources or All Projects) in the Filter box.

To create a custom filter, follow these steps:

1. Display the view in which you want to filter information.
2. Above the table, click Filter, Group, Search.
3. In the expanded section that appears, click Custom Filter.
4. In the More Filters dialog box, enter the field you want to filter by in the Field Name box (see Figure 24-5).

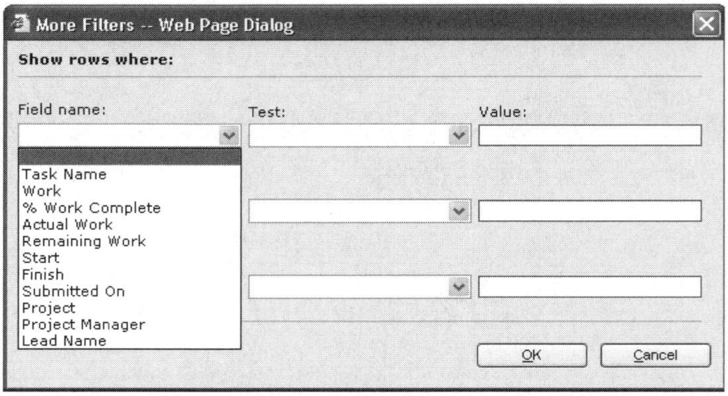

Figure 24-5. Click the field by which you want to filter your view information.

5. In the Test field, enter the test criteria, for example, Equals or Contains.
6. In the Value field, enter the value for the field and then click OK.

   The task list changes immediately to show only those items that meet your filter criteria.
7. To see all items in the table again, click All Tasks in the Filter box.

You can also select the AutoFilter check box to add the AutoFilter arrows to each column in the current view.

To collapse the Filter, Group, Search section, click the – (minus) button in the upper-left corner of the section.

Printing or Exporting a Table

NEW FEATURE!

In Project Web Access 2003, you can now print the table on the following pages:

- Tasks
- Projects
- Resources
- Updates
- Risks
- Issues
- Documents

You can also use this function to export the contents of the table to a Microsoft Office Excel 2003 workbook. To print or export a Project Web Access table, follow these steps:

1. Display the view containing the table you want to print.
2. Below the table, click Print Grid on the left or Export Grid To Excel on the right.

   The grid setup page appears (see Figure 24-6).

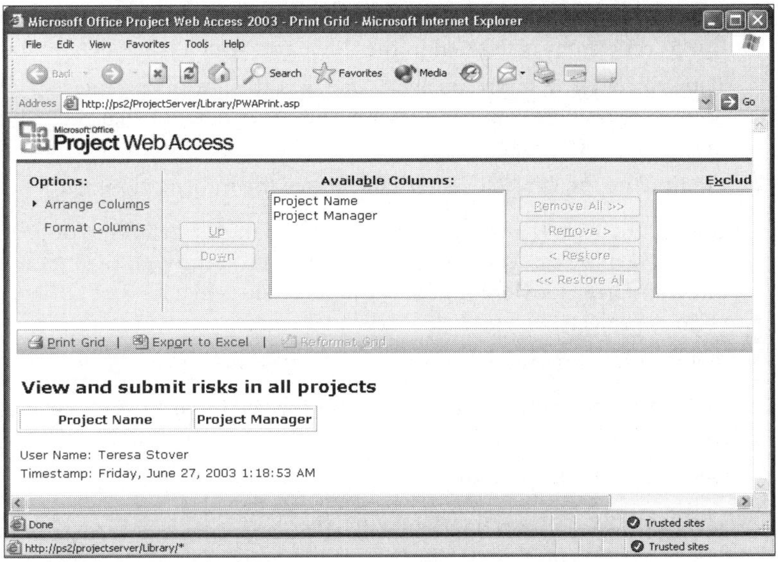

Figure 24-6. Set up the columns you want printed or exported.

3 Select field names in the Available Columns box and use the Up and Down buttons to rearrange the order of the columns as it will be printed or exported.

4 If you want to exclude any fields from the print or export operation, click its name in the Available Columns box and then click the Remove button.

This removes the column only for the print or export operation. The field is still present in the view itself.

A preview of the printed report or exported workbook appears in the lower half of the view.

5 Click Print Grid to send the report to the printer. Click Export To Excel to send the report to an Excel workbook.

Analyzing Your Project Portfolio

It's likely that you'll spend much of your time in the Projects area of Project Web Access. It's here where you can scrutinize various views of an individual project. This is also the place where you can analyze aspects of multiple projects to get the high-level picture of projects you need.

Reviewing Summary and Detail Project Information

You can see the summary list of all published enterprise projects and then drill down to examine the details of an individual project. To see the summary of enterprise projects, follow these steps:

1 In the Project Web Access navigation bar, click Projects. Make sure that View Projects In Project Center is selected in the side pane, which is the default for this page.

The Project Center appears. The table lists all enterprise projects, with each project occupying a single row and showing summary data for that project in the table and in the Gantt Chart area.

2 Manipulate the Project Center table to see the information you want.

Choose the view that shows the best information. Sort, filter, or group information. Hide and show categories of information. Scroll through the table or chart to find the information you're looking for. Compare values in a field of information among the various projects.

To see detailed information for any one of the enterprise projects, follow these steps:

1 Make sure the Project Center table is displayed, with View Projects In Project Center selected in the side pane.

2 Click the link for the project you want to review.

The project view appears (see Figure 24-7).

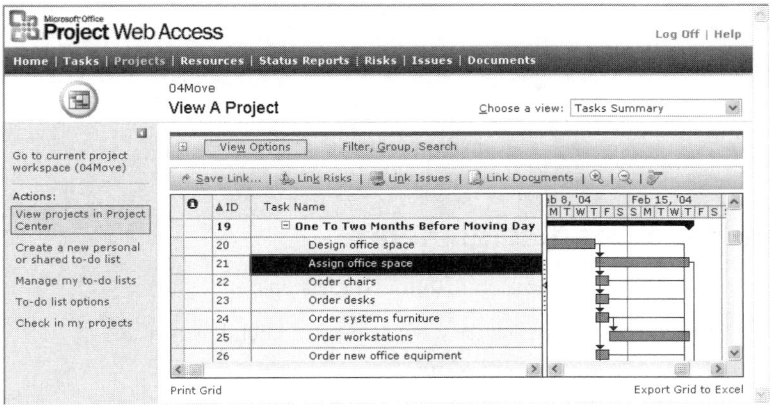

Figure 24-7. View individual project details.

Just as with the summary table, choose the view that shows the best information. Sort, filter, or group information. Hide and show categories of information. Scroll through the table or chart to find the information you're looking for. Compare values in a field of information among the various projects.

Opening Multiple Projects in Project Professional

If you're set up for enterprise project management using Project Professional and Project Server, you can use Project Web Access to group projects the way you need. This basically replaces the need for master projects and subprojects as used in standalone projects in Microsoft Project.

To open multiple projects in a single Project Professional window, follow these steps:

1. In the Project Web Access navigation bar, click Projects. Make sure that View Projects In Project Center is selected in the side pane.

   The Project Center appears, showing all enterprise projects.

2. Click several projects you want to view in a Project Professional window.

   Use the Ctrl or Shift key to select multiple projects at once.

3. Above the table, click Open.

   Project Professional opens and displays the full project information for each of the selected projects. Each project name is a summary task, with all tasks listed below it.

4. Work with the grouped project information in Project Professional as needed. When finished, click File, Close.

Analyzing Resource Information

The Resources area is a key location for managers needing to keep a close eye on the performance of the enterprise resource pool. In the Resource Center, you can review resource assignments, their current or future workload allocation, and their current or future availability for additional work.

Reviewing Resource Assignments

To review resource assignments, follow these steps:

1. In the Project Web Access navigation bar, click Resources.

   The Resource Center appears.

2. In the side pane, click View Resource Assignments.

   The View Resource Assignments page appears (see Figure 24-8).

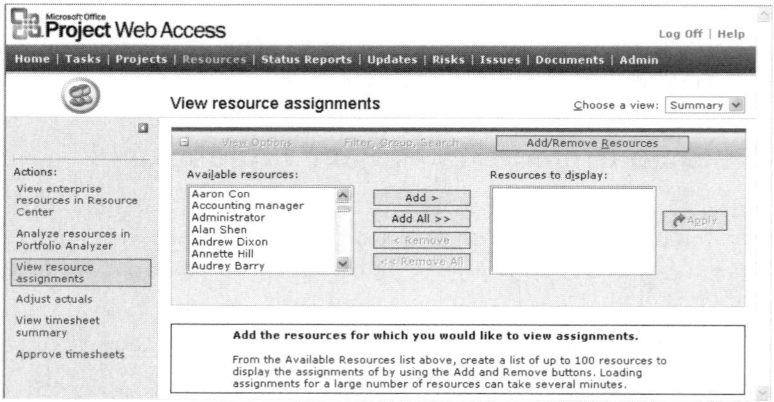

Figure 24-8. Select the resources for whom you want to review assigned tasks.

3. In the Available Resources box, click the names of the resource whose assignments you want to review.

   Use your Shift or Ctrl keys to select multiple resources as needed.

4. Click the Add button.

   The selected resources are added to the Resources To Display box.

5. Click the Apply button.

   A view appears, showing all tasks assigned to the selected resources.

Reviewing Resource Availability

To review resource availability, follow these steps:

1. In the Project Web Access navigation bar, click Resources.

   The Resource Center appears.
2. In the side pane, click View Enterprise Resources In Resource Center.

   All enterprise resources are displayed.
3. Scroll through the table to find the resource whose availability you want to check.

   Click in the Choose A View box to switch to a different resource view if necessary.

   Click View Options or Filter, Group, Search above the table to arrange the resources in the table to make it easier for you to find and work with the resources.
4. Select the resource whose availability you want to check and then above the table click View Availability.
5. In the Choose A View box, select a resource view that shows resource availability the way you need. Default views include the following:
   - Assignment Work By Resource
   - Assignment Work By Project
   - Remaining Availability
   - Work

Create a Status Report

You can use Project Web Access to design a status report for other project resources to complete and submit to you periodically. You set up the time period and the headings. At the designated time periods, the individuals write their status report and submit it to the project server. You can review the status reports individually or have the project server compile them for an integrated project status report.

You need to request the status report only when you first set it up. Resources see automated reminders in their Project Web Access Home page when a status report is coming due.

To set up a narrative status report, follow these steps:

1. In your Web browser, log on to Project Web Access and then click Status Reports in the navigation bar (see Figure 24-9).

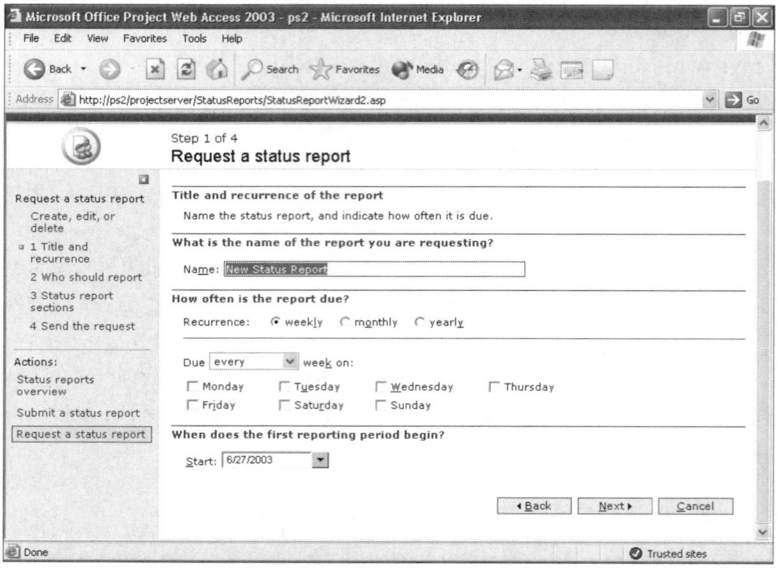

Figure 24-9. Click Request A Status Report to design a narrative periodic status report.

2 In the side pane, click Request A Status Report.

3 Complete the options on the page and then click Next.

4 Work through the succeeding pages to design the status report the way you need (see Figure 24-10).

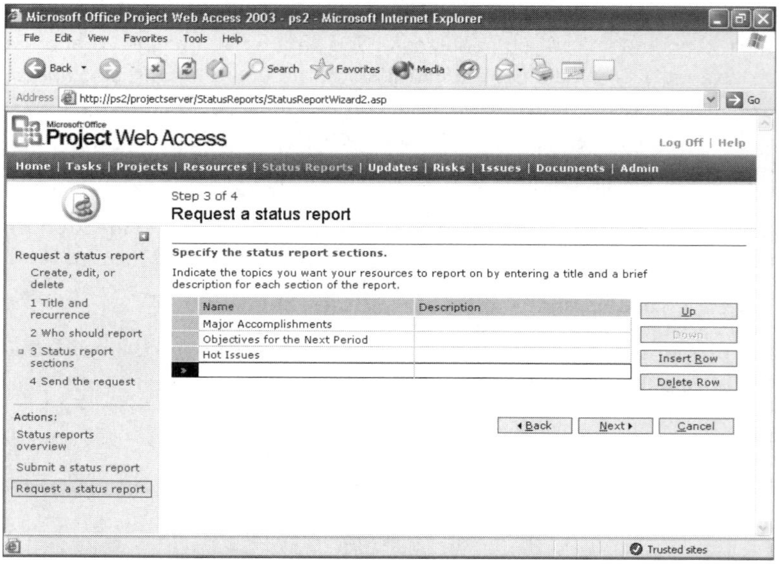

Figure 24-10. Specify the major topics for the status report.

5. Click Next after each page.
6. On the final page, click Send.

   The status report request, details, and schedule are sent to your specified resources.

Examining Projects Using Portfolio Analyzer

One of the primary capabilities of the Project Server enterprise features is that it can show information about every project in the entire organization. In large organizations, or in those that have very large numbers of active projects, it's generally not practical to review the details of every project throughout the organization. However, it's highly advantageous to see a high-level summary of project schedules, costs, and resource utilization. It's also helpful to be able to roll information from multiple projects together and to make comparisons between them.

Using Portfolio Analyzer, you can analyze schedule performance or resource utilization for a single project, multiple projects, or even all projects in the enterprise portfolio. Such analysis can provide a wealth of information, from whether you're spending too much on material and equipment costs to whether it would make good business sense to follow through on your proposal for a new ambitious project.

Portfolio Analyzer compiles project or resource information you request and presents the high-level summaries in a spreadsheet (*PivotTable*) or graph (*PivotChart*) format.

> **Note** Your project server administrator sets up the background facilities for you to use Portfolio Analyzer, including the *online analytical processing (OLAP) cube*. The basis for much of the analysis also depends on the setup of custom enterprise outline codes, including multivalue enterprise resource outline codes.
>
> Work with your project server administrator to make sure you have the OLAP cube and custom codes in place that will help you analyze project information the way you need.

To create a table or chart of summarized project or resource information using Portfolio Analyzer, follow these steps:

1. In the Project Web Access navigation bar, click Projects.

   If you're analyzing resource information, click Resources.
2. In the side pane, click Analyze Projects In Portfolio Analyzer.

   If you're analyzing resource information, click Analyze Resources In Portfolio Analyzer in the side pane.

   The Portfolio Analyzer page appears.
3. In the Choose A View box, select the view that displays the type of information you want to see in the Portfolio Analyzer results.

4. Set any additional options for what you want to show or hide by clicking View Options. To specify the fields you want to see, select the Show Field List check box and then drag fields you want onto the row or column in the PivotTable or PivotChart.

> **Tip** **Use Portfolio Analyzer from Project Professional**
>
> Portfolio Analyzer
>
> You can work with Portfolio Analyzer from Project Professional. Make sure that Project Professional is connected to Project Server. On the Collaborate toolbar, click Portfolio Analyzer.
>
> If the Collaborate toolbar is not showing, click View, Toolbars, Collaborate.

Running Scenarios Using Portfolio Modeler

With Portfolio Modeler, you can create alternate versions of a plan to model what-if scenarios: comparing, analyzing, and experimenting with different versions to help decide on the best course of action. These project models serve as a strategic planning tool, used to research and validate on model projects (rather than live projects). Portfolio Modeler is therefore used primarily by executives to evaluate the capacity of the organization to take on new projects.

Specifically, executives and resource managers can use Portfolio Modeler to plan on project resource allocation by basing assignments on skill requirements. Users can quickly view the effects of various staffing options at the schedule start, schedule finish, and resource allocation levels. With Portfolio Modeler, managers can quickly identify staff problems across projects in an organization and then model how staffing changes can potentially affect schedules, costs, and workloads. Model results can be saved as reports, which can then be used with the Resource Substitution Wizard in Project Professional to apply the model to live enterprise project plans.

> ## Inside Out
>
> **Don't model resources on live data**
>
> Use Portfolio Modeler only on alternate versions of a project, never on the live version—and certainly never on a project in which any actuals have been reported. Portfolio Modeler is intended only for strategic planning, not for projects that are live and in progress.
>
> If you run Portfolio Modeler on a live project with actual progress reported, resources who have reported actuals might be substituted out of the project, and this can change the overall scheduling of the project in significant ways.
>
> Portfolio Modeler is best used to help identify areas in which resource allocation might be improved.

To create a project model, follow these steps:

1. In the Project Web Access navigation bar, click Projects.
2. In the side pane, click Model Project With Portfolio Modeler.

The Portfolio Modeler page appears (see Figure 24-11).

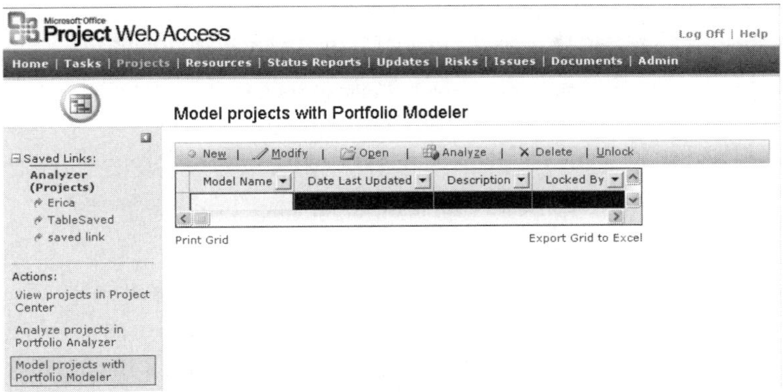

Figure 24-11. Use the Portfolio Modeler to run what-if scenarios on projects and resources.

3. On the Model Projects With Portfolio Modeler page, click New.
4. On the next page, under Model Name And Description, enter the name and description you want for your model.
5. Under Projects, select the projects you want to include in the model and then click Add.

   Your selected projects move to the Selected Projects box.
6. Under Resources, select the resources you want to include.

   You can include resources in the projects you selected for the model, any available enterprise resources at or below an RBS level that you indicate in the box, or specific resources you select in the Available Resources box.
7. Click Next.

   The Scheduling Context page appears. This page lists any other project files that have some relationship with the selected projects, such as cross-project links or a nonenterprise resource pool.
8. Select any related projects that you might want to include in the model and then click Next.

   The Choose Scheduling Options page appears, listing all projects and related projects you have selected for modeling to this point.
9. If you want to prioritize one project over another, increase its Priority value to be higher than the others.

   Projects with higher priority values have their resource requirements handled first, and therefore tend to get the better resource matches than projects with lower priority values.

   Priority values range from 1–1000, with 500 being the default.
10. Click Next.

    Your model is now created, and you can open it from the Portfolio Modeler page.

Portfolio Modeler

Tip **Use Portfolio Modeler from Project Professional**

You can work with Portfolio Modeler from Project Professional. Make sure that Project Professional is connected to Project Server. On the Collaborate toolbar, click Portfolio Modeler.

If the Collaborate toolbar is not showing, click View, Toolbars, Collaborate.

To open and analyze the results of a model you have created, follow these steps:

1. In the Project Web Access navigation bar, click Projects.

   The Project Center page appears.

2. In the side pane, click Model Project With Portfolio Modeler.

   The Model Projects With Portfolio Modeler page appears.

3. Select a project and then click Open or Analyze. Choose the projects and resources you want to include in this model.

For more details about using Portfolio Modeler, download the online book from the Microsoft Project Web site entitled "Microsoft Office Project 2003 Application Configuration Guide," and see Chapter 11, "Responding to Changes in Your Project."

To download the online book, go to *http://www.microsoft.com/downloads*, and then search for Project Server 2003.

Setting Up E-Mail Reminders and To-Do Lists

Project Web Access provides tools to add a layer of efficiency to your project activities. You can set up automated notifications so you can receive e-mail reminding you about various aspects of your project and progress tracking. You can also create a to-do list to keep track of things you need to do in Project Web Access.

Configuring E-Mail Notifications

To configure automated e-mail reminders to yourself, follow these steps:

1. In the Project Web Access navigation bar, click Home.
2. In the side pane of your Home page, click Alert Me About My Tasks And Status Reports.

   The Alert Me page appears (see Figure 24-12).

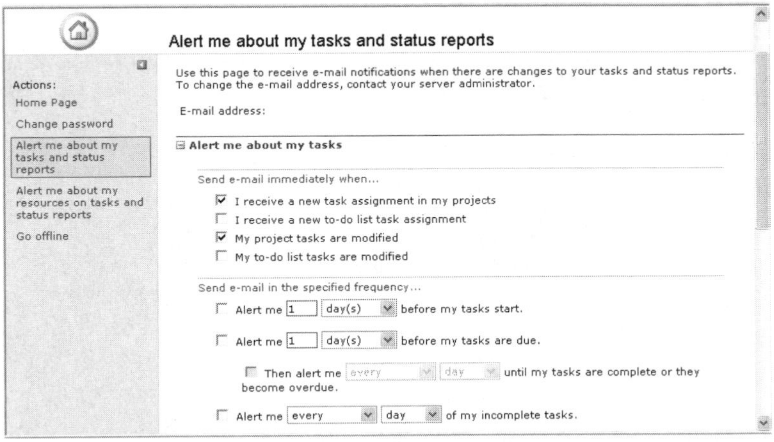

Figure 24-12. Specify any e-mail notifications you want to receive.

3. Review the options throughout this page and select the check boxes for the events for which you want to be notified via e-mail. Clear the check boxes for events for which you do not want an e-mail notification.

   You can set up e-mail notification options for upcoming tasks, overdue tasks, and status reports.

4. When finished, click Save Changes at the bottom of the page.

Creating To-Do Lists

While you review and analyze projects and resources in Project Web Access, you might have a number of activities you want to keep track of. They're probably not tasks that belong in a project plan; they're just a list of reminders to yourself. You can create a to-do list for yourself to keep track of these kinds of tasks.

To create a to-do list, follow these steps:

1. On the navigation bar, click Project.
2. In the side pane, click Create A New Personal Or Shared To-Do List.
3. Click Next.

   The To-Do List Options page appears (see Figure 24-13).

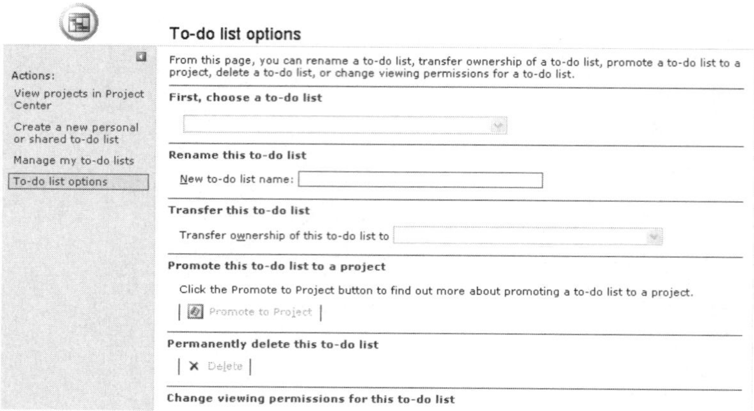

Figure 24-13. Set up a to-do list for yourself.

4 Work through the page to create your to-do list.

You can create multiple to-do lists, possibly for different categories. Your personal to-do lists are stored only in your own Microsoft Project Web Access site, and are not included in any public or project information.

> **Tip** **Assigning and publishing to-do lists for others**
> You can also create to-do lists for other users. You can create a to-do list and assign it to an individual user. You can also publish a to-do list for all users.

Managing Risks, Issues, and Documents

If your installation of Project Server is integrated with Windows SharePoint Services, you have three more collaboration features available in Project Web Access, as follows:

- Risk management, in the Risks area
- Issues tracking, in the Issues area
- Document control, in the Documents area

Risks, issues, and documents can be added, tracked, linked with tasks, assigned responsibility, and eventually closed. These all become an important aspect of managing the project as well as capturing important project archival information for use in planning future projects.

> **Note** By default, users with executive-level privileges are set up with the permission to view risks, issues, and documents. Depending on how the administrator has set up Project Server and Windows SharePoint Services, additional permission might be granted for executives to add and edit risks, issues, and documents.

Mitigating Project Risks

NEW FEATURE! *Risks* are events or conditions that can have a positive or negative impact on the outcome of a project. Because of this, project management and risk management go hand-in-hand. Users can record information about risks, update this information, and track the risk. Risks can be escalated to the right person for mitigation.

Risks can also be associated with specific tasks, resources, documents, issues, and other risks.

To work with the risk management features, follow these steps:

1. In the Project Web Access navigation bar, click Risks.

   The View And Submit Risks In All Projects appears (see Figure 24-14).

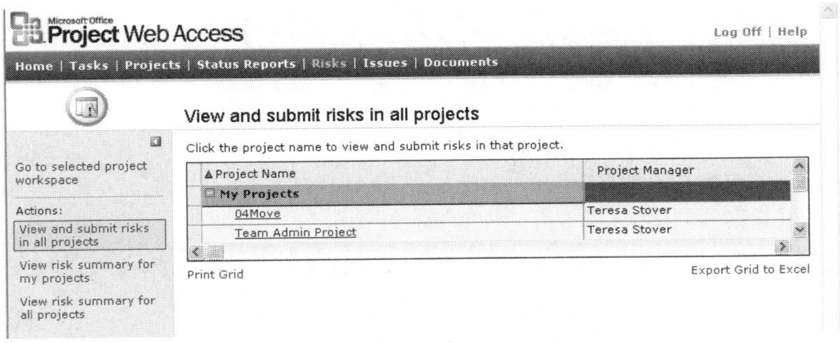

Figure 24-14. Click any of the projects to view or submit risks associated with that project.

2. Click the project to review risks or enter a new risk.

   If no risks are entered yet, the Risks: New Item page appears (see Figure 24-15).

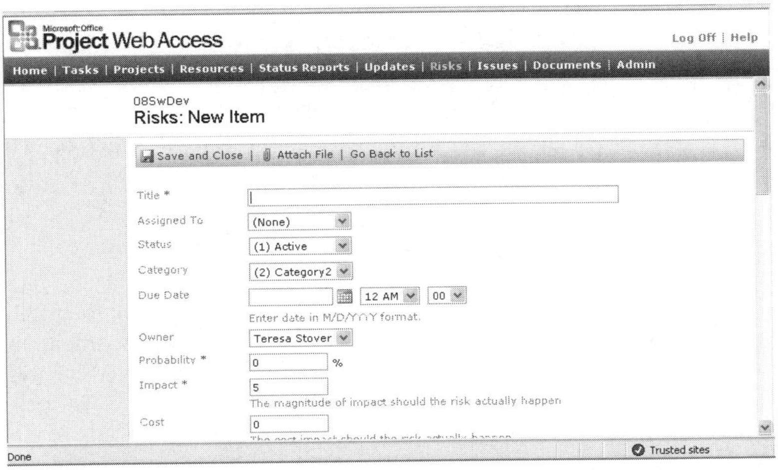

Figure 24-15. Use the Risks: New Item page to enter a new risk associated with the selected project.

3 Complete the page with the risk information. When finished, click Save And Close.

Monitoring Project Issues

Issues tracking is integral to project management and team communication because most issues either arise from task activity or will affect task activity. By tracking issues related to a project, communication is improved on project-related issues, ensuring that problems are handled before they become crises.

With the issues tracker, you can enter issues, assign ownership, track progress, record resolutions, and create related reports.

The issue page includes a due date, discussion of the issue, and date of resolution. Issues can be associated with affected tasks, documents in the document library, or other related issues.

To work with the issues tracking feature, follow these steps:

1 In the Project Web Access navigation bar, click Issues.

The View And Submit Issues In All Projects appears (see Figure 24-16).

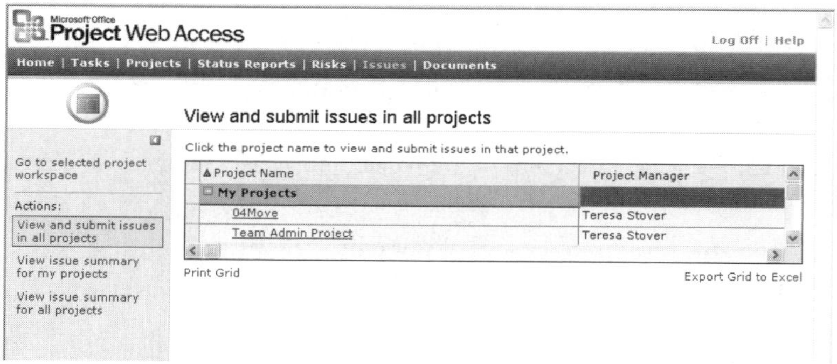

Figure 24-16. View and work with the project issues.

2 Click the project to review issues or enter a new issue.

If no issues are entered yet for the selected project, the Issues: New Item page appears.

3 Complete the page with the issue information. When finished, click Save And Close.

Controlling Project Documents

Through Windows SharePoint Services and Project Server, a document library can be established and associated with a project. The Project Web Access document library can be an excellent repository for project-related documents, including needs analyses, scope definition, product specifications, deliverable documents, team contact information, change control plan, status reports, and more.

A central location for public documents related to a given project can enhance collaboration and the project management process, ensuring that the entire project team has all essential information at their disposal.

Depending on how permissions are set, you might be able to add a document, view documents, and search for documents in the document library. When adding a new document, you enter the filename and location for the document, specify the owner and status (for example, Draft, Reviewed, Final, and so on), and enter any pertinent comments. Documents can also be associated with specific tasks.

After the project server administrator sets up and configures Windows SharePoint Services and the Document Library specific to your team, you can see documents directly from your Project Web Access site.

NEW FEATURE! New in Project 2003 is version control. Document versions can now be controlled using checkin and checkout processes. If a document is checked out, only the user who has checked it out can save to it. Multiple versions of a document can be compared and archived separately. When a document is linked to a project or individual tasks, the most current version of the document is linked.

To work with the document management features, follow these steps:

1. In the Project Web Access navigation bar, click Documents.

   The View And Upload Documents In All Projects page appears (see Figure 24-17).

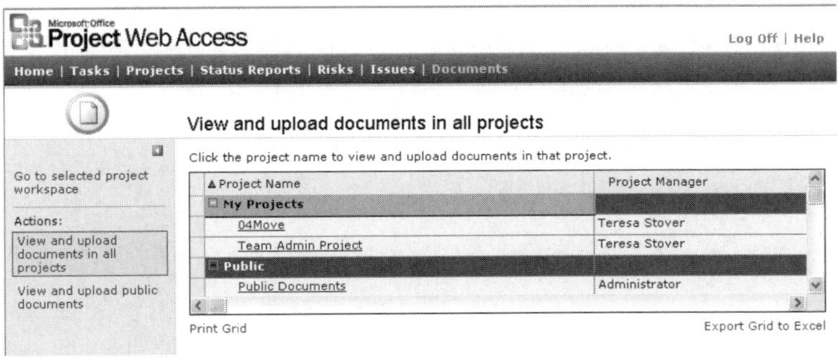

Figure 24-17. View and work with the document library.

2. Click a project to review its documents or to add a new document library.

Chapter 24

Part 8

Customizing and Managing Project Files

Chapter 25

Customizing Your View of Project Information

Organizations are as unique as people, and each project that an organization manages has its own particular needs. The solution to each new challenge requires a specific set of information, just as each step in managing a project does. You can control what information you see and how it is formatted, whether you want to satisfy your own preferences or meet the specialized needs of a particular project. Almost every aspect of Microsoft Office Project 2003 can be molded to your specifications, including the following:

- Views
- Tables
- Fields
- Groups
- Filters
- Reports

If you or your organization use outline codes, such as accounting codes to categorize tasks or skill codes to categorize resources, you can customize outline codes in Project 2003 for this purpose. You can adapt these codes to your organization's standards; apply them to project tasks and resources; and then sort, group, or filter information using your custom outline codes.

You can use these customized elements in one project or every project you create. This chapter describes how to customize all these elements and use them in your projects.

Customizing Views

Each view gives you a different perspective on your project information. The right view with pertinent data can simplify your project management tasks or uncover potential problems. You can specify which views you see, change the tables and fields that appear in a view, and control how information is categorized and displayed so you can look at your project information the way you want.

For more information about working with the built-in Microsoft Project views, see "Using Views" on page 95.

Changing the Content of a View

Microsoft Project includes a variety of standard views that present task, resource, and assignment information. When these standard views don't meet your needs, you can customize their content or create new views that are more suitable. In single pane views, you can specify which view, table, group, and filter to apply when the view appears; and for combination views, you can change which views appear in the top and bottom pane.

Note Even though views such as the Gantt Chart and Task Usage view are made up of two sides on the left and right, they're still considered single pane views.

To customize the content of an existing single pane view, for example, the Gantt Chart, Resource Sheet, or Task Usage view, do the following:

1 Click View, More Views.

2 In the More Views dialog box, click the view's name in the Views list (see Figure 25-1).

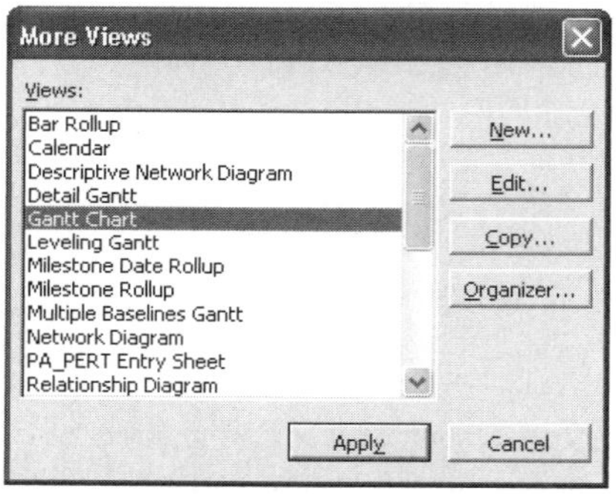

Figure 25-1. You can edit an existing view, copy an existing view, or create a completely new view.

3 Click the Edit button. The View Definition dialog box appears (see Figure 25-2). If you want to create a new view that is similar to the selected view, click the Copy button and type a new name in the Name box.

Tip **Create customized elements before you reference them**
If you plan to use customized tables, groups, or filters in a view, you must create those elements before you use them in a customized view. You must also create customized single pane views before you can include them in a combination view.

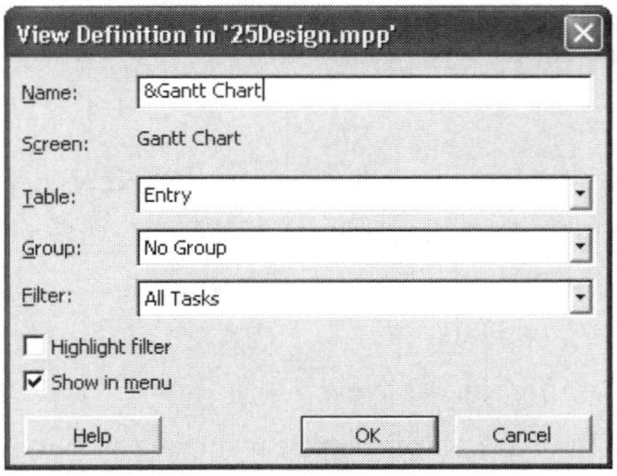

Figure 25-2. You choose a table, group, and filter when you customize a single pane view.

4. In the Table box, click the table that you want to appear in the customized view.
5. In the Group box, click the group that you want to use.
6. In the Filter box, click the filter that you want to apply.
7. If you want to highlight filtered tasks, select the Highlight Filter check box.

Inside Out

Tired of clicking More Views?

The View menu and the View bar include the views used most frequently by the majority of Microsoft Project users. However, if you prefer other views such as the Task Details Form or one of your customized views, you might get tired of clicking More Views every time you want to use them.

You can replace the default views with your favorites on the View menu and View bar. Click View, More Views. Click the view you want to add to the View menu and then click Edit. In the View Definition dialog box, select the Show In Menu check box. To remove a view that you don't use from the list, clear its Show In Menu check box.

You can also modify the order in which views appear. By default, task views appear first and in alphabetical order, followed by resource views in alphabetical order. In the More Views dialog box, click the view you want to move and then click Edit. In the Name box, add a number in front of the name to move it to the top of its respective list. If you prefix all the displayed views with a sequential number, they'll appear in numerical order.

You can prefix a view name with text to differentiate customized views from standard ones. For example, if you add the prefix "C-" at the beginning of the name of each customized view, the list will segregate your customized and standard views.

To customize the content of an existing combination view, for example, the Task Entry view or Resource Allocation view, follow these steps:

1. Click View, More Views.
2. In the More Views dialog box, click the view's name in the Views list.
3. To change the existing view, click the Edit button. To create a new view based on the existing view, click the Copy button.

   The View Definition dialog box appears.
4. In the Name box, type a new name for the view.
5. In the Top box, click the view that you want to appear in the top pane (see Figure 25-3).

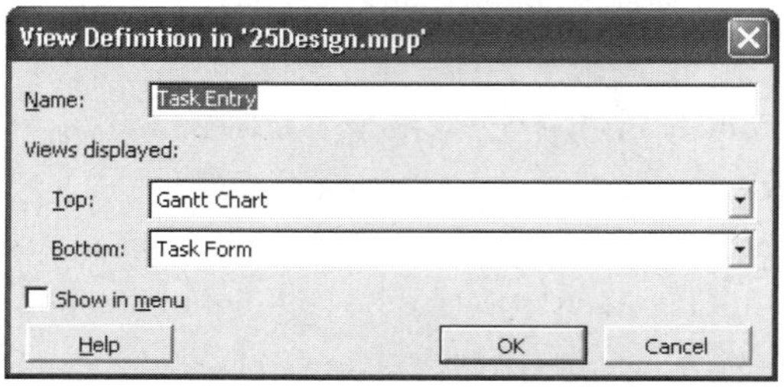

Figure 25-3. Specify which views are displayed in the top and bottom panes of a combination view.

6. In the Bottom box, click the view that you want to appear in the bottom pane.

> ## Inside Out
>
> **Change the table and view definition**
>
> Changing the table that appears in a view also changes the table in the definition of that view. That table appears the next time you display that view. However, applying a group or filter to a view does not change the group or filter selected in the View Definition dialog box. The view uses the group and filter you chose when you customized the view.
>
> When you customize an existing single pane view, the View Definition dialog box displays the type of view used, but you can't modify it. However, when you create a new single pane view, you can choose which type of view to use.

Creating a New View

If none of the existing views come close to meeting your needs, you can create an entirely new single pane or combination view. To do this, follow these steps:

1. Click View, More Views.
2. In the More Views dialog box, click New.

3 In the Define New View dialog box, select either the Single View or Combination View option and then click OK.

   The View Definition dialog box for the type of view you selected appears.

4 Specify the contents of the view, as described in the previous section, "Changing the Content of a View."

Tip **Applying a view quickly**

You can use the keyboard to choose a view from the View menu by assigning a keyboard shortcut. In the View Definition dialog box for the view, type an ampersand (&) before the letter in the view name that you want to use for the shortcut and then save the customized view.

When you want to use your keyboard shortcut, press Alt+V to open the View menu and then press the shortcut letter to apply the view. This works for built-in views as well as your custom views.

Use a different letter for each keyboard shortcut. If you choose a letter that is already in use by another menu entry, you might have to press the letter more than once to apply the view you want.

Changing the Font for a View

By default, the font used throughout the Microsoft Project views is Arial 8 points. If you prefer a different font or size for one or all text elements in a particular view, follow these steps:

1 Click Format, Text Styles.

2 In the Item To Change box, be sure that All is selected.

   This changes the font for all text elements in the current view in this project, including column and row headings, Gantt bar text, and all field data such as task and resource names.

3 Click OK.

Inside Out

No way to set an overall default font style

Suppose you have used the Text Styles dialog box to apply certain fonts to row and column titles, another style to milestone tasks, and yet another to critical tasks. However, when you switch from the Gantt Chart to the Task Usage view, you find that the fonts revert to their default style in that view.

Text styles apply only to the current view in the current project. You need to make the same changes in every view in which you want them to appear.

After you have applied your font changes to every view, you can also make these same changes available to all your projects. Copy your modified views to the global template (global.mpt) using the Organizer.

For information about copying views to the global template for use in other projects, see "Copying Customized Elements" later in this chapter on page 813.

Formatting a Gantt Chart View

The chart portion of the Gantt Chart view provides a graphical representation of your project schedule. You can emphasize information in your schedule by formatting individual Gantt bars or all Gantt bars of a certain type. Similarly, you can apply formatting to different categories of text or only to the text that is selected. Link lines and gridlines communicate information, but they can also clutter the Gantt Chart. Layout options and formatting for gridlines control how much you see of these elements.

Use the Gantt Chart Wizard

If you would rather not format each element in a Gantt Chart view, you can use the Gantt Chart Wizard to specify what information you want to see and how to format the Gantt Chart's elements. You can choose a standard type of Gantt Chart such as Critical Path or Baseline, choose from several predefined Gantt Chart styles, or create a custom Gantt Chart.

If you opt for a customized Gantt Chart, you can control which types of Gantt bars appear and customize the color, pattern, and end shapes for each type. You can choose to display resources and dates on the taskbars and choose exactly the fields you want to display. Finally, you can show or hide the link lines between dependent tasks.

Formatting the Appearance of Gantt Bars

You can modify the shape, fill pattern, and color of individual bars or all Gantt bars representing a particular type of information; for example, milestone tasks or summary tasks. You can also customize the marks that appear at the beginning and end of those bars. For example, you might want to accentuate critical tasks that aren't complete by making them red with red stars at each end.

To change the appearance of all Gantt bars of a particular type, follow these steps:

1. Click View and then click the Gantt Chart view whose bars you want to customize.

   Your modifications will apply to the Gantt bars in this specific Gantt Chart view only.

2. Click Format, Bar Styles.

   The Bar Styles dialog box lists all the Gantt bar types for the current view with the settings for their appearance (see Figure 25-4). For example, Gantt bars appear as a blue bar for normal tasks, whereas summary Gantt bars are solid black with black end marks at both ends.

Tip **Open the Bar Styles dialog box quickly**

You can also open the Bar Styles dialog box by double-clicking the background of the chart portion of a Gantt chart.

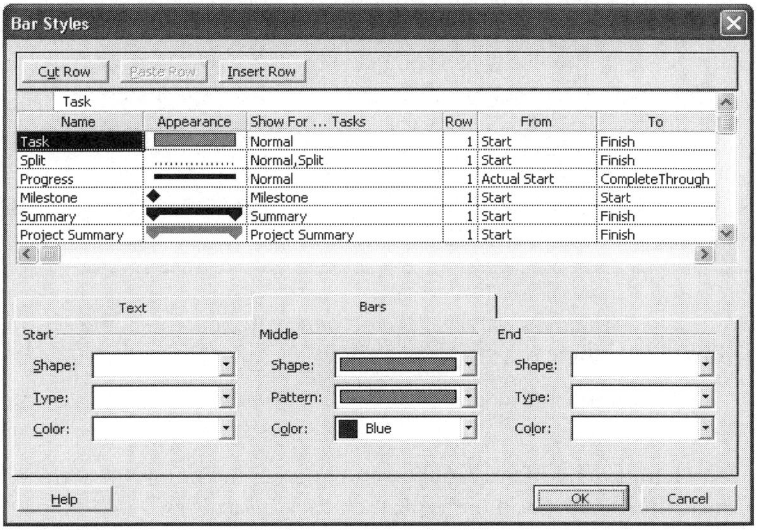

Figure 25-4. You can customize the appearance of the Gantt bar as well as markers at its start and end.

3. To change the look of a specific type of Gantt bar, click its name in the table.
4. Click the Bars tab, and then make the changes you want to the Start, Middle, and End of the bar.

   The settings for the start and end determine the appearance of the markers at the beginning and end of the bar, whereas the settings for the middle control the appearance of the bar itself.

To change the pattern, color, and shape of the Gantt bar for individual tasks (rather than all tasks of a particular type), do the following:

1. In the sheet portion of the view, click the task or tasks whose Gantt bars you want to change.
2. Click Format, Bar.
3. In the Format Bar dialog box, click the Bar Shape tab.
4. Make the changes you want to the Start (beginning marker), Middle (the bar itself), and End (ending marker).

Troubleshooting

Changing the bar style for one task changes the Gantt bars for all tasks

The Bar and Bar Styles commands on the Format menu sound similar, but they operate quite differently. The Bar command applies the changes you make to only the tasks that are currently selected. The Bar Styles command applies changes to all Gantt bars of a particular type; for example, critical tasks, incomplete tasks, or milestones.

This distinction is analogous to changing the formatting in a word processing document. You can select an individual paragraph and change the formatting to Arial 14, Bold. But if you want all headings to use this formatting, you can save time by creating a style and applying it to each heading paragraph.

In addition to changing the styles of Gantt bars, you can also define new types of Gantt bars. To do this, follow these steps:

1. Apply a Gantt Chart view.
2. Click Format, Bar Styles.
3. Scroll to the end of the list of Gantt bar types or click a row above where you want to insert your new Gantt bar type; then click Insert Row.
4. In the Name field, type the name of your new Gantt bar.
5. Click the cell in the Show For … Tasks column.
6. Click the down arrow in the box and then click the category of task for which this bar should be displayed. For example, if you're creating a style for tasks that are not finished, click Not Finished.

Tip **Create a Gantt bar style for multiple conditions**
If you want a Gantt bar style to appear when more than one condition exists, click the first condition, type a comma, and then click the second condition, such as "Critical, Not Finished." You can also create a Gantt bar that appears when a condition is not true. Type the word "Not" in front of a selected task condition, such as "Not Milestone," or "Critical, Not In Progress."

7. In the From and To columns, click the date fields that determine the beginning and end of the Gantt bar. For example, you might draw a progress bar from the Start date to the Complete Through date or a bar from the Actual Start date to the Deadline date for critical tasks that aren't yet finished.
8. Click the Bars tab and then specify the appearance for the Start, Middle, and End of the bar.

9 Click the Text tab and then click the box for the position, such as Left or Right, depending on where you want text to appear for the Gantt bar.

10 Click the down arrow in the box and then click the name of the task field whose content you want to appear for this Gantt bar type.

Tip **Create a bar style for flagged tasks**

If you want to call attention to tasks that don't meet any of the task conditions listed in the Show For... Tasks field, you can create a new bar style that applies only to marked or flagged tasks. When you mark or flag tasks, they appear in that bar style.

You can add the Marked field to the sheet portion of your Gantt chart and then set the value to Yes for each task you want to mark. If you are already using the Marked field, you can insert a column for one of the custom flag fields, such as Flag1, and set it to Yes for those tasks. In the Bar Styles dialog box, create a new bar style to show for the Marked or the custom flag field and specify its appearance and associated text.

Troubleshooting

A Gantt bar doesn't appear in the chart

A Gantt chart displays bars in the order that they appear in the Bar Styles dialog box. If Gantt bars with a narrower shape such as progress bars appear above the normal Gantt bars in the list, the wider Gantt bars hide the narrower ones.

If you rearrange the order so the narrower Gantt bars appear below the wider ones in the Bar Styles list, you can see both bars.

Inside Out

Stack the Gantt bars

Some tasks might meet the conditions for several types of Gantt bars. If this occurs, Microsoft Project draws a Gantt bar for the task for each condition that it satisfies. These bars might overlap each other and obscure some of the information you want to see.

To avoid this overlapping, you can stack up to four Gantt bars, one above the next, so they're all visible. To do this, in the Bar Styles dialog box, specify 1, 2, 3, or 4 in the Row field for each overlapping Gantt bar.

For example, suppose that you have created multiple baselines and want to review them in the Multiple Baselines Gantt. Use numbers in the Row field to stack the Gantt bars representing the different baselines.

Formatting the Appearance of Gantt Bar Text

Displaying task field values next to the Gantt bars makes it easy to correlate task information with bars in the chart. By displaying text next to Gantt bars, you can often reduce the number of columns needed in the sheet portion of the Gantt chart and display more of the chart portion.

To change the text for all Gantt bars of a particular type, follow these steps:

1. Click Format, Bar Styles.
2. Click the name of the Gantt bar type whose text you want to change.
3. Click the Text tab.
4. Click the box for the position, such as Left or Right, in which you want the text to appear for the Gantt bar.
5. Click the down arrow in the box and then click the name of the task field whose content you want to appear for this Gantt bar type.

To change the text accompanying the Gantt bar for selected tasks, do the following:

1. In the sheet portion of the view, click the task or tasks whose Gantt bar text you want to change.
2. Click Format, Bar, and click the Bar Text tab in the Format Bar dialog box.
3. On the Bar Text tab, click the box for the position—such as Left, Right, Top, or Bottom—where you want the text to appear for the Gantt bar.
4. Click the down arrow to the right of the box and then click the name of the task field whose content you want to appear for this Gantt bar (see Figure 25-5).

   For example, if you want text to appear to the right of the Gantt bar, click the Right box, click the down arrow, and then click the name of the field whose content you want to appear on the right end of this task.

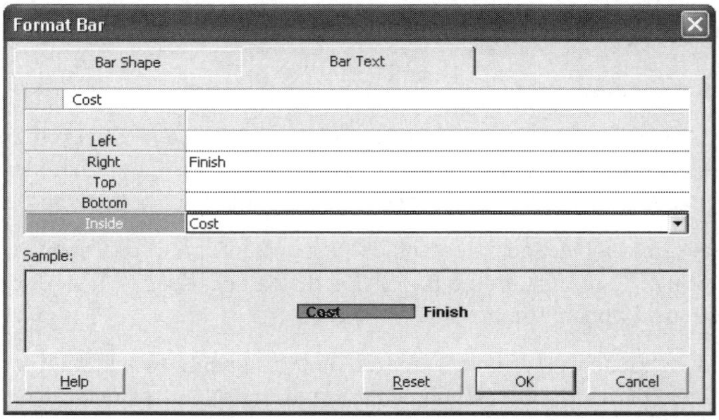

Figure 25-5. You can specify fields to display as text for selected Gantt bars.

Although you can change the text position and content for individual Gantt bars, you can't change the font, style, or color of the text. To change the text style for all Gantt bars of a particular type, follow these steps:

1. Click Format, Text Styles.
2. In the Item To Change box, click the type of task whose text style you want to change.

   For example, if you want the text accompanying all critical tasks to be 16-point red type, click Critical Tasks in the Item To Change box.
3. Make the changes you want in the Font, Font Style, Size, and Color boxes.

> **Tip** **Format text Styles and individual text**
> The Text Styles command on the Format menu formats the text for tasks of a particular type. To change the attributes of only the selected text, use the Font command instead. Click Format, Font and then choose the font, font style, size, and color.

Formatting the Layout of Gantt Bars

Link lines between dependent tasks show how tasks are related to each other. However, too many link lines can obscure the information you are trying to communicate. You might want to modify the appearance of link lines, the height of Gantt bars, or whether splits and rolled-up bars are displayed if the schedule is too cluttered. To change the layout of links and bars in a Gantt chart, do the following:

1. Click Format, Layout.
2. In the Layout dialog box, select the option for how you want the links between dependent tasks to appear.

   For example, you can hide the link lines, draw them as S-shapes between the ends of tasks, or display them as L-shapes from the end of one task to the top of another task.
3. Choose a date format to use when a date field is associated with a Gantt bar.
4. If necessary, choose the height of the Gantt bar.
5. Choose other layout options to roll up Gantt bars, draw the bar width in increments of whole days, or show splits.

   For example, if you roll up Gantt bars, summary tasks display information about their subordinate tasks. If you are fine-tuning your project schedule, you might want to view where splits occur or see the duration of tasks down to the hour.

Formatting the Appearance of Gridlines

Gridlines separate elements such as columns and rows in the sheet portion of a Gantt chart or the dates and tasks in the chart portion. For example, you might want to add horizontal lines to the chart to help correlate Gantt bars with their associated tasks in the sheet portion. To change the gridlines in a Gantt chart, follow these steps:

1. Click Format, Gridlines.

2 In the Line To Change box, click the element whose gridlines you want to add, remove, or change.
3 Elements for both the sheet portion and chart portion of the Gantt chart appear in the Line To Change list.

   The current style appears in the Normal area.
4 In the Normal section, change the line type in the Type box and the color in the Color box.
5 If you want to display lines at certain intervals, such as after every fourth item, click the interval in the At Interval section.

For information about modifying the timescale in the Gantt chart, see "Modifying the Timescale," later in this chapter on page 783.

Change the Format of a View

Formatting changes you make within a view apply only to the active view. For example, modifications you make to the chart, bar, or text styles, individual Gantt bars, or text formatting in the Tracking Gantt appear only when you display the Tracking Gantt. You can customize the formatting for each view without worrying about modifying all the others.

Also, changes you make to views in one project file apply only to that project file. When you create a new project file, it uses the default views.

If you want to make customized views available to other project files, see "Sharing Customized Elements Among Projects," later in this chapter on page 812.

Modifying a Network Diagram

Network diagrams display tasks as boxes, or nodes, with link lines showing the task dependencies. Because a network diagram doesn't include a task sheet like the Gantt chart, it's important to specify the information that you want to appear inside the boxes. You can customize the appearance of the boxes or how they are arranged within the diagram.

Formatting the Content and Appearance of Boxes

Just as you can change the appearance of Gantt bars for different types of tasks, you can modify the boxes in a network diagram depending on the task type. You can also control what task information appears inside those boxes.

To change the appearance and content for all boxes of a particular type, do the following:

1 Click View, Network Diagram.
2 Click Format, Box Styles.

The Box Styles dialog box lists all the box types for the current view and the settings for their appearance (see Figure 25-6).

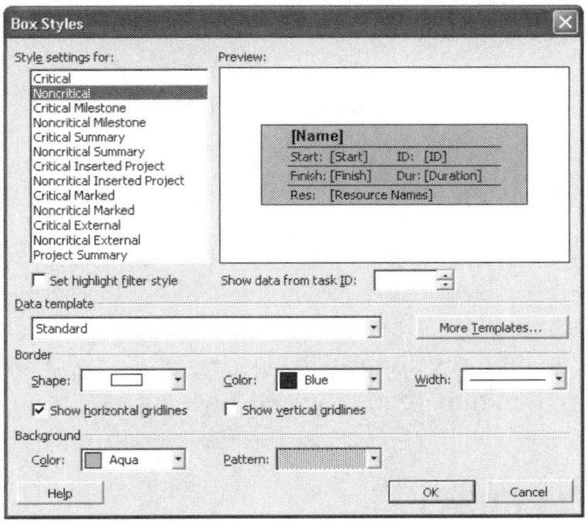

Figure 25-6. You can customize the appearance of a network diagram box as well as specify what task information appears inside each box.

3 To customize a specific type of box, click its name in the list.

4 To change the fields that appear within the box, click a data template in the Data Template box.

A preview of the box using the selected data template appears.

Tip **Show other information in a Network Diagram**

You can also modify or create new data templates for the boxes in the Network Diagram. For example, you might want to include a custom field in a data template. Click More Templates, click a template name, and then click Edit or Copy. To create a new template, click New. To insert a field into the data template, click the cell where you want to insert the field, click the down arrow, and then click the name of the field in the list.

You can also add fields that display graphical indicators to the template.

5 If necessary, change the shape, color, and width of the box border.

6 If you want to display horizontal or vertical gridlines between the fields inside a box, select the Show Horizontal Gridlines and Show Vertical Gridlines check boxes.

7 If necessary, choose a background color and pattern.

Caution Although you can select different colors and patterns for the box background, any combination other than solid white makes it difficult to read the task information.

To change the displayed fields and border appearance for individual boxes (rather than all boxes showing a particular type of project information), follow these steps:

1. Choose the boxes you want to format in the Network Diagram.
2. Click Format, Box.
3. In the Data Template box, click the data template you want to use.
   A preview of the box using the selected data template appears.
4. Make the changes you want to the shape, color, and width of the border.
5. Make the changes you want to the background color and pattern for the box.

Tip **Access the Format dialog box**
You can open the Format Box dialog box by double-clicking the border of a box. Double-clicking the background of a Network Diagram opens the Box Styles dialog box.

Formatting the Layout of Boxes

The Network Diagram is much like a flowchart of the tasks in a project. The layout options for the Network Diagram control how boxes are positioned and aligned, the distance between the boxes, the appearance of links, and other settings.

To change the layout of a Network Diagram, do the following:

1. Click Format, Layout.
   The Layout dialog box appears.
2. To position boxes manually by dragging, select the Allow Manual Box Positioning option.
3. In the Arrangement box, choose the order in which boxes are placed on the diagram.
   For example, you can arrange the boxes from the top left down to the bottom right of the diagram. You can choose to place critical tasks before others.
4. Choose the alignment, distance between rows and columns, and the width and height of the boxes.
5. Select link options such as whether to draw lines orthogonally or directly between boxes, whether to include arrows and link labels.
6. If necessary, choose link colors.

Tip **Fine-tune the display of the Network Diagram**
If you select the option to position boxes automatically, it's a good idea to also select the Adjust For Page Breaks check box in the Box Layout section. Otherwise, boxes located across a page break are printed on two pages in the diagram.

Summary tasks are difficult to distinguish in a Network Diagram, so you might want to clear the Show Summary Tasks check box. If you display summary tasks, it's best to select the Keep Tasks With Their Summaries check box.

Modifying the Resource Graph

The Resource Graph presents resource allocation, cost, or work over periods of time. The horizontal axis represents time; whereas the vertical axis represents units such as availability, cost, or work. You can choose the fields that you want to appear in the graph. You can also modify the appearance of bars and text of particular types and change the gridlines in the graph. However, you cannot modify the appearance of individual bars or text.

Modifying the Appearance of Resource Graph Bars

The Bar Styles dialog box for the Resource Graph contains four areas, each of which controls the appearance of bars for different sets of information. For example, if you graph overallocations, the two top areas display overallocations, whereas the bottom areas display allocations less than or equal to the maximum available units. The areas on the left side of the dialog box control the way group data appear. The areas on the right side of the dialog box control the appearance of data for one selected resource.

Follow these steps to modify the appearance of Resource Graph bars of a particular type:

1. Click View, Resource Graph.
2. Click Format, Bar Styles.

   Because the bars in the Resource Graph represent information that you don't see in the Gantt chart, the Bar Styles dialog box for the Resource Graph contains different settings than the Bar Styles dialog box for Gantt charts (see Figure 25-7).

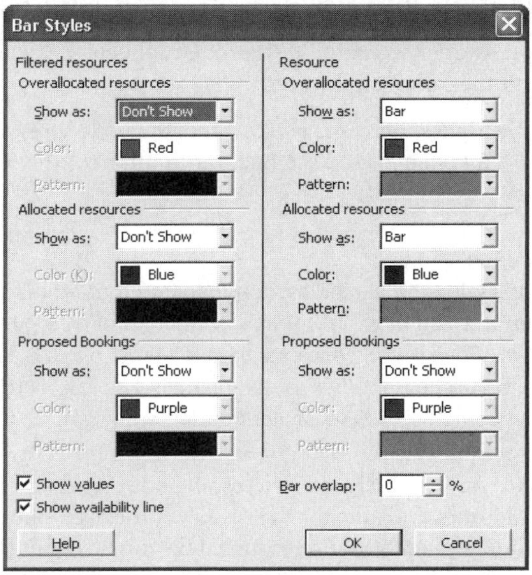

Figure 25-7. You can choose which field to display in the Resource Graph for individual resources and groups of resources.

3 In the Bar Styles dialog box, choose the types of data you want to show, for example, allocated resources or proposed bookings.

For any information you do show, specify the color and pattern for its representative bars.

> **Inside Out**
>
> **Determine what the Resource Graph shows**
>
> When the Resource Graph appears in the bottom pane below a task view, the graph shows the values for only one resource. When the Resource Graph appears below a resource view or in the top pane, it displays the values for all tasks. It can display the data for one resource or a group of resources; or compare data for one resource to a group. If you want to see only the data for the selected resource, click Don't Show in the Show As box for Filtered Resources. However, if you want to compare the values of the selected resource to other resources in a filter, click one of the other graph methods in the Filtered Resources area. To differentiate overallocations from regular assignments, choose methods, colors, or patterns in the Overallocated and Allocated areas of the dialog box.
>
> In addition, when you view any of the fields that relate to work or resource availability, you can select the Show Availability Line check box to display resource availability on the graph.

Changing the Information that Appears in the Resource Graph

To choose which values you want to see in the Resource Graph, click Format, Details. A shortcut menu appears with the following choices:

Peak Units. Represents the highest percentage of units assigned to a resource during each period on the graph. Units that exceed the maximum units for the resource appear as an overallocation.

> **Caution** **Peak units can be misleading**
> Peak units are helpful for analyzing the allocation of a resource that represents more than one person, such as Painters, which might have maximum units of 400 percent for a four-person painter pool. However, if one resource is assigned full-time to two 2-day tasks during one week, Peak Units equals 200 percent (two tasks multiplied by 100 percent allocation) even though the person can complete 4 days of work during one week.

Work. Displays the amount of work assigned to a resource during the period. If the hours exceed the number of hours available for the resource, the excess hours appear as an overallocation. The hours available for a resource take into account the resource calendar and the resource's maximum units.

Cumulative Work. Displays the total work assigned to the resource since the project began.

Overallocation. Includes only the hours that the resource is overallocated during the period, not work hours that fit in the resource's workday.

Percent Allocation. Represents the work assigned to a resource as a percentage of his available time.

Remaining Availability. Shows the number of hours that the resource is available. This graph is helpful when you are trying to find someone to work on a new task.

Cost. Displays the labor cost and per-use cost of a resource for the period. The total cost of a task appears in the period in which the task begins or ends, if resource costs accrue at the start or end.

Cumulative Cost. Shows the running total of the cost since the start of the project. This choice can show the total cost of a project when you display the value for a group that includes all the project resources.

Work Availability. Represents the number of hours that a resource could work based on his or her maximum units and resource calendar. It doesn't take into account any existing assignments.

Unit Availability. Displays the same information as Work Availability, formatted as a percentage.

> **Tip** **Modifying field formats**
> You can control how information is formatted in the Resource Graph.
>
> To change the unit for work, click Tools, Options and then click the Schedule tab. In the Work Is Entered In box, select the time unit you want for work.
>
> To change the currency format for costs, click Tools, Options and then click the View tab. Under Currency Options, specify the currency format you want.

To modify which information appears in the Resource Graph, follow these steps:

1. Right-click the background of the Resource Graph and then click the type of information to be displayed in the Resource Graph.

   For example, if you are trying to eliminate the overallocations for a resource, click Overallocation or Percent Overallocation. On the other hand, if you are looking for an available resource, click Remaining Availability.

2. If necessary, right-click the background of the Resource Graph, and then click Bar Styles to adjust the appearance of the information.

   For example, you can view overallocations for the selected resource and others in the same resource group (see Figure 25-8).

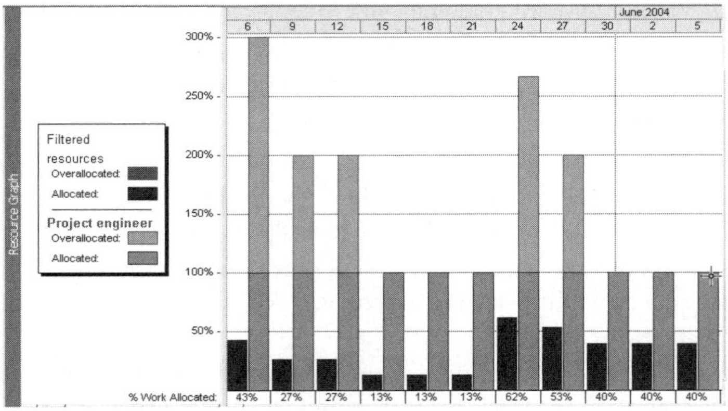

Figure 25-8. The Resource Graph can show information for one selected resource and a group of resources.

For information about modifying the text styles or gridlines in the Resource Graph, follow the steps described in "Format Text Styles and Individual Text" and "Formatting the Appearance of Gridlines," earlier in this chapter on page 771.

Modifying the Calendar View

You can customize the bar styles, text styles, layout, gridlines, and timescale for task bars in the Calendar view.

To modify the bar styles for a particular type of task, do the following:

1. Click View, Calendar.
2. Click Format, Bar Styles.

   Because the bars in the Calendar view represent information that you don't see in the Gantt chart, the Bar Styles dialog box for Calendars contains different settings from the Bar Styles dialog box for Gantt charts.
3. To change the appearance of a specific type of Calendar bar, click its name in the Task Type list; for example, Noncritical or Marked.
4. Under Bar Shape, specify the Bar Type, Pattern, Color, and Split Pattern for the Calendar bar.
5. In the Field(s) box under Text, click the field that you want to appear inside the Calendar bar.

   If you want to show the contents of multiple fields with the Calendar bar, separate the fields with a comma. For example, to see the task name and resource initials, select the Name field, type a comma, and then select Resource Initials (see Figure 25-9).

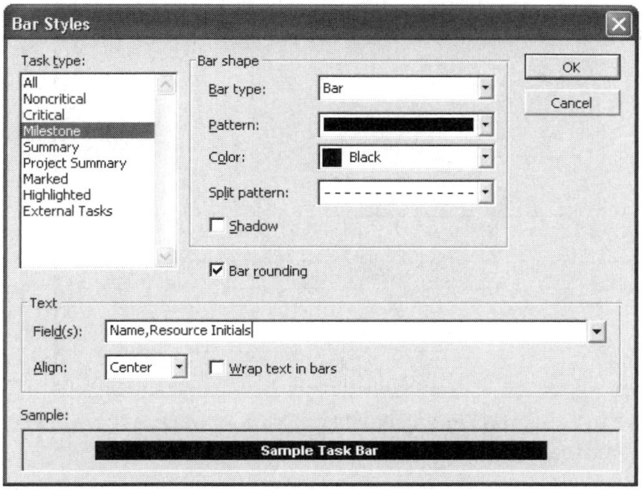

Figure 25-9. Use the Bar Styles dialog box for the Calendar view to specify bar formatting and field content for various types of Calendar bars.

To modify the arrangement of tasks in the Calendar, follow these steps:

1. Click Format, Layout.

   The Layout dialog box for the Calendar view appears.

2. To display as many tasks as you can in the Calendar boxes, select the Attempt To Fit As Many Boxes As Possible option.

   This option sorts tasks by Total Slack and then by Duration. Otherwise, tasks appear in the current sort order.

3. Select the Automatic Layout check box to reapply the layout options as you add, remove, or sort tasks.

To modify the timescale in the Calendar, do the following:

1. Click Format, Timescale.
2. In the Timescale dialog box, click the Week Headings tab and then choose the titles that you want to appear for months, weeks, and days in the calendar (see Figure 25-10).

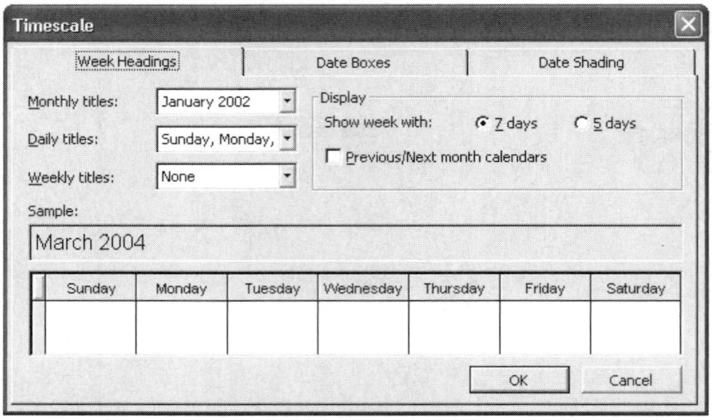

Figure 25-10. Use the Timescale dialog box for the Calendar view to specify the Calendar timescale's appearance.

3. Select the 7 Days option to display all days in a week, or select the 5 Days option to display the work days.
4. Select the Previous/Next Month Calendars check box to show a preview of the previous and following months in the view.
5. Click the Date Boxes tab to specify the information you want to appear in the heading for each date box.
6. Click the Date Shading tab to customize how working and nonworking time for base and resource calendars appear on the calendar.

For information about modifying the text styles or gridlines in the Calendar, follow the steps described in "Format Text Styles and Individual Text" and "Formatting the Appearance of Gridlines," earlier in this chapter on page 771.

Modifying a Sheet View

The Resource Sheet and the Task Sheet display information about your project resources and tasks in a tabular layout. The Task Sheet appears as the sheet portion of a Gantt chart. You can change the table that appears in the sheet view along with the height of rows and width of columns.

For more information about customizing text, see the sidebar, "Format Text Styles and Individual Text," earlier in this chapter on page 771.

To change the table in the sheet view, click View, More Views. Click a sheet view, for example, Task Sheet or Resource Sheet, and then click Apply.

Another method is to right-click the Select All box in the upper-left corner of the table (above row 1). A shortcut menu appears with tables for the sheet view. Click the name of the table that you want to appear.

For example, to see costs in the Task Sheet, click Cost on the shortcut menu. If the table you want doesn't appear on the shortcut menu, click More Tables and then double-click the table you want in the Tables list.

To resize a column in the sheet, use one of the following methods:

- Position the mouse pointer between two column headings until it changes to a two-headed arrow and then double-click the column edge to resize the column to fit all the values in the column.
- Position the mouse pointer between two column headings until it changes to a two-headed arrow and then drag the column on the left to the desired width.
- Double-click the column heading to display the Column Definition dialog box. Click the column width in the Width box or click Best Fit.

> **Tip** **Display column headings the way you want**
> As of Project 2002, text wrapping is provided for header cells in a table as well as manual header row height adjustment. To adjust the row height automatically to display the entire column title, click View, Table and then click More Tables. Click the table you want to modify and then click Edit. In the Table Definition dialog box, select the Auto-Adjust Header Row Heights check box.

You can change the height of one or more rows in a sheet.

For information about resizing all rows in a table, see "Customizing Tables," later in this chapter on page 785.

Do the following to resize individual rows in a sheet:

1. To make a row taller, position the mouse pointer between the two row headings (beneath the row's ID number) until the mouse pointer changes to a two-headed arrow and then drag downward.
2. To make a row shorter, position the mouse pointer between the two row headings (beneath the row's ID number) until the mouse pointer changes to a two-headed arrow and then drag upward.

For information about inserting, deleting, moving, and copying rows and columns in a table, see "Customizing Tables," later in this chapter on page 785.

Modifying a Usage View

Usage views, such as the Resource Usage and Task Usage view, display information divided across time periods. Usage views include a sheet view in the left pane and a *timephased* grid (the timesheet) with the field details in the right pane. You can customize the sheet and the timescale for the timesheet as you can in the Gantt Chart and other views. You can also choose which fields you want to see in the timesheet.

To select and format the timephased fields shown in the timesheet in a usage view, follow these steps:

1. Click View, Resource Usage or choose another usage view.
2. Right-click the timesheet, click Detail Styles, and then click the Usage Details tab.

   The Usage Details tab lists the different timephased fields you can display in the timesheet, such as Work, Actual Work, Overtime Work, and Cost (see Figure 25-11).

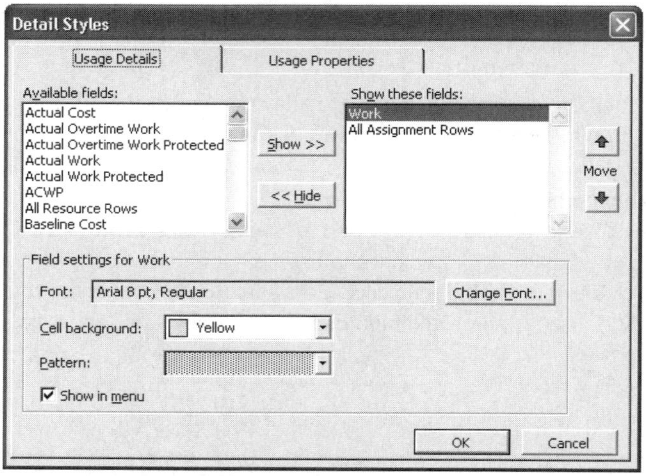

Figure 25-11. Choose the fields to display and their formatting in the Detail Styles dialog box.

3. In the Available Fields list, click the fields you want to add to the timesheet portion of the Usage View and then click Show.
4. To remove a field from showing in the timesheet, click its name in the Show These Fields list and then click Hide.
5. To change the order in which fields appear, click a field in the Show These Fields list and then click the Move up or down arrow buttons.

Move up

6. Choose the font, color, and pattern for the selected field if you want to change its appearance in the timesheet.

Tip **Adding fields in the timesheet**

To quickly add a field, right-click the timesheet and then click the field you want to add on the shortcut menu. A check box appears in front of the field name on the shortcut menu, and another row of timephased information appears in the timesheet for each task.

To remove a field from the timesheet, right-click the timesheet, and click the field you want to remove on the shortcut menu.

The Usage Properties tab in the Detail Styles dialog box includes the following options for formatting the detail headers and the data within the timesheet:

- If you want to align the data in the timesheet cells, click Right, Left, or Center in the Align Details Data box.
- If you can't see the field names on the left side of the timesheet, click Yes in the Display Details Header Column box.
- If the field names are missing in some of the rows, select the Repeat Details Header On All Assignment Rows check box.
- If the field names take up too much space, select the Display Short Detail Header Names check box.

For information about modifying the text styles or gridlines in a Usage view, follow the steps described in "Format Text Styles and Individual Text" and "Formatting the Appearance of Gridlines," earlier in this chapter on page 771. For information about formatting the sheet portion of the Usage view, see "Modifying a Sheet View," later in this chapter on page 780, and "Customizing Tables," later in this chapter on page 785. For information about formatting the timescale, see "Modifying the Timescale" below.

The values in the timesheet often exceed the width of the columns. Instead of adjusting the width of columns in the Timescale dialog box, you can resize them in the Usage view timesheet with the mouse. To resize columns in the timesheet, follow these steps:

1. Position the mouse pointer between two column headings in the timesheet until it changes to a two-headed arrow.
2. Drag the pointer to the left or right until the columns are the desired width.

   If the usage view is part of a combination view that's displaying a timesheet in both panes, changing the column width in one pane changes the width in the other pane so the timesheet columns always line up.

Modifying the Timescale

The timescale is a prominent feature in many Microsoft Project views, such as Gantt chart and usage views. You can display up to three timescales in a view. For each timescale, you can customize the units, the labels for time periods, and the label alignment. You can also display a calendar or fiscal year. In addition, you can choose how many timescales you want to use as well as the width of each period in the timescale.

Changes you make to the timescale apply only to the active view, but those changes become a permanent part of that view definition. Your timescale customizations appear each time you display that view.

To set the options for one or more tiers in the timescale, do the following:

1. Display a view that contains a timescale, such as Gantt Chart, Task Usage, or Resource Graph.
2. Right-click the timescale heading and then click Timescale on the shortcut menu.

   The Timescale dialog box appears.
3. The Timescale dialog box has four tabs (see Figure 25-12): Top Tier, Middle Tier, Bottom Tier, and Non-Working Time. The Middle Tier tab is displayed by default. In the

Show list under Timescale Options, click the number of tiers you want to display (one, two, or three).

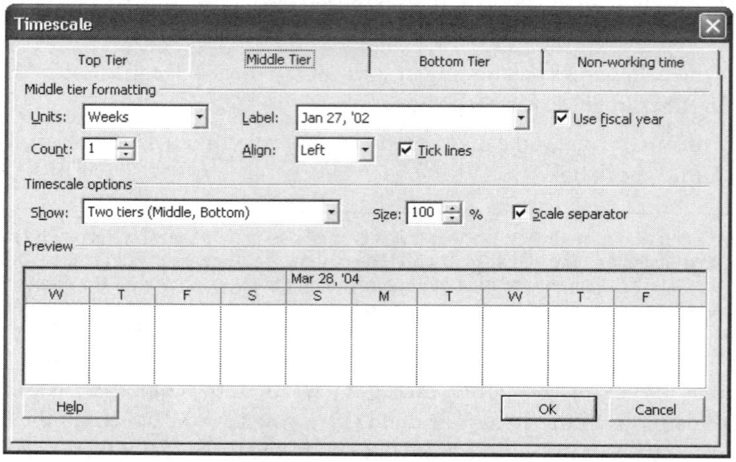

Figure 25-12. Customize the time periods that appear in a Gantt Chart, Task Usage, or Resource Graph view.

4 To change the width of the timescale columns, click a percentage in the Size box.
5 Select the Scale Separator check box to draw lines between each timescale tier.

To set the options for each timescale tier, follow these steps:

1 In the Timescale dialog box, click the tab for the timescale tier you want to customize.
2 In the Units box, specify the time unit you want to display for the current tier. For example, you might choose Quarters for the top tier if your organization's financial performance depends on this project.

> **Caution** The time unit in a lower tier must be shorter than the unit for the tier above it. For example, if the top tier time unit is months, the middle tier can't be years.

3 To display the fiscal year in the timescale, select the Use Fiscal Year check box.
4 To display an interval of more than one unit, choose the number of units in the Count box.

   For example, to display two-week intervals, click Weeks in the Units box and 2 in the Count box.

5 To change the label format, choose a format in the Label box; for example, 1st Quarter, Qtr 1, 2004, or 1Q04.
6 Click Left, Right, or Center in the Align box to position the label in the timescale.
7 If you chose to display more than one tier, click the tabs for the other tiers and repeat Steps 2 through 6.

Caution When you click the Zoom In or Zoom Out buttons on the Standard toolbar or click Zoom on the View menu, changes you make to the labels in the timescales disappear.

You can also control how nonworking time appears in the timescale. To set the nonworking time options in the timescale, do the following:

1. In the Timescale dialog box, click the Non-Working Time tab.
2. To display nonworking time using the same format as that for working time, select the Do Not Draw check box.
3. If you display the nonworking time, choose the color and pattern for the nonworking time shading.
4. Choose the calendar whose nonworking time you want to display in the Calendar box.

Tip **Changing nonworking time**
The Non-Working Time tab in the Timescale dialog box changes the appearance of nonworking time. To modify the schedule for nonworking time, click Tools, Change Working Time; or right-click the timescale heading and then click Change Working Time.

For more information about changing working and nonworking time, see "Setting Your Project Calendar" on page 70.

Customizing Tables

Sheet views, such as the Task Sheet and Resource Sheet, and Gantt Chart, display a table of data. If the information you want doesn't appear in the current table, you can switch tables or modify the table contents. You can customize the contents of a table directly in the view or through the Table Definition dialog box.

For information on switching the table applied to a sheet view, as well as working tables in general, see "Using Tables" on page 112.

Inside Out

Permanent changes to table definition

Table changes you make in the view change the table definition. If you insert or remove columns, modify the column attributes in the Column Definition dialog box, or adjust the column width using the mouse, the table definition changes to reflect those modifications.

Because it is so easy to make changes to a table in a view, it's important to remember that those changes become a permanent part of that table's definition. If you want to keep the current table the way it is, make a copy of it and then make your modifications to the copy.

Modifying the Columns in a Table

You can add, move, remove, or modify columns in any table. To modify the definition of an existing table, follow these steps:

1. Right-click the Select All cell in the upper-left corner of the sheet above row 1; then click More Tables on the shortcut menu.

   The More Tables dialog box appears with the current table selected.
2. Click the Edit button.

> **Tip** **Create a table quickly**
>
> To use the current table as a template for a new table, click Copy instead of Edit. To use a different table as a template, click that table's name and then click Copy.

3. The Table Definition dialog box shown in Figure 25-13 appears. If necessary, type a descriptive name in the Name box.

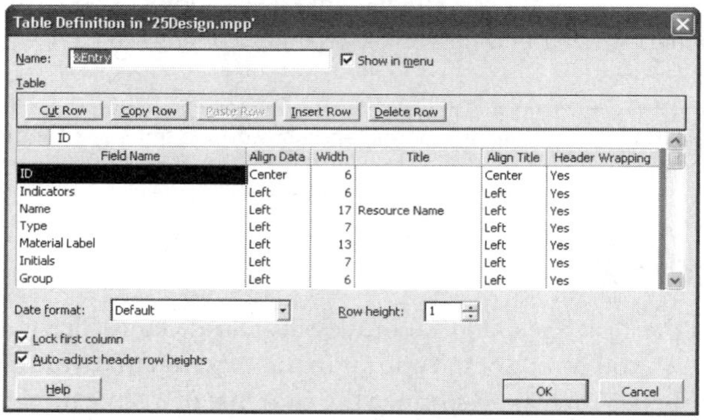

Figure 25-13. Customize the columns for a table in the Table Definition dialog box.

   If you want this table to appear on the Table menu, select the Show In Menu check box.

To move a column in the table, move fields in the rows in the Table Definition grid by doing the following:

1. Click the field name you want to move and then click Cut Row.
2. Click the row above where you want to insert the field.
3. Click Paste Row to insert the field at the new location.

You can add columns to the end of the table definition grid or insert them where you want. To insert a column into the table, follow these steps:

1. In the Table Definition dialog box, click the row in the grid above where you want to insert the field.
2. Click Insert Row to insert a blank row in the list.
3. Click the Field Name cell, and click the field name you want in the list.

Caution Pressing Enter is the same as clicking OK; either action closes the Table Definition dialog box. To complete the row with default entries, press Tab or click another cell in the list.

4 Specify the alignment of the data and the column heading as well as the width of the column.

   If you want the column heading text to wrap, click Yes in the Header Wrapping cell.

5 To display text other than the field name in the column header, type the text you want to appear in the column header in the Title cell.

Troubleshooting

You can't find the field you want to add in the Field Name list

When you're editing a task table, only task fields appear in the Field Name list. Likewise, when you edit a resource table, you can add only resource fields. Assignment fields appear only when you edit Usage views.

Similarly, if you can't find the table you want to modify, you might have the wrong type of view displayed. In the More Tables dialog box, select the Task or Resource option to display the list of task or resource tables.

To remove a column from a table, follow these steps:

1 In the Table Definition dialog box, click the field name for the column you want to remove.

2 Click Delete Row.

Modifying Other Table Options

You can customize other properties of a table in the Table Definition dialog box. For example, you can specify the format of dates or set a row height for all rows.

To set other table options, do the following:

1 In the Table Definition dialog box, click the format you want for any date fields in the table in the Date Format box.

   If you don't change this setting, the table uses the default date format for the entire project.

2 To change the height of the rows in the table, click a number in the Row Height box.

   This number represents a multiple of the standard row height.

3 To adjust the height of the header row to make room for the full column title, select the Auto-Adjust Header Row Heights check box.

Inside Out

Lock the first column for scrolling

If a table includes numerous columns, you might have to scroll in the sheet portion of the view to see them. But it's difficult to enter data in the correct cells when you can't see the task name column. You can keep a column in view by moving it to the first column and then selecting the Lock First Column option in the Table Definition dialog box.

To lock the Task Name column, in the Table Definition dialog box, click Name in the Field Name column and then click Cut Row. Click the first row in the Field Name list and then click Paste Row to insert the Name field in the first row in the list. Select the Lock First Column check box. The Task Name appears in the first column and does not disappear as you scroll.

Creating a New Table

If none of the existing tables even come close to meeting your needs, you can create a completely new table. To do this, follow these steps:

1. Click View, Table and then click More Tables.
2. In the More Tables dialog box, select the Task or Resource option to create a task or resource table, respectively.
3. Click New.

   The Table Definition dialog box appears with a default name in the Name box.
4. Enter a new descriptive name in the Name box.
5. If you want this table to appear in the View menu and View bar, select the Show In Menu check box.
6. Continue by adding the fields you want to appear in the table.

For information about how to add fields to a table, see "Modifying the Columns in a Table," earlier in this chapter on page 786.

Customizing Fields

The project database comes with a complete set of fields of varying data types. When you double-click a column heading or click Insert, Column, the Column Definition dialog box appears. In this dialog box, you can modify a few attributes, such as the title or alignment, for some of these built-in fields. Or you might change the font of the fields that appear in a row for a particular task. However, you cannot change what those fields represent or how they are calculated.

For more information about adding fields to tables, see "Using Fields" on page 120. For a complete list of available Microsoft Project fields and their descriptions, see Appendix B, "Field Reference."

If you want to track information that Microsoft Project does not monitor, you can create your own custom fields and add them to tables in your views. For example, you might want to track overhead costs that are calculated based on a combination of task duration, number of resources, and material resources consumed.

Microsoft Project provides several custom fields of each type for tasks and additional custom fields of each type for resources. In addition, there are sets of custom outline codes for both tasks and resources. Microsoft Office Project Professional 2003 provides similar sets of enterprise-level custom codes and custom outline codes. With Project Professional 2003, you can define project-related custom fields in addition to task and resource fields.

The custom fields are as follows:

Cost. Cost1 through Cost10 expressed in currency

Date. Date1 through Date10 expressed as a date

Duration. Duration1 through Duration10 expressed as time

Finish. Finish1 through Finish10 expressed as a date

Flag. Flag1 through Flag20 expressed as Yes/No flags

Number. Number1 through Number20 expressed as numeric data

Start. Start1 through Start10 expressed as a date

Text. Text1 through Text30 expressed as alphanumeric text up to 255 characters

Outline Code. Outline Code1 through Outline Code10 (the outline code format is defined by a *code mask*)

> **Caution** Even though the Start and Finish fields appear in the Custom Field list, Microsoft Project uses these fields to store the dates for interim baseline plans. If you intend to save interim baselines in your project, don't use the custom Start and Finish fields. Information in those fields will be overwritten when you save an interim baseline. Instead, use custom Date fields for your customized dates.

Customizing a Field

Custom fields already exist; you can't introduce new fields into the project database. Unlike the standard fields in the Microsoft Project database, you can modify the valid values for custom fields or specify how their values are calculated. You can control how their summary values are determined. If you don't want to display the values for a custom field, you can substitute graphical indicators.

Follow these steps to customize a field:

1. Click Tools, Customize, Fields.

   The Customize Fields dialog box appears.
2. Click the Custom Fields tab to display the options for a custom field (see Figure 25-14).

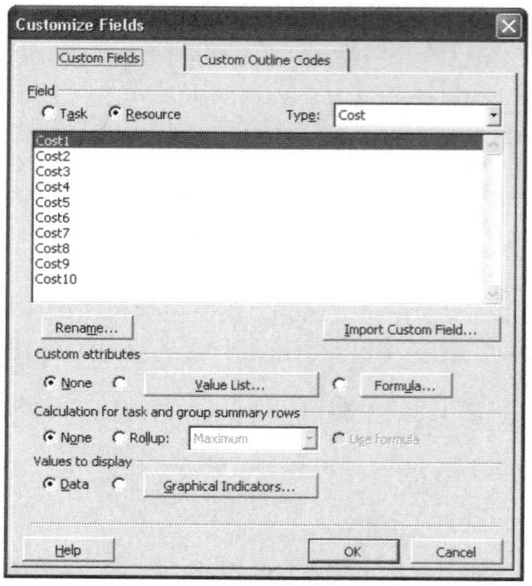

Figure 25-14. Create an alias, a list of values, a formula for calculation, or set additional options for a custom field.

3 Select the Task or Resource option to specify whether this will be a task or resource field.

4 Choose the type of custom field you want to customize in the Type box.

Troubleshooting

The custom field name isn't as informative as a column heading in a table

You can change the title that appears in a column heading by clicking the heading and typing text for the heading in the title box. For example, you might use a title such as Overhead Cost instead of Cost1 in the column heading. Changing the title in this way affects the heading only in that table. If you include the Cost1 field in another table, the column heading reverts to the field name.

You can create an alias for a custom field so the alias appears instead of the field name each time you use the field. In the Customize Fields dialog box, click Rename. Enter a descriptive name for the field. The alias and the original field name both appear in field lists.

Specifying the Values for a Custom Field

You can control the values that a custom field accepts. You can specify a list of valid values for a custom field or define a formula to calculate the result. If you do not specify a list of values or a formula, the custom field will accept any entry as long as it meets the requirements for the data type.

To specify a list of values that appears in a custom field list, do the following:

1 In the Customize Fields dialog box, click Value List.

The Value List dialog box appears (see Figure 25-15).

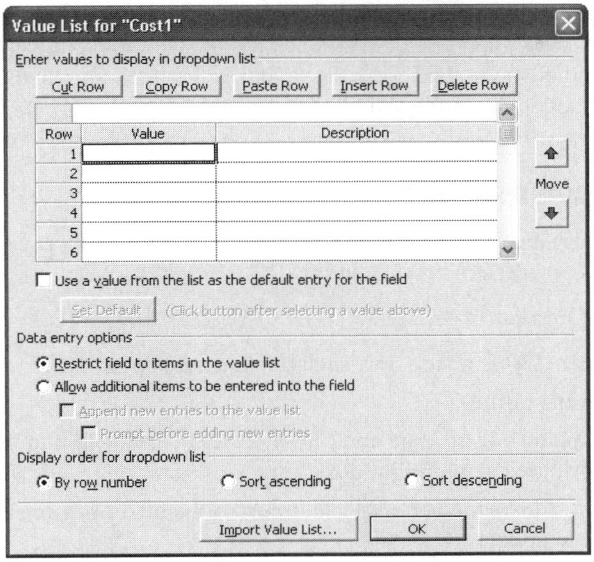

Figure 25-15. Specify the values to appear in a list for a custom field.

2 Click a blank cell in the Value column and then type the value. In the Description cell in the same row, add the corresponding description.

> **Tip** **Modifying custom field values**
> You can insert new values, remove existing values, or rearrange the values by clicking Cut Row, Copy Row, Paste Row, Insert Row, or Delete Row. You can also rearrange the order of the values by clicking the up and down arrows.

3 To specify one of the values as the default, select the Use A Value From The List As The Default Entry For The Field check box. Click the cell that contains the default value, and then click Set Default.

The default value appears in red.

4 To prevent users from entering values not in the list, select the Restrict Field To Items In The Value List option.

If you choose to allow other entries in the custom field, you can add them to the value list automatically by selecting the Allow Additional Items To Be Entered Into The Field option and Append New Entries To The Value List check box. It's good practice to also select the Prompt Before Adding New Entries check box to prevent typographical errors from creating new values in the list.

5 Select one of the options to order the values. The By Row Number option displays the values in the order you enter them in the list. You can also sort the values in ascending or descending order.

> **Tip** **Using existing values in a new custom field**
> If you already created a value list that contains the entries you want in another custom field or in another project, click Import Value List. Click the project that contains the value list; select the option for the type of field (Task, Resource, or Project), and then click the name of the custom field that contains the value list.

Creating a Calculated Field

You can calculate the value of a custom field by defining a formula made up of functions and other fields in the Microsoft Project database.

To define a formula for a calculated field, follow these steps:

1. In the Customize Fields dialog box, click the Formula option.
2. Click the Formula button.

   The Formula dialog box appears and displays the custom field name followed by an equal sign above the Formula Edit box.
3. To add a field to the formula, click Field, point to the field category, and then click the field you want to add.
4. To type a value in the formula, click the location in the formula where you want to insert the value and then type the text or number.
5. To add a function to the formula, click one of the function buttons; or click Function, point to the function category, and then click the function you want to add.
6. To direct the order that functions execute, insert parentheses in the formula (see Figure 25-16).

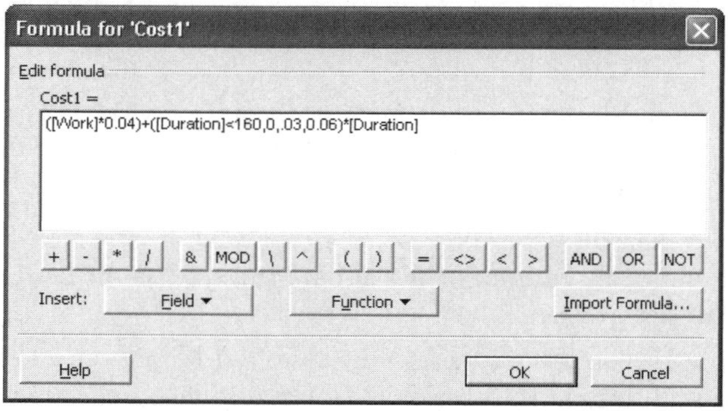

Figure 25-16. Build a formula using numerous functions and any field in the Project database.

Share formulas with other projects

You can share most customized elements between projects by copying them with the Organizer. Although the Organizer has tabs for most elements, a tab for formulas doesn't exist. To copy a formula between projects, you have to copy the custom field whose definition contains the formula.

For more information about sharing elements, see "Sharing Customized Elements among Projects" later in this chapter on page 812.

You can also import the formula from a custom field in another project into a custom field in the active project. In the Formula dialog box, click Import Formula. In the Import Formula dialog box, click the project that contains the formula; select the option for the type of field (Task, Resource, or Project), and then click the name of the custom field that contains the formula.

Calculating Group and Summary Values

By default, Microsoft Project does not calculate values for custom fields for summary tasks or for the rows containing rolled-up values for groups. However, you can specify how to calculate a value for summary rows. To use the same formula that you defined for the custom field, select the Use Formula option under Calculation For Task And Group Summary Rows in the Customize Fields dialog box. If you select the Rollup option, you can choose from several simple calculations including the following:

Average. The average of all nonsummary values underneath the summary task or group.

Average First Sublevel. The average of all the values of tasks one level below.

Maximum. The largest value of all nonsummary values.

Minimum. The smallest value for all nonsummary values.

Sum. The sum of all nonsummary values underneath the summary task or group.

When you work with a custom number field, the following calculations also appear when you select the Rollup option:

Count All. The number of summary and nonsummary tasks one level below the summary task or group.

Count First Sublevel. The number of nonsummary and summary tasks one level below the summary task or group.

Count Nonsummaries. The number of nonsummary tasks below the summary task or group.

Do the following to pick a mathematical function for a rollup value:

1. Select the Rollup option.
2. Click one of the functions in the Rollup list.

Working with Graphical Indicators

You can use graphical indicators to represent the text or values of a custom field. You can use these indicators to make values easier to understand or to hide numeric values from some audiences. For example, you might want to display a green light when a task is ahead of schedule; a yellow light when a task is slightly behind schedule; and a red light when a task is more than two weeks late.

To display graphical indicators instead of values for nonsummary rows, follow these steps:

1. Open the Customize Fields dialog box and the Custom Fields tab.
2. Under Values To Display, select the Graphical Indicators option and then click the Graphical Indicators button.

   The Graphical Indicators dialog box appears.
3. To assign graphical indicators to nonsummary rows, select the Nonsummary Rows option.
4. In the table, click the first empty cell in the Test column, click the down arrow, and then click the test you want to apply for an indicator; for example, Equals or Is Less Than.
5. Enter the value for the test in the Value(s) cell.

   You can enter a number or other string, or you can select a field whose contents become the value.

   For example, to display an indicator when a custom number field has a negative value, click Is Less Than in the list in the Test cell and then type 0 in the Value(s) cell. To display an indicator when a custom date field is greater than the baseline finish, click Is Greater Than in the Test cell and then click Baseline Finish in the Value(s) field.
6. Click the Image cell, click the down arrow, and then click the graphical indicator to display when the condition is true (see Figure 25-17).

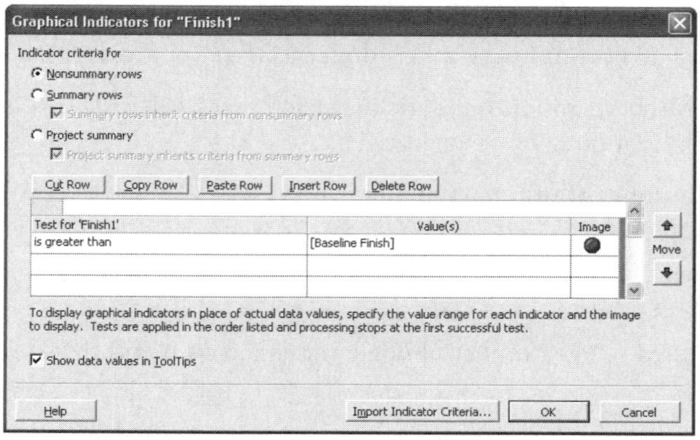

Figure 25-17. Set up criteria for displaying an icon that alerts you to specific conditions in the project.

7. To define graphical indicators when other conditions are true, repeat Steps 4, 5, and 6 in the next blank row in the table.

Tip **Display summary rows differently from nonsummary rows**
By default, summary rows and the project summary row both inherit the same conditions that you specify for nonsummary rows. If you want to use different conditions for summary rows, select the Summary Rows option and then clear the Summary Rows Inherit Criteria From Nonsummary Rows check box. Define the tests and indicators for summary rows as you would for nonsummary rows. To specify different conditions for the project summary row, select the Project Summary option and then clear the Project Summary Inherits Criteria From Summary Rows check box. Define the tests and indicators for the project summary row.

Customizing Groups

You can group tasks, resources, or assignments that meet a set of conditions. For example, you might group tasks by their schedule variance so you can concentrate on the ones furthest behind schedule. You might group resources by their level of availability so you can assign the resources who have the most free time. You can also choose to group assignments instead of tasks or resources; for example, to see which assignments are running over budget on hours. Group headings show subtotals for the values in the numeric fields for the group. For example, you might display assignments grouped by salaried and hourly employees and contractors, so you can see the total hours of work performed by each group. When you group these elements, subtotals for the groups appear in the Task and Resource Sheet as well as in the timesheet in Usage views.

For more information about applying existing groups, see "Grouping Project Information" on page 125.

Modifying a Group

If one of the existing groups doesn't meet your needs, you can modify it. If you want to keep the original group definition intact, you can instead copy an existing group and then modify it to create a completely new group. Do the following to customize a group:

1. Click Project, Group by, More Groups.
2. In the More Groups dialog box, click either the Task or Resource option to display the task or resource groups.
3. Click the group you want to modify in the list, and then click Edit or Copy.

   The Group Definition dialog box appears (see Figure 25-18).

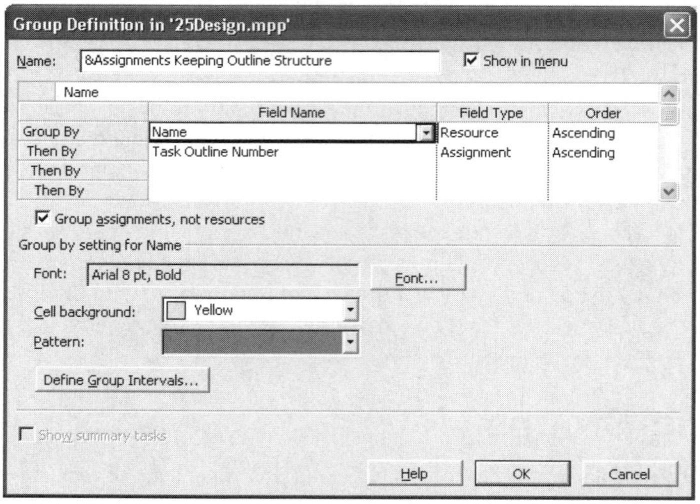

Figure 25-18. Group tasks, resources, or assignments by one or more fields.

4. If necessary, change the name of the group in the Name box.
5. Click the first empty cell in the Field Name column, click the down arrow, and then click the name of the field by which you want to group.

   The category for the field (Task, Resource, or Assignment) appears in the Field Type cell.
6. If necessary, change the grouping order.

   For example, you might want to use descending order to locate the resources with the most availability more easily.
7. To group assignments instead of tasks or resources, select the Group Assignments, Not Tasks check box for a task group or Group Assignments, Not Resources check box for a resource group.
8. To change the font, click Font. In the Font dialog box, choose a font, font style, font size, and color.
9. To change the background color, click a color in the Cell Background box.
10. To change the pattern for the group headings, click a pattern in the Pattern box.

Troubleshooting

You can't change the calculation for the value that appears in the group heading row

The group heading rows for standard fields display the sum of the values for the entries in the group. However, you might want to use a different calculation for the group heading row, such as the largest value or the average.

> Although you can't change the calculation for a standard field group summary, you can create a custom field equal to the standard field. Then you can calculate the group summary for the custom field using the other summary calculations. To do this, first create a calculated custom field. Then set the custom field equal to the standard field. Select the Rollup option and choose the calculation you want to use for the rolled-up value.

Groups often display elements in small sets, one set for each discrete value that exists in the field that you grouped. This process works well for fields such as Milestones that have only two values. For groups based on cost or work, the number of discrete values can seem endless. However, you can define intervals for groups. To do this, follow these steps:

1. In the Group Definition dialog box, click the field for which you want to define intervals.
2. Click Define Group Intervals. The Define Group Interval dialog box appears (see Figure 25-19).

   The default selection for Group On is Each Value.

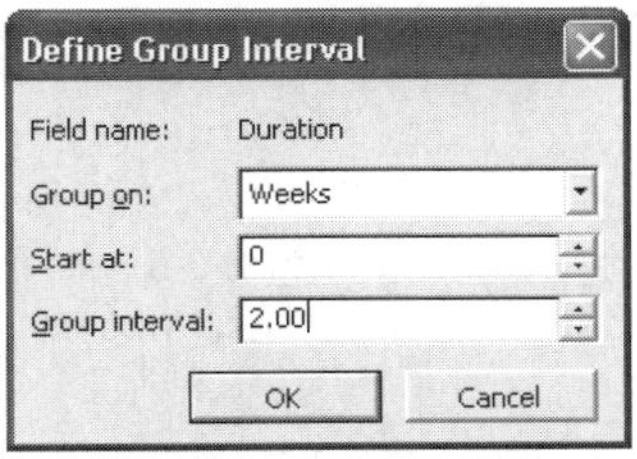

Figure 25-19. Set the starting value and size for group intervals.

3. Click the down arrow in the Group On box and then click the interval you want to use in the list.

   The intervals listed depend on the type of field. For example, the intervals for a field that represents work include units in which work is measured, such as hours, days, weeks, and months.
4. To start the interval at a specific number, type the number in the Start At box.
5. To define the interval size, type the number in the Group Interval box. To group assignments in intervals of two weeks worth of work, type 2.

Creating a New Group

When no groups exist that are similar to what you want, you can create a new group. To create a new group, do the following:

1. Click Project, Group By, More Groups.
2. In the More Groups dialog box, select the Task or Resource option to specify whether you're creating a task or resource group and then click New.
3. In the Name box, type a descriptive name for the new group.

4 Click in the first empty cell in the Field Name column, click the down arrow, and then click the name of the field by which you want to group.

The category for the field (Task, Resource, or Assignment) appears in the Field Type cell.

5 To group assignments instead of tasks or resources, select the Group Assignments, Not Tasks check box for a task group or the Group Assignments, Not Resources check box for a resource group.

6 Change the order of the grouping to Descending, if necessary.

Group Tasks with Overallocated Resources

You can create and apply a custom group that shows which tasks have overallocated resources assigned. This can help you determine which tasks are more at risk of missing their dates or generating overtime costs.

1 Click Project, Group By, More Groups.

2 In the More Groups dialog box, select the Task option and then click New.

3 In the Name box, type Overallocated.

4 Select the Show In Menu check box.

5 Click in the Group By row in the Field Name column, click the down arrow, and then type **ov** to scroll quickly through the list of fields. Click Overallocated.

6 Click OK.

Your new group appears in the More Groups dialog box.

7 Click Apply to initiate the Overallocated grouping to the current view. Click Close to close the dialog box without grouping.

Any time you want to apply the Overallocated grouping to a task view, click Group By on the Standard toolbar, and then click Overallocated. The view is grouped between those tasks that have overallocated resources assigned and those that do not.

Inside Out

Different "groups" in Microsoft Project

There are several types of groups in Microsoft Project. Each one serves a different purpose, so it's important to choose the correct one. A group resource represents several interchangeable resources. For example, you might define a resource called Carpenters, which represents five carpenters who can do basic carpentry. The Maximum Units for this resource would be the sum of the maximum units for each individual in the group resource, or 500 percent in this example.

A resource group represents a category of individual resources. You might define a resource group for employees and another for contractors so you can sort, filter, and view assignments using these categories.

Finally, a group that you apply using the Group By command on the Project menu categorizes and sorts tasks, resources, or assignments based on the values in any field in Microsoft Project.

Customizing Filters

Projects contain so much information that the data can simply get in the way when they're not pertinent. Filters restrict the tasks or resources that appear so you can more easily analyze your situation. Microsoft Project provides a number of standard filters that you can use as-is to weed out certain kinds of information and use as templates for your own customized filters. For example, the Incomplete Tasks filter displays only those tasks that are either in progress or not yet started, so you can focus on work yet to be done.

For more information about working with the built-in Microsoft Project filters, see "Filtering Project Information" on page 127.

Modifying a Filter

You can modify an existing filter. If you want to keep the original filter intact, you can also copy an existing filter and then modify it to create your new version. To customize a filter, follow these steps:

1. Click Project, Filtered For, More Filters.
2. In the More Filters dialog box, select the Task or Resource option to display the task or resource filters.
3. Click the filter you want to modify and then click Edit or Copy.
4. Click the Field Name cell you want to change, click the down arrow, and then click the name of the field by which you want to filter (see Figure 25-20).

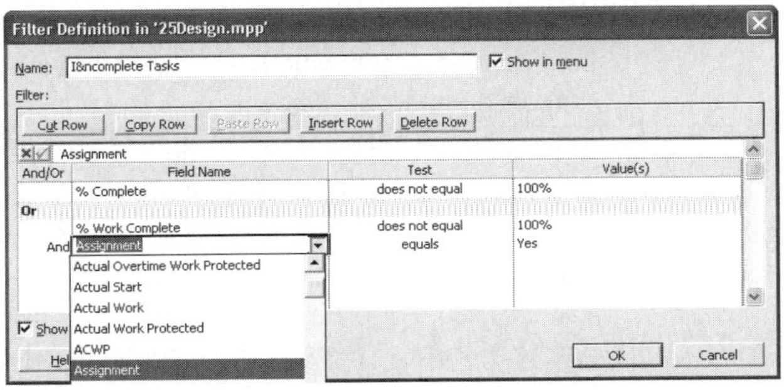

Figure 25-20. Modify the fields, tests, and values for a filter to display only the tasks that meet your criteria.

5. Click the Test cell, click the down arrow, and then click the name of the test you want to use for the filter.
6. Specify the value you want to use for the filter test in the Value(s) cell. You can type a value, click a field name from the list, or type a prompt to define an interactive filter.

For information about creating an interactive filter, see "Creating Interactive Filters" later in this section on page 804.

7. To display the summary tasks for tasks that pass the filter criteria, select the Show Related Summary Rows check box.

Troubleshooting

A filter doesn't display the correct tasks

Making changes to your project can cause what appear to be incorrect filter results. If you make changes to your project after a filter is applied, elements that no longer meet the filter criteria don't disappear until you reapply the filter. You can reapply the current filter by pressing Ctrl+F3.

Table 25-1 describes the tests you can use within a filter and provides an example of each.

Table 25-1. Filters

Filter Test	How You Can Use It
Equals	The values must be equal. For example, to filter for milestones, test whether the Milestone field equals Yes.
Does Not Equal	The values are different. For example, to show tasks with overtime, use the test Overtime Work field does not equal 0.
Is Greater Than	The Field Name value is greater than the entry in the Value(s) cell. For example, to show tasks that are late, check whether the Finish field is greater than the Baseline Finish field.
Is Greater Than Or Equal To	The Field Name value is greater than or equal to the entry in the Value(s) cell. For example, to show tasks at least 50 percent complete, test whether the % Complete field is greater than or equal to 50 percent.
Is Less Than	The Field Name value is less than the entry in the Value(s) cell. For example, to show tasks that are ahead of schedule, check whether the Finish field is less than the Baseline Finish field.
Is Less Than Or Equal To	The Field Name value is less than or equal to the entry in the Value(s) cell. For example, to show tasks that are under budget, test whether the Cost Variance field is less than or equal to 0.

Table 25-1. Filters

Filter Test	How You Can Use It
Is Within	The Field Name value is between or equal to the boundary values in the Value(s) cell. For example, to find the tasks within a range, test whether the ID is within the range specified in the Value(s) cell. To specify a range, type the starting value, type a comma, and then type the last value, such as 100,200.
Is Not Within	The Field Name value is outside the boundary values in the Value(s) cell. For example, to find the tasks that are not in progress, test whether the % Complete is not within 1%–99%.
Contains	The Field Name value is text that contains the string in the Value(s) cell. For example, to find the tasks to which a resource is assigned, test whether the Name field contains the resource name.
Does Not Contain	The Field Name value is text that does not contain the string in the Value(s) cell. For example, to find resources not in a resource group, check whether the Resource Group does not contain the name.
Contains Exactly	The Field Name value is text that must exactly match the string in the Value(s) cell. For example, to find tasks to which only a particular resource is assigned, check whether the Resource Name field contains exactly the resource's name.

Creating Filters

If you can't find a filter similar to what you want, you can create one. You can filter on any field or combination of fields in Microsoft Project, including custom fields that you defined. To create a new filter, follow these steps:

1. Click Project, Filtered For, More Filters.
2. In the More Filters dialog box, select the Task or Resource option to create a task or resource filter and then click New.
3. In the Filter Definition dialog box, type a descriptive name for the filter in the Name box.
4. If you want the new filter to appear on the Filtered For menu, select the Show In Menu check box.
5. Enter the field, test, and values that define your filter criteria.
6. To include the summary rows for the tasks or resources that meet the filter criteria, select the Show Related Summary Rows check box.

Tip **Use wildcard characters to locate the text you want**
You can compare a text field value to a string with wildcard characters when you use the Equals or Does Not Equal tests. Wildcard characters include the following:

- * represents one or more characters.
- ? represents any single character.

For example, DB* matches DB Developer, DB Administrator, and DB Designer. Des??? matches Design, but does not match Describe.

Create a Filter for Resource Booking Type

NEW FEATURE!

If you're using Project Professional, you might have added certain resources to your project as *proposed resources*. You can create a filter to find just proposed resources or just committed resources. Creating such a filter can be particularly helpful when you're finalizing your project team or the task assignments.

To create a filter for a booking type, follow these steps:

1. Click Project, Filtered For, More Filters.
2. In the More Filters dialog box, select the Resource option and then click New.
3. In the Name box, type a descriptive name for the filter; for example, **Proposed Resources** or **Committed Resources**.
4. Select the Show In Menu check box.
5. Click in the first row of the Field Name column and then type **bo** to scroll quickly through the list of fields. Click Booking Type.
6. Click in the Test column and then click Equals.
7. Click in the Value(s) column and then click Proposed or Committed.
8. Click OK.

   Your new filter appears in the More Filters dialog box.
9. Click Apply or Highlight to apply your new filter to the current view. Otherwise, click Close.

Any time you want to apply your new filter to a resource view, click Filter on the Formatting toolbar and then click Proposed or Committed.

Creating Comparison Filters

You can define filter criteria that compare the values in two different fields for the same task or resource. For example, to see whether a task started according to plan, you can filter for tasks in which the Actual Start date is less than or equal to the Baseline Start date.

To define a test that compares two fields, do the following:

1. Click the Field Name cell in the Filter Definition dialog box, click the down arrow, and then click the name of the field by which you want to filter.
2. Click the Test cell, click the down arrow, and then click the name of the test you want to use.
3. Click the Value(s) cell, click the down arrow, and then click the name of the field with which you want to compare the first field (see Figure 25-21).

   A field name in the Value(s) cell is enclosed in square brackets [ ].

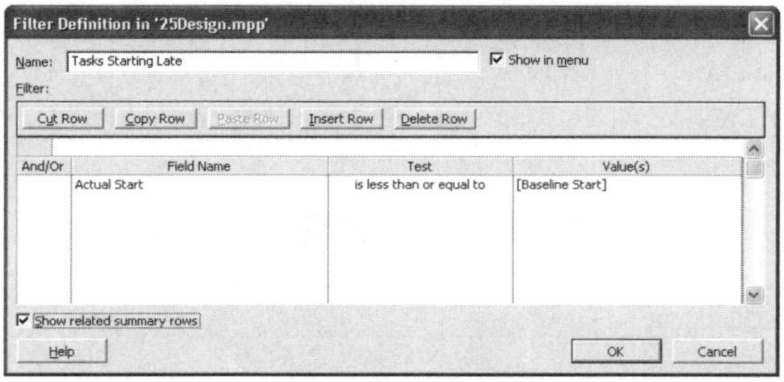

Figure 25-21. Create a filter that compares the value in one field against the value in another field.

Creating Filters with Multiple Tests

Sometimes it takes more than one or two criteria to filter the list to your satisfaction. You can create filters in which tasks or resources must meet at least one of the criteria.

To define multiple filter criteria, follow these steps:

1. In the Filter Definition dialog box, type a descriptive name for the filter in the Name box.
2. In the first row in the table, specify the field, test, and value for the first set of filter criteria.
3. In the second row, click the And/Or cell in the second row, and click And or Or.

   If you click And, the filter displays only elements that meet both criteria. The filter displays tasks that meet one or both of the criteria when you click Or.
4. Specify the field, test, and values for the second set of filter criteria.
5. Repeat Steps 2, 3, and 4 for any additional tests you want to define for the filter, defining each test on a separate row in the table and relating them with an And or Or.

When there are more than two sets of criteria, filters evaluate tests in the order in which they occur in the filter definition. The filter displays elements based on the results of the first two tests. It then compares those results to the outcome of the next test. The filter continues until there are no further tests to evaluate.

In some cases, you might want to adjust the order in which the tests are evaluated. For example, you might want to filter tasks first for those that use a particular resource and that aren't yet complete. Then you want to further filter the list for tasks that start and finish within a particular date range. You can group the filter criteria by clicking And or Or in the And/Or cell of an otherwise empty row.

Do the following to group criteria within a filter:

1. Define one or more tests for the first group of filter criteria.
2. In the next blank row after the first group of criteria, click the And/Or cell, and then click And or Or. Keep the rest of this row blank.

   This blank row containing only And or Or creates the grouping between the first set of filter criteria and the second set.
3. In the next row, define the tests for one or more additional filter criteria (see Figure 25-22).

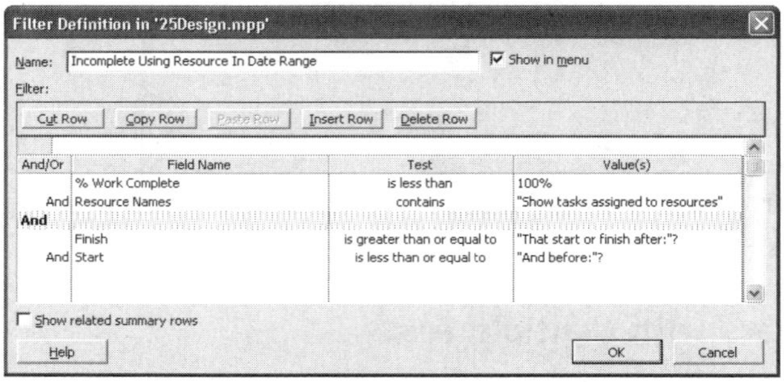

Figure 25-22. Control the order of test evaluation for a filter with And or Or operators.

Creating Interactive Filters

In many cases, you want to supply different values to a filter each time you use it. *Interactive filters* request values and then filter based on the values you provide.

To create an interactive filter, follow these steps:

1. In the Filter Definition dialog box for a new filter, type a descriptive name for the filter in the Name box.
2. Click the field and test for the filter.
3. In the Value(s) cell, type a text string followed by a question mark (see Figure 25-23).

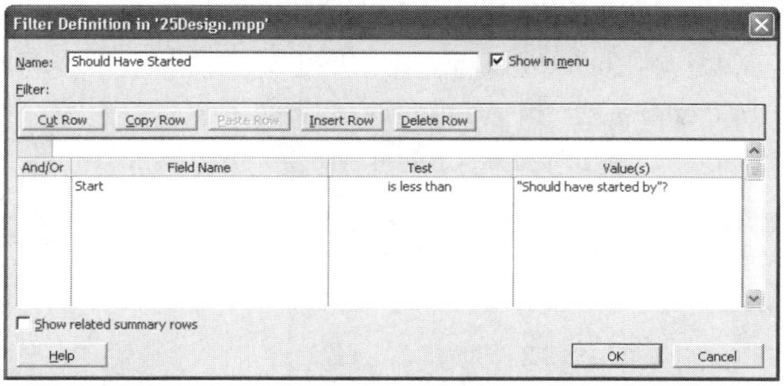

Figure 25-23. Create a filter that waits for user input.

When you apply your new interactive filter, the text string you entered appears as a prompt in a dialog box (see Figure 25-24). The question mark instructs Microsoft Project to pause until the user enters the value.

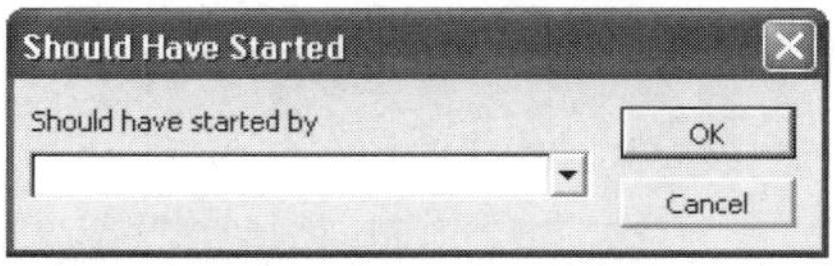

Figure 25-24. When you create an interactive filter, a dialog box appears, asking for the information you specified.

Customizing AutoFilter Criteria

AutoFilter is an easy way to filter by values in a single field. In addition, you can quickly create custom filters by saving an AutoFilter test. Create and save an AutoFilter when you want to quickly create a filter that operates on only one field at a time.

To create a custom filter using AutoFilter:

1. Display the sheet view whose rows you want to filter.

AutoFilter

2. Click AutoFilter on the Formatting toolbar. The AutoFilter arrows appear in the column headings for each field in the sheet view (see Figure 25-25).

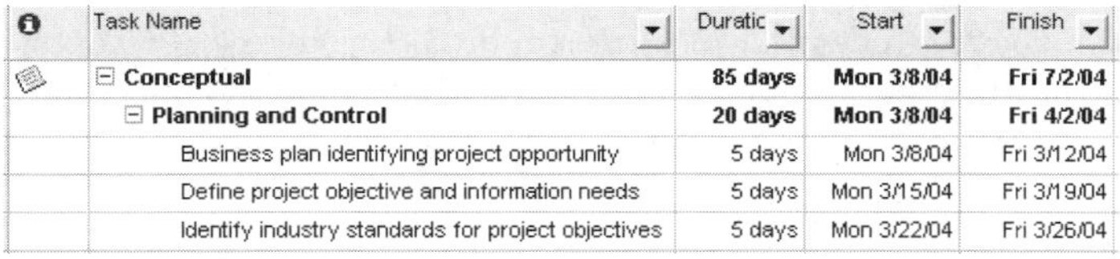

Figure 25-25. When you click the AutoFilter button, AutoFilter arrows appear in every column heading.

3. Click the arrow in the column whose information you want to filter by and then click Custom.

   The Custom AutoFilter dialog box appears with the field set to the current column.

4. Click the arrow in the first test box and click the criteria you want to apply.
5. In the first value box, click the arrow, and then enter a value or field name.
6. To add a second test, select the And or Or option.
7. Click the test and value for the second test (see Figure 25-26).

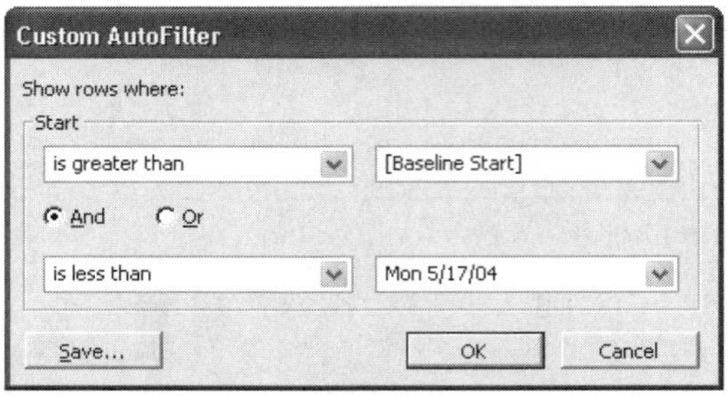

Figure 25-26. Customize and save an AutoFilter.

8. To save the AutoFilter test, click Save, which displays the Filter Definition dialog box.

   You can enter a filter name and make other changes before you save the filter.

> **Note** To turn off the AutoFilter arrows, click the AutoFilter button on the Formatting toolbar.

Working with Outline Codes

By default, the task outline delineates a hierarchy of tasks. A work breakdown structure (WBS) is a special hierarchy that separates the work for your project into manageable pieces that you can assign to project resources. But you might need to structure your tasks according to different hierarchies. For example, the accounting department might have a set of codes for tracking income and expenses by business unit.

In addition, your organization might need one, two, or several ways of looking at resource hierarchies. For example, your organization's resource manager might want to review the resource breakdown structure, whereas the procurement manager might require a bill that itemizes the materials for the project.

Using custom *outline code* fields in Microsoft Project, you can create up to 10 sets of custom task codes and 10 sets of resource codes, in much the same way you set up WBS codes. You can then sort, group, or filter your tasks or resource by any of these outline codes to see the tasks or resources displayed in that structure.

For information about setting up a task outline of summary tasks and subtasks, see "Sequencing and Organizing Tasks" on page 83. To set up and apply work breakdown structure codes, see "Setting Up Work Breakdown Structure Codes" on page 83.

Setting Up Outline Codes

Outline codes are customizable alphanumeric codes that provide a method of categorizing tasks and resources in your project. Microsoft Project does not recalculate custom outline codes as you modify the location or indentation of a task or resource because only you know the structure of tasks or resources you want to represent. To help others use your custom outline codes properly, you can create a lookup table so users can choose values from a list. You can eliminate invalid codes by restricting users to choosing only the predefined values.

An outline code can consist of several levels of uppercase or lowercase letters, numbers, or characters, along with a symbol to separate the levels of the code. The maximum length for an outline code is 255 characters.

Selecting the Outline Code

Follow these steps to select the custom outline code you want to start defining:

1. Click Tools, Customize, Fields and then click the Custom Outline Codes tab.
2. Select the Task or Resource option to specify whether you're creating a task or resource outline code.
3. Click the name of the outline code that you want to modify in the code list; for example, Outline Code1 or Outline Code8.
4. To rename the custom outline code, click the Rename button and then type the new name in the Rename Field dialog box.

   This name and the original field name appear in lists where the outline code appears.

Defining a Code Mask

The code mask is the template that delineates the format and length of each level of the outline code as well as the separators between each level. To define the code mask, do the following:

1. On the Custom Outline Codes tab of the Customize Fields dialog box, click the outline code for which you want to define a code mask.
2. Click the Define Code Mask button. The Outline Code Definition dialog box appears.
3. In the Sequence field of the first row, choose whether the first level of the code (or hierarchy) is a number, uppercase letters, lowercase letters, or alphanumeric characters.
4. In the Length field of the first row, specify the length of the first level of the code.

   A number in the Length cell indicates a fixed length for that level. If the level can contain any number of characters, click Any in the list.
5. In the Separator field of the first row, specify the character that separates the first and second level of the code.
6. Repeat Steps 3, 4, and 5 until all the levels of your custom outline code are set up (see Figure 25-27).

   As you enter the code mask for each succeeding level, the Code Preview box shows an example of the code.

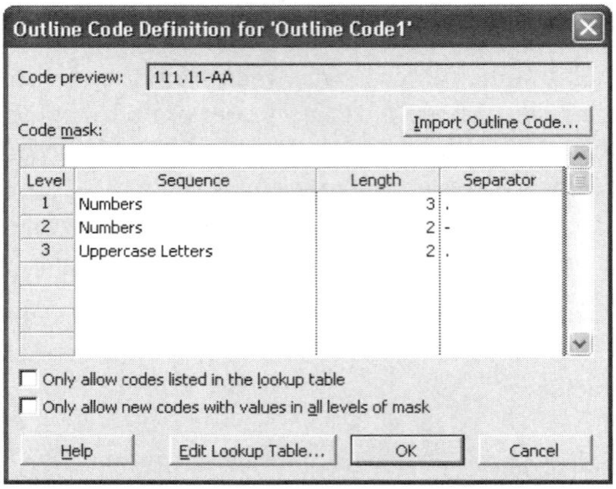

Figure 25-27. Define a custom outline code to display alternate hierarchies for tasks and resources.

At this point your outline code is ready to use. Any sequence of characters that fit your code mask can be entered in the outline code field you selected and defined.

Controlling Outline Code Values

You can define settings to help users enter the correct values and format for outline codes. To do this, follow these steps:

1. Be sure that the Outline Code Definition dialog box is open and the code mask defined for the selected outline code.
2. To restrict codes to only those listed in a lookup table, select the Only Allow Codes Listed In The Lookup Table check box.
3. If users can enter codes not in a lookup table, you can make sure they enter values in each level of the code by selecting the Only Allow New Codes With Values In All Levels Of Mask check box.

Defining a Lookup Table

If you want more control over how you or other users enter information in the outline code fields, you can set up a lookup table for them to choose from. A lookup table comprises a list of values for the outline code. To define a lookup table, do the following:

1. In the Customize Fields dialog box, click the outline code for which you want to create a lookup table.
2. Be sure that the code mask is defined for the selected outline code. Click Define Code Mask to set up or review the code mask.

   If you try to define a lookup table without a code mask, you'll see errors on each entry.
3. In either the Customize Fields dialog box or the Outline Code Definition dialog box, click the Edit Lookup Table button.

4 To make the hierarchy levels more apparent as you define lookup values, select the Display Indenting In Lookup Table check box.

With this check box selected, the values you will be entering will be indented according to their level in the hierarchy.

5 Click the first blank cell in the Outline Code column.

6 Type a value in the Outline Code cell.

The format and length of this value must match the first level of your defined code mask. For example, if you specified that the first level in the outline code's hierarchy must be numbers that are 3 characters in length, you must enter a 3-digit number or else an error alert will appear.

7 Click the Description cell and type a meaningful description of the entry.

Indent

Error Indicator

8 In the Outline Code cell in the second row, enter a value that conforms to the second level in the code mask. Click the Indent button to demote the entry to the next level of the code.

The outline code level appears in the Level column. The indent level, character types (number, uppercase letters, and so on), and then length of each entry must match your code mask. If the value you enter doesn't conform to the code mask defined for that outline level, the entry appears in red with an error indicator in the Level field.

9 Repeat Steps 5 through 8 to define additional values in the lookup table (see Figure 25-28).

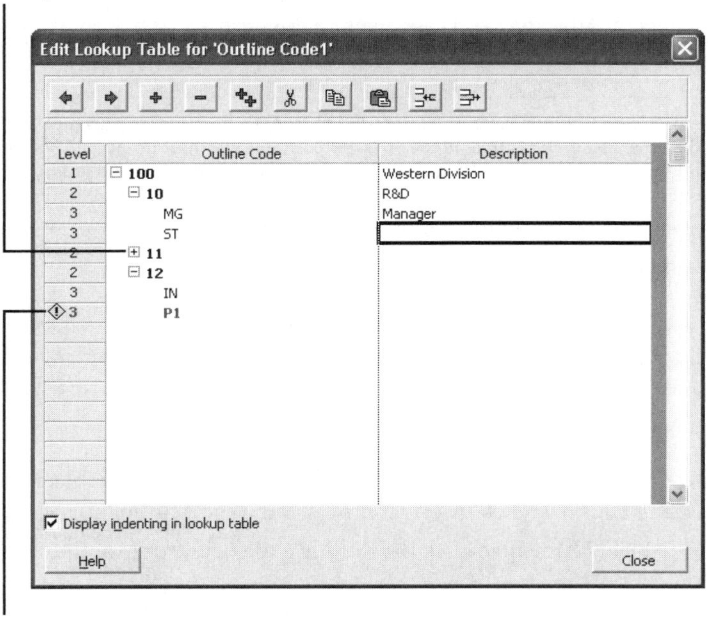

Figure 25-28. Define values in a lookup table to simplify outline code data entry.

10 Click the plus and minus signs that precede higher-level values to expand or collapse the outline levels.

Outdent

11 To promote the entry one level higher in the code, click the Outdent button.

12 When finished defining the lookup table, click Close.

The lookup table is saved with the outline code definition and code mask.

Tip **Modify values in a lookup table**
To insert a value in the outline, click the Insert Row button. You can also use the Delete Row, Cut, Copy, and Paste buttons to edit the values that already exist in the list.

Specify multiple properties for a single resource

NEW FEATURE!

If you're set up for enterprise project management using Microsoft Office Project Server 2003 and Project Professional, your project server administrator can identify enterprise resources as having multiple properties, such as skills, locations, or certifications. These multiple properties are set up with the Enterprise Resource Multi-Value (ERMV) fields, which are the enterprise resource outline codes numbered 20–29.

Your project server administrator sets up the multi-value codes and then assigns them to the enterprise resources. Project managers can then use the Build Team and Resource Substitution Wizard features to find enterprise resources that meet specific requirements for their projects. After they add resources to their project, they can use the multi-value codes to group or filter resources.

For information about administrator setup of the enterprise resource multi-value fields, see "Specifying Multiple Properties for a Resource" on page 613. For information about project manager use of the multi-value fields, see "Building Your Enterprise Project Team" on page 655.

Assigning Outline Codes

You can assign outline code values to tasks and resources as you would enter values for any other fields in Microsoft Project. You can type the values or, if you created a lookup table, choose one from a list.

To assign values for a custom outline code, follow these steps:

1 If your custom outline code doesn't appear in the current table, right-click a column heading and then click Insert Column on the shortcut menu.

2 In the Field Name box, click the outline code field (for example, Outline Code1) and then click OK.

   If you renamed the outline code in the Customize Fields dialog box, you'll see your field listed both by its new name and its generic name.

3 Click a cell in the custom outline code column.

4 If no lookup table exists, type the value in the cell.

When a lookup table exists, click the down arrow in the cell, and then click an entry in the list (see Figure 25-29).

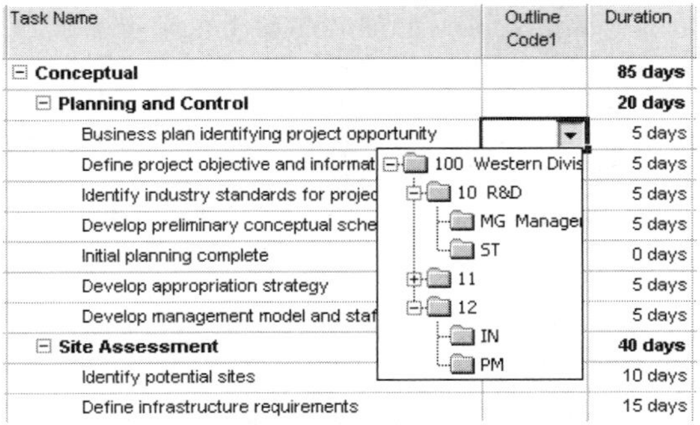

Task Name
Outline Code1
Duration
Conceptual
85 days
Planning and Control
20 days
Business plan identifying project opportunity
5 days
Define project objective and informat
5 days
Identify industry standards for projec
5 days
Develop preliminary conceptual sche
5 days
Initial planning complete
0 days
Develop appropriation strategy
5 days
Develop management model and staf
5 days
Site Assessment
40 days
Identify potential sites
10 days
Define infrastructure requirements
15 days
100 Western Divis
10 R&D
MG Manage
ST
11
12
IN
PM

Figure 25-29. Click the down arrow in the outline code field to choose from the lookup table.

> **Tip** **Determining the correct format for an outline code**
> Without a lookup table, there is no way to identify the format for the outline code. However, if you enter a value that doesn't conform to the code mask, an error message appears that includes the correct format.

Reviewing Your Tasks or Resources by Outline Code

Grouping, filtering, and sorting by outline codes is similar to changing the order of tasks and resources based on values in other fields. You simply apply a group, filter, or sort criterion that uses the custom outline code.

To quickly group tasks or resources using a custom outline code, do the following:

1. Click Project, Group By, Customize Group By.
2. In the Customize Group By dialog box, click the down arrow in the Field Name cell and then click the name of the outline code.
3. If necessary, change the value in the Order cell, the color and pattern of the group, and other group settings.

For information about customizing a group and creating a permanent group using a field, see "Modifying a Group," earlier in this chapter on page 795.

To quickly filter tasks or resources using a custom outline code, follow these steps:

1. Display the sheet view whose rows you want to filter.
2. On the Formatting toolbar, click AutoFilter.

   The AutoFilter arrows appear in the column heading for each field in the sheet view.

3 Click the arrow in the outline code column.
4 Click the value by which you want to filter or click Custom if you want to create a custom filter based on the outline code.

Note To turn off the AutoFilter arrows, click the AutoFilter button on the Formatting toolbar.

For information about customizing a filter, see "Customizing Filters," earlier in this chapter on page 799.

To sort your tasks or resource using an outline code, do the following:

1 Click Project, Sort, Sort By.
2 In the Sort By dialog box, click the down arrow in the Sort By box and then click the name of the outline code in the list.
3 If necessary, select the Ascending or Descending option to change the sort order.

Sharing Customized Elements Among Projects

If you customize elements—such as tables, views, fields, or filters—in one project, you will probably want to use those elements in a new project. Customized elements are stored in the project in which you create them, but you can copy these elements to other projects or templates using the Organizer. If you want a customized element available to every new project, use the Organizer to copy the element to the global template. In addition, you can use the Organizer to rename or remove elements from a project or template.

For information about using the global template, see "Working with the Project Global Template" on page 848. To use the enterprise global template, see "Standardizing Enterprise Project Elements" on page 621.

Working with the Organizer

The Organizer includes tabs for every type of customizable element in Microsoft Project. By clicking a tab, you can see the elements of that type that are available in two project files. These project files can be active projects or templates, so you can copy customized elements between active projects or from a project to a template, or even restore the original element from a template to a project.

You can copy, delete, or rename customizable elements including the following:

- Views
- Working times calendars
- Reports
- Toolbars
- VBA modules and macros
- Import and export maps

- Forms
- Fields
- Tables
- Groups
- Filters

To open the Organizer, click Tools, Organizer. An Organizer button to open the Organizer dialog box is also available in the following dialog boxes:

- More Views
- More Groups
- More Tables
- Custom Reports
- More Filters
- Customize Forms

Copying Customized Elements

No matter which type of element you copy, the procedure is the same. You choose a source file that contains the element you want to copy, choose a destination file into which you want to copy the element, and then copy the element.

Follow these steps to copy an element from a project to the global template:

1. Open the project that contains the element you want to copy.
2. Click Tools, Organizer to open the Organizer dialog box (see Figure 25-30).

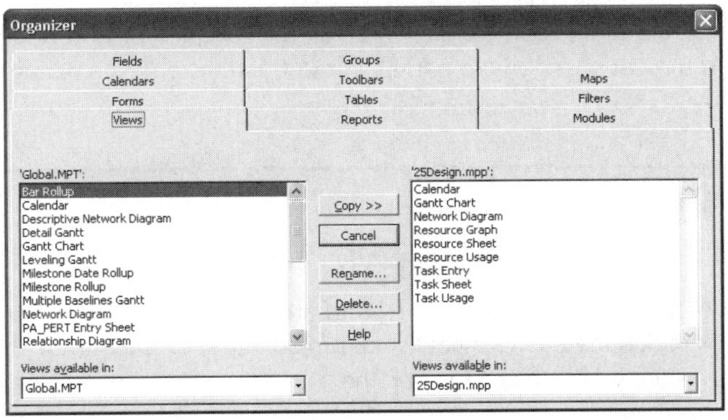

Figure 25-30. Copy customized elements between projects and templates, or rename and delete existing elements.

3. Click the tab for the type of element you want to copy.
4. In the <*Element*> Available In box on the right side of the dialog box, click the project that contains the element you want to copy.

   <*Element*> stands for the name of the current tab.

5. Click the name of the element you want to copy from the list of elements on the right side of the dialog box.
6. Click Copy. If an element with the same name already exists in the global template, Project asks you to confirm that you want to replace the element in the global template. Click Yes to replace the element in the global template with the one from the source project.

   To copy the element with a different name, click Rename and then type a new name.

To copy an element between two projects, do the following:

1. Open both the source and destination projects.
2. Click Tools, Organizer to open the Organizer dialog box.
3. Click the tab for the type of element you want to copy.
4. In the <*Element*> Available In box on the right side of the dialog box, click the source project.
5. In the <*Element*> Available In box on the left side of the dialog box, click the destination project.
6. Click the name of the element you want to copy from the list of elements on the right side of the dialog box.
7. Click Copy. If an element with the same name already exists in the destination, Microsoft Project asks you to confirm that you want to replace the element in the destination project. Click Yes to replace the element in the destination project with the one from the source project.

   To copy the element with a different name, click No. Then click Rename and enter a new name.

Caution You can't rename some built-in elements. In addition, you can't rename fields in the Organizer. You must change field names in the Customize Fields dialog box.

Inside Out

Custom toolbars apply to the entire application

Microsoft Project treats toolbars differently from other customizable elements. Toolbars apply to the application instead of a particular project, so they are stored in the global template by default. When you modify a toolbar, the modified version appears, no matter which project you open.

If you want to share a customized toolbar with someone else, copy it from the global template to a project file and then send the project file to that person. They can use the Organizer to copy the toolbar to their global template.

Removing Customized Elements

Although customized elements can simplify your work, extraneous elements in projects and templates can be distracting. When you copy a customized element to the global template, you no longer need it in the project in which you created it. If you created a customized element by accident, you can remove it using the Organizer. To do this, follow these steps:

1. Open the project that contains the element you want to delete.
2. Click Tools, Organizer to open the Organizer dialog box.
3. Click the tab for the type of element that you want to delete.
4. In the <*Element*> Available In box on the right side of the dialog box, click the project that contains the element you want to delete.

   <*Element*> stands for the name of the current tab.
5. Click the name of the element you want to remove from the list of elements on the right side of the dialog box.
6. Click Delete. In the confirmation box, click Yes to delete the element.

Renaming Customized Elements

You can rename customized elements using the Organizer. For example, you should rename a customized element in your project if you want to copy it to the global template without overwriting the original element in the global template. You can't rename some built-in elements. Fields are renamed in the Customize Fields dialog box.

Do the following to rename a customized element:

1. Open the project that contains the element that you want to rename.
2. Click Tools, Organizer to open the Organizer dialog box.
3. Click the tab for the type of element that you want to rename.
4. In the <*Element*> Available In box on the right side of the dialog box, click the project that contains the element you want to rename.

   <*Element*> stands for the name of the current tab.
5. Click the name of the element in the list of elements on the right side of the dialog box.
6. Click Rename.

   The Rename dialog box appears.
7. Type the new name for the element.

Restoring Customized Elements to their Default State

If you forget that changes you make to a table in a view modify that table's definition, you might customize a standard table accidentally. You can reverse the changes you made, but if you made a lot of changes before you realized your mistake, it's easier to restore the standard table. You can restore standard elements by copying them from the global template into your active project using the Organizer.

Follow these steps to restore a standard element:

1. Open the project to which you want to restore a standard element.
2. Click Tools, Organizer to open the Organizer dialog box.
3. Click the tab for the type of element that you want to restore.

> **Tip** **Restoring the table that appears in the current view**
> You can't restore a table if it appears in the current view. Either switch to a view that does not use that table, or right-click the All Cells box (the blank cell above the ID numbers) and click another table name on the shortcut menu.

4. In the *<Element>* Available In box on the right side of the dialog box, click the project to which you want to restore the standard element.

   <Element> stands for the name of the current tab. The global template appears on the left side of the dialog box by default.
5. Click the name of the element you want to restore in the list of elements in the global template on the left side of the dialog box.
6. Click Copy. When the confirmation dialog box appears asking you to confirm that you want to replace the element in the project, click Yes.

Chapter 26

Customizing the Microsoft Project Interface

Microsoft Office Project 2003 offers a plethora of commands to assist project managers with every aspect of managing a project. Menus, toolbars, and keyboard shortcuts provide easy access to commonly used features. However, you might find that the commands you use frequently are not easily available or don't appear on a menu at all, whereas commands you never use stake a prime position. As you use Project 2003 and identify the commands you use the most, you can customize the menus and toolbars to display your favorites. You can also assign keyboard shortcuts to access commands without removing your hands from the keyboard.

Microsoft Project provides forms for entering data into fields. Some forms, such as the Task Entry and Task Details Forms, are off-limits—you can't change them. However, there are several predefined forms you can modify or copy to fit your data entry requirements. You can also build your own forms if your needs are quite specialized.

Creating and Customizing Toolbars

Toolbars display commands without taking up much space. However, if you display several toolbars and each one includes commands you don't use, you give up screen area that you might prefer to use for the Gantt Chart or other project information. You can keep the space that toolbars take to a minimum by customizing existing toolbars or creating your own.

Tip **Display toolbars on one row or two**

You can display the Standard and Formatting toolbars on one line to reduce the space that these toolbars use. Right-click in the toolbar area and then click Customize. In the Customize dialog box, click the Options tab. Clear the Show Standard And Formatting Toolbars On Two Rows check box.

If some of the commands you want don't appear when these toolbars share a row, click the Toolbar Options arrow on the right end of the toolbar and then click the toolbar button you want.

Customizing Toolbars

If the built-in toolbars have most of what you need, it might be easier to customize those toolbars than to create your own. You can add, remove, or rearrange toolbar buttons. For example, you might add a few buttons to the Standard toolbar from the Resource Management and Tracking toolbars. You can also specify how toolbars display their command and the appearance of buttons.

Adding and Removing Buttons on a Toolbar

To add a button to an existing toolbar, follow these steps:

1. If the toolbar you want to customize is not visible, click View, Toolbars and then click the name of the toolbar.
2. Click Tools, Customize, Toolbars.

   The Customize dialog box appears.
3. Click the Commands tab.

   Categories of commands, such as File, Format, and Tracking, appear on the left side of the dialog box. The commands within the selected category appear on the right side of the dialog box (see Figure 26-1).

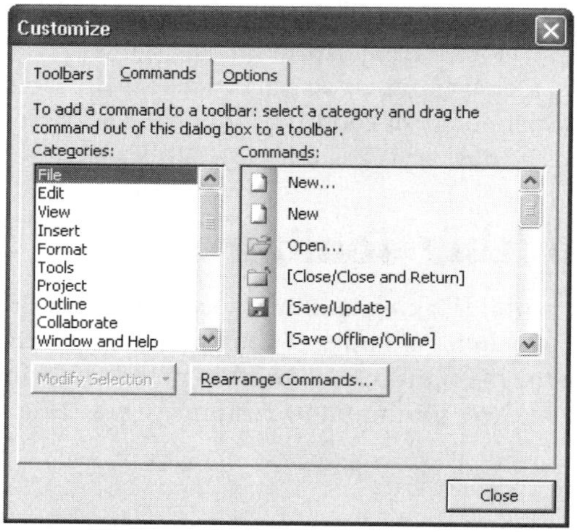

Figure 26-1. You can drag commands from the list in the Customize dialog box to a toolbar or menu.

4. Click the category of the command you want to add.

   If you don't know the category to which it belongs, select a generic or all-inclusive category, such as All Commands or All Macros.
5. Drag the command you want to add from the command list to the toolbar. The mouse pointer changes to an I-beam to indicate where the command will be placed. Move the mouse pointer until the I-beam is in the location you want and then release the mouse button.

Tip **Add a menu to a toolbar**

To add a built-in menu to a toolbar, open the Customize dialog box and click the Commands tab. Click Built-In Menus and then drag the menu you want from the Commands box to its new position on the toolbar.

To add a custom menu to a toolbar, click New Menu in the Categories box and drag the menu name from the Commands box to the toolbar. Right-click the new menu on the toolbar, type a name in the Name box on the shortcut menu, and then press Enter. After naming the menu, you can drag commands or menus to the new menu. Right-click a menu entry to modify the button images and text.

Working with Personalized Toolbars

Microsoft Project personalizes toolbars and menus by displaying only the commands you use most frequently. Initially, Microsoft Project loads menus and toolbars with commands popular with the majority of users. As you select commands on menus and toolbars, those commands appear near the top of a menu, whereas commands you rarely use disappear.

To access hidden toolbar buttons, click the Toolbar Options button at the end of the toolbar and then click the button you want. To access hidden commands on a menu, click the double arrows at the bottom of the menu and then click the command you want.

If you prefer to see all commands on a toolbar or menu at all times, you can turn off personalized menus. To do this, right-click any menu or toolbar and click Customize in the shortcut menu. In the Customize dialog box, click the Options tab. Select the Always Show Full Menus check box.

To remove a button from a toolbar, do the following:

1. If the toolbar you want to customize is not visible, click View, Toolbars and then click the name of the toolbar you want to customize.
2. Click Tools, Customize, Toolbars.

   The Customize dialog box appears.
3. On the toolbar, right-click the command you want to remove and then click Delete in the shortcut menu.

   The command is removed only from the toolbar. It's still available in the Customize dialog box.

Quickly Customize Toolbars

You can customize toolbars without using the Customize dialog box. If you want to hide or display buttons that appear on a toolbar by default, click the Toolbar Options button, point to Add Or Remove Buttons, and then point to the name of the toolbar you want to customize. A list of all the buttons associated with the toolbar appears (see Figure 26-2).

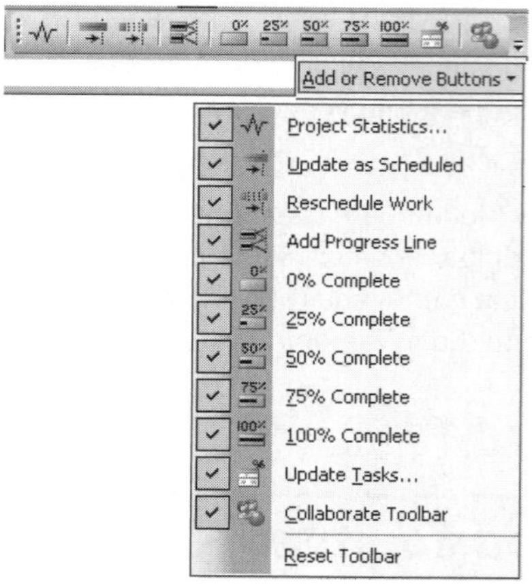

Figure 26-2. Click Toolbar Options on a toolbar to add or remove buttons on that toolbar.

The commands on the shortcut menu have the following characteristics:

- Commands that are preceded by a check mark are currently shown in the toolbar.
- Commands that do not have a check mark are hidden.
- Commands that are dimmed are not on the toolbar by default.

Clicking a command in the list toggles the command between hidden and visible. If you add a button to a toolbar, you can remove it only by using the Customize dialog box.

To rearrange the buttons on a toolbar, follow these steps:

1. Display the toolbar you want to customize by clicking View, Toolbars and then clicking the toolbar's name.
2. Click Tools, Customize, Toolbars.

   The Customize dialog box appears. You only need to open the dialog box; it doesn't matter which tab is showing.
3. On the toolbar, drag the button you want to move until the I-beam is in the location you want and then release the mouse button.

Troubleshooting

You can't remove buttons on a toolbar

The Add Or Remove Buttons command doesn't remove custom buttons you added to a built-in toolbar or any buttons on a custom toolbar. A custom toolbar's name is dimmed in the Add Or Remove Buttons shortcut menu, so you must click Customize to remove buttons from it. Buttons added to a built-in toolbar are dimmed on the shortcut menu.

To remove custom buttons on a built-in toolbar or any buttons on a custom toolbar, drag the buttons off the toolbar while the Customize dialog box is open.

Changing the Properties of a Toolbar

When you right-click a toolbar button while the Customize dialog box is open, a shortcut menu with commands for changing the contents and properties of a toolbar appears. The commands on this shortcut menu include the following:

Reset. Restores the original button, command associated with the button, and settings for the button on a built-in toolbar.

Delete. Removes the button.

Name. Displays a box in which you can enter a new name that appears in the ToolTip for the button.

Copy Button Image. Copies the selected button image to the Clipboard so you can paste it to another button.

Paste Button Image. Pastes the image on the Clipboard to the selected button. You can copy graphics from other applications or images from other buttons.

Reset Button Image. Restores the button image to the default.

Edit Button Image. Opens the Button Editor dialog box, in which you can edit the image.

Change Button Image. Displays a menu of images from which to select a new image.

Default Style. Displays only a button image on a toolbar and the button image and text on a menu.

Text Only (Always). Displays only text for the command in toolbars and menus.

Text Only (In Menus). Displays a button image on a toolbar and only text on menus.

Image And Text. Displays a button image and text in toolbars and menus.

Begin A Group. Adds a group divider to the toolbar.

Assign Macro. Opens the Customize Tool dialog box in which you can select a command for the button.

Troubleshooting

The toolbar doesn't appear where you want it

Toolbars might appear docked at the top, sides, or bottom of the screen; or they can float in their own window in the middle of the screen. To change the location of the toolbar, drag the toolbar to the top, side, or bottom of the screen.

To float the toolbar, drag it into the middle of the screen. Double-click the toolbar to toggle between docking and floating.

Creating Toolbars

If the commands you use most are scattered across several built-in toolbars, creating a toolbar of your favorite commands might be the best solution. You can also use the Organizer to copy an existing toolbar as a template.

To create a new toolbar, follow these steps:

1. Click Tools, Customize, Toolbars.

   The Customize dialog box appears.

2. Click the Toolbars tab and then click New.
3. In the New Toolbar dialog box, type the name of the toolbar you're creating.
4. Click OK.

   The toolbar name appears in the toolbars list in the Customize dialog box, and the empty toolbar appears onscreen (see Figure 26-3).

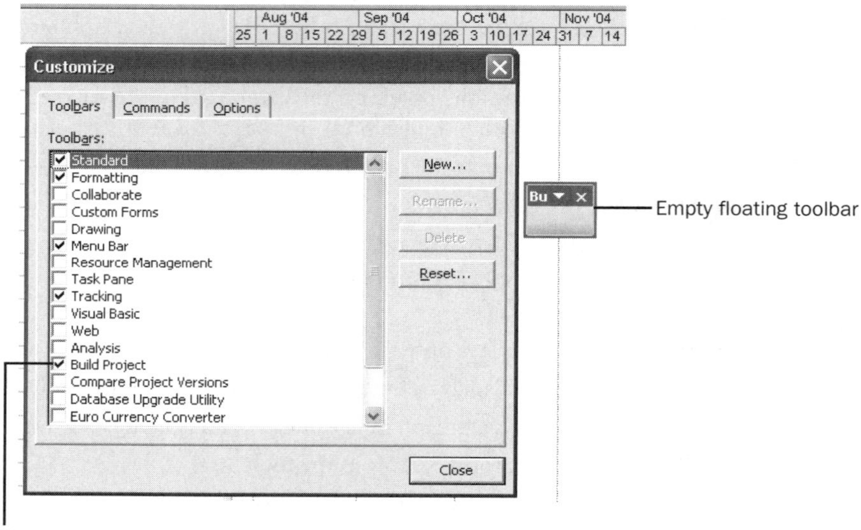

Figure 26-3. As soon as you name your new toolbar, it appears onscreen, ready to accept command buttons.

5. In the Customize dialog box, click the Commands tab.
6. Click the category of the command you want to add.
7. Drag the command you want to add from the command list to its location on the new toolbar.

   The command appears on the toolbar.

8. Repeat Steps 6–7 for all the command buttons you want to add to your new toolbar (see Figure 26-4).

   The commands on a single toolbar can be from different categories.

Figure 26-4. You can create a toolbar with the commands in any category you use frequently.

You can use the Organizer to make a copy of a toolbar so you can modify it to meet your needs. Because Microsoft Project saves toolbars and menus in the global template by default, you must copy the toolbar to your active project, rename it, and then copy the new toolbar back into the global template for editing.

For more information about the global template, see Chapter 28, "Standardizing Projects Using Templates."

To use an existing toolbar as a template for a new toolbar, do the following:

1. Click Tools, Organizer.
2. In the Organizer dialog box, click the Toolbars tab.

   Elements in the global template appear on the left side of the dialog box.
3. In the list for the global template, click the name of the toolbar you want to use as a template.
4. Click Copy to copy the toolbar to your active project.
5. Click the toolbar you just copied to the list for your active project and then click Rename.
6. In the Rename dialog box, type a unique name for the toolbar.
7. Click Copy again to copy the renamed toolbar back to the global template.
8. Click the toolbar in the list for your active project and then click Delete so the toolbar appears only in the global template list.
9. To change your new toolbar, follow the steps in the section "Customizing Toolbars" earlier in this chapter on page 818.

Troubleshooting

You can't find the custom toolbar you built

Customized menus belong to the application, not the active project, and are stored in the global template so that they are available whenever you use Project on your computer. If you go to a different computer and open the project that was open when you created the custom toolbar, that toolbar does not appear on the Toolbars menu.

To see the custom toolbar on another computer, you must either copy the global template to this computer or use the Organizer to copy the toolbar. Use the Organizer to copy the toolbar from the global template on the one computer to the project file itself.

Deleting Toolbars

You can't delete built-in toolbars. You can delete only toolbars that you created. Follow these steps to delete a user-defined toolbar:

1. Click Tools, Customize, Toolbars.

   The Customize dialog box appears.

2 Click the Toolbars tab and then click the name of the user-defined toolbar you want to delete.

3 Click the Delete button. Click OK in the dialog box that prompts you to confirm the deletion.

Tip **Use the Organizer to delete toolbars**

To delete one or more toolbars without displaying each one, click Tools, Organizer. Click the Toolbars tab. Click the name of the custom toolbar and then click Delete.

Troubleshooting

You can't delete a toolbar

Although you can't delete the toolbars that are built into Microsoft Project, you can reset them to their original configuration. The Delete button is dimmed when you select a built-in toolbar in the Customize dialog box. To reset a built-in toolbar, click the toolbar in the list and then click Reset. Click OK in the dialog box that prompts you to confirm your actions.

Resetting a toolbar removes any customizations you made, including any custom buttons you created. To save custom buttons, copy them to another toolbar before you reset the current one.

Modifying Button Images

You can modify the image of a button on a toolbar. For example, if you created several Print buttons, each of which prints to a different printer, you can modify a button's image to indicate which printer it uses. You can move the image around within the boundaries of the button or change the colors of the cells that make up the image.

Do the following to modify a button image:

1 Right-click a toolbar and then click Customize.

The Customize dialog box appears.

2 Right-click the button you want to edit and then click Edit Button Image.

The Button Editor dialog box appears (see Figure 26-5).

3 To modify the image, click a color in the Colors area. If you want to erase colored boxes in the image, click the Erase box.

4 In the Picture area, click individual cells or drag the mouse pointer over cells to change their color.

As you change the image, you can see what the image looks like in the Preview area.

5 To move the image within the Picture area, click a directional arrow in the Move area.

If the image fills the Picture area in one or more directions, the directional arrows might be dimmed.

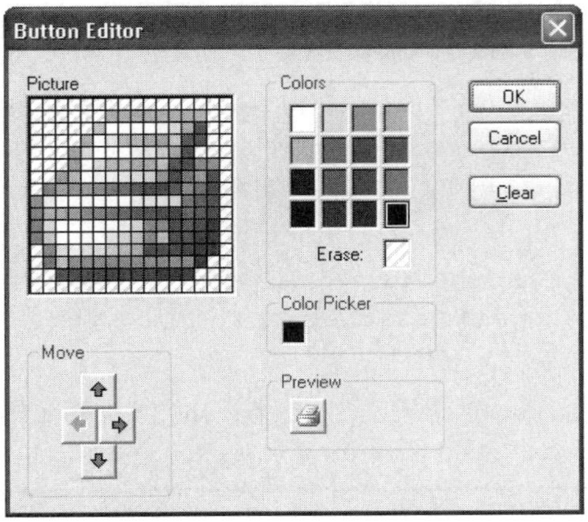

Figure 26-5. You can modify the image that appears on a toolbar button.

Creating and Customizing Menus

Menus are simply toolbars with a different presentation style, and they can contain commands or other menus. Although toolbars are thriftier with space, menus can display a description of the commands or submenus.

Tip **Share modified toolbars and menus**

Toolbars and menus belong to the entire Microsoft Project application, not just to a particular project. They are stored in the global template by default. When you modify a toolbar or menu, the modified version is available no matter which project you open.

To share a customized toolbar with someone else, copy it from the global template to a project file and then send the project file to that person. He or she can use the Organizer to copy the toolbar to their global template.

You can add, remove, or rearrange commands and submenus on a menu. You can also specify whether the menu displays buttons or text, and change the appearance of buttons as you do for toolbars.

To add a menu to another menu, follow these steps:

1 Click Tools, Customize, Toolbars.

The Customize dialog box appears.

2 Click the Commands tab. Scroll to the bottom of the Categories list and click New Menu.

New Menu is the only command in the New Menu category.

3 Drag the New Menu command to the location where you want to insert it (see Figure 26-6).

Figure 26-6. You can insert a menu or command on a menu bar.

Creating Keyboard Shortcuts

You can assign a keyboard shortcut to any command on a menu. With the Customize dialog box open, right-click the menu or command for which you want to define a keyboard shortcut. In the Name box on the shortcut menu, type an ampersand (&) before the letter you want to use as the shortcut.

Use a different letter for each keyboard shortcut. If you choose a letter that is already in use by another menu entry, you might have to press the letter more than once to select the command you want.

To choose a command using a keyboard shortcut, click a menu to display its commands. Press the shortcut letter for the command you want to select.

To add a command to an existing menu, follow these steps:

1. Click the Commands tab in the Customize dialog box.
2. Click the category of the command you want to add to the menu.
3. Drag the command from the command list to its new location.

Tip **Drag menus and commands where you want them**

When you drag New Menu or any other command to a menu bar, an I-beam pointer appears. Drag the command until the I-beam is where you want to place the command or menu and then release the mouse button. If you want to insert a command in a menu on the menu bar, drag the command to the menu where you want to insert it. When the commands for that menu appear, drag the mouse pointer to its new location and release the mouse button.

To remove a command from a menu, do the following:

1. Click Tools, Customize, Toolbars.

   The Customize dialog box appears.
2. Right-click the command you want to remove from the menu bar and then click Delete. If you want to remove a command from a pull-down menu underneath the menu bar, navigate to the command you want to remove, right-click it and then click Delete.

Tip **Rearrange commands on a menu**

You can rearrange the commands on a menu and modify their properties in the same way that you customize buttons on a toolbar. With the Customize dialog box displayed, drag a command or menu to its new location.

To modify the properties of a command or menu, right-click it and then click the command you want on the shortcut menu, as described in the section "Changing the Properties of a Toolbar" earlier in this chapter on page 821.

Creating and Customizing Forms

Custom forms are dialog boxes that display Microsoft Project fields for data entry. Don't confuse *custom forms* with built-in *form views* such as the Task Entry view. Form views are built in to Microsoft Project and show a set of predetermined fields. On the other hand, custom forms are like dialog boxes that you create. You specify the fields of information you want on the form, where they are to be placed, and how they are accessed.

To use a custom form, you first select the tasks or resources you want to edit with the form. Then you open the form and enter values into the fields. When you click OK on the form, the changes are applied to the selected tasks or resources, and the form disappears.

> **Tip** **Enter field values using a table**
>
> If you want to enter field values without having to open and close a custom form, you can add the fields you want to a table. You can then edit the values in the sheet portion of a view.

Creating Forms

You can create a new custom form or copy an existing form and then edit it. You can add fields, text, and buttons to the form. You can also add group boxes to separate items within the form.

Follow these steps to create a new form:

1. Click Tools, Customize, Forms.

   The Customize Forms dialog box appears (see Figure 26-7).

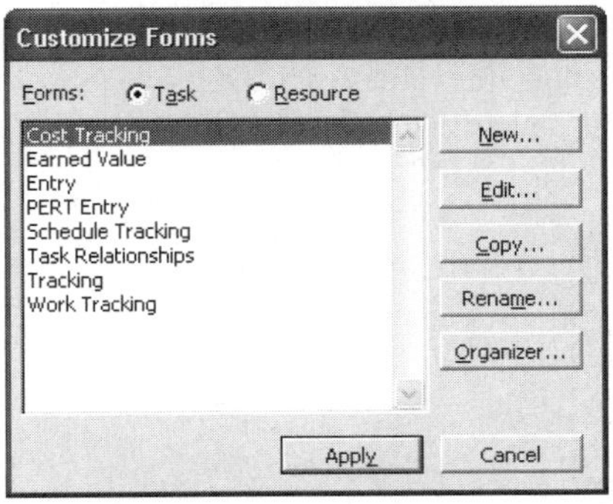

Figure 26-7. Use the Customize Forms dialog box to work with an existing form or create a new one.

2. To create a new custom form, click New.

   To use an existing form as a template, click the form in the list and then click Copy.

3. In the Define Custom Form dialog box, type a new name for the form. If you want to open the form with a keyboard shortcut, type the letter in the Key box.

Caution Microsoft applications use many letters of the alphabet for other commands, such as C for Copy, X for Cut, and P for Paste. If you select one of these reserved characters for a shortcut key, a warning appears that instructs you to select another letter.

4 When you click OK, the Custom Form Editor opens (see Figure 26-8).

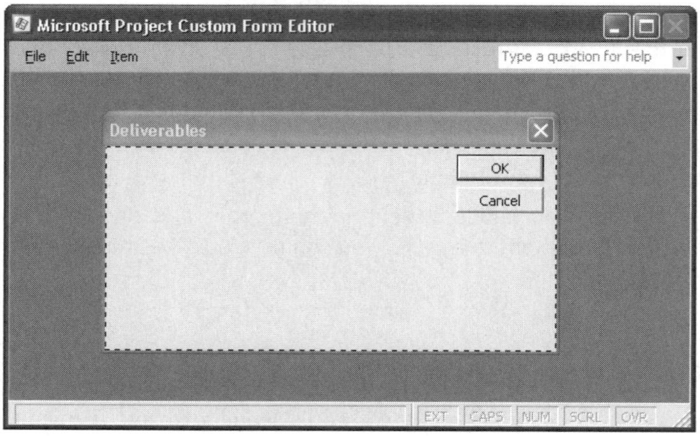

Figure 26-8. You can specify the size and position of the dialog box for a custom form as well as its contents.

5 To change the size of the form, drag a corner or one of its edges until the form is the size you want.

6 To change where the form appears when it loads, drag the title bar of the new form to the location onscreen you prefer.

If you want to specify an exact size and location for the form, double-click the form. In the Form Information dialog box, enter values in the X and Y boxes to specify the form's location. Enter values in the width and height boxes to specify the form's size (see Figure 26-9).

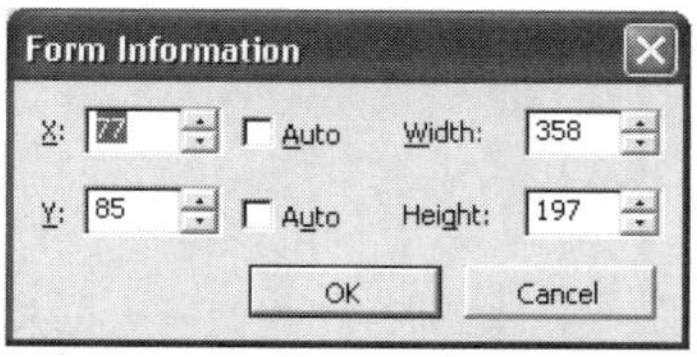

Figure 26-9. Specify the precise location and size of your form in the Form Information dialog box.

Tip **Specify the size of your form**

The values in the X and Y boxes represent pixels on your screen. If your screen resolution is 1280 by 1024, a form with a width of 640 and height of 512 would take up half the screen.

Adding Fields

Custom forms display fields that contain information about the selected tasks or resources. By default, you can view or edit any of the fields in a form. However, you can restrict a field so that it can't be edited.

To add a field to a form, follow these steps:

1. In the Microsoft Project Custom Form Editor window, click Item, Fields.

   The Item Information dialog box appears (see Figure 26-10).

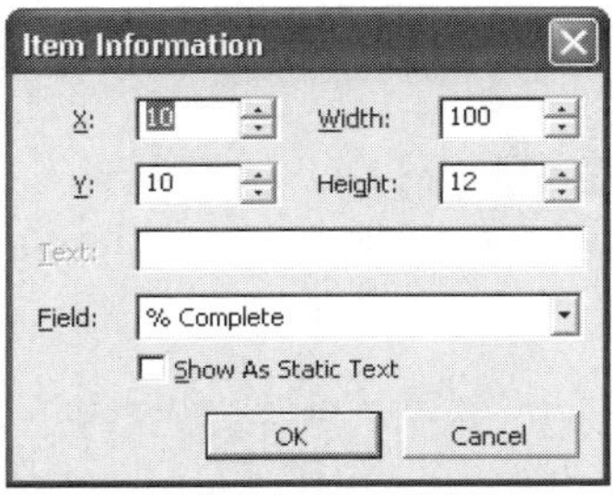

Figure 26-10. You can specify the size, position, and field name as well as whether users can edit the field value.

2. To specify the location of the field, enter values in the X and Y boxes.
3. To specify the size of the field box, enter values in the Width and Height boxes.

> **Tip** **Resize a field box by dragging**
>
> After a field box is added to your form, you can easily resize it by dragging one of its edges or corners. You can also move the field box by dragging the center of the box to the new location.

4. In the Field box, click the field that you want to appear in the box.

   Click the down arrow and then type the first character or two to move quickly to the field you want.
5. To prevent users from editing the field, select the Show As Static Text check box. A value appears in the field, but users can't edit those values.
6. Click OK.

   The field box appears in the form as specified. Make any adjustments you want to the size and position of the field box.
7. Repeat this procedure for all field boxes you want to add to your custom form.

Adding Text

You can add text to label the fields or convey other information to the user. To add text to a form, do the following:

1. In the Custom Form Editor window, click Item, Text.

   A new blank text box appears within the form you are editing.

2 Double-click the text box to display the Item Information dialog box.

3 Type the text you want to appear on the form in the Text box and then click OK.

The text appears in the form (see Figure 26-11). If necessary, drag the text to the position you want.

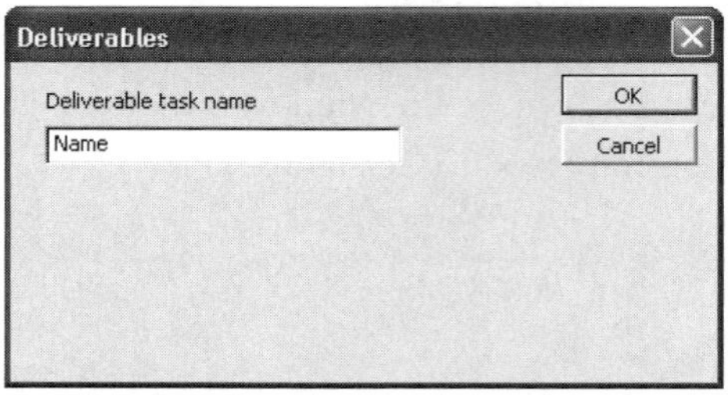

Figure 26-11. Start to create a new form with field boxes and text boxes.

Follow these steps to modify text:

1 To change the size of the text box, drag one of its edges or corners.

2 To reposition the text box in the form, drag the center of the text box to the location you want.

3 To change the text itself, double-click the text box.

Adding Buttons

A new form includes OK and Cancel buttons by default. However, if you removed one of these buttons earlier and want to replace it, you can add buttons to the form. To do this, follow these steps:

1 In the Custom Form Editor window, click Item, Button.

The New Button dialog box appears.

2 Select the option for the button that you want to add to the form.

You can add only an OK or Cancel button.

3 Click OK in the New Button dialog box to add the button to the form.

4 Drag the button where you want it to appear in the form.

Tip **Forms can't contain more than one OK or Cancel button**

A form includes an OK and Cancel button by default. You can't add another OK or Cancel button to the form. The only time you can exercise the Item, Button command is after you delete one of those buttons.

Adding a Group Box

If a form contains a lot of fields, you can make the form more readable by grouping related fields. You can add a group box to the form and then move the items you want to group into it.

To add a group box to a form, do the following:

1. In the Custom Form Editor window, click Item, Group Box.

   The group box appears in the custom form.
2. Drag the group box to the location you want in the form.
3. To resize the group box, drag one of its edges or corners.
4. To change the text that appears at the top of the group box, double-click the group box. The Item Information dialog box appears. Type the new label in the Text box.
5. Move any other items you want into the group box.

For information about creating forms using Visual Basic for Applications, see "Creating UserForms" on page 926.

To save your new form, click File, Save. You cannot name the form from the Custom Form Editor, but you can do so in Microsoft Project in the Customize Forms dialog box. To return to Microsoft Project, click File, Exit.

Editing Forms

Follow these steps to edit an existing form in Microsoft Project:

1. Click Tools, Customize, Forms.

   The Customize Forms dialog box appears.
2. Click the name of the form you want to edit and then click Edit.
3. Make the changes you want in the Custom Form Editor window, as described in the section "Creating Forms" earlier in this chapter on page 827.
4. When finished, click File, Save.
5. Click File, Exit to close the Custom Form Editor window and return to Microsoft Project and the Customize Forms dialog box.

Renaming Forms

Do the following to rename an existing form:

1. Click Tools, Customize, Forms.

   The Customize Forms dialog box appears.
2. Click the name of the form you want to rename and then click Rename.
3. Type the new name in the Define Custom Form dialog box.

Displaying Custom Forms

You can use the Customize Forms dialog box when you want to use one of your forms. However, if you plan to use a custom form frequently, you can add a button to a toolbar or assign a shortcut key to open it.

To open a custom form from the Microsoft Project menus, follow these steps:

1. Select the tasks or resources you want to edit.
2. Click Tools, Customize, Forms. The Customize Forms dialog box appears.
3. Click the name of the form you want to display and then click Apply (see Figure 26-12).

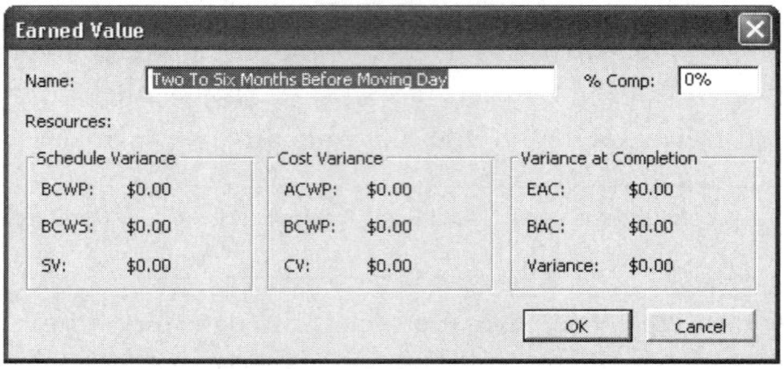

Figure 26-12. Select the task or resource form you want to edit, and then click Apply to display the form.

To add a form as a toolbar button, follow these steps:

1. Click Tools, Customize, Toolbars.
   The Customize dialog box appears.
2. Click the Commands tab. Click the All Forms category.
3. Drag the form you want to add from the command list to the toolbar.

For more information about adding buttons to toolbars, see "Adding and Removing Buttons on a Toolbar" earlier in this chapter on page 818. For information on defining a keyboard shortcut for a form, see "Creating and Customizing Forms" earlier in this chapter on page 827.

Chapter 27

Automating Your Work with Macros

One of the easiest ways to increase your day-to-day productivity with Microsoft Office Project 2003 is to use macros. Macros can automate repetitive, tedious, or complex tasks, freeing your time for more important tasks such as managing your projects.

This chapter focuses on macros you might use to automate tasks that you need to do frequently. Typically, macros are created by recording the steps in a task, which means that little (if any) programming is required.

For more information about advanced macro tasks, such as using them as part of larger solutions to customize or extend the Project 2003 interface and functionality, see Part 9, "Programming Custom Solutions."

Understanding Macros

Washing the dishes—what a chore. Pick up a dirty plate, wash it with soapy water, rinse it off, and then dry it. It's the same every time. But with a dishwasher, all the tedium of washing, rinsing, and drying is automatically handled by the machine, leaving you free to do better things with your time. (Now if you could only get the kids to empty it without being told…) Similarly, you don't want to perform the same tedious series of commands week after week; you just want a specially formatted report to print every Friday. What you need is a macro.

What Is a Macro?

Basically, a macro is a shortcut that performs a series of commands. Rather than manually performing each step necessary to complete a task, you simply tell the software what each step is, what needs to be accomplished in each step, and in what order the steps must occur. Then you designate some way to set this series of commands in motion.

In the past, creating a macro usually involved one of the following two problems:

- The macro language was powerful but arcane, which resulted in a complicated process that took a lot of time to learn.
- The macro language was easier to understand but limited in the range of tasks it could perform, making for a very frustrating experience.

In Microsoft Project, however, you have the best of both worlds with Visual Basic for Applications (VBA). A subset of the highly popular Visual Basic programming language, VBA is both powerful and easy to understand. What's more, the tools available in Microsoft Project make creating macros about as easy as can be. Most macros can be created without ever seeing, much less writing, VBA code.

Why Use Macros?

When you use Microsoft Project (or any other business productivity software) you use it because it makes doing your job easier and more efficient. One of the reasons that software can make you more productive is that the features it has are, in a sense, a collection of macros that accomplish tasks that the software designers feel can be accomplished more effectively by using a computer. More importantly for this discussion, these "macros" perform tasks that the designers learned their customers want. But what the designers can't do is create *all* the features that *every* customer wants. This is where macros can prove so useful.

Because individual users can create a macro to accomplish some particular task, you can essentially customize the software by adding "features" that support the particular way you do your job.

For example, let's say that you do have to print a certain report every Friday. Before you can print anything, you have to do the following:

- Choose the right view of your project data.
- Choose among several filters to exclude unwanted tasks.
- Choose how and in what way you will sort the data.
- Choose the report format you need.

After you open the right project, you might have to click your mouse well over a dozen times before you can print the report. With a macro to perform all those steps for you, printing the report would be reduced to only a few mouse clicks.

Just because macros can be used to perform a complex series of steps doesn't mean that every macro has to be elaborate. Maybe you have certain simple things you do in Microsoft Project all the time, such as creating WBS code masks. By recording a macro and creating a new toolbar button for it, you have a convenient one-click method of opening the WBS Code Definition dialog box.

For more information about creating new toolbar buttons to run macros, see "Creating Toolbar Buttons" later in this chapter on page 843.

Creating Macros

The easiest and quickest way to create a macro, especially one that will be used to automate a lengthy series of steps, is to record the steps that make up a task. Recording a macro is just what it sounds like: Start the macro recorder, perform the series of actions you want the macro to do, and then stop the recorder. In most cases, there's no need to edit the VBA code generated by the recorder.

For more information about creating macros by writing VBA code directly, including how to edit macros, see Chapter 31, "Writing Microsoft Project Code with Visual Basic for Applications."

Understanding the Record Macro Dialog Box

Before you can record a macro, you must first get your project environment ready for recording by setting the conditions that are required for the steps in the macro to occur. Such conditions might include something obvious such as opening a particular project, but can also include steps such as selecting a certain task or resource. You should also have a clear plan for what you want to record; any mistakes you make while the macro recorder is running will be included in the macro. Now you're ready to begin recording.

Click Tools, Macro, Record New Macro. The Record Macro dialog box appears (see Figure 27-1), in which you can enter information about the macro (such as a name and a description) and assign it a shortcut key.

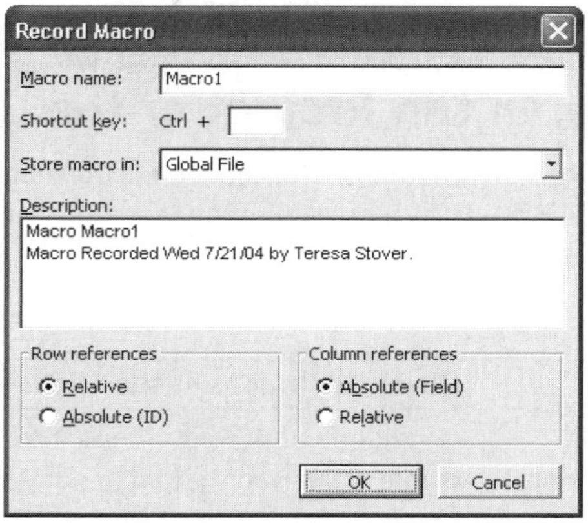

Figure 27-1. The decisions you make in the Record Macro dialog box determine not only when you can use a macro, but also aspects of how it will behave when it runs.

For more information about assigning keyboard shortcuts to macros, see "Creating Keyboard Shortcuts" later in this chapter on page 843.

There are three settings in the Record Macro dialog box that are even more important than the name of the macro or the keyboard shortcut you might use to run it:

Store Macro In. Use the choices in the drop-down list to specify where the macro will be stored. If you choose This Project, the macro is stored in the file with the project that is currently open and will be available only when that project is open. If you choose Global File, the macro is stored in the global file (Global.mpt) and is available whenever Microsoft Project is running, regardless of whether a particular project (or any project at all) is open.

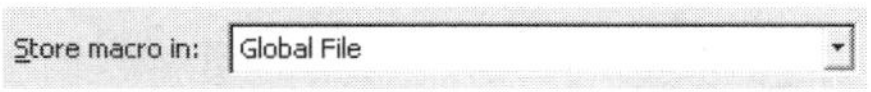

Row References. Accept the default setting of Relative if you want Microsoft Project to record relative row references. Thus, when the macro is run, it will always attempt to move the same number of rows from the selected cell after the macro encounters the command to select a new cell.

For example, suppose that a cell in row 1 is selected and you select a cell in row 4 while recording the macro. From then on, every time the macro is run and encounters the command to select a new cell, it always moves three rows from whatever cell was selected before the macro was run.

Select the Absolute option if you want be certain that a particular row—based on the selected cell's row ID—will be selected when a macro runs. In the example just given, your macro will always select a cell in row 4, regardless of which cell is selected before the macro is run.

Column References. Unlike row references, the default setting for column references is Absolute, based on the selected field. No matter where fields are positioned, absolute column references select the same column every time. Relative column references work just like relative row references.

Where the Macros Are: In the Project or the Global

When creating a new macro, you need to decide whether you will be storing the macro in the current project or in the project global file. Which is best? Well, that depends. Table 27-1 lays out the conditions and recommendations for different situations.

Table 27-1. Where to Store the Macros

Store the Macro in the Project If	Store the Macro in the Global If
Certain very specific conditions must be met in the project plan in order for the macro to run successfully. For example, you might need to select a particular task before running your macro or you might need to select a varying group of resources.	Conditions aren't as stringent for the macros. Many formatting macros can fit this category.
You're distributing the project to others and want the project to be fully self-contained, without also having to provide the global.	The macro is entirely for your own use, or for the use of individuals using the same project plan on the same computer. Or if you all have access to the global, through a network share, for example.
You're not expecting to need to edit the macros.	The macro is used in multiple projects or by multiple users, and you know you might need to adjust the macros and want to make the change just once. When you edit a macro in the global, the change is implemented the next time any user accesses the global to open his project. That is, you don't have to edit the macro 30 times for 30 different users on 30 different computers.

Table 27-1. Where to Store the Macros

Store the Macro in the Project If	Store the Macro in the Global If
You've set up a number of keyboard shortcuts, and you're concerned about the limited number of keyboard shortcuts in the global and keyboard shortcuts in the project getting in each other's way.	Keyboard shortcuts are not a big issue in your macros, or if you're certain that macros in the project plan and the global file use different keyboard shortcuts.

Another note about keyboard shortcuts and the global file: because all the macros in a particular project must share the available keyboard shortcuts, toolbar buttons, and names, only one macro in a project can use Ctrl+A as a keyboard shortcut, for example. This rule also applies to the Microsoft Project global file, which is open whenever Microsoft Project is running. If you use Ctrl+A as a keyboard shortcut in the global, no other macro in the global file can use that shortcut. If you store your Ctrl+A macro in the project file, however, you can have another macro, stored in another project, which also uses Ctrl+A as its keyboard shortcut.

Absolute Column References Can Be Tricky

The decision to use absolute column references might seem like a no-brainer, but absolute column references are based on the selected field. Because fields can be moved, you might sometimes get unexpected results.

For example, suppose that you recorded a macro using absolute column references in a project you share with someone else. When you recorded the macro, you selected the third column, which contained the Start field. At some point, however, your co-worker opened the project and inserted the Duration field as the third column.

The next time you run the macro, the fourth column gets selected because that's the new location of the Start field. If you assumed that the third column would always be selected because absolute column references are "safe" and that's where you always put the Start field, your macro is now broken.

Knowing When to Say "When"

Knowing when to stop the recorder can be as important as the recording environment itself. For an automatic procedure like a macro to be truly trustworthy—and therefore useful—it should have an ending point that is intuitive, or at least easy to remember.

For example, the Bold button on the Formatting toolbar is basically a macro to automate clicking Font on the Format menu and then clicking Bold in the Font Style list. If you have already selected a word, you know that clicking the Bold button formats the word a certain way and then stops. If you haven't selected a word, you know that the Bold button turns on a certain kind of formatting for anything you type until you click it again to turn that formatting off. Both endings are so easy to remember that they've probably become intuitive for you.

The same should be true for any macro you record. It should be easy for you to remember what conditions must be met before you can run the macro, what the macro will do, and when it will stop. A macro that performs a 20-step procedure for you is no good if you're afraid to run it because you can't remember what it might do along the way.

Add the Visual Basic Toolbar

If you record new macros frequently or prefer to run macros by selecting them by name rather than using a keyboard shortcut or a toolbar button, you might find it convenient to use the Visual Basic toolbar:

To display the Visual Basic toolbar, click View, Toolbars, Visual Basic. You can also simply right-click in the toolbar area of the screen and then click Visual Basic on the shortcut menu. The same commands that are available by pointing to Macro on the Tools menu are available here.

Recording a Macro

Let's return to the idea of a weekly report, as described earlier in this chapter. The report that you print every Friday requires you to do the following:

- Change the view to the Tracking Gantt.
- Apply a filter to display only incomplete tasks.
- Sort the tasks by finish date in ascending order.
- Print the results using the Slipping Tasks report.

Tip **Set up favorable conditions for successfully recording the macro**

Before recording your macro, make sure that all your planned steps will take you through to the end of the process you want to program.

In the following example, you need to open a project that actually contains slipping tasks. If there are no slipping tasks, a report is not generated, and you can't record the steps for printing the report and closing the dialog boxes.

You've decided to automate these tasks by recording them in a macro. Follow these steps to record the macro:

1. Click Tools, Macro, Record New Macro.

   The Record Macro dialog box appears.

2. In the Macro Name box, enter a name for your new macro, for example, **Friday_Report**.

A macro name cannot contain spaces, but you can use the underscore character to represent spaces if you want. Although the macro name can contain letters, numbers, and the underscore character, it must begin with a letter. Also, the macro name cannot use any word that Microsoft Project reserves as a keyword.

3. In the Store Macro In box, click This Project.
4. In the Description box, change the first line to a descriptive name, for example, **Weekly task report**.
5. Because the macro won't be selecting cells, make sure that the Row References option is set to Relative and the Column References option is set to Absolute (Field).
6. Click OK to begin recording.

   If you are showing the Visual Basic toolbar, the Record Macro button changes to the Stop Recorder button. Otherwise, there's no indication that you're in the macro recording mode.

> **Note** Remember, everything you do when recording will be written into the macro that you are creating, including any mistakes.

7. Click View, Tracking Gantt.
8. Click Project, Filtered For, Incomplete Tasks.
9. Click Project, Sort, By Finish Date.
10. Click View, Reports.
11. Double-click Current Activities, double-click Slipping Tasks and then click Print.
12. Click OK in the Print dialog box and then click Close in the Reports dialog box.
13. Stop the recorder by clicking Tools, Macro, Stop Recorder. If you're showing the Visual Basic toolbar, you can also click the Stop Recorder button.

Stop Recorder

> **Note** We chose to store this macro in the open project, but it's a good example of a macro that could be stored in the global file as well. Because all the macro does is change the way the data in a particular project is displayed and then print a report, you could record the steps to open the right project at the beginning of the macro. You could then print the report anytime Microsoft Project is running without having to manually open the project first.

Troubleshooting

Why doesn't your macro select the right cell?

If your macro is supposed to select cells as it runs, but selects the wrong ones or even causes an error, one of the following items may be the cause:

- The macro was recorded using one combination of settings for absolute or relative column or row references, but the actual conditions under which the macro is run require a different combination.

You can either rerecord the macro by using a combination that better suits the situation under which the macro is run, or you can edit the macro code in the Visual Basic Editor and then change it manually.

If you change the reference settings manually, the following table shows the different values that should be used when changing the type of column and row references:

Reference	Absolute	Relative
Column	The value for the Column argument is the name of the field in quotes.	The value for the Column argument is a positive number, indicating the number of the column.
Row	The value for the Row argument is a positive number, indicating the number of the row, and the RowRelative argument is False.	The value for the Row argument may be either a negative or positive number. The RowRelative argument is either True or is missing (the default value is True).

Note The columns for the row number and the Indicators field (if showing) are both counted when using relative column references. The first "normal" column is actually column 3 when manually editing column references in a macro.

- The macro assumes that a particular cell or item has been selected before the macro is run.

  You could always try to remember that the proper cell is selected before running the macro, but rerecording the macro (or editing it in the Visual Basic Editor) to select the proper cell before it does anything else solves the problem and also makes the macro more robust.

- The column (or row, if it is for a subtask) containing the cell to select may have been hidden or the row may have been deleted.

  Most of the solutions to this problem involve writing complicated Visual Basic code, so the best solution, until you're more comfortable working with the Visual Basic Editor to edit your macros, is to simply make sure that the proper conditions are met before running your macro. Using column references can also help you spot this problem early on because your macro will cause an error on the line that refers to the missing column and make it easier for you to guess at what the problem is.

Looking at Macro Code

For many people, knowing how to record and play back a macro is sufficient for most of their needs. But what if you made a minor mistake while recording a macro? What if you recorded a complex macro that referenced a project by filename and then the filename was changed? Although you might not ever need to know how to write VBA code, much less create an entire macro with it, the first step to making simple changes or corrections is to understand how simple and logical the macro code can be.

For more information about the Visual Basic Editor, see "Using the Visual Basic Editor" on page 906.

If you were to start the Visual Basic Editor that is included as part of Microsoft Project and open the Friday_Report macro, this is the code you would see:

```
Sub Friday_Report()
' Macro Weekly task report
' Macro Recorded Tue 3/5/04 by Steve Masters.
    ViewApply Name:="Tracking Ga&ntt"
    FilterApply Name:="I&ncomplete Tasks"
    Sort Key1:="Finish", Ascending1:=True
    ReportPrint Name:="Slipping Tasks"
End Sub
```

It's quite short and reasonably simple. You might already have made some guesses about what different sections of the code mean, such as information that also appears in the Microsoft Project interface. Table 27-2 gives descriptions of each line in the VBA code.

Table 27-2. Breakdown of Code in the `Friday_Report` Macro

Macro Code	What It Means
`Sub Friday_Report()`	The beginning of the macro. `Sub` is short for subroutine, which is what a macro really is. The text that follows is the name of the macro.
`' Macro Weekly task report` `' Macro Recorded Tue 3/5/02 by Steve Masters.`	Any line that starts with an apostrophe is a comment and is ignored by Visual Basic. You can use comments anywhere in a macro to remind yourself of what the different parts do.
`ViewApply Name:="Tracking Ga&ntt"`	This line changes the view to the Tracking Gantt. The ampersand (&) comes before the letter that acts as an access key on the View menu.
`FilterApply Name:= "I&ncomplete Tasks"`	This line applies a filter to display only incomplete tasks.
`Sort Key1:="Finish", Ascending1:=True`	This line sorts the tasks by finish date in ascending order.
`ReportPrint Name:= "Slipping Tasks"`	This line prints the Slipping Tasks report.
`End Sub`	The end of the macro, like the period at the end of a sentence.

If, after recording the macro, you decide that you prefer to sort the tasks in descending order, it doesn't take that much time or trouble to record the macro all over again. But it takes even less time to simply edit the macro and change `True` to `False` in the line `Sort Key1:= "Finish", Ascending1:=True`.

Chapter 27

Follow these steps to start the Visual Basic Editor:

1. Click Tools, Macro, Macros.

Tip Pressing Alt+F8 is another way to display the Macros dialog box.

2. In the Macro Name list, click the name of the macro you want to edit.
3. Click the Edit button.

   The Visual Basic Editor starts and displays your macro code (see Figure 27-2). You can now begin editing the macro code.

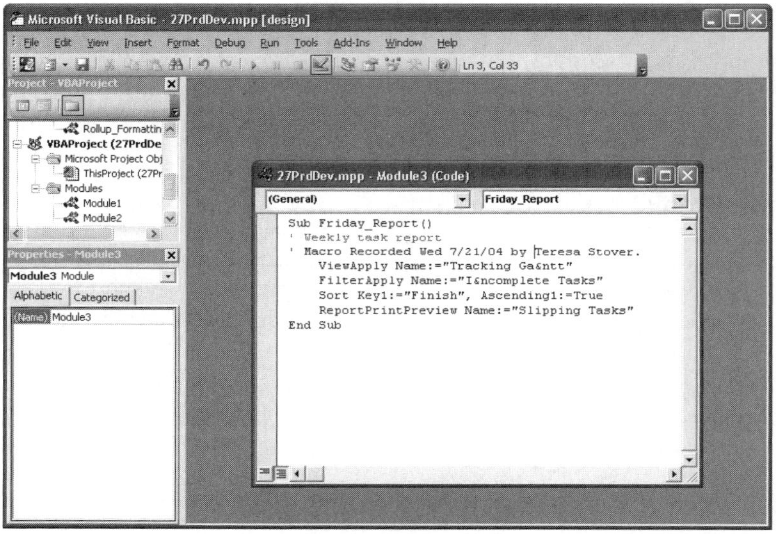

Figure 27-2. Open VBE to review and edit your macro code.

Running Macros

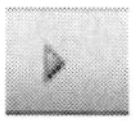

Run Macro

There are three standard methods for running a macro. First, you can run a macro by selecting it from the list of available macros in the Macros dialog box. In the Macros dialog box, select the name of the macro you want to run and then click the Run button.

The other two methods are to press a keyboard shortcut assigned to a macro and to click a toolbar button created for a macro.

Creating Keyboard Shortcuts

Key commands such as Ctrl+C are the oldest and most common shortcuts to access software features, especially for displaying dialog boxes or performing some quick action. Unfortunately, as more and more keyboard shortcuts are assigned to software features, fewer of these simple combinations are left over to be used for macros.

In Microsoft Project, a keyboard shortcut for a macro must be a combination of the Ctrl key and a letter. Because Microsoft Project has many built-in keyboard shortcuts, the only letters available for macro shortcuts are A, E, J, M, Q, T, and Y.

You can assign a keyboard shortcut to a macro when you record it, as described in "Creating Macros" earlier in this chapter. You can also assign a keyboard shortcut to a macro any time after you create it by using the Macro Options dialog box.

Follow these steps to open the Macro Options dialog box:

1. Click Tools, Macro, Macros.
2. In the Macro Name list, click the name of the macro you want to modify.
3. Click the Options button.

   The Macro Options dialog box appears (see Figure 27-3).
4. Add a shortcut key combination and then click OK.

   You can also edit the macro description if you want.

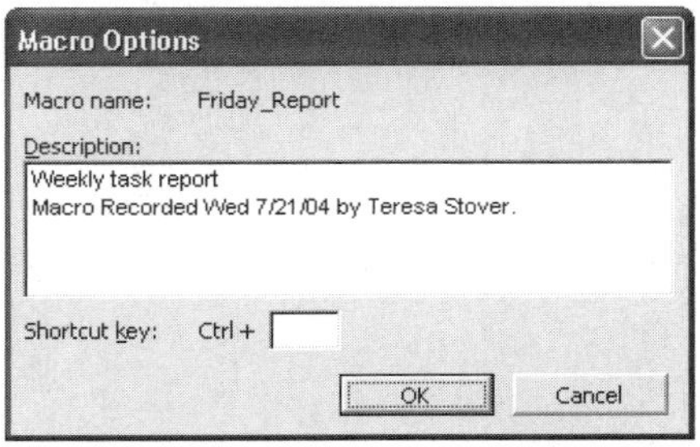

Figure 27-3. Change a macro's description or shortcut key with the Macro Options dialog box.

Tip **Use keyboard shortcuts for frequently used macros**

To gain the most advantage of the quick access provided by keyboard shortcuts, assign them to frequently used macros that perform simple tasks such as opening a dialog box.

Creating Toolbar Buttons

The most common shortcut for running a macro is to create a toolbar button for it. This is true for the following reasons:

- You don't have to memorize a key combination.

- You can display the name of the macro as part of the button.
- You can add it to both a menu and a toolbar, and you can group it with other buttons that are related in some way.

Note **Customize menus just like toolbars**

Beginning with Microsoft Project 2000, menus are treated just like toolbars; you can add, modify, or even delete menus and menu commands as desired.

A macro is not associated with a toolbar button when you record it. Instead, you actually customize the Microsoft Project interface by using the Customize dialog box.

Follow these steps to create a new toolbar button for a macro:

1. Click View, Toolbars, Customize. You can also simply right-click in the toolbar area and then click Customize on the shortcut menu.

   The Customize dialog box appears.

2. Click the Commands tab and then click All Macros in the Categories list (see Figure 27-4).

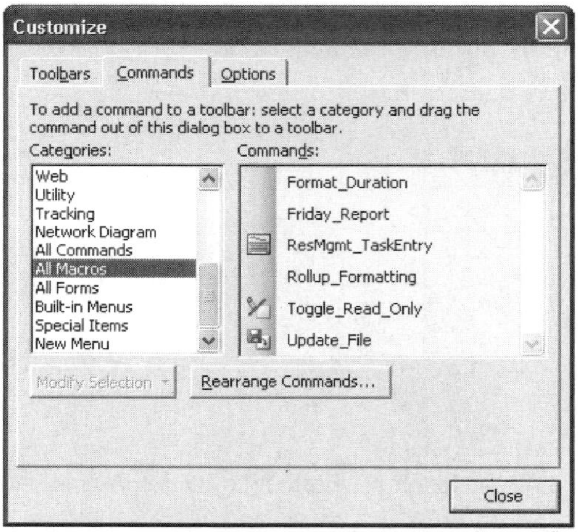

Figure 27-4. Open the Customize dialog box to choose a macro to add as a toolbar button.

3. Click the name of a macro in the Commands list and then drag it to the desired location on any toolbar or menu (see Figure 27-5).

Figure 27-5. Add your macro to any toolbar or menu in Microsoft Project.

When you create a toolbar button for a macro, the button initially displays just the name of the macro. You can modify the new button in many ways, including renaming it, assigning an image to it, or changing its display style. You can even edit the image used for a button or draw your own.

Chapter 27

Follow these steps to assign an image to the button:

1. Click View, Toolbars, Customize.
2. While the Customize dialog box is open, click the toolbar button for which you want to display an image.

   When the Customize dialog box is displayed, clicking a toolbar button doesn't run the macro or command; instead, it selects the button. When selected, the button has a black border.
3. In the Customize dialog box, click the Commands tab.
4. Click the Modify Selection button.
5. Point to Change Button Image and then click the graphic you want to use for your selected toolbar button.

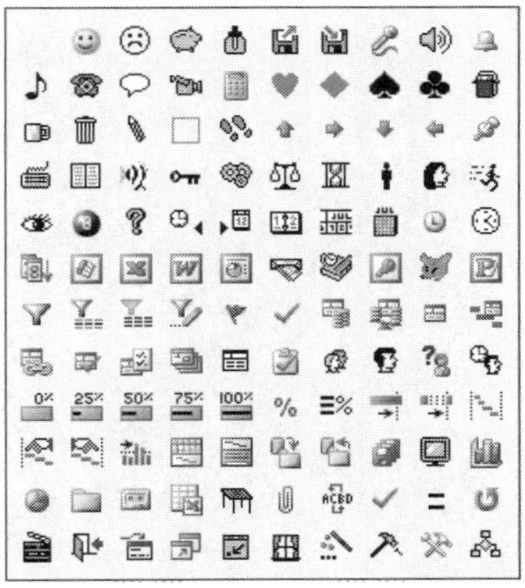

6. Click the Modify Selection button again and then click Default Style.

   The button displays the image you selected, but the name of the macro appears only as a ScreenTip when you move the mouse pointer over the button.

Note **Change the button name**

The Name box on the Modify Selection menu is used for both the caption and the ScreenTip of the button you're modifying. You can change this text to whatever suits you without also changing the name of the macro itself.

For more information about customizing Microsoft Project toolbars and menus, see Chapter 26, "Customizing the Microsoft Project Interface."

Chapter 28

Standardizing Projects Using Templates

With each project you manage, you learn more and more. You practice effective project management methods and see what works and what doesn't. You gain more knowledge about project management in your specific discipline or industry. Likewise, as you continue to manage projects with Microsoft Office Project 2003, you increase your proficiency with it as a productivity tool for planning, tracking, and communicating your project information.

You can record some of the knowledge you gained from hard-won project management experience by using Project 2003 *templates*. As you enter the closing processes of a project, saving the project file as a template for future use can be one of your most valuable project closing activities. Templates are special project files in which various types of project information can be stored for use with future projects, either by you or by other project managers.

You can also use templates to save yourself from reinventing that old wheel. Obtain project templates already developed by industry experts and adapt them for your own project requirements, thereby saving time and giving yourself a leg up on planning your next project.

Whether a template is based on your own project experiences or someone else's, it can contain the following types of information:

- Tasks
- Durations
- Sequences and tasks
- Resources dependencies

Templates are also a great means of setting standards. If your organization follows a specific methodology in each project, if certain review processes are required at certain stages, or if a specific format is mandated for progress reports, those requirements can all be reflected in the template. Similarly, any custom features that reflect organization standards or that you've designed to make your project work more effectively can also become a part of your template.

Understanding the Template Types

There are three types of templates in Microsoft Project:

- **Project template.** The project template might contain task and resource information that you can use as a basis for starting a new project. It's often based on past project experiences in the organization or in the industry. For example, there are software project templates, commercial construction templates, product development templates, and so on.

  There are a wide variety of project templates available, both within Microsoft Project and from third-party sources. You can use such a project template as the basis for a new project you're creating. If you're closing a project, you can save and adapt your plan as a project template file for you or others to use and benefit from your experience.

- **Project global template.** The project global template, also referred to as the *global.mpt* file, is a template that contains elements and settings pertinent to how you use Microsoft Project. Such elements include views, tables, groups, filters, and reports for customized ways of looking at project information. The project global template can include calendars, macros, and toolbars for specific methods of executing Microsoft Project commands and functions. The project global template can also include general Microsoft Project program settings to set defaults for editing, scheduling, and calculations, to name a few.

  The project global template is automatically attached to every project file you work with. As the user and project manager, you have control over the content of your project global template, although you can share it with others if you want.

- **Enterprise global template.** If you're set up for enterprise project management using Microsoft Office Project Professional 2003 and Microsoft Office Project Server 2003, the *enterprise global template* is also automatically attached to every enterprise project you check out. Think of it as a global template over the project global template, or the "global global." This template dictates standards being enforced and customizations made available throughout the enterprise; for example, custom fields, views, and macros. These standards provide for customization and consistency across all projects in an organization. The standards propagated through the enterprise global template also make it possible for project information throughout the enterprise to be compared and analyzed to one another in meaningful ways.

  Because the enterprise global template affects all projects throughout the enterprise, only users who have certain permissions can check out and modify the enterprise global template. Many organizations give that responsibility to one or two project server administrators or portfolio managers.

For more information about the enterprise global template, see "Working with the Enterprise Global Template" on page 622.

Working with the Project Global Template

The project global template, or *global.mpt*, is an integral part of every project file. Essentially, the project global template is a collection of default settings for a variety of elements throughout a project file. These elements include the following:

- Views
- Custom fields and outline codes
- Tables
- Toolbars
- Groups
- Forms
- Filters
- Macros and VBA modules
- Reports
- Import/export maps
- Base calendars

As you alter settings in your project by customizing your view and calendar settings, modifying tables, and creating sets of custom fields, for example, those changes initially apply to just the current project. If you want your custom settings available to any project opened on your local computer, you can add them to the project global template using the Organizer (see Figure 28-1). Those new settings become your new defaults.

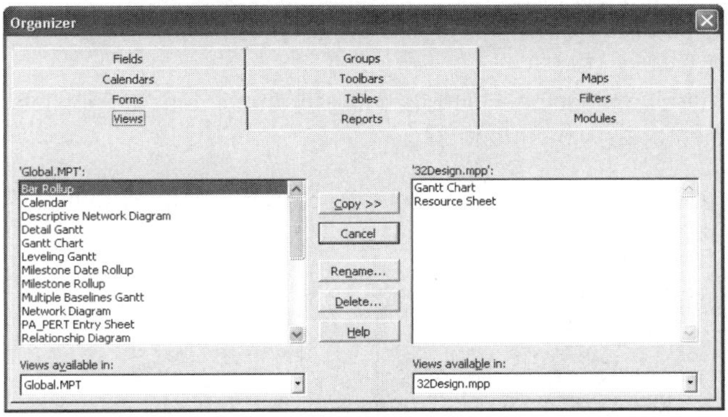

Figure 28-1. Use the Organizer to copy customized elements to the project global template to make those elements available to other projects.

For more information about the Organizer, see "Sharing Customized Elements among Projects" on page 812.

The project global template also contains your Microsoft Project-wide settings, which you access by clicking Tools, Options. In the Options dialog box, various categories of options are available, like View, Schedule, Calculation, and so on. Certain settings apply just to the current project file; others apply to Microsoft Project as a whole and change the project global template. You can use the Set As Default button to add current project settings to your project global template (see Figure 28-2).

Chapter 28

These options are saved to the project global template.

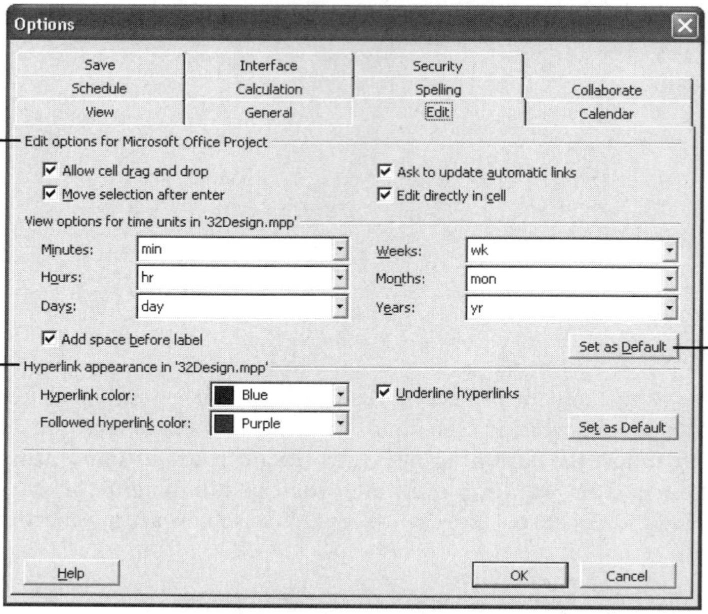

Click Set As Default to apply current settings to the project global template.

These options apply only to the current file.

Figure 28-2. Any group of options specified as being for the current file applies only to that file unless you click the Set As Default button.

Settings that do not specify that they apply only to the current file apply to Microsoft Project in general (see Figure 28-3).

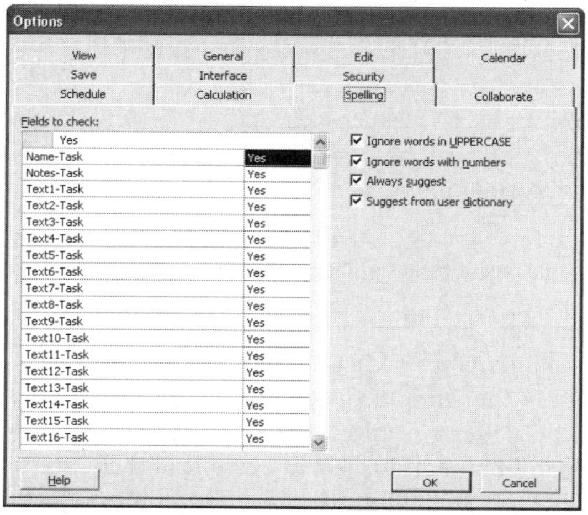

Figure 28-3. The settings on the Spelling tab apply to your spelling checker options in Microsoft Project in general. Changes here update the project global file.

When you change a Microsoft Project setting, every new file you open from that point on will reflect that change. When you change a local project setting and then set it as a default, it will apply to any new projects, but it will not change the setting for other existing projects.

Working with Project Templates

A project template is a standardized starting point for a new project. A template can contain task information, resource information, or both. It might be very broad in scope, showing just major phases and generic resource names, for example. Or the template can be highly detailed, with multiple outline levels of tasks, their durations, task dependencies, and specific resource information.

Microsoft Project comes with a set of built-in templates for a variety of industries and applications. Microsoft Project templates are available from third-party sources as well, such as professional societies and standards organizations. You can also create your own templates based on previous projects you have completed. It's a good practice to adapt and save the plan of a completed project as a template for future use in your organization, either for yourself or for others.

For more information about using a project plan as template, see "Creating Your Own Project Template," later in this chapter on page 857.

A project template serves as a knowledge base for a certain type of project. It is meant to save you time when planning your new project and to let you build on past project experiences. The project template can also help set and enforce organizational standards. It can disseminate custom features and elements, such as specially designed reports, company-specific base calendars, modified views, and so on.

Starting a New Project Using a Template

Whenever you start a new project, you're given the opportunity to choose a template. If you start a project with a template, your new project file is populated with information from that template. You then adapt that information to meet your project's specific requirements. When you save the file, you're saving a new project file, rather than overwriting the existing template file. This way, the template remains available for use in its more generic format.

Built-In Templates

The following templates are supplied with Microsoft Project:

- Commercial construction
- Engineering
- Home move
- Infrastructure deployment
- New business
- New product

- Office move
- Project office
- Residential construction
- Software development
- Software localization

There are additional built-in templates for the deployment in your organization of specific Microsoft products, such as Windows XP, Exchange Server, and more.

Microsoft Project online Help provides comprehensive details about each template provided. In the Help box, type **templates** and then click the Available Templates link (see Figure 28-4).

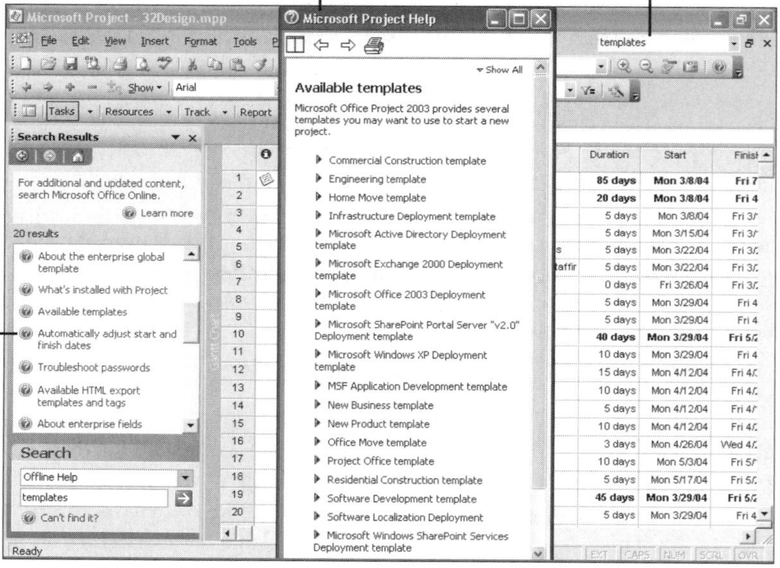
The corresponding Help topic is displayed when a search result is selected.
Enter a key phrase in the Help box.
Help Search Results appear in the left pane.
Microsoft Project Help
Available templates

Figure 28-4. Read about any of the built-in templates to see whether it fits the type of project you need to build.

Creating a New Project with a Template

To create a new project from a template, follow these steps:

1 Click File, New.

Note If you just click the New button on the Standard toolbar, you won't get the choices you need in the Project Guide.

2 In the New Project pane, under Templates, click the On My Computer link.

3 In the Templates dialog box, click the Project Templates tab (see Figure 28-5).

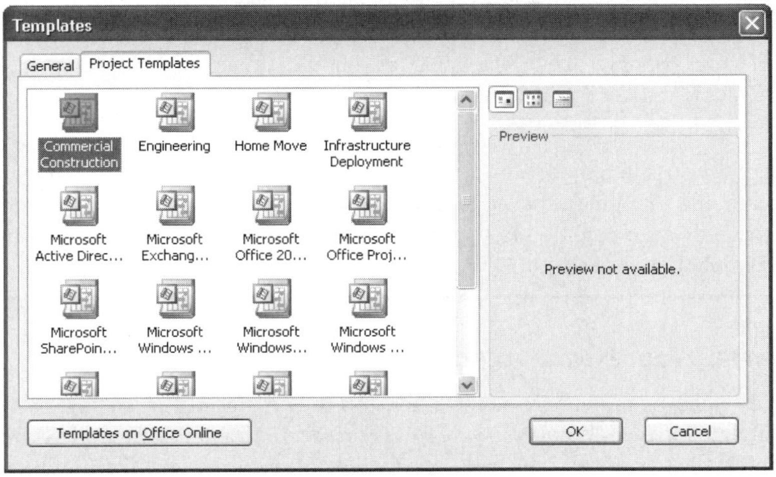

Figure 28-5. All built-in templates are listed.

4 Click the project template you want to use and then click OK.

A new project plan appears, based on the template you chose (see Figure 28-6). If this is the first time you've chosen a template, Microsoft Project might need to install it. This just takes a few moments.

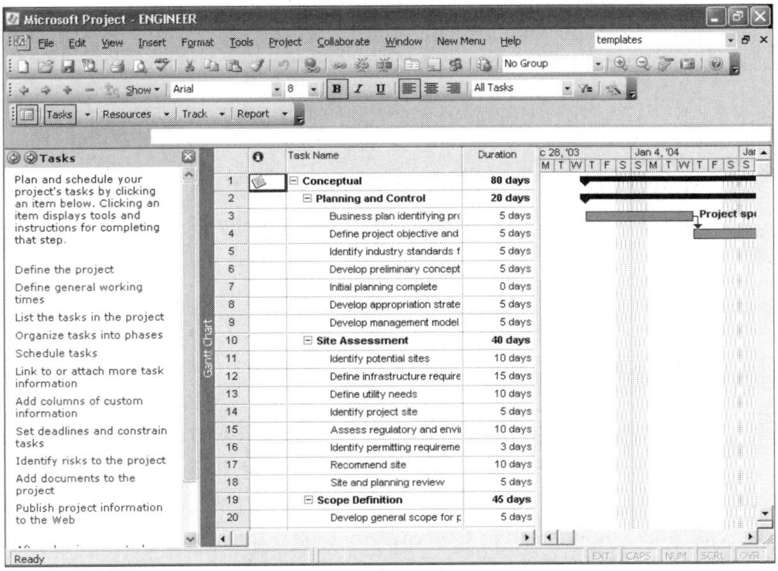

Figure 28-6. A new project file is created based on your selected template.

Create a New Project from an Existing One

You can use an existing project as the basis for a new project. To do this, click File, New. In the New Project pane, under New, click the From Existing Project link. Browse to find the project you want to use as the basis for your new project and then open it. When you save this file, Microsoft Project makes sure that you give it a different name, so the original file remains intact.

When you use a project file as the basis for a new project plan, you might need to do a little more adaptation than with a regular template. For example, you probably need to remove all date constraints and any actuals, and you might need to remove resource information as well.

Saving Your New Project

The original template file has an extension of *.mpt*, indicating that it is a Microsoft Project template file type. When you save a new project file based on a template, by default your new project file is saved as a normal *.mpp* (Microsoft Project plan) file. To save a project based on a template, do the following:

Save

1. On the Standard toolbar, click Save.
2. In the Save As dialog box, choose the drive and folder in which you want to save the new project.
3. In the File Name box, enter a descriptive name for your project and then click the Save button.

Adapting the Template to Your Project

Review your new project file for the types of information included and the level of detail. Review as follows:

- In the Gantt Chart or other task sheet, review the list of tasks. Determine whether you need to add more tasks or remove extraneous ones.
- Check to see whether durations are filled in for the tasks. If they are, see if they seem close to the durations you will expect in your new project.
- Review the chart portion of the Gantt Chart or the Network Diagram and see whether task dependencies have been set up. Review their appropriateness and their complexity.
- Display the Resource Sheet and see whether there is any resource information. There might be generic resources. If you're using a template generated within your organization, you might see names of actual individuals.

Based on this review, you can see how much adaptation you'll need to do to tailor this template to your project.

> **Tip** **Use the Adjust Dates tool to update the project start date in a template**
>
> If you're building a new project plan based on a template, use the Adjust Dates tool to bring the scheduled project start date in the template to your own project's start date.
>
> Click View, Toolbars, Analysis to show the Analysis toolbar. Click the Adjust Dates button on the Analysis toolbar. In the Adjust Dates dialog box, enter your project start date and then click OK.

Downloading a Project Template

You can download additional templates for different industries and endeavors from the Office Online Web site. To do this, follow these steps:

1. Click File, New.
2. In the New Project pane, click the Templates On Office Online link.

   Your Web browser launches and goes to the Office Online Web site (see Figure 28-7).

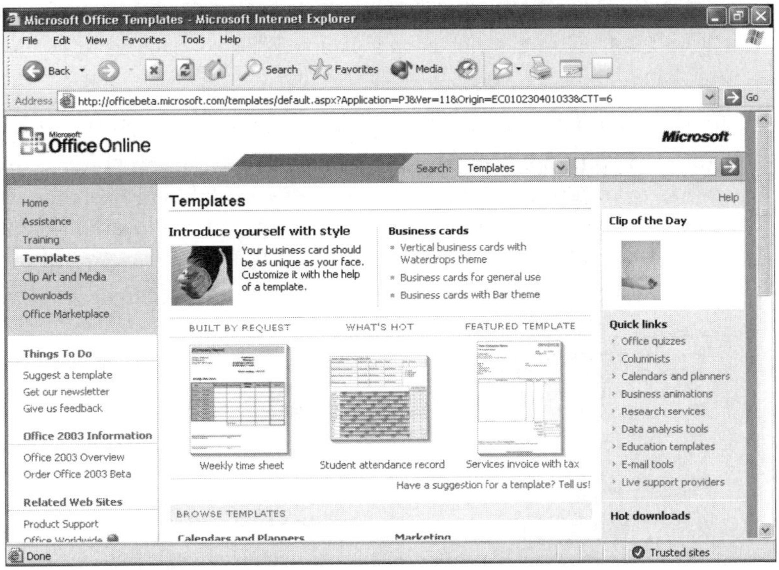

Figure 28-7. The Office Online Web site contains more templates, as well as clip art, training, and articles that are continually being updated and expanded.

3. Under Meetings And Projects, click Project Management.

   The Project Management templates page appears (see Figure 28-8).

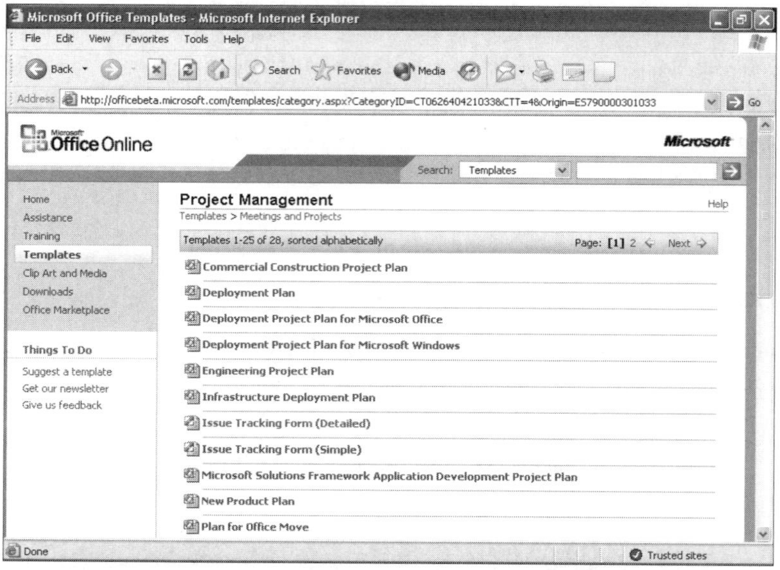

Figure 28-8. Use this Web page to find and download more project management templates.

4 To select or just preview a template you might want to download, click its name in the list. Note the application icon beside each template name, and be sure to select one with the Microsoft Project icon. Other templates related to project management are also listed for other applications such as Microsoft Office PowerPoint 2003 and Microsoft Office Access 2003.

A preview of the selected template appears (see Figure 28-9).

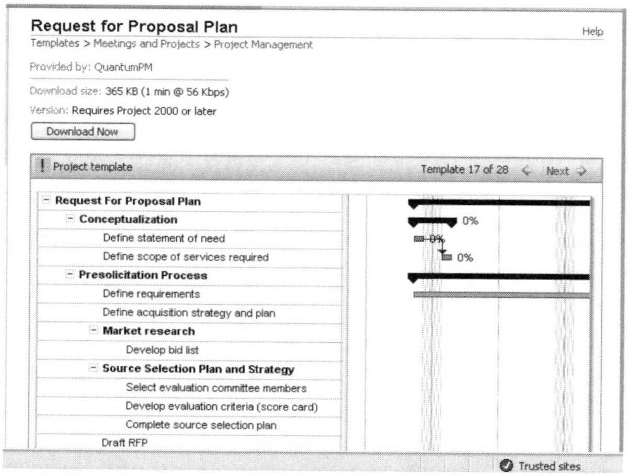

Figure 28-9. If a template fits your bill, click Download Now to copy it to your computer.

Chapter 28

5 If you like the template, click Download Now. Follow the steps to copy the template onto your hard drive.

When finished, the downloaded template is loaded into Microsoft Project as a new project plan based on that template. You can immediately adapt that template to the specifics of your project.

Creating Your Own Project Template

After you plan and track a few projects to completion using Microsoft Project, you'll see that you're recording valuable information in your project plans. Of course, you'll archive your project plan for historical purposes. However, you can also use an existing or completed project plan as the basis for a template that will save you and others a great deal of time when planning future projects.

By creating your own template, you can save task and resource information, format settings, project-specific options, calendars, macros, and other elements that you've used successfully in other projects. Any Microsoft Project file can be saved as a template.

To save an existing project file as a template for future use by you or other project managers, follow these steps:

1. Open the project file you want to save as a template.
2. Click File, Save As.
3. In the Save As Type list, click Template (*.mpt).

   The filename changes from the .mpp extension to .mpt, indicating that a copy of the regular project plan file will be saved as a template file. Also, the file is moved to the Templates folder. As long as your template is stored in this folder, it will appear in the Templates dialog box.
4. Click the Save button. The Save As Template dialog box appears (see Figure 28-10).

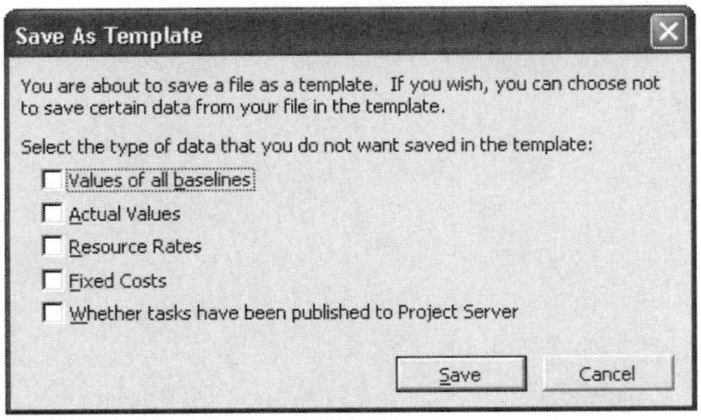

Figure 28-10. The file might include tracking and other specific information not appropriate for a template. Select the information you want to exclude from the template.

5. Select the check box for any item you do not want to be saved as part of the template and then click the Save button.

   The file is saved as a template in your Microsoft Templates folder on your computer's hard disk.

Copy Templates that Others Have Created

If you want to use templates that others in your organization have created or if you obtain templates from a third-party source or an industry standards organization, copy the file into your Microsoft Templates folder. Storing the template in the right folder ensures that you'll see the templates listed in the Templates dialog box.

If you're using Windows XP or Windows 2000, the path is C:\Documents and Settings \<Name>\Application Data\Microsoft\Templates.

If you're using Windows 98, the path is C:\Windows\Application Data\Microsoft \Templates.

By default, the Application Data folder is hidden in Windows XP and Windows 2000. To show hidden files and folders, in Windows Explorer, click Tools, Options. Click the View tab. In the Advanced Settings box, double-click Hidden Files And Folders if necessary to show its options. Select the Show Hidden Files And Folders option.

To check that your new template appears in the Templates dialog box, do the following:

1. Click File, New.
2. In the Project Guide, under New From Template, click the General Templates link.

   Your new template should be listed on the General tab (see Figure 28-11).

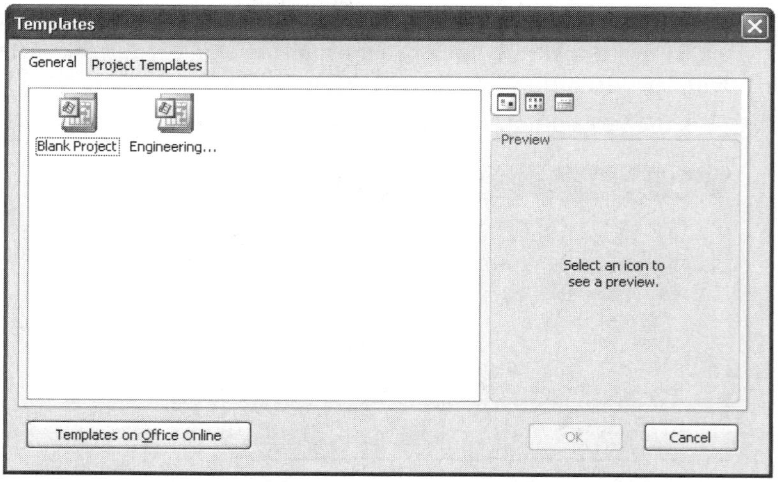

Figure 28-11. The General tab of the Templates dialog box contains any templates you've created.

Tip **Change the location where templates are stored**

By default, templates stored in the Microsoft Templates folder appear in your Templates dialog box. You can store templates in a different folder, however, and direct the Templates dialog box to find them in the new location. Changing the location of the templates can be useful if a set of templates has been developed for your organization and they've been placed on a file server for multiple project managers to use and perhaps update.

To change the location of the Microsoft Templates folder, click Tools, Options and then click the Save tab. Under File Locations, click User Templates and then click the Modify button. Browse to the new location and then click OK.

Review the new template file and see whether there is any other information that should be removed. Here are some suggestions:

- Display the task sheet and apply the Constraints table. See if there are any date constraints that should be changed to As Soon As Possible or As Late As Possible.
- Review the task dependencies shown in the template. Determine whether they're useful or should be removed.
- Review the Resource Sheet. Decide whether you want to keep specific resource information or replace it with generic resource names. Also decide whether you should change maximum units and other availability information, and whether the cost information should be retained or deleted.
- Review tasks, resources, and assignments to see whether there are any notes that should be removed.

After you finish adapting the template, click Save on the Standard toolbar. Your changes are made to the template.

Updating an Existing Template

If you need to update the information in an existing template, you cannot simply open the template and save it; it will save a copy of the template as a regular project (*.mpp*) file. To update and save information in the template itself, follow these steps:

1. Click File, New.
2. In the New Project pane, under Templates, click the On My Computer link.
3. In the Templates dialog box, double-click the template you want to update.
4. Make the changes you want to the template.
5. On the Standard toolbar, click Save.

   The Save As dialog box appears.
6. In the Save As Type list, click Template (*.mpt).

   The current folder switches to the Templates folder. The template you just edited should appear in the list of files.
7. Click the template, and then click the Save button.

A prompt appears, indicating that you're about to replace the existing file (see Figure 28-12).

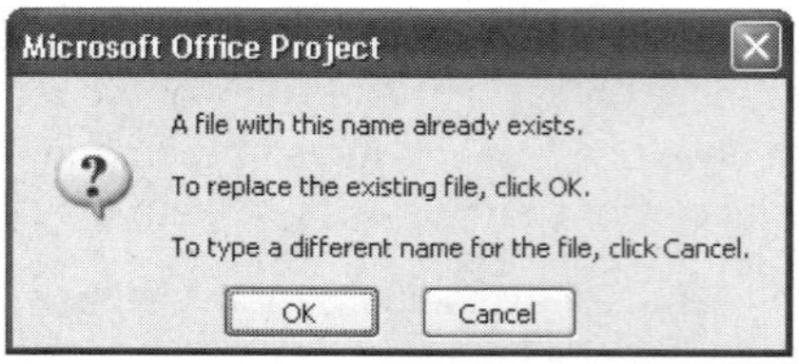

Figure 28-12. Microsoft Project warns you that you're about to replace the existing template file, but that's exactly what you want to do.

8. Click OK. The Save As Template dialog box appears.
9. Click the Save button. Your changes are saved to the template file.

> **Warning** If several project managers use the same project template, be careful when you're updating templates because your changes can affect many projects.

Closing a Project

After the planning, executing, and controlling processes of the project, the final process is the closing of the project. At this point, you've fulfilled the goals of the project and it's now complete. In the closing process of the project, you can analyze project performance with concrete data about schedule, cost, and resource utilization. You can also identify lessons learned and save acquired project knowledge.

Analyzing Project Performance

Review your overall project and compare your baseline plan to your actual plan. You can review variances in the schedule, in costs, and in assignment work. Any large variances can help point out problem areas in the project. Some helpful reports for such analysis include the following:

- Project Summary
- Overbudget Tasks
- Top-Level Tasks
- Overbudget Resources
- Milestones
- Earned Value
- Budget

To generate one of these reports, click View, Reports and then double-click Overview or Costs.

For more information about generating reports, see Chapter 12, "Reporting Project Information."

Recording Lessons Learned

Whether or not you will continue to be involved in this type of project, others are likely to benefit from the experience and knowledge you've gained. At the end of your project, gather your team together and conduct a "postmortem" session, in which you can objectively discuss what went well with the project and what could be improved next time.

It's often helpful to have team members prepare notes in advance. In larger projects, you might find it more practical to conduct a series of meetings with different groups of team members and stakeholders, perhaps those who were responsible for different aspects of the project.

Be sure to have a concrete method for recording the discussion points. After the session, compile the lessons learned report, including solutions to identified problem areas.

Project Management Practices: Administrative Closure

As you complete each major milestone or phase, you've probably been getting formal acceptance of that phase by the sponsor or customer. The sponsor reviews the deliverables and checks that the scope and quality of work are completed satisfactorily and then signs off his or her acceptance of that phase.

When you reach the end of the project, you get your final acceptance and signoff, which at this point should be a formality because the sponsor has been involved and signing off on the interim deliverables all along.

This final project acceptance is part of the administrative closure of the project. Administrative closure also includes analyzing project success and effectiveness, and archiving documents and results. At this point, contracts are closed and budget records are archived. Employees should be evaluated and their skills in your organization's resource pool should be updated to reflect the increase in skills and proficiencies they've gained as a result of working on this project.

A complete set of project records should make up the project archives, and these archives should be readily available for reference for future similar projects.

If the project plan is your repository for project-related documents, add your lessons learned report to the closed project. You can embed the document in the plan, create a link to the document, or add it to the document library through Microsoft Office Project Web Access 2003 and Project Server 2003.

For more information about adding a document to a project, see "Attaching Project Documentation" on page 73. For information about using the document library, see "Controlling Project Documents" on page 691.

In addition to archiving the document with the rest of the project historical records, include it with your planning materials for the next project. Be sure to keep your solutions in the forefront so you can continue to improve your project management processes.

Saving Acquired Project Knowledge

Through the planning and tracking of your project, it's likely that you've recorded a mass of valuable information about the following:

- Task durations
- Task and resource costs
- Work metrics (units per hour completed, and the like)

You might want to collect information about planned or actual durations, work, and costs to use as standards for planning future projects.

These durations and work metrics can be included in a project template based on the closing project. Save the project plan as a project template for future use by you or other project managers in your organization who will be working on a similar type of project. In your template, you can remove actuals, resource names, and constraint dates, for example. But the tasks, durations, task dependencies, base calendars, and generic resources can be invaluable in a project template. In addition, any custom solutions you've developed—such as views, reports, filters, and macros—can also become a part of your template. Through the efficiencies you built into your project plan, you're laying the groundwork for future efficiencies.

Chapter 29

Managing Project Files

It's a very basic concept: When you save a project file, you're ensuring that it'll be there when you need to open and work on it again. In a nutshell, managing project files involves saving, finding, and opening your project files. The majority of the time, that's all there is to it. But you can't open a file if you can't find it. You want to be sure you know where you put your files; if you're at a loss, you need to know the best techniques for searching for and finding them quickly.

You also want to guard against data loss in the event of a system crash by saving your file often enough and having a recent backup file handy. Another safeguard is password protection. These are all aspects of sound file management, which are covered in this chapter.

Opening Project Files

After you save a project, you can open it again and continue working. You can open a file stored on your own computer or on a network drive. If you're working in an enterprise environment, you can open your project file from the Microsoft Office Project Server 2003.

You can open many different types of files in Microsoft Office Project 2003, including database, spreadsheet, or text files.

Opening a Saved Project

You can open files from your local machine as well as from a network drive. If you're running Microsoft Office Project Professional 2003, you can also open a project file from a project stored in the Project Server 2003 database.

Opening a Project from Your Local Computer or a Network Drive

To open a project from your local computer or a network drive, do the following:

Open

1. On the Standard toolbar, click Open.

   The Open dialog box appears with your default folder selected (see Figure 29-1).

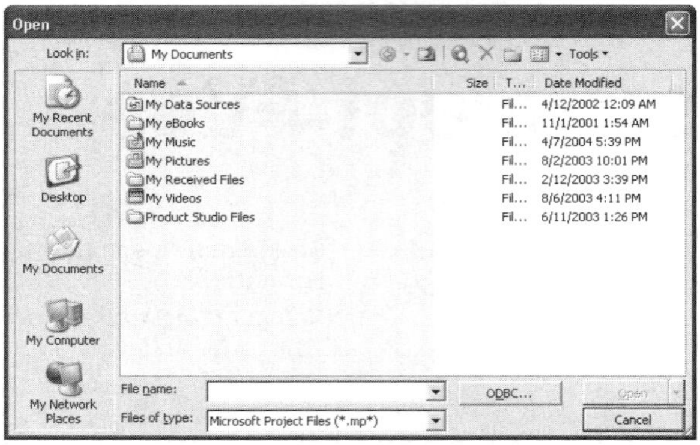

Figure 29-1. The Open dialog box shows the list of available project files in the selected location.

You can also click File, Open to display the Open dialog box.

2 In the Look In box, click the drive or folder where the project file resides.

3 If necessary, double-click the folder that contains the project file.

4 Double-click the project file you want to open. You can also click the project and then click Open.

Open options

When you open your project, you have three options for the way the file opens: Read-Write, Read-Only, or Copy. In the Open dialog box, click the arrow to the right of the Open button to choose which option you want in the list:

Open. Opens the project file normally; that is, in Read-Write mode. This mode is selected by default when you simply click the Open button (rather than the Open arrow).

Open Read-Only. Opens the project in Read-Only mode. You can view the project, but you can't save it. To save any changes you make to a Read-Only project file, you need to save the file with a different name by using the File, Save As command.

Open As Copy. Opens a copy of the project file you selected. "Copy (1) of" is added in front of the filename. If you open a second copy, it will be named "Copy (2) of," and so forth. Any changes you make appear only in the copy of the file, not in the original file.

Opening a Project from Project Server

To open an enterprise project file, you must open the project from Project Server. Opening an enterprise project is also referred to as *checking out* the file, which prevents anyone else from changing the file while you are working on it. However, others can still view the read-only file.

Note This section applies only if you're working with Project Professional 2003 set up for an enterprise environment.

To open a project stored in the Project Server database, follow these steps:

1. Click File, Open.
2. Enter your user ID and password, if prompted, and then click OK.
3. The Open From Microsoft Project Server dialog box appears (see Figure 29-2). Make sure the Read/Write To Check Out option is selected.

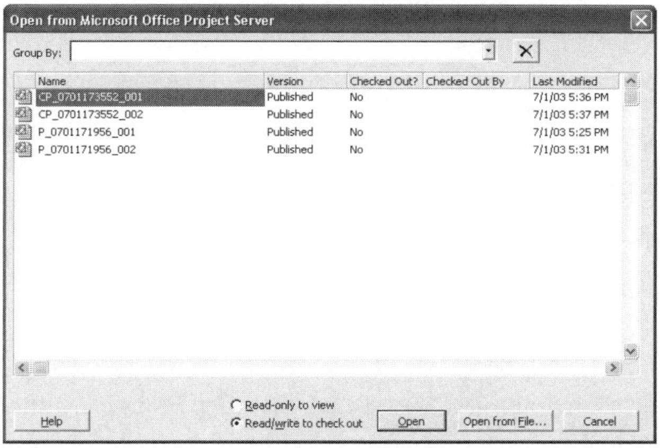

Figure 29-2. The Open From Microsoft Project Server dialog box shows the projects stored on Project Server that you are authorized to check out or view.

4. Double-click a project's name.

   The project file opens in Microsoft Project.

If you want to work with the project while not connected to Project Server, click File, Save Offline and then specify the location where you want to save the project. If there are other users with accounts on the same server, they cannot edit the file until you click File, Save Online (which saves it to Project Server).

For more information about working with enterprise projects, see "Creating a New Enterprise Project" on page 645.

Opening Projects Created in Previous Versions of Microsoft Project

In Microsoft Project 2003, you can easily open project files created in earlier versions of Microsoft Project. If the file was created in Microsoft Project 2002, 2000, or Microsoft Project 98, it can be opened directly in Microsoft Project 2003 with no additional steps required.

If the project file was created in a version of Microsoft Project earlier than Microsoft Project 98, it must first be saved as an MPX file before Microsoft Project 2003 can open it as a project file. The MPX file format is a record-based ASCII text file format available in Microsoft Project.

Note In addition to the MPX file format, you can open a variety of file formats other than the standard Microsoft Project Plan (MPP) file format.

For more information, see "Saving and Opening with Different File Formats," later in this chapter on page 872.

Searching for Files

Have you ever been unable to find a file? The search can be frustrating and painful, and it is often a big waste of time. A new file-finding feature is built into Microsoft Project 2003 that simplifies finding lost files.

To search for a file, do the following:

1. On the Standard toolbar, click Open.

   If you are logged in to Project Server, the Open From Microsoft Project Server dialog box appears.
2. If you're logged on to Project Server, click the Open From File button to display the Open dialog box.
3. In the Open dialog box, click Tools, and then click Search.

   The Search dialog box appears (see Figure 29-3).

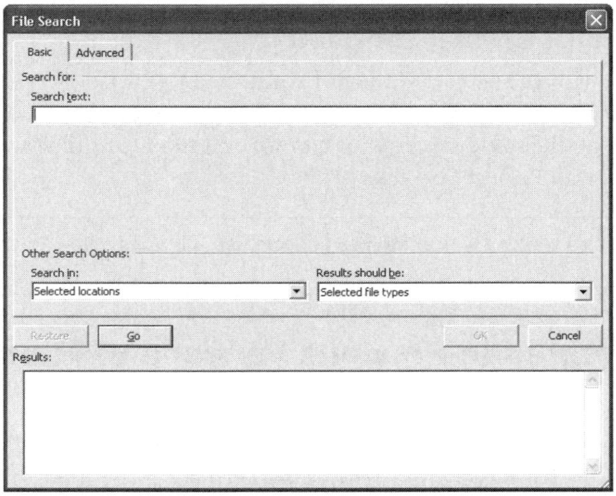

Figure 29-3. Use the Search dialog box to enter and execute basic or advanced search parameters.

4 Make sure that the Basic tab is displayed.

5 In the Search Text box, type a portion of the filename you want to search for.

For example, if you know that your filename contains the word "software" or "deployment," as in "Software Deployment Project," enter one or more of those words.

6 In the Search In box, select the check boxes for the drives, network drives, and folders in which you want to search for the file.

7 In the Results Should Be box, select the check boxes for the types of files you want to search for; for example, Project Files and Web Pages.

Add project summary information

All projects can be associated with a title, subject, author, manager, and other information. When you add project summary information to your project, you are adding levels of detail that can be used for reports and searches. For example, if you search for a project's author and the author has indeed been identified for a project, that project is returned as a result of the search. You can also use these fields when creating customized reports. For example, if you want to create a set of reports about projects managed by a specific project manager, the Manager field needs to be completed for each project.

To add project summary information to your project, do the following:

1 Click File, Properties.

The Properties dialog box appears (see Figure 29-4).

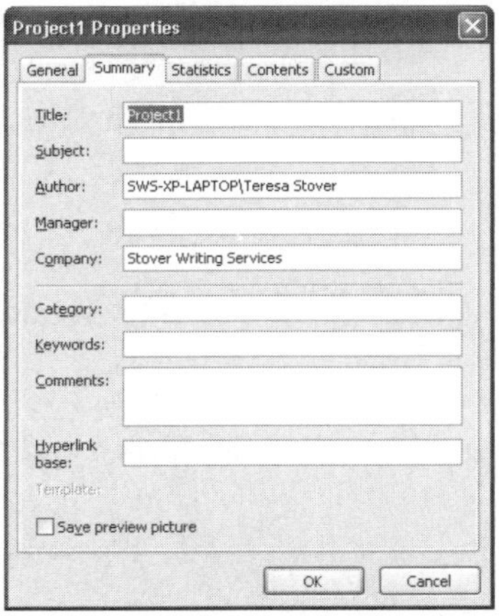

Figure 29-4. Information you add to the Properties dialog box can be used in reports and searches.

2 If necessary, click the Summary tab.

3 Enter any summary information in the fields provided; for example, Title, Subject, Author, Manager, and Company.

Chapter 29

Inside Out

Your project file size has ballooned

You might find that the size of your project file has ballooned, which can happen if you select the Save Preview Picture check box.

If you experience trouble with enormous file sizes, look in the Properties dialog box and clear the Save Preview Picture check box.

Sometimes a basic search on the filename doesn't return the file you need or it returns too many files. You can perform an advanced search, which includes a specific property and value for the file. The properties in an advanced search are the ones you can enter in the file's Properties dialog box. Properties include author, comments, company, creation date, manager, subject, and more. For example, you can search for a project file by the name of its author or by its creation date.

To perform an advanced search for a file, follow these steps:

1. In the Search dialog box, click the Advanced tab.
2. In the Property box, click the property of the file for which you want Microsoft Project to search.
3. In the Condition box, click the condition of the property you have selected, corresponding with the value you will select.

   Examples of conditions are: Is (Exactly), Includes, Equals, More Than, At Most, and so on.
4. In the Value box, type the value of the property and condition you selected.
5. Click the Add button.

Tip **Narrow the search**
Add more than one set of criteria, and use the And and Or options to include or exclude an additional set of criteria from the previous set.

6. In the Search In box, select check boxes for the drives, folders, and network drives in which you want to search for the file.
7. In the Results Should Be box, select the check boxes for the types of files you want to search for; for example, Project Files and Web Pages.
8. Click Search.

Saving Files

Saving a project file ensures that it's stored on a hard disk for future access. The hard disk might be on your own computer, on your company's network, or on the Project Server for an enterprise project. Saving files to a consistent location can make finding your primary and backup files very easy.

Saving a New Project to Your Local Computer or Network Drive

Do the following to save a project file to a drive on your local computer or to a network drive:

1. On the Standard toolbar, click File, Save As.

   The Save As dialog box appears (see Figure 29-5).

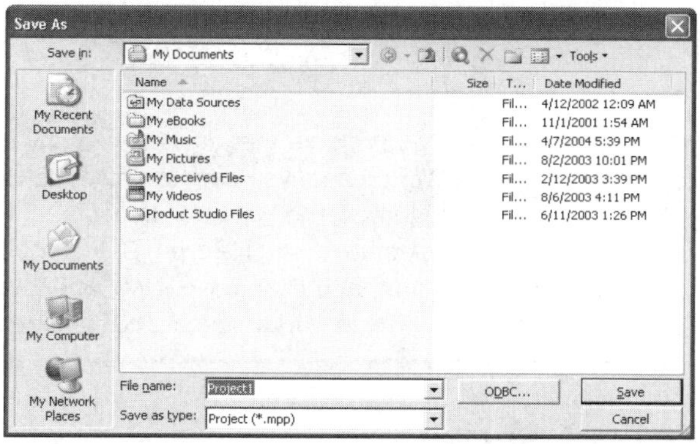

Figure 29-5. The Save As dialog box displays the contents of the default folder.

2. In the Save In box, click the drive or folder where you want to save the file.
3. If necessary, double-click the folder in which you want to save the file.
4. In the File Name box, type the name of the file.
5. Click Save.

Save

After saving a file with a name and in a specific location, be sure to save continually during your work session. A good rule of thumb is to save about every five minutes, or anytime after you make significant changes that you wouldn't want to lose in the event of a system failure or power outage. On the Standard toolbar, click the Save button or press Ctrl+S.

You can have Microsoft Project automatically and periodically save your file so you don't have to remember to do so. **See "Saving Project Files Automatically" later in this chapter on page 875.**

Save options

Depending on what you're trying to do, there are different ways to save your project file:

Save. When you click File, Save, Microsoft Project displays the Save As dialog box, in which you name the file and select the location where it is to be saved. For projects that are already saved, the Save command simply saves your changes to the existing file.

Save As. When you click File, Save As, the Save As dialog box appears, in which you name the file and select the location where it is to be saved. Use this dialog box to save new project files as well as create an alternate or backup copy of your project or save it as a different file type.

Save As Web Page. When you click File, Save As Web Page, the Save As dialog box appears with Web Page (*.html; *.htm) selected as the file type. Saving the current view as a Web page enables you to post to your project's Web site on the Internet or your intranet. Select the location of the Web page to be saved, enter the name, and click Save.

Save Workspace. When you open all the projects that you want to save and open together, and then click File, Save Workspace, you can combine individual projects into a group that's always opened together. The Save Workspace As dialog box appears with Workspace (*.mpw) selected as the file type. Select the location of the workspace to be saved, enter the name, and click Save. Now whenever you open a workspace file, all the projects saved in this workspace are opened at the same time.

Saving a Project to Project Server

When working with an enterprise project, you first open the project from Project Server. When you are finished with the project, you save and *check in* the file to the Project Server database.

Note This section applies only if you're working with Project Professional set up for an enterprise environment.

To save a file to Project Server, follow these steps:

1. If you are already connected to Project Server, click File, Save. If you are not connected to Project Server, click File, Save Online.

   The Save To Project Server dialog box appears (see Figure 29-6).

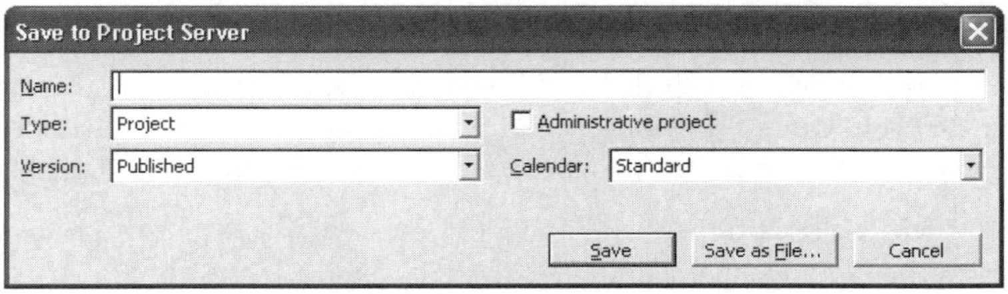

Figure 29-6. The Save To Project Server dialog box enables you to save project plans in the enterprise environment.

2 Indicate whether the project is a Project or a Template.

3 Select a Version.

Published is the default version.

4 Select the Calendar associated with the project.

Standard is the default calendar.

5 Click Save. The project is now saved on Project Server and will be available for others to open. Note that you must close the project on your computer before others will be able to open this project.

> **Tip** **Save the enterprise project offline**
> If you want to save the project offline, click Save As File. Other users will not be able to open this project until you save it to Project Server.

What's in a filename?

In Microsoft Project, you can name a project just about anything you want, as long as the name doesn't exceed 255 characters. Any combination of uppercase and lowercase letters can be used because Microsoft Project does not recognize case in filenames. The following symbols cannot be used in a filename:

- Asterisk (*)
- Less-than symbol (<)
- Backward slash (\)
- Question mark (?)
- Colon (:)
- Quotation mark (")
- Forward slash (/)
- Pipe symbol (|)
- Greater-than symbol (>)
- Semicolon (;)

Specifying the Default Save Location

If you have a drive or folder dedicated to your project management files, you might want to make that your default save location. This default location will be the folder that is presented first whenever you open or save a project file. To set the default folder, do the following:

1. Click Tools, Options.
2. In the Options dialog box, click the Save tab (see Figure 29-7).

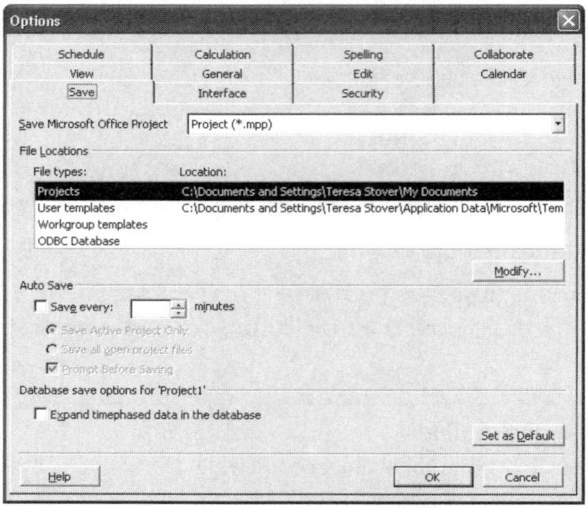

Figure 29-7. Use the Save tab in the Options dialog box to set defaults for saving project files.

3. Under File Locations, click the Modify button. The Modify Location dialog box appears.
4. Browse to the drive and folder where you want your new project files to be saved by default. Click OK.
5. In the Options dialog box, click OK.

> **Tip** **Set the default file type**
> If you regularly save your project files as something other than an MPP file (for example, a Microsoft Project Database or Microsoft Project 98 file), you can change the default file type from MPP to your file type of choice. Click Tools, Options, and in the Options dialog box, click the Save tab. In the Save Microsoft Project Files As box, select the file type you want to use as the default.

Saving and Opening with Different File Formats

A file format is an arrangement of data in a file that specifies the file type and defines the file in a way that allows any application that can open the file to open it correctly. When you create and save a regular project file, it's saved as an MPP file with the *.mpp* extension. The .mpp extension indicates that this is indeed a regular project file.

However, you can save project files in other file formats. You can also open files with other file formats in Microsoft Project. Table 29-1 details the file formats supported by Microsoft Project for saving, opening, or both.

Table 29-1. Supported File Formats

File Format	Extension	Notes
Microsoft Project Plan	.mpp	Saves the file as a Microsoft Project Plan file, which is the default file type for projects being saved or opened.
Microsoft Project template	.mpt	Saves the file as a Microsoft Project template file. The template can then be used as a basis for new projects. When you open a file based on a template, you can change and save those changes to the template file.
Microsoft Project workspace	.mpw	Saves open project files as a Microsoft Project workspace file. When you open an MPW file, all associated projects are opened in a single step.
Microsoft Project Exchange	.mpx	Opens a file created in a version of Microsoft Project earlier than Microsoft Project 98. This is a record-based ASCII text file format that Microsoft Project 2003 can read, allowing early Microsoft Project files to be converted to Microsoft Project 2003 files.
Microsoft Project database	.mpd	Saves the project file as a Microsoft Project database. This file type can be opened in Microsoft Access or any other application that can open the MPD file format. This format replaces the older MPX file format as the standard interchange format for Microsoft Project data.
Web page	.html	Saves the current view as a Web page. The file can then be published to an Internet or intranet Web site.
Microsoft Project 98	.mpp	Saves the Microsoft Project 2003 file so that it can be opened by Microsoft Project 98. Any feature in Microsoft Project 2003 that is not in Microsoft Project 98 (for example, enterprise fields and additional baselines) is not saved in this format.
Microsoft Access database	.mdb	Saves the file as a Microsoft Access database. The file can then be opened in Microsoft Access. You can also open Access files in Microsoft Project. To save a Microsoft Project file in an ODBC format, click the ODBC button in the Save dialog box and follow the instructions in the Select Data Source dialog box.

Table 29-1. Supported File Formats

File Format	Extension	Notes
Microsoft Excel workbook or PivotTable	.xls	Saves the file as a Microsoft Excel workbook or as a Microsoft Excel PivotTable. The file can then be opened in Microsoft Excel. A PivotTable is a table that combines and compares large amounts of data, and in which you can rotate columns and rows to modify the source data to create different views. You can also open an Excel file in Microsoft Project.
Text (Tab delimited)	.txt	Saves the file as a text file using tabs to separate the data. This is ideal for using the project information in a third-party application or on another operating system. You can also open a text file in Microsoft Project.
Text (comma delimited)	.csv	Saves the file as a text file that uses commas to separate the data. This is ideal for using the project information in a third-party application or on another operating system. You can also open a CSV file in Microsoft Project.
eXtensible Markup Language	.xml	Saves the file as XML data. When Microsoft Project saves data as XML, the structure is determined by the Microsoft Project XML schema. You can also open an XML file in Microsoft Project. An XML file must conform to the Microsoft Project XML schema for Microsoft Project to understand and open it. For more information about the Microsoft Project XML Schema, see Projxml.htm on the Microsoft Project 2003 installation CD.

Note Opening a file from a different file format in Microsoft Project can be referred to as importing the file. Likewise, saving a project file with a different file format can be referred to as exporting the file. There's often more to the import and export process than simply opening or saving the file. Sometimes you need to create an import/export map.

For more information about importing and exporting, see "Importing and Exporting Information" on page 497.

Safeguarding Your Project Files

After your hard work creating, updating, and tracking your project file, you want to make the file as secure as possible. The further you get into the life cycle of the project, the more information you have in the project plan. The more information stored there, the more devastating a file loss can be.

Saving Project Files Automatically

Although it's not hard to remember to click the Save button every few minutes while working, you can also have Microsoft Project remember for you. You can set Microsoft Project to automatically and regularly save your file every few minutes. This can decrease your risk of losing recent work.

To have Microsoft Project automatically save active and open projects, follow these steps:

1. Click Tools, Options.
2. In the Options dialog box, click the Save tab.
3. Under Auto Save, select the Save Every check box, and then enter how often (in minutes) you want Microsoft Project to automatically save your active or open projects.
4. If you want Microsoft Project to save only the active project, select the Save Active Project Only option.
5. If you want Microsoft Project to save the active project along with any other open projects, select the Save All Open Project Files option.

Inside Out

Turn off the autosave prompt

It can be handy to be notified when your application will perform an action that you might not otherwise be aware of. However, you might find the Prompt Before Saving feature annoying. You've already instructed Microsoft Project to save your file at a frequency that you specified. If you don't want to be asked whether or not you want to save at every specified interval, clear the Prompt Before Saving check box. However, if you frequently experiment with what-if scenarios in your project file, you might want to be prompted before it saves one of your experiments.

Backing Up Your Project Files

It's always a good policy to have at least two copies of any important computer file. This way, if the file is inadvertently deleted or somehow is corrupted (or if you get a little crazy with your what-if scenarios), you have another file to go back to.

Note You cannot create backups of project files if the project is stored on Project Server or if you are running Project Professional in online mode.

To automatically create backups of active project files, do the following:

1. Click File, Save As.
2. In the Save As dialog box, click Tools and then click General Options.

   The Save Options dialog box appears (see Figure 29-8).

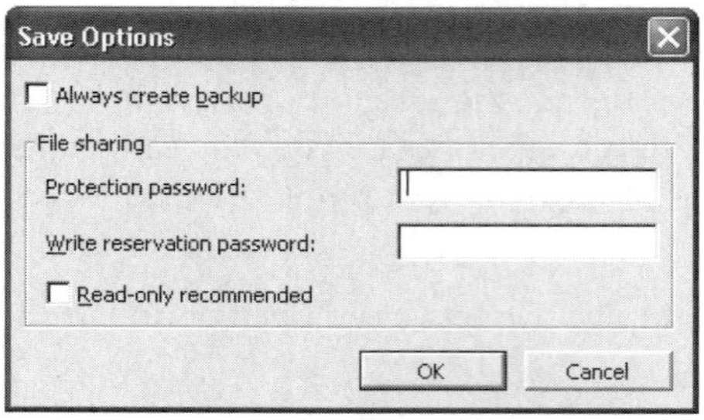

Figure 29-8. Use the Save Options dialog box to set up file backups and passwords.

3. Select the Always Create Backup check box.

The backup copy adopts the same filename as the original project file, but has a different extension. BAK is appended to the filename of all backup copies. For example, the backup file of "deployment.mpp" is "deployment.bak."

To restore a backup file as a regular project file, follow these steps:

1. On the Standard toolbar, click the Open button.
2. In the Open dialog box, browse, if necessary, to the drive and folder where the backup file is stored.
3. Be sure that All Files (*.*) is selected in the Files Of Type box.

   Otherwise, files ending in .bak will not appear in the list.
4. Find the backup file and double-click it.

   Microsoft Project opens the backup file.
5. Click File, Save As.
6. The Save As dialog box appears.

   If necessary, browse to the location where you want to save the restored backup project file.
7. Enter a new filename for the restored backup file.
8. Make sure that Projects (*.mpp) is selected in the Save As Type box.
9. Click Save.

> **Tip** **Keep a backup on a separate drive**
> Your project BAK file is a great contingency in case your project file is accidentally deleted or corrupted. However, if both the project and the backup are saved on the same drive and that drive crashes, your backup will be lost as well. Remember to periodically save a backup to an alternate drive.

Protecting Your Project Files with a Password

If you are not using Project Server as a central location for your company's project files, saving your project files to a public network folder is one way to have centralized project files. This enables your company to back up critical files more regularly and reliably. It also provides a convenient location for your co-workers to collaborate on projects. However, it can also allow unauthorized individuals access to files with sensitive or confidential information. Perhaps your project is in its initial phase and you aren't ready to share it with the rest of the company. Or maybe a project has information that should be seen only by a small group of people in your organization. If this is the case, consider assigning a password to prevent unauthorized access to sensitive project files.

> **Note** You cannot protect a project file with a password if it is stored on Project Server or if you are running Project Professional in online mode.

There are two types of passwords: Protection and Write Reservation. To assign a password to a project, do the following:

1. Click File, Save As.
2. In the Save As dialog box, click Tools and then click General Options.
3. In the Save Options dialog box, enter the password in either the Protection Password or Write Reservation Password text box.

   With a protection password, users can open the project file only if they know the password.

   With a write-reservation password, users can view the project file, but they cannot change it.
4. Click OK.
5. In the Confirm Password dialog box, type the password again. Click OK.

> **Tip** **The Read-Only Recommended option**
> If you want to remind users to open the project as Read-Only without locking out users who might have forgotten the password, consider the Read-Only Recommended check box. If you select this check box, the next time a user goes to open this file, a message suggests that the user open the file as read-only unless they need to save changes to the file. It then provides the option of opening the file as Read-Only or not.

Responding to a Microsoft Project Problem

If you encounter a problem with Microsoft Project, such as the program freezing or experiencing a "fatal error," you can send the details of the problem to the Microsoft Project development team. When the error happens, a dialog box is displayed, providing the option to restart Microsoft Project and view the details of the error report. If you want to provide information on the problem to Microsoft, click Send The Report To Microsoft. If you don't want to provide the information, click Don't Send.

Depending on the severity of the error, you might be able to continue working in Safe mode, at least to get to the point where you can save your file.

Inside Out

Don't send your proprietary project

Depending on the nature of the error you encounter, your entire project file could be sent to the Microsoft Project development team. If your project contains confidential information, be sure to click Don't Send.

Part 9

Programming Custom Solutions

Chapter 30

Understanding the Visual Basic Language

Before discussing the Microsoft Office Project 2003 object model, the Visual Basic Editor, and other aspects of and tools for creating and editing code-based solutions in Project 2003, you must first understand some of the elements and principles of Visual Basic:

- Objects, properties, methods, and events
- Data types
- Variables
- Decision and loop structures
- Procedures
- Scope

As you develop your Visual Basic skills and move on to writing more advanced code, there are some general principles of software development that make writing code easier, faster, and less prone to error:

- Using naming conventions for procedures and variables
- Writing modularized code
- Writing formatted code
- Writing efficient code
- Trapping errors

Finally, although much of the discussion presented here is necessarily at a relatively high level, given the overall focus of this book, the intent of this chapter is to provide an overview of the Visual Basic concepts you'll need to take full advantage of VBA in Microsoft Project without being forced to look for a separate reference. After you're comfortable with the information presented here, you should find that most of what remains to be learned in Visual Basic is simply an extension of what you already know.

Note Although *Visual Basic for Applications* is used to collectively describe the programming language and environment included with Microsoft Project, the language itself is Visual Basic. For the remainder of this chapter, *Visual Basic* is used to refer to the language and its elements.

For more information about these and many other Visual Basic concepts, see the topics under the heading "Visual Basic Conceptual Topics" in the table of contents of the Microsoft Visual Basic Help files.

The Microsoft Developer Network (MSDN) at *http://msdn.microsoft.com/* is also an excellent resource for programming guidelines, tips, and examples.

Installing VBA Help

By default, the Help files for VBA are automatically installed the first time you use them. Follow these steps if you want to install them now:

1. Insert the Microsoft Project 2003 CD-ROM into your computer's CD or DVD drive.
2. Click Start, Control Panel and then double-click Add/Remove Programs.

Note The name of this item might be slightly different for your operating system.

3. Click Microsoft Project in the list of installed programs and then click Change.
4. Click Add Or Remove Features and then click Next.
5. Expand the Office Shared Features item and then expand the Visual Basic for Applications item.
6. In the Visual Basic Help list, click Run From My Computer.
7. Click the Update button.

This installs several Help files, including those for the Microsoft Project object model, concepts and language reference specific to VBA in Microsoft Office and related programs, general Visual Basic concepts and language reference, and Microsoft Forms.

Understanding Objects, Properties, Methods, and Events

Objects, properties, methods, and events, along with variables and procedures, form the core of how you interact with Microsoft Project, whether it's by using a macro or creating an entire VBA program within Microsoft Project.

Tip Standard Visual Basic and general programming terms are italicized the first time they are discussed in this chapter.

Objects

An *object* is a discrete identifiable thing. It can be something generic, such as a window or a toolbar; or it can be something specific to Microsoft Project, such as a project or a resource. Most objects have at least three common *properties*, such as the following:

Name This is the name of the object, such as "project" or "calendar."

Application This is a way to access the object that represents the software itself.

Parent This is a way to access the object that precedes the object in the *object model.*

Objects also usually have properties specific to their types. For example, a Task object has properties that return the start and finish dates. Because objects form the basis of how you interact with Microsoft Project, they also have *methods* and *events*.

A *collection* is a group of objects, almost always of the same type: A Tasks collection, not surprisingly, is made up of Task objects. Collections typically have the following features:

An Add method This is a way to add a new object to the collection.

An Item property This is a way to access a particular object in the collection.

A Count property This is the number of objects in the collection.

Perhaps confusingly, a collection is also an object, which means that a collection can have all the same features of an object, including properties (such as Name, Application, and Parent) and methods.

Parents and Children: The Object Model Hierarchy

An object model is a system of objects that provides a programmatic model for interacting with an application. Object models in VBA are represented in a hierarchical "tree" fashion with the Application object (the object representing the program itself) as the root. All other objects and collections are children of the root object.

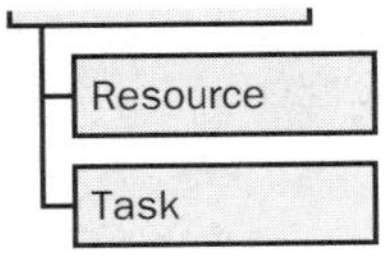

In Microsoft Project, for example, collections such as the Windows, Projects, and Tables collections—as well as the Cell and Selection objects (and others)—are *child objects* of the Application object. For each of those child objects, then, the Application object is not only the root of the object model, but the *parent object*.

Other than the Application object, which has no parent, every object and collection has a parent object. Objects usually have child objects (the Project object has Resources and Tasks collections, for example), and collections always have children: Each object in the collection is a child of the collection itself.

Properties

A property is an aspect or characteristic of an object. A property can be simple, such as the name of the object. A more complex property might be a collection of child objects. Properties are either *read-only*, which means that they only provide information; or *read/write*, which means they can also be changed as needed.

For example, the Name property of a Project object is read/write because you can always rename a project. The Parent property, though, which returns a reference to the Application object, is read-only.

Methods

A method is just a way of telling an object to do something. The Application object, for example, has an AppMinimize method. When you *call* (or "invoke") the AppMinimize method, you're telling Microsoft Project, represented by the Application object, to minimize its window.

Many methods return information about the results of the action, such as when the AppMinimize method returns a value of True or False to tell you whether Microsoft Project was minimized successfully.

Some methods can accept *arguments*, which are ways of supplying additional information to the method. The Tasks collection's Add method, for example, has optional Name and Before arguments, so that you can specify a name and position for the new task as you create it. For example, the following code creates a task called "Write chapter" as the third task (the new task is inserted before what was the third task) in a collection of tasks:

```
ActiveProject.Tasks.Add "Write chapter", 3
```

Calling Methods That Return Values

If a method returns a value, you can call the method with parentheses or without them:

- Calling a method with parentheses returns either a value or a reference to an object, so you must do something with the result or an error will occur. The following code returns a *reference* to the Task object it just created:

  ```
  ActiveProject.Tasks.Add("Write chapter", 3)
  ```

  Without additional code to work with the returned object, this code will result in a syntax error.

- Calling a method without parentheses means that the method takes action and discards the return value. The following code creates a task:

  ```
  ActiveProject.Tasks.Add "Write chapter", 3
  ```

For more information about methods that return values (*functions*), see "Understanding Procedures" later in this chapter on page 888.

For more information about working with optional arguments, see "Named Arguments" later in this chapter on page 897.

Events

An event can occur (*fire*) when an object does something as the result of a method or user action, which can *trigger* the event. Sometimes, several events can fire in sequence. Events can contain calls to methods, which can then cause even more events to fire.

For example, when the following code creates a new task, it triggers the Application object's ProjectBeforeTaskNew event:

```
ActiveProject.Tasks.Add "Write chapter", 3
```

If you want to prevent the task from being created, you can use the event's Cancel argument to do so.

In another example, closing Microsoft Project with an unsaved project file open causes several events of the Project object to fire:

Project_BeforeSave. This fires just before Microsoft Project asks if you want to save the project.

Project_BeforeClose. This fires just before the project closes.

Project_Deactivate. This fires as the closing project is about to *lose focus*.

Note Several Application-level events also fire in this example.

Understanding Data Types

When you create (*declare*) a variable or function by specifying a data type, you are letting Visual Basic know that the variable will always contain a certain kind of data. This is known as an *explicit declaration*. Although not technically required in Visual Basic, it is an excellent programming practice because:

- *Implicit declarations* (creating a variable without specifying its data type) result in the Variant data type. Whereas each of the other data types use varying amounts of memory, Variants always use the same comparatively large amount of memory regardless of the data they store. This can result in an inefficient use of memory. For example, storing True or False information in a Variant instead of a Boolean variable uses eight times as much memory.
- If you always use explicit declarations and mistype the name of a variable, Visual Basic recognizes that it's a mistake and gives you a warning. If you use an implicit declaration, Visual Basic just assumes it's a new variable, which can cause unexpected results in your code that are hard to fix because you might not notice the typo.

- Using the functions included with Visual Basic when converting data from one type to another makes your code easier to understand and maintain.

Tip **Avoid implicit declarations**

Put the following line at the beginning of every class, user form, or code module to have Visual Basic warn you if you accidentally make an implicit declaration:

```
Option Explicit
```

To make sure that you always use explicit declarations, you can select the Require Variable Declaration check box in the Visual Basic Editor. This check box is on the Editor tab of the Options dialog box, which you can open by clicking Tools, Options.

Table 30-1 lists data types. Although it is not a complete list, it is probably sufficient for the majority of code you will write in VBA.

Table 30-1. Data Types

Type	Description
String	Used to store any kind of alphanumeric information. Numbers stored in Strings are treated as text, so sorting numbers in a String variable means that 10 comes before 2.
Long	Used to store numbers in the range –2,147,483,648 to 2,147,483,647.
Integer	Used to store numbers in the range –32,768 to 32,767. Integers use half as much memory as Longs.
Boolean	Used to store True or False information. If you pass a nonzero number to a Boolean variable, the variable becomes True. If you pass a Boolean value of True to a numeric variable, the variable becomes –1. False always becomes 0, and vice versa, when you pass values between Boolean and numeric variables.
Object	Used to store references to objects. Object variables declared as Object are referred to as being *late-bound*. Late-bound variables are sometimes necessary, such as when your code must work with several different types of object. Code that uses late-bound references, however, can run slower than references declared for a specific *class*, such as a Project, Resource, Task, and so on. Binding an object variable to a specific class is known as *early binding*. (The term *object variable* is sometimes used to generically describe a variable that stores a reference to an object, even if the variable was declared as a specific class of object.)

For more information about declaring variables, including prefixes and other naming conventions, see "Naming Conventions" later in this chapter on page 894.

Understanding Variables

Variables are simply places where information is temporarily stored while a program is running. A variable has a value only when you *assign* one to it, either through direct interaction (clicking a button on a dialog box, for example) or by the action of code in your program.

Variables are used when interacting with users, tracking details while the program is running, and passing information among different parts of the program. They are also used to represent individual items in a collection of items, such as when working one-by-one through a collection of tasks in a project.

A Boolean variable, for example, is declared as follows:

```
Dim blnStatus As Boolean
```

An *array* is a special type of variable that can store many related values at one time. (Because an array has to be declared like any other variable, all the data in an array has to be the same data type. The exception, of course, is an array declared as Variant.) In fact, an array can store a nearly unlimited number of values—limited primarily by the amount of memory in your computer—in up to 60 dimensions.

Arrays are a lot like temporary spreadsheets, in which each "cell" (*element*) in a "column" (*dimension*) is a single piece of data. Each time you add a dimension, it's like adding another column to your "spreadsheet." The final dimension in an array declaration (or the only dimension in a one-dimension array) is the number of rows in your spreadsheet.

Note By default, the dimensions in an array are 0-based, which means that the first element is numbered 0 instead of 1. When you declare the size of the array, you subtract 1 from the desired size to determine the *upper bound* of the array.

Examples of array declarations are shown in Table 30-2.

Table 30-2. Array Declarations

Description	Declaration
One-dimension Long array of fixed size (1 column with 5 rows)	`Dim lngOneDArray(4) As Long`
Two-dimension Integer array of fixed size (5 columns with 10 rows)	`Dim intTwoDArray(4, 9) As Integer`
Two-dimension Integer array of fixed size using 1-based (not zero-based) dimensions	`Dim intTwoDArray(1 To 5, 1 To 10) As Integer`

Table 30-2. Array Declarations

Description	Declaration
One-dimension String array of variable size	Initial declaration: `Dim strVarArray() As String` Specification of initial size: `ReDim strVarArray(4)` Specification of new size, while retaining existing data: `ReDim Preserve strVarArray(9)`
Two-dimension String array of variable size	Initial declaration: `Dim strVarArray() As String` Specification of initial size: `ReDim strVarArray(4, 9)` Specification of new size, while discarding existing data: `ReDim strVarArray(4, 19)`

Constants are similar to variables in that they store data, but the value of a constant is specified when you declare it and never changes while your code is running. In this sense, they are like read-only properties.

At first glance, constants might not appear very useful, but they are valuable tools for writing *self-documenting code*. For example, the Microsoft Project constant "pjFinishToStart" is a much more meaningful description of the link type for a task than 1, which is the value it represents.

A typical String constant might be declared as:

```
Const c_strName As String = "Some text"
```

For more information about self-documenting code, see "Writing Code That Is Easily Understood" later in this chapter on page 894.

Understanding Procedures

For all intents and purposes, everything that happens in your code happens in procedures. *Functions* and *subroutines* (*subs*) are both types of procedures you can write. Both contain Visual Basic code (*statements*), and both can accept input (*arguments*).

The only real difference between functions and subroutines is that functions can directly return information to the *calling procedure* by assigning a value to the name of the function. This means you can use functions like variables, so functions should be declared as a certain data type, just like any other variable.

For example, the following code has a sub AddTask that calls a function strNewTask:

```
Function strNewTask(strName As String, intBefore As Integer) As String
    ActiveProject.Tasks.Add strName, intBefore

    If ActiveProject.Tasks(intBefore).Name = strName Then
        strNewTask = "Success!"
    Else
        strNewTask = "Failed to create task!"
    End If
End Function
```

```
Sub AddTask()
    MsgBox strNewTask("Write chapter", 3)
End Sub
```

The Sub and End Sub, Function and End Function statements define the boundaries of the sub or function. As you can see, the statement declaring the function declares it as a particular data type, whereas the sub does not.

This code contains several other items worth noting:

- The function has two arguments, strName and intBefore, which are declared just like any other variables, even though they are part of the function declaration.
- To return a value from a function, you must first assign a value to the name of the function, as in the following line:

  ```
  strNewTask = "Success!"
  ```

- The MsgBox function takes several arguments, one of which is a String that contains the text to display in the dialog box. (It is itself a function because it can return information about which button the user clicked; by calling it without parentheses, we're discarding the Integer value that it would otherwise return.) Instead of being supplied as text in quotes (a *string literal*) or even as a "traditional" variable, the argument is supplied as the return value of the function strNewTask.

Understanding Scope

Scope is a term used to describe when and where a variable or procedure is available. There are three levels of scope:

Procedure. Variables declared at this level (using the *Dim* keyword) are only available within the procedure. Also referred to as *local.*

Module. Variables and procedures declared at this level (using the *Dim* keyword or—for improved readability—the *Private* keyword) are available anywhere within a form, class, or module. Also referred to as *private.*

> **Note** Declaring a variable with module-level scope should not be confused with the idea of simply declaring a variable in a module. By default, variables declared in a module are available only within the module (module scope), but declaring a variable with the *Public* keyword makes it available everywhere (global scope).

Global. Variables and procedures declared at this level (using the *Public* keyword) are available throughout your program. Also referred to as *public.*

The value stored in any variable is temporary, dependent upon where it was declared. When a variable *goes out of scope* it is reset to its default value, such as 0 for numeric variables. In the case of a local variable, for example, it goes out of scope when the procedure in which it is declared has been completed.

Understanding Decision Structures

Decision structures control whether other statements *execute*, according to the results of *conditional statements*. In the function strNewTask, for instance, there was an If...Then...Else decision structure that determined what to set for the function's return value, based on the results of a test.

There are four different decision structures, each suitable for different situations, but they are all very similar:

If...Then. The simplest of all decision structures, the If...Then statement takes just one action if just one condition is met. If the condition is not met, the statement does nothing:

```
If ActiveProject.Tasks(1).PercentComplete = 100 Then MsgBox "Task complete!"
```

If the first task's PercentComplete property is not 100, the line is skipped.

> **Note** Unlike the other decision structures, If...Then can either be a single-line statement or a *block*. An If...Then statement is one test, one action, and one line of code. An If...Then block is still one test, but it can perform many actions over several lines of code.

> **Note** Because a decision block is essentially a miniature procedure, it must have some sort of ending statement. The End If statement at the end of a decision block works just like the End Sub or End Function at the end of a procedure.

If...Then...Else. A more common form of decision structure is the one used in the function strNewTask, If...Then...Else. Unlike the If...Then statement, this structure performs a test to determine not whether it should take action, but which action it should take. Something will always happen because meeting the condition results in one action, and anything else results in the second:

```
If ActiveProject.Tasks(1).PercentComplete = 100 Then
    MsgBox "The task is complete!"
Else
    MsgBox "The task is not finished."
End If
```

In this situation, if the task's PercentComplete property is 100, the dialog box appears just as it does for the If...Then statement. The difference here is that anything less than 100 also displays a dialog box.

If...Then...ElseIf. A variation on the If...Then...Else type is the If...Then...ElseIf block. In this variation, there can be any number of ElseIf statements, each of which performs a further refinement of the test defined in the original If...Then statement. For example:

```
If ActiveProject.Tasks(1).PercentComplete = 100 Then
    MsgBox "The task is complete!"
ElseIf ActiveProject.Tasks(1).PercentComplete >= 50 Then
    MsgBox "The task is more than half finished."
ElseIf ActiveProject.Tasks(1).PercentComplete > 0 Then
    MsgBox "The task has started, but is less than 50% complete."
```

```
Else
    MsgBox "The task has not started!"
End If
```

Select Case. This is another way to test for a large number of conditions, but in a more readable way than an If…Then…ElseIf block.

```
Select Case ActiveProject.Tasks(1).PercentComplete
    Case Is = 100
        MsgBox "The task is complete!"
    Case Is >= 50
        MsgBox "The task is more than half finished."
    Case Is > 0
        MsgBox "The task has started, but is less than 50% complete."
    Case Is = 0
        MsgBox "The task has not started!"
End Select
```

> **Note** The *Is* keyword used here is only required because these Case statements are also comparisons, which means they have to be compared with something. Typically, the Select Case statement contains a reference to a variable, and each Case statement represents a different possible value.

As you can see, using the Select Case structure makes it much easier to find the different conditions for displaying a dialog box. In fact, the statement

```
Case Is = 0
```

is even more explicit than is strictly necessary because we've already eliminated every other possible value for the PercentComplete property. In this instance, a simple

```
Case Else
```

would have been sufficient, and is probably just as readable.

> **Tip** **The more explicit, the better**
> The value in using an explicit construction instead of the Case Else statement can be shown by simply asking this question: What if you didn't know that the range of possible values for the PercentComplete property was 0–100?

Understanding Loop Structures

Unlike decision structures, which control *whether* other statements execute, loop structures control *how often* other statements execute.

There are just three loop structures, even though the last in this list has several variations:

For…Next. A For loop is used to work through a known number of items. The number of times the loop should run is specified by means of a counter variable, which typically increments by 1 each time the loop repeats.

The following code loops through a task's resource assignments and displays the name of each resource in its own dialog box:

```
Dim intCount As Integer

For intCount = 1 To ActiveProject.Tasks(1).Assignments.Count
    MsgBox ActiveProject.Tasks(1).Assignments(intCount).ResourceName
Next intCount
```

Tip **Use the Count property**
Even though the number of items in a For loop must be known, that number doesn't have to be known by you, the programmer. In this code, the Assignments collection's Count property is used to supply the value for intCount.

You can use the Step argument to increment by values greater than 1, or you can use it to decrement the counter. If you decrement your loop, of course, the initial value of the counter must be set to the number of items, instead of to one. This code works like the previous example, but in reverse order:

```
Dim intCount As Integer

For intCount = ActiveProject.Tasks(1).Assignments.Count To 1 Step -1
    MsgBox ActiveProject.Tasks(1).Assignments(intCount).ResourceName
Next intCount
```

For Each...Next. This is essentially a For loop for objects, although it can also be used for items in an array. In this case, the code behaves identically to the first For...Next example, but uses an object variable instead of a numeric counter:

```
Dim objAssign As Assignment

For Each objAssign In ActiveProject.Tasks(1).Assignments
    MsgBox objAssign.ResourceName
Next objAssign
```

Quite often, loop structures contain decision structures. The following code loops through every task in a project and displays a dialog box stating whether the task is complete:

```
Dim objTask As Task

For Each objTask In ActiveProject.Tasks
    If objTask.PercentComplete = 100 Then
        MsgBox "The task is complete!"
    Else
        MsgBox "The task is not finished."
    End If
Next objTask
```

Do...Loop. A Do loop is really a combination of an If...Then statement and a For loop for which you don't know how many items there are. It executes code an undetermined number of times, but is limited by the results of a test it performs for each repetition.

The two most common forms of a Do loop are the Do While...Loop and Do Until...Loop structures. A Do While loop runs code as long as the condition is True, whereas the Do Until loop runs code only while the condition is False (that is, until it's True). Compare the following two examples:

```
Sub WhileTest()
    Dim intCount As Integer

    intCount = 1
    Do While intCount <= 10
        MsgBox intCount
        intCount = intCount + 1
    Loop
End Sub

Sub UntilTest()
    Dim intCount As Integer

    intCount = 1
    Do Until intCount > 10
        MsgBox intCount
        intCount = intCount + 1
    Loop
End Sub
```

In each case, 10 dialog boxes appear, incrementing from 1 to 10. The difference is that the Do While loop runs while the variable is less than or equal to 10. The Do Until loop runs until the variable is greater than 10.

Note Unlike a For loop, it's possible that the statements in a Do loop won't be executed because the result of the conditional test might never be true. If the variable intCount in the two procedures had been set to 11 instead of 1, neither loop would run.

The other two variations of a Do loop are the Do...Loop While and Do...Loop Until structures. Whereas the more "traditional" Do loops test the condition statement before proceeding, these variants perform their actions and then test to see whether a condition is true. The following code always displays a dialog box, even though the condition is never true:

```
Dim intCount As Integer

intCount = 100
Do
    MsgBox intCount
    intCount = intCount + 1
Loop While intCount <= 10
```

Writing Code That Is Easily Understood

Recording a simple macro here or there might not seem much like programming, but after you start creating them by hand, recording and editing more complex macros, or even writing what amount to full-fledged computer programs, some general principles of software development become more important. One of these principles is using a consistent system of coding conventions.

Coding conventions result in code that is *self-documenting*, which is to say, written in such a way that it describes what it is and what it's used for. Different aspects of self-documenting code can be accomplished through several methods, some of which have been touched on earlier in this chapter:

- Naming conventions
- Constants for procedures and variables
- Explicit declarations
- Named arguments
- Modularized code
- Formatted code

You know that your coding conventions work when someone unfamiliar with your code can rely upon the code itself to "explain" what procedures do, what type of data they accept or return, which variables have local or global scope, and so on.

Tip **Use comments**
Use comments liberally throughout your code. Strictly speaking, of course, comments have nothing to do with self-documenting code, but they are used to make your code as readable and easy to understand as possible.

Comments in Visual Basic begin with an apostrophe ('). Anything that comes after the comment character, even if it's in the middle of a line of code, is considered a comment and is ignored by Visual Basic. (An apostrophe that is inside a set of quotation marks is not treated as a comment character.)

Naming Conventions

Using a system of naming conventions is one of the easiest things you can do to make your code self-documenting. Using naming conventions means doing two things: using descriptive names for procedures and variables; and using prefixes that describe the data type, scope, and function of the procedure or variable.

Assigning descriptive names to procedures and variables doesn't have to mean that names will be long and complicated. All that is required is that the name indicate roughly what the procedure is used for or the type of information represented by the variable. Mixed case should be used to make the name easier to read, such as AddTask, FormatTableForPrinting, or TaskName.

Prefixes can be used to describe many things about the procedure or variable, such as type, scope, and function. In fact, there is a commonly used system of prefixes for Visual Basic, examples of which are shown in Tables 30-3 through 30-6.

Table 30-3 shows prefixes that describe data types, such as strTaskName.

Table 30-3. Data Types

Prefix	Type of Variable
bln	Boolean
str	String
int	Integer
lng	Long
obj	Object
var	Variant

Table 30-4 shows prefixes that describe controls, such as cmdOK and txtTaskName.

Table 30-4. Controls

Prefix	Type of Control
chk	Check box
cmd	Command button
frm	Form
lbl	Label
lst	List box
mnu	Menu
opt	Option button
txt	Text box

Table 30-5 shows prefixes that describe scope, such as the local variable strTaskName and the global gstrTaskName.

Table 30-5. Scope

Prefix	Type of Scope
no prefix	Procedure (local)
m	Module (private)
g	Global (public)

Table 30-6 shows prefixes that describe function, such as c_gstrTaskName for a global String constant and a_intTaskList to describe a local Integer array.

Table 30-6. Function

Prefix	Type of Function
c_	A constant
a_	An array

The following example of a sub and a function, taken from the discussion on procedures earlier in this chapter, illustrates the use of prefixes and descriptive names:

```
Function strNewTask(strName As String, intBefore As Integer) As String
    ActiveProject.Tasks.Add strName, intBefore

    If ActiveProject.Tasks(intBefore).Name = strName Then
        strNewTask = "Success!"
    Else
        strNewTask = "Failed to create task!"
    End If
End Function

Sub AddTask()
    MsgBox strNewTask("Write chapter", 3)
End Sub
```

Suppose that you were reading the code for the first time, the two procedures weren't right next to each other, and all you saw was AddTask. Suppose further that AddTask was written as follows:

```
Sub AddTask()
    MsgBox strNewTask(strTaskName, intTaskNum)
End Sub
```

Because of a consistent pattern of naming conventions, you can infer a lot about strNewTask, including:

- strNewTask is a function.
- Functions use a prefix, and subs do not.
- The function returns a String.
- The prefix *str* denotes a String variable.
- The function takes at least two arguments.
- You do not know, however, if either argument (or both) is optional.
- The first argument requires a String representing the name of a task.
- The prefix *str* denotes a String variable, and the name of the variable indicates the type of information it contains.
- The second argument requires an Integer representing the position of the new task in the task list.

  The prefix *int* denotes an Integer variable and the name of the variable indicates the type of information it contains.

Declarations

As described earlier in this chapter in the discussion on data types, variables (including functions, which you can think of as a special type of variable) can be declared implicitly or explicitly. Although there's nothing fundamentally "wrong" with using implicit declaration, explicit declaration is generally a good idea because:

- Using the right data type is simply a matter of using the right tool for the job. The smaller a data type is (the less memory it uses), the faster it runs.

> **Note** Although there might be situations in which you don't know the data type returned by a called procedure, which might make you inclined to rely upon implicit declaration, you should still explicitly declare the variable as Variant. Doing this doesn't create any performance gains, but you still get the other benefits of explicit declaration.

- Explicit declaration means if you mistype a variable name, Visual Basic recognizes the error and warns you of the mistake. Implicit declarations mean that any variable name not already known by Visual Basic results in a new variable.
- If you want to declare a variable with module-level or global scope, you have to explicitly declare the variable with the Dim, Private, or Public keywords.
- It's easier to find and understand the uses for variables that are explicitly declared, especially if they are consistently grouped at the beginning of a module or procedure.

Named Arguments

When supplying arguments for a method, each argument is separated from the next with a comma; for example:

```
ActiveProject.Tasks.Add "Write chapter", 3
```

When it comes to self-documenting code, however, that code isn't especially descriptive. You can probably guess that "Write chapter" is the name of the new task, but it's harder to guess what the 3 is for. This is one way in which *named arguments* can be valuable.

Using named arguments means that instead of supplying just the values for each argument, you precede each value with the name of the argument. The argument name is then separated from the argument value with a colon and an equal sign:

```
ActiveProject.Tasks.Add Name:="Write chapter", Before:=3
```

It is now clear that the name of the new task is "Write chapter" and that it appears before the task that is currently third in the task list.

Named arguments are also used for methods that have many optional arguments, some of which you aren't using. Without named arguments, you must supply a comma as a placeholder for each optional argument, so that the arguments you are using appear in the expected order and position. This results in code that can be quite cryptic:

```
Application.WBSCodeMaskEdit , , , 2, "-"
```

The only way to find out what the two values are being used for is to look up the method in Help. If you use named arguments, however, you don't need to use placeholder commas and the code is very descriptive:

```
Application.WBSCodeMaskEdit Length:=2, separator:="-"
```

When you use named arguments, you can specify them in any order you choose. The code in the previous example could have been written with the two arguments in reverse order:

```
Application.WBSCodeMaskEdit separator:=-, Length:=2Constants
```

Constants are an important and useful feature of Visual Basic that makes code self-documenting. In fact, Visual Basic is full of constants, including what is probably the most common constant of all: vbCrLf. This constant, which represents a carriage-return and linefeed, is used to format text for display. The following code displays a sentence in two lines:

```
MsgBox "Here is a long sentence, " & vbCrLf & "broken into two lines."
```

The vbCrLf constant is much more user-friendly, not to mention convenient, than the old method of using `Chr$(13)` & `Chr$(10)` to do the same thing.

As mentioned earlier in this chapter, constants are frequently used to represent fixed numeric data, such as the Microsoft Project constant "pjFinishToStart." The name of the constant, especially when you know that it's a member of the PjTaskLinkType *enumeration* ("enum"), is very effective at describing what kind of link is being applied with the LinkPredecessors method, for example. Using just the numeric value of pjFinishToStart doesn't provide you with any real information at all.

You can create your own constants much as you would a variable, except you use the Const keyword and immediately assign a value to it:

```
Const c_lngMyFinishToStart As Long = 10
```

Modularized Code

When you record a macro, all the code generated by the macro recorder is written into one procedure. As you learn to write code by hand and begin to write more complex procedures, you might be inclined to continue this practice. Breaking your code into separate components for easily identifiable tasks, however, makes reading, debugging, maintaining, and modifying your code much simpler.

Looking again at the AddTask and strNewTask procedures, for example, you can see that there's no reason the functions of the two procedures couldn't have been combined into one. Keeping them separate means that AddTask could be modified to perform additional tasks by simply calling new procedures in addition to strNewTask, such as SearchForUnassigned-Resources and AssignResources.

Another aspect of modular code is that it makes writing new code faster and easier. A procedure that searches for overallocated resources, for instance, could be called from many other procedures rather than rewriting the same code for every procedure that needed it.

Formatted Code

Part of what makes something easy to read—whether it's a book, a Web site, or computer code—is its layout. Formatting your code for readability doesn't just make things easier on your eyes; it makes writing and debugging your code easier, too. As with naming conventions, there are some practices that have been standardized for Visual Basic:

- Indenting, typically 4 spaces, is used to help differentiate the "contents" of a construct from the statements that define the construct. For example, the contents of a sub are indented from the Sub and End Sub statements. Similarly, the contents of a decision structure are indented from, for example, the If...Then and End If statements.
- Grouping declarations of variables and constants at the beginning of modules and procedures makes them easier to find.
- Using blank lines before and after procedures, variable declarations, and decision and loop structures makes them easier to find and read.
- Using multiple, indented lines for If...Then statements not only makes it easier to differentiate the condition from the action taken when the condition is met, but simplifies the work necessary to add additional actions.

  For example, the line

  ```
  If ActiveCell.Task.PercentComplete = 100 Then MsgBox "Task complete!"
  ```

  from the discussion of If...Then statements could have been written as

  ```
  If ActiveCell.Task.PercentComplete = 100 Then
      MsgBox "Task complete!"
  End If
  ```

  Although Visual Basic supports placing multiple statements on one line, each separated from the others with a colon (:), doing so makes your code much harder to read.
- Breaking long lines into multiple lines with an underscore (_) prevents excessive horizontal scrolling. The line continuation character can be used only after an operator (such as the &, +, And, and Or operators) or between arguments of a procedure. For example:

  ```
  ViewEditCombination Name:="Check Resources View", Create:=True, _
    TopView:="Gantt Chart", BottomView:="Resource Sheet"
  ```

  and

  ```
  If blnThis = True And blnThat = True And blnThose = False And _
    blnOthers = True Then
      MsgBox "Hey!"
  End If
  ```

> **Tip** When using the line continuation character, it's customary to indent the continued lines by two characters.

- When breaking long lines of quoted text into multiple lines, the & operator and the line continuation character must be used outside of the quotation marks or they will be considered as part of the text:

```
MsgBox "This is a very long line of text and would scroll " & _
  "horizontally for quite a ways, which is why it was broken " & _
    "into several lines of code."
```

Writing Efficient Code

There are some people who would say that in this age of cheap computer memory and stunningly fast processors, efficient code isn't as important as it used to be. Perhaps they're right in a strict sense, but the idea of efficient code is more than just code that doesn't require much memory and uses as few processor cycles as possible. Efficient code also means using the best data type for the job, using object references wisely, and writing "smart" code.

Inside Out

Visual Basic is high level and compiled, which means that what you write is converted by a *compiler* into machine code for use by the computer. Modern compilers are amazingly good at optimizing the compiled code, but you are (in theory, at least) giving up some level of efficiency by not writing machine code directly. The tradeoff is that it is much, much faster and easier to write in a compiled language.

Visual Basic is also what's known as a high-level language, which means that it doesn't support methods for working with memory and the computer's processor that are available in a low-level language such as C.

Writing efficient code is as much an art as a science, and a full discussion of it is far beyond the scope of this book. There are, however, some simple things you can do to make your code more efficient:

- When working with objects, use early-binding as much as possible.

  As discussed earlier in this chapter, early-binding means declaring object variables of a specific class such as Project, Resource, Form, or CommandBar. Object variables that are early-bound run faster than those that are late-bound, or that are declared simply As Object.
- When you're done working with an object variable, get rid of it. When you're finished with an object variable, set it equal to the keyword *Nothing*. This clears the object reference and frees up memory. For example:

```
Dim objAssign As Assignment

For Each objAssign In ActiveProject.Tasks(1).Assignments
    MsgBox objAssign.ResourceName
Next objAssign

Set objAssign = Nothing
```

Tip Object variables that are local in scope will be automatically cleared when the procedure ends and they go out of scope.

- When making multiple calls to an object, use the With and End With statements.

  This code makes the Office Assistant feature visible and causes it to perform an animation action:

```
Assistant.Visible = True
Assistant.Sounds = True
Assistant.Animation = msoAnimationGetAttentionMajor
```

  As you can see, there are three calls to the Assistant object. Each time Visual Basic encounters one of those calls, it has to create another internal reference to the Assistant object. The following construction performs the same action and is much more readable, and Visual Basic has to create only one internal object reference:

```
With Assistant
    .Visible = True
    .Sounds = True
    .Animation = msoAnimationGetAttentionMajor
End With
```

- Always close connections to external objects.

  When working with connections to data sources or other applications, you should always be sure to close the connection when you are finished with it. The reason for this becomes obvious when working with other applications programmatically. When you use Automation to access the Microsoft Excel object model from Microsoft Project, for example, you are actually starting Excel invisibly. If you fail to close the connection when you are done, Excel continues to run—and take up memory—until the computer is shut down.

For more information about Automation and working with other applications programmatically, see Chapter 31, "Writing Microsoft Project Code with Visual Basic for Applications."

- Increase the upper bound of a dynamic array in chunks.

  When you redimension the upper bound of a dynamic array, avoid doing so individually for each new element. Instead, make a reasonable guess of how many additional elements are likely to be necessary and enlarge the array accordingly.

Tip **Track your elements**

To know when you're running out of available elements from the last time the array was redimensioned, you'll need to create a variable that tracks how many elements are already in use. If you don't, and you assign a value to an element that hasn't been created, you'll receive a "subscript out of range" error message.

- When determining which data type to use, choose the best one for the job.

  As discussed earlier in this chapter, in a general sense, using a specific data type is faster and almost always uses less memory than when using a Variant. More specifically, there are several different numeric data types, each suitable for a different range of values, and each using more or less memory than the others.

> **Note** You need to be aware of the individual limitations of each numeric data type when determining which type to use. For example, assigning a value greater than 32,767 to an Integer or assigning any negative value to a byte causes an overflow error.

Trapping Errors

Try as you might to be perfect, you will introduce errors into your code. Many of them will be simple typing or syntax errors that will be caught by Visual Basic. Still others will be errors of action, in which your code works differently from what you intended, that you will catch when testing your code. The remainder consists of situations that you didn't think would arise or actions you didn't think your users would take. It is for this last class of errors that error trapping is so important.

Take the following procedure, for example:

```
Sub DisplayTaskNames()
    Dim objTask As Task

    For Each objTask In ActiveProject.Tasks
        MsgBox objTask.Name
    Next objTask
End Sub
```

It seems harmless enough because it just iterates through the tasks in the current project and displays each task name in a dialog box. But the code has a fatal flaw, assuming that there is a task on each line of the Gantt Chart, Task Sheet, or other task view. If there is a blank line, Visual Basic raises an error because there is no Task object where it expects to find one.

In this instance, there are two ways to handle the situation. The first solution is to plan for this quirk of Microsoft Project by testing for a Task object before attempting to act upon it. The If…Then statement in the following code avoids the assumption:

```
Sub DisplayTaskNames()
    Dim objTask As Task

    For Each objTask In ActiveProject.Tasks
        ' When an object Is Nothing, there is no object.
        ' If an object isn't Nothing, there must be
        '   an object.
```

```
        If Not (objTask Is Nothing) Then
            MsgBox objTask.Name
        End If
    Next objTask
End Sub
```

This is an example of code being "smart." By testing for a known but only potential problem, you have effectively trapped an error before it happens.

The following code is more representative of error trapping because it uses the On Error statement and features an actual error handler, although the fact that it knows what error might occur makes it a little artificial:

```
Sub DisplayTaskNames()
    Dim objTask As Task

    ' If an error arises, execution of the code skips
    '   ahead to the label "ErrorHandler."
    ' If the error is handled successfully, execution
    '   returns to the line that follows the line
    '   where the error occurred.
    On Error GoTo ErrorHandler

    For Each objTask In ActiveProject.Tasks
        MsgBox objTask.Name
    Next objTask

ErrorHandler:
    ' Knowing that a blank line instead of a Task object results
    '   in error code 91, you can clear the error and move on.
    If Err.Number = 91 Then
        Err.Clear
        Resume Next
    End If
End Sub
```

For more information about error handling and the Err object, see the "On Error Statement" topic in Microsoft Visual Basic Help.

Error trapping doesn't necessarily mean writing error handlers that allow your code to fail gracefully, usually by telling the user about a problem and asking them to fix it. Instead, error trapping can be thought of in the larger context of "preemptive debugging." If you do a good job of planning ahead, true error handlers are sometimes unnecessary. Trapping errors can be as simple as writing code that enforces rules.

Suppose that part of your code queries the user for a number between 1 and 10. What if the user doesn't provide a number? Will your code fail because it expects an answer, or will it test for a blank value and re-query the user for a response? What if the user enters a letter or other invalid character, instead of a number? By thinking about the potential situation and planning ahead, you have avoided an error condition.

Tip Humans being human and therefore unpredictable, code that interacts with a user typically requires the most planning and error handling.

Although there is much still to learn about Visual Basic, you should now have a solid base of knowledge upon which you can further develop your skills in Microsoft Project or anywhere else that supports a Visual Basic–based language.

For more information about using Visual Basic in Microsoft Project, see Chapter 31.

Chapter 31

Writing Microsoft Project Code with Visual Basic for Applications

If you read Chapter 27, "Automating Your Work with Macros," or if you've ever created a macro in Microsoft Office Project 2003, you already know that Visual Basic for Applications is one of the most powerful features of Project 2003. But there is much more to VBA (as it is more commonly called) than creating macros to automate repetitive, tedious, or complex tasks.

> **Note** Although Visual Basic for Applications is used to collectively describe the programming language and environment included with Microsoft Project, the language itself is Visual Basic. For the remainder of this chapter, Visual Basic is used to refer to the language and its elements.

For additional information about Visual Basic, see Chapter 30, "Understanding the Visual Basic Language."

After reading this chapter, you will be able to:

- Edit or expand upon macros you have recorded.
- Find and fix errors in your macro code.
- Create your own forms and dialog boxes for user interaction.
- Access Microsoft Project features from other programs, such as Microsoft Office and Visio, or even from Web pages.
- Use external libraries to provide additional capabilities to your macros.

For more information about working with external data and other items outside the VBA environment, see Chapter 32, "Working with Microsoft Project Data."

Before you can tap into the power of Visual Basic for Applications, though, you need to learn more about the Visual Basic Editor and development environment.

Using the Visual Basic Editor

One of the major components of VBA is the Visual Basic Editor. The editor is the development environment you use when writing, editing, and debugging code. It is also where you create forms (*UserForms* in the context of VBA) for interacting with the users of your code, and create references to external objects and libraries.

The discussion in this section is focused on just two aspects of the Visual Basic Editor: the windows and the Tools menu. Other elements of the editor are described as part of larger discussions later in the chapter.

> **Tip** **Visual Basic and programming terminology**
> Standard Visual Basic and general programming terms are italicized the first time they are discussed in this chapter.

Windows

When you open the editor—either by clicking Tools, Macro, Visual Basic Editor, or by pressing Alt+F11—just two windows are visible:

- The Project Explorer shows all the modules, UserForms, and other items in your VBA project, including references to other projects.

> **Note** Unless otherwise noted, in this chapter the term "project" means VBA project, whereas the term "plan" is used to refer to Microsoft Project files.

When you open the editor, two VBProject objects are listed. The first object, the ProjectGlobal project, contains all the code, UserForms, and modules associated with the Global file. The second object, the VBAProject project ("VBAProject" is the default name of any new project), contains the same items associated with the open Microsoft Project plan.

Initially, the This Project object is selected in the Project Explorer. This Project represents the plan itself, including events associated with the plan (see Figure 31-1).

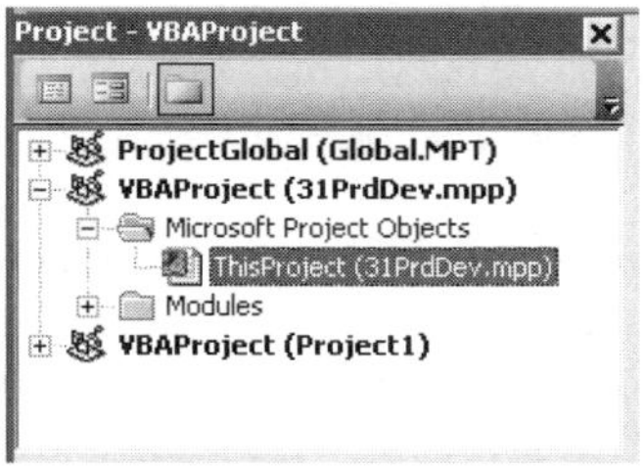

Figure 31-1. View all the items in your project by using the Project Explorer.

For more information about plan-level events, see "Working with Events" later in this chapter on page 919.

- The Properties window lists the properties for the selected item (see Figure 31-2). You can use the Properties window to easily change design-time properties, such as the name or style of an object, which can only be modified by using the editor.

> **Tip** **Run-time properties**
> Some of the properties listed in the Properties window are also run-time properties, which means they can be changed by your code while it is running.

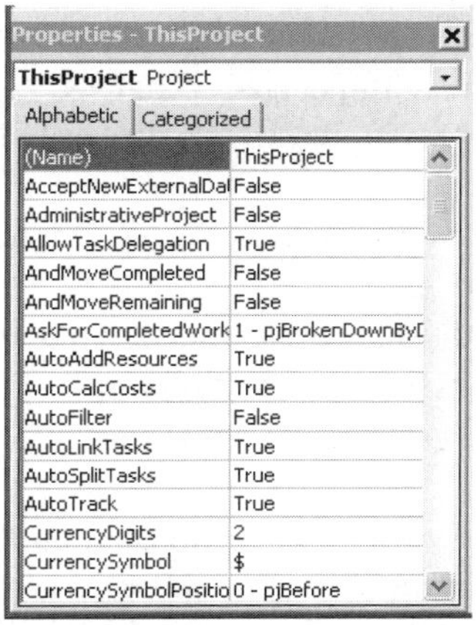

Figure 31-2. The Properties window shows the properties of the selected project and each of the items (UserForms, modules, and so on) that are contained in it.

Also of major importance is the Code window, in which you spend the majority of your time when using the editor. All Visual Basic code attached to a plan or a UserForm, or in a module or class, appears in the Code window. To open the Code window, simply double-click an item in the Project Explorer. (To view code for a UserForm, right-click and then click View Code.)

There are four controls associated with the Code window:

Objects box. For all items in the Project Explorer, this box displays the word (General). For VBProject objects and UserForms, it also displays the name of the object (Project or UserForm). Finally, for UserForms, the Objects box also displays the name of each control on the UserForm.

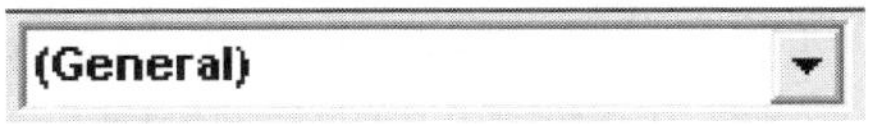

Objects

Procedures/Events box. For all items in the Project Explorer, this box displays the word (Declarations) and the names of procedures. For VBProject objects and UserForms, it also displays the names of events associated with the object selected in the Objects box.

Procedures/Events

Procedure View

Procedure View button. Displays just one procedure at a time in the Code window. This button is located in the lower-left corner of the Code window.

Full Module View

Full Module View button. Displays all procedures in the Code window, each separated by a horizontal line. Full Module is the default view for the Code window, and it is also located in the lower-left corner of the Code window.

The following windows are also part of the editor, but will be discussed in more detail later in this chapter:

Immediate. Any code entered in this window is immediately evaluated and run. Code entered in the Immediate window is not saved. It is frequently used as a sort of scratch pad, especially when debugging.

Locals. Displays information about all local (procedure) variables and their values. Used when debugging.

Watch. Displays information about watches that have been created. A watch is any expression that can be evaluated to produce a value. Used when debugging.

UserForm. Displays a UserForm. Used when creating or editing the visual elements of a UserForm.

Toolbox. Displays controls that can be placed on a UserForm, including ActiveX controls and other insertable objects you might have added to your project from external sources. Used when creating or editing the visual elements of a UserForm.

Object Browser. Displays information about the objects, properties, methods, events, and constants (the object model) that are available in type libraries referenced by your project or that you create in procedures. (Type libraries are files with the .olb, .tlb, or .dll extensions.) Used when writing code or learning about the features of an object model.

Tools Menu

One of the most powerful functionalities of the VBA environment is its capability to extend itself beyond the bounds of the host program. Two of the commands that provide this functionality, adding references to other object models and additional controls for UserForms, are found on the Tools menu. Also on the Tools menu are the following commands for customizing the editor and adding Help files, password protection, and digital signatures to your project:

References. Opens the References dialog box (see Figure 31-3), in which you make connections to external libraries, including the object models of other applications.

Libraries that are referenced by a project are indicated by the check box next to the library name. Clearing the check box of any library that you are not using in your project results in faster compilation of your project because unused object references must otherwise be verified.

> **Note** The "Visual Basic for Applications" and "Microsoft Project 11.0 Object Library" libraries are always referenced by Microsoft Project and cannot be removed.

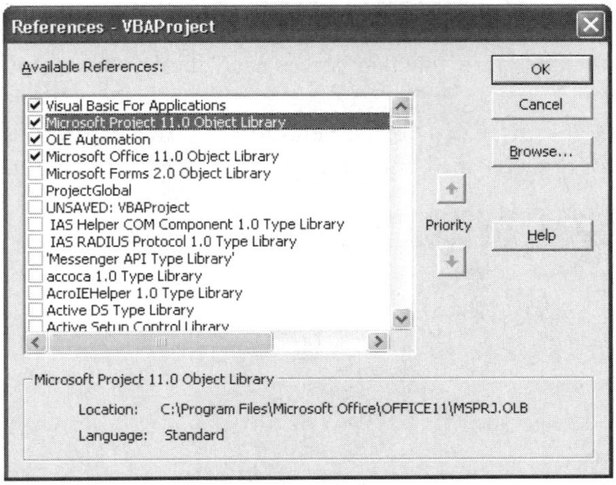

Figure 31-3. The References dialog box controls which objects are available to your project. Selections here determine which object models display in the object browser.

The Priority buttons change the order in which libraries are searched for objects. You should change the priority of a reference only if the same object name is used in more than one referenced library.

Note References are specific to each project.

Additional Controls. Opens the Additional Controls dialog box (see Figure 31-4), in which you select additional custom controls to use on your UserForms. This command is available only when creating or editing the visual elements of a UserForm.

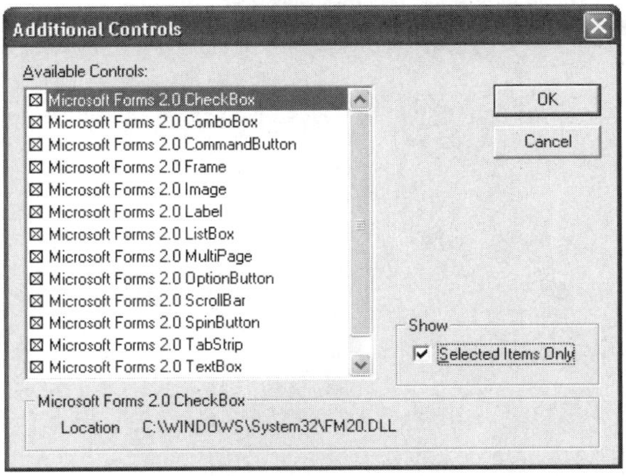

Figure 31-4. Selections made in the Additional Controls dialog box determine which controls appear in the Toolbox window.

Note Although any control that appears in the Available Controls list can be added to the Toolbox, not all controls are authored so that they can be used outside their intended environment.

Options. Opens the Options dialog box (see Figure 31-5), in which you select visual, behavior, and other options for the editor that suit your needs or preferences.

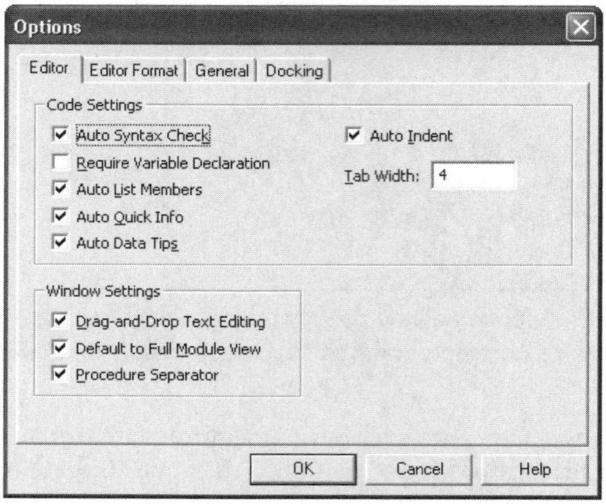

Figure 31-5. Selecting the Require Variable Declaration check box on the Editor tab of the Options dialog box enforces explicit declaration of variables.

VBAProject Properties. Opens the Project Properties dialog box (see Figure 31-6). Don't confuse the Project Properties dialog box with the Properties window. You can use the Project Properties dialog box to modify the properties of a VBProject object, including giving it a description and connecting it to a Help file.

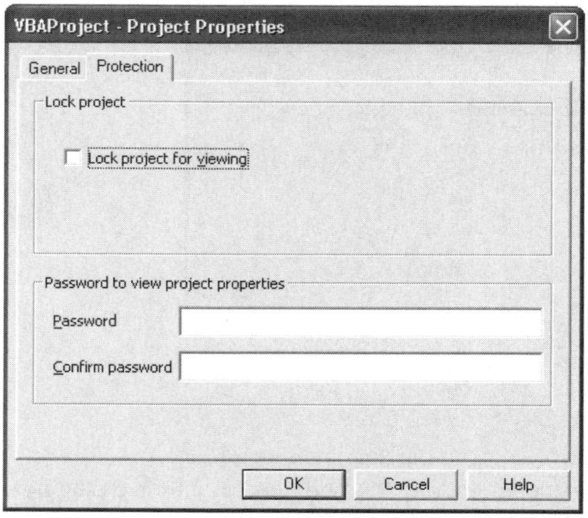

Figure 31-6. Specifying a password without also selecting the Lock Project For Viewing check box protects the Project Properties dialog box only.

Tip **Project information in the object browser**
The project name and description also appear in the object browser, which can be especially useful when searching for specific procedures in larger projects.

You can prevent other people from viewing or modifying your project by clicking the Protection tab, selecting the Lock Project For Viewing check box, and then providing a password.

Note The name of this command changes according to the name of the selected project. "VBAProject" is the default name of any new project.

Digital Signature. Displays the Digital Signature dialog box (see Figure 31-7), in which you can digitally sign a project with a certificate.

Figure 31-7. The Digital Signature dialog box for a project signed with a certificate created by using SelfCert.exe is shown here.

Digitally signing a project lets other users of your project know that it originated with the signer and has not changed since it was signed. You can use the SelfCert program, found in the Program Files\Microsoft Office\Office11 folder, to create your own certificate.

For more information about digital signatures, including how to obtain a digital certificate from a commercial Certificate Authority, search for "About digital signatures" in Microsoft Project Help.

Note In an environment in which the macro security level is set to High on all computers, a self-signed project can be deployed but cannot be run because it does not have a secure-enough certificate. You must use a certificate issued by a Certificate Authority in this situation.

Tip **Deploy a project under High security**

One way to deploy a project in a High security environment is to send the source code to users as text, instruct them how to paste it into the Visual Basic Editor, and then use SelfCert to certify the code using their own local certificate.

Finding the Right Help

Microsoft Project includes four different Help systems for VBA, and it might not always be clear where the content you're reading originated. Sometimes, you might know which Help system contains the information you need, but you might not be able to figure out how to open that specific Help file.

To get assistance with	Do the following
General Visual Basic concepts and language reference	Click Help, Microsoft Visual Basic Help in the editor.
Concepts and language reference common among Microsoft Office and related programs (including Microsoft Project)	Click a Microsoft Office–specific item in code or in the object browser and then press F1.
Members of the Microsoft Project object model	Click a Microsoft Project–specific item in code or in the object browser and then press F1.
UserForms	Click a UserForm, a control on a UserForm, or an item in the Properties window, and then press F1.

Understanding the Microsoft Project Object Model

Now that you have a foundation in Visual Basic concepts and know your way around the development environment, you're almost ready to begin creating customized solutions in Microsoft Project. The final piece of the VBA puzzle to familiarize yourself with is the object model.

But how do you familiarize yourself with an object model? Should you just dive in and start writing code, trusting that you'll figure out the object model as you go? Should you start reading the Help files that are included with Microsoft Project? Or should you use the object browser to (literally) browse the object model? The answer to all three of these questions is Yes. Choose the option that best suits your particular requirements and situation.

What Is an Object Model?

As described in Chapter 30, an object model is a system of objects that provides a programmatic model for interacting with an application. That's a bit of a mouthful, but what it means is that the object model is your portal to the features of Microsoft Project. The features of the object model, in concert with the power of Visual Basic, provide you with the ability to make Microsoft Project do virtually anything you want.

Inside Out

Not everything is in the object model

The object model is amazingly full-featured, but it is important to understand that it's not the Visual Basic "version" of all the features in Microsoft Project. As with every program that exposes one to programming, the object model does not always have a one-to-one correlation to what you can see or do in the user interface. It is just those portions of the program that seem useful for macro writers and other developers. This is why, even if new items have been continually added as the programming environment in Microsoft Project has developed, you can still occasionally find features that are not fully accessible (or not available at all) through the object model.

Learning a mature object model like that of Microsoft Project is made easier by relationships, both in the object model and in the Microsoft Project interface:

- Items that are important in the program are important in the object model, too. For example, the most important objects in the object model, aside from the Application, are the Project, Task, Resource, and Assignment objects.
- Relationships between items in the object model match those same relationships in the program itself.
- The hierarchical nature of the object model makes finding these relationships much simpler.

Note For more information about working with Microsoft Project's object model from another program, see "Extending and Automating Microsoft Project" later in this chapter on page 932.

Useful Tools When Learning the Object Model

Although there are many different ways to learn your way around the object model, there are three tools that can make doing so much easier:

Auto List Members. This option for the Visual Basic Editor (enabled by default) automatically lists all methods, properties, events, and children for an object as you type your code.

Besides saving additional typing—you can just select the item you want from the list—this option can help you learn about a relevant portion of the object model as you work (see Figure 31-8).

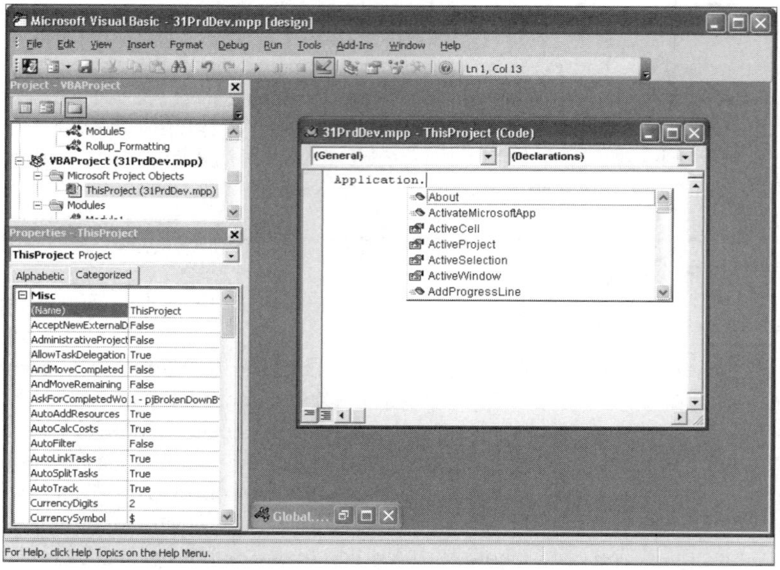

Figure 31-8. The Auto List Members box, shown here displaying part of the list for the Application object, is great way to learn about the object model as you work.

> **Tip** **How object-oriented code relates to the object model**
>
> When you see a period between two object names in Visual Basic code, such as Application.Projects or ActiveCell.Task.Assignments, you have "branched" from one section of the object model to another.
>
> If you think of the object model as a tree with the Application object as its root, this "dot syntax" of object-oriented code is not only a useful reminder that you've moved from one "branch" to another, but it can actually help you understand the relationships between items in the object model.

Microsoft Project Visual Basic Reference. Whether you use it with the object browser, use it while writing code, or just browse its contents, the Visual Basic reference for Microsoft Project contains everything you need to know about the object model.

There are graphical representations of the object model hierarchy, full explanations of the members of the Microsoft Project object model—including links to Help topics about the other object models automatically referenced by a project—and many examples showing the object model "in action."

Object Browser

Object Browser. The object browser (see Figure 31-9) displays all the items (properties, methods, events, and so on) in every object model that is referenced by your project. Open it by pressing F2 or clicking the Object Browser button.

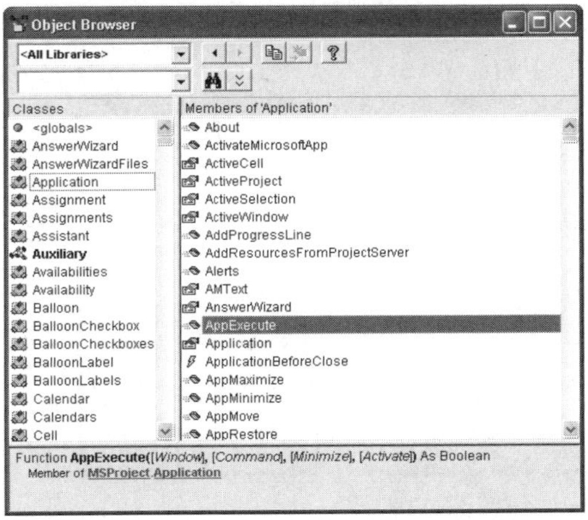

Figure 31-9. The object browser displays information about the libraries referenced by your project.

The object browser has three panes. The pane on the left is a list of classes. A class can be one of several things, including an object, collection, module, type (a user-defined data type), or enumerated data type (a collection of constants; usually referred to as an *enum*).

Clicking a class displays a list of members for the class in the pane on the right. In the figure just shown, one of the members of the Application object is selected.

Finding the Default Member of a Class

The icons next to a class or member name provide information about the item, such as whether it's a method or a property. A method with the following icon:

or a property with the following icon:

is the default member of its class.

Although default members can be used simply by referring to their class, doing so can sometimes make your code less readable. For example, although `CostRateTable(2)` is much less readable than `CostRateTable.Index(2)` because the default property for most objects is Name, using `Tasks(4)` (or any collection name) instead of `Tasks.Item(4)` is a common practice.

The Details pane at the bottom of the Object Browser (see Figure 31-10) lists specifics about the selected item, such as whether a property is read-only or read/write, the numerical value for a constant, or the arguments for a method.

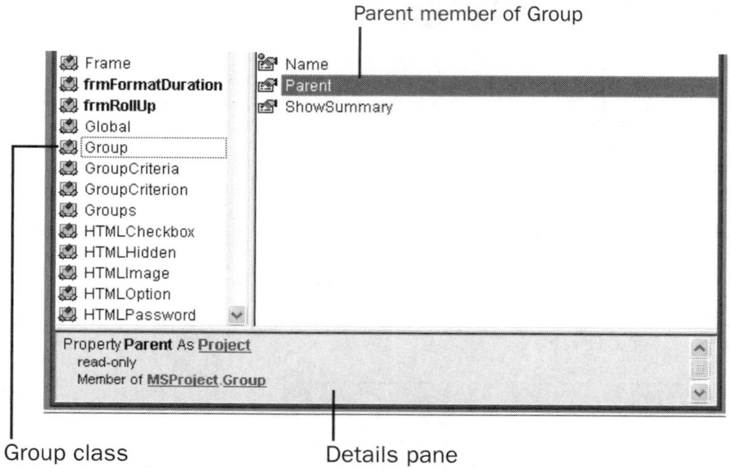

Figure 31-10. For properties or methods that return objects, the name of the object is a link in the Details pane.

It can be useful, especially if several libraries are referenced by your project, to filter the list of items shown in the object browser. You might also want to search for specific items by name or by part of a name. Use the Library and Search Text boxes (see Figure 31-11) to filter the list of items referenced by your project and search for specific items, respectively.

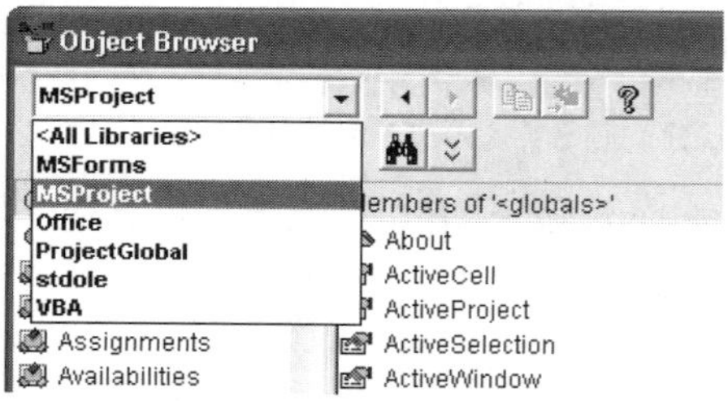

Figure 31-11. Use the Library box to filter items in the object browser and the Search Text box to find specific items.

> **Note** By default, the Search Text box performs "loose" searches, which means that searching for task returns items such as Task, TaskDependency, ExternalTask, DefaultTaskType, and so on.
>
> To return only exact matches for a search, right-click anywhere in the Object Browser window and then click Find Whole Word Only.

Creating Macros

Chapter 27 describes how to create a macro by recording the steps that make up a task. Although creating macros this way is easy enough and does work, it's not the most effective way to write Visual Basic, especially as your development skills grow. Creating macros in the Visual Basic Editor also enables you to use many more tools to develop Visual Basic solutions than are provided by recording actions in the Microsoft Project interface.

Writing a Macro in the Editor

Writing macros directly in the editor can seem a little daunting if you don't have much experience with programming or if you aren't comfortable with the object model. There are few tools to help you start (other than the Add Procedure window, which you can find by clicking Insert, Procedure), so one way to begin is to simply record a macro and then edit it in the Visual Basic Editor.

For the purposes of this discussion, though, you can simply follow these steps to create a macro in the editor directly:

1. Create a new project and then open the Visual Basic Editor by pressing Alt+F11.
2. Double-click the ThisProject object in the Project Explorer.

   The Code window opens with the cursor in the upper-left corner.
3. Type the following code in the Code window:

```
Function strNewTask(strName As String, intBefore As Integer) As String
    ActiveProject.Tasks.Add strName, intBefore

    If ActiveProject.Tasks(intBefore).Name = strName Then
        strNewTask = "Success!"
    Else
        strNewTask = "Failed to create task!"
    End If
End Function
```

Note Be sure to capitalize variable names exactly as they are shown here.

As you enter the code, you will notice some things that the editor does:

- As you type `strName As` in the function definition, a list displays classes and data types. As you start typing `String`, the list scrolls until String is selected (see Figure 31-12). You can continue typing the word, select String from the list, or press Ctrl+Space to complete the word.
- When you press Enter at the end of the line containing the function definition, several things happen at once: As the word "function" is capitalized, a blank line and End Function are inserted, and Visual Basic keywords (Function, String, Integer, and so on) are colored blue.
- When you press Enter at the end of a line containing an equals sign (=), the editor puts spaces around the equals sign.

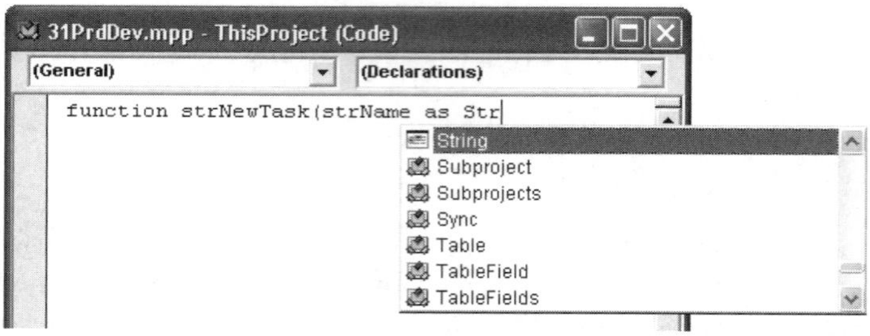

Figure 31-12. The Auto List Members feature scrolls through an alphabetical list of possible matches for data types and constants as you type.

4 Type the following code in the Code window:

```
Sub AddTask()
    Dim strTaskName As String
    Dim intTaskNum As Integer

    strTaskName = InputBox$("Type a name for the new task:")
    intTaskNum = CInt(InputBox$("Type the position for the new " & _
      "task in the task list:"))

    MsgBox strNewTask(strTaskName, intTaskNum)
End Sub
```

As you enter this code, the same actions occur as when you entered code for the function, but something really interesting also happens: Typing `strnewtask(` causes the Quick Info feature to list information about the arguments and return value for `strNewTask` (see Figure 31-13).

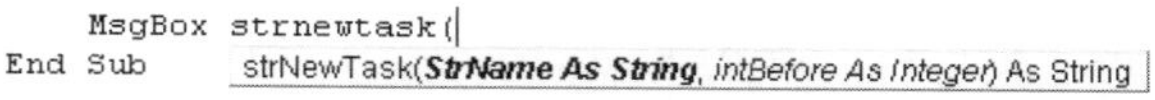

Figure 31-13. The Quick Info feature lists details about procedures you create and about items in the object model.

Returning to the Microsoft Project interface and opening the Macros dialog box (click Tools, Macro, Macros) shows the AddTask procedure as a new macro.

> **Tip** **Switch between Microsoft Project and the Visual Basic Editor**
> After the Visual Basic Editor has been opened, Alt+F11 toggles between Microsoft Project and the editor.

Deciding Where to Create and Store Procedures

The discussion so far has been about creating procedures in the ThisProject object for the VBAProject project, but that might not always be the best place to create procedures. In deciding where to create procedures, you should think about what the code is meant to do and whether you want to distribute your code to other people.

Depending upon your needs and the type of code you're writing, you should create procedures in the following areas:

- The ProjectGlobal project, if you want your procedures available for every plan you work with. Procedures in the ProjectGlobal project are associated with the Global file, which is opened every time you start Microsoft Project.
- The VBAProject project, if the procedures are used only for that particular plan. Procedures in the VBAProject project are associated with that particular plan and are available to anyone who opens the plan.
- A code module, if you want to be able to easily distribute the code to other people. Modules can be easily distributed because they are not associated with any particular plan and can be imported into a project as needed. Also, because they are not associated with any plan, modules are a good place to store general "utility" code.

Note To add an existing module to a project, right-click the project in the Project Explorer, click Import File, and then browse to the file that you want to insert.

Working with Events

Macros require user action to start, but you might occasionally need code to start automatically. For example, every time a shared plan is saved, you might want to store information about the person who saved it. In a situation like that, you need code that is run from an *event procedure*.

An event procedure is any code that is tied to an event, such as when a plan is saved or a task is deleted. When the event *fires*, the code is activated. Anything you can do in a "regular" procedure you can also do in an event procedure, including calling other procedures and making references to other object models.

For more information about events in UserForms, such as Click events for buttons, see "Creating UserForms" later in this chapter on page 926.

In Microsoft Project, there are events attached to the Application and Project (representing an open plan) objects (see Figure 31-14). You can find the events by looking for the event icon in the object browser or by expanding the Events item in the Contents tab of the Microsoft Visual Basic Reference.

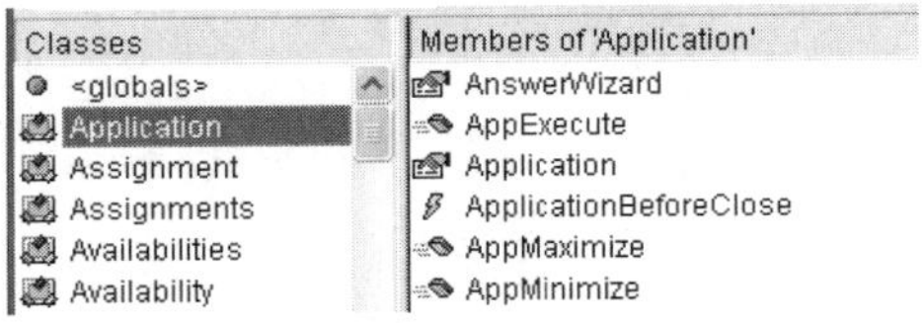

Figure 31-14. The ApplicationBeforeClose event is a member of the Application object.

> **Note** **Sort items by type**
> To sort items in the object browser by type instead of simply alphabetically, right-click anywhere in the object browser and then click Group Members.

Creating Application Event Procedures

Creating Application event procedures is a three-step process. The first step is to create a class module that contains an Application object variable declared with events. *WithEvents* is a Visual Basic keyword that means the variable should respond to events. You can only use WithEvents in class modules.

The second step is to *bind* the class containing your event procedure to the Application object. You do this by first declaring a variable that represents the class module and then writing a procedure that assigns the variable to the Application object.

For the last step, you need to decide how to run the code that binds the class to the Application object. You can either write the binding code directly in a project-level event procedure or if you want to keep your code more modular, you can write it anywhere you like and then simply call it from a project-level event.

Follow these steps to create an event procedure for the Application object:

1. Right-click anywhere in the Project Explorer and then click Insert, Class Module.
2. In the Code window for the new class, enter the following code:

```
Public WithEvents objMSProjectApp As Application
```

> **Note** The variable represented here by objMSProjectApp can be named anything you like.

3. In the Objects box, select objMSProjectApp.

   The editor creates a blank procedure for the NewProject event. If you want to write a procedure for a different event, click it in the Procedures/Events box.
4. Write your event code as you would for any other procedure.

   For example, the following code prevents a particular resource from being assigned to tasks. (Note that the procedure declaration must be entered on one line in the Visual Basic Editor, not on three as shown here.)

```
Private Sub objMSProjectApp_ProjectBeforeAssignmentChange(ByVal asg As
Assignment, _
  ByVal Field As PjAssignmentField, ByVal NewVal As Variant, _
    Cancel As Boolean)

    If Field = pjAssignmentResourceName And _
      NewVal = "Patricia Doyle" Then
        MsgBox "Patricia is no longer available for assignment!"
        Cancel = True
    End If
End Sub
```

5. Change the Name field in the Properties window for the class from Class1 to clsAppEventProcedures.
6. In any module except the class module in which you wrote the event procedure, enter the following code in the Code window:

```
Dim clsAppEvents As New clsAppEventProcedures

Sub BindEventToApplication()
    Set clsAppEvents.objMSProjectApp = Application
End Sub
```

7. Double-click ThisProject in the Project Explorer to open the Code window, click Project in the Objects box, and then type the following code in the Project object's Open event:

```
BindEventToApplication
```

Creating Project Event Procedures

To create an event procedure for the Project object, the code must be written in the ThisProject object, rather than in a code module. Events for the Project object are attached to the plan, which ThisProject represents.

Follow these steps to create an event procedure for the Project object:

1. Double-click ThisProject in the Project Explorer to open the Code window.
2. In the Objects box, click Project.

   The editor creates a blank procedure for the Open event. If you want to write a procedure for a different event, click it in the Procedures/Events box.
3. Write your event code as you would for any other procedure.

   For example, the following code adds information to the plan's summary task about who saved the plan, and when, each time it is saved:

```
Private Sub Project_BeforeSave(ByVal pj As Project)
    Dim strName As String

    strAlias = InputBox("Please enter your name: ")
    pj.ProjectSummaryTask.AppendNotes vbCrLf & "Saved by " & _
      strName & " on " & Date$ & " at " & Time$ & "."
End Sub
```

Debugging Macros

You will occasionally make mistakes in your code. Many will be simple syntax or typing errors that are caught by the Visual Basic compiler. Most of the rest become obvious when you examine your code (the "duh" factor). Sometimes, however, you'll find a situation in which something is going wrong and you can't immediately figure out why. Your next step is to use the debugging tools available in the editor.

For more information about debugging, including some concepts and general principles, see "Trapping Errors" on page 902.

Although most of the features discussed here are true debugging tools such as breakpoints, there are other features of the editor that are useful when debugging, but also have uses outside a debugging situation.

Using Breakpoints

A *breakpoint* is a place in your code where you want to temporarily break out of the run-time environment without actually ending your program, so that you can examine the code during execution. A breakpoint (and you can have as many as you want at one time) is a lot like a Pause button.

The F9 key toggles a breakpoint for the selected line of code, which is marked (using the default colors) by a brown dot in the margin and brown background for the line of code (see Figure 31-15). You can create breakpoints only in lines of executable code, which excludes blank lines, comments, and even lines where you declare a variable.

```
Function strNewTask(StrName As String, intBefore As Integer
    ActiveProject.Tasks.Add StrName, intBefore

    If ActiveProject.Tasks(intBefore).Name = StrName Then
        strNewTask = "Success!"
    Else
        strNewTask = "Failed to create task!"
    End If
End Function
```

Figure 31-15. If a new task is successfully created in this function, this breakpoint never gets hit and execution proceeds normally.

Note Press Ctrl+Shift+F9 to clear all breakpoints from your code.

Tracing Execution

After your program has been paused, you need to see what's going wrong with your code. This can mean watching your code run line by line (*tracing*) to see where, for example, it takes a different path through a decision structure than what you expected.

The following tools are available when tracing code:

- The F8 key steps into a procedure, which is the most detailed mode of tracing. If the procedure you're tracing makes a call to another procedure, execution transfers to the called procedure just as it would normally, but in break mode.
- After you've stepped into a procedure and have decided that you no longer need to trace through it, you can step out (Ctrl+Shift+F8) to return to the calling procedure.

- Stepping over (Shift+F8) is to treat a call to another procedure as a stand-alone statement; that is, to trace the code that calls another procedure without actually tracing the code in the called procedure.
- Using the Run To Cursor option (Ctrl+F8) essentially creates a temporary breakpoint. Code runs from the current location to the cursor, where it re-enters break mode. This is useful if you stepped into a procedure and want to skip over large sections of it without stepping out of it, but don't want to create an actual breakpoint.

> **Note** Pressing F5 while tracing execution returns to normal execution, unless another breakpoint is encountered before the program ends.

Using Watches

Watches are used to keep track of values automatically while debugging. A watch is anything that can be evaluated to produce a value, which means it can be an expression such as ActiveProject.Tasks(intBefore).Name = strName, or simply the name of a function or variable (see Figure 31-16).

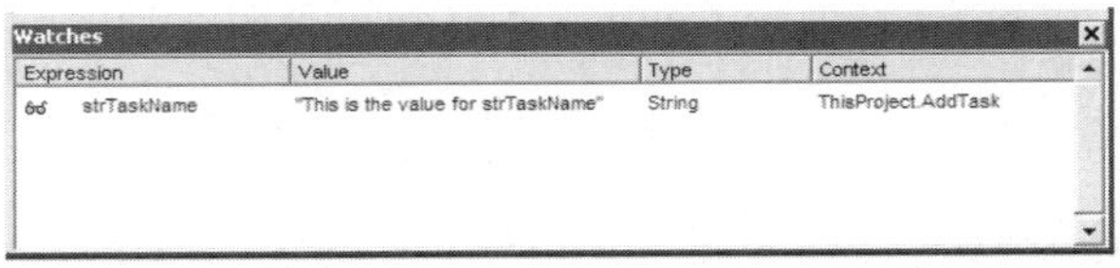

Figure 31-16. The Context column shows that the scope for the variable is local, existing in the AddTask procedure of the current module. If the active statement were in another procedure, the Value column would display <Out of context>.

> **Note** **Use Auto Data Tips as a watch**
> The Auto Data Tips option (enabled by default) works like an ad hoc watch by providing information about the value of a variable (including the value of properties) when you move the mouse pointer over it while in break mode.

You can use watches in two ways:

- To simply watch the value of an expression while debugging.
- To define a condition, rather than simply a line of code, that should force entry into break mode.

You can add watches while in design mode or break mode. Although you can manually enter the expression you want to watch in the Add Watch window (see Figure 31-17), it's easier to simply highlight the variable or expression by right-clicking in the Code window and then clicking Add Watch.

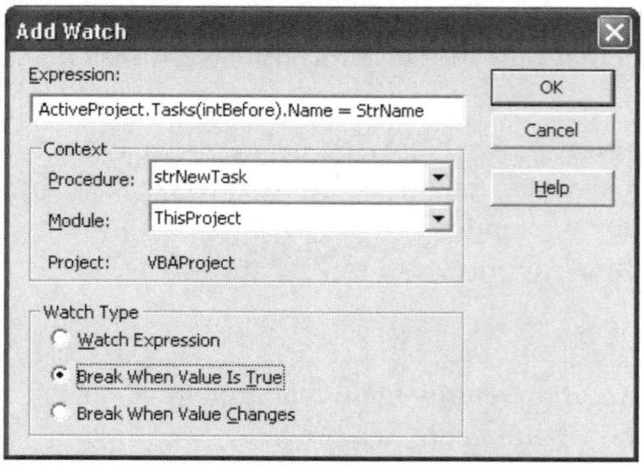

Figure 31-17. Set the Watch Type to specify whether you want to watch the expression or test its value to determine when to enter break mode.

Using the Locals Window

The Locals window acts like a dynamically generated list of watches for the current procedure. As execution moves from one procedure to another in break mode, the Locals window is updated to show a list of local variables and their values (see Figure 31-18).

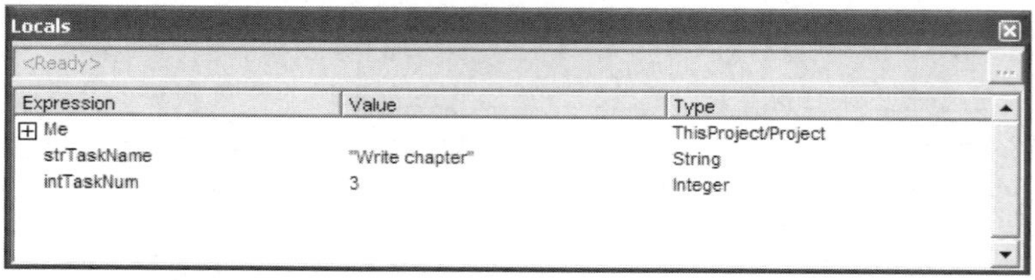

Figure 31-18. Click the plus sign (+) next to the expression "Me" to see the value of every property, variable, and function referenced by or defined in your project.

If a variable can be assigned a value in more than one location in a procedure (such as when a different value is assigned to the same variable, depending upon which path is taken through a decision structure), it is listed once for each possible assignment. Assuming that the procedure runs successfully, only one of these occurrences will have an entry in the Value column by the time execution moves out of the procedure.

Unlike the Watches window, which is read-only, you can modify items in the Value column to test different actions taken by your code. If you had a decision structure in your code, for example, that took different actions according to the value of a local variable, you could do the following:

1. Insert a breakpoint at the beginning of the structure and then run your macro.
2. When execution enters break mode, step through the decision structure to see the results.

3. At the end of the decision structure (or at any time before execution moves to a different procedure), change the value of the variable in the Locals window to something else.
4. Select the line with the breakpoint, use Ctrl+F9 to force execution to return to that line, and then step through the decision structure again.

Using the Immediate Window

The Immediate window (Ctrl+G), which can be used when debugging or at design-time, is a very versatile feature of the editor: Think of it as a "scratch pad" for code.

In design mode, you can enter a question mark (?) and any expression into the Immediate window to be evaluated. Typing ?8*7 and pressing Enter, for example, returns 56 just below the expression in the Immediate window. You can even enter small procedures to be evaluated, although they must be entered as one line, such as the following:

```
for x = 1 to 3: msgbox x: next x
```

In break mode, you can do anything you can in design mode, plus you can do the following:

- Find the value of variables:

  ```
  ?strname
  ```

> **Tip** **When capitalization matters**
> Capitalization in the Immediate window doesn't matter unless you have multiple variables with the same name but different capitalization.

- Assign new values to any local, module-level, or global variable:

  ```
  strname="some new value"
  ```

- Evaluate expressions:

  ```
  ?ActiveProject.Tasks(intBefore).Name = strName
  ```

> **Note** **Edit and re-evaluate an expression**
> You can edit an existing expression in the Immediate window and then press Enter to re-evaluate it, without having to type the expression anew.

Debugging with Navigation Tools

There are a few other features in the editor that, although frequently used while debugging, are actually tools for navigating within your code. They are most useful in modules that contain many procedures, in which finding a particular item can sometimes be difficult.

Bookmarks (see Figure 31-19) can be used to mark a location in your code. Unlike breakpoints, bookmarks can be used anywhere, including blank lines.

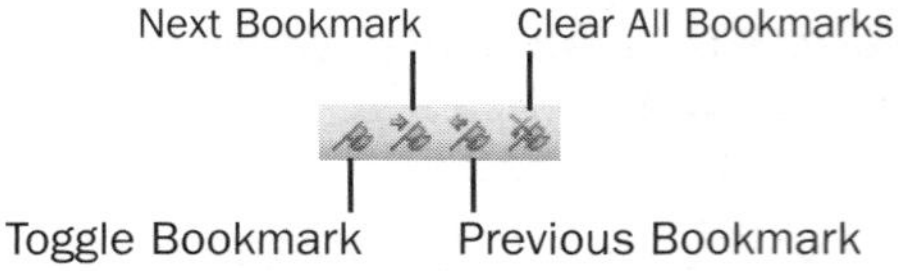

Figure 31-19. Use the bookmark controls on the Edit toolbar to toggle, move between, or delete all bookmarks.

The Definition command (press Shift+F2 or right-click the Code window) moves focus to the location where the procedure or variable under the mouse pointer is defined. If the item is a member of a type library referenced by your project and not defined in your code, focus moves to the appropriate location in the object browser.

The Last Position command (press Ctrl+Shift+F2 or right-click in the Code window) returns focus to the previous location after using the Definition command or changing code. The Last Position command loops through as many as eight locations.

Creating UserForms

Writing macros and other code to accomplish things you need to do is a major part of using VBA, and UserForms are another. UserForms, which are the visual counterpart to Visual Basic procedures, provide you with the ability to interact with your users as if your creation was part of Microsoft Project itself.

> **Note** All the normal rules and principles for working with Visual Basic code, including events and debugging, also apply to working with UserForms.

Creating a Simple Form

To begin designing a UserForm, click Insert, UserForm. A blank UserForm appears (see Figure 31-20) in place of the Code window (if showing) with the Toolbox window floating somewhere near it (see Figure 31-21). At the same time, the information in the Properties window changes to show properties for the new UserForm.

> **Note** For the remainder of this section, UserForms are simply referred to as forms.

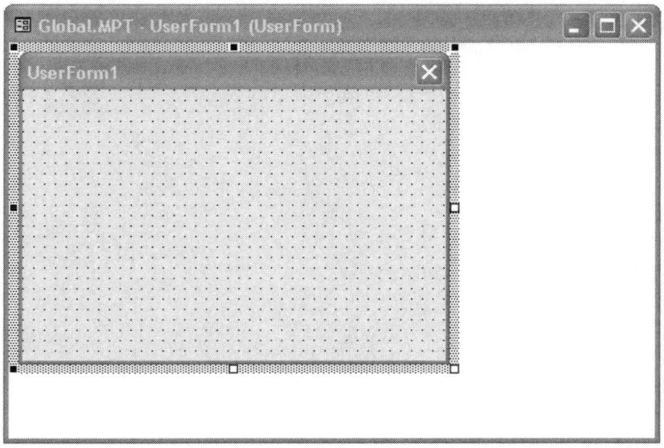

Figure 31-20. A new UserForm window is the visual counterpart to a blank Code window.

Figure 31-21. Use the Toolbox to place visual components on your UserForm. You can use Tools, Additional Controls to place more "tools" in the Toolbox.

Follow these steps to change some of the default properties of the form:

1. In the Properties window, change the value for the Name field from `UserForm1` to `frmWelcome`.

   This changes the name of the form in the Project Explorer and is how you refer to the form, when necessary. Also, if you export it, `frmWelcome.frm` will be the filename of the form.

2. Change the value for the Caption field from `UserForm1` to `Welcome!`.

   This is what appears in the title bar of the form when it is running.

3. Click the Font field and then use the Browse button to change the base font for the form from 8 point Tahoma to 10 point Arial (see Figure 31-22).

   Although changing the font in the form doesn't have any visible effect, any controls you add to the form will use the font you specified as their default font. Changing the font now is quicker and easier than changing it for each control individually later.

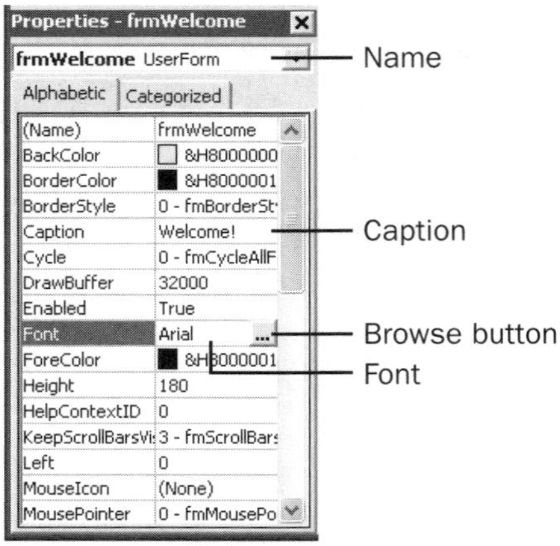

Figure 31-22. Start designing your UserForm by changing certain properties.

Now that you've created a form and modified some of its properties, the next task is to add controls. Follow these steps to add two buttons, a label, and a text box:

TextBox

Label

Command-Button

1. In the Toolbox window, click the TextBox button and then draw a rectangle on the form.
2. In the Properties window, change the value for the Name field from `TextBox1` to `txtName`.
3. In the Toolbox window, click the Label button and then draw a rectangle just above the text box.
4. In the Properties window, change the value for the Name field from `Label1` to `lblName`.
5. Change the value for the Caption field from `Label1` to `Enter your name:`.
6. In the Toolbox window, click the CommandButton button, draw a rectangle to the right of the label and the text box and then click the CommandButton button again to draw another button just below the first.
7. Click the first button, change the value for Name from `CommandButton1` to `cmdOK`, and then change the value for Caption from `CommandButton1` to `OK`.
8. Click the second button, and give it the name `cmdCancel` and the caption `Cancel`.
9. Adjust the position of the controls and the size of the form (see Figure 31-23).

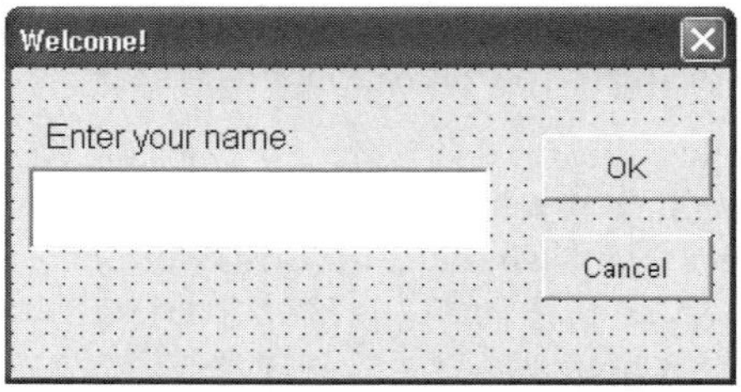

Figure 31-23. This is what the completed frmWelcome should look like after the controls have been positioned and the form sized appropriately.

Adding Code to Your Form

Before your new form can be used to do anything, you must write event procedures for the controls on it. For the form created in the previous section, you need to write code only for the two buttons.

The button `cmdCancel` needs code to close the form's window, in case the user doesn't want to use the form. The quickest way to open the Code window for a form or control is to double-click the item while in design mode. If you double-click the Cancel button on the form, the Code window opens to the `cmdCancel_Click()` event procedure. Type the following code into the Cancel button's vClick event:

```
frmWelcome.Hide
```

> **Note** **The Me keyword**
> The Me keyword always refers to the class (a form is a kind of class) in which it is used. Instead of `frmWelcome.Hide`, for example, you could simply use `Me.Hide`.

The `cmdOK` button is where all the action is for this form. The OK button takes the name the user entered in the `txtName` box and adds it to the status bar at the bottom of the Microsoft Project window.

With the Code window open, click `cmdOK` in the Objects box to gain access to the `cmdOK_Click()` event. Type the following code into the OK button's Click event:

```
Application.StatusBar = "What would you like to do now, " & _
  txtName.Text & "?"
```

This code sets the Application object's StatusBar property to be the text in quotes, plus the value of the `txtName` box's Text property.

Because you want the form to close after the user clicks the OK button, add the same code you added to the Cancel button's Click event:

```
Me.Hide
```

Integrating Your Form into Microsoft Project

You now have a form with controls and event procedures that perform actions when the controls are used, but no one will ever see the form until you determine how the form is activated. With many types of forms, it's enough that the user runs a macro, which then displays one or more forms as it runs.

For this form, though, you want to automatically display the form every time a particular plan is opened. Follow these steps to create an event procedure for the Project object that will display your form every time the plan is opened:

1. In the Project Explorer, double-click ThisProject.

   The Code window opens.

2 In the Objects box, click Project, and then type the following code into the Project object's Open event:

```
frmWelcome.Show
```

3 In the Procedure/Events box, click BeforeClose and then type the following code into the Project object's BeforeClose event:

```
Application.StatusBar = False
```

Because code tied to the Project object is changing an application-level property, you need this additional code to "clean up" the effects of using the form by resetting the StatusBar property to its default value (see Figure 31-24).

What would you like to do now, Mr. Jones?

Figure 31-24. The Microsoft Project status bar after someone has used the form.

Note The first form your users see when opening the plan is actually the macro virus security dialog box. If a user selects the Disable Macros button, none of the event procedures run and your form doesn't display.

For more information about Project events, see "Creating Project Event Procedures" earlier in this chapter on page 921.

Three Birds, One Stone

If you like the idea behind the example of displaying a form every time a specific plan was opened, but want something a little more robust, you can avoid three of its potential detractions by working with the Global file (the ProjectGlobal project) instead of a particular plan (the VBAProject project):

- To make the code frmWelcome.Show run every time Microsoft Project starts, expand the ProjectGlobal project and double-click the ThisProject object instead of the ThisProject object under the VBAProject project.
- Because the StatusBar property is reset to its default when Microsoft Project closes, you don't need the BeforeClose event code.
- Because of the special nature of the Global file, users don't see the macro virus security dialog box. This means there is no chance that the user will choose to disable the code that displays your form.

A more sophisticated version of this example is one that adds a new menu item or toolbar that can be used to access the forms you have created. This method integrates your forms with the Microsoft Project interface even more closely, although you probably wouldn't bother doing so for a simple, limited-use form such as the one you just created.

Follow these steps to create two Project event procedures that add a new item to the View menu (see Figure 31-25) that, when clicked, displays the frmWelcome form:

1. Double-click ThisProject in the Project Explorer to open the Code window.
2. In the Objects box, click Project, and then type the following code into the Project object's Open event:

```
Dim objViewBar As CommandBar
Dim objNewItem As CommandBarButton
Dim intTotalItems As Integer

Set objViewBar = Application.CommandBars("View")
intTotalItems = objViewBar.Controls.Count

If objViewBar.Controls(intTotalItems).Caption <> "Show my UserForm" Then
    Set objNewItem = objViewBar.Controls.Add(Type:=msoControlButton)
    objNewItem.Caption = "Show my UserForm"
    objNewItem.BeginGroup = True
    objNewItem.OnAction = "frmWelcome.Show"
End If

Set objNewItem = Nothing
Set objViewBar = Nothing
```

3. In the Procedures/Events box, click BeforeClose, and then type the following code into the Project object's BeforeClose event:

```
Dim objViewBar As CommandBar
Dim intTotalItems As Integer

Application.StatusBar = False

Set objViewBar = Application.CommandBars("View")
intTotalItems = objViewBar.Controls.Count

If objViewBar.Controls(intTotalItems).Caption = "Show my UserForm" Then
    objViewBar.Controls(intTotalItems).Delete
End If

Set objViewBar = Nothing
```

Because code tied to the Project object is changing two application-level items, you need this additional code to "clean up" when the plan is closed by resetting the StatusBar property to its default value and removing the Show My UserForm command from the View menu. This procedure ensures that Microsoft Project is in its default state when other plans are opened.

Note Until the plan is closed, the new View menu item is visible from every other open plan. Clicking it from one of those plans, however, results in an error.

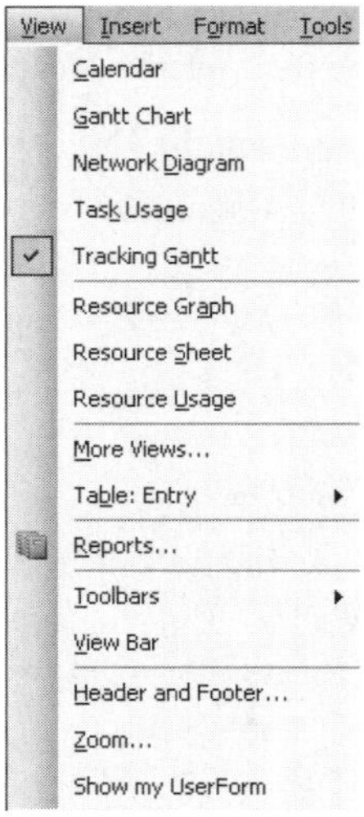

Figure 31-25. The new Show My UserForm command appears at the bottom of the View menu.

Extending and Automating Microsoft Project

As mentioned in the discussion of the Tools menu earlier in this chapter, one of the most powerful functionalities of the VBA environment is its capability to extend itself beyond the bounds of the host program, which can be done in two main ways:

- Referencing external type libraries (files with the .olb, .tlb, or .dll extension) or ActiveX controls (files with the .ocx, .dll, or .exe extension) to provide additional functionality to your code and forms.
- Using Automation to run other programs from Microsoft Project or to run Microsoft Project from other programs.

> **Note** The Microsoft Project Developer Center at *http://msdn.microsoft.com/project/* contains a great deal of useful information about advanced programming with Microsoft Project, including links to the Microsoft Project Software Development Kit.

Working with External References

Working with external references usually means either adding ActiveX controls to your forms or using external type libraries to do things that aren't part of the object model for the program you're using. The Microsoft Web Browser control, for example, is an ActiveX control commonly added to forms, whereas a reference to one of the Microsoft ActiveX Data Objects (ADO) libraries might be used to provide easy access to data sources.

Using ActiveX Controls

Working with ActiveX controls is probably the easiest way to use external references. Controls that have been *registered* on your computer (this happens automatically when controls are installed on your computer) appear in the Additional Controls dialog box (click Tools, Additional Controls) and can be added to the Toolbox. After a control appears in the Toolbox, you can use it just as you would any of the *intrinsic controls* in the Microsoft Forms library that is included with Microsoft Project.

All ActiveX controls have common properties for a name, physical dimensions and position, tab order, and so on, in addition to whatever properties and methods they supply as part of their specialized functionality. All the general information you know from working with the intrinsic controls also applies to new controls, enabling you to concentrate on working with the new capabilities the control provides.

Note Many ActiveX controls also have type libraries associated with them, which appear in the object browser. These libraries might be listed in the Library box by the filename of the library instead of by the name of the control as it appears in the Additional Controls dialog box.

Using External Libraries

An external type library (sometimes called a "helper library") is really nothing more than an object model that doesn't have a visual element and doesn't represent the Visual Basic aspect of another program. Type libraries are installed in association with a program or the operating system.

After you add a reference to a library (click Tools, References), the objects, methods, properties, events, and constants defined in the library appear in the object browser. There are no special rules for working with an external type library and you can use its members as you would the members of the Microsoft Project object model.

The following code is an example of working with an external type library. It uses the Microsoft ActiveX Data Objects 2.6 Library to access the values of certain fields for each record in a Jet (Microsoft Access) database:

```
Sub ReadDataFile(strFileName As String)
    ' The Connection object is found in the ADO library
    ' The New keyword in a variable declaration creates an object
    '  reference at the same time as the variable is declared
    Dim conData As New Connection
    ' The Recordset object is found in the ADO library
    Dim rstTopic As New Recordset
    Dim strSelect As String
    Dim bytCount As Byte

    ' Connect to data source
    ' ConnectionString is a property of the Connection object
    conData.ConnectionString = "Provider=Microsoft.Jet.OLEDB.4.0;Data Source=
"& _
      strFileName
```

```
    ' This Open method is for the Connection object
    conData.Open

    ' Select the records and open a recordset
    strSelect = "SELECT * FROM Topic"
    ' This Open method is for the Recordset object
    rstTopic.Open strSelect, conData

    ' Move to the first record in the Recordset object
    rstTopic.MoveFirst

    ' Read through each record to find the values I want
    For bytCount = 1 To rstTopic.Fields!byt1.Value
        rstTopic.MoveNext

        ' gudtText is a global, user-defined collection object
        gudtText.blnNumbered.Add rstTopic.Fields!byt1.Value
        gudtText.bytMatchNode.Add rstTopic.Fields!byt2.Value
        gudtText.bytNumber.Add rstTopic.Fields!byt3.Value
        gudtText.strText.Add rstTopic.Fields!str2.Value
    Next bytCount

    ' Close the reference to the Connection object
    conData.Close

    ' Clean up the object references
    Set rstTopic = Nothing
    Set conData = Nothing
End Sub
```

Automating Microsoft Project

Automating a program such as Microsoft Project means that you control the program remotely, even invisibly, as if you were actually using the interface. This means, for example, that you can use the Spelling Checker feature of Microsoft Word in Microsoft Project or the math functions of Microsoft Excel from within Microsoft Project. In fact, you can even automate Microsoft Project from a Web page.

Automating with a Library Reference

Programs that support making references to the Microsoft Project object model, such as Microsoft Word, provide the easiest access to Automation:

- Setting a reference to a library by using the References item on the Tools menu automatically provides the connection between the host application and Microsoft Project.
- Many of the tools available when writing Visual Basic code in Microsoft Project are typically available in the host's development environment, such as the Auto List Members option. (Obviously, writing Automation code from a VBA-enabled program provides all the tools available from Microsoft Project because they both use the Visual Basic Editor.)

Follow these steps to create a simple example of automating Microsoft Project from any Microsoft Office program:

1. Press Alt+F11 to start the Visual Basic Editor.
2. In the References dialog box, scroll through the Available References list and then click the Microsoft Project 11.0 Object Library.
3. Create a new procedure and type the following code into it:

```
MSProject.Visible = True
MSProject.FileNew

MSProject.ActiveProject.Tasks.Add "task 1"
MSProject.ActiveProject.Tasks.Add "task 2"
MsgBox MSProject.ActiveProject.Tasks.Count

MSProject.Quit pjDoNotSave
```

An obvious difference from typing this code in Microsoft Project itself is the MSProject class, which represents the Microsoft Project Application object. In every other respect, though, writing code that uses members of the Microsoft Project object model in another application looks and "feels" just as it would in Microsoft Project.

Automating without a Library Reference

Automating Microsoft Project when you can't directly link to the object model, such as when using Automation from a Web page or some similar environment, follows the same principles as when using a reference. It does, however, require more code and, more importantly, more research.

The additional code is necessary because the host application doesn't have the connection provided by the library reference. You must write code that creates a new *instance* of Microsoft Project as an object reference before you can use the members of the object model.

The additional research is necessary because the host application doesn't know anything about the Microsoft Project object model, which affects your code in two major ways:

- The code you're typing is essentially treated like text (there's no link to the object model to verify members of objects or automatically list arguments for methods, for example), so you must be reasonably comfortable with the object model (or at least have easy access to information about it).
- You must use the numeric values of any constants defined in the Microsoft Project object model because the host application can't know what values the constants map to without an active reference to the object model. (In this situation, it's common to declare constants of the same name as used by Microsoft Project so your code is as readable as it would be if you had a library reference.)

Follow these steps to create a simple example of automating Microsoft Project from any program that supports Visual Basic or Visual Basic Scripting edition (VBScript):

1. Define an object variable and then use the CreateObject method from the Visual Basic (or VBScript) core object library to make a connection to Microsoft Project:

```
Dim Proj As Object

Set Proj = CreateObject("MSProject.Application")
```

Note This is an example of a late-bound object reference. For more information about late-binding, see Chapter 30.

2. Enter the code that provides the functionality for your procedure, replacing "Application" (when writing a procedure in Microsoft Project) or "MSProject" (using Automation with a library reference) with the object variable defined in step 1:

```
Proj.Visible = True
Proj.FileNew

Proj.ActiveProject.Tasks.Add "task 1"
Proj.ActiveProject.Tasks.Add "task 2"
MsgBox Proj.ActiveProject.Tasks.Count
```

3. When entering the code for the Quit method, use the numeric value of the `pjDoNotSave` constant:

```
Proj.Quit 0
```

4. Discard the object variable's reference to Microsoft Project:

```
Set Proj = Nothing
```

Note **Using the Visual Basic Editor**
If it is more convenient, you can enter this code in the Visual Basic Editor of any Microsoft Office program, and it behaves just as it would in a Web page or the like. If you do use the Visual Basic Editor, make sure that the project doesn't have a reference to the Microsoft Project library.

Chapter 32

Working with Microsoft Project Data

Okay, so you're well-versed in using Microsoft Office Project 2003 to create projects, delegate tasks, set up resources and assignments, work with calendars, customize project fields and global settings, and more. What you might not know yet is how Project 2003 keeps track of all this information, including where and how it is stored. You also might not know the ways in which you can view or use this information outside of Microsoft Project.

This chapter introduces key concepts about the databases associated with Microsoft Project, including the types of tables and data these databases include, and the different ways you can view these data.

Microsoft Project data are found in the following locations:

Microsoft Project database. This is the primary storage location for Microsoft Project data. It is an integral part of any Microsoft Project plan and it contains all the data associated with a project. Data stored in the Microsoft Project database can be accessed by opening the following:

- Any file that Microsoft Project can open (depending on the type of file, it might need to be converted to a Microsoft Project 2003 file).
- A file from Microsoft Office Project Server 2003.

The project file in another application that can open the file; for example, a Microsoft Project database file opened in Microsoft Office Access 2003.

If you are using the enterprise features with Microsoft Office Project Professional 2003 and saving project data to the Project Server 2003 database, the Microsoft Project database also stores enterprise project information.

Project Server database. The Project Server database stores settings for Microsoft Office Project Web Access 2003, including security settings, resource views, and some enterprise project data. Data and settings in this database can be accessed only by project server administrators with permission to access the database. The entire database can be viewed by an authorized Microsoft SQL Server user. Certain settings stored in this database can be accessed by authorized users of Project Web Access 2003. Other users access subsets of data indirectly when using Project Web Access views or when checking projects into or out of Project Server using Project Professional 2003.

For more information about Project Web Access and enterprise project management, see Chapter 20, "Understanding the Project Workgroup and Enterprise Model."

OLE DB. Object Linking and Embedding (OLE) is an object-based technology that can be used to share information by providing a uniform approach to how the data is stored and accessed between applications. OLE DB is a set of Component Object Model (COM) objects that provide database functionality by providing uniform access to data stored in an information container (a Microsoft Project file, for example). OLE DB allows you to access the data in the file (using an OLE DB Provider) much in the same way that you access data in a database. OLE DB provides many of the benefits of a database without requiring the existence of a database to use the data.

In this context, OLE DB is a provider of data, a Microsoft Project file contains the actual data, and Access 2003 is a tool that you can use to access the data.

Introducing Common Database Elements

A *database* is a collection of information broken into categories or groups of data that have predefined relationships to each other. Each group of data, in turn, is a collection of specific details that is distinct from other groups of data; for example, task information is distinct from resource information. If you can imagine a project as a set of tasks, a set of resources, and a set of assignments, you're already on your way to understanding how the Microsoft Project database fits together.

All the databases used by Microsoft Project share some common elements, including general types of data that are stored in each database. All Microsoft Project databases contain information about the following:

Projects. Project tables link all related information (tasks, resources, assignments, and so on) to a specific project. Project tables also define unique information related to a particular project. In addition, project tables store some global settings such as those found in the Options dialog box (Tools, Options) and the Properties dialog box (File, Properties).

Tasks. Task tables define all the fields and relationships in Microsoft Project that make up a task, such as the task name, start date, finish date, duration, and assigned resources.

Resources. Resource tables define all the fields and relationships that make up a resource, such as the resource name, e-mail address, hourly rate, and availability dates.

Assignments. Assignment tables link tasks and resources and other related information, in addition to defining unique information related to a particular assignment, such as assignment delay, assignment work, and total cost for the assignment.

Calendars. Calendar tables contain all working times calendars used by projects, resources, tasks, or assignment availability in a project.

Custom Field Information. Each database has a different way of storing customized information. In general, you can create custom fields—including code, date, duration, flag, number, and text fields—for both local and enterprise projects.

Application Settings. Global settings, such as those stored in the project global template and the enterprise global template, are typically stored in project-related tables.

The three databases have a number of unique tables. Some of these unique tables track data that can be accessed only from within that database, or have a specific purpose for using project data outside of Microsoft Office Project Standard 2003 or Project Professional; for example, the security and view tables in the Project Server database. Some just track data in a different way than another database does. For example, the custom fields in the Project Server database are separated out into their own individual tables; whereas in the OLE DB, these same fields are included within the Task, Resource, Assignment, and Project tables.

In addition to the general types of information stored by all three databases, the Microsoft Project database and Project Server database also track the following information:

Internal Tables. These tables store strings of data; for example, the words that appear in the user interface in Microsoft Project or Project Web Access. Internal tables are also used by Microsoft Project to link "behind-the-scenes" information.

Security Tables. These tables are used to determine which users have access to Project Web Access and other specific features available when Project Server, Project Web Access, and Project Professional are used together. These security tables also determine the specific areas within this enterprise project management workspace that users can view, and whether a user can log on to Project Server to check out a project.

Display Settings. These settings are used in Project Web Access to control the appearance of Gantt charts and other views. These settings are similar to those you can control with the Microsoft Project global template. The difference is that information stored in this database is modified using Project Web Access. Note that the enterprise project global template is an actual project stored in the database. If you checked out the enterprise global template and made changes, you would be changing these display settings in the database.

Notifications and Reminders. Project Web Access has automated notifications and reminders that are tracked with unique tables in the Project Server database. This service requires a Simple Mail Transfer Protocol (SMTP) mail server.

Enterprise Views. Project Web Access can be used to create, store, and display project views. This is the administrative table that stores the settings used to create the views and a large number of dedicated view tables. In general, the type of information stored in these view tables is very similar to the type of information contained in the Microsoft Office Project 11 OLE DB Provider.

Storing Data in a Database

Information in a database is stored in a set of predefined tables, each made up of a set of predefined columns. A table can have an unlimited number of rows. Think of rows as a collection of data with a set of individual components, also known as *records*. Think of columns as all the individual components that make up a collection of data, also known as *fields*.

To demonstrate what this means in a project database, each task displayed on a separate row in a table is a different task record. Each of the columns intersecting that task record's row represent the task's fields; for example, the task name, duration, start and finish date, and assigned resources. In the same way, each resource is a different resource record.

To view your project information as an Access database, follow these steps:

1. In Microsoft Project, open the project whose information you want to use in Access.
2. Click File, Save As.
3. In the Save As Type box, click Microsoft Access Database (*.mdb).
4. In the File Name box, enter a name for the project database in Access.

   By default, the name of the Access file is adopted from the project filename. The filename extension changes from .mpp to .mdb.
5. Click Save.

   The Export Wizard appears.
6. In the first Export Wizard page, click Next.
7. In the Export Wizard – Data page, be sure that the A Full Project option is selected (see Figure 32-1) and then click Next.

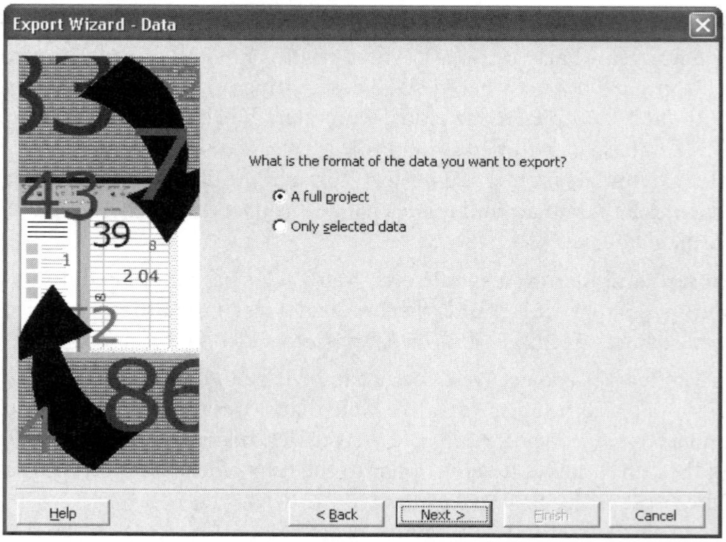

Figure 32-1. The Export Wizard walks you through the process of exporting your project to the Access database format.

8. In the Export Wizard – Project Definition page (see Figure 32-2), click Finish.

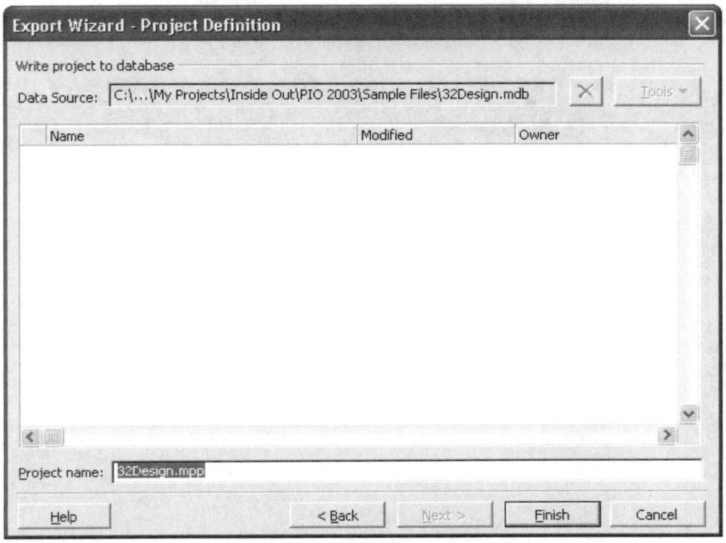

Figure 32-2. Click Finish in the third Export Wizard page, and you're ready to open your project data in Access.

9 In Access, click File, Open and browse to the location of the project database you just exported. Select the project file with the .mdb filename extension and then click Open.

The project database opens, showing all the tables that were exported from the Microsoft Project database into Access (see Figure 32-3).

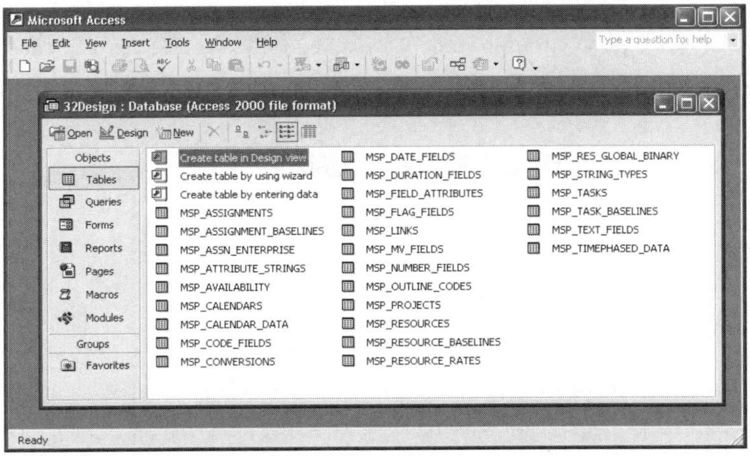

Figure 32-3. The Access Database window lists each table in the exported project database.

10 Double-click the MSP_TASKS table (see Figure 32-4).

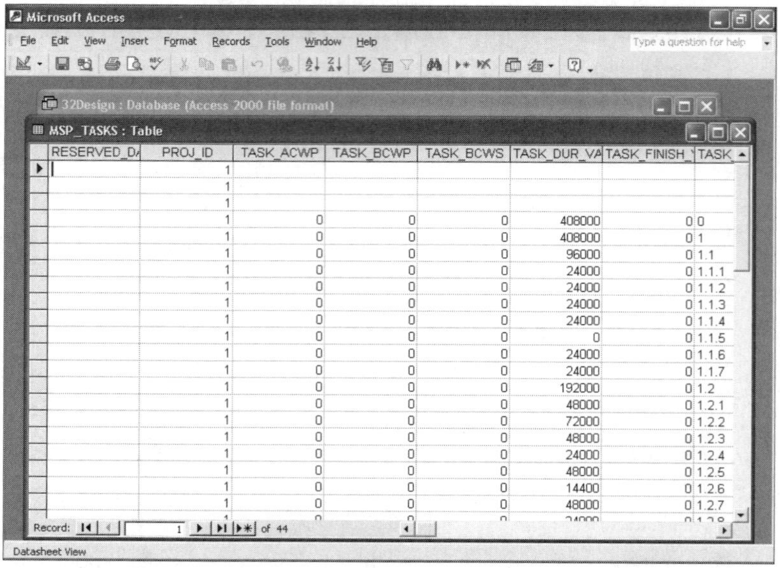

Figure 32-4. Every unique task in your project has its own row in the MSP_TASKS table.

11 Scroll through the table to see how the project information appears in the database table. Open other tables in the database to get a better idea of how the project database appears in Access.

Notice that each column has a different name, such as TASK_NAME or TASK_DUR_IS_EST. Each task occupies a different row in the table. Locate the TASK_NAME column to see the names of your project's tasks. Note that this field is not at the far left of the table, as you expect to see it in Microsoft Project (see Figure 32-5).

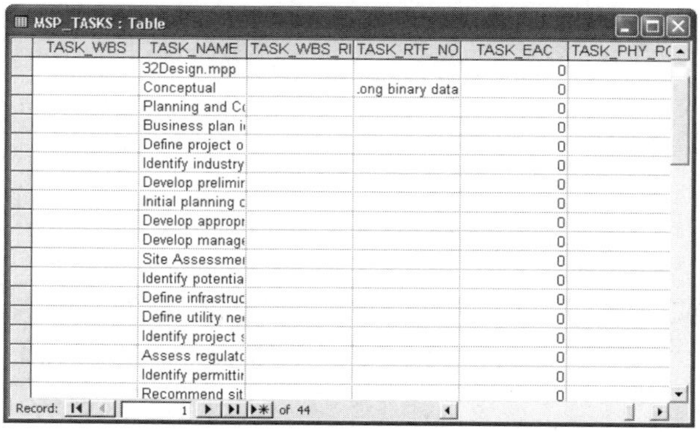

Figure 32-5. The TASK_NAME field is probably closer to the right edge of the table.

For more information about exporting Microsoft Project files to other applications, see "Importing and Exporting Information" on page 497.

Notice also the TASK_UID column, which assigns each task a unique ID number. No other task in the entire database can share this value. Obviously, a project with hundreds of assignments and resources and thousands of tasks will be a very large table in Access. Giving a unique ID number to each row in each table in the database is the simplest way to keep everything organized. The unique ID number is also used to identify relationships in the database; for example, which tasks and resources are part of an assignment. If your database has dozens of projects, the unique ID number is used to identify which tasks and assignments are part of a specific project.

You can open any of the tables in the Microsoft Project database. You can also change information in your project plan and see it instantly reflected in the Microsoft Project database. To open a project database table and change project information, follow these steps:

1. With your Microsoft Project database opened in Access, open the MSP_PROJECTS table (see Figure 32-6).

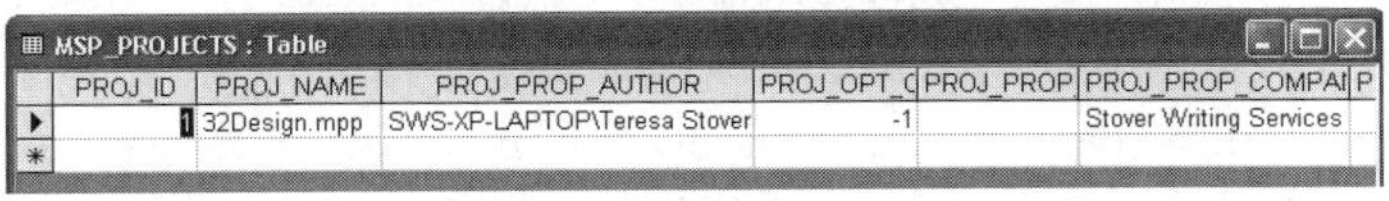
MSP_PROJECTS : Table

PROJ_ID	PROJ_NAME	PROJ_PROP_AUTHOR	PROJ_OPT_C	PROJ_PROP	PROJ_PROP_COMPA	P
1	32Design.mpp	SWS-XP-LAPTOP\Teresa Stover	-1		Stover Writing Services	

Figure 32-6. The MSP_PROJECTS table is used to store all project-related data.

2. Find the PROJ_PROP_AUTHOR column.

   Your name might be there, depending on how Microsoft Project is set up.
3. Go to Microsoft Project and make sure the same file is open.
4. In Microsoft Project, click File, Properties. Enter or modify your name in the Author field and then click OK.
5. Return to Access and review the PROJ_PROP_AUTHOR field.

   You'll see that the field has changed to reflect the edit you made in Microsoft Project.

   If you don't see the change, close and then reopen the MSP_PROJECTS table to refresh it.

It might seem that you could change your name in the field in Access, save it, and then have it appear in Microsoft Project. However, data updates don't work this way in this instance because the project saved as an Access database acts as a read-only data source, not a read/write data source; Access provides read-only access to a Microsoft Project file saved as a database.

Microsoft Access yes/no values

Using -1 and 0 in a database is a simple way to define an either/or situation. If a column contains data that can be either true or false, yes or no, or any other choice between two options, often the database will display a 1 or a 0, or a 0 or a -1, depending on how the database is set up. In this case, Access displays 0 and -1 for either/or values. The higher number represents the positive or true value; the lower number represents the negative or false value.

Understanding Data in the Database

A *database* is made up of lots of little pieces of data. In the case of Microsoft Project, there are task names, task durations, calendars, resource costs, and so on. Each of these pieces of data that has a column in a database table also has a *data type* associated with it. Data types are used to define the way the data is stored in the database. For example, a resource cost field needs to hold a number that might not be a whole number, so it needs a data type that allows a number such as 20.50. A task name field needs to hold whatever name the project manager gives it, so this field needs to be able to accept alphanumeric text data.

There are generalized types of data. Basically, four major areas are required: numbers, dates, text, and yes/no data. The OLE DB uses just these basic data types because it's a relatively simple database when compared to the Microsoft Project and Project Server databases, which use more than four data types. For example, the Project 11 OLE DB Provider uses Number for all fields that store non-date numbers; in the Microsoft Project and Project Server databases, numbers are represented by more specific data types such as Int (integer, requiring 4 bytes of storage), Decimal, Float (approximate numbers), Smallint (integer, requiring 2 bytes of storage), or Tinyint (integer, requiring 1 byte of storage), and so on.

A data type restricts the type of data allowed in that field in the database and helps keep the right data in the right place. The following sections describe general data types; specific data types are mentioned also.

Yes/No Data

The *Yes/No* data type is used when you must choose between two options. Examples include the following:

- True or False
- Yes or No
- Schedule From Start or Schedule From Finish

Fields in the Project OLE DB Provider use the *Boolean* data type to define this data. In the Microsoft Project and Project Server databases, the fields that contain the same data are either Bit, Smallint, or Tinyint data types. These three data types are used to represent small amounts of data:

- Bit stores either a 0 or a 1.
- Smallint can store integers ranging from -32,766 to 32,766.
- Tinyint can store integers ranging from 0 to 255.

Dates and Times

Date and time data types are stored in either Date (Project OLE DB Provider) or Datetime (Microsoft Project and Project Server databases) fields. They both display their data like this: mm/dd/yy hh:mm:ss AM/PM. For example: 06/01/04 12:00:00 AM for midnight, June 1, 2004.

Note To see an example of this data type in your project database in Access, look at the TASK_EARLY_FINISH field in the MSP_TASKS table.

Text Data

The *text* data type data is, quite simply, alphanumeric text; that is, any letters and numbers. It can be the name of a project, a resource, or a task. It can be the text that describes an option in the user interface. In the Project OLE DB Provider, Text is the data type that stores this data. In the Microsoft Project database, the data types Char, Varchar, and Text are used to store this data. In the Project Server database, the data types Char, Nvarchar, and Text are used to store this data.

Typically, the Text data type allows the maximum number of characters (up to 2,147,483,647); whereas Char, Varchar, and Nvarchar have their maximum allowable characters defined in the database using (n) to define the maximum length. For example, the Project Name field cannot store more than 255 characters. In the Microsoft Project database, the data type for this field is Varchar(255).

Specific Values

A specific value data type is information that contains a certain value predetermined by Microsoft Project. For example, a specific value can be an integer that represents a selection you have made in the user interface. It can be a single number or a large, seemingly random number that represents a duration or an amount of work.

Inside Out

How duration field values are stored

If the field stores a duration value, it will store the duration as the result of a calculation: minutes x 10. For example, 10 hours would be stored as 10 hours x 60 minutes x 10, or 6000. A work value is stored as minutes x 1000. So 2 hours worked would store as 2 hours x 60 minutes x 1000, or 120,000.

In the Project OLE DB Provider, the Number data type is used to represent these types of data. In the Project Server database, the data types Decimal, Integer, Smallint, and Tinyint are used to represent these types of data.

In the Project Server database, the data types Decimal, Float, Integer, Smallint, and Tinyint are used.

How the Project database stores values

If you want to see an example of the way the Microsoft Project database stores specific values based on settings you choose in the user interface, do the following:

1. In Microsoft Project, open the project you exported as the database.
2. Click Tools, Options.
3. On the View tab of the Options dialog box, change Decimal Digits to 1 and Placement to something other than the default.
4. If necessary, open the project in Access.
5. Open the MSP_PROJECTS table.
6. Find the PROJ_OPT_CURRENCY_DIGITS and PROJ_OPT_CURRENCY_POSITION fields.

   Notice the values in the database and notice the values in the View tab of the Options dialog box. In the case of PROJ_OPT_CURRENCY_DIGITS, the value corresponds to the value shown in the Options dialog box (0, 1, or 2). In the case of PROJ_OPT_CURRENCY_POSITION, the value is 0, 1, 2, or 3; which represents $1 (before), $1 (after), $ 1 (before, with space), or $ 1 (after, with space), with 0 being the first item available in the list.

Miscellaneous Data

There are some data types that store unique types of data. These data types are used sparingly. For example, image data types are used to store binary data in the Microsoft Project and Project Server databases. There is also a Uniqueidentifier data type in the Project Server database that tracks globally unique IDs.

Understanding Project OLE DB Provider Data

Use Access to take advantage of the capabilities of the Project OLE DB Provider. After you use the Project OLE DB Provider to connect to a project file in Access, you can access OLE data stored in a Microsoft Project file. Use the Microsoft Project data to create custom reports or break out and manipulate specific pieces of data. You can use this data across a wide variety of data sources, including relational databases, spreadsheets, and the Internet.

> If you want to know more about OLE DB, see "Working with External References" on page 932. You can also visit *www.msdn.microsoft.com*. In the Search MSDN box, enter **What OLE Is Really About** and then click Go. Under Technical Resources, click the link to this article.

Project Server uses an OLE DB add-on called OLE DB for Online Analytical Processing (OLAP). This allows Project Web Access to present data using Microsoft Office Web PivotTable and PivotChart reports.

There are many possibilities for using OLE technology with a Microsoft Project file. For example, you can use ActiveX Data Objects (ADO) to access specific fields in a Microsoft Project file using an OLE DB Provider.

> For more information about using OLE DB, see Microsoft Access and Microsoft Office Excel 2003 online Help. You might also find *Microsoft OLE DB 2.0 Programmer's Reference and Data Access SDK* helpful. You can also visit *www.msdn.microsoft.com*. In the Search MSDN box, enter **Choosing Your Data Access Strategy** and then click Go. Under Technical Resources, click Choosing Your Data Access Strategy (OLE DB Technical Articles).

All the data you enter in your project plan can be exposed using the Project OLE DB Provider. The presentation of this data can vary, depending on the application you use to expose it, but it will always break out into a consistent grouping of data.

The following tables are exposed by the Project OLE DB Provider:

Assignments. This table contains all assignment information in the project, including references to all related tasks and resources.

Availability. This table stores the amount of time, start date, and finish date for each time period that each resource is available to work. Each unique time period is stored as a separate row.

For example, suppose that a resource is available for 4 hours on Monday and all day Friday. In this case, there would be two rows for this resource: one for the time period on Monday and one for the time period on Friday. If the resource were only available for 2 hours in the morning and 2 hours at the end of the day on Monday, these two time periods would be divided into two separate rows as well.

Calendar. These three tables store all calendar-related information, including the time periods covered by the calendars, whether a calendar is a working times calendar or a base calendar, and exceptions.

Cost Rates. This table stores the costs associated with resources and assignments.

Custom Field. These tables store date, duration, number, text, field, and flag information that has been customized. Some of this information is available only for enterprise projects.

Predecessors. This table links tasks to their predecessor tasks, including the amount of lead or lag time; the duration of the lead or lag time; and whether the task relationship is start-to-start, finish-to-start, start-to-finish, or finish-to-finish.

Project. This table stores all project-related information, including project-level settings available in the File, Properties and Tools, Options dialog boxes.

Resources. This table stores all information about each resource in the project.

Successors. This table links tasks to their successor tasks, including the amount of lead or lag time; the duration of the lead or lag time; and whether the task relationship is start-to-start, finish-to-start, start-to-finish, or finish-to-finish.

Tasks. This table stores all information about each task in the project.

Task Splits. These tables track the start and finish dates for a task that has been split. There is also a separate table for baseline task splits.

NEW FEATURE!

Timephased. These are 15 unique timephased tables, five each for assignments, resources, and tasks. Each table is broken down by minute, hour, day, week, and month.

Inside Out

No Data Access Pages for Project 2003

With earlier versions of Microsoft Project and Microsoft Access, you could create a Data Access Page (DAP), which enabled dynamic Web page reports that could be viewed in Microsoft Internet Explorer. DAP was made possible by the Project OLE DB Provider. However, the Project OLE DB Provider is not installed in Access 2003; therefore, DAP is no longer available.

There is an alternative, though. If you're set up with Project Server, you can use the Project Web Access to create dynamically updated Web reports for project information. All the reporting that a DAP could do is built in to Project Server, through the use of the SQL Server OLE DB Provider.

You can also use ActiveX Data Objects (ADOs) to connect to the Project OLE DB Provider. Refer to pjoledb.htm on the Companion CD for the procedure.

For more information about creating dynamic Web reports for project information in Project Web Access, download the online book *Microsoft Office Project Server 2003 Administrator's Guide*. Go to *http://www.microsoft.com/downloads* and search for Project Server 2003.

Also, refer to the Microsoft Project Software Development Kit (SDK). Go to *http://msdn.microsoft.com/project*, click Microsoft Project 2003, and then click SDK Documentation.

Understanding the Microsoft Project Database

The Microsoft Project database can be viewed in Access or Excel 2003 if you open a project file saved in the proper format. When viewed in either Access or Excel, the Microsoft Project database has more tables than you would see in a project file that has been accessed using the Project OLE DB Provider. Nevertheless, whether you view project data through the Microsoft Project database or the Project OLE DB Provider, you're seeing almost exactly the same set of data.

If you open a project database in Access, you see a large collection of tables. The Microsoft Project database includes the following tables:

MSP_ASSIGNMENTS. This table stores all assignment-related details. A separate table is used for summary assignments (called MSP_ASSN_ENTERPRISE). This is the same type of information stored in the Assignments table in the OLE DB.

MSP_AVAILABILITY. This table stores the amount of time, the start time, and the end time for each time period that a resource is available to work. This is the same type of information stored in the Availability table in the OLE DB.

MSP_CALENDARS and MSP_CALENDAR_DATA. These tables store all calendar-related information, including the time periods for the calendars, whether a calendar is a working calendar or a base calendar, and exceptions (see Figure 32-7).

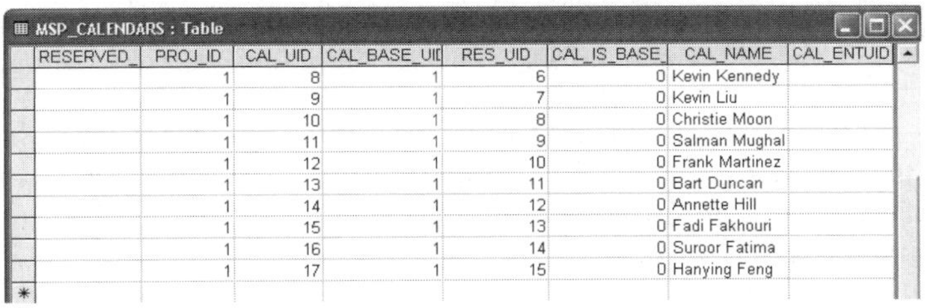
MSP_CALENDARS : Table

RESERVED_	PROJ_ID	CAL_UID	CAL_BASE_UI	RES_UID	CAL_IS_BASE	CAL_NAME	CAL_ENTUID
	1	8	1	6	0	Kevin Kennedy	
	1	9	1	7	0	Kevin Liu	
	1	10	1	8	0	Christie Moon	
	1	11	1	9	0	Salman Mughal	
	1	12	1	10	0	Frank Martinez	
	1	13	1	11	0	Bart Duncan	
	1	14	1	12	0	Annette Hill	
	1	15	1	13	0	Fadi Fakhouri	
	1	16	1	14	0	Suroor Fatima	
	1	17	1	15	0	Hanying Feng	

Figure 32-7. The MSP_CALENDARS table is used to store all calendar-related data.

MSP_n_FIELDS. These tables store custom field information related to dates, durations, flag, number, text, code, and more. Substitute CODE, DATE, DURATION, FLAG, NUMBER, or TEXT for the *n* in the table name. Some of this information is available only for enterprise projects.

MSP_n_BASELINES. These tables store baseline data related to assignments, resources, and tasks. Substitute ASSIGNMENT, RESOURCE, or TASK for *n* in the table name.

MSP_LINKS. This table stores predecessor and successor task information, including links to other enterprise projects. This is the same type of information that is stored in the Predecessor and Successor tables in the Project OLE DB Provider.

MSP_OUTLINE_CODES. This table stores custom information related to outline codes. This is the same type of information that is available when you click Tools, Customize, Fields and then click the Custom Outline Codes tab in the Customize Fields dialog box.

MSP_PROJECTS. This table stores data related to the project as a whole, including information set in the Properties and Options dialog boxes.

MSP_RESOURCES. This table stores all information about each resource in the project.

MSP_RESOURCE_RATES. This table stores the costs associated with each resource or assignment.

MSP_TASKS. This table stores all information about each task in the project.

MSP_TIMEPHASED_DATA. If you choose to expand timephased data in Microsoft Project (click Tools, Options; choose the Save tab in the Options dialog box; and select the Expand Timephased Data In The Database check box), the expanded timephased data is saved to this table.

To view the contents of any of the tables, just double-click the table.

Understanding the Project Server Database

The Project Server database is used to store data that helps enable collaboration between project managers and team members, manage Project Web Access administrative settings, manage users and set their security privileges for accessing Project Web Access and Project Server, and store the data used to create project and resource view tables.

You can access information stored in the Project Server database by connecting Project Professional to Project Server or by logging on to Project Web Access.

For more information, see Chapter 22, "Managing with Project Professional and Project Server."

After Project Server is installed and running, its administration is done mainly through the Admin tab in Project Web Access. The project server administrator can create new users and groups of users, set permissions for users, create views, and manage the default settings for all users of Project Web Access.

If you want to know more about the individual tables and fields in this database, see pjsvrdb.htm on the Companion CD.

Partitioning Your Database on Separate Servers

NEW FEATURE! Server scalability and performance are improved in Project Server 2003, through database partitioning. You can partition the Project Server 2003 database across two or three servers, either during Project Server Setup or later using database scripts provided on the Project Server CD. Partitioning the Project Server database uses the linked server capabilities of Microsoft SQL Server 2000.

During setup, the Views database tables can go on one server while the Project database and services can go on one or two other servers. The improved distribution increases the number of users that the database can accommodate by dividing the workload of the Project Server application across a greater number of servers.

Three distinct sets of Project Server database tables are available to be configured as a partition using the linked server capabilities. Each set of tables has a specific role in the Project Server database:

MSP_. Tables that begin with MSP_ are the core data tables for most types of project data.

MSP_WEB_. Tables that begin with MSP_WEB_ are the core data tables for all types of Project Server data, including Project Server security, administrative settings, data links between Project Server and Windows SharePoint Services, and more.

MSP_VIEW_. Tables that begin with MSP_VIEW_ store project data that has been published to the Project Server database from Project Professional. This is the information that is used in Portfolio Analyzer and in Project Center views.

When you partition the database, you have three options:

Implement a 2-way partition during Project Server Setup. You can partition the database during setup. One server will get the MSP_ and MSP_WEB_ database tables; the other will get the MSP_VIEW_ database tables.

Implement a 2-way partition after Project Server Setup. You can run a 2-way partition after setup. One server will get the MSP_ database tables plus either the MSP_WEB_ or MSP_VIEW_ database tables. The other server will get the MSP_WEB_ or MSP_VIEW_ database tables (whichever set of tables wasn't included with the MSP_ tables).

Implement a 3-way partition after Project Server Setup. You can run a 3-way partition after setup. The MSP_, MSP_WEB_, and MSP_VIEW_ database tables will each be placed on their own server.

Caution Deciding to partition the Project Server database calls for careful planning and foresight. After you partition the Project Server database and begin publishing projects to the Project Server database, you're committed. Although not impossible, it's very difficult to undo the partition and restore the Project Server database on a single SQL Server 2000 server. In addition, extra steps might be required for your organization's disaster-recovery plan.

Experimenting with Project Server Using the Sample Database

NEW FEATURE!

Project Server 2003 includes a sample database containing a custom set of project, resource, and reporting data. This sample database has been created so that you can play with Project Server features without having to create a set of demonstration data yourself.

The Project Server sample database can help you better understand and plan for various enterprise project management (EPM) features such as the enterprise global template, enterprise resource pool, Portfolio Analyzer, Portfolio Modeler, and Project Server security. With the sample database, you can immediately jump in and begin using these features. In addition, instructions available on the Project Server installation CD walk you through the processes that project managers and resource managers go through while using Project Server.

The Project Server sample database requires special steps to be performed during installation. The sample database is designed to be installed on a single server along with Project

Server, Windows SharePoint Services, SQL Server 2000, and Analysis Services. The Project Server sample database requires Windows Server 2003. Microsoft Office Word 2003 is required in order to use the Windows SharePoint Services Documents, Issues, and Risks feature. (Word 2003 is not required to use Project Server 2003 outside the sample database.)

For more information about setting up and configuring the Project Server sample database, read the files pjsvr.chm and sampledb.htm on the Project Server CD.

Part 10

Appendixes

Appendix A

Installing Microsoft Office Project 2003

Microsoft Office Project 2003 has two editions: Microsoft Office Project Standard 2003 and Microsoft Office Project Professional 2003. This appendix includes procedures and guidelines for setting up Project (both Standard and Professional versions) as a stand-alone desktop tool.

Project 2003 continues using server-based solutions, as introduced in Microsoft Project 2002. You can use the collaboration features of Microsoft Office Project Web Access 2003 and Microsoft Office Project Server 2003 with Project Professional. Note that Project Server and Project Web Access interaction with Project Standard 2003 are not available; you can only use Project Professional to create and work with project data saved to the Project Server database.

If you connect Project Professional to Project Server, you can use the enterprise features, which include enhanced project standardization through use of the Enterprise Global Template, resource management through the use of the Enterprise Resource Pool, Portfolio Modeler, Resource Substitution Wizard, and Build Team from Enterprise features; and project analysis across an entire organization using Portfolio Modeler, Portfolio Analyzer, and Project Server data views. This appendix will explain some guidelines regarding the setup of Project Server and Project Web Access, and connecting Project Professional 2003 to Project Server. For specific Project Server and Project Web Access setup assistance for small deployment scenarios, refer to the Pjsvr.chm file that can be accessed from Project Server Setup or found on the Project Server CD-ROM.

Installing Project Standard and Project Professional 2003

This section includes information and procedures for setting up Project Standard 2003 or Project Professional 2003 as a stand-alone desktop project management solution.

Project Standard and Project Professional System Requirements

Before you install Project Standard 2003 or Project Professional 2003, make sure that your system meets the minimum requirements. If you are planning on working on large projects with hundreds of tasks, summary assignments, and resource pools, it is recommended that you have up to an additional 128MB of RAM available. The system requirements for a computer running Project Standard or Project Professional include:

- Intel Pentium 233MHz (minimum) or higher processor. Intel Pentium III class processor (or better) is recommended.
- 128MB of additional RAM beyond the requirements of your operating system (minimum) is recommended.
- 130MB of available hard disk space (hard disk usage will vary depending on configuration; custom installation choices may require more or less hard disk space).
- Super VGA (800x600) or higher resolution monitor.
- Microsoft Internet Explorer 5.01 with Service Pack 3 or later, Microsoft Internet Explorer 5.5 with Service Pack 2 or later, or Microsoft Internet Explorer with Service Pack 1 or later. For the best experience, use Internet Explorer 6.0.
- Project Server 2003 and Project Professional 2003 required for enterprise project and resource management capabilities. Project Server 2003 has a separate set of system requirements.
- To use Microsoft Office Project Web Access 2003 with Project Professional 2003, you need 5MB additional hard disk space, plus Microsoft Outlook 2000, Outlook 2002, or Microsoft Office Outlook 2003 if you plan on importing project tasks to an Outlook calendar.

Note If you want to use non-enterprise (workgroup style collaboration) or enterprise project and resource management, you will also need to connect Project Professional to Project Server.

See "Microsoft Office Project Server 2003 Setup Issues" later in this appendix on page 962 for more information.

You can run Project Standard 2003 and Project Professional 2003 on any of the following operating systems:

- Microsoft Windows XP Professional (recommended)
- Microsoft Windows XP Home
- Microsoft Windows 2000 Professional

Setting Up Project 2003 for the First Time

To set up Project Standard or Project Professional on a computer where there is no previous version of Project installed, follow these steps:

1. Close any other applications that are running.
2. Place the Project Standard or Project Professional CD in your computer's CD-ROM drive.

If Project Standard or Project Professional Setup doesn't start automatically, click the Start button on the Windows taskbar and then click Run. Type X:\setup.exe (where X is the name of your CD-ROM drive) and then click OK.

After Microsoft Office Project Standard 2003 Setup or Microsoft Office Project Professional 2003 Setup is running, continue through the following steps to complete installation.

> **Note** If you are upgrading from a previous version of Project, follow the steps detailed in "Upgrading from a Previous Version of Project," later in this appendix on page 958.

3. In the Product Key window, enter your 25-character product key in the Product Key boxes. Click the Next button.
4. In the User Information window, enter your User Name, Initials, and Organization. Click the Next button.
5. In the End-User License Agreement window, review the agreement and then select the I Accept The Terms In The License Agreement check box. Click the Next button.
6. In the Type Of Installation window, select the installation option you want: Typical Install, Complete Install, Minimal Install, or Custom Install. Select the Typical Install option to install Project 2003 with the default settings and most commonly used components. Click the Next button. Skip to Step 7 if you selected either Install Now, Minimal Install, or Complete Install.

> **Note** If this window says Upgrade Now, there is a previous version of Project already installed on this computer.
>
> Refer to "Upgrading from a Previous Version of Project" later in this appendix on page 958.

7. If you choose a Custom installation, the Advanced Customization window appears. Click the plus or minus signs to expand or collapse the tree. Click the down arrow next to the component to change its installation status to Run From My Computer, Run All From My Computer, Installed On First Use, or Not Available (which means the item is not installed—you can install it later). Click the Next button.

   The hard disk space required by the customized installation of Project Standard or Project Professional is updated in the lower right corner of the Microsoft Office Project 2003 Setup window when you add or remove features from the installation.
8. The Summary page appears. Click the Install button.

   The Now Installing Microsoft Project Professional window appears. This window tracks the progress of the installation.

   When the installation is finished, the Setup Completed window appears. You can use the Web to check for the latest product updates from Microsoft and you can delete any installation files required by Setup that are no longer needed. Click Finish. You can now run Microsoft Office Project 2003 by clicking Start, All Programs, Microsoft Office, and then Microsoft Office Project 2003.

Installation Options

You have five ways to install Project: Upgrade Now, Typical Install, Complete Install, Minimal Install, and Custom Install. Any custom component can be added or removed later by placing your Project CD-ROM into your CD drive and running setup.exe. The five installation options do the following:

- Upgrade is available if you have a previous version of Project installed on your computer. Previous versions of Project will be removed unless you select the Complete Install, Minimal Install, Typical Install, or Custom Install option when upgrading to Project 2003.
- Typical Install installs Microsoft Office Project 2003 with the most commonly used components. You can install additional features on first use or add them later using Add/Remove Programs in the Control Panel.
- Complete Install installs all files available to be installed, including components that are not normally used during the day-to-day use of Project by the majority of users.
- Minimal Install installs Project 2003 with just the minimum number of files required to run Project.
- Custom Install enables you to install components of Project that are not normally installed by selecting from the following options: Run From My Computer, Run All From My Computer, Installed On First Use, and Not Available.

Upgrading from a Previous Version of Project

How is upgrading from a previous version of Project different from a clean installation? If you choose to replace your old version of Project when upgrading to Project Standard 2003 or Project Professional 2003, you may not be able to open project files created in versions of Project earlier than Microsoft Project 2000 because the data structure in Project 2003 has been enhanced and expanded with new fields, details, and capabilities. This means that older versions of Project cannot read a file created in Project Standard 2003 or Project Professional 2003. Files created in Microsoft Project 2000 and Microsoft Project 2002 can be opened in Microsoft Project 2003 because the databases are compatible; files created in versions of Project earlier than Microsoft Project 2000 must be saved in an MPD file format before you can open them in Project Standard 2003 or Project Professional 2003.

For more information about saving a project file as an MPD file format, see "Saving and Opening with Different File Formats" on page 872.

If you have a previous version of Project installed on your computer when you run Project Standard 2003 or Project Professional 2003 Setup, you have some choices that are different than the steps described in "Setting Up Project 2003 for the First Time."

To upgrade an older version of Microsoft Project to Project 2003, run Microsoft Office Project 2003 Setup. Be sure to close down any other applications that you might have running. Place the Microsoft Office Project 2003 CD in your computer's CD-ROM drive. If Microsoft Office Project 2003 Setup doesn't start automatically, open the contents of the CD-ROM and double-click setup.exe. After Microsoft Office Project 2003 Setup is running, continue through the following steps to complete installation.

The process is basically the same as installing a new copy of Project, except that you will be given two options during the setup process:

- Upgrade to Project 2003. Select Upgrade to upgrade to Project 2003 and remove all previous versions of Project.
- Keep or remove previous versions of Project. If you want to keep previous versions of Project on your computer, you must select Custom Install, Typical Install, Minimal Install, or Complete Install instead of Upgrade.

Activating Project 2003

Project 2003 runs with full product features 50 times before it requires activation. The Microsoft Office Project 2003 Activation Wizard runs the first time you run Microsoft Project, and it will guide you through the activation process.

You can activate Project over the Internet or by phone. If you choose to activate by phone, the activation process could take longer.

To activate Project, do the following:

1. Start Microsoft Office Project 2003. The Microsoft Office Project 2003 Activation Wizard appears if you have not yet activated Project.
2. On the Activation Wizard page of the Microsoft Office Project 2003 Activation Wizard, select either I Want To Activate The Software Over The Internet or I Want To Activate The Software By Telephone. Click the Next button.
3. On the next page, click Register Now to register your copy of Project 2003 (optional). Click Close to finish activating Project 2003.

Running Maintenance Mode

After Project has been installed successfully, you can add or remove optional features, perform repairs, or uninstall the entire application using Maintenance Mode. To use Maintenance Mode, place your Project CD-ROM in your CD-ROM drive to run Project Setup. The Maintenance Mode Options window appears.

You can now add or remove features, make repairs, or uninstall Project by selecting one of the following options:

- Add Or Remove Features
- Reinstall or Repair
- Uninstall

The following sections detail each of these options.

Adding or Removing Features

To add or remove features of Project, do the following:

1. Place your Project CD-ROM in your computer's CD-ROM drive. The Maintenance Mode Options window appears. If this window does not automatically appear, browse to your Project CD-ROM and run setup.exe.
2. Select Add Or Remove Features.
3. Click the Next button.

   The Advanced Customization window appears.
4. To add a feature, click the arrow next to the feature you want to add, and change Not Available to either Run From My Computer or Installed On First Use.

   Installed On First Use makes the feature available, and you can run this feature from Project at a later date. You might be required to insert the Project CD-ROM or access the network drive from which you originally installed Project to use the added feature. Because of this, you should select the Installed On First Use option only if you will have access to the Project CD-ROM or network location at the time you run this feature.

   Run From My Computer installs the feature on your computer's hard disk. You will not be asked to provide the Project CD-ROM when you first run this feature.
5. To remove a feature, click the arrow next to the feature you want to remove and change the Run From My Computer or Installed On First Use setting to Not Available. Click the features you want to add or remove and click the Update button.

   Project Setup will perform the actions you indicated. Setting a feature to Not Available will remove the feature entirely. You cannot use this feature until you add it using the steps described earlier.
6. When finished adding or removing features, click the Update button.

Repairing Microsoft Project

Occasionally, you might notice that Microsoft Project isn't running as well as it should. This problem can be caused by many factors, including frequently installing or uninstalling software or continuously using an application.

You can repair your Microsoft Project installation by running Maintenance Mode Options and selecting the Reinstall or Repair option. To repair your copy of Microsoft Project, do the following:

1. Place your Microsoft Project CD-ROM in your computer's CD-ROM drive.

   The Maintenance Mode Options window appears. If this window does not automatically appear, browse to your Project CD-ROM and run setup.exe.

2. Select Reinstall or Repair.
3. Click Next.

   The Reinstall Or Repair Project window appears.
4. Select Reinstall Project to restore your copy of Project to its original settings.
5. Select Detect And Repair Errors In My Project Installation to search for the source of the problems you might be experiencing with your current installation of Microsoft Project.
6. Click the Install button to restore your copy of Microsoft Project to its original settings or to detect and repair errors.

Uninstalling Microsoft Project

You can use Maintenance Mode to uninstall Microsoft Project from your computer. To uninstall Microsoft Project, do the following:

1. Place your Microsoft Project CD-ROM in your computer's CD-ROM drive.

   The Maintenance Mode Options window appears. If this window does not automatically appear, browse to your Microsoft Project CD-ROM and run setup.exe.
2. Select Uninstall Microsoft Project.
3. Click the Next button.
4. Click Yes to uninstall Microsoft Project or click No to cancel.

Working with an Administrative Installation Point

If you need to make Project available for installation by multiple users on a network, consider creating an administrative installation point. This installation point provides any user who needs to install a copy of Project with a way to install it by finding the location on the network and running setup.exe.

Creating an Administrative Installation Point

To create an administrative installation point, do the following:

1. Click Start, Run.
2. Enter your CD-ROM drive letter.
3. Type setup.exe.
4. Enter /a.

For example, if your CD-ROM drive letter is D, the line you enter to create an administrative installation point is d:\setup.exe /a. You then specify the location to use as an administrative installation point. Anyone who runs setup.exe from the administrative installation point can install Microsoft Project.

This feature is available only for versions of Microsoft Project that have one of the following MSI files in the root directory of the CD-ROM:

- prjstde
- prjproe

Adding Your Company Name to the Default Installation

You can add your company's name to the Project Setup program in an administrative installation point by adding COMPANYNAME="xx" (where "xx" is your company's name, including the quotation marks) to the command line when creating an administrative installation point. For example:

```
D:\Setup.exe /a COMPANYNAME="Microsoft"
```

There are many command-line options available in Project Setup. For a complete list, see the Microsoft Office Resource Kit at *http://www.microsoft.com/office/ork*.

Microsoft Office Project Server 2003 Setup Issues

If you want to store projects in a database, use Microsoft Office Project Web Access, or take advantage of enterprise project management and resource management features, you need to install Project Server and configure it for your organization. To properly install Project Server, you should have a solid working knowledge of Microsoft SQL Server 2000 and know how to configure your computer as an administrator. In addition, your organization should commit resources to planning your enterprise project implementation in order to ensure that you get the maximum benefit from your Project Server deployment.

Project Server provides timesheet, reporting, collaboration, and analysis tools and stores this information in a database that includes global settings for Project Web Access and Project. Project Server is protected by a security layer that restricts access to only those authorized to send and receive data from the database. Most users connect to Project Server either directly through Project Professional 2003 or by using Project Web Access.

The following applications are used along with Project Server:

Project Web Access. This application is required for online workgroup project collaboration. Project Web Access provides a Web interface to information stored in Project Server. Users log onto Project Web Access with a user name and password stored in Project Server. Team members can work with their individual assigned task information and view overall project information. Resource managers and team leads can maintain resource information and delegate tasks. Managing stakeholders can view overall project information. Administrators can set up and modify Project Server user accounts and settings.

Note For more information about using Project Web Access, see Chapter 21, "Managing Your Team Using Project Web Access."

Windows SharePoint Services. This application enables the document library, risks-tracking, and issues-tracking features of Project Web Access and Project Professional. Documents, risks, and issues can be accessed from the Documents, Risks, and Issues pages in Project Web Access or from the Collaborate menu in Project Professional. This information is stored in a different database from Project Server and can be managed from within the Admin area of Project Web Access.

Microsoft SQL Server 2000. This is the database application required for use with the Project Server database. All the database tables and stored procedures used by Project Server are stored here. Some users of Project data need permission to create, update, or modify data stored in a database stored in Microsoft SQL Server 2000. For more information about the contents of the database, see Pjsvrdb.htm and Pjdb.htm, located on the Microsoft Office Project Server 2003 installation CD.

Microsoft SQL Server Analysis Services. This application must be installed in order to use the enterprise Portfolio Analyzer features of Project Professional and Project Web Access. Microsoft SQL Analysis Services must have the same Service Pack updates as those installed for Microsoft SQL Server 2000.

Microsoft Office Web Components (OWC). This application is required to use the work with views and information in views of Project Web Access.

Project Professional 2003. This is the client application interface for Project Server. Users with appropriate permissions can check out, modify, and save the Enterprise Global Template and Enterprise Resource Pool; publish project plans to Project Server; and perform other related enterprise project and resource management tasks.

Making Decisions about Your Project Server Setup

Before your project server administrator sets up Project Server, you need to make a few decisions. Your organization requires a lot of information before deploying Project Server. Some questions to consider:

- How many people do you expect to use Project Server, including from Project Professional and from Project Web Access?
- Can users use Project Server authentication, Windows NT authentication, or both?
- Do users from outside your corporate intranet require access to Project Web Access or Project Server?
- Will you be using Project Web Access for team collaboration?
- Will you be using the Windows SharePoint Services Document Library, Risks and Issues features as part of your Project Web Access setup?

- Will you be using enterprise features? Which enterprise features?
- How often do you want to build or update OLAP cubes?
- If you're using enterprise features, do you want to set up Analysis Services for the Portfolio Analyzer and Portfolio Modeler feature?

Advanced Resources for Microsoft Project

The following online books are available for free in the Microsoft Download Center at *http://www.microsoft.com/downloads*:

- *Microsoft Office Project Server 2003 Enterprise Features Guide*
- *Microsoft Office Project Server 2003 Configuration Planning Guide*
- *Microsoft Office Project Server 2003 Disaster Recovery Guide*
- *Microsoft Office Project Server 2003 Installation Guide*
- *Microsoft Office Project Server 2003 Application Configuration Guide*
- *Microsoft Office Project Server 2003 Administrator's Guide*

Microsoft Project no longer supports the following:

STS 1.0. Users need to run the Microsoft Project Server migration tool to migrate STS 1.0 subwebs into STS 2.0 sites.

Microsoft Project Server accounts. Project 11 and STS 2.0 support Windows accounts only.

Different Windows accounts. The STS features work only with the current Windows account.

Microsoft Office Project Professional 2003 integrates with Windows SharePoint Services to provide document management, issue tracking, and risk management. Microsoft SharePoint Team Services v. 1.0 is no longer supported.

Enterprise Project Management System Requirements

With the enterprise features of Project Professional 2003 (when connected to Project Server 2003), you have access to powerful standardization, customization, resource management, and executive analysis capabilities across your entire organization.

To be able to use enterprise features in Project Professional 2003, you need to connect Project Professional 2003 to Project Server 2003. In addition, you need the following components:

- Microsoft SQL Server 2000 Service Pack 3 or later.

  This component must be installed before installing Microsoft Project Server. You should always ensure that you have applied the latest service packs for SQL Server and that you have the most recent security updates.
- Microsoft SQL Server Analysis Services, Service Pack 3 or later.

  This component is required to use the enterprise Portfolio Analyzer and Portfolio Modeler features.

Appendix B

Field Reference

This appendix lists all the fields available in Microsoft Office Project 2003, broken down by type of data:

- Currency
- Date
- Duration
- Enumerated
- Indicator
- Integer
- Outline Code
- Percentage and Number
- Text
- Yes/No (Boolean)

In addition, the following special categories of fields are grouped together for your reference toward the end of this appendix:

- Custom
- Earned Value
- PERT Analysis

Each row in the following tables contains the name of a field in Project 2003 and the category in Microsoft Project to which the field belongs; for example, tasks, resources, and so on. Each row contains a description of the field and the name of the field when it's exposed using the Microsoft Office Project 11.0 OLE DB Provider. Each row also includes the name of the field when you open a project as a database, for example, when you save a project as a Microsoft Office Access database and open it in Access.

Fields are listed in this appendix if the field in the database contains the same data entered or added through Microsoft Project. Some fields listed in this appendix that can be accessed using the Project 11.0 OLE DB Provider do not have a corresponding field in the Microsoft Project database. These "missing" fields are actually the results of calculations based on values stored in other fields. For example, the Cost Variance field contains the difference between a baseline cost and total scheduled cost. The Cost Variance field can be assigned in Microsoft Project and exposed using the OLE DB Provider, but it doesn't have its own field in the Microsoft Project database because Cost Variance is the result of a calculation (Cost – Baseline Cost).

Most fields in Microsoft Project can be found in the following OLE DB Provider or Microsoft Project database tables:

- **Assignment.** Fields are stored in the Assignments table in OLE DB and in the MSP_ASSIGNMENTS table in the Project database.
- **Assignment (Timephased).** Fields are stored in the Minute, Hour, Day, Week, and Month assignment-timephased tables in OLE DB.
- **Resource.** Fields are stored in the Resources table in OLE DB and in the MSP_RESOURCES table in the Microsoft Project database.
- **Resource (Timephased).** Fields are stored in the Minute, Hour, Day, Week, and Month resource-timephased tables in OLE DB.
- **Task.** Fields are stored in the Tasks table in OLE DB and in the MSP_TASKS table in the Microsoft Project database.
- **Task (Timephased).** Fields are stored in the Minute, Hour, Day, Week, and Month task-timephased tables in OLE DB.
- **Custom.** Fields are stored in the tables they are associated with in OLE DB; for example, custom assignment cost fields are in the Assignments table.

Custom Fields in the MSP_PROJECTS Database

Although custom fields are stored in the OLE DB Provider tables, custom fields are stored in the following tables in the MSP_PROJECTS database:

- MSP_ASSIGNMENT_BASELINES
- MSP_DATE_FIELDS
- MSP_DURATION_FIELDS
- MSP_FLAG_FIELDS
- MSP_NUMBER_FIELDS
- MSP_OUTLINE_CODES
- MSP_RESOURCE_BASELINES
- MSP_TASK_BASELINES
- MSP_TEXT_FIELDS

Data stored in the MSP_PROJECTS database tables aren't as easy to use as the custom fields in the OLE DB Provider because custom fields in the Project database are defined by multiple fields; and the tables can contain data for assignments, resources, and tasks.

If you're set up for enterprise project management using Microsoft Office Project Professional 2003 and Microsoft Office Project Server 2003, you have access to enterprise resource multivalue fields. As its name implies, these multivalue fields can contain multiple values and are stored in the MSP_MV_FIELDS table in the Microsoft Project database.

Note Each of the five timephased tables for assignments, resources, and tasks are named *n*TimephasedBy*X* where *n* is assignments, resources, or tasks; and *X* is Minute, Hour, Day, Week, or Month.

For more information about working with fields and adding them to tables, see "Using Tables" on page 112 and "Using Fields" on page 04xx. For more information about custom fields, see "Customizing Fields" on page 788 and "Working with Outline Codes" on page 806.

For detailed information about each individual field, including calculations, best uses, and examples, refer to the Fields Reference section of Project Help. To do this, click Help, Microsoft Project Help. Click Table Of Contents and then click Reference. Click Fields Reference, click Table Of Contents, and then click Reference. Click Fields Reference.

For more information about the OLE DB provider tables and the Project database tables, the fields in these tables, and how to understand the data in these tables and how it links to assignments, resources, or tasks, see Pjdb.htm—included on the Microsoft Office Project Standard 2003 or Project Professional 2003 installation CD.

Field Types

The fields listed in the following tables (Currency, Date, Duration, Enumerated, Indicator, Integer, Outline Code, Percentage and Number, Text, and Yes/No) are grouped by data type, as follows:

- Currency fields
- Date fields
- Duration fields
- Enumerated fields
- Indicator fields
- Integer fields
- Outline code fields
- Percentage and number fields
- Text fields
- Yes/No (Boolean) fields

Currency Fields

Table B-1 lists all currency and currency rate fields available in Microsoft Project.

For more information about working with costs, see Chapter 8, "Planning Resource and Task Costs," and "Monitoring and Adjusting Costs" on page 338. For more information about analyzing project information with earned value, see Chapter 13, "Analyzing Project Information."

Table B-1. Currency Fields

Field	Available Categories	OLE DB Provider	Microsoft Project Database	Description
Actual Cost	Assignment	AssignmentActualCost	ASSN_ACT_COST	The actual costs associated with resource work or fixed costs for tasks.
	Assignment (Timephased)	AssignmentTime-ActualCost		
	Resource	ResourceActualCost	RES_ACT_COST	
	Resource (Timephased)	ResourceTimeActualCost		
	Task	TaskActualCost	TASK_ACT_COST	
	Task (Timephased)	TaskTimeActualCost		
Actual Fixed Cost	Task (Timephased)	TaskTimeActualFixedCost		The actual fixed cost expenses charged over time.
Actual Overtime Cost	Assignment	AssignmentActual-OvertimeCost	ASSN_ACT_OVT_COST	The actual overtime costs.
	Resource	ResourceActual-OvertimeCost	RES_ACT_OVT_COST	
	Task	TaskActualOvertimeCost	TASK_ACT_OVT_COST	
ACWP	Assignment	AssignmentACWP	ASSN_ACWP	The earned value actual cost of work-performed (ACWP).
	Assignment (Timephased)	AssignmentTimeACWP		
	Resource	ResourceACWP	RES_ACWP	
	Resource (Timephased)	ResourceTimeACWP		
	Task	TaskACWP	TASK_ACWP	
	Task (Timephased)	TaskTimeACWP		
BAC	Assignment	AssignmentBaselineCost	ASSN_BASE_COST	The earned value Budget At Completion (BAC). Same as the Baseline Cost field.
	Assignment (Timephased)	AssignmentTime-BaselineCost		
	Resource	ResourceBaselineCost	RES_BASE_COST	
	Resource (Timephased)	ResourceTime-BaselineCost		
	Task	TaskBaselineCost	TASK_BASE_COST	
	Task (Timephased)	TaskTimeBaselineCost		

Table B-1. Currency Fields

Field	Available Categories	OLE DB Provider	Microsoft Project Database	Description
Baseline-Cost	Assignment	AssignmentBaselineCost	ASSN_BASE_COST	The total planned cost for work performed, plus fixed costs.
	Assignment (Timephased)	AssignmentTime-BaselineCost		
	Resource	ResourceBaselineCost	RES_BASE_COST	
	Resource (Timephased)	ResourceTime-BaselineCost		
	Task	TaskBaselineCost	TASK_BASE_COST	
	Task (Timephased)	TaskTimeBaselineCost		
Baseline1-10Cost	Assignment	AssignmentBaseline1-Cost10		The baseline costs for Baseline 1 through Baseline 10.
	Assignment (Timephased)	AssignmentTimeBaseline1-Cost-10		
	Resource	ResourceBaseline1-Cost10		
	Resource (Timephased)	ResourceTimeBaseline1-Cost-10		
	Task	TaskBaseline1Cost-10		
	Task (Timephased)	TaskTimeBaseline1-Cost-10		
BCWP	Assignment	AssignmentBCWP	ASSN_BCWP	The earned value budgeted costs of work performed (BCWP) costs.
	Assignment (Timephased)	AssignmentTimeBCWP		
	Resource	ResourceBCWP	RES_BCWP	
	Resource (Timephased)	ResourceTimeBCWP		
	Task	TaskBCWP	TASK_BCWP	
	Task (Timephased)	TaskTimeBCWP		

Table B-1. Currency Fields

Field	Available Categories	OLE DB Provider	Microsoft Project Database	Description
BCWS	Assignment	AssignmentBCWS	ASSN_BCWS	The earned value budgeted cost of work scheduled (BCWS) costs.
	Assignment (Timephased)	AssignmentTimeBCWS		
	Resource	ResourceBCWS	RES_BCWS	
	Resource (Timephased)	ResourceTimeBCWS		
	Task	TaskBCWS	TASK_BCWS	
	Task (Timephased)	TaskTimeBCWS		
Cost	Assignment	AssignmentCost	ASSN_COST	The total scheduled cost for an assignment, including expected costs and those already incurred.
	Assignment (Timephased)	AssignmentTimeCost		
	Resource	ResourceCost	RES_COST	
	Resource (Timephased)	ResourceTimeCost		
	Task	TaskCost	TASK_COST	
	Task (Timephased)	TaskTimeCost		
Cost Per Use	Resource	ResourceCostPerUse	RES_COST_PER_USE	The cost for each unit of work performed by a resource.
Cost Variance	Assignment	AssignmentCostVariance		The difference between the base-line cost and total scheduled cost.
	Resource	ResourceCostVariance		
	Task	TaskCostVariance		
Cost1-10	Assignment	AssignmentCost1-10		The values for the custom Cost1 through Cost10 fields.
	Resource	ResourceCost1-10		
	Task	TaskCost1-10		
Cumulative Cost	Assignment (Timephased)	AssignmentTime-CumulativeCost		The cumulative cost for all work performed on all assigned tasks, as distributed over time.
	Resource (Timephased)	ResourceTimeCumulative-Cost		
	Task (Timephased)	TaskTimeCumulativeCost		

Table B-1. Currency Fields

Field	Available Categories	OLE DB Provider	Microsoft Project Database	Description
CV	Assignment	AssignmentCV		The earned value Cost Variance (CV), which is the difference between the budgeted (baseline) cost and the actual cost of work performed.
	Assignment (Timephased)	AssignmentTimeCV		
	Resource	ResourceCV		
	Resource (Timephased)	ResourceTimeCV		
	Task	TaskCV		
	Task (Timephased)	TaskTimeCV		
EAC	Task	TaskEAC	TASK_EAC	The earned value estimate at completion (EAC), which is the expected total cost of a task.
Fixed Cost	Task	TaskFixedCost	TASK_FIXED_COST	The expense for a nonresource task.
	Task (Timephased)	TaskTimeFixedCost		
Overtime Cost	Assignment	AssignmentOvertimeCost	ASSN_OVT_COST	The total scheduled overtime cost for an assignment, resource, or task.
	Resource	ResourceOvertimeCost	RES_OVT_COST	
	Task	TaskOvertimeCost	TASK_OVT_COST	
Overtime Rate	Resource	ResourceOvertimeCost	RES_OVT_COST	The total overtime cost for a resource on all assigned tasks.
Remaining Cost	Assignment	AssignmentRemaining-Cost	ASSN_REM_COST	The costs associated with completing remaining scheduled work.
	Resource	ResourceRemainingCost	RES_REM_COST	
	Task	TaskRemainingCost	TASK_REM_COST	
Remaining Overtime Cost	Resource	ResourceRemaining-OvertimeCost	RES_REM_OVT_COST	The remaining overtime costs for a resource.
Standard Rate	Resource	ResourceStandardRate	RES_STD_RATE	The standard rate for nonovertime work performed by a resource.

Table B-1. Currency Fields

Field	Available Categories	OLE DB Provider	Microsoft Project Database	Description
SV	Assignment	AssignmentSV		The earned value schedule variance (SV), which is the difference between BCWP and BCWS measured in cost terms.
	Assignment (Timephased)	AssignmentTimeSV		
	Resource	ResourceSV		
	Resource (Timephased)	ResourceTimeSV		
	Task	TaskSV		
	Task (Timephased)	TaskTimeSV		
VAC	Assignment	AssignmentVAC		The earned value variance at completion (VAC), which is the difference between BAC and EAC, measured in cost terms.
	Resource	ResourceVAC		
	Task	TaskVAC	TASK_VAC	

Date Fields

Table B-2 lists all date fields available in Microsoft Project.

For information about working with the project schedule and associated date fields, see Chapter 9, "Checking and Adjusting the Project Plan," and "Monitoring and Adjusting the Schedule" on page 327.

Table B-2. Date Fields

Field	Available Categories	OLE DB Provider	Microsoft Project Database	Description
Actual Finish	Assignment	AssignmentActualFinish	ASSN_ACT_FINISH	The actual date and time when a task is completed.
	Resource	ResourceActualFinish	RES_ACT_FINISH	
	Task	TaskActualFinish	TASK_ACT_FINISH	
Actual Start	Assignment	AssignmentActualStart	ASSN_ACT_START	The actual date and time when a task began.
	Resource	ResourceActualStart	RES_ACT_START	
	Task	TaskActualStart	TASK_ACT_START	
Available From	Resource	ResourceAvailableFrom	RES_AVAIL_FROM	The start date that a resource is available to start work on a project.

Table B-2. **Date Fields**

Field	Available Categories	OLE DB Provider	Microsoft Project Database	Description
Available To	Resource	ResourceAvailableTo	RES_AVAIL_TO	The end date that a resource is no longer available to work on a project.
Baseline Finish	Assignment Resource Task	AssignmentBaselineFinish ResourceBaselineFinish TaskBaselineFinish	ASSN_BASE_FINISH RES_BASE_FINISH TASK_BASE_FINISH	The originally planned completion date for assignments or tasks.
Baseline Start	Assignment Resource Task	AssignmentBaselineStart ResourceBaselineStart TaskBaselineStart	ASSN_BASE_START RES_BASE_START TASK_BASE_START	The planned beginning date for an assignment or task.
Baseline 1-10Finish	Assignment Resource Task	AssignmentBaseline1-Finish-10 ResourceBaseline1-Finish-10 TaskBaseline1Finish-10		The baseline finish values for Baseline1Finish through Baseline10Finish.
Baseline 1-10Start	Assignment Resource Task	AssignmentBaseline1-Start-10 ResourceBaseline1-Start-10 TaskBaseline1Start-10		The baseline start values for Baseline1Start through Baseline10Start.
Complete Through	Task	TaskCompleteThrough		The most recent date that actuals have been reported on a task.
Constraint Date	Task	TaskConstraintDate	TASK_CONSTRAINT_DATE	The date associated with a task constraint.
Created	Task	TaskCreated	TASK_CREATION_DATE	The date and time that a task was first added to this project.
Date1-10	Assignment Resource Task	AssignmentDate1-10 ResourceDate1-10 TaskDate1-10		The values for the custom Date1 through Date10 fields.

Table B-2. Date Fields

Field	Available Categories	OLE DB Provider	Microsoft Project Database	Description
Deadline	Task	TaskDeadline	TASK_DEADLINE	The date by which a task must be completed.
Early Finish	Task	TaskEarlyFinish	TASK_EARLY_FINISH	The earliest date that a task can finish, based on predecessor and successor tasks, constraints, and delays.
Early Start	Task	TaskEarlyStart	TASK_EARLY_START	The earliest date when a task can start, based on predecessor and successor tasks, constraints, and delays.
Expected Finish	Task	TaskFinish2		The expected finish date of a task for PERT Analysis calculations.
Expected Start	Task	TaskStart2		The expected start date of a task for PERT Analysis calculations.
Finish	Assignment Resource Task	AssignmentFinish ResourceFinish TaskFinish	ASSN_FINISH RES_FINISH TASK_FINISH	The date that a task is scheduled to be completed.
Finish1-10	Assignment Resource Task	AssignmentBaseline1-Finish-10 ResourceBaseline1-Finish-10 TaskBaseline1Finish-10		The values for the custom Finish1 through Finish10 fields.
Late Finish	Task	TaskLateFinish	TASK_LATE_FINISH	The latest date that a task can finish, based on predecessor and successor tasks, constraints, and delays.

Table B-2. Date Fields

Field	Available Categories	OLE DB Provider	Microsoft Project Database	Description
Late Start	Task	TaskLateStart	TASK_LATE_START	The latest date when a task can start, based on predecessor and successor tasks, constraints, and delays.
Optimistic Finish	Task	TaskFinish1		The optimistic finish date of a task for PERT Analysis calculations.
Optimistic Start	Task	TaskStart1		The optimistic start date of a task for PERT Analysis calculations.
Pessimistic Finish	Task	TaskFinish3		The pessimistic finish date of a task for PERT Analysis calculations.
Pessimistic Start	Task	TaskStart3		The pessimistic start date of a task for PERT Analysis calculations.
Preleveled Finish	Task	TaskPreleveledFinish	TASK_PRELEVELED_FINISH	The finish date for a task before resource leveling.
Preleveled Start	Task	TaskPreleveledStart	TASK_PRELEVELED_START	The start date for a task before resource leveling.
Resume	Task	TaskResume	TASK_RESUME_DATE	The date when the remaining portion of a split task is scheduled to resume.
Start	Assignment Resource Task	AssignmentStart ResourceStart TaskStart	ASSN_START RES_START TASK_START	The date when a task or assignment is scheduled to begin.
Start1-10	Assignment Resource Task	AssignmentStart1-10 ResourceStart1-10 TaskStart1-10		The values for the custom Start1 through Start10 fields.

Appendix B

Table B-2. Date Fields

Field	Available Categories	OLE DB Provider	Microsoft Project Database	Description
Stop	Task	TaskStop	TASK_STOP	The date when a split task is to temporarily stop. This is associated with a subsequent Resume date field.
Summary Progress	Task	TaskSummaryProgress		The progress made on a summary task.

Duration Fields

Table B-3 lists all duration fields available in Microsoft Project.

For more information about durations, see "Setting Task Durations" on page 138.

Table B-3. Duration Fields

Field	Available Categories	OLE DB Provider	Microsoft Project Database	Description
Actual Duration	Task	TaskActualDuration	TASK_ACT_DUR	The amount of time that actual work has been performed on a task, up to the current date.
Actual Overtime Work	Assignment	Assignment-OvertimeWork	ASSN_OVT_WORK	The amount of overtime work already completed by a resource on a task.
	Assignment (Timephased)	AssignmentTime-OvertimeWork		
	Resource	ResourceOvertime-Work	RES_OVT_WORK	
	Resource (Timephased)	ResourceTime-OvertimeWork		
	Task	TaskOvertimeWork	TASK_OVT_WORK	
	Task (Timephased)	TaskTimeOvertime-Work		

Table B-3. Duration Fields

Field	Available Categories	OLE DB Provider	Microsoft Project Database	Description
Actual Work	Assignment	Assignment-ActualWork	ASSN_ACT_WORK	The amount of work already completed by a resource on a task.
	Assignment (Timephased)	AssignmentTime-ActualWork		
	Resource	ResourceActualWork	RES_ACT_WORK	
	Resource (Timephased)	ResourceTime-ActualWork		
	Task	TaskActualWork	TASK_ACT_WORK	
	Task (Timephased)	TaskTimeActualWork		
NEW FEATURE! Actual Overtime Work Protected	Assignment	Assignment-ActualOvertime-WorkProtected	ASSN_ACT_OVT_ WORK_PROT	The amount of actual overtime work reported by a resource and retained on Project Server, regardless of whether the project manager changes the amount in the project plan.
	Assignment (Timephased)	AssignmentTime-ActualOvertimeWork-Protected		
	Resource	ResourceActualOver-timeWorkProtected	RES_ACT_ OVT_ WORK_PROT	
NEW FEATURE! Actual Work Protected	Assignment	AssignmentActual-WorkProtected	ASSN_ACT_WORK_ PROT	The amount of actual work reported by a resource and retained on Project Server, regardless of whether the project manager changes the amount in the project plan.
	Assignment (Timephased)	AssignmentTime-ActualWorkProtected		
	Resource	ResourceActualWork-Protected	RES_ACT_WORK_ PROT	
	Task	TaskActualWork-Protected	TASK_ACT_WORK_ PROT	
Assignment Delay	Assignment	AssignmentDelay	ASSN_DELAY	The amount of time between when a resource is assigned work and when a resource begins work.

Table B-3. Duration Fields

Field	Available Categories	OLE DB Provider	Microsoft Project Database	Description
Baseline Duration	Task	TaskBaselineDuration	TASK_BASE_DUR	The amount of time originally planned to complete a task.
Baseline Work	Assignment	AssignmentBaseline-Work	ASSN_BASE_WORK	The number of work resource hours originally planned for a task.
	Assignment (Timephased)	AssignmentTime-BaselineWork		
	Resource	ResourceBaseline-Work	RES_BASE_WORK	
	Resource (Timephased)	ResourceTime-BaselineWork		
	Task	TaskBaselineWork	TASK_BASE_WORK	
	Task (Timephased)	TaskTimeBaseline-Work		
Baseline1-10 Duration	Task	TaskBaseline1-Duration-10		The baseline duration values for Baseline 1 through Baseline 10.
Baseline1-10 Work	Assignment	AssignmentBaseline1-Work-10		The baseline work values for Baseline 1 through Baseline 10.
	Assignment (Timephased)	AssignmentTime-Baseline1Work-10		
	Resource	ResourceBaseline1-Work-10		
	Resource (Timephased)	ResourceTime-Baseline1Work-10		
	Task	TaskBaseline1-Work-10		
	Task (Timephased)	TaskTimeBaseline1-Work-10		
Cumulative Work	Assignment (Timephased)	AssignmentTime-CumulativeWork		The amount of work over a period of time.
	Resource (Timephased)	ResourceTime-CumulativeWork		
	Task (Timephased)	TaskTimeCumulative-Work		

Table B-3. **Duration Fields**

Field	Available Categories	OLE DB Provider	Microsoft Project Database	Description
Duration	Task	TaskDuration	TASK_DUR	The amount of working time between a task's start and finish dates.
Duration Variance	Task	TaskDuration-Variance	TASK_DUR_VAR	The difference between a task's baseline duration and total scheduled duration.
Duration1-10	Assignment	Assignment-Duration1-10		The values for the Custom Duration1 through Duration10 fields.
	Resource	Resource-Duration1-10		
	Task	TaskDuration1-10		
Finish Slack	Task	TaskFinishSlack		The difference between a task's early start and late finish dates.
Finish Variance	Assignment	AssignmentFinish-Variance	ASSN_FINISH_VAR	The difference between the baseline start date of a task or assignment and its current finish date.
	Task	TaskFinishVariance	TASK_FINISH_VAR	
Free Slack	Task	TaskFreeSlack	TASK_FREE_SLACK	The amount of time that a task can be delayed before it will delay a successor task.
Leveling Delay	Assignment	Assignment-LevelingDelay	ASSN_LEVELING_DELAY	The amount of delay caused by resource leveling.
	Resource			
	Task	TaskLevelingDelay	TASK_LEVELING_DELAY	

Table B-3. Duration Fields

Field	Available Categories	OLE DB Provider	Microsoft Project Database	Description
Negative Slack	Task			The amount of time that a task is behind schedule. This time must be recovered to prevent delays for successor tasks.
Optimistic Duration	Task	TaskDuration1		The optimistic task duration for PERT Analysis calculations.
Over-allocation	Assignment (Timephased)			The amount of work that exceeds the amount of time a resource is available.
	Resource (Timephased)	ResourceTime-Overallocation		
	Task (Timephased)			
Overtime Work	Assignment	Assignment-OvertimeWork	ASSN_OVT_WORK	The amount of work assigned to a resource that is charged at a resource's overtime rate.
	Assignment (Timephased)	AssignmentTime-OvertimeWork		
	Resource	Resource-OvertimeWork	RES_OVT_WORK	
	Resource (Timephased)	ResourceTime-OvertimeWork		
	Task	TaskOvertimeWork	TASK_OVT_WORK	
	Task (Timephased)	TaskTime-OvertimeWork		
Pessimistic Duration	Task	TaskDuration3		The pessimistic task duration for PERT Analysis calculation.

Table B-3. Duration Fields

Field	Available Categories	OLE DB Provider	Microsoft Project Database	Description
Regular Work	Assignment	Assignment-RegularWork	ASSN_REG_WORK	The amount of work assigned to a resource that is charged at a resource's standard rate.
	Assignment (Timephased)	AssignmentTime-RegularWork		
	Resource	ResourceRegularWork	RES_REG_WORK	
	Resource (Timephased)	ResourceTime-RegularWork		
	Task	TaskRegularWork	TASK_REG_WORK	
	Task (Timephased)	TaskTimeRegularWork		
Remaining Availability	Resource (Timephased)	ResourceTime-Remaining-Availability		The amount of available resource time not currently allocated to any task in a given time period.
Remaining Duration	Task	TaskRemaining-Duration	TASK_REM_DUR	The amount of time required to complete a task.
Remaining Overtime Work	Assignment	AssignmentRemaining-OvertimeWork	ASSN_REM_OVT_WORK	The amount of scheduled overtime work remaining on unfinished tasks.
	Resource	ResourceRemaining-OvertimeWork	RES_REM_OVT_WORK	
	Task	TaskRemaining-OvertimeWork	TASK_REM_OVT_WORK	
Remaining Work	Assignment	Assignment-RemainingWork	ASSN_REM_WORK	The amount of work remaining on a task.
	Resource	ResourceRemaining-Work	RES_REM_WORK	
	Task	TaskRemainingWork	TASK_REM_WORK	

Table B-3. Duration Fields

Field	Available Categories	OLE DB Provider	Microsoft Project Database	Description
Start Slack	Task	TaskStartSlack		The amount of time that a task can be delayed without affecting a successor task's start date or a project's finish date. Calculated by measuring the difference between a task's early start and late start dates.
Start Variance	Assignment	AssignmentStart-Variance	ASSN_START_VAR	The difference between the baseline start date and the current scheduled start date.
	Task	TaskStartVariance	TASK_START_VAR	
Total Slack	Task	TaskTotalSlack	TASK_TOTAL_SLACK	The amount of time that a task can be delayed without affecting the project's finish date.
Work	Assignment	AssignmentWork	ASSN_WORK	The total scheduled amount of work assigned to a resource.
	Assignment (Timephased)	AssignmentTimeWork		
	Resource	Resource	RES_WORK	
	Resource (Timephased)	ResourceTimeWork		
	Task	TaskWork	TASK_WORK	
	Task (Timephased)	TaskTimeWork		

Table B-3. Duration Fields

Field	Available Categories	OLE DB Provider	Microsoft Project Database	Description
Work Availability	Resource (Timephased)	ResourceTime-WorkAvailability		The maximum amount of time that a resource is available to be assigned work during a specified time period.
Work Variance	Assignment	AssignmentWork-Variance		The difference between baseline work and scheduled work.
	Resource	ResourceWork-Variance		
	Task	TaskWorkVariance		

Enumerated Fields

Table B-4 lists all fields that store enumerated values in Microsoft Project.

Table B-4. Enumerated Fields

Field	Available Categories	OLE DB Provider	Microsoft Project Database	Description
Accrue At	Resource	ResourceAccrueAt	RES_ACCRUE_AT	The way in which resource costs are accrued: at the start, at the end, or prorated across the span of the project.
Base Calendar	Resource	ResourceBase-Calendar	RES_CAL_UID	The base calendar to be used with a particular resource.
Workgroup	Resource	ResourceWorkgroup	RES_WORKGROUP_MESSAGING	The collaboration method used to communicate with resources on a project team.
NEW FEATURE! Booking Type	Assignment	Assignment-BookingType	ASSN_BOOKING_TYPE	The booking type for a resource, either Committed or Proposed.
	Resource	Resource-BookingType	RES_BOOKING_TYPE	

Table B-4. Enumerated Fields

Field	Available Categories	OLE DB Provider	Microsoft Project Database	Description
Constraint Type	Task	TaskConstraintType	TASK_CONSTRAINT_TYPE	The type of constraint applied to a task.
Cost Rate Table	Assignment	Assignment-CostRateTable	ASSN_COST_RATE_TABLE	The cost rate table used for a particular assignment.
Earned Value Method	Task		TASK_EVMETHOD	The method (Percent Complete or Physical Percent Complete) used to calculate earned value budgeted cost of work performed (BCWP).
Fixed Cost Accrual	Task	TaskFixedCost-Accrual	TASK_FIXED_COST_ACCRUAL	The way in which fixed costs are accrued: at the start, at the end, or prorated across the task duration.
Priority	Task	TaskPriority	TASK_PRIORITY	The relative importance of the task scheduling; used to determine priority for task leveling.
Resource Type	Assignment	Assignment-ResourceType	ASSN_RES_TYPE	The type of resource (work or material) assigned.
Status	Task	TaskStatus		The current status of a task: Complete, On Schedule, Late, or Future Task.
Task Calendar	Task	TaskCalendar	TASK_CAL_UID	The base calendar to be used with a particular task.
(Resource) Type	Resource	ResourceType	RES_TYPE	The type of resource: either work or material.

Table B-4. Enumerated Fields

Field	Available Categories	OLE DB Provider	Microsoft Project Database	Description
(Task) Type	Task	TaskType	TASK_TYPE	The type of task: fixed work, fixed units, or fixed duration.
Work Contour	Assignment	Assignment-WorkContour	ASSN_WORK_CONTOUR	The way in which work is distributed over the length of an assignment.

Indicator Fields

Table B-5 contains information about indicator fields, which are used to provide additional information about assignments, tasks, and resources, using a simple visual icon.

Table B-5. Indicator Fields

Field	Available Categories	OLE DB Provider	Microsoft Project Database	Description
Indicators	Assignment Resource Task	Various Various Various	Various Various Various	Indicators that provide additional information about assignments, tasks, and resources.
StatusTask Indicator				Indicators that provide information about whether a task is complete, on schedule, late, or planned.

Integer Fields

Table B-6 lists all integer fields available in Microsoft Project.

Table B-6. Integer Fields

Field	Available Categories	OLE DB Provider	Microsoft Project Database	Description
ID	Resource Task	ResourceID TaskID	RES_ID TASK_ID	The position of a task or resource in relation to other tasks or resources.
Outline Level	Task Level	TaskOutlineLevel		The task's location within the project outline.

Table B-6. Integer Fields

Field	Available Categories	OLE DB Provider	Microsoft Project Database	Description
Predecessors	Task	Task-Predecessors		The Task ID for a predecessor task.
Resource ID	Assignment			The position of the resource within the project, in relation to other resources.
Successors	Task	Task-Successors		The Task ID of a successor task.
Task ID	Assignment			The position of the task within the project, in relation to other tasks.
Unique ID	Assignment	Assignment-UniqueID	ASSN_UID	The unique ID of an assignment, resource, or task.
	Resource	Resource-UniqueID	RES_UID	
	Task	TaskUniqueID	TASK_UID	
Unique ID Predecessors	Task	TaskUniqueID-Predecessors		The unique ID of a predecessor task.
Unique ID Successors	Task	TaskUniqueID-Successors		The unique ID of a successor task.
WBS Predecessors	Task	TaskWBS-Predecessors		The work breakdown structure code of the predecessor tasks.
WBS Successors	Task	TaskWBS-Successors		The work breakdown structure code of the successor tasks.

Outline Code Fields

Table B-7 lists all outline code fields available in Microsoft Project.

Table B-7. Custom Outline Codes

Field	Available Categories	OLE DB Provider	Microsoft Project Database	Description
Outline Code 1-10	Resource	ResourceOutline-Code1-10		The values for the custom OutlineCode1 through OutlineCode10 fields.
	Task	TaskOutline-Code1-10		

Percentage and Number Fields

Table B-8 lists all percentage and number fields available in Microsoft Project.

Table B-8. Percentage and Number Fields

Field	Available Categories	OLE DB Provider	Microsoft Project Database	Description
Assignment Units	Assignment	AssignmentUnits	ASSN_UNITS	The number of resource units assigned to a task, expressed as a percentage of a resource's total availability.
CPI	Task Task (Timephased)	TaskCPI		The earned value cost performance index, which is the ratio of the difference between BCWP and ACWP.
Cumulative Percent Complete	Task (Timephased)			The progress of a task measured as a percentage of the total work required to finish the task, as distributed over time.
CV Percent	Task Task (Timephased)	TaskCVP		The earned value Cost Variance percent (CV%), which is the ratio of CV to BCWP, expressed as a percentage.
Max Units	Resource	ResourceMax-Units	RES_MAX_UNITS	The maximum number of units a resource is available to be assigned to tasks in the project.
Number1-20	Assignment Resource Task	Assignment-Number1-20 Resource-Number1-20 TaskNumber1-20		The values for the custom Number1 through Number20 fields.
Objects	Resource Task	ResourceObjects TaskObjects	RES_NUM_OBJECTS TASK_NUM_OBJECTS	The number of objects, such as an inserted graphic or a linked file, associated with either a task or resource.
Peak	Assignment Resource	Assignment-PeakUnits Resource-PeakUnits	 RES_PEAK	The number of units that represents a resource's largest assignment (in units) or the number of units required to complete an assignment.

Appendix B

Table B-8. Percentage and Number Fields

Field	Available Categories	OLE DB Provider	Microsoft Project Database	Description
Peak Units	Assignment (Timephased) Resource (Timephased)	AssignmentTime-PeakUnits ResourceTime-PeakUnits		The number of units that represents a resource's largest assignment (in units) or the number of units required to complete an assignment, shown for a specific time period.
Percent Allocation	Assignment (Timephased) Resource (Timephased)	AssignmentTime-PercentAllocation ResourceTime-PercentAllocation		The percentage of a resource's total available units compared with assigned units.
Percent Complete	Task Task (Timephased)	TaskPercent-Complete	TASK_PCT_COMP	The ratio of a task's total duration to completed duration.
Percent Work Complete	Assignment Resource Task	TaskPercentWork-Complete	TASK_PCT_WORK_COMP	The ratio of a task's total work to completed work.
Physical Percent Complete	Task		TASK_PHY_PCT_COMP	A percent complete value that can be used as an alternative to regular percent complete for the purposes of calculating BCWP and other earned value fields.
SPI	Task Task (Timephased)	TaskSPI		The earned value schedule performance index (SPI), which is the ratio of BCWP to BCWS.
SV Percent	Task Task (Timephased)	TaskSVP		The earned value schedule variance (SV%), which is the ratio of SV to BCWS.
Task Outline Number	Assignment	TaskOutlineNumber	TASK_OUTLINE_NUM	Indicates a task's position in the outline.
TCPI	Task	TaskTCPI		The earned value To Complete Performance Index (TCPI), which is the ratio of remaining work to remaining funds.
Unit Availability	Resource (Timephased)	ResourceTime-Unit-Availability		The number of units a resource is available to be assigned work, expressed as a percentage of a resource's total units.

Text Fields

Table B-9 lists all text fields available in Microsoft Project.

Table B-9. Text Fields

Field	Available Categories	OLE DB Provider	Microsoft Project Database	Description
Code	Resource	ResourceCode		The information about a resource entered as a code, abbreviation, or number.
Contact	Task	TaskContact		The name of the person responsible for a task.
E-mail Address	Resource	ResourceEmail-Address		The e-mail address for a resource.
Group	Resource	ResourceGroup		The name of the group that a resource is part of.
Hyperlink	Assignment	Assignment-Hyperlink		The title of a hyperlink associated with an assignment, resource, or task.
	Resource	Resource-Hyperlink		
	Task	TaskHyperlink		
Hyperlink Address	Assignment	Assignment-Hyperlink-Address		The hyperlink address of a hyperlink associated with an assignment, resource, or task.
	Resource	Resource-HyperlinkAddress		
	Task	TaskHyperlink-Address		
Hyperlink Href	Assignment	Assignment-HyperlinkHref		The combination of the Hyperlink Address and the Hyperlink Sub-Address fields.
	Resource	Resource-HyperlinkHref		
	Task	TaskHyperlinkHref		
Hyperlink SubAddress	Assignment	Assignment-Hyperlink-SubAddress		The location within a document associated with the Hyperlink Address field.
	Resource	ResourceHyperlink-SubAddress		
	Task	TaskHyperlink-SubAddress		
Initials	Resource	ResourceInitials	RES_INITIALS	The abbreviation of a resource's name.

Table B-9. Text Fields

Field	Available Categories	OLE DB Provider	Microsoft Project Database	Description
Material Label	Resource	Resource-MaterialLabel	RES_MATERIAL_LABEL	The name of the unit of measurement associated with a material resource.
Name	Resource Task	ResourceName TaskName	RES_NAME TASK_NAME	The name of a resource or task.
Notes	Assignment Resource Task	AssignmentNotes ResourceNotes TaskNotes	ASSN_RTF_NOTES RES_RTF_NOTES TASK_RTF_NOTES	The notes about an assignment, resource, or task.
Outline Number	Task	TaskOutline-Number	TASK_OUTLINE_LEVEL	The number that identifies a task's position in a project's outline; this number is entered automatically by Microsoft Project.
Phonetics	Resource	Resource-Phonetics	RES_PHONETICS	The phonetic information about a resource name; used only in the Japanese version of Microsoft Project.
Project	Assignment Resource Task	Projects Projects Projects	The PROJ_NAME field in the MSP_PROJECTS table contains the name of a project. Match the PROJ_UID in the MSP_ASSIGNMENTS, MSP_RESOURCES, or MSP_TASKS tables to the PROJ_UID in the MSP_PROJECTS table to identify the project name.	The name of the project.
Resource Group	Assignment Task	ResourceGroup ResourceGroup		The name of a group to which a resource belongs.

Table B-9. Text Fields

Field	Available Categories	OLE DB Provider	Microsoft Project Database	Description
Resource Initials	Assignment	ResourceInitials in the Resources table	RES_INITIALS in the MSP_RESOURCES table	The initials of a resource assigned to a task.
	Task	ResourceInitials in the Resources table	RES_INITIALS in the MSP_RESOURCES table	
Resource Names	Assignment	ResourceName in the Resources table	RES_NAME in the MSP_RESOURCES table	The name of a resource assigned to a task.
	Task	ResourceName in the Resources table	RES_NAME in the MSP_RESOURCES table	
Subproject File	Task	TaskSubprojectFile		The name of an inserted project, including the path to the project.
Task Name	Assignment	TaskName	TASK_NAME	The name of a task.
Task Summary Name	Assignment	Assignment-TaskSummary-Name		The name of a summary task.
Text1-30	Assignment	Assignment-Text1-30	MSP_TEXT_FIELDS	The values for the custom Text1 through Text30 fields.
	Resource	ResourceText1-30	MSP_TEXT_FIELDS	
	Task	TaskText1-30	MSP_TEXT_FIELDS	
WBS	Assignment Task	TaskWBS	TASK_WBS	The work breakdown structure codes used to represent a task's position within the project.
Windows User Account	Resource	ResourceNT-Account		The Microsoft Windows user name for a work resource.

Yes/No Fields

Table B-10 lists all Yes/No fields available in Microsoft Project. Yes/No fields, which are set either by the user or by Microsoft Project, indicate the state of a task, resource, or assignment as being on or off or being true or false. Yes/No fields are also referred to as *Boolean* fields.

Table B-10. Yes/No Fields

Field	Available Categories	OLE DB Provider	Microsoft Project Database	Description
Assignment	Assignment Resource Task			Indicates whether this is an assignment.
Can Level	Resource	ResourceCanLevel	RES_CAN_LEVEL	The setting that specifies whether leveling can be performed on the resource.
Confirmed	Assignment Resource Task	Assignment-Confirmed ResourceConfirmed TaskConfirmed	ASSN_IS_CONFIRMED	The setting that specifies whether a resource has accepted an assignment using an electronic team collaboration method.
Critical	Task	TaskCritical	TASK_IS_CRITICAL	The setting that specifies whether the task is on the critical path.
Effort Driven	Task	TaskEffortDriven	TASK_IS_EFFORT_DRIVEN	The setting that specifies whether the task is effort-driven.
Estimated	Task	TaskEstimated	TASK_DUR_IS_EST	The setting that specifies whether a task's duration is estimated.
External Task	Task	TaskExternalTask	TASK_IS_EXTERNAL	The setting that specifies whether the task is an external task.
Flag1-20	Assignment Resource Task	Assignment-Flag1-20 ResourceFlag1-20 TaskFlag1-20		The setting that specifies whether the custom fields Flag1 through Flag20 are on or off.
Group By Summary	Resource Task	TaskSummary	TASK_IS_SUMMARY	The setting that specifies whether a task is a summary task.
Hide Bar	Task	TaskHideBar	TASK_BAR_IS_HIDDEN	The setting that specifies whether Gantt and Calendar bars are hidden for a task.
Ignore Resource Calendar	Task	TaskIgnore-ResourceCalendar	TASK_IGNORES_RES_CAL	The setting that specifies whether a resource's calendar is taken into account in conjunction with a task calendar.

Table B-10. Yes/No Fields

Field	Available Categories	OLE DB Provider	Microsoft Project Database	Description
Inactive	Resource			The setting that specifies whether an enterprise resource has been made inactive.
Level Assignments	Task	TaskLevel-Assignments	TASK_LEVELING_ADJUSTS_ASSN	The setting that specifies whether assignments can be split or delayed to resolve resource overallocations.
Leveling Can Split	Task	TaskLevelingCan-Split	TASK_LEVELING_CAN_SPLIT	The setting that specifies whether resource leveling can cause a task split on the remaining work on a task.
Linked Fields	Assignment	AssignmentLinked-Fields	ASSN_HAS_LINKED_FIELDS	The setting that specifies whether an assignment, resource, or task has OLE links to it from within the project, another project, or an external application.
	Resource	ResourceLinked-Fields	RES_HAS_LINKED_FIELDS	
	Task	TaskLinkedFields	TASK_HAS_LINKED_FIELDS	
Marked	Task	TaskMarked	TASK_MARKED	The setting that specifies whether a task is identified, or *flagged*, as requiring further attention.
Milestone	Task	TaskMilestone	TASK_MILESTONE	The setting that specifies whether a task is a milestone.
Overallocated	Assignment	Assignment-Overallocated	ASSN_IS_OVERALLOCATED	The setting that specifies whether resources have been assigned work beyond their work capacity or availability.
	Resource	Resource-Overallocated	RES_IS_OVERALLOCATED	
	Task	TaskOverallocated	TASK_IS_OVERALLOCATED	
Recurring	Task	TaskRecurring	TASK_IS_RECURRING	The setting that specifies whether a task is recurring.

Table B-10. Yes/No Fields

Field	Available Categories	OLE DB Provider	Microsoft Project Database	Description
Response Pending	Assignment Resource Task	Assignment-ResponsePending Resource-ResponsePending TaskResponse-Pending	ASSN_RESPONSE_PENDING	The setting that specifies whether a response to an update has been received through an electronic team collaboration method.
Rollup	Task	TaskRollup	TASK_IS_ROLLED_UP	The setting that specifies whether information on the subtask Gantt bar is rolled up to the summary task bar.
Subproject Read Only	Task	TaskSubproject-ReadOnly		The setting that specifies whether a subproject of a task is read-only.
Summary	Task	TaskSummary	TASK_IS_SUMMARY	The setting that specifies whether the task is a summary task.
TeamStatus Pending	Assignment Resource Task	AssignmentTeam-StatusPending ResourceTeam-StatusPending TaskTeam-StatusPending	ASSN_TEAM_STATUS_PENDING	The setting that specifies whether a response to a progress request has been received through an electronic team collaboration method.
Text Above	Task			The setting that specifies whether text appears above or below the summary Gantt bar.
Update Needed	Assignment Resource Task	AssignmentUpdate-Needed ResourceUpdate-Needed TaskUpdateNeeded	ASSN_UPDATE_NEEDED	The setting that specifies whether an update message should be sent to resources to notify them of updates to their assigned tasks through an electronic team collaboration method.

Special Field Categories

The fields listed in the following tables (Custom Fields and Custom Outline Codes, Earned Value, and PERT Analysis) are all included in the tables found earlier in this chapter. In this case, these fields are listed by their function in the project plan.

Custom Fields and Custom Outline Codes

Custom fields can be used to create your own cost, date, duration, finish, flag, number, outline code, start, and text fields in Microsoft Project. The number of customizable fields of a given type can range from 10 to 30. When using Microsoft Project or the OLE DB Provider, you will see the fields listed with the type and the number of the custom field. When you're viewing the custom fields using Microsoft Access or Microsoft Excel, each custom field is stored in a unique table that contains all the data required to identify the custom field or custom outline code and where it is being used within a project. The table name is listed in the Microsoft Project Database column. Table B-11 shows custom fields.

For more information about working with custom fields, see "Customizing Fields" on page 788 and "Working with Outline Codes" on page 806.

Table B-11. Custom Fields

Field	Available Categories	OLE DB Provider	Microsoft Project Database	Description
Cost1-10	Assignment Resource Task	AssignmentCost1-10 ResourceCost1-10 TaskCost1-10		The currency values for the custom Cost1 through Cost10 fields.
Date1-10	Assignment Resource Task	AssignmentDate1-10 ResourceDate1-10 TaskDate1-10		The date values for the custom Date1 through Date10 fields.
Duration1-10	Assignment Resource Task	AssignmentDuration1-10 ResourceDuration1-10 TaskDuration1-10		The duration values for the custom Duration1 through Duration10 fields.
Finish1-10	Assignment Resource Task	AssignmentFinish1-10 ResourceFinish1-10 TaskFinish1-10		The date values for the custom Finish1 through Finish10 fields.
Flag1-20	Assignment Resource Task	AssignmentFlag1-20 ResourceFlag1-20 TaskFlag1-20		The Yes/No values for the custom Flag1 through Flag20 fields.

Table B-11. Custom Fields

Field	Available Categories	OLE DB Provider	Microsoft Project Database	Description
Number1-20	Assignment Resource Task	AssignmentNumber1-20 ResourceNumber1-20 TaskNumber1-20		The numeric values for the custom Number1 through Number20 fields.
OutlineCode1-10	Resource Task	ResourceOutlineCode1-10 TaskOutlineCode1-10		The values for the custom OutlineCode1 through OutlineCode10 fields.
Start1-10	Assignment Resource Task	AssignmentStart1-10 ResourceStart1-10 TaskStart1-10		The date values for the custom Start1 through Start10 fields.
Text1-30	Assignment Resource Task	AssignmentText1-30 ResourceText1-30 TaskText1-30		The text values for the custom Text1 through Text30 fields.

Earned Value Fields

Earned value fields are used to measure the cost of work and are based on a task's baseline cost. Table B-12 shows earned value fields.

For information about working with earned value, see Chapter 13.

Table B-12. Earned Value Fields

Field	Available Categories	OLE DB Provider	Microsoft Project Database	Description
ACWP	Assignment	AssignmentACWP	ASSN_ACWP	The earned value actual cost of work performed (ACWP).
	Assignment (Timephased)	AssignmentTimeACWP		
	Resource	ResourceACWP	RES_ACWP	
	Resource (Timephased)	ResourceTimeACWP		
	Task	TaskACWP	TASK_ACWP	
	Task (Timephased)	TaskTimeACWP		

Table B-12. Earned Value Fields

Field	Available Categories	OLE DB Provider	Microsoft Project Database	Description
BAC	Assignment	Assignment-BaselineCost	ASSN_BASE_COST	The earned value Budget At Completion (BAC). Same as the Baseline Cost field.
	Assignment (Timephased)	AssignmentTime-BaselineCost		
	Resource	Resource-BaselineCost	RES_BASE_COST	
	Resource (Timephased)	ResourceTime-BaselineCost		
	Task	TaskBaselineCost	TASK_BASE_COST	
	Task (Timephased)	TaskTimeBaselineCost		
BCWP	Assignment	AssignmentBCWP	ASSN_BCWP	The earned value budgeted costs of work performed (BCWP) costs.
	Assignment (Timephased)	AssignmentTimeBCWP		
	Resource	ResourceBCWP	RES_BCWP	
	Resource (Timephased)	ResourceTimeBCWP		
	Task	TaskBCWP	TASK_BCWP	
	Task (Timephased)	TaskTimeBCWP		
BCWS	Assignment	AssignmentBCWS	ASSN_BCWS	The earned value budgeted cost of work scheduled (BCWS) costs.
	Assignment (Timephased)	AssignmentTime-BCWS		
	Resource	ResourceBCWS	RES_BCWS	
	Resource (Timephased)	ResourceTimeBCWS		
	Task	TaskBCWS	TASK_BCWS	
	Task (Timephased)	TaskTimeBCWS		
CPI	Task	TaskCPI		The earned value cost performance index, which is the ratio between BCWP and ACWP.
	Task (Timephased)			

Table B-12. Earned Value Fields

Field	Available Categories	OLE DB Provider	Microsoft Project Database	Description
CV	Assignment	AssignmentCV		The earned value Cost Variance (CV), which is the difference between the budgeted (baseline) cost and the actual cost of work performed.
	Assignment (Timephased)	AssignmentTimeCV		
	Resource	ResourceCV		
	Resource (Timephased)	ResourceTimeCV		
	Task	TaskCV		
	Task (Timephased)	TaskTimeCV		
CV Percent	Task	TaskCVP		The earned value Cost Variance percent (CV%), which is the ratio of CV to BCWP, expressed as a percentage.
	Task (Timephased)			
EAC	Task	TaskEAC	TASK_EAC	The earned value estimate at completion (EAC), which is the expected total cost of a task.
Earned Value Method	Task		TASK_EVMETHOD	The method (Percent Complete or Physical Percent Complete) used to calculate BCWP.
Physical Percent Complete	Task		TASK_PHY_PCT_COMP	The percent complete value, also known as earned value percent complete; an alternative to BCWP.
SPI	Task	TaskSPI		The earned value schedule performance index (SPI), which is the ratio of BCWP to BCWS.
	Task (Timephased)			

Table B-12. Earned Value Fields

Field	Available Categories	OLE DB Provider	Microsoft Project Database	Description
SV	Assignment	AssignmentSV		The earned value schedule variance (SV), which is the difference between BCWP and BCWS measured in cost terms.
	Assignment (Timephased)	AssignmentTimeSV		
	Resource	ResourceSV		
	Resource (Timephased)	ResourceTimeSV		
	Task	TaskSV		
	Task (Timephased)	TaskTimeSV		
SV Percent	Task	TaskSVP		The earned value schedule variance (SV%), which is the ratio of SV to BCWS.
	Task (Timephased)			
TCPI	Task	TaskTCPI		The earned value To Complete Performance Index (TCPI), which is the ratio of remaining work to remaining funds.
VAC	Assignment	AssignmentVAC		The earned value variance at completion (VAC), which is the difference between BAC and EAC, measured in cost terms.
	Resource	ResourceVAC		
	Task	TaskVAC		

PERT Analysis Fields

PERT Analysis is a technique used to evaluate task durations using best-case (optimistic), expected-case (expected), and worst-case (pessimistic) scenarios based on a task's duration, start date, or finish date. All PERT Analysis fields use Custom fields to store the information. Table B-13 shows PERT Analysis fields.

For information about working with PERT Analysis, see "Setting Task Durations" on page 138.

Appendix B

Table B-13. PERT Analysis Fields

Field	Available Categories	OLE DB Provider	Microsoft Project Database	Description
Expected Finish	Task	TaskFinish2		The expected finish date of a task for PERT Analysis calculations.
Expected Start	Task	TaskStart2		The expected start date of a task for PERT Analysis calculations.
Expected Duration	Task	TaskDuration2		The expected duration of a task for PERT Analysis calculations.
Optimistic Finish	Task	TaskFinish1		The optimistic finish date of a task for PERT Analysis calculations.
Optimistic Start	Task	TaskStart1		The optimistic start date of a task for PERT Analysis calculations.
Optimistic Duration	Task	TaskDuration1		The optimistic duration of a task for PERT Analysis calculations.
Pessimistic Finish	Task	TaskFinish3		The pessimistic finish date of a task for PERT Analysis calculations.
Pessimistic Start	Task	TaskStart3		The pessimistic start date of a task for PERT Analysis calculations.
Pessimistic Duration	Task	TaskDuration3		The pessimistic duration of a task for PERT Analysis calculations.

Appendix C

Online Resources for Microsoft Project

This appendix includes links to resources on the World Wide Web related to Microsoft Office Project 2003 and project management.

Microsoft-Sponsored Resources

The following is a list of Microsoft Web sites that can provide further assistance and information in your work with Project 2003:

Microsoft Project Home Page

http://www.microsoft.com/office/project Official site for Microsoft Project. Includes sales information, product specifications, deployment kits, and downloads. It also includes links to other resources for Microsoft Project and project management and developer resources.

Microsoft Office Online

http://office.microsoft.com To go to the Web site quickly, press F1 to open the Microsoft Office Online side pane in Microsoft Project. Click Connect To Microsoft Office Online. Your Web browser launches and goes to the Microsoft Office Online Web site.

This site contains step-by-step assistance, training modules, downloadable templates and clip art, articles, links, tools, and more for all Microsoft Office products, including Microsoft Project.

Office Online Templates

http://officeupdate.microsoft.com/templategallery In addition to the project template files supplied with Microsoft Project, additional templates are continually being added to the Microsoft Project Web site. To see these templates, in Microsoft Project, click File, New. On the New Project page of the Project Guide, click Templates On Office Online. To navigate to the Web site yourself, enter the Web site address, click the Meetings And Projects link, and then click the Project Management link.

Microsoft Project Knowledge Base

http://support.microsoft.com Microsoft Product Support Services maintains a knowledge base of articles about Microsoft Project. You can search this knowledge base to find answers to your specific questions about Microsoft Project or to troubleshoot a problem you're experiencing. Enter the Web address, and then in the Search The Knowledge Base box, type **Project 2003**.

Microsoft TechNet

http://www.microsoft.com/technet/prodtechnol/project Microsoft TechNet includes technical articles and resources designed specifically for information technology professionals and system administrators. Browse a category in the left pane. Or, in the Search box, enter the item or topic you're searching for.

Microsoft Download Center

http://www.microsoft.com/downloads The Microsoft Download Center includes resources available for you to download. To find downloads available for Microsoft Project, under Search For A Download, click Microsoft Project in the Product/Technology box and then click Go.

Microsoft Community Newsgroups

http://support.microsoft.com/newsgroups Join an online community and participate on a newsgroup devoted to Microsoft Project issues. Under Community Newsgroups in the left pane, click Office and then click Project. The newsgroup categories are listed. You no longer need to use newsreader software to participate in a newsgroup; you can simply use the Web-based newsreader. These newsgroups offer help and discussion with other Microsoft Project users, including Microsoft Most Valuable Professionals (MVPs).

Microsoft Project Solution Providers

http://www.msprojectpartner.com This site enables you to find companies worldwide that can help you develop and implement custom project management solutions for your organization, as well as project management training services. You can search this site for a specific solution provider by name, by type of service provided, by country, by category, and more.

Microsoft Developer Network

http://msdn.microsoft.com/project The Microsoft Project center within the Microsoft Developer Network (MSDN) Web site contains programming guidelines, tips, and examples for developing solutions for Microsoft Project. The site includes articles of interest to developers, code samples, downloads, links to user groups and newsgroups, and more. Also included are links to the Microsoft Project Software Development Kit (SDK) and Project Resource Kit (PRK).

Microsoft Office Project 2003 Software Development Kit (SDK)

http://msdn.microsoft.com/project At this URL, click the Microsoft Office Project 2003 SDK link. The Microsoft Office Project 2003 Software Development Kit contains tools and information for Microsoft Project solution providers, value-added resellers, and other developers interested in extending and customizing the features of Project 2003, Microsoft Office Project Server 2003, Microsoft Office Project Web Access 2003, and the enterprise features. The SDK also includes articles regarding the use of the Component Object Model (COM) add-ins, Web parts, the online analytical processor (OLAP) cube, and more.

Index to Troubleshooting Topics

Index

Symbols & Numeric

A

E

H

I

J-K

L

M

N

O

P

S

U

W

About the Authors

Teresa S. Stover is a technical communications consultant who specializes in Microsoft Project and project management. As the owner of Stover Writing Services since 1987, she manages documentation projects for multiple clients, including Apple Computer, National Semiconductor, Boeing, MetLife, Unisys, and most significantly, the Microsoft Project User Assistance team. For these clients, she has developed books, online help, tutorials, and multimedia productions. Having won seven Society for Technical Communications awards, including a Best In Show, Teresa's other books include titles on Windows, Office, Team Manager, and Microsoft Money. When not writing in her Victorian home office in southern Oregon, Teresa conducts workshops on computer, business, and project management topics. She is also a disaster volunteer for the American Red Cross and "plays store" most Saturdays at her husband's shop, Stovepipe Antiques. Teresa can be reached at sws@echoweb.net.

James A. Scott is a rare case of a history major done good. A strong fascination with computer technology and software development quickly pulled him back from the dark side in the mid-1990s and led him down the path toward technical writing. Since then, he has been involved with technical writing, creating Web sites (both copy and code), working with XML when it was almost brand new, and finding ways to enjoy being handed increasingly difficult subjects to write about. During off-times, James can usually be found somewhere in the vicinity of a football (soccer) field.

Stephen T. Adams has been writing Basic since it was an acronym, back in the 1970s. Originally training to be an intelligence analyst with the CIA, he changed directions in 1990 and began a career in the software industry. He has worked in product support, in software testing, and as both an editor and a writer, publishing his first book in 1992. Steve was an award-winning technical writer for Microsoft Project from 1996 until 2002, when he took a developer position at Microsoft. An avid auto racing fan, Steve can occasionally be found tearing it up at the local track, where he likes to pretend he's the next Ayrton Senna.

crosoft Press

Inside **security information** *you can trust*

Microsoft® Windows® Security Resource Kit

ISBN 0-7356-1868-2 Suggested Retail Price: $49.99 U.S., $72.99 Canada

Comprehensive security information and tools, straight from the Microsoft product groups. This official RESOURCE KIT delivers comprehensive operations and deployment information that information security professionals can put to work right away. The authors—members of Microsoft's security teams—describe how to plan and implement a comprehensive security strategy, assess security threats and vulnerabilities, configure system security, and more. The kit also provides must-have security tools, checklists, templates, and other on-the-job resources on CD-ROM and on the Web.

Microsoft Encyclopedia of Security

ISBN 0-7356-1877-1 Suggested Retail Price: $49.99 U.S., $72.99 Canada

The essential security reference for computer professionals at all levels. Get the single resource that defines—and illustrates—the rapidly evolving world of computer and network security. The MICROSOFT ENCYCLOPEDIA OF SECURITY delivers more than 1000 cross-referenced entries detailing the latest security-related technologies, standards, products, services, and issues—including sources and types of attacks, countermeasures, policies, and more. You get clear, concise explanations and case scenarios that deftly take you from concept to real-world application—ready answers to help maximize security for your mission-critical systems and data.

Microsoft Windows Server 2003™ Security Administrator's Companion

ISBN 0-7356-1574-8 Suggested Retail Price: $49.99 U.S., $72.99 Canada

The in-depth, practical guide to deploying and maintaining Windows Server 2003 in a secure environment. Learn how to use all the powerful security features in the latest network operating system with this in-depth, authoritative technical reference—written by a security expert on the Microsoft Windows Server 2003 security team. Explore physical security issues, internal security policies, and public and shared key cryptography, and then drill down into the specifics of the key security features of Windows Server 2003.

Microsoft Internet Information Services Security Technical Reference

ISBN 0-7356-1572-1 Suggested Retail Price: $49.99 U.S., $72.99 Canada

The definitive guide for developers and administrators who need to understand how to securely manage networked systems based on IIS. This book presents obvious, avoidable mistakes and known security vulnerabilities in Internet Information Services (IIS)—priceless, intimate facts about the underlying causes of past security issues—while showing the best ways to fix them. The expert author, who has used IIS since the first version, also discusses real-world best practices for developing software and managing systems and networks with IIS.

To learn more about Microsoft Press® products for IT professionals, please visit:

microsoft.com/mspress/IT

Press products are available worldwide wherever quality computer books are sold. For more information, contact your book or computer retailer, software reseller, or local Microsoft :e, or visit our Web site at **microsoft.com/mspress.** To locate your nearest source for Microsoft Press products, or to order directly, call 1-800-MSPRESS in the United States. (In all 1-800-268-2222.)

crosoft
Press

The practical, portable guides to
Microsoft Windows Server 2003

Microsoft® Windows® Server 2003 Admin Pocket Consultant
ISBN 0-7356-1354-0

The practical, portable guide to Windows Server 2003. Here's the practical, pocket-sized reference for IT professionals who support Windows Server 2003. Designed for quick referencing, it covers all the essentials for performing everyday system-administration tasks. Topics covered include managing workstations and servers, using Active Directory® services, creating and administering user and group accounts, managing files and directories, data security and auditing, data back-up and recovery, administration with TCP/IP, WINS, and DNS, and more.

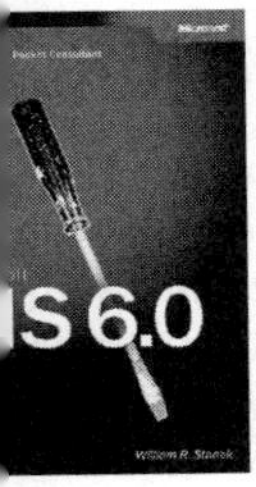

Microsoft IIS 6.0 Administrator's Pocket Consultant
ISBN 0-7356-1560-8

The practical, portable guide to IIS 6.0. Here's the eminently practical, pocket-sized reference for IT and Web professionals who work with Internet Information Services (IIS) 6.0. Designed for quick referencing and compulsively readable, this portable guide covers all the basics needed for everyday tasks. Topics include Web administration fundamentals, Web server administration, essential services administration, and performance, optimization, and maintenance. It's the fast-answers guide that helps users consistently save time and energy as they administer IIS 6.0.

learn more about the full line of Microsoft Press® products for IT professionals, please visit:

microsoft.com/mspress/IT

ft Press products are available worldwide wherever quality computer books are sold. For more information, contact your book or computer retailer, software reseller, or local Microsoft fice, or visit our Web site at **microsoft.com/mspress.** To locate your nearest source for Microsoft Press products, or to order directly, call 1-800-MSPRESS in the United States. (In call 1-800-268-2222.)